John Jamieson, David Donaldson

Supplement to Jamieson's Scottish Dictionary

John Jamieson, David Donaldson

Supplement to Jamieson's Scottish Dictionary

ISBN/EAN: 9783337233860

Printed in Europe, USA, Canada, Australia, Japan

Cover: Foto ©Paul-Georg Meister /pixelio.de

More available books at **www.hansebooks.com**

SUPPLEMENT

TO

JAMIESON'S SCOTTISH DICTIONARY

WITH MEMOIR, AND INTRODUCTION

BY

DAVID DONALDSON, F.E.I.S.

ALEXANDER GARDNER,
PAISLEY; AND 12 PATERNOSTER ROW, LONDON.

1887.

INTRODUCTION.

IN the following work I have attempted to complete the SCOTTISH DICTIONARY compiled by Dr. JAMIESON. By far the larger portion of the work consists of materials collected during a long and varied course of reading extending over many years; and the remaining portion consists of additional forms, meanings, and illustrations of words recorded in the DICTIONARY, and of corrections and improvements of a large number of its meanings and etymologies.

These materials have been drawn chiefly from works that have been issued since the DICTIONARY was published; and many of them were quite unknown to the author of that work. Besides new and more correct editions of various important works which he used, I have specially to note the publications issued under the direction of the Deputy Clerk Register of Scotland, by the Burgh Records Society, and by the Scottish Text Society,—works which cover the whole period of Scottish history during which the vernacular was written and spoken by all classes of society. But, a large number of words have been gleaned from books used by Dr. JAMIESON; and not a few from works which he must have read with very considerable care. A full list of the books read or consulted during the progress of the work will be found at the close of this Introduction.

In the remarks which I have to make on the great work of Dr. JAMIESON, I do not feel called upon to say much regarding the elaborate Dissertation with which it is prefaced : first, because the question, which it was meant to settle, has long ago been settled in quite another way, and all competent scholars are now agreed that the language of the Scottish Lowlands is simply a form of Northern English or Northumbrian; and second, because the main subject which it discusses, viz., the language of the ancient Picts, has no practical bearing on the question in dispute; for, "Whatever might be the race or language of the Picts, it is difficult to deduce the origin of the Scoto-Northumbrian dialect from them—for this weighty reason, that two of the three millions who speak it inhabit districts where that people never had a permanent settlement during any known period

INTRODUCTION.

of their history." * Indeed, that once famous Dissertation can now be considered only a notable feat of literary card-building: more remarkable for the skill and ingenuity of its construction, than for its architectural correctness, strength and durability, or practical usefulness.

That the language of the Scottish Lowlands is in all important particulars the same as that of the northern counties of England, will be evident to any unbiassed reader who takes the trouble to compare the SCOTTISH DICTIONARY with the Glossaries of Brockett, Atkinson, and Peacock. And the similarity is attested in another way by the simple but important fact, that regarding some of our Northern Metrical Romances it is still disputed whether they were composed to the north or the south of the Tweed. No doubt, the vocabularies are not in every respect identical: but the differences are of the same kind, as exist at the present day between the dialects of Fife and Forfar, and are not so strongly marked as those that exist between the dialects of Fife and Aberdeen. In verbal forms, grammatical construction, and all other distinguishing characteristics, they are one and the same language. And to this conclusion all competent scholars have given their consent.

But whatever differences of opinion existed or may still exist regarding the origin and relation of the Scottish language, there has been remarkable unanimity regarding the greatness and value of Dr. JAMIESON's DICTIONARY. When first issued it was greeted with immense enthusiasm, and was accorded the highest praise. The vast learning and research, the extensive and multifarious reading, and the exact discrimination between meanings and shades of meaning which it displayed, at once attested the greatness of the author's ability and the excellence of his work. For general correctness of reference and exactness of quotation it has never been surpassed: and to this feature of the work I feel bound to add my testimony; for, having followed the author in most of the fields in which he worked, I have always found him faithful to his authority, and scrupulously exact in presenting it. Errors and defects no doubt there are in his DICTIONARY; but they are largely to be accounted for by the difficulties of the task, the incorrectness of many of the versions from which he had to work, and the fact that many of the works which he consulted were then only in MS. Few authors even of the present day could do so much or so well; and, all things being taken into account, the wonder is that the errors and mistakes are not much more numerous.

In those days, and for long after, the works of our earliest Scottish writers were, as a rule, imperfectly edited; for, with but few exceptions, editors did not much concern themselves to obtain a correct representation of the original MS. or

---

* Garnett's Philological Essays, p. 46.

INTRODUCTION. vii.

earliest known text of the work on which they were engaged. This gave rise to many false readings and false forms of words, which were entered in the DICTIONARY, and thereby attested and perpetuated as genuine terms. In every other page of this SUPPLEMENT the reader will find an example and correction of these mistakes. And here I may call attention to a whole series of false forms of words which have originated through ignorance of a very simple matter, viz., an ancient method of forming a certain contraction. In many early Scottish MSS. *kk* is written in a contracted form very like *lk*; but all the same the scribe meant *kk*, which represents *kk* or *uk*, according as the preceding vowel is sounded short or long. Ignorant of this form of contraction, editors have copied the apparent *lk* instead of the real *kk*, and thereby introduced forms of words which really did not exist. Thus originated *balk*, a joist or spar, *colk*, a cock, *rolk*, a rock, *olk* and *oulk*, *wolk* and *woulk*, a week, and various others which are explained in the following pages. And regarding these words it may be noted in passing, that in none of them is the letter *l* sounded. The first to point out and explain this remarkable series of false forms was Professor Skeat of Cambridge, who made them the subject of an important address to the Philological Society early in 1886.

A considerable number of corrections both of meaning and etymology will be found in the new edition of the SCOTTISH DICTIONARY issued a few years ago ; but the original plan of that edition, and the arrangements for its publication, did not permit more than a partial treatment of this section of the work. And when it was found that an additional volume would be required to overtake the supplementary matter that had been collected, it was resolved to reserve the more important corrections and improvements for that volume. By this arrangement the present work has been made doubly useful : for it forms a supplement both to the old and to the new edition of the DICTIONARY.

Regarding the materials of this work, I may state generally that a large portion consists of words previously recorded, but explained only in separate glossaries or scattered explanatory notes. Another portion consists of variants, peculiar forms, or corruptions of words explained in the DICTIONARY ; but, as a rule, entries of this kind are treated simply as cross-references. A very large number of the words, however, are here recorded for the first time, at least as Scottish words, and of many of them the explanation will be found nowhere else. And the number of such words would have been much larger had I recorded all that I have collected ; but I have purposely passed over all words that are vulgar in form or gross in meaning, as unsuitable for a work intended as an aid to polite learning. Besides, the insertion of such words could serve no good end, and would certainly tend to confirm the idea that coarseness is a characteristic ele-ment of the Scottish tongue : an idea which, unfortunately, certain glossaries have caused many to entertain.

Purposely, also, I have refrained from adding to or enlarging upon that class of words to which *kabbie-labbie, hush-mush, hippertie-skippertie, nippertie-tippertie* belong. Of such words a large number of examples might easily have been added ; but for all useful purposes the list supplied by the DICTIONARY is sufficiently numerous ; and however interesting such words may be as examples of peculiar combination, they are decidedly of a low class, and are used only among the vulgar. And I may here state regarding a number of very peculiar words explained by JAMIESON, that they are at least questionable, and in some cases mere inventions. Specially so are such words as *breckum-trullie* recorded as used in Ayrshire ; for it is well known that several of them were supplied to the correspondent in that district by way of hoax. They certainly never were in general use even among the vulgar, and they are not worthy of a place in the DICTIONARY.

In the arrangement, grouping, and illustration of the words I have as far as possible followed the plan of the DICTIONARY. In every case where the word has different meanings, the primary one is first given, and the others follow in suitable order : for each of them authority is given and exact references whereby it may be easily verified, or when no authority is given, it is to be understood as in common use. In the references and cross-references the reader will be guided by the following simple rule : words printed in Roman type represent words in the DICTIONARY, and those printed in Italic represent words in the SUPPLEMENT ; while those which are enclosed within square brackets represent words that were added in the new edition.

The statement of the etymology, however, will be found much more simple and uniform than that of the DICTIONARY, and much more concise ; for, the symbols which are used furnish in every case an exact reference to some authority. Thus, the symbol " Icel." means not merely Icelandic, but that the word with which it is connected is taken from Vigfusson's Icelandic Dictionary. For explanation of these symbols see the List of Abbreviations. Still, I have in every case given the actual or probable source of the word, and the authority for the form and interpretation of it which are given ; and when no authority is stated it is to be understood that the word is taken from the book referred to by the etymological symbol. In very many cases cognate forms are given for the sake of further illustration ; but they form no part of the direct history of the word. Again, when the etymology is disputed, or when the word has been used in some important discussion, I have simply stated the fact and referred the reader to the works in which the subject is treated. In a dictionary for general use such discussions are entirely out of place ; to the ordinary reader they are simply confusing, and to the scholar they are too often mere impedimenta. It

INTRODUCTION. ix.

was in this portion of his work that Dr. JAMIESON was led into most of his mistakes. His proneness to discussion often induced him to consider points that had no practical bearing on his subject, to see resemblances that were little better than fancies, and to trace relations that were sometimes impossible. In confirmation of this statement see his etymologies of Tiller, Trone, Torfeir, and Vaudie, and compare them with the corrections which are now given. But, even in our severest criticism of his mistakes and shortcomings, we must be just, and remember how much straighter and smoother the way has been made for us, and how few finger-posts he had to guide him in those paths where we now have many.

As promised in the fourth volume of the new edition of the DICTIONARY, and as a fitting accompaniment to this supplementary volume, a short memoir of Dr. JAMIESON is also given, which, we trust, will be acceptable to the reader.

Having thus sketched the purpose and plan of my work, there remains only the pleasant duty to perform of acknowledging my indebtedness to the many friends who have assisted me in its production. To one and all I tender my most sincere and hearty thanks.

To Professor Skeat of Cambridge I am specially indebted for most valuable assistance in many ways while the work was in progress, and for important additions and corrections while it was passing through the press. Our friendship of more than a quarter of a century enabled me to consult him in every difficulty; and at all times his assistance was promptly and generously given. However much he might be pressed in his own literary work, he never failed in readiness to assist me in mine; and without that assistance the work would have lacked much of its fulness and correctness of details, especially in the section of etymology.

To Dr. Dickson, Curator of the Historical Department of the General Register House, Edinburgh, I am greatly indebted for explanation and illustration of very many of the words, and for most important suggestions regarding the arrangement of the materials. To his careful revisal of the proofs also, I am indebted for several of the most interesting corrections and additional meanings; and I am very grateful for the unwearied patience, and care, and kindness he displayed in all his communications.

To Dr. Marwick, Town Clerk of Glasgow, my best thanks are due for the access to important books and records which he so kindly granted, and for the unfailing courtesy and kindness of his assistants during my frequent visits to his repositories. And in this connection I have specially to thank Robert Renwick, Esq., editor of the Burgh Records of Stirling, for the many and important services which he rendered by making and verifying extracts from the various MSS. published by the Burgh Records Society, by revising the proofs of my work as it was passing through the press, and by supplying materials for several additional entries.

My best thanks are due also to J. W. Cursiter, Esq. of Kirkwall, for several contributions of materials connected with the language and customs of Orkney and Shetland, which have been of immense service to me in many ways. Also, to David Nicolson, Esq. of Wick, I tender sincere thanks for the use of his MS. Notes on the Dialect of Caithness, and of his transcript of Notes and Additions to JAMIESON'S DICTIONARY made by the late Rev. Charles Thomson, one of Dr. JAMIESON'S contributors. Both contributions supplied valuable materials for my work.

To Sir Herbert Maxwell, Bart., M.P., I tender most cordial thanks for several valuable contributions of words peculiar to the South of Scotland, which he voluntarily prepared for me at a time when leisure was scant and precious. My only regret is that his engagements did not permit him to undertake more.

From Dr. Alexander Laing of Newburgh-on-Tay I received several important contributions regarding the Fifeshire dialect, which I have been able to turn to good account; and for these and various other favours I thank him most sincerely. And similarly to James B. Murdoch, Esq., of Glasgow, who has assisted me in various ways, and to all the friends who, by supplying books, by correspondence, or by any other means have helped to further my work, I now tender sincere and hearty thanks.

And now I commit my work to the public with the earnest desire that it may prove useful, and with the sincere wish that, however manifold its defects, it may be accepted as an honest endeavour to accomplish a very difficult task.

MEMOIR OF DR. JAMIESON.

TOWARDS the close of his long and busy career, Dr. Jamieson so far yielded to the entreaties of his friends as to throw together some memoranda of the principal events of his life; but, although they were written with great simplicity and candour, in a reflective spirit, and with considerable graphic force, the work as a whole was found to be unsuitable for publication. From these materials, however, a short but very suitable memoir of the author was compiled for the second and somewhat condensed edition of the SCOTTISH DICTIONARY, issued in 1840-1; and since then, other two accounts of his life have been published.[1] But as that memoir was in substance furnished by the surviving relatives of Dr. Jamieson, it has been selected for our present purpose; and having been slightly recast in order to adapt it to the present time, it is now presented to the public as the most reliable that can be given.

JOHN JAMIESON was born in Glasgow on the 3rd of March, 1759, and was the only son of the Rev. John Jameson, first pastor of the Associate Congregation in Havannah Street (now Duke Street), Glasgow. His mother was the daughter of Mr. Cleland, a merchant of Edinburgh, who had married Rachel, the daughter of the Rev. Robert Bruce of Garlet, son of the second brother of Bruce of Kennet. This excellent man, the great-grandfather of Dr. Jamieson, suffered persecution as a Presbyterian minister during the troubles of Scotland. Dr. Jamieson's paternal grandfather was Mr. William Jameson, farmer of Hill House, near Linlithgow, in West Lothian; a person of respectable connexions, being related to several of the smaller landed proprietors of the county, and to some of the wealthy merchants of the flourishing commercial town of Borrowstounness. But although both his son and his grandson were Seceder ministers, he was himself a strict Episcopalian,—a fact which, from the then prevailing horror of Episcopacy entertained in Scotland, Dr. Jamieson's father seems to have been unwilling to avow, for the Doctor only learned it at an advanced age from his friend Sir Alexander Seton, who recollected William Jameson of Hill House,

---

[1] One appeared in Tait's Edinburgh Magazine for August, 1841; and the other, in the posthumous volume of Dr. Jamieson's Dissertations on the Work of the Spirit, published in 1844. A brief account of this volume is given near the close of the present memoir.

as the sole and very zealous churchwarden of his uncle, the vicar of Riccarton, some eighty years before.

In early life, for some reasons which he describes as puerile, instead of following the orthography of his ancestors, he adopted the different spelling of Jamieson, which it was judged best that he should retain; but he made his family resume the original name of Jameson.

The future lexicographer received his first lessons at a school kept by his father's precentor, named Macnair, a person apparently very incompetent for the task of tuition, and with whom he seems to have been placed more with a view to the advantage of the teacher than of the pupil. After this imperfect course of elementary instruction, and according to the practice then general, and not yet quite obsolete in Scotland, of leaving the English language to shift in a great measure for itself, he was sent in his seventh year to the first class of the Latin grammar-school of Glasgow, then taught by Mr. Bald. He was a master of a stamp not unfrequently met with in those times, being an excellent boon companion, and possessed of great humour, but more than suspected of a leaning in favour of the sons of men of rank, or of those wealthy citizens who occasionally gave him a good dinner, and made liberal *Candlemas offerings*. This partiality having been manifested by unjustly withholding the highest prize of the class from the not rich Seceder minister's son, as Mr. Bald himself afterwards admitted, the boy was withdrawn at the end of the first year. He was then placed under a private teacher named Selkirk, who is described as a worthy man, and under his guidance and the unremitting care of his father at home he made such progress, that he was deemed fit to enter the first "Humanity" or Latin class in the University of Glasgow when only nine years old. Dr. Jamieson, in commenting upon this his very early appearance at the college, gently expresses his regret that his excellent father should have so hurried on his education, and justly remarks, that however vividly impressions may seem to be received by a young mind, they are often so superficial as to be altogether effaced by others which succeed them. The professor of the Humanity class was the Rev. George Muirhead, of whom his pupil entertained the most affectionate recollection, and an "indelible veneration." Muirhead was himself a character; and though something of a pedant, an enthusiastic scholar. He entered with his whole soul into the business of his class. Classical reading, but above all, *Virgil*, was his passion. While a country minister, he had, it was said, purchased a piece of ground to improve in the way prescribed by the "Georgics," which system of husbandry produced its natural consequences. Once that young Jamieson wished to borrow an amusing, though still a Latin Book, from the library belonging to the class, Muirhead addressed him with considerable sternness:—

"John! why would you waste your time on books of that kind?"

"What would you have me to read?" inquired John, with all humility.

The Professor then replied, with great fervour, and to the utter astonishment of the boy—" Read Virgil, sir ; read him night and day—read him *eternally !*" That he did so himself was evident from the black and well-thumbed state of his own copy of Virgil. The other professors were glad when the Session closed, that they might either be off in every direction whither inclination led, or left at leisure for any favourite study or pursuit; but "good old George never left the college, and seemed to have no enjoyment save in stalking like a ghost through the courts and piazzas, solitarily occupying the scenes in which all his earthly delight was concentrated." This "original" boarded with the celebrated brothers Foulis, who, as Printers to the University, were allowed a house within its precincts.

During his second year at the Latin class, young Jamieson also attended the first Greek class, which was then taught by Dr. James Moor, the well-known author of the Greek Grammar which bears his name. Though a man of talent, he was very inferior to Muirhead as a teacher; and his habits were such as to deprive him of that authority over his class which is necessary to maintain order and incite application. To Jamieson, at least, the course was almost entirely lost.

So early in life as this period, the future antiquary was beginning to show a taste for old coins, and other curious objects, on which he expended his pocket-money ; and a vein for poetry at the same time evinced itself. Both predilections were congenial to those of Professor Moor, with whom Jamieson became so far a favourite, that he kindly explained the coins the boy brought to him, and would show him his own valuable collection, acquired while he had travelled with the unfortunate Earl of Kilmarnock. In short, under Moor his pupil seems to have made progress in everything save his proper business, the Greek language. His boyish negligence was partly to be ascribed to the ill-health of his father, who had been struck with palsy, and who subsequently laboured under the effect of repeated shocks. Deeply and repeatedly does the Doctor, in his recollections, regret his idleness—precious time trifled away that could never be recalled. This regret is, however, oftenest to be found in the mouths of those who, like him, have been the most diligent and unremitting in study and in business, and who best know the value of time.

During his attendance on the prelections of Professor Muirhead, his mind received that bias which influenced the literary pursuits of his after life. "The Professor," he says, " not satisfied with an explanation of the words of any classical passage, was most anxious to call the attention of his pupils to the peculiar force of the terms that occurred in it ; particularly pointing out the shades of signification by which those terms, viewed as synonymous, differed from each other. This mode of illustration, which at that time, I suspect, was by no means common, had a powerful influence in attracting my attention to the classical works, and even to the formation of language in general ; and to it I most probably may ascribe that partiality for philological and etymological research in which I have ever since had so much pleasure. I have yet in my possession some of the notes which I took down, either during the class hours or afterwards, from my first attendance on the Humanity class."

The precarious state of his father's health made the studies of an only surviving son, already destined to the ministry, be pushed forward with anxious rapidity. The friendly Professor Muirhead disapproved and remonstrated; but there was too good reason for the precipitance. Jamieson's father afterwards informed him, that he was much afraid that, having been long a prisoner from complicated disease, he would be early taken away; and, as he had nothing to leave his son, he was most desirous to forward his classical and professional education. He was accordingly next session sent to the Logic class, though, as he remarks, "a boy of eleven years of age was quite unfit for studying the abstractions of logic and metaphysics." This year also he considers "entirely lost," and that "it might be blotted out of the calendar of his life." A second year spent in philosophical studies was employed to little more purpose; and though he now studied under the eminent philosopher, Dr. Reid, he had become, during his father's continued illness, too much, he says, his own master to make any great progress "either in the Intellectual or Moral Powers." He took some pleasure in the study of *Mathematics;* but over *Algebra,* on which he consumed the midnight oil, the boy, very naturally, often fell asleep. His classical and philosophical studies were certainly begun in very good time; but it is yet more surprising to find the Associate Presbytery of Glasgow admitting him as a student of theology at the age of fourteen! The Professor of Theology among the Seceders at that period was the Rev. William Moncrieff of Alloa, the son of one of the four ministers who had orignally seceded from the Church of Scotland, from their hostility to Patronage, and who subsequently founded the Secession Church. Though not, according to his distinguished pupil, a man of extensive erudition, or of great depths of understanding, Moncrieff was possessed with qualities even more essential to the fulfilment of his important office of training young men in those days to the Secession ministry; and from the suavity of his disposition, and the kindness of his manners, he was very popular among his students. After attending Professor Moncrieff for one season at Alloa, young Jamieson attended Professor Anderson (afterwards the founder of the Andersonian Institution) in Glasgow, for Natural Philosophy: for which science he does not seem to have had any taste. While at the Glasgow University, he became a member of the different literary societies formed by the students for mutual improvement. These were then the *Eclectic,* the *Dialectic,* and the *Academic;* and he was successively a member of each of them. Their meetings were held in the college class-rooms, and were well attended by students and visitors; and sometimes the professors graced the ingenuous youths with their presence, as an encouragement to diligence.

The Doctor relates many beautiful instances of the mutual respect and cordial

regard which then subsisted among the different denominations of the clergy of Glasgow, and which was peculiarly manifested towards his father during his severe and protracted illness. Comparing modern times with those better days, he says :—
"If matters go on as they have done in our highly favoured country for some time past, there is reason to fear that as little genuine love will be found as there was among the Pharisees, who from sheer influence of party, in a certain sense still 'loved one another,' while they looked on all who differed from them in no other light than they did on Sadducees. May the God of all Grace give a merciful check to this spirit, which is not from Him!"

Dr. Jamieson was himself, throughout the whole course of his life, distinguished by a liberal and truly catholic spirit. His friends and intimate associates were found among Christians of all denominations, though he conscientiously held by his own opinions. If he ever lacked charity, it appears to have been towards the Unitarians, a fact perhaps to be accounted for by his early controversy with Macgill and Dr. Priestly. Episcopalians and Roman Catholics were among his friends, even when his position, as the young minister of a very rigid congregation of Seceders in a country town, made the association dangerous to him, as being liable to misconstruction by his flock.

From his earliest years, Dr. Jamieson seems to have had the happy art of making friends of the wise and the worthy, and especially of persons distinguished for natural powers of the mind, or for great literary attainments. He had the no less enviable power of retaining the regard he had attracted, and of disposing every one with whom he came into contact to forward his views, whether these were for personal or public objects. A really remarkable degree of interest seems to have been taken in his prosperity, and in that of his large family, at every period of his life. From boyhood he had been cordially received into what may assuredly be called the best society at that period known in Scotland,—namely, that of eminent friendly professors, clergymen distinguished by talents and piety, and religious families among the ancient gentry.

Dr. Jamieson, while attending the Theological Lectures of Mr. Moncrieff at Alloa, often enjoyed the hospitality of the Rev. Mr. Randall of Stirling, the father of his friend, Dr. Randall Davidson, afterwards of Muirhouse. The worthy minister of Stirling, whom he represents as of a very generous and cordial nature, would fain, as a friend, have advised the young and active-minded student to leave the Secession, and direct his views to the Established Church, which held out a more inviting prospect to a youth of talents ; for such Jamieson, even then, must have appeared to strangers. The recommendations of Mr. Randall must have been the more tempting, that the cause of the Secession was then viewed with great dislike, and its adherents exposed to the reproach of the world, which youth bears with so much difficulty. But the strong desire of his father, his own convictions, and every kindly influence that had grown up with him, bound him to that cause; and he stood by it through good and through evil report, nor did he ever repent the sacrifice which he had made.

After he had attained the dignity of a student in Theology, instead of condescending to resume the *red gown* of the Glasgow student, he repaired to Edinburgh to prosecute his studies, and lived, while there, in the house of his maternal grandfather, Mr. Cleland. He attended the prelections of the eminent Dugald Stewart, then only rising into fame. He also studied the Hebrew language in a private class; and was admitted a member of a Society of Theological Students, who met once a-week in the class-room of the Hebrew Professor in the University. "A man of great learning and piety, adorned by singular modesty," was this private Professor, who bore the honorary descriptive title—or nickname —of the *Rabbi* Robertson.

During the young student's residence in Edinburgh, he made many valuable and desirable acquaintances, and acquired some useful friends. Of this number was the venerable Dr. John Erskine, who continued the friend of Jamieson for the remainder of his honoured life. He venerated and loved the Evangelical Dr. Erskine, but he also felt great respect for his Moderate colleague, the celebrated Principal Robertson, the Historian. Robertson was long the leader of the Moderate party in the Church Courts; and though a conscientious Seceder, and one in a manner dedicated from his birth to the service of the Secession Church, young Jamieson, on witnessing the masterly manner in which Robertson conducted business in the Church Courts, felt, in his own words, "That if he were to acknowledge any ecclesiastical leader, or call any man a master in divine matters, he would prefer the Principal in this character to any man he had ever seen; for he conducted business with so much dignity and suavity of manner, that those who followed seemed to be led by a silken cord. He might cajole, but he never cudgelled his troops."

After attending the Theological class for six sessions, the candidate for the ministry was, at the age of twenty, appointed by the Synod to be taken on trials for license; and in July 1779, he was licensed by the Presbytery of Glasgow. In the Secession Church at that time, when a young man obtained license he was immediately put on duty, and was appointed to preach within the bounds of the presbytery every Sunday in the year. This was indeed a most important part of his training for the regular ministry; though it allowed very little time for the preparation of sermons between the closing of his public theological studies and the commencement of his itinerancy. In the wide district in which Jamieson's duties lay, there were, at the time, many vacancies, and also the germs of new congregations; so that the scenes of his labours on successive Sabbaths lay often far apart.

Dr. Jamieson's first appearance as a preacher was at Colmonell, in Carrick in Ayrshire, then a very dreary and poor place. From the first he seems to have been popular, and this small isolated congregation wished to obtain the young preacher as their pastor; but to this he gave no encouragement, deeming it his duty to leave such matters to the regular authorities, applied to through the forms usual upon such occasions. His next appointment was to the Isle of Bute, and Cowal in Argyleshire. The picture which he gives of characters and of manners, more than a century ago, and their contrast with those of present times, is not a little striking. The venerable Doctor, in old age, relates, "I found my situation on this beautiful island very comfortable. The place of preaching was in Rothesay. I lodged at a farm-house in the parish of Kingarth; and I never met with more kindness from any man than from —— ——, the minister of the parish." This was not at all in accordance with the Doctor's subsequent experiences of the Established ministers in other parishes, and particularly when he came to be settled in Forfar. A nephew of the minister of Kingarth had written from Glasgow, apprizing him of the young Seceder preacher's invasion of his parish, and recommending the encroacher to his kindness. The Doctor continues, "I had no sooner taken up my residence than he came to call for me, and urged me in the most strenuous manner to come to his manse. When I expressed my sense of his great kindness, declining to receive the benefit of it as delicately as I could, he told me that if I persisted in my refusal, he would attribute it solely to *bigotry;* as he supposed I could have no other reason for preferring the accommodation of a cottage to that of his house, save my unwillingness to reside under the roof of a *kirk minister.*" To convince him of the reverse, the young Seceder finally agreed to spend *one* night at the manse; a proceeding probably somewhat hazardous, from the jealousy of such intercourse sometimes felt by the dissenting flocks. This clergyman belonged to a class of Moderates which has for ever passed away. He went out daily with his dog and gun, and often stepping into the cottage, surprised the Seceder preacher poring over his next Sabbath day's discourse.

Dr. Jamieson passed over to Cowal in the depth of a severe winter, and was received in a wretched smoky hovel, without even glass to the aperture through which light was received; and there he had to eat, sleep, and study. These were not the palmy days of the Secession Church, whose followers have now reared comfortable and often handsome edifices for worship in every district of Scotland, and provided liberally for the subsistence of their ministers. The young preacher was submitting most christianly or philosophically to dire necessity, when he received a kind invitation from an elderly lady to take up his abode in the mansion of Achavuillin, then belonging to a family of the name of Campbell, though it has long since changed its fine Celtic appellation with its proprietor, and become the modern Castle Toward. There the stranger was treated with the hospitality which characterized the country and the period. The master of the house was then in America with his regiment; for the war of the revolution still raged: but his mother did the honours of his house; and some of the younger inmates even accompanied the preacher to his romantic place of worship, which might have been that of the Druids, once so well known in the same locality. "It was," says the Doctor, "in the open air, by the side of a rivulet: the congregation being assembled on a slight acclivity, at the bottom of which it ran. I stood in the hollow, having a large moor-stone for my pedestal, the ground being covered with a pretty deep layer of snow, which had fallen in the night. For my canopy I had a pair of blankets stretched on two poles. The situation was sufficiently romantic ; for, besides the circumstances already mentioned, the sea flowed behind, and the mountains of Argyleshire terminated the prospect before. Notwithstanding the severity of the weather, I never addressed a more sedate auditory, nor one apparently more devout."

In the beginning of 1780, Mr. Jamieson was appointed by the Associate Synod (the Supreme Court of the Secession) to itinerate in Perthshire and the neighbouring county of Angus. After preaching for several Sabbaths in Dundee, in which there was then a vacancy, he made so favourable an impression, that the congregation agreed to give him a call to be their pastor. But Forfar, his next preaching station, was to be his resting-place, and for many years an ungenial and dreary sojourn. To Forfar he was at that time, of course, a total stranger ; and in old age he touchingly relates :—" Though I were to live much longer than I have done since that time, I shall never forget the feeling I had in crossing the rising-ground, where I first had a view of this place. I had never seen any part of the country before. The day was cold, the aspect of the country dreary and bleak, and it was partly covered with snow. It seemed to abound with mosses, which gave a desolate appearance to the whole valley under my eye. I paused for a moment, and a pang struck through my heart, while the mortifying query occurred—' What if this gloomy place should be the bounds of my habitation?' And it was the will of the Almighty that it should be so."

The congregation of Forfar was at that time but newly formed, and had never yet had any regular minister, being, by orders of the Presbytery, *supplied*, as it is termed, from Sabbath to Sabbath by young probationers and others.

Three calls were at the same time subscribed for the popular young preacher ; from Forfar, from Dundee, and from Perth, where he was wanted as a second or collegiate minister. The congregation of Dundee was large and comparatively wealthy, but the call was not unanimous.

Either Dundee, or the second charge in Perth, would have been a much more agreeable and advantageous appointment for Mr. Jamieson; but the Synod allotted him the small, poor, and ill-organized congregation of Forfar, which with difficulty managed to allow him a stipend of £50 a-year. It is to be hoped that the motives of the Ecclesiastical Court in this choice were pure, and that, as Perth and Dundee might be considered comparatively safe even with inferior candidates, they were induced, as a matter of policy, to send a popular, active, and able young man to a new locality, where the congregation required to be consolidated. However this might be, Mr. Jamieson felt, and not without some degree of bitterness, that the decision was most unfavourable to him in every respect. He had lived enough in towns, and among the better classes, and had seen enough of the difficulties of his father with a stipend nearly double, to be fully aware of the utter inadequacy of that allowed him. With regard to society, he could maintain little social intercourse with the uneducated persons composing his congregation, and beyond them he was not only without any connexions in the place, but had to contend with coldness and dislike, arising from that prejudice against the Secession before alluded to, and which appears to have been very strong in Forfar. Some ludicrous instances are given of petty persecution from that cause, particularly on the part of the minister of the Established Church, who seems to have considered Jamieson, and the Episcopalian clergyman of the place, as two refractory parishioners, and to have assumed an air of insulting superiority strangely misplaced.

On the whole, it is not easy to conceive a position more trying in every respect than that of the young minister at his outset in Forfar; and a man of less energy, although of equal talents, would probably have been altogether lost in it. There was, however, one bright side : he was affectionately, nay, anxiously wished for by the whole of his congregation ; and this unanimity afforded some consolation to him, as well as to his father,—the latter recollecting that, although he had been opposed in his call to Glasgow by only two persons, the two had proved thorns in his side as long as they lived. Besides, Mr. Jamieson knew that he was in the path of duty; and, piously resigning "his lot into the hands of the All-Wise Disposer of events," with the assurance which followed him through life, "that his gracious Master would provide for him in the way that was best," he looked forward to the future with firmness.

The struggle was severe at first, but by degrees he became better known and better appreciated. He acknowledged with marked gratitude the obligations he owed, in that respect, to Mr. Dempster of Dunnichen, a gentleman of high character and considerable influence in the county, which he represented for some time in Parliament. This amiable person was his first, and proved through life his fastest friend. Until this acquaintance with Mr. Dempster, which was brought about by an accidental call, his only enjoyment was in visiting at intervals several respectable families in Perth and its neighbourhood, or the hospitable manse of Longforgan in the Carse of Gowrie, then a residence combining every charm. But the friendship and influence of Mr. Dempster procured similar enjoyments for him nearer home. At Dunnichen, indeed, he was a welcome guest at all times, and there he became acquainted, through the cordial introduction of Mr. Dempster, with all the landed aristocracy of the county. This enlargement of Mr. Jamieson's circle of social intercourse was further aided and confirmed by his marriage, about a year after his settlement in Forfar, with the daughter of an old and respectable proprietor in the county, Miss Charlotte Watson, youngest daughter of Robert Watson, Esq. of Shielhill in Angus, and of Easter Rhynd in Perthshire. Mr. Jamieson, when very young, had frequently heard a friend speak with affectionate admiration of the family of Shielhill,—of their hospitality, and of their regard for

c

religion,—the latter a quality not very common at the time amongst the landed proprietors of that part of the country. He was thus predisposed to esteem the whole family, some of whom he had, before coming to Forfar, seen in his father's house at Glasgow.

It must have appeared almost madness to think of marriage with so very limited an income, even allowing for the greater value of money at that time; but the bachelor state was deemed incompatible with the ministry in Scotland; and, besides, prudential motives do not always prevent a young man from falling in love. The union, however, which soon took place, and which lasted for more than half a century, proved in all respects a most auspicious one. Mr. and Mrs. Jamieson had no doubt for a long period much to contend with from limited means and a very numerous family; but the untiring industry of Mr. Jamieson soon made up for all other deficiencies.

Mr. Jamieson's confidence in Providence, and in his own energies, thus began to reap its reward. To loneliness at home, and indifference if not neglect abroad, there now succeeded strong domestic attractions, and the esteem and regard of respectable neighbours.

Shortly after his marriage, he began to work seriously for the Press, and he continued for upwards of forty years to be a constant and even voluminous writer. While yet a mere stripling, he composed some pieces of poetry for Ruddiman's Weekly Magazine, which we notice only because they were his first appearance as an author. We next find him communicating, in a series of papers to the Literary and Antiquarian Society of Perth, of which he was a member, the fruits of his researches concerning the antiquities of Forfarshire. These papers led Mr. Dempster to recommend his writing a history of the county, and the suggestion gave impulse and direction to his local inquiries, although it was never fully complied with. But the publication which first seems to have obtained for him some literary reputation, and the character of an orthodox and evangelical minister, was his reply, under the title of "Socinianism Unmasked," to Dr. Macgill of Ayr, whose peculiar heresy had lately been broached.

This work paved the way for his favourable reception in London, which he visited for the first time in 1788-9. He carried to London with him a collection of sermons, afterwards published under the title of "Sermons on the Heart," which became very popular. With the exception of this work, his other writings do not seem to have yielded him in general much profit, although they added to his reputation. Letters given him by Dr. Erskine and others procured for him an extensive acquaintance, particularly in the religious circles and with the evangelical ministers of the metropolis. It was thus he became acquainted with the pious and benevolent Mr. Thornton, the eccentric Ryland the Baptist minister, John Newton, Venn, and Cecil. There also he found antiquarian and literary associates, while his poem on the "Sorrows of Slavery," brought him under the notice of the abolitionists, and led to an acquaintance with Wilberforce and Granville Sharpe.

The consideration he enjoyed in these metropolitan circles, and particularly amongst his religious friends, must have been augmented by his "Reply to Priestley," for which he received the diploma of Doctor of Divinity from the College of New Jersey, the first honour of the kind that had been conferred upon a Seceder.

Dr. Jamieson repeated his visits to London at different times, officiating there for his friend Dr. Jerment, while that gentleman went to see his connexions in Scotland. On these occasions, he extended the circle of his general acquaintance, and appears also to have discovered several distant relations mixing in good society. One of them was a distant female cousin, Lady Strange, the widow of the celebrated engraver, who to her last day took pride in her broad Scotch, and otherwise retained all the warmth of early national feeling. When the Doctor, till then a stranger to her, made his formal obeisance, "the good old lady," he says, "ran up to me with all the vivacity of fifteen, and taking me in her arms, gave me a hearty embrace." She was one of those whose heads and hearts are continually occupied with plans for serving their friends; and her influence, of which she had a good deal, was ever zealously exerted to promote Dr. Jamieson's interests. One of her schemes was that he should leave the Secession and look for promotion in the Church of England; but such an idea, it may well be believed, had still less chance of being for a moment harboured by him, than that before mentioned of his entering into the Church of Scotland, although he had now been lingering on for more than a dozen of years on the same pittance of £50 a-year.

During this long lapse of time, his greatest enjoyment, beyond his own fireside, was still found in the society and steady friendship of Mr. Dempster. "Many a happy day," he writes, "have I spent under the roof of this benevolent man. We walked together; we rode together; we fished together; we took an occasional ride to examine the remains of antiquity in the adjacent district; and if the weather was bad, we found intellectual employment in the library,—often in tracing the origin of our vernacular words in the continental languages."

The Doctor had not yet projected his great work, the Dictionary; the first idea of which arose accidentally from the conversation of one of the many distinguished persons whom he met at Mr. Dempster's residence; Dunnichen being long the frequent rendezvous of not merely the most eminent men of Scotland, but of such learned foreigners as from time to time visited the country. This was the learned Grim Thorkelin, Professor of Antiquities in Copenhagen. Up to this period, Dr Jamieson had held the common opinion, that the Scottish is not a language, and nothing more than a corrupt dialect of the English, or at least of the Anglo-Saxon. The learned Danish Professor first undeceived him,—though full conviction came tardily,—and proved to his satisfaction that there are many words in our national tongue which never passed through the channel of the Anglo-

Saxon, nor were even spoken in England. Before leaving Dunnichen, Thorkelin requested the Doctor to note down for him all the singular words used in that part of the country, no matter how vulgar he might himself consider them; and to give the received meaning of each. Jamieson laughed at the request, saying, "What would you do, Sir, with our vulgar words; they are merely corruptions of English?" Thorkelin, who spoke English fluently, replied with considerable warmth, "If that *fantast*, Johnson, had said so, I would have forgiven *him*, because of his ignorance or prejudice; but I cannot make the same excuse for you, when you speak in this contemptuous manner of the language of your country, which is, in fact, more ancient than the English. I have now spent four months in Angus and Sutherland, and I have met with between three and four hundred words purely Gothic, that were never used in Anglo-Saxon. You will admit that I am pretty well acquainted with Gothic. I am a Goth; a native of Iceland, the inhabitants of which are an unmixed race, who speak the same language which their ancestors brought from Norway a thousand years ago. All or most of these words which I have noted down, are familiar to me in my native island. If you do not find out the sense of some of the terms which strike you as singular, send them to me; and I am pretty certain I shall be able to explain them to you." Jamieson, to oblige the learned stranger, forthwith purchased a two-penny paper book, and began to write down all the remarkable or uncouth words of the district. From such small beginnings, made more than twenty years before any part of the work was published, arose the four large quarto volumes of his DICTIONARY and SUPPLEMENT, the revolution in his opinion as to the origin of the Scottish language, and that theory of its origin which he has maintained in the learned Dissertations which accompany the Dictionary.

It would not now be easy, we apprehend, to explain the difficulties, discouragements, and privations under which that great undertaking was prosecuted for a long series of years. The author had now a large family to maintain and to educate, and he was even embarrassed with debts inevitably incurred, while the prospect of remuneration for his labours was distant and uncertain. How he and Mrs. Jamieson struggled through their accumulating difficulties, might probably have puzzled themselves on looking back to explain; but he was strong in faith, and also active in endeavour.

On the death of Mr. Adam Gib, Dr. Jamieson received a call from the Seceder congregation of Nicolson Street, Edinburgh, to be their minister. But the Synod again opposed both the wishes of the congregation, and Dr. Jamieson's interests and obvious advantage; and that, too, at a period when his removal to the capital would have been of the greatest advantage to his literary projects, and to the professional education of his elder sons. He very naturally felt with acuteness this second frustration of his reasonable hopes; but, as before, he quietly submitted. A few years more elapsed, and Mr. Banks, the successor of Mr. Gib, having gone to America, the doctor was again unanimously called, and the Synod then thought fit to authorize his translation. The change from Forfar to Edinburgh was, in every point of view, a happy and auspicious event. His stipend was probably quadrupled at once : he was restored to early connexions and literary society, and obtained every facility for prosecuting his philological and etymological researches. Shortly after this he learnt that the Rev. Mr. Boucher, Vicar of Epsom, was engaged in a work of somewhat similar character; and mutual friends advised that the one should buy the other off, and obtain the accumulated materials for the use of his own work. Any reward for his labours, however inadequate, was then an important consideration with Dr. Jamieson; and for a time he thought of giving up his treasures for £250; but the dislike which he had felt from the beginning, at the idea either of compromise or co-operation, afterwards fortified by suspicions that Mr. Boucher's view of the Scottish language would degrade it to the level of the English dialects, and the conscientious conduct of the friend of the vicar, the late Bishop Gleig of Stirling, who was too well aware of the real value of Dr. Jamieson's manuscripts to sanction such a sacrifice, ultimately and happily put a stop to the negotiation. The subsequent death of the Rev. Mr. Boucher, before the publication of his work, left the field clear for our national lexicographer. It is not merely as patriotic natives of Scotland, that we rejoice in this circumstance, but as the friends of sound literature; and as prizing yet more highly than the learning displayed, that fund of innocent and delightful entertainment and instruction, spread before us in the pages of the Scottish Dictionary ;—those imperishable records of our history, our literature, and our usages, which may enable all future generations of our countrymen, and their off-sets in every distant land, to think and feel as *ancient* Scots; and which will keep open for them the literary treasures of their fathers--the pages of their Burns and Scott, and of those other works which, but for this master-key, must soon become sealed books.

The people of Scotland certainly never took so great an interest in any work that had appeared in their country as they took in the Dictionary. It was every one's concern; and after the first two volumes had been published, and had set many thousand minds at work to add to, or endeavour to render more perfect, this national monument, from the palace and the castle to the farm-house and the cottage the learned author found devoted and often able auxiliaries in completing his great undertaking. Those who could not assist him with *words*, yet circulated his prospectuses, and procured subscribers to the work. Through the interest and exertions of Lord Glenbervie, the duty on the paper for printing the Dictionary was remitted, in virtue of a provision entitling the publishers of works on *Northern Literature* to a drawback on the paper used. Among his friends of a later period, none were more zealous than the late Duchess of Sutherland, through whose interest or recommendation he was afterwards chosen one of the ten Associates of the Royal Literary Society, instituted by George the Fourth. Each Associate was entitled to a pension of one hundred guineas. The Society, which numbered among its members Coleridge and D'Israeli, fell with George the Fourth, which occasioned no little disappointment and hardship to some of the Associates. The fact, as it regards Dr. Jamieson, serves to bring to light a circumstance highly honourable to both the parties concerned. The Doctor had by this time, in consequence of advancing age and indifferent health, resigned the charge of his congregation on a retiring salary of £150; and other sources of annual income had been dried up at the same time. He would, therefore, willingly have had the pension restored by Government, and addressed himself to Earl Spencer with that view. The Earl, unable to effect any change in the councils of King William, generously and in the most delicate terms offered to continue the Doctor's allowance out of his own pocket, and at once sent an order on the house of Sir William Forbes & Co. for the first half-yearly payment. This munificence on the part of a stranger to one having no possible claim upon him, save as a man of letters, whom he might imagine to be placed in difficulties in his old age by a measure of financial economy, made a deep impression on Dr. Jamieson's mind; and it may well be supposed, that although he declined the proffered assistance, he did so with much feeling, and with expressions of sincere gratitude. The correspondence about this affair must have left warm feelings of mutual regard and satisfaction in the minds of both these excellent men; indeed, so much was this the case, that Earl Spencer left him by will a legacy of £100 per annum, as a mark of his esteem and respect. In 1833 the pension was in Dr. Jamieson's case restored through some secret court influence; Earl Grey, then Premier, himself announcing that the Doctor had been placed on his Majesty's Civil List for a pension to the amount of that which he had lost by the dissolution of the Literary Society instituted by George the Fourth.

Dr. Jamieson's severest affliction had been in seeing the greater part of his numerous family descend to the grave before him: some in infancy and childhood, but others in the prime of life and of usefulness. Of seven sons who reached manhood, only one survived him. Three died in India; of whom two had arrived at distinction in the medical service. His second son, Mr. Robert Jameson, an eminent member of the Scottish bar, long in lucrative practice, and entitled to look forward to the highest honours of his profession, was cut off a few years before his venerable parent. But his last, and the heaviest blow of all, was the loss of Mrs. Jamieson, a lady equally remarkable for the good qualities of her head and of her heart, and who had shared his lot for fifty-five years.

In the latter years of his life, Dr. Jamieson suffered much from bilious attacks, for which he was recommended to try the waters of different noted Spas in Scotland. From such stations as Pitcaithley, the Moffat Wells, or Inverleithen, he was in the habit of making rounds of visits to those families of the neighbouring nobility and gentry who had been among his earlier friends. The banks of the Tweed between Peebles and Berwick had ever been to him a more favourite and familiar haunt than even the banks of his native Clyde; and many of the happiest days of his later summers were spent amidst the lovely scenes of "Tweedside," and among the friends and relatives which he possessed in that classic district. He had always been fond of angling ; and in the Tweed and its tributary streams, he socially pursued the " gentle craft," almost to the close of life. Of the houses which he had long been in the habit of visiting on Tweedside, none seems to have left a more indelible impression on his memory than Ashestiel, the happy intermediate residence of Sir Walter Scott, whom Dr. Jamieson had first visited in his little cottage at Lasswade, and,—for the last of many times,—in the lordly halls of Abbotsford only a very short while before Scott went abroad, never again to return—*himself.*

One of the most important public affairs in which Dr. Jamieson was ever engaged, was bringing about the union of the two branches of the Secession, the Burghers and Antiburghers. Those only who understand the history of these great divisions of the Seceders, and their mutual jealousies and dissensions, can appreciate the difficulty and the value of the service of again uniting them, and the delicacy, sagacity, and tact which it required. To this healing measure, which he had deeply at heart, Dr. Jamieson was greatly instrumental.

Notwithstanding his bilious and nervous disorders, the Doctor seems, considering his laborious and often harassing life, to have enjoyed up to a great age a tolerable measure of health. His "*Recollections,*" to which he appears to have added from time to time as memory restored the more interesting events and reminiscences of his earlier years, seem to have terminated abruptly in 1836. He died in his house in George's Square, Edinburgh, on the 12th of July, 1838, universally regretted, esteemed, and beloved for his learning, piety, and social qualities, and as one of the links which connected Scottish society with the past.

Besides the different books which Dr. Jamieson edited, such as Barbour's Bruce, and Blind Harry's Wallace, in two volumes quarto, Slezer's *Theatrum Scotiæ,* with a memoir of the author, and other works,—among the more important of his multifarious original writings are the following :—

Socinianism Unmasked	1786.
The Sorrows of Slavery. A poem.	London, 1789.
Sermons on the Heart, 2 vols. 8vo.	London, 1790.
Congal and Fenella. A metrical tale, in two parts. . .	London, 1791.
Reply to Dr. Priestley, 2 vols.	1795.
Eternity. A poem.	1798.
Remarks on Rowland Hill's Journal. . . .	1799.
The Use of Sacred History, 2 vols. 8vo. . . .	1802.
An Important Trial in the Court of Conscience, 12mo. .	1806.
An Etymological Dictionary of the Scottish Language, 2 vols. 4to.	Edinburgh, 1808.
Abridgment of Dictionary, 8vo.	1818.

An Historical Account of the Ancient Culdees of Iona. . Edinburgh, 1811.
Hermes Scythicus, or the Radical Affinities of the Greek and
 Latin Languages to the Gothic, 8vo. . . . Edinburgh, 1814.
Supplement to Dictionary of the Scottish Language, 2 vols. 4to. Edinburgh, 1825.
Historical Account of the Royal Palaces of Scotland. . Edinburgh,

Besides these works, he left in MS. carefully prepared for the press, a series of Dissertations on the Reality of the Spirit's Influence, on which he had been engaged for more than fifty years. Shortly before his death he entrusted the work to two of his dearest friends, and instructed them to dispose of it to the best advantage, and to devote the proceeds to the fund for aiding the orphans and decayed ministers of the Secession. For various reasons the work was not published till 1844, and its success has been very limited.

Dr. Jamieson at different periods received literary honours. He was a member of the Society of Scottish Antiquaries, and long acted as one of its secretaries. He was a member of the Royal Physical Society of Edinburgh; of the American Antiquarian Society of Boston; and of the Copenhagen Society of Northern Literature; and, while it existed, he was a Royal Associate of the first class of the Literary Society instituted by George IV. At a comparatively early period of his career he received, as has been mentioned above, the degree of Doctor in Divinity, with a regular diploma from the College of New Jersey, in the United States of America.

LIST OF BOOKS, MANUSCRIPTS, AND EDITIONS QUOTED IN THIS WORK.

A.

AASEN's Norsk Ordbog, Christiania, 1873. Referred to by Norw.
Accounts of the Lord High Treasurer of Scotland, vol. i., A.D. 1473-1498, ed. Thomas Dickson, LL.D. Edin., 1877. Scot. Record Series.
Acts of the Lords Auditors of Causes and Complaints, 1466-1494, ed. Thomas Thomson. Edin., 1839. Scot. Record Series.
Acts of the Lords of Council in Civil Causes, A.D. 1478-1495, ed. Thomas Thomson. Edin., 1839. Scot. Record Series.
Acts of the Parliaments of Scotland, ed. Thomas Thomson and Cosmo Innes, 12 vols. Edin., 1814-1875. Scot. Record Series.
Ælfric's Glossary, printed in Wright's Vocabularies.
Æneid of Virgil Translated into Scottish Verse by Gawin Douglas, Bishop of Dunkeld, ed. George Dundas. Edin., 1839. Bann. Club Series.
—————— ed. Thomas Ruddiman. Edin., 1710.
Agricultural Surveys of the Counties of Scotland., Edin., V. Y.
Alliterative Romance of Alexander, ed. Rev. Joseph Stevenson, M.A. London, 1849. Roxburghe Club Series.
Ancient Ballads and Songs of the North of Scotland, ed. Peter Buchan, 2 vols. Edin., 1828.
Ancient Laws and Customs of the Burghs of Scotland, 1124-1424, ed. Cosmo Innes. Edin., 1868. Burgh Rec. Soc. Series.
Ancient Mysteries Described, by W. Hone, London, 1823.
Ancient Scottish Ballads, ed, G. R. Kinloch. Edin., 1827.
Ancient Scottish Poems from the Bannatyne MS., ed. Sir D. Dalrymple. Edin., 1770.
Ancient Scottish Poems—The Gaberlunzie-Man, and Christ's Kirk on the Green, ed. John Callander, Esq. of Craigforth. Edin., 1782.
Ancient Scottish Prophecies in Alliterative Verse, reprinted from the ed. of 1603. Edin., 1833. Bann. Club. Series.
Anglo-Saxon—Ettmüller, L., Lexicon Anglo-Saxonicum. Leipzig, 1851.
Anglo-Saxon Chronicle, ed. B. Thorpe, 2 vols. 1861.
Annals of Dunfermline, ed. E. Henderson, LL.D. Glasgow, 1879.
Antiquaries of Scotland, Transactions of the Society of Edin., V. Y.
Archæological and Historical Collections relating to the Counties of Ayr and Wigton, 4 vols. 1879-84.
—————— relating to the County of Renfrew, vol. i., Paisley, 1885.
Arnot's Criminal Trials. Edin., 1785.
Atkinson's Glossary of the Cleveland Dialect. London, 1868.
Awntyrs of Arthur : see Robson's Met. Rom. ; Laing's Anc. Pop. Poetry; Sir Gawayne; and Pinkerton's Scot.

Poems Reprinted. Pinkerton called it Sir Gawan and Sir Galaron of Galloway.
Ayenbite of Inwyt, or Remorse of Conscience, by Dan Michel of Northgate, ed. R. Morris. E.E.T.S., 1866.
Aytoun, Prof. W. E., The Ballads of Scotland, 2 vols. Edin., 1859.
—————— Lays of the Scottish Cavaliers. Edin., 1864.

B.

Bailey, N., Universal Etymological English Dictionary, seventh edition. London, 1735.
—————— English Dictionary, vol. ii. London, 1727.
Balfour, David, Oppressions in Orkney. Edin., 1860. Mait. Club Series.
—————— Odal Rights and Feudal Wrongs. Edin., 1860.
Ballad Minstrelsy of Scotland, Romantic and Historical. Glasgow, 1871.
Ballantine, James, The Gaberlunzie's Wallet. Edin., 1874.
Banffshire Dialect, ed. Rev. W. Gregor, Trans. Phil. Soc., 1866.
Bannatyne Club Publications.
Buke of the Howlat ; Robene and Makyne and Testament of Crosscid ; King James the Sext ; Palice of Honour ; Diary of James Melvill ; Spalding's Troubles in Scotland ; Pitcairn's Criminal Trials ; Scottish Prophecies in Verse ; Diurnal of Remarkable Occurrents ; Memorable Transactions in Scotland ; The Seven Sages; Sir Gawayne ; The Æneid of Virgil; Booke of the Universal Kirk ; Origines Parochiales ; Black Book of Taymouth.
Bannatyne MS., 1568, in Advocates' Library, Edinburgh. Glasgow, 1873-1881. Hunt. Club Series.
Barbour's Bruce, ed. John Pinkerton, 3 vols. London, 1790.
—————— ed. John Jamieson, D.D. Edin., 1820. This edition is based on the Edin. MS.
—————— ed. Cosmo Innes, in Spalding Club series. Aberdeen, 1856. This ed. is based on a collation of the various MSS. and printed editions.
—————— ed. W. W. Skeat, LL.D., in E. E. T. S. series. London, 1870-1877. This edition is based on the Camb. MS.
—————— Legends of the Saints, ed. Dr. C. Horstmann, Berlin, and pub. by Henniger Bros., Heilbronn.
Bellenden's Historie and Cronikis of Scotland. Edin., 1536.
—————— Translation of the First Five Books of Livy. Edin., 1822.
Black Book of Taymouth, with other papers from the Breadalbane Charter Room, ed. Cosmo Innes. Edin. 1855. Bann. Club Series.

d

Blame of Kirkburiall, Tending to Perswade Cemiteriall Civilitie, by Mr. William Birnie, minister of Lanark, A.D. 1606, ed. W. B. D. D. Turnbull, Esq. Reprint, London, 1833.
Blind Harry's Wallace, ed. James Moir, M.A. Edin., 1885-6. Scot. Text Soc.
———————— ed. Dr. Jamieson. Edin. 1820.
Blount's Law Dictionary, second edition. London, 1691.
Book of Customs and Valuation of Merchandises in Scotland, 1612; see Halyburton's Ledger, in Scottish Record Publications.
Book of Days: A Miscellany of Popular Antiquities, ed. R. Chambers, LL.D., 2 vols. Lond. and Edin., 1866-8.
Book of the Universal Kirk of Scotland: Acts and Proceedings of the General Assemblies of the Kirk of Scotland since 1560, ed. Thomas Thomson, 3 vols. Edin. 1839-45. Bann. Club Series.
———————— ed. Alex. Peterkin. Edin., 1839.
Bosworth's Anglo-Saxon Dictionary, London, 1838.
———————— Compendious Anglo-Saxon and English Dictionary, London, 1848.
Brachet's Etymological French Dictionary, tr. by G. W. Kitchin. Oxford, 1873.
Brand, John, M.A., Observations on Popular Antiquities, with additions by H. Ellis, 3 vols. London, 1848.
Bremen Wörterbuch, 5 vols. Bremen, 1767. Referred to by L. Ger.
Brewer, Rev. Dr., Dictionary of Phrase and Fable, third edition. London, n. d.
———————— The Reader's Handbook of References. London, 1880.
British Animals, History of, ed. John Fleming, D.D. London, 1842.
Brockett, J. T., Glossary of North Country Words, third edition, 2 vols. Newcastle, 1846.
Buchan Dialect—Poems,&c., including Ajax Speech to the Grecian Knabbs, and Ulysses' Answer, &c. Edin., 1785.
———————— Footdee in the Last Century, and The Goodwife at Home. Aberdeen, 1872.
———————— Douglas, rendered by George Smith: see Douglas, a Tragedy, etc.
Buchan, Peter: see Ancient Ballads and Songs.
Buik of the Croniclis of Scotland, or a Metrical Version of the History of Hector Boece, by William Stewart; ed. W. B. Turnbull, 3 vols. London, 1858. Rolls Series.
Burgh Records of Aberdeen, from 1398 to 1625, ed. John Stuart, LL.D., 2 vols. Aberdeen, 1844-8. Spald. Club Series.
———— of Aberdeen, from 1625 to 1747, ed. John Stuart, LL.D., 2 vols. Edin., 1871-2. Burgh Rec. Soc. Series.
———— of Edinburgh, from 1403 to 1643, ed. Dr. Marwick, 4 vols. Edin., 1870. Burgh Rec. Soc. Series.
———— of Glasgow, from 1573 to 1581, ed. John Smith, Esq., 2 vols. Glasgow, 1832-4. Mait. Club Series.
———— of Glasgow, from 1573 to 1660, ed. Dr. Marwick, 2 vols. Glasgow, 1876. Burgh Rec. Soc. Series.
———— of Peebles and Important Charters, from 1165 to 1710, with Preface by W. Chambers, Esq., LL.D. Edinburgh, 1873. Burgh Rec. Soc. Series.
———— of Prestwick, from 1472 to 1782, ed. John Fullarton, Esq. Glasgow, 1834. Mait. Club Series.
———— of Stirling, from 1519 to 1666, ed. Robert Renwick, Esq. Glasgow, 1887. Printed for the Glasgow Stirlingshire Soc.
Burgh Schools of Scotland, History of, by James Grant, M.A. London, 1876.
Burguy's Glossaire. In tome III. of Grammaire de la Langue D'Oïl, par G. F. Burguy, 2me edition. Berlin and Paris, 1870.

Burns, R., Poems, Songs, and Letters (Globe edition), 1868.
Burns, R., Poetical Works, ed. Rev. R. A. Willmott. London, 1866.
———————— Poetical Works, ed. W. S. Douglas, 2 vols. Kilmarnock, 1871.

C.

Cædmon, ed. B. Thorpe; published by the Society of Antiquaries, London, 1832.
Calendar of Documents Relating to Scotland, preserved in H. M. Public Record Office, London, ed. Joseph Bain. Vol. I., 1108-1272, Edin. 1881. Scot. Rec. Series.
Catholik and Facile Traictise, by Jhone Hamilton. Paris, 1581.
Chambers's Etymological Dictionary of the English Language, ed. J. Donald. Edin., 1880.
Chambers, Robert, LL.D., The Scottish Ballads, collected and illustrated by. Edin., 1829.
———————— The Scottish Songs, collected and illustrated by. Edin. 1829.
———————— The Romantic Scottish Ballads, their Epoch and Authorship. Edin. 1859.
———————— Popular Rhymes of Scotland. Edin. 1842.
———————— Songs of Scotland Prior to Burns. Edin. n. d.
———————— Miscellany of Popular Scottish Poems. Edin. 1869.
———————— Book of Days: a Miscellany of Popular Antiquities, 2 vols. London and Edin., 1866-8.
Charters of the Royal Burgh of Ayr, printed for the Ayr and Wigton Archæological Association. Edin., 1883.
———— of the Friars Preachers of Ayr, printed for the Ayr and Wigton Arch. Assoc., Edin. 1881.
———— of Edinburgh, 1143-1540. Edin. 1871. Burgh Rec. Soc.
———— of Peebles; see Burgh Records of Peebles.
———— of the Royal Burgh of Stirling, 1124-1705, printed for the Provost and Magistrates of the Burgh, Glasgow, 1884.
———— of the Abbey of Crossraguel, 2 vols. Ayr and Galloway Archæological Association, 1886.
Chaucer, Canterbury Tales, six-text edition, ed. F. J. Furnival. Chaucer Soc.
Chaucer, Canterbury Tales, ed. Tyrwhitt, with reprints of Chaucer's Minor Poems, &c. London, E. Moxon, 1855.
Child, Prof. F. J., English and Scottish Ballads, 8 vols. London, 1861.
Cochran-Patrick, LL.D., R. W., Coinage of Scotland, 2 vols. Edinburgh, 1880.
———————— Ancient Mining in Scotland. Edinburgh, 1878.
Cocke Lorelle's Bote. London, 1817. Roxburghe Club.
Colkelbie Sow; see Laing's Anc. Pop. Poetry of Scotland, or Bannatyne MS. in the Hunterian Club Series.
Collections for a History of the Shires of Aberdeen and Banff, ed. Joseph Robertson. Aberdeen, 1843. Spald. Club.
Complaynte of Scotlande, re-edited by James A. H. Murray (E.E.T.S., extra series), 1872-3.
Cornhill Baron Court Book; see Ayr and Wigton Arch. Coll., vol. iv.
Cotgrave, R., French and English Dictionary, with another in English and French, ed. Robert Sherwood. London, pr. by Adam Islip, 1632.
Court of Venus, by John Rolland in Dalkeith, 1575, ed. Rev. W. Gregor, LL.D. Edin., 1884. Scot. Text Soc.
Coventry Mysteries, ed. J. O. Halliwell. Shakespeare Society, 1841.

Criminal Trials in Scotland from 1488 to 1624, ed. Robert Pitcairn, 4 vols. Bann. Club.
Cromek's Reliques of Robert Burns. London, 1808.
—— Remains of Nithsdale and Galloway Song. London, 1809. [By Allan Cunningham.]
—— Select Scottish Songs, 2 vols. London, 1810.
Cunningham, Allan, Songs of Scotland, Ancient and Modern, 4 vols. London, 1825.
Cursor Mundi, ed. Dr. R. Morris (E.E.T.S., Parts I-V.), 1874-8.
Cyclopædia of English Literature, by R. Chambers, LL.D.; third edition, revised by Dr. Carruthers, 2 vols., Lond. and Edin., 1876.

D.

Danish.—Ferrall and Repp's Danish and English Dictionary, 2 vols. London, 1873.
—— Molbech's Danish Dialect Lexicon, Kjöbenhavn, 1841.
Dialect of Cleveland; see Atkinson.
—— Lonsdale, Glossary of, ed. R. B. Peacock. London, 1869. Other Dialects are noted under E.D.S.
—— Southern Scotland, ed. J. A. H. Murray, LL.D. London, 1873.
Diary of Mr. James Melvill, Minister of Kilrenny, 1556-1601, Edin., 1829. Bann. Club.
Diez, F., see Romance Languages.
Diurnal of Remarkable Occurrents in Scotland since the death of King James the Fourth, ed. Thomas Thomson. Edin., 1833. Bann. Club.
Documents Illustrative of the History of Scotland from 1286 to 1306, ed. Rev. Joseph Stevenson, M.A., 2 vols. Edin., 1870. Scot. Record Series.
Douglas, Gavin, Works of, ed. J. Small, 4 vols., Edin., 1874.
Douglas, a Tragedy by John Home, rendered in the Buchan Dialect by George Smith. Aberdeen, 1824.
Ducange.—Lexicon Manuale ad Scriptores Mediæ et Infimæ Latinitatis, ex glossariis C. D. D. Ducangii et aliorum in compendium accuratissime redactum, par W.-H. Maigne D'Arnis. Paris, 1866.
Dunbar, William, Poems of, ed. David Laing, 2 vols. Edin., 1834.
—— ed. John Small, LL.D. Edin., 1884-5. Scot. Text Soc.
Duncan's Appendix Etymologiæ, A.D. 1595, a Scottish Glossary selected from Duncan's Latin Grammar, ed. John Small, M.A. E.D.S. Series.
Dutch.—New Pocket Dictionary of the English and Dutch Languages. Leipzig, C. Tauchnitz.
—— Kilian, C., Old Dutch Dictionary. Amsterdam, 1642.
—— Sewel, W. A., Large Dictionary, English and Dutch. Amsterdam, 1754.

E.

Early Britain—Celtic Period, by Prof. J. Rhys, M.A. London, 1882.
—— Roman Period, by Rev. H. M. Scarth, M.A. London, n.d.
—— Anglo-Saxon Period, by Grant Allen, B.A. London, n.d.
Eastwood and Wright's Bible Wordbook—a Glossary of Old English Bible Words, by J. Eastwood and W. Aldis Wright. London, 1866.
E.D.S.—English Dialect Society's Publications: including Ray's Collections, Glossaries of Cumberland, Whitby, East-Yorkshire, Mid-Yorkshire, West-Yorkshire, Holderness, Swaledale, &c.
Edward the Fourth, Wardrobe Accounts of, ed. Sir N. H. Nicolas. London, 1830.
E.E.T.S.—Early English Text Society's Publications: including Ælfred, Alexander, Alliterative Poems, Ayen-bite, Barbour, Chaucer, Complaynte of Scotland, Early English Homilies, Ellis, Floriz, Gawayne, Genesis, Hali Meidenhad, Havelok, Joseph, King Horn, Knight de la Tour, Lancelot, Legends of the Holy Rood, Levins, Lyndesay, Mort Arthure, Partenay, Piers Plowman, Troybook, Will. of Palerne, &c.
Elizabeth of York, Privy Purse Expenses of, ed. Sir N. H. Nicolas. London, 1830.
English Glossary, Supplementary, by T. L. O. Davies, M.A. London, 1881.
English Plant Names from the Tenth to the Fifteenth Century, by John Earle, M.A. Oxford, 1880.
Ettmüller; see Anglo-Saxon.
Etymological Dictionary of the English Language, by Rev. W. W. Skeat, LL.D. Oxford, 1882. Supplement, 1884. Also, Concise Etym. Dict. of the Eng. Lang., by the same author, second edition, Oxford, 1885.
Etymological Geography, by C. Blackie, with Preface by Prof. J. S. Blackie. London, 1875.
Exchequer Rolls of Scotland, 1264-1469, ed. John Stuart and George Burnett, 7 vols., Edin., 1878-1884. Scot. Record Series.

F.

Family of Rose of Kilravock, ed. Cosmo Innes, Edin., 1848. Spald. Club.
Farmers' Ha', and Ha'rst Rig, by Dr. C. Keith, see Misc. Pop. Scot. Poems.
Field Book of Sports and Pastimes of the United Kingdom. Lond., 1833.
Flora Scotica, ed. W. J. Hooker, LL.D., 2 parts. London, 1821.
—— ed. Rev. John Lightfoot, 2 vols. London, 1792.
Flügel, Dr. J., Practical English and German Dictionary. Leipzig, 1879.
Flyting of Polwart and Montgomery: see Watson's Collection, or Poems of Alex. Montgomery.
Folk-Etymology, A Dictionary of Verbal Corruptions, ed. Rev. A. S. Palmer. London, 1882.
French.—Dictionnaire International Français-Anglais, par M. M. H. Hamilton et E. Legros. Paris, 2 vols., 1872.
—— Littré, E., Dictionnaire de la langue Française, 4 vols., with Supplement. Paris, 1877.
—— See also Burguy and Cotgrave.

G.

Gaelic.—Dictionary of the Gaelic Language, by Macleod and Dewar. Glasgow, 1839.
Galt, John, Works of; including Annals of the Parish, The Provost, Sir Andrew Wylie, The Entail, The Ayrshire Legatees, and Lawrie Todd.
Gawan and Gologras; see Sir Gawayne.
Gawayne and the Green Knight, an Alliterative Romance Poem, ed. Dr. Richard Morris. E.E.T.S., 1869.
Genesis and Exodus, The Story of, ed. Dr. Richard Morris. E.E.T.S., 1865.
Glasgow.—Memorabilia of the City of Glasgow, 1588-1750. Glasgow, 1868.
—— Records of the Incorporated Trades in Glasgow; including the Bonnetmakers, Coopers, Cordiners, Dyers, Glovers, Hammermen, Maltmen, Masons, Skinners, Tailors, Weavers, and Wrights. Glasgow, V. Y. Also, MS. Minutes of the Incorporations of Coopers and Wrights from the middle of the sixteenth to the middle of the eighteenth century.
Gloucester, Robert of, Chronicle, ed. Thomas Hearne, M.A., 2 vols. Oxford, 1724.
Gothic.—A Mœso-Gothic Glossary, by Dr. Skeat. London, 1868.
Greek.—Liddell and Scott's Greek-English Lexicon, London, 1865.

Grein, C. W. M., Bibliotheca Anglo-Saxonica, vol. 3 and 4, forming a dictionary for Anglo-Saxon Poetry. Gottingen, 1861-5.
Gude and Godlie Ballates, reprint of edition of 1578, ed. David Laing. Edin., 1868.
Guest, E., History of English Rhythms, 2 vols. London, 1838.

H.

Halliwell, J. O., Dictionary of Archaic and Provincial Words, 2 vols., fifth edition, London, 1865.
Halyburton.—Ledger of Andrew Halyburton, Scot. Conservator in the Netherlands, A.D. 1492-1503, together with the Book of Customs, &c., in Scotland, 1612, ed. Cosmo Innes, Edin., 1867. Scot. Record Series.
Hamilton, Janet, Poems and Ballads. Glasgow, 1873.
Hamilton.—The Catechism Set Forth by Archbishop Hamilton, St. Andrews, 1551. Reprint, with Preface by Prof. Mitchell, D.D. Edin., 1882.
——————Edited with Introduction and Glossary by T. G. Law. Oxford, 1884.
Hampole, Richard Rolle de.—Pricke of Conscience, a Northumbrian Poem, ed. Dr. R. Morris, (Phil. Soc.) London, 1863.
Harp of Renfrewshire : a Collection of Songs and other Poetical Pieces : (originally published in 1819). Paisley, 2 vols., 1872.
Harp of Caledonia, a Collection of Songs Ancient and Modern, ed. John Struthers, 3 vols. Glasgow, 1819.
Havelok the Dane, ed. Dr. W. W. Skeat and Sir F. Madden. E.E.T.S., extra series, 1868.
Haydn's Dictionary of Dates, thirteenth edition, by B. Vincent. London, 1868.
Helenore, or The Fortunate Shepherdess, by Alex. Ross, A.M., ed. Dr. Longmuir. Glasgow, 1868.
Henryson, R., Poems and Fables, with Notes and Memoir by David Laing. Edinburgh, 1865.
——————Moral Fables, reprinted from Hart's ed., ed. D. Irving, LL.D. Edin., 1832. Mait. Club Series.
Herd, David : see Songs Ancient and Modern.
Hermes Scythicus, or the Radical Affinities of the Greek and Latin Languages to the Gothic, by John Jamieson, D.D., F.R.S.E. Edinburgh, 1814.
History of the Troubles in Scotland, from 1624 to 1646, by John Spalding, 2 vols. Edin., 1830. Bann. Club.
Hogg, James, Tales and Stories, 2 vols. Glasgow, 1884.
——————The Queen's Wake. London and Edinburgh, 1870.
——————See Jacobite Relics.
Howlat, Buke of the, by Holland, ed. D. Laing. Edinburgh, 1823. Bann. Club.
——————————— ed. D. Donaldson. Paisley, 1882.

I.

Icelandic—Icelandic-English Dictionary, by R. Cleasby and G. Vigfusson, Oxford, 1874 : with an Appendix containing a list of words etymologically connected with Icelandic, by Dr. W. W. Skeat. 1876.
Innes, Cosmo, Sketches of Early Scotch History. Edinburgh, 1861.
——————Scotland in the Middle Ages. Edinburgh, 1860.
——————Scotch Legal Antiquities. Edinburgh, 1872.
——————Scottish Surnames. Edinburgh, 1860.
Innes, Thomas.—Critical Essay on the Ancient Inhabitants of Scotland. Reprinted from the original edition of 1729. Edinburgh, 1879.
Irish-English Dictionary, by E. O'Reilly : with a Supplement by J. O'Donovan. London, 1864.

Irving, David, The History of Scottish Poetry from the Middle Ages to the Close of the Seventeenth Century. Edinburgh, 1861.
Italian and English Dictionary, by John Millhouse, 2nd ed., 2 vols. London, 1857.
Isumbras, Romance of, in the Thornton Romances, ed. J. O. Halliwell. 1844.

J.

Jacobite Relics of Scotland, ed. James Hogg, 2 vols. (reprint). Paisley, 1874.
James First of Scotland, the Life and Death of, ed. Rev. Joseph Stevenson. Edin., 1837. Mait. Club.
James the Sext, the Historie and Life of, ed. Thomas Thomson, Esq. Edin., 1825. Bann. Club.
Jamieson, J., Scottish Dictionary, abridged by John Johnston ; ed. John Longmuir. Edinburgh, 1867.
Johnny Gibb of Gushetneuk, in the Parish of Pyketillim, by W. Alexander. Edin., 1873.

K.

Kilian's Old Dutch Dictionary. Amsterdam, 1642.
Kingis Quair, by James I. of Scotland, ed. Rev. W. W. Skeat, L.L.D. Edin., 1884. Scot. Text Soc.
Knox, The Works of John Knox, ed. David Laing, 6 vols. Edin., 1847-64. Wodrow Soc.

L.

Laing, David, LL.D., Works edited by :—
——————Alexander Scott's Poems. Edinburgh, 1821.
——————Alexander Montgomery's Poems. Edinburgh, 1821.
——————Select Remains of the Ancient Popular Poetry of Scotland. 1822.
——————History of Roswall and Lillian. Edinburgh, 1822.
——————Book of the Howlate by Holland. Bannatyne Club, Edinburgh, 1823.
——————Fugitive Scottish Poetry of the Seventeenth Century. Edinburgh, vol. i., vol. ii., 1853.
——————History of Sir Egeir, Sir Gryme, and Sir Graysteill. Edinburgh, 1826.
——————The Knightly Tale of Golagras and Gawane, and other Ancient Poems. Edinburgh, 1827.
——————Ancient Scottish Prophecies in Alliterative Verse. Bannatyne Club, Edinburgh, 1833.
——————Dunbar's Poetical Works, 2 vols. Edinburgh, 1834, with Supplement, 1865.
——————The Seven Sages, by John Rolland of Dalkeith. Bannatyne Club, Edinburgh, 1837.
——————Works of John Knox, 6 vols. Wodrow Society, Edinburgh, 1846-1864.
——————Sir Degarre, a Metrical Romance of the 13th Century. Abbotsford Club, Edinburgh, 1863.
——————Diary of Alexander Brodie of Brodie, 1652-1685. Spalding Club, Aberdeen, 1863.
——————Poetical Works of Robert Henryson. Edinburgh, 1867.
——————The Gude and Godly Ballates, Edinburgh, 1868.
——————Wyntoun's Chronicle, 3 vols. (Historians of Scotland). Edinburgh, 1871-2.
——————Sir David Lindsay's Poetical Works, 3 vols. Edinburgh, 1879.
Laird of Logan, Anecdotes and Tales illustrative of Scottish Wit and Humour. Glasgow, 1878.
Lancelot of the Laik, ed. Dr. W. W. Skeat. E.E.T.S., 1865.
Langtoft.—Peter Langtoft's Chronicle, by Robert of Brunne, ed. Thomas Hearne, M.A., 2 vols. Oxford, 1725.
Latin.—Latin-English Dictionary, by J. T. White and J. E. Riddle, fifth edition. London, 1876.
Layamon's Brut, ed. by Sir F. Madden, 3 vols., (Soc. Antiq.) 1847.

Leighton, R.—Bapteesement o' the Bairn, Scotch Words, and Loss o' the Whittle. London, 1872.
Leo, Prof. H.—On the Local Nomenclature of the Anglo-Saxons, translated by B. Williams. London, 1852.
Leslie's Historie of Scotland, translated in Scottish by Father J. Dalrymple, ed. Father E. G. Cody, O. S. B., part. i. Edin., 1885. Scot. Text Soc.
Levins, Manipulus Vocabulorum, ed. H. B. Wheatley. E.E.T.S., 1867.
Liber Albus, Liber Custumarum, and Liber Horn; ed. H. T. Riley, M.A., 3 vols. London, 1860-2. Rolls Series.
Liddell and Scott; see Greek.
Littré; see French.
Low German; see Bremen Wörterbuch.
Low Latin; see Ducange.
Lyndesay, Sir D., Works of. E.E.T.S., 1865-8.
———— Poetical Works, ed. David Laing, 3 vols. Edin., 1879.
Lyric Gems of Scotland, First and Second Series. Glasgow, n. d.

M.

Mackenzie.—Grievances and Oppression of Orkney and Shetland. Edin., 1836.
Macphail, S. R., History of the Religious House of Pluscardyn. Edin., 1881.
Mallet's Northern Antiquities, translated by Bishop Percy, 8vo. London, 1847.
Maetzner.—An English Grammar : Methodical, Analytical, and Historical; by Prof. Maetzner, Berlin. Translated by C. J. Grece, LL.B., 3 vols. London, 1874.
Maitland Club Publications :—
Henryson's Fables; Burgh Records of Glasgow; Burgh Records of Preatwick; Life and Death of James First; Lancelot du Lak; Rob Stene's Dream; Oppressions in Orkney; M. C. Miscellany.
March, F. A.—Comparative Grammar of the Anglo-Saxon Language. London, 1870.
Marsh, G. P.—Lectures on the English Language, ed. Dr. W. Smith. London, 1862.
Maxwell, A., History of Old Dundee : drawn chiefly from the Town Council Register. Edinburgh, 1884.
Memorials of Transactions in Scotland, from 1569 to 1573, by Richard Bannatyne, Secretary to John Knox, ed. Robert Pitcairn. Edin., 1836. Bann. Club Series.
Million of Potatoes; see Misc. Pop. Scot. Poems.
Milton. — The Poetical Works of John Milton, with Verbal Index by C. Dexter Cleveland, new edition. London, 1865.
Minot, L., Poems of, ed. T. Wright. Lond., 1859.
Minstrelsy of the Scottish Border, ed. Sir W. Scott, 4 vols. Edin., 1830.
Miscellany of Popular Scottish Poems, including Peblis to the Play, Wife of Auchtermuchty, Piper of Kilbarchan, Farmers' Ha', Har'st Rig, Watty and Meg, Loss o' the Pack, Will and Jean, Siller Gun, Million of Potatoes, Tint Quey, &c., ed. Robert Chambers. Edin., 1860.
Miscellany of the Spalding Club, 5 vols. Aberdeen, V. Y. Spald. Club Series.
Miscellany of the Wodrow Society, vol. i. Edin., 1844.
Morte Arthure. ed. E. Brock, E.E.T.S., reprint, 1871.
Motherwell, William.—Minstrelsy Ancient and Modern. Glasgow, 1827.
———— Poetical Works of, ed. James M'Conechy. Paisley, 1881.

N.

Nares, R.—Glossary to the Works of English Authors, new edition, by Halliwell, and Wright, 2 vols. London, 1859.

Neil's Tour through Orkney and Shetland. Edin., 1806.
North Countrie Garland, ed. James Maidment. Edin., 1824.
Norwegian.—Ivar Aasen's Norsk Ordbog. Christiania, 1873.
Notes and Sketches of Northern Rural Life in the Eighteenth Century. By W. Alexander. Edin., 1877.
Nursery Songs, collected by David Robertson. Glasgow, 1844.

O.

Old Church Life in Scotland, by Rev. Andrew Edgar, First and Second Series. Paisley, 1885-6.
Old Country and Farming Words, ed. James Britten, F.L.S. London, 1880.
Old Glasgow from the Roman Occupation to the Eighteenth Century, by A. Macgeorge, Glasgow, 1880.
Old Dutch; see Kilian and Sewel.
Old French; see Cotgrave, Burguy, and Roquefort.
Old Norsk Ordbog, ed. Johan Fritzner. Christiania, 1867.
Orcadian Sketch Book, W. T. Dennison. Kirkwall, 1880.
Orfeo and Heurodis; see Laing's Anc. Pop. Poetry of Scotland.
Origines Parochiales Scotiae : The Antiquities Ecclesiastical and Territorial of the Parishes of Scotland, ed. Cosmo Innes, 3 parts. Edin., 1850-5. Bann. Club.
Orkneyinga Saga, translated by Hjaltalin and Goudie, ed. Joseph Anderson. Edin., 1873.
Ormulum, ed. R. M. White, 2 vols., Oxford, 1852.
Ornithological Dictionary, by Col. G. Montagu, F.L.S., ed. James Rennie, A.M. London, 1831.

P.

Palice of Honour, by Gawin Douglas, Bishop of Dunkeld. Edin., 1827. Bann. Club.
Palsgrave, Lesclaircissement de la Langue Francoyse, par Maistre Jehan Palsgrave, reprint, Paris, 1852, parts, 1846-7.
Paterson, James, The Ballads and Songs of Ayrshire, 2 parts, 1846-7.
Peacock, E.—Glossary of Words used in the Wappentakes of Manley and Corringham, Lincolnshire. Eng. Dial. Soc., 1877.
Peebles to the Play; see Misc. of Pop. Scot. Poems.
Percival; see Thornton Romances.
Percy, Bishop.—Reliques of Ancient English Poetry, 3 vols. London, 1839.
Peterkin's Notes on Orkney and Zetland. Edin., 1822.
———— Rentals of Orkney. Edin., 1820.
Philological Essays of Rev. R. Garnett. London, 1859.
Philological Society's Transactions, for various years.
Philology of the English Tongue, by John Earle, M.A. Oxford, 1871.
Picken, David.—Poems and Songs. Paisley, 1875.
Pictures of Old England, by Dr. R. Pauli. London, 1861.
Piers Plowman. — The Vision of William concerning Piers the Plowman. A, B, and C text, ed. Dr. W. W. Skeat. E. E. T. S., 1867-1873. Notes to the three texts, 1877.
Pinkerton, John. — Ancient Scottish Poems from the Maitland MS., 2 vols. London, 1786.
———— Select Scottish Ballads, 2 vols. London, 1783.
———— Scottish Tragic and Comic Ballads, 2 vols., 1781.
———— Scottish Poems Reprinted, 3 vols. London, 1792.
Piper of Kilbarchan; see Watson's Collection, and Misc. Pop. Scot. Poems.
Pitcairn, Robert.--Criminal Trials in Scotland, from A.D. 1488 to A.D. 1624, 4 vols. Bann. Club.

Planché, J. R.—History of British Costume, third edition, 8vo, London, 1874.
Poetry and Humour of the Scottish Language, Charles Mackay, LL.D. Paisley, 1882.
Popular Ballads and Songs, ed. Robert Jamieson, 2 vols. Edin., 1806.
Privy Purse Expenses of Henry VIII., ed. Sir N. H. Nicolas. London, 1827.
—————— Princess Mary, ed. Sir F. Madden. London, 1831.
Privy Council of Scotland, Register of, vols. 1-7.
Prompt. Parv.—Promptorium Parvulorum sive Clericorum Dictionarius Anglo-Latinus Princeps, ed. A. Way, A.M. Lond., 1865.
Pystyl of Swete Susan; see Laing's Anc. Pop. Poetry of Scotland.

R.

Rab and his Friends; Extracted from "Horæ Subsecivæ," by Dr. John Brown, F.R.S.E.
Ramsay, Allan.—Poetical Works, 2 vols. Paisley, 1877.
—————— Evergreen, 2 vols. Glasgow, 1876.
—————— Tea Table Miscellany, 2 vols. Glasgow 1876.
—————— Scots Proverbs. Edin., 1776.
Rauf Coilyear; see Laing's Anc. Pop. Poetry of Scotland.
Ray, John.—Collection of English Words not generally used. Re-arranged and edited by Dr. W. W. Skeat. Eng. Dial. Soc., 1874.
Reader's Handbook of References, ed. Rev. Dr. Brewer. London, 1880.
Regiam Majestatem : The Auld Laws and Constitutions of Scotland, ed. Sir John Skene. Edin., 1774.
Register of the Privy Council of Scotland, 1545-1607, ed. J. H. Burton and Professor Masson, 7 vols. Edin., V. Y. Scot. Record Series.
Registrum Magni Sigilli Regum Scotorum, A.D. 1306-1546, 3 vols. Scot. Record Series.
Reminiscences of the Pen Folk, by David Gilmour, second edition. Paisley, 1873.
Reminiscences of Scottish Life and Character, by Dean Ramsay, LL.D., fourteenth edition. Edin., 1867.
Richardson, C.—Dictionary of the English Language, 2 vols. London, 1863.
Richthofen's Altfriesisches Wörterbuch. Göttingen, 1840.
Ritson, Joseph, Ancient Popular Poetry. London, 1833.
—————— Ancient Songs and Ballads, 2 vols. London, 1829.
—————— Metrical Romances, 3 vols. London, 1802.
—————— Scottish Songs, 2 vols. London, 1794.
Robene and Makyne, and Testament of Cresseid by Robert Henryson, ed. George Chalmers. Edin., 1824. Bann. Club.
Robert de Brunne, Handlyng Synne, ed. F. J. Furnivall. Rox. Club, 1862.
Robert of Gloucester's Chronicle, ed. T. Hearne, 2 vols. Oxford, 1724.
Robinson, F. K., A Glossary of Words used in the Neighbourhood of Whitby. Eng. Dial. Soc., 1875-6.
Robson, J., Three Early English Metrical Romances. Camden Society, 1842.
Rob Stene's Dream, a Poem, printed from a MS. in the Leighton Library, Dunblane, ed. W. Motherwell. Glasgow, 1836. Mait. Club.
Romance Languages.—Etymological Dictionary of the Romance Languages, chiefly from the German of F. Diez, ed. T. C. Donkin, B.A. London, 1864.
Roquefort, J. B. B., Glossaire de la Langue Romane, 2 vols., Paris, 1808, with Supplement, 1820.

S.

Scotch Legal Antiquities, Lectures on, by Cosmo Innes. Edinburgh, 1872.
Scotland under Her Early Kings, by E. W. Robertson, 2 vols. Edin., 1862.
Scots Poems, Watson's Collection of, in 3 parts, 1706-1711, reprint Glasgow, 1869.
Scott, Alex., Poems of, reprint. Glasgow, 1882.
Scottish Ballads, Historical and Romantic, ed. John Finlay, 2 vols. Edinburgh, 1808.
Scottish Poems of the 16th Cuututy, ed. Sir J. G. Dalyell, 2 vols. Edin., 1801.
Scottish Poets, Modern, ed. D. H. Edwards. Brechin, 7 vols., V.Y.
Scottish Proverbs, collected and arranged by A. Henderson, ed. James Donald, F.R.G.S., Glasgow, 1881.
—————— collected and arranged by Alex. Hislop, Glasgow, 1862.
—————— collected by Allan Ramsay, Edinburgh, 1776.
Scottish Text Society Publications—The Kingis Quair, Court of Venus, Dunbar's Poems, Blind Harry's Wallace, Leslie's History of Scotland, Sir Tristrem.
Scottish Gaël; or Celtic Manners, by James Logan : ed. Rev. A. Stewart, 2 vols. Inverness, 1876.
Scottish Gallovidian Encyclopedia, ed. John Mactaggart; reprint, Glasgow. 1876.
Scott, Sir Walter, Select Poetry of, 6 vols. Edinburgh, 1849.
Scottish Record Publications—
Acts of Parliaments of Scotland, ed. Thomas Thomson and Cosmo Innes, 12 vols. Edinburgh, 1814-75.
Acts of the Lords of Council in Civil Causes, A.D. 1478-1495.
Acts of the Lords Auditors of Causes and Complaints, A.D. 1466-1494.
Registrum Magni Sigilli Regum Scotorum, A.D. 1306-1546.
Register of the Privy Council of Scotland, 1545-1607.
Exchequer Rolls of Scotland, 1264-1409.
Accounts of Lord High Treasurer, 1473-1498.
Ledger of Andrew Halyburton, 1492-1503.
Documents Illustrative of the History of Scotland, 1108-1272.
Sempill Ballates.—The Poems of Robert, James, and Francis Semple. Edin., 1870.
Seven Sages, a Poem in Scottish Metre by John Rolland of Dalkeith, ed. D. Laing; reprinted from the ed. of 1578, Edin., 1837. Bann. Club.
Seven Sages, in English Verse, ed. Thos. Wright. London (Percy Society), 1845.
Sewel's Old Dutch Dictionary. Amsterdam, 1754.
Skeat, Prof. W. W.—Specimens of Early English ; Specimens of English Literature ; Piers Plowman ; Tales from Chaucer ; Mœso-Gothic Glossary ; English Words related to Icelandic ; Concise Etymological Dictionary ; Etymological Dictionary of the English Language.
Shakespeare's Works, Glossary to, by Rev. A. Dyce. London, 1880.
Shirrefs, Andrew, Poems chiefly in the Scottish Dialect. Edin., 1790.
Sibbald, J.—Chronicle of Scottish Poetry, from the Thirteenth Century to the Union of the Crowns, 4 vols. Edinburgh, 1802.
Siller Gun, by J. Mayne ; see Misc. Pop. Scot. Poems.
Sir Gawan and Sir Galaron of Galloway ; see Pinkerton's Scot. Poems Reprinted, but much more correctly in Sir Gawayne, and in Laing's Ancient Pop. Poetry of Scotland, where it is called The Awntyrs of Arthur.
Sir Gawayne ; A Collection of Ancient Romance Poems, ed. Sir F. Madden, Edin., 1839. Bann. Club.
Sir Tristrem, ed. George P. M'Neill, LL.B. Edin., 1886. Scot. Text Soc.

Skene, W.F., Celtic Scotland: A History of Ancient Alban, 3 vols. Edin., 1876-1880.
Skinner, Rev. John.—Songs and Poems. Peterhead, 1859.
Slang Dictionary. London, 1874.
Social Life in Former Days; chiefly in the Province of Moray: by E. D. Dunbar, 2 vols. Edin., 1870.
Songs Ancient and Modern, Heroic Ballads, &c., ed. David Herd, 2 vols. Glasgow, 1869. Reprint of ed. 1776.
Songs of Scotland Prior to Burns, ed. R. Chambers, LL.D. Edin., n. d.
Spalding's Memorialls of the Troubles in Scotland, A.D 1624-1645, ed. John Stuart, LL.D., 2 vols., Aberdeen, 1850. Spald. Club.
Spalding Club Publications:—
Burgh Records of Aberdeen, Collections of Aberdeen and Banff, House of Rose of Kilravock, Spalding's Troubles in Scotland, The Brus, Thanes of Cawdor, S. C. Miscellany.
Spanish and English Dictionary, by F. C. Meadows, eighth edition, London, 1856.
—————— by M. Velasquez de la Cadena, London, 1878.
Specimens of Early English, A.D. 1298-1393, by Dr. Morris and the Rev. Dr. Skeat, new edition, revised for the second time, Oxford, 1873.
Specimens of English Literature. A.D. 1394-1579, by the Rev. Dr. Skeat. Oxford, 1879.
Sproull, John (commonly called Bass John), Miscellaneous Writings of; and Wodrow's account of his trial and imprisonment. Privately printed, Glasgow, 1882.
Stevenson, R. L., Kidnapped. Edin., 1886.
Stirling, Charters and Other Documents Relating to, A.D. 1124-1705. Glasgow, 1884.
—————— Extracts from the Burgh Records, 1519-1666. Glasgow, 1887.
Stratmann.—Dictionary of the Old English Language, compiled from writings of the 12th, 13th, 14th and 15th centuries, by F. H. Stratmann, third edition. London, 1878.
Strutt's Sports and Pastimes of the People of England, ed. W. Hone. London, 1841.
Swedish.—The Tauchnitz Swedish and English Dictionary. Leipzig, 1875.
—————— Rietz's Swedish Dialect Dictionary. Lund, 1867.
—————— Ihre's Suio-Gothic Glossary, 2 vols. Upsal, 1769.
Sweet, H.—Anglo-Saxon Reader. Oxford, 1876.
—————— History of English Sounds. London, 1874 (E. D. S.).
Symmie and his Bruder; see Laing's Anc. Pop. Poetry of Scotland, or Bannatyne MS. in the Hunterian Club Series.

T.

Tannahill, Robert, Poems and Songs, ed. D. Semple, F.S.A. Paisley, 1876.
Taylor, I.—Words and Places, third edition. London, 1873.
Tennant, William.—Anster Fair, and other Poems. Edin., 1814.
—————— Papistry Stormed, or the Dingin' down o' the Cathedral. Edin., 1827.
Thanes of Cawdor: Papers selected from the Charter Room of Cawdor, and ed. by Cosmo Innes. Aberdeen, 1859. Spald. Club.
Thom, William.—Rhymes and Recollections of a Handloom Weaver. Paisley, 1883.

Thornton Romances, ed. J. O. Halliwell, Camden Soc., London, 1844.
Thorpe, B.—Analecta Anglo-Saxonica. London, 1846.
Tooke, John Horne, Diversions of Purley, ed. R. Taylor. London, 1857.
Towneley Mysteries, (Surtees Society), London, 1836.
Trench, R. C., English Past and Present, seventh edition. London, 1870.
—————— On the Study of Words, thirteenth edition. London, 1869.
—————— A Select Glossary, fourth edition. London, 1873.
Trevisa, John of, tr. of Higden's Polychronicon. Record Series.
Troybook, ed. Panton and Donaldson, E. E. T. S.
Tytler, P. F., History of Scotland from the Accession of Alexander III. to the Union, 4 vols., 8vo, Edin., 1864.

V., W., Y.

Vieyra's Portuguese and English Dictionary, 2 vols. Paris, 1837.
Virgil's Æneis, translated into Scottish Verse by the famous Gawin Douglas, Bishop of Dunkeld, ed. Thomas Ruddiman. Edin., 1710. See also under Æneid.
Wackernagel's Altdeutsches Handworterbuch. Basle, 1861. Referred to by O. H. Ger. and M. H. Ger.
Wallace.—Blind Harry's Wallace, ed. from the Edinburgh MS. by John Jamieson, D.D. Edin., 1820.
—————— ed. James Moir, M.A. Edin., 1884-6. Scot. Text Soc.
Watson's Collection of Scots Poems, in three parts, 1706-11, reprint, Glasgow, 1869.
Watson, Walter, Poems and Songs of. Glasgow, 1877.
Watty and Meg, and Loss o' the Pack; see Alex. Wilson's Poems, or Misc. Pop. Scot. Poems.
Webster, N., New Illustrated Unabridged Dictionary, ed. C. A. Goodrich and N. Porter. London, 1880.
Wedgwood, H., Dictionary of English Etymology, second edition. London, 1872.
Welsh and English Dictionary, by W. Spurrell, second edition. Carmarthen, 1859.
Whistle Binkie, or the Piper of the Party, 2 vols. Glasgow, 1878.
Whitelaw, Alex., Book of Scottish Ballads, with Historical and Critical Notices. Glasgow, 1855.
—————— Book of Scottish Song, with Historical and Critical Notices. Glasgow, 1855.
Wife of Auchtermuchty; see Ramsay's Evergreen, and Misc. Pop. Scot. Poems.
Will and Jean; see Misc. Pop. Scot. Poems.
William of Palerne, ed. Dr. Skeat, (E.E.T.S., extra series), 1867.
Williams, R.—Lexicon Cornu-Britannicum. Llandovery and London, 1865.
Wilson, Alexander, Poems and Literary Prose, ed. Rev. A. B. Grosart, 2 vols. Paisley, 1876.
Winzet's Tractates for Reformation of Doctrine and Manners in Scotland. 1562-3. Reprint, Edinburgh, 1835. Mait. Club.
Witchcraft in Scotland, History of, by C. K. Sharpe, Glasgow, 1884.
Withering's British Plants, ed. W. MacGillivray, LL.D. London, 1856.
Wright, T., Vocabularies, Anglo-Saxon and Old English, ed. R. P. Wülcker, 2 vols. London, 1884.
Wyntoun, The Orygynale Cronykil of Scotland, by Andro Wyntoun, ed. David Laing, 3 vols.. Edin., 1872-9. (Hist. of Scotland).
York Mystery Plays, ed. L. Toulmin Smith. Oxford, 1885.

ABBREVIATIONS USED IN THIS WORK.

I.—ETYMOLOGICAL REFERENCES.

A.-S.	Anglo-Saxon; as in the Dictionaries of Bosworth, Etmüller, and Grein; and in Wright's Vocabularies edited by Wülcker.	*M. E.*	Middle English (English from the thirteenth to the fifteenth centuries inclusive); as in Stratmann's Old English Dict., 3rd edition, 1878.
Celt.	Celtic; used as a general term for Irish, Gaelic, Welsh, Cornish, &c.	*M.H. Ger.*	Middle High German; as in Wackernagel's Wörterbuch, 1861.
Corn.	Cornish; as in Williams' Dict., 1865.		
Dan.	Danish; as in Ferrall and Repp, 1861.	*Norw.*	Norwegian; as in Aasen's Norsk Ordbog, 1873.
Du.	Dutch; as in the Tauchnitz Dutch Dict.		
E.	Modern English; as in Webster's Dict.	*O. Du.*	Old Dutch; as in Kilian, 1642, or Sewel, 1754.
Fr.	French; as in Hamilton and Legros, 1872. See also the Dictionaries by Brachet and Littré.	*O. Fr.*	Old French; as in the Dictionaries by Cotgrave, Burguy, or Roquefort.
Fries.	Friesic; as in Richthofen, 1840.	*O. H. Ger.*	Old High German; as in Wackernagel's Wörterbuch, 1861.
Gael.	Gaelic; as in Macleod and Dewar, 1839.		
Ger.	German; as in Flügel, 1861.	*O. Sax.*	Old Saxon; as in the Héliand, ed. Heyne.
Goth.	Mœso-Gothic; as in Skeat's Glossary, 1868.		
Gr.	Greek; as in Liddell and Scott's Lexicon, 1849.	*Port.*	Portuguese; as in Vieyra, 1837.
Icel.	Icelandic; as in Cleasby and Vigfusson, 1874.	*Scand.*	Scandinavian; used as a general term for Icelandic, Danish, Swedish, and Norwegian.
Ir.	Irish; as in O'Reilly, 1864.		
Ital.	Italian; as in Millhouse, 1857.	*Span.*	Spanish; as in Meadows', 1856.
Lat.	Latin; as in White and Riddle, 1876.	*Swed.*	Swedish; as in the Tauchnitz Dict.
L. Ger.	Low German; as in the Bremen Wörterbuch, 1767.	*Swed.dial.*	Swedish dialects; as in Rietz, 1867.
		Teut.	Teutonic; used as a general term for Dutch, German, and Scandinavian.
L. Lat.	Low Latin; as in the Lexicon Manuale (abridged from Ducange) by Maigne d'Arnis, 1866.	*W. or Welsh.*	Welsh; as in Spurrell, 1861.

II.—OTHER ABBREVIATIONS.

acc.	accusative case.	*nom.*	nominative case.
adj.	adjective.	*obs.*	obsolete.
adv.	adverb.	*orig.*	original, or originally.
A. V.	Authorised Version of the Bible, 1611.	*part. pr.*	participle present.
Bann. C.	Bannatyne Club Series.	*part. pt.*	participle past.
cf.	confer, i.e. compare.	*pl.*	plural.
comp.	comparative.	*prep.*	preposition.
conj.	conjunction.	*pret.*	preterite.
dat.	dative case.	*pr. t.*	present tense.
der.	derivative.	*prob.*	probably.
dimin.	diminutive.	*pron.*	pronoun.
E. D. S.	English Dialect Society Series.	*q. v.*	quod vide = which see.
E. E. T. S.	Early English Text Society Series.	*Rec. Soc.*	Burgh Records Society Series.
f. or fem.	feminine.	*s. or sb.*	substantive.
frequent.	frequentative.	*sing.*	singular.
gen.	genitive case.	*Sp. C.*	Spalding Club Series.
i.e.	id est, that is.	*S. T. S.*	Scottish Text Society Series.
imper.	imperative mood.	*superl.*	superlative.
inf.	infinitive mood.	*s. v.*	sub verbo = under the word.
interj.	interjection.	*syn.*	synonym, or synonymous.
lit.	literally.	*tr.*	translated, or translation.
Mait. C.	Maitland Club Series.	*v. or vb.*	verb.
m. or masc.	masculine.	*var.*	variant.
n. or neut.	neuter.		

Abbreviations not explained in these lists will be readily understood by referring to the List of Books and MSS.

SUPPLEMENT

TO THE

ETYMOLOGICAL DICTIONARY

OF

THE SCOTTISH LANGUAGE.

A.

A, AA; AE, AU, AW, O, OW, *s.* Water; and applied in various ways to the sea, a river, stream, spring, fountain, &c., of which there are abundant traces remaining in almost all the districts colonised by Norsemen or Danes; as in Laxa, salmon river; Brora, bridge river; Thurso, Thor's river; &c.

The terminations *au, aw, o, ow,* are forms of Gael. *abh,* water; as in the Awe in Scot., and the Ow in Ireland.

A.-S. *ëa,* water.

A', AW, *adj.* and *s.* 1. All: with applications as in E.

2. Every; as, "*A'* body sais sae," every one says so. And when followed by a *pl. s.,* it means *every* with the sense of *each*; as, "*a' folks,*" every body, each and all.

This latter application may be well illustrated by the notice given long ago to the scholars of a country school, when winter had set in, and the school fire was to be set a going next day. The teacher having intimated the welcome news before dismissal, wound up with the stern laconic order,—"Noo, min'! a' *bairns* brings a peat the morn."

AABER, *adj.* Eager to obtain a thing, Gl. Shetl.

Icel. *æfr,* vehement; Dan. *ivrig,* Sw. *ifrig,* eager.

To AABIN, ABIN, *v. a.* To half-thresh a sheaf before giving it to horses; Orkn.

"The sheaf being held in the hands is raised upwards; then, by a sudden downward stroke, against some fixture, the bulk of the best grain is knocked off." J. W. CURSITER.

The sheaf when so treated is called an *aaber, aber,* or *abir, i.e.,* a halfer, from Goth. *halbs,* a half; Icel. *hálfr*; Dan. *halv. Aabin,* then, is to halve the sheaf between man and beast.

AABIR, AABER, ABIR, *s.* A sheaf of grain half-threshed; lit. a halfer or halved one, Orkn. V. *Aabin.*

AAR, AUR, *s.* A scar, S.; an animus or ill-feeling, a grudge, Ayrs., Orkn. V. *Aur.*

AARNIT, AURNIT, *s.* The pignut; the root or tuber of Bunium flexuosum, Linn. Clydes. V. ARNUT.

A.-S. *eorthe-hnut*; Dutch, *aardnoot*; E. *earth-nut.*

AB, *s.* Check, hindrance, impediment, Orkn. To AB, *v. a.* and *n.* To hinder, keep back, place at a disadvantage; also, to pain, cause pain, ibid.

This is prob. a contr. of *aback,* and an adaptation to colloquial use. Mr. Cursiter gives it as common in Orkney.

ABAISING, ABAISIN, ABASIN, *part. pr.* Abusing, hurting, ill-treating by word or act; South and West of S.: *abeising,* Aberd. Used also as a *s.*

ABANDOUN, *adv.* Abandoned, left to myself, all alone.

Without comfort, in sorowe *abandoun.*
  Kingis Quair, st. 25.

O. Fr. "*A bandon,* at large;" Cotgr.

ABASING, ABAYSING, ABAYSYNG, *s.* Drawing back, cowardice, dismay. V. ABAYS.

Of sic confort men mycht thaim se,
And of sa richt fair contenyng,
As nane of thame had *abasing.*
  Barbour, xvii. 322.

Thre sper-lynth, I trow [weill] mycht be
Detuix thame, quhen sic *abasing*
Tuk thame, but mar, into a swyng,
Thai gaf the bak all, and to-ga.
  Ibid., xvii. 573, C. MS.

To ABAUNDOUNE, *v. refl.* To behave oneself boldly, fight recklessly. V. ABANDON.

Thar men mycht se, that had beyn neir
Men *abaundoune* thame hardily.
Barbour, xvii. 143. SKEAT.

ABAUNDANLY, *adv.* In disorderly manner, straggling; also, recklessly, boldly. V. ABANDONLY.

Thai yschit all *abaundanly*
And prikit furth sa vilfully
To wyn the ladis at thai saw pas.
Barbour, viii. 461. SKEAT.

Bot quhen the nobill renownyt kyng,—
Saw how the Erll *abaundonly*
Tuk the playn fald, &c.
Barbour, xi. 629. SKEAT.

ABAYSING, ABAYSYNG, *s.* Cowardice, dismay, abasement, Barbour, xi. 250. V. *Abasing.*

ABBREID, *adv.* Abroad, Bann. MS., p. 348, l. 40. V. ABREID.

ABEET, *conj.* Albeit, although, Ramsay.

ABEISING, ABEISEING, *part. pr.* Loc. pron. of *abusing*, hurting, ill-treating by word or act, Abord.

". . . and for *abeiseing* hir face, and making the same bla," &c. Burgh Recs., Aberd., 6 Sept., 1641.
Fr. *abuser*, to abuse; from Lat. *abusus*.

ABELYET, *part. pt.* Dressed, fitted up. V. ABULYEIT.

"Item, gevin to a currour passand to the Bischope of Dunkeldin to mak his innys be *abelyet* for the ambaxatouris, ii s. vj d." Accts. Lord H. Treas. Scot., i. 52. DICKSON.

ABELYEMENT, ABILYEMENT, *s.* V. ABULIEMENT.

ABESIE, *s.* An abbacy, Lyndsay, Thrie Estaitis, l. 1218.

To ABID, *v. a.* To wait for. Barbour, xviii. 65. V. *Abyde.*

ABIRGOUN, *s.* Habergeon, Bann. MS., p. 174, l. 14.

ABIT, *v. a.* A form of *abideth*, abides, awaits, Kingis Quair, st. 133.

Another form is *abyt*. The term is used by Chaucer, in Cant. Tales, l. 10643; and the author of the Quair has many loans from that source.

ABOK, YABOK, *s.* A name given to a *gabbing*, talkative, or impudent child, West and South of S. V. GABBY.

ABONE, ABOON, *prep.* and *adv.* Above, S.

ABONE BROE, ABOON-BREE. Above water. Of a person in difficulty, or one who has a very small income, it is commonly said,— "He can hardly keep his head *abone-broe.*"

ABOUT THE BUSS, *adv.* Lit., about the bush: round about; not direct, downright, or straight-forward. Of an honest, earnest man it is said,—"He never gaes *about the buss;*" S.

Frae we determinit to doo,
Or else to clim zou Cherrie-tree,
Thai bade *about the buss.*
Montgomery, Cherrie and Slae, s. 46.

For Authors quha alleges us,
Thai wald not gae *about the buss*
To foster deadlie feid.
Ibid. Id., s. 77.

"To beat about the bush" is the usual form of the phrase in England.

ABOVIN, ABOVYN, ABOUN, ABOWYNE, *prep.* Above. A.-S. *abufan.*

And be the croun that was set
Abovin his hed on the basnet.
Barbour, xii. 38. SKEAT.

ABOVIN, ABOWYN, *adv.* Above, superiorly, as victor; *at thar abovin*, in the better case, having the upper hand; Barbour, xiv. 204.

Stand [on] fer and behald vs to.
Gif thou seis me *abovin* be,
Thou sall haf vapnys in gret plentè.
Barbour, v. 599. SKEAT.

To ABOYSE, *v. a.* To abuse.

"Item, at thai *aboysis* thar seruice whar thai haf dispec at the assise noys thaim be streit keping of the law," &c. Chalmerlan Air, ch. 10.

ABSCENITIE, *s.* Obscenity, unclean thing, filth, refuse.

". . . that natures *abscenities* be decently couered and ouerrailed with her mother's mouldes." Blame of Kirkburiall, ch. vi.

ABSCIDIT, *part. pt.* Cut off, cut up, mangled; Colkelbic Sow, l. 845.

Lat. *abscidere*, to cut off.

To ABSCONSE, *v. a.* To hide, conceal.

That ye may wellis gif to my febill ene,
To testifie with teris my wofull cace,
And with your murning weid *absconse* my face.
Sempill Ballates, p. 162.

ABSOLUTE, *adj.* Unconditional; hence, imperative, compulsory.

". . . yet the necessitie was neuer *absolute*, as we shew before; no not in the lawfull place, let be in the Kirk." Blame of Kirkburiall, ch. xix.
Lat. *absolutus*, from *absolvere*, to set free.

To ABSOVE, ABSOUE, *v. a.* To absolve, free from, set free; pret. and part. pt. *absovit, absouit.* Burgh Recs. Aberdeen, 18 Apr., 1539.

Lat. *absolvere.*

ABUF, ABUFF, ABUFFIN, *adv.* Above, over all, Barbour, xii. 172. V. *Abovin.*

ABUNE, ABOUN, ABONE, *prep.* Above, over, *abune a'*, out of all character, unreasonable. V. *Abovin.*

"And ilke broustare sal put hir alewande ututh hir house at hir wyndow or *abune* hir dur, that it may be senbill communly til al men," &c. Burgh Lawis, ch. 63.

> Magre thair fayis, thai bar thaim swa,
> That thai ar gottyn *aboun* the bra.
> *Barbour*, xviii. 454.

The phrase *abune a'* is common all over S. ; it is so used in Orkn. and Shet. as well.

ABY, *adv.* and *prep.* Lit., on by, beside, aside by: also, besides, beyond, same as *forby*.

> And sum thair bene, waittis on the Quene,
> Bot gaip ay quhill they get hir :
> And war echo heir, I tak na fair,
> The Feynd *aby* we set hir.
> *Sempill Ballates*, p. 76.

" *The Feynd aby*," beside the fiend, at deil's distance, like an outcast.

The term is still used in both senses ; but perhaps more frequently as *forby* ; as in the common colloquial phrase, ' abune and *aby* a' that,' above and beyond all that.

To **ABY**, *v. a.* To buy, pay for, atone, pay dear for, buy dear. V. ABY.

> Let thame be punyst and thar cryme *aby*.
> *Douglas, Eneados*, Bk. x. ch. 1.

Dr. Jamieson's rendering of this term is defective with all its fulness.

A.-S. *abycgan*, to buy, pay for, recompense ; also re-buy, redeem.

To **ABYDE**, *v. n.* To wait for, to face, remain. V. *Abid*.

> Wes nane of thame that wes so wicht
> That cuir durst *abyde* his fere.
> *Barbour*, xv. 63.

This is the reading of the Cambridge MS., the Edin. MS. has *abid*, q. v.

ABYTE, *s.* Dress, habit, Dunbar, Bann. MS., p. 328, l. 28. V. ABBEIT.

To **AC**, **AK**, *v. a.* and *n.* V. ACT.

ACAMY, ACAMIE, *adj.* Small, diminutive : used also as a *s.*, and applied to any small diminutive person or animal ; South and West of S., Orkn.

This is prob. a corr. of *atomy*, short for *anatomy* in the sense of a skeleton.

ACCEPTIONE, *s.* Distinction, difference ; like E. *exception*, as applied to persons.

". . . makkis na *acceptions* of persons," &c. Compl. Scotland, p. 152. E.E.T.S.

O. Fr. *acception*, an acception ; also, a respect or distinction of persons in judgment ; Cotgr.

ACCIDENTIS, ACCIDENCE, *s. pl.* Money on hand, sums that have come dropping in day by day ; occasional income : generally used in the pl. V. ACCEDENS.

". . and pay for the samyn of the reddiest of the *accidentis* that is in their handis," &c. Burgh Recs. Aberd., 21 Feb., 1592. Sp. C.

Lat. *accido* ; from *ad*, and *cado*, to fall.

To **ACCLAIM**, ACCLAME, *v. a.* To claim or demand as one's right. Blame of Kirkburiall, ch. xiii. V. ACCLAME.

ACCOMBENT, *s.* Accompaniment or companion at feasts or meals.

". . that so they might reserue their dead friends extant to be ordinar *accombents* with them at their tables." Blame of Kirkburiall, ch. iv.

Lat. *accumbens*, reclining, used as a *s.*: *accumbere mensae*, to recline at table.

ACCORDIS, ACCORDING. *Accordis to*, is agreeable to ; *according for*, fitting, requisite, necessary for ; *according to*, pertaining to, connected with.

". . and allow as ye think *accordis* to resone." Accts. Lord H. Treas. Scot., i. 166. DICKSON.

". . and al odir stuf *according for* hir to the clere owte red to pass hir voyage," &c. Ibid., i. 125.

". . to bring again certane thingis to the King *according to* artilyery, powder, schot, and sic thing." Ibid., i. 60.

The term *acordant* was similarly used in E. ; as, "*acordant* to resoun," Chaucer, Prol. 37.

To **ACCRESE**, ACCRESCE, ACCRESS, *v. a.* and *n.* To increase, grow ; yield interest. V. ACRESE.

ACCRESE, ACCREIS, ACCRECE, *s.* Increase ; interest yielded, Burgh Recs.

ACH, *inter.* Ah ! Generally expressive of pain or disgust, Bann. MS., p. 1010, l. 231. S.

Gael. *ach*, id.; Ger. *ach* ; Sw. *ack*.

ACHEAT, ACHET, *part. pt.* Escheat, escheated. O. Fr. *eschet*, *eschete*.

". . his gudis sal be *achet*." Burgh Recs. Aberd., 27 Jan., 1481.

ACHEN, AIKEN, *s.* A small bivalve found in sandy bays. V. *Aichan*.

ACHER, *s.* An ear of corn ; *icker*, Burns, Ayrs. V. ECHER.

"—— and drew ane *acher* furth of the laid, and said," &c. Trials for Witchcraft, Spald. Mis., i. 114. A.-S. *œchir*, id.

ACHT, AGHT, *s.* Possession ; duty ; right. V. AUCHT.

This term under various spellings is so used all over Scot. from Shetl. to the Cheviots.

ACHTAD, ACHTAND, ACHTANDE, *adj.* Eighth. V. AUCHT.

". . the *achtad* part of rig," i.e., the eighth part of a bushel. Burgh Recs. Prestwick, p. 23.

". . was accusit of destructione of iij *achtande partis* of pes be his gude," &c. Burgh Recs. Prestwick, 2 May, 1503.

ACKWA, ACKA, ACCA, *s.* A contr. form of *aquavitae*, whiskey : " a dram o' gude *ackwa*; " " prime *acca*; " West of S.

ACKWART, *adj.* Contrary, hindering : also, difficult, troublesome, unfortunate, disastrous ; Blame of Kirkburiall, ch. xii. V. ACQUART.

In the sense of *unfortunate, disastrous,* &c., this term is still used throughout the Lowlands of Scotland and in the North of England. A good illustration of its colloquial use in the North of England is given in George Stephenson's naive reply to his examiner before a Parl. committee concerning the dangers of trains running at high speed. To the supposition of a cow straying on the line before such a train, George's ready answer was, "*It wad be ackart for the coo.*" Burns used the form *awkart*.

ACOYSSING, *s.* Exchange, excambion.

"Gif forswith thai mak *acoyssing* or a change of land amang thaim selff ilke ane of thaim sall geyff twa pennyis." Burgh Lawis, ch. 52.

O. Fr. *acoiser, acoisier, aquiser, aquoiser,* lit., to appease, satisfy; hence, to buy, purchase, exchange; from *coit,* a doublet of *quitte,* from Lat. *quietus,* quiet; Burguy. Here we have an explanation of the old custom of striking hands and crying *quit* or *quits* at the conclusion of a bargain, purchase, or exchange.

ACQUISITION, *s.* The act of acquiring by purchase or barter; purchase.

"For the Jewes doe comprise all titular rights vnder one of three: *acquisition,* like Abrahams (in the conqueis of the caue, Gen. 23.); Heredation, like Isaac's (succeeding thereto); lucrifaction, like Jacob's, whose wealth was the winning of his owne haud-hammers." Birnie's Blame of Kirkburiall, ch. xix.

Fr. *acquisition,* id.; and from the same source as *acoyssing,* q. v.

ACQUORN, Accorn, *s.* An acorn; Compl. Scot., p. 144, E. E. T. S.

ACQUYT, *pret.* Freed: short for *acquytit.*

Quhen euir thai met thaim on the se,
He sent and *acquyt* him planly;
And gave the trewis wp openlye.
Barbour, xix. 237.

To **ACRE,** Ackre, Aikur, *v. a.* To buy, sell, let, deal, or work, by the acre, i.e., at a fixed rate per acre; part. pr. *acrein', ackrin'.*

In agricultural districts of Scot. this was a common method of disposing of growing crops, and of arranging for harvesting crops.

To **ACT,** Ac, *v. a.* and *n.* 1. To act, do, transact, S.

2. To enter or enrol as an act; synon., *to buik.*

". . than comperit Archbald Dickyson and askyt at the balyeis that thai wald caus the clerk *to ac* that deliuerans in the common buk on hys expensis." Burgh Rec. Peebles, 21 July, 1479.

3. To become surety or responsible for another.

". . William Tait and James Mathiesone became *actit* conjunctlie and seuerablie for William Mathiesone," &c. Burgh Recs. Poebles, 1 Mar., 1629.

4. To appoint, command, sentence, summon.

". . and vnderlye the saidis lawes als oft as he salbe requyrit or *acit* thairto," &c. Burgh Rec. Peebles, 1 Mar., 1620.

Ac, *s.* An act, law, rule, record.

". . caus the clerk to mak an *ac* thairapon," &c. Burgh Rec. Peeb., 14 Jan., 1481.

Ack is used for *act* in England also.

Actit, Ackit, Acit, *part. pt.* Enacted; appointed or resolved to be the law; also, entered in the books of the burgh as law or judgment; recorded. Hence, made or become surety for another; sentenced, summoned. V. *Act, Ac.*

This term under various spellings is common in all our Burgh Records, and in those of the higher courts.

Actor, Auctor, *s.* An author, writer; Compl. Scot., p. 25, E. E. T. S.

To **ADDRESS,** Addres, *v. a.* 1. To dress, prepare, fit, or plan. In Golfing, to prepare or make ready for striking the ball: part. pres. *addressing.*

". . their ceremonies consisting in three points: First, in mourning for the dead; next, in *addressing* the corpse for the grave; and last, in his conuoyance thither." Blame of Kirkburiall, ch. vii.

2. To array, collect, and set in order.

He gat soyne vittyng that thai weir
Cumand on him, and war so neir,
His men *addressit* he thame agane,
And gert thame stoutly tak the plane.
Barbour, xiv. 263. Skeat.

The meaning is similar to that of *dress* in *dressing the lines:* indeed the Edin. MS. reads *dressyt.*

O. Fr. *addresser,* from *dresser,* to erect, set up, arrange.

Addres, Address, Addressement, *s.* Redress, adjustment, arrangement.

". . quhidder thai get ane *addressement* or nocht, and to take the next-best, and gif it be found that thai get ane sufficient *addres,*" &c. Burgh Rec. Peebles, 16 Feb., 1570.

". . gif they can haif ane *address* of my lord Regent grace," &c. Burgh Rec. Peebles, 16 Feb., 1570; also 12 Apr., 1570.

Addressement, *s.* Same as *Address,* q. v.

To **ADDUCE,** *v. a.* To lead on, entice, wheedle, beguile: part. pt. *adduced.*

". . as he did punishe the seducing serpent with a curse, the inducing Eua with a crosse of subjection . . ,the oueransly *adduced* Adam with the care and sweatty labours of this militant lyfe," &c. Blame of Kirkburiall, ch. xix.

ADJUTORIE, *s.* Aid, help, assistance; helper, assistant; Dunbar, Ballad to Lord Stewart, l. 25.

Lat. *adjutorium,* help; *adjutor,* helper.

ADMIRALITE, *s.* Oversight; act or right of inspection or examination: an old form of right of search.

". . askis and requiris *admiralite* of our saide schip, to the gret tribill of our said seruitor," &c. Burgh Recs. Aberd., 25 Dec., 1497.

ADO, *v.* 1. To do; *aw ado,* ought to do; Charters of Edinburgh, 12th and 20th Sept., 1423.

It is also used in the same sense in Barbour, x. 349; and this use is still common in the West of S., as in—
"Ye hae nathing *ado* wi' that."
Ado is short for *at do*, to do.

2. As a *part.*, doing, adoing, being done; as, "There's little *ado* in the market the day," West of S.

3. As a *s.*, worth, concern, importance; as, "A matter of more *ado*," Blame of Kirk-buriall, ch. xi.
Also used as in E. in the sense of bustle, trouble, difficulty, &c.

ADOUN, *adv.* Down, down by, S. Same as E. *adown*.

ADUERSAR, ADUERSOUR, *s.* Adversary, enemy, assailant; pl. *aduersouris*, Barbour, xvii. 736. Also, the opposite party in an action at law, Stirling Charters, 1508, Peebles Recs.

To ADVERT, ADUERT, *v. a.* To turn towards, to direct. Lat. *advertere*.
Till Jupiter his mercie list *aduert*.
Kingis Quair, st. 25. SKEAT.
Dr. Jamieson rendered this term, "to avert, to turn aside," which is wrong. Probably he was misled by his first reading of the passage he gives in illustration :—
Fra my sinnes *advert* thy face.
Poems, Sixteenth Cent., p. 116.
And Dr. Laing made the same mistake in editing "The Gude and Godlie Ballates." V. his Gloss.
To advert is lit. to turn to or towards; then, to direct to or towards, to grant or send; then, to direct, and hence, to control: but it is generally used in the secondary meanings. In the passage last quoted it means simply *to direct, to turn;* and in the first passage, *to grant* or *send*.

ADVERTENCE, *s.* Ability or power to advert to; direction, control, power to control. Kingis Quair, st. 108.

ADUORTIT, *part. pt.* Miscarried, Sempill Ballates, p. 163.
Fr. *avorter*, to miscarry : Lat. *abortire*, id.

ADZOOKS, *interj.* An exclamation of surprise, disgust, scorn: properly, a minced oath, being a corr. or veiled form of *godsake*, or even a stronger oath; Renfrews., Ayrs.
And rang'd in mony a glorious line,
Appear the bouncin' lasses;
Whase shape, *adzooks*,
An' killing looks,
An' claes like o'ening cluds;
Wad hermits fire
Wi' fond desire,
To leave their caves an' woods.
Alex. Wilson's Poems, p. 83.
This term is not unknown in E., as the following passage, written in 1834, shows—
And says I, "Add-zooks!
There's Theodore Hooks,
Whose sayings and doings make such pretty books."
Lines by the author of "Ingoldsby Legends."

AEFALD, *adj.* Single, simple; hence, straightforward, honest, upright, S. V. AFALD.

AER, AAR, AIR, *s.* A stony, pebbly beach; also, a smooth beach, a sandbank, the seashore. V. AIR.
This term is confined to Orkney and Shetland, and may be traced to Icel. *eyrr*, a gravelly bank; O. Norse *eyri*, the sea-shore where no grass grows. V. Gl. Orkn. and Shetl.

AESSIEPATTLE, ASSIPATTLE, *s.* A name applied to a neglected child; one who sits or pattles among the ashes, Orkn. and Shetl. V. ASHIEPATTLE.
In the central and southern districts of S., the term becomes *assiepet*, q. v.

AETEN, *adj.* Oaten, Ramsay. V. AITEN.

AETH-KENT, *adj.* Easily - known, well-known; also, easily recognised, Shetl. V. EITH.
This term is still widely spread in S.; and consequently is variously pronounced. However, there are two leading forms, *aeth* or *aethly-kent*, and *eith* or *eithly-kend* or *kent*.
A.-S. *łath*, easy; and *cennan*, to ken, make known, causal of *cunnan*, to know.

AFFAMYSIT, *part. pt.* Famished, starved.
Affamysit for falt of fude.
Lyndsay, Exper. and Court., l. 5490.
Fr. *affamer*, to famish.

To AFFANE, *v. a.* To attempt, essay, try; Alex. Scott, Bann. MS., p. 686, l. 1. V. AFAYND.

AFFECTION, *s.* Self-will, opinionativeness, obstinacy; the act of following one's own inclination.
"But now most men alss are so deeply addicted to *affection*, that they neyther make count nor question how or where they should bury," &c. Blame of Kirk-buriall, ch. v.
This is a peculiar application of Lat. *affectio*, the nature or condition of a thing: it implies much the same idea as *affinity*, as applied in chemistry.

AFFEER, AFFERE, *s.* Demeanour: a form used for *effer, effeir*, q. v. Barbour, vii. 126, Herd's Ed. V. AFFEIR.

AFFERIT, AFFERT, *part. pt.* Afraid, made afraid, Bann. MS., p. 93, l. 12. V. AFFERD.

To AFFERME, *v. a.* 1. To affirm, declare.

2. To confirm, constitute, make legally binding.
Quhen this cunnand thus tretit wes,
Aud *affermit* with sekirnes.
Barbour, iv. 178.
". . . ner the les the soytis salbe callyt and the court *affermyt*." Chalmerlan Air, ch. 3.

AFFETTERIT, *part. pt.* Fettered, enthralled: Henryson, Orph. and Eur., l. 603.
A.-S. *fetor, feter*, a fetter.

To **AFFEY**, *v. a.* To trust, Bann. MS., p. 691, l. 5. V. AFFY.

AFFIRMANT, AFFIRMAT, AFIRMAT, *s.* One who holds the Bishop's courts, and has the right of confirmation.

". . becaus that Robert Elect *affirmat* of Abirdon has schavine hym vnkindly," &c. Burgh Recs. Aberd., 7 Nov., 1431.
Lat. *affirmare.*

To **AFFLUDE,** *v. a.* To injure the look or appearance of anything, Dan. pro. *aflöd,* id. Gl. Orkn. and Shetl.

Many of the etymologies in this work are perplexing, and not to be relied on; this is a specimen. No authority is given; and nothing like it is to be found in Aasen. Perhaps *afflöde,* to skim off the cream, is intended.

AFFMAKING, *part.* and *s.* Lit. making or taking off; hence, lessening, dealing out, selling off; and generally applied to a load or stock of goods.

". . dischairging the bringeris of fir to the towne frome *affmaking* of thair loadis," &c. Burgh Recs. Aberd., 15 Aug., 1632.

This act forbad country people selling off their loads of fire-wood, fir branches, &c., outside the town; as, by so doing they escaped payment of the dues demanded by the town. *Affmaking* is the opposite of *upmaking,* gathering together.

AFFRAYIT, AFFREYIT, AFRAYIT, *part. pt.* Made afraid, dismayed, afraid.
Cumand on thaim sa sudanly,
Thai all *affrayit* be gretumly.
Barbour, ii. 291.

AFFRAYITLY, AFFRAITLY, *adv.* Timidly, in terror; in a frightened way; Barbour, vi. 296.
The laif fled full *affrayitly.*
Barbour, vi. 434. SKEAT.

AFFRUG, AFRUG, *s.* Back-roll, return: "*affrug* o' the sea, a spent wave receding from the shore;" Gl. Shetl.

Prob. from Dan. *af,* off, and *ryk,* a rug, jerk, pull; *afrykke,* to twitch or pull off; Sw. *afrycka.*

AFFSET, *s.* 1. Hindrance or stoppage of a person at work, or of the work on which he is engaged; also, the cause of the hindrance or stoppage, and the time during which it lasts; as, "We've ha'en an *affset* every month this simmer. This ane 's the want o' wattir for the mill: an' last pay my *affset* was three days."

2. An attack of illness or whatever unfits a person for work; also, the cause of it, the consequence of it, &c.; as, "John's ha'en a sair *affset* this while: it was a fivver. Aye, he'll fin' that *affset* (i.e., the effects of it) for mony a day."

3. Ornament, decoration, beautifying; chief attraction, crown or completion of a work, the best of all; as, "That window o' floura is a gran' *affset* to the room." "That's his best pictur, it's the *affset* o' a' the lave."

In these senses the term is still used over the greater part of Scot. At first sight there seems to be no connection between the last sense and the first and second; but a little consideration will solve the difficulty, and it will be seen that they are simply the bad and the good senses of *affsetting* or departure from the usual, ordinary state of matters. An *affset* from work or health is a serious matter to the worker; and an *affset* or increase of beauty touches even the most sordid nature. For the first and second senses one might use for syn. the term *dounset*; while for the third the terms *outset* and *upset* in their best meanings, would be the most agreeable.

These are additional meanings to those of the DICT.

To **AFFY,** *v. a.* To trust; pret. and part. pt. *affyit,* trusted, believed; *affy* also means to inspire or give confidence; Douglas, Encados, Bk. xi., ch. 8.
In commownys may nane *affy,*
Bot he that may thar warand be.
Barbour, ii. 502.

AFFYANCE, *s.* Trust, confidence; Douglas, Palice of Honour, st. 7.
Fr. *afier,* Lat. affidare, to trust, confide.

AFIRMAT, *s.* V. *Affirmant.*

AFOIR, *adv.* and *prep.* Before, Aberd. Burgh Recs., vol. ii., p. 210. V. *Afore.*

AFORDALE, *adv.* To the fore, remaining on hand, laid aside for future use; also, still alive. V. AFFORDELL. It is also used as an *adj.*

". . that fall the fre mone the towne has *afordale,*" &c. Burgh Recs. Aberd., 26 Jan., 1544, Sp. C.

AFORE, AFOR, AFOIR, *adv., prep.,* and *adj.* Before; as, "He ran on *afore,* and wan there *afore* the time, wi' the *afore*-han' siller,".S.

Fore-han' is, however, more common.
My Lan' *afore* 's a gude auld has-been.
Burns, The Inventory, l. 8.

Lyndsay used three forms of this term, *afore, affore, afforow. Afore* is still colloquial in the north of England; and *afern* was used by Chaucer, Rom. Rose, l. 3951.
A.-S. *onforan,* in front.

AFRAYIT, *part. pt.* V. *Affrayit.*

AFTERLING, EFTERLING, *adj.* Later, of later date; late in order of time or succession.

"Againe, for the processe of *afterling* practise, we finde it precise to the paterne as the owne positiue law." Blame of Kirkburiall, ch. xvi.

"Whose *afterling* entry falling out in the dreg of all tymes, doth render it not onely suspect," &c. Ibid., ch. xiii.

AFTERSHOT, *s.* After-thought, later-invention, product, result.
"The searcher will finde it but an *aftershot* of antiquitie; as the back-treading of tymes will teach." Blame of Kirkburiall, ch. xiii.
In the process of distilling whisky, the strong spirit which comes away first is called the *foreshot* or *foreshots;* and that which comes last, the *aftershot* or *aftershots.*

AFT-HANKS, *s.* That part of a boat where the bands come together at the stem and stern, Gl. Orkn. and Shetl.
Perhaps the same origin as *hunks* and *hunkers.* Icel. *húka,* to sit with bent legs; *hokra,* to go bent.

AGANE, AGAIN, AGIN, GANE, GEN, GIN, *prep.* Against; also, by, by the time of, on, at; thus, " Fortune 's been sair *agane* him;" "It'll be ready *agane* Saturday;" "I'll be back *agane* gloamin, or agane e'en;" "If a' gangs weel, he'll be here *gane* Martimes." V. *An, prep.*
Agin is merely a variety of *agane;* and *gane, gen, gin,* are contracted forms of it. *Againt* and *gaint,* with the meaning *against* are also used in various districts of the West of S.
All these varieties are from A.-S. *gean, ongean,* opposite, against: implying opposition made or taken up; motion towards and up to a certain point; also, duration or passing of time to a certain point; the point in each case being indicated by the noun or phrase following. (See the examples given above.) Hence the other meanings, *by, by the time of, on, at, about,* which have lived on in the Scot. dialect, and have almost, if not altogether, died out in the English.

AGANESAID, *part. pt.* Gainsaid, resisted.
". . for it is to wit that all domes falsit or *aganesaid* in burrow courts salbe determinyt and declarit in Hadingtoune, throw foure burgess vysaste and sufficiandest of ilk ane of thire burrowis, Borwik, Roxburgh, Edinburgh, Striueling, befor the chalmerlain withoutyne delay." Fragments of Old Laws, 52.

AGANEWARDE, *adv.* Contrarywise.
"The Kyngis borowman may hafe batayle of abbotis borowmen and of pryouris and of erlys borowmen and barounis, bot nocht *agaynwarde.*" Burgh Lawis, 13.

AGANIS, AGANYS, *prep.* Against, Barbour, vii. 12, xiv. 316. A.-S. *ongean.*

AGIN, AGANE, *adv.* and *prep.* Again, against; by, by the time of; by and bye; in opposition to; also, a second time, as "ye'll better no do that *agin!*" Clydes. V. *Agane.*
Agin is common in England as a prov. form.

AGIT, *adj.* Aged, well up in years, S.
Off *agit* folk, with hedis hore and dolie.
Kingis Quair, st. 83.
Still the common pron. of *aged.*

To AGMENT, *v. a.* To augment, enlarge, increase, extend; as, "We man *agment* his aliment." West of S. Used by Lyndsay, Exper. and Court., l. 2998.

AGMENT, *s.* Augment, increase, Ayrs.
Fr. *augmenter,* Lat. *augmentare,* to enlarge, increase. The *s.* is prob. older than the *v.* V. Skeat's Etym. Dict. under *Augment.*

AGO, *part. pt.* Gone, decayed, dead; also used as a pres. part., going, astir, fast going, fading, dying out.
Gentrice is slane, and pietie is *ago,*
Allace! gude Lord, quhy tholis Thow it so?
Henryson, Dog, Scheip, and Wolf, l. 167.
A.-S. *dgán,* gone, past.

AGONE, *part. pt.* as *adv.* Ago; *agone syne mony a yere,* long ago many a year, or many a long year ago. Kingis Quair, st. 196, Skeat.

To AGREGE, *v. a.* To follow up, prosecute, press; Burgh Recs. Aberd., 29 July, 1530, Sp. C. V. AGGREGE.

AGREST, *adj.* Rustic, rural; Compl. Scot., p. 16, E.E.T.S.

AHAME, *adv.* At home, within doors; as, "Ye better bide *ahame* the day;" a contr. of *at hame.* Ayrs., Gall.

AIBLINS, *adv.* Perhaps. V. ABLINS.
This form is used in the poems of Burns, Alex. Wilson, and most of the minor poets of the West of S. Ramsay, however, appears to have used *ablins.* V. The Gentle Shepherd.

AICHAN, AIKEN, ACHEN, *s.* A small bivalve (*Mactra subtruncata,* Da Costa), found in sandy bays of the Frith of Clyde.
Prob. so named on account of its likeness to an acorn: A.-S. *dc,* an oak; *deen,* oaken.
Myriads of *aichan* shells were dug up near Dumbreck, by the workmen engaged in cutting the canal between Glasgow and Paisley.

AIKIS, *s.* An axe; pl. *aikisis;* Burgh Recs., Aberd., 1 June, 1547, Sp. C. V. AIX.
This form represents the common pron., which is similar to that of the earliest times; Gothic *akwisi,* an axe; O. Northumb. *acase.*

AIL, AILL, *s.* Ailment, sickness; ill of whatever kind.
Be that sum pairte of Mawkynis *aill,*
Outthrow his hairt cowd creip;
He fallowit hir fast thair till assaill,
And till hir tuke gude keip.
Henryson, Robene and Makyne, l. 77, Bann. MS.

AILE, AILL, *s.* Ale.
"Item, at the pottis at thai haf contenis nocht samekle cler *aile* withoutyn berme." Chalmerlan Air, 10.
"Also, gif the bailies keep the assise of bred, *aill,* and flesches." Inquiries, Chalmerlan Air, 5.

AILL-BOT, *s.* An ale-barrel; kept as store for the household ale.
". . item, ane *aill-bott,* vj s. viij d.," &c. Burgh Recs. Glasgow, 28 Jan., 1588-9.

AILSHIE, ALSHIE, s. A familiar name for Alexander, S. V. ELSHIE.

"—— a speech worthy of *Ailshie* Gourlay, or any other privileged jester," etc. Scott, Antiquary, ch. 43.

AIN, AINE, adj. One.

"Also, gif any man halds in his ovene mae servants than *aine* master, twa servants, and ane knave." Inquiries, Chalmerlan Air, 51.
Ovene, bakehouse; *master*, journeyman.

AIRANDS, AIRANS, s. pl. Errands, messages, business, avocation.

". . vnder the payne of putting in the netherhole incontinent, exceptand folkis of honesty passand thair leifull *airands*, and at thai haif bowetts or candillis within thair [hands] in taikin thairof." Burgh Rec. Edin., 17 Nov., 1498.

AIRD, s. The earth, ground, soil.

". . Kepand the *aird* and schriff thairof on—delvit or cassin vp," &c. Burgh Recs. Aberd., 25 Nov., 1590. Sp. C.
This form is according to local pron.

AIRGH, AIRCH, adj. Averse, reluctant, hesitating; synon. *swithering*. V. ARGH.

AIRISKAP, ARSCHIP, ARSCAP, s. Heirship, heritage, inheritance. V. AYRSCHIP.

". . the quhilk forsaid gudis the said Edam gaf to James Brown for his *airiskap* or the dividing of the barnis gudis." Burgh Rec., Prestwick, May 13, 1743.
". . the quhilk suld be *arschip* till her sone," &c. Burgh Rec., Prestwick, Oct., 1515.
". . the said Jonet than incontinent deliverit the *arscap* tyl John his schon." Burgh Rec., Peebles, 28 Mar., 1457.

AIRNS O' A PLEUCH. Irons of a plough; the iron portions of the old plough. V. PLEUCH IRNES, PLEUCH AIRNS.

To AIRT, v. a. and n. 1. To set or place in or towards a certain direction; as, "Lay them open, an' *airt* them east an' west."

2. To move, walk, or work in a certain direction, or towards a certain point: hence to tend, wend, try, persevere; as, "He's dune weel, an's *airtin* to the cn' o' his wark." "I *airtit* hard to get awa' wi' the laird; but I saw him *airtin* hame an' oor by;" i.e., an hour ago.

These are meanings additional to Dr. Jamieson's.

AISK, s. and v. Drizzle. V. *Ask*.

To AISLE, AIZLE, v. a. To sun, to dry in the sun. V. ASOL.

AISLE, AIZLE, ISEL, s. 1. A red-hot ember, a fragment shot from a fierce woodfire, a gleaming point; as, "Fra the hill we saw the licht in the windo like a bricht, far-awa *aisle*," Ayrs. V. EIZEL.

2. A mass of red-hot embers, a red-hot, gleaming or glowing fire; as, "Draw the fire thegither an' mak a fine *aisle*," Ibid.

3. As an adj.; red-hot, gleaming, glowing; as, "Ye man keep the fire in a fine *aisle* tid, or *aisle* heat," Ibid.

Under *eizel*, both meaning and etymology are defective; and the full force of the passages quoted is not brought out.
A.-S. y̆sel, y̆sele, a fire spark, spark, ember, hot ashes; and such are the meanings of the term still.

To AISLE, ISEL, v. n. To become a mass of red-hot, glowing embers; to gleam, to glow: part. pr. *aislin'*, *iselin'*, *islin'*.

AISLIN', ISELIN', ISLIN', part. pr. Becoming a red-hot glowing mass; gleaming, glowing; as, "Let the fire alane; it's *aislin'* fine. I like the gluff o' an *aislin'* fire," Ayrs.

In Banffshire this term is used colloquially in a metaphorical sense. Mr. Gregor, in his Gloss. of the district, gives *isle*, anger, and *to isle*, to be angry; but, from the illustrations he gives, I suspect the definitions ought to be, *state of anger*, i.e., of red-hotness, and *to be in such a state*, which would quite accord with the primary meanings. The illustrations will make this quite evident:—

"He wiz in an *isle* at 'im for deein' that,"
"He wiz jist *islin'* at 'im, fin he widna dee fat he bade 'im."

AISTLAR, s. Ashlar work; a hewn stone; used also as an adj., as, "*aistlar* wa's," i.e., walls of ashlar work.

". . with gunbollis and duiris of *aistlar*," &c. Burgh Recs. Aberd., 20 Feb., 1532, Sp. C.

AITHER, conj. Either; as, "Aither you gang or I gang," Clydes.

AITHER, AYTHER, conj. and pron. The one or the other, each of two, one of two: as, "Ye'll get *aither* o' them ye like;" "jist see thae twa *aither* wi' ither how thai gae on!" "There's but twa left; an' I mun hae *aither* o' them."

A.-S. œgther, a contracted form of œghwœther, aye whether, in the sense of *whichever*.

AIT-MELE, s. Oatmeal.

"Item, for viij. bollis of *ait mele* ; for ilk boll xj. s." Accts. Lord H. Treas. Scot., 1497, I. 343, Dickson.
A.-S. *ata*, oat or oats, and *melu*, *melo*, meal: Dan. and Du. *meel*, Swed. *mjöl*.

AITRIE, AITTRIE, adj. Cold, bleak, grim; generally applied to the weather. Used also as a s., cold, bleak weather; Gl. Orkn. & Shet. V. ATRY.

This is merely a softened form of *atrie*; but in sound nearer the origin. Icel. *eitr*, poison.

AIVING, part. Being in doubt, hesitating, considering, Shetl.

AIVILOUS, AIVALOUS, *adj.* Doubtful, uncertain, Ibid.

Icel. *efa, ifa*, to doubt, to be in doubt; *efan, ifan*, doubt; *efan-ligr, ifan-ligr*, doubtful.

AIZLE-TEETH, *s. pl.* Double teeth, grinders. V. ASIL.

This is a common name in the West and South of S., and in some districts of the North of E. Icel. *jaxl*, a molar; in Shetl. still called a *yackle*. Sw. *oxeltander*, molars.
In Renfrew. and Lanarka. the pron. is *assle* or *aisle teeth*. The Cleveland Gloss. gives *assle-tooth*.

TO AK, AC, ACK, *v. a.* and *n.* V. *Act.*

AK, *s.* An oak, A.-S. *ac.* V. AIK.

"Item, the ferd day of March, [1496] gevin for xxxᵗⁱ sparris, to mak a paraling of *ak* for the gunnys; for ilk spar iiij. s.," &c. Accts. Lord H. Treas. Scot., l. 322, Dickson.

AKER, *s.* An acre; pl. *akeris.*

". . . a confirmacioune of vj. *akeris* of land wyth the pertinentis, wythin the schirefdome of Edinburgh," &c. Accts. Lord H. Treas. Scot., i. 218, Dickson.

AKERBRAID, *s.* The breadth of an acre; generally applied to space or distance; Chryst Kirk, Bann. MS. p. 284, l. 70.

ALABAST, *s.* Alabaster.

Schir Arch[i]bald his sone gert syne
Of *alabust* bath fair and fyne
[Ordano] a towne full richly,
As it behufit till swa worthy.
  Barbour, xx. 588, Camb. MS.

The Edin. MS. has *alabastre*. Gr. *alabastos*.

ALANE, ALLANE. It *alane*, the mod. *its lane*, of itself, without any other means, help, or inference; lit. *it al ane*, it all by itself.

". . . sa that it walde haue fallin donne *it allane*, suppois the said William had never put hande to his house." Burgh Recs., Aberd., 20 Oct., 1503.

ALANA, ALANIE, A'LANY, *adv.* and *interj.* All alone, all alone now! A term of advice or encouragement used by a mother or nurse when teaching an infant to stand or walk, S.

This term is interesting on account of its being one of the oldest in our language. The earliest Saxon settlers used it, in almost the same tones as now, in the first homes they made in our land. It is pure Northumbrian Anglo-Saxon, *al dna*, all alone.

ALBEID, *conj.* Albeit, although; Sempill Ballates, p. 239. V. ALDUIST.

ALBLASTRIE, ALBLASTRYE, *s.* Weapons of the arbalest or crossbow kind used in war or hunting; also the art or practice of shooting with them. L. Lat. *arbalista*, a crossbow; *arbalisteria*, crossbow artillery.

. . . . . the elk for *alblastrye*.
  Kingis Quair, st. 156.

(Sup.)   D

For *alblastrye* may mean, "famed in the practise of shooting;" since, on account of the speed of the animal and the thickness of its hide, to shoot an elk would require great skill and address in the use of the crossbow. Or it may mean "for resisting shot of crossbow," or simply, "for resisting shot"; as in speaking of armourplate we say, "It must be steel for shot," i.e., for resisting shot. Prof. Skeat evidently adopts the latter rendering : ". . *for alblastrye* means 'against warlike cross-bow bolts and darts." V. Kingis Quair, p. 87. Regarding the capability of elk-hide to resist pointed weapons, he, however, quotes the following important statement:—". . shields and targets were made of the skin of the elk, which were thick enough *to resist the point of the sharpest spear.*" E. Phipson, Animal Lore, p. 122.

ALD, ALDE, AULD, *s.* 1. That which is old; as, "The *ald* is better that the new." This is the old form of the *adj.*

2. The past or olden time; as "Stories of *ald.*"

3. Old age; as, "*Alde* an' ill are sair to bide."

4. Old people, and people of the past or olden time; as, "The *auld* like best the proverbs o' the *ald.*"

5. Parents, when compared with children; thus, "As gangs the *ald*, sae rins the young."

The term is still used in all these senses; but in *s.* 2, perhaps *eild* is more common.
In Roland's rendering of the story of the Seven Wise Masters, the term occurs frequently.

As for that time I laid on side my holye,
And in my hand sue uther volume tuke.
Of lychter dyte and storeis of the *ald*,
That seir auld men befoir in tymes had tald.
  S. Seages, l. 260.

Quod scho, it is ane Proverb of the *ald*,
Quhilk I oft times in mirriues hes hard tald.
  Ibid., l. 277.

A.-S. *cald*, old.

ALDERS, ALDERIS, AULDERS, *s. pl.* Ancestors, forefathers, people older than ourselves; parents, as regards their children; South and West of S.

When changes are pressed on an unwilling person, a very likely reply will be—"It sairt our *alders*, it may weel sair us ;" i.e., it served our forefathers, &c. A common expression of respect for old age in a mixed company is,—"We'll let the *aulders* gang first." And a mother, in answer to the clamours of hungry children at meal-time, will say,—"Jist ye bide gin yer *alders* are sairt," Clydes.

ALE-CAP, *s.* Originally, the horn or wooden vessel from which ale was drunk, but latterly the name was applied to any kind of vessel used for that purpose; it is also used as a general term for ale-drinking, carousing, &c.

Ale-cap wi' lass he ne'er had kis't.
  Alex. Wilson's Poems, p. 369, Ed. 1876.

Yill-caup, the form used by Burns in the Holy Fair, was certainly the pron. with which Wilson was best acquainted, and which he commonly used.

ALECK, ALICK, *s.* A familiar form for Alexander; same with Sandy, Sanny, Sawny, Saunders.
  Blind *Aleck* next appears,
  Whose head for many years,
  A hot-bed of poesie has been.
  Finlay, Street Oratory, Whistle Binkie, i. 257.

ALERING, ALLERING, ALRINE, ALRYNE, *s.*
1. The passage or channel behind the battlement of a building, which served to collect the waters that fell upon the roof; *alure,* Prompt. Parv.
  ". . . mending of the battelling and *alering* of the tolbuith," &c. Burgh Recs., Aberd., 18 June, 1554, Sp. C.
  When the battlement was low or the roof came near to it, a channel was cut in the passage to lead the water to the gargoilles, hence—

2. The water-channel round the roof of a building.
  "Item, gevin to ane man to clenge the *allering* of the tolbuith, and to beir the red of it away, ij^s vj^d "
  Accts. Burgh of Edin., 16 Feb., 1554. Recs. Soc.

3. The term was also applied to the battlement or crown of a building, and to a parapet wall.
  The touris to take and the torellis,
  Vautes, *alouris*, and the cornellis.
  Kyng Alisaunder, l. 7210.
  Into her cité thai ben y-gon,
  Togider thai assembled hem ichon,
  And at the *alours* thai defended hem.
  Gy of Warwike, p. 85.
  See Halliwell under *alour,* and Prompt. Parv. under *alure ;* also, Du Cange under *Alatoria, Allorium.*
  The form *alure* occurs in Robert of Gloucester. But *alering* and *alrine* or *alryne* are the Scot. forms of the term, and the modern *rin* or *rins,* as the name of the channels cut round the roof of a building, may be short for *alrin, alrins.*
  Fr. *alleure, allure, allés,* a passage, way.

ALEWAND, AILWANDE, *s.* The sign hung out by brewers and sellers of ale. In Chaucer, *ale-stake.*
  "And ilke broustare sal put hir *alewande* ututh hir house at hir wyndow or abune hir dur, that it may be seabill community til al men, the whilk gif scho dois nocht scho sal pay for her defalt iiijd." Burgh Lawis, 63.
  "Item, at thai put nocht furth thair *ailwande* to certify the cunnaris of the ayl as thai solde." Chalmerlan Air, 10.
  A.-S. *ealo,* Icel. *öl,* ale ; Icel. *vöndr,* a shoot of a tree, a rod.

ALFE, AILF, *s.* Lit. elf; but applied to a mischievous, ill-natured, or cantankerous child; also to a troublesome person of small stature; as, "He's an *alfe* o' a wean that ;" "Did ye hear that *ailf* o' a body ?" Clydes.
  A.-S. *ælf,* an elf.

ALFISH, AILFISH, *adj.* Cross, fretful, mischievous, ill-natured, Ibid. E. *elfish.*

ALICREESH, ALICREES, ALICRIS, *s.* Licorice, Spanish licorice, Clydes., South of S.
  This was the common name for it as late as the beginning of this century. It is now called *black-sugar, sugar-ali,* and sometimes *licry.*
  Prob. a corr. of O. Fr. *liquerice,* licorice; Ital. *legorizia, lecurizia.*

ALIE-BOWLIS, *s.* The game of bowls as played in alleys, rinks, or runs.
  " . . . abuse done be scolleris and printicies haunting the yairdis quhair *alie bowlis,* Frenche kylis, and glaikis ar usit, to thair grit hurt and deboscherie," &c. Burgh Recs., Glasg., 14 Apr., 1610. V. ALAIS.

ALIENARE, ALIENOUR, *s.* Alien, stranger; but generally applied to a person living outside the burgh bounds.
  Those living in the town or burgh were called *touns-folk* or *burghers ;* those in the outlands, *outlanders* or *out-tounsfolk ;* and those outside the burgh bounds, were *alienaris* or *alienouris.* Dr. Jamieson's definition of *alienare* is therefore defective.

ALIKEWAYES, ALYKEWAYES, ELYK-WAYES, *adv.* Likewise, in like manner, also, in addition. Burgh Recs., Edin., ii., 89. V. ELIKWISS.

ALISURIS, *s. pl.* Prob. a misreading of *alienuris* or *alinouris,* aliens, strangers, persons living outside the burgh bounds. Burgh Recs., Aberd., 7 July 1497. V. *Alienare.*

ALK, *s.* The common guillemot, Shetl.; the black-billed Auk, Orkn.
  The term *Alk, Auk,* is applied to different birds of the Alca family ; perhaps in each case the bird so called is the species best known in that district. In the South of Scot. *auk* is, in one case at least, corr. into *hawk :*
  V. *Allan-hawk.*
  Dan. *alke,* Icel. and Swed. *alka,* an auk.

ALKIN, ALKYN, ALKYND, ALLKIN, ALL-KYN. Of every kind: *allkyn thyng,* things of every kind. Barbour, i. 134, 191 ; xiii. 717 ; xvi. 311. V. ALLKYN.
  In the Edin. MS. this word appears like *allryn,* the *k* being carelessly formed. Dr. Jamieson read it so and entered it in his Dict.; but there is no such word. See footnote in Prof. Skeat's Ed. of Barbour.
  " . . . the kyngis bailyeis sall halde rycht betuen thaim of *alkyn* manere of querelle," &c. Burgh Lawis, ch. 25.

ALL, AW, A', *adj.* Every; still in common use, as "He sells a' kin' o' thing," or "*all* kind o' things ;" West of S.
  " . . . the world lay besotted, and swattering in *all* sorts of superstition," &c. Blame of Kirkburiall, ch. xiii.
  This use of *all* is peculiar. In E. it is followed by the plural number ; but in S., even when *the* is used, the noun that follows is in the singular ; as, "He has a' *the* kin' o' things needed. The E. structure, however, is also used.

ALLAN HAWK, *s.* The Aulin or Arctic Gull, *Larus parasiticus;* prob. called *hawk* from its habit of pursuing smaller gulls till they disgorge their food. *Hawk,* however, may be a corr. of *awk.*

On the shores of the Solway Frith the Arctic Gull is known by this name : in the northern islands it is called *Scouti-aulin, Dirten-allan,* and sometimes simply *Allan.*
Neil, in his Tour through Orkney and Shetland, in describing this bird says,—"They pursue and harass all the small gulls till they disgorge or vomit; they then dexterously catch what is dropped ere it reach the water," p. 201. V. AULIN, SCOUTI-AULIN.

ALLEDGEANCE, ALLEGANCE, ALLEGANS, ALEGENS, *s.* Allegation, declaration. Lawis of the Barons, ch. 40. V. ALLEGIANCE.

ALEGANS, ALLEGANS, *s.* Allegation, declaration, Burgh Rec., Peebles, 10 May, 1462. V. ALLEGIANCE.

ALLER, *gen. pl.* Of all; *thar aller,* of them all, Barbour, i. 137. A.-S. *ealra,* gen. pl.

Given in the DICT. as an adv. meaning *wholly,* &c., and explained by various statements; but it is evidently a poetic use of an A.-S. form that even in Barbour's time had become obsolete.

ALLEVIN, *adj.* Eleven, Aberd. Burgh Recs., S.

ALLEVINT, *adj.* and *adv.* Eleventh, Ibid. S.

ALLGAT, ALLGATE, *adv.* Always, by all means, Barbour, xii. 362. V. ALGAIT.

ALLICOMGREENYIE, *s.* A game played by young girls at country schools, Gall.

They form themselves into a circle, faces toward the centre; one goes round on the outside with a cap, saying—
" I got a letter from my love,
And by the way I drop'd it, I drop'd it."
She drops the cap behind one of the party, who must pick it up and try to catch the other who runs out and in and cross the circle as quickly as possible. If the follower breaks the course, that is, does not run in the footsteps of the other, she fails. Then the one caught, or the one who fails, stands in the circle, face out, and the other goes round as before. The game ends when the last of the circle fails, or she begins it anew. V. Gall. Encycl.

ALLICOMPAIN, ALLICOMPAN, *s.* A corr. of Elecampane, a medicinal plant greatly esteemed by country people in the West and South of S.

The Elecampane or Inula Campana,—the *Inula Helenium* of the Materia Medica is in many districts believed to be a certain cure for almost every kind of pain, wound, or bruise.

ALLIE, *s.* A familiar form of the proper name Allan, West of S.

But aye when Elspa flate or things gaed wrang
Next to my pipe was *Allie's* sleekit sang.
Alex. Wilson's Poems, p. 20, Ed. 1876.

Allie here represents Allan Ramsay, whose songs were then in great repute.

ALLRYN. A misreading of *Alkyn,* q. v.

ALL-WELDAND, ALL-VELDAND, *adj.* Almighty; lit. *all-wielding.*

For had nocht god *all-veldand*
Set help intill his awne hand,
He had ben ded vithouten dreid.
Barbour, v. 577, Camb. MS.

Than lovit thai god fast, *all-veldand,*
That thai thar lord fand haill and feir.
Ibid., vi. 314, Ibid.

ALLYA, ALLYE, *s. pl.* Allies, alliance, Compl. Scot., p. 78, 182 ; *allye,* Barbour, xvii. 319, Camb. MS. Edin. MS. reads *elye.*

ALLYACE, ALLYAS, *s. pl.* Men of the same family or alliance. V. ALYA.

And ilk schield in that place
Their tennent or man wace,
Or ellis thair *allyace,*
At thair awin will.
Houlate, l. 610, Bann. MS.

Asloan MS. has *allyas.* .
Fr. *allier,* Lat. *ligare,* to tie, *alligare,* to unite.

ALMES, ALMESS, *s.* A corr. of *almous,* alms, q. v.; and used also as short for *almous-house,* alms-house.

". . the *almess* collectit ilk day," &c. Burgh Recs. Aberd., 23 Sept. 1600, Sp. C.
". . ludging within the *almes* and seikhous," &c. Ibid., 7 Oct., 1612, Sp. C.

ALMUSHOUS, *s.* An almshouse, hospital. Burgh Rec. Peebles, 25 Oct. 1462. V. ALMOUS.

ALONGWIS, ALONGOUS, ALLONGHOUSE, *prep.* Along, alongst; right or straight along.

" . . . in order, and doun *allonghouse* the haill toun to the mercat place." &c. Burgh Recs. Aberd., 17 July, 1612.

ALRICH, ALRISH, ALRISHE, *adj.* Lit., elvish, spirit-haunted ; hence, weird, lonesome, dreary, terrible, frightful. V. ELRICHE.

" . . . bogils or Gaistes . . . wandring in a vagrant estate about graves and *alrish* deserts," &c. Blame of Kirkburiall, ch. xii., xvii.
Lyndsay has "the *alrich* Queene of Farie." Thrie Estaitis, l. 1544.
This is the same term, only in another form, that Burns used in his Address to the Deil, st. 8.

When wi' an *eldritch,* stoor quaick, quaick,
Amang the springs.

ALRYNE, *s.* The passage or channel behind the battlement of a building; the channel or water-course on the roof of a building; also, a parapet or parapet wall. V. *Alering.*

"Thy tour and fortres lairge and lang,
Thy nychbours dois excell.—
Thy *alryne* is a nervall greit,
Upreiching to the hevin.
                    Maitland Poems, p. 255.

Dr. Jamieson left this term undefined; but in an elaborate note to the quotation above, he said,—"This apparently signifies a watch-tower, or the highest part of a castle;" and after giving an etymology to suit, his conclusion is,—"Thus, it may here signify the highest point or pinnacle," &c.
Both meaning and etymology are alike worthless, and this note must therefore be deleted. *Alryne* in a contr. for *alering* or *aluring*, with the meaning of M.E. *alure*; Prompt. Parv.: Fr. *alleure*, *allure*, *allée*; Cotgr. And in this passage, describing the ancient castle of Lethingtoun, it means *battlement* or *parapet*. For its various applications, v. *Alering*.

ALSA, ALSUA, *conj.* Also; A.-S. *ealswá*.
". . . to the saide first day of Decembre *alsa* inclusive," &c. Accts. Lord H. Treas. Scot., i. 1. DICKSON.
The form *alsua* occurs frequently in the Burgh Laws of Scotland: thus in ch. 7,—
"And *alsua* of this alswele as of other he aw and sall be demyt be his peris in burgh be law of burgh."

ALSAMEN-BREAD, ALSAMYN BRED, *s.* Prob. bread baked of whole flour. V. ALSAME.
". . . at thai bak nocht ilk kynd of bred as the law of burgh requeris, that is to say, wastell, symnel, alsamyn, samyn bred, and demayn." Chalmerlain Air, ch. 9.

ALSE, AUSE, AWS, *s.* Ashes. V. As.
". . . al men ar eird ande *alse*." Compl. Scot., p. 152, E.E.T.S.
A very old form of this word is *askes* which occurs in the Romance of Havelok, and is still used in the South of S.; it is now applied to the cinders of a spent fire;—at least it was so when I have heard it used, as in the expression, "*naething left but askes*." The fine dust or powder being called *alse* or *ause*.
Icel. *aska*; A.-S. *æsce*, ash.

ALS-TIT, ALSS-TITE, *adv.* As soon as possible, Barbour, v. 80. Icel. *títt*, soon.

ALSWELE, ALSWEIL, ALSS-WEILL. 1. As a *conj.*, as well as, and also, together with.
". . . the mutis wythin the kyngis burgh *alwele* mutis of landis as of othir thyngis," &c. Burgh Lawis, ch. 47.

2. As an *adv.*, as well, Barbour, i. 124.

ALTAR-MEN, *s.* Officiating priests, ministers at the altar; a similar form to *churchmen*.
"Gods Altar-mens trauels in his own trueth ought to be steil-bowed," &c. Blame of Kirkburiall, Dedication, p. 1.

ALTELYERIE, *s.* A corr. of *artillery*, ordnance.
". . . witht the peice of *altelyerie* callit ane ring dog," &c. Burgh Recs. Glasg., 11 Mar. 1577-8.

ALTHOYT, *conj.* Although.
". . . and than thai aw oustom and mall *althoyt* thai haf the samyn fredom that has the barounis of baronyis." Fragments of Old Laws, ch. 26.

To ALY, ALYE, ALYIE, *v. a.* To alienate, dispose. V. ANALIE.
". . . that acho nother sel na *aly* that arscap." Burgh Recs. Peebles, 28 Mar. 1457.

ALYAR, ALYER, *s.* One who alienates.
". . . of ony borouagis to be analyt befor at it be lauchfully profferit to the nerrest of the blude of the *alyar*." Chalmerlan Air, ch. 4.

AMATON, *s.* A thin, bony person; a mere skeleton, Gall. *Amitan*, a weak, foolish, or silly person, Dumfr.
Both forms are prob. corr. of *anatomy*.

AMEDONE, AMIDON, *s.* A kind of starch, used for dressing the finer ruffs and frills worn by ladies, commonly called *stiffing*.
"Gilliane Vau Narsone, a Fleming in Leith, who had the privilege for 21 years of making *amedone* and of selling it at 40d. the pound, complained to the Privy Council against Thomas Fleming of Edinburgh for making and selling of the said *amedone* or *stiffing*," &c. Register, Priv. Council, 1601, vi. 268.
Dutch, *ameldonk*, starch.

AMERCIAMENT, *s.* A fine; Burgh Lawis, ch. 44. V. AMERCIAT.

AMER-TREE, EMMER-TREE, *s.* A beam of wood or bar of iron built in the chimney, or set over the fire, to which is attached a chain for suspending pots, &c. Prob. for *ember-tree*; Orkn.
Evidently the same as the *rannel-tree*, *rantle-tree*, *rannle-bauks*, of the centre and south of Scot. This beam or bank was made of the *rannle* or rowan tree, to protect the hearth or house from the cantrips of witches.

To AMESE, *v. a.* To mitigate, appease, satisfy; Lyndsay, Complaint to the King, l. 42. V. AMEISE.

To AMIT, AMITT, *v. a.* To set aside, give away; also, demit, resign, lose.
". . . we mak, *amittis*, and frely giffis ouer," &c. Charters of Peebles, 15 Dec. 1473.
In this quotation *mak* is most probably a mistake for *makis*; a misreading of the transcriber. The MS. is very much decayed.
". . . he sall tyne and *amitt* the said burss," &c. Burgh Recs. Aberd., 29 Jan. 1623. "*Burss*," bursary.
Lat. *amitto*, to let go, set free.

To AMONIS, *v. a.* To exhort. V. AMMONYSS.

AMONESTYNG, *s.* Exhortation, advice. V. AMMONYSS.

Quhen he to thame of his ledyng
Had maid ane fair *amonestyng*
Till do weill, &c.
Barbour, xx. 412, Camb. MS.
Edin. MS. reads *monestyng,* q. v.

AMP, *s.* Fear, Shetl. Norw., *ampe,* trouble.

To AMPILL, *v. a.* To amplify. V. *Ample.*

To AMPLE, AMPILL, *v. a.* To amplify, extend, enlarge, augment.

" . . . and to eik, *ampill,* change, or correct the samyn als oft as neid beis," &c. Burgh Recs. Aberd., 9 Jan., 1543, Sp. C.
O.Fr. *amplier,* short for *"amplifier:* amplifie, inlarge," &c. Cotgr.

AMYT, *s.* An amice; a priestly vestment, Accts. Lord H. Treas. Scot., i. 64, 177. V. AMITE.

AN, *conj.* A contr. for *than;* similar to *at* for *that;* as, "It's mair *an* ye deserve." South and West of S.

It occurs frequently in the earlier Burgh Records.

AN, *prep.* By, about the time of; and often implying before: as, "I'll be back *an* gloamin;" "It 'll be a' by *an* ye come back," all will be over by the time, or before, you come back. Ibid.

An may be a contr. form of *agane, gane, gin,* q.v.; or simply a form of *on,* at the time, by.

To AN, *v. a.* To give, grant, concede, bestow, send.

Miche gode I wold him *an.*
Sir Tristrem, p. 42, st. 66.

Y take that me Gode *an.*
Ibid., p. 144.

Misled probably by the Glossary to this poem, Dr. Jamieson gave the definition and etymology of this word entirely wrong. It means *to give, grant, bestow;* and is from A.-S. *unnan, ic đn*; O. Ger. *geunnan;* Ger. *gönnen,* to give or grant freely.

ANALYT, *part. pt.* Alienated. V. ANALIE.

ANAMELIT, ANAMALYT, ANAMULET, *part. adj.* Enamelled. Accts. Lord H. Treas. Scot., i. 81; Barbour, xx. 305, Camb. MS.

Between 1538 and 1542 large amounts of native gold were used for the coinage of Scotland, and for making and mounting various articles for the royal household. Among these were " . . . ane dragoun *anamulet,* and ane target of the Kingis awin gold for his Majesty." Early Records of Mining in Scotland, Intro., pp. 15-16, COCHRAN-PATRICK.

ANATHEMATICALL, *adj.* By or with anathema; *"anathematicall* excommunication," excommunication with cursing.

". . . that kinde of vncleannes was punished with *anathematicall* excommunication." Blame of Kirkbariall, ch. xviii.
Gr. *anathema,* anything devoted, especially to evil.

ANCIENT, *s.* An ensign; the officer who carries the colours of his company. V. *Anseinye.*

". . . the saids capitanes to chuise thair awne lievetentis, *ancientis,* and uther inferiour officiaris," &c. Burgh Recs. Aberd., 4 Sept. 1644.

This form occurs repeatedly in these records. It is from Fr. *enseigne,* from Lat. *insigne,* a badge, flag. Shakespeare used this term in both its senses of standard and standard-bearer; as in 1 Hen. IV., iv. 2.; Oth. i. 1, ii. 1, 3.

ANCIENTE, *s.* Antiquity, ancientness. Barbour, vi. 252. V. ANCIETY.

ANCIENTRY, AUNCIENTRY, *s.* Antiquity, ancientness; as, "They claim great *ancientry* o' name and bluid;" also, old-fashionedness, precociousness; as, "The *ancientry* o' that bairn I dinna like; he talks like a gran'-father," Clydes.

ANDE, AINDE, *s.* Breath. V. AYND.

ANDLESS, AINDLESS, AINLESS, *adj.* Breathless. V. AYNDLESSE.

ANDER, *s.* A porch, Shetl. Icel. *önd,* id.

To ANDOO, *v. n.* To keep a boat in position by rowing gently against wind or tide, Orkn. and Shetl.

Lit. to *undo* the effect of wind or tide by rowing against it: Icel. *önd,* against.

ANDRUM, ANTRUM, AUNTRIN, ANTERIN, AUNTERIN, *s.* The name given to the afternoon or early evening repast; also, the time allotted to it; called also, *four-hours, é'enshanks,* and *anterin-time.*

These are corruptions of A.-S. *undern,* the third hour, i.e., 9 a.m.; but the term was afterwards applied to the third hour after noon, and by-and-bye to *afternoon* and *evening.* Under various forms it is found in many of the English dialects; for particulars see Halliwell's Dict. under Aunder.

The Scot. corruptions may be traced thus: *antrum* and its varieties from *andrum;* and this for *andorn,* which in turn is a corr. pronunciation of *undern.*

The term *drum,* as applied to ladies' afternoon tea, is a modern contraction of *andrum.*

The afternoon repast was also called *andersmeat* by our forefathers; and this must be a very old term, as even in Gothic we find *undaurni-mats,* uudern-meat.

ANE, *adj.* and *s.* One, some one, somebody, as, "Sae, *ane* telt me to gae up by," i.e., some one told me, &c. South and West of S.

A' ANE. All one, quite the same, immaterial; as, "It's *a' ane* whether ye gang or I gang, Ibid. Cf. prov. E., "It's *all one* to me."

AR ANE, WAR ANE. This phrase is still common, meaning of one mind, plan, or purpose, united.
That all *war ane* faine wald I wis,
Bot yit thocht sum againis yow faill,
This actioun haill sa honest is,
With Godis grace it sall preuaill.
Sempill Ballates, p. 21.

IN ANE. At once, immediately. E. *anon.*
Dame Nature the nobillest nychit *in ane*,
For to ferm this fetherem, and dewly hes done.
Houlate, l. 887, Bann. MS.
This phrase is also used in the sense of *in one*; *in one set, lot, or piece*; *united, whole*; as, "The pairts were a' *in ane* when ye got it;" i.e., were in their proper place or order, connected.

OUR ANE, OOR ANE. Lit. our one; but applied to husband, wife, son, daughter, lad, lass, or sweetheart, instead of the name, and sometimes as the name of him or her; as, "*Oor ane* boght me a gran' goun at the fair." West of S.
A common salutation by a country lad to his lass on giving her a present is,—"Hae! that's for ye'r *our ane;*" i.e., because you are, &c.

ANERYS, *adj.* Single, only, own.
This form is due to adding the masc. gen. suffix *es* to *anre*, which is the A.-S. gen. fem. of *án*, one.
"A burges may thruch his *anerys* vuyce put hym till athe at nytis hym his dett, what man sum evir he be." Burgh Lawis, ch. 28.
"*Nytis,*" denies.

ANEW, *s.* A ring or bracelet, a clasp; also, a tendril of a creeping plant, a twist or curving spray in a garland or chaplet of flowers, a sprig, a curl; pl. *anewis*.
A chapellet with mony fresche *anewis*.
Kingis Quair, st. 160.
Jamieson's explanation of *anewis* is not sufficiently full and clear, and does not present the fine figure of the poet correctly. The *anewis* mean the rings or wreaths composing the chaplet, or, the sprays or clusters ringed or twined into it; hence, the passage suggests a chaplet with many fair, fresh wreaths, or, with many fresh sprays twined. In short, one like that worn by the fair Joan when the poet first saw her. V. st. 46, 47, of the Quair.

ANGALUCK, *s.* An accident, a misfortune, Shetl.
Dan. *angaae*, to concern; and *lykke*, luck.

ANGELLIS, *s. pl.* Angels, angel nobles; coins. The Angel or Angel Noble was an English gold coin current in Scotland, and valued at 24s.
". . . tauld in presens of the Chancellare, Lord Lile, the Prior of Sanctandros, in a pyne pig of tin. In the fyrst, of *angellis* twa hundreth foure score and v *angellis*," &c. Accts. Lord H. Treas. Scot., i. 79.
"Item, that samyn nycht [22 Aug. 1497] giffin to Schir Robert Ker, als he had lent the King to the cartis, tua vnicornis, tua *angellis:* summa iiij lib. ijs viij d." Ibid., i. 353, DICKSON.

Rating a unicorn at 18s., the angel was then worth 23s. 4d.

ANGERIE, *s.* A crowd, multitude, Shetl.
Prob. from Icel. *ör-grynni*, a countless multitude; VIGFUSSON.

ANGRIE, *adj.* Angry, enraged, mad.
The Husband than woxe *angrie* as ane hair.
Henryson, Fox, Wolf, and Moon, l. 12.
The phrase "*angrie as ane hair*," like its modern form "mad as a March hare," had even in Henryson's time a wide range of application.
"*Husband,*" husbandman, ploughman.

ANGYEOUN, *s.* An onion. Burgh Recs. Aberd., ii. 127. V. INGOWNE.

ANGYR, *s.* Affliction, vexation. Barbour, i. 235. As an *adj.*, grievous, distressing. Ibid., xx. 490. V. ANGIR.
The adj. form *angry*, as used by Barbour, means *adverse, troublesome*, v. 70; *vexatious*, xvii. 24.

ANGYRLY, ANGIRLY, *adv.* Angrily. Barbour, iv. 321, Edin. MS.; Ibid., viii. 486, Camb. MS.

ANKER, ANKYR, *s.* An anchor; pl. *ankyrs*. Barbour, iii. 691.
"And gif the schippis duellis and makis resting and tweeches the erd with *anker,*" &c. Custome of Schippis, ch. 1.

ANKER-HALD, *s.* Anchorage; bottom fit for anchoring, bottom.
For *anker-hald* nane can be fund,
I pray zow cast the leid-lyne owt.
Sempill, Flemyng Bark, s. 7.

ANKER, ANKYR, *s.* 1. A dry measure, similar to the firlot, still used in Orkney and Shetland in measuring potatoes; one third of a barrel.

2. A liquid measure formerly in use in all districts that traded with the Dutch: it was equal to ten wine gallons. In Orkney and Shetland it was reckoned equal to 38 Danish quarts.

3. A small barrel used by smugglers for carrying their brandy on horseback, &c.: also, the small barrel, open at one end, used for holding the oatmeal in daily use, and for various other household purposes, was called an *anker*, as in the following extract from an inventory of household goods belonging to a burgess of Aberdeen:—
"Item, ... thre hand axis, a brogit staf, a litil *ankyr*, a gyrdil, a bakbrede, a brewyne fat," &c. Burgh Recs. Aberd., 26 Apr. 1477.
The *anker* is still so used in secluded districts of the South and West of S.; and is a *big* or a *wee*, a *muckle* or a *little anker*, according to its size or capacity.
Dan., Dutch, Ger. *anker*, a measure.

ANNA, ANNAT, *s.* The first year's income of a benefice: Accts. Lord H. Treas. Scot., i. 197. V. ANN.

In Scotland, the fifth penny of the *annat* belonged to the king; consequently this casualty could not be exacted without his consent.

ANNALIIT, *part. pt.* Disponed, alienated, pledged, gifted, founded. Burgh Recs. Aberd., 1563. V. ANALIE.

This term occurs in all our Burgh Recs., and under various forms. It is most frequently met with in connection with deeds of gift and foundation, and in records of bargains for loans and exchanges.

ANNES, ANNIS, *adv.* Once, one time. Burgh Rec. Peebles, 20 Oct. 1564. V. ANES.

ANNET, ANNAT, *s.* V. *Anna.*

ANNS, *s. pl.* Awns, beards of barley or grass; also, chaff of oats, barley, &c. V. AWNS.

Icel. *ögn,* Dan. *avne,* chaff.

ANNUAL, *s.* A yearly present, payment, or tax.

"Item, to the beidmen of the Trinetie College for thair *annuall* xli."
"Item, to Sir Johne Bauld for the *annual* of the grammer sculc, awing be the toun xl. s." Accts. Burgh of Edin., 1552-3, Recs. So.

ANNUAL-RENT, *s.* Yearly payment to landlord or creditor; yearly income from property or money; rent, interest, S.

This term is employed in all these senses in an entry in the Burgh Recs. of Aberd., dated 1 Dec. 1624; but, generally, it means *interest,* as in the following passage:—
". . . lyes out of payment, alsweill of principall as *annual-rent,*" &c. Burgh Recs. Aberd., 5 Feb. 1640. Recs. So.

ANORDINAR, ANORDNAR, ANORNAR, UNORDNAR, UNORNAR, *adj.* Inordinate, enormous, unusual, extraordinary; as, "They gied *anordnar* ransoms for cowts the day." West and South of S.

These are various corruptions of *inordinar ;* from *in,* neg., and Fr. *ordinaire,* ordinary.
By-ordnar is similarly used, but has generally a wider range of meaning.

ANOTAMELL, ANTOMELL, *s.* Anatomy, art of dissection, dissection, subject for dissection.

". . . that is to say, that he knaw *anotamell,* nature and complexion of euery member humanis bodie," &c. Burgh Recs. Aberd., 1 July, 1505.
". . . and that we may have anis in the yeir ane condampnit man eftir he be deid to mak *antomell* of," &c. Ibid.

ANOURNMENTS, ANOWRNMENTS, *s. pl.* Adornments, decorations. Charters of Peebles, 4 Feb., 1444-5. V. ANORNE.

ANOY, *s.* Err. for *Not,* employment, business. Barbour, xiii. 173, Edin. MS. V. NOTE.

ANOY, *s.* Annoyance, harm. Barbour, viii. 371. Pl. *anoyis,* troubles, hardships. Ibid., i. 304.

O. Fr. *anoier, anuier;* Fr. *ennuyer,* te annoy, vex, trouble. It. *noia,* trouble; Sp. *enoja,* offence, injury.

To ANSCHIR, *v. a.* To answer, reply; Henryson, Bann. MS., p. 1005, l. 58.

ANSCHIR, ANSCHEIR, *s.* An answer, reply; Ibid., p. 958, l. 41.

ANSEINYE, ENSEINYE, *s.* 1. An ensign, flag, banner of a company. V. ANSENYE.

"Ordanes tua new cullouris to be *enseinyeis* to be bocht vpon the tounes charges," &c. Burgh Recs. Glasg., 2 Apr. 1627.

2. An ensign, an officer who carries the regimental colours.

"Ninian Andersone, *anseinyie* for the craftis," &c. Ibid., 18 Mar. 1601.

3. A company of soldiers. Ibid., 18 Mar. 1601.

In the Burgh Recs. of Aberdeen there are some very strange forms of this word, as, *antaingzies,* in p. 305, and *anzangzes,* in p. 308 of vol. ii., Spal. Cl.; and *ancient,* in pp. 14, 28, and 72 of vol. iv., Rec. Soc. In the Burgh Recs. Glasg., vol. i., p. 471, the form is *hanseinyie,* as if for *hand-sign.* The entry is interesting on account of its particulars, and runs thus:—
"June 11, [1583]. Item, depursit for coillis, peitis, candle, and some boyes wadgis, ane polk to the *hanseinyie,* and for mending of the cheinyeis of the knok, vj li. vj s. viij d."
This term is a corr. of Fr. *enseigne,* from Lat. *insigne,* a badge, flag.

To ANT, *v. a.* To attend to, to attend, obey; Shetl.

Icel. *ansa,* id.

ANTECESSOUR, ANTECESTRE, *s.* An ancestor; Henryson, Bann. MS., p. 1005, l. 26; Compl. Scot., p. 186, E.E.T.S. V. ANTYCESSOR.

ANTICK, ANTIK, *adj.* Ancient, oldfashioned, antique.

"But in this also we are more *antick* nor antiquity." Blame of Kirkburiall, ch. vii.
Fr. *antique,* from Lat. *antiquus,* ancient.

ANTINMAS, *s.* Prob. Anthony's mass, twenty-four days after Christmas, Shetl.

St. Anthony, the patriarch of saints, is commemorated in various ways all over Europe. His day in the Calendar is 17th January, or twenty-four days after Christmas, as stated in the Gloss. Orkn. and Shetl. V. Chambers' Book of Days, i. 124.

ANTOMELL, *s.* Anatomy, subject for dissection. V. *Anotamell.*

ANTRUM, AUNTRUM, s. The afternoon or early evening repast; also, the time fixed for it, sometimes called *anterin-time*, and *aunterin-time*. West and South of S. V. *Andrum*.

This term is a corruption of A.-S. *undern*, the third hour, which under various forms occurs in many of the English dialects.

ANWELL, s. Annual, yearly rent or payment; pl. *anwellis*. Charters of Peebles, 4 Feb. 1444-5, Lanark Recs., 1505.

Anwell is properly an *adj.*, and as such is still in use; as, *the anwell meetin'*.

ANYESTER, s. A name given to a two-year-old sheep, or rather to one in its second year, Shetl.

ANYING, ANANYING, *part*. Owing, a corr. of *awning*, *awnin'*, also in use, Gall.

ANYS, *adv*. Once. Barbour, i. 272. V. ANIS.

APANE, APAYN, *adv*. At a pinch. Barbour, ix. 64, 89. V. APAYN.

Dr. Jamieson's meaning of *apayn* is entirely wrong. Fr. *à peine*, at or under penalty, in extremity, in desperation, at a pinch. See note in Prof. Skeat's Ed., pp. 573-4.

APARALE, APARAILE, s. Preparation; apparatus, fittings. V. APPARELLE.

Till ordane till mak *aparale*
For till defend and till assale.
Barbour, xvii. 241, Camb. MS.
. . . . certi=hard I neuir say,
That Inglis men mar *aparaile*
Maid, then thai did [than] for bataill.
Ibid., xi. 51, Edin. MS.

APIN, APPIN, *adj*. and v. Open; also as an *adv.*, openly; as, "It was done *apin* afore al men." V. APPIN.

APPYNLY, *adv*. Openly. Compl. Scot., p. 133, E.E.T.S.

APLOCHS, s. pl. Remnants, remains of any work or repast, West and South of S. V. ABLACH.

In olden times scarcely a field of grain was shorn, or a meadow mowed, but portions were left in corners uncut to secure the favour of the warlocks; these portions were called *aplochs*. Modern farming, however, recognises neither *aplochs* nor *warlocks*.

Gael. *ablach*, carrion, the remains of a creature destroyed by ravenous beasts; hence, *ablaoich*, a term of contempt, applied to persons and things.

APNYT, *pret*. For *opnyt*, opened. V. *Apin*.

Thair yattis haff thai *apnyt* sone.
Barbour, xvii. 136, Edin. MS.
Camb. MS. has *opnyt*.

APNYT, *v. n*. For *hapnyt*, happened, Bann. MS., p. 1014, l. 370; in p. 1004, l. 28, the form *appinnit* occurs.

APONLANDE, APOLAND, UPLANDIS, UP-OLANDE, *adj*. Belonging to the country, living outside the burgh.

"And gif he be a burges *aponlande* he sal geyf viii s,"
&c. Burgh Lawis, ch. 40.
". . . men *upolande* may borow thair pundis thryis fra wolk to wolk . . . And gif the *uplandis* man throuch frawartschyp of hym selff will nocht borow his punde," &c. Burgh Lawis, ch. 34.
In M.E. *upland* and *uplandish* are not uncommon.

APO-SYNAGOGIE, s. Separation or excommunication from the synagogue; Blame of Kirkburiall, ch. xviii. V. under *Arch-synagogue*.

To APPARDON, APPARDOUN, *v. a*. To pardon.

Appardoun me of this,
Gif ocht be to displeiss yow,
And quhair I mak a miss,
My mynd salbe to meiss yow.
Alex. Scott, Bann. MS., p. 844, l. 145.

APPELLACIONE, s. An appeal. V. APPELL.

"Item, gevin to Henry Mare, iiij^{to} Februarij, passande to Sanct Andros, a notare for the intimacione of the Kingis *appellacione* fra the Bischop of Sanctandros, to his expensis, xxiiij s." Accts. Lord H. Treas. Scot., i. 47. DICKSON.

APPERANCE, APPERANS, s. Apparent fitness, aptness.

Monye alleageance lele, in lede nocht to lane it,
Off Aristotle and ald men scharplye thai schewe;
The prelatis thair *apperance* proponyt generall.
Houlate, l. 269, Bann. MS.
O. Fr. *apparoir*, Lat. *apparere*, to be open to view.

APPILL OREYNYEIS, s. pl. Oranges.

"Item, for bering of the *appill oreynyeis* to the hous fra the schip, iij. s." Accts. Lord H. Treas. Scot., i. 330, DICKSON.
This entry is under date 24 Aprile, 1497, and refers probably to a present of oranges for King James IV., which had just arrived at the port of Leith.
Pomegranates were in like manner then called *appill garnetis*.

APPINNIT. V. APNYT.

To APPLAUD, APPLAWD, *v. a*. To settle, devote, or apply, by public vote or consent; hence, to vote, devote; part. pt. *applaudit*.

". . . and the money gottin for the samyn to be *applaudit* to the commond weill of this guid toun," &c. Burgh Recs. Aberd., 6 Jan. 1561.
Fr. *applaudir*, to applaud.

APPOSIT, *adj*. Opposite, Compl. Scot., p. 55, E.E.T.S.

APPOSITIONE, s. Opposition, Ibid., p. 55.

To APPOST, *v. a*. To arrange, dispose, put in order for defence, fortify. Lat. *appositus*, apt, fit. V. APPOSIT.

How & what way ye suld *appost* your bordour,
Maddeis counsall is verry excellent.
Sempill, Exhortatioun to the Lordis, s. 14.

APPOVENTABYLL, *adj.* Terrible, causing or striking terror.

The thounder raif the cluddis sabyll,
With horrabyll sound *appoventabyll.*
Lyndsay, Exper. and Court., l. 1416.

Fr. *epouvantable,* terrible ; from *epouvanter,* to scare ; formerly *espouvanter,* originally *espaventer,* from Lat. *expaventare,* deriv. of *expavere.* V. Brachet's Etym. Dict.

APPROFFYT, *part.* Proven, proved. Burgh Rec. Peebles., 5 Oct. 1461.

APPROWIN, *part. pt.* Approved, accepted.

"—receavit and *approwin* be the counsell," &c. Burgh Recs. Aberd., 17 Oct. 1649.
Another form is *approffyt*: both are used in these Records, and are common elsewhere.
Jamieson gave only the form *appreue.*
Fr. *approuver,* to approve.

APPURVAIT, *part. pt.* Provided, prepared.

Held with him-self a gret menye,
Swa that he mycht be *appurvait*
To defend, gif he war assayit.
Barbour, ix. 424. Cam. MS.
Edin. MS. has "*be ay purwayit.*"

AQUARIE, *s.* Aquarius, one of the signs of the zodiac ; Kingis Quair, st. 1.

AQUITE, AQUITIE, *s.* Equity, fair play.

". . . conform to justice, *aquite,* and guid custom," &c. Burgh Recs. Aberd., 3 Aug. 1548.
Fr. *equité,* "equitie, equalitie," Cotgr.

To AQUYTE, *v. a.* To acquit, free. V. *Acquyt.*

". . . he sall nocht fecht, bot thruch the athis of xii men suilk as hym sclff is he sall *aquyte* hym." Burgh Lawis, ch. 22.

ARAISIT, *part. pt.* Raised, lifted up. Kingis Quair, st. 75, Skeat.

ARAND, *part. pr.* Ploughing. Compl. Scot., p. 44. V. AR.

Goth. *arjan,* to plough ; Lat. *arans,* ploughing. M. Eng. *earing.*

ARAYMENT, *s.* Order, setting forth, arrangement, preparation.

". . . apon the *arayment* and utbris necessaris of the play to be plait in the fest of Corpus Xristi nixttocum." Burgh Recs. Aberd., 21 May, 1479.
O. Fr. *arraier, arroier,* to order, arrange, Burguy ; *arroyer,* Cotgr.

ARBYTRE, *s.* Arbitrament, decision. Lat. *arbiter,* a judge, umpire.

And he suld swer that, bot fenyeyng,
He suld that *arbytre* disclar
Off thir twa that I tauld of ar.
Barbour, l. 75.

ARCH-SYNAGOGUE, *s.* The chief or ruler of the synagogue.

"The which [i.e., profanation] as the *arch-synagogues* of olde did punishe with apo-synagogie ; so should Kirk-pastors now ding it with the discipline rod." Blame of Kirkburiall, ch. xviii.

(Sup.) c

To ARESTE, *v. n.* To pause, condescend.

For it was hale his beheste.
At thair alleris requeste,
Mycht dame Nature *areste*
Of him for to rewe.
Houlate, l. 857, Bann. MS.

This sense of the vb. is peculiar.
Fr. *arrester,* to bring one to stand, from Lat. *restare,* to remain behind, stand still ; Sc. *reist.*

ARG, *adj.* Eager, fierce, Shetl.

Icel. *örthigr,* stalwart, brisk, in the sense of braving, or defying ; as in the expression, "*örthgaak upp sem leo,* to rise to one's feet like a lion ;" Cleasby.

ARGOSIE, *s.* Anger, fury, ibid.

ARGERIE, *s.* A crowd, multitude, Shetl.

Icel. *ör-grynni,* a countless multitude ; Cleasby.
The term *angerie,* used in Orkn., is prob. a corr. form of *argerie.*

To ARGEWE, ARGIE, *v.* To argue ; to contend with, to fret against, to chide. V. ARGIE.

. . . In my mynd
My folk I wold *argewe,* bot all for noght.
Kingis Quair, st. 27.
The term is still used in S. in all these senses ; but most of them are now obsolete in E. In Ayrs., Renfr., Lanarks., a mother still says to her quarrelsome children : "Ye'll *argie* ither fra morn ti' nicht ; ye're never done wi't." And the terms *argie-bargie, argie,* and *bargie,* are applied to such contentions.
O. Fr. *arguer,* to argue, plead ; to contend with.

To ARIFFE, *v. n.* To arrive. Barbour, iv. 559.

ARIWYNG, *s.* Arrival. Ibid., v. 122.

ARLED, *part. pt.* Secured by part payment or part possession ; infeft ; *arled in,* secured or taken possession of for the party who has right of entry. V. ARLE.

". . . for the Innes of eternity are alreadie *arled in* for our farther assurance, by our two faithful furriours, Enoch and Elias," &c. Blame of Kirkburiall, ch. iii.

ARMINE, ARMYNE, *s.* Ermine, fur. V. ARMING.

With menever, martrik, grice, and ryche *armyne.*
Lyndsay, Papyngo, l. 1047.
Low Lat. *arminea,* ermine.

ARMYNG, *s.* Armour, arms, Barbour, iii. 614. V. ARMYN.

Used also as an *adj.,* meaning pertaining to or form-part of armour, as *armyng hois, armyng doublet, armyng schone,* hose, doublet, shoes, to be worn with armour. Accts. Lord H. Treas. Scot., pp. 256, 257, 269, Dickson.

ARRAGE, *s.* Feudal service with draught-cattle, i.e., *avers ;* also, the right of such service; Compl. Scot., pp. 124, 125, E.E.T.S. V. ARAGE.

This term is short for *average* : Low Lat. *averagium,* id. V. Du Cange.

ARRAVIS. *s. pl.* Arrows.
And defend welll the vp-cummyng,
Sen he wes varnysit of Armyng
That he thair *Arravis* [thurt] nocht dreid.
Barbour, vi. 121, Cam. MS.

ARRAY, *s.* Garb, fashion, pattern, style; also, uniformity; *in array,* in uniform; *of array,* of one pattern, uniform, alike.
Thaire tabartis ar noght bothe maid of *array*.
Kingis Quair, st. 110.
Prof. Skeat suggests that *maid* should here be omitted, and *array* read *a ray*, i.e., one order, style, pattern.

ARRES, *s.* Arras, tapestry; so named from Arras, in Artois, N. of France, where it was first made; used also as an *adj*.
". . and for the tursing of the *arres* clathys to the Abbay and the Freris at the parliament," &c. Accts. Lord H. Treas. Scot., i. 53, Dickson.

ARREST, ARREIST, AREIST, *s.* The legal seizure of a person's wages in payment of debt; also, the decree or authority for such seizure; same as E. *arrestment*. S.
The ordinary E. meanings of this term are current in S. also.
O. Fr. *arrest*, an arrest, an execution served upon a man's person or goods, &c. Cotgr.

ARSCAP, ARSCAPAT, *s.* Heirship, inheritance, Burgh Rec. Peebles. V. AYRSCHIP.
The form *archap* occurs in these same Records under date 13 April, 1457; and *airiskap* in Prestwick Recs., p. 22.
The term is frequently used as an *adj.*; as, "—the *arschip* gudis," heirship goods, or goods inherited; Burgh Recs. Edin., 25 July, 1548.

ARSDENE, *s.* Archdean, arch-deacon. The opposite to *soddene*, i.e., subdean, in P. Plowman.
Vpoun the sand yit I saw, as thesaurare tane
With grene awmouss on hede, Schir Gawane the Drake;
The *Arsdene* that aurman ay precband in plane,
Correctour of Kirkmen was clepit the Clake.
Houlate, l. 211, Bann. MS.
Given *Arseene* in the DICT.
Dr. Jamieson corrected some of the mistakes in the passage as published by Pinkerton; but *Arseene*, and *kirkine* for *kirkmen*, he retained. In the Bannatyne MS. the word at first sight appears like *Arseene*, and it is so given in the very carefully prepared edition of the MS. issued by the Huuterian Society; but closer inspection shows it to be *Arsdene*, and that the misreading is caused by the d being imperfectly formed under the turn of the s. In the Asloan or Auchinleck MS., which is beautifully written, the word is clearly *archedene*.

ARSET, *adv.* Backwards, stern foremost; same with *arslin, arselins,* q. v., Gall.

ARSOUN, *s.* Bow of a saddle, saddle-bow. Barbour, xvi. 131; *forther und hynder arsoun,* front and back bow of saddle.

Arsoun is sometimes used for the saddle itself; but properly the saddle had two arsouns, one in front and one behind, called the *fore* or *forther arsoun,* and the *hynd* or *hynder arsoun*. Hence—
In the *arsouns* before and behynde
Wer twey stones of ynde,
Gay for the maystrye.
Sir Launfal, l. 955.
Jamieson's mistake with this word is as ludicrous as it is wide of the mark. He must have been, as Prof. Skeat mildly puts it, "strangely misled by the sound of the former part of the word." V. Note, Barbour, p. 777, E. E. Text Soc.
Fr. *arçon,* saddle-bow.

ARTICLES, *s. pl.* 1. The subjects to be discussed, and the laws to be passed, by the Scot. Parliament were called *articles*.
"The three estates of the realm having been assembled, certain persons were elected for the determination of the *Articles* to be proposed to them by the king, leave of returning home being given to the other members of the parliament." Tytler's Hist. Scot., vol. ii., p. 51, Ed. 1864.

2. Lords of the Articles, or short, "The Articles," the members who formed the Committee of Parl. for determining the Articles; also, the Committee of Parliament, which was usually called "The Articles."
"That name suspect of religione be chosen upon the Articles." Book of the Universal Kirk, p. 400, Ed. 1839.
Some idea of the duties of this Committee, and of the mode of its election, may be gathered from the following extracts from Tytler's Hist. of Scotland.
"Parliament was then prorogued to the 17th of March, whilst tho committee known by the name of *the Lords of the Articles,* continued their sittings for the introduction of such statutes as were esteemed beneficial to the general interests of the kingdom." Vol. iii., p. 9, Ed. 1864.
Regarding the opening of Parl., and the preliminary proceedings that followed, see the account given by the same author in vol. iii., pp. 126-7. These being ended,—
"The Lords of the Articles were next chosen, the order of which, says Randolph, 'is that the Lords Spiritual choose the Temporal, and the Temporal the Spiritual,—the Burgesses their own.'" Vol. iii., p. 127.
From which we learn that Scot. laws were framed not by Parliament, but by a select committee of Parliament, while all the other members were at home and engaged on their own affairs.
In the Complaynt of Scotland the term *artiklis* is applied to the conclusions, terms, or particulars of a treaty; v. p. 97, E.E.T.S. ed. The indenture of an apprentice is still called his articles; and the Captain of a ship takes charge of its Articles.

ARUELL, *s.* A funeral feast. V. ARVAL.

To **ARYVE,** ARRYFE, ARYWE, *v. n.* To arrive, reach. V. *Ariffe*.
"Gyf ony schyp *aryve* at the havyn of Berwyk or ony vthyr havyn wythin the Kynryk of Scotland," &c. Customc of Schippis, ch. 1.
Aryve and its part. pt. *arywyt* are used by Barbour, iii. 389, 637.

AS, *conj.* That: *quhare as*, where that, Kingis Quair, st. 40.

This use of *as* is still common in the South and West of S. It is also often used as a rel. pron. for *that:* but this use is common in various districts of England as well.
When preceded by a comparative, *as* means *than;* as, " *mair as,*" more than; Compl. Scot., pp. 5, 13, 14, &c. V. As.

ASCHIN, *adj.* Ashen, of ash-wood.
" Item, giffin for ane *aschin* tre, to be toppis to the Kingis pallyounis, xiiij s." Accts. Lord H. Treas. Scot., i. 285, Dickson.
A.-S. *æsc,* Icel. *askr,* Dan. and Swed. *ask,* an ash.

ASIAMENT, *s.* Easement, convenience, accommodation ; Burgh Recs. Aberd., 31 May, 1488. V. AISMENT.

To ASICH, *v. a.* A form of Assyth, q. v. It occurs in Burgh Recs. frequently. Forms like this arose from mis-reading *t* as *c.* In M. E. MSS. instances are manifold. V. *Assich.*

ASISE, ASIS, s. Assize. V. *Assis.*

ASK, AISK, *s.* 1. Drizzle; small particles of dust, or snow, half-fog half-rain ; Orkn. and Shetl.

2. A wooden dish for holding ashes, ibid.

To ASK, AISK, *v. n.* To rain slightly, to drizzle, ibid.
Icel. *aske,* A.-S. *æscan,* ashes.

ASKAR, *adv.* In scorn, contempt, derision, or despite ; with mocks, jeers, or raillery.
Thay gart mee stand fra thame *askar,*
Evin lyk a beggar at the bar,
And fleimit mair or lesse.
Lyndsay, Thrie Estaitis, l. 1401.
Prob. relying on the Bannatyne MS. reading *afar,* Dr. Laing rendered this term, *at a distance, away from,* which cannot be correct ; for it contradicts the statement of the last line, and is not in keeping with the sense of the passage.
No doubt *askar* is from O. Fr. *eschar, escar, esker,* from *escharnir, escarnir, eschernir, eskernir,* to blame, rail at, mock, jeer, insult : *à eschar,* in derision. V. Burguy's Gloss.
With this meaning the sense is clear, and the picture complete ; for the passage reads thus : " They made me stand aside with scorn, just like a beggar at the bar [of an ale-house] ; and they pushed, drove, or turned me out more or less."

ASLARS, ASLAURRIS, *s. pl.* Ashler stones.
V. ASHLAR.
". . that he sall furnys in hewing vj° fete of *aslaurris* to the furnessing and completing of the towre of the Tolbuith," &c. Burgh Recs. Edin. 19th Mar., 1500-1.

To ASOL, ASSOL, AISLE, *v. a.* To sun ; to dry, mellow, or season in the sun ; generally applied to yarn, clothes, &c., that are best dried in the sun ; Ayrs.

ASOL, AISLE, ASSOL, *s.* Sunning, drying, mellowing, or seasoning in the sun ; also, the act or the state of sunning, &c. ; as, "The claes 'll be gettin' a fine *aisle* day ;" " Run noo, an' set the claes to the *asol,*" Ibid.

ASOLIN', AISLIN', *part. adj.* Sunning; sundrying ; fit or suitable for sunning ; in the state, act, or process of sunning : as, "It's a gran' *aislin* day: see an' put out a' the *asolin'* things first," Ibid.
O. Fr. *assoler,* to sun ; to season, harden, or dry in the sun : *assolé,* sunned ; seasoned, &c. in the sun. Cotgr.

ASOOND, *adv.* In a swoon, Shetl.

ASOYLE, ASOILS, *v. a.* A contr. form of *assoilyie* and it corr. *assoilsie,* to acquit, free, absolve ; also, resolve, answer, reply to, unriddle.
Dr. Jamieson represents Douglas as using *assoilyie* improperly in the sense of *resolve,* &c. This is certainly an error, and one into which he would not have fallen had he considered or compared this term with *soilye,* to solve, resolve ; V. DICT. In the sense used by Douglas, and many other writers, the prefix *a* or *as,* is here simply intensive. It is a French usage in which Scottish writers delighted ; indeed it is a marked peculiarity of the language as compared with English. But even E. writers so used the term, as in

Asoyle my qwestyon anon ryght
Thy brother Abel, wher now is he ?
Ha don, and answere me as tycht.
Cov. Myst., p. 38.
These contracted forms are still used colloquially in reference to law cases.

ASPERT. Prob. a mis-reading of *affert* or *afferit,* frightened, made or caused to be afraid.
This term occurs only in the following passage of the *Kingis Quair,* which is evidently more or less corrupt.
" Though thy begynnyng hath bene retrograde,
Be froward opposyt quhare till *aspert,*
Now sall that turn and luke on the dert."
K. Q., st. 170.
So it stands in the only MS. that has come down to us ; and various attempts have been made to get at the meaning of the author, but without success. The latest, and by far the best, editor of the poem, Prof. Skeat, calls it "the hopelessly difficult phrase *quhare till aspert,* the meaning of which is unknown, and which must be corrupt." He renders the line, *Be froward,* &c., " by means of the perverse hostile men, whereunto (they were) exasperated ;" but confesses that his rendering of it "is very obscure, though less forced than any other explanation," p. 90.
Dr. Jamieson proposed *harsh, cruel,* as the meaning of *aspert ;* but his note shows that he was not satisfied with it ; and, indeed, no one has accepted it. And the same may be said more or less certainly of all the other proposals.
Seeing then that the passage as it stands defies explanation, I began with it as a passage corrupted in the transcribing ; then after testing it word by word, I concluded that the most likely places where a trans-

criber would go wrong, and especially one who did not know the language well, were *quhare till*, *aspert*, and *dert*. Then, a careful study of the context suggested that *quhare till* is a very likely mis-reading of *quha here till*, who hitherto; *asperi*, of *affert* or *afferit*, frightened, overawed; and *dert*, of *deirt*, *derit*, or *deerit*, daunted, injured, wronged, oppressed.
The passage so restored would be,—
" Though thy begynnyng hath been retrograde, Be froward, opposyt, quha heretill affert ; Now sall that turn and luke on the deirt."
Which certainly improves the scansion, and does not force the sense ; *opposyt* being read as it is commonly pron. *opsit* ; and *turn*, or *deirt*, as disayllabic.
The meaning of the passage then is : " Though thy beginning has been backward or unfortunate through [the working of] froward, adverse men, who hitherto frightened thee ; now shall they turn and look upon thee as an injured one." And we know that such a change did take place very soon after this passage was written, and almost as suddenly as is implied. In the early summer of 1423 James was writing his *Quair* in despondency, and almost without hope of freedom ; and by the end of August a commission was at work arranging for his return to Scotland as lawful king. See Tytler's Hist. of Scot., vol. ii., ch. 1.

ASPOSIT, ASSPOSIT, *part. pt.* 1. Disposed, inclined, able. V. ASPOSIT.

2. Appointed, directed, enjoined.
" . . . ane chaplane . . . daylie doand mes at the said altar quhan he is *assposit*." Burgh Rec. Peebles, 20th Jan. 1520.
Assposit occurs in this sense under date 15 Oct., 1481 ; and *espposit* occurs under date 28 Mar., 1457, bearing the first sense.

ASPYNE, *s.* A long boat. V. *Espyne*.
The meaning of this word is somewhat vague and indefinite in the DICT., but the derivation is correct. The Cam. MS. reads *esypne*, which may be directly traced to Icel. *espingr*, Sw. *esping*, a ship's boat. V. Prof. Skeat's Gl. to Barbour.

ASSALE, ASSAY, ASSAYE, *s.* Assault, attack, attempt. Barbour, Douglas, Lyndsay. V. ASSAILYIE.
. . . . the toun wes hard to ta
Vith oppyn *assale* be struith or mycht, Tharfor he thoucht to virk vith slicht.
Barbour, ix. 350. Cam. MS.
Edin. MS. has *sawt*.
Assale and *Assay* are also used as *vb*.

ASSBACKET, ASBACKET, ASEBACKET, *s.* An ashbat ; West and South of S. V. As, Ass.
This is a dimin. of *assback*, a *back* or tub for ashes. The term *back* is still applied to a kind of brewer's tub, and has been corr. into *bat* ; in the same way *bat*, a winged mammal, is corr. from M. E. *bakke*, *backe* ; Sc. *bauckie*, and *bauckie-bird*.

ASSEISIT, *part. pt.* Settled, entered on possession, fixed.
. . . . . . Mars in Capricorne ;
And Cynthia in Sagittar *asseisit*.
Lyndsay, Papyngo, l. 130.
In law, a person is still said to be *seised* or possessed of property : there is also the term *seisin* or *seizin*, possession of property.

To ASSEMMYLL, ASSEMBILL, *v. n.* To assemble, Barbour, xvii. 341 ; to advance to battle, Ibid., ii. 294 ; to join battle, encounter, attack, Ibid., xii. 267, 543 ; *assemmyl on*, to attack, Ibid., xiii. 7, Camb. MS. V. ASSEMBLE.

ASSENTATIONE, *s.* Flattery; in the sense of assenting to every thing said by a superior. Compl. Scot., p. 3.
O. Fr. *assentation*, "assentation, flatterie, colloguing," Cotgr.

To ASSICH, ASICH, *v. a.* To compensate, to give compensation, part. pt. *assichit*. V. ASSYTH, of which it is a corrupt form.
" . . . he wants his mere, and the saidis persons acht til upricht and *assich* him for hir." Burgh Recs. Aberd., 19 July, 1480. Sp. C.

ASSIGE, *s.* Siege. Burgh Recs. Aberd., 2 Oct., 1546. V. ASSEGE.
In another entry during the same month it is written *sage*.

ASSIGNAIS, ASSIGNAS, *s. pl.* Assignees. Charters of Edinburgh, 8 Nov., 1482. Burgh Rec. Edin., p. 230.

ASSIS, *s. pl.* Ashes, potash. V. AS.
" . . . ilk barell of tasill twa peniis, of a barel wyth *assis* twa peniis," &c. Assize of Petty Customs, ch. 11.

ASSIS, ASSYIS, ASISE, *s.* Assize, a statute fixing the weight, measure, or price of anything. Fr. *assise*, a set rate ; from Low L. *assidere*, to set, fix, settle.
" A man may profe sesing of lande boucht wyth in the burche efter the law and the *asise* mayd be Dauid King of Scotland this maner," &c. Fragments of Old Laws, ch. 10.
" Item, at thai keip nocht, na gerris keip the *assis* of breid and aile, wyn and flesche lauchfully." Chalmerlau Air, ch. 4.

ASSISORIE, *s.* Assessorship ; the post, duties, or work of an assessor. Burgh Recs. Edin., vol. iii., p. 5. Recs. So.

To ASSOLYE, *v. a.* To absolve ; pret. and part. pt. *assoleit*. Barbour, xx. 295, Camb. MS. V. ASSOILYIE.
This vb. is still used in Scotch Law.

ASSONYE, ESSONYE, *s.* An excuse for absence, a law term. V. ASSONYIE, *v.*
" . . . and quha that dissobeyis and absentis hym in the tym withoutin leif or a resonable *assonye* he sal payo," &c. Burgh Rec. Edin., 2 Dec. 1474.

ASSOUERIT, *part. pt.* Browned, ripened.
This wes in-till the harvist tyde
Quhen feldis, that var fair and vyde, Chargit with corne *assouerit* var.
Barbour, x. 187, Camb. MS.

ASS [21] ATH

O. Fr. *sor*, Fr. *saur*, brownish red.
"*Saurir*, to turne iuto a sorrel colour," Cotgr. V.
Prof. Skeat's Barbour, p. 646.

ASSOWERYT, *pret.* Felt assurance, felt secure, trusted.

For in his noble gouernyng,
And in his hey chewalry,
Thai *assoweryt* rycht souerauly.
Barbour, xi. 309, Edin. MS.

O. Fr. *asseurer*, to secure, from Lat. *assecurare*.

ASSWETIT, *part. adj.* Accustomed: Lat. *assuetus*.

In gamis glaid he was rycht weill *asswetit*,
Rycht featlie on the fluire alswa could dance.
Sempill Ballates, p. 2.

ASSYTHER, *s.* A law officer whose duty was to see that offences were suitably punished or atoned for, an assessor. V. ASSYTH.

"Item, for breid and drink feched furth to the *assytheris*, xxx s." Accts. Burgh of Peebles, 15 Dec. 1629.
This refreshment was given to the *assytheris* at a burning of witches, and appears to have been a refreshment all round; for the same entry continues thus:—
"Item, feched furth thairof to the hangman and wiches, xviii s."

To ASTERT, *v. n.* To start, bound, set off; also, to start up or aside; and hence to avoid, shun, escape, Kingis Quair, st. 40, 44. V. ASTART.

ASTLAYR, ASTLER, *adj.* Ashler. V. ASHLAR.

" . . . xii^c hewyn stanys *astlayr* and coynyhe swilk as fallys to that werk," &c. Charters of Edinburgh, 29 Nov. 1387.
Used also as a *s*, as in the following:—" . . . and he sall furnys ill' fute of the *astler* weill hewin on all faces for ij d the fute," &c. Burgh Recs. Edin., 19 Mar. 1500-1.

To ASTONEY, *v. a.* To amaze, astonish, dismay, Barbour, i. 299, Herd's Ed. V. STONAY.

ASTRASIMENT, *s.* A corr. or errat. for *astransimeut*, distraint, seizure of goods for debt.

" . . . tane in *astrasiment* of payment of a Hamburgh barel of salmond," &c. Burgh Recs. Aberd., 16 Jan. 1469.
O. Fr. *astraindre*, also *rastraindre*, to distrain: *astrenilement*, *rastrendement*, distraint, Burguy.

ASUA, *conj.* Also, as well as: a corr. of *alsua*, Burgh Recs. Aberd., 12 Sept. 1489.

ASUR, AISUR, *s.* and *adj.* Azure, Houlate, l. 346; *aisser*, Mait. Cl. Misc., iii. 372.

ASYSS, *s.* Assize, Barbour, xix. 55, Edin. MS. V. *Assis*.

AT, *prep.* From, of, at the hands of; also, by, or in accordance with, like to.

"Item, giffin to the Prothonotar, at the kingis command that he tuke up *at* Anthoine Keth, lxxxxvilj. lib. vjs. viijd." Accts. Lord H. Treas., Scot., i. 364, Dickson.
" . . . the faithfull after Constantine in founding of kirks, taking the type *at* Ierusalems temple," &c. Blame of Kirkburiall, ch. vi.

AT AL, AT ALL, AT A', *adv.* 1. In all things, in all respects, in every way, at best.

So used by Douglas in his Prol. to *Eneados*, Bk. I.
"My waverand wit, my cunnyng feble *at all*."

2. In or at any thing, in any respect, in any way, at any time, on any account; in this sense it is similar to *ava*', and still in common use. "He can do na gude *at a'*." "Wark disna concern him *at a'*." "Ye'll aye fin' me at hame; I ne'er gae out *at a'*."
In this sense it is generally preceded by a negative term.

3. It is also used in the sense of rightly, correctly, properly, well; and hence, with comfort, satisfaction, or credit, &c. "Tell me hoo to do't; I canna do't *at a'*." "Withoot a new goun, I couldna gang wi', nor sit beside thae gran' folk *at a'*."
In senses 2 and 3 the meaning is intensified by repeating the phrase: as, "I canna gang there *at a'*, *at a'*." V. AT ALL.

ATAE, ATOO, *adv.* Unto, towards; hence, close, shut; as, "Come in atae," i.e., come in towards (the fire). And to a person going out,—" Draw the door atae," draw the door close, shut the door on leaving. West of S., Orkn.
In Orkn. the form is *atto*. Gl. Orcadian Sketch Book.

ATEMPTAT, *s.* Contempt; act of contempt; an illegal aggression. V. ATTEMPTAT.

" . . . in the committing of the said enormitie and heycht *atemptat*," &c. Burgh Recs. Aberd., 4 May, 1562.
Fr. *attentat*, an illegal aggression, alieni juris violatio; and in this sense it occurs frequently in the Privy Council Register.

ATEN OUT O' PLY. Animals that are very lean and in poor condition, although they have had abundance of food, are said to be *aten out o' ply*, eaten out of plight or condition. South and West of S. V. PLY.

ATENTIC, *adj.* Authentic. Compl. Scot., p. 3. V. ATTENTIK.

ATHER, ATHIR, *adj.* and *pron.* The one or

the other, each, each of two, both. V. *Aither*.
But *ather* ran at uther with sic haist.
Lyndsay, Justing betuix Watsoun and Barbour, l. 21.
This form is repeatedly used by Lyndsay, and in various senses.

ATIS, *s.* Oats; A.-S. *áta*, pl. *átan.* V. AIT.
"Item, to Dave Caldewell, the saim da, be a precep, to by him a chalder of *atis*, vj. lib." Accts. Lord H. Treas Scot., I. 131, Dickson.

ATESTRAE, AITSTRAE, *s.* Oat-straw, a stem or straw of oats; West and South of S.

ATONIS, *adv.* At once. V. ATANIS.

ATOUER, OUTOUER, OUTOUR, *prep.* Above, beyond, farther, farther than. V. ATOUR, *Outouer.*
"All action that is *atour* the statute of the Lord, . . . that is aboue or *at ouer* the statute of God," &c. Blame of Kirkburiall, ch. xx.

To ATRAY, ATREY, ATTRAY, *v. a.* To trouble, frighten, torment, harass; part. pt. *atrayed, atreyed, attrayed.* V. TRAY.
A.-S. *trege,* vexation, shame, loss; M. Eng. *treie, trey.* Hence *tregian,* to vex, trouble, grieve.

ATSET, *s.* The commencement of the ebb-tide, Shetl.

To ATTACH, *v. a.* To charge, arrest, summon. Fr. *attacher*, from Lat. *tango*, to touch.
" . . . charge you that incontinent ye *attach* all strangers whais names . . . sall present to you in writ, placing them under safe and sure pledges that they shall compeir," &c. Chalmerlan Air, ch. 2.

ATTACHIT, ATTACHYT, *part. pt.* Attached, charged, summoned, arrested.
"Gif that a burges be *attachyt* ututh the burgh for det or for ony mysgilt," &c. Burgh Lawis, ch. 51.
" . . . sic as has brokyn the pece of the fayr, he sal be *attachyt* and aykerly kepyt till the motis of that ilke fayr," &c. Burgh Lawis, ch. 86.

ATTACHMENT, ATACHEMENT, *s.* Charge, summons, arrest; also, the legal document authorizing the charge, &c.
"The sergeand shall swear . . . that he will lawfully attach and faithfully present his *attachments.*"
Oaths of Officers, ch. Sergeand.
" . . . the said Andro callit thrys and nocht enterit, than the seriand Thomas of Loch prufit his *atachement,*" &c. Burgh Rec. Peebles, 20 Jan. 1476.

ATTANIS, *adv.* At once. V. ATANIS.

ATTEICHIT, *part. pt.* Attached, charged, incriminated, inculpated. V. ATTEICHE.
Be thow *atteichit* with thift, or with tressoun. .
Henryson, Parl. of Beistis, l. 183.
Fr. *attacher,* to attach; but here used in its legal sense.

ATTER, AUTER, *s.* An altar; also, in the sense of *altarage* it is common in the earlier Burgh Records.

ATTERIGE, ATTRAGE, *s.* Altarage.
" . . . that the *atteriges* salbe desairnit in the patronis handis," &c. Burgh Recs. Peebles, 7 Apr., 1567.

ATTER, ATER, ETTER, *s.* Poison, poisonous matter, purulent matter from a sore, Clydes. V. ETTIR.
A.-S. *átor,* also *áttor,* poison; hence *attercop,* the old name of a spider.

ATTILE, ATTILE-DUCK, *s.* A water-fowl; also called the Pochard or Poker. Orkn., Neill's Tour. V. ATTEILLE.

To ATTLE, ATTEL, ATEL, *v. a.* and *n.* Lit. to go towards, to approach; hence, to aim at, purpose, intend, propose, direct, direct one's way, journey. V. ETTLE.
Icel. *œtla,* to intend.
Both *attle* and *ettle* have been used from the earliest times; they occur in Will. and Werwolf, Cov. and Town. Mysteries, Gawaine Romances, and our Scot. Burgh Records, and they are still used.

ATTLE, ATEL, *s.* Aim, purpose, intention, attempt. V. ETTLE.

ATTRAYED, *part.* Troubled, frightened. V. *Atray.*

ATWEEN-LICHTS. The distance between neighbours' houses, Shetl.

To AUAILYE, AVALYE, *v. n.* To avail, be of use. V. AVAIL.

To AUANCE, *v. a.* To advance, help, help forward, prosper. Kingis Quair, st. 50, 79, 156. V. AVANCE.

AUCHE, *s.* A haugh, flat land. Gael. *augh,* id.
" . . . a fre lonyng throw the sayd *auche* to Glentras as efferis to the town to haf of law," &c. Burgh Rec. Peebles, 14 Dec. 1475.

AUCHEN, *adj.* Flat, level; also used as a *s.* meaning field, fertile land.
Various names of places in S. are derived from *Auche :* as, Auchleven, in Aberdeenshire; Auchens, Auchinleck, and Auchindrane, in Ayrshire; Auchinearn and Auchingray, in Lanark; Auchidinny, in Mid-Lothian; Auchtermuchty and Auchterdoul, in Fife; and Auchterarder, in Perth.

AUCHT. 1. *Aucht and Want,* use and wont, usual, customary. V. AUCHT.
" . . . for xiiij*ꬰ* merks yeirly, to be payet at the termes *aucht and want,*" etc. Burgh Rec. Edin., 1466.
" . . . asiamentis, profitis, ande deviteis, *aucht and wont.*" Burgh Recs. Aberd., 1488.

2. **Aucht of ressoun**, reasonable duty, or satisfaction.

". . . redy to do to the said letteris the *aucht of ressoun*." Burgh Recs. Aberd., 12 Jan. 1544.

AUCHTSUM, *adj.* Eightsome, consisting of eight persons or things.

He was bot *auchtsum* in his rout,
For of danger he had no dout.
 Lyndsay, Sq. Meldrum, l. 1225.

A.-S. *eahtasum*, eightsome : from *eahta*, eight.

AUCHTY, *adj.* Eighty. S. A.-S. *eahta*, eight.

AUCTOR, AUCTOUR, AWCTOR, AUTOUR, *s.* Author, originator; Henryson, Douglas: Bann. MS. pp. 948, 959, 847.

AUD, *adj.* Old; a corr. of *auld*, q.v.

AUDIENS, *s.* Audience, hearing; Complaynt of Scot., p. 31: open court, Henryson.

Thair suld no man for wrang or violens,
His aduersar punneis at his awin haud,
Without process of law in *audiens*.
 Henryson, Wolf and Lamb, l. 67, Bann. MS.

Dr. Laing's ed. gives "Without proces of law and *evidence ;*" the other is the better reading.

AUDIT, *s.* A horizontal shaft or level forming an approach to a mine or a means of draining it; Early Recs. of Mining in Scotland, p. 107 : *adit*, Derbyshire Lead-Mining Terms, Dial. Soc. Lat. *aditus*.

AUDITURE, *s.* Audience, congregation, company of listeners.

". . . and the nixt day following the *auditure* was so sclender that many wondered." Knox's Reformation in Scot., I. 136, Wood. Soc.

Fr. *auditoire*, an audience, from Lat. *auditorium*.

AUENTURE, *s.* V. AVENTURE, and *Aventure*.

To AUERT, *v. a.* and *n.* The older form of *aduert*, to attend, attend to, inquire; examine ; also, to acquaint; advise, warn. V. *Advert*.

The O. Fr. form was *avertir*, which is given as *advertir* by Cotgrave. Mod. Fr. *avertir*.

". . . to quietlye *auert* quhair they heir noyis of strangearis or seiknes, and to *auert* the prouest and bailzies thairof," etc. Burgh Recs. Aberd., 27 July, 1530.

"*Heir noyis of,*" get information regarding : same as "*hear tell of,*" and "*get word of.*"

AUERTENCE,*s.* Attention, oversight, examination; also, information, notification, warning. Burgh Recs., Aberdeen, 17 May 1531.

AUERTY, AVERTY, *adj.* Prudent, cautious, well-advised; Barbour, viii. 162, xviii. 439. V. AWERTY.

AUHTING, *part.* Owing. Burgh Rec. Peebles, 18 June, 1565. V. AUGHTAND.

AUING, AVING, AWING, *part. pr.* Owing. Burgh Recs. Aberd., 18 March, 1532. V. AVAND.

AUL', *adj.* Old ; so pron. in the South and West of S.

AULFARRAN, *adj.* Sagacious.

AULFARRAN, *adj.* Sagacious.

AULD SAUNDERS, AULD SANNERS, AULD SANNY, *s.* A name for the deil, Satan; Clydes. V. *Saunders*.

AULD WIFE, *s.* 1. An old woman, S.

2. A name given to a talkative, gossiping person,—one whose speech and manners are similar to those of an old woman; also to one who makes much of little things, S.

3. The cowl or cover of a chimney-can, used as an aid-vent.

So called on account of its likeness to an old woman's head enveloped in a flannel cap.

In ordinary cases the chimney-can or *pig* has set on it a top or *tap :* hence the term *pig-tap*. But where the ventilation is imperfect, the *tap* is removed and an *auld-wife* is substituted. During high winds both *old-wives* and *pig-taps* are apt to be thrown down, and street walking at such times is somewhat dangerous. Hence the severity of a storm, and one's courage in braving it, came to be represented by the expression, "raining *auld-wives* and *pig-taps,*" which became corrupted into "raining *auld-wives and pike-staffs.*"

AUM, AWM, *s.* Alum ; so pronounced by the people all over Scotland, like *caum*, *cawm*, for calm.

To AUM, AWM, *v. a.* To soak with alum, as in the process of making tinder, awm't or white leather, &c.; also, to beat soundly, thrash, punish,—in the same sense as E., to tan, to tan one's hide.

AUM LEATHER, AUM'T LEATHER, *s.* Called also *white leather;* leather prepared by soaking in a solution of alum, and used for gloves, for lining shoes, &c., S.

AUMERALE, *s.* Admiral. V. AMYRALE.

". . . Gilbert Meignes, vnder *aumerale* in name of the toone," etc. Burgh Recs. Aberdeen, 18 Feb. 1445.

O. Fr. *amirail*, *amiral ;* but from Arab. *amir*, a prince, an emir.

AUNCIETY, AUNCIETIE, *s.* Antiquity, ancientness ; Blame of Kirkburiall, ch. xix. V. ANCIETY.

The form *anciente* occurs in Barbour, vi. 252; and in various districts of the West of S. the forms *ancientry*, *auncientry* are still used in the same sense.

AUNTY, *s.*   1. A vulgar name for a loose woman, one who keeps a brothel.

In a similar sense it was used by Shakespeare in Winter's Tale, iv. iii. 11.

2. A vulgar name for the bottle, a debauch.

It's guid to be social and canty,
It's cheering to coup aff our horn—
But makin' ower free wi' our *aunty*
Is sure to bring trouble the morn ;
For *aunty's* a dangerous kimmer,
And no to be dallied wi' aye,
She'll turn to bleak winter our simmer,
And sprinkle our baffets wi' grey.
Alex. Rodger, Whistle-Binkie, ii. 237.

The term *aunty* was commonly applied to an unmarried woman who kept an inn or public house, and hence its application to the drink obtained in such places. In the West of S. it is still a common saying when a person is seen in liquor—"*He's been seein' his aunty.*"

AUR, AURR, AWR, *s.*   The mark left by a cut or wound, S.   V. ARR.

While the cut or wound is healing the mark is called a *scar* ; when it is completely healed the mark is called an *aur*.

Icel. *arr, örr*, Dan. *ar*, Sw. *ärr*, a seam, scar or mark of a wound.

To AURGLEBARGIN, *v. n.*   To wrangle, contend ; same as *tirr-wirr*, Ramsay.   V. ARGLEBARGLE.

The tendency to drop the *l* in words of common use is illustrated by this word ; its common pron. is *argiebargie*, or *argo-bargo*.

AUTENTICAL, *adj.*   Authentic, authenticated.   V. ATTENTIK.

". . . the auld *autentical* acts of the burcht," etc. Burgh Rec. Prestwick, 31 Jan. 1576-7.

AUTHENTIKLY, *adv.*   Authenticated, with attestation.

"And ordanis that ilk burgh tak the copy of this act *authentikly* vnder the clerkis signe and subscriptioun manuell," etc. Burgh Rec. Edin., 10 Nov. 1500.

To AVAILL, *v. a.*   To lower. Barbour, xvii. 620, Camb. MS.   V. AUALE, AWAIL, AVAILL.

AVAK, AVAIK, *adj.* and *adv.*   Lit. vacant, empty, unfilled ; hence, incomplete, unconcluded ; also, unpaid, unsettled ; in arrears, behind hand.

". . . the said vicar to persew the saidis personis that lyis *avak* in contemptioun afor the spiritual jurisdiction," etc. Burgh Recs. Aberd., 24 May, 1546.
Fr. *vaquer*, from Lat. *vacare*, to be vacant.

In its literal sense the term is applied to a house or farm or property that is unoccupied ; in the second sense it is applied to a lease or an engagement that is not yet concluded ; in the third sense, a rent, a debt, etc., that remains unpaid ; in the fourth sense, to the person who has not paid his rent, debt, etc., as in the passage quoted.

AVAL, *adj.*   Fallen down, helpless, not able to rise.   V. AVAILL.

When an animal has fallen on its back or side so that it cannot raise itself, it is said to be *aval*. Ewes with lamb are sometimes in this state, and, if not assisted by the shepherd, they soon become the prey of corbies and hoodies.

AVALYE, *v.*   *Avalye que valye*, avail what may avail, whatever may be the result, Barbour, ix. 147, Camb. MS.   V. AVAIL, AUAILYE.

Fr. *vaille que vaille*, Lat. valeat quantum valeat.

AVAWARD, *s.*   Vanguard.

And knaw suthly on quhat maneir
Their *avaward*, that was so stout,—
War reboytit so suddandly.
Barbour, xii. 179, Camb. MS.

Fr. *avant*, before, and O. Fr. *warde*, guard, guard ; the modern form is *avant-garde*.

To AVENT, *v. a.*   To give air to, to cool, to vent.   V. AWENT.

AVENTOUR, AVENTURE, *s.*   Venture, hazard, risk ; adventure, exploit ; fortune, chance, luck ; and in a general sense, accident, mischance.   V. AUNTER, AVENTURE.

WILD AVENTOURIS, WYLD AVENTURIS, *s.*   Free ventures, foreign ventures ; the name given to foreign vessels that brought goods into port on venture.

". . . gif it sall happin the toun to bald the common mylnis . . . and the *wild aventouris* into thair awin handis this yeir intocum," etc. Burgh Recs. Edin., 16 Oct. 1515.

". . . the comptar chargis him with the dewte of the *wyld aventuris* set to him the yeir of his office for the sowme of sevin hundreth merks." Treas. Accts., Burgh Recs. Edin., 1553-4.

AVERAGE, AVERISH, *s.*   V. under *Avery*.

AVERTY, *adj.*   Prudent, cautious, well advised.   Barbour, viii. 162, Camb. MS.   V. AWERTY.

AVERY, *s.*   The supply of provisions for the horses.   V. AVERIE.

Dr. Jamieson rendered this word "live stock, as including horses, &c.," and in doing so followed too closely Du Cange's meaning of M. Lat. *averia*, from which this word is derived. Whatever this term may have originally included, its Scot. derivative *avery*, *averie*, was used in the sense given above ; it related to—not the horses, but provender for the horses. And the chief of the department was the *avenar*, or Master of the Avery. V. Accts. Lord H. Treas. Scot., i. 231, Dickson.

In various districts of S. the term *average*, corr. into *averish* and *avery*, is applied to the stubble and grass left in corn fields after harvest, because it generally is the portion of the *avers* or horses. *Average* and *averish* are common in the North of E. also ; v. Brockett's Gloss.

AVISE. *On avise*, tell of, consider.
And othir mo that I can noght *on avise*,
King is Quair, st. 97, Skeat.

AVISE, *adj.* Prudent, considerate. V. AWISE.

AWA, *prep.* as *adj.* Reduced, failed, broken in health, wealth, or position ; as, " He's *awa* to skin an' bane," i.e., reduced to a skeleton. He's clean *awa* wi't noo; naebody trusts him, i.e., he is completely broken in credit, &c.

In the phrase, *awa' i' the head*, deranged, beside one's self, as given by Dr. Jamieson, *awa* implies an extension of the idea expressed above.

AWA, *interj.* Implying contradiction, ridicule, banter, coaxing, &c.; as, " Hoot, *awa'* man! ye're clean wrang." As in the case of *ava*, the meaning is intensified by repetition, S.

AWA-GAIN, AWA-GAUN, *s.* Departure, leave-taking, death. V. WA-GAIN.

To AWAILYE, AWAILE, *v. n.* To avail, to be of use, Barbour. V. AWAILL.

To AWAL, *v. a.* To lower, let down, descend. V. *Availl*.

Thai that with-in the castell wer
Had armyt thaim and maid thaim boun ;
And sone thair brig *awalit* doun,
And ischit in-till gret plenté.
Barbour, xv. 134, Edin. MS.

Fr. *avaler*, to lower.

AWALK, AWAUK, *v. n.* To awake. Lyndsay, Thrie Estaitis, 7, 273.

AWALL, AWAILL, *s.* Value, equivalent. V. AWAIL.

" ... sax potionis of wyne, or the *awall* of of the samyn," etc. Burgh Recs. Aberd., 16 Apr., 1526.

AWANSEMENT, *s.* Advancement, promotion ; Fr. *avancer*.

He tretyt thaim so wisly ay,
And with sa mekill luff alsua,
And sic *awansement* wald ma
Off thair deid, that the mast cowart
He maid stoutar then a libart.
Barbour, xv. 522, Edin. MS.

AWANT, AWAUNT, AUANT, *v.* and *s.* Vaunt, laud, praise. Addit. to Awant.

Fr. *vanter*, id.: the prefix being simply intens. The terms are used by Rolland, after Chaucer.

AWAR, *s.* Owner, Burgh Recs. Aberd., 27 Feb. 1507. V. AWNER.

To AWARD, *v. a.* To ward off, to protect or defend from attack or violence, to guard against.

"But *to award* the malignance of any gain-said affection, I stronghold myself under your Marqueeships Mecenatisme." Dedication, Blame of Kirkburiall.
This term is from the Teut. root *War*, to protect,
(Sup.) D

defend ; A.-S. *warian, woerian, gewoerian*. V. Skeat's Etym. Dict. under AWARE and WARY.

To AWARE, *v. a.* To guard, protect, or defend against ; also, to avoid, shun, prevent, save from. V. AWARD.

" Against the poyson of this Papistry, there are two preseruatiue considerations that may *aware* it." Blame of Kirkburiall, ch. xii.
"But *to aware* that sore sin of profanation, there are," etc. Ibid., ch. xviii.
A.-S. *gewoerian*, to protect; from *woer, gewoer*, aware, cautious. V. Skeat's Etym. Dict.

AWAYWARD, AWAYWART, *adv.* In flight, in retreat, retreating.

The Erll with the schirreff met he
Awayward with thar gret menye.
Barbour, xvi. 584. Camb. MS.
Edin. MS. has *awaywart*.

AWCHT, *pret.* Owed, ought to do, Barbour, i. 255 ; deserved, Ibid., iii. 59. V. AUCHT.

AWENAND, *adj.* Comely, suitable, advantageous, Barbour, iii. 41. V. AVENAND.

AWER, *s.* A cart-horse, draught-horse ; Alex. Scott, Bann. MS., p. 843, l. 110. V. AVER.

To AWISE, AWYSE, *v. a.* To advise, counsel, instruct, assure ; put for *avise*, Fr. *aviser*, Mod. E. *advise*.

As he *awisyt*, now have thai done.
Barbour, ii. 29 .
Ic ask yow respyt for to se
This lettir, and thairwith *awyseit* be
Till to-morn, that ye be set.
Barbour, i. 620.

AWIS, AWYS, EWIS, *s.* Advice, counsel, instruction, direction. Fr. *avis*.

" The baillies be *awis* of the counsall," etc. Burgh Rec. Peebles, 4 Oct. 1568.
" In the fyrst, feyt be the *awys* of the Thesaurar, the Comptrorollar and Master Alexander Inglys in Leythe," etc. Accts. Lord H. Treas. Scot., I. 245, Dickson.
" . . . by *ewis* and consent of the haill craft," etc. Burgh Recs. Peebles, 30 Sept. 1506.

AWISEMENT, *s.* Consideration, time for considering. Barbour, ii. 297. V. *Awise*.

AWMENER, *s.* A purse, a bag for alms.

And quhen he fled wes, as yhe her,
Thai fand in-till his *awmener*
A letter—
Barbour, viii. 490, Camb. MS.

Edin. MS. has *coffer*.
O. Fr. *aumosniere*, Fr. *aumônière*, a bag for alms.

AWN, AWNE, *adj.* Own. Barbour, vi. 636, Camb. MS. V. AWIN.

AWNTYR, *s.* Adventure, hap, risk. Barbour, xix. 761, Edin. MS.

Awentur is the most common form of this word in our earlier prose. Cf. *Awntyrs of Arthur*.

AWR [26] AZE

AWRIGE, *s.* The tips of the little ridges laid by the plough are called the *awrige* of the field ; when the grain is sown the *awrige* is harrowed over to cover the seed, West and South of S.

The *awrige* "is the angular points, as it were, above the level of a ploughed ridge." Gall. Encycl. This is prob. the E. *arris*, O. Fr. *areste*, Mod. Fr. *arête*: cf. the *arête* of a glacier.

AWSE, *s.* Err. for *avise*, advice. Burgh Recs. Aberd., 2 June, 1539.

AWTEAL, ATTEAL, *s.* A small teal, not much larger than a snipe.

In the South of S. this bird is called the *Awteal;* in Orkney and Shetland, the *Ateal* or *Atteal.* Dr. Edmonstone calls it *Anas Ferina*, Pochard, Greatheaded Wigeon, or *Ateal;* and Mr. Low, after describing the teal, says :—"I have seen another bird of the teal-kind here called *Atteal.* It is found in our lochs in great numbers in winter ; is very small, brown or dusky above, and a yellowish belly," etc. Fauna Orcadensis, p. 145. V. ATTEILLE.

To **AWYIT,** *v. a.* and *n.* To await, to wait upon ; to superintend, to manage. Burgh Recs. Aberd., vol. ii. pp. 33, 48, Sp. C.

In pp. 115, 120 of same vol. the same verb occurs under the form *avayting*, awaiting, waiting on. These are purely local forms.

AWYN, AWNE, *adj.* Own. V. AWIN.

AWYNAR, AWANAR, AWAR, *s.* Owner. Burgh Recs. Aberd., 27 Feb. 1507. V. AWNER.

These three forms occur in the same record.

AWYR DE PAIS, AWYR DE PAIIS, *adj.* or *s.* Avoirdupois, a weight of which the pound equals 16 oz. Fr. *avoir de pois*, goods of weight.

". . . and of al maner of thingis of *awyr de paiis*, of ilk c. pund at the outgang twa penüs," etc. Assize of Petty Customs, ch. 7. Burgh Rec. Edin., I. 241.

To **AWYSE,** *v. a.* To advise, assure ; part. pt. *awysit*, well advised. V. *Awise*.

AWYS, *s.* Advice. Fr. *avis*. V. *Awis*.

AWYSILY, *adv.* Advisedly, warily. V. AWISELY.

AWYSS. Errat. for *a wyss*, a way, a wise, Barbour, iii. 526, x. 542, Edin. MS.

AXIS, *s.* An attack, a sudden fit or seizure, as of pain or sickness, Kingis Quair, st. 67 ; pl. *axes*, pains, aches, qualms, Orkn.

Both the definition and the etymology of this term as given by Dr. Jamieson are wrong. It is merely the O. Fr. *acces*, as in the phrase, "*acces de fiebvre*, a fit of an ague," Cotgr. V. Gloss. Kingis Quair, Skeat's Ed.

AY, *adv. Ay quhill*, always till, on till, until.

"Item, for the costis maide in Edinburgh vpon xxxvj of [Lutkyn's] folkis that wes takin in Leytht *ay quhill* thai wer justyfiit, xxxvj lib." Accts. Lord H. Treas. Scot., i. 118, Dickson.

This Deyf Lutkyn was the noted Danish pirate Lutkyn More, who for years infested the North Sea and plundered many a Scottish vessel. He and a number of his men were at length captured and brought to Leith ; and, as the above entry records, 36 of them were afterwards *justyfiit*, i.e., executed. V. Introduction to the L. H. Treas. Accts.

AYFALDLY, *adv.* Lit. *one-fold-ly* ; hence, with one end, aim, or desire ; with one consent, earnestly, unanimously. Burgh Recs. Aberd., 28 Jan. 1494. V. AFALD.

To **AYME AT,** *v. a.* To cover, include, embrace, have to do with. Still in use in West of S.

"For although the ten words of Moses tables seeme onely *to ayme at* the ten broad sinnes, that negatively they inhibite, yet there are none of their infinite broode and of-spring, that may not be particularly repledged to his mother kinde, and so incurre the reuerence of some one of the Decalogue lawes." Blame of Kirkburiall, ch. v.

This peculiar use of the phrase *to aim at* is suggested by the idea of covering the object with the weapon aimed at it ; but even that starting-point is far apart from the earliest meanings of the vb. *to aim*. Its first form is Lat. *œstimare*, to estimate, which in O. Fr. became shortened to *œsmer* and *esmer ;* and the latter form began to be used in the sense of "to aime or levell at," Cotgr. From this form our modern *aim* was derived. In Prompt. Parv., p. 190, *Gessyn* or *amyn* are given as Eng. for Lat. *estimo*, *arbitror*, *opinor*.

AYTH, AYTHE, *s.* An oath. V. AITH, ATHE.

AZE, *s.* A large blazing fire, Shetl. V. *Aisle*.

Icel. *usli*, a conflagration ; Vigfusson, A.-S. *y'sel*, a fire spark, hot ember.

B.

BA', BAW, s. A ball, S.
They yowff'd the *ba'* frae dyke to dyke
Wi' unco speed and virr ;
Some baith their shou'ders up did fyke,
For blythenees some did flirr
Their teeth that day.
Skinner, Christmas Ba'ing, s. 2.
Yoweff'd, struck, drove. V. Youf.
Fr. *balle*, It. *balla*, Low. Ger. *bal*, Icel. *böllr*.

BA' MEN, BAWMEN, s. pl. Ball-players; but generally applied to football-players; Skinner's Christmas Ba'ing, st. 34.

BA' SILLER, BA' MONEY, BOWL-MONEY, BOW-MONEY, s. Originally the money claimed from a marriage-party for the purchase of a football for the community; and in some districts, for bowls : now, it is simply a largess called for by, and sometimes given to, the crowd of young people gathered at the place where the marriage is to be celebrated.

Wherever a marriage is about to be celebrated (in Scot. it is usually in the home of the bride), a crowd of young people very quickly gathers, and the cry for *Ba' Money* is raised almost with enthusiasm. As party after party arrives, the shout is revived; and when the company is supposed to be gathered, the cry is kept up with deafening din till the demand is gratified, or till it becomes evident that nothing is to be given. When it is given, the largess is usually in the form of coppers—farthings, halfpence, and pennies—and is thrown among or beyond the crowd in handfuls, or all at once from a hat. The scramble which follows is eager and ludicrous in the extreme, and the result, even to those who are most successful, is often as painful as it is profitable. Whatever each one gets is kept or spent at pleasure.

In some districts of Ayrshire this largess is called *Ba' Siller ;* in Lanarks. and Renfrews., *Bowl Money, Bow Money.*

The following passage from Brockett's Gloss. shows that the custom is well known in the North of England :
"*Ball-Money*, money demanded of a marriage company, and given to prevent being maltreated. In the North it is customary for a party to attend at the church gates, after a wedding, to enforce this claim. The gift has received this denomination, as being originally designed for the purchase of a football." P. 23, Ed. 1846.

GOWF-BA', s. An old name for the game of shinty, and also for the ball used in the game; Wat. Watson's Poems, West of S.

The term is now almost confined to the ball used in the game of golf.

BAA. A word used in lulling a babe to rest; as in the old song *Rocking the Cradle*, "Hushie *baa* babie lye still."

BAA, s. The calf of the leg ; the sole of the foot ; the palm of the hand. S. V. BAW.

Though thus generally applied, the *baa* of the foot is properly the rounded portion of the sole lying at the base of the great toe ; and the *baa* of the hand, the rounded portion of the palm lying at the base of the thumb.

BABBS, BEBBS, s. Particles of loose skin that rise on the face when the beard has not been shaved for two or three days, West and South of S.

"*Babbs* ; that vile luce or slimy matter a razor scrapes off the face in shaving," Gall. Encycl.

BABITY BOWSTER. The name of an old song, tune, and dance : a corr. of Bab at the Bowster : *Bab* being the common pron. of *bob*, to bow or curtsey, to dance ; West of S.

In "Songs of Scotland prior to Burns" Dr. R. Chambers gives the following form of the song as sung by girls playing on the streets of Glasgow :

Wha learned you to dance,
Babity Bowster, Babity Bowster,
Wha learned you to dance
Babity Bowster brawly ?

My minny learned me to dance,
Babity Bowster, Babity Bowster,
My minny learned me to dance,
Babity Bowster brawly.

Wha ga'e you the keys to keep,
Babity Bowster, Babity Bowster,
Wha ga'e you the keys to keep,
Babity Bowster brawly ?

My minny ga'e me the keys to keep,
Babity Bowster, Babity Bowster,
My minny ga'e me the keys to keep,
Babity Bowster brawly.

This song is still sung by young girls at play in the West of Scotland ; but there is also an older form, which is often lilted while the dance proceeds. It is the same with *Bumpkin Brawly*, q. v., simply substituting *Babity Bowster* for that name.

Merry meetings of young people are generally wound up by singing and acting Babity Bowster ; and balls are closed with the dance of that name.

To BACHLE, BAUCHLE, v. a. To carry about for sale, to hawk goods in town or country ; part. pt. and pret. *bachlit, bachleit, bauchlit.* V. BACHLEIT.

Dr. Jamieson left this term unexplained, but gave the correct etymology of it. Both forms occur in the Burgh Records of Edinburgh, I. 29, 43. The extract quoted under *Bachleit* affords a good example of the use of the verb.

BACHLER, BAUCHLAR, s. A hawker, a pedler.

". . . mak the said personis or personis to be pvnyst as efferis ; and richt swa of the *bauchlaris* of the said labour," &c. Skidner's Seal of Cause, Burgh Recs. Edinburgh, i. 29.

BACHLES, *s. pl.* Old shoes; also the lumps of snow which collect on the shoes in walking over fresh snow; West and South of S. V. BAUCHLES.

BACHYT, *part. adj.* Infected, diseased, unclean. V. BAUCH.

"The inquest fyndis Alex. Symsoun *bachyt*, and ordains hym to bald hym wythine hymself quhil the next court." Burgh Rec. Prestwick, 7th July, 1541.

BACK, BAK, BAKKE, *s.* The name given to the ridge or central strip of a hide, skin, or fur.

"Foynes *backes* the dozen, iiij li." Halyburton's Ledger, p. 306.
Foyne or *Fouine*, the foumart or beech-marten: O.Fr. *faine*, a beech tree.
For convenience in working, and to suit the purposes for which the several parts were adapted, hides, skins, and furs were often cut up into distinct parts : especially when they were large. Tanned hides and skins were divided into backs and bellies. Furs were divided into backs, bellies or wombs, gills, legs, and tails. V. Halyburton's Ledger, pp. 305-7.

BACKBAN, BACKBIN, *s.* A backband; another name for the *backwiddie* or *rigwiddie*; the chain or band that crosses the back of a horse when yoked in a cart, S.

BACK-CREELS, *s. pl.* Wicker baskets formed to fit the human back; the contr. form *creels* is also common.

Before wheel-barrows came into common use, *back-creels* were used in cleaning out byres, stables, etc.; and in such *creels* manure, etc., were carried to the fields. Their use is not yet unknown in some parts of the Northern Hebrides and of Orkney and Shetland.
In the Lowlands *back-creels* are now used chiefly by fish-wives for carrying their fish to market.

BACKIEBIRD, BAUCKIE-BIRD, *s.* The bat, West and South of S. V. BAK, BAUKIE.

When lyart leaves bestrew the yird,
Or wavering like the *bauckie* bird,
Bedim cauld Boreas' blast.
Burns, The Jolly Beggars, s. 1.

M. E. *bakke*, a bat; cf. Dan. *aftenbakke*, i.e., evening bat.

BACK OUT OWRE, BACK-OUT-OUR, *adv.*
1. Backwards, backover; as, "He fell clean *back-out-owre*."
2. Back to a place, and implying return; as, "I'll rin *back-out-owre* and get your bag."
3. Back from, away from; as, "Come *back-out-owre* the fire this minit!" Come back from the fire immediately.

BACK-TREAT, *s.* An entertainment given to a newly married couple by their young friends after the honeymoon, Orkn.

BAES, *s. pl.* Cattle, beasts, Shetl. V. *Beas*.

To **BAFF,** *v. a.* A term used in golfing; to strike the ground with the sole of the clubhead in playing; and such a stroke is called a *baff*. Addit. to BAFF, *v.* and *s.*

BAG, *s. Bag irnis, Bag hirnys,* the metal mountings of a bag: *irnis* or *irons* including both framework and fittings.

"Item, to Gilbert Fisch for j pare of *bag hirnys* to the King, price xxxv s." Accts. L. H. Treas. Scot., I. 28.
"Item, to thre men that fand the *bag irnis* of gold; to ilk ane xl s," &c. Ibid, I. 270, Dickson.
In the Acta Dom. Concilii, p. 131, in a list of "*gudes of areschip*" we find the phrase, "a bag with *siluer irnis*."

BAGGIE, *adj.* and *s.* Big bellied: same with *Baggit*; but often used as a *s.*, meaning a person with a big belly; Ayrs., Gall.

BAIBERREIS, *s. pl.* Bayberries; fruit of Laurus nobilis, from which Oil of Bays is extracted; Halyburton's Ledger, p. 288.

To **BAIBLE,** *v. a.* To sip often, tipple; also, to drink carelessly or with spilling; West of S. Similar to E. *bibble*.

BAIBLING, BAIBLIN, *part. adj.* Tippling; boozing.

BAID, *pret.* Abode, remained, waited. Henryson, Testament of Cresseid, l. 490, Fox and Wolf, l. 177. V. BIDE.

BAID, *s.* Delay, tarrying; also, place of abode, dwelling; Henryson, Dog, Scheip, and Wolf, l. 145. V. BADE.

BAIGNET, BAIGINET, BEGNET, *s.* A bayonet.

In lines extended lang and large,
When *baiginets* o'erpower'd the targe,
And thousands hastened to the charge.
Burns, Sherra Moor, s. 3.

This weapon is said to have been invented at Bayonne in France (whence the name) about 1670. It was adopted by the British in 1693. V. Haydn's Dict. Dates.
The invention at Bayonne may be quite correct, and the date given may indicate when the weapon was first fitted to a gun; but the term *bayonnette* was in use long before that, meaning "a kinde of small flat pocket dagger, furnished with knives; or a great knife to hang at the girdle like a dagger." Cotgrave's Dict., 1611. V. Suppl. to Skeat's Etym. Dict.

BAIK, *s.* A biscuit, Loth., West of S.; *flour-baiks*, Burgh Rec. Edinburgh, i. 215. V. BAKE.
There were and still are various kinds of *baiks*, named from their shape, colour, kind of flour of which they were made, &c.

BAILLIE DAYS, *s. pl.* Days during which farmers were bound to labour for their lairds: so called in the South of S.

BAI [29] BAK

This form of service is now almost unknown in the Lowlands, but is still common in many districts of the Highlands and Islands.
"*Baillie days* were mentioned in tacks : so many days of *baillie harrowing*, so many of *baillie peating*, and so on. They were very troublesome days to farmers, and those *baillie works* brought *kempin* to great perfection ; for, when the labourers of many farmers met, they behaved little better with each other than when strange herds of oxen meet, goring and frothing about who should have the mastery." Gall. Encycl.
Baillie days were days devoted to the *Bailiff* or Steward,—that is for work under his order and supervision.

BAIN, BANE, *adj.* Prompt, ready, willing; hence, obedient, ready to start, prepared, ready or eager for the call, &c. V. BAYNE.

The explanation of this term as given under *bayne*, is defective. The idea of ready, willing, hearty, or eager service, which it always implies, is not set forth. See the passages quoted. In Mid. Eng. it meant obedient, submissive, etc.

Thou wast ever to me fulle *bayn*.
Town Myst., p. 39.
To his byddinge I wilbe *bayne*.
Chest. Myst., p. 69.

BAIRD, *s.* A noisy, turbulent person; generally applied to a scold. V. *Bard.*

To BAIRGE, BARGE (with *g* like *j*), *v. n.* To speak in a loud and angry manner; to scold, rail, or taunt loudly ; also, to drive about like one in anger; as, " She jist likes to gae *bairgin* about;" West and North of S. V. BERGE.

BAIRTUITHE, *s.* A boar's tusk. V. BAIR.

Between 1538 and 1542 a considerable quantity of native gold was used in Scotland. "Large amounts were used for the coinage of the gold bonnet pieces, and for sundry other purposes, such as making a '*bairtuithe*' (mounting a boar's tusk to be used as a coral) for the Prince, a shrine for 'ane bane of St. Audrian of May," etc. Early Records of Mining in Scotland, Intro., p. 15, Cochran-Patrick.

BAISING, BASSING, *s.* and *adj.* Basin. V. BASING.

Fr. *bassin*, O.Fr. *bacin* and *bachin*.

BAISING-SILUIR, BASSIN-SILUIR, *s.* A gratuity given to certain servants of the king's household, especially to the yeomen of the wine and ale cellars, and the porters. V. BASING.

"Item, to Robert Douglas of the wyne cellar, to his *basing siluir* at Newyeremes, x li."
"Item, to Sande Balfour of the aile sellar, to his *basing siluir*, v li."
"Item, to the portaris, clikwis, to thare *baising siluir*, x li." Accts. L. H. Treas. Scot., A.D. 1495, i. 268.

BAIST, BAISTE, *part. pt.* Abashed, confused, cowed, afraid. V. BAISED.

Bees noghte *baiste* of yone boyes, ne of thaire bryghte wedis.
Morte Arthure, l. 2857.

To BAIST, BASTE, BAST, *v. a.* To beat, drub, drive off ; hence, to defeat, overcome ;

and in the pass. voice, to be awed, cowed, terrified. V. BAIST.

The secondary meaning only is given in the DICT. The term is still used in its primary sense both in Scot. and North of Eng.
"Baist, baste, to beat severely ;" Brockett.

BAIT, *s.* The supply of food for a horse, a feed ; also, the time or place for feeding; Henryson, Wolf, Fox, and Cadgear, l. 108. V. BAYT, *v.* For *bait*, boot, V. *Bat.*

BAITH-FATE, BATH-FAT, *s.* Bathing vat or tub.
". . viij eln of brade clatht . . . to covire a *baith-fate* to the Quene," &c. Accts. L. H. Treas. Scot., l. 30.
". . iij elne of brade cloth for a schete to put about the Quene in the *bath-fat*," &c. Ibid. 6th Oct., 1473, Dickson.
A.-S. *bathian*, to bathe ; *baeth*, a bath, and *fat*, a vat, Du. *vat*.

To BAIVER, *v. n.* To gad about, make much ado about little things; to run after shows, weddings, displays of finery, &c.: mostly used in the part. form *baiverin*, West of S.

BAIVERING, BAIVERIN, *part. adj.* Gadding about ; taking interest in trifles, displays, finery, &c.; as, "She's grown a daidlin, *baiverin* gawkie."

BAJAN, BAIJAN, *s.* A novice, a beginner in any trade, art or science : a form of Bejan, q. v.

To BAJAN, BAIJAN, *v. a.* To initiate a beginner or apprentice. V. BEJAN, *v.*

BAK, *s.* The back ; *gaf the bak*, turned their backs, fled ; *ta the bak*, to flee, take to flight. Both phrases are common in Barbour.

To BAK, *v. a.* To bake. V. BAKE.
"The thrid, at thai bak nocht ilk kynd of bred as the law of burgh requeris," &c.; Chalmerlan Air, ch. 9.

BAKBRED, BAKBREID, BAKBROD, *s.* A bakeboard, a kneading board, West of S. V. BAIKBRED.

BAKSTULE, BAKSTWLE, *s.* A bake-stool ; a large stool or small table on which cakes or bannocks were kneaded and formed; Burgh Recs. Prestwick, p. 23.

BAKHUDE, *s.* Hiding or skulking behind backs. In certain games favoured by young people the hunted or pursued one tries to elude the pursuer by hiding behind his companions, and dodging from one to another : this is called *backhide* or *backhude*.

And for dreddour that he suld bene arreist,
He playit *bakhude* behind fra beist to beist.
Henryson, Parliament of Beistis, l. 178.

BALANDIS, *s. pl.* Balances. The same form is used for the singular also.

"That thai present that tym al thar mesuris, *balandis*, wechtis, elnwandis, and all other instruments of whatsumever kynd," &c.; Chalmerlan Air, ch. 1.
Prob. a corr. of Lat. *bilanx*, consisting of two dishes.

BALDIE, BALDY, *s.* A familiar form of Archibald, West of S. V. BAULDIE.

BALDKYN, BALTKEN, *s.* A baldachin, or canopy of state borne over a king or high state-official; also, the rich cloths of which it is formed: *baltkenis mortuaris*, mortuary baldachins, or, the rich funereal drapery for catafalques before the altar. Inventory St. Salv. Col. St. Andrews, Mait. Club Misc., iii. 199.

O. Fr. *baldachin, baldaquin, baudequin*, a canopy or cloth of estate, Cotgr.

BALDSTROD, BALESTROD, *s.* A bawd, unclean person; Colkelbie Sow, l. 166, Bann. MS.

Not defined in DICT.; but in the note which is added the meaning suggested is correct, and the etymology nearly so. V. Cleasby and Vigfusson's Icel. Dict. under *baliz*, bold, and *sertha*, *sarth*, from which comes *stretha* (used of dogs and beasts), and *stred*, to which Dr. Jamieson refers.

The term occurs in Wright's Vocabularies as *bawdstrot, bawolstrott*, and *baustrott*, and is applied to both sexes, pp. 605, 693, 695.

BALE, BAILL, *s.* Sorrow, misery, evil, disaster, destruction, Gol. and Gaw, l. 719.

A.-S. *bealu*, sorrow.

BALE-FEIR, BALOFEIR, *s.* Lit. a bail-companion; fellow-surety; associate in bail, bond, or bargain.

". . . and to furnis ane vther bigger als sufficient as himself . . . and for payment to the said John Ottirburne and his *balofeir*, with their servand," &c.
Burgh Recs. Glasgow, i. 240.
Printed *balofeir* in Recs. Soc. issue; but probably it should be *baleseir*. However, the original record is very much decayed, and most difficult to decipher.
O.Fr. *bailler*, to keep in custody, used as a law term, and A.-S. *gefera*, from pt. tense of *faran*, to go.

BALINGARE, *s.* A kind of vessel. V. BALLINGAR.

"Of ilk crayer, bushe, barge, and *balingare*, v. s." Custom of Ships and Boats at Leith in 1445; Burgh Rec. Edinburgh, p. 8.

BALK, *s.* A beam, rafter; a pole or perch for fowls, a spar for a cage-bird. V. BAUK.

BALK-SPARRIS, *s. pl.* The tie-beams of a roof that unite the rafters. Accts. L. H. Treas. Scot., i. 381.

BALK, *s.* A ridge or strip of land left unploughed; Henryson, The Twa Mice, l. 24. V. BAUK.

BALK-BRED, BALK-BRAID, *s.* The breadth of a *balk* or ridge of unploughed land.

BALTKEN, *s.* V. BALDKYN.

To BAMF, *v. n.* To stump, dump, toss, or tumble about; part. *bamfin*; part. pt. *bamfd*.

"He wont to be *bamfin* aff the heads wi' collier briggs whiles, and they under close-reefed tap-sails. Seldom ever was he out any long voyage with his boat, but the water bruik on him or he got back;" &c.
Gall. Encycl.

BAMF, *s.* A person with broad, flat, clumsy feet: one who goes about stumping and tossing his feet about.

BANCKE, *s.* V. *Bank*.

BAND, *pret.* Bound. Accts. L. H. Treas. Scot.

BAND, *s.* That part of a hinge which was fastened on the door.

Jamieson makes it *a hinge*. The old-fashioned hinge consisted of a hook, affixed to the door-post, and a band (with a loop at the end to fit the hook) fastened to the door. Hence hinges are described as "hooks and bands."

BANDELERIS, BANDELEIRIS, *s. pl.* Bandoleers; leathern belts worn by ancient musketeers for sustaining their musket and carrying charges of powder; sometimes the belt was called a *bandoleer*, and the small leathern cases for powder attached to it, *bandoleers*. V. Cotgrave's Fr. Dict.

"Item, fyve muskettes with thair *bandeleris* all worth xxx. li." Commissary Records of Glasgow, quoted in Burgh Rec. Prestwick, p. 145.
This term occurs also in the Burgh Records of Peebles, 6 July, 1648, as *bandeleans*.

BANDIT, *part. adj.* Bound with metal bands.

". . . fundin in a *bandit* kist like a gardeviant," &c. Accts. L. H. Treas. Scot., I. 82.

BANDIT STAFE, *s.* An official baton; so called because bound with bands of metal. Often mentioned in Burgh Recs.

BAND LEDDER, *s.* Leather for binding or edging.

"Item, for *band ledder* to the Queens furringis of hir gownis, v s." [Apr. 1474.] Accts. L. H. Treas., I. 36.

BANDKYN, *s.* Errat. in DICT. for *Baudkyn*; but definition is correct. V. *Baldkyn*.

BANDON, BANDOUN, *s.* Subjection, thraldom, bondage.

Quhen that scho lukit to the serk,
Scho thoct on the persoun:
And prayit for him with all hir harte,
That lowsit hir of *bandoun*.
Henryson, *Bludy Serk*, l. 84.

BANDONIT, *part. pr.* Subdued; kept in subjection, kept aloof.

The shepherd, mourning over his faithful dog now dead, is represented as saying :—
For all the belstis befoir *bandonit* bene,
Will schute upon my beistis with iro and tene.
Henryson, Wolf and Wedder, l. 20.

This term is wrongly rendered "*abandoned*" in Dr. Laing's edit. of Henryson.

O. Fr. *bandon*, from Low Lat. *bandum*, an order, decree; also written *bannum*. Hence Fr. *à bandon*, by license, at liberty. V. BRACHET, Etym. Fr. Dict., and Skeat, Etym. Dict., under ADANDON.

BANERECH, *s.* Money payable on account of *band*, i.e., bond or covenant; the person engaging to pay was called a *bander*, q.v.

". . . for wrangus wythhaldin fra hym of viij. s. of *banerech* or thairby," &c. Burgh Rec. Prestwick, 6 Oct., 1544.

Gael. *bann*, a bond, bill, and *riadh*, interest.

BANESTIKILL, *s.* A fish; the three-spined stickle-back; Henryson, Wolf, Fox, and Cadgear, 1. 52. V. BANE-PRICKLE; BANSTICKLE.

BANIS, BENIS, BENYS, BEINS, *s.* A fur; perhaps vair, a fine ermine.

"Item, coft fra Will. Sinclare, v mantill of *banis* to lyne a syde gowne to the King, . . . vj Octobris [1493], price of the mantill xiiij s.," &c.; Accts. L. H. Treas. Scot., i. 15.

"*Mantillis of banis*" is rendered "a kind of mantle," in the DICT. This is a wild guess. The mantil was a certain number of skins of fur. V. MANTIL in Supp. *Banis* is supposed to have been the *vair*, or fine ermine.

BANK, BANKE, BANCK, BANCKE, *s.* An order, injunction, prohibition, proclamation, call, summons.

The meaning of this term as given by Dr. Jamieson is quite misleading, and the etymology is altogether wrong. V. BANCKE.

In the Burgh Recs. of Glasgow, vol. II., the following entry frequently occurs :—" Ordaines ane *bank* to be sent throw the toune be touck of drum," &c. This was the usual method of publishing the orders of the magistrates, of calling the burgesses to conference, and of notifying the arrival of supplies of food, &c.

Bank is a corr. of O. Fr. *ban*, from Low Lat. *bannum*, a proclamation: whence also E. *ban*, pl. *banns* of marriage.

BANKIT, *s.* A banquet, feast, festival, public rejoicing. Fr. *banquet*, id.

This term occurs frequently in the Burgh Records, and is generally applied to the entertainment and ceremonies on an occasion of public rejoicing, such as a coronation, royal marriage, King's birthday, &c. A good idea of a *bankit* in olden times, and of how much and of what kind of enjoyment our forefathers included under that term, may be obtained from the following record.

On 30th March, 1603, the glad tidings reached Aberdeen, "that vpon the tuentic fourt day of Marche instant, his Maiestie, our Kyng and Souerane, wes proclamit and declarit Kyng of Inglaud." Instantly the provost, bailies, and counsel met, and resolved to honour the event by public thanksgiving and a *bankit*; "and for this effect ordained the baill towne to be warnit be sound of trumpet and drum to assemble instantlie in thair paroche kirk, and thair give thankis and praeis to God for the foresaid glad tydings of his Maiestie's preferment, successioun, and electioun to the said kingdom of Ingland; and efter the ending of thanksgiving, and of the exhortatioun, ordanis bonefyris to be sett on throcht all the streittis of the towne, the haill bellis to ring, the croce to be deckit and hung, the wyne and spycerie to be spent abundantlie thairat, a numer of glassis to be cassin, and the haill youthis of the towne to tak thair hag-buttis and accompanie thair magistrates throcht the haill rewis of the towne, pas the tyme in schuting thair muskattis and hagbutis til lait at nicht, the townis haill mvnitioun and artailyrie to be chargit and schott, and all godlie mirines and pastyme vsit that may expres the joy and glaidnes of the people, and ordanis the deane of gild and thesaurer to furneis the wyne, spycerie, and glassis to the end foirsaid in all decent and cumlie forme, and the expensis to be deburset be thame thairon, the counsall ordanis the same to be allowit in thair comptis."

A later entry records that when said *comptis* were reckoned the expenses were found to amount to £53 6s. 8d. V. Burgh Records, vol. II. pp. 236-8.

BANNA, BANNO, *s.* Contr. or corr. of *bannack* and *bannock*, a sort of cake, q. v.

BANTIN, BANTON, BANTIN COCK, *s.* A Bantam, Bantam cock: applied to a strutting little man fond of fighting; Gall., Ayrs.

BANYST, *part. pt.* Banished, Barbour, iv. 522.

To BAR, BARRE, *v. a.* To debar, hinder, prevent; to exclude.

To BAR UP, *v. a.* To shut up or out'from, imprison, isolate: hence, to shut out, cut off, banish.

". . . as reprobated are with God *barred up* from hope." Bl. of Kirkburiall, ch. VI.

BAR, *s.* A flail: properly, the swing or movable portion of the flail, West and South of S.

To BAR, BARRIE, *v. a.* To thrash; also, to swing a flail properly; as, "It's no ilka ane can *bar*," every one can't swing a flail properly.

Barrie is properly a freq. form : *bar* being used to express simply the act or process, and *barrie* to express continued action : thus, "I'm thinkin' *to bar* some bear the morn," I intend to thrash some barley to-morrow : "I've *barried* some nine hours the day," I have thrashed for nearly nine hours to-day.

Icel. *berja*, to beat, thrash. In Cleasby and Vigfusson's Dict. this term is said to be unknown in Eng. This is a mistake; *berry*, to thrash corn, is still used in the North of E. V. Brockett's Gloss.; and *bar, barrie*, are still used in South and West of S.

BARRIED, *part.* and *adj.* Thrashed; as an *adj.*, stiff and sore as after a day's thrashing.

BARMAN, *s.* A thrasher, one accustomed to the *bar* or flail.

The *barmen* did rattle their flails ow're the bawks,
The millers did hushoch their melders in haste,
And hung the best braws that they had on their backs,
To flash at the funny bonello.
Gall. Encycl., p. 78.

BARAT, BARET, s. Contention; The Houl-ate, l. 332, Asloan MS. V. BARRAT.

BARD, BAIRD, s. A bold, turbulent woman; a scold; Burgh Recs. Édin., iv. 510. V. BARDACH.

This term is still used in many districts of S. It is common in Orkn. and Shetl., and throughout the greater part of the Lowlands.

BARDY, BARDIE, adj. Bold, fierce, turbulent. V. BARDACH.

BARD, s. A bold headland, the top of which projects beyond the base, Shetl.

Icel. *barth*, brim, projection : hence the projecting headlands of the island of Mousa, and of Bressay, are called the Bard of Mousa, and the Bard of Bressay.

BAREL, BARIL, s. A measure: the twelfth part of a *last*.

"Item, for bering of xxvᴵˣ vj barellis of bere, that the Countas of Ros gaif to the King, and threscore barellis of mele, xx s." Accts. L. H. Treas., i. 359. This measure was used for grain, flour, meal, fish, and hides. V. LAST.

BARELL-FERIS, s. pl. Barrel irons. V. BARELL-FERRARIS.

BARELL-FERRARIS, s. pl. For *Barell-ferruris*, barrel-ironwork or barrel-irons, iron hoops for barrels. Fr. *fer*, iron, an iron: hence an iron hoop. V. FERRARIS.

Dr. Jamieson's rendering of this term does not satisfy the sense of the passage in which it occurs. The rendering given above was proposed by Prof. Skeat in his edition of Barbour, p. 594. It certainly makes the passage clear. *Barrel-feris* is the reading of the Camb. MS.

BARFORS, s. Errat. in Edin. MS. for *barfrois* or *berfrois*, a tower, watch-tower; Barbour, X. 708. V. *Burfray, Berfroiss.*

BARFRAY, BARFRY, s. A belfry, tower. V. *Berfroiss.*

BARGE, BAIRGE, BERGE, s. A moveable shutter constructed with parallel boards that open and shut like a venetian blind; used in drying-sheds, West of S.

M. H. Germ. *bergen*, to protect; *berc*, protection. Du. *bergen*, to save, make or keep safe, lock up. The *barges* or *berges* when open admit the air, and when shut protect from rain, etc.

BARKAND, BARKANDE, part. Tanning; Burgh Lawis, ch. 93. V. BARK.

BARKARIS, s. pl. Tanners; Chalmerlan Air, ch. 28. V. BARK.

BARKIT, BARKED, part. adj. Tanned. V. BARK.

"Item, that thai mak schone, butis and vther graitht of the lethir or jt be *barkit*." Chalmerlan Air, ch. 22.
". . . no stranger bringing *barked* hides for sale

shall sell them within house," &c. Lawis of the Gild, ch. 45.

BARKCATT, s. A fender, guard, defence, protection; a frame-work of timber set in front of a sea-wall or harbour to protect it during the process of building or repairing.

". . . and als protestit that in cais ony skayth or danger come to the pannellis [of Newhaven harbour], that ar put vp, in defalt of *barkcattis*, considdering the said Johne will intromet thairwith, that the falt thairof be nocht imput to him." Burgh Recs. Edinburgh, 2 Nov., 1556, II. 254.

O. Fr. *bariquade, barriquade*, "a barricade, a defence of barrels, timber, pales, earth, or stones, heaped up, or closed together : and seruing to stop up a street, or passage, and to keepe off shot, &c." Cotgr.

Prob. from Sp. *barricado*, from *barrica*, a barrel ; whence the E. *barricade*.

Halliwell gives *barriket*, a small firkin.

BARKIN, s. Barking; coughing: used also as an *adj*.; as, "a *barkin*' hoast," a short, hard, rapid cough, resembling the bark of a dog; Burns, Scotch Drink.

BARLAY, BARLIE. V. BARLEY.

BARLIE-FETTERER, s. "An instrument of many edges used for taking the beard off the grain barley;" Gall. Encycl.

BARMEKIN, BARMEKYN, s. A rampart. V. BARMKYN.

BARMSKIN, s. Lit. bosom-skin; a leather covering for the breast, a large leather apron ; Orkn. and Shetl.

The large leather apron worn by tanners and curriers is called a *bramskin*, q. v.

Sw. and Dan. *barm*, the bosom or breast, and Sw. *skinn*, Dan. *skind*, a skin or hide.

BARMWHIN, BARMWHUN, s. A thick close branch of whin on which barm was laid to preserve it for brewing. It was hung up in a dry, airy place, Gall. Encycl.

BARONY, s. Lands held of the Crown, and erected *in liberam baroniam*, with jurisdiction both civil and criminal within its bounds.

"Item, componit with Vmfra of Murray of Abirkerny for the resignacione of certane landis, and gevin of thame to him agane in *barony* lyand within Stratherne, jᶜ lib;" Accts. L. H. Treas. Scot., i. 3, DICKSON.

BARRET, s. Strife. V. BARRAT.

To BARTYN, v. a. To strike, dash, break to pieces; Gol. and Gaw., l. 719. V. BRYTTYN.

A form of *bryttyn*, to smash ; from A.-S. *bryttian*, to break into pieces.

BASAND, s. and adj. Sheep-skin dressed like Spanish leather, basil.

"Item, for ane done *basand* skyn, to be halk hudis to the King, iij s." Accts. L. H. Treas. Scot., i. 365.

BASLAR, *s.* A baselard: a long dagger or sheathed knife, worn suspended from the girdle; *baselarde,* Prompt. Parv.
"Item [the first day of November, 1495, in Edinburgh], bocht to the King fra the Franche cutlar, ij *baslaris,* price xlviij s." Accts. L. H. Treas. Scot., i. 227.
The basclard was worn by knights when not in armour, by the higher class of civilians, and sometimes even by ecclesiastics.
O. Fr. *bazelaire, badelaire.*

BASSING, *s.* V. *Baising.*

BASTALYE, BASTULRY, *s.* A bastile, fort, citadel; occurs frequently in Burgh Recs. meaning a blockhouse. V. BASTAILYIE.
Fr. *bastille,* a fortress.

BASTERO, *s.* Prob. a misreading of *baston,* a baton; Burgh. Recs. Edin., 8 Nov., 1494. V. BASTOUN.

BAT, BAIT, *s.* Boot, abatement, deduction; Halyburton's Ledger. V. BOOT.

BAT, BATE, *conj.* Both; this is the local pron.; Burgh Recs. Aberdeen, i. 427.

BATALL, BATELL, BATTAILE, BATTELL, *s.* A battle, fight; *battalyhe,* Barbour, N., 725.

BATALL-WRICHT, BATTEL-WRYCHT, *s.* A braggart, braggadocio, bully.
In breth as a *batall-wricht* full of bost blawin'.
The Houlate, l. 916, Asloan MS.
Lit. a *battle-wright,* feud-provoker: like *bully-rag.* However, the line is usually read with *wricht* as an adjunct to *full.*

BATTAILLYNG, *s.* Battle array; Barbour, viii. 47, Edin. MS.

BATCHIE, BATCHY, *s.* A baker, West of S.: from *batch,* the quantity of bread put into the oven at one time.

BATERIE, *s.* V. *Battry.*

BATIT, BAYTIT, *pret.* Took refreshment on a journey. Icel. *beita,* to bait.
"Item, for the Kingis hors met in Bigar, passand to Quhithirne, quhare the King *batit,* xiiij d.," Accts. L. H. Treas. Scot., i. 355 [A.D. 1497].
"Item, that samyn day [3 Nov. 1496] quhare the King *baytit* abone llay, for hors corne, ij s.," ibid. i., 305.

To BATTELL, BATTAILLE, *v. a.* To battlement, to build a battlement or parapet, to ledge, top, or crown.
".. the said Andrew sall big and hew ane rod on baythe the syddis of the said brig, and *battell* the said brige on baythe the syddis of the samyn with hewn wark," &c.; Burgh Recs. Aberdeen, 9 Aug., 1609.
O. Fr. *bastille,* a building, from *bastir,* to build.

(Sup.) E

BATTAILLYT, *part. pt.* Embattled, furnished with battlements, Barbour, ii. 221.

BATTER, *s.* A spree, booze, drinking-bout, Clydes.
I had a hat, I had nae mair,
I gat it frae the hatter;
My hat was smash'd, my skull laid bare,
Ae night when on the *batter.*
Alex. Rodger, Song in Whistle Binkie, l. 211.
This is a humorous application of *batter,* to lay a stone obliquely, or off-the-straight: a term in masonry. Similar terms in masonry are also used to express this state, as *slued,* and *skued,* q. v

BATTRY, BATERIE, *s.* Kitchen utensils.
".. of a duaane of pannys of *battry* at the furth passyng twa pennies, at the entrying nocht," &c. Assize of Petty Customs, ch. 9.
"Off the custome of cordwain, *baterie,*" &c. Burgh Rec. Edinburgh, p. 242.
Halliwell states that in Suffolk this term means *a tea kettle.*
L. Lat. *bateria,* cooking utensils; Du Cange.

BAUBEE, BAUBIE, BAWBEE, *s.* A halfpenny. V. BABIE, BAWBIE.

To BAUCHLE, *v.* BAUCHLAR, *s.* V. *Bachle, Bachler.*

BAUDKYN, *s.* Entered in DICT. as BANDKYN; but defin. is correct. V. also *Baldkyn.*

BAUDMINNIE, BALDMINNIE, *s.* The plant Gentian, believed to have properties that can kill the foetus in the womb; hence its name *Bawd-money.* V. BAD-MONEY.
"*Baudminnie*—An herb having the same qualities as the Savingtree." Gall. Encycl.

BAUDRIC, BADRICK, BADRICHE, *s.* A band, bandage, belt, scarf, baldric; *bawderyke,* Prompt. Parv.
O. Fr. *baldret, baldre, baldrei,* from Lat. *balteus,* a belt: Burguy. In Mod. Fr. *baudrier,* a sword belt, a girdle.
The term occurs in Chaucer and Shakespeare; in the latter as *baldrick*; and in the All. Rom. Alexander, l. 1782, it is *badriche,* a band or bandage; but in the Gloss. it is left unexplained.

BAUDRIE, *s.* Bawdry, lewdness, uncleanness, wickedness; Seven Sages, l. 333.
O. Fr. *bauderie,* id.; from *baud,* bold, gay, wanton.

BAUK, *s.* Err. for *Bank,* an order, proclamation, prohibition; Burgh Recs. Glasgow, 22 May, 1647. V. *Bank.*

BAULD, *adj.* Bold; Montgomery. V. BALD.

BAUM, BAWM, *s.* Balm, an herb; also balm, an ointment, a perfume; S. E. *balm.*

To BAUM, BAWM, *v. a.* To balm, scent, perfume; to embalm; hence, to preserve; S.

BAUMING, BAUMIN, *part.* and *s.* Balming, embalming; perfume, S.

BAWLMYT, BAWMYT, *part. pt.* Embalmed, Barbour, xx. 286.

BAUTHLE, *s.* A corr. of *battle,* E. *bottle,* a bundle: still used in the expression, *a buttle o' strae.* Pl. *bauthles, bauthlis, battles,* bundles, implies one's moveable or personal property. V. BATTLE.

My brelat that wes gret belld, bowdyn wes sa huge,
That neir my barel out brist or the band makin ;
But quhen my billis and my *bauthles* wes all braid selit,
I wald na langar beir on bridill, bot braid vp my heid.
  Dunbar, Twa Mariit Women, l. 347.

"My billis and my bauthles," all my belongings, property, both gifted and personal : *billis* being frequently used for *deeds, title deeds, infeftments.*
Fr. *boteler,* to make up in bundles.

BAWDRONIS, *s.* A common name for a cat; Henryson, Uplandis Mous and Burges Mous, l. 168. V. BAUDRONS.

In the West of S. this term has been corrupted into *pautrons,* as in the old nursery rhyme,—
"Pussy, pussy, *pautrons,* whare hae ye been," &c.

BAWK, *s.* V. *Balk.*

BAWSAND, BAWSENT, BAWSINT, BASSAND, *adj.* Streaked or patched with white on the face: applied to horses and cattle. V. under BAWSAND.

Dr. Jamieson is quite astray in his etymology of this term, and Sibbald whom he corrects is right. It is from O. E. *bawsin,* a badger, as the following neat analogy by Mr. Garnett abundantly shows :—
"*Brock* is a badger ; *bawsin,* ditto ; *brock-faced* (ap. Craven Glossary, and Brockett), marked with white on the face like a badger ; *bawsin'd,* ditto." Philol. Essays, p. 68.
Baucynes, badgers, occurs in Will. & Werwolf, p. 83.

BAWSIE, *s.* A horse or a cow having a white strip or patch on the face. V. *Bawsand,* BASSIE.

The term is also used as a familiar name for an old horse,—a douce, canny, old beast; Clydes.

BAWTIE, BAWTY, *s.* and *adj.* A familiar name for a dog: as an *adj.,* round, plump, thriving; as, a *bawtie* bairn. V. BATIE.

"Board na' wi' *bawty* or he'll bite you."
  Scotch Proverb.

Whenever our *bawty* does bark,
Then fast to the door I rin,
To see gin ony young spark
Will light and venture but in.
  Slighted Nansy, Herd's Collection, ii. 82.

BAYD, *pret.* of Bide; also as *s.* V. *Bide.*

BAZELL LEATHER, *s.* Tanned sheepskin: still called *basil;* Halyburton's Ledger, p. 318.

The usual name in Scot. is *basil,* or *bazel;* but the correct form is *basan,* or *basen :* O. Fr. *basane, basane,* sheep leather dressed like Spanish leather, and coloured red, green, or yellow, &c., for shoes, or the covering of books ; Cotgr. The modern term is a corr. from the French, which was adapted from the Span. *badana,* a dressed sheepskin ; and that in turn came from the Arab. *bitânat,* applied to such leather because it was used to line leathern garments. V. Skeat's Etym. Dict., Suppl.

BE, *v.* Let be, or *let alone,* not to mention, without reckoning ; over and above, as well as, besides.

". . the necessitie was neuer absolute ; no not in the lawfull place, *let be* in the Kirk"; Blame of Kirk- buriall, ch. xix.
". . whereof my labor were infinite, *let be* vaine, to descryue " ; Ibid., ch. iv.

The meaning of this very common phrase is not fully given in the DICT.; and a few words of explanation are here necessary.

In negative sentences, like that in the first quotation given above, the phrase is equal to *and far less,* or *and far less so ;* in positive or affirmative sentences it is equal to *as well as, and more than that,* or, *over and above,* as in the second quotation.

BE TO, BE TA. Must, in the sense of intending, being resolved or determined to be or do. Different, therefore, from *bi te, bu ta,* behoves to, which implies action or influence from without causing the necessity.

"And if thou *be to* ly at the altar, how wantst thou a Priest to say thy soule Masse ? " Blame of Kirkburiall, ch. xi.

Be to, pron. *be ta,* is still in common nse : thus, one speaking about a dour, stubborn neighbour, will say, "Aye, richt or wrang, he *be ta* get it," *i.e.,* he had made up his mind and he must get it.

While *be ta, bi ta* or *bu ta, bit ta* or *but ta,* have often the same meaning, and are generally pronounced alike, they are quite different terms: *bi ta* or *bu ta* are corr. of *bus to,* behoves to ; and *bit ta* or *but ta,* corr. of *bud to,* behoved to. V. under Boot, *Be't, Bit.*

BEAKEN, *s.* A beacon, signal. V. BEKIN.

". . . set as on the shalde shoare lyke *beakens* to warne the shipwreake of soules " ; Bl. of Kirkburiall, ch. xvii.
A.-S. *beácen,* a sign.

BEAMED, *part. adj.* Filled, saturated, prepared for the purpose, accustomed to, ready for ; Orkn. Addit. to BEAM, *v.*

BEAR, BEARE, BERE, *s.* A bier ; also, a shell or coffin.

The bier was a frame on which dead human bodies were carried to the grave : A.-S. *bǽr,* from *beran,* to bear ; Lat. *feretrum,* from *ferre,* id. And when it became customary to enclose each body before burial, the shell or coffin was called the bier : that which was carried, or that in which the dead body was carried, to the grave,—the old frame or bier not being then required. The persons who carried the bier were called *bearers,* or *bear-men,* q.v.

"So (I doubt not) if now they had life in their boulke, they would yet ryue sheets, breake *beares,* tumble downe tombes, with Paul's spirit at Listra, to testifie their reclamation of such profanity." Blame of Kirkburiall, ch. xiii.

BEAR-MEN, BERE-MEN, *s. pl.* Carriers of the bier; carriers of the dead.

"Now the last funerall duety appertained to the Vespilones, or *bear-men,* whose peculiare calling was (beeing followed in ranks by the Acoluthists their

friends, wherof now the Roman Bishops hes bereft them) to carry their corps in their coffins to the grave." Ibid., ch. vii.
The following interesting particulars regarding the burial of the dead during a time of pest are given in the Burgh Records of Edinburgh, under date 15 Oct., 1568 :—
"Item, that the thesaurer caus mak with all diligence for euery ane of the baillies, clengeris, and the buroaris of the deid, ane goun of gray with Sanct Androis cors, quhite, behind and before, and to euerie ane of thame ane staff with ane quhite clayth on the end, quhairby thay may be knawin quhaireuer thay pas.
"Item, that thair be maid tua clois beris with foure feit colourit our with blak, and ane quhite cors with ane bell to be hanging vpoun the heid of the said beir quhilk sall mak warning to the pepill." Vol. iii., p. 254.

BEAS', *s. pl.* A contr. for *beasts*, cattle; but also used as a term for lice.

An' if the wives an' dirty brats
E'en thigger at your doors an' yetts,
Flaffan wi' duds an' grey wi' *beas*',
Frightin' awa your ducks an' geese.
Burns, Address of Beelzebub.

BEASENIN, BEASNIN, *s.* Called also *beestie-milk:* the fat thick matter drawn from a cow's udder immediately after she calves; Gall., Ayrs.
This is prob. a corr. or local pronunciation of *beestin* or *beistyn* from the A.-S. *by'sting.* V. BEIST, BEISTYN.

To BEAT, *v. a.* To mend, repair. V. BEIT.

BEATIN, BEATING, *s.* 1. Mending, repairing: also, the act of mending, West of S. V. BEITING.

2. That which is used for mending or repairing; in weaving, the thread used in mending a flaw or break in the web; Alex. Wilson's Poems, p. 68, Ed. 1876.
The passage in which this term occurs is not fit for quotation. The word is still in common use.

To BECALL, *v. a.* To call upon, challenge, demand: also, accuse, impeach.

Be thu kaysere or kynge here, I the *becalle*
To fynde me a freke to fyghte one my fille.
Avent. Arthure, 1. 410.

To BECLATTER, *v. a.* To tire with clattering, to praise overmuch. V. CLATTER.

Hout awa, Johnny, lad ! what maks ye flatter me ?
Why wi' your praises sae meikle beapatter me ?
Why sae incessantly deave and *beclatter* me,
Teasing me mair than a body can bide ?
Alex. Rodger, Song in Whistle Binkie, i. 148.

To BECOME, *v. n.* To occur, happen, befall.

Induryng this first monarchie
Become that wofull miserie
Of Sodome, &c.
Lyndsay, Exper. and Court., l. 3388.
A.-S. *becuman,* to come to be, to come about.

BED, BEDE, *pret.* of Bide. Addit. to Bed. V. Baid.

BED, BEDE, BEDDING, *s.* V. Baid.
Bedding, meaning place of abode, occurs in Dunbar and Kennedy, l. 208. V. *Berdless.*

BE'D, BED, BEID, pron. *beed.* A coll. form for *be it*; as, "That canna *be'd.*" Dunbar, Freiris of Berwick, l. 532.
The tendency to soften and to drop the dentals *t* and *d*, when terminal, prevails in various districts of Scot., but especially in the West, where *be'd* for be it, *do'd, da'd,* or *di'd,* for do it, *ha'd* or *haid* for have it, &c., are the usual forms of common speech. Traces of this tendency are found in the works of our earliest poets; and the terms *beid, dude, haid, said,* occur in the popular poems of the fifteenth and sixteenth centuries. The prevalence of this pronunciation in those times is attested py Alex. Scott's "Ballat maid to the Derisioun and Scorne of Wantoun Wemen," with its refrain, " I sall not *said* agano."
In Lanarkshire and Renfrewshire schoolmasters have great trouble in training their pupils to sound *t* and *th*; and the words went, thrice, water, butter, are usually pronounced *wend, hrise, wahher, buhher.* And yet the same persons add a softened *t,* almost *d,* to the words once, twice, thrice, and pronounce them *wonste, hwiste, hriste,* with *h* broadly guttural.

BEDAL, BEDDEL, *s.* Beadle, an inferior officer of court; commonly called beagle, q.v.
" Nane aldirman, bailye, na *beddel* sall bake brede na brew ale to sell wythin thair awin propir house duraude the tym that thai stand in office." Burgh Lawis, ch. 59.

BEDELL, BEDALL, *s.* A person who is bedrid. V. BEDRAL.
". . . colloct and gadder the cherite and almous . . . and distribue amangis the *bedellis* and pure folk eftir thair discretioun." Burgh Rec. Peebles, 21 June, 1501.

BED-FELLOW, *s.* Applied to a husband, a fellow-lodger, a fellow-traveller. Addit. to BEDFALLOW.

BED-FELLOWSHIP, *s.* Companionship, fellowship, company.
" We shall be blessed with the *bed-fellowship* of Iesus in our buriall lare, whereeuer it be." Blame of Kirkburiall, ch. viii.

BEDIS, BEIDIS, BEYDIS, *s. pl.* Beads.
" Item, in a box beand within the said blak kist, the grete *bedis* of gold contenand sex score twa *bedis* and a knop." Accts. L. H. Treas., i. 80.
" Item [22 August, 1497], for ane par of *bedis* to the King, xv s." Ibid., i. 353.
These were boads for saying the rosary: usually called, as in the second extract, a pair of beads, or a pair of paternosters.
"They were of various materials—wood, amber, ooral, lapis lazuli, crystal, silver, and even of gold, and varied in number from ten to one hundred and fifty or even a largor number. Each tenth bead was followed by one larger and more ornamental, called a gaude, which served to reckon the paternosters, while the common beads counted the aves. Usually they were in two lengths, one of fifty, the other of ten ''aves.'' The shorter was worn suspended by a ring from the finger, the longer was slung over the shoulder, hung on the arm, or suspended from the girdle.'' Note by Mr. Dickson ; V. Gloss.

A PAIR OF BEDIS. A set, stand, or string of beads.

When a cleric was infeft in office the patron or superior presented him with a set of beads as sasine thereof.

"The sside day [28 June, 1509] the provost, bailyeis, counsale, and communitie, presentit Master Johne Merschell to the gramar scolis of the said burghe for all the dais of his liwe, and admittit him to the saide scolis be gift of *a pair of bedis*, with ale comoditeis, fredomes, and profites pertaining thairto." Burgh Recs. Aberd., i. 80.

BEDIT. For "*bed it,*" abode it. V. BED.

BEDRAIT, BEDRIT, *pret.* Befouled with ordure; Dunbar and Kennedy, l. 450. V. BEDRITE.

BEDRENT, *adj.* and *s.* Applied to a person who is bedrid; Burgh Recs. Edinburgh, i. 79. V. BEDRAL.

BEDSEIK, *adj.* Confined to bed through sickness; so sick as to be unable to rise from bed; Trials for Witchcraft, Spald. Misc., i. 84.

BED-STOCK, *s.* The strong bar or frame of wood forming the front of a bed. S.

Before I lie in your bed,
Either at *stock* or wa'.
Old Song.

BED-STRAY, BED-STRAE, *s.* Bed-straw, the straw with which a bed, or mattress of a bed, is stuffed: also the plant Galium, of which there are many species. S.

When the term indicates a plant, *G. verum*, Common Yellow Bed-straw, or *G. Aperine*, Goosegrass, or Cleavers, is meant, generally the latter.

To BEDUNG, *v. a.* To cover with dung; to manure; also, to smirch, spatter, or foul with dung: part. pa. *bedunged.*

"For our Kirk-courtes or yardes are ordinarily *bedunged* by pestring and pasturing brute." Blame of Kirkburiall, ch. vi.

BEED-LADY, *s.* Lit., a lady supported by alms or in a bead-house; but, as in the quotation given below, applied to the ladies of a family of rank provided for by the heir; hence, ladies-dependent. V. BEDIS.

". . . of these two your dayly *beed-Ladies;* your Mother, to wit, the mirrour of all godly graue matronisme, and your Spouse now the yong fruteful Matriarch of that multi-potent Marquesad." Blame of Kirkburiall, Dedication to the Marquis of Hamilton.

BEEL, BIEL, *s.* Shelter, abode. V. BEILD.

To BEEMFILL, BEEMEFILL, *v. a.* To fill up completely, as in packing a box: hence, to back up, bolster, confirm, maintain.

". . . alledging to a most anuncient custome of keeping the predecessor lare in buriall. To *beeme-fill* the which, they may bring (I confesse) some canons of counsels," &c.

". . . he wold procure an inacted law to *beem-fill* the Kirk acts against Kirkburiall," &c. Blame of Kirkburiall, ch. xix.

This verb is derived from *beamfill* or *beamfilling,* the chips of stone or brick used in filling up the spaces or chinks that are left in the walls of a house after the beams have been planted.

BEEN-HOOK, *s.* The harvest work which a tenant was bound to give to his landlord in part payment of rent; Gloss. Orkn. and Shetl. Similar to the Bonnage-Heuk of more Southern districts.

BEER-BUNTLIN, *s.* Beer-bunting; a bird: called in north-eastern counties the *corn-buntlin;* West and South of S. V. BUNTLIN.

"*Beerbuntlins.* Birds as large as thrushes, and somewhat like them in plumage; common amongst grain, particularly *beer,* when growing," &c. Gall. Encycl.

BEES, BEIS, *v.* An old form of the pres. ind. and subj. of the vb. *to be;* used in all the persons of both numbers. Not confined to the third pers. sing., as stated in DICT. V. BEIS.

This form is still in use, and is a record of the old Anglian dialect. It is sometimes found (like A.-S. *béo*) with a future sense, as in the first example given below. It occurs frequently in the Townley Mysteries, which are supposed to have been acted at Widkirk Abbey in Yorkshire: thus,—
For mekille in heven *bees* youre mede, p. 316.
Alle *bees* done right at the wille, p. 324.
Wyt thou welle thou *bees* to late, p. 326.

BEEST, BESTE, *s.* A beast; generally applied to cattle: pl. *beestis, bestis, bestys.* V. BEST.

". . . at thai sek nocht the kingis merkat ilk merkat day on the manor of the byting of *beestis* to be etin, that is to say of oxin, of mutone, and swine." Chalmerlan Air, ch. 7.

BEESTIE, BEESTIE MILK, *s.* V. BEIST, *Beasenin.*

BEETOCK, *s.* A sword; properly, a dirk or dagger carried in the hose or boot.

For gin she'll thocht ta thing was richt,
She would her *beetock* draw, man,
An' hegg't like . . . till ance the Bill
Was made goot Gospel law, man.
Alex. Rodger, Highland Politicians, s. 2.

Gael. *biodag,* a dirk, or dagger.

BEEVIT, *part. pa.* Errat. for *brevit,* recorded, written, declared, accounted, esteemed. V. BREVE.

This strange blunder is due to Pinkerton: v. DICT. But Jamieson's note is a wild guess and wide of the mark.

Fr. *bref,* from Lat. *brevia,* short. Ducange gives *breviare,* in breves redigere, describere; and Cotgrave gives *brief,* a writ.

BEFORE. *Of before,* formerly, in former times, of old; *yitt as of before,* still as formerly, for the present as in past times; Burgh Rec. Edinburgh, 3 October, 1505.

BEFORE THE HAND, BEFORE HAND. Before the point or time of requirement: generally applied to money, and in relation to gathering, spending, or using it. It commonly means on hand, not required; before being due, before an equivalent has been given or received; and is a translation of Lat. *præ manibus*.

Although both forms of the phrase have generally the same meaning, *before the hand* is always the form used in reference to money or goods on hand and not specially required; and *before hand* is always applied to what is got or given before being due, as, *before hand wages*, or *wages before hand*. A good example of the use of the first form is given in the following passage:
". . . and knawing thamoselfis to haue na common gude *before the hand*, and to be greitlie superexpendit and thair common renttis thirlit, sua that it sall nocht be able to thame to help repair and big the saidis warkis according to thair honour and commoun weill, except the merchanttis and craftismen may be persuadit to repair the proffit of the commoun mylnis for this present yeir allanerlie," &c. Burgh Recs. Edin., 19 Mar., 1567-8.
The *warkis* here referred to were the re-building and repairs occasioned by a severe storm which had raged in the district shortly before that date.

BEGAINE, *part. adj.* V. BEGANE.

BEGARY, *s.* Decoration, adornment. Ad. to BEGARIE, *v.*

Thocht now in browdir and *begary*,
Sche glansis as scho war Quene of Fary.
Rob Stene's Dream, p. 4.

BEGET, *v.* A corr. of *begeck*, deceive, befool, jilt.

I suld haue maid him in the stour to be full hard stad
And I had witten that the Carll wald away steill;
Bot I trowit not the day that he wald me *beget*.
Rauf Coilzear, l. 607.
V. BEGECK.

BEGGAR'S BED, *s.* The bed which in farm and country houses was allotted to beggars; it was generally made up in the barn. S.

He wadna ly intil the barn, nor yet wad he in byre,
But in ahint the ha' door, or else afore the fire.
And we'll gang nae mair a roving, &c.
The *beggar's bed* was made at e'en wi' guid clean straw and hay,
But in ahint the ha' door, and there the beggar lay.
And we'll gang nae mair a roving, &c.
The Jolly Beggar, *Herd's Coll.*, ii. 27.

BEGGAR PLAITS, *s. pl.* Creases in the skirts of garments.

So called because beggar's weeds are generally plaited in this manner by the owner's lying or sitting on them. V. Gall. Encycl.

BEGIN, *s.* A form of *biggin*, a building, house; Burgh Recs. Aberdeen, i. 72. V. BIGGING.

BEGIRT, *part. pa.* A corr. of *begarit*, trimmed, ornamented; "an black cloak *begirt* with velvit;" Burgh Recs. Aberdeen, i. 458. V. BEGARIE.

BEGNET, *s.* A bayonet. V. *Baignet*.

BEGOUD, BEGUDE, BEGUD, BEGUID, *pret.* and *part.* Began. *To beguid*, to be begun; Aberd. V. BEGOUTH.

Mirk the lift was, drousy cluded,
An' the starns *begoud* to glow'r.
Alex. Wilson's Poems, p. 105, Ed. 1876.

Begoud is often used as a part. in the West of S., especially when preceded by the aux. *have*; as, "He hasna *begoud* to't yet."

BEHED, *pret.* Local for *behaved*; as, "bot sua hes *behed* himself in tyme bygane;" Burgh Recs. Aberdeen, i. 355. V. BEHAD.

BEHEVIN, BEHEUIN, *part. pt.* Behewn, hewn in two; Barbour, xvii. 755, Camb. MS.; *to-hewyn*, Edin. MS.

BEHOWYT, BEHAUIT, BEHUD, BEHUYED, BEHUYIT, *pret.* Behoved, it behoved; Burgh Recs.

BEHUIFULL, BEHUFFULL, *adj.* Needful, necessary, requisite; A.-S. *behofian*, to stand in need of.

". . . at thai walter nocht na *behuifull* thing to thaim that he aucht to find," &c. Burgh. Rec. Edinburgh, 13 Dec., 1463.
The form *behufull* occurs in Charters of Peebles, 20 January, 1520, p. 51, and in the Burgh Recs. of that town of date 23 July, 1480.

BEICH. *On beich*, at a distance, aloof; "I byd *on beich*," I stay at a distance, I stand aloof; Alex. Scott's Poems, p. 73, Ed. 1882.
This is another form of *abeigh*, *abeech*, q.v.; like *astray* and *on stray*.

BEID. For *be it.* V. *Be'd.*

To BEID, *v. n.* Errat. for *Bide*, to wait for; Barbour, viii. 183, Camb. MS.

BEIDMAN, *s.* A resident in a bede-house, or one who is supported from the funds appropriated for this purpose. V. BEDEMAN.

BEID-WOMAN, *s.* A woman who resides in a bede house or hospital. V. BEDIS, BEDEMAN.

". . . Jonat Andersoun, *beid-woman* in Kingiscace . . . ane boll meal for the Beltane term last by past," &c. Burgh Rec. Prestwick, 27 Nov., 1606.

BEIK, *s.* Like E. *beak*, is variously applied in the sense of a projecting point; V. DICT. Pl. *beiks*, *beikis*, is often applied to projecting teeth, tusks, and specially to the corner teeth of a horse.

I haif run lang furth in the feild,
On pastouris that ar plane and peild;

I mycht be now tane in for eild,
My *beikis* ar spruning hô and bauld.
    Dunbar, Petition of Gray Horse, l. 40.
V. BEIK.

BEIKYN, *s.* A beacon; pl. *beikynnis*; Burgh. Recs. Aberdeen, i. 150. V. BEKIN.

BEILD, *s.* A poet. form of *beil*, bale, sorrow, misery; *to do beild*, to work havoc, destruction, ruin.

It is so used by Dunbar in his Welcum to Lord Bernard Stewart, l. 61, where he compares him to Hannibal.
    Bold Hannibal in batall *to do beild.*

BEILDIT, BELDIT, *part. pt.* Sheltered, housed; surrounded, protected, favourably situated; *beildit in blis*, surrounded with every comfort, perfectly happy, happy-hearted. V. BELDIT.

Then Schir Gawayne the gay, gude and gracius,
That euer was *beildit* in blis, and bounte embracit.
    Gaw. and Gol., s. 31.

i.e., "That was always happy hearted and a pattern of kindness."
Dr. Jamieson's rendering of *Beldit* is very defective. This was pointed out by Sir F. Madden in his Gloss. to the Gawain Romances, q.v.
A.-S. *byldan*, to build, house, furnish, shelter.

BEIR, *s.* 1. Beer, barley; Lyndsay, Douglas. V. BEYR.

2. Beer.

"Item, to Andro Bertoune, for tua pipe of ceder and *beir;* the price of all ix lib." Accts. L. H. Treas. Scot., i. 343.

At this time, 1497, beer was chiefly imported from Germany; very little was made in Scotland, and even what was made was for the most part brewed by foreigners. V. Introduction to L. H. Treas. Accts., Dickson.

To BEIR, *v. a.* To bear, carry; *we beir ws,* we behave; Barbour, xiv. 275; *beird*, pret., betook himself, proceeded, went. V. *Bear.*

Quhair the Coilyear bad sa braithlie he *beird.*
    Rauf. Coilyear, st. 14.

BEIR, BERE, *s.* A bier. V. *Bear.*

BEIR-MEN, BERE-MEN, *s. pl.* V. *Bear-men.*

BEIT, *s.* A bundle, sheaf; *in beitis set,* set or laid out in sheaves; Henryson, Preiching of the Swallow, l. 206. V. BEET.

To BEJAIP, BEJAPE, *v. a.* To befool, deceive; Dunbar. V. JAIP, JAPE.

BEK, *s.* and *v.* V. BECK.

To BEKKLE, *v. a.* To distort, put out of shape; Shetl. Similar to Bachle, q.v.

BELD, BEILD, *adj.* Bold, daring.

War kene knychtis of kynd, clene of maneris
Blyth, bodyit, and *beld,* but baret or boast.
    The Houlate, l. 332, Asloan MS.
Bann. MS. has *beild.*

BELD, BELL, *adj.* Bald, bald-headed, S.

BELD CYTTIS, BELL KYTIS, *s. pl.* Bald Kites; prob. the Bald Buzard or Marsh Harrier, *Circus Rufus*, is meant in Houlate, l. 640.

"Basardis and *Beld Cyttis,* as it might be," &c.
By some strange mistake Dr. Jamieson rendered this term as *Bald Coots,* a meaning quite foreign to the passage iu which the term occurs. Besides, *coots* are never called *cyttis* or *kytes*—the reading of the two MSS.; but that name was and still is given to birds of the falcon family, which the poet here describes.

BELL, *s.* A bald place, a spot of baldness: also, a patch of white, as in the forehead of a cow or horse. Addit. to BELL.

". . to haf sauld to Johnne Masone ane hors, blak-broune inowitt, with ane *bell* in the forrett, for the sowme of fywe merkis, vjs. viijd.," &c. Burgh Recs. Aberdeen, 23 Mar., 1555.

Gael. *bal, ball,* a spot, mark, freckle.

BELENE, *v. n.* Errat. for the following.

To BELEUE, BELEWE, BILEUE, *v. n.* To tarry, remain, wait, linger; Sir Gawan and Sir Gal., i. 6: pret. *belewyt*, continued; Barbour, xiii. 544: A.-S. *belifan,* to remain behind.

This entry is substituted for *Belene* in the DICT. Dr. Jamieson was misled by his text. The mistake regarding *belewyt,* under *to beleif,* is quite different.

BELEWYT, *pret.* Remained, continued; Barbour, xiii. 544, Edin. MS.

Under *To Beleif* Dr. Jamieson quotes this passage, and renders *belewyt,* gave up, as from A.-S. *belaevan.* It is not so, but from A.-S. *belifan,* to remain. *Beleue* or *bileue* in this sense is used by Chaucer in his Squieres Tale. See Prof. Skeat's note, Barbour, p. 777.

BELIF, BELIFE, BELIFF, *adv.* Soon, quickly: forms of *belyve* used by Barbour: A.-S. *be,* by or with, and *life,* life.

To BELIGGER, *v. a.* To beleaguer, besiege, invest; Blame of Kirkburiall, ch. xix.

BELL, *s.* A familiar form of Isabel or Isabella.

A wife he had, I think they ca'd her *Bell.*
    Alex. Wilson, Rab and Ringan, l. 21.

BELL, *adj.* and *s.* V. *Beld.*

BELLAMTYM, *s.* A form of Beltane, q. v., Burgh Rec. Peebles.

BELLAMY, *s.* A boon companion; Dunbar.
Fr. *belle ami, i.*

BELLIBAN, *s.* The band of leather or stretch of rope passing under the belly of a horse and secured to the two shafts of the cart, to give stability in loading: E. *belly-band.*

To BELLISHE, v. a. To embellish, adorn, beautify; Blame of Kirkburiall, ch. x.

BELL-WEED, BELL-WARE, s. A coarse sea-weed; Fucus vesiculosus, Linn.; called also *Kelp-ware*. West of S.

BELLY-GOD, s. One who makes a god of his belly, a glutton: used also as an *adj.*, as in the term *belly-god-beastes*, applied to monks and nobles before and after the Reformation.

" . . we may be laide in a comely, closse, clean, competent Kirk-ilo or yarde, that so associating our aelues with the predecessor saints, and not byked in with the *belly-god-beastes* that blindes the world," &c. Blame of Kirkburiall, ch. xiv.

In his Hist. of the Reformation in Scotland, John Knox calls the Bishop of Ross, " that *belly-god*, Maister Dauid Panter." V. Laing's Ed., i. 262.

BELLYS, BELLIS, s. Bellows; Burgh Rec. Peebles, 28 Jan., 1463.

BELSTRACHT, adv. Straight on one's belly, straight forward, full-stretched, prostrate; as, " He fell *belstracht* down." West of S. V. BELLY-FLAUGHT.

A.-S. *belg*, the belly, and *streccan*, to stretch. *Boltraught* is the form in Will. and Wer., l. 1852.

BELT. To bear at the belt, to have always at hand or in readiness.

" . . some reasones . . . . . that men may in familiar vse, as it were, beare the same about *at their belt*." Blame of Kirkburiall, ch. xx.

BEMASKED, part. adj. Masked over, or decked out for the purpose of concealing the reality; Blame of Kirkburiall, ch. xix.

BEMYS, BEAMES, s. pl. Trumpets. V. BEME.

A.-S. *byme*, a trumpet.

BENE, BEYNE, KING OF. The king or leader of the festivities of Twelfth Night. V. BANE, KING OF BANE.

" Item, on Uphaly da, [1489], to the Kingis offerande, xviijs. Item, to the King of Bene, the saim da, xviijs." Accts. L. H. Treas., i. 127.

" Item, to Jhonne Goldsmyth, be a precept, for his expens quhen he was King of Beyne," v. li. [a.d. 1497]. In the cake made for Twelfth Day it was customary to insert a bean, and he who obtained the portion of the cake containing it became king of the evening's festivities. In earlier times the banqueting was continued for many days. (V. Brand's Notes to Bourne, p. 205).

When the portion fell to the lot of a lower officer of the court or household, it was customary for the company to contribute under the name of offerings to the King to defray the expenses incurred by the proper tenure of that high office. No doubt the gifts referred to in the records quoted above, were made by James IV. for that purpose. Similar gifts are recorded of Edward III. of England. V. Strutt's Sports and Pastimes, p. 343, ed. 1841.

BENIS, BENYS, BEINS, s. pl. V. *Banis*.

This term frequently occurs in Halyburton's Ledger:

BENNELS, BENNLES, s. pl. The name given to the various kinds of reed-grass and reeds which are used for making mats. It is also applied to the dry withered weeds collected for fuel, South of S. Addit. to BENNELS, q.v.

To BENSE, v. n. To stride, strut, or bound boldly, West of S. V. BENSELL.

This term is similar to E. *bounce*, when so applied. The ders. *bensing*, *bensie*, are used as *adjs.*

BENT SILUER, s. Payment for rushes, bent grass, &c., used for covering the floors of rooms. Correct. and Addit.

" Item, to Andro of Balfour for his bent *siluer* to the Kingis chalmiris al the yere, xiij li. vj s. viij d." [A.D. 1473-4.] Accts. L. H. Treas., i. 66.

Dr. Jamieson in rendering this term has gone far astray. He identifies it with *Bleeze Money*, and represents it as paid only to schoolmasters, and by way of gratuity. Perhaps this idea of gratuity suggested to him the strange supposition regarding the origin of the term with which the article closes. He asks—" Can *bent* be corr. from Fr. *benit*, q. blessed money, as being claimed on some Saint's day ? " Why ! bent grew before there was a saint to bless or be blessed ! and bent *siluer* was a payment regularly made to those persons who provided bent for covering the floors of rooms. In some districts the schoolmasters claimed the payments monthly all the year round; in others only during the summer months. Latterly, and until the impost ceased, the second method was followed all over Scotland. *Bleeze Money* was the payment for fuel and lights during the winter months.

In the Burgh Records of Aberdeen there is a most interesting entry from which one may gather various particulars regarding bent *siluer* in the beginning of the seventeenth century. On 24th October, 1604, "the prouest, baillies, and counsall" of Aberdeen met to consider certain " greiffis gevin in be a gryt number of the communitie of this burgh, complaining on Maister Dauid Wedderburne, maister of thair grammer schooll, for certane abuses and extortionis baith enterit and raisit in the said school, by all gude ordour or forme," &c. One of those "*greiffis*" was—" Item, for tackiug aucht pennies monethlie of eiverio bairne for *bent siluer*," which, after much careful and " cannic " consideration (for Maister Wedderburne was present by command), the council unanimously resolved to answer by the following law:—" Item, that anis ilk moneth during thir four monethis following in the symmer seasone allanerlie, viz., May, Junij, July, and August, the bairnis that gangis not to the bent thame selffis, sall pay ilk ane of thame aucht pennies to the maister for bying of bent."

By this judicious consideration of the interests of both parties concerned, the dispute regarding bent *siluer* was for the time settled.

Interesting particulars regarding this school-tax are given in Grant's Hist. of the Burgh Schools of Scot., pp. 173, 475-6.

BENYS, BENIS, s. pl. Beans; applied to the seeds and to growing crop.

" . . . . wyth whete or wyth vthir corne, or wyth pese, *benys*, or salt," &c. Custome of Schippis, ch. i.

BER, s. Beer, barley. V. BEAR.

BERAND, *part. pr.* Roaring, snorting, bellowing. V. BEIR, *v.*

BERD, BEIRD, BRED, BREID, BREDE, *s.* A board, plank, a piece of thin flat wood, a table; the plate, box, or other vessel for receiving alms for the poor; also, daily food, victuals. V. BURD.

BERDED, BEIRDED, BREDED, *adj.* Boarded, covered with boards, made of boards or planks, West of S.

BERDLESS, BERDLES, BEIRDLESS, *adj.* Boardless, i.e., destitute, starving.

For thew hes nowthir for to drink nor eit,
Bot lyk ane *berdles* baird, that had no bedding.
Dunbar and Kennedy, l. 208.
"*No bedding*," no biding-place, abode, home.

BERDLASS, *adj.* Beardless; Barbour, xi. 217.

BERFROISS, *s.* A tower, watch-tower; O. Fr. *beffroi, berfroit,* a watch-tower, from which has come E. *belfry.* V. *Barfray.*

Lap fra a *berfroiss* on the wall,
Quhar he emang his fayis ell
Defendit him full douchtely.
Barbour, x. 708, Camb. MS.
He buskit to ane *barfray*.
Twa smal bellis rang thay.
Gol. and Gaw, l. 777.
In Edin. MS. miswritten *bar fora,* q.v.
Although this term has come to us through the French, it is of H. M. Germ. origin, being from *bercvrit, bervrit,* a tower for defence or protection, which was first applied to the movable tower used in sieges to enable the attacking party surely and safely to throw missiles into the city. H. M. Germ. *bergen,* to protect, and *vrit* or *frid,* a place of security, a tower. It was afterwards applied to the watch-tower within the city walls, in which at a later date a clock was erected, and a bell for the sentinel to sound in time of danger. From this arose the application of the term to a bell-tower. V. Burguy's Gloss., Wedgwood's Etym. Dict., and Skeat's Etym. Dict. Suppl.

To BERE, BEYR, *v.* and *s.* V. *Bear.*

BERING SWERD, *s.* A sword of state.

"Item, . . . j quarter of rede crammasy vellus for the coueriug of the litil *bering swerd,* price xx s."
Accts. L. H. Treas. (1474], i. 26.

BERFUTE, *adj.* Bare-footed; "bla *berfute* berne," Dunbar and Kennedy, l. 210. V. BAREFIT.

BERGE, BARGE, *s.* A barge, a small trading vessel.

"Of ilk creare, busche, *berge,* and ballinger, v. s." Toll on Ships and Boats at Leith (1423). Burgh Rec. Edinburgh, i. 4.

BERGE, *s.* A shutter. V. *Barge.*

To BERIS, BERYS, *v. a.* To bury; a corr. of *Bery*; part. pt. *beryst,* buried; Charters of Peebles, 3 Sept., 1450.

BERISING, *part.* and *s.* Burying, buriall. V. BERY.

"Item, for the expensis of the *berising* of Georg of Douglas at the Kingis command, [a.d. 1494], ix li. x s."
Accts. L. H. Treas., i. 238.
In Abp. Hamilton's Catechism the form *berissing* is occasionally used; and *berisch,* as inf. form also occurs.

BERIST, BEREST, *s.* Breast; pl. *beristes*; Burgh Recs. Aberdeen, i. 413.

This form represents the pron. in those districts where the *r* is prominently sounded.

BERM, BERME, *s.* V. BARM.

"Item, at the pottis at thai haf contenis nocht samekle cler aile withoutyn *berme*." Chalmerlan Air, ch. 10.

To BESPICE, BESPISE, BESPYCE, *v. a.* To spice, embalm.

". . . the Indean with Got-seame did besmeare, the Schithean swallied, the Egyptian pickled with bryme, but the Gerrons, a Schithian sect, after exinteration, *bespyced* their gutlesse goodsirs;" &c. Blame of Kirkburiall, ch. iv.
". . . the Pollinctors embalmed and Sandapillarianes *bespised* the corps of the great," &c. Ibid. ch. vii.

BEST, BEEST, BEIST, *s.* A single skin of fur. Addit. to BEST.

"Item, fra Thom. Cant, xxiiij *bestes* of groce to lyne a typpat to the King," &c. Accts. L. H. Treas., Scot., l. 17.
This use of the term is common in Records of Inventory and Expense.

BESTIE, BEASTIE, BEESTIE-MILK, *s.* Same with Beist, and *Beasenin,* q. v.

BEST CHEIP, *adj.* Best bargain, best for the money. V. under *Cheip.*

BEST RESPECTS, *s. pl.* Used colloquially in the sense of "immediate friends;" as, "Hoo's a' your *best respects* the day?" Orkn.

A peculiar application of the valedictory phrase of a familiar epistle.

To BESWIK, BESWIKE, BISWIKE, *v. a.* To cheat, deceive. V. BESWEIK.

BESYD, *adv.* Aside, astray.

Peraventure my schcip ma gang *besyd*
Quhill we haif liggit full neir.
Henryson, Robene and Makyne, l. 43.

BE'T, BE'T TA, BE'D, BE'DA. Forms of *bud, bud-te,* behoved, behoved to, must, had to, Clydes.

Spring, thochtlose gilpy, leuch and sang,
The very birds join'd in the chorus,
Till winter-har'd Winter found ere lang
She be't tie up her bull-dog Bor'as.
James Manson, Song in Whistle Binkie, ii. 127.

BET, *v.* Prob. a mistake for *Let,* stop, stay, hinder; Barbour, i. 254. V. Skeat's ed.

To BETAK, BETAKE, *v. a.* 1. To resort, apply, have recourse to; as, "Weel, weel!

sin ye'll no richt me, I'll *betak* me to the Court o' Session;" pret. *betook*, part. pt. *betane, betaen*, West of S.

This verb is still used in the West of S.; but it is seldom found in Scotch or English authors later than the seventeenth century. Shakespeare and Milton used it in this first sense only.

2. To overtake, hunt, capture; as, "If ye gang fast ye'll *betak* him within an hour."

3. To beset, waylay, pounce upon; as, "When a' the ills o' eild *betak* ye." "The deil *betak* ye." "The drunk, the late, and the lazy the bogles *betak*." Ibid.

4. To hand over, commit; as, "Weel, weel, I'll jist *betak* ye to the bogle!" said by way of threat to a troublesome child. Ibid.

This application of the term is a very old one; see Havelok, l. 1407, Town Myst., p. 230, Cov. Myst., p. 70, 72. And Barbour, in recounting the terror which the Black Douglas spread throughout the Border Marches of England says—

And yelt haf Ik herd oftsis tell,
That he so gretly dred was than,
That quhen wiffis wald thar childre ban,
Thai wald suen with ane angry face
Betake thame to the blak dowglas.
Barbour, xv. 538, Hart's Ed.

Betak is still used in all these senses in the West and South of S. A.-S. *betǽcan*, to show, betake, commit, send, follow, pursue.

BETANE, *part. pt.* Lit. overtaken: hence, beset, waylaid, in difficulties, in straits, hard bested. V. *Betak, Betake.*

Thar was a baroune maknauchtan,
That in his hart gret kep has tane
[Vnto] the Kingis chewalry,
And prisyt hym in hert gretly.
And to the lord off lorne said he;
"Sekyrly now may ye see
Betane the starkest pundelan,
That euyr your lyff-tyme ye saw tane.
Barbour, iii. 159.

Dr. Jamieson's difficulty with this word arose perhaps from not sufficiently considering the circumstances of the situation in which Bruce is represented at this point of the story; and his rendering of *betane* as enclosed, shut up, is incorrect. Prof. Skeat pointed out this error in his edition of Barbour, pp. 650, 777-8, and gives *pursued* as the meaning: which is so far correct, but not the full meaning; for it does not bring out the real point of Macnauchtan's enthusiastic remark to the Lord of Lorne regarding the extraordinary prowess of Bruce, and his marvellous skill and dexterity when surprised and attacked by fearful odds. A glance at the circumstances of the parties will make this clear.

As Bruce's attack on the clansmen of Lorne had failed, he ordered his forces to retreat. They did so in good order, and he took position in their rear to protect them during the pursuit. While passing through a narrow defile, he was beset by three of the boldest and strongest of the enemy, who had sworn to kill him. The struggle was fierce and desperate; but Bruce was equal to the occasion, and rid himself of his opponents by cutting down one after the other of the band. This feat so terrified the rest of the pursuers, that they were glad to keep out of his reach : or, as the poet puts it,—

"'That efter him dar na man ga."

(Sup.) F

Bruce then rode after his men and brought them to a safe encampment for the night.

The prowess of the Scottish king was witnessed by the Lord of Lorne and some of his chiefs, among whom was one Macnauchtan, who was so impressed and stirred by the matchless heroism of the Bruce, that he could not contain himself. So, turning to the Lord of Lorne as Bruce rode off to guide and protect the retreat, he said, "You see there, surprised and beset though he be, the greatest pundelan that ever you saw foiled." *Tane*, having here the sense of *taken aback*, *put out*, *foiled*, as in the common saying, "I was quite *tane* when I saw him :" and *pundelan*, meaning probably *pounder* or *mallet-hand*, or as Prof. Skeat suggests, "*fist of wood*," which "may have been an epithet of a hero, like Fierabras; cf. Goetz with the iron hand." V. *Pundelan*.

While the above was in proof a friend suggested to me that *betane* might be an error for *begane*, gone off, with the sense of escaped.

BETAUGHT, *pret.* and *part. pa.* V. BETAUCHT.

BETEICHE, *v. a.* V. BETECH.

BETILL, *s.* A beetle, a potstick; The Houlate, l. 787, Asloan MS.: in Bann. MS. *bittill*, q. v.

BETISE, BETHYS, *prep.* Between, betwixt.

". . . John Tyry was mayd burges on Sant Lukis day, and sal pay for his fredom xxli s. ; and x s. of that to pay *bethys* this and Qwysonday nixt to com, and x s. be Machalmus next folouand ; plegis hymself." Burgh Recs. Peebles, 18 Oct., 1456.

The form *betise* was common in the West of S., especially among elder people, about forty years ago. It is prob. a corr. of *betwis*, *betwise*, which represent the common pron. of *betwix*,—local for *betwixt*. Indeed, the dropping of final t and d is a marked peculiarity of the Western district, where there is also a strong tendency to slip or at least smother those letters when they occur in the body of the word.

BETT, *pret.* Beat; Henryson, Preiching of the Swallow, l. 208. V. BET.

BETTERIN, BETTRYN, *part. pr.* and *s.* Mending, improving, enriching; whatever is used for the purpose of enhancing the value of goods; Halyburton's Ledger, p. 120.

BETUIX, BETUICH, *prep.* Betwixt, between. V. BETWEESH.

BEUERYN, BEVEREN, *part. pr.* Trembling, wavering, full flowing: "with his *beveren* berde," his full flowing beard; Awnt. Arthur, s. 28 ; "with *beueryn* lokkes," with locks flowing or wavering in the wind; Morte Arthur, fol. 91b. V. BEVEREN.

Explanation defective and uncertain in the DICT. A.-S. *bifian*, to tremble; and cognate with Germ. *beben*.

BEUGH, BEW, *s.* A bough of a tree; A.-S. *bóg, búh*, from *búgan*, to bow or bend.

Syne ilk branch and *beugh* bowlt thaim till.
The Houlate, l. 607, Asloan MS.

Bann. MS. has *bew*. Montgomery uses pl. *bews*.

BEUK, s. A book; Burns, Jolly Beggars, Compl. Scot. p. 67, E.E.T.S. V. BUIK.
"*The Beuk*," the Bible, is common in Scot. Church-literature of last century.

BEURE, *pret.* of *bere*. Bore; Henryson, Aige and Yowth, l. 14. V. BEAR.

BEUST, s. Grass two years old; applied also to grass which, having stood through winter, is somewhat withered; hence the adj. *beusty*, half-withered; Gall.

BEUSTY, *adj.* Applied to grass which is dry and sapless, or somewhat withered; Ibid.
"'Is there a Galloway farmer who does not know what a tuft of *beusty* grass is? Not one." Gall. Encycl.

BEVAR, s. A frail old person, one who trembles or totters. V. BEVER, v.
The *bevar* hoir said to this berly berne.
  Henryson, Aige and Yowth, l. 41.

BEVNE, BEUN, *prep.* and *adv.* A form of *bune*, *boon*, a contr. of *abune*, *aboon*, *aboven*, above, beyond, higher up or farther on than; Aberd., Banff.
". . . to ony part beneath the Braidgutter, ane penny Scots money, and *bevne* the Braidgutter, tua pennies," &c. Burgh Recs. Aberdeen, 22nd June, 1498.
From an Act fixing the charges for carrying goods from the harbour to the burgh.

BEWSCHERIS, BEWSCHYRIS, s. pl. Lit. fine gentlemen, i.e., knights, nobles, gallants. Fr. *beau sire*, contr. of *beau seigneur*.
Than busk thaj but bliu, monye *bewscheris*,
Graithess thame, but growching, that gait for to gane.
  The Houlate, l. 148, Bann. MS.

BEYR, s. and v. V. BEIR, BERE.

To BEYT, v. a. To mend, repair; also supply. V. BEIT.

BEYTING, s. Repair. V. BEITING.

BIAND, *part.* Buying; Chalmerlan Air, ch. 8. V. BY.

To BIBBLE, v. n. To shed tears; also to cry and sob; part. pr. *bibblin*, weeping and sobbing; Aberd., Gall. V. BUBBLE.
In the counties of the Forth and Clyde Basins we find the form *bubble*, as in the common phrase *to bubble an' greet*; and in the South of Scot., particularly in Galloway, we find *bibble*. In Aberd. both forms are in use; in and around Aberdeen it is *bibble*; while in the Buchan district it is *bubble*.

To BICK, BYKE, v. n. To weep and sob, to whinge; West and South of S. Add. to BICK.
Bick is applied to the short, quick sounds made by a child when sobbing and crying; *byke* is applied to the long drawn sobs that come after the crying has ended. Hence the saying, "I'd rather see a bairn *bickin* than *bykin*."

To BID BETTER, v. To desire, wish, or pray for anything better. Addit. to BID.
An' that there is, I've little swither
  About the matter :—
We cheek for chow shall jog thegither,
  I'se ne'er *bid better*.
  Burns, Ep. to Major Logan, s. 8.

BIDDING, BIDDYNG, s. 1. Command; Barbour, xvi. 312. V. BID.

2. Invitation, request; as, "Dinna need a second *biddin'*;" "I got a *bidding* to the wedding."
Bidden occurs in both senses in the Bible, and was so used by the best authors till the beginning of the seventeenth century. V. Bible Word-Book, p. 66. From A.-S. *beódan*, to command.

BIE, s. A contr. for *bield*, a shelter.

BIEN, s. Wealthy, plentiful, well-provided. V. BENE, BEIN.
This form of the term was adopted by Ramsay, Ferguson, and Burns. Even in rendering his stock of Scottish Proverbs, Ramsay used it; for example—"Provision in season makes a *bien* house." S. Prov., p. 59.

BIGGONET, s. V. BIGONET.
This form of the word is the more common; the other is the more correct.

To BIG ON, v. a. To increase, to secure, i.e. the guards: a term in curling; West and South of S.
The term is thus explained in the Gallovidian Encyclopedia:—"If a stone lies near the *cock*, and guarded, yet thought to need a double guard, if not a triple, the order from that side that has *in* the stone, is commonly *to big on*,—to guard away—to "*block the ice.*" P. 55.

BIKE, BYKE, BICHT, s. The bend of a hook; also, the hook at the end of the chain by which a pot is suspended over a fire, or, the hook or bend of the crook; West of S. Similar to E. *bight*.
A.-S. *byge*, a bend, bending, corner.

To BIKKYR, BIKKER, v. a. and n. To skirmish, annoy; Barbour, xvi. 102; Welsh, *bier*, a battle. V. BICKER.

BIL, BILL, BYL, s. A letter, billet, order for payment; *compt bill*, an account; Accts. L. H. Trens., i. 19, 24, 93, 379.

BILFODDER, BILFUDDER, s. Belly-fodder, food, provisions: generally applied to the grass, &c. cut from banks and hedges to supply cattle; West and South of S.
A.-S. *bylg*, the belly, and *fodder*, food. This is an old term; it occurs in Will. and Wer., l. 1858.

BILL-AIX, s. A light hatchet for chopping twigs and branches; West of S; *bullax*, Banffs.; *balax*, Aberd. V. BALAX.

BILLHUIK, s. A hedge-bill, a bill-hook; West and South of S.

BILLOITTES, s. pl. Bullets; Burgh Recs. Peebles, 20 Sept., 1648; *billots, billets*; West of S.

BILT, s. A short, dumpy person; AYRS., Gall.; adj. *biltie*, is also used. V. BILTIE.

BILLY, s. A brother, companion, fellow; pl. *billies* has generally the sense of fellows, chields, folk. V. BILLIE.

To BIN, v. a. To bind, wrap, tie, tether: " He was neither *to bin* nor haud," i.e. he could not be controlled, he was mad with rage; pret. *ban, bun;* part. pt. *bun*; West of S.

BIN'IN, BINNIN, *part., adj.,* and *s.* Binding, band, tether : as, *bin'in* corn, a *binnin* rape, the cow brak fra the *bin'in*, i.e. the tether ; West of S.

BINDIS, s. pl. Bundles, bales; goods made up in bales.
" — vesiater and serchare of the skynnis and *bindis* thairof within the said burgh," &c. Burgh Rec. Edinburgh, 4 July, 1517.

BINWUD, s. Bindwood, a local name for the woodbine or honeysuckle ; Gall.
Sing hey for the *Binwud* tree,
O! sing how for the *Binwud* tree ;
For there the lads and the lasses wad meet,
And daff 'neath the *Binwud* tree.
Song : Gall. Encycl., p. 70.

BIR, s. A cry or whizzing sound made by birds. V. BIRR.
The foullis ferlie tuke thair flicht anone,
Sum with ane *bir* thay braidit ouer the bent.
Henryson, Preiching of the Swallow, l. 173.

BIRLAT, s. A lady's hood, the stuffed rondelet of a hood ; also, a standing neck or ruff of a gown.
" Item, [1473], fra Will of Kerketle, ij elne j quarter of satyne for tippatis, colaris, and *birlatis,* price elne xxx s." &c. Accts. L. H. Treas., i. 74.
Fr. *bourlet,* as above. The term was applied not only to ladies' hoods, but also to those worn by graduates, lawyers, &c. V. COTGRAVE.

To BIRSLE, v. n. To bristle ; to become suddenly hot, angry, or defiant; Gall.
From *birse,* a birstle, q. v. A.-S. *byrst.*
Birsle and *bristle* is a similar transposition to *firth* and *frith.*

BIRSYNET, s. A corr. of *brisket,* the breast of an animal; Burgh Recs. Edin., iv. 5.
Fr. *brichet, brechet,* the brisket ; Welsh, *brysced,* id.

BIRUN, *part. adj.* Bypast, overdue. V. BYRUN.

BISSOM, BISSUM, BIZZOM. V. BYSSYM.

BISSY, *adj.* Cross, ill-tempered, angry ; easily provoked to anger, excitable, Orkn.
Generally applied to animals when tormented by flies ; but sometimes the application to individuals is not less suitable : *bissy* being simply the Lowl. Sc. *birsy*.

BIT, BIT TA. Same as *Be't, Be't ta*, q. v.

BITHOCHT, *pret.* Bethought, considered, reflected ; *I bethocht me*, I reflected ; *it bithocht me,* it struck me, flashed on my mind, West of S.

BIWIST, s. Food, meal, provision.
Fell antour that he prayd Crist
To eet wit him at his *biwist*.
And Crist that scknes fra him kest.
Metr. Hom., p. 16.
A.-S. *biwist,* id.

BIZZARD, s. A buzzard. Falco buteo, Linn. Often, but wrongly, called *the bizzard gled*.
Here is Satan's picture,
Like a *bizzard gled,*
Pouncing poor Redcastle,
Sprawlin' as a toad.
Burns, Buy Braw Troggin.
The *bizzard* and the *gled* are properly two distinct birds ; but the term *gled* is applied to all the birds of the buzzard and kite family, in the same sense as hawk is applied to both falcons and hawks.

BIZZIE, s. Bedding for a cow; Orkn. V. BYSS.

BLACK-BIDES, s. pl. Bramble-berries.
This name for bramble berries was given by Dr. Jamieson as *Black-boyds ;* but it is not so pronounced in the districts in which the name is still used.
Bide may be from Gael. *bideag,* a crumb, morsel, small thing ; because the berry consists of a great number of small vessels.

BLACK BOOK, BLACK BOOKS. A term used to imply disfavour, displeasure ; also, debt. Used in South of England dialects also.
A person who has offended a friend or neighbour in some way, commonly expresses himself by saying, " I ken I'm in his *black-book* : " i.e. I know I have offended him, or, I am in disfavour with him. Also, a person who owes money to another is said to be in his *black-books* for so much.

BLACK JAUDY, s. Dirty faced lassie ; but generally applied to those girls who go from house to house doing the lowest kitchen work,—servants of servants: dim. of *jaude,* E. *jade*.
Ilk tree-legg'd laddie, Ilk club-taed laddie,
Ilk oily leary,
Ilk midden mavis, wee *black jaudy,*
A' dread an' fear ye.
James Ballantine, Wee Raggit Laddie, s. 7.
This term of contempt is prob. only an oblique use of Sc. *yad, yaud,* an old horse.

BLACK-NEB, *s.* A name for the carrion-crow; also called *blackie,* South and West of S. Addit. to BLACK-NEB.
This foul bird is known by the same name in the North of England. V. Brockett's Gl.

BLACK-PISH-MINNIES. *s. pl.* Black pismires, Gall.

BLADDS, *s.* A disease like small-pox, Shetl. Germ. *blattern.*

BLAE-BOWS, *s. pl.* Blue flax-bells, the flowers of flax; Gall.

BLAES, *s. pl.* Marks left by measles, small-pox, &c.; also marks of bruises, wounds, &c.
"The children were well at night and found dead in the morning, with a little blood on their noses and the *blaes* at the roots of their ears, which were obvious symptoms of strangling." Renfrewshire Witches, p. 150, Ed. 1877.

BLAISTRY, *adj.* Blustery, blustering; driving wet.
      . . . . . Winter snell,
Couldna sit down and see sic waistry,
Sae out she spak' wi' gousty yell,
And storm'd and grat sleet cauld and *blaistry.*
James Manson, Song in Whistle Binkie, ii. 127.

To **BLAIT,** *v. n.* To bleat.
The selie Lamb culd do na thing bot *blait;*
Sone wes he deid; etc.
Henryson, Wolf and Lamb, l. 85.
A.-S. *blætan,* Dutch *blaten,* to bleat; Lat. *balare.*

BLAND, BLANDE, *s.* Blend, mixture; *in bland,* blended, mingled; as, "quhite and red *in blande.*" V. BLANE, *v.*

BLANDA, *s.* Lit. blended grain; bear and oats mixed and sown together, Orkn. and Shetl. V. BLANDED BEAR.

BLANDA MEAL, *s.* Meal made from *blanda;* Gl. Orkn. Shetl.

To **BLANDISE, BLANDYS,** *v. a.* To coax, flatter, wile; Court of Venus, iv. 104.

BLASTIE, *s.* A hasty, impetuous, head-strong person or animal; an unmanageable creature. Almost like E. *bluster.*
The fourth a Highland Donald hastie,
A d——d red-wud Kilburnie *blastie.*
Burns, The Inventory.
A.-S. *blǽst,* a blast, from *bládcan,* to blow, hence, to bully.

BLASTING, *s.* Puffing, blowing; boasting, S. V. BLAST.

BLATE, *adj.* Arduous, difficult, long and weary, productive of little. Addit. to BLAIT.
But yet his battle will be *blate,*
Gif he our force refuse.
Montgomery, Cherrie and Slae, s. 87.

BLATHER, *s.* V. BLETHER.

BLAUD, *s.* A large or great piece of any thing, West of S.; a great or sudden blast of wind is also called a *blaud,* Ibid. V. BLAD.
An' sets a' laughing at his *blauds* o' rhyme.
Alex. Wilson's Poems, p. 22, Ed. 1876.

To **BLAUD,** *v. a.* To slap, beat, punish, mal-treat; also, break or knock to pieces, i.e., drive to *blauds.* V. To BLAD.
This day M'Kinlay taks the flail,
An' he's the boy will *blaud* her.
Burns, The Ordination, s. 2.
Blaud is the form and pron. of this word in the West of S.; *blad,* in the East; and these forms illustrate a well marked peculiarity of the dialects of those two districts of the country. In the East the vowel sounds are sharp and clear; in the West, long and broad; and the consonant sounds differ accordingly.

To **BLAW FISH,** *v.* To dry fish by ex-posure to the wind; to cure fish without salt; hence the terms *blawn fish, blawn cod,* &c. Gl. Orkn. Shetl.

To **BLAW FLESH.** To inflate it in order to make it appear richer and more solid.
Blawin' was a very common charge against fleshers in olden times, and the magistrates had often to inter-fere to prevent that trick of the trade. The following is a specimen :—
"Item, it is statut and ordanit that all flescheouris bring thair flesche to the mercet croce, . . . and that thai *blaw* nane thairof, nor yit let it doune nor score it," &c. Burgh Rec. Peebles, 15 July, 1555.
A hundred and twenty years earlier the magistrates of Aberdeen passed a similar law; and entries of the same kind are repeatedly met with in all our Burgh Records. These enactments prove that the mutton and beef of those days were inferior in quality and poor in substance.
For other tricks of the fleshers see *Letting Doun Flesh, Scoring Flesh,* and *Breking Pais.*

BLAW YE SOUTH. A veil'd and minced oath, capable of almost any of the meanings implied by such language.
The muckle devil *blaw ye south*
If ye dissemble.
Burns, Earnest Cry, s. 4.
This peculiar expression has long been common in the West of S., and is met with in the epistolary com-positions of many of the poets belonging to that dis-trict. Perhaps it is a record of the old enmity between the Scots and the English, and originally implied "blow you to England," i.e., send you among your worst enemies.

BLEBANE, *s.* A form of *Pleban,* q. v.

BLECK, BLEK, *s.* 1. A person of a dark or black complexion, a blackamore, a negro; also, a blackguard, a rascal. West and South of S.

2. A particle of any black matter, as of coal, soot, &c.; pl. *blecks, bleks,* is generally applied to those flakes of soot which rise

from a smoky fire, and are so common in the atmosphere of large towns during damp weather; Ibid.

3. Pl. *blecks*, mildew, smut; often called *blecks amang wheat;* Ibid.

BLEK-TUB, *s.* A tub for holding blacking, i.e., the iron liquor used by curriers for staining the surface of upper leather.

"—— item, a *blek-tub* furnyst, ane vly barrell with ane vly chopin," &c. Burgh Recs. Aberdeen, 17 Feb. 1541, Sp. C.

BLEDDER, BLEDDIR, BLETHER, *s.* A bladder; Compl. Scot., p. 65, E.E.T.S.

BLEDDER-CHEIKIS, BLETHER-CHEEKS, *s. pl.* Cheeks puffed out like a bladder; Dunbar, Compl. to King, l. 23. Syn. *buffy-cheeks*.

BLEECH, *s.* A smart stroke or blow with the open hand, or with any flat surface; called also a *bilch* or *bilsh*; when given with a stick or cane it is called a *bilt, guilt,* or *whilt:* a common but vulgar term.

BLEER'T AND BLIN'. Bleared and blind, unfit to see or to be seen.

Duncan sigh'd baith out and in,
Grat his een baith *bleer't and blin'*,
Spak o' lowpin o'er the linn;
Ha, ha, the wooing o't.
Burns, Duncan Gray, st. 2.

O. Swed. and Dan. *plire*, and *blire*, to blink; and Swed. and Dan. *blind*, A.-S. *blind*, without sight.

BLENKYNT, *pret.* Blinked, glanced; Barbour, viii. 217; shone, Ib. xi. 190.

This term is formed from the stem *blink*, with suffix *nen*, Goth. *nan*, which is often used to form verbs of a neuter or passive sense.

BLENSHOUIN, *s.* Thin gruel; same with Blenshaw, q.v., Perths.

To BLERE, BLER, *v. a.* V. BLEAR.

BLESIS, *s. pl.* Blazes, flames; Barbour, iv. 129, 138. Edin. MS.

BLESS YOUR BANES, BLIS YOUR BANIS. Lit. *bless your bones*, but commonly used to express a wish or prayer for comfort and prosperity to the party addressed, or a promise of future benefits in return for present favour or aid. As, " Bless your banes for that ;" i.e., Good luck to you for that favour. " I'll bless your banes for that yet ; " i.e., " I'll do you a good turn for that some day ; " or, " I'll do as much for you again."

The expression is very old, and prob. originated in the idea of benefits obtained through pilgrimage to shrines, relics, and bones of saints. The modern application is much more limited than the ancient one, as the following example from Henryson will show :—

Sen I bot playit, be gracious me till,
And I sall gar my freindis *blis your banis*.
The Wolf and the Wedder, l. 125.

BLESSIT, *adj.* Bare, bald, white spotted; generally applied to animals having bald or white spots or patches on their skin. In Orkney and Shetland a white faced horse or cow is called a *blessit.*

This is prob. the same as *blassit,* [*blasmit,* blazed, having a blaze on the face or forehead ; from Dan. *blisset,* id., also white faced.

BLETHER, BLEDDER, BLATHER, *s.* A bladder; also, a person who talks long or loudly, but to little purpose. Addit. to BLETHER.

May gravels round his *blather* wrench.
Burns, Scotch Drink, st. 17.
An' bid him burn this cursed tether,
An' for thy pains thou'se get my *blather.*
Ibid., Death of Poor Mailie.
. . . . he be spent
As tume's a *blether.*
Alex. Wilson's Poems, ii. 39.

A.-S. *blædr,* Swed. *blåddra,* a blister, bladder.

BLEWING, *part.* as *s.* Blowing or raising the price of an article, regrating.

" . . . in amerciament of court for the *blewing* of meil and selling to alienatis." Burgh Recs. Aberdeen, i. 425, 7th June, 1497.

This is prob. only a fig. use of the *v. to blow,* to inflate.

BLEW-STONE, *s.* A bluish-coloured stone of which tombstones were made ; hence, a tombstone.

" . . . and yherly to pay xl s. quhill he bryng hame the *blew stane* til his fadre, and that to be raisit be the sight and ordinance of his modre, and of Schir Adam, and Thomas his brother, til syng for his fadre saule at Sancte Duthawis altar." Burgh Recs. Aberdeen, 19th Feb., 1450.

The stone referred to was probably a mountain limestone.

BLIBBANS, *s. pl.* Strips of any soft or slimy matter ; mostly applied to the larger sea weeds that cover rocks at ebb tide ; Gall.

The term is also applied to large shreds of greens or cabbage which careless or slovenly cooks put into broth. Quite a common grumble of the ploughman to the maid, as he leaves the kitchen after the breakfast, is, " Now, Jenny, min', nae *blibbans* in the kail the day."

BLIN, BLYN, *s.* Delay, hindrance ; deceit, guile : *but blin,* at once, straightway, without fail ; Houlate, l. 148. V. BLIN, *v.*

BLINCHAMP, *s.* A game or amusement of country boys in the South and West of S. It consists in *champing* or breaking birds' eggs blindfold. *Blin-Stane,* Clydes.

The amusement is thus described in the Gall. Encycl. :
" When a bird's nest is found, such as a *Corbie's* or

Hoodicraw's, or some such bird that the people dislike, the nest is herried and the eggs laid in a row a little from each other on the grass. One of the players is then blindfolded, and with a stick in hand marches forth as he thinks right to the egg-row, and strikes at it. Another tries the *champing* after him; and so on, until they thus blindfolded break them; hence the name *blindchamp*." P. 75.

BLINCHT (*c* as *s*), *part. adj.* Blanched, pale-faced, sickly looking.

And there will be Geordie M'Cowrie,
And blinking after Barbra and Meg,
And there will be *blincht* Gillie-Whimple,
And peuter-fac't flitching Joug.
Fr. Sempill, The Blythsome Wedding, s. 5.

BLINK, *s.* A ray, gleam, glow; a glance, glimpse, also, the time occupied by it; hence, a short time, a little while; a kindly glance, also the influence of it; a gleam of hope or prosperity during adversity, &c. V. BLENK.

This term is common in E. in the sense of a glance, gleam, or glow of light; as, a *blink* of sunshine, the ice-*blink*.

BLINKER, *s.* One who blinks, jinks, cheats, or decoys in whatever way; one who shirks or evades his fair share of drink in a company of merry-makers; also applied by Burns to an exciseman, because he cheats the home-maker of liquor whenever he can. A term of contempt. V. BLINK, *v.*

Dr. Jamieson questioned the correctness of Burns' definition of this term as one of contempt. V. DICT. He would not have done so had he remembered the following passages: and besides, the term is still so used in the West of S.

Ochon for poor Castalian drinkers,
When they fa' foul o' earthly jinkers,
The witching, curs'd, delicious *blinkers*
Hae put me hyte,
And gart me weet my waukrife winkers
Wi' girnin' spite.
Burns, Ep. to Major Logan.

Here the *blinkers* are the ladies, of whom he speaks as decoyers, jilters, &c., who have driven him crazy. The next example requires no explanation:

Thae curst horse-leeches o' the Excise,
Wha mak' the whisky stells their prize;
Haud up thy han', Dell! ance, twice, thrice!
There, seize the *blinkers!*
An' bake them up in brunstane pies
For poor d—d drinkers.
Ibid., Scotch Drink.

BLINKIN, *part. pr.* Winking, smirking, peeping; looking on in a stupid, half-dazed, idle manner; as, "*Blinkin* baudrons by the ingle sits."

Here stands a shed to fend the show'rs,
An' screen our countra gentry;
There, racer Jess an' twa three w——
Are *blinkin* at the entry.
Burns, Holy Fair.

BLINKS. *The Blinks* were short periods of revival and refreshing which the persecuted hillmen enjoyed between the years 1669 and 1679—from the granting of the Act of Indulgence to the murder of Archbishop Sharp. V. BLENK, *s.* 9.

"When men listened to a minister who was risking his life to preach to them, and when they saw on the rising grounds around sentinels watching for the approach of enemies before whom they themselves might fall, they could not but give unusual heed to the word spoken. The result was that deep impressions were often made, and that that decade was ever afterwards remembered as a time of blessing and revival. It was the season of *The Blinks*, as they were called." Walker, Scot. Church Hist., pp. 80-1.

BLIN-STANE, *s.* Same as *Blinchamp*: only, a stone is used instead of a stick: Clydes.

BLOCK THE ICE. A curling term with same meaning as "*Big on*," *q. v.*; run up guards round a well-placed stone, to prevent an opponent taking it out; West and South of S.

BLODWITE. V. BLUIDVEIT, *Bludwite.*

BLONKS, *s. pl.* Horses, steeds.

This term is not explained in DICT.; but a passage is given in illustration, of which the following line is the only one worth quoting :—

As spreitles folks on *blonks* houffit on hicht.
King Hart, i. 22.

The note on *houffit* is a mistake and altogether misleading. The word means tarried, lingered, hovered, or hung about, and occurs frequently in Bruce, Wallace, and similar poems. *Blonks*, too, is simply the pl. of *blonk*, which is correctly explained in the preceding article. The term originally meant a white or gray horse (Fr. *blanc*), but was afterwards used as a general name for that animal. V. Guest, Eng. Rhythms, p. 459, note 5, ed. 1882.

BLOTS, *s.* Foul, dirty, or spent water; Orkn. Shetl. V. *Blouts.*

To BLOWT, BLOUT, *v. a.* and *n.* To belch or throw out with force; applied to liquids, as, "The bung bowtit out, and the yill *blowtit* after't;" West of S. Cf. *Bluff.*

In a passage of the Insulted Pedlar, Wilson uses this term with great skill: unfortunately quotation is unsuitable.

BLOUTS, *s. pl.* The noise made by porridge, broth, &c. when boiling over a strong fire; the portions ejected from a pot or cauldron of fiercely boiling water, &c.; also, the foul water thrown from a washing tub; West of S.

"Keep your *blouts* for your ain kail yard," is still said to a person who is making a present of some useless or used-up article. The expression refers to the thrifty practice of using the *blouts*, or dirty soap suds, as *guidin* or manure for the kail-yard.

BLUCHANS, *s. pl.* Name given to those small fish which children catch in rock pools in the South of S. V. BLICHEN.

Most prob. this is another form of *Blichen*, a little thing, a fragment, and connected with Gael. *bloigh*, *bloidh*, a fragment, a wee thing.

BLUD, BLUDE, *s.* Blood. V. BLUID.

"Item, giff ony of the brether of the gyld thru violence drawis *blud* of ane othir, he sall amend wyth xx *s.*," &c. Lawis of the Gild, ch. 7.

BLUDWITE, BLUDWYTE, BLUDEWETE, BLUIDWEIK, BLODWITE, BLODWYTE, BLODEWITE, *s.* The fine or amerciament for bloodshed; also, the right to uplift this fine within a certain district. Addit. to BLUIDVEIT.

For particulars regarding this term see Skene, De Verb. Signif., and Cosmo Innes, Scotch Leg. Antiq., p. 60.

BLUE, *s.* A vulgar name for whisky, and other spirits; West of S.

Misfortunes on ilk ithers' backs,
Come roarin' whyles aroun' me ;
For comfort to the *blue* I rax,
Or aiblins they might drown me.
 Alex. Wilson's Poems, p. 98, ed. 1876.

Blue ruin, the Eng. slang term for gin, is now often applied to whisky in S.

BLUE, *adj.* True-blue, complete, thorough, perfect, out and out; as, "a *true-blue* Scot;" Burns, Earnest Cry.

Almost the only material from which a dyer can obtain a fast-blue is indigo; but its costliness has made the workman try various substitutes which produce results apparently equal to those of the costlier dyestuff. Such colours having been found to be all more or less fugitive came to be called "*not the true blue*;" and the frequency of the experience no doubt led to the adoption of the term *true-blue*, as equivalent to complete, thorough, real, and as an emblem of constancy. This use of the term is very old. V. Chaucer's Squieres Tale, l. 644, and note, Clar. Press, ed.

To **BLUFF, BLUGH,** *v. a.* and *n.* To blow in jerks or puffs from the mouth, to blow small objects by means of a tube; as, to *bluff* peas. V. PLUFF.

About the end of autumn schoolboys often amuse themselves by *bluffing* haw-stones at each other by means of a small tin tube, called a *bluffer*, or *blugher*, *pluffer* or *plugher*. In country districts the tube is made from a stalk of the cow-paranep or water-dropwort.

BLUFFER, BLUGHER, *s.* See note above.

BLUMF, BLUMPH, *s.* A dull, stupid person who can't or won't express himself, Gall. and Ayrs.; same with *Sumph*, q. v.

BLUNKER, *s.* A bungler, one who spoils everything he meddles with; Scott, Guy Mannering, ch. 3. Errat. in DICT.

This may be a corr. of *bungler*, or of *blunderer*, most prob. of the former by transposition. It certainly has no connection with *blunks*, blank pieces of cloth for printing, with which Dr. Jamieson related it; and even were it so formed, it could not mean *a printer*, as he stated. It may, however, be related to *blunk*, a vulgar corr. of *block*, which is often applied to a big, stout,

stupid person, by way of contempt; West and North of S.

BLUNKS, *s. pl.* A corr. of *blanks*; and when the pieces of calico are printed they are said to be filled. Addit. to BLUNKS.

To **BLUSH, BLUSCH, BLYSCH,** *v. n.* To look, gaze, stare.

The kynge *blysched* on the beryne with his brode eghne.
 Morte Arth., l. 116.
A better barbican that burne *blusched* upon never.
 Green Kn., l. 793.

Blink and *blush* are often used synon.; but they really are quite different terms; *blink* is to glance, and *blush* is to gaze, or look boldly.

BLUSH, BLUSCH, *s.* A look, gaze; also, a gleam, glow, gush of light.

To hide a blysful *blusch* of the bryght sunne.
 Green Kn., l. 520.

BLUTTER, *v.* and *s.* A corr. of Blatter, q. v.

BLUTTER, *s.* A rash and noisy speaker. Addit. to BLATTER.

A common term still in the West of S.

BLWMYS, *s. pl.* Blooms, flowers. Barbour, v. 10.

BLYD-MEAT, BLYID-MEAT, *s.* V. BLITHEMEAT.

To **BLYN, BLYNE,** *v. n.* To cease; Dunbar, Twa Mariit Wemen, l. 428. V. BLIN.

BOATSTICK, BOITSTAIK, *s.* The pole of a small boat; used for punting or for setting a light sail. The mast of a small fishing boat is still called *the stick*.

"... tuik in his hand ane grit aik trie, being the *boitstaik* of his boit, and offerit maist barbarouslie to stryk the said Thomas thairwith, wer not he wes hinderit be uther guid nychtbouris," &c. Reg. Priv. Council, vi. 238.

A.-S. *bát*, a boat, and *sticca*, a stick,'staff, pole.

BOCHLE, *s.* A var. of *Bauchle*, but generally applied to a female with large, clumsy feet; also, to one who is continually bothering about; Gall.

BOCHT, BOUCHT, BOYCHT, *pret.* and *part. pt.* Bought; Accts. L. H. Treas., i. 28, 93, 235.

BOCKIE, *s.* A bogle, goblin, Orkn. and Shetl. A colloquial form of Bogle.

BODACH, *s.* An old man; but used by Scott and others in the sense of a spectre, bugaboo; sometimes also as a familiar name for the devil.

Gael. *bodach*, an old man.

BODDLE, *s.* A coin. V. BODLE.

BODUM, BODOUM, *s.* Bottom, bottom of a tub, barrel, or other such vessel; also used for the vessel itself, and for ship, vessel, craft.

The application of this term to a ship, vessel, &c., which is still common, is of long standing. In the Burgh Recs. Aberdeen, of date 23 May, 1522, is the following :—
"That the gudis now being in Aberdene, quhilkis wer inbrocht one ane Hollanderis *bodum*, allegit to be ane Frenchman price," &c.

BODWIN NALIS, *s. pl.* Prob. errat. for *bodum nalis*, bottom nails, *i.e.*, nails for bottom planking, or sheathing of vessels; Accts. L. H. Treas., i. 254.

BODYN, *part. pt.* Bidden, urged, challenged; Barbour, vii. 103.

The sense of this form as here used is bidden to battle, challenged to fight; A.-S. *beddan*, to bid, part. pt. *boden*.

BOFFET, BOFFET-STULE, *s.* A kind of foot-stool. V. BUFFETSTOOL.

This term is still used in various districts of England.

BOGBEAN, *s.* A flowering plant common in bogs and marshes: Menyanthes trifoliata, Linn., E. *buckbean*.

This marsh-plant, so named from its bean-like appearance, is often called the marsh trefoil. It has a beautiful flower, and is much favoured by herbalists. In the West of S. a decoction of bogbean and strong ale is used as a cure for jaundice; and Withering, after describing the plant, says, "This beautiful plant is possessed of powerful medicinal properties : an infusion of the leaves is extremely bitter, and is prescribed in rheumatisms and dropsies; it may be used as a substitute for hops in making beer." British Plants, ed. Macgillivray, p. 131.

BOIRBREVE, BORBREIVE, *s.* Lit. a *birth-brieve*, or formal certificate of descent, granted to merchants or gentlemen who had settled or intended to settle abroad. It was a means of securing their social position in their new abode, and was granted under the great seal or the seal of a burgh.

". . . the previe seall, callit the seall of caus, quhairwith the testimoniallis and *boirbrevis* that pnssis to uther pairtis beyond sey ar seallit," &c. Burgh Recs. Aberdeen, 26 Nov. 1593.

Du. *geboortebrief*, a birth-brieve: for specimens of which, V. Misc. Spalding Club, vol. v.

BOISE, BOIS, BOISS, *s.* A bottle, jar. V. Boss.

BOIST, BOAST. *Boist be blawin*, the threatening be blown past, danger or difficulty be gone or got over; Lyndsay, Thrie Estaitis, l. 2287, Bann. MS., Court of Venus, iv. 306.

But barrat or bost, without strife or bullying; Houlate, l. 332. V. BOIST.

BOITSTAIK, *s.* V. *Boatstick*.

BOKIE-BLINDIE, *s.* Blind-buck: a game similar to Blind Man's Buff; Orkn. Shetl. V. BLIND HARIE.

BOLL-KAIL, *s.* Cabbage : common pron. is *bow-kail*; Corshill Baron Court Book, Ayr and Wigton Arch. Coll., iv. 185.

BOLLE CUSTOM, *s.* Dues levied on grain brought to port or market; a duty of so much per boll; Burgh Rec. Edinburgh, 1453, i. 14.

BOM, BOME, BOMSPAR, *s.* A boom, spar, or beam; also, a spar for a gate, or for shutting in.

". . to mak yettis of tre vpoun the tua eist portis, and als to mak *bomis* at the west end of the castelget and wther places of the town neidfull." Burgh Recs. Aberdeen, 17 Oct., 1562.

"*Bomsparres* the hundreth, xli." Halyburton's Ledger, p. 291.

Sw. *bom*, Du. *boom*, Germ. *baum*, a boom.

BOMBART, BOMBARD, *s.* A large gun, a cannon.

"Item, [A.D. 1496], for ij bowschis to a *bombart* quhele, vs." Accts. L. H. Treas., i. 294.

"Item, that samyn day, [10th Apr. 1497], giffin to Johne Mawar, elder, in part payment of the quhelis making to the *bombardis* and Mons, iiij. lib." Ibid., i. 328, DICKSON.

M. Lat. *bombarda*. Before the invention of cannon this name was applied to the balista.

BONAT, BONET, *s.* A sail. V. BONETT.

BOND, *s.* A boundary, limit; pl. *bondis*, bounds, boundaries.

"Item, gif the merkis and *bondis* of the burgh be weil kepit til ilk man." Chalmerlan Air, ch. 28.

O. Fr. *bonne*, a limit, boundary, from L. Lat. *bodina*, *bonna*, a bound, limit. Gael. *bonn* is prob. related to this root, if not a contracted form of it. V. *Bound*, Skeat's Etym. Dict.

BONDE, BOND, BOOND, *s.* 1. A bondman, serf.

"Gif ony man fyndis his *bonde* in the fayre, the whilk is fra hym fled, with the pece of the fayr is lestande he may nocht of lauch chace na tak hym." Burgh Lawis, ch. 88.

This word has generally been derived from the verb *to bind*; but it is also connected with L. Lat. *bondagium*, a form of tenure : hence *bondman*, or in earlier times *bonde*, one holding under this tenure.

2. A husbandman; and in Shetl. is still used in the sense of peasant, small farmer.

A.-S. *bonda*, from Icel. *bóndi*, a husbandman, from *búa*, to till. V. Skeat's Etym. Dict.

To **BONE,** *v. a.* To pray, beseech, implore; to solicit, crave. V. BONE, *s.*

This term is common in O. E. in the sense *to pray*, &c.; as in the formulary, "Lef fader ic the *bone*." But as it passed into everyday use the meaning degenerated to *solicit, crave, beg;* and in the West of

BON [49] BOR

S. It is now used in the sense of *to button-hole, to dun;* as, "I'll *bone* ye for my fairin the morn."

BONELLO, *s.* A corr. of Bonalais, q. v. Gall.

BONTETH, *s.* V. BOUNTETH.

BOO, *v.* and *s.* V. *Bu.*

Boo-Cow, BOO-MAN, *s.* V. under *Bu.*

BOOIN, BOUIN, BUIN, *s.* Forms of BOWIN, q. v.

To BOOK, BEUK, BUIK, *v. a.* To enter, enrol, register, record in the books of a burgh, kirk-session, presbytery, &c. Addit. under BOOK, *v.*

BOOKING, BOOKIN, BEUKIN, BUIKIN, *s.* 1. Enrolment, recording; generally applied to the act of recording in the books of a burgh, kirk-session, presbytery, &c.
Booking, as defined in DICT., refers to kirk-session books only.

2. The feast or merry-making held in the home of the bride after the act of *booking* has been accomplished.

3. A peculiar tenure of certain lands in the burgh of Paisley; also, a holding under this tenure.
"Conveyances of such lands are similar to those of proper feudal or burgage subjects, except that, in place of the obligation to infeft, they contain an obligation 'to book and secure.' . . . The Register of *Bookings* is kept in the Burgh by the Town Clerk, and the Register books remain permanently under his custody." Bell's Law Dict.
This form of tenure is now peculiar to Paisley.

BOOL, BOUL, *s.* A ball, marble, bullet, cannon ball, &c. S.
". . . the maisteris of artillierie to provyd *boolis, slottis,*" &c. Burgh Rees. Aberdeen, 17 Oct. 1542.

BOOLIE, BOWLOCH, *adj.* Crooked, deformed, bandy-legged, West of S. V. BOWLIE.

BOOLIE, BOWLOCH, *s.* A person who is deformed or bandy-legged. V. BOWLIE.
While both forms are used in the West of S., *Bowloch* is the one most common in Gall.

BOOND, *s.* A peasant, a small farmer; Shetl. Sw. and Dan. *bonde,* id. V. *Bonde.*

BOONDSFOLK, *s.* Peasantry, countrypeople; Shetl.

BOORTREE, BOORTRIE, *s.* V. BOURTREE.
Also used as an *adj.,* as, a *boortrie* bush, a *boortrie* gun.

To BOOTCH, BOUTCH, BITCH, *v. a.* To botch, bungle, muddle; West of S. E. *botch.*
O.L. Germ. *botsen,* Dutch *botsen,* to beat, repair.
(Sup.) G

BOOTCH, BOUTCH, BITCH, *s.* A botch, bungle, muddle; Ibid.

BOOTCHER, BOUTCHER, BITCHER, *s.* A botcher, bungler, muddler; Ibid.

BOOTIE, BOOTY, *s.* A square of flannel doubled cornerwise, and worn over head and shoulders by women; Orkn.
Prob. so called because *boot* or bent double, and then bent over the head of the wearer; or it may be simply *boot,* about. V. BOUTOCK.

BOOTING, *s.* Booty. V. BUITING.

BORBREIVE, BORBRIEF, *s.* V. *Boirbreve.*

BORCLATHIS, *s. pl.* Board-cloths, tablecloths; Halyburton's Ledger, p. 159.

BORDONIT, *part. pt.* Bordered, braided, embroidered; Court of Venus, i. 119.
A corr. of *bordurit,* bordered, edged, tipped, or of *brodurit,* embroidered: like *brodinstar, browdinstar,* an embroiderer.
Bord still means border, edge; the ornamental strip of which a border is made; the braid with which an edge is bound or welted: and a *bord* is often called a *bording* or *bordin.*

BORDURE, *s.* A border, rim, edge.
. . . . his basnett birneschet full bene, With a *bordure* aboute, alle of brynte golde.
Awnt. Arthur, l. 30.
Mis-read *brandur* in Pinkerton's edit.

BORLY, BORLIE, *adj.* Stout, strong, largebodied. V. BURLY.

BORN, BORNE, *s.* This term represents, 1. a burn, scald; 2. a burn, stream; 3. a barn, granary; Burgh Rees. Aberdeen, Glasgow, Prestwick, etc.

BORN-BROTHER, BORNE-BRITHER, *s.* Brother by the same father, step-brother.
". . . excommunicate Ishmael who could not abyde his *borne brother* Isaac during the lyfetyme of their common father Abraham," etc. Blame of Kirkburiall, ch. xv.

BOROW, *s.* A burgh; Burgh Laws, ch. 31. V. BURCH.

BOROWAGE, BUROWAGE, BURRAIGE, *s.* A burgh-holding. Used also as an *adj.,* implying burghal, pertaining to a burgh.
"That is to say that ilke burges sall geyff to the kyng for his *borowage* at the deffendis, for ilke rud of land v d be yhere." Burgh Lawis, ch. 1.
". . . with liberteis, priuileges, & fre *burowage* like as," etc. Charters of Peebles, 28 Oct., 1473.
". . . takkisman of the *burraige* custum of Peeblis set to him by the baillies," etc. Burgh Rees. Peebles, 1 Feb., 1571.

BOROW-GREFF, *s.* V. *Burgh-Greve.*

BOROWMEN, *s.* Burgh-men, burgesses; Burgh Lawis, ch. 13.

BORRELL-LOONS, s, pl. Wild or mischievous country lads; Sir W. Scott.
O. Fr. *borel* (=Fr. *bureau*) from Lat. *borellus*, coarse, rude, vulgar.

To BORROW, v. a. To pledge, pawn, put away, lay aside. Addit. to BORROW.
It makis me all blythnes to *borrow*;
My panefull pnrs so prikillis me.
Dunbar, To the King, l. 4.

BOSIE, BOSY, s. An endearing form of *bosom*.
O! dinna me tak
Frae that *bosy* awa;
Dinna ask your wee laddie
To try the stirk's sta'!
Ballantine, The Stirk's Sta'.

BOSIT, part. adj. Hollowed; in the form of a case or cover; also, embossed. V. BOS.
". . . sal be made a brase for his lair in *bosit* werk," etc. Charters of Edinburgh, 11 Jan., 1454-5.

BOSSIE, BAUSSIE, s. V. BASSIE.

BOST, s. V. BOIST, *Boist*.

BOT. 1. As a *conj.*, but, lest, unless.
2. As a *prep.*, without, except.
3. As an *adv.*, only.
Both defin. and etym. of this term as given in DICT. are misleading. It is simply a form of E. *but*, which is fully explained in Wedgwood's Etym. Dict.

BOT, s. A bolt, or staple; pl. *bottis*, Burgh Rec. Peebles, 1626-7: the term is still applied to those kneed bolts on which doors and window-shutters are hung.
"Item, for a *bot* of irne, and leyd, and til a masson to mak a hoylle and put the bot in, viij d." Accts. L. H. Treas., i. 184.

BOTCARD, s. Errat. in DICT. for *Bottard*, q.v. The definition, however, is correct.

BOTKIN, s. A small knife; originally a small dagger; Dunbar, Freiris of Berwik, l. 176.
This term occurs in Chaucer as *boydekin* or *boydekyn* (var. ed.); and in Shakespeare as *bodkin*, Ham. iii. 1: it generally meant a small dagger. Gael. *biodag*, a dirk, dagger: from which *bodkin* or *botkin* is formed as a dimin.

BOTTANO, s. A kind of linen; Halyburton's Ledger, p. 318. V. BOTANO.

BOTTARD, BATTARD, BATTER, s. A small cannon. V. BATTART.

BOUCHER, s. Butcher, hangman.
Syne furth him led, and to the gallous gals,
And at the ledder fute his leif he tais;
The Aip was *boucher*, and bad him sone ascend,
And hangit him: sae he maid his end.
Henryson, Parl. of Beistis, l. 300.
O. Fr. *boucher*, *bouchier*, a butcher, slaughterman, and hence a hangman.

BOUGE, BOWGE, BOUGIE, s. A bag, travelling bag, portmanteau. Hence its secondary meaning, the allowance of provisions from the king or lord to the knights, squires, &c., who attend him in an expedition; cf. Skelton's poem called "The Bowge of Court." Addit. to BOUGE.
This term is not properly defined in the DICT. For other forms, v. Gloss. Halyburton's Ledger.

BOUGH, BOWGH, BUGH, s. Budge, lamb's fur, lambskin with the wool dressed; Halyburton's Ledger, p. 37, 74. V. BUGE.

BOUKE, s. Errat. in DICT. for *bonke*, bank, brae, hill-side, or height; pl. *bonkes*.
A simple but strange mistake; as the phrase "*bonkes so bare*" is of frequent occurrence in these poems. The passage corrected is—
To byker at thes baraynes in *bonkes* so bare.
Sir Gawan and Sir Gal., i. 4.
The form *boncke* occurs in Layamon, but in Ormulum and later works it is *banke*. It is said to be from A.-S. *banc*; but only *banca* is found, meaning *bench*. V. Skeat's Etym. Dict.

BOULK, BOULKE, BOWK, s. Body, frame, bulk, size; Blame of Kirkburiall. V. BOUK.

BOULGETE, BOWLGIET, BOUGIET. V. BULGET.
These are diminutive forms of *bouge*, which in Halyburton's Ledger are applied to various kinds of bag, mail, or case for covering or packing goods.
O. Fr. *boulgette*, *bougette*, *bouge*, a budget, wallet, &c. Cotgr. E. *budget*.

To BOULT, BOUT, BOWT, v. a. To bolt or clean grain, meal or flour; E. *bolt*.
"Exeerno, 'to sift or *boult*," Duncan's Appendix Etymologiæ, 1595.

BOULT, BOUT, BOWT, BOUAT, BOUET, s. A bolter or sieve for grain, etc.

BOULTCLAITH, s. Bolting cloth; Halyburton's Ledger, p. 291. V. BOUTCLAITH.

BOULTIT, BOUTTIT, BOUT, part. pa. Bolted, sifted, cleaned; applied to grain.
". . . breid that be guid stuf, fresche, veill *boultit*, and without mixtiour, and veill bakin;" etc. Burgh Recs. Aberdeen, 9th August, 1540, Sp. C.
The contr. form *bout* is still common in the West of S.; as in testing meal or flour a farmer will say—
"Aye, that's bonnie, *weel-bout* stuff."

BOURCHT, s. Surety, bail. V. BORGH, BORCH.
". . . ilke ane of the foresaide masonnys is othiris *bourcht*," etc. Charters of Edinburgh, 29 Nov., 1387.

BOUSING, part. pr. Drinking, swilling.
While we sit *bousing* at the nappy,
An' getting fou and unco happy.
Burns, Tam O' Shanter.

BOUSSIE, BOOSSIE, adj. Flabby, puffed up; Whistle Binkie, i. 293. V. BOUZY.

BOUT, BOWT, *s.* A bolt, round, roll; a roll of cloth especially of fustian, canvas, etc., containing twenty-eight ells; West of S.: pl. *bouttis*, Halyburton's Ledger.

BOUT, BOWT, *s.* and *v.* V. *Boult.*

BOUTGATE, BOUTGANG, BOUTGAIN, BOUTING, BOUTIN, *s.* Lit. a going about, the extent of an *about* or a round: hence, the act of making it; the distance traversed, the time occupied, or the work done, during the round. Thus, in mowing, a *boutgate* or *bouting* is the space gone over or the work done with one sharp, i.e., one sharpening of the scythe; in ploughing it means two furrows, the out and the return one. From these come the secondary meanings, a turning round in action, a turning back, doubling, circumventing; a complete or sudden change, alteration, vicissitude; a round about or circuitous way. Addit. to BOUTGATE.

". . . that neyther prescription of tyme, vsucapion of person, nor *boutgate* of circumstance can giue a regresse, if this greedie world could be induced to beleue." Blame of Kirkburiall, ch. xix.
This term is not sufficiently explained in the DICT. The definitions are based on secondary meanings.

BOW, *s.* and *v.* Buoy, Shetl.; but in many of the fishing districts of Scotland the term is so pronounced.

BOWALLIS, *s. pl.* Prob. an errat. for BOWNDIS, bounds.

". . . thairfor the counsell, seeing the fornamet thric persones remaning obstinat, and travelland dalye to raise vproir, sisme, and diuisioun within this burght and *bowallis* thairof . . . gif remeid war nocht provydit for correcting of the saidis licentius persones, . . . it was ordanit, consentit, and grantit to, that na burgess of gild set ony duelling houss or boitht bo ony of thame, nor keip secretis witht thame, or gif thame ony labour or manuall exercitioun of thair craft in tyme cuming," etc. Burgh Records Aberdeen, 19 Feb., 1581.
The term occurs again near the close of this record in a similar sense, which tends to confirm the rendering given above.

BOW - DRAUCHT, *s.* A bow-shot, an arrow's flight; Barbour, vii. 19.

BOWING CHAFFS. Lit. bending chafts, i.e., distorting the features, pulling faces, making grimaces; Orkn.

BOWLGET, BOWLGIET, *s.* V. *Boulgete.*

BOWLIS, *s. pl.* 1. Balls, knobs.

"Item, giffin for ij tynnyt bandis 'and viij *bowlis* for trestis for the oosting burd, xxxij d." Accts. L. H. Treas., i. 295.

2. A game, called also *lang bowlis*, and nine pins. V. LANG-BOWLIS, and KILE.

"Item, that samyn nycht, in Sanctandros, to the King to play at the *lang bowlis*, xviij s." Accts. L. H. Treas. (28 Apr., 1497), i. 332.

BOWL-MONEY, BOW-MONEY, *s.* Same as *Ba' Siller*, q.v., Renfrews., Lanarks.

BOWRTRE, BORTREE, *s.* V. BOURTREE.

BOWSCH, *s.* The bush of a wheel. V. BUSH.

"Item, for ij *bowschis* to a bombart quhele v s." Accts. L. H. Treas., i. 294.

BOWSIE, BOWSE, *s.* The name of a huge, misshapen, hairy monster invoked by foolish mothers and nurses to frighten obstinate and troublesome children.

This silent, ugly, awful monster, with piercing eyes, and ears that can hear the slightest sound, whom no door or lock can keep out, and who comes and goes like the wind, is represented as ever on the watch for bad children, whom he seizes and carries off to his darksome den, to become his servants, or to be kept till they are fit to be devoured.
The *Boo-Cow* and the *Bowsie* are the two great horrors of infancy and early childhood : the first is the *roaring* monster for crying, noisy, vicious children ; and the second is the *horrible and ugly* monster for cowing the refractory and disobedient ones.
The term *Bowsie* is prob. from Fr. *bossu* (Lat. *gibbosus*), crooked, hunch-backed, deformed ; and in order to make the creation more terrible, the characteristic of Swed. *buskig*, bushy, hairy, was added. But this creation, like that of the *Boo-Cow*, was prob. suggested by the Bible description of the devil.
As might be expected, however, the Boo-Cow and the Bowsie are often confounded in nursery story and practice : sometimes through ignorance, and sometimes on purpose to make the creation more terrific.

BOWSSLEIT, *s.* and *adj.* The name of a kind of nail: prob. the kind commonly used in building the small boats of the time : Dutch *buis*, a small boat.

"Item, the xix. day of Januare, [1496], giffin to Johne Lam, in part of payment of v^m nalis, ane thousand of singil *bowssleit*, and iiij^m wraklene, iiij li." Accts. L. H. Treas., i. 310.
As this word is rather indistinct in the MS., and may be read *bowssplelt*, it may mean *flat-boat* nails, or small flat-headed nails ; which is somewhat confirmed by the *wraklene*, which were large flat-headed nails. V. WRAKLENE.

BOWSTAFIS, BOWSTINGIS, BOWSTEYNGIS, *s. pl.* Strips of wood from which bows were made. *Bowstingis* is sometimes misread *bowstringis*, as in the passages given below. V. BOWSTING.

"Of fremen . . . of ilk hundredth . . . . *bowstreyngis*, viij d."
"Of vnfremen . . . of the hundredth *bowstringis*, xvjd." Customes of Guidis ; Burgh Rec. Edinburgh, i. 44, 46.
"Of the hundir *bow-stafis*, viij d. ;" Ibid. 25. Sept., 1445.
Bowstingis were sold by the hundred or by the score ; *bowstrings*, by the dozen. V. Halyburton's Ledger, p. 291.

BOWYT, BOWT, BOOT, *part*. and *adj*. Bent, crooked; a *bowt* saxpence: *boot*-backit. V. BOW'D.

"Item, on Ywle da, [1489], to the King himself takin furth off the Thesaurarie purss, vij angellis and a half angel, ix li."
"Item, til him, the saim da, ane angell qubilk he *bowyt* and put abowte his beydis, xxiiij s." Accts. L. H. Treas., i. 126. Dickson.

This bending or *bowing* of "*ane angell*" by the King, and then putting it about his beads, is an example of a custom which prevailed all over the country even to the beginning of this century. During a time of sickness, or hardship, or perplexity, a person would "*bow*" or bend a gold or silver coin, and promise that, in the event of recovery or deliverance, he or she should present that coin at the shrine of the saint whose aid was invoked. If the person had no faith in saints, the coin was promised to be laid on "*the brod*," i.e., the plate at the church door for collections for the poor. Many persons are still possessed by the notion that a *bowyt* or crooked coin has luck attached to it.

BOYIS, *s. pl.* Gyves, fetters: *in boyis*, in bonds, fettered; Barbour, x. 763. Another form is *in the bows*, in the stocks. V. Bows.

Dr. Jamieson appears to have been uncertain regarding this term. He is, however, correct both as to meaning and derivation; but, as Prof. Skeat has pointed out, the latter would be improved by tracing the term to O. Fr. *buie*, a fetter, from Lat. *boia*, id.

BOYTACH, *s.* A bunch or bundle: applied also to a small dumpy animal, that has difficulty in walking, Gall. V. *Bodach*.

BRABANER, BRABONER, *s.* A weaver, a customer weaver; Burgh Rec. Prestwick, 16 Jan., 1550-1, Hist. Old Dundee, p. 50.

This is certainly a very old term. Originally applied to the cloth-workers from Brabant, who settled in the larger towns on the east coast, it soon became restricted to the chief handicraft which they followed, viz. weaving. And this application would be all the more easy to the native population, because their term for a weaver was almost identical in sound. In the Gael. a weaver is a *breabadair*, pron. *brabadar*, a kicker, i.e., a treddler; or, it may be a driver or kicker of the shuttle; or, the idea may include both movements: Gael. *breab*, to kick.

It is interesting to trace this word through the various changes it has undergone as a proper or family name. In our Burgh Records, among such names as Smith, Miller, Skinner, Walker, Baxter, and Litster (afterwards Lister), we occasionally find the name Brabner; and in the Aberdeen Records of the 15th and 16th cents. it appears under the forms of Braboner, Brabaner, and Brabner. A century later it assumes the form Brebner; and by and bye it becomes Bremner, a name which is still common in the north of Scotland, and by no means uncommon in populous districts of the western and southern counties.

To BRACE, BRASE, *v. a.* Short for embrace, to hold, clasp, or bind tightly; hence to enfold, enclose, shut up.

Hir mervallus haill madinheed
God in hir bosum *braces*,
And hir divinite fra dreid
Hir kepit in all casis.
Henryson, Salutation of the Virgin, l. 50.

O. Fr. *brace*, Fr. *bras*, an arm: from which came the v. *brace*, to clasp with a band, as with closed arms; hence, to tighten, as, *to brace* a drum by means of its bands; also, to enfold, enclose, shut up, which is the sense in the passage quoted.

BRACE, BRASE, *s.* 1. A bracer or guard for the left arm of an archer; Cherrie and Slae, st. ix.

2. The coping, covering, or head-piece of an ornamental recess, a monument, or other mural erection in churches, graveyards, etc.

3. An enclosure for the dead, an ornamented covering of a tomb, a monument for the dead shaped like a sarcophagus.

". . in the quhilk Ile thare sal be made a *brase* for his lair in bosit werk, and aboue the *brase* a table of bras with a writ specifeand the bringing of that rellyk be him in Scotland with his arms;" etc. Charters of Edinburgh, 11 Jan. 1454-5.

Addit. to BRACE.

BRADE, BRAID, *s.* Deceit, deception, delusion, figment, fancy.

". . for to presume vpon the prerogatiue of buriall, for being in Kirk-place, it were a brain-sick *brade*." Blame of Kirk Buriall, ch. xix.

A.-S. *brægd*, deceit fiction.

Palsgrave has "*brayde* or hastynesse of mynde, *colle*," i.e. passion, anger; but in Green's Works, ii. 268, the term occurs in the sense of *craft, deceit*; and Shakespeare uses *braid* as an *adj.* in the sense of *deceitful*. V. Dyce, Gl. Shak.; Halliwell, Prov. Dict.; and Hearne, Gl. Langtoft.

BRAID, BRAYD, *v.* and *s.* V. BRADE.

BRAID, *s.* A board, table, etc. V. *Bred*.

BRAIDLINGIS, BRADELINGS, *adv.* Broadwise, abreast; in a mass, all at once.

"Now, Kirkburiall althogh it be now come without blush, yet it brake not in *bradelings*, but as it were by degrees and some shame." Blame of Kirkburiall, ch. xiii.

Icel. *breithr*, Goth. *braids*, A.-S. *brád*, broad.

BRAIGGLE, *s.* "Any old, unsafe article—as a large gun with a large lock." Gall. Encycl. Called also a *briggle*, a *brikkle*; and when the article is much out of order, or its parts loose, a *rickle*.

Prob. both forms are corr. of *brickle*, an old form of *brittle*.

BRAIG-KNIFE, BRAIG-KNYFE, *s.* A carving knife, a flesher's knife.

"George Speir, fleschour, . . . for breking vp the kirk dwrris the tyme of the sessioun, and drawing of ane *braig knyfe* to the beddell of the kirk," etc. Burgh Recs. Glasgow, i. 329, Recs. Soc.

Gael. *breac*, to carve; pron. *brechg*. The knife referred to is still called a *breck-knife, brecking-knife*. V. *Brek*.

BRAIK, *s.* V. BRAKE.

BRAIKEN, *s.* The bracken. V. BRACHEN.

BRAIN-PAN, Brane-pan, s. The skull; Blame of Kirkburiall, ch. x.: syn. *harn-pan.*

BRAIRDED DYKES, s. pl. Hedges or fences stuffed with whins or other brushwood to prevent cattle getting through to the growing crop; West and South of S.

BRAISSARIS, s. pl. V. Braseris.

To BRAITHE, v. a. To boil down; i.e., to make *brae* or *bree* of; Orkn.

BRAMMO, Bramo, s. Milk and meal stirred together: used as a hasty meal; Orkn. A mess of oatmeal and water; Gloss. Shetl.

Evidently *brammo* is what is known in the more southern counties as *dramock* or *brose*.

BRAMSKIN, s. A form of *Barmskin*, q. v.

BRAND, part. adj. Brawned; Dunbar, Twa Mariit Wemen, l. 429. V. Branit.

BRANDED, part. pt. Errat. for *brauded*, broidered, embroidered. V. Dict.

This mistake is due to the careless transcript published by Pinkerton. V. Gloss. to Gawain Romance, Bann. Club.

BRANDER, Brandur, Brandering, s. Frame, framework; support for scaffolding, as trestles, &c.; also the scaffolding surrounding a building; Spald. Club Misc., V. 50, 65. Addit. to Brander, q. v.

Pl. *branders* is now generally applied to the trestles or supports of a scaffold, &c., and *brandering* to the whole scaffolding or supports for the builders. *Brandering* and *brandreth*, with its corr. *brandraucht*, *brandrauth*, are often applied to the frames or framework to which panelling is attached. V. *Brandering*.

To Brander, v. a. To support by trestle or framework: to build or lay supports for scaffolding, &c.; also, to form a foundation for building by planting strong framework on piles driven into the ground; part. pt. *branderit, brandert.* Addit. to Brander, v.

" —— aud the said brig to be staggit and *branderit* sufficiently in deipnes vnder the channall, to mak a sufficient ground to big vpoun." Burgh Recs. Aberdeen, 15 Aug., 1610.

Brandering, Brandreth, Brandrauth, Brandraucht, s. Framework; trestles or supports for tables, scaffolding, &c.; framework foundation for building, panelling, &c. Burgh Recs. Aberd., Edin., Glasgow. Addit. to Brandreth, q. v. V. *Brander, s.*

The form *brandraucht* occurs in Accts. Burgh of Edinburgh, 1554-5, Recs. Soc.

BRANDUR, s. Errat. for *bordure*, a border, edge, or rim. V. Dict. under Branded.

BRANEWOD, adj. Stark mad, furious, mad with rage. V. Brayn-Wod.

The bard wox *branewood* and bitterly coud ban.
Houlate, l. 811.

This form occurs in Christ Kirk, s. 22, where it may be read either as a s. meaning firewood, or as an *adj.* with meaning as above. V. Dict.

BRANLING, Branlin, s. V. Bramlin.

BRASE, s. and v. V. *Brace.*

BRASEL, Braseill, Brasyll, Brissell, Blew Brissell, s. Brazil-wood; used for dyeing red colours: the Caesalpinia Braziliensis of commerce.

"*Brasyl* at the outtryng aw nathyng, bot at the outgang ilk hundreth of *brasyll* sall pay twa peniis," &c. Assize of Petty Customs, ch. 7.

The term also occurs in various forms in Halyburton's Ledger.

It is a curious fact that the country of Brazil is named from M.E. *brasil*, already in use before A.D. 1400.

BRATTIE, s. Dimin. of Brat, an apron; used as a name for clothing in general; as, " the bit and the *brattie*," food and clothes. S. V. Brat.

BRATTISH, Bartise, s. A brattice or wooden partition dividing rooms; also applied to the wood-work ventilators in mines; West of S.

This term is common in mining districts of the N. of England. V. Brockett's Gloss.

BRAUDED, part. pt. Broidered, embroidered; "*brauded* with brente golde;" Awnt. Arthur, s. 29.

Misread *branded* in Pinkerton's edit.

BRAWNET, Brounet, s. A dark brown colour; generally applied to animals, as, " a *brawnet* horse." In Gall., *brawnet* ; in Ayrs. and Lanarks., *brounet.*

"A colour made up of black and brown, mostly relating to the skins of animals. A 'nowt beast o' a *brawnet* colour' takes a south-country man's eye next to that of the 'slae black.'" Gall. Encycl.

Fr. *brunet*, brownish : dim. of *brun*, brown, from O. H. Ger. *brûn*.

To BRAY, Brey, Brea, v. a. To beat, pound, reduce to powder. Addit. to Bray.

This term is so used all over S., and in the N. of E. (V. Brockett's Gl.); but the common F. meaning is to pound in a mortar. O. Fr. *breier, brehier* (Fr. *broyer*), from M. H. Ger. *brechen*, to break.

BRAYAND, Breiying, part. Crying, bawling, squalling.

" . . . sua at that man sall have wytnes of tua loll men or of women nychtburis that herde the chylde cryand or grotand or *brayand*." Burgh Lawis, ch. 41.

BREAD, Brede, s. Breadth; as, *a hand-brede, an acre-brede.* V. Breid.

". . . undertakis to big the brig, as said is, of the hight, *bread*, and wyndnes as the same presently standis," etc. Burgh Recs. Aberdeen, 15 Aug., 1610.
A.-S. *brædu*, id. M. E. *brede*. *Breadth* is a comparatively modern Eng. form.

BREASKIT, BRISKIT, *s.* V. BRISKET.

BREASTIE, *s.* Dimin. of breast; a familiar or kindly term used in speaking to children or to pets.
Wee, sleekit, cowrin, tim'rous beastie
O, what a panic's in thy *breastie*.
Burns, To a Mouse, st. 1.

BRECBENNACH, *s.* V. BREKBENACH.

BRECHANS, *s. pl.* The wooden hames used with the *wassie* or straw collar in Orkn. and Shetl.
Lit. protectors, or protecting crooks: Icel. *bjarga*, A.-S. *beargan*, to protect; or as a corr. of *bergh-hames*, protecting splints or crooks. They are similar to the *hames* of the Lowlands, where the collar to which they are attached is called a *brecham*.

BRECK AN EGG, BRACK AN EGG. A phrase in curling, meaning, to strike a stone with force just sufficient to crack an egg at the point of contact.
At the close of a round, when the stones are well gathered near the cock, and it is difficult to run in another without doing damage, a friend of the player about to throw will lay his brush on a certain stone and cry, "Noo, John, ye see this ane? Weel, jist *breck an egg* on't, man, an' we'll win."

BRECKAN, BRECKIN, *s.* A fern. V. BRACHEN.

BRECKANY, *adj.* Full of or covered with ferns; as, *breckany* braes.

BRED, BREDE, *adj., adv.,* and *s.* V. BRAID.

To BREDE, *v. n.* To spread, spread out, expand; Barbour, xvi. 68.
A.-S. *brǽdan*, id.

BRED, BREDE, BRAID, BROD, *s.* 1. A board; a package e.g., of skins, tied between boards; a certain number of skins so packed. Addit. to BRED.
A bundle of skins was called a *bred* or a *brede*: thus—"Item, for lynyng a gowne to the King, a *bred* of bwge, vi li. xiij s. iiij d." Accts. L. H. Treas., i. 135.

2. The plate, box, or ladle carried round to receive the offerings during church service: the plate set at the entrance to a church to receive the collection for the poor: also, the offerings thus received.
". . . ordanit that Sanct Nicholace *braid* siluer be given to the sustentatioun of the seik folkis of the pest, during the tyme thairof, . . . and als ordanit Andro Losoun to gif the *braid* siluer he gat on Sonday last was, to be distribuit to the seik folkis." Burgh Recs. Aberdeen, 11 Oct., 1546.
Before the Reformation all offerings were received in the *bred, braid,* or *brod,* carried round near the close of the service; and on "*solemp days*" it was the duty of the provost and bailies to carry the *bred ;* but after the Reformation the *bred* was used only for the collection for the poor, and it was set on a stool at or near the entrance to the church, and was presided over by an elder.

3. A window board, or window shutter; as, "It's growin dark, gae out an' put on the *breds*," or "put ta the *breds*," West of S.
The moon has rowed her in a cloud,
Stravaging win's begin
To shuggle and daud the *window-brods*,
Like loons that wad be in.
Wm. Miller, Gree Bairnies Gree, s. 1.

The street windows even of dwelling houses long ago were guarded by shutters, or *breds* or *windo-brods*, hung by one side to the window-cheek, and folded back to the wall during day time: in shutting, these were simply swung round, or *put ta*, and bolted. Another kind, also in one piece, fitted close to the window frame, and could be *put on* or taken off as required.

4. A spar, bolt, bar, guard: as, "He closed the yett an' shot the *breds ;*" S.

To BRED, BRAID, *v. a.* 1. To board, spar, or cover with wood, S.

2. To bar, spar, bolt.
". . . to cloise the toun and *bred* the portis of the same, and oupmak all wydis and waistis," etc. Burgh Recs. Aberdeen, 21 March, 1526.

BREDEFU', *adj.* Full to the *brede*, i.e., board or lid, border, or brim; like the form "full to the bung;" completely filled. In M. E. *bretful*, Halliwell.
The term is still used in West of S.
Sw. *brädd*, brim ; *bräddful*, full to the brim : Dan. *bredfuld*, a brimfull.

BREEKUMS, *s.* Small or scanty breeches, boys' breeches. V. BREEKS.
Although the *breekums* on thy fuddy
Are e'en right raggit.
James Ballantine, Wee Raggit Laddie, st. 1.

To BREEL, *v. n.* To drink plentifully, to fuddle; another form of *Birl*, q. v. Ayrs., Gall.
And sure it wad been baith a sin and a shame,
For ony ava to hae draunted shame ;
The deil a ane did sae, fu' gladly they came,
And *breel'd* at the lairdie's bonello.
Gall. Encycl., p. 78.

BREEST-BANE, BREIST-BANE, *s.* The breast-bone of a fowl, the *merry-thought*. Gall. Clydes.
Pu'in' the *breest-bane* is an amusement enjoyed by young people all over the country ; and it is as well known in Eng. also. Description is therefore unnecessary.

BREIDHOUS, *s.* A pantry.
In a list of payments made by the Lord High Treasurer during the year 1404-5, "*be preceptis deliueris*," we find the following :—

"Item, to William Douglas of the *breidhous*, xxx li." Accts. L. H. Treas., i. 237.

BREIF, Breiff, Breff, Breive, *s.* "A writ issuing from Chancery in name of the King, addressed to a judge, ordering trial to be made by a jury of certain points stated in the brieve." Bell's Law Dict.

"Item, gevin to Richert Wallas, currour, to pass with lettres to summound the barones and frehauldiris of the schirefdomes of Inuernes, Elgin, Forrais, Banff, and Abirdone, to the seruing of the *breif* of ydeotryc vpone the Erle of Suddirland in Inuernes, xx s." Accts. L. H. Treas., i. 238.

BREIRD, *v.* and *s.* V. Braird, Breer.

To BREK, Breck, *v. a.* Besides the ordinary meanings of *break* in use in E., there are several special or peculiar applications of it in Scot. of which the following are the most noteworthy.

1. To cut up, part into pieces, portions, or quantities; as, *to brek* a bouk or carcase, *to brek* a salmon, *to brek* bulk.

Brek; in this sense, is common in M. E.

2. To cut off bit by bit, to part or take in small; hence, to retail, sell by retail : as, "I dare na sell the bouk, I man *brek* it to the neebours a' roun'."

3. To portion, apportion, divide proportionally; hence, to stent or tax.

". . . ordanis viij personis of them that is ellis brokin anentis the payment of the pulder *to brek* thame that brak the laif efter Beltane, and in the mein tyme to gif to the gunneris ane quarter of puldor, and xx li. to be *broking* to the brig werk and puldor." Burgh Recs. Peebles, 25 Apr., 1571.

"*To brek the taxt*," i.e. to apportion the tax, or to fix each person's share of it, is a phrase which frequently occurs in our Burgh Records ; and the persons who performed the duty were called "*brekaris of the taxt*."

4. To depart from, or do contrary to, a fixed standard or law; as, "to *brek* the measure," to give less than the proper measure, or to trade with a false or diminished measure ; "to *brek* the pais," lit. to break the weight, i.e., to give less than the due weight, or less than was bargained for ; "to *brek* price," to sell an inferior article at the price of the good and sufficient, or to charge higher prices than those fixed by law.

In every burgh the price of ale, bread, and flesh, was fixed at stated times ; and the parties who did not conform to the rates were dealt with for *breking measure, pais*, or *price*.

Brekar, Breckar, *s.* 1. One who divides or portions a thing into its several parts; as, "a bouk or carcase *brekar*," who cuts it up into its various parts, and lays them out for further use. Of this class there were the brekar of flesh, and the brekar of salmon, etc. V. *Brek*.

2. One who sells his goods in small portions, or by retail, a huckster or retailer.

3. One who divides or apportions a tax among the members of a community, according to their means, was called "a *brekar* of the tax."

"The counsale ordanis the *brekaris* of the xl li. taxt, diuisit for the commone effaris and welth of the toune," etc. Burgh Recs. Peebles, 19 May, 1572.

BREKBENACH, Brecbennach, *s.* The name of the battle ensign of the Abbot of Arbroath. V. Dict.

It has been suggested with great probability (Proc. Antiq. of Scot., 2nd Ser. ii. 435) that the Latin word *vexillum*, by which the Brekbanach is described, has misled antiquaries generally into the belief that it was a banner; the likelihood being that it was a reliquary such as the Breac Moedoc and other known Celtic *vezilla* or battle ensigns. Addit. to *Brekbenach*.

BRENT, *s.* Spring : also used as an *adj.*, belonging to the spring-season ; Orkn.

BRESCAT, Brescat Brede, *s.* Biscuit.

Perhaps from Fr. *bresca*, O. Fr. *bresche*, L. Lat. *brisca*, a honey-comb ; Dicz : but more probably a corr. pron. of *biscuit*.

"Item, to Andro Bertoune, for.ij^m *brescat brede* to him, [the Duke of York, in 1497]." Accts. L. H. Treas., i. 343, Dickson.

This supply was for the Duke of York's ship then lying at Ayr, and formed but a small item of the expenses incurred by the King's favour for Perkin Warbeck.

To BRET, Brett, *v. n.* To strut, stride, or bounce along ; Orkn. Prob. the local form of Braid, q. v.

Icel. *bregtha*, to start.

BREUST, Brost, Broust, *s.* V. Browst.

Brekstar, Brostar, Brorstar, Brouster, *s.* V. Browster.

To BREVE, Breue, *v. a.* To record, state, relate, or describe briefly ;· to account, reckon, esteem, deem ; also, in the general sense of to speak of, to tell, inform ; Gaw. and Gol. s. 22, 23 ; Wallace, ix. 1941.

These meanings are additional to those given under the *v. Brief, Breve*, etc.

To BREVIATE, Breuiat, *v. a.* To summarize, to write or state in outline.

BREVIATLY, Breuiatlie, *adv.* Concisely ; in brief time, space, or manner; off hand, without reflection, hurriedly ; Court of Venus, i. 770, S. T. S.

BRIDLIN' RAPES, *s. pl.* The ropes used to hold down the thatch on stacks of grain, and roofs of houses in country districts; West and South of S.
When the stacks have been built and covered, ropes of straw are fixed vertically over the thatch : these are called *owrgaun rapes.* The *bridlin rapes* are then carried round and caught on the vertical ones, and the covering is made secure.

BRIERIE, BREERIE, *adj.* Birky, troublesome, bold and restless : like a thorny brier bush always fretting one. Addit. to BREERIE.
Stourie, stoussie, gaudy *brierie,*
Dinging a' things tapsalteerie ;
Jumping at the sunny sheen,
Flickering on thy pawky een.
John Crawford, Mother's Pet, s. 3.

BRIG, BRIGGER, BRIGDER, *s.* The portion of twisted hair to which a fishing-hook is tied ; also, the tapering line of twisted hair to which a cast of flies is attached ; West of S. : *brigder,* Shetl.
A.-S. *bregdan, bredan,* to braid, plait, weave.
Prob. it is to such a *brig* that reference is made in the expression, *a brig o' ae hair,* i.e., a tie or tome of the lightest texture possible : perhaps, also, a tie or line of gut.

BRIGAN, BRIGGAN, *s.* A brigand, robber; Burgh Recs., Aberdeen, i. 338. Sp. C. V. BRIGANER.

BRIGACIE, *s.* Brigandage, V. BRIGANCIE.

To BRIGANT, *v. a.* To waylay and rob.
Brigantis sik bois and blyndis thame with a blawa.
Dunbar and Kennedy, l. 436.

BRIGHOUSS, *s.* A bridge-house, a tollhouse; Barbour, xvii. 409. V. BRIG.

BRIGINTINE, BRIGINTYNE, BRIGINT, *s.* A brigandine, a jacket of mail worn by archers and cross-bowmen; it was also called a *brigat*; Accts. L. H. Treas., i. 143.
" Item, . . . ½ elne of vellous to the Kingis *brigintynis,* price xxv s." Accts. L. H. Treas., i. 19.
"Item, ij ½ elne of vellus to the coueringis of *brigintynis,*" etc. Ibid., i. 24.
"The brigandine was a jacket composed of rings or small plates of metal sewed on leather, or quilted between folds of canvas or fustian. Those worn by men of rank were covered with rich stuffs, as the extracts just given indicate." Ibid. Gloss.
Fr. *brigandine.*

BRIGINTARE, *s.* A maker of brigandines, an armourer.
"Item, gevin to Johne Clement the *brigintare,* be a precept subscriuit with the Kingis hand vndir the signete, for his Mertymes fee, x li." Accts. L. H. Treas., i. 65, Dickson.

To BRIK, *v. a.* To break, burst, bud; part. pr. *brikand,* budding, Dunbar. V. *Brek.*

BRINT ANNUELLIS, *s. pl.* There are three applications of this term :—
1. The lands and tenements within the burghs and towns of Scotland, " burnt be the auld enemies of England."
2. The annuals or yearly duties belonging to such lands and tenements.
3. The Act of Parl. " maid [in 1551] anent the annuelles of landes burnt be our auld enemies of England within burrowes." V. BRYN.
". . . for xiiij s. of annuel quhilk is infeft for doing yerelie of the said dirige . . . conforme to the actis made be the Thre Estatis of the *brint annuellis,*" etc. Burgh Rec. Peebles, 2 Dec., 1555.
For particulars see Scot. Acts, Mary, 1 Feb., 1551. This Act settled the manifold disputes between landlords and tenants that arose after the ruthless havoc wrought by the English invasion under Somerset in 1547.

To BRISE, BRYSE, *v. a.* To crush, rend, burst with force; pret. *bris,* part. pt. *briz, brist*; Shetl., Orkn., West of S. V: BRIST.

BRIS, *s.* A crush, rent, crack, rupture; Ibid.
Fr. *briser,* to break.

BRISSEL, BLEW BRISSELL, *s.* V. *Brasel.*

BRISSLE, *v.* and *s.* A form of BIRSLE, q. v.

BROCHAN, *s.* The plaid worn by Highlanders; Gael. *breacan,* id.
". . . were they a' rouped at the Cross—basket hilts, Andra Ferraras, leather targets, brogues, *brochan,* and sporrans." Scott, Rob Roy, ch. 23.
"Particoloured dresses were used by the Celts from the earliest times; but the variety of colours in the *breacan* was greater or less according to the rank of the wearer. The *breacan* of the Celtic king had seven different colours ; the Druidical tunic had six ; and that of the nobles four." M'Leod and Dewar's Gaelic Dict., p. 84.

BROCHES, *s. pl.* Spurs. Add. to BROCHE.

BROCHT AND HAMBALL. A corr. of *Brogh* or *borgh of hamald,* surety for goods passing from the seller to the buyer ; Burgh Recs. Aberdeen, i. 283. V. under HAMALD.

BROCK, BROKS, *s.* Refuse, trash. V. BROK.
" I gat neither stock nor *brock* "—neither money nor meat. Scot. Proverb.

BROCK, *s.* A badger ; Gael. *broc.*
In some districts this term is applied to a person of filthy habits. "He's a dirty *brock,*" and " He smells like a *brock,*" are statements still in common use.
Wi' yowlin' clinch aul' Jennock ran
Wi' aa'r like ony *brock ;*
To bring that remnant o' a man,
Her foistest brither Jock.
Alex. Wilson, Callamphitre's Elegy, s. 8.

BROCK-FACED, *adj.* Faced like a badger,

i.e., striped with white, S. Syn. *bawsand, bausint.*

BROCK-HOLES, *s. pl.* Badger holes: dens or abodes of the badger; West and South of S.

BROCKIT, *adj.* Like a badger in colour, black and white: applied to animals. Also applied to a person of filthy habits; as, "Ay, badger he is! *brockit*, barken't, saur't an' a';" West of S. V. BROCKED.

BROCKSHOLE, BROKSHOLE, *s.* Lit. badger's hole or den: the common name for the blackhole of a prison, into which only the vilest criminals were put.
"Ane kie of *brokshole* with ane slott in the innersyd," &c. Burgh Rec. Peebles, 22 Jan., 1650.

To BROD, BROUD, BRODER, BROUDER, BROWDER, *v. a.* To braid, broider, embroider; hence, to ornament, adorn, deck, array; part. pt. *brodyn, broudin, broudyn, browdyn, broderit, brouderit, browdrit, brodrit,* broidered, embroidered.
"Item, a frontall of reid say *brodrit*, cost 13 s." Halyburton's Ledger, p. 159.
The birth that the ground bure was *browdyn* on bredis.
Houlate, l. 27. Bann. MS.
This term is given as *Brondyn* in the DICT.: an errat. of the text from which the passage was taken.
A.-S. *bregdan*, to braid; part. pt. *brogden*, braided. Fr. *broder*, to embroider; lit. to work on the edge, to edge; *broder* being a doublet of *border*, from Fr. *bord*, an edge, hem, or selvage. V. *Broider*, in Skeat's Etym. Dict.

BRODUR, BRODURE, *s.* An embroiderer; *broduris silk,* embroiderer's silk; Halyburton's Ledger, p. 249.

BROWDIR, *s.* Bordering, fringing, embroidery.
Thocht now in *browdir* and begary,
Sche glansis as scho war Quene of Fary.
Rob. Stene's Dream, p. 4, MS.

BROWDSTAR, BROWSTAR, BROSTAR, BRUSOURE, *s.* An embroiderer; contr. for *Browdinstar*, q. v. V. BROUDSTER.
All these forms of the word occur in the Accounts of the Lord High Treasurer. They form a fine example of the process of contraction by which words in frequent use are simplified.

BRODS, WINDOW-BRODS, *s. pl.* V. *Brod.*

BROGIT-STAF, *s.* A pike-staff. V. under BROG.
Called also a *broddit-staff*, q. v.

BROICH, *s.* Broach: "*on broich*," broached, tapped, with open tap, without stint.
All dentals delr wes thair but dowt,
The wyne *on broich* it ran.
Alex. Scott's Poems, p. 24.

(Sup.) H

Before the days of taps or spigots, wine, ale, or other liquor was drawn from the barrel by removing a neatly-fitting wooden pin, called *a broach.*

To BROILYIE, *v. n.* To brawl, Barbour, iv. 151, Edin. MS.: the com. form is *Brulyie,* q. v.

BROK, BROKE, *s.* V. *Brock.*

BROKEN UP, BROKKIN VP, *part. ph.* Broken out, started, begun: as, "—— the pest is laitlie *brokkin vp* in St. Jhonestoun;" Burgh Recs. Edin., iv. 351, Sept. 1584.
This phrase occurs frequently in the Burgh Recs., and may still be heard among the working classes in the West of S. V. BREAK-UP.

BROKIN, *part. pt.* of *Brek,* q. v.

BRONDYN. Errat. for *Broudyn,* part. pt. decked, arrayed, q. v. V. DICT.

BRONT, *s.* Countenance, appearance, bearing, carriage.
Benyng of obedience and blyth in the *bront.*
Houlate, l. 160, Asloan MS.
Icel. *brún*, the eye-brow; A.-S. *brú*, Gael. *brd,* the brow; Bret. *abrant*, eye-brow. See *Brow* in Skeat's Etym. Dict.

BROOLYIE, BROULYIE, BROOLYIMENT, *s.* A quarrel, contention, commotion, storm. V. BRULYIE.
In keeping with that interposition of letters common in country districts this word is often pron. *broozle,* or *broosle* in the South of S.

BROSTAR, BROSTARE, *s.* V. BROWSTER.

BROUDYN, BROWDIN. V. BROWDYN, *Brod.*

BROUGH, BRUGH, BRUFF, *s.* 1. A circle, ring; applied also to a crowd; West of S. V. BOURACH.

2. Applied to the rings or circles drawn round the *tee* in curling. Ibid. V. BRUGH.

BROUGH OR BRUGH ABOUT THE MOON. The hazy ring or ruff which surrounds the moon in certain states of the atmosphere. Its appearance is said to indicate a coming storm of rain or snow; Ibid.

BROUN, BROUNE, *part. adj.* Brewing, fit for brewing; local pron. of *brewin'* ; Ayrs.
". . . for thair abstracted multouris of *broune* malt," etc. Corshill Baron Court Book. Arch. and Hist. Coll. Ayr and Wigton, ut. 95.

To BROWDER, *v. a.* To embroider; pret. and part. pt. *browderit,* Henryson, Testament of Cresseid, l. 417. V. under BROD.

BROWDIR, BROWDSTAR, *s.* V. under *Brod.*

BROWKIN, *part. pres.* V. *Bruk.*

BROWN, BROWNE, part. pt. V. BROWIN.

BRUCH, BRUGH, s. A burgh, town; bruch and land, town and country; Lyndsay. Thrie Estaitis, l. 1802. V. BURCH.

BRUGLING, BRUGLIN, part. adj. Striving, struggling; hence contending, contentious, haughty, vain-glorious. V. BRUGHLE.

". . . the occasion of the brugling brags of men, and of the contemp also of Gods hous and seruants." Blame of Kirkburiall, ch. xv.

To BRUK, BRUKE, BRWK, BROWK, v. a. To use, wear, possess, enjoy; Barbour, v. 236, xx. 132; part. pr. bruking, brukyn; "brukyn and joysing," possessing and enjoying, an old law term regarding property, and implying penceable possession of it; browkin, Chart. Peebles, 5 Feb., 1505-6. V. BRUIK.

BRUK, BRUKE, s. A brook, stream; Henryson, Wolf and Lamb, ll. 17, 35.
A.-S. broc, brooc, Dutch broek, a marsh, a pool.

BRULIE, BROULIE, adj. and s. Scroll, draft, outline, skeleton; as, "Brulie Minutes."

Of the Session Records of the Parish Kirk of Mauchline, some of the volumes are stated to be "unbound and incomplete; some are scroll books and are headed, 'Brulie Minutes;' some are duplicates," etc. Old Church Life in Scotland, p. 2. V. BRULTIE.
Fr. brouillon, a scroll or first draft of a document: from brouiller, to mix up confusedly.

BRUNIE, BRUNIES, s. V. BROWNIE.

BRUSOURE, s. V. Browdstar, under Brod.

BRYBE, s. Short for bribery, corruption, influencing by benefits; "brybe and boist," corruption and intimidation; Court of Venus, iv. 300, S. T. S.

Gloss, gives confusion as the meaning; but this is a mistake. The term is simply M. E. bribe, bryba used for bribery: just as we use gun for gunnery, machine for machinery.
O. Fr. bribe, "a peece, lump, or cantill of bread given to a beggar." Cotgr. And bribe is so used by Chaucer, C. T. 6058.

BRYBRIE, s. Beggary, evil-doing, villany; Dunbar and Kennedy, l. 63. V. BRIBOUR.
Lit. the work or conduct of a sorner, or low fellow.

BRYGATE, s. V. Brigintyne.
This appears a strange contraction of the word brigintyne, or brigantine; but it is obtained by the same process as brusoure from broudinstar. For the different steps in the process see under Browdstar.

BRYM, s. 1. Border or margin of a river, lake, or sea. V. BRIM, adj.
Lawch by a brym he gert thame ta Thair herbry, &c.
Barbour, xiv. 339, Camb. MS.
Edin. MS. has by a bourne, by a burn.

2. River, lake, flood; Henryson, Paddok and Mous, l. 38.
In M. E. brim, brym, has sometimes the first meaning; but oftener it implies the surf or surge of the sea; and sometimes, the sea, ocean, flood.

BRYNT, pret. and part. pt. Burnt; Burgh Lawis, ch. 50. V. BRYN.

BRYTH, BRYTH, s. A form of byrth, size, extent, burden; Burgh Recs. Aberdeen, i. 173, Sp. C. V. Byrth, birth.

BÛ, s. pl. Cattle: the term occurs in the old deeds in Orkn. and Shetl. Norw. bu, id.

To BU, BUE, BOO, v. n. To low, bellow; to imitate the cry of cattle; to utter a loud long inarticulate sound as a call, or for the purpose of terrifying; also, to speak in a loud monotonous tone and to little purpose, as, "He boo'd awa' for an hour, an' tell'd us nathing." Addit. to BU, BUE.

Bu, BUE, BOO, s. A coll. name for a bull,—a cow being called a bu-lady; a bellow, a low, a loud long inarticulate sound; also, short for bu-cow, boo-man, bugaboo, and as a general name for an object of terror. Addit. to BU, BOO.

BU-COW, BU-KOW, BOO-COW, BOO-MAN, BOO, s. Names for that great terror of infancy, the roaring monster that finds out and carries of bad children, and devours them in darkness. Addit. to BU-KOW, BU.

The first term is lit. the roaring terror, goblin, or monster; the second implies the same being, just as the bad man implies the devil; and the third term is a shorteued form of these names.
The roaring monster, or monster that roars for his prey, is invoked by foolish parents and nurses to terrify obstinate crying children; but, as stated in DICT. bu-ko o and bu are applied in a general sense to any scarecrow or object of terror. The dread monster, however, though a creation of mothers and nurses, was probably suggested by the Bible description of the devil. These names are as well known and as much used in the North of Eng. as they are in Scot. V. Brockett's Gloss.

BUIL, s. A division or stall in a stable or byre; also, a sheepfold, a byre; Shetl.

To BUIL, v. a. To house cattle; to drive cows into a byre, or sheep into a fold; Ibid.

To BULWAVER, v. n. To go astray like cattle; Ibid.

BUC-HORN, s. A goat-horn; a musical instrument much favoured by shepherds in olden times. Prob. the same as Ramsay called Stock-and-horn, q. v. Compl. Scot., p. 42, E. E. T. S.

In the Gloss. to the Compl. Dr. Murray renders this term *buckhorn*, without explanation. The passage referred to mentions the *buc-horn* as a mnsical instrument; and a similar passage in p. 65 evidently refers to the same instrument as "maid of ane gait horne." For a description of this instrument, V. STOCK-AND-HORN, and CORN-PIPE.

To BUCK, BUCKWORK, *v. a.* To break or pound ore for smelting. Addit. to BUCK.

BUCKER, BUKKER, *s.* An instrument like a causewayer's dumper or dolly, used by miners for breaking or crushing ores.

BUCKERAR, BUCKHERRAR, BUCKKERER, *s.* One who breaks metal with a bucker or dumper.

"Waschers with the seiff, *Buckeraris* or breakers of mettell," etc. Early Records of Mining in Scotland, p. 143.
These terms were used in the mining districts of England also. V. Derbyshire Lead-mining Terms, Eng. Dial. Soc.

BUCKBEARD, *s.* A kind of whitish or grey lichen found growing on rocks on the edge of woods, generally near water. Gall., Ayrs.

This growth, which is named from its resemblance to the beard of a buck, "is often seen in the form of a wine-glass, or inverted cone, and looks very beautiful. It is not used now-a-days for any thing, but anciently the witches found it a useful ingredient in a charm mixture." Gall. Encycl.

BUCKIES, BUCKIBERRIES, *s. pl.* Name given to the fruit of the brier in the South and West of S.

Dan. *bukke*, Sw. *bocka*, Du. *bukken*, to bow, bend, or swe'l out.
"There are three species of *buckiberries* in the country: a long green kind, good to eat, grows on lofty bushes; another much like them, but grows on higher bushes, and never ripens well; and a third kind, about the size of a sloe, and of the same colour, which grows on a dwarfish brier, thought to be somewhat poisonous." Gall. Encycl.

BUCKSKIN, *s.* Lit. a kind of leather made from the skins of bucks: but the term was used as a name for a soldier in the American army during the War of Independence, and was afterwards applied to American settlers or planters.

Cornwallis fought as lang's he dought,
Au' did the *buckskins* claw, man.
    Burns, When Guilford Good.

—— I'se hae sportin' by an' by
For my gowd guinea;
Tho' I should herd the *Buckskin* kye
For't in Virginia.
    Ibid., Ep. to John Rankine.

"The *Buckskin Kye*," the cattle of an American planter. The meaning of the last two lines is, "Though I should be banished to the Virginia plantations on account of it." Such banishment was unfortunately too well known by Scotsmen during the times of religious persecution: but not for Burns's offence.
The prevalence of buckskin clothing in the Revolutionary army originated the names *buckskin boys* and the *buckskins*, which the British applied to the American soldiers in contempt.

BUDDILL, BUDDLE, *s.* A rocker or cradle used by miners in washing gold or silver ores.

"Buckeraris, waschers with the seiff, dressaris and wascheris with the *buddill*, wascheris with the canves, schoilmen," etc. Early Records of Mining in Scotland, p. 143.

BUDGE, BWGE, *s.* Dressed lamb or kid skins; also, lamb's fur; Accts. L. H. Treas., i. 227. V. BUGE.

BUDGEL, BUNGEL, *s.* Lit. a bag, a poke, and sometimes so used; but generally it implies a bundle, pack, budget. Prob. only corr. of *bundle*; West and South of S. V. BENJEL.

BUDIE, *s.* A basket made of straw; Shetl.

Sw. and Dan. *bod*, a store-house, magazine: Gl. Shetl. gives Dan. pro. *bodel*, a straw basket.

BUFE, BOIF, *adv.* and *prep.* Above: a contr. for *abuve*, *aboif*, q. v. Sometimes used as a *s.* as, *fra bufe*, from above, Henryson, Salutation of the Virgin, l. 20.

A.-S. *dbufan*, above: compounded of *an*, on; *be*, by; and *ufan*, upward. The form *be-u/an* occurs in the laws of Æthelstan. V. Skeat's Etym. Dict.

BUFFEL STUIL, *s.* Prob. a corr. of Buffet-Stool, q. v.; Burgh Recs. Edin., iv. 540.

BUGE STAFF, BUGH STAFF, *s.* A pike staff; a pike, halbert, or light spear.

". . . and to the said Johne Simple a bed a *buge staff* price vj s viij d," etc. Acta Dom. Aud., 16 Oct., 1483, p. 123.
"Item, gevin to a man in Edinburgh at the Kingis commande, xiij° Augusti [1473], for the couering of *bugh staffis*, xij s." Accts. L. H. Treas., i. 43, Dickson.
Fr. *vouge*. "a hunting or hunter's staffe; a boares speare." Cotgr.

BUGHT, BUCHT, *s.* A bend, curvature, fold, tangle; an enclosure, a pen or fold for sheep; also a cave or hollow among rocks used for the same purpose. V. BOUCHT.

To BUGHT, BUCHT, *v. a.* To bend, fold, enclose, tangle; to pen or fold sheep. Addit. to BOUCHT, *v.*

BUGHTIN-TIME, BUCHTIN-TIME, *s.* V. BOUCHTING-TIME.

BUGILL, *s.* An ox, draught-ox; Kingis Quair, st. 157, Henryson, Parl. Beistes, l. 106.

O. Fr. *bugle*, a wild ox; 'from Lat. *buculus*, a bullock, dimin. of *bos*, an ox or cow.

BUGRIE, *s.* Sodomy.

BUGRIST, *s.* A vile lewd person, Sodomite: "*bugrist* abhominabile," Dunbar and Kennedy, l. 526.
O. Fr. "*bougrerie*, buggerie, Sodomie ;" Cotgr.

To BUIK, and BUIKIN. V. *Book, Booking.*

BUIRD, BURD, *s.* A bord or border, edging; braid, brading; also, embroidery; Court of Venus, i. 119. V. BORD.

BUIRDING, BUIRDIN, *s.* Boards, covering of boards; as, "the *buirdin* o' the rufe," "the shop was jist a run up o' *buirding* ;" West of S. V. BURD.

BUIRDLY, *adj.* V. BURDLY.

BUIT, BUTE, BUT, *s.* Boot, advantage, profit; hence, help, amends; na *buit*, no help for it, nothing better, no amends, no profit.
I counsall thee mak vertew of ane neid :—
Their was na *buit*, bot furth with thame scho yeid.
Henryson, Testament of Cresseid, l. 481.
A.-S. *bót*, help, amends ; hence *bétan*, to help ; and cf. *bet*, better.

To BUIT, BUTE, *v. a.* To profit, advantage, help, assist, amend ; " Quha sall me *bute* ?" Henryson, Lyoun and Mous, l. 136.
To buit, E. *to boot*, as used in bargain making, is not a *v.*, as some have stated ; it means "for an advantage or profit ;" hence, " in addition, over and above."

BUIT, *part. pt.* Bowed, decked with bows of ribbon.
Her goun sukl be of all guidnes,
Begareit with fresche bewtie,
Buit with rubanis of richtausnes,
And persewit with prosperitie.
Bann. MS., fol. 228 b ; p. 657, Hunt. C.

BUK, BUCKRAME, BUKRAM, BWKRAM, *s.* Buckram, a kind of cloth ; Accts. L. H. Treas., i. 37, 188, 203, Dickson ; Halyburton's Ledger.
It has been supposed by some that this cloth was originally made of goat's hair ; but, at a very early period it appears to have been made of fine cotton, and worn only by persons of rank. Sir Robert Cooke, vicar of Hagley, bequeathed in 1537, "a *bocram* shert" and "a payer of *bocram* shettis." (Bury Wills, p. 129, Camd. Soc.). In later times the cloth appears to have been made of flax, and therefrom it was less esteemed.
Fr. *bougran*, contse stiffened stuff with open interstices ; from It. *bucherare*, to perforate. Others derive it from *boc*, a goat; hence, *buckram* is stuff made of goat's hair. V. Diez, Rom. Dict.

BUKKIE, BUKKY, *s.* V. BUCKIE.

BULB, BULBOCH, *s.* A disease among sheep ; when infected, they drink water until they swell—become like a bulb—and burst, Gall. Encycl.

BULE, pl. BULIS, *s.* V. BOUL.

BULLACE, BULLISTER, *s.* A large sloe, wild plum ; West of S.

The name is also applied to the bush on which this fruit grows ; O. Fr. *bellocier*, id. Cotgr., *belloce*, Roq.

BULLION, *s.* A name for gold or silver lace ; but when used in pl. *bulliones*, it generally means little balls, knobs, or bosses of gold or silver for ornamenting articles of dress, &c.
"*Bulliones* for purses, the groce contening tuelf dozen," etc. Halyburton's Ledger, p. 293.
Fr. *bouillon*, from L. Lat. *bullio, bulliona*, a mass of gold or silver ; Du Cange. In its second meaning, the term may be derived from Lat. *bulla*, a boss.

BUMMLE, *v.* and *s.* A corr. of *bungle*, botch, blunder, with all its varieties of application ; West and North of S.

BUM-PIPE, *s.* A vulgar name for the plant Dandelion ; prob. because its long tubular flower-stalks are made into *bum-pipes* by children. Syn. *Pisstebed*, corresponding to the French name *Pissenlit*.

BUMPKIN BRAWLY. An old song: also the tune of the song, or the dance to which that tune is played, Gall.
The song is :—
Wha learn'd you to dance,
You to dance, you to dance,
Wha learn'd you to dance—
A country bumpkin brawly ?
My mither learn'd me when I was young,
When I was young, when I was young,
My mither learn'd me when I was young,
The country bumpkin brawly. .
The tune of this song is always played to the dance which ends a ball in the South of S. Words, tune, and dance are almost the same as in the "*Cushion*" or "*Babity Bowster.*"

BUNDIN, BUNDYN, *part. pt.* Bound ; Barbour, v. 300, vii. 115 : A.-S. *bindan.*

BUNEUCII, BUNNEUCH, BUNYEUCH, *s.* Diarrhœn: generally used in the pl. *buneuchs*, purgings. V. BUNYOCH.

BUNJEL, BUNYED, *s.* A burden of straw, hay, or fern, Gall.: prob. a corr. of *Bundle.*

BUNKER, BUNKART, *s.* 1. A rough heap of stones or refuse ; Fife, Banff.

2. A term in golfing, applied to a sand-pit or a patch of rough stony ground. A ball in such a position is said to be *bunkered.*

BUNNIS, *s.* Pl. of BUN, a cask, q. v.

BUNSE, BUNCH, *s.* Applied to a girl or young woman who is squat and corpulent, Gall., Ayrs. V. BUNCH, *v.*

To BUNT, *v. n.* To cast about, cater, beg,. work.
Tho' I was born armless, an' aye unco wee,
My Maggie was muckle an' *bunted* for me.
James Ballantine, Naggy and Willie, s. 1.

Gael. *buinnig*, to win, gain, acquire ; from *buin*, to treat, bargain, or take away.

BUOCK, *s.* A pimple ; Orkn.
Icel. *bogna*, to become curved or bent ; allied to *bogi*, a bow ; A.-S. *boga*, Ger. *bogen*.

BUR, BURE, *pret.* 1. Bore, carried ; *bur the flour*, was the loveliest, lit. carried off the prize. Henryson, The Bludy Serk, l. 9. A.-S. *beran*.

Other forms of this expression are *bure the bell*, drawn from the custom of silver bells as the prize at races ; and *bure the gre*, won or held the highest place, drawn from the custom of seating the honourable guest on the dais, which rose a step or two above the level of the floor.

2. Pressed, forced, drove ; *bur thame bakwart*, drove them back ; Houlate, l. 498, Bann. MS.

To **BURBLE, BURBEL,** *v. n.* To bubble, boil, or boil, like water from a spring ; to purl. West of S. Add. to BURBLE, q. v.
Burbyll, Prompt. Parv. ; *burbly*, bubbling, Lydgate, Minor Poems, p. 181.

BURBLE, BURBEL, *s.* A bell or bubble on water ; a purl, purling, Ibid.

BURD, *s.* A var. of *bourd*, meaning a pleasant device, a bit of flattery. Addit. to BOURD.

Qubilk was that thay wald Venus make content
De sum new *burd*, and hir plesour fulfill.
Court of Venus, iv. 418.

BURD, BWRD, *s.* Board, maintenance ; Accts. L. H. Treas., i. 180. Dickson. Addit. to BURD.

BURD ALEXANDER, *s.* V. BORD ALEXANDER.

BUREIT, *part. pt.* A corrupt form of *Beryit*, or *Beriet*, buried ; Houlate, l. 530, Bann. MS. ; the Asloan MS. has *Beryit*.

BURELIE, *adj.* V. BURDLY, BURLY.

The later form *burly* came to mean merely large and strong : the idea of stateliness being dropped, as, "He's a *burly* chap." In this sense it was used by Henryson, in his "Ressoning betwixt Aige and Yowth," l. 20, "with breist *burly* and braid."

BURGANDYNE, *s.* A brigandine ; Burgh Recs. Edinburgh, 10 Aug., 1498. V. *Brigintyne*.

BURGH AND LAND. Town and country ; Dunbar. V. LAND.

The country district of a parish is still called the *landwart* district.

BURGH-GREVE, BUROW-GREFF, BUROW-GREYFF, *s.* A magistrate of a burgh.
"The *burow-greff* may nocht thruch rycht do na man to aithe for brekyn of assyse, bot gif ony man plenyeis hym of othir." Burgh Laws, ch. 38.

The form *borow-greff* is also used in this old law book. A.-S. *burh*, *burg*, a fort, from *beorgan*, to protect ; and *geréfa*, a steward, a bailiff.

BURIALL BEERE, *s.* Prob. an errat. for *Buriall-lare*. V. next entry.

"—— there can be nothing more incompatible nor the same thing to be made an *buriall-beere*, and to remain a kirk both at once," &c. Blame of Kirkburiall, ch. xvii.

BURIALL-LARE, *s.* Burial-place, last resting-place, grave. V. LARE.

"—— blessed with the bed-fellowship of Jesus in our *buriall lare.*" Ibid., ch. viii.

BURNBECKER, *s.* A name given to the *water-ousel*, and also to the *water-wagtail*.

"This bird is a frequenter of burns or streams of water ; it keeps its body in continual motion, *beckbecking* : hence the name *burnbecker*." Gall. Encycl.

BURNMEN, *s. pl.* Water-carriers ; also called *burn-leaders* : men who carried water from burns and wells to supply the brewers, dyers, skinners, &c., in a manufacturing town. Burgh Recs. Edin., 4 May, 1580.

The entry referred to records one of many enactments of the magistrates of Edinburgh forbidding the *burnmen* or *burn leaders* to take water from the public wells during a time of drought.

The record informs us that a considerable number of women made their living by carrying water to the inhabitants : they are called *wemen watter bereris*. After forbidding the water-carriers, both men and women, to take water from the wells, it discharges "the women of the said tred in all tymes heirafter," and commands "the nychtbouris to scrue thame selffis be that feyit and boushald scruandis as thai sall half ado."

To **BURN NITS.** This is one of the superstitious customs observed on Hallowe'en, and greatly favoured by the younger members of the company convened for the occasion. See Burns, Hallowe'en, s. 7-10.

Not the least attraction of this charm is that the performers can divine regarding the future of their friends as well as regarding their own. And the performance of the charm often occasions a display of feelings which interested parties know how to read, and on which much future speculation may be founded. The charm is worked thus :—The party places two nuts in the fire, one after the other, naming (aloud or in secret) the lad and lass to each particular nut as it is placed ; and according as the nuts burn quietly together, or start aside from each other, so will the course and issue of the courtship of the persons represented be. V. Burns, Hallowe'en, note to st. 7.

BUROWAGE, BURRAIGE, *s.* and *adj.* V. under *Borow*.

BURREAW, BURRIAWE, BURREOUR, *s.* V. BURIO.

BURRO RUDIS. V. BURGH ROODS.

BURROWSTOUN, BURRATOUN, s. V. BORROWSTOUN.

BURSE, BURS, BURSS, s. Lit. a purse, and often so applied; but generally used as short for a bursary for a student; Burgh Recs. Aberd., ii. 365, 381. V. BURSARY.

BURSAR, BURSOUR, s. A purser, treasurer, receiver of monies collected; Ibid., i. 123. Addit. to BURSAR.

BURSEN KIRN, s. Lit. a bursten kirn: harvesting accomplished with great labour and difficulty.

"Thus, if the last of the crop cannot be got cut by the shearers for all they can work until night be set in, then they say they have had a bursen kirn; they have burst themselves almost before they got the last cut or girn shorn." Gall. Encycl.

To BUSH, BUSH UP, v. a. and n. To move nimbly about, work heartily; also, to make clean and tidy, brighten up: in the latter sense, bush up is generally used; West of S.

This term is used much like E. push; and is prob., like buss, another form of busk, q. v.

BUSING-STANE, BUSIN-STANE, s. The stone set up as a partition between cows in a byre: lit. stalling stone. "You twa wad need a busin-stane atween ye:" addressed to quarrelsome children. West of S. V. BUSE.

In Lanarkshire this partition is called a weir-buse, q. v.

To BUSK FLIES. To dress fly hooks. V. To BUSK HUKES.

BUSKY, BUSKIE, adj. Bushy; poet. form of Bussie, q. v. E. bosky. V. under BUSS.

BUSPIKAR, BOYSPIKAR, BYSPIKAR, s. A large spike-nail, used in ship-building. Accts. L. H. Treas., i. 253, 334, 357.

Du. buis, a small ship, and spijker, a nail.

BUSSOME, BISSOUME, s. Besom, broom; pron. buzzom, bizzum.

And Jonet the weido on ane bussome rydand.
Dunbar, Birth of Antichrist, l. 34.

A.-S. besma, besem, Du. bezem, Ger. besen, a broom, a rod. "The original sense seems to have been a rod; or perhaps a collection of twigs or rods." Skeat, Etym. Dict.

BUT, BOUT, s, V. BAT, Bot.

BUT, BWTE, s. Bute; a Scottish pursuivant, who took his designation from the island of Bute. Pron. buit.

"Item, the xj day of Nouember, in Lythqus, to But to pas to Berwyk with lettores, xxiiij s." Accts. L. H. Treas., i. 124.

BUT AND BEN, adv. In the same entry, or, on the same landing, of a dwelling house; in opposite sides of the same entry or landing; as, "Ken her! we leeve but an' ben wi' ither;" Clydes. Addit. under BUT.

BUTE, s. and v. Advantage, profit. V. Buit.

BUTHIS, s. pl. Booths, shops; Burgh Laws. V. BOTHE.

BUTHMAN, s. The keeper of a booth or covered stall, a shopkeeper; Dunbar, Tailyeour and Sowtar, l. 19.

BUTIS, s. pl. Butis of leather, pieces of tanned leather. V. under BUTT.

BUTTEREGE, BUTTRISH, s. A buttress; Burgh Rec. Edin., iii. 35, 36; pl. buttereges, and in West of S. pron. buttrishes.

O. Fr. bouteretz, bouterets, buttresses; from bouter, to thrust. In discussing the origin of the term buttress, Prof. Skeat says, with reference to some quotations by Wedgwood, "It thus appears that b..ttress=bouterets, and is really a plural! The Fr. plural suffix -ez or -ets was mistaken, in English, for the commoner Fr. suffix -esse, Eng.-ess." Suppl. Etym. Dict., p. 789.

BUTTRIE, s. Lit. the place for butts or bottles. The place or passage for the buckets in a draw-well; also, the buckets and the apparatus for working them.

The Cabok may be callit covetyce,
Qnhilk blomis braid in mony mannis ee,
Wa worth the well of that wickit vyce;
For it is all hot frand and fantasie,
Dryvand ilk man to leip in the buttrie,
That dounwart drawis unto the pane of hell.
Christ keip all Christianis from that wickit Well.
Henryson, The Fox and Wolf, l. 222.

In his Gloss. to Henryson Dr. Laing renders buttrie, "scullery, pantry;" which is wrong. In the fable of "The Uplandis Mous" and "The Burges Mous," l. 44, the term is certainly so applied; but here the application is quite different, and must be either to the moveable buckets or to the passage in which they move; for all the references are to a draw-well and the working of the buckets. Besides, the term buttrie, butterie, like all Fr. words so terminating, is capable of various applications; like boucherie, which may mean the trade of a butcher, a butcher's shop, stall, or stock, a slaughter-house, or indiscriminate slaughter. O. Fr. boute, Fr. botte, a cask; from which bouteille, a bottle, a hollow vessel, bouteillerie, a collection of such vessels, a place for storing them, for making or selling them, a cupboard or a table to set them on; and thence M. E. botelerie, E. buttery, with various applications.

BUTTS, BUTTIS. A pair of buttis, the distance between the two targets set up for the practice of archery, a bow-shot, bow-draught; Burgh Records Aberd., ii. 324.

Butt is, in the first place, the target itself; but

when archery was more than a genteel pastime, distance was generally reckoned in this manner. The record ref rred to above also gives "distant thairfra *ane halff pair of buttis* or thairby"; and farther on, "*within ane quarter pair of buttis* or thairby." Pp. 324-325. Addit. to BUTT.

BUYR, *pret.* Bore. V. BUIRE.

BUYT-TREIS, BUIT-TREES, *s. pl.* Boot-trees, or lasts for boots; Burgh Recs. Aberdeen, i. 176.

BWGE, *s.* V. BUGE.

BWNTE, *s.* Goodness; Barbour, x. 294. A corr. form of *bovnte*, in Camb. MS.; Edin. MS. has *bounte*.

BYKIR, BYKKIR, BYKKYR, BYKYR, *s.* and *v.* V. BICKER.

BYKNYS, *s. pl.* Beacons for guiding vessels into harbour or past a dangerous coast.

". . . for the outtaking of the greit stanis in the hevin and redding of the channell betuix the *bykuys.*" Burgh Recs. Edinburgh, 31 May, 1504.

A.-S. *bedcen,* a sign, a nod.

BYLAND, *s.* Lit., a side land, adjoining land; and in this sense it is still used; also, a portion of land jutting out into the sea, a peninsula.

"Ardrossan Castell in respect it is situated on a swelling knope of a rock running from a toung of land advancing from the maine land in the sea, and almost environed with the same; for *Ross* in the ancient Brittish tounge signifies a *byland* or peninsula." Timothy Pout, MS. in Advocates Library, written about 1620.

This term is given in Halliwell's Dict. with a note that it was probably introduced by Harrison in his Descriptione of Britaine, which was published in 1577. This may be correct as regards the meaning *peninsula*; but in the sense of *out*-land, additional or side-l nd, the term is certainly very much older. It is a common name in the upland districts of the West and South of S. for those patches of marsh or bog land from which the farmer is allowed to cut hay for his cattle : such land being *by,* beside or additional to, the farm proper.

BYLE, BILE, *s.* A boil, a sore; pl. *bylis,* pimples, pustules, marks of leprosy; Henryson, Test. Cres., l. 395.

The same forms are used in Piers Plowman. A.-S. *byl, by'le,* Du. *buil, bule,* Dan. *byld,* a blain, blister.

BYMARK, *s.* Private mark, merchant or trade mark: also, emblem, arms, motto.

". . . and ilk ane of thair craftis to hane thair *bymarkis* on thair awin bannaris that thai m ik principale oust vpoun for the keiping of the samyn;" etc. Burgh. Rec. Edinburgh, 15 May, 1509.

BYNALL, *s.* A tall lame man, Gall. Encycl.

BY-NAME, BYE-NAME, *s.* Originally the epithet to one's name, which almost every one had; this was common on both sides of the border. The term now means a nickname, and is so used from Shetland to the Humber. Syn. *to-name.*

In his Gloss. of North Country Words, Brockett gives the following example of *by-names* from Maitland's Complaynt. Of the Liddesdale thieves he says:

Ilk ane of thame has ane to-name
Will of the Lawis,
Hab of the Schawis,
To make thair wawis
They think na schame.

The *by-name* was an absolute necessity in clans, fishing villages, &c , where there were many persons of the same name. I remember an instance of a grandfather, his son, and three grandsons, each named Tam Wylie, who were usually spoken of as Auld Tam, and Wee Tam, Tailor Tam, Nailer Tam, and Bowlie Tam. To the boys of my time these were the persons' nicknames ; but to our parents and the older people the *by-names* were simply distinctive.

BYND, BYNDE, *s.* A bundle or a packet of a certain size, or fixed number of articles; a *bynd* of skins containing twenty-four skins. Addit. to BIND.

". . . of a *bynde* of skynnys of schorlyng, that is to say twenty four, a penny," etc. Assize of Petty Customs, ch. 5.

BYNT, *s.* Bent, bent-grass; also the common or waste land on which it grows; Burgh Rec. Prestwick, 9 Oct., 1525. V. BENT, *Bent-Siluer.*

BY-ORDINAR, BY-ORD'NAR, *adj.* Extraordinary, far above common; Clydes. V. *Anordinar, Unordinar.*

Wi' a face like the moon, sober, sonsy, and douce,
And a back, for it's breadth, like the side o' a house,
'Tweel, I'm unco ta'en up wi't, they mak' a' sae plain :—
He's just a town's talk—he's n *by-ord'nar* wean.
Wm. Miller, The Wonderfu' Wean, Whistle Binkie, ii. 316.

BY-PUT, BY-PIT, *s.* A temporary substitute, a pretence; also, a slight repast before meal-time; S.

BYRNE-JRNE, BYRN-AIRN, *s.* A burning or hot iron; an iron for branding goods, cattle, criminals. V. BIRN, BURN-AIRN.

". . and ane *byrne-jrne* to be put vpone thair chekis that brukis ony of the *aidis statutis,*" &c. Burgh Recs. Aberdeen, 27 July, 1529. Sp. C.

BYRNYS, *s. pl.* Breastplates. V. BIRNIE.

BYRTHEN, BYRTHENE, BYRTHING, BYRDING, BYRTH, BYRTHT, BYRN, *s.* A burden: also burden, as applied to capacity of vessels, Burgh Recs. Aberdeen, i. 173. V. BIRTH, BIRDING.

BYRTHENSAK, *s.* 1. Theft of goods which the thief could carry off on his shoulder.

2. A court for the trial of such cases of theft: the baronial right to hold such courts; Scotch Leg. Antiq., p. 246. Addit. to BERTHINSEK.

Jamieson's etym. of this term is incorrect: should be A.-S. *byrthen*, a burden, a load carried, and *sacu*, cause, dispute, law-suit. From *sacu* comes E. *sake*.

BYRYNS, BYRYNNIS, *s. pl.* V. BYRUNIS.

BYSMARE, BYSMER, *s.* Reproach, dishonour: hence applied to a lewd or immoral person. Addit. to BISMARE.

BYSPIKAR, BOYSPIKAR, *s.* V. BUSPIKAR.

BYSS, BUSS, BYSSIE, *s.* Bedding for cattle, straw, etc.; also, the soft, dry material with which a bird's nest is lined; Shetl., Orkn.

BY-THAN, BITHAN, *adv.* By that time, before that time, then; as, "Next year! I may be dead *by-than.*"

By then is a common phrase throughout England; and its pron. varies according to the dialect used.

BY-TIME, *s.* Odd time, odd hours, intervals of leisure; as, "I've aye a book for *by-time*; "At a *by-time,*" now and then, occasionally, S.

C.

CAAR, CARRIE, *adj.* and *s.* Left, left-handed; a person who is left-handed; Ayrs. V. CAIR, KER.

Caar, carrie, and *carrie-handit* are still in use; also the synon. *kippie.*
Gael. *caerr,* left.

CABIL-STOK, CAIPSTOK, *s.* A capstan, Compl. Scot., p. 40, E.E.T.S., Burgh Recs. Edin., ii. 61.

The form *caipstok* of the Edin. Recs. is a corr. of *caibstok,* a shortened form of *cabil-stok,* i.e., the *stock* or holding frame for the *cable.*

CACH, *s.* The game of tennis, or a game similar to it. V. CAITCHE.

"Item, that samyn day [10th May, 1496], in Struielin, to the King to play at the *cach* vi li. x s." Accts. L. H. Treas., i. 275. Dickson.
This game was a favourite amusement in the time of James IV. and James V.; and the place where it was played was called the *cachpule.* Ibid., Gl.

CACKER, *s.* V. *Calker, Cauker.*

CA'D, *pret.* and *part. pt.* Called; as, "They ca'd him Tam." V. CALL.

CA's, *s.* and *v.* Calls; as, "He *ca's* in every Friday." V. CALL.

Necessity's demands and *ca's*
War very gleg.
Alex. Wilson, The Insulted Pedlar, s. 9.

To CADGE, CAGE, *v. a.* To hawk or peddle wares; to carry bundles or loads; also, to go about from place to place collecting articles for sale, as eggs, butter, poultry, &c. Addit. to CADGE, CACHE.

CADGED, *adj.* Used in all the senses given above.

CADGER, CAGEAR, *s.* One who hawks peddles, carries, or collects, as stated above; a porter, a messenger; Accts. L. H. Treas., i. 252.

Dr. Jamieson's statement that *cadger* properly denotes a fish carrier, is certainly incorrect, or applies to certain districts only.

CADGING, *part.* and *s.* Used in all the senses given above.

CADGER-POWNIE'S DEATH. Death through starvation, or through neglect and starvation.

Then up I gat, an' awoor an aith,
Tho' I should pawn my pleugh and graith,
Or die a *cadger pownie's death*
At some dyke back,
A pint an' gill I'd gie them baith
To hear your crack.
Burns to Lapraik, st. 7.

CADIE, CADDIE, CAD, *s.* 1. The name given to the lad who carries the clubs of a golf-player, and, if necessary, gives him advice regarding the game.

2. A boy's cap; generally applied to a glengary; Renfrews., Lanarks. Addit. to CADIE.

CADIOUM, CADDIOUM, *s.* A cask, a barrel: generally applied to one of large size, and to a tun or vat.

". . . and viij s. and daling of thair aill, and striking out of thair *caddioum* bodoum, for the third falt." Burgh Recs. Aberdeen, i. 210, s. c.
If this is not a corr. of *caldron,* it may be from Lat. *cadus,* a cask.

CAFFUNYEIS, *s. pl.* Prob. gaiters, leggings.

"Item, that samyn day [26th January, 1496] payit to Thom Home for butis, schone, pantovinis, and *caffunzeis*, tane to the King agane Zule; that is to say, a pare of butis, thre pare of singil solit schone, ij pare of *caffunzeis*, a pare of pantovinis, a pare of doubil solit schone, and ij pare of *caffunzeis* to thaim, xxix a. vj d." Accts. L. H. Treas., i. 311. Dickson.
Gael. *calpa*, calf of the leg, pl. *calpannan*; similar to the E. *leg, leggings*. Another form is *calpa na coise*.

CAGEAR, *s*. A cadger. V. under *Cadge*.

To CAGHT, CAUCHT, CAUGHT, CHAWCHT, CACHT, *v. r*. To purchase, buy; pret. and part. pt. same as pres. A corr. of *caft, coft*.
For Conyie ye may *chawcht* hir.
    Alex. Scott, Wantoun Wemen, st. 4.

CAGIELIE, CAGIE, *adj*. Fondly, lovingly, jocosely; Whistle Binkie, ii. 238. V. CAIGIE.

CAIN, *s*. V. CANE.

CAIN, KEN, *s*. A denomination of weight used for cheese, equal to 300 stone; also, the quantity of cheese made by a farmer during one season. West of S.
"It is not uncommon in Ayrshire for a farmer's wife and one female servant, besides milking the cows, washing clothes, etc., etc., to make in one summer a *ken* of cheese; a *ken* consists of 300 stone, trone weight." Ure's Agriculture in Dumbarton, pp. 76-77.
Gael. *cinneas*, growth, produce: from *cinn, cinnich*, to grow, increase, multiply; M'Leod & Dewar.

CAIP, CAPE, *s*. A cope, an ecclesiastical vestment. Errat. in DICT.
The examples given by Jamieson refer to this vestment, not to the common *cape* or short mantle.

CAIPSTOK, *s*. V. CABIL-STOK.

CAIRFULL, *adj*. Sad, sorrowful, mournful, anxious, melancholy; Douglas, Virgil, vi., ch. 7; Henryson, Test. Cres., l. 310.
A.-S. *caru, cearu*, sorrow, care, Grein; Goth. *kara*, sorrow.

CAIRSAY, *s*. A woollen stuff. V. KERSEY.

CAIS, KAIS, *s. pl*. Jackdaws. V. KAY.

CAKE FIDDLER, CAIK FIDLER, CAYK FYDLAR, *s*. Lit. a cake-wheedler, one who works or obliges for the gain it brings, a self-seeker, a parasite: Douglas. V. CAIK FUMLER.
This term is given in DICT. as *caik-fumler*, which is found to be a misreading of *caik fidler*. V. Small's Ed. of Douglas, iv. 248. *Fiddling* is still used for fawning, feigning work or kindness, &c., in order to gain an end; and *feedlin, fidlin*, is the Aberdeenshire pron. of *wheedling*.

To CALANGE, CALENGE, CALLANGE, *v. a*. To claim, challenge, accuse, speak against, revile. Same as *Challange*, q. v.
(Sup.) I

CALANYE, CALANYEAR, CALANYOUR, *s*. V. under *Chalange*.

CALANYE, CALENYE, CALLANYE, CALLENYE, *s*. Same as *Chalange*, q. v. Pl. *cullenyeis*, Halyburton's Ledger, p. 268.
Both *v*. and *s*. have very many applications, but as law terms their usual form is *Chalange, Challange*, q. v. The form *Calanye* or *Callenye*, generally implies evil speaking, false charges.

To CALCUL, CALCULD, *v. a*. To calculate; pret. and part. pt. *calculd*; Rob Stene's Dream, p. 27.

CALDWAR, CALDWARD, CALWART, *adj*. Coldish, somewhat cold; West of S., Shetl. V. CALD.

CALF, *s*. Chaff; Henryson, Preiching of the Swallow, l. 233. V. CAFF.

CALF, *s*. and *adj*. Infield grass, enclosed or protected pasture; generally it means grass, pasture, as in the phrase, *crop and calf*, crop and grass. V. CALF-SOD, CALF-WARD.
O man! but mercie, quhat is in thy thocht!—
Thow has aneuch: the pure husband richt nocht
Bot croip and *calf* npon ane clout of land.
    Henryson, Wolf and Lamb, l. 123.

To CALF, CALFET, CALFIN, CALFIND, *v. a*. To caulk, close; *calf, calfet*, Sempill Ballates, p. 230; *calfin, calfind*, Accts. L. Treas., i. 378. V. COLF.
These are shortened forms of Fr. *calfater*. In Bann. MS. Sempill's poem has *calf*, afterwards altered to *calfèd*. V. Hunterian Club Ed., p. 349.

CALFATER, CALFUTER, *s*. A caulker.

CALIMANCO, *s*. A kind of cloth; a corr. of Lat. *camelaucum*; Halyburton's Ledger, p. 327.
The term occurs in the list of "Customs, &c., in 1612," under the sect. "*wroyht silk*" goods.

CALK, CAULK, CAUK, *s*. Chalk; also, a chalk mark. Addit. to CAWK.

To CALK, CAULK, CAUK, *v. a*. To chalk, to mark with chalk, also, to write with it.
The cunnar or taster having valued the ale shall "*calk* apoun a dur alsmony scoris with *calk* as the galoun salbe salde of the saide aile." Burgh Recs. Prestwick, p. 17. Maitland Club Series.

To CALK, CAUK, CAWK, CALKER, CAUKER, *v. a*. To fix iron plates or guards on the heels of boots or shoes, to point or sharpen horse-shoes to prevent slipping during frost.
A.-S. *calc*, a shoe, borrowed from Lat. *calceus*, a der. of *calx*, the heel; *calcare*, to tramp, tread, press or press out by means of treading on; hence, the idea of pressing or driving home, ramming, cramming, &c., which is implied in *calking* the seams of a ship, the plates of a boiler, &c.
Both Irish and Gael. have *calc*, to calk, press, &c.;

but prob. like the A.-S., adopted from the Lat.; certainly, in neither case is the term derived from the Celtic word for the *heel*.

CALK, CAUK, CAWK, *s.* *Calking;* a sharpening of a horse's shoes on account of frost; as, "I man gie the horse a *calk* the day." The form *calking* is also used.

CALKER, CAUKER, CAWKER, *s.* 1. An iron plate or guard for the heel of a boot or shoe.

2. One who makes those iron heel-plates, a maker or sharpener of horse shoes, also, a nailer or maker of iron furnishings for shoemakers.

Calk and *calker* are also used in their ordinary E. meanings. And in Dumfries, the name *calker* or *cauker* is applied to a country blacksmith, and to a worker in rod and plate iron; prob. because a large portion of his work is in connection with shoes for man and horse.

CALLENYE, CALLANYE. V. under *Chalange*.

CALLET, *s.* A wench, jade, doxy, trull, drab, scold, &c.; a term of contempt. Particular meanings are represented by the adj. prefixed. Cf. Gael. *caile*.

I'm as happy with my wallet, my bottle, and my *callet*,
As when I used in scarlet to follow the drum.
Burns, Jolly Beggars.

Here's our ragged brats and *callets!*
Ibid.

The term is common in North of Eng. V. Brockett's Gloss. It was used also by Skelton and Shakespeare.

To **CALLOW**, *v. n.* To calve, Shetl. V. *Calve*.

CALPE, CALPES, CALPICH, *s.* V. CAUPE.

CALSHES, *s.* A portion of dress for boys. For younger boys it is a sort of slip-dress buttoned behind, forming jacket and trousers; for older boys it forms vest and trousers, and a jacket is worn above.

The taylors too maun fung awa',
Or else they'll bar'ly mak it;
For bien fo'ks callans maun be braw,
Wi' *calshes* an' a jacket.
Wat. Watson, Chryston Fair, st. 3.

O. Fr. *calçons, calsons,* close linen breeches, under slops.

CALSIE, CALSAY, *s.* and *v.* V. CAUSE.

CALWE, CALI, CAWE, CAW, *s.* A calf, West of S. V. CA'.

Used also as a *v.*: *cawe* and *caw* are the most common forms, prob. because they best represent the pron.; as, "The coo *caved* the day." *Callow* is the form used in Shetl.

Pl. *calwis, cawes, caws, caus:* all these forms occur in the Burgh Recs. of Prestwick; also the form *kawis.*
". . . of a last of hert hydys aucht peniis, of a dakyr of hynd *calwis* thre half peniis," &c. Assize of Petty Customs, ch. 5.
". . . ony personne or personis that apprehendis *caws* within his corne," &c. Burgh Recs. Prestwick, 15 Oct. 1554.

CA'M, CAUM, *adj.* Calm, still, low, quiet, Keep a *ca'm souch*, keep silence, say nothing.

As *ca'm*, blae, bitter frosty day.
Alex. Wilson, Rabby's Mistake, s. 2.

CAME, *s.* A comb: applied to every sort of comb natural and artificial. Not confined to a honey-comb, as given in the DICT.
In the fable, the fox addressing the cock, says,—
Your beik, your breist, your hekill, and your *came*.
Henryson, Chanteclair and the Fox, l. 58.
A.-S. *camb*, a comb or crest; Dan., Swed., and Dutch, *kam*, id.

CAMMELOIT, *s.* V. CHAMLOTHE, *Chamelet.*

CAMMES, CAMES, *s.* Canvas: not gauze, as given in DICT.
Simply forms of *cammas*, a corr. of canvas: consequently the etym. suggested is wrong.

CAMPIS, *s. pl.* Long locks, tangles, tufts; Henryson, Paddok and Mous, l. 28. In the fable of the Lyoun and the Mous, l. 10, it is misprinted *lampis* in Laing's Ed., p. 159.

O. Fr. *campoles*, tendrils, twining or twisting fibres: a dimin. from Celtic *cam*, crooked. But *campis* may be short for *camp hairs*, lit. bent hairs, spelt *campe hæris* in Allit. Poems, ed. Morris, B. 1695, and not explained.

CAMSHEUCH, CAMSHOCH, CAMSHO, *adj.* Crooked, crippled, badly shaped; and when applied to temper or disposition, surly, gurly, thrawn, cross-grained, cantankerous. Addit. to CAMSCHO.

Still used in both senses. Common in the works of Alex. Wilson, and other poets of the West of S. It occurs also in Blame of Kirkburiall, ch. xix.

CAN, CANN, *s.* An open or closed vessel of metal, earthenware, or wood, in which liquids or semi-liquids are contained, carried, or kept ready for use.

This term has a much wider range of meaning in Scot. than in Eng., and is applied to almost every sort of vessel used for holding or containing liquids of semi-liquids. For example, milk-cans, oil-cans, paint-cans, are of all sorts, sizes, and materials; and the small tubs or vessels in which workmen mix and keep their supply of plaster, lime, paste, &c., are called plaster-cans, lime-cans, paste-cans, &c.
This application of the term *can* to any vessel used for storing, carrying, or holding in readiness, has been used since the earliest times of which we have record; but, whether the term is of Teutonic or Celtic origin is still disputed. Certainly, its wide and varied applications in the West of S. agree better with Gael. *can, cann* (which range in meaning from a reservoir or vessel in general, to a cup or drinking vessel in particular), than with any of the Teut. forms of the word. It may be noted too, that in Gael., when a drinking cup is specially meant the term *canna* (like Scot. *cannie*, a little can), and its pl. *cannachan* (like Scot. and Eng. *cannikin*, drinking cups), are used.

CANARE, KANER, s. A water-bailiff.
"For intruding themselves into the fishings of the water of Findhorne and Spey and removeing of his (the Earl of Murray's) *kaneris*, and placeing of thair awne *kaneris* therein." Reg. Priv. Council, vi. 383. Prob. Gael. *ceannard*, a chief, an overseer.

CANBUS, s. A corr. or misprint of *Canvas*. In the Assisa de Talloncis, ch. 8, it is *Cannes*. Addit. to CANBUS.
Jamieson left this term unexplained, but suggested *yourd-bottles* as the meaning: which is a mistake.

CANDLEMAS KING, s. The title and honour conferred on the boy who gave the highest gratuity to the schoolmaster at Candlemas: also, the boy who so excelled. Among the girls there was a similar title and honour, viz.: Candlemas Queen. V. CANDLEMAS CROWN.

CANE, CAIN, KAIN, CAN, CHAN, s. A burden or duty paid by the occupier of land to his superior. It consisted of a fixed portion of the produce of the land. Addit. to KANE.
The definition given in the DICT. is defective, and the explanation is misleading. Indeed, only a small portion of the article is correct. But in Jamieson's day the term was not properly understood, and it is only lately that a correct idea regarding it could be formed.
The following statements by Mr. Skene, the famous Celtic scholar and historian, are perhaps the simplest and clearest that have yet been given on the subject. Having stated various forms of Cane exacted by superiors both highland and lowland, he concludes that "it consisted of a portion of the produce of the land, in grain when it was arable land, and in cattle and pigs when pasture land. It was in fact the outcome of the 'Bestighi,' or food-rent of the Irish laws, and the 'Gwestva' of the Welsh laws, paid by every occupier of land to his superior. Over the whole of Scotland, except in Lothian, it was a recognised burden upon the crown lands and upon all lands not held by feudal tenure, but it ceased as soon as the possessor of the land was feudally invested." And regarding the name of this burden he says: "The Can or Chan was so termed from the Gaelic word 'Cain,' the primary meaning of which was 'law.' It was the equivalent of the Latin word 'canon,' and like it was applied to any fixed payment exigible by law." Celtic Scotland, iii. 231.

CANNEL, CANLE, s. A candle.
. . . . a "brilliant chandelier"
Was just a girr, that frae the laft hung down
Wi' *cannels* here an' there stuck on't a' roun.
Alex. Wilson, The Spouter, l. 160.

CANNIE, CANNY, CAUNIE, adv. Slowly, gently, carefully, frugally, honestly, prudently, discreetly, &c. V. CANNY, *adj.*
The adverbial use of this word is very common in the West of Scotland, and its applications are exceedingly varied. For example, 'I canna rin noo, I hae to gang *cannie*, rale *cannie*.' 'Slip out quite *canny*.' 'The twa auld bodies live gey *cannie*' (this may mean quietly, carefully, frugally, prudently, or comfortably).

The same ideas may be expressed by, 'The twa are gey *cannie* livin' auld bodies."
Some of the illustrations of *canny* as an *adj.* in DICT. are really adverbial; V. under s. 4, 8, 10.
Of its use by our poets the following example may suffice,—
And e'en envy his blessed fate,
Wha sat sae *canny*.
Alex. Wilson, Insulted Pedlar, s. 22.
Gat tippence worth to mend her head,
When it was sair;
The wife slade *cannie* to her bed,
But ne'er spak mair.
Burns, Death and Dr. Hornbook, s. 25.

CANTEL, s. Errat. in DICT. for *Cautel*, a trick, q. v.
This misreading of *cautel* was taken from Pinkerton's version of "The Houlate," copied from the Bann. MS. It appears also in the Hunterian Club ed. of that MS. but the Asloan MS., which is followed in Dr. Laing's version of the poem, gives *cautel*.
As the sense of the passage is evident, Dr. Jamieson's definition of *cantel* is what is implied by the right word, *cautel*; but in his note of explanation and etymology he is altogether wrong.

CANTLE, CANTIL, CANTEL, s. 1. A corner, projection, ledge, slice, portion broken or cut from a mass: as, "A *cantle* o' the rock hung owre us;" "a *cantle* o' cheese."

2. The crown, ridge, sheer, dividing line; as, "the cantle o' the cawsey," i.e., the line from which the causeway *cants* or rolls downwards to the side gutters, the crown of the causeway.
Addit. to CANTEL.

CANTRAIP, CANTRIP, *adj.* Uncommon, supernatural, magic, charmed. Addit. to CANTRAIP.
The term is so used in Burns' Tam o' Shanter, and his Epistle to Major Logan.

To CAP, CAUP, v. n. To bulge, twist, or warp, like green wood; pret. and part. pt. *capt, caupt*; West of S.
Gael. *cop*, to foam, heave up; *copan*, a boss, dimple, cup.

CAP, s. Short for capping, turning over, rising up, like a small boat on a rough sea: "at cup and koo," at rising and falling: Sempill Ballates, p. 231. V.

CAPPIE, *adj.* Cup-shaped, hollow; also, warping, given to warping, like green wood, as, "That timmer's unco *cappie*;" Ayrs.
The term occurs in the old nursery rhyme,—
Roun, roun, rosy, *cappie*, *cappie* shell !
The dog's awa to Hamilton to buy a new bell.

CAPADOS, CAPIDOS, s. V. CAPIDOCE.

CAPE, s. Cope; top. V. CAIP.
"High stood the gibbet's dismal *cape*."
Alex. Wilson, The Shark, s. 10.

CAPSTANE, *s.* Copestone; hence, the highest or last thing, point, or position in a series; the crown, 'the worst or the best, the finishing touch, completion. V. CAPE-STANE.

I've been poor, and vex'd, and raggy,
Try'd wi' tronbles no that sma';
Them I bore—but marrying Maggy
Laid the *capstane* o' them a'.
Alex. Wilson, Watty and Meg, s. 9.

CAPERCAILYE, CAPERCALYEANE, CAPULCAILYIE, *s.* The great cock of the wood. Errat. in DICT.

Jamieson's definition is wrong, and his discussion of the etym. only mystifies it. The explanation given by Pennant is certainly the correct one. The bird is called Capercailye and Capulcailye, which are simply var. of Gael. *capull-coille*, the great cock of the wood: lit. the horse of the wood; *capull*, a horse, being used fig. for *great*, and in that sense applied to any great creature of its kind. Cf. *capull-lin*, the great lint beetle. This is prob. the explanation of the term *capyl* or *capyll* as applied to a hen with a brood of chickens, and as a general name for a domestic hen. The term is so used in the Townley Mysteries. V. Gloss.

CAPERNUTIE, CAPERNUTED, *adj.* Slightly elevated, or under the influence of liquor. It is generally applied to that state called *talkin'-fou*. Addit. to CAPERNOITIE.

Of the stark aquavitæ they baith lo'ed a drappie,
And when *capernutie* then aye unco happy.
D. Webster, Whistle Binkie, l. 293.

CAPILL, CAPLE, *s.* A horse or mare. Henryson, Wolf, Fox, and Cadgear, ll. 78, 140. V. CAPYL.

CAPITBIRNE, CIPIBERNE, *s.* A hood, cape, or short mantle; Accts. L. H. Treas., i. 24, 22: *capy-berne*, Act. Audit., p. 112.* V. CAPITE BERN.

CAPPIE, CAPPIE-STANE, *s.* Steeth stone, sinker or bottom stone attached to the end of a fishing line, and serving as an anchor or grapnel; Shetl. Addit. to CAPPIE. V. STEETH-STONE.

Evidently a coll. form of *capstane*, meaning the terminal or limiting stone. V. *Capstane*.

CAPRAVENS, CAPRAVENIS, *s. pl.* Roof-spars, rafters; Halyburton's Ledger, p. 294. Errat. in DICT.

The meaning suggested in DICT. is wrong: so also the etym. The term is redundant, being the Dutch pl. *kapraven*, roof-spars, with the Eng. pl. termination added.

CAPTION, *s.* A law term meaning, 1. The act of taking a person who is to be arrested. 2. The warrant or authority for making an arrest, also called "*letters of caption.*" 3. The law which authorizes and regulates arrest. Addit. to CAPTION.

CAPTRENE, *s.* A cap, lid, or cover of wood: as is used for a large pot, vat, or tun.

". . . in duobus plumbis novis et duobus mascfattis et quatuor gylefattis et duobus *Captrenys*, c angys et ij tynis emptis apud Innercnlan, xxx s." Excheq. Rolls Scot., i. 15.

A.-S. *cæppe* (prob. borrowed from Lat. *cappa, capa*) a cap or cover, and *treowen*, wooden.

CAR, CAIR, *s.* Care, regard: also grief, sorrow, affliction; Barbour, xx. 586. V. CARE, *v.*

CARAGE, *s.* Prob. an Errat. for *corage* or *curage*, courage, bravery, boldness, spirit.

Off forebearis thay tuke *carage* and smell.
Henryson, Orpheus and Eurydice, l. 25.

Carage and smell, for *corage* and *smell*, boldness and sagacity. Dr. Laing, in his ed. of Henryson, renders *carage*, behaviour, which makes nonsense.
Fr. *courage*, courage, spirit, bravery.

To CARB, CERB, *v. n.* To fret, wrangle, quarrel: prob. a corr. of E. *carp*. In these senses Curb, Carbin, are used both as *s.* and *adj.*

CARD, CARDE, KARDE, *s.* A sort of woollen cloth.

"Et in empcione decem et octo peciarum de *card*." Excheq. Rolls Scot., i. 220.
"In empcione centum trijinta ulnarum de *karde*." Ibid. i. 117.

CARDAMUM, CARDY, *s.* A name for gingerbread, and other spiced cakes sold at country fairs. West of S., Fife.

So called on account of their spicing: cardamoms being used in all the varieties of cake, and forming the chief ingredient in some of them. These seeds are almost strictly medicinal with us now; but formerly were in common use for flavouring various kinds of food. They are still largely used for that purpose in India and other parts of Asia; and are still in favour in Germany for flavouring pastry.

CARDYVIANCE, *s.* A close cupboard, a safe for meat; Accts. L. H. Treas., i. 175. V. GARDEVIANT.

CARF, *s.* Generally pron. *scarf*: also used as a *v.* Addit. to CARF.

CARGAIT, *s.* Cart-road, country-road; Burgh Recs., Glasgow, i. 124, 132, Recs. Soc. V. CAR, and GAIT.

CARIAGE, CARYAGE, CARAGE, *s.* Lit. that which is carried; but generally a horseload, a cart-load; also, heavy goods, baggage; Barbour, xi. 238, xv. 19. Addit. to CARAGE.

CARIAGE-HORS, *s.* A pack-horse, a loaded sumpter-horse; Accts. L. H. Treas.

CARIAGE-MEN, *s. pl.* Carriers, sumpter-men, baggage-carriers; Barbour, viii. 275. V. CARYARE.

CARJOUR, CARYARE, s. A lighter; also a raft for carrying timber; Accts. L. H. Treas. i. 248, Dickson. Addit. to CARYARE.

CARION, CARIOUN, s. Dead, putrid, or putrifying flesh; a dead body: also, the human body as being liable to death; Douglas, Virg. Bk. viii. ch. 5, Blame of Kirkburiall, ch, 3.

To CARK, v. a. To load, pack; to make up in bales or bundles: pret. *carkit*; part. pa. *carkyt*. V. CARK.

"Giff ony alien schip come *carkyt* wyth wyn or tonnys wyth hony or oyle," &c. Custome of Schippis, ch. 2.
Northern Fr. *carker*, answering to Fr. *charger*.

CARLECHE, adj. Churlish, vulgar. V. CARLISH.

CARLES, CARLS, s. pl. A corr. of *Carols*, songs of joy or mirth, but generally applied to those sung at Yule-tide, chiefly on Hogmanay, the evening before the New-Year: app. also to the gifts bestowed on the singers, which were mostly small cakes baked for the occasion. V. CAROL-EWYN.

Hence the expression, "If ye come on Hogmanay I'll gie ye your *carles*." This relic of Scot. customs in catholic times is nearly extinct; but it still lingers in an attenuated form in various parts of Perthshire. In the West of S. the expression has become merely, "Come an' get your Hogmanay."
In Shetland *carl* is a name applied to a loose or licentious song. V. Gloss, Shetl.

CARPIN, s. and part. Talk, talking; narrative, narration. V. CARP.

CARRIT, CARVIT, part. adj. Carved, ornamented.
". . . ane stand-bed of *carrit* work ioynit with ane portell," &c. Burgh Recs. Prestwick, 21 Nov., 1587. Mait. Cl. Series.
A.-S. *ceorfan*, Du. *kerven*, Dan. *karve*, Swed. *karfva*, to carve.

CARRY, CARRY-HANDIT, adj. and s. Left handed. V. *Caar*.

CART, s. *Cartis of Were*, artillery carts, or carts for carrying guns; Accts. L. H. Treas., i. 50.
Clos Cartis, enclosed carts or ammunition waggons for carrying gun-stones and other ammunition, Ibid., pp. 280, 287, 291.
Serpentyn Cartis, carts for carrying the guns called serpentina or culverins, Ibid., pp. 291, 295.
Stane or *Stone Cartis*, carts for carrying stones for building or fortifying, Ibid., p. 338.

CARWELL, s. A carvel or caravel, a kind of ship; Douglas, Pal. Hon., Third pt.
Fr. *caravelle*, id. It was of the galley form, and had latteen sails.

CARWING-PRIK, s. Carving-fork, or such a substitute for it as is used in holding a round of beef to be sliced. Errat. in DICT.

CASCROM, CAS-CHROM, s. Lit. crooked foot; a crook-handled spade used by Highlanders, a kind of foot plough.

"It consists of a strong piece of wood, five to seven feet in length, bent between one and two feet from the lower end, which is shod with iron fixed to the wood by means of a socket. The iron part is five or six inches long, and about five inches broad. At the angle a piece of wood projects about eight inches from the right side, and on this the foot is placed, by which the instrument is forced diagonally into the ground and pushed along." The Scottish Gael, ii. 96.
Gael. *ca-*, a foot, and *chròm*, made crooked, or *cròm*, crooked. V. M'Leod and Dewar's Gael. Dict.

CASDIREACH, s. A long straight-handled delving spade used in the Hebrides; Scottish Gael, ii. 97.
Gael. *cas*, a foot, and *direach*, straight (Lat. *directus*).

CASE, CACE, CAIS, CAICE. *Case be*, lest, lest it may be: also used like *in case*, in the event, on condition, if so be that, if it happen; and sometimes with the meaning, perhaps, it may be; as, "An' *case be* ye meet him," i.e., and should, &c. "An' *case be* ye'll meet him," i.e., and perhaps, &c.

"Or a's sequester'd out an' in,
Case be he mak' a slopin—
The Shirra's warran' says, "Begin
An' mak' a muckle roupin'."
Wat *Watson's Poems*, p. 74.

CASSIDOUNE, s. Errat. for *Cristendome*. Barbour, xi. 471, Camb. MS.

CASSIT, part. adj. Chased, engraved, ornamented.
"Item, a *cassit* collere of gold made like suannis set in gold with xvj rubeis and diamantis and viij quhite suannis and set with double perle." Accts. L. H. Treas., i. 85. Dickson.

CAST, s. 1. A trench, ditch, cutting, or other channel for the passage of water.

2. A drive; a lift by the way: as, "It's a lang road, but twice owre I got a *cast* in a cart." Addit. to CAST.

To CAST on, v. a. To lay on, impose, assess, allocate.
"The Judge ordaines the birlaymen, with the halp of Robert Wilson in Hillhouse and the officer, to sight the quarrie and ground, and *to cast one* the skaith proportionallie, conforme to claime." Cornhill Baron Court Book, Ayr & Wigton Arch. Coll., iv. 168.

CASTELLAYNE, CASTELLANE, s. A castellan: a constable or keeper of a castle; Burgh Lawis, ch. 102. V. CASTLEMAN.

CASTLE-WARD, CASTLE-WAIRD, CASTLE-WARDE, s. A tax in lieu of garrison service.

A duty payable annually by certain lands, mostly in the Lothians and in the shires of Berwick and Lanark, in commutation of the obligation to furnish a contingent to the garrison of a certain castle.
(Exch. Rolls and Reg. of Great Seal passim.)
"The said Alexander and the langer levar of his sounnis beforesaide sall pay the castel-warde and the soyte," &c. Reg. Mag. Sig. 1424-1513, No. 473.

To CAT, CATHE, v. a. and n. To toss or drive by striking with the hand or with a light club or bat; also, to play handball; part. pr. *catting, cathing*, used also as n *s*. us the name of the game.
These are simply varieties of *catch, cache*; Du. *kaatsen*, to play tennis. Besides, *cat* or *catting* as a game is a variety of tennis. V. CAITCHE.

CAT, CATHE, *s*. A light bat used in tossing or driving a ball; also, a stroke with the bat, a toss of the ball. Also used as short for *catting*, playing at cat, and as the name of the game.

CATAIL, CATAL, CATALE, CATELL, *s*. Cattle; property, possession, wealth; also, like E. *chattels*, applied to small moveables; Barbour, iii. 735, v. 275, vi. 399, xviii. 249; Lawis of Gilde, ch. 1; Burgh Lawis, ch. 19.
M. Lat. *catalla*, cattle and all moveable property.

CAT-HAIR, CATS-HAIR, *s*. Names given to the streaky streaming clouds called *cirrus* and *cirro-stratus*. In Shetland called *Cats-Crammacks*.

CATITOIS, *s*. Err. for *cacitois*, a form of *cacoethes*, a bad habit, obscenity; Sempill Ballates, p. 234.

CATLING, *s*. Catgut; pl. *catlingis*, catgut strings for lutes, &c. Halyburton's Ledger, p. 321.

CATTER, *s*. Money, cash; Alex. Wilson's Poems, p. 35. V. CATER.

CATTIE, CATTY, *s*. Dimin. of Cat.
Is there ony that kens me my auld auntie Matty
Wi' 'r wee black silk cloak and her red collar'd *cattie?*
James Ballantine, Whistle Binkie, l. 189.

CATTIE-BARGLE, CATTIE-BARGIE, CATTIE-WURRIE, *s*. A noisy, angry quarrel among children; same as ARGLE-BARGLE, q. v.
The terms are also used literally as names for *a cat's quarrel*.

CATYF, *s*. A poor man, a miserable or wretched person, a churl.
I lukit furth a littill me befoir,
And saw a *catyf* on a club cumand,
With cheikis leyne and lyart lokis hoir.
Henryson, Ressoning betwixt Aige and Youth, l. 10.
O. Fr. *caitif*, poor, mean, poor-looking, occurs in the Chanson de Roland of the 11th cent., and is a doublet

of *captif*, a prisoner, from Lat. *captivus*. Regarding the changes in form and meaning see Brachet's Etym. Dict.

CAUL, adj. and *s*. Cold: a form of Cauld, q. v; Alex. Wilson's Poems, p. 411.

CAUSE', CAWSE', CAWSEE, CAWSEY, CAUSIE, CALSAY, *s*. A causeway or paved way: hence applied to a highway or public road, the central portion of a street set apart for horses and vehicles; and as a general term for street, lane, &c. Addit. to CAUSEY.

To CAUSIE, CAWSEY, CALSAY, CALSIE, v. a. To pave.

CANTLE O' THE CAWSEY. The centre, ridge, or 'crown of the causey,' q. v.
When he's fou he's stout and saucy,
Keeps the *cantle o' the cawsey*;
Hieland chief and Lawland laird
Maun gie room to Donald Caird!
Sir W. Scott, Donald Caird, st. 3.

CAUSIE-BURGESS, CALSAY-BURGES, *s*. A pedlar, hawker, street-merchant.
"Ordanis all *calsey burgesses* to haif na pairt of the hillis" [i.e., no share of the hill pasture or town's common]. Burgh Recs. Peebles, 26 May, 1609.
Poor tradesmen or dealers, not being burgesses, were not allowed to hold a booth or erect a stall for the sale of their wares, and were restricted to peddling or hawking them about in hand, or exposing them for sale on the causeway. V. *Bauchle*.

CAUSIE-MAKER, CALSIE-MAKER, *s*. A pavior, Burgh Recs. Aberdeen, i. 208, 258, Rec. Soc. The form *Causier* is now used all over the country, and sometimes *Causieman*.

CAUTEL, CAUTIL, CAWTEL, *s*. A trick, device, pretence, joke; craft, skill; Houlate, 1. 771, Asloan MS. Addit. to CAUTELE.

CAUTELOUS, adj. Wily, cunning; Henryson, Chanteclier and Foxe, l. 6. V. CAUTELE.

To CAVEL, CAVIL, v. a. To mix, mix up, mingle; *to cavil fish*, to take fish from the hooks of a long line as they are brought up, i.e., to mix all sorts and sizes; Orkn. and Shetl.

CAVILLATIONE, CAVILATIOUN, *s*. Cavilling, Compl. Scot., p. 167, E. E. T. S.; false or unjust charge, wrong-doing; Blame of Kirkburiall, ch. xix.
O. Fr. *caviller*, "to cavill, wrangle, reason crossly." Cotgr. Lat. *cavillari*, to banter.

CAWCHT, pret. Caught. V. CAUCHT.

CAWDROUNE, *s*. A caldron; Accts. L. H. Treas., i. 344. O. Fr. *caudron*.

CEBO, CEBA, s. V. *Cibo*.
To CEIS, CEISS, v. a. V. *Ces*.
CELLAT, s. A head-piece. V. SELLAT.
CENNYLL, s. A form of Canell, q. v.
CENS, CENSS, s. Incense, spices; contr. for Fr. *encens*, from Lat. *incensum*.
"Item, to the singaris that nycht [5 Jan 1497], that brocht the *cens* in to the King, xxxj s." Accts. L. H. Treas., i. 375.

CENTERS, CENTREIS, CENTREIS, s. pl. The cooms or frames used by builders in constructing arches; Burgh Recs. Aberd., ii. 300, 321. Sp. C.

CENTRAL, s. A sentry; prob. only a local pron.
". . . that na *centralis* remoif of the wautsche quhill utheris cum and be enterit in thair places." Charters, &c., of Peebles, p. 352, Rec. Soc.

CERTAIN, CERTEYNE, CERTIN, s. Certainty; as, "But for the *certain* o't, I canna speak;" "and this is the *certeyne*," Kingis Quair, st. 138, Skeat's ed. S. T. S.

To CES, CEIS, v. a. and n. To cease, stop, end. Fr. *cesser*; Lat. *cessare*, from *cedere*, to yield, give up.
". . . and whatsomeuer bruther of the gyld . . . cummys nocht to the place of the congregatioun or the ryngin of the bell *ces*, he salbe in his ameroiament." Lawis of the Gild, ch. 17.
Ceis is used as a v. in Houlate, l. 926.

CESSIOUN, SESSION, SESSYON, s. The Supreme Civil Court in Scotland; usually called *the Session*; Accts. L. H. Treas., i. 242, 269, Dickson.

CEYBO, CEYBA, s. V. *Cibo*.

CHADDER, CHALDER, CHELDER, s. A chalder, a measure of grain containing 16 bolls. In Orkney a weight equal to eighteen meills of malt, thirty-six meills of bear upon the bear pundlar, and twenty-four upon the malt pundlar; Wallace's Orkney.
The Scot. boll of meal is reckoned at 140 lbs. avoir. Fr. *chaudron*, a kettle: E. *chaldron*.

CHAFFIT, *pret.* and *part. pt.* Heated, as grain that has been exposed to wet; Douglas, Eneados, i., ch. 4, Small's Ed. V. *Chauf*.

CHAIP, s. The metal tip of a scabbard.
"Item gevin to Androu Balfoure, a ferding of ane noble to gilt a *chaip* to the Kingis swerd, vij s. vj d." Accts. L. H. Treas., i. 25.
Fr. *chape*, O. Fr. *chappe*, "a cope; also, the chape or locket of a scaberd," &c., Cotgr.; from Lat. *cappa*, a hooded cloak.

CHAIP, s. Purchase, etc. V. *Cheip*.

CHAIR, s. Chariot, carriage, car.
As king royall he raid upon his *chair*.
Henryson, Testament of Cresseid, l. 204.
Fr. *char*, O. Fr. *car*, *char*, a car; Lat. *carrus*, a sort of four-wheeled carriage which Cæsar first saw in Gaul; a Celtic word; Bret. *karr*, a chariot; O. Gael. *car*, Irish *carr*, a car, cart, waggon. V. Skeat's Etym. Dict. under CAR.

CHAK-WACHE, CHACK-WATCH, s. Checkwatch or inspector of the watch or guard; pl. *chak-wachys*, Barbour, x. 613. Also used as a v.
In Blind Harry's Wallace, viii. 817, the duty of the *chak-watch* is stated in a general way. A night attack of the English was being executed, but failed to surprise the enemy; for—
To chak the wache Wallace and ten had beyn Rydand about, and has thair cunmyng seyn.
A more particular account is given in Burgh Recs. Glasgow, ii. 113, Rec. Soc.

To CHALANGE, CHALLANGE, CHALLENGE, CHALLANCE, CHALLENCE, CALLANGE, CALLENGE, CALANGE, CALENGE, v. a. To claim, challenge, demand, sue, accuse, impeach, malign, revile, calumniate. The general meaning is to call in question; to charge, sue, or prosecute at law, to act as plaintiff; Chalmerlan Air, ch. v., Burgh Lawis, ch. 7, 10, 11.

CHALANGE, CHALENGE, CHALLANGE, CHALLENGE, CALANGE, CALENGE, CALLANGE, CALLENGE, CALLANYE, CALANYE, s. A claim, challenge, complaint, accusation, suit, charge; Burgh Lawis, ch. 15, 21, 75, 78.

CHALANGER, CHALENGEOUR, CHALLANGER, CHALLANGEAR, CHALLANGEOUR, CALANYEAR, CALANYOUR, s. 1. One who challenges, accuses, or arrests a person on account of some crime or wrong-doing; Burgh Lawis, ch. 74.

2. The official of a craft appointed to examine the goods and work of the several masters; to challenge faults of work, and to arrest bad or insufficient material. He was the inspector of the craft, and is frequently mentioned in Burgh and Guildry Recs.

3. A challenger, plaintiff, suitor, in a law court. V. CHALANCE.
". . . to eschew greitt trubill and daynger that hes bene sustenit in tymes bygane be *calanyears* quhilkis accept thame to the court of processis and dilatour, and wald nocht obey to the . . . court peremptour," &c. Burgh Recs. Edin., 6 Oct., 1492.
O. Fr. *calanger*, *calenger*, to claim, challenge, question, sue; Cotgr.

CHALMER, Chamer, Chavmir, *s.* The chamber or moveable breech-piece of a gun. Addit. to Chalmer.

"Item, that aamyn day [4 July, 1496], giffin to Johne Lain, smyth, for part of payment of making of gunchameris to gunnys that was in the Flour and wantit *chameris*, xl s." Accts. L. H. Treas., i. 281, Dickson.

CHAMELET, Chambelote, *s.* Camlet, a sort of cloth.

His chymers wer of *chamelet* purpure broun.
            Henryson, Evergreen, i. 186.

Dr. Laing's edition of Henryson reads this word *chambelote*.

Fr. *camelot*, from Arab. *khamlat*, camlet; Low Lat. *camelotum*. Dr. Jamieson gave this term from Fr. *chameau*, a camel; but this is a mistake.

CHANCER, Chanser, *s.* A form of *chancel*, Barbour, v. 356, 366.

Variations of this kind are not uncommon. *Channel* is often pron. *channer;* and channel stones are for short called *channers*, q. v.

CHANDLER, Chandlar, Chandelar, *s.* Chandelier, candlestick, Halyburton's Ledger, p. 295; *chandelar for precatis,* i.e., chandelier for tapers or taper-holders; Mait. Club Misc., iii. 200. Addit. to Chandler.

CHANGE-FOLK, *s. pl.* Publicans, keepers of inns and alehouses, &c. West of S. V. Change.

CHANGIT. Err. for *chanyit*, Houlate, l. 605, Bann. MS. V. *Chenyie*.

CHANNEL-STANE, *s.* An old name for the game of curling; called so on account of the stone with which it is played. Addit. to Channel Stane.

O for the *Channel Stane!*
The fell gude game, the *Channel Stane!*
There's no a game amang them a'
Can match auld Scotland's *Channel Stane!*
   James Hogg, Whistle Binkie, i. 347.

CHANON, Chanoun, Chanoune, *s.* A canon, a dignitary of the church; Accts. L. H. Treas., i. 334 : pl. *channounis,* Ibid., p. 1.

CHANONRYE, Channonry, Chennonrye, Channery, Chanry, *s.* The place of residence of the canons of a cathedral, a cathedral.

"Item, to the pure folk in the *Chanonrye* of Ros, at the Kingis commaund, vij s. iiij d." Accts. L. H. Treas., i. 325.

The following explanation is added by the editor, Mr. Dickson.

The *Chanonry* was properly the cathedral close or precinct; but the cathedral itself was sometimes so called, and Fortrose, the cathedral town of the diocese of Rose, was commonly known as the Chanonry of Rosa. The presbytery in which the parish of Fortrose is situated is still known as the Presbytery of Chanonry. In Houlate, l. 203, the term means a cathedral. Fr. *chanoine*, a canon, from Lat. *canonicus*.

CHANTER, Chantour, *s.* 1. The cantor, precentor or ruler of a choir, a cathedral canon who had charge of the music; Accts. L. H. Treas., i. 315, Dickson.

2. The pipe of a bagpipe on which the tune is performed. Errat. in Dict.

"The *chanter* is, like the other pipes, fixed in a head-stock, which is sufficiently large to contain the reed. This is formed of two thin slips of common reed or cane, fixed with much nicety to a small metal tube, which produce the sound by vibration. Those of the other pipes are formed of a joint of the reed, one end close, the other open, with an oblong slit for the passage of the air." Scottish Gael, ii. 304.

CHANTERIS, *s.* Errat. for *Chauceris*. The phrase *chanteris kuikis*, Bann. MS. fol. 91, a., as printed by Hailes, Sibbald, and Laing, is a misreading of *Chauceris kuikis*, i.e., drunken fellows like the cook described by Chaucer. V. Manciple's Prol., Cant. Tales.

Jamieson's attempt to explain *chanteris*, like all previous attempts, is altogether wrong. The correct reading was first given in the Hunterian Club version of the Bann. MS.; and the meaning of the phrase was first explained by Prof. Skeat in "Notes and Queries" of April 29, 1882. The chief difficulty in the extract from Alex. Scott's poem, as it stands in the Dict., having been thus cleared away, the line—
      "Sic Christianis to kis with Chauceris kuikis "
evidently means, "to rank or rate such Christians with drunken fellows like Chaucer's cook." V. Poems of Alex. Scott, ed. 1882, p. 11, and Note, p. 98.

CHAPLANRY, Chapilnary, *s.* The office, duty, service, or income of a chapel priest; chaplaincy; Burgh Recs. Aberd., i. 21, 30. Sp. C.

CHAPPET, *pret.* and *part. pt.* Beat, knocked, struck, chopped; as, "He *chappet* awa' like a nailer;" "He *chappet* at the door;" "The knock *chappet* twa;" "I *chappet* aff its head;" "*Chappet tatties* and *neeps*," beat or mashed potatoes and turnips. V. Chap, *v.*

To **CHAPS,** Chaups, *v. a.* To challenge, question, contradict; as, "Weel, I *chaps* that," meaning, I challenge or question the statement. Also, to accept, embrace, choose, select, claim; as, "*Chaps* ye," or, "I chaps ye," or simply, "Chaps,"—said when a person at once accepts an offer or bargain. Addit. to Chap.

This is another and more common form of *chap, chaup*, given in the Dict. with defective explanation. Prob. *chaps*, the first pers. sing. pres. of *chap*, to strike, was originally used by both parties when they struck their bargain, or rather when they struck hands in accepting the bargain; but, when the final s came to be dropped in the first pers. sing. pres. of verbs, and was still used in this one, *chaps* would come to be accepted as the verb in its simplest form, and would be treated accordingly. This explanation is confirmed by the striking of hands being still an accompaniment of the use of this term in bargain-making.

CHAR. Errat. for *charre* in Edin. MS. Barbour, xi. 123.

CHAR. Errat. for *thar*, it needs, it is necessary; Barbour, viii. 257, xii. 300. V. Skeat's ed., Gloss. and Notes.

CHAR, CHARRE, *s.* A cart-load, a charge: *a char of leid*, a cart load of lead, which was an uncertain quantity varying from 15 to 24 cwts.: syn. *fothir, fuddir, fiddir*, E. *fodder*. Addit. to CHAR. V. CHARRE.

Fotinellis, in first example under Char, is a misprint in Balfour for *fotmellis*, pl., of *fotmell*, usually written *fadmell*, a weight of 70 lbs.

CHARRE, *s.* Array of carts or waggons, baggage waggons; Barbour, xi. 123, Camb. MS. Cf. Fr. *charroi*, a baggage-train. V. CHAR.

The Edin. MS. reads *char*, which in the DICT. is so far correctly rendered *carriages*. *Charre* is certainly a better reading, being disyllabic and adapted to the rhyme. V. Skeat's ed., Gloss. and Notes.
O. Fr. *charee, charree*, a cart-load: Godefroy.

CHAR, *s.* On *char*, ajar: lit. on the turn, from A.-S. *on cyrre*, id. Douglas, King Hart.

N.B. The second example of *char* given in the DICT. is a mistake; the term there means a *chariot*, and the phrase *on char*, in a chariot. In Eneados iii. ch. 6, however, Douglas has "the dur *on char*," i.e. ajar. V. Small's ed. ii. 146, 23.

CHARD, *s.* A ridge or bank of sand in a links, Orkn.

CHARGEOUR, *s.* A large plate or dish; also, a flask or ladle for charging or loading guns: E. *charger*.

"Item, for ij dowbil platis of quhit irne to be gun *chargeouris*, xx d.
Item, for iiij ayngill platis to be *chargeouris*, xx d."
Accts. L. H. Treas., A. 1496.
Fr. *charger*, to load or charge; Lat. *carricare*.

CHARGES, *s. pl.* Expense, cost: *upon the charges*, at the expense. Addit. to CHARGES.

The explanation *rents* is insufficient, and in general wrong. The term is still in common use. A person asking the price or cost of an article says, "What's the charge?"

CHARITE, CHARITIE, *s.* V. CHERITE.

CHARTOUR, CHARTEROUR, CHERTOUR, *s.* A Carthusian monk, Houlate, l. 185.

CHASBOLL, CHESBOLL, CHESBOW, *s.* An onion. Fr. *ciboule*, "a chiboll or hollow leeke;" Cotgr. Addit. to CHASBOLL.
(Sup.) K

Chasboll, as used in the Compl. Scot. and quoted in DICT., certainly means an onion; and *Chesbow*, as used by Douglas, as certainly represents the Lat. *papaver*, a poppy. That these forms are merely varieties of the same word there can be no doubt. It is found also as *chebolle, chesebolle, chespolle, chybolle*; and was applied both to an onion and to a poppy. In Wright's Vocabularies, i. 786, it represents *sinolus, sipula*, a little onion: in 711, *sinollus*, id.: in 710, *sepa*, an onion: in 713, *papaver*, a poppy: in 644, both *papaver* and *sepula*. Halliwell gives *chesebolle*, a poppy, and *chibbals*, onions; and in Prompt. Parv. *chesebolle*, is rendered by *papaver*, a poppy, and *chybolle* by *cinollus*, a little onion.

How two plants so different in character came to be called by the same name, we can now only guess; but that they were so named explains the difficulty by which Jamieson was misled. The last para. of his article is of no value.

CHASE, *s.* *Brak a chase*, suddenly started or began a pursuit. Addit. to CHASE.

Jamieson's explanation of this phrase is unfortunate. The use of *break* in the sense of start, open, begin, is not uncommon. In conversation one *breaks* a new subject: in anger one *breaks out on* a person: in mining the workman *breaks* a new vein or seam, etc.

CHAT, CHATT, *s.* Same as CHACK, q.v.; its dimin. is CHIT, q.v.
Common in North of England also.

To CHAUF, CHAFF, *v. a.* To warm, chafe, heat; to make hot, or cause to become heated, like grain or hay that has been exposed to wet: hence, to spoil, mildew, corrupt: pret. and part. pt. *chauft, chaffit*.

Than was the quhiete, with fludis *chauft* and wete.
Douglas, *Eneados*, l. ch. 4.

Ruddiman's edit. has *chauft*; Small's has *chaffit*, which in the Gloss. is not well rendered by "*corrupted, drenched*."

Fr. *chaufer*, to heat, warm, chafe: from Lat. *calefacere*, to make warm or hot.

CHAULANCE, *s.* A challenge. V. CHALANCE.

To CHAUNER, CHAUNNER, *v. n.* To grumble, fret, chide, maunder; part. pres. *chaunrin*, often used as an adj., as, *chaunrin critics*, fault-finding critics; Alex. Wilson's Poems, p. 80. V. CHANNER.

This form of the word represents the pron. of it in the West of S.

CHAUNRIN, *part. adj.* Grumbling, complaining, fretting: West of S.

CHAUNT, *v.* To speak with a twang or strange accent, Orkn.

CHAWT, CHAWD, *v.* and *adj.* Chagrined, disappointed, filled with regret. Addit. to CHAW.

To CHEEP, CHEPE, *v. n.* To peep, chirp, as a bird; to speak in a low or subdued voice, to whisper; also, to creak as shoes. Addit. to CHEIP.

CHEEPS, *s. pl.* A common term for creaking shoes, but specially applied to dress-shoes, slippers, pumps.

Nor shall his *cheeps* and powder'd wig
Protect him frae a lashin'
Right keen this day.
Alex. Wilson, The Hollander, s. 2.

CHEESE. This important article of food is called *hung-cheese, laid-cheese,* or *wrought-cheese,* according to the manner in which the curd has been prepared.

HUNG-CHEESE. "It is called *hung* when the curds are tied up in a cloth or net, and, to get quit of the whey, are hung up instead of being put under the press." Ure, Agriculture of Dumbarton, p. 77.

LAID-CHEESE. "It is called *laid* when the curds are pressed at first very gently with the hand, great care being taken not to break them; and the whey as it rises is taken off with a skimming dish. This process is continued till the whey is extracted and the curds become solid. They are then broken into as large pieces as possible, and put into the chesset to be pressed. . . . Dunlop cheese is mostly of the *laid* kind." Ibid., p. 76.

WROUGHT CHEESE.. "It is called *wrought* when the curds are repeatedly broken with the hand in separating the whey. And when they become solid they are carefully broken with the hand and cut small with a knife; then they are squeezed in linen cloths and rubbed small with the hands till they become dry and pulverised and ready for the chesset." Ibid., pp. 74-5.

CHEIP, CHAIP, *s.* Barter, exchange price: *best cheip,* best bargain, best for the money: *gude cheip,* good bargain, good for the money: hence both terms came to mean *cheapest.*

". . . and quha can do best and *best cheip* let your lordschipis appoint him to refyne the kingis park," &c. Early Records of Mining in Scotland, p. 77.
Better-chaip, better bargain, better return for the money, was also used. V. Burgh Recs. Edin., iv. 160, Roc. Soc.
A.-S. *ceáp,* price: hence *ceápian,* to cheapen, to buy.

CHELD, CHELDE, *s.* A young man, page, servant; pl. *childer.* V. CHIEL, CHILD.
"Item [19 Nov., 1490], til a *cheld* to ryn to Patrik Home with a bil to kepe the day of trew at Gedwort, xijd." Accts. L. H. Treas.

CHELDER, *s.* A chalder. V. *Chadder.*

To CHENYIE, CHENYE, CHANYIE, *v. a.* To chain, link, join, connect; part. pt. *chenyeit, chenyit, chanyit,* Houlate, l. 604. Addit. to CHENYIE.

CHERITE, CHERITIE, CHERITEY, CHARITE, *s.* A to-boot or extra added to the quantity purchased on account of the dearness of the article, or in token of respect, favour, or good wishes for the purchaser; pl. *cheritvyss.*
This term appears to have puzzled Dr. Jamieson, and it was left by him undefined. In his notes and illustrations, however, he gave various suggestions regarding its meaning and etymology, which are altogether wrong, and very wide of the mark.
As stated above, the *charity* or *cheritle* was an extra added to the quantity given in return of service or for money; and prob. the custom of giving such extra is as old as bargain-making itself. Certainly it is well known, and of every day practice now; and the extra is called *boot* or *buit, till't, owre, bye,* in or *on,* and *to the bargain,* when spoken of in a general sense; but the extra given with bread is *to bread;* with flesh meat, a *bane* (which may be a bone, a scrap of lean or fat, a pluck, a kidney, or a trotter, according to the liking of the purchaser and the amount of the purchase); and for various other bargainings there are particular extras. When the extra, however, was given in money, it was called a *luck-penny, love-penny,* God's-*penny,* &c., whatever its value might be; and the term *cherity* was used specially in reference to the fixed extra allowed with quantities of victual, as of wheat, bear, malt, meal, &c. The *cherity* for each of these was one peck to the boll, that is, each boll contained 17 pecks,—16 by measure and 1 as charity. When *double cherity* was allowed the boll contained 18 pecks; and smaller quantities in proportion.
From our Burgh Records we learn that various attempts were made by the magistrates to put down this system of *charities,* but all were ineffectual. At last the subject was taken in hand by Parliament, and settled by various Acts passed between 1617 and 1625. These enacted that there should be one uniform system of weights and measures throughout the country, and that all *charities* should be abolished, In spite of these Acts the old custom was followed for many years after in our larger burghs, and under the new style of weights and measures; and in some of the more rural districts it continued to exist down to the middle of last century. The system of extras is apparently inherent in bargain-making, and the Acts of Parl. which made it illegal have only compelled parties to devise other means of carrying it out.
The passages quoted in DICT. sufficiently illustrate the use of the term; and in the Acts of the Scot. Parl., August 1621, will be found a good example of the act prohibiting *charities,* entitled " Anent the discharging of a peck to the boll." The following quotation is a record of one of the many attempts made by burghal authority to abolish the custom.
". . . that nay woman sal by meile in the mercat, bot gif scho mak price of it or scho gif her erllys, and that thai sall tak nay strakis nor *cheritoyss.*" Burgh Recs. Aberd., i. 431.
O. Fr. *charité,* charity, love, mercifulness, goodwill. Cotgr.

CHERTOUR, CHERTEROUR, *s.* V. CHARTOUR.

CHESYING, *part.* Choosing, election. V. CHESE.

CHESSIS, *s. pl.* Jesses; the bands of leather or silk with which hawks were tied by the legs; Accts. L. H. Treas., i. 366.

Chessis, yessis, or *jesses,* is a corr. of O. Fr. *jects* or *gects: geet* meaning a cast or throw, as at dice. "*Les gects d'un oyseau,* a hawkes jesses," Cotgr.

To CHEVE, CHIEVE, *v. a.* To achieve, accomplish, procure, prosper.
Fr. *achevir,* to master.

To CHIEVER, *v. n.* To storm, rage, scold, jangle, complain against.

He grat gryaly grym; and gaif a gret yowle, *Cheuerand* and chydand with churliche cheir.
Houlate, l. 54, Asloan MS.
Bann. MS. reads *hedand,* a contr. form of *hedinond,* scorning, deriding; which is certainly a mistake, as it mars the alliteration.
O. Fr. *sevir,* to rage, scold, jangle.

CHEVERON, *s.* A rafter, spar; pl. *cheueronys, cheverons*: Assize of Petty Customs, ch. 8: Burgh Recs. Edin., p. 242.
The *chevron* of heraldry, denoting an honourable ordinary, represents two rafters of a house meeting at the top: in building called a *couple.*

To CHEWES, CHEWIS, *v. a.* To choose, select; to pick out the best, to be a good judge of.
The Pitull and the Pype Gled crynd pewewe, Before thir princis ay past as pert purviouris,
For thai couth *chewis* chikunis and perches pultre.
Houlate, l. 644, Asloan MS.
The Bann. MS. reads *cheires,* but it is an alteration of the original *chewes.*
Icel. *kjósa,* A.-S. *cedsan,* Du. *kiezen,* to choose; M.E. *cheosen, chusen, chesen.*

CHIERE, *s.* A peculiar form of *chere,* cheer, demeanour, countenance, look; Kingis Quair, st. 161, S. T. S.

CHIFT, *s.* and *v.* Shift, change; Alex. Scott, Wantoun Wemen, st. 9.

CHILDROME, *s.* A corr. form of Schiltrum, q. v. Barbour, xii. 429, 433, Camb. MS. V. Skeat's Ed. Gloss. and Notes.

CHILDYNE, *s.* Childing, i.e., child-bearing, travail with child, Barbour, xvi. 274. V. CHILD-ILL.

CHIMNAYE, CHYMNAY, CHIMNEY, CHIMNIE, *s.* A grate, a fire-place. V. CHIMLEY.
In the list of moveable heirship fixed by an old Scotch law we find,—"... . a caldrone, a ketill, a brandreth, a posnet, a *chymnay,* a stop, a cruk." Burgh Lawis, ch. 116.
And in a claim of heirship raised in the Burgh Court of Glasgow, 17 Dec., 1574 :—
"Iteim, ane irne *chimnaye* witht raxis, weyand aucht stane wecht," &c. Burgh Recs. Glasgow, i. 33.
In many districts of S. the term is still so used.
The form *chymna* occurs in Accts. L. H. Treas., i. 22.

CHINGLY, *adj.* Like shingle or gravel; applied to small coals from which the dross or culm has been separated; West of S. Same as *chirlie* of Perths. Addit. to CHINGILY.

CHIRLIE, CHIRLY, *adj.* Well-shaped, of nice handy size; hence, suitable, handy. Appl. to pieces of coal, stone, or brick, that are suitable for general use. V. CHIRLE.

CHIRNEL, CHURNEL, *s.* A kernel or small hard swelling in the neck of a young person. Pl. *chirnele, churnels,* a name given to the ailment of swollen glands of the neck.
This ailment is also called *waxen chirnels,* a corr. of *waxing* (growing) *chirnels,* because it is common to young people during periods of growth.
A.-S. *cyrnel,* a diminutive from *corn,* grain.

CHISSET, CHISET, *s.* Same as Chessart, q. v.

To CHIVER, *v. n.* To shiver, tremble, shake. Boys call their bit of bread after bathing, their *chiverin piece,* or *chiverin chow;* corr. into *chivery chow.* It is also called a *chitterin piece,* or *chitterin chow;* corr. into *chittery chow:* Clydes. V. under CHITTER.

CHOLLE, *s.* Jowl, jaws. V. DIOT.
In the DICT. this term is left undefined. A note, however, is given explanatory of the passage in which the word occurs; but its statements are altogether wrong. Jamieson's mistake here is remarkable: because, a few lines higher up in the same column, he defines and explains the same term correctly.
In the passage quoted *chalous* means chafts or jowls, and *chyne* means chin. In Coventry Mysteries, p. 37, and in Prompt. Parv. occurs *chavyl-bone,* of which *chalous* is a pl. form.

CHUCK, CHUCKS, *s.* Short for CHUCKIE-STANE, CHUCKIE-STANES, q. v.; also, a girl's game played with five of these pebbles.
This game is played all over Scot., and is common in the North of Eng. V. Brockett's Gloss. Marbles and shells are sometimes used instead of pebbles.

CIBOW, CIBA, CEYBO, CEYBA, CEBO, CEBA, SIBO, SIBA, SEBO, SEBA, *s.* An onion. V. SEIBOW.
This word is often represented as *seibow,* and is so entered in the DICT.; but according to the etymology *cibow* is the better form. Fr. *ciboule,* from Lat. *cæpulla,* for *cæpa,* an onion.

CILHOUS, CILEHOUS, *s.* An outhouse, cellar vault: originally a shed consisting of a lean-to roof with wooden supports in front.
"Item, in ane *cilhous* nerrest the zett, certane vnthresschin beinis to the number of thrie thravis or tharby." Burgh Recs. Prestwick, 21 Nov. 1587. Du. *cel,* a cell, and *huis,* a house; Lat. *cella,* a cell or hut, Gk. *kalia.*

CINCOGISH, *s.* V. *Kincogish.*

CIN'ER, CINNER, *s.* A cinder.
An' lood the chimney wi' a tanle
O' bleezin coals an' *cin'ers.*
Alex. Wilson, Daybreak, s. 6.
Fr. *cendre,* It. *cenere,* from Lat. *cinis, cineris,* a cinder, is commonly given as the deriv. of this word; but

since the A.-S. has *sinder*, Icel. *sindr*, Swed. *sinder*, Dan. *sinder*, *sinner*, a cinder, it is more than probable that the term was introduced by our northern ancestors. See Skeat's Etym. Dict.

CLADDACH, CLEDDACH, *s*. A shingly beach, Gall.

Clidyoch, as given by Jamieson, is a corr. form of this form. V. DICT.

Gael. *cladach*, a shore, beach; a stony beach; M'Leod and Dewar.

This term is still used in Wigtonshire as the name for a shingly or stony beach; and it occurs in various place-names in that district; e.g., *Claddyochdow*, in Kirkcolm parish, *Clady House*, in Inch parish.

In Ireland also it is similarly used. A part of the town of Galway is called "the *Claddach*."

CLAER, CLARE, *s*. A corr. form of *claver*, clover.

CLAGGUM, CLAGGIE, *s*. A coarse sweetmeat, consisting of treacle hardened by boiling, and flavoured. Named from its tough, sticky character.

This favourite of all young folks has various names, of which the most common are *candy*, *blackman*, *gundie*, *claggie*, and *claggum*; and almost every town and village has a local name over and above, which is generally the name of a woman who has become famed for making the article. It is known and enjoyed all over Scot. and Eng.

To CLAITH, CLAYTH, *v. a.* V. CLATHE.

CLAKE, *s*, V. CLAIK.

CLAM, *s*. A clam or scollop-shell; also called a *clamp-shell*.

So called from the *clamping* or close sticking, closing, or adhering of the shells: clamping together like a vice. Some clams, however, stick to rocks. Du. *klampen*, to hold, stick together: *klampe*, *klam*, tenacious. Dan. *klamme*, a clamp. Jamieson's suggestion of O. Fr. *esclumme* as etym., is a mistake. V. Wedgwood's Etym. Dict.

CLAM, CLAME, CLAMBE, *pret*. Climbed; scrambled or struggled upward. S.

CLAMERSUM, CLAMMERSOME, *adj*. Contentious, fractious, discontented, and noisy; continually grumbling or fault-finding.

This term, as generally used, implies both *clamorous* and *ill-natured*.

CLAMYS, CLEMYS, *v*. Claims, desires, requires; Barbour, i. 417, ii. 104.

CLAPPER, CLAPPIR, *s*. 1. That which claps: hence applied to the tongue of a bell, the hopper of a mill, the tongue of a scold, etc.

2. A kind of hand-bell which lepers carried and rattled as they moved about in public. It was used by the night-watch also, and in earlier times by the town-crier, who was therefore called "*the clapman*."

To leir to clap thy *clapper* to and fro,
And leir efter the law of lipper leid.
Henryson, Testament of Cresseid, l. 479.

3. A noisy talkative person, a scold.

To CLAPPERCLAW, *v. a.* Lit. to claw with the clapper, i.e., to attack with the tongue: to rate, scold, or abuse. Addit. to CLAPPERCLAW.

CLAPPER-TONGUE, *s*. Loud noisy tongue, incessant talk; also applied to a female who is loud or voluble in speech, or who is much given to gossip; "She's a real *clapper-tongue*:" West of S.

A *clapper tongue* wad deave a miller.
Burns, Sic a Wife as Willie had.

CLAPPER-TONGUED, *adj*. Having a tongue like a clapper, i.e., noisy and constantly wagging; "She's a *clapper-tongued* lassie;" West of S.

CLAR, *s*. Short for *Clarsach*, q. v.

CLARCHE PIPE. Not a compound, but two distinct words. Read—

"With Clarche, Pipe, and Clarion."

Clarche, like *clar*, is short for *clarsach* or *clarsha*, a harp, and cannot be combined with *pipe*.

CLARSACH, CLARSHA, CLARISHOE, *s*. A harp.

"The harp proper was called clar, or *clarsach*, by the Scots and Irish, and was sometimes termed *siteam*, a word now obsolete." Scottish Gael, ii. 273.

Gael. *clarsach*, and for short, *clar*, a harp.

CLARSCHA, CLARESCHAW, CLARSCHAAR, *s*. A harper.

"Item, to Martyn, *clareschaw*, and to the toder Ersche *clareschaw*, xviij s." Accts. L. H. Treas., i. 117, Dickson.

This term is often confounded with *clarsach*, and rendered a *harp*. V. DICT.

CLASH, *s*. Gossip, scandal; pl. *clashes*, fabrications, lies; Alex. Wilson's Poems, pp. 18, 89; West of S. V. CLASH.

CLASHIN, *s*. Evil-speaking, insulting language, heckling in all its forms.

No ;—here am I, wi' vengeance big,
Resolved to calm his *clashin*';
Nor shall his cheeps nor powdered wig.
Protect him frae a lashin'
Right keen this day.
Alex. Wilson, The Hollander, s. 2.

CLASHIN, CLASHING, *part*. Soaking, dripping wet. V. CLASH, *v. n.*

Wi' waefu' heart, before it sank,
I heul't it oot a' *clashing*;
And now they're bleaching on the bank,
A melancholy washing
To me this day.
Alex. Wilson's Poems, p. 94.

This use of the word is very common in the West of S.

To CLATHE, CLAITHE, CLAITH, CLETHE, v. a. To clothe, dress: pret. and part. pa. *clatht, claitht, cleitht, clethd.* The forms *to claitht, to cleitht,* are also used ; Compl. Scot., p. 98, E. E. T. S. V. CLEED.

CLATHING, CLAITHING, CLEITHING, CLETHING, *s.* Clothing, dress; Houlate, l. 186, Asloan MS. V. CLEEDING.

Waesucks! for him that gets nae lass,¹
Or lasses that hae naething !
Sma' need has he to say a grace,
Or melvie his braw *claithing!*
  Burns, Holy Fair, st. 25.

CLATHT, *part. pt.* Clothed, clad.

To CLAUR, CLAUER, *v. a.* and *n.* To seize, clutch; pret. *claurd, claurt,* part. pt. *claurt, claured:* "*he let claur at me,*" he tried to clutch me; West of S.

A.-S. *clāwu,* Du. *klaauw,* a paw, claw, clutch, talon ; that by which a creature cleaves or holds on by. Cf. M. E. *cleafres,* claws.

CLAURT, *s,* A clutch, grasp, scratch, scrape ; thence the *v. to claurt, claut,* as in DICT. Addit. to CLAURT.

CLAUTET, CLAUTIT, CLAWTET, *pret. part. pt.* and *part. adj.* Scraped, cleaned : applied to dishes and food , as , " The bicker he *clautit* an' left na a seed." West of S. V. CLAT, CLAUT.

For soon as ilka dish was *clautet,*
He'd lift his looves an' een, an' fa' to't,
Owre plates an' banes
An' lengthen out a grace, &c.
  Alex. Wilson's Poems. p. 52.

CLAUTS, *s. pl.* Hands ; also finger-nails : properly the hands in the act of seizing; E. *clutches ;* as, " I'll try to keep out o' yer *clauts ;*" Clydes.

What dawds o' cheese, frae out yer *clauts*
Wi' fury ye hae worry'd.
  Alex. Wilson's Poems, p. 34.

This is an application of *clats* or *clauts,* handcards for teazing wool. V. CLAUTS.

CLAVERS, *s.* Goosegrass. V. *Clever.*

CLAVIE, *s.* Prob. synonymous with torch, flare.

This term is now known chiefly in connexion with a superstitious ceremony called "*the burning of the clavie,*" which is annually observed on New Year's Eve at the fishing village of Burghead on the Moray Frith, with the view of securing a good season's fishing. The *clavie* consists of a tar barrel, within which a fir prop about four feet in length is fixed, surmounted by the staves of a herring cask. It is set fire to with special formalities, and is, while still burning, carried in procession to a particular spot in the neighbourhood of the village. For a full account of this singular observance see Proc. Soc. of Antiq. of Scotland, vol. x., p. 647.

CLEIK, *s.* Short for *cleik-ful,* i.e., a haul, set, lot, number.

Jok, that wes wont to keip the stirkis.
Can now draw him ane *cleik* of kirkis.
  Dunbar, Remembir as of before, l. 67.

That is, the greedy place-hunter can now haul to himself a *cleik-ful* of livings.

To CLEKE, CLEEK, *v. a.* V. CLEIK.

CLEMMIL, *s.* Steatite, Orkn. (v. Neil's Tour, p. 75).

CLENE, CLEIN, CLEYNE. 1. As an *adj.,* clean, clear, fine, good, excellent, complete, thorough; also, empty, void ; Barbour, xi. 141, 427, xiii. 443.

2. As an *adv.,* wholly, entirely, completely, well; excellently ; Ibid, xvi. 462, xviii. 229 : *clene und law,* wholly and to the bottom, Ibid. x. 123.

CLETHE, CLEITHE, CLETHING, CLEITHING. V. under CLATHE.

CLEUE AND LAW. Errat. in DICT. for *Clene and Law.* V. under CLENE, *adv.*

This mistake is corrected and explained in Skeat's Barbour, pp. 578, 579.

To CLEVER, *v. n.* To clamber, Kingis Quair, st. 9; to cling, Ibid. st. 159. Addit. to CLEVER, *v.*

As used in this poem *clever* has a frequentative force, and Prof. Skeat says, " Better spelt *cliver* ; it is the frequentative of Icel. *klifa,* to climb." Gloss. Kingis Quair.

CLEVERS, CLEEVERS, CLIVERS, CLAVERS, *s.* Goosegrass, cleavers, *Galium aparine:* called also Robin-run-the-hedge.

The plant is named *Cleavers* or *Clavers* in North of Eng. also. V. Brockett's Gloss. It is so named on account of its *cliving* or climbing nature.

CLEVIN, *s.* A measure equal to 5 bolls ; but whether a measure of grain or of fodder only has not been ascertained.

"Redditus prebende de illo anno . . xᵏ et vj *clevins* et tres bolle prebende. Summe xiiijˣˣ *clevins* xj *clevins* et tres bolle prebende, que sunt in celdris iiijˣˣxj celdre et due bolle prebende." Exch. Rolls Scot. i. 7.

In p. 21 of same vol. the value of a *clevin* is clearly shown by a statement that 50 c.=15 chalders 10 bolls.

CLEW, CLOU, *s.* Short for CLOUSE, q.v.

CLEWCH, CLEW, *s.* A hollow between steep banks, a narrow glen or valley; Accts. L. H. Treas. i. 299; also, a precipice, high rocky bank; pl. *clewis,* like E. cliffs, shelving rocks ; also, gaps or glens among the rocks or in a hilly district, Douglas, Virgil, i. ch. 4. Addit. to CLEUCH.

CLEYNG, *s.* Errat. in DICT. for *Clethyng,* clothing. V. under CLATHE, *v.*

This explanation, suggested by me in the note appended to Dr. Jamieson's article, has been confirmed

CLIFT, s. A cliff, high and steep rock; a steep rocky hill side.

> The herd, maist like ane's finger wauks,
> Aboon yon fearfu' clift,
> Scarce seen this day.
> *Alex. Wilson's Poems*, p. 92.

A.-S. *clif*, a rock, headland, cliff; Icel. *klif*, a cliff. Not connected, as is sometimes stated, with the verb *cleave*, to split; but with A.-S. *clifian*, to cleave to, Icel. *klifa*, to climb. See Skeat's Etym. Dict.

CLIMMIN, CLYMIN, CLYMBYNG, *part.* and *s.* Climbing, ascent, Barbour, x. 595. Syn. *speelin*.

CLINSCHEAND, *part. pres.* Limping, stumping, walking like a lame person, or like one with a contracted leg; another form is *clinking*, and both forms are still used. Addit. to CLINCH.

> And winkand with ane eye, furth he wend;
> *Clinscheand* he come, that he nicht nocht be kend.
> *Henryson, Parliament of Beistis*, l. 173.

Clinch is still so used in West of S.: V. Gloss. Wilson's Poems. A lame persou, or one with a club-foot is often called *a hippity*, *a clincher*, or *a hippity-clincher*.

Clinch is a softened form of *clink*, to beat, strike, or knock sharply; and is applied to lame or club-footed persons on account of the beating or dumping manner in which they walk. V. Douglas' Virgil. V. ch. 5. Du. *klink*, a blow, *klinken*, to strike smartly, to sound; Dan. *klinge*, to sound, jingle, when struck; *klinke*, to clench, rivet; Sw. *klinka*, id.

CLIPPING HOUSE, *s.* V. CLIPHOUSS.

CLIVER, *s.* A footpath down a cliff, Orkn.

To CLOIT, CLOITER, *v. a.* To strike, thump, batter; different forms are *clod*, *clout*, West of Scot. Addit. to CLOIT.

CLOLLE, *s.* Errat. in DICT. for *Cholle*, jaws, q. v.

Defin. and etym. are wrong. The error originated in Pinkerton's version of the poem, which supplied the term.

To CLOOR, CLOUR, CLOWER, *v. a.* To dint, to make a mark or impression, to scratch; hence to make a welt, lump, or bump; and in a general sense, to beat, knock, or thump violently; to hurt, damage, or disfigure by so beating, &c. Addit. to CLOUR.

> Ye've lost a patriarch and mair
> Whase crown Death's lang been *cloorin*.
> *Alex. Wilson, Cullamphitre's Elegy*, s. 1.
> While he, silly doofart, said never a word,
> But aye his *cloner'd* cantle kept clawin', kept clawin.
> *Whistle Binkie*, ii. 234.

This term is not sufficiently explained in the DICT. Swed. *kula* means a den, cave, cavern; also a ball, bullet; that is, a hollow or dint, an elevation or lump; and *kullra* means to make a dint or a lump, to cause a hollow or an elevation; hence, to strike or beat with a club or stick, &c., to thump, thwack, crash; and in a general sense, to beat, knock, or thump in any way. Prob. *cloor*, to diut, to welt, and *cloor*, to scratch, are two distinct verbs: the one from Sw. *kula*, as already stated, and the other from Sw. *klo*, a claw, pl. *klor*. The act and result in each case are certainly very different.

CLOOR, CLOUR, CLOWR, *s.* A dint or hollow, a scratch; also, a bump or elevation, a welt. Also, a blow, stroke, crash. V. CLOUR.

Not used in Orkn. in sense of a blow, but only in the sense of a scratch as by a nail or sharp point.

CLOORIN, CLOURIN, *s.* Dinting; welting; also, beating, knocking, crashing, thrashing; West of S.

CLOOSE, CLEWS, *s.* Sluice. V. CLOUSE.

CLOSE, *s.* A passage, entry, blind alley.

CLOSE-FOOT, CLOSE-HEAD, CLOSE-MOUTH.

These terms may be best explained thus:—Close, like street, has two distinct meanings: 1. a passage; 2. the houses built along that passage. As a passage, its opening or entry from the street is called *the close-mouth* or mouth-of-the close; the part which passes through the fore-land, or leads to the back-houses, is called *the close-head* or head-of-the close; the part along which the back-houses are built is *the close* proper, and its termination is *the close-foot* or the foot-of-the close.

In the second sense—houses built along the passage, back-houses or back-row, the entry or passage through the fore-land, or from the street to the back-houses, is called *the close-mouth*; the place meant by Alex. Wilson in his picture of a rainy day—

> And hens in mony a caul' *close-mouth*
> Wi' hingin tails are dreepin'.

Then, the houses next to the close-mouth, or nearest the street, form *the close-head*; and those at the other end, or farthest from the street, form *the close-foot*. Thus it comes that the passage through a fore-land is sometimes called the *close-mouth*, and sometimes the *close-head*: being at the same time the mouth or entry to the back-houses, and the head of the close or passage. Similarly, the *close-head* may mean the head of the passage, or the houses at the head of the passage. It is in the latter sense that the term is used by Sir Walter Scott. Addit. to CLOSE, CLOSE-HEAD.

CLOSOUR, CLOSUR, *s.* 1. Enclosure, a park or place enclosed. V. CLOSEHIS.

"It is to wytt that gyf ony burges haf *closour* or yharde closurit, and ony bestis of his nychburia, hors ox or kow or ony other bestis entter tharin," &c. Fragments of Old Laws, ch. 36.

2. A case, cover, receptacle.

"Item, ane crem stok of siluer with ane *closour* of siluer." Mait. Club Misc., iii. 203.

O. Fr. *closure*, an enclosure; from Lat. *clausitura*. Another form is *closerie*.

CLOUT, CLUT, *s.* A cloth, patch, rag; hence, a little bit, a small portion. Addit. to CLOUT.

> . . . : the pure husband richt nocht
> Bot croip and calf upon ane *clout* of land.
> *Henryson, Wolf and Lamb*, l. 123.

To CLOVE, v. a. To break or split the fibres of flax preparatory to heckling it. V. CLUFF.

And skutch and *clove* and heckle lint and spin a pund of tow.
Old Song, The Weary Pund of Tow.

To clove, lit. to claw, to tear with claws; for lint was cloved by being struck on and drawn over a set of sharp spikes or hooks. By this process the fibres were split and prepared for heckling.

A.-S. *cleófan*, Du. *kloven*, Icel. *kljúfa*, Dan. *klöve*, to cleave, split. Cf. A.-S. *clá, cleó*, Icel. *kló*, Dan. *klo*, a claw.

CLOWER'D, *part.* and *adj.* V. CLOOR.

CLOWIT, *part. pt.* Nailed, fastened with nails, rivetted. Errat. in DICT.

A habirgeoun of burnist mailyeis brycht,
With gold ourgilt *clowit* thrynfald full tycht.
Douglas, Virgil, v., ch. 5.

Fr. *clouer*, to nail, fasten with nails.

Douglas here describes a hauberk of his own time, and represents it as "triple, tightly fastened with nails, i.e., riveted, and overgilt with gold." Both in this passage and the similar one in Bk. III., l. 467, he renders "*concertam hamis*" by *clowit*, nailed, riveted. On the authority of Ruddiman, Dr. Jamieson rendered this term "made of clews, woven"; and Mr. Small has repeated the mistake, but with a slight variation, by his rendering "sewed, made of clews." The context clearly shows that those meanings are inadmissible; for the hauberk is stated to have been so heavy that two strong servants could scarcely carry it on their shoulders.

CLUCH, *s.* Represents a pron. of CLEUCH, q. v. Rob Stene's Dream, p. 13.

CLUD, *s.* A cloud, pl. *cluds*; Alex. Wilson's Poems, pp. 42, 47.

CLUDED, *part. pt.* Clouded, covered with clouds, Ibid. p. 105.

CLUDY, CLUDDY, *adj.* Cloudy, obscured, dark; West of S.

A.-S. *clúd*, a round mass; hence *cloud* is allied with *clod* and *clot*.

CLUE, *s.* A clue as of yarn, &c.

Some sinfu' *clues*, the laft aboon,
Ye'll fin' row't in a blanket.
Alex. Wilson's Poems, p. 44.

Du. *klu wen*, a clew; A.-S. *cliwen*, a shortened form of *cliwen*, id.

CLUNG, *pret.* and *part. pt.* Dried up, shrunk, shrivelled, withered: synon. *geisined, creent, crined*. V. CLING.

CLUT, *s.* V. CLOUT.

CLUTE, CLOOT, *s.* Prop. half of the hoof of a cloven-footed animal; but generally a hoof. The pl. *cloots, clutes, cluits*, hoofs, is very often used for *feet* in speaking of cows and horses; and among country people the term is sometimes applied to human feet; West of S. Addit. to CLUTE.

While Mirran wi' her shoelin *cloots*
Ran yellochan an' greetin.
Alex. Wilson, Callamphitre's Elegy, s. 9.

The phrase "*shoelin cloots*"=shuffling feet, i.e. flat, ungainly feet.

CLYMBYNG, *part.* and *s.* V. CLIMMIN.

CLYNK, *s.* Stroke; sound, tinkle. V. CLINK.

". . . and forgather hastelie betwix the Tolbuith and the mele mercatt at the *clynk* of the commoun bell," &c. Burgh Recs. Edin., 19 Aug. 1524.

To CLYNSCH, *v. n.* V. CLINCH.

COAL-GUM, GUM, *s.* Small coal, dross. Addit. to COAL-GUM.

Coal-gum, or for short, *gum*, is occasionally used with the meaning of *coal-dust*, and *grime*, but its usual meaning is small-coal, dross, riddlings, as used for furnaces, etc. E. *culm*, from Fr. *ecume*, dross.

Coom is the name generally given to *coal-dust, grime*, etc. V. COOM.

COBLE, COBELL, COBBIL, COWBLE, COWBIL, COWBILL, *v.* A tub, barrel, or cistern sunk in the ground to collect rain or drain water. Addit. to COBLE.

"Ane devyse . . for sinkis to serve the baill houssis and to discend in tua *cobillis* or ane *cobell* as salbe thocht most convenieut." Aberd. Burgh Records, 6 March, 1616.

The form *cowbill* occurs repeatedly in Burgh Recs. Edinburgh, vol. i: v. pp. 187, 188, 189, where it means a malt-coble.

COCK, *s.* A familiar term equivalent to *fellow*, used only among friends in greeting or hearty praise; West of S.

A core o' as good hearty *cocks*
As e'er spent a saxpence o' siller.
Alex. Wilson's Poems, p. 11.

Rab was a gleg, smart *cock*, with powder'd pash,
Ibid., p. 24.

COCK-LOFT, *s.* The highest gallery in a church, S.

COCQUET, COKKET, *s.* A custom-house certificate that goods for export have been duly passed; also, the dues paid for passing such goods; also, the office where goods for export are passed.

"For the customares aw . . to haue their awin clerc at their awin expenses, whom over, customares and tronares alike, the same clerc of *cocquet* aucht to be controuller." Statutes of David II., 5 Dec. 1365.

This word is supposed to be a corruption of the words *quo quietus* which occur in the Latin form of the cocquet. V. Nares' Dict.

CODRUM, CODRE, *s.* Forms of CUDREME, q. v.

COELTS, *s. pl.* Woods, clumps of wooding, plantings, or as usually pron. *plantins*. Addit. to COELTS.

This term is left undefined in DICT.; but, in the accompanying note the meaning "*colts*, young horses," is suggested: but this rendering makes nonsense of the passage quoted. The word is an English adaptation of Gael. *coillie*, woods, short for *coilltean*, pl. of *coille*, a wood, forest: E. *holt*.

COGALL, Cogan, *s.* Prob. a misreading of *Tonegall*, q. v. Exch. Rolls Scot., i. 6, 7, 21.

The word *cogall*, which occurs frequently in the same connection in the abridgement by Lord Haddington's transcriber of the lost Rolls for the years 1263-6, in which *tonegal* also is found, is probably the same word written in the original in a contracted form and misread. It has the same meaning, viz., a weight equal to 6 stones.

To **COGHLE,** Coghil, *v. n.* To cough in a weak or exhausted manner; to gasp or blow like a person out of breath, or suffering from asthma: a dimin. of *cough*; West of S.

COILL-HUCHIS, *s. pl.* Coal pits, Burgh Recs. Prestwick, 5 Dec., 1489. V. Coilheuch.

COKALAND, *s.* V. Cockalan.

COKBATE, *s.* A cockboat, a small boat; Accts. L. H. Treas., i. 253. Cf. M. E. *cogge*, O. Dutch. *kogge*.

These terms, however, are borrowed, like the E. word, from O. Fr. *coque*, a cockle, an egg-shell; Cotgr.

COKKILSCHELL, *s.* A scallop shell.

"Item, a collare of *cokkilschellis* contenand xxiiij schellis of gold." Accts. L. H. Treas., A. 1488, i. 86. The reference is to the collar of the Order of St. Michael.

COKSAILL, *s.* A weather-cock.

". . . for mending of the *coksaill* quhen the wind blewe it doun, iiij s." Burgh Recs. Peebles, p. 414.

COLECT, Colleo, *s.* A collection, or contribution for a certain purpose, generally benevolent; also, a tax.

"Gif ony of the breder of gilde fall in puerte, the breder of the gilde sal help him of gudis of the gilde, or thai sal mak a *colect* throu the communite of the toun to the some of xx s.," &c. Fragments of Old Laws, ch. 2.

"And gif he [i.e., the leper] has nocht of his awne, the burges of that toune sal gar be gudderyt amangis thaim a *collec* to the valure of xx s.," &c. Burgh Lawis, ch. 58.

"Item, at thai [i.e., the baillies] put *colectis* vnreulfully and vndetfully nocht counsalit wit the comunite of the burgh." Chalmerlan Air, ch. 4.

Fr. *collecte*, from Lat. *collecta*.

COLEN, Colyne, *s.* and *adj.* Cologne: *colyne silk*, Cologne silk, Burgh Recs. Aberdeen, i. 234, Sp. C.

COLK, *s.* The eider duck, Orkn. (*v.* Neil's Tour).

To **COLL,** Cole, *v. a.* To cut, trim, or put into shape, to hollow out, to shape. Addit. to Coll.

This term is not properly defined in Dict. It does not mean to cut in general, nor to cut obliquely, as there stated. The primary idea is to cut or trim into shape; and this is implied in colling the hair, colling a candle, and colling a shoe or stocking . in each case it is cutting to a desired shape or form. Perhaps the best example in illustration is the phrase "*to coll a sey*," i.e., to cut out a nearly circular opening in a garment for the insertion of a sleeve, or to hollow out the armpit of a garment in order to relieve tightness: that is, in both cases, to cut out the required shape. Jamieson's etym. of the term is correct, and confirms the definitions now given. Besides, the term is still used in the North of E. with these meanings. V. Brockett's Gloss.

COLLEG, *s.* Colleague, associate, companion or fellow in office.

". . . ye accept the said office, and with your saidis *collegis* use and put the samyn to executioun deuly in all poyntis," &c. Burgh Recs. Edin., 8 Sept., 1519.

Lat. *collega*, one chosen or selected; Fr. *collègue*, a colleague.

COLLIE, Colly, *s.* 1. The line across the rink in curling; same as Coll, q. v.

2. A name given to a curling-stone that fails to pass the Collie; also to a failed ball in the game of bowls. V. Coll.

COLLOGUE, *s.* A conversation in whispers or secret, a private interview, a conference, confederacy.

O. Fr. *colloque*, a conference.

To **COLLOGUE,** *v. n.* To speak in whispers to each other, to converse secretly; to plot, plan, confederate.

COLMOTH, Colemoth, Colmouth, Colemie, Colmie, Colm, Comb, *s.* The coalfish, *Gadus carbonarius*, Linn.; for short, called a *colm, comb, com*; and when young, a *comamie, colminie*. Addit. to Colemie, Colmie.

This fish, which is still much used by the poorer classes, was salted and dried in large quantities for winter use. It is frequently mentioned in customs and Burgh Recs. V. Assize of Petty Customs, ch. 6. The *comamies* or young coal-fish appear to have been much prized; and they are mentioned by Scott as one of the dainties of May—

Butter, new cheis, and beir in May,
Comamis, cokkillis, curdis and quhay,
Lapstaris, lempettis, mussillis in schellis,
Grene lekis and all sic men may say,
Suppois sum of thame sourly smellis.
Alex. Scott, Of May, st. 7.

To **COLOR,** *v. a.* and *s.* To gloze, pretend regarding, represent falsely, palm off; hence the sb. *coloring*.

"The quhilk day the provest, baillies, and counsall, ordanis William Anderson till compeir befoir thame on Tyesday nixttocum for *coloring* of vnfremenies guidis," &c. Burgh Recs. Edin., 4 Mar., 1524-5.

COLRAIK, *s.* Surety. V. CULREACH.

COLYAR, COLYER, COLYEAR, COILYEAR, *s.* A collier, Accts. L. H. Treas., i. 389, 390; also, a coalman, hawker of coal, as, Rauf *Coilzear*, Ralph the coalman, or coal-ca'er.

Not Ralph *the collier*, as generally rendered; for he did not dig the coals, he only sold them. As he informed the Emperor,—
Iline ouer seuin mylis I duell
And leidis Coilis to sell.
st. 4.

COM, CUM, *v.* These forms occur as *pr. t., pa. t.,* and *pa. part.,* in each of the following applications.

1. Come, came; arrive, arrived.

2. Sprout, sprouted; like grain in growth, and in the process of malting. V. COME.

3. Stretch, expand, yield; stretched, &c.; like a cord under tension, metals under heat, &c.

COM, COME, CUM, *s.* 1. Coming, arrival, approach; Barbour, Wallace. V. COM.

2. Growth, germination. V. COM.

COMAMIE, COMINIE, *s.* V. under *Colmoth.*

To COMBURIE, *v. a.* To bury in company with.

"And so like some American Kings whose custome is to *comburie* their concubines with themselues, so must we our old-mans affections before we dissolue." Blame of Kirkburiall, ch. 16.

COME-AGAINST, *adj.* Repulsive, Orkn.

COME-KEIK, *s.* A novelty, Orkn.

COMMENTAR, *s.* Commentary, explanation; Blame of Kirkburiall, ch. 5.

COMMINITE, COMUNYTE, *s.* V. COMMONTY.

COMMON, *adj.* Public, belonging to or for the benefit of the public; as, *common clerk,* the town clerk; *common pyper,* the town piper; *common minstrel,* the town musician; Accts. L. H. Treas., i. 239, 375.

These officials are frequently mentioned in the Burgh Records of Scotland, especially the *common minstrels*, as most of the towns had one or more of those humble musicians, and the nature of their calling tended to bring them oftener before their masters, the magistrates, than was pleasant to either party.

To COMMON, COMMOUN, *v. n.* To have dealings with, commune, converse: part. pr. *commoning, commonyng,* used as a *s.* meaning intercourse, conversation; Douglas, Virgil, iv. ch. 1, Palice of Honour.

COMMON-GUDE, *s.* V. under *Gude.*
(Sup.) L

COMMONTY, *s.* Commonness, publicity; a common, public, or every day matter. Addit. to COMMONTY.

"Now this sepulchral communion for the *commonty* of it, none should contemn." Blame of Kirkburiall, ch. 10.

COMPACIENT, *adj.* Compassionate, Douglas, Virgil, i. ch. 9.

COMPLEIS, COMPLES, *s.* An accomplice, confederate; pl. *compleisis, complesis,* Burgh Recs.

Fr. *complice,* "a *complice,* confederate, companion in a lewd action;" Cotgr.

COMPREMYTTIT, *part. pt.* Engaged together, jointly sued; Burgh Recs. Prestwick, 2 June, 1541. V. COMPROMIT.

COMPRISER, *s.* Valuator, appraiser, arbiter. Addit. to COMPRYSER.

"James Smith in Kirktoune pursues Allan Langwill in Murehouse for eaten corne be the said Allanc his horse; Arthure Bryce, one of the *compriseris* thereof, being personallie present, declares the said skaith to his judgement wes three pecks, at seavin shilling four penies the peck, inde tuentie two shilling." Corshill Baron Court Book, Ayr and Wigtown Arch. Coll., iv. 109.

COMPTOUR-BURD, *s.* A counting-board; a board divided into squares to facilitate the counting of money; also called a *Covontour.*

This term occurs in a list of heirship goods, thus:—
". . ane flandres kist price vj s.; ane box, price iij s.; ane *comptour burd,* price a merk;" &c. Acta Dom. 1490, p. 176.

Fr. *comptoir,* a counting board; also, a coffer for money.

COMYN, *s.* Cumin, cumin seed; Petty Customs, ch. 7. Lat. *cuminum.*

CON. A form of *Can* used for Gan, as auxiliary verb, i.e., did: as, *con full,* did fall, fell; *con study,* did study, studied. V. CAN.

CON, CONE, *s.* A form of Can, ability, possibility; Court of Venus, iv. 279. V. CAN.

Printed *tone* in Court of Venus, p. 120, S. T. S.; but the context suggests that it may be a mis-print or a mis-reading of *cone.*

CONABILL, CONABLE, *adj.* Convenient, suitable; fit or able to be arranged; a contr. of O. Fr. *covenable* (=*convenable*), id. Barbour, iii. 290, v. 266. Other forms are *cunable, cunnable.* Errat. in DICT.

CONAND, CUNAND, *s.* V. CONNAND.

CONCEIT, CONCEAT, CONSEATE, CONSAIT, CONSATE, *s.* Lit. a conception, i.e., of the mind: hence, fanciful contrivance or arrangement; whim, delight; Houlate, ll. 284, 300.

". . . that not only for a religious respect were they separated from the places of God, but in a politick *conseate* also from their owne, in permitting no cittie buriall." Blame of Kirkburiall, ch. 16.
Then he march'd thro' the house, he march'd but, he march'd ben,
Like ower mony mae o' our great little men,
That I leugh clean outright, for I couldna contain,
He was sic a *conceit*—sic an ancient like wean.
The Wonderfu' Wean, Whistle Binkie, ii. 317.

CONCEITY, CONCEATY, *adj.* Ready, apt, quick-witted, appropriate; also, causing or yielding pleasure, taking one's conceit or fancy; as, "A blithe, *conceity*, wee thing." Addit. to CONCEITY.

"According to the *conceaty* resolution of Theodore in answer to the tyrant Lysimachus, that it was all one to him to putrifie aboue, or vpon, or within the earth." Blame of Kirkburiall, ch. 6.

CONCLAVE, *s.* Secret chamber, council-room.

Till he come quhair thir sisteris sat so schene
In sue *conclave* all maid of Christall cleir.
Court of Venus, ii. 501, S. T. Soc.
Fr. *conclave,* a conclave, closet; Cotgr. Lit. a locked up place.

CONCUBY, *s.* A concubine, Charters, &c. of Peebles, p. 269, Rec. Soc.

To CONDAMP, *v. a.* To condemn; pret. and part. pa. *condampnit*; Compl. Scot. p. 117, 119, E. E. T. S.

CONDAMPNIT, *part. pt.* Condemned, Lawis of the Gild, ch. 9.

CONDYT, *s.* A conductor, Kingis Quair, st. 113. Addit. to CONDIT.

CONFEKKIT, *part. adj.* Confected, prepared by art: "*confekkit* drynkis," fermented liquors.

". . . at that time the pepil drank nothir vyne nor beir, nor na vther *confekkit* drynkis." Compl. Scot. p. 145, E. E. T. S.
Lat. *confectus,* id.

CONFIRMACIONE, *s.* A charter or deed confirming a previous grant; ratification. Accts. L. H. Treas., A. 1473-4, i. 2.

"Item, ane *confirmacione* of ane charter to Johne Lord Semple of the landis of Montgrenane, xli."
"Item, ane charter of *confirmacione* of the ferd part of the landis of Glassill to Patrik Lindusaye, iij li."
Accts. L. H. Treas., A. 1494-95, i. 211.

CONFRARIE, *s.* Brotherhood, fraternity, association.

". . . statute and ordauit be the provest, baillies, counsale, and brether of the *confrarie* of the gild," &c.
Burgh Recs. Edin., 29 March, 1508.
Fr. *confrérie,* a fraternity; O. Fr. *confrairie,* Cotgr.

To CONFRONT, *v. a.* To arrest, stem, stay.

". . . except so far as by exemples we may *confront* our present confusions, whereat I aime." Blame of Kirkburiall, ch. 5.

CONGREW, *adj.* Congruous, harmonious; Court of Venus, ii. 77. Lat. *congruere,* to accord.

To CONJUNE, *v. a.* To conjoin: pret. and part. pa. *coniunit*; Compl. Scot., p. 77, 82, E. E. T. S. Lat. *conjungere.*

CONJUNCT-FEFTMENT, *s.* Joint infeftment, giving possession of property to husband and wife in common.

"Item, ane charter of *coniunctfeftment* to Alexander Reid and his wiff, v. li. vj s. viij." Accts. L. H. Treas., A. 1494, i. 211. Dickson.

To CONJURE, CONIURE, *v. n.* To conspire, rebel, or league against authority; Compl. Scot. p. 133, E. E. T. S.

CONJURATIONE, CONIURATIONE, *s.* Conspiracy, act of leaguing against authority; Ibid., p. 117.

CONNOYANCE, CONNYSAUNCE, CONYSANCE, *s.* V. COGNOSCANCE.

The term of which these forms are varieties implies cognisance in the ordinary as well as in the heraldic sense. Jamieson gave the latter only.

CONNRYNG, *s.* Prob. a mistake for *commyng* or *coumyng,* cumin.

Fr. *cumin,* Lat. *cuminum,* Heb. *kammon.*
"Alsswa the said halye gayf sessing with a penne of a pond of *connryng* of Wil Bully land aweet the Cors." Charters &c. of Peebles, p. 113, Rec. Soc.

CONNYNG, CONNIN, *s.* Experience, skill, ability, judgment.

". . and thai sall swer the gret athe that thai sall thar of suth say and na suth layne, at thar *connyng* and at thar knawlage, or thane be the worde of thar faderys," &c. Fragments of Old Laws, ch. 10.
Modified from Icel. *kunnadi,* knowledge, experience; from *kunna,* to know.

CONQUES, *v.* and *s.* V. CONQUACE.

CONQUEST, CONQUISHED, *part. pt.* Acquired, obtained by purchase; Accts. L. H. Treas., i. 3. Addit. to CONQUACE.

CONSAIT, CONSATE, *s.* V. *Conceit.*

To CONSIDER, *ger.* To be considered.

"The contrare kinde of exemples that negatiuelie are set down to exhort to abstinence from their imitation rests *to consider.*" Blame of Kirkburiall, ch. 17.
This application of the gerund is still used: as, "The letter is still *to write.*"

CONSINGAGE, COSINGAGE, *s.* V. COSINGNACE.

CONSPIRATIONE, *s.* Conspiracy, Compl. Scot., p. 113, 117. Fr. *conspiration.*

To CONSTREINYE, CONSTRENYE, CONSTREIGNE, v. a. To constrain, compel; Compl. Scot., p. 68, 125, E.E.T.S.

". . . that law will nocht *constreinye* na burges to tak ony ither borch for his punde than a burges bot gif he will." Burgh Lawis, ch. 32.

". . . bot gif it war sua that he war sa gretly *constreignit* throu nede, . . . for nede has na law." Ibid., ch. 101.

Fr. *constraindre*, from Lat. *constringere*.

CONSTRY, CONSTRIE, CONSTRE, s. V. CONSTERIE.

CONSUET, *adj*. Customary, usual.

"Item, gif thar be ony that has away woll skynnis or hiddes of the whilkis thai pay na custom aucht and *consuet*." Chalmerlan Air, ch. 28.

Lat. *consuetus*, accustomed.

CONSUET, s. Short for *Consuetude*.

CONSUETUD, s. Custom. Lat. *consuetudo*.

". . . but his wardane . . . sall geyff answer for hym and thole doine for hym eftir the *consuetud* and the consideracion of the worthi men of the toune." Burgh Lawis, ch. 80.

To CONTEMPIL, v. a. To contemplate, observe, watch; pret. *contemplit*; Compl. Scot., p. 37. 47, E.E.T.S. Fr. *contempler*.

CONTEMPLINE, CONTEMPLENE, *part*. and s. Contemplating, contemplation; Ibid., p. 46.

CONTENANCE, COUNTINANS, s. Demeanour, bearing; Kingis Quair, st. 45, 50, 82, Barbour. i. 392, 482; *be countinans*, apparently, to all appearance, Ibid., xi. 496. V. CONTENE.

Barbour uses both *contenance* and *contening* in the same sense, vii., 387.

CONTENTATIOUN, s. Satisfaction, compensation; Burgh Recs. Edin., 6th March, 1525-6. V. CONTENT.

CONTROWIT, *part. pt.* Contrived, invented, devised; Douglas, Virgil, ii., ch. 3, Edin. MS. V. CONTRUFE.

In Ruddiman's Ed. *contruuit* from *contrufe; controwit* is from the other form *controve*, which is given by Halliwell. The term is not correctly rendered in Small's Gloss. to Douglas.

CONVETH, s. A certain duty paid to a chief or superior.

The following statement will make Jamieson's explanation of this term complete.

"*Conveth* was the Irish ' Coinmhedha or Coigny,' and the ' Dovraeth ' of the Welsh laws ; and was founded upon the original right which the leaders in the tribe had to be supported by their followers. It came to signify a night's meal or refection given by the occupiers of the land to their superior when passing through his territory, which was exigible four times in the year; and when the tribe territory came to be recognised as crown land, it became a fixed food contribution charged upon each ploughgate of land.

"In the reign of Alexander the Third this word seems to have assumed the form of Waytings, and appears in the Chamberlain Rolls of his reigu as a hurden upon the Thanages." Skeno's Celtic Scotland, iii. 232.

CONVICT, CONVICK, CONVYKKYT, *part. pt*. Convicted, found guilty; used also for condemned, and as short for convicted and condemned.

". . . and thai be *convict*, thai sall pay amorcyment of viij s." Burgh Lawis, ch. 60.

"Isobel Cokkie in Kyntor, be vertew of this commission, *convick* and brunt, 19th Feb., 1596." Trials for Witchcraft, Spald. Misc., i. 84.

"And gif scho makis ivil ale . . . and be *convykkyt* of it, scho sall gif til hir mercyment viii s.," &c. Burgh Lawis, ch. 63.

CONVYNE, CONWYN, CONWYNE, COVYNE, COVYNG, s. Agreement, bargain, counsel, plot, design; used both in a good and in a bad sense; Barbour, iv. 111, v. 301, ix. 14, xiii. 122.

O. Fr. *covine*, agreement, contrivance.

CONYE, CONYIE, s. A double hook or cleek used by fleshers in suspending a carcase of mutton, beef, &c.

". . . ane *conye*, ane camroll, with ane obiuse." Burgh Recs. Aberd., i. 176, Sp. C.

CONYIE, CONYIIE, COYNYIE, *adj*. Cornered, angular, squared. V. COIN.

". . . xii[c] howyn stanys astlayr and *coynyhe* swilk as fallys to that werk." Charters of Edin., 29th Nov., 1387.

COPPIN, *part. pt.* Errat. in DICT. for *Croppin*, crept, q. v.

This mistake originated in Tytler's Ed. of The Kingis Quair. V. Note in Skeat's Ed., p. 92.

COOM, s. Dust from a mill, or from riddled seeds, i.e., from corn, Orkn.

COPILL, s. A couplet, Kingis Quair, st. 92, 93, S.T.S.

COPPIT, *adj*. Cup-shaped, hollow; Douglas, Virgil, xiii., ch. 4, Edin. MS.

Ruddiman's Ed. has *toppit*, topped, atop, borne aloft. The passage runs thus:—

. . . . . the snale
Schakand hyr *coppit* schell or than hir tale.

CORBAL, CORBELL, s. A projecting stone or piece of timber which supports a superincumbent weight; also used as short for *corbel-table*.

"Item, for sawing of twa geistis and *corbellis*, ilk geist x[d] and ilk *corbell* v[d]; summa ijs vj[d]." Accts. Burgh of Edinburgh, 26th Jan., 1554.

Fr. *corbeille*, a wicker basket; also, a corbel in masonry.

CORDALSAILYE, s. Prob. parapets or other projections corbelled out beyond the face of a fortified wall. V. *Saillie*.

"Licentiam edificandi castra, turres et fortalicia cum januis ferreis, le battelling *corbalsailye*, barmkynnis et carceribus." Reg. Mag. Sig., 1424—1513, No. 1639.

Fr. *corbeille*, a corbel, and *saillie*, a projection; like "*saillie de maison*, an outjutting room;" Cotgr.

CORCE, *s.* Cross. V. Cors.

CORDINAR, Cordonare, Cordynar, Cordenar, *s.* A shoemaker, Accts. L. H. Treas. i. 65, iii. 268, 285. E. *cordwainer*.

O. Fr. *cordoan, cordowan*, Cordovan leather; Roquefort. Low Lat. *cordoanum*, from *Cordoa*, a spelling of Cordova, in Spain. V. Skeat's Etym. Dict.

CORDOK, *s.* A place of detention for evil-doers; a lock-up, prison cell.

". . . Nov., 1554, for ix. snekkis with thair stapils to the ix. *cordokkis* of the tolbuith," &c. Accts. Burgh of Edinburgh, ii. 294.

Prob. from Gael. *coirtheach*, wrong-doing, wrong-doer, a guilty person.

CORD-TAWES, *s.* Taws of cord; i.e., a scourge of small cords.

". . . the Kirk . . . , as being a denne of theeues, deseruing the Lord's *cord-tawes*." Blame of Kirkburiall, ch. 13.

CORDWAN, Cordwane, *s.* V. Cordevan.

CORKIS, *s. pl.* Cork-heeled shoes.

This term occurs in a list of articles of dress obtained for the Queen and her ladies when preparing to start on a pilgrimage to Whithorn in August, 1473. The list is headed, "Thingis tane for the Queenis persone."

"In the first, to Caldwele of hire chalmire, to pay for patynis and *corkis*, xij s." Accts. L. H. Treas., i. 29. Dickson.

These are the "*corkit schone*" of our old ballads.

CORNLAND, Corneland, *s.* Arable, tilled, or cultivated land.

". . . prata, marresia, hortos terras arabiles, lie *corneland*, terras non arabiles lie *unland*." Reg. Mag. Sig.

CORNIS, *s. pl.* Corn crops. S.

CORONAT, *part. adj.* Crowned, Henryson, Lyoun and Mous, l. 58.

Lat. *coronatas*, id.; from Lat. *corona*, a crown.

CORPS-GUARDE, *s.* Body-guard; Blame of Kirkburiall, ch. 19.

CORRECTOR, Correctour, *s.* Rector, instructor, conductor; as, "*correctour* of the queir," rector of the choir; Burgh Recs. Aberd., 5 Oct. 1553, Houlate, l. 212.

CORRODY, Corody, *s.* A sum of money, or an allowance of food, drink, and clothing due to the King from a vassal for the maintenance of an accredited servant when passing through his lands. V. *Conveth*.

David I. of Scot. made frequent visits to the court of Henry I. of Eng., and on each occasion was provided for both in going and returning by grants of *corrody*. V. Calendar of Documents relating to Scotland, i. 2-6.

O. Fr. *conroyer, corroyer*, to furnish, provide.

CORSAY, Corsie, *s.* A kind of cap worn by women: called also a *courche*, a *curche*, a *curchey*; and like M. E. *courchef*, is der. from Fr. *couvre-chef*.

". . pulling of hir *corsay* of hir heid and rugging of hir hair." Burgh Recs. Peebles, p. 275, Rec. Soc.

CORTRIKYS, *s.* A kind of cloth made at Courtray, the Flemish name of which was Cortrijck, or Kortryk.

Following two entries as to the purchase of cloth of Ypres comes "Idem computat per empcionem de v poviis cum dimidio J ulua cum dimidia ulna *Cortrikys* et communis varii coloris et precii." Exch. Rolls, Scot. ii. 465.

CORUYN, Corvyne, *part. pt.* Carved out, cut from; Douglas, Virgil, 141, 9, Rudd. ed. Errat. in Dict, q. v.

Edin. MS. has *corvyne*, which proves Dr. Jamieson's rendering to be wrong. However, he only followed Ruddiman.

COSYNE, Cosyng, *s.* A cousin, near relation, Barbour, xii. 31; pl. *cosyngis*, Ibid. viii. 396.

COSYNAGE, *s.* Kin, kindred, relationship; Ibid. v. 135. V. Cosingnace.

COT-ARMOUR, Cotearmour, Coytarmour, Cot of Armis, *s.* A surcoat or tabard charged with armorial bearings; *cot-armour*, Barbour, xviii. 95; pl. *cot-armouris*, armorial devices, Ibid. viii. 231. These terms are also used by Barbour and Douglas, meaning a coat of mail.

"Item, [3 Sept., 1496] for ij. elne of dowbil rede taffaty, to be the Kingis *cotearmour*, xxxvj s." Accts. L. H. Treas., i. 292.

And on 3 Oct., 1488, ". . . for ix *coyt armouris* to the harroldis and purcyfantis, price of ilk peyce, sylk, golde, aysure, and the makin of thaim, v li; summa of the ix, xlv li." Ibid. i. 163.

O. Fr. *cote*, a coat; *armoirié*, graven or charged with arms. But, as a coat of mail, from *cote*, a coat; and *armure*, harness, armour.

COTHERLIE, *adj.* Kindly, affectionate; Orkn.

COTTON, Cottont, Cottonit, Cotonyt, *adj.* Dressed with a nap, having a soft nap; as, *cotton lamskinnis*, lambskins with the wool cottoned or dressed, Accts. L. H. Treas., i. 202: *cotonyt clath*, cloth dressed or finished with a long nap, Ibid. i. 164.

COTTONOY, *s.* An annoyance, Orkn.

COU, *v.* and *s.* V. Cow.

COU [85] COW

To COUCH, v. a. To lay, inlay, set, deck, adorn; pret. and part. pt. *couchit*, decked, Kingis Quair, st. 46.

COUCHIT, COWCHIT, *part. pt.* Inlaid; same as Coutchit, q. v., Douglas. E. *couched*.

COUDE, CODE, *s.* Chrisom-cloth. V. CUDE.

To COUER, *v. a.* To recover. V. COUR, COWER.

COUNTERFOOTE, *s.* Pattern, example, imitation. E. *counterfeit*. V. COUNTER-FACTE.

"For as the Lord said to his two disciples (that after the *counterfoote* of Elias, would haue comn anded a consuming fire to come downe against the inhospitall Samaritanes.)" Blame of Kirkburiall, ch. 16.

COUNTINANS, COUNTYNANS, *s.* V. *Contenance*.

COUP, COWP, *s.* V. COOP.

To COUP, *v. a.* To shoot or empty the load of a *coup* or cart. Addit. to COUP, *v.*

COUP, *s.* 1. A *coup* or cart-load; as, "*coups* of fuilyie," cart or horse-loads of manure, Ayr and Wigtown Arch. Coll., iv. 149.

2. The act, right, or liberty of emptying a cart-load.

3. A place for shooting or emptying cart-loads of earth, ashes, and rubbish.

Clay-holes, quarries, etc., that the owners desire to be filled up are advertised as *coups*.

FREE COUP, *s.* Liberty to *coup* or deposit rubbish free of charge; also, a place where this liberty may be had.

To advertise a *free-coup* at such a place is the usual method of notifying that rubbish is urgently required at that place for levelling purposes.

The foregoing applications of *Coup* are still used.

To COUPON, COWPON, CULPON, *v. a.* To cut into pieces, slice, cut up.

"For superstition is lyke some serpents, that though they be *couponed* in many cuttes, yet they can keepe some lyfe in all." Blame of Kirkburiall, ch. 11.

Fr. *coupon*, a slice : from *couper*, to cut.

COUPON, COWPON, CULPON, *s.* A shred, rag, cutting, pairing. Addit. to COWPON, q. v.

The form *culpon* occurs in Chaucer, meaning a little bunch or bundle.

To COUR, CURE, *v. a.* To cover, spread, protect, to serve with the male; part. pr. *cureing*, used also as a *s.*

"In the action persewed be the said Robert Edmund against Robert Alexander in Foggiehillok for half a croun for *cureing* a mare with the persewer stoned horse. The Judge decerned the defender to pay half pryce because the defender was oblidged to goe to another horse, quhich was proved at the bar." Corshill Baron Court Book, Ayr and Wigtown Arch. Coll., iv. 240.

COUR, CURE, *s.* A cover, dish; pl. *curis*, *cureis*, bake-meats, cooked meats, Houlate, l. 695.

Given as *Curer* in DICT., which is a misreading of Pinkerton's ed. Bann. MS. has *cureis*; Asloan MS. *curis*.

COURFYRE, CURFOYR, *s.* Curfew, evening-bell. Fr. *couvre-feu*.

"Ordanis the stepill and knok to be ordourlie and sufficientlie kepit, neit and wont, aud to regne (ring) xij houris, vj houris, and *courfyre* nychtlie." Burgh Rec. Peebles, p. 324. Rec. Soc.

The term occurs in Aberdeen Burgh Recs., 27 Oct., 1503 as *curfoyr*.

To COURAY, *v. a.* To curry, to dress or prepare tanned leather for the shoemaker.

"Item, whair thai suld gif thair lethir gude oyle and taulch, thai gif it bot watter and salt. Item, thai wirk it or it be *courait*, in greit hindering and sknith of the Kingis liegis." Chalmerlan Air, ch. 22.

O. Fr. *conroier*, later *couroier*, or as Cotgrave has it *conroyer, courroyer*, "to currie, tawe, or dresse, as leather."

Burguy gives the forms *conroier, conreier, conraer*, to equip, furnish, prepare, put in order: from the root *roi, rei, rai*, order, arrangement.

COURPLE, *s.* The crupper of a saddle; Accts. L. H. Treas., i. 388. V. CURPLE.

COURTICIAN, CURTICIAN, *s.* A courtier, courtesan; Compl. Scot., p. 133. Fr. *courtisan*.

COURTINGIS, *s. pl.* Curtains.

"Item, [A. 1474] fra Will of Rend to bind my Lordis *courtings* jj quarter of bukramo, price xij d." Accts. L. H. Treas., i. 41.

"*My Lord*" here mentioned was Prince James, afterwards James IV. of Scotland, and the bit of buckram became part of the furnishing of his cradle.

COUTH, COUTHIN, *s.* A two-year-old and a three-year-old coal-fish, Orkn.

COUTHY, COUTHIE, *adj.* V. COUTH.

To COVAIT, COWAIT, *v. a.* To desire, wish, crave; Court of Venus, iii. 184, 502.

To COW THE BENT. Lit. to crop the coarse grass of the common or of untilled land; to take what one can get, to live as one may. *Cow the Bent* implies living on poor fare, and hence poverty, disgrace, misfortune.

Milch cows are pastured on the best grass; less worth cattle are sent *to cow the bent*. When a person is disgraced or cast off, he is said to be sent *to cow the bent*. The life of poverty, disgrace, or misfortune, is often called a life of "*cow the bent*."

And sum day quhen he seis his skaith,
He will yow thank and rewaird baith,

And turn the fox bak to his rent,
And former style of *cow the bent.*
  Rob Stene's Dream, p. 5.

COWARDY, COWARDIE, *s.* Cowardice, faint-heartedness. Barbour, i. 26, 747, Edin. MS.

Camb. MS. reads *woidre,* stratagem, cunning, in ix. 747, which certainly makes better sense. V. Skeat's Barbour, Gloss., and note p. 579.

COWBEL, COWBILL, COWBLE, *s.* V. COBLE, Coble.

COWNTOUR, *s.* V. *Comptour-burd.*

COWNTOURIS, *s. pl.* Counters, called also *Nuremberg tokens,* used in calculations on the Counter or Comptour-board. Accts. L. H. Treas., i. 300.

COYNYE, *s.* and *adj.* Corner. V. COIN.

CRAAR, CRARE, *s.* V. CREARE.

CRABBING, *s.* Irritation, provocation, rage; Henryson, Orpheus and Eurydice, l. 503. V. CRAB.

CRABSTANE, CRIBSTANE, *s.* Kerbstone, border of street pavement; S.

CRAIKAND, *part.* Croaking, crying; Henryson, Preiching of the Swallow, l. 159. V. CRAIK.

CRAIG, *s.* Neck, throat. V. CRAG.

CRAKLING - CHEESE, *s.* Refuse of tallow pressed into the form of a cheese; used for feeding dogs, poultry, etc., S. Addit. to CRACKLINGS.

Tallow refuse is also called *crakkings;* and the cake or cheese *crakking-cheese;* West of S.

CRAK-RAIP, CRAK-RAPE, *s.* Crack-rope; one fit for the hangman's rope; a term of contempt applied to a thief or a rascal, expressive of what he deserves.

In dreid and schame our dayis we indure:
Syne widdie-nek and *crak-raip* callit als,
And till our hyre hangit up be the hals.
  Henryson, Tod's Confessioun, l. 48.

In Dr. Laing's ed. of Henryson this term is carelessly rendered "*hangman's rope.*"

Crak-raip or *crack-rope, crack-hemp, crack-halter,* are terms of contempt used both in Eng. and Scot., and generally applied to habit-and-repute thieves: but, like the term *widdie-nek* as used by Henryson, and *gallowsbird* of modern times, they were also applied to rogues, rascals, and miscreants of the worst kind, to express the end they will come to, or the punishment they deserve. Shakespeare certainly uses *crack-hemp* in this sense. Some writers, however, define *crack-raip* as one who has been hanged, but escaped by the breaking of the rope; for a man can't be hanged twice. But this meaning is, at least, not the one in which the term is commonly used; and prob. it has originated from the mistaken idea that *crack* means to break. In this connection it means to stretch or strain tight, to stretch to the utmost: just as we say the rigging, cordage, or timbers of a ship crack and shiver when straining in a storm.

CRAN, *s.* A crane; also, a vulgar name for a heron; Accts. L. H. Treas., i. 182, Dickson.

In Scot. records the word *cran* almost always means a heron, and during the fifteenth century this bird must have been common in Scotland, as it formed an important dish at great feasts. V. Gloss. to Accts. But the crane never was a native of Scotland, and has always been an exceedingly rare visitant.

Or like a *cran,* . . . .
That man take nine steps before she flees,
  Old Proverb.

A.-S. *cran,* Dan. *krane,* Swed. *kran,* id.

CRAN-CRAIG, CRAN-CRAIGIE, CRAN-CRAIGIT, *s.* and *adj.* Crane neck, one who has a long slender neck; also, crane-necked; as, "That *cran-craigie* beast cou'd never ca' coals," West of S.

V. *Cran,* a crane, and *Craig,* a neck.

CRAP - HEICH, CROP - HEICH, CROPE - HEIGH, *adj., adv.,* and *s.* Topmost, highest: *in the crop - heich,* in the highest place, Houlate, l. 408, Bann. MS.

CRARE, *s.* V. CREARE.

CRASIE, CRASY, CHRAISY, *s.* A kind of bonnet for women, a sun-bonnet, Clydes., Lothian. V. Gaberlunzie Wallet, p. 40.

CRAUDON, *s.* A craven. V. CRAWDON.

CRAW-POCKIES, *s.* The eggs of sharks, skate, and dog-fish, Orkn.

To CREAN, CREEN, CREIN, *v. a.* Forms of CRINE, to shrivel, &c., q. v.

CREANCE, CREANS, *s.* Credit. Fr. *créance.*

"And all manner of othir thingis till thair *creance* lent or laid iu wed within thair burghe jt sall fully be determyt and endit." Fragments of Old Laws, ch. 8.

CREANSOUR, *s.* A creditor. Fr. *créancier.*

"And gif he wil nocht it outquyte, it sal be salde and the *creansour* sall tak his dett." Burgh Lawis, ch. 79.

CREDENCE, *s.* Credentials, testimonials; evidence, attestation. O. Fr. *credence,* as *creance.*

Quhen thai consault had the cas and the *credence,*
Be the herald in hall huve thai nocht ellis.
  Houlate, l. 300.

CREAT, *pret.* and *part. pa.* Created, Compl. Scot., p. 34, 43, E.E.T.S.

CREESHIE, *adj.* V. under CREISCH.

CREMAR, *s.* A pedlar, a hawker of wares; Accts. L. H. Treas., i. 184. V. CREAMER.

According to the burgh laws the *cremar* was allowed to have an open stand or stall at certain fairs and markets but their usual stance was on the street, and if

possible near the door of a church, as noticed in the entry quoted above.
The burgess and guild-brother, who kept a booth or shop, had no favour for the *cremar;* and it was reckoned dishonourable for a booth-keeper to be a *cremar* as well. Indeed, in a dispute among the hammermen of Glasgow in 1045 regarding one of their brethren who had been *creaming,* the provost and magistrates were intreated to protect the craft ; and the petition presented by the guild craved them " to caus the said Robert keip himself and his wair within his owne buith and drope, and to cousider that no buithe keiper aught to be ane *creamer,*" etc. Burgh Recs. Glasgow, Vol. II., p. 77, V. *Drop.*

CREME-STOK, CREM-STOK, s. The chrismstock or vessel for holding the holy anointing oil.

"Item, ane *crem-stok* of siluer with ane closour of siluer and the laif of the graithe langamd thairto of euore." Reg. Vestments, &c. St. Salvator's Coll. St. Andrews, Maitland Club Misc., iii. 203.
O. Fr. *cresme,* the chrism.

CREMESYE, s. V. CRAMESYE.

CREN, s. A crane. V. CRANE.

CRENISHED, *part. pt.* Notched, serrated; broken or gapped along the top or edge, as a mouldering wall or rusty sword.

"The back dyick of the college yaird quhilk is *crenished* and speldit . . and lickle to faill." Aberd. Burgh Records, 28 Aug., 1646.
O. Fr. *crené,* nicked, notched, indented.

CRENYIE, *adj.* Small, dwarfish, Orkn.

CRESCHE, s. Grease. V. CREISCH.

" . . . falset in weyande of ony thyng suilk as well, nowte *cresche* or swyne sayme," etc. Burgh Lawis, ch. 68.

CREWIS, *s. pl.* Craves. V. CROO, CRUVE.

CRIIT, CRIOUR. V. under *Cry.*

To CRINGE, CRYNGE, CRENGE, CRAINGE, *v. n.* To cringe, crouch, shrivel, draw together, cower; as, "He sits *cringin'* at the fire."

He criplit, he *cryngit,* he cairfully cryd,
He solpit and sorrowit in sichingis seir.
Houlate, l. 956, Bann. MS.

As generally used this term seems to be a freq. of *crine,* to shrivel, grow less ; Gael. *crionan* : which, however, could not evolve the final *ge.* As used in Mod. Eng., it is said to be derived from A.-S. *cringan, cringan, crincan,* to sink in battle, fall, succumb. V. Skeat's Etym. Dict.

CROFF, CRUFF, s. A hovel, sty. V. CRUFE.

CROIP, s. Crop ; *croip and calf,* crop and grass, Henryson. V. under *Calf.*

CROKETS, CROKETTIS, *s. pl.* Ruffles, neck-ornaments, curls, tresses ; West of S. Addit. to CROCKATS.

Crockets were twists of hair originally. V. Halliwell.

To CRONE, CRUNE, *v. n.* V. CROYN, CROON.

CROOK, CRUIK, s. A crack or cleft in a rock, or in a rocky hill-side ; also, hollows under projecting rocks ; Barbour, x. 602, 605, Hart's Ed. E. *creeks.*

CROOKED, CRUKYT, *adj.* Deformed, lame, decrepid. V. CRUKE.

"Andrew Buchanan in Robertlane pursues Thomas Wylie in Meikle Corshill for curing of ane horse *crooked.*" Corshill Baron Court, Ayr and Wigtown Arch. Coll., iv. 107.

"Giff ony of our brether of the gilde in his eyld fall *crukyt* or pure or in ane vncurabill seyknes, and he haue nocht of his awin whar of he may be austenyt . . . he aalbe releffyt." Lawis of the Gild, ch. 12.

To CROON, CROUN, *v. a.* To hum or sing softly, as to an infant; to sing with subdued voice, as for practice when one is alone or pleased. V. CROYN.

Whiles holding fast his gude blue bonnet ;
Whiles *crooning* o'er some auld Scots sonnet.
Burns, Tam o' Shanter.

But blythely tak' the road, an' while journeying alang,
Croon cheerily to mysel' an auld Scottish sang.
Alex. Wilson's Poems, p. 410.

In the DICT. *croon* is represented as a neut. vb. only.

To CROON, CROUN, *v. n.* To emit low, sad, sorrowful tones, to sing a lament ; to mourn, lament; as, "She sits *croonin'* for her bairn that's gane." Addit. to CROON, CROYN.

Croon is also used to express playing or practising in a low or sad tone; as, "the shepherd *croonin* on his pipe." In this sense James Ballantine uses the term in his merry song, "The Auld Beggar Man."

He puff'd on the weaver, he ran to his loom ;
He shankit the snab bame to cobble his shoon ;
He skelpit the herd, on his bog-reed to *croon—*
Saw ye e'er sic a strong auld man !
Gaberlunzie's Wallet, p. 14.

CROON, CROONACH, s. The act of singing in a soft low voice, a song of sorrow or lamentation, a low sweet lullaby; Gaberlunzie's Wallet, p. 198. Addit. to CROON.

CROOPAN, s. The throat, Orkn.

CROOPAN, s. The tail crupper ; girth of a horse, Orkn.

CROP, CROPE, s. The top. V. CRAP.

CROP, CRUP, *pret.* Crept, did creep. Addit. to CRAP.

The forms *crap, crop, crup,* are still used as pret. of *creep ;* so also are the corresponding forms of the part. pt. *crappen, croppen, cruppen.*

CROPPIN, *part. pt.* Crept, Kingis Quair, st. 182, Skeat's Ed. S. T. S.

In the DICT. this word is given as COFFIN, from Tytler's ed.; but it is a misreading. See Note in Skeat's ed., p. 92.

Other forms of this part. pt. are *creepin, crappin, crippin, crep, crip, crap, crop.*

CROPE, *v.* and *s.* Croak. V. CROUP.

CROSE-GAIRD, CORCE-GAIRDIS, s. The cross-guard, the watch or watchmen at the burgh cross; Burgh Recs. Edin., iv. 187, Rec. Soc.

CROUF, s. A kind of hide, a stout shoe-leather.
"And thar is aucht for the canage of a last of hydys xij d, of a last of crouf j d." Fragments of Old Laws, ch. 27.

CROUNE, CROUN, CROVNE, CRONE, s. A crown, a gold coin of which there were various denominations current in Scotland, viz.:—

1. *Scottis Croune*, first struck by Robert III., which varied in value at different periods from 12s. to 13s. 4d.; but it was generally reckoned at 13s. 4d. Accts. L. H. Treas., i. 167.

2. *Franche Croune*, which varied in value from 12s. 6d. to 15s., but the usual value was 14s. This coin was very much used in Scotland; indeed, it appears to have been the favourite gold coin during the 15th and 16th cents. Ibid. i. 64, 167.

3. *Croune of the Sone*, i.e., crown of the sun, so called from its mint mark, and often mentioned in old accounts, was reckoned at 14s. value, Ibid. i. 302.

CROVE, CROOVE, s. A trap for fish, Aberd., Perths., West of S. V. CRUVE.

CROWNAIR, s. Coroner. V. CROWNARE.

CRUCHET, CRACHET, s. A little crook or cleek, Barbour, x. 41. Fr. *crochet*.

CRUDGEBAK, s. Crookback. In M. Eng. *crocheback*, *crouchback*.
A *crudgebak* that cairfull eative bura.
Douglas, King Hart, i. 116, ed. 1874.

CRUIK, s. V. CROOK.

CRUK, CRUKE, CRUIK, s. The strong iron hook used in suspending a large pot over a fire; also, the iron chain with a small hook called a *gab* attached, used in suspending a small pot. Prob. this confusion arose from the frequent use of both *cruik* and *gab* for suspending a small pot; Burgh Lawis, ch. 16. Addit. to CROOK.

2. A shepherd's crook or staff. By *heuk and cruk*, by reaping hook or shepherd's staff, that is, by tilling land or keeping flocks; and these being the primitive modes of earning a living, the phrase in early times would represent *by this way or that, by one way or other, by some means*. In like manner, *by heuk and cruk* would represent *by both ways*, and then *by all ways or means, by any or every way*.
The mair we get *by heuk and cruk*,
We aften grow the greedier.
Alex. Wilson, *The Shark*, s. 7.
Another meaning of *cruk, cruik*, is given under CROOK AND BANDS.

CRUKYT, adj. Decrepit. V. CROOKED.

CRULL, s. A confused heap, a complete smash, Orkn.

CRUMB, CRUMBE, s. A curve, bend, crook; hence, in a fish the point where the body bends or curves from the tail, the anal fin.
"Neither sall it be leasum to him to cutt the sal-mound above the *crumbe* or any parte therof," etc. Burgh Recs. Glasgow, 17 Feb., 1644. V. *Salmon Tail*.
This is an extract from the famous Glasgow "Law of Salmound Tails " to which appeal was often made during the 17th and early part of the 18th cents.
Gael. *cruime*, a bend, curvature; from. *crom*, crooked.

To CRY, v. a. To proclaim, publish, declare; as, "*To cry* a fair or a roup." Addit. to CRY, q. v.

To CRY A FAIR. To proclaim or give public notice regarding the holding of a fair.
In olden times this was a great and most important proclamation, and was made with all due ceremony on the evening of the day before the fair. To the people of the burgh the proclamation was made by a town-officer standing on the tolbuith stair, or on the steps of the cross: and to the landward or country people it was made by another officer who stood on the public green or common.
The following extract from the Burgh Records of Glasgow gives a full account of "the crying of a fair." It is dated 6 July, 1590.
"The peace of the fair was proclamit be David Coittis, mair of fie, vpoun the Grene, and be James Anderson, town officer, vpoun the tolbuith stair, oftir the forme and tennour vnderwrittin :—Forsamekle as the sevint day of Julij approcheand is the fair day of the burgh and citie of Glasgow of auld, heirfoir, I, in our Soverane Lordis name, and als in name and behalf of the baillies of the regalitie of Glasgw, and provost and baillies of the same, commandis and chargis and als in-hibits and forbiddis all our Soverane Lordis lieges that nane of thame tak vpoun hand to molest or trouble ony persone or persouis repairand to the said fair, remane-and thairin, or passand thairfra, for ald feid or new, for auld dett or new, or brek the peace of the said fair be way of tuilzie or trublance, for the space of aucht dayis nixt thairefter, vnder the pane of ten pundis ilk fault vnforgevin." Burgh Recs. Glasgow, i. 154, Rec. Soc.

To CRY A ROUP OR SALE. To proclaim or publish it by the bellman or town officer.
In towns the bellman passed through the streets with his proclamation : but in country districts with scattered population he cried a roup or sale at the church door as the people came out.
O auctioneers he was the wale,
And rairly he could *cry a sale*
On Sabbath, when the kirk did scale,
And neir did spare.
Fisher's Poems.

CRIIT, CRIYT, CRYDE, CRIDE, *pret.* and *part. pt.* Cried, proclaimed; proclaimed in church.

". . . giffin to ane wif that brocht cheriis to the King and *criit* on him for siluer, iiij s." Accts. L. H. Treas., I. 349.

". . . [3 Feb., 1493] . . Johne Keyr, messinger, passand with the Kingis lettrez in Galoway and Carryk to ger wapynschawingis be *cryit*," etc. Ibid., i. 319.

In West of S. this term is pron. *cride* (*i* as in *pride*), and *cryde* (*y* as in *dyed*): generally *cryde*, when it ends a phrase or sentence, and *cride*, when it is followed by other words.

Before the Registration Act came into force, the fee paid to a Session Clerk for proclamation of banns was called *cryin siller*.

CRIOUR, CRIER, *s.* An inferior officer of a burgh, a town-officer, a sergeand, a beadle.

"The *criouris* [seriandis] sal be chosyn communly be the consent of all the burges, and thai aw to be lele men and of gude fame, and thai sal suer fewte to the King and the aldirman and the bailyeis of the toune and to all burges in full court." Burgh Lawis, ch. 71.

The *crier* was, as the extract judicates, an officer of court, and an officer of the burgh; indeed, the name by which he was best known and is still called, a *town's officer*, includes both duties. He acted as crier at the common courts, and passed through the town with bell or drum to publish notices and proclamations; on great occasions he led the procession of magistrates and carried a bright polished halberd, and on market days he kept a sharp eye on the weights and measures, and passed round the stalls with the *customers* when they uplifted their dues or petty customs. He was therefore a well-known and important person in the burgh of olden times; but his duties and his honours have been greatly diminished of late by Burgh Improvement Acts.

CRYKE, CRUIK, *s.* V. *Crook.*

CRYSME, *s.* Consecrated oil; also, unction, anointing. Blame of Kirkburiall, ch. 14.

CUBBIE, *s.* A small cassie or basket, often made of heather; Orkn.

CUD, CUDE, *s.* 1. Cud; *chewt their cude*, ruminated, reflected, mused, meditated.

Owre a broad wi' bannocks heapet, Cheese, and stoups, and glasses stood;
Some were roaring, ithers sleepit,
Ithers quietly *chewt their cude*.
Alex. Wilson, Watty and Meg, s. 4.

2. Stuff to chew, food.

Thy *cud*, thy claithis, thy coist, cumis nocht of the.
Houlate, l. 978, Bann. MS.

A.-S. *cwidu*, and later *cudu*, cud, from *cedwan*, to chew. Gael. *cuidh*, food.

CUDDIE, *s.* A ditch or cutting to lead the drainage of a district to a river; also, an overflow connection between a canal and a river. Addit. to CUDDIE, q. v.

Except during the time of flushing or overflow the water in the *cuddie* is stagnant or nearly so.

The term is a corr. of O. Fr. *conduit*, an aqueduct, a canal. V. CUNDIE.

(Sup.) M

CUDICHE, CUDDECHT, CODDECHT, CODDACHEICH, *s.* A term synon. with *Conveth*, q. v.

This word frequently occurs in rentals of lands in the Highlands and Islands, and signifies a night's victuals or entertainment: from Gael. *cuidh*, food, and *oidhche*, night.

CUDYOCH, CUDYEOCH, *s.* V. CUDEIGH.

CUIL, CUYL, *adj.* and *v.* Cool, North of S.: *cule*, West of S. V. *Cule, v.*

To CUILYE, *v. a.* To entice, beguile; another form of CULYE, q. v.

O. Fr. *guiller*, "to cousen, beguile, deceiue;" Cotgr.

CUIR, *s.* Task, office, duty, Court of Venus, Prol. 246; thought, desire, Ibid., i. 421. E. *cure*.

To CUIR, *v. a.* To value, esteem, regard.

For sic storyis I *cuir* thame not ane prene.
Court of Venus, iii. 546, S. T. Soc.

O. Fr. *cure*, from Lat. *cura*, care.

CUIT, *s.* The ankle. V. CUTE.

CUITIKINS, CUTIKINGIS, *s. pl.* V. CUTIKINS.

To CUITER, CUTTER, *v. a.* and *n.* Same as CUTER, to cocker; also, to coax, wheedle, caress, fondle, whisper lovingly; Whistle Binkie, I. 155, II. 66. Addit. to CUTER, KUTER.

CUITERER, CUTTERER, *s.* A coaxer, wheedler, fawner, fair-speaker; West of S.

CULD, *v. aux.* Did, Compl. Scot., p. 63, E. E. T. S.

This peculiar use of *culd* arose from confounding the auxiliary *gan* (=did) with *can*, and then using *culd* as its past tense.

To CULE, *v. a.* and *n.* To cool, to become cool.

"He may *cule* his outes a wee," i.e., he must wait a little.

"Keep your breath to *cule* your parritch;" said to one who is angry without cause.

Schir Ranf caucht to *kule* him, and tak mair of the licht
He kest vp his vesseir,
With ane cheualrous cheir.
Rauf Coilyear, s. 65.

A.-S. *cól*, cool; Dan. *köl*, Swed. *kylig*, Ger. *kuhl*.

CULE, CUIL, CUYL, *adj.* and *s.* Cool, cold, become cool or cold, of sufficient coolness. As a *s.* like E. cool, cold, implying, state, condition, etc.

Are ye no gaun to waeken the day, ye rogue?
Your parritch is ready and *cule* in the cog.
W. Miller, Sleepy Wee Laddie, st. 1.

CULPON, *s.* A shred. V. COWPON, COUPON.

CULUM, *s.* A tail, fundament.
The *culum* of Sanct Bryda cow,
The gruntill of Sanct Antonis sow,
Quhil bure his baly bell.
Lyndsay, Thre Estaitis, 1. 2102.
Lat. *culus,* fundament.

CULVERIN, CULUERENE, CULVRIN, *s.* Originally a hand gun of a yard long; afterwards a cannon of the second order, long in proportion to its calibre; also called a serpentine; Accts. L. H. Treas., I. 122, 131. V. CULRING.
Fr. *couleurrine,* from *coleuvre,* an adder; Lat. *colubra.*

CUM, COM, *v.* and *s.* V. Com.

CUM, CUMB, COOM, KIM, *s.* A tub, cistern, as, "a milk-*cum* or *kim* ;" also, a large ladle for baling a boat; West and South of S.

CUMMEN, COOMEN, KIMMEN, *s.* Lit. a small *cum* or *kim,* a small or shallow tub, a ladle, a skimmer. V. KIMMEN.
Gael. *cum,* to keep, hold; *cuman,* a milking pail, a circular wooden dish without a handle; M'Leod and Dewar.

CUMBLY, *adj.* Comely, Barbour, xi., 132, Edin. MS.

CUMFETHIS, *s. pl.* A corr. of CONFECTS, sweetmeats, q. v. It represents a pron. which is still common.

CUMMERIT, CUMMYRIT, CUMRAIT, CUMRAYIT, *pret.* and *part. pt.* Cumbered, encumbered, harassed, overwhelmed; Barbour, xi. 198, xiv. 298, xiii. 127, xiv. 550, xvii. 123.

CUMRAW, CUMROW, *s.* A comrade, companion, neighbour.
". . . for keiping gud nychtburcheid to thair *cumrowis,*" etc. Burgh Recs. Prestwick, 24 Apr,, 1572.
This form may be only the local pron. of E. *comrade.*

To CUMSEIL, COMSEIL, *v. a.* To line the roof and walls of a room with wood, to ceiling and wainscot, to lath and plaster; Old Church Life in Scotland, p. 38. V. COOM-CEIL'D.
This may be a compound of *con,* altogether, and M. E. *syle,* to ceil, to cover with boards, line, etc., and used to imply the lining of a room with wood or with lath and plaster: but more prob. it is *coom-ceil* with extended meaning adapted to modern usage. In most cases the lining is laid or fitted on *cooms* or frames.

CUNGLES, *s. pl.* Coarse gravel, roundish water-worn stones; E. *shingles.* V. CHINGLE.

CUNGLY, *adj.* Gravelly; covered with shingles or roundish water-worn stones; as, "a *cungly* shore;" Ayrs., Orkn. V. CHINGLIE.

CUNNAR, CONNAR, *s.* A tester, taster. V. CUN.
"Item, at thai put nocht furth thair ail wande to certify the *cunnaris* of the ayl as thai solde. Item, at thai sell ail nocht the *cunnar* beand present, na yit cunnand efter hend." Chalmerlan Air, ch. 39.
In the Record edition of Acts of Parliament and in the Ancient Laws and Customs of Scotland issued by the Burgh Record Society, these words are given as *tunnaris, tunnar, tunnand,* the transcriber having probably misread *c* as *t.* Cf. E. *ale-conner.*
The following extracts explain the use of the *alewand,* and how the ale was *cunned.*
"And ilke broustare sal put hir alewande ututh hir house at hir wyndow or abuue hir dur that it may be seabill communly til al men, the quhilk gif scho dois nocht scho sal pay for hir defalt iiij d." Burgh Lawis, ch. 63.
". . . the bailyeis sall pass throu the towne with thair officeris and *cunnaris* and cwnd and vese the aill, and mak the price how the aill salbe sauld fowr tymes in the yeir," etc. Burgh Recs. Peebles, 8 Nov., 1571.
Then the *cunnar,* having valued the ale, and declared it in the presence of the bailies and their officers, did "calk apoun a dur alsmony scoris with calk as the galoun salbe saulde of thair aille." Ibid., p. 17.
In those days ale was an important article of food, and it was necessary to protect it from the 'tricks of trade' as well as the greed of the seller; hence the following law, which held good in every burgh.
"And scho [i.e., the broustare] sall mak gud ale and approbabill as the tym askis. And gif scho makis ivil ale and dois agane the custume of the toune and be convykkyt of it, scho sall gif til hir mercyment viii s. or than thole the lauch of the toune, that is to say he put on the kukstule, and the ale sall be geyffin to the pure folk the tua part, and the thryd part send to the brethyr of the hospitale. And rycht sic dome sal be done of meide as of ale." Burgh Lawis, ch. 63.

CUNNING, *s.* A rabbit. V. CUNING.

CUNTRE, COUNTRE, *s.* Encounter, attack; Douglas, Virgil, vii. ch. 9, Edin. MS. V. COUNTYR.

CUNYE, CUNYEE, CUNYIE, *s.* Coinage. Used also as an *adj.*; as, "the *cunyee* siluir of the pennyis." Accts. L. H. Treas., I. 312. Addit. to CUINYIE.

CUNYEING, *part.* as a *s.* Coining; as, "in the *cunyeing* of fifty tua Trois pundis and ane halue vnce of brokin siluer vesschell," etc. Accts. L. H. Treas., I. 168.

CUNYEIT, *pret.* and *part. pt.* Coined; Ibid., i. 313.

CUNYER, CUNYEOUR, CUNYIER, *s.* A coiner; *fals cunyer,* a false coiner, a maker of base money. V. CUNYIE-HOUSE.
"Item, for twa horss to carry the *fals cunyers* to the gallows, and name bringing of their legs and heids, and girding of thair bodeyis, xxij s." Accts. Burgh of Edinburgh, 1553-4.

"... and the said sitter to be brocht bak to us and to be diliuerit to the *maister cunyeour*," [i.e., master of the mint] etc. Burgh Recs. Edinburgh, 1554, II. 204.

CUP, *s.* A term in golfing applied to a small cavity or hole in the course, prob. made by the stroke of a previous player.

To CUP, *v. a.* In golfing it means to mark or break the ground with the club when striking the ball; also, to strike the ground with the club when driving a ball.

CUPPIL, CUPPLE, *s.* A stone of butter and a stone of skimmed milk cheese sold together.

"In 1737 a Lochunyoch farmer sold 14 *cuppil* of butter and cheese for £33 : 4 : 0 Scots." Notes on Lochwinnoch by Dr. Crawford.

CURAS, CURACE, *s.* A cuirass; Douglas, Virgil. Fr. *cuirasse*.

CURAT, *s.* A curator, preceptor.

"Henry of Culan . . . of lauchful aige, out of tutoury and has chosine til his *curatis* to gowerne him." Burgh Recs. Aberd., 12 July, 1463.

CURBULYE, *s.* Lit. boiled leather: jack or jacked leather, leather that has been thickened and hardened in the dressing; Douglas, Virgil, v. ch. 7, Edin. MS. In Ruddiman's ed. *corbulye*, q. v.

CURCHE, CURCHEY, *s.* A woman's cap. V. COURCHE, *Corsay*.

Pl. *curchis* occurs in Burgh Recs. Aberdeen, i. 309, Sp. C., but is misprinted *curclus*. Unfortunately there are very many such mistakes in this most interesting series of Burgh Records.

CURE, *v.* and *s.* Cover. V. *Cour*.

CURER, *s.* Errat. in DICT. for *Cure*. V. under *Cour*, *s.*

CURFOYR, *s.* Curfew. V. *Courfyre*.

CURIALL, *adj.* Of or belonging to a court, hall, or seat of judgment; Court of Venus, i. 793, S. T. Soc. Fr. *curial*, id., from Lat. *curia*.

CURROR, CURROUR, CURROURE, *s.* A courier, messenger; Accts. L. H. Treas., I. 267, 45, 52.

O. Fr. *courier*, *coureur*, a runner; from O. Fr. *courre*, from Lat. *currere*, to run.

CURTICIAN, *s.* A courtier. V. *Courtician*.

CUSSIT, *s.* A small chest or box, Orkn.

Prob. a variation of *chesset*, Lowlands.

CUSTUMABILLY, *adv.* Customarily, Barbour, xv. 236.

CUSTUMAR, *s.* A collector of customs, Chalmerlan Air, ch. i. V. CUSTUME.

CUTTIT, *part. adj.* A *cuttit hors*, a gelding; Accts. L. H. Treas., I. 381.

CUTTOCH, CUTTACH, *s.* A young cow of between one and two years; between a stirk and a quey. V. CUDDOCH.

The kye's gane to the birken wud
The *cuttochs* to the brume,
The sheep's gane to the high hills,
Thay's no be hame till nune.
Old Ballad.

Gael. *cutach*, short; alluding to the horns of the animal at that age.

CUVIE, *s.* The fleshy part of a horse's tail, Orkn.

CUVIE, CUFIE, COUFIE, *s.* An iron ring used for passing down over fishing-lines so as to save the sinker, etc., when the hooks get entangled on the bottom, Orkn.

CWNNAR, *s.* A taster. V. *Cunnar*.

CYRE, *s.* Leather, Barbour, xii. 22, Edin. MS. Fr. *cuir*.

Jamieson's ed. reads *tyre;* but it is simply a misreading of *cyre* in the Edin. MS. The Camb. MS. has *qwyrbolle*, a corr. of *cuir bouilli*, jacked leather. V. Skeat's Barbour, p. 582.

CYTE, CYTTE, KYTE, *s.* A kite: a bird of the hawk family; also called *bald kite*, Houlate, l. 640. V. *Beld Cyttis*.

D.

D, 'D. An abbreviation for *it* after a verb; as, *nee'd*, see it; *tell'd*, tell it.

The first form is combined with the verb, and is often found in songs and ballads : as in "I sall not said agane," which forms the refrain of Alex. Scott's ballad on *Wantoun Wemen*.
This abbrev. for *it* is found in the earliest stages of the Northumbrian dialect, as in Hampole and Barbour; and it is still in common use on both sides of the Tweed.

DACKER, *adj.* Hesitating, uncertain, undecided: applied to a person who can't make up his mind, and to the weather when unsettled; Lanarks., Renfrews.

DACRE, *s.* A decade. V. DAIKER.

To DADE, *v. a.* To lead a young child; to guide or teach it to walk. Errat. in DICT.

Jamieson's explanation is wholly wrong, and so is the etymology. He does not even show that the word is Scottish. To *dade* is to support a child in leading-strings, and to teach him to walk; Cf. DODD and DUDDLE. Halliwell has "*dade*, to lead children beginning to walk." But Drayton uses it as if with reference to a child, in the sense "to toddle." Thus the child is "no sooner brought to toddle about, but it at once trips away from its mother;" and again, "as Isis gently advances." See *Deedle* and *Doodle* in Skeat's Etym. Dict.

DADGEON-WABSTER, *s.* A customer-weaver, a weaver of linen or woollen stuffs for country neighbours, West of S.

DAFT, *adj.* Originally mild, gentle, innocent; hence weak, weak-minded, silly; and in this sense it was, and still is, well known in village life. Addit. to DICT.

Jamieson's long note on the etym is mostly wrong. In M. E. *daft* and *deft* were synon. They were "formed from the base *daf*, to fit, appearing in A.-S. *gedafen*, fit." V. DEFT in Skeat's Etym. Dict.
In Rolland's Court of Venus, prol. l. 74, S. T. S. ed., *daft* occurs with the meaning, weak, purposeless :—

And he that hes of Watter the natoure,
Is *daft*, and doyld, drasie with small effect.

DAG, DAGG, DEG, *s.* A gun, hand-gun, pistol.

DAG-HEAD, DEG-HEAD, DOG-HEAD, *s.* The hammer, snap, or dog-head of a gun or pistol. V. DOG-HEAD.

DAGMAN, DAGMEN, *s.* Same as *Dag-Head;* Sempill Ballates, p. 334.

DAILY-DAY, *adv.* Every day, continually, constantly; prob. a corr. of *day-by-day*.

DAINE, *adj.* Lit. worthy; hence, modest, &c. Same as DANE, q. v.

Under *dane* Jamieson accepts the etym. which under *duine* he rejects. They are forms of the same word. O. Fr. *dain*, from Lat. *dignus*, worthy.

DAINTY, *adj.* Large, plump, &c.

The following note is a corr. of the etym. V. DICT. "The suffix in M.E. *dainteth* or *deinteth* has nothing to do with *tide*, time. It is due to the O. Fr. *daintet*, older form of *daintee;* and *daintet* is simply the Lat. acc. *dignitatem;* just as we have O. Fr. *charitet*, love, from *caritatem*, &c., so also M. E. *bountith*, O. Fr. *bontet*, M. E. *bounty*." Skeat.

DAIVERT, *adj.* V. DAVERT.

DAIVERTLY, DAIVERTLIKE, *adv.* Same as DAIVILIE, q. v.

DALINES, *s.* Prob. a misprint of *dalmes*, damask: "velvott, *dalines*, feytyng clayth," Burgh Recs. Edin., 2 April, 1516, Recs. Soc.

Prob. *feytyng* is a mistake for *seytyng*, satin. It occurs also in p. 153 of same vol.

DALING, *s.* A doling out or dividing. V. DAILL.

". . . and viij s. and the *daling* of thair aill for the secund fault." Burgh Recs. Aberdeen, I. 210.

DAMAS, DAMYSK, *s.* V. DAMMES.

DAMIE, *s.* Poet. for *dame*, lady, lass; Burns, Ep. to Dr. Blacklock, st. 5.

In this case Burns applied the term *damies* to the fabled nymphs of Castalia.

DAMNATOUR, *s.* Adjudgment, judgment or finding against one, condemnation; sentence of guilty. Fr. *damnatoire*.

"Anent the selanderous wordis spokin be Jane Foirside . . . and conform to sne decreit and *damnatour* gewin thairvpoun of the foirsaid selanderous wordis." Burgh Recs. Glasgow, 25 July, 1584, Rec. Soc.

To DAMNIFIE, DAMPNIFE, *v. a.* To damage, injure, spoil: part. pa. *dampnifeit, damnifit, damnefeit,* damaged, hindered, impoverished; Burgh Recs. Aberdeen, 1 April, 1606. Lat. *damnificare*. V. DAMPNE, DAMPNIS.

". . . quhairby we sould be hinderit and *dampnifeit* in our proffit," &c. Early Records of Mining in Scotland, p. 57, Cochran-Patrick.

DAMS, PLUM-DAMS, DAMSELS, *s. pl.* Popular names for damsons, small black plums: originally called DAMASCENE PLUMS.

Prunes and preserved plums were also called *plumdams*, and the term is frequently found in Household Accts. with those meanings.

DANDIE, DANDY, *s.* Originally, a weak, light-headed person: "a noodie, a ninnic;" Cotgr. Hence the other meanings which are secondary. O. Fr. *dandin.* Addit. to DICT.

To DANGLE, DANNLE, DENGLE, DENNLE, DINGLE, DINNLE, DUNGLE, DUNNLE, *v. a.* and *n.* To swing, vibrate, shake, quiver; to throb, beat, tingle, pringle, thrill, smart, shoot or quiver with pain. Addit. to DANYEL, DINLE.

Dangle and *dungle* (generally pron. *dannle, dunnle*), imply powerful or wide-spread motion or sensation: *dengle*, and *dingle* (pron. *dennle, dinnle*), are used like their diminutives, and limit the motion or sensation in kind, intensity, and locality. Regarding the etym. of the terms see under DANYEL.

DANLEDOOSIE, DINLEDOUSIE, *s.* V. DINGLEDOUSIE.

DANNERS, DAUNERS, *s. pl.* V. DANDERS.

DANSKIN, DANSKENE, DANSKEINE. *s.* Dantzic. Errat. in DICT.

This word has been explained by Jamieson and others as a name of Denmark; but this is found to be a mistake. V. Gloss., Accts. L. H. Treas., I., Dickson.

DANT, DANTE, DANTEE, DAINTE, DAINTIE, DENT, DENTIE, *s.* Dainty, pleasure, joy, respect, regard, affection, honour. Addit. to DANT. V. DENT.

These are simply varieties of M. E. *deinte, deintee*, from O. Fr. *daintie*, which Cotgr. connects with an older form *dain*, the original form of Fr. *digne*, from Lat. *dignus*.

Dant was left undefined by Jamieson; but in his note he suggests the correct meaning. The term is often used in Barbour, and with various meanings. V. Skeat's Gloss.

DANTIT, DAUNTET, *pret., part.,* and *adj.* Subdued, cowed, crushed, heartless; Whistle Binkie, ii. 30. V. DANT.

DAPLAR, *s.* A dish, platter. V. DOUBLER.

To DARE, DER, DEIR, DERE, *v. a.* To be bold enough, as, "We *dare* be poor," Burns; to risk, venture; to challenge, defy, forbid, as, "He dar'd or der'd him to do't;" to keep under, abash, intimidate, cow, terrify, as, "Death *dares* or *dere's* us a'." Pret. *dart, daurt, deirit, deirt, dert.*

To DARE, DEIR, DERE, *v. n.* To shy, shrink, fear, or be afraid, quake, tremble, start, startle; as, "He'll *dare* or *dere* at his ain shadow;" also, crouch, hide, lie hid: part. pt. *dart, deirt, dert.* Addit. to DARE.

By frythis and fellis,
That the dere dwellys,
And darkys and darys.
Avontyrs of Arthur, st. 4.

"*Darkys and darys*," lurks and lies hid. Jamieson left this term undefined, but referred the reader to his explanation of DURKEN. No assistance, however, can be got there, for his rendering of both words is wrong. *Dare* as here used is to lie hid, and is prob. allied to E. *daze* and *doze.*

M. E. *daren* means also to be dazed, to lurk, and is sometimes a mere duplicate of *darke*. Stratmann gives various examples, and Lat. *latere* as the most common meaning : see his O. E. Dict.

DART, DAURT, DERT, *part.* and *adj.* Frightened, terrified, cowed : hence, crushed, heartless, dull; or shrinking, trembling, starting or easily stupified.

His *dart* oxin I compt thame not ane fle :
Yone wer mair melt for sic ane man as me.
Henryson, Foxe that begylit the Wolf, l. 172.

DARK, DARKE, *s.* and *v.* V. DARG.

To DARK, DERK, DIRK, DURK, DARKEN, DERKEN, DIRKEN, DURKEN, *v. a.* and *n.* To make, grow, or keep dark; as, "Come hame when it *darks*," i.e., grows dark; also, to hide, conceal, lurk, lie hid; part. pt. *dirkit*, Dunbar, Bann. Poems, p. 22 ; *dirknyt*, Douglas, Virgil, iii. ch. 8. V. DIRKIN, *Durken.*

By frythis and fellis,
That the dere dwellys,
And darkys and darys.
Avontyrs of Arthur, st. 4.
"*Darkys and darys*," lurks and lies hid. V. DARE. *Derkin* in a *den*, and *dirkit in a den*, are expressions still used by boys while playing at those games in which hiding-places or dens are used ; and by *derkin* they mean hiding, lurking, lying concealed. The running to, and running into the den is *derning ;* but the lying hid there during the search is *derking* or *dirking.*

This meaning of *dark* is very old. In William and the Werwolf it occurs repeatedly, as in ll. 17, 44, 1834, 2543, 2851.

DARLOCH, *s.* A quiver. V. *Dorlach.*

This form represents a common lowland pron. of Gael. *dorlach*, a sheaf, case, or quiver of arrows, and is used in the account of the Conflict in Glenfruin given in Pitcairn's Criminal Trials, II. 432.

To DARREN, *v. a.* To contest, fight out, decide by combat: a form of DEREYNE, q. v. Errat. in DICT.

As a further correction of this error the following note is appended :—
"Explanation wrong; it is simply Chaucer's verb *darreyne*, to fight out. See Morris's Glossary to the Knight's Tale. The word is *daryne* in Small's edition, and is there wrongly explained ; besides which, *stryfe* is misprinted *striee*. The line means 'to fight ont the strife with huge enith or mace.' The rejected French etymology is the right one." Skeat.

To DASCAN, *v. n.* To enlarge, discourse, comment; hence, reason, ponder. E. *descant.* Addit. to DICT.

Jamieson's definition of this term is defective, and his etymology is wrong. As Prof. Skeat has pointed out, the word is just E. *descant*, of which Das Kane, given farther on, is another form. There, however, Jamieson is right.

DASS, *s*. A stack. Not explained in DICT.
The three entries of Dass in Dict. ought to form only one; for they deal with the same term under different applications.
"*Dass*, in North E. *dess*, a stack, from Icel. *des*, a stack; whence Icel. *hey-des*, a hay-stack, misspelt *hendys* in note to *Dass*, just above. The quotation is wrongly punctuated; the semi-colon after "just out" should be a comma, and the comma after "braes" should be a semi-colon." Skeat.

DAUCHIE, *adj.* V. DAUKY, DAGH.

DAUD, DAWD, *v.* and *s.* V. DAD.

DAUDIN', DAWDIN', *part., adj.*, and *s.* Striking, beating, battering.
The hail comes rattlin and brattlin snell an' keen,
Daudin' an' blaudin', tho' red set the sun at e'en.
W. Miller, Spring, st. 2.

DAUMERT, *adj.* Stupid, stupified, stunned.
V. DAMMERTIT.

To **DAUNER**, DAUNNER, DAUNDER, *v.* V. DANDER.

To **DAUR**, *v. a.* V. DARE.

DAVE, *s.* Short for David.

DAVELIN, *s.* Errat. for *Devalin*, or *Devaling*, q. v. The definition is correct.

To **DAVER**, *v. a.* and *n.* V. DAIVER, DAUER.

DAVIELY, *adv.* Languidly. V. DAIVILIE.

DAWNT, DAWNTYT. V. DANT.

DAY OF TREW. A diet or meeting to treat of a truce: pl. *trewes*, now E. *truce*.
". . . . with lettres to diners personis on the Bordouris, for the *day of trew* to be haldin eftir the diets of Anwic." Acots. L. H. Treas., 4 Oct., 1473, I. 45, Dickson.
This use of the term *day* was common in the border districts of Scot., and was extended to a meeting for settlement of disputes between parties living on opposite sides of the Tweed. It is so used in the opening of the Song of the Rid Square.
The seventh of July, the suith to say,
At the Rid Square the tryst was sett;
Our wardens they affixt a *day*,
And as they promised so they mett.

DEAD, *adj.* 1. A term used in golfing: applied to a ball—1st, when it falls without rolling; 2nd, when it lies so near the hole that the "put" is a *dead* certainty.

2. A term used in quoiting, bowling, and similar games: applied to the quoits, bowls, &c., of opponents which lie equidistant from the tee; so called because they are lost to both sides, and don't count. V. under *Deid*.

DEASK, DEASIT, *adj.* Besotted, Orkn.: prob. local for *dased*, *dasit*. V. DASE.

To **DEBAUSCH**, DEBOSH, DEBUSH, *v. a.* and *n.* These are merely variants of the same word, and mean to mar, spoil, waste in any way. O. Fr. *desbaucher*.

DEBLAT, DIBLET, *s.* Lit. a little devil; a young devil, an imp.; pl. *deblatis*, imps. Accts. L. H. Treas., I. 68, 239, Dickson.
A *deblat* and satyrs, personated by boys dressed in character, "appear to have formed a conspicuous feature in the fantastic retinue of the St. Nicholas bishop." Gloss. to Treas. Accts.
O. Fr. *diableteau*, "a little diuell, a yong diuell;" Cotgr.

DEBTFULLY, DETFULLY, *adv.* Duly, as in duty bound, thankfully. V. DEBTFULL.

To **DECERNE**, DESCERN, *v. n.* To sit or act as judge in a contest or dispute, to adjudicate in. Addit. to DECERN, q. v.
Glaydly I wald his fader stude heyrby,
This interprys to *decerne* and aspy.
Douglas, Virgil, x. ch. 8, Small's ed.
This word is omitted in the Gloss. of this ed. Ruddiman's ed.-reads *derne*, prob. for *derene*, to declare the right, act as umpire: O. Fr. *deresnier*, Burguy.
O. Fr. *decerner*, to determine, adjudicate: Lat. *decernere*.

To **DEE**, DE. Of the many strange expressions used to indicate the occasion, the mode, and the effect of one's death, the following are some of the more striking:—

1. To *Dee a Cadger-pownie's death*, to die of starvation and neglect; Burns' Epistle to Lapraik, st. 7.

2. To *Dee the death o' Jenkins' hen*, to die unmarried: Jenkins had only one hen. V. JENKINS' HEN.

3. To *Dee in one's shoon*, to die on the gallows, to be hanged; Whistle Binkie, I. 205.
It has been handed down by tradition that Charlie Graham, a noted tinker, knocked off his shoes on the gallows that no one might be able to say "he died wi' his shoon on." He was executed at Perth in the beginning of this century. A. L.

4. To *Dee a fair strae-death*, to die in one's bed; Burns, Death and Dr. Hornbook. V. STRAE-DEATH.

DEID, DEDE, *s.* 1. Misfortune, disaster, misery, affliction. Addit. to DEID and DEDE.
Off thy *deid*, quod the Paip, pitie I hawe.
Houlate, l. 118.
This term is applied colloq. and poet. to any grave trouble, disease, disaster, or misery of a deadly character.

2. Pl. *deids*, lost ones, ones that don't count: a term in quoiting, bowling, and similar games of skill, applied to the quoits, bowls, &c., of opponents which lie equidistant from the tee.

"*It's deids*," i.e., it is a case of *deids* or nothing for either side, is called out by the leading players when two opposing quoits, bowls, &c., are found to be equidistant from the tee.

DEID-KIST, DEDE-KIST, *s.* A coffin.

"An old maiden lady died at Barr Castle while on a visit to the family. The bedroom that she had occupied was in one of the turrets, the ascent to which was by a narrow, dark, winding stair. The minister took an early opportunity of calling at Barr to condole with the family; and when near the gateway he met the laird apparently in deep sorrow, and at once began to administer consolation. Having listened for a short time, the laird somewhat abruptly said :—" Man, what's a' this lang palaver for ? I ken weel eneuch she's dead, and kent she was deein. It's no that I care for ; its no that ava ; but how are we to got up wi' the *deid-kist*, or doun wi' the corp ? Can ye tell me that ?'" Laird of Logan, Gloss.

DEID AND WEIR. *The aventure of deid and weir*, the risk or hazard of death and war.

This condition was frequently attached to agreements of purchase or sale of public property, &c. "The gaitt dichting and dewteis thairof is sett this yeir in tocum with the aventure of *deid and weir* to Alexander Pennecuik for the sowm of xx li." Burgh Recs. Edin., 2 Aug., 1527, Rec. Soc.

To DEEDLE, *v. a.* and *n.* Lit. a frequent. of *dade*, to train an infant: hence its apparently different meanings to dandle, to sing, &c. *Doodle* is another form. V. Dade.

Frequently in amusing her charge a nurse may be heard using the variants *deedle*, *dadle*, *doodle*, either in combination or separately. And a meaningless lilt, rhyme, or song, run over in nurse fashion, is called a *deedie-doodle*: so also is a badly played tune on a flute, violin, or other instrument.

Jamieson's etym. of this term is wrong.

To DEFADE, *v. a.* To cause to fade, to weaken, despirit ; Kingis Quhair, st. 170: part. pt. *defadide*, Morte Arthure, l. 3305.

Fr. *de-*, prefix, with causal sense ; *fade*, "unsavoury, tasteleese, weak ;" Cotgr.

To DEFALK, *v. a.* To deduct, remit ; part. pt. *defalkit ;* Burgh Recs. Edin., 20 Feb., 1524-5. V. DEFAIK.

DEFALT, DEFAUT, *s.* Failure ; but generally implying neglect, carelessness, slovenliness, wrong-doing.

"Item, I wanttyt out of my hous in her *defalt* and sleuht, ane plaid of ix. elln, the price xxiiij. s." Burgh Recs. Aberdeen, I. 175.

DEFAWTYT, *part. pt.* Defaulted; found in default i.e. culpable ; Barbour, i. 182. Addit. to DICT.

Pinkerton's meaning is wrong, and Jamieson's note is not quite clear. There is no difficulty, however, regarding the term.

DEFEIS, *s.* A discharge, acquittance, Accts. L. H. Treas., I. 166. Short for DEFAISANCE, q. v.

DEID, *s.* Deed, act, action, mode of action ; Barbour. i. 302, v. 278, xvi. 323.

To DEILL, DELE, DAIL, *v. a.* and *n.* To deal blows, strike, beat, hammer ; Barbour, iii. 32 ; to have to do, bargain, buy or sell, as, " I'll no *dele* wi' you." Addit. to DELE, DAIL.

To DEIR, *v. a.* To make dear, make dearer, to raise the price of.

". . . that na neichtbour tak in hand to by the saidis victualis or tymmer to regrait and *deir* agane upoun the nychtbouris." Burgh Recs. Edin., 7 Oct., 1462, Rec. Soc.

A.-S. *dedre*, precious, high in price.

DELF, *s.* A peat-hag, a quarry ; pl. *delvis* ; Fife, West of S. Addit. to DELF.

This term with the meaning *a quarry* was common in M. E.; "*delves or quarries*" occurs in Wycliffe's version of the Bible, 2 Chron. 34.

DELIGATE, DELIGAT, DILIGAT, DILLAGAT, *adj.* Corr. of *delicate*, delicious, dainty, select, selected, first-rate, splendid ; Sempill Ballates, p. 227. DICT. gives the form DILLAGATE, q. v.

DELITABILL, DELETABILL, DELICTABILL, *adj.* Delightful, pleasant, pleasing ; Barbour, i. 1. O. Fr. *delitable*.

DELIUERANCE, DELEVERANCE, *s.* 1. A legal decision, judgment ; Accts. L. H. Treas., I. 106, 270.

2. Payment : pl. *deliueransis*.

". . as is contenit in the buke of the Comptaris *deliueransis* to the Masteris of Werk." Ibid., I. 74, Dickson. Addit. to DELIVERANCE.

To DELLUT, *v. a.* To screen, hide, protect. V. DILL.

" . . . to set wechis baith within the toyne and without, to *dellut* thame fra thair ennemyes." Burgh Recs. Aberdeen, I. 114.

Cf. Icel. *dylja*, Swed. *doelja*, to hide.

To DEMBLE, DIMBLE, *v. a.* To dip, immerse ; also, to set or root young plants : Aberd., Orkn. ; like *dimple* and *dibble*, q. v.

To DEME, *v. a.* To deem, judge, adjudge, doom, condemn ; Barbour, i. 213, iv. 328 ; part. pt. *demyt*, *demt*, *dempt ;* imper. *demys*,

judge ye; Ibid., vi. 283; but later form is *dem*, q. v.
A.-S. *déman*, to judge.

To DEMERIT, DEMARIT, *v. a.* To merit, deserve.
". . . vndir pane that thai sall *demarit* as brekaris of commoune ordinance." Burgh Recs. Aberdeen, I. 20.

DEMPT, *pret.* and *part. pt.* V. *Deme*.

DEMPTION, *s.* A great quantity; as, "a *demption* of rain," Orkn.

DENNLE, *v.* and *s.* V. *Dangle*.

DENS, DENSS, *adj.* Addit. to DENCE, q. v.

To DEPAS, *v. n.* To depart, leave; to cause to depart.
". . the *sojarris* . . to *depas* incontinent of the toune." Burgh Recs. Peebles, 5 May, 1559, Rec. Soc.

To DEPEND, *v. n.* To await consideration, to be entered on the roll: a law term.

DEPENDANCE, *s.* Waiting, the state or position of waiting to be brought forward: a law term applied to a case when entered on the court-roll.
". . . that anes the actioune may be put under *dependance* befoir onie parliament." Burgh Recs. Aberdeen, Dec. 4, 1605.

DEPENDARE, *s.* A dependant, retainer; pl. *dependaris*.
". . . the said Captane James, nor nane of his servandis and *dependaris*, nor na vtheris quhome he may stope or lat." Burgh Recs. Aberdeen, Feb. 3, 1604.

To DEPREHEND, *v. a.* To apprehend, seize, capture; Knox, Hist. Ref. Scot., I. 261.

DEPUT, *part. pt.* Deputed, set apart; "*ordanit* and *deput* for the samyn," Burgh Recs. Edin., 28 March, 1525, Rec. Soc.

To DERE, DEIR, DEYR, *v. a.* V. *Dare*.

DERIT, DEIRT, DERT, *part. adj.* V. *Dare*.

DERIGE, DIRIGE, DYRIGE, *s.* That part of the Office for the Dead beginning "Dirige Domine," &c.: also frequently used as name of this office; Accts. L. H. Treas., I. 178, 229, 200. Addit. to DERGY. V. under OBIT.

To DERNE, *v. a.* Prob. a contr. form of *derene*, lit. to declare the right, act as umpire in a contest or dispute. O. Fr. *derainer*, *deresnier*, id. Addit. to DERNE, q. v.
Jamieson left this word undefined, but suggested a meaning which is unsuitable. Explanation is given under *Decerne*, q. v.

DERT, *part.* and *adj.* V. under *Dare*.
Jamieson's suggestion regarding the meaning of this term is certainly wrong. The rendering now proposed is at least probable, and agrees with the particulars of the situation implied. V. *Aspert*.

DERTHING, *s.* Dearth, scarcity: also, hoarding up victuals in order to raise the price; Burgh Recs.

To DERUB, DEROB, *v. a.* Lit. to disrobe, to strip, rob, cheat: *part. pa.*, *derubit*.
"For quhat can ony man say gif I be *derubit* of my rycht, susteuing the grit lose and skayth that I haif gottin, bot it war his Majesties dishonour." Early Records of Mining in Scotland, p. 67.
Fr. *derober*, to strip, rob, steal: from Lat. *dis*, away, and *robe*, q. v. in Brachet's Etym. Dict.

DESALY, *adv.* Dizzily, Barbour, vi. 629.
A.-S. *dysig*, foolish; O. Du. *duyzigh*, dizzy.

To DESCROY, *v. a.* Put for DESCRIVE, to describe. Barbour, xiii. 185, Edin. MS.

DESOLAT, *adj.* Destitute, utterly in want; "*desolat* of prouisioun," destitute of food, Burgh Recs. Peebles, 15 Aug. 1608, Rec. Soc.

DESSPOSIT, *part. pt.* Bound by agreement, covenanted; same as *esposit*, q. v.
". . . present dayly the alter quhen he is *dessposit* as efferis." Burgh Recs. Peebles, 15 Feb., 1476, Rec. Soc.

DESTANE, *s.* Destiny, Barbour, v. 428.

DET, *s.* Debt, money due; pl. *dettis*, sums owing, sums due; *the Kingis dettis*, sums due to the King, Accts. L. H. Treas., I. 220, 241, 267. M. E. and O. Fr. *dette*.

DETBOUND, DETBUND, *part. pt.* Impledged, mortgaged.
". . . the hous quhilk wes *detbound* to the said Jhone of before the doun casting thairof," &c. Burgh Recs. Edin., 20th Jan., 1541-2. Rec. Soc.
Jamieson's statement regarding this term is a mistake, and his definition represents only a secondary meaning.

To DETEENE, *v. a.* To detain, hinder; also, to retain, keep.
". . . to dedicate the same thing a Kirk, and yet *deteene* it a buriall." Blame of Kirkburiall, ch. 19.

DETERMYNAT, *adv.* Assuredly, certainly. Barbour, i. 129.
O. Fr. *determiner*, to determine, conclude.

DEVALING, DEVELING, *s.* Covering of centres or cooms used in building arches.
Lit. bowing, curving, from *deval*, to incline, slope, bow. It consists of narrow planks or boards laid as a covering over the centres or frames on which arches are built. The term is wrongly given as DAVELIN in DICT.
". . . tymber to be centries, *develing*, irne, lead,

etc., to be furneist be the toune." Burgh Recs., Aberdeen, 29 March, 1615.
O. Fr. *devaller*, to lower or let down; Cotgr. Cf. Fr. *avaler*.

DEVAT, DEWAT, *s*. A turf. V. DIVET.

To DEVAWL, *v. n.* V. DEVALL.

DEVIS, DEVYS, DEVYSE, *s*. A plan, design, Burgh Recs., Treas. Accts.; testament, will, Lyndsay, Papyngo, l. 730: *at devyse*, with skill or exactness, Douglas, King Hart, st. 16. Fr. *devis*.

DEVISOUR, DEVYSOUR, DEWISOUR, *s*. A factor, agent, steward, manager, Barbour, xx. 72. V. DEVISE.

DEVOYEN, *part. pt.* Devoided, emptied, cleared. V. DEUOID.
". . . that all the tovn be *devoyen* of the swyn croftis." Burgh Recs. Aberdeen, I. 70.

DEVULGAT, DIVULGAT, *part. pt.* Divulged.

DEW, DEWE, *adj.* Able, worthy, valiant; a poet. form of Dow, q. v.; Houlate, l. 575.

DEWLY, *adv.* Readily, promptly, properly, thoroughly; Houlate, l. 888.

DIACLE, *s*. A small dial worn with articles of personal ornament; "*diacles* of wode, the dozen, xij s.; of bone, the dozen, xlviij s." Customs and Valuations, Halyburton's Ledger, p. 297; Accts. L. H. Treas., I. 83. Addit. to DIACLE.

DIASPINET, *s*. Diapered or variegated silk; Excheq. Rolls Scot., I. 380.
In Latin it appears as *diaspinetum* and *diaspretum*: compare O. Fr. *diaspre*, diaper, and its modern form *diapre*.

DICH, DICHING. Pron. of Dicht, Dichting V. DICHT.

DICTON, *s*. A motto, inscription. V. DITON.

DID, *pret*. Put, placed, threw.
He tuk a culter hate glowand—
And went him to the mekill hall,
That then with corn was fyllyt all,
And heych up in a mow it *did*.
Barbour, iv. 117.
This meaning of the v. *do* was not uncommon. The confession of a wrong-doer in a burgh court usually ended with "and I *do* me in your will," i.e., I put myself in your hand, or your judgment. See also Court of Venus, 2. 785. V. under *Doid*.

DIET, DIETE, DYET, *s*. 1. An appointed day for meeting, muster, justice, etc.; also, the meeting, muster, etc.: hence the phrase, "to desert the *diet*."
(Sup.)

2. A day's work; Accts. L. H. Treas., I. 246.
3. A service, supply, course; as, "a *diet* of worship:" a repast, meal; as, "a diet of meat." Pl. *diets, dietis, dyetes*, courses, dishes; Awnytyrs of Arthur, st. 15. Addit. to DIET.

DIGHT, DICHT, DICH, *s*. A wipe, rub, scrub; also short for *dighting*, a rubbing, scrubbing, cleaning, dressing. V. DICHT, *v.*

To DILASCH, *v. a.* To discharge; Reg. Priv. Council, VI. 259. V. DELASH.

DILCE, DILSE, DULCE, *s*. V. DULSE.

To DILDER, DIDDER, *v. a.* and *n*. To shake, jerk; also, to dribble, ooze, trickle, glide: hence, to trifle, waste time, work carelessly; West of S., Orkn.

DILDER, DIDDER, *s*. A smart jerk, shake, jolt.

DILIGAT, *adj.* V. DELIGAT.

DIMINUTE, *adj.* Diminished, lessened. Lat. *diminutus*.
Gif that ye find ocht throw my negligence
Be *diminute*, or yit superfluous,
Correct it at your willis gratious.
Henrysone, Prologue to Fables, l. 41.

DINEN, DEINEN, *s*. Dinner; also, a meal, sufficient for a meal; West of S., Orkn. V. DINE.
In Orkn. and Shetl. a full meal, a bellyful is called a *deenin*: and in Shetl. "to get one's *dienen*," is to be well served. V. Gloss.

DINGLE, *v.* and *s*. Thrill, throb. V. DINLE.
Dingle, with meanings like those of E. *tingle*, is common in West of S. and in Orkn. and Shetl.

DINNEL, *v.* and *s*. V. DINLE.

DIOCY, *s*. A diocese, Burgh Recs.

To DIRD, *v. a.* To beat, thump, dump, in order to solidify, as when filling a sack of grain; as to drive or cast violently. Addit. to DIRD, *s*.
O. Fr. *dourder*, to beat, thump.

DIRDER, *s*. A driver, whipper-in; as a *dog-dirder*, dog-breaker, kennel-attendant.

To DIRKEN, *v. n.* To lurk; to peer, pry. Addit. to DICT. V. *Dark, v.*
In both entries the meaning has been missed. In the passage by Fergussou the meaning is *to lurk*; in the other it is *to pry*.

To DISCOMMODE, *v. a.* To inconvenience, disturb, annoy.

DISCOMMODITIE, *s*. Inconvenience, annoyance. Burgh Recs. Aberdeen, 2 July, 1595.

N

DISCUS, *s.* Conclusion, settlement; and prob. an old law term applied to the final statement and finding of the judge.

". . . to attend vpone the said actioun, vntil the finall end and *discus* thairof." Burgh Recs. Aberdeen, 5 March, 1616.
Lat. *discussio*, examination.

DISFAMETE, *s.* Impoverishment, want.

". . . Our heretage of Caidmour hes lying waist without teling or sawing to the greit *disfamete* and hunger of xvnj[xx] of houshalderia." Charters, &c., of Peebles (Burgh Rec. Soc.), 281.

To DISGEEST, DISJEEST, *v. a.* To digest: part. pr. *disgeestin, disjeestin,* digesting; also used as a *s.* digestion.

This corruption is common all over Scotland, and in many parts of England.

To DISGRES, *v. a.* To fleece, strip, rob.

". . . may persaue hie intentioun and meaning alwayis to be *to disgres* me and my richt of the samin tak, takand vpoun him to querrell my rycht," &c. Early Records of Mining in Scotland, p. 67.
O. Fr. *desgresser,* a form of *desgraisser,* "to unfatten, ungrease, rid of fat, make leane; also to rifle;" Cotgr.

DISIONE, *s.* V. DISJUNE.

To DISPERSON, *v. a.* Same as MISPERSON, q. v.; part. pr. *dispersoning,* used also as a *s.*, Burgh Recs. Aberdeen, I. 416; Glasgow, I. 77, Rec. Soc.

To DISPESCHE, *v. a.* To despatch, send or drive away; Burgh Recs. Edin., III. 12, 102. O. Fr. *depescher.*

To DISPIT, *v. a.* To dispute, contend, oppose, call in question.

And till gud purpoiss *dispit* and argow,
A sylogysme propone, and elk exclud.
Henryson, Cock and Jasp, l. 45.

To DISPRISE, DISPRYSE, *v. a.* To attack with intent to injure, maliciously surprise and assault; part. pr. *disprysing,* used also as a *s.*, meaning assault and battery.

"The quhilk day William Paterson [and] Patrick Lowiesoun convict be ane assyse vpoun the *disprysing* of William Todrig, baillie, invadand him with cruell wawponns and drawin swordis, for the quhilk caus thai sall be had to the trone and thair hands to be straken throch, and that is gevin for dome." Burgh Recs. Edin., 20 Oct., 1500, Rec. Soc.
O. Fr. *despriser,* lit. to take, handle, or deal with contemptuously, and, like *mespriser,* with similar meaning, applied to every variety of wrong-doing to a neighbour, from simple disrespect to assault and battery. From O. Fr. *des* or *dis,* from, away from; hence, badly, wrongfully; and *priser,* from Lat. *prehensus,* part. pt. of *prehendere,* to take, seize. In various instances the prefix *dis* has been adopted in Scot. instead of *mis,* as in this word *disprise;* but in some cases both forms are used, as, *dispersion* and *misperson, distrust* and *mistrust,* the last two are in E. also.

DISTRENYEABILL, DISTRINYABILL, *adj.* Able or fit to be distrained. V. DISTRINYIE.

DIVET-SPADE, *s.* Same as FLAUCHTER-SPADE, q. v.

DOB, *adj.* and *s.* Short for *doble,* double, equal, equidistant; pl. *dobs,* things that are equal or equidistant. Orkn.

When two persons playing at pitch-and-toss place their pitchers equidistant from the tee, they are said to be *dobs,* and require to throw again.

To DON, *v. n.* Short for *to double,* to do or play over again, as when the players are equal. Orkn.

DOCHLY, *adv.* Errat. for DEWLY, q. v.

This mistake was made in Pinkerton's version of the Houlate, taken from the Bann. MS., which reads *dowly,* afterwards altered to *dewly.* Asloan MS. has *dewly.*

DOCHTLESS, DOUGHTLESS, *adj.* Powerless, worthless, unworthy, of little value. V. DOCHTY.

"A *dochtless* dawtie gets a beggar's dower." Old Proverb.

DOCUMENT, *s.* Evidence, attestation. V. DOCUMENT, *v.*

". . . be verray *document* of thaim that herd and saw the begyning of that bargan." Charters, &c., of Peebles (Burgh Rec. Soc.), p. 132.
The writing at the end of an instrument in which the notary sets forth his name and authority, is called his *Docquet.*

To DODDER, DOTHER, *v. n.* To totter, to walk in a weak or trembling state, to move about in an aimless or stupid manner. V. DOTTAR, DODD.

The form *dod* is also used to express the feeble and unsteady motion of an old person:—"He's hardly able to *dod* out an' in now."

DODDER'D, DOTHERD, *adj.* Tottering, frail, feeble, stupid; "He's auld an' dodder'd noo."

Dodder and *dodder'd* are common in the North of Eng. V. Brockett. In some parts of E. the quaking-grass is caleld *dodder-grass.*

DOGONIS, *s. pl.* Simply the pl. of *dogon,* which is the same word as *dugon,* a term of contempt. Errat. in DICT.

Both defin. and etym. of this term are wrong; but both are correctly given under DUGON, q. v.

DOGS-HELPER, *s.* A person of mean appearance, Orkn.

DOID. A form of *do it,* and sometimes of *I do it.* A more common Scot. form is *dude* or *duid.* Addit to DICT.

This term was left undefined by Jamieson; and regarding his note of explanation Prof. Skeat writes:—
"Explanation and etymology are quite wrong. *Doid = do it;* and *do it on* is short for *I do it on,* which in M. E. means, 'I refer it to.' This phrase is common in Piers Plowman. See the Glossary, p. 597, col. 2, l. 6."

DOKSILVER, *s.* Dock-dues, harbour-dues; Burgh Recs. Edin., II. 239, Rec. Soc.
This was a charge collected by the water-bailie of the port of Leith. It is thus defined in Stirling Charters, 1641, p. 151 :—"portus et textrine monotis *lie heavin silver et dock silver.*"

DOLIE, DOOLIE, *adj.* V. **DOLLY.**

DOLVEN, DOLLIN, *part. pt.* Buried. V. **DOLLYNE.**
The phrase *deid and dollin,* in Dunbar's Mariit Wemen, l. 410, occurs as *ded and doluen* in William and the Werwolf, ll. 2630, 5280.

DONIE, *s.* Lit. dun-coloured one; and in this sense it is used as a name for a hare. Addit. to **DICT.**
The following is Prof. Skeat's explanation of the term. Dr. Jamieson's note is wrong.
"The etymology is easy. It stands for *dun-y,* from *dun,* its colour. So also E. *donkey* for *dun-ik-y.*"

DOO, *s.* A dove, etc. V. **DOW.**

DOOKAT, DOOKET, *s.* V. **DOWCATE.**

DOOFART, DOFART, *adj.* and *s.* V. **DOWFART.**

DOOK, DOOKER, DOOKAR. V. under **DOUK.**

DOOKING, DOOKIN, DOUKIN, *s.* Dipping, plunging, bathing, diving, drenching: also, the amusement of ducking for apples.

DOOR-STANE, DOOR-STEP, *s.* The threshold of a door: called *door-stanes, doorsteps,* when consisting of two or more steps.
In North of Eng. the same terms are used. V. Brockett's Gloss.

DOORWARD, DURWARD, *s.* Door-keeper, usher, guard of the presence chamber. V. **DURWARTH.**

DORCHE, *s.* A form of **DUERCH,** a dwarf, Houlate, l. 650, Asloan MS.

DOREN. A form of *dereyne,* to contest, fight out, settle by combat. V. **DEREYNE.**
This term was left undefined; and Jamieson's suggestion regarding its meaning is wrong. The following note gives full and satisfactory explanation.
"By the common error of *o* for *e,* this is merely for *deren,* a better form of *darren.* See note on *Darren* above. The editions rightly have *direnye,* another spelling of *dereine;* the final *ye* is the peculiar way of printing the suffix, which is often (still worse) printed as *ze.*" Skeat.

DORLACH, DARLOCH, *s.* A bundle, truss, package; portmanteau, or other form of travelling bag or case; also, a sheaf of arrows, a quiver. Addit. to **DORLACH.**
Of the two entries of this term in the DICT., the first is correct so far as it treats, but the second is wrong. On the authority of Sir W. Scott Jamieson accepted the word as different from the Gael. *dorlach;* but it is the same word, and the passages quoted might have kept him right on that point: indeed the term is found only in lists of the arms, or records of the fights and forays of Highlanders, and in Acts of Parl. relating to the Highlands. For examples of its use, *v.* DICT.; and for the form *darloch, v.* Pitcairn's Crim. Trials, II. 432.
Gael. *dorlach,* a handful, a bundle; a sheaf of arrows, a quiver; M'Lood & Dewar.

DORMANTS, DORMANS, DORMONDS, DORMOUNDS, DORMERS, *s. pl.* The sleepers or joists of a house on which flooring is laid, Burgh Recs., Edin., I. 45, 243. Fr. *dormeur.*

DORMY, *adj.* A term used in golfing; applied to a player when he is as many holes ahead of his opponent as there are holes still to play.

DORNTOR, *s.* V. *Dortor.*

DORTOR, DORTON, DORNTOR, DORNTON, DORTS, DORT, *s.* A slight repast, refreshment; food taken between meals; West of S. V. **DORDERMEAT.**
"A herd in the parish of Beith complained that other herds got a *dortor* like a *dortor,* but he got a dochtless *dortor,*" i.e., a miserably small one. Laird of Logan, Gloss.
These are some of the many forms which have sprung from A.-S. *undern,* short for *undern-mete,* afternoon meal. Jamieson gives *dordermete,* as used in Angus; Ray, in his Collection of North-Country Words, gives *aandorn, aunder, dondinner, doundrins,* and *orndorns,* as names for afternoon refreshments; and Thoresby in his letter to Ray gives *earnder,* forenoon drinking, as used in Yorkshire. *Dortor* and its variations, however, as used in the West of S., mean generally a repast or refreshment between meals; though these are perhaps most frequently applied to the *mid-day* piece given to farm servants, and to young people when engaged in out-door work.

DORTOUR, DORTOR, *s.* A dormitory, bedroom; also, a posset or sleeping draught taken at bed-time, like our modern *nightcap.*
Fr. *dortoir,* a bedroom; and in the second sense the term is short for Fr. *dormitoire,* "a sleep-procuring medicine." Cotgr. Both terms are from Lat. *dormitorium,* a dormitory.

DOTACIOUN, *s.* Gift, endowment. V. **DOTAT.**

DOTTLE-TROT, *s.* Also called "the oldman's walk:" the rapid, short-step walk of an old person; Perths., Forfars. V. *Dodder.*

To **DOUBLE, DOWBIL, DOWBILL,** *v. a.* To line a gown, cloak, &c. Fr. *doubler.* Addit. to **DOUBLE.**
". . . . . iij elne and dimid. of scarlet to be a lang gowne to the Duk. . . . . . . viij elne of blak dammysk to *dowbil* it with," &c. Accts. L. H. Treas., I. 203. Dickson.

DOUBLER, DOUBLAR, DOWBLER, DUBLAR, DUPLAR, DOBLERE, DIBLAR, DAPLAR, *s.*

A large dish or platter, generally of wood or pewter, of which there were three sizes, *little-doubler*, *doubler*, and *grete-doubler*: Acta Audit., p. 82; Accts. L. H. Treas., I. 71; Burgh Lawis, ch. 116. Addit. to DIBLER, and DUBLAR, q. v.

Dr. Jamieson must have been uncertain regarding this term, as it was left undefined in both the forms in which it is given. It is from O. Fr. *doublier*, a dish, and represents one of the platter-shape. In M. E. *dobeler*, *doblere*, which in Prompt. Parv. and Wright's Glossaries represent Lat. *parapses*, *parapsis*, a dish or platter; and in the latter work the *grete-doblere* represents *cathinus*, a similar dish of larger size.

According to the old Burgh Laws the *doubler* was one of the articles of heirship, which passed to the successor; being accounted one of "the necessaire thyngis pertenand til his hous." Burgh Lawis, ch. 117, Rec. Soc.

DOUN, *adv*. In reduction or abatement; as, "Gie me a saxpence *doun* o' the price." It is also used as a *s*.; as, "How muckle *doun* will ye gie?" i.e., what or how much reduction will you allow?

Both senses have been long in use.
"Geviu to Jamos Andersoun, fermarare of the towne myln, *doun* of his ferme be ressoun of the greit dronaht, xxj li." Accts. Burgh of Glasgow, 22 Aug., 1573.

DOUN-SITTING, DOUN-SETTIN, *s*. Settlement by marriage, but specially implying the house and plenishing; as, "She's got a gran' *doun-sittin*."

DOURIER, *s*. and *adj*. Dowager; Hist. Estate of Scotland, p. 85, Wodrow Soc. Misc. V. DOWRIER.

DOWKET, *s*. A dovecot. V. DOWCATE.

DOWNIE, *s*. V. DAUNIE.

DOYCHLE, DOICHLE, *s*. A dull, stupid, sleepy person; a sloven. V. DOIL'D.

To DOYCHLE, DOICHLE, *v. n*. To walk or work in a stupid or dreamy state.

DOYLDE, *adj*. Stupid. V. DOIL'D.

DOYN, DONE, DOON, DOONS, DUNZE. Forms of the part. pt. *done*, used as very, in a great degree. Jamieson's explanation of these forms is round-about and faulty. A simpler and more satisfactory one is given in the following note.

"*Doyn* is merely the p. p. *done*, used in a very peculiar way; see *Dones* in Glossary to P. Ploughman, and Notes to the same, p. 419. Hence *sa done* is so done, so made; hence, in such a manner or way, and finally, to that degree. Sa done *tyrsum* is, tiring to that degree. So *doons severe*, severe to that degree. *No that dunze strong*, not to that degree strong, not so strong; and so on. The passage cited from P. Plowman is quite to the point." Skeat.

To DRAIGLE, *v. a*. and *n*. To trail along wet dirty ground, or over wet grass, &c.; to make or become wet or dirty by so doing; also, to bespatter with mud, to be soaked with rain. E. *draggle*.

Jenny's a' wat, poor body,
Jenny's seldom dry;
She *draiglet* a' her petticoatie,
Coming through the rye.
Burns, Coming through the Rye.

Draigle is prob. a dimin. of *drake*, to drench, soak, Icel. *drekkja*, to drown, swamp; Goth. *dragkjan*, to give to drink.

DRAIGLE-TAIL, DRAIGLE-TAILED, *adj*. Applied to females whose dress is fouled with wet or mire, or who are careless or slovenly in dress or bearing. *Draigle-tails* is a common name for such a person.

DRAIGLIN, DRAIGLING, DRAIGLE, *s*. A soaking with rain, wet, or mire; a spattering with mud; a wet, dirty condition, as, "What a *draigle* ye're in!"

DRAP, *s*. A raindrop: the eaves of a house; the line of raindrop from the eaves. Addit. to DRAP.

The last of these meanings may be illustrated by the answer of a selfish cocklaird who was called to account for some act contrary to good neighbourhood:— "I can, and I wull do as I like inside my ain *drap*." V. *Dreep, Drop*.

DRASIE, *adj*. Drowsy, sluggish, lazy; listless, dispirited.

For Flewme is flat, slaw, richt slipperie and sweir,
And *drasie*, to spit can not forbeir.
Court of Venus, prol. l. 17, S. T S.

That is, "a phlegmatic person is so dead-lazy that he can't be at the trouble even to spit."

And he that hes of Watter the natoure,
Is daft, and doyld, *drasie* with small effect.
Ibid., prol., l. 74.

That is, he is "listless and has little outcome."
In the Gloss. this word is rendered *dripping*; this is a mistake.
A.-S. *drúslan*, *drúsan*, to be sluggish.

DRAUNT, DRAUNTIN'. V. DRANT.

To DRAW, *v. a*. A term in golfing; to drive widely to the left hand. Syn. *hook*, *screw*.

To DRAW A STRAE BEFORE THE CAT. To wheedle, cajole, blind, or amuse a person in order to gain some end.

"Than," said the Wolf, in wraith, "wenis thow with wylis,
And with thy mony mowis me to mak?
It is an auld dog douties that thow begylis;
Thow wenis *to draw the stra befoir the cat?*"
"Schir," said the Foxe, "God wait, I mene nocht that," &c.
Henryson, Wolf, Foxe, & Cadgear, l. 60.

DRAWIN, *part. pt*. Withdrawn, passed.

Thair with dame Natur hes to the bevin *drawin*.
Houlate, l. 942.

To DREEP, v. n. To drip, ooze, strain; part. pr. *dreepin*, used also as a *s.*, and as an adj.; part. pt. *dreepit*.

While rains are blattrin' frae the south,
An' down the lozens seepin';
An' hens in mony a caul' closs-mouth
Wi' hingin' tails are *dreepin'*.
Alex. Wilson's Poems, p. 82, ed. 1876.

DREEP, *s.* Drip, dripping, as from a roast, from the eaves, &c.: also, the eaves; and where drops from the eaves fall on the ground, as, "Yo mun bide within your ain *dreep*." V. *Drap*.

DREG, *s.* The last or least worth of anything; hence, the basest, vilest. Addit. to DREG.

". . . . falling out in the *dreg* of all tymes, wherein the world lay besotted and swattering in all sorte of superstition." Blame of Kirkburiall, ch. 13.

DREG-BOAT, DREG-BOTE, *s.* 1. A dredger, a kind of fishing-boat.

"Of ilk *dreg-boat* and hand-lyne bot cummand in with fiech," &c. Burgh Recs. Edin., 16 Nov., 1471, Recs. Soc.

2. A boat or great-punt carrying a dredging machine, used for deepening a harbour, river, &c.; also, a boat or punt for the receiving and carrying away the dredgings of such a machine.

3. A track-boat, a canal boat drawn by a horse.

DREID, DREED, DREDE, *s.* Dread, fear, doubt, suspicion, suspense. Addit. to DREAD.

DREIDLES, DREEDLES, DREDLESS, adj. and adv. Without fear, doubt, or wavering; doubtless, unhesitatingly.

Mak a fair foule of me,
Or ellis *dreidles* I due,
Or my end day.
Houlate, l. 116.

DRENG, *s.* A dependant. V. DRING.

To DRIDDLE, v. n. To work, walk, or act in a feeble, unsteady, or uncertain manner; generally applied to the doings of old people, of the lame, and the lazy.

Gipsies and tinkers are said "*to driddle* about to get work, and *to driddle* at it when they do get it;" and of lazy loafers it is said, "they winna work, they'll only *driddle*." And as expressive of the weakness and unsteadiness of old age Burns used this term with fine effect in his Epistle to Major Logan—

Hale be your heart! Hale be your fiddle!—
To cheer you through the weary widdle
O this wild warl',
Until you on a crummock *driddle*
A gray-hair'd carl.

"*To driddle* on a crummock," to :otter along on a staff.

The nouns *driddle, driddling, driddler*, are also used in the same senses as the verb. V. Whistle Binkie, I. 159.

DRIFT, *s.* Track, trail, way, passage; passing away, lapse; also a mining term, meaning a passage cut or driven between two shafts, ways, or rooms. Addit. to DRIFT.

Poor hav'rel Will fell aff the *drift*,
An' wander'd thro' the bow-kail.
An' pow't, for want o' better shift,
A runt was like a sow-tail
Sae bow't that night.
Burns, Halloween, st. 4.

Track or *trail* is the meaning usually given to *drift* as here used; but it is quite possible that Burns meant *drove* or *company*, and referred to the party who had gone out hand in hand "to pou their stocks." That application of the term was quite common in Burns's day, and is still used in Ayrshire.

In the sense of *passing away* this term is frequently met with in sermons, &c., even of last century; as in the phrase "the *drift* of time," i.e., the lapse of time.

DROGAT, DROGIT, *s.* A coarse woollen cloth: E. *drugget*, Fr. *droguet*.

DROILT, DRULT, adj. Weak, feeble, awkward: also used as a *s.* and applied to a feeble or awkward person; Orkn. and Shetl.

To DROILT, DRULT, v. n. To walk or work awkwardly; Ibid.

DROILTIE, DRULTIE, *s.* and adj. Applied to a feeble, awkward, or slovenly person; Ibid.

To DROKE, DROOK, v. a. V. DRAKE.

DROKE, DROOK, DROKIN, DROOKIN, *s.* A drench, soaking: a drenched or soaking state; as, "The beast's in a *droke* o' sweat," i.e., streaming with perspiration; West of S., Orkn.

The form *drookin* is more widely used. A person drenched with rain is said to have got "a complete *drookin*."

DROTES, *s.* Errat. in DICT. for *Dyetes*, diets, repasts, courses.

As given in first sense the term, its definition, and etym. are correct; but in the second sense all are wrong; for, in the passage quoted the word *drotes* is a misreading of *dyetes*, repasts. V. DICT.

DROWPAND, DROUPAN, DRUPIN, adj. Drooping, bowing, bowed down; crushed, sad, demure, feeble; Houlate, l. 188. V. DROWP, *s.*

To DRUSH, DROSH, v. n. To crumble, crush, fall to pieces; to spoil, go wrong, fail. V. DRUSH, *s.*

DRUTE, *s.* A lazy, slovenly, heartless person. V. DRUTLE.

Shame fa' the fallow that did do't,
He's naething but a wortbless *drute*.
Fisher's Poems.

DRY-TAPSTER, s. One who sells but does not brew ale; Burgh Recs. Edin., II. 5, Rec. Soc. V. TOPSTER.

DUBLAR, s. V. Doubler.

DUCHTY, DUCHTIE, adj. V. DOUGHTY.

DUFFIE, DUFFY, adj. Blunt, blunt-pointed, round-headed; Orkn. Addit. to DUFFIE.

DUIE-OYE, s. A great-great-grandchild, Orkn.

DUILL, s. Grief, sorrow: pl. *duilles, duillis*, mourning for the dead, also short for *duleweeds*, mournings, Blame of Kirkburiall, ch. 7; another form is *dule-claes*, widow's-weeds. Addit. to DULE.

DULSACORDIS, s. A musical instrument, prob. a dulcimer; Houlate, l. 762.

DULSET, DULSATE, s. A musical instrument: prob. a small dulcimer, Houlate, l. 762.

DUMMYGRANE, s. Corr. of *Demigrane*, the name of a rich glossy silk; Sempill Ballates, p. 238.

O. Fr. *demigraine*, also *migraine*, "scarlet or purple in graine;" Cotgr.

DUNGIN, DWNGIN, part. pt. V. DONGIN.

DUNNLE, v. and s. V. Dangle.

To DUNT, v. a. 1. To crush, mark, or indent by striking; like *to dunkle*; as, "Ye've *duntit* the lid o' the tin can."

2. To compact, shake together, by striking the mass on the ground; as, *to dunt* a sack of grain. Addit. to DUNT.

To DURE, v. n. To endure, abide, continue, last; Houlate, l. 169.

To DURKEN, v. n. To lie hid, lurk: lit. to be made dark. "Thei *durken* and dare," they lurk and lie hid. Errat. in DICT. V. *Dark*, and *Dare*.

The explanations of this term given by Jamieson, Sibbald and Pinkerton are worthless; but they had not correct versions to work on. Sir F. Madden pointed out this mistake, or series of mistakes, in his Gloss. to Sir Gawayn.

DUSANE, DUSAIN, GREIT DUSANE, s. An old name for the magistrates of a burgh, the town council. Prob. so called because it originally consisted of twelve members.

The origin of this name, and the composition of the body which it represents are not known with certainty; but the name continued to be applied to the town council of Edinburgh long after that body numbered above thirty members. A record dated Oct. 1416 states,—". . . aldermannus pro presenti anno, one

dene of gild, two appreciatores vini, two seriandi gilde, four appreciatores carnium, one bursator, thirty two of lie *dusane*." Under date, Oct. 1418, "the *dusane* is callit 'duodecim consules et limitatores;'" and an entry dated 19 Oct. 1492, gives some particulars regarding the meetings and regulations of this important body at that time. It runs thus:—"It is ordanit be the hale *dusane* of the town that gif any of the *dusane* beand wairuit cumis nocht betymes for the halding of the counsale in the wirking of the commoun proffeitt, that he sall pay for ilk defalt vj [pennies?] vn[for]gevyn, to be drukken be the *dusane*, and gif the dene or baillies or any of thame cummis nocht within dew tyme thai sall dowbill als mekill vnforgevin. Item, it is ordanit that ilk dusane day the commoun proffeitt be spokin of and sene to or ony playntis or vther thingis be hard." Burgh Recs. Edin., I. 2, 62.

In Peebles there were, in 1463, twenty-one persons "chossyng the *doussane* for the reformation of the town;" and in 1574 the old name was still retained, although the body then consisted of twenty-five members. Burgh Recs., pp. 150, 172, Rec. Soc. Now, as all the free burghs of Scot. had the same form of government, these facts suggest the probability that the name of the governing body in a burgh was, down to the close of the 16th cent., the same as it had been fixed at the foundation of the burghal system; and that it was then so fixed on account of the number of members required to form the body.

DUSSIE, DUSCHET, s. Coll. forms of *dulcet*, a musical instrument of the dulcimer kind; Sempill Ballates, p. 205, 207. V. DULSET.

DWERCH, DORCHE, s. A dwarf. V. DUERCH.

DWINE, v. and s. V. DWYNE.

DYAMAND, DYAMOND, s. Applied to anything that is shaped like a diamond or lozenge; cubes of iron used as shot; blunt diamond-shaped heads for tilting-spears; Accts. L. H. Treas. I. 310, Dickson.

"Item [10 Sept. 1496] for a waw of irne to be *dyamondis* for guncast, xxv. s." Ibid. p. 293.

O. Fr. and M.E. *diamant*, from Lat. *adamas, adamantis*, which was borrowed from the Greek. V. Trench's Select Glossary.

DYCE, DYSS, DIS, s. Dice; also applied to anything that is dice or diamond-shaped, as *dis of irne*, cubes of iron like dice; *dis hedit*, having a square or diamond-shaped heart; Accts. L. H. Treas., I. 133, 295, 357.

DYET, s. A diet, repast, course; Awntyrs of Arthur, st. 15.

DYKIE, s. Short for *dyke-sparrow*, a hedgesparrow; West of S.

DYSCHOWYLI, adj. Lit. with hair in disorder, like a lady going to or rising from rest: hence, in disarray. O. Fr. *deschevelé*. Addit. to DICT.

Jamieson's definition gives in a general way the meaning implied in the passage quoted; but it does not give the correct meaning of the term.

DYS [103] EDD

"The etymology is obviously wrong; it is merely the E. *dischevelled*, with the hair untidy; from O. Fr. *chevel*, hair, Lat. *capillus.*" Skeat.

DYSMEL, *s.* V. DISMAL.

DYVOUR, DYVOR, *s.* Cheat, rogue, rascal, neer-do-well; Wattie and Meg, st. 21. Addit to DYVOUR.

This term is still used in West of S. as an epithet of opprobrium, and synon. with *blackguard*.

E.

E, EE, EIE, E'E, *s.* Eye; look, look-out, watch; regard, liking, desire, craving; as in "a kindly *ee*, a lang *ee*, a constant *ee*." Addit. to E.

AFORE E. Before one's eyes, in one's heart or mind.

". . . eldaris qnha has the feir of God *afore e.*" Burgh Recs. Peebles, p. 279, Rec. Soc.

To HAVE E. To look, watch, watch over; to consider, be interested in, try to assist or benefit.

". . . the counsale regardand and *haveand eie to* the burges barnes of the said towne, and to schaw thame fauour." Burgh Recs. Glasgow, I. 59, Rec. Soc.

To EAGGLEBARGIN, *v. n.* To wrangle, contend, quarrel, Ramsay. V. ARGLE-BARGLE.

Pron. also *Eaggle-baggle* in the Lothians; *argie-bargie* in Fife and Perths.; and *argy-bargo* in the West of S. In Ayre. *argie-bargie* is also in use. These variations show that this word has nothing to do with *haggling* in a *bargain*, as Dr. Jamieson suggested; but *argle-bargle* and all its varieties illustrate the Scottish tendency to drop or change the liquids in words that are much used.

EARLEATHER, *s.* V. *Eirledder*.

EASE, EIS, EISS, ESS, *s.* Ease, leisure, satisfaction, comfort, favour; Barbour, i. 228, vii. 302: *at eiss*, at leisure, Ibid. xv. 542: *male ess*, disease, Ibid. xx. 73, Camb. MS., and in Edin. MS. *malice*.

To EASE, EIS, EISS, *v. a.* To comfort, satisfy, Barbour, v. 291.

EASED, *part. pt.* Rested, satisfied; well furnished or provided.

"So then, seeing our nobles now may be, as of olde they were then, so honourablie *eased* with ones princely Iles or tombes, why should they wilfully incurre vnnecessar profanation, by burying in Kirks?" Blame of Kirkburiall, ch. 10.

O. Fr. *aisé*, pleased, satisfied. But in this case *eased* is used in the senso of *aisé* in the phrase *aisé en son meanage*, which Cotgrave renders "well furnished with all houshold prouision."

EASY, ESIE, ESY, *adj.* Light, moderate, not great, costly, or extravagant: as, "Now,

mak your price *easy.*" It is also used as an *adv.*: as, "They're bein folk, but they live quite *easy*," i.e., without much cost or display. Comp. *easier*, superl. *easiest*, *esiest*.

Braid burdis and benkis our beld with bancouris of gold,
Cled our with clene clathis,
Raylit full of riches,
The *esiest* was the arress,
That ye se schold.
Houlate, st. 52.

"*Esiest*," least worth, least expensive.

EASTIN, ESTIN, *adj.* and *adv.* Eastern, eastward, Dunbar; Compl. Scot., p. 61, E. T. S.

EATEN CORN, EATTEN CORNE, ETTEN CORNE, *s.* Oats eaten by domestic animals trespassing.

"Alexander Dickie persued Barbara Fultoun for sevein peckis of *eatten* corne this last summer." Corshill Baron Court Book, Ayr and Wigtown Arch. Coll., IV. 75.

EBBIE, *s.* The abbrev. of Ebenezer; it is often further abbreviated into Ebb, which in West and South of S. is pron. Aib.

EBURE, *s.* V. EUOUR, EVER.

ED, EODE, *pret.* Went. V. YED, YEDE.

To EDDER, *v. a.* To rope a stack. V. ETHER.

EDDIE, *s.* The abbrev. of Edward; it is often further shortened into Ed, which is corr. into Ned.

To EDDLE, ETTLE, *v. a.* and *n.* To earn, win by labour, work for: as, "Ye'll just get what ye *eddle* for, or what ye *ettle*."

EDDLES, EDDLINS, ETTLES, ETTLINS, *s. pl.* Earnings, wages, recompense, retribution; fruits of one's labour: as, "Wait a wee, your *eddlins* 'll ourtak ye." "Ye'll get your *ettlins* for that yet."

Icel. *ödlask*, to win, gain as property; Cleasby. In the North of E. the forms are *addle*, *aidle*, *eddle*. V. Brockett's Gloss.

'EE, *pron.* A coll. form for *thee* and *ye*, and sometimes for *thou* and *you;* as, "I mann tell '*ee*." "Is tat '*ee*?" i.e. is it you?
This was a common form in the West of S. thirty years ago, and may still be heard in rural districts. The modern form is *ye*.

EEN, EIN, *adj.* and *v.* Even. V. EVIN.

EENSHANKS, *s.* Afternoon repast; also called *four-hours*, from the time at which it was taken. V. FOURHOURS.
This repast is also named *antrim, antrin, andorn,* and of late years *drum*: but all are from *undern*.
Eenshanks is a corr. of *een* or *eenin*, evening, and *shenk*, drink, refreshment. The term still exists in the South of Scot. See *nuncheon* in Skeat's Etym. Dict.

EERAN, EERIN, EARAND, *s.* An errand, message, business; Whistle Binkie, i. 253; pl. *eerans, eerins*, duties, daily work outside one's own house, purchases.
In some districts the applications of the pl. form are peculiar. The husband's *eerans* or *turns* are his daily work or round of duties; but the wife's *eerans* are her messages or purchases, and her *turns* are her round of domestic duties.

EETCH, EITCH, AITCH, *s.* An adze, a carpenter's tool.

EFREST. Errat. in DICT. for *Esiest*, q. v.
This error was made by the transcriber of Pinkerton's version of the Houlate. Jamieson's note on the word suggests a meaning quite the reverse of that which the correct word implies. V. under *Easy*.

EFT, EFF, *adv.* After, afterwards, again; Barbour, vi. 378. Addit. to EFT.

EFT-CROP, EFF-CROP, *s.* 1. After-crop, also called tail-crop, i.e., the grass that springs up among the stubble after the crop is cut. V. *Averish*.

2. A crop of the same kind as the ground yielded last year. V. *Eff-crop*, *v*.

To EFF-CROP, *v. a.* Lit. to after-crop, i.e., to take two successive crops of the same kind from a field.
". . tenants were restricted not to *eff-crop* the infield (i.e., not to take two successive crops of oats), nor to fourth-crop the out-field till *baugh-ley*." Robertson, Agriculture of S. Dist. Perthshire, p. 23.

EFTERHIN, EFTIRHIN, *prep.* and *adv.* Another form of EFTERHEND, EFTIRHEND, q. v.
This term often implies *next after*, and sometimes *over and above, in addition to*, when used as a prep. As an adv. it often implies *soon* or *immediately afterwards*.

EFTERINS, EFTIRENS, *s.* Lit. afterius, that which comes after, the result, consequence, effect, settlement, penalty, reward. V. EFTIR-FALLIS.

To EGLE, EGGLE, *v. a.* A corr. of *ettle*, to intend, design, aim, attempt; part. pr. *egling*.
". . put furth his hand *egling* to mak him ane gait." Burgh Recs. Peebles, 3 May, 1537.

EIK, EKE, EK, *adv.* Also.

EILINS, EELINS. 1. As an *s. pl.*, equals in age. V. EILDINS.

2. As an *adj.*, of equal age; as "Your laddie's *eilins* wi' our lassie." West of S.

To EIND, EYND, EIN, *v. a.* and *n.* To breathe, whisper; devise, imagine. V. EIND, *s.*

To EIND-ILL, EINDILL, EYNDILL, EINIL, *v. n.* and *a.* Lit. to breathe ill: to devise, imagine, whisper, or spread evil thoughts; to be jealous, suspicious, or vengeful; to suspect, defame, slander. V. EYNDILL.
Thay lichtly sone and covettis quickly;
They blame ilk body and thay blekit;
Thay *eindill* fast and dois ill lickly;
Thay sklander saikles and thay suspectit.
Alex. Scott's Poems, p. 71, ed. 1882.
The form *indill* was also used. V. under *Eldning*. This word has been printed *kindill* by Lord Hailes in his extracts from the Bannatyne MS., and *eindill*, which is the correct reading, by the Hunterian Club, and by the editor of the 1882 ed. of Scott's Poems. The context, however, suggests that it should be printed *eind-ill* : and when it is thus separated into its parts the whole passage becomes plain and pithy.

To EIR, EYR, *v. a.* To plough, till, cultivate; pret. *eirit*, Henryson, Foxe and Wolfe, l. 22; *eyrit*, Douglas, Virgil, xii. ch. 9; part. pr. *eirand*. V. ERE, AR.
In the Gloss. of Laing's ed. of Henryson *eirit* is rendered "waxed." This is a mistake.

EIRDE HOUSES. V. under ERD.

EIRS, EERS, *s. pl.* The kidneys. V. EARS, NEIRS.

EIR-LEDDER, ERLEDDER, *s.* The loin-strap, a portion of the harness of a draught-horse; also called the *eir-strap* or *neir-strap*, because it passes over the region of the kidneys; Accts. L. H. Treas., I. 295, and Gloss.
Jamieson's suggestion regarding the etym. of *eirledder* is a mistake. The word is a corr. of *neerledder*, from M. E. *neer*, a kidney : O. H. Germ. *neiro*, O. Icel. *nyra*. V. STRATMANN.

EIRLEDDER-PINS, ERLEDDIR-PYNNYS, *s. pl.* The pins of iron on the shafts of a cart to which the eir-leathers were fastened; Accts. L. H. Treas., Gloss.

EISTLET, EISLIT, EISTELLIT, *adv.* and *adj.* Eastward; West of S. : " be *eistellit* the same," Burgh Recs. Glasgow, I. 389, Rec. Soc. V. EASTILT.

EK, *adv.* and *v.* V. *Eik*, EIK.

ELABORED, *part. pt.* Industriously worked, built, or fashioned. O. Fr. *elaboré.*

". . . Pharas Conchres . . . having a sepulchrall Pyramide *elabored* by the panofull taske of God's people." Blame of Kirkburiall, ch. 9.
This word is not uncommon in E. works of the same period. In Urquhart's Rabelais, Author's Prologue, we find the phrase "most perfectly *elaboured* by nature."

ELCROOK, ELCRUIK, *s.* Lit. an eel-spear or leister, but generally applied to the large flesh fork used by cooks.

"Item, ane peulder dische, ane trunschoor, ane *elcruik* and ladill, price thairof xx. s." Burgh Recs. Glasgow, i. 129.
". . . of Laik patrones they become lawlesse publicans, lyke Hophnees with *elcrookes* to minche and not Samueles to mense the offerings of God." Blame of Kirkburiall, ch. xix.

ELCRUIK, *s.* A crock or earthen vessel for holding oil; also a crock. V. EULCRUKE.

In the Burgh Rec. Soc. version of the law quoted by Jamieson this vessel is called simply "*a cruk;*" but the same article is meant,—an *oil-crock.*

ELDIS. Errat. in DICT. for *Clois*, closely.

In the list of Errata printed at the end of his Gloss., Ruddiman gives *clois* as the correct reading; *eldis* was therefore set aside, not overlooked. Small's ed. reads *clois.*

ELDNING, ELDNYNG, *part.* Rousing, firing up, making jealous; Dunbar, Mariit Wemen, l. 126; as a *s.*, jealousy, Ibid., ll. 119, 204. Addit. to ELDNING, q. v.

A.-S. *elnian*, to strengthen. V. Jamieson's note, in which he suggests that *eyndlyng* is the same with *indilling.* This is confirmed by the Maitland MS. reading *endling* in l. 204. V. *Eind-ill.*

ELENCH, *s.* A summary, abstract, recapitulation, conclusive summing up.

"Now here ere I end, for the more populare application, I will contriue an *elench* of some former reasones in sylogistick forme; by the which self-momus may see Kirk-buriall blame vndenyablie induced." Blame of Kirkburiall, ch. 20.
Lat. *elenchus*, an index of a book; in logic, the conclusion or summing up of an argument.

ELF-ARROW-HEADS, *s. pl.* Same as ELFSHOT, q. v.

ELSCHENER, ELSCHONER, ALSCHONER, *s.* V. ELSHENDER.

ELSHIN, ELSHON, ELSIN, ELSON, *s.* An awl. V. ELSYN.

EMBROUDIN, ENBROUDIN, *part. pt.* Embroidered or bordered; trimmed or decorated with an ornamental border; decked, adorned. V. BROWDIN.

(Sup.)   O

Endland a ryuer plesant to behold,
Enbroudin all with fresche flowris gay.
Kingis Quair, st. 152, Skeat's ed.
Broudin or *browdin* is a more common form, and still in use.

EMERANT, *s.* Errat. in DICT. for *Emeraut:* but the definition is correct. Also, in the following entry Emerant, Emerand should be *Emeraut, Emeraud:* the *ut, ud=lt, ld.*

EMMELDYNG, *s.* Prob. a misprint of *emmeldyng*, lit. outside or edge - refuse; butcher's offal, scrap, or carcase paring: also applied to a strip, rag, or tatter hanging from a piece of dress. Another form is EMMLE-DEUG, q. v.

Jamieson entered this word with its quotation, but gave neither defin. nor etym. for it. That it is a misprint is almost certain; and by substituting *u* for *n* the passage becomes clear, but remains coarse.
The term is a compound of Gael. *iomall* (pron. *emall*), outskirt, border, edje, and *diliagha*, the refuse of persons or things; M'Leod and Dewar.

EMMLE-DEUG, *s.* Another form of *Emmeldyng* in last entry, q. v. Addit. to DICT.

The definition given in DICT. is secondary, and the etym. suggested is wrong. See explanations given above.

EMMORAUT, *s.* and *adj.* Emerald: another form of *emeraut.* V. under *Emerant.*

This form is often misprinted *emmorant*, through misreading *u* as *n.*

To EMPESCHE, EMPESH, *v. a.* V. EMPASH.

EMPHASE, *s.* Emphasis, force of expression or meaning; Blame of Kirkburiall, ch. 6. O. Fr. *emphase*, id.

EMPIRE, *adj.* Empyrean, empyreal; "the hauyn *empire*," the highest heaven, Compl. Scot., p. 49, E. E. T. S. Fr. *empyrée.*

To ENCHAIP, *v. a.* To buy, bargain, trade. do business; Rauf Coilyear, st. 25. Errat. in DICT. V. under *Encheve.*

Jamieson's suggestion regarding the meaning of this term does not suit the passage quoted. *Enchaip* may be from O. Fr. *enchapter*, var. of *achapter*, later *acheter*, to buy, procure, trade; Lat. *alcaptare.* Or it may be formed with Fr. prefix *en*, and M. E. *chep*, cheap, barter, traffic.

To ENCHEVE, ENCHEIF, ENCHIEF, *v. a.* To achieve, accomplish, go through with; hence, to win, conquer, triumph. A corr. of *achieve.*

That I haue said I sall hauld, and that I tell the plane;
Quhair ony coilyear may enchaip I trow till *encheif.*
Rauf Coilyear, st. 25.
That is, "Where any collier may trade I trust to succeed." V. *Enchaip.*
Encheve and *eacheve* are variants of *achieve*, borrowed from the O. Fr., which gives many similar forms; as *encuser* and *escuser* for *accuser.* V. BURGUY.

To ENCHEVE, ENCHEIF, ENCHIEF, EN-
CHEWE, v. a. To eschew, shun, avoid, shy
at; Douglas Virgil, v. ch. 8.

These are simply variants of *escheve, escheue*. Douglas in his translation of Virgil uses both forms, but *escheve* more frequently. In Bk. v. ch. 8, both forms occur within the course of a few lines. V. ESCHEVE.

To ENCHIEF, v. a. V. *Encheve*, ESCHEVE.

Jamieson's first suggestion regarding this term is correct, although given with considerable doubt. Explanation is given under *Encheve*.

To END, v. n. To come to an end, to die;
Barbour, xi. 553.

ENDING, END-DAY, s. End, end of life, death;
Barbour, ii. 197 : *end-day*, Houlate, l. 117.

Enday, day of ending or of death, as used by Wyntown, is used also in the general sense of *ending*.

ENDUE, ENDEW, adj. Due, owing, unpaid.

". . . for borrowed money *endew* be hire."
Corshill Baron Court Book, Ayr and Wigtown Arch. Coll., iv. 90.

ENDURAND, *prep.* During. V. INDURAND.

ENEL-SHEET, s. Lit. an *end-day sheet*, a winding-sheet. V. ENDAY.

Forbye a dainty *enel-sheet*,
Twa cods, whilk on the bouster meet,
An' slips anew to mak' complete
A beddin' o' the kin' O.
Wat. Watson's Poems, p. 59.

The *enel-sheet* was a double sheet of fine linen which thrifty females selected and carefully preserved in fold ready to be used as a covering for their dead body before it was put in the coffin. It was a special requisite of a bride's outfit, and decked her bed on the marriage night : after which it was carefully laid past to be used again only as her last earthly covering.

To ENFORCE, v. a. To force, force open, forcibly enter, violate. Fr. *forcer*.

"And although to beligger the lodgings of men, . . . they wil looke ere they loup ; yet to *enforce* the Kirkhouse (as if God had no gunnes) there are many of small feare." Blame of Kirkburiall, ch. 19.

To ENGENER, v. a. To engender, beget;
pret. *engeneret*, Compl. Scot., p. 153, E. E.
T. S. Fr. *engendrer*.

ENGYEOUN, ANGYEOUN, s. An onion,
Burgh Recs. Aberd., p. 127.

ENLANG, ENLANGIS, ENLANGS, INLANGIS,
adv. Endwise, end foremost, from end to
end, right on, without break or pause.
Addit. to ENDLANG, q. v.

These forms are frequently met with ; but they represent simply the various pron. of *endlang, endlangis*.

ENLANG, ENLANGIS, prep. Along, by way
of : forms of *alang, alangs*, and like them
used also as *adv*.

". . . ane penny for ilk beist passand *enlangis* the brig." Burgh Recs. Glasgow, I. 167, Rec. Soc.

To ENLUMYNE, v. a. To illumine ; part.
pt. *enlumynyt*, Barbour, xx. 229. Edin.
MS.

To ENNOY, v. a. To annoy; part. pt.
ennoyit, annoyed, troubled ; Douglas, Virgil,
V. ch. 11.

ENPARING, s. Impairing, diminution, lowering ; Douglas, Virgil, xiii. ch. 11.
O. Fr. *empire*.

ENSENS, s. Incense, Compl. Scot., p. 7.
E. E. T. S. Fr. *encens*.

To ENSENCE, v. To offer incense, Dunbar.

ENSENYE, s. Insignia ; "the *ensenye* of the fleise," Compl. Scot., p. 149, E. E. T. S.
Addit. to ENSEINYIE.

ENSPRETH, s. and adj. V. INSPRAICH.

To ENSURE, v. a. To make sure, rely ;
Douglas, Virgil, v. ch. 8. O. Fr. *seur*, sure.

ENTECHMENT, s. Teaching, learning, experience ; Douglas, Virgil, xi. ch. 4.

A.S. *tæcan, tæcean*, to show, teach.

ENTENT, s. 1. Intention, purpose, message.
In hons and in half hee
To tell his *entent*.
Howlate, l. 143.

2. As a law term, judicial finding or assent ; hence, concurrence, consent.

That sen it uychlit Nature, thair alleris maistriss,
Thai coud nocht trete but *entent* of the temperale.
Ibid., l. 277.

O. Fr. *entente*, intention ; M. E. *entente*. In law the *entent* or *intent* of any disputed point was determined by the judges.

To ENTER, v. a. To commence, set to work, as, "We'll *enter* the men on the ditch the morn ;" to begin to work, or set to work for the first time, as "to *enter* a hawk," to fly it at quarry for the first time ; Accts. L. H. Treas., I. 360, Dickson : to take on trial, to undergo probation, as, " We *enter* prentices for a month before indenture." O. Fr. *entrer*.

". . . beast or body, education should aye be minded, I have six terries at hame. . . I had them a' regularly *entered*, first wi' rottens—then wi' stoats or weasels—and then wi' the tods and the brocks—and now they fear naething that ever cam wi' a hairy skin on't." Guy Mannering, ch. xxii.

ENTRE, ENTRA, s. Entry to office, duty, possession, inheritance ; the succession of an heir, Accts. L. H. Treas., I. 6, 315 ; compearance, as, " souerte for the *entre* of a man to the Justice aire," Ibid. I. 217. O. Fr. *entrée*.

To ENTERMET, *v. n.* To intermeddle, intromit; pret. and part. pt. *entermettit.* O. Fr. *entremettre.*

". . to pass and summonde the folkis that *entermittit* with the brokin schip." Accts. L. H. Treas., i. 101, Dickson.

To ENTIRE, ENTYRE, *v. a.* To inter, bury; part. pt. *entirit, entyrit*; Barbour, xix. 224; Douglas, Virgil, xi. ch. 4. Lat. *in terra.*

ENTIRE, *s.* Interment, burial; Douglas, Virgil, vi. ch. 2.

ENWYT, *part. pt.* Witnessed, attested, proven.

". . the said Jhone Myller denyit ony strykon of hym, bot yt was *enwyt* be secht of his ourisman." Burgh Recs. Prestwick, 2 June, 1541, Mait. c.

ENY, *adj.* Any; Barbour, x. 200.

EQUE, *s.* A closed or balanced account; hence, acquittance, receipt; so called from the phrase, "*et sic eque,*" which was written at the foot of an account when it was closed or settled; Burgh Rec. Glasgow, II. 41.

". . produceit the townes *eque* vpoun the payment of thair burrow mailles in exchequer." Burgh Recs. Aberdeen, i. 118, Rec. Soc.

EQUIVOCATION, *s.* The method, manner, or act of calling different things by the same name: also, a name applied or common to different things.

". . it [i.e. the grave] hes yet scauen names more, that, by scripturall *equivocation,* are common with hell." Blame of Kirkburiall, ch. 17.
"As by weighing the scripturall *equinocations* that are bestowed ou both kirk and graue." Ibid.
Lat. *equus,* equal; and *vocatis,* a calling.

ER, *v. aux.* Are; Douglas, Barbour.

ERAST, ERASTE, *adj. superl.* Earliest, readiest, soonest or easiest got at; hence, first. Addit. to ERAST.

". . . to do this with the *eraste* pennyes that may be gottyn of the comoune rentaile." Burgh Recs. Aberdeen, 5 Sept., 1452, Sp. C.
". . . a promise of the *erast* chapilnary that vakit at was at thar gift." Ibid., 20 July, 1456.

ERB, EIRB, *s.* An herb; Compl. Scot. p. 67, E. E. T. S.

ERE, *adv.* Formerly. V. ER.

To ERIE, EARIE, *v. n.* To fall behind, to be lacking or awanting: part. pr. *eriand, eareand,* used also as a *s.* meaning amount lacking, deficit.

". . . and quhair that will not serve, the *eareand* to be supplied out of the collectionis for the poore at the kirk dooris." Burgh Recs. Aberdeen, 4 June, 1619, Sp. C.

O. Fr. *erier, eriere,* var. of *ariere,* Mod. Fr. *arrière,* behind, backward : from Lat. *ad retro.* V. Burguy's Gloss.

ERLEDDER, *s.* V. under *Eirs.*

ERRAS, *s.* Arras, Accts. L. H. Treas. I. 52.

ERROUR, *s.* An erroneous verdict of an inquest, Accts. L. H. Treas., i. 210; *assis of errour,* an assize summoned to correct such a verdict and retour, Ibid., i. 214, Dickson.

ERSCHE, ERYSCHE, ERIS, *adj.* Belonging to the Highlands of Scotland, Celtic; Accts. L. H. Treas., I. 177, 233, 266. V. ERSE.

ERSCHMAN, *s.* A Highlander, a Celt; Ibid., I. 288.

ERCHRYE, ERCHRYNE, *s.* The Celtic people; the country of the Erse or Irish. V. ERSE.

Thir ar the Ireland kingis of the *Erchrye.*
Houlate, l. 801, Bann. MS.
The Asloan MS. reads *Irischerye.*

ERSE, ERS, *s.* 1. Bottom. V. ARSE.

". . . and that the meill be als gud in the sek *ers* as is in the mouth thairof." Burgh Recs. Peebles, 5 Dec., 1571.

2. Hinder end; tail, as in the tail-board of a cart, the tail of a plough, which are called the *erse*-board, and the *erse* o' the plough or the plough-*erse.*

Erse is the common form, and represents the pron. in Scot.; the form *arse* is similarly used in various districts of Eng.

ERWEST, *s.* Harvest, harvest time, Burgh Recs. Prestwick, p. 21, Mait. Club.

ESCAPE, *s.* A fault, slip, mistake, error in translation.

Spotswood, in his account of the Burntisland Assembly when discussing the subject of a new translation of the Scriptures, and a new metrical version of the Psalms, tells how King James urged the necessity of the undertaking by pointing out "sundry *escapes* in the common translation," etc. V. Note in Reg. Privy Council, VI. 237, and full account in Spots., pp. 463. 465.
Shakespeare used this term in the sense of violation or transgression of lawful restraint; Tit. Andron., iv. 2; a sense of modern E. *escapade.*

ESCHAMIT, *part. pt.* Ashamed, Compl. Scot., p. 43, E. E. T. S. M. E. *aschamed.*

A.-S. *áscamod,* p. p. of *áscamian,* to make ashamed; Skeat.

To ESCHEIF, ESCHIEF, *v. a.* V. ESCHEVE.

ESCHELLIT, ESCHELLETT, *s.* A small hand-bell or clapper, such as was used by lepers. O. Fr. *eschellette.*

This term has left undefined by Jamieson, and the suggestion he made regarding its meaning is certainly wrong. The meaning now given renders the passages quoted in the DICT. clear and intelligible.

O. Fr. *eschellette,* "a little hand-bell, such as Cryers vse ;" Cotgr. It is a dimin. of O. Fr. *eschiele, eschelle,* a little bell; Burguy: or, as Cotgrave gives it, of *eschalle,* "a little ringing or tinging bell."

ESCHET, ESCHETE, ESCHETIT, *part. pt.* Escheated, forfeited; Accts. L. H. Treas., I. 10, 67, Burgh Recs.

ESCHET, ESCHETE, ESHET, *s.* Forfeiture, Compl., Scot., p. 133, E. E. T. S.; forfeit; pl. *eschetis, eschaetis,* forfeited goods, Accts. L. H. Treas., I. 11, Dickson : *eshet,* Burgh Recs. Aberd., I. 436.

O. Fr. *eschet,* p. p. of *escheoir,* to fall out, to fall or come unto ; Cotgr.

ESHUED, *pret.* and *part. pt.* Shunned. V. ESCHIEVE.

ESIE, ESIEST. V. under *Ease.*

ESPOSIT, ESSPOSIT, *part. pt.* Promised, pledged, bound by promise or agreement. Another form is *asposit,* q. v.

". . . and geyf it hapnys the sayd Jonot to byg thar land that John sal suple tharto has he is *essposit.*" Burgh Recs. Peebles, p. 118, Rec. Soc.

O. Fr. *esposer,* to espouse, in the sense in which it is used in the phrase '*to espouse* a cause,' i.e., to become pledged to follow or support it. Burguy gives the forms *esposer, espuser, espouser,* from Lat. *sponsare,* to pledge oneself, to become surety. The form *asposit,* which is more common in our Burgh Records, is found in almost every engagement of a new chaplain by the magistrates ; he is to perform certain stated duties as he is *asposit,* i.e., bound by his agreement or promise, pledged to do. Jamieson's definition of the term is thus defective.

Dessposit is used in exactly the same sense and circumstances in Burgh Recs. Peebles, 15 Feb., 1476.

ESPYNE, *s.* A long-boat. V. ASPYNE.

ESS, *s.* Ease. V. *Ease.*

To ET, ETE, *v. a.* To eat ; pret. *et, ete, ett, eyt, eyte,* Barbour, ii. 495, iii. 539, vii. 169 ; part. pt. *etin, etyn,* Ibid., vii. 170.

To ETHER, EDDER, *v. a.* To rope a stack of grain, &c. V. DICT.

The defin. of this term in DICT. is correct, but the etym. is wrong. There is no such word as *heatherinn* in A.-S. The verb is derived from the *s. ether,* A.-S. *edor,* a fence, enclosure, &c. V. ETHERINS.

EUR, VRE, *s.* Ore. V. URE.

EUUSE, EVUSE, EWUSE, *adj.* and *adv.* Forms of *ewous,* near, contiguous, q. v.

These forms occur in the same record, and all are misprinted with n for u. V. under EWOUS.

To EVANCE, *v. a.* To advance, forward, in the sense of paying, lending, or sending money.

"[The bailies and council] ordane James Ros . . . *to evance* euery ane of thame the sowme of xxvj li. for fulfilling of thair promys maid to my said Lord Regenttis Grace," etc. Burgh Recs. Edin., 1 July, 1575.

EVER, *s.* V. EVOUR, EUOUR.

EVIN, EWIN, EWYN, EIN, EEN, *adj.* Even, smooth, level, straight, equal ; of equal rank, worth, or ability.

EVIN, EVYN, EWYN, *adv.* Evenly ; level, in a level position ; in a line with, on equal terms or footing, all alike, straight.

To EVIN, EWIN, EWYN, EIN, EEN, *v. a.* 1. To even, equal, match, mate ; as, "Ne'er a man'll *evin* till her ;" part. pt., *evind, eend, eind.*

2. To direct, speak of, charge, or lay to one's charge ; as, "Sic a thing was never *eind* to him," i.e., intended for, hinted to, or attributed to him. Addit. to EVEN, q. v.

EVINING, EWYNNING, *s.* Evening, levelling ; the act of levelling.

". . consentit to the *ewynning* of thair Castelbill, and yking the same about." Burgh Recs. Aberdeen, i. 110, Sp. C.

A.-S. *efen, euen,* even, level ; M. E. *euen.*

EVIN, EVYN, EWIN, EWYN, *s.* Eve, evening, eventide ; Barbour. 1. 106, xvii. 335, xix. 719. *Ewn,* and *ein* are also used.

A.-S. *æfen.*

EWEST, *superl.* Nearest. Errat. in DICT. V. under *Ewous.*

EWIL-CRUIK, *s.* A corr. of *aval-crook,* also pron. *awal-cruik,* and *havil-cruik* : lit. a lowering crook, or crook for lowering a pot suspended over the fire. It consists of a set of links or rings and a small movable hook.

". . ane taingis, ane *ewil cruik,* ane pair of pot bulis," &c. Burgh Recs. Aberdeen, I. 336, Sp. C.
Fr. *avaler,* to lower or let down.

EWIS, *s.* Advice, counsel. V. AUISE.

". . dekin of the wobstairis by *ewis* and consent of the haill craft." Burgh Recs. Peebles, 30 Sept. 1566.

EWOUS, EUOUS, EUUSE, EVUSE, EWISE, *adj.* and *adv.* Near, close, contiguous : compar. *mair ewous;* superl. *ewest, maist ewous.*

". . being committit to *ewous* and nar this burgh." Burgh Recs. Aberdeen, II. 82, Sp. C.

". . houssis callit the townis housaia, . . and that maist *ewous* to the tolbuith." Ibid., p. 120.

". . one of your landis liand mair *evuse* to ws, or interchange the saidis landis with wtheris haiffand landis liand mair *ewuse* to ws." Ibid., I. 117.

The form *maist ewest,* which frequently occurs in Burgh Records, Charters, etc., is really a double superlative ; and prob. it was this form which misled Jamieson to adopt *ewest* as the primary *adj.* He certainly knew that *e west* was used, as it still is, in the sense of nearest, next, (V. note) ; but perhaps he had not found the simpler form *ewous,* or had taken it to be a corr. of *ewest.*

Perhaps *ewous* is a corr. of *newous*; cf. A.-S. *néawist*, neighbourhood, nearness, and Prov. E. *newstness*, nearness.

EXCEPAND, *part.* and *prep.* Excepting, except; Compl. Scot., p. 95, E. E. T. S.

To EXCERCE, *v. a.* V. EXERCE.

EXECUTION, EXECUCIOUN, *s.* As a law term implies carrying out or causing to take effect; hence, *the execucioun of a summons* is the serving of it; Accts. L. H. Treas. i. 239.

To EXEME, EXEMPNE, *v. a.* To examine, prosecute, sit in judgment on, test or try; Lyndsay, Kitteis Confessioun, l. 7. Addit. to EXAME, EXEM.

For quhill he gadderis and growis riche,
He settis you to *exeme* sum wiche.
Rob Stene's Dream p. 19.

This peculiar form of *examine* appears to have been pron. *exame* or *exem*; as it is made to rhyme with *yame*, which prob. was then, as now, pron. *gem* (*g* hard).

EXEQUIES, *s.* Funeral rites or services, burial; Blame of Kirkburiall, ch. xi. 16.

EXERCITIOUN, *s.* Diligence, constant careful practice; Lyndsay, Thrie Estaitis, l. 3339. Addit. to EXERCITIOUN.

EXIES, *s.* The same as *axies*, *axis*, an attack of sickness, q. v.

M. E. *axes*, O. Fr. *acces*, Lat. *accessus*, an attack; as in *accessus febris*, a febrile attack, which Cotgrave renders by "*access de fiebure*, a fit of an ague."

EXINTERATION, *s.* Disemboweling. V. DISINTRICATION.

To EXPONE, *v. a.* To lay out, expend, bestow; part. pt. *exponit*. Lat. *exponere*.

". . . the mony and proffeit of the said land . . . nocht to be *exponit* in othir vasis." Burgh Recs. Aberdeen, i. 118, Sp. C.

EXTENTAR, *s.* V. EXTENTOUR.

EXTRET, EXTRETE, EXSTREIT, EXTREYT, *s.* The certified lists of the compositions, fines, etc., levied at the justice-aires; Accts. L. H. Treas., i. 316, 217, 113, 201: also, the money so levied, Ibid. i. 316, Dickson. Low Lat. *extractus*, an extract, record, statement.

EYRD, *s.* Earth. V. EIRD, ERD.

EYRIT, *part. pt.* Ploughed, Douglas, Virgil, xii. ch. 9.

F.

FABULATOUR, *s.* Reader or reciter, story-teller. Lat. *fabulator*.

". . . that ilk class [of scholars] find onlio ane candill in the nicht, and he that happinnis to be *fabulatour* to bring his candill with him." Rules for Grammar School of Aberdeen, Burgh Recs., 24 Oct., 1604, Sp. C.

FABURDON, *s.* Full-part song or harmony. Addit. to FABURDON, q. v.

Under Bourdon, in Littré abrégé par Beaujean, the term is thus defined :—"Fauxbourdon, musique dont toutes les parties se chantent note contre note."

FACELESS, *adj.* Timorous, cowardly; without heart or courage.

Thair land, thair honour, and triumphand fame
Salbe dispersit in dispyte of Inuy,
Quhen *faceless* fuillis sall not be settin by.
Sempill Ballates, p. 30.

FACHALOS, *s.* A night's lodging and entertainment: the duty of entertaining for a night a messenger of the king, chief, or superior.

Skene in his Celtic Scotland, Vol. III., p. 234, defines it as "probably the Irish 'Fochtfels,' which is explained as 'the first night's entertainment we receive at each other's house.'" It was a tax or burden on lands in Galloway held under the King. A different but less satisfactory explanation is given by Cosmo Innes in Legal Antiquities, p. 70.

FADE, FAID, *s.* A leader, guide; applied to the chief or director in games, sports, &c. Errat. in DICT.

"For ouen as in a sea-fairing flot, the formest by saile doth fuir before with lantern and flag, as *fade* whom the rest shonld follow." Blame of Kirkburiall, ch. 16.

A.-S. *fadian*, to set in order, arrange, direct.

Dr. Jamieson was quite astray regarding the meaning and etym. of this word; and his mistakes have been repeated by Mr. Small in his Gloss. to Douglas. The word was not uncommon in the West of S. some years ago, and may still be used.

FADER-HALF, FADYR-HALF, *s.* Lit. father's-half, father's side.

". . . his heritage sal be in yemsell of his frendis on the *fodyr-half* till the leill elde of the ayre." Burgh Lawis, ch. 98, Rec. Soc.

FADMELL, FODMELL, *s.* A weight or mass of lead equal to 70 lbs.

Prob. the bar of lead was so called because it measured a foot in length. Dan. *fod*, a foot, and *maal*, a measure.

To FAIK, FAKE, v. a. and n. V. FALK.
The various entries of *Faik* in DICT. should have been combined; for they represent mere varieties of meaning and use. The same variation obtains in the pron. of the common name of the Razorbill. "In the Hebrides this bird is called *falk* or *faik*." Neill's Tour, p. 197.

FAILYEIT, adj. Infirm, broken-down in body or mind; as, "ane ald *failyeit* preist," Accts. L. H. Treas., I. 324. Fr. *faillir*. V. FAILYE.

FAINFU, adj. Affectionate, kind and careful, gladsome; Orkn.
Icel. *feginn*, glad. A.-S. *faegen*. M. E. *fayn*.

To FAIT, v. a. To make, construct, fit; to supply, provide: part. pr. *faiting*.
". . . hinging of the said bell and *faiting* all wark thairto," &c. Burgh Recs. Glasgow, i. 482, Rec. Soc.

FAKFALLOW, s. Comrade, bosom-friend, boon-companion. V. FAIK, FAKE.
Troll By be his maister frakly will ryd,
And with ane hude on his heid hovis him besyd;
Cheik for cheik also and *fakfallow* lyk,
And with aue quarrell to riche and to pure ay reddy to pyk.
Myne Ordour of Knavis, Bann. MS., p. 446, Hunt. Soc.

FAKIN, part. pr. Wanting. V. FAIK.

FALCON, FALCOUNE, FALCOWN, s. The name of a small cannon carrying shot of about 2½ lbs. weight; Burgh Recs. Aberd., I. 253.

To FALD, v. a. To fold, double, turn down, fold up; as "to *fald* the claes." Addit. to FALD.

FALDIT, part. and adj. Folded, doubled, closed, shut; as, "wi' doors *faldit*," i.e. shut; *faldit neiffis*, closed fists, Burgh Recs., Glasgow, I. 145, Rec. Soc.

FALDIN-BED, s. A bed constructed so that it may be folded up when not in use, and set aside like a chest or press.

To FALK, FAIK, FAKE. 1. As a v. a., to lower, diminish, abate, deduct, halt, fold, compress; part. pt. *falkyte*, deducted, Accts. L. H. Treas., I. 245; pret. *faikit*, as, " My feet has never *faikit*," i.e., halted.
"Thar sal be chosin four discrete persounes to *falk* the tax of men that has tholit skath oft." Burgh Recs. Aberdeen, 18 Feb., 1445.

2. As a v. n., to fall short, to be lacking or defective; to fail, droop, wither. Addit. to FAIK.
"Na," quod the Taid, "that proverb is not trew";
For fair thingis oftymis ar fundin *faikyn*."
Henryson, Paddok and Mous, l. 58.
L. Lat *falcare*, to cut or lop with a sickle: from Lat. *falx*, a sickle. V. under *Faik*.

FALL, FA', FAW, s. Short for *fall-trap*, *faw-trap*; and applied to any kind of trap for catching animals. Addit. to FALL.

FALL-TRAP, s. A trap which encloses by the falling of a movable slip or cover; a mouse-trap, rat-trap, &c.
I haif housis anew of greit defence;
Of cat nor *fall-trap* I half na dreid.
Henryson, Uplandis Mous and Burges Mous, l. 90.
Fall-trap became shortened to *fall*, *fa'*, or *faw*, which by-and-bye came to mean a trap, and to be applied to any kind of trap. Hence any kind of mouse-trap is still called a *mouse-faw*; of rat-trap, *ratton-faw*, &c.

To FALOW, FALLOW, v. a. To mate, match, associate, connect, unite. Addit. to FALOW.
It passis fer all kynd of pestilence,
Ane wickit mynd with wordis fair and sle;
Be war thairfoir with qnhom thow *fallowis* thee.
Henryson, Paddok and Mous, l. 138.

FALOWSHIP, FALOUSCHIP, FALOSCHIP, s. Fellowship, society; partner, owner. V. FALOW.
The use of this term in the latter sense is very old. An example occurs in the Custuma Portuum, ch. 1, in a passage stating the custom to be paid by a ship loaded with grain.
"And giff the corne or ony vthyr be of ayndry *faloschippys* [i.e., belong to different owners] ilk *faloschip* sal gyf ij bollis of the best," &c.

To FALT, FAUT, FAUTE. 1. As a v. n., to fail, err, do wrong, offend against the law.
"And gif he *faltis* twyis he sall be chastyte twyis for his fortaute." Burgh Lawis, ch. 19, Rec. Soc.

2. As a v. a., to lack, be destitute of; as, "to *falt* the fode." Awntyrs of Arthur, st. 25.

3. To find fault with, accuse; also, to find guilty of fault or wrong-doing.
Falt is properly to fall short of what is right and lawful; *forfalt*, to do contrary to right or law, to transgress.
The various entries of *Falt* and *Faut* in DICT. should have been thus combined. Several additions are here given.

To FALYE, v. n. To fail. V. FAILYE.

FAMILIARE, FAMELYAR, adj. Belonging to one's *familia* or household; household, family: not confidential (as usually explained). Addit. to FAMILIAR.
Jamieson adopted the definition generally given, which is wrong. The word occurs often in our Burgh Recs., and always with the meaning given above. For example:—
". . . . . . the said Sir Thomas Kenedy was in the kyngis resprit at the byschop of Sanct Androis has of the kyngis as *famelyar* tyl him." Burgh Recs. Peebles, 9 June, 1460.
"Wit ye was to haif takin vnder oure speciale mainteinance . . . . . . oure louittis all the merchandis and inhabitautis of oure burgh of Peblis and the fredome thairof, and all and sindry thair landis, rentis, possessiouns, ... corne,

FAM [111] FAY

catall, *familiare servandis, factoures, procuratouris, ... and all and sindry thar gudis,"* &c. Charter of James IV. in 1509, Recs. of Peebles, p. 42, Rec. Soc.

FAMULIT, *pret.* Stammered, stuttered: hence, "*famulit hir facultie*," mumbled over her utterance. Addit. to FAMULIT.
Dan. *famle*, to hesitate, falter. Jamieson's first etym. is wrong.

FAN, *s.* A wreath or drift of snow; Orkn.
That which has been fanned or drifted by the wind.
Lat. *vannus*, a fan. Cf. Fr. *van*.

FAN, FAN', *pret.* Pron. of *fand*, found.
He *fan* Death's fearfu' grapple-airns,
An' that he cou'dna free them.
Alex. Wilson's Poems, p. 43, ed. 1876.

FAND, FANT. Represents the pron. of *fand it*, found it; as, "He socht it till he fand out."
Fand is the result of softening *t* in *fan't*, which is short for *fand it*. There is a large number of similar forms, as *bede* for *be it*, *dude* for *do it*, *said* for *say it*, *paid* for *pay it*, &c.

FANGAR, *s.* Catcher; as in *fisch-fangar*, fish-catcher, Houlate, l. 181. V. FANG, *v*.

FANT, *adj.* Faint, weak-hearted, timorous; "nothir febill nor *fant*," Dunbar, Tua Marriit Wemen, l. 86. M. E. *feint*.
O. Fr. *feint*, p. p. of *feindre*, to feign.

FAREFOLKIS, *s. pl.* V. DICT.
Regarding the etym. of *fairy*, all the opinions quoted by Jamieson are wrong except the last one, viz., O. Fr. *faerie*, enchantment. The proper word for a fairy or elf is *fay*, from Lat. *fatum*. V. Skeat's Etym. Dict.

FARNE, *part. pt.* A form of *faren*, fared. Dunbar, Mariit Wemen. V. FAIR.
A.-S. *faran*, to go; pp. *faren*.

FARROW, FARRY, FARRA, *adj.* Applied only to cows: as, a *farrow-cow*, one that gives milk during the winter. V. FERRY-COW, FORROW-COW.

FAS, FASSE, *s.* A tuft, lock, curl, knop, drop, tassel, fringe; pl. *fassis*, edging, fringes, tassels, Accts. L. H. Treas., I. 22, 228. Addit. to FAS, FASSIS.
A.-S. *fæs*, a fringe, hem.

FASE, FASS, *adj.* False. V. FAUSE.

FASLY, *adv.* Falsely; Dunbar, Bann. MS., p. 161, l. 27, Hunt. Soc.

FASTENING, *s.* V. FESNYNG, FESTYNANCE.

FAT, FATE, FATT, *s.* A vat, tub, Accts. L. H. Treas., I. 30. Addit. to FAT.
A.-S. *fæt*, a vat.

FATGUDE, *s.* A tax levied in Orkney and Shetland: the term used for the quantity of butter or oil paid to the superior.
"*Fatgude*, a term used in Zetland for the butter or oil paid to the Donatary." Balfour, Odal Rights and Feudal Wrongs, p. 114.

FAULD, *s.* 1. The open field, meadow, pasture. V. FAULDS.
By firth, forrest, or *fauld*.
Henryson, Robene and Makyne, l. 96.

2. A fold, sheep-fold; also, the flock folded, as in the fine song of Ramsay, "The Waukin o' the Fauld."
"*The waukin o' the fauld*" is the night-watch that is kept at the ewe-bughts or fold to prevent the weaned lambs from getting back to their dams.

FAUSE, *adj.* Sleekit, sly, double; Orkn. Addit. to FAUSE,

To FAUT, FAUTE, FAWTE, *v. a.* and *n.* V. *Falt*.

FAUTIE, FAUTY, *adj.* Faulty, wrong-doing, guilty; Burgh Recs. Prestwick, p. 18: also used as a *s.*
"And by all meanes compell and reproue the *fautie* and vicious;" etc. Conf. of Faith of Swiss Churches, p. 18, Wodrow Soc. Misc.

FAUTIFU, *adj.* Fault-finding; difficult to please: Orkn.
O. Fr. *fautier*, *faultif*, faulty, blame-worthy; Cotgr.

FAVELLIS, *s. pl.* Errat. in DICT. for *Forellis*, q. v.

FAVOROUS, FAUOROUS, *adj.* Pleasant, delightful, kindly; Court of Venus, i. 591, ii. 712: also, comely, becoming, Ibid., iv. 110.

FAWD, *s.* A fold. V. FAULD.

FAWIN-ILL, *s.* The falling sickness, epilepsy. V. FAW.
Fluxis, hyvis, or buttit ill,
Hoist, heidwark, or *fawin ill*,
Rowlis Cursing, Bann. MS., p. 300, Hunt. Soc.

FAX, *s.* Hair of the head, locks. Errat. in DICT. A.-S. *feax*, id.
Jamieson's mistakes regarding the meaning and the etymology of this term have unfortunately been repeated in the Gloss. to Small's ed. of Douglas, and in the Gloss. to The Court of Venus, S. T. Soc.

FAY, *s.* Deed, conduct, life. Fr. *fait*, from Lat. *factum*.
Be thow atteichit with thift or with tressoun,
For thy misdeid wrangous and wickit *fay*.
Henryson, Parl. of Beistis, l. 184.
Prof. Skeat suggests that *fay* may here mean faith, belief. Fr. *foi*, Anglo-Fr. *fei*, *fey*. If so, *wickit fay* may be rendered false belief: cf. Chaucer, Clerkes Prologue, l. 9.

FAYAND, *pret.* A vulgar pron of *faynd*, made shift, found means: which is the pret. of *fayn, fen*, the common pron. of *faynd, fend*, to make shift, find means. V. FAYND, FEND.
Quhilk oft *fayand* with forss his fa till offend.
Houlate, 1. 593, Bann. MS.
Asloan MS. has *fandit*.

To FAYT, *v. a.* To pretend. Addit. to FAYT, q. v.
Not defined in DICT. The term is formed from the s. *faitor* (a pretender), which is the O. Fr. form of Lat. acc. *factorem*: M. E. *faitour*.

FEACHT, *s.* An expedition, foray: *feacht and sluaged*, expedition and hosting, the right or duty of the tribal members to follow their chief to foray and war; Skene's Celtic Scotland, III. 234.
Gael. *feachd*, an army, host, levy; M'Leod and Dewar.

FEAL, FEEL, *adj.* Faithful, honest; lit. true to one's pledge or promise. O. Fr. *feal*, from Lat. *fidelis*. Addit. to FEALE.
"That he will be leel aud *feel* to our Lord the King, and to the community of that burgh in which he is made burgess." Oath of a Burgess.
In the original Latin form of the oath the words *leel* and *feel* are in the vernacular.

FEAL, FEALL, *adv.* Faithfully, Corshill Baron Court Book, Ayr and Wigtown Arch. Coll., IV., 221.

To FEARD, *v. a.* To adorn, Bl. of Kirk., ch. 7. V. FARD.

FEARD, FEIRD, FERD. 1. Coll. forms of *fear it*; as, "The law, he winna *feard*."
2. Afraid, frightened, terrified; as, "Dinna be *feard*."

FEAT, FETE, FETT, *adj.* and *adv.* Neat, smart, becoming, well done: also, neatly, becomingly, nobly, Houlate, l. 518.

FEATED, *part.* and *adj.* Fitted, adapted, suited. V. FEAT.
". . . better *feated* for wowing nor woing, that heires or widowes never dallies more nor vnder their duilles." Blame of Kirkburiall, ch. 7.

FEATLY, FEATLIE, *adv.* Fitly, fittingly, suitably; Bl. of Kirk., ch. 3; also, neatly, gracefully, as, "She dances aye sa *featly*."
Fr. *fait*, from which comes E. *feat*, a deed well done.

FECHAR, FESHAR, FISHER, *s.* One who fetches, brings, carries, or conveys; as, "the *fecharis* of the said victualis." Burgh Recs. Aberdeen, I. 264. V. FECH.

To FECHT WI' NOWT. To take part in a bull-fight, or to be present at one.

Or by Madrid he taks the rout,
To thrum guitars, an' *fecht voi' nowt*.
Burns, Twa Dogs.

FEDRAM, *s.* Feathers, plumage. V. FEDERAME.

FEE, *s.* Fief. Lat. *feodum*. V. FE.

To FEEL, FEIL, FELE, *v. a.* To perceive by the sense of taste, or of smell; to taste, to smell; as, "Don't you *feel* the bitter flavour of the orange;" "I can't *feel* the scent at all."
The Foxe the flewar of the fresche herring *feillis*.
Henryson, Wolf, Foxe, and Cadgear, l. 80.

To FEEM, FEME, *v. n.* To gush, pour, stream; West of S., Orkn. V. FEIM, FAME.
. . while sa't tears *feem*
Sae sair fae baith his een.
Dennison, Orcadian Sketch Book.
Femed, in the sense of *foamed*, occurs in the Green Knight. See Gloss. Gawayne Romances.

To FEIFFLE, FIFFLE, *v. n.* To work in a clumsy or foolish manner; Orkn. Similar to FUFFLE, q. v. Icel. *fifl, fyfl*, a fool.

FEIFFLAN, FIFFLIN, *adj.* Clumsy; Orkn.

FEIR, *s.* The rate or average of prices: the written engagement or terms of engagement of a servant; and when it relates to a public servant, it is sometimes called "the act of *feir*," Burgh Recs. Glasgow, I. 65. V. FEIRIS, FIARS.
This term most commonly means the average price of grain during one year; and the pl. *feiris*, ur *fiars*, is still used in that sense only.
Under Fiars Jamieson first accepts and afterwards rejects the correct etym. of this term, which is O. Fr. *feur*, a rate or price set on a thing: Lat. *forum*.

FEITHO, *s.* A polecat, Henryson. V. FITHOWE.

FELDIFAIR, *s.* Lit. *field-farer*, i.e. one who lodges in the fields, a tramp, wanderer, outcast.
Quod hie, Madame, I sene the day and hour,
Ye wald haif thollit me to byid in your Bour.
(Quod scho) that is past, gude nicht now *feldifair*,
Fair on fond fuill, thow gettis heir no fauour:
Thow art no Page for to do vs plesour.
Rolland, Court of Venus, iv. 718.
The bird named the Red-Shank or Fieldfare, is generally called the Feltifare. In adopting the term here Rolland perhaps plays on the name.

FELL, *adj.* Many, very many; as "*Fell* of the fals folk," Houlate, l. 522. V. FEIL.
This word is still used both as an *adj.* and an *adv.*
V. FELL.

To FELL, *v. a.* To let fall, lower; hence, to abate, deduct, as in price or payment. Addit. to FELL.

The definition given in DICT. is secondary and defective; the etym., however, is correct; but A.-S. *fellan*, to make to fall, cast down, is perhaps more direct.

FELLING, *part.* and *s.* Lowering, down-bringing; abatement, deduction.

"Also, if any one buy . . merchandise, and give God's penny or any silver in arles, he shall pay to the merchant from whom he bought the said merchandise according to the rate before agreed upon without *felling* or herlebreaking." Lawis of the Gild, ch. 27, Rec. Soc.

FELLIT, *pret.* Knocked down, overthrown, killed, Houlate, l. 511. E. *felled.*

To FELYE, FELYIE, *v. n.* V. FAILYIE.

FENCE, FENS, *s.* An arrestment for debt; a prohibition. Addit. to FENCE.

". . . for the lousen of ane *fence* mad be Sande Knycht in the handis of Riche Finlay of ane payr of boys." Burgh Recs. Prestwick, 2 June, 1544, Mait. C.

To FENCE, FENS, *v. a.* To poind or arrest for debt ; to prohibit by law; pret. and part. pt. *fencet, fencit, fensit.* Addit. to FENCE.

". . . he hes causit *fens* and put under arreistment certane victuall." Burgh Recs. Prestwick, p. 145, Mait. C.
". . . for this geyr quhilk was *fencet* in his hand be Jhone Ondirwood officer." Ibid., 20 Nov., 1570.
". . . bot to *fens* the same fra doing thairof." Burgh Recs. Glasgow, 6 Aug., 1596, Rec. Soc.
Fence is simply a shortened form of *defence.* V. DICT.

FENIS, *v. pres. t.* Feigns. V. FENYE.

FEPPIL, *v.* and *s.* V. FIPPIL.

FERDIN, FERDING, FERDYNE, *s.* 1. A fourth part; Accts. L. H. Treas., I. 25, 335. V. FERD.

2. Prob. the quartering of a town or burgh, i.e. the dividing of it into quarters for the purpose of rating the inhabitants for taxes: "the keeping of the *ferdyne*," the keeping of the rolls of the quarters.

". . . the said Schir Walter sal haf of the towne the keping of the *ferdyne*, and twa merks yeirlie tharfor, . . . the twa merkis yeirlie for the keping of the *ferding* to be pait to the said Schir Walter," &c. Burgh Recs. Aberdeen, 13 Jan., 1484.

FERDINGMAN, *s.* V. *Ferthingman.*

FERE, *adj.* FERE, *s.* V. DICT.

Delete first entry, and set quotation under the second, as *fere* certainly means *companion*, mate. V. Gloss. Kingis Quair, Skeat's ed. Under second entry, in para. of etym., delete all after the third sentence : the statements are mere fancies, and wrong.

FERE, FEIR, *s.* Fear, doubt, hesitation, uncertainty. Addit. to FERE, q. v.

This term was not defined in DICT., but Jamieson suggested the correct meaning. Small's ed. of Douglas reads *fere*, fear; hence, "in *manere fere*" implies in doubt, uncertain.

(Sup.) P

FERIAR, FERYAR, *s.* A ferryman, Accts. L. H. Treas., I. 275, 334.

To FERK, FIRK, *v. n.* To proceed, drive on; as in walking, riding, working. Hence, to strive, struggle ; also, to hitch or move about in a restless, jerking manner ; Orkn.

He *ferkied* in the am'ers sae,
That a' his folk began tae prae,
And tenk him for the Gyre.
Dennison, Orcadian Sketch Book.

This term occurs in the Gawayne Romauces, and is rendered "to proceed, ride," in the Gloss.

FERKY, FIRKY, *adj.* Pushing, plodding, hardworking; resolute, determined ; West of S.

FERM, *adj.* Firm, fast, constant ; Fragments of Old Laws, ch. 29, Burgh Rec. Soc.

To FERME, *v. a.* Short for *afferme,* to affirm, declare, testify ; *as fermes anew,* as many persons affirm, Houlate, l. 525. Addit. to FERME, q. v.

FERMOUR, FERMOR, FERMAR, *s.* A tenant; one holding at a yearly *ferme* or rent ; a tacksman of public taxes or customs. Addit. to FERMORER.

"A fewfermar may nocht mak a *fermour* of ony lande, bot it be first gevin vp to the first ourlord and he sal mak him *fermour* or malor, and than at the first that *fermour* sal haf the fredome of the burgh, for ij men bath at anis and to gidder may nocht haf it of the samyn burrouagis." Fragments of Old Laws, ch. 11, Rec. Soc.

FERMYSON, FERMYSONE, FIRMYSOUN, *s.* The season when male deer were not allowed to be killed ; Awntyrs of Arthur, st. 1.

Cowel and Blount define *fermison* as the winter season of killing deer; but, as is indicated in the opening of the Awntyrs of Arthur, only females were then killed, and in Sir Gawayne and the Green Knight ll. 1156-7 we are told—

For the fre lorde had defende in *fermysoun* tyme
That thair schulde no mon mene to the male dere.

L. Lat. *firmatio*, privilege, protection ; hence *firmationis tempus,* the close season for males, was also called the *doe season.*

FERRY-LOUPER, *s.* The name given by the peasantry of Orkney to a settler or incomer: one who has crossed from the mainland.

FERS, *s.* Errat. in DICT. for FORS, q. v.

This is a mistake in Tytler's ed. Laing's ed. of Henryson reads *force.*

FERTER, *s.* A contr. form of FERETERE, a bier, q. v.

FERTER-LIKE, *adj.* Fit for one's coffin ; in modern phrase, at death's door, like a ghost. Errat. in DICT.

While Jamieson adopted the meaning given in the

Gloss. to Poems in the Buchan Dialect, he confessed his dissatisfaction with it, and suggested the correct Ballates, p. 76.
one.

FERTHING-MAN, FARTHINGMAN, FER-DINGMAN, FARDINGMAN, *s.* An officer or magistrate of a burgh having charge of a quarter; the modern bailie. Errat. in DICT.

FEST, *adj.* Fast, firm, steadfast, true; as, in the expression, "*fast friends.*"
That was the Turture trewest,
Ferme, faithfull and *fest,*
That bure that office honest.
Houlate, l. 128.
A.-S. *fæst,* Dan. and Swed. *fast,* fast, steadfast.

FETE, FETT, *adj.* and *adv.* V. FEAT.

To **FETER,** *v. a.* To fetter, to fasten, fix, hold: part. pt. *fetrit,* fastened, held close.
Thair mantillis grein war as the gress that grew in May sessoun,
Fetrit with thair quhyt fingaris about thair fair sydis.
Dunbar, Twa Marriit Wemen, l. 25.
Lit. to fasten by the feet; hence the phrase to lay one by the heels. A.-S. *fetor,* a shackle: M. E. *feter.*

FETHT, *part. pt.* Infeft: represents the common pron. of FEFT, q. v.
". . . quhilk deyit *fetht* & sessyt of tuay rud of mos." Burgh Recs. Prestwick, 2 Dec., 1563, Mait. C.

FETHREME, *s.* Feathers, plumage. V. FEDDERAME.

FETTILLIE, *adj.* With vigour, skill, or ability; dexterously. V. FETTLE.
And belliflaucht full *fettillie* thame flaid.
Henryson, Paddok and Mous, l. 128.

FEWTIR, FEWTIRE, FEUTER, FEUTRE, *s.* The rest for the spear or lance: in *fewtir,* in rest; *kest in fewtir,* set in rest, couched, Rauf Coilyear, st. 63. Errat. in DICT.
Jamieson's defin. and etym. of this term are quite wrong, as Sir F. Madden pointed out in his ed. of William and the Werwolf. The term occurs not unfrequently in the Morte Arthur, the Gawayne Poems, and Alexander Romances.
O. Fr. *feltre, feutre, fautre,* the feutre or spear-rest, a part of a war-saddle; Burguy. Low Lat. *filtrum, feltrum,* felt, thick matted stuff.

FEY, FEE, FIE, *adj.* V. DICT.
Under sense 3, Jamieson's statement that Fr. *fée,* fatal, is from the same source as Sc. *fey,* predestined, is a mistake. Fr. *fér,* is from Lat. *fatum;* Sc. *fey* is from Icel. *feigr,* A.-S. *fæge,* as he states in the same note. Skeat.

FEYND, FEYNT, *s.* The fiend, devil. V. FIENT.
The expressions "*feynd mak care,*" and "*feynd may care*" are still in common use; and, while they differ in but one letter, they have very different meanings. The first is an imprecation that the devil may make or send sorrow, vexation, mischief; and the second is an expression of light-hearted unconcern regarding consequences, or of total disregard of the subject in hand: "the fiend may care, but I don't!" An example of

the use of the first form is found in the Sempill Ballates, p. 76.

FEYTING, FEYTYNG, *s.* Prob. err. for *seyting, seytyng,* satin; Burgh Recs. Edin., I. 153, 159, Rec. Soc.

FIALLIS, FIEALLIS, *s. pl.* Wages, hire. V. FEALE.

FIERD, *s.* V. DICT.
Fierd is probably a firth, Dan. and Nor. *fjord:* but in this passage it evidently means a ford, passage, and is a corr. form of *furd, faird,* A.-S. *ford.* It prob. represents a vulgar pron. of that term. Jamieson's explanation is misleading.

FIGONALE, *s.* A small basket in which figs and other dried fruits are packed: "a *figonale* of fruct," Houlate, l. 833.
Span. *figs,* Fr. *figue,* from Lat. *ficus,* a fig.

FIGORY, *adj.* Figured, flowered. Fr. *figuré.*
". . . to purfel a govne to my Lady of blac satyne *figory.*" Accts. L. H. Treas., I. 73, Dickson.

To **FIND,** FIN', *v. a.* To perceive by the sense of touch, of taste, or of smell; as, "Do you *fin'* ony cauld the day?" "I canna *fin'* the taste o't." "I *fin* na smell ava."
This use of *find* is common in the North of Eng. also. V. Brockett's Gloss.

FINDING, FYNDYN, *part.* and *s.* Procuring, providing: "on his ain *finding,*" providing for himself, able to support himself.
". . . what tyme he be passit fra his fadre burde till his awne *fyndyn.*" Burgh Lawis, ch. 14, Rec. Soc.

FINDY, *adj.* Solid, heavy; well-found, as applied to grain when the ear is well filled. Addit. to DICT.
Not from the v *find,* as suggested by Jamieson, but from A.-S. *findig,* heavy, firm.

FIOLD, *s.* A hill; upland pasturage; Orkn. Originally an open down. V. FOLD. In the South of S. and North of E. called a *fell;* M. E. *fel.* Icel. *fjall, fell,* a hill; Swed. *fjäll,* Dan. *field,* a fell.

To **FIRE,** *v. a.* To cast, throw; as, "to *fire* a stone," West of S., Orkn.

FIRMANCE, FIRMANS, FIRMYN, *s.* 1. Short for *affirmance,* affirmation, ratification or acknowledgement of duty to a superior; act or deed implying such duty or subjection; also generally obligation, binding arrangement. Addit. to FIRMANCE.
". . that nane neighbour duellaud within the said burgh sal mak ua *firmans* to the said Robert Elect, na yet to nane of his factoris on his behalf." Burgh Recs. Aberdeen, I. 411, Sp. C.

2. A place of confinement, a prison; custody. Addit. to FIRMANCE.

". . . he sall nocht be had ututh the fredome of the burgh, nouthir to castel na til nane othir *firmyn*, bot gif it be that he hafe na borowis." Burgh Lawis, ch. 117, Rec. Soc.

FIRRE, FYRRE, adv. Farther, further; Gawayne Rom.
A.-S. *fyrra*, comp. of *feor*, far.

FIRRET, s. A ferret, weasel: pl. *firrettis*, Assize of Petty Customs, ch. 2, Rec. Soc.
O. Fr. *furet*, a ferret; Cotgr. Low. Lat. *furetus*.

FIRY-FARY, s. V. FERIE-FARIE.

FISSEIS, s. Chilblains; Orkn.
Perhaps from Lat. *fissura*, a fissure or crack, from *fissus*, p. p. of *findere*, to cleave.

To FIT, FITT, FUT, v. a. To adjust or balance an account; also, to examine, test, or audit accounts: to *fitt and cleir*, to balance and settle an account, Burgh Recs. Glasgow, II. 269.
The part. *fitting* is frequently used as a s.: as, "the *fitting* of eques," the balancing of accounts. Icel. and Icel. and Norw. *fitja*, to knit together: M. Eng. *fitten*, to arrange.

FIT-CHAPMAN, CHOPMAN, s. A packman, pedlar; a travelling merchant, one who traverses the country carrying his wares in a pack; Burgh Recs. Aberdeen, II. 54, 266, 273, Sp. C.

FIT-SYDE, adv. On an equal footing; but often used in the sense of quits, avenged, and sometimes like upsides; as, "I'll be *fit-side* wi' you for that yet:" Burgh Recs. Glasgow, I. 304, Rec. Soc. V. FOOTSIDE.

FITHEL, FYTHEL, FYDILL, s. A fiddle, Houlate, l. 761, Asloan MS. A.-S. *fithele*.

FITHELAR, FYTHELARE, s. A fiddler, Accts. L. H. Treas., I. 326, 274.

To FLA, FLAE, FLEY, v. a. To flay, strip off, skin; pret. *flew, flaid, fleyd*.
Ga feche him hither and *fla* his skyn of swyith.
Henryson, Wolf and Wedder, l. 26.

FLAGH, FLACH, FLAW, FLEW, pret. Flew, fled, passed quickly.

FLAGHT, FLACHT, s. 1. Flight; as, "The rogues were in full *flaght* to the border."

2. Flash, glare; a flash of lightning is called a *flaght* o' fire, or, a *fire-flaght*. Pl. *fluchtis*, sparks of fire carried by the wind, Burgh Recs. Glasgow, I. 333. V. FIRE-FLAUCHT.

3. Glance, a momentary view; as, "I got but a *flacht* o't as it gaed by."

4. A flight ot birds. V. FLAUCHT.

FLAIK, s. The frame, rack, board, or table of a stall erected on market-days to display the dealer's wares: pl. *flaikis*, Burgh Recs. Glasgow, II. 24, 168.

FLASCHE, FLASS, s. A bunch, sheaf, bundle; "a *flasche* of flanis," i.e., a sheaf of arrows, Henryson, Test. Cresseid, l. 167.

FLAT, adj. A term in golfing, applied to a club of which the head is at a very obtuse angle to the shaft.

To FLAWME, v. a. To baste. V. FLAME.

To FLAY, FLAE, v. a. To frighten, terrify; also, to scare, drive away; West and South of S. V. FLEY.
Fley and *fleg* are more common forms; but *flay* is the prevalent form in North of E. V. Brockett's Gloss. It occurs in the Towneley Mysteries, pp. 30, 150.

FLEID, part. pt. Afraid, terrified. V. under FLEY.

FLEIDNES, s. Fright, terror, Henryson. V. FLEYITNES.

FLEOCK, s. A fly; Orkn. A dimin. of FLEE, q. v.

To FLESH, FLESCH, v. a. To scrape or clean the flesh-side of skins preparatory to tanning or tawing them; part. pr. *fleshing*, used also as a s.
The first process in leather-dressing is steeping the skins or hides in a strong solution of lime in order to swell and harden them. In the next process each skin is stretched on a curved beam, and thoroughly scraped, first on the grain or upper side to rid it of its hair or tufts of wool, then on the flesh or under-side to strip off the particles of fat or flesh adhering to it. The first part of the process is called *hairing*; the the second, *fleshing*; and both operations are performed by means of large curved knives called *irons* or *beaming-knives*.

FLESHING-BUIRD, FLESCHING-BUIRD, s. The large curved beam on which skins or hides are stretched in order to have the particles of fat and flesh scraped from their inner or flesh-surface; Burgh Recs. Aberdeen, I. 176, Sp. C.

FLESHING-IRON, FLESCHING-IRNE, s. A large curved knife with a handle at each end, used in scraping and cleaning the flesh-side of skins or hides; Burgh Recs. Aberdeen, I. 176, Sp. C.

FLESH-HOUSE, FLESCHOUS, s. Flesh-market, fleshmarket-house.
"Item that the fleschowaris dicht and mak clene the *fleschous* ilka ouke on Friday." Burgh Recs. Aberdeen, 4 June, 1444.

FLET, *adj.* Lit. flat, plain. Addit. to FLET, q. v.

FLEW, *pret.* Flayed, stript, skinned. V. *Fla.*

With that in hy the doggis skyn of be *flew,*
And on the scheip rycht softlie couth it sew.
Henryson, Wolf and Wedder, l. 39.

In the Gloss. to Laing's ed. of Henryson this word is rendered "fled;" but this is a mistake.

FLEWAR, *s.* Odour, scent, Henryson. V. FLEOURE.

FLINDRIKIN, *s.* A form of *Flanderkyn,* a native of Flanders. Used also as an *adj.;* as, "a *Flindrikin* meir," a mare of Flemish breed. Addit. to DICT. V. FLANDERKIN.

FLOCHT, *s.* Fluster, flurry, excitement: *on flocht,* in a flutter either of joy or fear. Errat. in DICT.

For I am verray effeirit and *on flocht.*
Henryson, Wolf and Wedder, l. 107.

Jamieson's meanings of this term are all correct except the first one, which is here corrected. The phrase *on flocht* is still used with these meanings.

To FLOT, FLOTE, FLOYT, FLOYTE, *v. a.* To trim in a particular way, perhaps with *fluting.*

". . . vij quarteris of grete brade claith, to *flot* a doublat to the King." Accts. L. H. Treas., I. 21, Dickson.

The other forms occur in pp. 16, 21, 23.

FLOTING, *s.* Prob. fluting; trimming.

". . . to by stufe and *floting* for the Kingis doublat of broune purpure dammask, vj s. viij d." Ibid., p. 23.

FLOTE, *s.* A band, company, following; All. Rom. Alexander, ll. 770, 1210. Addit. to FLOTE.

FLOURE-JONETTE, *s.* Great St. John's-wort. Errat. in DICT.

The flower of the broom does not suit the poet's description of the *floure-jonette:* but the flower of Great St. John's-wort does. V. Kingis Quair, p. 70, Skeat's ed. S. T. S.
O. Fr. *jaulnette,* "Hardway, S. Peter's-wort, square S. John's grasse, great St. John's-wort;" Cotgr.

FLOUSE, *s.* V. FLOSH.

FLOW, FLO, *s.* A basin, sound, or arm of the sea; Orkney. Addit. to FLOW, q. v.

"Scalpa *Flow* is a sea basin amongst the Orkneys, nearly, enclosed by Pomona, Burray, S. Ronaldshay, Walls, and Hoy, and containing many smaller islands. Length 15 m., breadth, 8 m." Johnston's General Gazetteer.

Icel. *flói,* a bay or large firth. Deep water in a bay is also called *flói,* opp. to the shallow water near the coast. Cleasby.

FLUTHERY, *adj.* Flabby, soft, not firm; Orkn. Also, boggy, marshy; South of S.

Lit. of the nature of a *flow,* or *flow-moss,* which, though appearing to be firm, is really a quagmire. V. FLOW, FLOW-MOSS.

FOIRJUGEIT, *part. pt.* V. *Forjugit.*

FOIRPART, *s.* Front. V. FOREPART.

FOIRSTAIR, *s.* V. *Forestair.*

FOLLOWER, FOLLOWAR, FOLOWER, FOLOUAR, *s.* Applied to any young domestic animal while dependent on or companying with its mother; as, "a hen and its *followers,*" "a cow and its *follower,*" etc. Addit. to FOLOWER.

This term occurs frequently in Burgh Records.

To FONDE, *v. a.* and *n.* To begin, attempt, try; to resolve, plan, commence, as when one enters on a journey, expedition, or undertaking. See quotations in DICT. Addit. to FONDE, q. v.

FORBORNE. *part. pt.* Withheld, excluded: "Yea, and the fire hes not bene *forborne,*" Blame of Kirkburiall, ch. 4.

FORBYAR, *s.* V. FORE-BYAR.

FORCAST, *s.* A corr. of *farcost,* a small trading vessel; Fragments of Old Laws, ch. 20, Burgh Rec. Soc.

FORCOP, FORCAUP, *s.* The Lawman's salary for the Thing circuits: a tax paid by the Odallers in Orkney and Shetland. Addit. to FORCOP, q. v.

Although Jamieson left this term undefined he certainly had a correct though vague idea of its meaning. His etym., however, is worthless. The following statement by Balfour of Trenaby is both full and clear.
"*Forcop,* Norse *thing-för-kaup,* itineris forensia merces; the Lawman's salary for the Thing circuits; afterwards charged by the Donatary, first against the Crown, and again against the parishes on various pretexts, sometimes of Odal usage, sometimes of feudal claim; but according to Dufresne, '*For-capium,* exactio, tributum haud debitum, per vim et contra jus captum.'" Odal Rights and Feudal Wrongs, p. 115.

FORD, FORDE. A coll. form of *for it;* as, "I dinna care *ford.*"

The quhilk I stand *ford* ye nocht understude.
Henryson, p. 43. l. 8, Laing's ed.
Both forms of the word occur in the Sempill Ballates: *ford,* in p. 92, and *forde* in p. 37.

FORE, *interj.* A warning cry of golfers to a person standing or moving in the way of the ball. A contr. of *before.*

To FOREBARGAIN, FOIRBARGAIN, FORBARGIN, *v. n.* To bargain or arrange for before hand; pret. and part. pt. *foirbargained.*
Burgh Recs. Glasgow, II. 312, Rec. Soc.

This word is still used, generally in the sense given above, sometimes in the sense of *to bespeak,* and sometimes of *to arle.*

FORECOTT, FORECOTT-HOUSE, s. A front cot-house or cottar's house; Corshill Baron Court Book, Ayr and Wiglown Arch. Coll., IV. 140.

FORE-GERE, s. Fittings for attaching the front horses of a team; Accts. L. H. Treas., I. 300.

FORE-LOOFE, s. V. DICT.
Prob. Skeat has pointed out that *loofe*, as here used, is closely connected with E. *leave*, in the sense of permission; but it has nothing to do with *loof*, the palm of the hand, which Jamieson quotes from Ihre. Under *forleff*, which is simply another form of the same word, he gives the correct etym., Su. Goth. *loefwa*, to promise, or lit. to give leave.

FOREMAK, s. Preparation; but generally used in the sense of display, show, or bustle made in preparing for an event; Orkn.

FOREPART, FOIRPART, s. The front.; as, "the *foirpart* of the land," Burgh Lawis, ch. 105: the first portion, instalment, or payment; as, "the *forepart* of the stent," Burgh Recs.

FORE-RAW, FOIR-RA, s. The foreyard of a ship. Compl. Scot., p. 40, E. E. T. S.
Cf. Dan. *raa*, a sail-yard.

To FORESEE, FOIRSEE, FOIRSIE, v. a. 1. To see, speak or arrange with a person beforehand.
". . . that na maner of persoun within the burgh pas heir eftir to the saide realme of England without thai first *foirsie* the pronest and bailleis, that thair names may be sett doun in roll." Burgh Recs. Glasgow, I. 348, Rec. Soc.

2. To search for, seek out, select, secure, or arrange for beforehand.
". . . to provyde and *forsie* for convenient ludgeing within this burgh to the commissionaris of burrowis quha ar to meit heir the tyme forsaid." Ibid., I. 337.

3. To oversee, superintend, direct; as, "To *foresee* the men and the wark till it be endit."

FORE-SPAR, s. A swingle-tree for a front horse of a team; pl. *fore-sparris*. Accts. L. H. Treas., I. 298.

FORESTAËR, FOIRSTAER, s. A forestaller. Syn. *forebyar*.

FORESTAIR, FOIRSTAIR, s. A front outer-stair, a stair projecting into the street.
Your stinkand Scule that standis dirk,
Haldis the lycht fra your Parroche Kirk ;
Your *foirstairis* makis your houssess mirk,
Lyk na cuntray bot heir at hame.
Dunbar, *To the Merchants of Edinburgh*, 1. 17.

FORETOP, FORTOPE, FOIRTOP, s. Top or crown of the head, the brow or forehead;

the forelock or front hair of a man, the fronts or false hair of a woman.
Ruschit baith to the bard and ruggit his hair—
Thai fylit him fra the *fortope* to the fut thar.
Houlate, 1. 824, Asloan MS.

FORE-TOWIS, s. pl. Traces for attaching the front horses of a team, Accts. L. H. Treas., I. 300.

FOREWERK, s. The barbican or fortified gateway of a castle.
"Item, that samyn day [8 May, 1497], . . . in part of payment of the bigging of the *forewerk* of Dunbar." "Item, the ix day of Maij, giffin to Thom Barknr, to pas to Dunbar to tak the mesure of the irne yet of it to mak it, xx s." Accts. L. H. Treas., I. 334, Dickson.

FORFALDED, FORFALDIT, part. pt. Hanging in folds, crumpled; hence, as applied to the ropes or sails of a boat, drooping, hanging loose. V. FALD, v n.
Bot fra the feill your bowling once begin
To mak *forfalded* flapping on the mast,
Cast lous the fuksheit, the bonuet, and the blind,
Let hir ly by, ye must abyd the blast.
Bann. MS., p. 1080, Hunt. Soc.

To FORFALT, FORFAUT, FORFAUTE, v. n. To do wrong, to transgress or violate the law, to offend, trespass. Addit. to FORFALT.

FORFALT, FORFAUT, FORFAUTE, s. Wrongdoing, trespass, offence, transgression; *in forfaute*, under charge of wrongdoing, guilty of breaking the law. Addit. to FORFALT.
"Gif ony man or ony woman in the burgh be in *forfaute* of brede or ale, nane sall hafe tharof a do bot the borow greffis. And gif he faltis twyis he sall be chasty te twyis for his *forfaute*." Burgh Lawis, ch. 19, Rec. Soc.
O. Fr. *for*, and E. *fault*, from Lat. *fallere*.

To FORGRYP, v. a. To unload, discharge, or deliver cargo.
"Gif ony burges of Scotland that is qwyt of custum hyre a schyp to *forgryp* wyth wyne corne or ony vthyr marchandys to the toun of Berwyk." Custome of Schippis, ch. 3, Rec. Soc.
Low Lat. *forgorpire* (i.e., foris guerpire), to give up possession, Ducange.

FORINGIT, part. pt. Errat. in DICT. for *Forjugit*, q. v.
This mistake was made in Tytler's ed. of The Kingis Quhair, and appears in every later ed. of that work except the one prepared by Professor Skeat for the S. T. S. in 1884 : there the word is correctly printed *furiugit=forjugit*.

FORJUGIT, part. pt. Unjustly doomed or condemned; Kingis Quair, st. 3, Skeat's ed., S. T. S.
O. Fr. *forjuger*, to judge or condemn wrongfully; Cotgr.

FOROTH, prep. V. FOROUTH.

FOR-RAIKIT, FOR-RAKIT, *part. adj.* Worn out with long travel or wandering about; as, "I'm weary *for-raikit;*" West of S. V. RAIK.
As commonly used the term implies travelling about from place to place as packmen do. It occurs in the Townley Mysteries in a similar sense.

FORRET, FORRAT, FORRIT, FURRIT, *adv.* Forward. 1. In *direction :* on, onwards, as, "gang *forret.*" Coll. Eng. *forrud.*

2. In *place, position :* in front, before, in advance, as, "He man aye be *forret,* gang where he may."

3. In *time :* in advance, before, fast, as, "The clock is ten minutes *forret.*"

4. In *manner :* on, more and more, gradually better, as, "He'll soon be well; he's ha'din *forret* every day."

5. In *degree :* on, advanced, towards or near the end, as "How far *forret* is he wi' the wark?"
Addit. to FORRET, q. v.

FORREYN, *s.* A foreigner; pl. *forreyns.*
". . . all the burges of the burgh, alswel *forreyns* as deynseens." Chalmerian Air, ch. 3, Rec. Soc.

FORRON, *part. pt.* V. FORRUN.

FORROW, *prep.* and *adv.* Before, in front of, outside, without. V. FOROUT, FOROUTH.
He said, "Fair Lady, now mone I Do, treatly ye me trow :
Tak ye my sark that is bludy,
And hing it *furrow* you.
Henryson, The Bludy Serk, l. 76.

FORRUN, FOIRRUN, FORRON, *part. pt.* Run out, exhausted with running, Henryson. V. FORROWN.

FORS, FORSS, *s.* Lit. a cascade, waterfall. Addit. to FORS, q. v.
This term has nothing to do with *force,* as Ihre suggests. It is like Icel. *fors, foss,* a cascade; and is allied to Swed. *frusa,* to gush.

FORSCHENT, *part. pt.* Degraded, broken down, trampled on. V. SCHENT.
As blasphemar of God Omnipotent,
Bot ony law thair I condampnit was
Amang thair folk defowlit and *forschent.*
Anon. Bann. MS., p. 83, Hunt. Soc.

FORSPOKYN, *part. pt.* 1. Bespoken, pleaded, sought. V. FORESPEAKER.
". . . thocht it be ututh the courte na *forspokyn* thar in, it sall suffice wele inoch." Burgh Lawis, ch. iii.

2. Bewitched. V. under FORSPEAK.
Occurs in same sense in the Townley Mysteries, p. 115.

To FORSWRNE, *v. a.* Errat. in DICT. for *Forsume,* q. v.
A misreading by Pinkerton.

To FORSUME, *v. a.* To misspend, waste, consume; Douglas, K. Hart, ed. Small, I. 107.
A compound of *for,* implying wrongly, and Lat. *sumere,* to take, use, spend.

FOR-THI, FORTHY, *conj.* V. DICT.
"Really—A.-S. *forthy,* or *forthi,* where *thi* is the instrumental case of *the.*" Skeat.

FORTHOUGHT, *pret.* Rued, repented. V. FORTHINK.

FOSS, *s.* A ditch, a fosse; Burgh Recs. Aberdeen, 2 Apr., 1481. Addit. to FOS.

FOTINELLIS, *s. pl.* Errat. for *Fotmellis,* explained under *Char,* q. v. V. FADMELL.

FOTMEL, *s.* A weight of 70 lbs. V. *Fadmell.*

FOUD, *s.* V. DICT.
The following is an important addition to the explanations given by Jamieson :—
"*Foud,* Norse *fogeti,* Dan. *fogud,* quæstor Regius, Collector of the King's Skatt, Skylids, Mulcts, etc., afterwards Chief Judge, and ultimately Sheriff of the Foundrie of Zetland." Balfour, Odal Rights and Feudal Wrongs, p. 115.

FOUELLIS, *s. pl.* Lit. fuel, materials or supplies for burning; but also applied to victuals, supplies for food; King Hart, st. 8, Small's ed.
Pinkerton misread this word *favellis,* and suggested that it meant *savours;* and on his authority Jamieson adopted that reading, but evidently with some doubt, for he left the word undefined.
The term occurs in Barbour iv. 64, 170, Camb. MS. as *fowaill,* fuel; and in Prompt. Parv. as *fowayle,* with same meaning; but in a note the editor quotes a passage from Richard Cœur de Lion (l. 1471) to show that the word had also the more general sense of provisions, needful supplies. It is in this sense that it occurs in King Hart.
L. Lat. *foallia,* fuel : but the Scot. *fovellis* may have been adopted from O. Fr. *fuelles,* recorded by Roquefort with the meaning of brushwood, firewood.

FOUL, *s.* A full, a firlot. V. FOU, FOW.

FOURSOME, *adj.* A term in golfing, applied to a match in which two play on each side. Addit. to FOURSUM, q. v.

FOY, *adj.* Foolish, silly; prob. a corr. of Fr. *fol.*

FOY, *s.* Merry-making, entertainment, treat; Ayrs. Addit. to FOY, q. v.
"He said the said balyies was *foy* takaris [i.e., treat takers], and held na courtis na did na justice in the toune." Burgh Recs. Prestwick, 6 Feb., 1496-7, Mait. C.

To FOYNE, v. n. To feint, thrust, as in fencing; Douglas, Virgil, v. ch. 8, ed. Small.
O. Fr. *foigne*, a long staff or pole ; hence, *to foin*, to thrust.

FRA, *prep.* Arising from, occasioned by, on account of, because of. Addit. to FRA.
"Item, the xxᵗⁱ day of Nouember, till ane man to pas to the Lard of Franche *fra* a traytoure he tuke." Accts. L. H. Treas., I. 98, Dickson.
A.-S. *fram, fra*, which is still used to express the origin or occasion of an act.

FRACA, *s.* Disturbance, uproar, quarrel; a loud or angry altercation, blustering dispute ; South and West of S.
Fr. *fracas*, crash, din : from *fracasser*, to shatter ; Lat. *frayor*.
Although of French origin, form, and pron., this term has been in use for a long time, and is now used familiarly by persons who know nothing of French.. Even in Burns's day it was used as it is now, although to serve his own end he wrote it *fracas* and rhymed it with *Bacchus*.
It is often pron., especially in the East of S., *forca*, as if the first syllable wore *for*.

FRAEL, *s.* A frail, a basket made of rushes; also called a *fraer*; Assize of Petty Customs, ch. 12, Rec. Soc. Low Lat. *frælum*, M. E. *frayle.* V. FREARE.

To FRAIN, FRAYNE, *v. n.* To enquire. V. FRANE.

To FRAIST, FRAST, *v. a.* To seek, enquire, ask. Addit. to FRAIST.
Fraist is frequently so used in the Gawayne Romances. Icel. *freista*, to ask, inquire.

FRAUDFULLY, *adv.* Fraudulently, Burgh Lawis, ch. 45, 91, Rec. Soc.

FRAWARTSCHYP, *s.* Frowardness, contrariety ; Burgh Lawis, ch. 34, Rec. Soc.

FRE, *adj.* V. DICT.
Combine the two entries under this form ; they are really the same word. Del. the etym. under the second entry ; it is altogether misleading. V. FRELY.

FREHAULDIR, *s.* A free-holder, Accts. L. H. Treas., I. 238.

FREIS, *adj.* Flowered, ornamented ; with a flowered or ornamented border; with a raised, flowered, or ornamental pattern, like flowered-silk, which is called *frese silk, fresed* or *fraised* silk. Addit. to FREIS, q. v.

FRESIT, *part. pt.* Woven, worked, or ornamented with a raised or flowered pattern. Addit. to FRESIT, q. v.
". . ane kaip of clayth of gold *fresit* with reid veluott :—item, ane kaip and chesapill with tinua-

killis, haill furniat of gold, *fresit* on grene veluett." Burgh Recs. Aberdeen, I. 320, Sp. C.
These terms were left undefined by Jamieson : but the suggestion which he made regarding their probable meaning is quite correct.
O. Fr. *friser, frizer*, "to frizle, crispe, curle, braid ;" Cotgr. : *frizons*, "frizled or raised worke of gold or silner wire ;" Ibid. Sp. *frisar*, to raise the nap on cloth ; Diez. And the same idea of raised work is implied by E. *frieze*, a horizontal broad band occupied with sculpture.

To FREIT, *v. a.* To eat into, eat up, devour; corrode, cause to decay ; Henryson, Cock and Jasp, l. 76. E. *fret.* V. FRET.
Freit, fret, in M. E. *freten*, is from A.-S. *fretan*, to eat up, which is a contr. of *for-etan*, id.

FREITTEN, FRETTEN, *part. pt.* Seamed, pitted, deeply marked ; as, pock-*freitten*, pock-marked.

FRENSWN, *adj.* Misprint in DICT. for FRENSWM (friend-some).

FRERE-KNOTTIS, *s. pl.* Ornamental forms or figures in goldsmith's work, in imitation of the knotted cords of the Franciscans; called also Cordelier Knots. Addit. to FRERE-KNOTT.
"Item, a chenye of gold maid in fassone of *frere knottis*, contenand fourti foure knottis." Accts. L. H. Treas., I. 83, Dickson.
And regarding another chain found in the same "*kist*," there is the following entry :—
"Item, sax pecis of the said chenye of gold of *frere knottis*." Ibid., p. 84.
These entries show that the *frere-knottis* were much more common than Jamieson supposed, and that they were not confined to figures and settings of precious stones.

FRESCUS, *adj.* Fresh, hale, strong. Lit. full of freshness : hence, unimpaired, sound, vigorous ; as, "of fre will and *frescus* mynd," Burgh Recs. Prestwick, 24 April, 1486, Mait. C.

FRETE, *s.* A fret, an ornament of network; the hair-net of gold or silver wire, often jewelled, generally worn by ladies in the fifteenth century. Errat. in DICT.
"Item, a *frete* of the Quenis oure set with grete perle sett in fouris and fouris." Accts. L. H. Treas., i. 84, Dickson.
Jamieson's suggestion that the *frete* was "prob. a ring, band, hoop," is a mistake. It was a covering for the hair, and an important article of a lady's headdress during the 15th cent. It is mentioned by Chaucer in his Legend of Good Women, and in The Flowre and the Leaf ; and Planché in describing a lady's dress at the close of the 14th cent. says :—
"The hair was still worn in a gold *fret* or caul of network, surmounted frequently by a chaplet of goldsmith's work, a coronet, or a veil, according to the wearer's rank or fancy." British Costume, p. 181, ed. 1874.

FRETHIN, FRETHN, FREYTHING, *part.* and *s.*
V. FREITH.

FRIM-FRAM, *s.* A variant of *flim-flam*, a trifle, whim, fancy, invention. Addit. to FRIM-FRAM.

FRIMPLE-FRAMPLE, *adv.* In a confused, promiscuous, or tangled manner.

FRITH, FRYTHE, *s.* An enclosed wood; pl. *frithis, frythis,* "by *frythis* and fellis." Awntyrs of Arthur, st. 1.

FRITTLE, *s.* Errat. in DICT. for *Succour.*
Another of the errors into which Jamieson was led by the careless transcripts of Pinkerton. In this case the alliteration shows that a wrong word has been adopted. The etym. and remarks by Jamieson are therefore worthless.
Both the Bann. and the Asloan MS. read *succour.*

FRONE, *s.* V. DICT.
Etym. is simply Fr. *fronde,* a sling; Lat. *funda.*

FRONSIT, *part. pt.* Wrinkled. V. FROUNSIT.

FROSNIT, *part. pt.* A var. of *fronsit, frounsit,* wrinkled, furrowed; hence, old and careworn. V. FROUNSIT.
His face *frosnit,* his lyre was like the leid,
His teith clatterit and cheverit with the chin.
  Henryson, Test. Cresseid, l. 155.
In the Gloss. to Laing's ed. of Henryson *frosnit* is rendered *frosted,* which does not express the meaning of the poet. The context shows that the passage is a description of the appearance of "hoary Saturn," without any remark regarding the cause of it. Besides, in any case a *frosted* face is a very inapt expression. But, *frosnit* is not from A.-S. *frósan,* to freeze, but from O. Fr. *froncer,* to wrinkle, and is another form of *fronsit,* which Henryson uses in his fable of the Paddok and the Mous, in the phrase "his *fronsit* face." Indeed, Sibbald's reading of the passage is a "His face *fronsit.*" Chron. Scot. Poetry, i. 162. Cf. E. *flounce.*

FUDDER, *s.* V. DICT.
In note on etym. delete all the second sentence. Fr. *foudre* is from Lat. *fulgur.* The Goth. origin is a mistake.

FUKSHEIT, FUKSCHEIT, *s.* The sheet or rope that fastens the *fuksail,* i.e., fore-sail; Bann. MS., p. 349, Hunt. Soc.
Cast lous the *fuksheit,* the bonnet, and the blind :
Lat hir ly by, ye must nbyd the blast.
  Ibid., p. 1080, Hunt. Soc.

FULYEIT, *part. pt.* Defaced, worn, worn out: "*fulyeit* in labour," useless or worthless for work; Dunbar, Twa Marriit Wemen, l. 86. V. FULYIE.

FUND, FUNDE, FUN', FUN, *pret.* and *part. pt.* Found, gathered, experienced.
And as thai talkit at the tabill of mony taill *funde,*
They wauchtit at the wicht wyne, and waris out wourdis.
  Dunbar, Twa Mariit Wemen, l. 39.

FUND, FUNT. Short for *fund it,* found it.
Fund is the result of softening *t* in *fun't,* which is short for *fund it.* V. *Fund.*

FUNDING, *part.* and *s.* Founding, laying the foundation, commencing; Accts. L. H. Treas., I. 336. V. FUNDMENT.

FUNYIES, FWNYIES, *s. pl.* The fur of the polecat or fitch; also polecat skins. Addit. to FUNYIE.
". . . vj mantillis of *funyies* to lyne the sammyne [gowne]. Accts. L. H. Treas., I. 225, Dickson.
". . . for iij mantellis of *funyeis* to lyne the gowne of claytht of gold that wes the Kingis." Ibid., I. 190.
Fr. *fouine, foyne,* the polecat.

FURCHE, *s.* The two hind quarters of an animal: as, "a *furche* of venyson," Accts. L. H. Treas., I. 181. Fr. *fourche.*

FURE, *pt. subj.* Might go, should go. Addit. to FUR, FURE.
Fane wald I wit, quod the fyle, or I furth *fure.*
  Houlate, l. 79.
. A.-S. *faran,* Sw. *fara,* Dan. *fare,* to go, wend.

FURRIT, *pret.* and *part. pt.* Furred, lined, or trimmed with fur; dressed in fur.
The quhyrrand Quhitret with the Quhaisill went
The Feltho that hes *furrit* mony fent.
  Henryson, Parl. of Beistis, l. 117.

To FURSET, FURSETT, *v. a.* To set forth, further, carry out, execute. Addit. to FURTHSET.
". . proclamatioun charging hir hynes liegis of Murray and Narne to mete hir hynes at Strabogy for *fursetting* of hir hynes seruice." Family of Kilravock, p. 238, Sp. C.

To FURSTAND. *v. a.* To supply, furnish: also, to guarantee. Lit. to *forth-stand.*
"Johne Ratray promest to cause warkmen enter to the Castell hill one Monnonday nyxt cumis . . the toun *furstand* him expensis to do the samyn, and Maister Androv Talidef promest him xxs. of vnlawis to do the samyn." Burgh Recs. Aberdeen, I. 122, Sp. C.

FUTE, FUT, *s.* The stand for a glass, cup, vase, etc. Accts. L. H. Treas., I. 85. Addit. to FUTE.

FUTGANG, *s.* V. FITGANG.

FUTE-MANTIL, FWT-MANTIL, *s.* Housings of cloth which reached nearly to the feet of a horse.
The foot-mantle was considered a mark of great dignity and state, and was worn by the king and his nobles on great occasions of state, such as a coronation procession, a riding of parliament, &c. In the Treasurer's Accounts of payments in connection with the preparations for the coronation of James IV. in 1488, the following entries occur.
"Item, for the elne of velus til a *fut mantil.*"
"Item, thre elne of bucram to lyne it with." Accts. L. H. Treas., I. 147, Dickson.

FUTE-SCHETE, *s*. A narrow sheet spread across the foot of a bed. It was sometimes of plain, sometimes of costly material, as fur, cloth of gold, &c. Accts. L. H. Treas., I. 24, 32.

FUTTIT, *pret*. and *part. pt*. Footed, marched, Sempill Ballates, p. 38. V. FIT.

To FUYR, *v. a*. To carry. V. FURE.

FYAN, FYANE, *s*. A fugitive, outlaw: lit. one who has fled from justice. O. Fr. *fuyant*.

". . the said Androw beand captyve and presonar incarcerat in the said toune of Hull as *fyane* and enemy to Ingliss natioune." Burgh Recs. Aberdeen, I. 283, Sp. C.

FYKE, FYKING. V. under FIKE.

FYLE, *s*. A vile creature. Errat. in DICT.

This term occurs in Havelok, l. 2499, with the same meaning as in the passage quoted. Lat. *vilis*, vile, mean.

FYNDYN, *s*. Providing. V. *Finding*.

FYR-BURDIS, *s. pl*. Boards or planks of fir, Accts. L. H. Treas., I. 246.

To FYTE, *v. a*. V. DICT.

This form represents the local pron. of *white*, to cut; and *fyte*, *qultyte*, *white*, are variants of E. *thwite*, A.-S. *thwitan*, to cut.

G.

GAADYS, *s pl*. Gauds, gems, pearls, precious things; string or strings of beads, which are still called *hanks of beads*, and in olden times were *hanks of gaudies*. Addit. to GAADYS, q. v. V. GAUDEIS.

Not defined by Jamieson, who evidently did not understaud the proverb in which the term occurs. The saying is used to express an ironical estimate of the value of a pretentious, boastful person's remarks. In explanation of the latter part of the proverb, Prof. Skeat suggests a reference to the story of the good girl from whose mouth fell pearls and diamonds.

To GAAR, GAUR, *v. a*. To scratch, seam, or cut into; as, "His arms are *gaur'd* yet wi' the beast's claws;" West of S.

Gael. *geàrr, geur*, to cut, seam, furrow.

GAAR, GAUR, *s*. A scratch, seam, or cut made by drawing a sharp point over a smooth surface; West of S.

GADGE, GAGE, GEDGE, GEGE, *s*. 1. A standard measure, a standard of measurement; Burgh Recs. Glasgow, I. 153, Rec. Soc.

2. Search, scrutiny, look-out; watch or hunt for what will benefit oneself; as, "He's aye on the *gadge*," West of S.

To GADGE, GEDGE, *v. a*. 1. To measure; to test measures by the standards, also, to adjust them.

2. To search, look-out, watch for contraband goods; to look out, watch, hunt for gifts, benefits, &c.

(Sup.)   Q

GADGER, GAUGER, GAGER, *s*. 1. An exciseman, one who gauges excisable goods, and searches, etc., for contraband.

2. One who is always on the look-out for gifts or benefits: "a greedy *gadger*."

The latter sense is comparatively modern, and evidently has been suggested by the duties and methods of the *gauger* in cases of contraband goods.

GADGERY, GAUGERIE, GAUGRIE, GEDGRIE, JEDGRY, JEDGERIE, *s*. Standards of weights and measures; Chalmerlain Air, ch. 1: the testing and attesting of weights and measures; Blue Blanket, p. 105.

Before weights and measures can be issued for use they must be tested or compared with the legal standards, and attested or stamped by the keeper of the standards.

O. Fr. *gauger, gaugir*, to gauge or measure: Low Lat. *gaugia*, the standard measure of a wine cask; Ducange.

GAIN, GAAN, *adv*. Pretty, tolerably, very, quite; as, "*gain* weel, *gaan* near, *gain* cheap." V. GEY.

Used to express indefinite degree of comparison, and sometimes used for *gayly*, *geyly*. It is common in the North of E. also, and similarly used. V. Brockett's Gloss.

Prob. an abbrev. of *gay and*: but etym. is doubtful.

GAIN, *adj*. Fit, near. V. GANE.

GAIRDONE, *s*. Guerdon, recompense. Addit. to GAIRDONE, q. v.

Na growme on ground my *gairdone* may degraid.
Henryson, Aige and Yowth, st. 3, Bann. MS.

Not defined in DICT., and the meaning suggested by Jamieson is wrong.

Lord Hailes misprinted *growme* as *growine*, which no doubt helped to mislead Jamieson, although he had a correct idea of the word it represented. In Laing's ed. of Henryson the word is printed *grome*.
O. Fr. *guerdone*, a recompense : from L. Lat. *widerdonum*, which is compounded of O. H. G. *wider*, back, again, and Lat. *donum*, a gift. V. Skeat's Etym. Dict.

GAIT, *s*. Lit. a going : hence pasturage for cattle in a common during summer; one *gait* being rated to maintain a cow; two *gaits* a horse; and half a *gait* a calf. Also called *gang*. South and West of S.

This term is still used in some districts of the North of E. V. Peacock's Gloss.

GAIT, GA'D, GAUT (*ga* as in gall), *part. adj.* Marked with *gaws* or welts. V. *Gawed*, *Gawit*.

GAIT GLYDIS, *s. pl.* Worn out old horses with scarred and fretted hide. Addit. to DICT.

Tuelf *gait glydis*, delr of a preine.
Maitland Poems, p. 183.
Not defined by Jamieson; but the meaning of *gait* which he suggested is wide of the mark. The expression is still used.
In The Country Wedding, Herd's Coll. Scot. Songs, II. 91, ed. 1869, the following line occurs:—
An auld *ga'd glyde* fell owre the heugh.
It may be noted in passing that this song as given by Herd is really a more modern version of The Wowing of Jok and Jenny, preserved in the Bann. MS.

GAL, GAYL, *s*. Gable, which is still pron. *gale*, or *gail*, in various districts of S.
". . hir maaster and scho sal lay thar grath in the *gal* on Sir Jon Lochys to mak thar yet sekyr." Charters, &c. of Peebles, Burgh Rec. Soc., p. 132.
"*Grath*," fixtures for the "*yet*," or gate referred to.
V. GRAITH, *s*.

To GALAY, *v*. V. DICT.
This word is certainly not related to A.S. *gælan*; but it is prob. from O. Fr. *galler*, to sport, make merry, &c. (V. Cotgr.), and hence related to *galliard*.

To GALE, GEAL, *v. n*. To tingle. V. GELL.

GALER, GALLER, GALION, GALLION, *s*.
1. A gallery, balcony. O. Fr. *galerie*.

2. A galley, a French war vessel.
When the French vessels, which brought Queen Mary to Scotland, were about to return home, she granted 100 crounis of the sun "to six pilots of the twa *galeris*;" and £66 13s. 4d. to "Monsieur Tynnance, to be distributit amangis the officiaris of the twa *galeris*;" and 200 crounis of the sun to M. Tynnance for his own use. (V. Treasurer's Accts.)
And these entries are explained by the following record of 1 Sept., 1561 :—". . the said Monsieur Domell ·[d'Aumale] depairtit with the twa *gallionis*, quhilk brocht the Quenis Grace hame, to France." Diurnal of Occurrents, p. 67.
O. Fr. *gallere*, *galere*, a galley; Cotgr.

GALLEAN-HEID, *s*. A gallery-head, gargoyle or gurgoyle : a projecting spout to throw the water from the gutter of a building, or refuse water, etc., from a room. These spouts were generally carved into grotesque heads or figures of animals, like those which support a gallery: hence the above name.
". . . with ane small spout in ilk chalmer to convoy the vrine throch the wall, and with *gallean heidis* convenient for the wark, as aalbe fund necessar and expedient." Burgh Recs. Aberdeen, II. 341, Spald.

GALYARD, GALLIART, *s*. A sprightly dance, Compl. Scot., p. 66, E. E. T. S. Also the name of a favourite Scot. dance. Addit. to GALYEARD.

GAMOND, *s*. A dance, step, movement : "ane gay *gamond* of France," Lyndsay, Thrie Estaitis, l. 452. Addit. to GAMOUNT.

GANE, *s*. V. DICT.
Del. Jamieson's note. The term is simply M. E. *gane*, open mouth, yawn ; *gab*, as in Burns' Tam o' Shanter, is syn. for the word in both quotations.
A.-S. *ganian*, to gape, yawn : from *gán*, pret. of *gínan*, to gape widely. Icel. *gína*.

GANG, GENG, GING, *s*. 1. Family, flock, band, retinue : applied both to persons and animals, as to a chief and his followers, a flock of sheep, a fox and its cubs, &c.

2. A set, stand, supply, fixed number: as, "a *gang* of horss schone." Burgh Recs. Aberdeen, II. 38, Sp. C.
A.-S. *genge*, a flock : Icel. *gangr*, a going, a band or flock, like E. *gang*, in "a gang of gipsies."

To GANG *in a gate*. Lit. to go in one way : to be of one mind, act together ; Houlate, l. 285.

GANGAND-GAIT, GANNIN-GAIT, *s*. The foot-path of a public road; also, the footpath through fields to a farm house : so called to distinguish them from the cart or carriage way or *gait*; West of S.

GANANDEST-GAIT, *s*. The shortest road, or the easiest to travel.
To zone busteous Belrne that bolstit me to byde
Amang the gulzart gromis, I am bot ane Gest,
I will the *ganandest gait* to that gay glyde.
Rauf Coilzear, s. 61.

GAN-WAY, GANG-WAY, *s*. Same as *Gangand-Gait*.

GARATOUR, *s*. A watchman, a watchtower. V. GARRIT.
Schir Golngros' mery men menskful of myght,
In greis and *garatouris* graithit full gay ;
Sevyne score of schelldis thai schew at ane sicht.
Gawan and Gol., st. 38.

Jamieson's reference of this term to Greis, greaves for the legs, is a mistake : so also is his statement, given under that heading, that *garatouris* "probably denotes armour for the thighs." In the passage quoted above *greis* means steps, stairs, or platforms on battlements ; and *garatouris* means watch-towers. V. Gloss. Gawayne Romances.
The proper and usual meaning of *garatour* is watchman.

To GARD, GARDE, *v. a.* To hem, bind, trim, in order to prevent the edge from fraying; to braid, to ornament with trimmings or facings; Accts. L. II. Treas., I. 202. Fr. *garder.*
Occurs in Shak., Merch. Ven. ii. 2, 164; &c.

GARD, GARDE, *s.* A hem, border, trimming, facing.
This word, both as a *v.* and as a *s.*, occurs frequently in inventories, and other notices of dress. It is common in Eng. also. V. Halliwell's Dict.

GARDELOO, *s.* V. DICT.
For O. F. *gure,* read O. F. *gare.*

GARDENAT, GARDNETT, GARDMET, GARDMAR, *s.* Varieties and corruptions of GARDNAP, q. v.
These forms occurs frequently in Burgh Records, Inventories, &c.

GARDENER'S GARTENS, *s. pl.* V. DICT.
For *garters* read *gartens.*

GARDEVIANT, GARDYVIANCE, GARDYVYANSS, *s.* A close cupboard, an ambry or safe for meat ; Accts. L. H. Treas. Scot., I. 82, 99, 175. Addit. meaning.
The forms *gardewiat* (Aberdeen B. Recs., I. 259, Sp.C.), and *gardlewyot* (Peebles Burgh Recs., p. 262, Rec. Soc.), may be vulgar corr. of this term ; but more prob. they are mistakes in the reading or printing of it : in both cases the meaning is "a cabinet or escritoire." Fr. *garde-viande,* a cup-board : not *garde-de-viande,* as in DICT.

GARDEVINE, *s.* V. DICT.
For *gar-de-vin* read *garde-vin.*

GARDNAP, *s.* V. DICT.
In quotation, for "*deiche gardnap,*" read "deiche *gardnap*" (i.e. dish, gardnap).
For Fr. *garne-nappe,* read Fr. *gar-de-nappe ;* and del. last sentence of note.

GARRAY, GARRIE, GARRY, *s.* Preparation, array ; bustle, confusion, noise, &c., of a number of persons preparing for some sport or undertaking ; Peblis to the Play, st. 2. Often pron. *gurry,* as in speaking of a disorderly housewife or servant, "She's aye in a *gurry,*" i.e. bustle and confusion. Addit. to GARRAY.
In the Towneley Mysteries, p. 64, *garray* is used with the meaning *force, troops, army ;* a meaning which E. *array* sometimes has still.

GARRON, GARROWN, *s.* A spar, pole, shaft : syn. *rung.* Addit. to GARROWN.
". . *garrons* to be barrowis," i.e. poles for making shafts for hand-barrows ; Burgh Recs. Edinburgh, II. 324, Rec. Soc.
Left undefined in DICT., but suggestions regarding meaning and etym. are given. On both points they are wrong. The term is allied to O. Fr. *garrot,* which Cotgrave defines as "the cudgell wherwith a carrier, &c., winds up, and straines hard, the cord he binds his packe withall."

GARSON, *s.* Treasure, reward, gift, present. Errat. in DICT.
Garson, garysoun, are forms of *garsom, gersom,* later *grassum, gressum,* q. v. See also notes under GERSOME in DICT.
Jamieson was mistaken regarding both the meaning and the etymology of this word. It occurs in the Allit. Rom. Alexander, ll. 1074, 1662 in the expression "*gevos garsons* of gold and of gude stanes."

GATING, *part. pr.* Waiting, watching, looking on. ADDIT. to GATING, q. v.
"O. F. *gaiter,* also *waiter,* to watch ; *wait* and *gait* are mere doublets. Jamieson's etymology is all wrong." Skeat.

GAUDÉ-DAY, *s.* V. DICT.
"Better *gaudy-day.* Not in use 'at the universities :' for it is unknown at Cambridge. But *gauldy-day*—annual fast-day is the regular term at Oxford, and is commonly cut down to *gaudy.*" Skeat.

GAUGERIE, GEOGRIE, *s.* V. *Gadgery.*

GAUKIE, *s.* V. DICT.
A better etym. is Icel. *gaukr,* a cuckoo, Scot. *gowk.* M. E. *goky* is from A.S. *gcác.*

GAVIL, GAVEL, GAVYL, GEVIL, *s.* Railing, hand-rail ; syn. *ravil, raivel.*
". . for making of the *gavil* of the tolbuith stair." Burgh Recs. Edinburgh.
This term is still used in various districts of Scot.

GAWDIES, GAADYS, GALDEIS, GOWDEIS, *s. pl.* The smaller beads of a rosary. Addit. to GAUDEIS, q. v.

GAWED, GA'D, GAWIT, GAWT, GAUT, GAIT, *part.* and *adj.* Galled, fretted ; marked with welts, frets, scars, or wounds, as, "a puir *gawt* glyde," a poor worn-out old draught-horse. V. GAW, and under *Gait.*

GAYLY, GAYLIES, *adv.* Pretty well, fairly well ; "How's a' wi' ye ?" "On, *gayly !*" V. GEILY.
But hear, my Lord Glengarry, hear,
Your hand's owre light on them, I fear ;
Your factors, grieves, trustees, and bailies,
I canna' say but they do *gaylies.*
Burns, Address to Beelzebub.

To GEAL, *v. n.* V. GELL.

GEASONE, *adj.* Scarce, rare, seldom found Errat. in DICT.
Jamieson evidently confounded this word with

gissen, geysen, leaky, shrunk : from Icel. *gisinn*. Whereas it is from A.-S. *gæsne*, scarce, rare. "*Geasone* is a common M. E. word, meaning *scarce*. See *gesen* in Gloss. to P. Plowman, and the Notes." Skeat.

GEBLET-DOOR, (*g* hard), *s*. A recess in the wall of a room to admit a small press, or to form an enclosure for private purposes; Burgh Recs. Aberdeen, II. 341, Sp. C. E. *gablet*.
Geblet, gablet, dimin. of *gable*, is in architecture, a small ornamental gable or canopy formed over a buttress, niche, etc.

GEDDART STAFF, **GEDWARD STAFF**, *s*. Forms of *Jeddart-Staff*. V. **JEDBURGH STAFF**.

GEDLING, *s*. Fellow, knave; Rauf Coilyear. Addit. to **GEDLING**.

GEDOUN, *s*. A form of Guidon, a banner, q. v.; Reg. Mag. Sig. Scot., 1513-1546, note, p. 733.

GEERS (*g* hard), *s. pl.* The props and cross planks used to support the roof of a coalmine; West. of S. Also in North of E. V. **GEER**.

GEHL-ROPE, *s*. V. **DICT**.
The etym. of this term is not A.-S. *ge-heald*, but Swed. *göling*, a top-rope.

GEIR, *s*. A form of Gair, q. v.; Hist. Old Dundee, p. 242.

GEKGO (*g* soft), *s*. A form of *Jacko*, a jackdaw, q. v.; Douglas, Pal. Hon., i. 21, Small's ed.
In Gloss. to this ed. the term is rendered "*a cuckoo;*" evidently confounding it with *gukgo*, a cuckoo, which also occurs in Douglas (v. Virgil, xii. prol.), and is generally written *gukkow*.

GELCOT, *s*. A jacket, Burgh Recs. V. **GALCOTT**.

GELL, **GELD**, (*g* hard), *adj*. A pron. of *yeld*, *yell*, barren, not giving milk. V. under **YELD**.
This pron. is still common in the West of S. and must have been long in use; for the form *yeld* occurs in the Towneley Mysteries, pp. 75, 81.

GEM, **GEMME**, (*g* hard), *s*. Represents the common pron. of *game*; Douglas, Virgil, iv. prol.; also, recreation, enjoyment, gambling; Rob Stene's Dream, p. 8.

GEMMEL, **GEMMELL**, *adj*. Twin, double; Accts. L. H. Treas. Scot., I. 376, Dickson. Lat. *gemellus*. So also by Douglas, Virgil, x. 7; but as a *s*. meaning two-part harmony, in Palice of Honour.

In modulation hard I play and sing Faburdoun, pricksang, discant, countering, Cant organe, figuratioun, and *gemmell*.
Small's Ed., I. 20.

GENT, *adj*. Comely, fair, neat : still used as short for *genteel*. V. **GENTY**.

GENTRE, **GENTRIE**, *s*. Nobleness, nobility, generosity : also used like *gentrice*, q. v.
And thame restor agane of hys *gentre*, To suffir thame begravin for to be.
Douglas, Virgil, xi. ch. 3.

GENYELL, *s*. Pron. of **GANYEILD**, q. v.

GENYIE, *s*. V. **DICT**.
In l. 6, for *Reid of Reidswire*, read *Raid of Reidswire*.

GEROFLEIS, **GEROFLEE**, **GERRAFLOUR**, **GIRAFLOUR**, **GIRRAFLOUR**, **GILOFER**, **GILOFRE**, *s*. A gillyflower; Sempill Ballates, p. 77 : *Gerafloure*, Kingis Quair, st. 190. O. Fr. *giroflée*.

GERSING, **GERSIN**, *s*. Pasturage. V. **GERS**, *s*. and *v*.

GESLIN, **GESLING**, (*g* hard), *s*. A gosling. V. **GAISLIN**.

GESSERANT (*g* soft), *s*. A coat of mail composed of small oblong plates or scales overlapping each other, a jazerant; Kingis Quair, st. 153, Skeat's ed. Addit. to **DICT**.
Both Tytler's and Jamieson's renderings of this word are wrong, and fail to bring out the poet's comparison of the scales of the fish glittering in the sun like the scales on such a coat of mail. V. **Gesserawnte** and Jesseraunt in Halliwell's Dict.
O. Fr. *jaseran*, "a coate or shirt of great and close-woven maile;" Cotgr.

GEST, **GESTE**, *s*. Deed, action, history, tale; Douglas, Virgil, i. ch. 11. Addit. to **GEIST**, q. v.

GET, *s*. Yield, produce; also, booty, prey.
In the first sense the term is used in connection with net and creel fishing; and in the second sense it is applied to the food carried by birds of prey to their young.

GETLING, **GETTLIN**, **GEDLING**, *s*. Lit. a dim. of *get*, a child, but in that sense applied only to one begotten in bastardy. Most commonly a term of opprobrium like fellow, knave, vagabond, and confounded with *gadling*; also used colloq. like bairn, child, etc., as applied to a timorous or cowardly person. Addit. to **GAITLING**.

GETT, *s*. A form of *gait*, a road, way: *common-gett*, highway, public road, street, causeway; Burgh Recs.

GEVIL, **GEVILL**, *s*. A hand-rail. V. **GAVIL**.

GEWELING, *s.* Javelin; Burgh Recs., Aberdeen, II. 27, Sp. C.

GIBBET, GYBBATE, (*g* soft), *s.* The *swee* or chimney crane for suspending a pot over the fire; Burgh Recs. Aberdeen, I. 408, Sp. C. V. SWAY, SWEE.

The term is still so used in various districts of Scot. Smaller pots whre suspended by means of the *crook* (a series of links), and *gab* (a movable hook); but the largest pots were hung on the *swee* itself, or were attached to it by a strong double hook called the *gibbet-gab.*

GIBBET-PAN, *s.* A name given to the largest pot or pan used in cooking: so called because it generally hung on the gibbet or *swee*: also called *kail-pat*, and *guse-pan*.

To GIDE, GYDE, GID, *v. a.* To guide; Accts. L. H. Treas. Scot., I. 248, 294, Dickson.

GIGLY (*g* soft), *adj.* Unsteady, shaky, likely to be upset or overturned; West of S. V. *Jeegly.*

GIGOT, *s.* V. JIGOT.

GILAVER, GELAVER, (*g* hard), *v.* and *s.* Gossip. V. *Glaver.*

GILLET (*g* hard), *s.* A gelding, a riding horse; Henryson, Parl. Beistis, l. 103.

Bann. MS. reads *Jonet.*

GILLIVER (*g* soft), *s.* 1. A form of GILL-FLIRT, q. v.

2. A gilliflower. V. *Gerofleis.*

GIMELL, GIMMAL, *adj.* and *s.* V. *Gemmel.*

GINGEBRACE, GINGEBRAS, GYNGIBRACE, *s.* Ginger-bread, spice-cake.

This term occurs frequently in the Exchequer Rolls of Scot. It was common in the West of Scot. not many years ago, and has not yet quite passed away.

GINKER, *s.* A dancer, Fr. *ginguer.* Addit. to GINKER, q. v.

GINNEL, *s.* A runlet or narrow channel for water, a street gutter: "Bairns like to plouter in the *ginnels.*" West of S.

This term is similarly used in the North of E. V. Peacock's Gloss.

A.-S. *gin*, a narrow opening or channel, has been given as the etym. of this word; but more prob. *ginnel*, like *kennel* with same meaning, is simply a corr. of M. E. *chanel, canel*, O. Fr. *chanel, canel*, from Lat. *canalis*, a cutting, trench, channel.

GIRAFLOUR, GIRRAFLOUR, GERRAFLOUR, *s.* V. *Gerofleis.*

To GIRG, GERG, GARG, GURG, *v. n.* To jerk or gurgle, as when one walks with water-logged boots. Addit. to GIRG.

GIRNAR, GIRNER, (*g* hard), *s.* Same as GIRNALL, q.v.

GIRTH, *s.* A course of washing: also, a supply of water prepared for washing clothes, etc. Spald. Misc., I. 87, 1597.

GIRTH, GIRTHE, GURTHE, *s.* A hoop, band: com. pron. *girr;* Burgh Recs. Prestwick, p. 137, Mait. C. V. GIRD.

GISE, GYSE, (*g* hard), *s.* Fashion, custom; Douglas, Virgil, v. ch. 2: appearance, dress, garb; also, disguise, and hence *giser*, *gysar*, in its later meanings. Addit. to GYSE.

GISSEN, GISSEIN, GESYNE, (*g* soft), *s.* Childbirth, parturition. Addit. to GIZZEN, q. v.

GISSEIN-LAIR, *s.* Child-bed; place or time of parturition. V. JIZZEN-BED.

"Thow lent to Meryeoun Nasmyth ane pair of heid scheittis in hir *gissein-lair*, in the quhilk thow pat in thi witchecraft." Trials for Witchcraft, Spald. Misc., I. 86, 1597.

GITHORN, GYTHORN, GITHERN, *s.* A guitar; Douglas, Virgil, xiii. ch. 9; Houlate, l. 758.

GLAIVE, GLAUE, GLAYF, *s.* A sword, a scymitar; Scott's Antiquary, ch. 40.

GLAM, *s.* Noise, cry, clamour: generally applied to a loud prolonged cry, as of a crowd or a pack of hounds; as, "the *glam* of the ratches."

Glamer given by Jamieson is properly a freq. of *glam*, and implies a combination of various sounds. Indeed *glam* and *glamer* are forms like *chat* and *chatter*. For etym. see under GLAMER.

To GLAMMER, GLAMER, *v. a.* To shout after, rail at, scold.

". . openly *glammerand* him saiand scho auld ger banys the said Schir John out of this toune." Burgh Recs. Aberdeen, 16 June, 1490, I. 46, Sp. C.

GLASSBANDS, *s. pl.* Strips or bands of lead for securing the panes of glass in a window; Burgh Recs. Glasgow, I. 67, Recs. Soc.

GLASSIN. 1. As an *adj.*, made of glass, glass, glazed: "the haill *glassin* wyndoes;" Burgh Recs. Aberdeen, II. 348, Sp. C.

2. As a *s.*, glazing, filling with glass, mending the glass-work: "the repairing and *glassin* of the wyndoes;" Ibid., II. 349, Sp. C.

3. Glass-work, panes of glass, glass.

To GLAVER, GLAIVER, *v. n.* To chatter, babble, talk foolishly, gossip: part. *glaverin'*.

Another form is *gilaver*. West and South of S.

GLAVER, GLAIVER, *s.* An idle, foolish, or gossiping talk or story: also, one who is addicted to such gossip. Ibid.
Prob. a variety of *claver*: cf. Germ. *klaffen*, to chatter. Still, the term is common in the North of Eng. also, and is found in Alliter. Rom. Alexander, l. 5505, meaning a gabble, chattering.

GLEBARD, *s.* A glow-worm; Henryson, Parl. Beistis, l. 115. M. E. *globerd*; Wright's Voc., *glouberd*.
This is prob. an instance of *e* for *o*: a miswriting which is not uncommon in MSS.

GLEW, GLEE, *s.* Result, outcome; hence, fate, destiny; Barbour, vi. 658. See also *glewis* in Kingis Quair, st. 160, Skeat's ed. Addit. to GLEW.

To GLIFF, GLIFT, GLYFTE, *v. n.* To glance, to look in a quick, hurried, or startled manner; to glint, gleam, or glare, like a flush of sunshine or a flash of light : *pret., gliffed, glifte, glyfte.* V. GLIFF, *s.*

Fu' lang he glower'd at Jenny,
But she barely *gliffed* at him;
Then he tried to think he didna care,
But he trimmled in lith an' lim'.
Old Song.

He *glyfte* vpe with hys eghne that graye were and grete.
Awntyrs of Arthur, st. 28.

GLIFNIT, *pret.* Glanced. V. GLIFFIN.

GLITNIT, *part. adj.* Clotted, dabbled, fouled. V. GLIT, GLITTIE.
And all his hair was *glitnit* full of bluide.
Douglas, Virgil, ii. ch. 5.
Slime or ooze in the bed of a stream, also, the vegetation that collects on stones in half-stagnant water is still called *glit* in the West of Scot.

To GLOIR, GLORE, *v. a.* To glorify; Douglas, Pal. Hon. prol. Addit. to GLORE.

GLONDERS, *s. pl.* V. DICT.
"In the *glunners, glunters*, or *glunts*," in the glooms or sulks. These forms are still used in South and West of S.; *glunners* being the loc. pron. of *glonders*, like *wonners* for *wonders*.
"Evidently similar to *glunter*, which J. gives a few pages further on. *O* and *u* constantly interchange when *m* or *n* follows." Skeat.

To GLOPPE, GLOPPEN, GLOPNE, *v. n.* To wail, bewail, mourn with choking sighs; *pret. glopt, glupt, glopned, gloppened, gloppenyde*; Awntyrs of Arthur, st. 7. Errat. in DICT.
Jamieson's defin. of this *v.* is certainly wrong, as Sir F. Madden pointed out; and with the knowledge implied in his note, the mistake is a strange one. *To gloppe, gloppen*, is to gulp and wail like one in intense sorrow; and the *v.* had also a transitive sense, "to cause to gulp and wail," as in Morte Arthur, l. 2580—
Thowe wenys to *glopne* me with thy grete wordes.

Hence came the later meaning of the word, to frighten, to perplex or terrify: and so we find *glope* in the Towneley Mysteries, p. 146, meaning a surprise. V. Halliwell's Dict.

To GLOTTEN, *v. n.* To clot, curdle, lapper: pret. and part. pt. *glottent, glottnit.* Douglas, Virgil, v. ch. 6.

GLUFF. Be ane *gluff*, by a glove: a symbol of investiture, and of delivery. Addit. to GLUFF.
"The saide day [27 Aug., 1493], comperit ane richt nobile and honorable mane Alexander Iruyne of Drvm, . . . *gaff*, grantit, and assignit *be ane gluff* to Dauid Irwyne, his sone, all and hale his gudis beand within the landis of Coule," &c. Burgh Recs. Aberdeen, I. 51, Sp. C.

To GO *afore*, GAE *before*, *v.* To fall over.
This phrase is peculiar to Orkney. If a man falls over the pier, he is said to have "*gaen afore* the quay." J. W. C.

GNEDE, *adj.* Sparing, scanty; "It nas to large ne *gnede*," it was neither too large nor too little.
Misprinted *guede* in Sir Tristrem, and so given by Jamieson; but see explanation under *Guede*.

GOD'S PENNY, GODDIS PENNY, *s.* An old name for an earnest or arle penny, used in bargain making. Also, the silver penny or fine which a vassal paid to his superior on entry to a holding.
". . . at the entrie of all schips bringand in any vittaillis or tymmer at the port of Leyth, that the thesaurer of the towne that happinis to be for the tyme proffer a *goddis penny* and bye the same vpoun a competent pryce, gif he can, to the behuif, vtillity, and proffeitt of the nichtbouris of the towne." Burgh Recs. Edin., 1490, Rec. Soc.
Both name and custom were common in North of Eng. also. V. Brockett, Halliwell.

GOIF, GOYF, GOF, GOVE, GOW, GOWE, *s.* The pillory. V. under GOFE.
To be put in the *goif* or *gow*, was lit. to be set forth to public gaze, or to the contempt of one's fellows: see *v. goif, goue,* to gaze. Jamieson connects it with Icel. *gapa*, to stare with open mouth ; Germ. *gaffen.*

To GOIF, GOYF, GOVE, *v. a.* To punish by the *goif* or pillory ; Burgh Recs. Edin., I. 73, 201, Rec. Soc.

To GOLDER, GOLLER, GULLER, *v. n.* To talk in loud, boisterous, or domineering manner; West of S. V. GOLDER.

To GOLF, *v. n.* To champ or snort, as an enraged pig does while rushing along: part. pr. *golfing, golfand*, used also as a *s.*: both forms occur in Colkelbie Sow. Errat. in DICT.
Jamieson's defin. is certainly wrong. The word is still used in the West of S.

GOLFING, GOLFAND, s. Champing or snorting of an enraged pig.
And syne thay war ourthrawin most and leist,
For sory swyne for thair *golfing* affraid,
Till that the pig brak fra thame in a braid.
Colkelbie Sow, l. 740, Bann. MS.

GOLLAND, GOLLAN, s. Ragwort, a yellow flower common in moist meadows; Orkney.
Lit. *the golden one:* cf. *marigold.* It has the same name in the North of Eng. V. Brockett's Gloss.

GOLT, s. A drain, ditch. V. GOT, GOTE.

GOMERIL, s. The stick on which a pig is hung when scraped and cleaned; South of S.
This is evidently a corr. of *cameral, cammeril, camrel,* q. v.

GOODSIR, s. Forefather. V. GUDSYR.

GOOSE-NESTS, s. pl. Recesses formed in the interior walls of houses for the comfort and convenience of the geese while sitting on their eggs; Orkney.
"They are mentioned in a 17th cent. specification in my possession : but the custom is now nearly obsolete." J. W. C.

GORGET, GORGYT, s. 1. Lit., little throat-guard: a piece of armour to protect the neck; Douglas Virgil, x. ch. 7.
The Gloss. in Small's ed. renders *gorgyt,* "the throat."

2. Pl. *gorgets,* a kind of pillory: an instrument of punishment commonly called the *jougs.*
"Upon the first mercat day he shall sit in the stockes in tyme of mercat betuixt ten and twelve houres befoire noon of the day; and that he shall upoun the Sounday thairefter stand in the *gorgets* at the kirk of Balmaghie at the gathering of the congregation." Minute Book, War Com. of Covenanters in Kircudbright, 1640, 1641, p. 40.
Fr. *gorge,* the throat.

GOT, GOTE, s. V. DICT.
Gote, a canal, drain, has no connection with *gutter,* a run for catching drops from the eaves of a roof. The one is from Du. *goot,* from L. Lat. *gota,* a canal, conduit; the other from O. Fr. *gutiere,* from Lat. *gutta,* a drop.

GOT-SEAME, GOT-SAME, s. V. *Gut-same.*

GOUGE, s. A wench; Scott, Fair Maid of Perth, ch. 12. V. GUDGET.
O. Fr. *gouge,* id.

GOUPHERD, *part. pt.* Goffered, i.e. crimped, puckered, or impressed with goffering irons. Addit. to GOUPHERD, q. v.
This is simply a bad spelling of E. *goffered* or *gauffered* (V. Webster's Dict): hence, the etymology is wrong. Under Gowfre, however, Jamieson has given it correctly.

GOVIS, GOWES, GOWE, s. V. GOFE, *Goif.*

GOWK, s. V. DICT.
As noted under *Gaukie,* the best etym. for this term is Icel. *gaukr,* a cuckoo.
Regarding the form *golk,* Prof. Skeat explains that it is simply an example of *gokk* written with *lk* for *kk* : a practice that is not uncommon in MSS.

GOWK'S-SPITTLE, s. V. DICT.
In English *cuckoo-spittle.*

GRADELY, GRAIDLY, *adj.* and *adv.* Orderly, skilful, proper; completely, decently. V. GRAID, GRAITH.

To GRAISLE, GRASLE, GRASSIL. 1. As a *v. n.,* to grate, grind, crackle; Douglas, Virgil, i. ch. 2: also, to frizzle, crackle, crumple; West of S.
2. As a *v. a.,* to grind, champ, gnash; Ibid., viii. ch. 4, iii. ch. 10.
O. Fr. *gresiller,* to wriggle, frizzle, crumple, crackle. V. Cotgr. Dict.

GRAITH, *adj.* V. DICT.
Prof. Skeat has pointed out that this term is not from the A.-S., but from Icel. *greithr,* ready; and that the Icel. has *adj. s.,* and *v.,* all three, viz. *greithr,* ready, *greithi,* arrangement, and *greitha,* to arrange.

GRANE, s. 1. Branch, &c. V. GRAIN.
2. Pl. *granis,* spikes as in grass or corn in the ear; Houlate, l. 26. Addit. to GRAIN.
Dan. *grein,* a branch ; Icel. *greina,* to divide.

GRANIS, GRANYS, GRAYNIS, *s. pl.* Grains or kernes, cochineal, a dye-stuff ; Burgh Recs. Edin., I. 241, Rec. Soc.: in *grayne,* dyed with grains, dyed-fast, fast-coloured; Accts. L. H. Treas., I. 155.
Cochineal (*coccus ilicis*), Ital. *grana,* produced the best and fastest colour of its kind : hence, *in grane, in grayne, ingrain,* came to mean fast-coloured, fast-dyed, fast.

To GRATIFIE, *v. a.* Lit., to show favour or respect for one : to give a gratuity, present, or reward in addition to wages; part. pt. *gratifeit, gratifiit.*
". . . and be ressone thai ar recommendit be his Majestie for thair guid service the tyme of thair attendance upoun his Hienes service, thairfoir the saidis proveat, baillies, and counsall hes ordanit the saidis hagbutteris to be *gratifeit* with the soume of ane hundreth merkis, by and attour the soume of money aett doune for ane daylie wage to thame," &c. Burgh Recs. Glasgow, I. 135, Rec. Soc.

GRAY, s. A light wind, a gentle breeze; Orkney.
Prob. so called from its effect on the surface of a calm sea : Dan. *graane,* to grow gray or cloudy, to lower.

GRAYBEARD, s. A form of stoneware jug. Addit. to GRAYBEARD, q.v.
Prob. so) named from its spout being fashioned like an old man's face with a long pointed beard. The jug is still common.

GREIS, s. pl. Under this heading in DICT. delete quotation from Gawan and Golagros, which is misplaced; also the last para. from *Garatouris*, which is wrong. V. under *Garatour*.

To GRENE, v. n. V. DICT.
The best form of etym. for this term is Icel. *girna*, to desire, or A.-S. *gyrnan*, to yearn, be desirous. "I'm just *girnan* to get it," is a common expression in the West of S. when a person is longing for something that he likes.

GREWLINGIS, adv. V. GROFLINS, *Groflins*.

GRIES, s. V. DICT.
Delete this entry entirely: it is altogether wrong. The expression *stanerie greis*, lit. stony steps or flats, means *gravelly beds* or *slopes*: they are still called *staner beds* in the West of S.

GRIPPER, GRIPPER-OWRE-OUILLES, s. A midwife, Orkney.
The second form is confined to the South Isles of Orkney.

GROFE, GROFFE, s. The belly. V. GROOF.

GROFLINS, GROFLINGIS, GROOFLINS, GROOLINS, adv. Lying on the belly or with face downwards. Syn. *on groufe, agroufe*. Addit. to DICT. V. GRUFE, GROUFE.

GROWCH, v. and s. V. GRUCH.

GRUGSY, adj. Dirty, coarse-looking, slovenly; gen. applied to an untidy woman, Orkney. Prob. a var. of *Grousum*, q. v.

GRULINGIS, adv. Gol. and Gawane, st. 79. Short for *Grufelingis*. V. GROFLINS.

GRUNE, MS. *grunye*. V. DICT.
Regarding this entry the following note by Professor Skeat is important:—
"It ought to be noted that the Edin. MS. has not got *grunye*, as J. says. I believe I read it as *grune*; and I ought to have noted it as the reading of that MS. The Camb. MS. has *grund* like the editions."
Grune means "groin," snout, ness, or headland; Fr. *groin*, "snout," Cotgr. The place particularly meant is not quite certain, as any headland might have been so called. But there is evidence that Corunna was also called "the Groyne;" and Corunna may therefore be meant. See Notes and Queries, 6 S. xi. 416, 23 May, 1885.

GRUNSEL, s. The common pron. of groundsel (*Senecio vulgaris*, Linn), or ragwort.
So pronounced in North of Eng. also.

GRUPPY, adj. Close-fisted. V. GRIPPY.

GRYLLES, s. pl.. Errat. in DICT. for *Gylles*, glens. V. GILL.
A misreading in Pinkerton's version. In the same line there is another,—*grenes* for *greues*, groves. V. GREUE.

GUEDE. V. DICT.
This entry is altogether wrong. The following explanation is by Professor Skeat:—
"*Guede* is simply a misprint for *gnede*, sparing, scanty. 'It nas to large ne *gnede*,'—it was neither too big nor too little. This correction is made in Stratmann's Dict., s. v. *gnede*. There is no such word as *guede*, but *gnede* is common: Mätzner gives 13 quotations for it. And see *gnedy* in Gloss. to P. Plowman."

GUFF, GUFT, s. A whiff, puff; also, a slight breeze, light wind; West of S. Addit. to GUFF, q. v.

GUHYT. L. Gyhyt, pret. Lit. guided it, i.e. arranged, disposed, or managed it. V. DICT. for quotation.
Jamieson's explanation and etym. of this term are wrong. The form *gyhyt* is for *gy-it*, guided it, as explained above; and *guhyt* is for *guy-yt*, another form of *gy-it*.
Gy or *guy*, to guide, is from O. Fr. *guier*, id.; and the form *gy* is common in Chaucer. See explanations of GUIDE in DICT.

GUIDS, GUDIS, GUDES, s. pl. Cattle, live stock; Burgh Recs. Prestwick, Peebles, &c. V. GUD.
Peacock in his Gloss. of Lonsdale gives *goods* as a common term for cattle in that district of the North of E.

GUKKIT, adj. V. GOWKIT, GUCKIT.

GULSET, s. Jaundice, Compl. Scot. V. GULSA.

GULSCH, GULSH, s. A glutton; one who eats greedily; applied also to one who is over-corpulent. West of S. V. GULSHY.

GUMPTIOUS, adj. Self-important, forward, pretentious, fault-finding, quarrelsome. V. GUMPTION.

GUNNALS, GUNNLES, s. pl. 1. Gills. V. GINNLES.

2. Jowls, great hanging cheeks; West of S.

GUNNALD, GUNNLED, adj. With great jowls or hanging cheeks. Used also as a s. and applied to persons and animals; Ibid.

Mony long tuthit bore,
And mony galt come befoir,
And mony grit *gunnald*;
Gruntillot and Gamald.
Colkelbie Sow, l. 227.

Left undefined in DICT. The suggestion given is wrong. Cf. Icel. *gin*, the mouth of a beast, *gjölnar*, the gills of a fish.

GUSE-PAN, s. A pan for stewing a goose: also, a name for the largest pot or pan used in cooking. Addit. to GUSE-PAN. V. *Gibbet-pan*.

GUT-SAME, GOT-SAME, GOT-SEAME, s. Gut-fat, tallow, lard; *got-seame*, Blame of Kirkburiall, ch. 4.

GYDING (*g* hard), *s.* Occupation, employment, work: syn. *prettik, prattik*.

". . . young fallowis and young husis, haffand na prettik nor seruice to life vpon . . . pas in service or sum honest *gyding* to sustene them vpon, vnder the payne of banesing this towne for yeir and day." Burgh Recs. Edin., 3 Oct., 1505, Rec. Soc.

GYLL (*g* hard), *s.* A glen. V. GILL.

GYLOMYS, GYLUMIS, (*g* hard), *s. pl.* Guiding ropes used in lifting heavy blocks or bales with a crane, windlass, &c.; Burgh Recs. Edinburgh, II. 325, Rec. Soc. Syn. *gy-tows*, which is still used.

A compound of *gy*, to guide, and *lome*, a utensil, instrument. V. under GY, *v.*

GY-TOWES, GY-TOWS, *s. pl.* Same as *Gylomys*, q. v.

H.

HABERGEON, HABIRGEON, *s.* Dimin. of *hauberk*: a piece of defensive armour for the neck, consisting of the gorget only when made of plate, and of sleeves and gorget when composed of chain; Douglas, Virgil, iii., ch. 6 : *habbiegoun*, Lyndsay, II., 178, Laing's ed.

The *habergeon* was really a breast-protector.

HAENA, HENNA, HINNA. Common and coll. forms of *have not*.

While some puir creatures *haena* where to lay
Their heads, nor yet as much as for a meal would pay.
Alex. Wilson's Poems, p. 321, ed. 1876.

Henna and *hinna* represent the common pron. in the West of S. *Henna* and *hanna* are the forms in the North of E. V. Brockett's Gloss.

HAFFLINS-WAYS, HALFLIN-WISE, *adv.* In a slight measure, more or less; also, half-heartedly, undecidedly, reluctantly, as, " She *haflin-wise* consented." V. HALFLIN.

But, faith ! the birkie wants a Manse,
So, cannilie he hums them ;
Altho' his carnal wit an' sense
Like *hafflins ways* o'ercomes him
At times that day.
Burns, Holy Fair, st. 17.

HAG-MATINES. V. DICT.

Certainly *hag* must be deleted. It mars both sense and measure, and the line is complete and clear without it. Prob. the scribe had begun to write *haly* a second time, and, observing his error, left the word unfinished and undeleted.

HAID. Have it : a coll. form still in use.

His bois thay war of the reid Skarlet maid—
Begaryt all with sindrie silkis hew,
Of nedill wark richt richelie all resplaid,
Of biggest bind as he thocht best to *haid*,
Or ladyis hand with nedill culd it sew.
Rolland, Court of Venus, i. 122, S.T.S.

To **HAIK,** *v. a.* To beat, batter, drive or knock out of one's way. Addit. to HAIK, q. v.

(Sup.) R

But an auld cripple sailor cam' hame frae the Main,
Wha had left hame a callant, an' Nanny a wean,
An' he swore he wad lay my back laigh on the plain,
But I *haikit* him weel, an' wad do it again.
James Ballantine, Whistle Binkie, II. 3.

To **HAIK,** *v. n.* To tramp, trudge, or wend one's way : the act implies considerable exertion or endurance. Addit. to HAIK.

The Musk, the lytill Mous with all hir micht
With haist scho *haikit* unto that hill of bicht.
Henryson, Parl. of Beistis, 1. 124.

HAIPIT, *part. pt.* Heaped; Burgh Recs. Aberdeen, I. 191 : *happit*, West of S. V. HAP.

HAIRSE, *s.* A bier; also, a carriage for a dead body. Addit. to HAIRSE, q. v.

This form simply represents the pron. of E. *hearse*. M. E. *herse*, a frame for lights in a church, a bier, a carriage for the dead.
The etym. given in DICT. is wrong. V. under *Hearse*.

To **HAISLE,** *v. a.* To sun-dry. V. *Aisle*.

Haisle is still common in Ayrshire, and is generally used in reference to clothes or clothes.

To **HAISRE, HAIZRE, HAZRE, HAZE,** *v. a.* To half-dry or partially dry cloth or clothes in the open air, i.e., to dry such articles on the surface only.

Haisre is used in various districts of S. besides Ayrs., which is given in DICT. It is properly a dimin. of *haise*, to dry on a hedge, to hedge-dry clothes, and hence to dry clothes in the open air, or, as in Halliwell's Dict., "to dry linnen, etc." But although still so used in the East of Eng., *haze* has lost its original meaning in Scot., and is now used only as a contr. form of its dimin. *haisre*.

HAISERD, HAIZERT, HAZED, *part. pt.* Half-dried, partially-dried, dried on the surface. Addit. to HAIZERT, q. v.

The etym. suggested in the DICT. is incorrect and wide of the mark. As stated above, *haisre* is a frequent. of *haise*, or as more commonly spelled *haze*, to lay on a hedge, to hedge-dry; from O. Fr. *haie, haye,* a hedge.

HAIVLES, *adj.* Destitute. V. HAFLES.

HAK, HAYK, *s.* A hook; reaping-hook, fishing-hook, &c.; Accts. L. H. Treas., I. 100; Burgh Recs. Prestwick, p. 51, Mait. C.
Icel. *haki,* Swed. *hake,* Dan. *hage,* Du. *haak,* a hook.

HALFATT, *s.* V. HAFFIT.

HALFERS, s. Half-share; but generally interpreted *half-mine.* V. under HALFER.
When one of a party unexpectedly finds a piece of money or other article of value, the first in calling "*halfers*" is supposed to have a right to share to that extent with the finder.

HALF-LADE, *s.* A large cassie, or straw basket, used in Orkney. V. CASSIE.
Lit. a half-load; and so called because two of these baskets, when filled and slung on a pack-saddle, form a load for a pony.

HALF-ONE, *s.* A term in golfing; a handicap of a stroke deducted every second hole.

HALIS, *s.* A hall or covered market for the sale of provisions, etc. Errat. in DICT.
The definition and explanation given in the DICT. are altogether wrong. As pointed out by Prof. Skeat the term *halis* is simply the pl. of O. Fr. *hale,* a hall, a covered market; as Cotgrave explains it, "An open Market house or hall standing on pillers;" and then he adds—"*Les hales.* Such a Market house, hall, or Shambles wherein flesh and other victuals are sold."
Mod. Fr. *halle,* a market; of German origin; Brachet.

HALSLOCK, HALSLOK, *s.* and *adj.* V. HASLOCK.

HALVED, *part. pa.* A term used in golfing; applied to a match which results in a drawn game; also applied to a hole, when each party takes the same number of strokes to play it.

To **HAM,** *v. n.* A form of HUM, q. v.
The term is so pron. in Orkney.

To **HAMEL, HAMBLE,** *v. a.* V. HUMMEL.
This form of the word is used in Orkney.

HAMILT, *adj.* A form of Hamald, q. v.; Whistle Binkie, II. 15.

HAMLIN, HAMLAN, *s.* A cross, wile, trick; pl. *hamlins, hamlans,* applied to the doubling, tricks, and pretences of a fox. V. HAMMLE.

To **HAMMER,** *v. n.* To stutter, stammer, or hesitate in speaking, S.

HAN'-DARG, *s.* Handiwork, hand-labour; also, what one wins by labour. V. DARG.

Himsel, a wife, he thus sustains,
A smytrie o' wee duddie weans,
An' nought but his *han' darg* to keep
Them right an' tight in thack an' rape.
Burns' Twa Dogs.

HANDLING, HANDLIN, HANLIN, *s.* A discussion, altercation, quarrel: a merry-making, a meeting of friends or opponents for discussion; a soiree is often called a *tea-hanlan;* West of S.

To **HANDFAST,** *v. a.* V. HANDFAST.

HANDSHARP, HANDSCHAIRP, *adj.* Barehanded, scantily possessed or supplied, straitened; "*handschairp* in thair geir," straitened in their circumstances; Spald. Misc., I. 95.

HANG, *pret.* Hung; this form is still used. V. HING.
There saw I stand, In capis wyde and lang
A full grete nowmer; bot thaire hudis all,
Wist I noght quhy, atoure thair eyen *hang.*
Kingis Quhair, st 81, ed. Skeat, S.T.S.
With bow In hand, that bent full redy was,
And by him *hang* thre arowis In a cas.
Ibid., st. 94.

HANGING, *adj.* A term in golfing applied to a ball which lies on a downward slope.

HANING, HANYNG, HAINING, *adj.* Close, hedged, preserved; *hanyng tyme,* cropping time, while the fields or crops were enclosed in order to keep out cattle; also, close time, while the common was closed in order to preserve the grass. V. HAIN, HANE.
". . . not to suffer ony of thair bestial to gang lows pasturand . . . vnles the samyn guddis be sufficientlie tedderit in *hanyng tyme.*" Burgh Recs. Prestwick, 2 Oct., 1603, Mait. C.
". . . the Vanelaw [a common of the burgh] to be proclamit waist, seute, and *hanyng.*" Burgh Recs. Peebles, 25 Apr., 1571. Rec. Soc.

HANKLE, HANCLE, *s.* A form of HANTLE, q. v.

HANSEL-WIFE, *s.* The woman who distributes the hansel at a marriage, generally, the bride's mother; Orkney. V. HANSEL, under HAND.

HANT, *s.* Short for *hantle,* number, plenty, abundance. V. HANTLE.
I Nil it gif without ane gold Besant.
Forsuith, said he, of sic I haue na *hant.*
Rolland, Court of Venus, i. 804, S.T.S.

HANT, *s.* Custom, practice, habit; lit. haunt. "Ye'll ne'er turn an auld cat fra ill *hants.*"

HARBRY, HERBERIE, *s.* Harbourage, shelter, accommodation, lodging, entertainment; Houlate, l. 945, Bann. MS, Addit. to HARBERIE.

HARDLEYS, HARDLIES, adv. Hardly, scarcely; commonly pron. *harlies*; a vulgar form of *hardly*.
Common in North of E. also. V. Brockett's Gloss.

To HARM, v. n. To fret, grumble, be peevish or ill-natured; Orkn.
In the West of S. *hirm* is used in the same senses.

HARMIN, s. Fretfulness, peevishness, grumbling; Ibid.
Dan. *harm*, vexation, grief: *harmes*, to grieve, to be sorrowful.

To HARNAS, HERNES, v. a. To mount, garnish, ornament, decorate; part. pt. *hernessit*, Accts. L. H. Treas., I. 83, Dickson. Addit. to [HARNAS].
"In the fyrst, a belt of crammassy *hernessit* with gold and braid." Ibid.

HARNESS, HARNISH, s. and adj. Shawls of a particular pattern; Alex. Wilson's Poems, p. 60, ed. 1876: *harness-weaver*, *harnish-weaver*; West of S.

HARROBLE, s. A bar or spar of a harrow; pl. *harrobles*; Orkn.
Dan. *harve-bul*, a harrow-bar; Larsen. A compound of *harv*, a harrow, and *bul*, a bar or spar. Icel. *herfi-bulla*.

HARROKIT, HARRIKIT, adj. and s. Hairbrained; a form of HALLOKIT, q. v. West of S.
This term is pron. *harrygaud* and *haddygaud*, in North of E. V. Brockett's Gloss.

HARSKY, adj. Of a rough, coarse nature; but generally used like *harsk*, rough, coarse; Henryson, Paddok and Mous, l. 46. V. HARSK.

HARTH, adj. Sharp-pointed, protruding; like the bones of a lean animal. A form of HARSK, q. v.
Thy hanchis burklis, with hukebanis *harth* and haw.
Dunbar and Kennedy, l. 131, S.T.S.

HAS-BEEN, HES-BEEN, s. A thing of the past; applied to any thing that formerly was useful or valuable, but is now worn out or decayed. Addit. to HAS-BEEN.
Imprimis then, for carriage cattle,
I have four brutes o' gallant mettle
As ever drew afore a pettle;
My Lan' *afore* 's a gude auld *has-been*,
An' wight an' wilfu' a' his days been.
Burns, The Inventory, l. 8.
Lan-afore, the fore horse on the left hand in the plough.
"And although it [the liberty of Kirkburial] was long held as indifferent in the doylde dayes, yet being now but vnuwhile, and as an *hes-beene*, should neuer be more." Blame of Kirkburiall, ch. 19.
This term is also used in Shropshire.

HASEWAITHE, s.
". . . una cum le wrak, wattell, waithe, et *hasewaithe*." Reg. Mag. Sig., 1424-1513, No. 1376.

HASLETS, HAUSLETS, s. pl. The inwards of an animal; the heart, liver, and lights: also called *pluck*, and *numbles*.
O. Fr. *hastilles*, "Th' inwards of a beast; as a hog's haslet, calues gather, sheepes plucke. etc." Cotgr.

HASSBILES, s. pl. A skin disease peculiar to infancy: it produces patches of dry scab on the head; Orkn.
Dan. *haus*, the skull, and *byld*, a boil: Norse *haus*, and *bolde*: Icel. *hauss*, and *bóla*.

HATESUM, HAITSUM, adj. Hateful, hated; causing or yielding hate; Douglas, Virgil, Bk. XI., ch. 4.

HATRANCE, s. Hatred; also, hindrance, as in the phrase, "moy nor *hatrance*," i.e., help nor hindrance. V. HATRENT.
". . noyther for fauour, priar, nor price, moy nor *hatrance*, but efter thair saull and conscience, as thai wald ansuyr to the great God, to the kingis grace, and towne of Abirdene, tharvpone." Burgh Recs. Aberdeen, I. 171, Sp. C.

HAUDIN, HADIN, s. Generally applied to a house or land held on lease; as, "a big *haudin*," a large farm: it is also applied to one's income or means of living, i.e., *upholding*. Addit. to HALDING, HADDIN.
I can say for mysel', tho' my *haudin* 's been sma',
That I'm weel up in years noo, yet guddlin' awa':
My frien's hae been kind, an' I freely admit,
"I hae aye been provided for, an' sae may I yet."
Walter Watson's Poems, p. 134.

To HAUGH, HAWK, v. a. and n. V. HAUCH.

HAVIL-CROOK, s. A form of *avail-crook*, lowering-crook: the iron chain and hooks used for suspending pots over a fire. The term sometimes includes both the *swee* and the *crook*. Burgh Recs. Aberdeen, I. 451, Sp. C. V. AVAILL, AVALE.
Fr. *avaler*, to lower.

HAW, adj. Hollow, shrunk, wasted: "with hukebanis harth and *haw*," i.e., sharp and shrunk; Dunbar and Kennedy, l. 181. The common form is *How*, q. v.

HAW-GAW, HAUGAW, HAUKA, s. A rag or refuse gatherer, a midden-raker.
This term is composed of *hauk*, to rake, to use the *hauk* or dung-fork, and *gaw*, a furrow, drain, dungstead.

HAWYNE, s. Haven, harbour; Burgh Recs. Aberdeen, I. 38, Sp. C.
A.-S. *hæfene*, Icel. *höfn*, Dan. *havn*, a harbour.

HAYND, *s.* Breath; Douglas, Virgil, Bk. vii., ch. 9. A form of AYND, q. v.

HAZARD, *s.* A general term in golfing for a piece of bad ground, such as a bunker, whin, etc.

To HAZE, *v. a.* Now used as a contr. form of *Haisre*, q. v.

This word originally meant "to lay on a hedge," to hedge-dry cloth or clothes, and by and bye simply to dry clothes in the open air, or, as in Halliwell's Dict., "to dry linen, etc." Hence came the dimin. *haisre*, to half-dry or partially dry clothes. *Haze*, however, has lost its original meaning, and is now used as a contr. form of its dimin. *haisre*.

HEARSE, HERSE, *s.* A frame for lights, candle or taper-holder: "ane bracine *hearse*," a chandelier of brass; Burgh Recs. Aberdeen, III. 69, 121, IV. 219, Rec. Soc.

The *herse* was an open framework of wood or metal which was placed, during a funeral service, as a canopy over the coffin and covered with lighted tapers. Also, a similar permanent framework of metal occasionally placed over recumbent monumental effigies, on which lighted tapers were placed at the celebration of the obit and anniversary of the deceased, and on some other occasions.
So named from its resemblance to a triangular harrow. Lat. *hirpex*, a harrow, whence O. Fr. *herce*, M. E. and Mod. Fr. *herse*. V. Skeat's Etym. Dict.

HEARSE, HAERSE, *adj.* Hoarse. V. HAIRSE.

HEART-AXES, *s.* V. DICT.

The etym. given in DICT. is wrong. The *axes* is not A.-S. *ece*, ache, but the Fr. *accés*, an attack of illness.

HEAVY - HEIDIT, HEVIE - HEIDIT, *adj.* Drowsy, listless, dull, gloomy, apathetic.

The last and worst is callit,Melancoly :
Soure, sorrowful, Inuious, cauld and dry :
Drowpond, dreidfull, gredie, and vntrew :
Heuie-heidit, and feindill in game or glew.
Rolland, *Court of Venus*, Prol. 31, S.T.S.
"Having a big heavy head;" Gloss. This is a mistake. Also *feindill*, which is rendered "ill-natured," is a misreading of *seindill*, seldom.

HEBAWDE, *s.* An owl.

Hornit *Hebawde*, quhilk clepe we the nycht owle.
Douglas, *Virgil*, vii. Prol., ed. Small.

HECK, HEIK, HIKE. A carter's call to his horse when he wishes it to draw towards him, i.e. to turn to the left. For "turn to the right," he calls "jee."

A common saying regarding a stubborn, intractable person is, "He'll neither *heck* nor *jee*." V. JEE.

HECKLE, *s.* Short for *heckle-pin*, a pin or tooth of a heckle, a sharp steel spike, Burns, Address to the toothache, st. 3. Addit. to HECKLE.

To HEDE AND HANG. To behead and hang; to punish with the utmost severity.

Sum say is ane King is cum amang us,
That purposis *to hede and hang* us.
Lyndsay, *Thrie Estaitis*, l. 3219, ed. Laing.

This phrase may refer to the beheading and subsequent suspension of the body in chains, or, more probably, to the two forms of capital punishment, decapitation and hanging: if so, the meaning is to inflict capital punishment, to execute.

HEEL, *s.* and *v.* The *heel* of a golfing club is the part of the head which is nearest to the shaft; and *to heel* is to strike or hit with this part.

HEGGERBALD, HEGGIRBALD, HAGGARBALD, *s.* Lean and scraggy one, lank and towsie loun. Lit. an *adj.*, meaning marked or formed like a heron. V. HEGRIE.

Fowll *heggirbald*, for hennis thus will ye hang.
Dunbar and Kennedy, l. 149, Laing's Ed.

Jamieson left this term undefined, but suggested a meaning which does not suit the sense of the two passages in which the word occurs. The one now given does Icel. *hegri*, a heron, Swed. *häger*: and *bald*, M. E. *balled*, marked or formed, from Gael. *bal*, a spot or mark.

HEIDING-SWERD, *s.* Beheading sword.

". . . . . ordanis Robert Glen, thesaurer, to ressaue fra Williame Makcartnay his tua handit sword to be vsit for ane *heiding-sword*, becaus the auld sword is failyeit, and to gif him five pound thairfor."
Burgh Recs. Edin., 3 Feb., 1564-5, Rec. Soc.

HEID-ROUME, *s.* Head or outer boundary of a feu or toft, i.e. the outer boundary of a head-room. Addit. to HEID-ROUME, q. v.

In 1572 the inhabitants of Peebles resolved to enclose the town with a wall; and that it might be built as speedily as possible they "statute and ordanit euery ane to big thair awne *heid-roome* betuix the Tolbuth to Peblis brig, and sua about the south syde of the toone to the Est Work; the haill commuuite to help to big it with dry stanis sa sone and as fare as is within thameselffis, and quhair superabundance of stanis is to help vtheris thairwith that mistaris, and this to be done within viiij nychtis."

To HEIF, *v. n.* To heave, labour; Douglas, King Hart, I. 116, ed. Small. E. *heave*.

A.-S. *hebban*, to lift, raise, elevate; Du. *heffen*, Dan. *hæve*.

HEISK, HISK, *adj.* Heady, nervous, excited, crazie; Orkn.

Norse *heak*, somewhat heady. Cf. Dan. *hidsig*, hotheaded; from *hidse*, to heat.

HEK, *s.* V. HECK.

HEKLIT, HEKILLIT, *part. pt.* Formed or fashioned like a monk's cowl.

His hude was reid *hekilit* atouir his croun,
Lyke to ane Poeit of the auld fassoun.
Henryson, *Testament of Cresseid*, l. 244.
His hude of scarlet bordourit weill with silk,
On *hekillit* wyis, untill his girdill doun.
Ibid., Prol. *Lyoun and Mous*, l. 32.

Prof. Skeat explains the term thus:—"It means a hood furnished with or fashioned like a monk's cowl, which completely covered the crown. Icel. *hökull*, a priest's cope : whence *hekla*, a kind of cowled or hooded frock, mount Hecla (Hekla) with its hood of snow. A.-S. *hæcile*, Gothic *hakul*; M. E. *hakel*, in Gawayne (Stratmann)."

HELE, *s.* Health, healing, cure, consolation, well-being, welfare ; "in guid *hele* and prosperitie," Burgh Recs. Aberdeen, I. 28, Sp. C. ; "confort and *hele*," Kingis Quair, st. 74 ; "hertis *hele*," heart-ease, consolation, Ibid., st. 169, 191, ed. Skeat. Addit. to HEIL, q. v.

To HELP, *v. a.* To improve, mend, repair, renovate ; pret. and part. pt., *helpit* ; Burgh Recs. Edinburgh, III. 279, Rec. Soc.

". . . thair ar sindrie defectis in the letter of gildrie, quhilk by gude advyse and deliberatioun mon be *helpit* and reformit." Burgh Recs. Glasgow, I. 341, Rec. Soc.

". . . quhilk stane wes ordanit to be *helpit* in the sauser mark thairof." Burgh Recs. Aberdeen, II. 322, Sp. C. This was one of the march-stones of the burgh, and its marks had become defaced.

HELY-HOW, *s.* V. under How.

HEMS, HEMMIS, *s. pl.* V. HAIMS.

HEND, HENDE, *adj.* Gentle, courteous ; Houlate, l. 325 : also, bright, comely, fair, as "*hendest* of hewis ;" Ibid., l. 893.

It is also used as a *s.* ; see under Heynd : and sometimes as an *adv.*, meaning carefully, kindly, lovingly, as in—

He gart hallowe the hart, and syne couth it hyng, About his hals full *hende*, and on his awne hart. *Houlate*, l. 477, Asloan MS.

Addit. to HEYND, HEND, q. v.

HEN-LAFT, *s.* The joists or *bauks* of a house ; also, the space above the joists.

Country houses long ago were generally of but one story, with thatched roof and open ceiling. The joists or *bauks*, being the recognised place for the poultry to roost during night, were called the *hen-laft*. And as household and other implements, and articles that were cumbersome or not much in use, were stowed away upon or above the joists, they were said to be kept in the *hen-laft*. And many a mother has brought order out of disorder by threatening to send the naughty ones "to bide in the *hen-laft*."

HEP, *pret.* and *part.* Heaped, piled up ; *hepmessour*, heaped - measure, heap - measure ; Burgh Recs. Aberdeen, I. 335, Sp. C.

HERBERE, *s.* A garden-plot or bed ; Kingis Quair, st. 31, 32. Addit. to HERBERE, q. v.

As pointed out by Prof. Skeat in his ed. of The Kingis Quair, the latter half of Jamieson's note on this term is a mistake. Delete from "It would seem," &c.

HERE, *s.* V. HEER.

HEREDATION, *s.* The act of inheriting ; also, right by inheritance : Blame of Kirkburiall, ch. 19. V. ACQUISITION.

Lat. *hæres*, an heir.

HERES, HERS, *s. pl.* Payments, rewards, dues ; as the dues payable to a miller and his men ; Burgh Rces. Edinburgh, IV. 306, Rec. Soc.

A.-S. *hyr*, hire, wages ; Swed. *hyra*, Dan. *hyre*.

HERKNERE, *s.* Listener : "the *herknere* bore," the keen or quick-eared boar, Kingis Quair, st. 156, ed. Skeat, S. T. S.

HERLIE, HERELY, HEIRLY, *adj.* and *adv.* Lordly, like a lord or chief, proudly ; Houlate, l. 846, 898. Addit. to HERLICH.

HERN, HARN, *s.* and *adj.* Linen : "*hern*-thread, *hern*-weaver, *harn*-weaver." Short for HARDIN, q. v.

HERNESSIT, *part. pt.* Ornamented. V. *Harnas.*

HERON-SEW, *s.* A young heron. Errat. in DICT.

Jamieson's mistake arose from confounding *heron-sew* and *heron-shaw*. They are different words. *Heron-sew* was in M. E. *heronsewe*, a young heron, and has this meaning in the passage quoted in the DICT. It comes from O. Fr. *heronceau*, having the same meaning. But *heronshaw*, or, as Cotgrave wrote it, *herneshaw*, means "a shaw of wood wherein herons breed." See his definition of *haironniere*, a heronry.

The pl. form *heronis sewis*, in the passage quoted in DICT., is doubly wrong : it ought to be only one word, *heronsewis*. The writer evidently took it to mean "heron's young ones."

HET, *adj.* Hot. *Gie him 't het*, give him it hot, i.e. scold or rate him soundly, beat him severely.

Yon ill-tongued tinkler, Charlie Fox, May taunt you wi' his jeers and mocks ; But, *gie him 't het*, my hearty cocks ! E'en cow the cadie. *Burns, Earnest Cry and Prayer.*

HET-SEIKNES, *s.* The rash, nettle-rash ; also called "*the hets;*" a skin eruption common among children ; Burgh Recs. Edinburgh, II. 16, Rec. Soc.

HETTLE, *adj.* V. DICT.

"This is not a corruption ; it is simply the A.-S. *hetol*, malignant." Skeat.

HEUCH, HEUGH, &c., *s.* V. DICT.

In senses 3, 4, and 5, at least, *heuch* is equivalent to A.-S. *holh*, a cavity ; and no doubt it was for this word that Dr. Leyden wrote *heolh*, as noted under sense 3.

HEULD, HEUD, *adj.* Kindly, gracious : *heuld-horn*, the gracious or grace-cup, Orkn.

"Sometime after the guests retired to bed, the lady of the house made a round of the bed-rooms, offering every guest a drink of warm, spirituous liquor. This was called the "*heuld*-drink," which was presented in a small horn vessel, called the "*heuld* horn." The vessel was smaller than the common drinking horn used at table, and held rather more than an ordinary tumbler." *Orcadian Sketch Book*, Note, p. 63.

Dan. *huld*, faithful, loyal : also, secret, private.

HEVED, HEVEDE, &c., s. V. DICT.
"Regarding the etymon of the term denoting the head, of course Horne Tooke is quite wrong ; the A.-S. heáfod (=Lat. caput) is distinct from hebban, the pp. of which is hafen." Skeat.

HEW, HEWCH, HUCHE, s. A shaft, mine, coal-pit. V. HEUCH.
". . and that his gracis subjectis micht hawe a securitie to tak thair hewis." Early Records of Mining in Scotland, p. 65.

To HEW, HEWE, v. a. To show, describe, declare, tell.
It war tyrefull to tell, dyte or addres
All thar deir armis in dewlye desyre.
Bot part of the principale netterthelos,
I sall haist me to hewe hartlie but hyre.
Houlate, l. 424, Asloan MS.
A.-S. *hiewan*, to form, shape, show.

HEWIT, part. pt. Errat. in DICT. for *Hewvit*, hoofed.
This is a misreading in Ruddiman's Douglas. Small's ed. reads *hovit*.

HEYDIN, HEYTHING, &c., s. V. DICT.
A better explanation of the origin of this term is Icel. *hæthing*, scoffing, mockery ; *hætha*, to scoff; from *háth*, scoffing.
Jamieson's statement that the *Strother* mentioned by Chaucer in the "Reeve's Tale" is certainly *Anstruther* in Fife, is a mistake.
The language employed by the speakers is undoubtedly that of the West Riding of Yorkshire; and Dr. Whitaker in his History of Craven long ago pointed out this fact, and conclusively showed that what Chaucer alluded to could be none other than Long Strother or Longstroth-dale in the north west part of the deanery of Craven. V. Garnett's Philol. Essays, p. 70.

HEYND, HENDE, adj. V. DICT.
Of the rival etym. suggested for this term, the following note indicates the best :—
"*Heynd* is from A.-S. *gehende*, near at hand, a derivation of hand. For the development of the sense compare M. E. *hende*." Skeat.

HICH, v. and s. V. HITCH.

HICHT, HEICHT, adj. Poet. and coll. form of *hichty*, high, haughty, insolent; and sometimes simply *heich*, high, with subjoined *t*, like *witht* for with.
Than Venus was cummerit in cairis kene,
With mind dement vneis scho micht sustene
The wordis scharp quhilk echo thocht al to *hicht*
Sayand, schaip ye to Cupid King nocht hiene?
Rolland, Court of Venus, iii. 291, S. T. S.
Sum ar sa proude, aud as ar put to *hicht*
In love and fauour of thair fair Lady bricht.
Ibid., Prol. 158.

HICK, s. A form of HECH, q. v.: "*hicks* an' hums," Whistle Binkie, II. 232.

HIDDERSOCHT. For *hidder socht*, brought hither, brought back. Addit. to HIDDERSOCHT.
Not one word, but a phrase applied to a person or thing that, having gone astray or been lost, has been sought for, found, and brought back to its place or owner.

HIDLINS, adj. and adv. V. HIDDLINS.

To HIKE, v. a. and n. To swing, sway, toss up and down ; part. *hiking*, used also as a s., as, "the *hiking* o' the boat." Addit. to HYKE, q. v.
A nurse *hikes* a child when she sits swaying it backwards and forwards, and when she tosses it up and down in her arms.
The word is common in the North of E. also. V. Brockett's Gloss.
Icel. *hvika*, mod. *hika*, to falter, sway, quake.

HILTER-SKILTER, adv. V. DICT.
In reduplicated words generally only one half of the word is significant; the other is merely a rhyming addition. Here the significant part is *skilter*, from Icel. *skildr*, part. pt. of *skilja*, to separate, break up, part.

To HINCH, HENCH, HAINCH, v. n. To halt, limp; West and South of S. V. HENCH.
All these forms are still in use ; and the older form *hink* is not yet quite obsolete ; but it is now generally used in the sense of to hesitate, hang, pause. For example, a lame person *hinches* as he walks along, and a stammerer *hinks* in his speech. V. HINK.
The variations presented by *hinch, hench, hainch, hink*, are found in *clinch, clench, clainch, clink*.
Icel. *hinka*, to limp.

HINCH, HENCH, HAINCH, s. A halt, limp ; lameness.

HINCHER, HENCHER, HAINCHER, s. A lame person; also called *hippity-hincher, hippity-haincher*. V. HAPPITY.

HINGAND-LOCK, HYNGAND-LOK, s. A padlock.
"Item, for tua *hingand lokkis* to the thesaure kist, iiij s. ij d." Accts. L. H. Treas., 2 Nov., 1497, Dickson.

HINGEN, v. pres. pl. Hang.
And lo ! quhy so thai *hingen* down thaire hudis,
Kingis Quair, st. 88, ed. Skeat, S.T.S.
This is not a Scot. form ; it is an imitation of the language of Chaucer. This plural termination occurs frequently throughout the poem.

To HINK, HYNK, v. n. To hesitate, lag, droop, fall off, fail. Addit. to HINK, q. v.
This term is really the old form of *hinch, hench, hainch*, to limp, halt ; and although not defined by Jamieson, its etym. is correctly indicated. V. under *Hinch*, &c.
Icel. *hinka*, to limp.

To HIRCHELL, HIRCHLE, v. n. V. HIRSILL, HIRSLE.

HIRDUM-DIRDUM, s. and adv. V. DICT.
Jamieson's suggestion gives no explanation of this term, which seems to be merely a reduplication formed from *dirdum*, din, loud and confused noise ; hence, *hirdum-dirdum*, great noise and confusion, and as an adv., uproariously, topsy-turvy.

The original sense of *dirdum* occurs in the passage quoted under HIRDY-GIRDY, q. v.

HIRDY-GIRDY, HIRDIE-GIRDIE, *s.* and *adv.* V. DICT.

The defin. in DICT. does not imply the contention, clamour, and uproar which form the prominent features of a *hirdy-girdy*, and which generally put men and things topsy-turvy. The etym., too, is equally defective.

The term is a reduplication from *gurr*, to growl, and *hur*, to snarl. Hence its application to angry, noisy quarrel, and its use as an adv. to express *uproariously* and *topsy-turvy*. See quotations in DICT.

E. *hurdygurdy*, a harsh, grating musical instrument, has the same origin. V. Skeat's Etym. Dict.

HIREGANG, *s.* Hire of oxen; expense of hiring.

". . . proficuum . . . cujuslibet bovis annuatim extenden. in le *hiregang* et laboribus ad 6 firlotas farine." Reg. Mag. Sig., 1424-1513, No. 1465.

To HIRM, *v. n.* To be peevish or fretful; to grumble; part. *hirmin*, used also as a *s.*, West of S. V. *Harm, v.*

This is a dimin. of *Harm*, q. v.: Dan. *harm*, vexation; *harmes*, to grieve.

HIRNE, HYRNE, *s.* V. DICT.

A.-S. *hyrne*, a corner: from *horn*. The affinities which Jamieson rejects are now generally accepted.

HIT, *pron.* V. DICT.

Jamieson's suspicion of the correctness of Tooke's derivation of this term was well founded. *Hit* is simply the neuter of A.-S. *he*.

"No one now believes in Horne Tooke's marvellous derivation from Goth. *haitan*." Skeat.

HITTIN, *part. pt.* Hit, beaten, licked. This form is still in use.

For William wichttar wes of corss
Nor Sym, and better knittin,
Sym said he sett nocht by his forss,
Bot hecht he sowld be *hittin*.
Alex. Scott's Poems, p. 24, ed. 1882.

HOAST, *s.* and *v.* Cough: *barkin' hoast,* a short, hard cough, like the barking of a dog; Burns, Scotch Drink. V. HOST.

HOGHEID, HOGGIT, HUGGIT, *s.* A hogshead, barrel, "a *hogheid* of beiff;" Burgh Recs. Glasgow, I. 123, Rec. Soc.

HOGMANAY, HOGMENAY, *s.* V. DICT.

The following note by Professor Skeat regarding the explanation of this term given in the DICT., may be accepted as an admirable summing up of the discussion :—

"If the French phrase *au gui menez* is genuine, the derivation of *hogmanay* from it is nearly certain; and this adaptation being accepted it follows, of course, that the phrase itself is of no very high antiquity. It ought, however, to be noted that all speculation as to the origin of the word *gui* may be spared; for it is neither Celtic nor Scandinavian, but simply the Fr. spelling of Lat. *uiscum*, mistletoe. Besides, the phrase *au gui menez* is devoid of all sense when detached from the accusative cases which *menez* governs.

"*Trololay* is the same as *truly-loly* in Piers Plowman: and the phrase in Cotgrave is not *Ay guy* (as misprinted), but *Au guy.*"

HOIF, HOFF, &c. V. DICT.

Under senses 3 and 4 the A.-S. word ought to be *hof*, not *hofe*.

HOIP, *s.* A hollow between hills. V. HOP, HOPE.

This form represents the pron. of the term in Tweeddale.

HOLE, *adj.* and *s.* Whole, complete; *all hole*, in every particular, wholly, entirely. V. HALE.

". . . we rejecte and refuse this monckely chastite, and *all hole* this slouthful and slouggishe sorts of lyfe of supersticious men," &c. Conf. of Faith of Swiss Churches. Wodrow Soc. Misc., I. 22.

A.-S. *hál*, Icel. *heill*, Dan. *heel*, Sw. *hel*, whole. Regarding the spelling with initial *w*, see Skeat's Etym. Dict. under Whole.

HOLINE, HOLEN, *s.* and *adj.* Holly; "of the *holine* hew," in colour like the holly, dark-green; Court of Venus, i. 88, S.T.S. Addit. to HOLYN.

HOLLAN BOOLS, HOLLAN'S BOOLS, *s. pl.* Dutch marbles: striped or variegated bowls greatly prized by boys.

Gnnnie! Myste's ta'en my ba',—
Flyting Mysie, flyting Mysie,
And flung my *Hollan's Bools* awa',—
Cankert, flyting Mysie:
The bonnie ba' ye made to me,
The bools I bought wi' yon bawbee,
She's gart them o'er the window flee=
Cankert, flyting Mysie.
Alex. Smart, Whistle Binkie, II. 377.

HOLLIS-PECE, *s.* A kind of small cannon.

". . . for delinerance agane to the said towne of thair artailzaric either following; that is to say, ane falcown, kilis pece, *hollis pece*, and thre serpentinis." Burgh Recs. Aberdeen, I. 195, Sp. C.

HOLT, *s.* V. DICT.

The two entries under this heading ought to have been combined. The various meanings given belong to A.-S. *holt.*

HONG, *pret.* Hung.
and with this *hong*
A mantill on hir schularis, large and long.
Kingis Quair, st. 160, ed. Skeat, S.T.S.

HOODOCK, *adj.* Like a hoody or carrion-crow; foul and greedy.

The harpy, *hoodock*, purse-proud race,
Wha count on poortith as disgrace.
Burns, Epistle to Major Logan, st. 7.

To HOOK, *v. a.* A term in golfing; to drive the ball widely to the left hand; same with *Draw*, q. v.

HOOL. Lap the *hool*; Burns, Halloween. V. COUP FRAE THE HOOL.

HORNEL, *s.* In DICT. misprinted *Kornel.*

HORNER, *s.* A worker in horn : a maker of horn spoons, cups, combs, etc. Burgh Recs. Aberdeen, III. 218. *Hornare,* Prompt. Parv.

In early times horning was an important craft in Scotland, and almost every large town had its Horner's Lane or Horner's Close, where the work was carried on. But now, through improvements in metal-working and machinery, the craft is all but extinct. A few of the simpler branches of horn-work are still followed by tinkers and gipsies.

HORT, *s.* A hurt, wound, sore. V. HORT, *v.*

The herknere bore; the holsum gray for *hortis.*
Kingis Quair, st. 156, ed. Skeat, S.T.S.
Gray, the badger. V. note under GREY.

HOSTISH, *s.* A hostelry, an inn; *hostish houses,* lodgings for travellers; Burgh Recs. Aberdeen, IV. 22, Rec. Soc.

Prob. a corr. of Fr. *hospice,* from Lat. *hospitium,* a place where strangers are entertained.

HOTE, *pret.* Called, said, declared; part. pt. *i-hote,* said to be, declared to be, Douglas, Palice of Honour, I. 17, ed. Small.

The form of the part. pt. is generally *yhote* in M. E.; but the prefix is seldom used in Scot.; it occurs, however, repeatedly, and in both forms, in the Kingis Quair. V. Gloss.

A.-S. *hátan,* to call, name, be called.

HOTE, HOIT, *part.* and *adj.* Prepared, adapted, fitted, suited, ready; Douglas, I. 17, 27, III. 183, 10, Small's ed. In last passage Ruddiman reads *hote.*

HOUFE, *s.* A large basket made of coarse wattle, used for carrying fish; Burgh Recs. Aberdeen, IV. 47, Rec. Soc.

In Orkney a similar basket made of straw is called a *huvie.* Prob. both terms are from Dan. *hov,* a bag-net, landing-net, bag. In Orkney a *huvie* is still used as a bag-net for trout. V. *Huvie.*

HOUK, *s.* V. DICT.

This word is not of Scandinavian but of Greek origin: adapted from Gk. *holkas.* See *hulk* in Skeat's Etym. Dict.

HOUP, HOUPE, *s.* A hoop, bundle, parcel, portion; Burgh Recs. Edinburgh, IV. 25. Addit. to HOUP, q. v.

HOUT, *s.* A wood, wooding, a clump of wooding; Douglas, Virgil, vii., Prol. A form of HOLT, q. v.

A.-S. *holt,* a wood; Du. *hout.*

HOUTIPAS, *s.* Lit. height and breadth: hence, guage, standard, model, pattern, sample.

". . . thairfoir the saidis baillies, counsall, and communitie, being thairwith ryplie adwysit, hes aggreit and condiscendit all in ane voce that the haill treis [i.e. barrels] that are to be sett vp aalbe of the quantitie of fyvtene gallounes, and the *houtipas* treis nocht to be translatit, and that ane gadge salbe appointit be the toun for that effect." Burgh Recs. Glasgow, 23 June, 1590, I. 153, Rec. Soc.

O. Fr. *haut et bau,* height and breadth.

HOVE, HOV, *s.* A hoof; pl. *hovis,* Douglas, Virgil, xii., ch. vi. *Hovit,* hoofed, Ibid. vii., ch. xiii.

HOW, *adv.* Why, for what reason or purpose. Still in use.

"And if thou be to ly at the Altar, *how* wantst thou a Priest to say thy soule Masse?" Blame of Kirk-buriall, ch. 11.

HOWBEID, *adv.* and *conj.* However, howsoever, though it may be; Sempill Ballates, p. 238. E. *howbeit,* which Lyndsay also uses.

Be not displeisit quhatevir we sing or say,
Amang sad mater *howbeid* we sumtyme relyie.
Lyndsay, Proclam. Thrie Estaitis, l. 22, Bann. M.S.

HOWDY, *s.* V. DICT.

For this term no satisfactory etymon has yet been offered. Regarding the one given by Jamieson, Prof. Skeat says:—"Any connection with Icel. *jóth,* a baby (which is the word which J., by these alterations, renders *iod*), is quite out of the question."

HOWSELYNGE, HOWSLYNGE, *part.* and *s.* The giving or receiving the sacrament; the Eucharist, the Sacrament.

"There is twayne whiche are named in the Church of God Sacramentes, Baptyme, and *Howslynge*;" etc. Conf. of Faith of the Swiss Churches. Wodrow Soc. Misc., I. 18.

". . . the Holy Supper of thankes, called *Howselynge,*" etc. Idem., p. 20.

"*Hooselyn* wythe the sacrament." Prompt. Parv.
"To howsylle, *communicare.*" Cath. Ang.

A.-S. *húsel,* an offering, oblation, sacrament; *húslian,* to administer the sacrament.

HOWTIDE, *s.* Ebb-tide, low-water, low-water mark. V. HOW.

". . descendens ad aquam de Annand et ab aqua de Annand ad aquam de Edin in lie *howtide.*" Reg. Mag. Sig., 1424-1513, No. 1376.

HOWYN, *part. pt.* V. DICT.

Howyn, lit. lifted : hence, lifted at the font. It is the part. pt. of the verb to *heave.* In Icel. *hefja,* means "to baptize"; see Vigfussen.

HUCH, *s.* A small heap. V. HUTCH.

HUCHE, *s.* A form of HEUCH, q. v. Alex. Scott's Poems, p. 28, ed. 1882.

HUD, HUDE, *s.* A hood, a covering for the head; "toppit *huddis* on heid," wearing peaked hoods, Houlate, l. 186.

HUDDS, *s.* Lit. hoods. V. DICT.

This term was left undefined; but it is simply the pl. of Hud explained on previous page. Indeed the two entries ought to be combined.

HUD-PYKE, *s.* V. DICT.
The etymology suggested for this term is not satisfactory. If *pyke* means to pick up, gather, collect, then, a *hud-pyke* may be a person who picks up odd or stray trifles and stows them away in his hood,—in short, a scrap-gathering save-all. But, if *pyke* means to steal, to pilfer, then, a *hud-pyke* may be one who pilfers from his neighbour's hood, i.e., one who steals the merest scraps and odd-things, a mean thief. Prof. Skeat inclines to the latter meaning: for he suggests, "*Hood-pike*=one who steals from a hood, in which no one would put away anything of much value, but might just put away temporarily things of slight value."

HUGGIT, HOGGIT, *s.* V. *Hogheid.*

HUIK, HUIKE, HUKE, HEWK, HAYK, HAK, *s.* A hook, a fishing-hook, a reaping-hook; also, a reaper, S. V. HEUCK.

HUKE, *s.* A frock, dress; a loose walking dress like a close-fitting mantle. V. HAIK.

And forto walk that freschë mayes morowe,
An *huke* sche had vpon hir tissew quhite.
Kingis Quair, st. 49, ed. Skeat, S. T. S.

Du. *huik,* a cloak; O. Fr. *huke,* "surquanie, froc;" Palsgrave. The *surquanie* or *souquenie* is explained by Cotgrave as a "frock, gaberdine." V. Gloss. Kingis Quair.

HULLOK, *s.* Hollock, a kind of sweet wine used in the sixteenth century; Burgh Recs. Aberdeen, II. 176, Sp. C., Halyburton's Ledger, p 335.

HUNDRED, HUNDER, *s.* A measure of garden-ground in Orkney, 15 ft. by 18 ft. in extent: ground sufficient for the growth of a hundred plants of kail.
In each plot or hundred the plants are set 18 inches apart, or in ten rows of twelve each. *Hundred,* therefore, means the long hundred or six score.

To HUNKER, *v. n.* To stoop, submit, yield, endure. Addit. to HUNKER.

But ought that we may do or say,
Waes me, they winna heed it;
We just mann *hunker* till the day
Their help 'll no be needit.
Walter Watson's Poems, p. 57.

HURCHIN, *s.* Urchin, dwarf, little fellow.
But *hurchin* Cupid shot a shaft,
That play'd a dame a shavie.
Burns, Jolly Beggars.

To HURD, HURDE, *v. a.* To hoard, stow or store away, conceal, hide; Burgh Recs. Edinburgh, III. 223, Rec. Soc. V. HURD, *s.*

HURDAR, HURDER, *s.* A hoarder; one who stores away or conceals his money or goods. Ibid., III. 168, Rec. Soc.

HURKIE, *adj.* Lazy, careless or slovenly in work; applied also to work that is unpleasant, troublesome, or unmanageable; West of S. V. [HURK, *v.*]

To HURKLE *down, v. n.* To submit, yield, give in. Addit. to HURKILL, q. v.
(Sup.)   S

But death cam' athort him, and sairly forfoughten,
He *hurkl'd down* quietly—prepared for to dee.
Whistle Binkie, I. 385.

HURLY-BED, HURLIE-BED, *s.* A trucklebed, trundle-bed; a bed set on *hurlies* or wheels and pushed under another: also called a *whirly-bed.*
In the houses of the working-classes the *hurly-bed* is an important piece of furniture. During the day it stands under a larger bed: at night it is *hurled* out to receive its occupants: and in the morning it is *hurled* back again.

HUSCHE, *s.* Issue, outlet. V. ISCHE.

To HUSHOCH, HUSHLE, *v. a.* To work in a hurried or careless manner, to dress or work slovenly, West and South of S.
The barmen did rattle their flails ow're the bawks,
The millers did *hushoch* their melders in sacks,
And hung the best braws that they had on their backs,
To flash at the funny bonello.
Kirrcormock's Bonello, Gall. Encycl., p. 78.

HUSHOCH, HUSHLOCH, *s.* A confused heap, tangled mass; hurried, careless, or slovenly work; also, one who works in a hurried, careless, or slovenly manner, Ibid.

HUSHOCHY, HUSHLOCHY, *adv.* and *adj.* In a hurried, careless, or slovenly manner; all of a heap: as an *adj.,* hurried, &c., Ibid.
Allied to E. *hustle,* from Du. *hutselen,* to shake up and down in a tub, bowl, or basket. A freq. form is *hotsen,* from which come our *hotch,* and *hotter,* q. v.

HUSSY, HUSSIE, HIZZY, *s.* 1. Housewife, mistress, housekeeper; pl. *husseis, hussis, hizzies;* Burgh Recs. Edinburgh, II. 30.

2. Woman, female; but in this sense generally applied to a stout, healthy young woman.
An' buirdly chiels and clever *hizzies*
Are bred in sic a way as this is.
Burns, The Twa Dogs.

This term, in both senses, is generally pronounced *hissie;* but it is not generally used in a contemptuous way, as stated by Jamieson: and even when it is so used, the contempt is communicated to it either by the tone of the speaker or by some qualifying word. V. HISSIE.

HUTH, *s.* Hollow, basin; Bann. MS., fol. 156 a. V. HUTCH.

HUVIE, *s.* A large straw basket used as a bag-net for trout; Orkney. V. *Houfe.*
Dan. *hov,* a bag-net, landing-net, bag.

HUYFE, *s.* A haunt; Douglas, III. 151, ed. Small. V. HOIF.

HYLAIR, *adj.* Agreeable, pleasant; Court of Venus, i. 157; well pleased, Ibid., ii. 480.

HYRE, *s.* Hurry, haste; Houlate, l. 424.
O. Swed. *hurra,* to whirl or swing rapidly, whence *hurry,* hurry, haste.

HYTE, *adj.* V. HITE.

I.

I. A prefix used in the *pret.* and *part. pt.*: also written Y, q. v. It is properly not a Scot. form, and does not belong to the Anglian dialect; but it was introduced by our earlier poets in imitation of Chaucer. It occurs frequently and in both forms in the works of James I., Gawin Douglas, and some of the later poets.

IAPE, *s.* and *v.* V. JAIP.

IBLENT, *pret.* and *part. pt.* Blinded, became blind.

Me thoght that thus all sodeynly a lyght
In at the wyndow come quhare that I lent,
Off quhich the chambere-wyndow schone full bryght,
And all my body so It bath ouerwent,
That of my sicht the vertew hale *Iblent.*
Kingis Quair, st. 74, ed. Skeat, S. T. S.
" Chaucer has *blente,* blinded, Troil, v. 1194 ;" Skeat.

IBUND, *part. pt.* Bound; Douglas, Virgil, Bk. iv. Prol.

ICH, *pron.* Each; Douglas, Virgil, Bk. x., ch. 2. A.-S. *ic.*

ICHANE, *interj.* Ochone; Douglas, Virgil, Bk. ix., ch. 8.

IENEPERE, *s.* V. JENEPERE.

IETE, *s.* Jet. V. *Jete.*

I-FALLYN, *part. pt.* Fallen: *I-fallyng,* Kingis Quair, st. 45, ed. Skeat.

I-HOTE, *part. pt.* Called, named, said to be: Douglas, Pal. Hon., I. 17, 27, ed. Small. V. *Hote.*
A.-S. *hâtan,* to call, name, be called.

ILAID, *part. pt.* Laid; Kingis Quair, st. 120.

ILEST, *s.* V. EELIST.

ILL-BIND, *s.* A bad shape or form: applied to articles of dress; West of S. V. [ILL-VYND].

ILL-MINTED, ILL-MINTIT, *part. adj.* Ill-meant; said or done with evil intention; West of S., Orkn. V. MINT.

ILL-THIEF, *s.* A name for the devil.
The *ill-thief* blaw the Heron south !
And never drink be near his drouth !
Burns, To Dr. Blacklock, st. 2.

ILOKIN, *part. pt.* Locked, enclosed, shut up; Kingis Quair, st. 69.
A.-S. *loca,* a fastening; Icel. *loka,* a lock : Goth. *galukan,* to shut up.

IMANG, IMANGIS, IMANGS, IMAN, *prep.* Among, amongst; also as an *adv.*, together, in one mass, as " Mix them a' *imangs ;*" *imang hands,* in hand, at command, in process, on the anvil; *imangs them, imangis themsells,* in their own hands, together, in common. West and South of S.
A.-S. *gemang,* among ; but prob. the prep. *gemang,* among, and the *adj. gemœne,* common have got mixed.

To IMBUIKE, IMBUKE, *v. a.* To register, enrol; also to retain in the register or on the roll.
" If ministers leave the Synod they are not to be *imbuiked* for their stipends." Records of Presbytery and Synod of Glasgow, 4 Apr., 1587, MS.
"That the said commissioners *imbuke* Mr. Alexander Rowat, minister at Ruglen." Ibid., 15 Jan., 1594.

IMODST, IMOST, *adj.* Unwilling, reluctant, hindering; Orkn.
Perhaps from Dan. *imod,* against, contrary to ; Sw. *emot.*

IMPERATIVE, IMPERATIUE, *s.* A command, order, demand.
"For as the Lords lawes are either *imperatiues* of good or inhibitiues of ill." Blame of Kirkburiall, ch. 16.
O. Fr. *imperatif,* imperious, commanding.

To IMPETRATE, IMPETRAT, *v. a.* To obtain by suit or entreaty.
" . . . to pass to the gouvernor and lordis of the realme, to *impetrat* letteris of justice and aggenis the said complaints." Burgh Recs. Aberdeen, I. 102, Sp. C.
Lat. *impetrare,* to obtain by entreaty: cf. O. Fr. *impetrer,* "to get by prayer, obtaine by suit ;" Cotgr.

IMPETRATION, IMPETRACIOUN, *s.* Acquirement by suit, the act of obtaining by entreaty.
" . . . and als to fortefy supple and help the saidis communitie of merchandis gild brethir for the *impetracioun* of quhatsumeuir priuilege or fredomes thocht to thame profitable at our Souerane Lord the King, lordis of parliament and counsall." Burgh Recs. Edinburgh, 10 Dec. 1518, Rec. Soc.

IMPIGNORAT, *part. pt.* Pledged, pawned.
"The tocher Kilravock gave with his daughter was nyne hundred merks ; for payment whereof he gave the lands of Kinstearie, *impignorat* to him for 300 merks." Family of Kilravock, p. 58, Sp. C.
Lat. *pignerare,* to pledge, pawn.

IMPLASTER, EMPLASTER, *s.* A plaster for wounds.
" . . . vnguents, drogs, *implasteris,* and vther mendicamentis." Burgh Recs. Edin., IV., 420.
Emplasteres occurs in p. 489 of same vol.

IMP [139] INF

Lat. *emplastrum*, a plaster for wounds. The form *plaister* is from O. Fr. *plaistre*.

IMPNE, *s.* A hymn, poem: pl. *impnis*, Kingis Quair, st. 196, S.T.S. V. YMPNE.
O. Fr. *ymne* (later *hymne*), a hymn ; Lat. *hymnus*, from Gk. M. E. *ympne*.

IMPORTURAIT, *part. pt.* Painted or pictured over with figures.
Importurait of birdis and sweit flouris,
Curious knottis, and mony hie deuise.
Douglas, Palice of Honour, I. 71, 19, ed. Small.
O. Fr. *pourtrait*, portrayed : Low Lat. *protrahere*, to depict.

IMPROBATION, *s.* V. DICT.
Misprinted Inprobation.

To **IMPRYVE,** IMPRIVE, *v. a.* V. IMPRIEVE.

IMPUT, *part. pt.* Imputed, Burgh Recs. Aberdeen, II. 15, Sp. C.

IMRIE, *s.* V. DICT.
Not from Gael., but from Icel. *eimr*, reek, vapour, and hence applied to smell.

IN, *prep.* On, in course of, during ; as, " a house *in* fire."

INTO, *prep.* In. V. INTILL.
The kyng sat *into* parleament.
Barbour, i. 602.
Not unfrequently a noun preceded by *into* expresses an adverbial sense ; as, "*into* party," partly, partially, Barbour, v. 115, 129.

INACTED, INACTIT, *part. pt.* Enacted, passed by authority ; Blame of Kirkburiall, ch. 19.

To **INAWE,** *v. a.* Same as INAWN, q. v.
Inawe is the correct form of the word ; *inawn* represents a vulgar pronunciation. V. *Out-awe*.
Inawn, a comp. of *in* and *awn*, own, used for *aw*, owe. The Scot. confusion of *aw* and *awn*, is very similar to the Eng. confusion of *owe* and *own*. Many old authors used *owe* where modern authors use *own*.

To **INBALM,** *v. a.* To embalm the dead ; Blame of Kirkburiall, ch. 7.

INBRECK, INBREK, *s.* A portion of infield pasture-land newly broken up or tilled ; Orkn. V. *Outbreck*.

IN-BURGESS, *s.* A burgess resident within the Burgh; Burgh Recs. Aberdeen, I. 37, Sp. C.

INCIDENCE, *s.* Incidental matter, unimportant particulars ; Kingis Quair, st. 7, S. T. S.

INCLINATION, INCLINATIOUN, *s.* Tendency, influence. Lat. *inclinatio*.
Thir four causis diuers variatiounis
In mans corps be sindrie *inclinatiounis*
Of the Planeitis ringand vnder the heuin.
Rolland, Court of Venus, Prol. l. 33.

INCOMPETABILL, *adj.* Incompetent, insufficient ; Douglas, Virgil, Bk. viii. prol.

INCUMMYN, INCUMMYNG, *s.* Coming in, inroad, invasion. Addit. to INCOMING.
". . . . with open proclamacione for the convocacione of the Kingis liegis again the *incummyn* of the Duc of Gloisater at the West Marche and Myddil."
Accts. L. H. Treas., 27 April, 1474, I. 49, Dickson.

IN-CUNTRIE, *s.* and *adj.* Inland.
". . . . maid a perfyte conques of that ylle, and reducit the samyn to als gryt obedience as ony pairt of the mane and *in-cuntrie*." Burgh Recs. Aberdeen, II. 232, Sp. C.

IND. V. DICT.
Prof. Skeat has pointed out that this *ind* is exactly parallel to Shakespeare's *end*, to inn, to get in, as used in Coriolanus, v. 6, 37. See Mr. Wright's note on the passage in Clar. Press ed., p. 253.

INDEGEST, *part.* and *adj.* Undigested, crude, immature ; Kingis Quair, st. 14, S. T. S. : rash, imprudent, Douglas, Virgil, Bk. xi. ch. 8. Lat. *digestus*.

INDEWIT, INDEUIT, *part. pt.* Endowed ; Burgh Recs. Aberdeen, II. 195, 196, Sp. C.

INDITE, *part. pt.* Indited, named, called.
First doun thay kest Moyses Pentateuchon,
With his storyis and Paralipomenon,
Judith, Hester, Ruth, Regum *inditc*.
Rolland, Court of Venus, iv. 3, S. T. S.
Most probably *his storyis* is a misprint for *historyis*, which the sense demands. There are very many such mistakes throughout this work.

To **INDOT,** *v. a.* To bestow, give away.
". . . the said Schir Patrik sall *indot*, gyf, and infeft certane landis . . in honor of God." Charters, &c., of Peebles, 20 Jan., 1520, p. 50, Rec. Soc.
Lat. *in*, and *dotare*, to give, bestow.

INDUCING, *part.* and *adj.* Enticing, beguiling, egging on.
"He did punishe all by proportion (the seducing serpent with a curse, the *inducing* Eua with a mutuall subjection, and the oquereasily adduced Adam with the care and sweatty labours of this militant lyfe.")
Blame of Kirkburiall, ch. 19.

INEMYE, INYMYE, *s.* Enemy ; Kingis Quair, st. 24, 156, S. T. S. Lat. *inimicus*.

INMYTEE, *s.* Enmity ; Ibid. st. 87 ; *inimitie*, ill-will, hatred, Burgh Recs. Aberdeen, I. 302, Sp. C.

To **INFANG,** *v. a.* To haul in, shorten. Addit. to INFANG. V. FANG.
Himself *infangis* the le scheit of the saill.
Douglas, Virgil, Bk. v. ch. 1, ed. Small.

INFATIGABLE, *adj.* Indefatigable ; Douglas, Bk. vi. ch. 5. O. F. *infatigable*.

INFECTION, *s.* Insinuation, evil suggestion or surmising, injurious statement.

[Declairand] thus be seir opinionis,
That lufe is foundit all of detractionis,
Mau to desaif with foull lust mundiall,
And is the way of the stait Infernall.
This and siclik with diuers *Infectionis*,
He diuulgatis as luge Imperiall.
Rolland Court of Venus, i. 746, S. T. S.

Lat. *infectus*, coloured, tinged; *inficere*, to put in, dye, stain.

INFELICITIE, INFELICITEE, *s*. Misfortune; Kingis Quair, st. 4, S. T. S.
O. Fr. *felicité*, happiness; Lat. *felicitas*.

INFIRMAT, *part. pt.* Confirmed, attested, proved.
". . qubilkis thingis, gif thai be *infirmat* of verite, ar richt displeasand." Burgh Recs. Aberdeen, I. 43, Sp. C.
O. Fr. *infirmer*, to make firm or sure, confirm: from Lat. *firmare*, to make firm.

To INFORS, *v. a.* To give force to; to rouse, strengthen. O. Fr. *enforcir*.
Infors thi wyndis, sink all thair schippis in feir,
Or scattir wyde quhair into cuntreis seir.
Douglas, Virgil, Bk. i. ch. 2, ed. Small.

INFORTUNATE, *adj.* Unfortunate, Kingis Quair, st. 24, S. T. S. V. INFORTUNE.

To INFOUND, *v. a.* To mould or form within, to infuse.
Creat within me and *infound*
Ane hart immaculat and mound.
Alex. Scott's Poems, p. 4, ed. 1882.
O. Fr. *infondre*, to infuse, fill in; Lat. *infundere*.

INFRE, *adj.* and *s.* Unfree; unfreemen. Applied to tradesmen who are not burgesses; "*infre* pakeris and pelaris," Burgh Recs. Glasgow, I. 114, Rec. Soc. V. UNFREE.
The form *unfre* occurs in the same Record.

To INGENER, *v. a.* To engender, beget; Douglas, Virgil, Bk. i. ch. 1; to stir up, cause, as, "to *engener* discord," Burgh Recs. Aberdeen, I. 343, Sp. C.; pret. and part. pt. *engenerit*.
O. Fr. *engendrer, engenrer,* to engender, procreate, produce; Burguy; Lat. *ingenerare*.

INGERS (*g* hard), INGRES, *s.* Grass or grass fields lying within the bounds of a town or village; Burgh Recs. Prestwick, 7 May, 1500, Mait. C.
The bill-pasture or common of a burgh is often called the *outgrass*.

INGON, *s.* An onion. V. INGOWNE.

INGRAIT, *adj.* Disagreeable, displeasing. Rolland, Court of Venus, ii. 296, S. T. S.

INGRATIOUS, *adj.* Grating, unpleasant, jarring.
". . . the *ingratious* discord in the eare of the least string, will mar al the mirth." Blame of Kirkburiall, ch. 5.

To INGRAVE, *v. a.* To engrave; part. pt. *ingrave*, engraven; Douglas, Virgil, Bk. v. ch. 5. O. Fr. *ingraver*.

INHERDANCE, *s.* Adherence, complicity.
". . . in thar helpyiug and supple with thair *inherdance*, warr folowaris and makaris of the said soite."
Burgh Recs. Aberdeen, 15 June, 1448, I. 17, Sp. C.
O. Fr. *inherence*, an inherence, a cleaving, &c.; Cotgr. Lat. *inhærens*, part. pr. of *inhærere*.

INHERDAND, *part. pr.* Adhering, clinging; Douglas, Virgil, Bk. x. ch. 13.
These terms occur more frequently as Anherdaus, Anherdand, Anerdant. V. ANHERD.

INHONESTIE, *s.* Indecency; refuse, rubbish. V. HONESTY.
"To tak of euery flescheonr occupeand his stok on the hie gaitt with flesche or fische, for the clengeing of thair *inhonestie* and filth of the same four pennies ilk quarter." Burgh Recs. Edinburgh, 27 Sept. 1509, Rec. Soc.

INIMITIE, *s.* V. under *Inemye*.

INJUR, *s.* Injury; Burgh Recs. Aberdeen, I. 321, Sp. C.

INLOK, *s.* Prob. an ordinary lock placed on the inside of a door, as distinguished from a "hanging lock" or padlock usually placed on the outside. Addit. to INLOKIS.

INMETTING, *part.* Measuring or meting out, selling by measure.
". . . awa that na wyne be resauit by *inmetting* with tavernaris stowppis." Burgh Recs. Edin., 31 Jan. 1543-4, Rec. Soc.
A.-S. *metan*, to measure.

INORE, *s.* Errat. in DICT.; a mis-reading of *inoghe*, enough.
This is another example of the carelessness of Pinkerton's transcriber, or of the incorrectness of the version which he transcribed; and it is not the only one in the passage which Jamieson quoted. In the four lines there are not less than four errors. Compare the version in the DICT. with the following :—
The bryghte byrdis and balde,
Had note *ynoghe* to by-halde
One that freely ta fawlde,
And one that hende knyghte.
Jamieson accepted *inore* as a genuine word; hence, both his meaning and etym. are worthless.

To INQUIET, *v. a.* To disturb, annoy; Burgh Recs. Aberdeen, I. 34, 417, Sp. C.

INSET, INSETT, *s.* Same as INSEAT, q. v.
The term is so written and pron. in Lanarks. and Stirl. Walter Watson in his "Answer to the Unco Bit Want" has
The mem I sall speak to my father,
To big us an *inset* an' spence;
Some plenishin' ayne we will gather,
An' get a' thing manag't wi' mense.
Poems, p. 67.

INSUSPECT, *part. pt.* Unsuspected, not to be suspected: "the *insuspect* auncients," the ancients who are above suspicion, or who cannot be suspected; Bl. of Kirkburiall, ch. 13.

INTEIR, *adj.* and *adv.* Entire; entirely; Alex. Scott's Poems, pp. 13, 81, ed. 1882.

INTERALLIS, INTERELLIS, *s. pl.* Entrails; Burgh Recs. Edinburgh, I. 114, II. 104, Rec. Soc.
Low. Lat. *intralia*, intestines : O. Fr. form *entrailles.*

INTEREST, INTREST, *part. pt.* Dishonoured, hurt, injured, wronged; Burgh. Recs. Glasgow, I. 109, Rec. Soc.

". . . seing dyvers of the cuntriemen and of the inhabitantis of this burght ar grytumlie *intrest* in the wynter day, throw the insufficiencie and hoillis in the said calsey." Burgh Recs. Aberdeen, II. 181, Sp. C.
O. Fr. *interess*, "dishonoured, hurt, or hindered by ; " Cotgr.

INTERLAQUEAT, *part. pt.* Entangled, captivated. Lat. *laqueatus*, id.
[Thy] minde it is sa *Interlaqueat*, [Sa fet]terit in the Net of lufe l'rophane.
Rolland, Court of Venus, l. 419, S. T. S.

To INTERLY, *v. a.* To undergo, endure. V. UNDERLY.

". . . to byde and *interly* the sentence," Burgh Recs. Prestwick, 12 Dec., 1558, Mait. C.

INTERLY, *adv.* Wholly, completely, entirely : a form of *enterly.*

To INTERMELL, *v. n.* To meddle or mingle with, deal or have to do with ; Court of Venus, ii. 172 ; also, to have carnal connection with, Ibid., iii. 521, 682, S. T. S. Addit. to INTERMELL.

INTERPRISAR, *s.* A person undertaking or engaged in a work.

". . . that nane molest nor cummer the *interprisaris* of the said wall." Burgh Recs. Peebles, p. 320.
O. Fr. *enterpris*, part. pt. of *enterprendre*, to undertake. L. Lat. *interprendere.*

INTERRUPTIONE, *s.* The act of breaking or interrupting the course of prescription. Lat. *interruptio.*

". . . of the quhilk house Williame Gray baillie, tuik doune ane dovet in takine of lauchfull *interruptione*, and fand the said hallf pennie hous and lands . . . to appertaine in propertie to the said towne of Aberdeine." Burgh Recs. Aberdeen, II. 323, Sp. C.
By so doing the bailie claimed the house as the property of the burgh, and so prevented the occupier from claiming it after the lapse of the period of prescription. This act was "analogous to the practice of the Roman law, which admitted of an interruption to any work or building by a *jactus lapilli*, the throwing down of one of the stones of the new work in presence of witnesses." Erskine's Institutes.

IN-TOLL, *s.* Entering into possession of burghal property : for short called *entry:*

also, the payment made to the bailie who transfers such property, by the party entering into possession of it.

"In our older burgh usages, burghal subjects were transferred by the bailie taking a penny for *in-toll* and a penny for out-toll." Innes, Leg. Antiq., p. 91.
The law of transference here referred to forms No. 52 of The Burgh Lawis, ed. Rec. Soc.

INTORTIVE, INTORITIVE, *adj.* Twisted, contumelious, cross, ill-tempered.
Bandownit with baill and full of brukilnes, With diuers faltis and wordis *Intoritiue*, Quhilk to Venus was all tald on bellue.
Rolland, Court of Venus, ii. 963.
Lat. *intortus*, twisted ; from *intorquere*, to twist.

INTRANT, *adj.* Entering on ; about to be entered on ; "thy *intrant* duelling," your new abode, the house you were entering into or taking possession of ; Spalding Club Misc., I. 135. V. INTRANT, *s.*
This term occurs in one of the charges of the Dittay against Jonat Leisk, a witch, whose case is recorded in the Trials of Witchcraft published in the above named vol.

To INTREIT, *v. a.* To treat, entertain, pleasure ; part. pt. *intreit*; Court of Venus, ii. 909, S. T. S.

". . . and to *intreit* hir in bed and buird, luf and kyndnes, godlie and fauourable, as it becumis ane mareit man to do to his wyf." Burgh Recs. Aberdeen, 1562, I. 345, Sp. c.
O. Fr. *entraiter*, to treat ; from Lat. *tractare*, to handle ; Burguy.

INTRESS, *s.* Entry. V. ENTRES.

INTREST, *part. pt.* V. *Interest.*

To INTUMULATE, *v. a.* To entomb, bury; Blame of Kirkburiall, ch. 19. Lat. *tumulare.*

To INUNCT, *v. a.* To anoint, smear ; part. *inunctand*, anointing, smearing.
Was nane other mayr happy nor expert, To graith and til innunct a castyng dart.
Douglas, Virgil, Bk. ix. ch. 12, ed. Small.
Invnctand venemus schaftis the ilk tyde.
Ibid., Bk. x. ch. 3.

INUNCTMENT, *s.* Ointment.
Precyus *invnctment*, salve, or fragrant pome.
Douglas, Virgil, Bk. xii. Prol.

INUNDIT, INUNDATE, *part. pt.* Inundated, flooded. Lat. *inundatus.*

"Item, for twa hundreth faill to lay the schoole flore whilk wes *invndit* with the water." Accts. Burgh of Peebles, 1631-2, p. 417, Rec. Soc.

INVER, INNER, Mouth of a stream or river, confluence of a river : cf. *Inver-ary.*

". . . quhill it eum to the first marche . . at the *inver* of the Blind burn quhair the same euteris in the Blackburne, direct forganes or aneut the said *inver.*" Burgh Recs. Aberdeen, II. 324, Sp. C.
Gael. *inbhir*, confluence of a river.

INVEROUN, *adv.* Round about, all round; Douglas, Virgil, Bk. xiii. ch. 5.
The form used by Barbour is INWEROUND, q. v.

INVESTIGABILL, *adj.* Unsearchable, inscrutable.
O Lord, thy ways beyn *investigabill.*
Douglas, Virgil, Bk. x. Prol., ed. Small.
Lat. *in,* not; *vestigare,* to track, trace.

To INVETERATE, *v. a.* Lit. to make or become old: hence, to establish, confirm, through age, use, or practice; Blame of Kirkburiall, ch. 13: part. pt. *inveterat,* established; Ibid., ch. 8: used also as an *adj.* with its modern meaning; Ibid., ch. 14.
Lat. *inveteratus,* retained for a long time.

INVICTAND, *part. pr.* Errat. in DICT. for *Inunctand,* anointing, smearing, q. v.
Had Jamieson given the whole of Ruddiman's note on this term its meaning would have been clear. The note runs thus:—"Either it should be *Invectand,* i.e. carrying, from *invectare,* i.e. *portare,* in vett. Gloss. apud Voss. ; or *infektand,* i.e. *infecting;* or *inunctand,* i.e. *anointing* or *besmearing with poison.*" V. Rudd. Gloss. Douglas.
Virgil has "calamos armare veneno," which, according to the Elphynstoun MS., Douglas rendered by "*Invinctand venemus schaftis.*" V. Small's ed. of Douglas, III. 289, 13.

INVINCENT, *part. adj.* Fettering; inthralling, captivating.
Lauds, renerence, helth, vertew, and honouris—
To the Venus I rander euermoir,
And nocht causles: with superabundant
Mirth, melodie, thow dois my hart refloir,
As *Invincent,* victour, and triumphant.
Rolland, Court of Venus, i. 296, S. T. S.
"As captivating, victorious, and triumphant."
In Gloss. rendered "*unconquered:*" this is a mistake, and mars the sense of the passage. The term is from Lat. *invincire,* to fetter.

INVITOR, *s.* Inventory; Burgh Recs. Aberdeen, I. 320, 323: this form represents the common pron.

INYON, INGON, INGYON, *s.* An onion: also called au *ingon,* West of S. V. INGOWNE.
"Item, to certane puir men for *inyons* was takin fra them for fear of the plage, xxx li. ix s." Accts. Burgh of Glasgow, 1635-6.
Inion is not uncommon in London, where the following E. proverb is popular:—
"Different people have different opinions,
Some like apples, some like *inions.*"

IOLIOUS, *adj.* Jolly. V. JOLIOUS.

IOROFFLE, *s.* V. JEROFFLERIS.
This form occurs in Kingis Quair, st. 178, ed. Skeat, S. T. S.

To IOSE, *v. a.* To enjoy. V. JOIS.

IPER (*i* as in *snipe*), *s.* Any foul liquid, ooze, mud, or sewage; Orkn.
Sae than he bent the auld wife in,
A' draigled ower wi' *iper,*
An' wi' a feedy, laid her doon
Apo' twa steuls tae sipe her.
Dennison, Orcadian Sketch Book, p. 125.

IRSCH, IRSCHE, IERSCHE, IRISCHE, *adj.* and *s.* Forms representing various pron. of *Erse,* Celtic, Gaelic, Irish; the language of the Celt, also the Celtic people or population; Dunbar and Kennedy, ll. 49, 345, 350.
V. ERSE.

ISCHE, *s.* Issue; pl. *ischis, ischeis,* emptyings, cleansings, as the contents of the stomach and entrails of a slaughtered animal; Burgh Recs. Edin., II. 253, Rec. Soc. Addit. to ISCHE.

ISLARE, *s.* and *adj.* V. ASHLAR.

IT, *pron.* Used in sarcasm or slighting for *he.*
Our Whipper-in, wee blastit wonner,
Poor worthless elf, *it* eats a dinner,
Better than ony tenant man
His Honor has in a' the lan'.
Burns, Twa Dogs.

ITHAND, *adj.* Constant and keen, continuous and blustery; *ithand wedderis,* stormy weather, fierce stormy wind. Addit. to ITHAND, q. v.
Ithand wedderis of the Eist drnif on sa fast,
It all to-blaisterit and blew that thairin baid—
Thair wis na Knicht of the Court quhat way the King raid.
Rauf Coilyear, st. 3.
The Icel. term from which *ithand* is derived is not *idin,* as in DICT., but *idhinn,* assiduous. See the explanation given in Gloss. to Skeat's Barbour, s. v. Ythand, p. 753.
The A.-S. words referred to by Jamieson have no connection with *ithand.*

I-THANKIT, *part. pt.* Thanked; Kingis Quair, st. 190, S. T. S.

IUGE, *s.* Judge; Kingis Quair, st. 82, S. T. S.

IUNYT, *part. pt.* Joined; Kingis Quair, st. 133, S. T. S. V. JUNE.

I-WONE, *part. pt.* Won; Kingis Quair, st. 108, S. T. S.

IYMP, *s.* Douglas, Virgil, Bk. i. prol. V. JYMP.

J.

JACK, *s.* A jacket, jerkin, coat of mail.

"And that ilk man, that his gudes extendis to twentie markis, be bodin at the least with a *jack*, with sleeves to the hand, or splents, and ane pricked hat, a sword and a buckler, a bow, and a schaiffe, gif he can get it." Accts. James II., No. 56, 1456, ed. 1682.

O. Fr. *Jaque*, "a Jack, or coat of maile," Cotgr.

The *jack* was a piece of defensive body-armour in the form of a jacket or surcoat usually of leather, sometimes strengthened with plates or scales of metal and quilted.

JACKO, JECKO, GEKGO, *s.* A name applied to the jackdaw: a dimin. of Jack. It is sometimes applied to a magpie also, West of S. V. under *Gekgo*.

JADGE, *s.* A gauge. V. JEDGE.

To JAG, *v. a.* V. DICT.

This word is prob. of Celtic origin. Cf. Gael. *dealg*, a prick, thorn, prickle; *dealgach*, prickly, thorny. However, the etym. suggested by Jamieson is certainly wrong.

To JAIP, *v. a.* V. DICT.

A much simpler etym. for this word is thus given by Prof. Skeat:—

"*Jaip* is from a by-form of O. Fr. *gaber*, to mock: from Icel. *gabba*, to deceive."

JAKE, *s.* V. JACK.

To JANGLE, JANGIL, *v. n.* To chatter, clatter, dispute in a noisy manner. Addit. to JANGLE, q. v.

"The iargolyne of the swallow gart the iay *iangil*." Compl. Scot., p. 39, E. E. T. S.

"Ye *jangle* an' skirl when ye fa' in wi' ither and grow pack; but the colour o' a ribbon or the shape o' a button 'll mak ye *jangle* in earnest, an' fa' out wi' ither for a week." West of S.

JAUDY, *s.* Dimin. of *jaude*, E. *jade*, a term of contempt for a woman; *jaudy*, a girl, lassie; but generally implying a girl of rude or wild disposition, or dirty, slovenly habit. Hence, *black-jaudy*, q. v.

Jaude is often used in a kind, familiar way in speaking of or to a smart growing girl: much in the same style as *wench* is used in the North of E. A mother will say with evident pride,—"Our Meg's growin' a ticht, braw *jaude*, so she is!"

In a similar strain Burns describes Nanny in Tam o' Shanter. After calling her a "winsome wench and walie," and stating some of her famous exploits, he winds up with the half-tender explanation,—

"A souple *jade* she was and strang."

JAUNER, *s.* and *v.* V. JAUNDER.

To JAUPIE, *v. n.* To break or scatter into *jaups* or small portions, as when a liquid is suddenly shaken out of a dish. V. JAUP.

Ilk auld wife stoyterin' wi' her drappie,
In teapot, bottle, stoup, or cappie,
Fu' snugly fauldit in her lappie,
Wi' couthy care,
Thou gar'st the hidden treasure *jaupie*
A' in the air.
James Ballantine, The Wee Raggit Laddie, st. 11.

JEAST, JEIST, *s.* Joist. V. JEEST.

JEDDART JUSTICE, *s.* V. DICT.

Jeddart represents the popular pron. of *Jedworth, Jedward,* old names of Jedburgh. For these forms see Index V., p. 761 of Skeat's ed. of Barbour.

JEDGRY, *s.* Standards of weights and measures; the testing and attesting of weights and measures: the dues arising from this office. Addit. to JEDGRY. V. *Gaugerie*.

To JEEG, GIG, *v. a.* To jerk, tilt, shake, rock. Addit. to JEEG, q. v.

When a' the lave gae to their play,
Then I maun sit the lee-lang day,
And *jeeg* the cradle wi' my tae,
And a' for the girdin o't.
Burns, Duncan Gray, First Version.

JEEG, *s.* A jerk, tilt, shake, rock, swing.

JEEGLE, *s.* A slight jerk, shake, or rattle: used both as a dimin. and as a frequent. of *jeeg*.

To JEEGLE, *v. a.* To jerk, shake, rattle lightly or rapidly: "I canna write if ye *jeegle* the table sae." Addit. to JEEGLE, q. v.

JEEGLY, *adj.* and *adv.* Jerky, shaky, unsteady; unsteadily.

JEEL, JEIL, *s.* Jelly; as in *calf-foot jeel*.

Now Johnnie was a clever chiel,
And there his suit he press'd sae weel,
That Jenny's heart grew saft as *jeel*,
And she birled her bawbee.
Song, Jenny's Bawbee.

Fr. *gelée*, frost, also, jelly; Cotgr.

JEOPARDIE, *s.* V. JUPPERTY.

JETE, IETE, *s.* Jet; Kingis Quair, st. 157, S. T. S.

JEVELLOUR, *s.* A jailor. V. JAUELLOUR.

JINGO RING, *s.* A girl's game; also called Merry Metanzie, q. v.

Tho' weel I lo'e the budding spring,
I'll no misca' John Frost;
Nor will I roose the simmer days,
At gowden autumn's rest;
For a' the seasons in their turn
Some kindred-for pleasures bring,
An' han' in han' they jink about
Like weans at *jingo-ring*.
William Miller, Hairst, Wh. Binkie, II. 346.

There are various forms of this game : some are short and simple ; others, long and intricate, like the one described in the last para. under MERRY-METANZIE, q. v. This form is played in various districts of the West. of S., and is a source of great amusement to the players.

All the varieties of the game, however, agree in their method of play, which is as follows :—The parties engaged join hands and form a circle ; then move round in quick lively step, singing the introductory verse—a form of which is given under MERRY-METANZIE ; then, as each verse proceeds, the motion and actions of the party are adapted to the particulars of the song.

A very good specimen of the game, including song, music, and directions for playing, is given in "Sangs for the Bairns," a valuable little work ed. by Andrew Stewart, Dundee.

To JIVE, v. a. To fetter, shackle ; hence, to arrest, capture. E. *gyve*, id.

Argyle was ta'en, and a' his men ran away.
When Douglas *jived* him,
Rived him,
Drived him,
And of all hopes his stars had deprived him.
Hogg's Jacobite Relics, I. 176.

Welsh. *gefyn*, a fetter, gyve ; Gael. *geimheal*, id.

JOGS, JOGES, JOGIS, s. V. JOUGS.

JOLIOUS, IOLIOUS, adj. Jolly, full of jollity.

So Ioyous is, so Iocund for to vse,
So *Iolious* repleit of all plesance.
Rolland, Court of Venus, i. 315, S. T. S.

O. Fr. *jolif, joli*, jolly : from O. Norse *jol*, a great feast : whence Swed. *jula*, to feast, and E. *Yule*. V. Burguy's Gloss.

JONET-FLOUR, s. V. JONETTE.

Jonet is from O. Fr. *jaulnet*, yellowish (dim. of *jaulne*, Mod. Fr. *jaune*, yellow), and was applied to different flowers : see Notes in DICT., and s. v. Jaulnette, in Cotgrave. Hence, when there is no qualifying or distinguishing term along with the name, it is almost impossible to determine which flower is meant. The Jonet-flower, however, that is referred to in the passage from the Kingis Qubair, is represented as having beautiful plumes, and this characteristic feature is found in only one of the flowers that bear the name, viz., the Great St. John's Wort, which has its stamens parted and grouped in most beautiful tufts or plumes. A single glance at that flower will convince the reader that it was to it the poet referred ; and this opinion is confirmed by Cotgrave's definition of *Jaulnette*, as "Harding, . . great S. John's Wort." V. Skeat's ed. of The Kingis Quair, p. 70, where the foregoing explanation first appeared.

JOROFFLE, s. A gilly-flour. V. JEROFFLERIS.

JOSE, JOSING, JOYSING. V. JOIS.

JUBISH, DUBISH, adj. Doubtful, suspicious ; having reason to doubt, suspect, or fear. Both forms are used in West of S.: the first is common iu Orkn. Corrupt forms of *dubious*.

"Patie was unco sweir tae rise ; and sweir was he tae tak the lock aff o' the haas-iron ; for he was terrably *jubish* o' Brockie's muckle fit. For ye see hid was t'onght a muckle smolie on ony aen wha was joggid, gin he deud no kick the offisher whin he tenk him oot." Dennison, Orcadian Sketch-Book, p. 33.

JUDAS CROIS, JUDAS CROCE, s. The centrepiece of the Paschal candlestick used in churches.

"Item, for the mending of the sepulture, the chapell dure, and *Judas crois* [in the Kingis chapell Striuilling], iiis." Accts. L. H. Treas., 1494-5, I. 228, Dickson.

"The paschal candlestick in churches, which was usually of brass, had seven branches, from the seventh or middle one of which a tall thick piece of wood painted like a candle, and called the Judas of the Paschal, rose nearly to the roof, and on the top of this was placed at Eastertide the paschal candle of wax." Ibid., Gloss.

To JUGGILL, v. a. To beguile, hoodwink, deceive.

Thairfoir he *juggillis* yow, quo I.
For Juggillaris, that all men begylis,
Divertis thair eis with subteill wylis,
Sum uder obiect to behauld
Till thay haif wrocht the thing thay wauld.
Rob Stene's Dream, p. 16, Mait. C.

O. Fr. *jogler, jugler,* to deceive cleverly ; Lat. *joculari*, to jest, make fun of ; Burguy.

JUGGS, &c., s. pl. V. DICT.

A much simpler and more satisfactory etym. for this word is given in the following note.

"*Juggs* is simply the Fr. *joug*, a yoke, and so derived from Lat. *iugum* at second hand. The E. *jug*, a cant term for a prison (also called jocosely a *stone jug*), is the same word. The *yoke* is the iron collar." Skeat.

JUIP, JUYP, s. V. JUPE.

JUPE, s. V. DICT.

The Fr., Ital., and other terms given by Jamieson for this word are all of Arabic origin : see Littré, Scheler, and Brachet. The Arabic word is *jubbat, jubbet* (final *t* is not sounded), an under-garment, a waistcoat quilted with cotton. V. Richardson's Dict., p. 494.

JUPERTY, JUPERDY, s. A feat or display of magic or sleight-of-hand, a pretence, deception. Addit. to JUPPERTY.

He couth werk wounderis quhat way that he wald :
Mak of a gray gus a gold garland ;
A lang sper of a betill for a berne bald ;
Nobillis of nut schellis, and siluer of sands.
Thus jowkit with *juperdys* the jangland Ja.
Houlate, l. 789, Asloan MS.

O. Fr. *jeu parti,* a divided or drawn game : hence the idea of risk, chance, skill, &c.

K.

KAEST, *s.* A dunghill, sink; Orkn. V. **KEUSS**.

KAIM, *s.* A low ridge, etc. V. DICT.
This word in all its applications is the same as *comb*, and is not allied to Fr. *cime*, which is from Gk. *kuma*. It is from A.-S. *camb*, a comb, crest, ridge; Dan. Sw. Du. *kam*, Icel. *kambr*. See COMB in Skeat's Etym. Dict.

KAIPIT, *part. pt.* Coped, covered, topped; Burgh Recs. Glasgow, I. 148.

KAIR-SKYN, *s.* A calf's skin. Misprint in DICT.

KAKA, *s.* Wild hemlock; Orkn.

KALENDIS, *s. pl.* Kalends, beginnings; "*kalendis* of comfort," Kingis Quair, st. 177.
Worschippe, ye that loueris bene, this may,
For of your blisse the *kalendis* are begonne,
And sing with vs, away, winter, away !
    Ibid., st. 34, Skeat's ed., S.T.S.
This is an imitation of Chaucer's *kalendes of hope*, Troil., ii., 7, and *kalendis of eschaunge*, Id. v. 1646.

KALSHES, *s. pl.* V. KILCHES, *Calshes.*

KAMSTARY, *adj.* V. CAMSTERIE.

KANER, KAINER, *s.* Overseer, bailiff, water-bailiff. V. *Canare.*
"Item, to the Lairdis *Kaner* for keiping of the yair anno lxxxv. [1590] thre bollis victuell, inde ix. lib."
Thanes of Cawdor. p. 193, Sp. C.
This term is still used in North of S. as the name of a water-bailiff.

KAR-GAIT, *s.* A cart-road; Burgh Recs. Prestwick.

KAUCH (gutt.), KEACH, KIAUGH, CAIGH, *s.* Fighting, struggling, battle, bustle, anxious exertion, anxiety about one's family or business. Addit. to KAUCH, q. v.
His wee-bit ingle blinkan bonilie
His clean hearth-stane, his thrifty Wifie's smile,
The lisping infant prattling on his knee,
Does a' his weary *kiaugh* and care beguile,
And makes him quite forget his labor and his toil.
    Burns, Cottar's Saturday Night, st. 3.
The first ed. read *kiaugh and care;* but in the ed. of 1793 the phrase was altered to *carking cares*. In latest eds. the original reading has been adopted.
Jamieson's etym. of *kauch* is wrong. The word is of Celtic origin, being from Gael. *cathaich* (pron. *kdech*), to fight; *cathachadh* (pron. *kiacha*), fighting, struggling; from *cath*, a fight.

(Sup.)   T

KAVEL, KEVEL, *s.* A lot. V. CAVEL.
An interesting illustration of the legal phrase "*by kavel or lot*," occurs in Erskine's Institutes, in the passage which tells how a Sheriff "kens a widow to her terce." It runs thus :—"She cannot possess any lands exclusive of the heir till the Sheriff ken her to her terce, by dividing the lands between the heir and her. In this division, after determining *by kavel or lot* whether to begin by the sun or the shade, i.e., by the east or the west, the Sheriff sets off the first two acres for the heir, and the third for the widow; and on the division of the whole in this manner, the widow, by herself or her procurator, takes instruments in the hands of a notary public."

KAVIE, *s.* V. CAVIE.

KEAPING-STANE, *s.* Coping, covering. Addit. to KEAPSTONE.
". . . and the *keaping-stane* to be of outlairis, frie wark, and boulted with irne fra the eist end to the wast end on ilk syd." Burgh Recs. Aberdeen, II. 300, Sp. C.

KEBBUCK-HEEL, *s.* The end-piece or remnant of a cheese. V. KIBBUCK.
O wives be mindfu', ance yoursel
How bonnie lads ye wanted,
An' dinna, for a *kebbuck-heel*,
Let lasses be affronted
On sic a day !
    Burns, Holy Fair, st. 25.

KECHAN, *s.* Same as KEECHIN, q. v.; Alex. Wilson's Poems, p. 67, ed. 1876.
Wrongly rendered *yeast* in Gloss.

KEDDIE, *s.* A little kid; "ane lamb *keddie*," a young lamb, Witchcraft, Spald. Club. Misc., I. 129.

To **KEDGE**, *v. a.* To fill, stuff, gormandise: "*kedged* like a king" is a common saying after a good meal.

KEDGE-KYTE, *s.* Lit. a fill-belly; a glutton, a coarse or greedy person at table; also applied to a big-bellied person.

KEELD, KELDE, *part. pt.* Marked with keel or ruddle; "the lambs are a' *keeld*." V. KEEL.
Thow has thy clamschellis and the burdoun *kelde*.
    Dunbar and Kennedie, L 431.

KEEVE, *s.* V. DICT.
A.-S. *cyfe*, from which this word is derived, is prob. borrowed from Lat. *cupa*, a vat. *Keeve* is a form of KIVE, q. v.

the sowen-seeds were stoepod and prepared; a *saut-kit*, or barrel, for storing salt; and various others. But in every case the *kit* was a wooden vessel for holding the stock, store, or supply of the article it contained; and the store or supply it held, as also the quantity required to fill it, was also called a *kit*.

KITTIE, COOTIE, *s.* A dimin. of *kit*; a small tub or shallow wooden vessel that can be easily carried about by hand; West of S.
O. Dn. *kitte*, a tub; Mod. Du. *kuip*.

KITLING, KITLIN, *s.* A kitten. V. KITTLING. Icel. *ketlingr*, a kitten.

KITTIE, *s.* V. DICT.
The various uses of this term prove that Callander's etym. is correct. *Kittie* is certainly a dimin. of *Kate*; and it is so used in P. Plowman, B. xviii. 426.

KIVE, *s.* Same as *keeve*, a tub, q. v.
Kive is the more correct form; as the word is derived from A.-S. *cyfe*. V. *Keeve*.

KLYPE, KLYTE, *v.* and *s.* V. CLYPE, CLYTE.

KNABBIE, *s.* Lit. a small *knab* or knob; a short bit of wood to pass through the eye of a rope used as a stall-tether; same as *Knool*; Orkn. V. MUNKIE.

KNAIF, KNEYF, KNAVE, *s.* A child, servant. V. KNAW.
Used also as an *adj.*; as in KNAVE-BAIRN, q. v.

KNAIFSCHIP, *s.* V. KNAVESHIP.

KNAIP, *s.* A servant. V. KNAPE.

KNAP, *s.* Knop, knob, cover, projection; as, "The *Knap* of hir elbow," Burgh Recs. Glasgow, II. 242, Rec. Soc. Addit. to KNAP, q. v.

KNAPPISKUA, *s.* V. KNAPSCHA.

KNAPPOLD, *s.* V. KNAPPEL.

KNAPPY, *adj.* In small roundish lumps, abounding in small lumps; Orkn.

KNAUCHT, *part. pt.* Caught, adopted; Douglas, Virgil, i. ch. 5.

To KNAW. *v. a.* To make known, confess, own. Addit. to KNAW, q. v.
". . . the said Thomas sal fyrst syt done on his kne and tak the nakit nyff that he hurt the said William with in his haude, and opynly *knaw* that he has offendit til him, and deliuer him the said knyf, to do with it that he will." Burgh Recs. Aberdeen, 2 Dec., 1467, I. 27, Sp. C.

KNAWIN, *part. pt.* Made known, declared, adjudged, allotted, put in possession.
". . . ther is now cammyn befor yow the dochtir of the fyrst wyff clamande the said lande as sir thairto and to be *knawin* be yow to the samyn and richt." Ibid., 20 Mar., 1468, I. 28, Sp. C. V. NOTE under KEN, *s.* 6.

KNAWING, *s.* Knowledge; *tofore knawing*, foreknowledge; Kingis Quair, st. 148, Skeat's ed., S.T.S. V. KNAW.

KNAWLEGEING, *s.* Knowledge, information, means of knowing or learning.
Yit nevertheles we may half *knawlegeing*
Of God Almychtie be his creatouris.
Henryson, Preiching of the Swallow, l. 29.

KNEEF, *adj.* Active. V. DICT.
The etym. of this term is correct enough; but the assertion that Fr. *naif*, is derived from Lat. *gnavus*, is utterly wrong; they have no connection whatever. Fr. *naif* is from Lat. *nativus*. V. LITTRE' and BRACHET.

To KNEISTER, *v. n.* To creak; applied also to the sound made in smothering a laugh; *part. pr. kneisterin*, as in *kneisterin shoon*, creaking shoes.
Prob. allied to Dan. *knuse*, to bruise, crush; Icel. *knosa*, A.-S. *cnysian*.

To KNICK *with nay*. V. NECK, NYKIS.

To KNIP, KNYP, *v. a.* To crop, nibble; as, "*to knip* the grass;" part. pt. *knyp*, Douglas, Virgil, xii. prol.; but commonly *knipt* or *knypt*.
Icel. *hneppa*, to cut short. Cf. E. *nip*.

To KNITT, KNYTT, *v. a.* To combine, strengthen; Kingis Quair, st. 194; part. pt. *knet*, knit, twined; Ibid., st. 31. Addit. to KNET, q. v.

KNITTEN, *part. pt.* Knit, compacted, built. This form is still used.
For William wichttar wes of corss
Nor Sym, and better *knittin*,
Sym said he sett nocht by his forss,
Bot hecht he sowld be hittin.
Alex. Scott's Poems, p. 24, ed. 1882.

To KNOOL, KNULE, NOOL, *v. a.* To beat with the knuckles or closed fist, to thrash; also, to beat or nag on the knuckles, as in the game of marbles called Nags, q. v. West of S.
Knool is simply a contr. form of *knuckle*.

To KNOOL, KNULE, KNUL, NOOL, *v. n.* To knuckle down or place the closed fist on the ground to receive nags; also, to bow, yield, submit, fawn, cringe: part. pt. *knoolt, knuled*, is frequently used as an *adj.*, meaning crushed, dispirited, henpecked; but generally written *noolt, nuled*, q. v.

KNORHALD, *s.* Prob. the same as KNAPPEL, q. v.
Oak-wood cut into battens or staves is called *knappel*, or *knorral*; and the battens are called *knappalds, knappolds, knapholts*; hence, *knorral* should give *knorralds* or *knorhalds*.
"Et pro duobus millibus bordarum, xxij li. Et pro ducentis *knorhaldis* vj li." Exchequer Rolls.

KNU [149] LAD

KNUCKLE-DUMPS, s. pl. V. NAGS.

KOO, s. A form of *kook*, the act of cowering, stooping, inclining forward; "*at cap and koo*," at rising and falling, applied to the motion of a ship at sea; Sempill Ballates, p. 231. V. KOOK, *Cap.*

KORT, *adj.* Short; "ane *kort* sleif," Burgh Recs. Aberdeen, I. 175, Sp. C.
O. Fr. *cort*, from Lat. *curtus*, short. E. *curt.*

KOSCHE, *adj.* Hollow; and as applied to a tree decayed, as, "the mekle *kosche* fir tree," Douglas, Virgil, v. ch. 8.
Gael. *cosach*, abounding in hollows, recesses, crevices; M'Leod and Dewar.

KOUHUBIE, s. A cow-herd; Douglas, Virgil, viii. prol. V. COWHUBBY.

To KOW, v. a. To eat greedily, to munch; Orkn. V. Cow.

KOW, s. The custom or tax of a cow claimed by the Church on certain occasions. Addit. to Kow, q. v.

In illustration of the manner and the spirit in which this old claim was exacted by the Church, see the second quotation under UMAST CLAITH in DICT. The following passages state how this vexatious exaction was abolished.

On that, sir Scribe, I tak ane instrument
Quhat do ye of the corspresent, and *kow*?
Lyndsay, Thrie Estaites, l. 2819.

We will decerne heir, that the Kingis grace
Sall wryte unto the Paipis Holines :
With his consent be proclamatioun,
Baith corspresent and *cow* we sall cry doun.
Ibid., l. 2832.

An interesting statement regarding "the corspresent and kow" of the vicarage of Tain is given in Orig. Paroch., II. pt. 2, p. 427. It show show the "crying donn" of these old Church claims affected the vicar.

"The said haill provestrie consisteit in offrandis, and the vicarage of Tain, of the whilk vicarage the kirk kow and clayth with the pash offrandis ceiss, and only restis teind lamb and teind lynt, quhilk will not extend to xx lib. or thairby."

The passage quoted in DICT. occurs at l. 3903. Jamieson left this term undefined; but in a note he gave Pinkerton's rendering, which is wrong.

KOY, *adj.* V. DICT.
Ruddiman is certainly correct in making this term the same as E. *coy*; Fr. *coi*.

KRÆM, KRAME, s. Booth, shop. V. CREAM, CRAIM.
This form is not common, but was used by Sir W. Scott in Rob Roy, ch. xiv.

To KREEST, v. a. To press, squeeze; Orkn.

KREEST, s. Pressure, crush; applied also to a falsetto voice, a forced cry, groan, Ibid.
Dan. *kryste*, Swed. *krysta*, to squeeze.

To KRINE, KREEN, v. a. and n. V. CRINE.

KUAFE, s. A coif or net.
Her brycht tressis envolupit war and wound
Intill a *kuafe* of fyne gold wyrin threid.
Douglas, Virgil, iv. ch. 4, Small's ed.
O. Fr. *coif*, *coiffe*; Low Lat. *cofia*, a cap; in M. H. Ger. *kuffe*, *kupfe*, a cap worn under the helmet.

KUNER, s. A taster. V. *Cunnar.*

KUSSEN, *part. pt.* V. *Kissen.*

KYLES, s. pl. A game of chance, called also nine-pins; also, the pins used in the game. Addit. to KILES, q. v.

The great Argyle led on his files,
I wat they glanc'd for twenty miles ;
They hough'd the Clans like nine pin *kyles*.
Burns, Shirra-Moor, s. 2.

KYMMEOUN, s. Same as KIMMEN, q. v.

KYNE, s. Kindred; Douglas, Virgil, i. ch. 3, Small's ed. A.-S. *cyn.*

KYRSET, s. KIRKSETT, *Kerset.*

KYTLE, v. and s. Tickle. V. KITTLE.

L.

LACHT, s. A vulgar pron. of laft, a loft, q: v. V. also *Laft.*

LADLE, LADILL, s. 1. A burghal duty charged on grain, meal, and flour, brought to market for sale; also, the proceeds or income obtained from that duty.

The Ladle was an important item of the Common Gude in old market burghs, and was farmed or set yearly to the highest bidder. At first, and for centuries, the duty was paid in kind—a ladleful from every boll, but latterly it was commuted to a money payment.

"The casualities of the mercat, callit the *Ladill*, is sett to Robert Millare, meleman, quhill Whitsonetysday nixtocum, for the sowme of nyne acoir merkis money, to be payit at the termes vait and wont; souertie for payment thairof, Johne Wilsoun, merchant; the termes are third in hand, third at myd terme, and the rest at Beltane." Burgh Recs. Glasgow, 1 June, 1574, I. 14, Rec. Soc.

2. The dish or vessel used as the measure in exacting this duty; also, the box used in churches for receiving the collection.

LAW [152] LEA

Lawdis is here used like *laudery*, loose-living, which Jamieson has wrongly connected with the A.-S. verb to drink, pour out. Both terms are much more closely allied to E. *lewd*. V. *Laudery*.

LAWRENCE, LAURENCE, LOURENCE; LAWRIE, LAURIE, LOURIE; LAWRY, LAURY, LOURY, *s*. 1. Various forms of the common name for the fox; the first set represents the name in full; the others the colloquial forms of it.

. . . Behald thais sympill scheip,
But bird or bound that sould thame kepe;
I lang for blude latt ws go byte,
And quenche our hungry appetyte.
O quhat a pray, sa fair and fatt !
Quod *Lawrence*, sirs, thank me for thatt !
Rob Stene's Dream, p. 16.

All the varieties of the full name occur in this satirical poem on Chancellor Maitland; but the form generally adopted by authors is *Lourence*. Most frequently, however, the term occurs in the contracted and colloquial forms *laurie*, *lourie*; and the frequency with which it occurs, together with the number of authors who use it, testify that the name has been in common use all over the country for centuries past.

Dr. Jamieson's remarks upon this word (under the form *Lowrie*), and specially his statement regarding the etymology of it, are practically of little worth; indeed, the greater part of the article is quite outside of the subject, and even what relates to it is not satisfactory. The name is derived from O. Fr. *larronceau*, " a pilferer, filcher, little theefe ;" Cotgr. The aptness of the term quite explains its acceptance and general adoption all over Scotland. Besides, the shorter forms Laurie, Lawry, Lourie, are represented in O. Fr. by the forms *larron*, and *lerre*, thief, plunderer. V. Cotgrave's Dict.

2. The great bell of a church was called Laurence, Lourie, Lang Lourie.

In olden times this bell was rung on important occasions only; but after the Reformation it was used as the workman's call-bell in the morning, and the bed-bell at night. V. Burgh Recs. Glasgow, I. 292.

" And he [the sacristan] sale ger ring curfoyr continuale, at hour and tyme aucht and wont. A tour he sal nocht ring *Laurence* of the saule messe nor menyngis, bot for the nobill and honorabill personis of the town, without leif of the alderman and the counsale." Burgh Recs. Aberdeen, I. 72, Oct. 1503, Sp. C. See also III. 40.

In cathedral and other large churches the bells were generally dedicated to favorite or patron saints; but in Scotland the great bell was commonly allotted to St. Laurence, and went by his name. In many of our large towns the bell rung at ten o'clock, night, is called Lourie, lang Lourie, big Lourie; and its call is still, at least acknowledged to be, the signal for respectable people to retire homeward from calls or amusements.

LAWRY, LAWR, *s* Laurel, the emblem of excellence, victory, &c. Fr. *laurier*.

. . . thow suld be hye renownit,
That did so mony victoryse opteyn ;
Thi cristall helme with *lawry* suld be crownyt.
Dunbar, *Welcum to Lord B. Stewart*, l. 67.

LAWTOCHE, *s*. Loyalty. V. LAUTE, LAWTA.

To LAY *tae* or *to*, *v. a*. Besides the primary meaning, put, bring, or place together, this

v. is used with the sense of (1), to lay on, exert, apply, expend; as, "Ye may *lay tae* the water now," i.e., let on or apply the water, as in starting a mill; " Begin now, and *lay tae* your hale strength," i.e., exert or expend it.

2. To close, shut; as, "*Lay tae* the lid now," i.e., close it; "*Lay tae* the door ahint ye," shut it.

3. *To lay a hand tae* or *to*, *to lay one's hand tae* or *to*, to commence, begin, take part in; to undertake, become responsible for; as, "I have not *laid a hand tae't* yet ;" " Na, na, I canna *lay my han*' to that wark, nor will I provide siller for't."

LAY-TAE, LATHIE, *s*. 1. A hold-fast built into the wall of a byre at the head of each stall, and to which the cow is closely tied up: in Orkney called a *lathie*.

2. A contest of any kind; as, " The twa cast-out, and had a grand *lay-tae*; but I jist let them hae't to ;" West of S.

To LAYNE, *v. a*. To conceal, hide; "noght to *layne*," not to hide anything, to tell the whole truth. V. DICT.

The three entries under this heading ought to be combined : they represent the same word under slightly different meanings. In the first entry the definition is wrong; in the second, which has no definition, the statements are in part correct: in the third, the definition is correct, but needless difficulties are raised regarding its application. In all three entries, however, the etymology is wrong, almost entirely.
The origin of the term is Icel. *leyna*, to hide, conceal.

LAYS, *s. pl.* Leas; or short for *lasors*, *leasures*, *lesures*, low grassy lands, pastures. V. LESURIS.

Upon that night when Fairies light
On Cassilis Downans dance,
Or owre the *lays* in splendid blaze,
On sprightly coursers prance.
Burns, *Halloween*, st. 1.

To LAYT, *v. a*. To look for, seek, seek after. Addit. to LAYT, q. v.

Del. the note under this term: the suggestion is a mistake.
This term is not common in S., and is now almost confined to the southern and border districts. Its compound *forleit*, to forsake, desert, is still used in various districts. V. FORLEIT in DICT.
Icel. *leita*, to seek, search ; Dan. *lede*.

LEADER, LEDAR, *s*. A driver, carter, carrier ; " *ledares* of burne," water-carriers, carriers of burn-water; Burgh Recs. Edinburgh, II. 141, Rec. Soc.

Water for culinary purposes was called *spring* or *well-water*, and *hard-water ;* and that used for washing, cleansing, &c., was called *burn* or *river-water*, and *soft-water*. Until comparatively late years the occu-

LEA [153] LEK

pation of water-carrier was followed by a large number of men and women ; some carried by hand, i.e., in pails, stoups, large tin cans, or a stand*; some by barrow, i.e., in a barrel set on a barrow ; and some by cart—those were the *leaders*. The quantity taken at each load by these carriers was called a *gang*.
"The stand was a barrel open at one end, and carried between two by means of spokes, as a hand-barrow is.

LEAME, *adj*. Splendid, gaudy. V. LEME, *v.* and *s*.

"For as Lucanus to Cesar sayes (who after the Pharsalian defeate of Pompey his host did inhibite to burne, that is after the Romane vse to bury the slane), *Capit omnia tellus quæ genuit, coelo tegitur qui non habet venam*. The which transuersed meanes—.
The earth is ready to receiue her broode,
And heauens will couer when *leame* tombes cannot do'ide.
Blame of Kirkburiall, ch. 2.

To **LEAP**, LEIP, *v. a*. To parboil. V. LEEP.

LEARY, *s*. A lamplighter. V. LEERIE.

LECTION, LECTIOUN, *s*. Election, choice.
". . . and than the court fensyt about, ilke man be his awn vos gaf thair *lectioun* to the sayd Schir John, and gaf hym lof thairtyll." Burgh Recs. Peebles, 14 June, 1462.
Lat. *lectio*, election, choice. Cf. the *lectio senatus* of the Romans.

LEDIN, LEDNE, LIDNE, *adj*. Lead, leaden, for or suited for lead ; as, "*ledin* nalis," nails used in fastening lead.
". . . for casting of the *lidue* gutters and mend-of thame." Burgh Recs. Edinburgh, II. 367, Rec. Soc. "Item for plantiour nalis, *lidne* nalis, and dur nalis to the lacht [i.e., loft] and uther wark." Ibid., II. 366.
A.-S. *leid*, Dan. and Sw. *lod*, lead ; M. E. *leed*.

LEENGYIE, *adj*. V. DICT.
This is simply a var. of "Lenyie," and should be combined with it : both forms are still used.

LEET, *s*. One portion of many, etc. V. DICT.
In last para. of this entry, A.-S. *hlete* should be A.-S. *hlét*.

LEEVIN LANE. V. DICT.
This expression is not peculiar to Ayrs. : it is common in various districts, even in Orkney also, where it is pron. *leevin leen*.

To **LEEZE**, LEESE, *v. a*. V. LEIS, LEIS ME.

LEFFEN, *s*. The name given to a farm or township in the Western Isles consisting of a halfpenny land.
"In the Islands the township usually consisted of what was called a penny land, but occasionally of the halfpenny land, termed *Leffen*. These penny lands, however, were of different sizes." Skene's Celtic Scotland, III. 371.
Gael. *lethphein*, comp. of *leth*, half, and *peighinn*, a penny.

LEG-DOLLAR, LEGED-DOLOUR, LEGGIT-DOLLOR, *s*. A coin of the United Provin-
(Sup.) U

ces worth about fifty-eight shillings, Scots. Errat. in DICT.
"Johne Rankine persewed Johne Ross, taliyour, for withholding from him ane *leged dolour*, at 5 a., anent the niffer of ane horse." Corshill Baron-Court Book, Ayr and Wigton Arch. Coll., IV. 104.
Not "a dollar of Leige," as suggested by Jamieson, but so called from its having the "impression of a man in armes with one leg, and a shield containing a coat of armes covering the other leg, upon the one syd, which does usually pass at the rate of fiftie-eight shillings Scots money." Coinage of Scotland, by R. W. Cochran-Patrick, Vol. II. p. 158, No. xlv. Addit. to LEG-DOLLOR.

LEGENCE, *s*. Licence, permission, liberty.
". . . and the *legence* gevin to vnfremen to saill with merchandeise, and we and occupy the fredome of this gud tounc." Burgh Recs. Aberdeen, I. 94, Sp. C.
Lat. *legare*, to send, depute, appoint, and hence allow in the sense of make lawful ; *leg* being here the stem of *lex*, a law.

LEG-HARNES, *s*. Greaves, armour for the legs ; Douglas, Virgil, xii. ch. 7.

LEIDSTERNE, *s*. Loadstar, pole-star. V. [LODE-STERNE.]
And sik Arcturus qubilk we call the *leidsterne*.
Douglas, Virgil, i. ch. 1, Small's ed.

To **LEIND**, *v. n*. To go, wend ; also, to consort, connect, ally. Addit. to LEIND, q. v.
Thay wald with nobill men be nemmit,
Syne laittandly to lawar *leindis* ;
So find I thair affectioun
Contrair thair complexioun.
Alex. Scott's Poems, p. 71, ed. 1882.
"*To lawar leindis*," to men of lower rank they go of their own accord, i.e., they connect themselves, consort, cohabit. Jamieson's etym. is correct, viz., *lenda*, to land, settle, take up one's abode ; but it also means "to close with one another ;" Cleasby and Vigfusson ; and the term has a much wider range of meaning than is represented in the DICT. It means "to go, wend," in Allit. Rom. Alexander, II. 379, 393 ; "to rest, tarry for a season," Ibid., l. 221, Barbour, iii. 747, v. 125 ; "to consort, cohabit," as in the example from Scott ; "to abide, dwell," as in quotations in DICT., q. v.

LEINE, *s*. Misprint for Leme. V. DICT.

To **LEIR**, LEAR, *v.a*. To learn ; to teach. V. LARE.

LEISK, LESK, *s*. The groin. V. LISK.

To **LEK**, *v. n*. To leak, drain, filter.

LEK, *s*. 1. A leak ; the drop from a tap or spigot ; also, leakage ; as, "Set a can to kep the *lek*. The *lek* rins to a gallon a week."
2. The pit in which a tanner soaks the bark, and from which the tan-liquor is drawn off for use.
It is so called because the liquor leaks or filters from it into a side-chamber called the *lek-ee* ; and from this well it is drawn off to the tan-pits.

LEKNESS, s. Leakiness, leaking.
" . . and cum within the hawin and port of the said burgh be ane north eist wind and *lekness* of ane of thair saiil achippis." Burgh Recs. Aberdeen, I. 439, 16 July, 1508, Sp. C.
Icel. *leka*, to drip, dribble, leak ; Dan. *læke*, Du. *lekken ;* M. E. *leken.*

LE-LANE, LEA-LANE, *adv.* All alone, lonely, in loneliness ; " my *le-lane,*" all by myself, with no one near me, or with no one belonging to me.

LEMANRIE, LAMENRIE, LAME, *s.* The arts, practices, or delights of lovers ; hence, free-love, carnal delight, fascination of love ; also, illicit love, harlotry, adultery. Addit. to LEMANRY, LAMENRY, q. v.
Gif siclik lufe cunnnis of your *Lamenrie,*
Your luif and lust heir planelic I deny.
    Rolland, Court of Venus, iii. 481, S. T. S.
With ardent lufe scho holdis me at hart,
In clene curage and vailyeant victorie,
Scho feidis me with fude of *Lamenrie,*
Scho cleithes me with cloikis of curtesie.
    Ibid., i. 397.
In last extract misprinted *Lameurie ;* and in Gloss. is defined as "sorcery," in both passages. Such a meaning is impossible in either passage, and is not implied by the term itself. Glamoury, in the sense of the fascination of love, love-spells, might serve to represent some of the applications of the term. V. LEMANE, LEMMAN.
The contracted form *lame* occurs in Henryson. Pract. Medecyne, l. 20.

To LEME, *v. n.* V. DICT.
"The E. *gleam,* though so often confused with *leme,* is in no way allied to it. *Leme* is A.-S. *léoma ;* gleam is A.-S. *glǽm.*" Skeat.

LENCE, *s.* Lit. a lance, i.e., a prick ; "*worth a lence,*" worth a prick, worth speaking of, in the least, at all.
This four scheldis of pryce in to presence
War chenyeit so chevalrus, that no creatur
Of lokis nor lynx mycht lous worth a *lence.*
    Houlate, l. 606, Asloan MS.

To LENCH, *v. a.* and *n.* To spring, bound ; as, "He *lenched* owre the burn like a grew."
West of S. Addit. to LENCH, q.v.

LENCH, *s.* A spring, bound, leap.
"As for Ieroboams Prophet . . the sense is, that being preuented by death (as he was by the lyons *lench*) he should neuer see home nor ly in his common laire by a peaceable death." Blame of Kirkburiall, ch. 19.
Fr. *lancer,* to hurl, fling ; *lance,* a lance ; from Lat. *lancea.*

LENTEN, *s.* Spring, the spring season ; Orkn. Addit. to LENTREN, q. v.

To LEP, *v. a.* To lap, lick up ; pret. and part. pt. *lepit.* Addit. to LAIP, q. v.
". . quhilk bluid quhen the doggis had *lepit* theirof they iustantly deit." Trials for Witchcraft, Spald. Misc. I. 120.
Icel. *lepja,* A.-S. *lapian,* Dan. *labe,* to lick up.

LEPRON, LEPROUN, *s.* A young rabbit or hare.
"Provyding that the conyngis and *leprones* be sparit betwix [ ] and Alhallowmes," Burgh Recs. Edinburgh, II. 231.
O. Fr. *leporin,* of or belonging to a hare ; *lapereau,* a young rabbit ; Cotgr.

LERIT, LEIRIT, LEYRYT, *pret.* and *part. pt.* Learned, instructed, taught. V. LARE.

LESSURE, *s.* V. *Lichory.*

LESTY, *adj.* Skilful, expert, ingenious : " the *lesty* beuer" ; Kingis Quair, st. 157, Skeat's Ed. V. LISTE.
A.-S. *list,* art.

LET. The following uses of *let* have been overlooked in the DICT.

To LET *aff, v. a.* To fire, shoot ; as, " He *let aff* the gun." Like LET *gae* or *go,* s. 2, q. v.

To LET *doun, v. a.* 1. To descend : as, " Noo jist *let* yersel *doun* the stair canny," i.e., descend cautiously.

2. To demean, degrade : as, "I winna *let* mysel *doun* sae for twice the siller."

3. To lower, reduce, drain ; as, "*to let doun flesh,*" to reduce overfed mutton or beef by bleeding the animal for hours before slaughtering it.
"That all flescheouris bring thair flesche to the mercat croce, and that thai blaw nane thairof, nor yit *let* it *doune,* nor score it, vnder the pane of viij. s."
Burgh Recs. Peebles, 15 July, 1555, Rec. Soc.
"It is statute and ordanit that thair be na muttoun scoirit on the bak nor na pairt thairof, nor yit *lattin doun* before, bot ane scoir owder befoir or behynd, wnder the pane of viij. s. ilk falt ; and that na martes be bowbredit nor *lattin doun,* under the same pane."
Burgh Recs. Glasgow, 6 Oct. 1574, I. 26, Rec. Soc.
The "*lettin doun of flesch*" was a trick of the fleshertrade common all over the country, and practised for centuries in spite of the stern enactments of the magistrates, and the heavy fines inflicted in order to put it down. It was a barbarous, cruel method of reducing the ramp flavour of the flesh of animals—mostly sheep —that were deemed too fat. Slight incisions were made in the tail or in the lower part of the breast of the animal, and it was left to bleed slowly for some hours before it was put to death. When the bleeding was at the tail, the animal was said to be *lettin* or *lattin doun behind ;* and when it was at the breast, it was said to be *lattin doun before.* This cruelty is now unknown in the trade ; but half a century has not passed since it ceased to be perpetrated.

To LET *gae* or *go, v. a.* To let loose, set, send ; as, " He *let go* the dog at him." Addit. to LET *gae* or *go,* q. v.

To LET *oot,* LAT *oot, v. a.* To open, open up ; as, "*to let oot* a girran," to lance or open up a boil : also, to widen, enlarge ; as, "*to lat oot* a sleeve or a skirt."

LETRIN, LETRON, LETROWN, s. V. LET-
TERON.
Letrin is evidently borrowed from O. Fr. letrin, which is derived, not from Lat. lectorium, as stated by Jamieson, but from L. Lat. lectrinum, which is from Gk. lēktron. Prob. he was misled by finding lectorium as one of the synon. of leterone in Prompt. Parv. The terms, however, have no etym. connection.
The primary sense of the word is bed, couch; hence, rest for a book; but it has no connection with Lat. legere.

LEVER, s. Errat. in DICT. for lyre, complexion, countenance.
A mistake in Pinkerton's version. Del. the note: for lonched is a misreading of louched, bending down, drooping. V. Sir Gawayne, Gloss.

LEVER. Lever lourd, rather by far, very much rather, preferred rather.
Enough of blood by me's been spilt;
Seek not your death frae me;
I'd lever lourd it had been mysel
Than either him or thee.
Gil Morice, st. 48.
Lit. rather rather; but, while lourd is often used like lever or leifer, it is much more frequently used as a pret. or part. pt.; and this is confirmed by the use of loor, lour, which occurs nearly always with a verbal meaning. It is in this acceptance that the last meaning, "preferred rather," has been given above. See examples under Lour.

LEVEREST, LEAVEREST, LIEFEREST, adv. Rather, much rather: superl. of lief, and used as a strong form of Lever, q. v. Orkney.

LEVERIE, s. Leave or permission from the owner: still in use. Addit. to LEVERE', q. v.
The term occurs in the mystery-play of Christ's entry into Jerusalem, in the question of the porter to the disciples.
Sale, what are ye that makis here maistrie,
To loose thes bestis withoute leverie?
Yow semes to bolde—
York Mystery Plays, p. 203, l. 65.
In the Gloss. it is rendered delivery.
O. Fr. livrée, delivery, that which is delivered, given, or granted. V. Cotgr. Dict.

LEVIN, LEWYN, s. Living, means of living, sustenance, provision: lewyn, Burgh Recs. Peebles, 13 Dec., 1456, Rec. Soc.

LEVYNE, LEWYN, s. A kind of light canvas.
"Et in empcione triginta quinque ulnarum de levyne."
Exch. Rolls, Scot. II. 444.
"De qua computat in panno coloris, tela lata et stricta, canubio grosso et subtili sive lewyn." Ibid, p. 371, where it is misprinted lelbyn.

LEYRYT, pret. Learned, were learning; Burgh Recs. Peebles, 19 Jan., 1466. V. LARE, Lerit.

LIBRAR, LIBRARE, s. Library; a house, room, or press, in which books are kept; Burgh Recs. Edinburgh, IV. 183. Fr. libraire, id.

This term is scarcely found in our Records before the beginning of the 18th cent.: till then, the word most commonly used was bibliotheck; and a librarian was called a bibliothecare.

LICHER (ch soft), LICHOUR, LYCHOUR, s. A lecher, lecherous person; Dunbar, Tua Maryit Wemen, l. 174; Douglas, Virgil, iv. prol.
Pron. lucher and loocher (ch soft) in West of S.

LICHEROUS, adj. Lecherous, lascivious; Sempill Ballates, p. 200.
Now to reforme thair fylthy licherous lyvis,
God gife the grace aganis this guld new yeir.
Alex. Scott, New Yeir Gift to Quene Mary, st. 8.

LICHORY, LYCHORY, LUCHRIE, LESSURE, s. Lechery, lasciviousness; Dunbar, Tua Maryit Wemen, l. 445: luchrie, Alex. Scott's Poems, p. 9, ed. 1882: lessure, Henryson, Pract. Medecyne, l. 20.
O. Fr. lecheor, lecher, lit. one who licks up, a man addicted to gluttony and lewdness: lescheur, lecherous: from O. H. Ger. lechón, to lick. V. Skeat's Etym. Dict.

LICHIS, s. pl. Lights, tapers, altar-lights; this pron. is still common.
". . . deuisit and ordand all the takismen of the watteris of this guid towne to pay and deliuer yeirlie at the natiuitie of our Lord, calliit Yowill, the lichis of wax, to the honour of God, our lady, and thair patroun Sanct Nicholace, conforme to thair auld vse and consuetud; that is to say, euery takisman of the raik and Done, thre lichis . . . to be gevin to the lichis of our altaris of our lady croce in the loft, and Sanct Nicholace," etc. Burgh Recs. Aberdeen, I. 149, 15 Dec., 1533, Sp. C.
The term occurs repeatedly in this entry, and throughout these Recs., but is sometimes misprinted lithis.

LICHT-HORSEMEN, s. pl. Plunderers, reivers, raiders: like the moss-troopers of the border; Burgh Recs. Aberdeen, III. 118, Rec. Soc.

LICK, s. A small quantity of anything; as, a lick of salt, a lick of sugar: and a piece of work that has been carelessly or imperfectly done, or has had slight attention bestowed on it, is said "to have got a lick and a promise."

LIDDER, LIDDERNES, s. Sloth, laziness. "Ill! he's jist ill wi' the lidder," i.e., oppressed with laziness: liddernes, Rauf Coilzear, s. 61. V. LIDDERadj.

LIDDERON, LIDRONE, s. A lazy, slovenly, or careless person; South and West of S. V. LADRONE.
The etym. of lidder given by Jamieson is impossible: that suggested by Ruddiman is certainly correct. A.-S. ly'thre, ly'ther, bad, wicked: to which Germ. liederlich, careless, etc. is allied. V. under LIDDER.

LIE, s. A term used in golfing:—(1.) The inclination of a club when held on the ground in the natural position for striking. (2.) The situation of a ball—good or bad.

To LIE. The following peculiar uses of this verb are common all over the country.

To LIE by, v. n. 1. To lie aside, apart, or away from others of the same kind; as, "Let that ane *lie by* till it's sortit."

2. To lie or remain unused, to stand idle; as, "Let the lame horse *lie by* for a week."

3. To commit adultery. V. LY-BY, s.

My Father was ane Erle and had ane wyfe,
Thocht he abusit his body and *lay by*.
Sempill Ballates, p. 134.

4. To keep off, stand back or away from, let alone; as, when a shepherd calls in his dog from the sheep, he orders it to *lie by*.

To LIE *owre near*. To be too fond of; as, "That cat *lies owre near* the fire to be a good hunter: also, to be too much cared for or fondled; as, "That lass *lies owre near* her mither to make a guid wife."

LIEGE, s. A subject. V. DICT.

The derivation of *liege*, from Lat. *ligatus*, bound, as given by Jamieson, was long and commonly accepted, but is now discarded. That it has come through the Fr. *lige*, *liege*, is certain; and that *lige* is allied with *ligatus* by early French writers is also certain; but careful comparison has shown that this connection was a mistake, and has caused confusion in the various meanings of the term; and that the history of the term before this confusion, points undoubtedly to O. H. Germ. *ledic*, *lidic* (Mod. Germ. *ledig*), free. Littré gives the origin of the term as uncertain: but Burguy and Brachet quite certainly give it as Germ. *ledig*. Taking this acceptation of the term, a *liege* lord was a lord of or over *lieges*, forming a *free* band or band of *free*-men; for, his *lieges* or *liege*-men, though bound to him in the strictest manner, were *free* from all astrictions or service to the soil, and therefore *free* to follow him wherever he called or led. V. Skeat's Etym. Dict.

LIFEY, adj. Cheery, merry, entertaining; also, active and pushing in business. Addit. to LIFEY, q. v.

This term is still current in various districts of the country, and is generally used in the senses given above.

LIFILY, LIFILIE, adv. With life and spirit; heartily, merrily.

LIFINESS, s. Liveliness, energy, spirit, mirth.

LIKAME, s. Body. V. LICAYM.

LIKAMY-DOCKS, LIKMY-DOCKS, s. An old name for the pillory, jougs, gyves, &c.

Long after the pillory, the jougs, and all such modes of punishment had been abolished, this term was used to impress the youthful mind with ideas of dreadful punishment consequent on wrong-doing, and especially on prowling about in forbidden places. The strange jail-like name of the place or thing (the meaning of which was carefully concealed), and the vague, dire consequences threatened, roused an indescribable terror in the offender, which no known reality could produce. Natives of the West of S. will no doubt recognise the term, and smile as they recall the terror it inspired.

LIKE, LYKE, adj. 1. Looking, with the appearance of; as, *ill-like*, ill-looking; *good-lyke*, good-looking; *hame-like*, with the appearance of home, or homely-looking. Addit. to [LIKE, adj.]

I grant I had ane Douchter was ane Quene,
Baith gude and fair, gentill and Liberall,
Doit with vertewis and wit Naturall;
Prignant in Spreit, in all things honourabill,
Lusty, gude *lyke*, to all men fauourabill.
Sempill Ballates, p. 164.

2. Similar, equal, even.

In the game of golf, when both parties have played the same number of strokes, they are said to be *like*, and they say to each other *like-as-we-lie*. V. Golfer's Handbook, p. 34.

3. As a s.; *like, the like*, even (as opposed to odd), the even stroke, are terms in golfing. Also, the match, the equal, one in every respect similar, as, in matching ribbon, cloth, etc. one shows the pattern and asks, "Ha'e ye *the like* o' that?"

In golfing, the stroke which makes a player equal with his opponent is called "*the like*." "If your opponent has played one stroke more than you—i.e., 'the odd,' your next stroke will be '*the like*.'" Golfer's Handbook, p. 35.

4. As an adv. implying desire, intention, necessity, or constraint; as, "Weel, just say I'm *like* to gang the morn," i.e., I am purposing or intending to do so: "If ye do that ye're *like* to pay for it," i.e., you will be bound, compelled, or constrained to do so; West and South of S.

This use of *like* is common in the North of E. also. V. Brockett's Gloss.

LILLY-LOW, s. Lit., a little flame, but used in nursery parlance for a bright light, a bonny light, "a bonnie wee low."

Dan. *lille*, little, and *lue*, a light, flame. Under Low, s., in DICT., this term is discussed; but neither meaning nor etymology is correct.

LIME-CRAIG, LYME-CRAIG, s. A lime quarry, a limestone-cliff; Burgh Recs. Glasgow, II. 177, Rec. Soc.

LIND. *Leif on lind*, leaves on the trees; Dunbar and Kennedie, l. 196. Addit. to LIND.

This phrase is used in expressions denoting length of time, greatness of number, etc.; as, "Last while there's *leif on lind*," i.e., as long as leaves grow on trees; "Ma nor there is *leif on lind*," i.e., more numerous than the leaves on the trees, or than leaves in a forest.

LINE, LYNE, *s.* Lint. V. LIN.

LINGLE, *s.* and *v.* V. LINGEL.

LINGY, *adj.* and *s.* Applied to the greasy surface that settles on stagnant water; Orkn.

LIPNIT, LYPNIT, *pret.* and *part. pt.* of LIPPEN. Trusted, expected; Douglas, Virgil, Bk. v. ch. 14, Small's ed.

To LIRT, LIRTE, *v. a.* To deceive, beguile; more commonly *belirt*; syn. *gowk, begowk*; West. of S.

LIRT, LIRTE, *s.* Cheat, deception, fooling, go-by; "He gied her the *lirt*," i.e., the slip, go-by, or, he befooled her; syn. *gowk.*

LIS, *interj.* Alas! *lis-a-lis*, alas, alas! Prob. only the local pron. of E. alas! Orkn.

LISOME, *adj.* Lawful: a form of Lesum, q. v. Burgh Recs. Glasgow, II. 260.

LIST, LYST, *s.* Border, hem, edge; syn. *roon, rund*, Ayrs. *rung*; Kingis Quair, st. 178.

LITHLESS, *adj.* Cheerless, comfortless; cold and hard. V. LITHE, *adj.*

The mitherless bairnie creeps to his lane bed,
Nane covers his cauld back or haps his bare head;
His wee huckit heelies are hard as the airn,
An' *lithless* the lair o' the mitherless bairn.
W. Thom, The Mitherless Bairn.

LIVRA, *s.* Vent: the opening in the roof of a house for the smoke to escape by; Orkn. and Shetl. E, *louver.*

Such smoke-vents may still be seen in various districts of the Highlands and in the Hebrides. Regarding those in the far north, see Hibbert's Shetland, p. 115.
Icel. *ljóri*, Norse *liore*, Dan. *ljore*, Sw. *liure*, the louver or smoke vent in the roof of a house, where the fire is made in the middle of the floor.

LOB, *part. pt.* Gelded, libbed: *lob-aver*, a gelded horse, Dunbar, Tua Maryit Wemen, l. 387. V. under LIB.

LOCALITIE, *s.* Apportionment of a levy or impost on a town or district for the support of soldiers, or purposes of war; Corshill Baron Court Book, Ayr and Wigton Arch. Coll., IV. 172. Addit. to LOCALITY.

The *locality* was taken sometimes in money, sometimes in food, clothes, silver-plate, etc., according to circumstances. The term was often used in the general sense of *cess, impost.* V. Book of War Committee of Kirkcudbright.

LOCHE, *s.* Bakin - *loche*, Alex. Scott's Poems, p. 27, ed. 1882. V. BAKIN-LOTCH.

LOCHT, *adj.* A form of *lotch*, thick, stout, substantial.

"Ninian Gilhagy is fand in the wrang for iniuring and boisting the haill officeris, calling thame false beggares, lymmeris, and lownes, and that he suld belt tua of thaime with ane *locht* rung." Burgh Recs. Glasgow, I. 199, Rec. Soc.

LOGGERAND, *adj.* Loose-hanging, long and unshapely, sprawling. V. LOGGAR.

Hir hingand browis, and hir voce sa hace
Hir *loggerand* leggis, and hir harsky hyde.
Henryson, Paddok and Mous, l. 45.

LOIK-HERTIT, *adj.* Kindly disposed: Dunbar, I. 79, ed. Laing. V. LUIK-HARTIT.

LOIKMAN, *s.* V. LOCKMAN.

LOKIN, LOCKIN, LOKYN, *part. pt.* Locked, enclosed, enfolded; Kingis Quair, st. 135; interlocked, closely folded, as, *lokyn-gowan*, the globe-flower; but the common form is *lucken* or *lukin*, q. v.

LONE, *s.* Errat. in DICT. for *lorre*, a laurel: a form of LORER, q. v.

A misreading in Pinkerton's version. Del. note: its suggestions are altogether wrong.

LONGEIT, *pret.* V. DICT.

May be read *lougeit*, lodged, as stated by Jamieson, and this reading agrees better with the context. It is so printed in the Hunterian Club issue of the Bannatyne MS.

LONGEOUR, LOUNGER, *s.* A sluggard, lazy one; "lurkand like a *longeour*," Douglas, Virgil, viii. prol. O. Fr. *longard.*

LONYE, LUNYE. *s.* Loin. V. LUNYIE.

LOO, *s.* Milk horn, i.e., the porous bone inside the horns of cattle; Orkn. In Shetl. called SLO, q. v.

LORE, *part. pt.* Errat. in DICT. for *loghe*, low. V. under *Lorre.*

LORN, *part. pt.* Lost, destroyed, ruined; Douglas, Virgil, xii. ch. 6.

A.-S. *loren*, lost; *part. pt.* of *leosan*, to lose.

LORRE, *s.* A laurel. V. LORER.

Under a *lorre* they light loghe by a felle.
Avontyrs of Arthure, st. 3.

Misread *lone* by Pinkerton: and for *loghe* he gave *lore.* In the version printed by Laing the line runs thus:—

Sythen vndir a *lorere* scho lyghte lawe by a felle.

LOTE, *s.* Feature, aspect, countenance; variant of *late.* V. LAIT.

LOUGEIT, *pret.* Lodged, abode, lived; Colkelbie Sow, l. 593, Bann. MS., Hunt. C.

LOUN, LOON, *s.* V. DICT.

The etym. of this term is left very uncertain. Most of the suggestions are only guesses; indeed, the only statement that is reliable is the one by Sibbald, that the derivation is from Teut. *loen*, a stupid, dull, foolish person. To this must be added O. Du. *lome*, Mod. Du. *loom*, slow, inactive. And that *m*, not *n*, is the older root letter is shown by its appearance in all the cognate languages. V. LOON, in Skeat's Etym. Dict., also in Wedgwood's.

To LOUR, LOOR, v. a. To like, prefer, wish desire; pret. and part. pt. *lourd.*
I *loor* by far she'd die like Jenkin's hen,
Ere we again met yon unruly men.
Ross's Helenore, p. 234, ed. 1868.
I wad *lourd* have had a winding sheet,
And helped to put it owre his head,
Ere we again met yon unruly men.
Minstrelsy Border, I. 106.
Seek not your death frae me;
I'd lever *lourd* it had been mysel,
Than either him or thee.
Gil Morice, st· 48.
This v. is formed from the comp. of *leif,* willing. V. under LEVER.

LOUR, s. Lucre, gain, profit, pay, reward. V. DICT.
A lase that luvis bot for *lour.*
Colkelbie Sow, l. 148, Bann. MS.
Not defined in DICT. The rendering of this line there given is wrong. Perhaps a corr. from Lat. *lucrum ;* but more prob. from Gael. *luach,* value, pay ; Irish *luach,* price, wages.

LOVAGE, LOUAGE, s. Praise, adoration: "for the *lovage* of God;" Burgh Recs. Edin., l. 58, 80, 214, Rec. Soc. V. LOUE.

LOVERY, LUFRAY, s. Corrupt forms of livery, bounty, or gift given to a servant at certain times in addition to wages, or as part of them. V. LEVERE'. Addit. to LOVERY, q. v.
Not defined in DICT., but the correct meaning is suggested in the accompanying note. The etym., however, is not Su.-G., but Fr. *livrée,* that which is delivered, stipend, donation, livery. It is correctly given under LEVERE', q. v.

To LOWE, v. a. To make low, humble, fawn, submit; Douglas, Palice of Honour, Pt. I. st. 6. V. *Laue.*

LOWING, LOWINS, LOUIN, LO'IN, s. Allowance, supply; also, reward or punishment due to one. Addit. to [LOWANCE], q. v.
". . . and has na *lowing* to vphald the samyn and daly chaplane thairat bot our ouklie penny gaderyt amangis the brethir of the said craft." Burgh Recs. Edinburgh, 17 Sept., 1533, Vol. II.
". . . for having his Majestie's Lieutenant at Inuernes the tuentie day of September nixt to cum, thairfra to pas vpon Lewis with fourtie dayes *loin,* and to report bak answer to the consall." Burgh Recs. Aberdeen, II. 229, Aug. 1602, Sp. C.
The term is still so pron. by elderly people in the West and South of S.; as, in speaking of a beggar, "She comes every week for her *lowins ;*" or, of a widow, "Her gnidman left her a gude *lotn.*"
Fr. *allouer,* to let out for hire: from L. Lat. *allocare,* to allot.

LOWIS, s. pl. Lochs; represents the pron. of *louchis.* V. LOUCH.

LOWNIT, adj. Still, calm, serene; "the *lownit* air," Doug., Virg., v. ch. 4. V. LOWN.
Icel. *logn,* serene, tranquil.

LOWRANE DAY, LAURNE DAY, s. St. Laurence-day, 23rd August; Spalding C. Misc., I. 136.

LOWS, LOWSE, adj. Loose. V. LOUSE.

To LOWT, v. and s. V. LOUT.

LUBER, LUBOR, s. A lazy fellow, an idle beggar: a term of contempt; Sempill Ballates, p. 67.
Gael. *lobhar,* a leper, worthless fellow: comp. of *lob,* to rot, and *fear,* man, person: a contemptuous term. M. E. *lobre, lobur.*

LUCHER (*ch* soft), s. A form of *lecher,* a lecherous person; West of S. V. *Licher.*

LUCHRIE, s. Lechery; Alex. Scott's Poems, p. 71, ed. 1882. V. under *Licher.*
Printed "*luthrie*" in Lord Hailes' Bann. Poems, p. 196, st. 10.

LUCIVE, adj. Bright, shining, glossy.
Thoch now in browdir and begary,
She glansis as scho war Queine of Fary,
With costly furis *lucive* and sable,
With stanis and perle fnnvmerable;
All gold begaiue, a glorious growme,
Slamb ouer with faird and fyne perfwme.
Rob Stene's Dream, p. 4, Mait. C.
By the editor of the poem *lucive* is defined as a s., meaning, "A kind of fur: supposed to be that of the otter"; but both sense and structure are better satisfied by reading it as an *adj.* with the meaning given above. The statement implies that the furs were either *bright, shining,* in contrast to sable, i.e., *white* and sable, or, that they were *bright, shining,* in addition to sable, i.e., *glossy* and black: the first meaning, however, is the more likely.
Prob. an adaptation of Lat. *lucificus* in the sense of *lucidus,* bright, shining.

LUCKS-TU. Generally used as an *interj.,* look, observe, note, remember; West of S., Orkn.
This expression is not a contr. form of *lookest-thou,* but simply the old pron. of the older Anglian form *looks-thou* or *loks-thu:* similar to *has-tu, hears-tu, is-tu, says-tu, sees-tu,* etc., which are still used. *Tu* was the common pron. of *thou,* when it followed the verb; and in various parts of the country it was prevalent till within comparatively late years: but though still common in Orkn., and used by elderly country people in the West of S., it is rapidly becoming obsolete.

LUCRIFACTION, s. The act of winning or gaining by one's own exertions; Blame of Kirkburiall, ch. xix. V. LUCRIFIE.

LUF and LIE. A sea term; to hug the wind closely; Sempill Ballates, p. 230. V. under LUIFE.

LUFFE, LUF, LUIF, LOOF, s. Hand: as, "He gied me his *lufe* on't," he gave me his hand by way of pledge; implying that they had struck hands over the business. Addit. to LUFE.
In many parts of the country the old *bargain-fest,*

"There's my *lufe*, I'll ne'er beguile ye," may still be heard at the conclusion of a bargain. Another and perhaps older form of the saying is, "There's my thoom, I'll ne'er beguile ye."

To LOOK TO ONE'S LUFE. To glance aside, to withdraw one's attention from work or duty for a moment, to attend to anything else while one's lord or master is near.

I dar nought luk to my *luf* for that lens gib,
He is sa full of ielusy and engyne fals.
    Dunbar, Twa Maryit Wemen, 1. 120.

The same idea is expressed, but in slightly different terms, a few lines further on.

I dar nought keik to the knaip that the cop fillis,
For eldnyng of that ald schrew that euer on euill thynkis.
    Ibid., 1. 125.

LUIF DROWRY, *s.* Love-pledge, token or assurance of love.

A Sidonian steid
Of cullour quhite, quham Dido, the fair lady
In hir remembrance gaif hym lu *luif drowry*.
    Douglas, Virgil, v. ch. 10.

LUKISMES, LOUKISMES, LUXMESS, *s.* The feast of St. Luke, 18th Oct.; one of the terms at which payments of accounts was made; Burgh Recs. Glasgow, I. 153, Rec. Soc., Burgh Recs. Prestwick, p. 15, Mait. C., Ayr and Wigton Arch. Coll., IV. 95.

LUKKIN, *part.* and *adj.* Close-fitting, webbed. V. LUCKEN.

LUNGSUCHT, LUNSAUCHT, LOUNGSOCHT, *s.* Lung-disease, a disease of cattle, now called *pleuro-pneumonia*.

". . . thou confessis to be a spreit, and puttis four stanis in the four nokis of the ward [i.e., an enclosure prepared by the witch or warlock], and charmes the samen, and thairby haillis the guidis, and prescrvis thame fra the *lunsaucht* and all vthor diseasis." Trials for Witchcraft, Spald. C. Misc., I. 120.

The curious reader will find a full account of charming for *lungsucht*, murrain, and other diseases of cattle, with various forms of charm and directions for using them, in the Appendix to the Preface of Kalendars of Scottish Saints.

A.-S. *lunge*, pl. *lungan*, the lungs, and *sucht*, disease. The lungs are so named on account of their lightness ; and in Scot. are called, for the same reason, the *lichts*.

LURE, LARE, LAAR, *s.* Flesh, lean flesh. V. under LIRE.

LUSH, *s.* A stroke, blow, cut, as with a wand or cane. V. LEISCHE.

To LUSH, LUSCH, *v. a.* and *n.* To dash, rush, encounter ; to strike at, lunge, beat, batter.

Sa wondir frely thai frekes fangis the fight,
Thai *luschit* and laid on, thai luflyis of lyre.
    Gol. and Gawane, st. 78, l. 5.

This term was overlooked both by Pinkerton and Jamieson, although it occurs frequently in the romances of Arthur and Gawayne. In Morte Arthur, l. 1459, we find—

With lufly launces one lofte they *luschene* to gedyres.
Again in l. 2224—
He laughte owtte a lange swerde and *luschede* one faste.

Prob. only a variant of *lash*, M. E. *lasche ;* but it is a very old form, as it occurs in the York Mysteries, both as a *s.* and as a *v.* See pp. 252, 292. As used in the Gaw. Rom., *lush* is onomato-poetic, and has, like *dush, thwack*, etc. originally at least, a reference to the nature of the sound caused by the blow, and therefore to the nature of the substances striking and struck. It is still so used in the South and West of S.

LUSOME, LUESOME, LOESUM, *adj.* Comely, winsome, worth loving. Addit. to LUFSOME, LUSOME.

LYAM, *s.* A cord, rope. V. LIAM.

LYKAME, LICAME, *s.* Body. V. LICAYM.

LYMB, LYME, *s.* Limbus, place of torment, purgatory : also, a prison, dungeon, thraldom.

Ane vthir place quhilk purgatory representis,
And, dar I say, the *Lymb* of faderis auld.
    Douglas, Virgil, vi. prol.

Fra rule, ressoun, and richt, redles I ran ;
Tharfor I ly in the *lyme*, lympit, lathast.
    Houlate, l. 969, Asloan MS.

In Bann. MS. "*lymb*."
Lat. *limbus*, a border ; *limbus patrum*, a place on the border of hell, where the patriarchs abode till Christ came to free them. Hence the phrase *in limbo*, meaning in prison.

LYMIT, LYMYT, LEMIT, LYMMIT, *part. pt.*
1. Adapted, fitted ; Douglas, King Hart, i. st. 3. Addit. to LYMMIT, q. v.
2. Engaged, appointed, set apart.

". . the quhilk to do we commit to you and to your seruandis and factouris that sall be *lymmit* be you thairto." Charters of Edin., 10 May, 1506, Rec. Soc., Burgh Recs. Aberdeen, I. 444, 445, Sp. C.

Loft undefined by Jamieson. The suggested meaning and etym. are incorrect.
Lat. *limitare*, to appoint, adapt, fit, engage ; Dan. *lempe*, id.

LYMMER, *s.* A rascal. V. LIMMAR.

In old Scot. laws the term was applied to a thief or reiver. It is still in use, but applied generally to a vicious or worthless woman, as in Wattie and Meg.

Ye'll sit wi' your *limmers* round you !
    Alex. Wilson's Poems, p. 7, ed. 1876.

LYMMERFULL, *adj.* Rascally, full of rascality, villainous.

Thow hes ane perrellous face to play with lambis :
Ane thowsand kiddis, wer thay in faldis full strang,
Thy *lymmerfull* luke wald fle thame and thair dammis.
    Dunbar and Kennedie, l. 152.

LYMPIT, *part. pt.* Made limp and weak, disabled, rendered powerless. Addit. to LYMPIT, q. v.

Not defined by Jamieson ; but his suggestions regarding meaning and etym. are nearly correct. Icel. *limpa*, weakness ; *lemja*, to thrash, flog, beat, so as to lame or disable : like vulgar E. *lam ;* Cleasby and Vigfusson.

LYNE, *part. pt.* Lain; "the samen has *lyne* wast above the fyftie yeiris," Burgh Recs. Glasgow, II. 321, Rec. Soc.

LYNE, LINE, *s.* Lint. V. LIN.

LYRE, *s.* Complexion, countenance, face. Addit. to LYRE, q. v.
Bot of his *lyre* was laithlie and horribill,
And had selkness quhilk was uncurabill.
Rolland, Seven Sages, l. 318.

M.

MAGHT, MAUGHT, MAUGHTS, *s.* V. MAUCHT.

MAGNIFICKLY, *adv.* Splendidly, perfectly; Bl. of Kirkburiall, Dedic.

MAID METER, MAD METIR, *s.* Rhyming couplets, rhyme.
Of the Cumean Silyl the poet says :—
Of prophecie scho did write buikis nine
In *maid meter* and vers Rethoricall.
Rolland, Court of Venus, ii. 511, S. T. S.
The form *mad metir* is sometimes rendered "doggerel" and "foolish or silly metre"; but this is a mistake. The poetry is, no doubt, sometimes poor enough; but the term does not convey that meaning.

MAIL, MAYL, MAYLE, MAYLL, *s.* A trunk, case, or bag for travellers; Halyburton's Ledger, p. 12.
Fr. *malle,* a trunk: from O. H. Ger. *malha.* V. Brachet's Dict.

MAIL, *s.* Tribute, etc. V. DICT.
Jamieson's etym. of this term is misleading. The "A.-S. *mal*, tribute," is purely imaginary; so also is "Isl. *mala*,"—at least as a direct form. Besides, the term was common in Celtic Scotland long before the period of Saxon influence; and, although in some of its meanings it has got mixed up with Fr. *maille* (which Littré and others derive from it. Lat. *medallia*, as stated in DICT.), it is to Celtic that we must look for its origin. Most prob. Gael. *mal,* rent, tribute, tax. Irish *mal,* tribute.

MAIN, MAYNE, MANE, *adj.* Chief, fine, best; as, *mayne-flour,* fine flour, best flour, of which mane-bread was made; Burgh Recs. Edinburgh, I. 220, Rec. Soc. Addit. to MANE, q. v.

MAINSHOTS, MAINSCHOTTIS, MAYNSCHOTES, *s.* The finest or best produce: applied to flour and spirits.
The lowest class of flour was called *foreshots* or first flour, and the finest or best was *mainshots,* of which manchet or mane-bread was made. In the case of spirits, the first that flowed from the still was a rank strong liquor called *foreshots*; after which came the best produce or *mainshots*; and the last or weakest liquor was called the *aftershots.*

MAINTO, MENTO, *s.* V. DICT.
This is almost certainly a corr. from Lat. *memento* (remember me; imper. of *memini,* I remember), with the common Scotch meaning *mind,* be *indebted;* as when one who has received a benefit says to the benefactor, "I'll *mind* yo for that," i.e., "I'll be indebted to you for that," or, "I'll do as much for you again."

MAIR, *s.* A first magistrate, etc. V. DICT.
Mair with this meaning ought to form a separate entry; it is a totally different word from *mair,* a sheriff's-officer. It is the Fr. *maire,* a mayor, from Lat. *major,* and is quite a modern word compared with the other, which is the old Gael. *maor,* an officer of justice. It was introduced into Scot. with the formation of guilds and corporations of burghs, etc.; but it very soon gave place to the term provost, which still continues in use. In the Statuta Gilde the term occurs in the preface and in ch. 38 (Records version), as Lat. *maior,* and is rendered in the Scot. translation *mair,* and *mayor.* See under *Maor.*

MAIS, MAISE, *s.* Six hundred: a term used in counting herrings; Accts. L. H. Treas., I. 382, Dickson. Addit. to MAZE, MESE, q. v.
As stated under MAZE and MESE the number is five hundred, but (as is not there explained), they are *long hundreds:* hence, a *maise* of herrings, is 600 herrings. That it was always so rated in Scotland has not been ascertained; but it certainly was so as far back as the 16th cent. In France, in the 13th cent., the *maise* of red-herring—*hareng sor*—was fixed at 1020, of white-herring—*hareng blanc*—at 800: a rating and variation which suggest that the *maise* was originally a measure, not a number as explained by Skene in his Verb. Sign. See Preface to L. H. Treas. Accts. p. ccvii., Dickson.
Gael. *maois*, "a large basket or hamper, a certain number of fish, five hundred herrings." M'Leod and Dewar.
Cf. Breton *maes*, a pannier, measure, which was adopted into O. Fr. as "*meisse,* panier où l'on met les harengs"; Roquefort.

MAISTER, MASTER, *s.* A title given to those, chiefly churchmen, who had taken the master's degree in arts; Accts. L. H. Treas., I. 1, 19, Dickson. Addit. to MAISTER, q. v.
Also, insert in s. 4 of this term in DICT. after the word farmer, "or other employer."

MAISTERSTIK, *s.* Lit. master-piece; trial-piece, or sample of one's skill and ability in his craft. V. STICKE.

Before a craftsman obtained the freedom and privileges of his craft, he had to produce his *masterstik* in proof of his skill and ability.

". . . the person creven to be admittit free of his craft first compone with the said deinis of gild, and be admittit frie be the toun, the *maisterstik* of the person to be admittit being exhibit and producit in judgement." Burgh Recs. Aberdeen, II. 34, Sp. C.

To MAIT, MAYT, *v. a.* To tire out, run down, capture; Douglas, III. 255. 1., Small's ed: part. pt. *mat, mate, mayt,* wearied, discouraged, confounded; Gaw. Romances. Addit. to MATE, q. v.

This term occurs in The Cherrie and the Slae, st. 16, in the phrase "*stail or mait,*" which is a phrase in the game of chess; and in that game *mate* is often used as short for both "to checkmate," and "to be checkmated." It occurs in the latter sense in the Kingis Quair, st. 168.

"Help now my game, that is in poynt *to mate.*"

MAIT, MATE, *s.* Checkmate; Kingis Quair, st. 169, Skeat's ed.

Mait, mate, short for *checkmate,* is from O. Fr. *mat,* short for *echec et mat,* which, like the game of chess with which it is connected, is of Persian origin. See under *Echec* in Littré.

To MAK. To the various senses of this v. represented in the DICT., add the following:

1. *To mak costis,* to defray costs; Accts. L. H. Treas., I. 277, Dickson; *to mak expensis,* to defray expenses; Ibid. pp. 46, 201.

2. *To mak furth,* to complete, equip; Ibid. 261, 339.

MAKELES, MAKLES, *adj.* Matchless. V. MAIRLESS.

MAKRELLE, *s.* A bawd, base woman; Douglas, II. 170, 30, Small's ed. Fr. *maquerelle.*

MALDY, MAUDY, *s.* A coarse woollen cloth of a grey or mixed colour: so called because it was like the material of a shepherd's *maud* or plaid. It was also called plaiding, and home-made.

"In the first, ane cloik of *maldy,* price thrie pundis; ane coit of the samyn hew, price fourtie schillinge; ane dowblet of [caulct], ane pair of gray breikis, ane pair of *maldy* schankes, ane lynning serk, &c." Burgh Recs. Glasgow, I. 128.

The greater part of the clothing worn in rural and Highland districts, even to a comparatively late period, was made of this *maldy*; and the cloth was to a great extent, indeed in some households entirely home made. The sorting, dressing, and dyeing of the wool, and the spinning of it into yarn, occupied a great deal of the time and care of the females in every household; and, when not woven at home, the yarn was given out to workmen called *customer* or *dadgeon weavers,* by whom

(Sup.) W

it was converted into cloth. When of the grey or mixed colour, and of the quality used for shepherds plaids, both yarn and cloth went by the name of *maldy,* or, as commonly pronounced, *maudy*; hence we have in the extract given above, "a cloik of *maldy,*" and *maldy* schankis" or stockings.

MALING, MALYN, *s.* A farm. V. MAILIN.

MALLURE, *s.* Evil, ill. V. MALHURE.

Fr. *malheur,* misfortune, evil; but *malheur* is not from Lat. *mala hora,* as Jamieson states, but from *malum augurium*; and *bonheur,* not from *bona hora,* but from *bonum augurium.* Lat. *augurium* (augury, presage), became *agur, aûr, eûr,* and latterly *heur,* luck, fortune. V. Littré, and Brachet.

MALTALENT, MAILTALENT, *s.* Ill-will, spite, passion, rage; Douglas, Virgil, i. ch. 1, heading, x. ch. 12, Small's ed. V. MATALENT.

O. Fr. *mal-talent,* despite, ill-will; Cotgr.

To MAMMER, MAMER, MEMER, *v. n.* To mumble, talk to oneself; also, to stammer, speak indistinctly. V. *Memer.*

MANAS, MANNAS, MANIS, MANNIS, *s.* A threat, threatening; *mannance,* Douglas, II. 177.7, Small's ed.

To MANAS, MANNAS, MANIS, MANNIS, *v. a.* To threaten; pret. *manasit,* Burgh Recs. Aberdeen, I. 407; part. *manysand,* Douglas, II. 82.6. Addit. to MANNES.

Fr. *menace,* a menace, threat; *menacer,* to threaten: from Lat. *minacia.*

MANDRAG, *s.* Lit. a mandrake; but used as a term of contempt for a deformed or worthless man,—a mere semblance of a man; Dunbar and Kennedy, l. 29.

That the plant mandrake is so called because its root presents the rude outline of a man is a mere fancy; but the resemblance may account for the use of the word as a term of contempt.

A.-S. and Lat. *mandragora,* the plant mandrake.

MANG, MANGS, MANGIS, *prep.* Among, amongst; South and West of S. V. *Amongis.*

To MANG, *v. a.* V. DICT.

The passage from Piers Plowman given in illustration of s. 6 of this term is quite a mistake. As Prof. Skeat has pointed out, it has nothing whatever to do with *mang.* The spelling *manzed* is a mere misprint for *mansed,* which is short for *amansed,* and *amansumed,* excommunicated, and hence cursed. V. Murray's New Eng. Dict., s. v., AMANSE.

MANNA, MAUNNA, MUNNA. Forms of MAUNA, q. v.

MANTIL, MANTILL, MANTLE, *s.* A package of skins of fur, containing from thirty to one hundred pieces, according to the kind of fur and size of the skins or parts of skins used; Accts. L. H. Treas., I. 15, 190, Dickson.

The package was prob. so named because it contained sufficient for the lining of a mantle; and the number of pieces it contained necessarily varied considerably, according to the kind of fur it contained, and because it sometimes consisted of whole skins, and sometimes of special parts of skins. See the varieties mentioned in the Book of Customs and Valuation of Merchandise in 1612, given in Halyburton's Ledger. In that work the words *mantil* and *pane*, though not identical in meaning, are used to denote the same number of skins. See note in Gloss. to Accts. L. H. Treas., I. 425.
Regarding other kinds of packages, see under *Bred, Pane, Timmer*.

MANTILL-WALL, MANTALE-WALL, s. A screen-wall, Douglas, Virgil, xii. prol. l. 24, Burgh Recs. Glasgow, I. 12, Rec. Soc.

To **MANURE, MANNOR, MANOR,** v. a. 1. To work, cultivate, administer, dispense: as, "to manor lan'," to cultivate the soil.

Leslie, in describing the southern counties of Scotland, says:—
"In thame ar mony noblemen, and almaist all, bot chieflie the mersmen, thay *manure* justice, and thay studie to politike affaires." Leslie, Hist. Scot., p. 10, S.T.S.

2. To use, have the use of, possess, enjoy.

"Allsua the gud wif sal *mannor* thir thyngys qwil acho lefis." Burgh Recs. Peebles, 13 April, 1457, p. 119, Rec. Soc.
Manure originally meant to work or till by hand, and is a contr. form of *manœuvre*, from Fr. *manœuvrer*. See Trench's Select Glossary.

MAOR, MAYR, s. Originally an officer equivalent to our sheriff's-officer. Addit. to **MAIR,** q. v.

While the duty of the *maor* was to execute the mandates of the sheriff, the office was hereditary, and he was generally called the *mair* of fee. When the district of the sheriff was large it was sub-divided into two or more mairdoms: for example, the sheriffdom of Angus had four bailliaries, and each had its own *mair*. In some cases the office was attached to certain lands in the district, and infeftment in these was accompanied by infeftment in the office: as, when Archibald, Earl of Argyll, and *dominus de* Craignichie, infeft Donald M'Illechallum "in the lands of Corworanbeg, and also of the office of sergeantry or maorship of the tenandry or mairdoly of Craignish." Innes' Legal Antiquities, p. 78-9.
Particulars regarding the casualties and fees connected with this office are also given in the work referred to.

MAIR-DEPUT, s. Deputy-mair, sub-mair, or officer of the sheriff.

". . . that the forsayd Johnn Dauidson, beyng ane *mair deput* of Abirdene for the tyme, disobeyit the forsayd Willame Rolland eldar, shirof deput of Abirdene for the tyme, and myspersonet hym with mony ewill wordis, . . and boistit the said shiref with ane knyff at his awn buitht dur." Burgh Recs. Aberdeen, 1539, I. 162, Sp. C.

MAORMOR, s. The great maor; an official title of dignity in Celtic Scotland.

"The *maormors* were the greatest officers of great districts, and it is to them, and not to the Thanes, that Shakspeare, in Macbeth, should have made young Malcolm address his speech—'Henceforth be Earls!' The *maormors* of Moray, Buchan, Mearns, and Angus, were exactly *Comites* or Counts : and, when the great change took place about the time of Canmore, they became Earls, and some of their descendants are so still." Innes' Legal Antiq., p. 79.
"*Maormor* is an ancient title among the Celts, found in misty and hardly historical Irish annals, but now made Scotch history by the Book of Deir." Ibid.
Gael. *maor*, "an officer of justice, a bailiff, a catchpoll, messenger: inferior officers in various capacities are so called." M'Leod and Dewar.
Maormor is comp. of Gael. *maor*, as above, and *mor*, great.

MAPPA-MOUND, s. The world, globe, earth; Rob Stene's Dream, p. 17. Addit. to **MAPAMOUND,** q. v.

MARABAS, s. and *adj.* A kind of bonnet, a large flat cap: "ane *marabas* bonnet," Burgh Recs. Edinburgh, II. 91.

O. Fr. *marrabaise*, "Bonnet à la mar. A flat cap;" Cotgr.

MARCIALL, *adj.* Of the month of March : "the sanctis *marciall*," Kingis Quair, st. 191, Skeat.

MARIOLYNE, MARGELEN, s. Sweet marjoram, Douglas, II. 61, 11, Small's ed.; *margelen*, Sempill Ballates, p. 77. Fr. *marjolaine*.

MARK, s. A land measure in Orkney: not of extent but of valuation proportioned to the taxation, and regulating both rights and burdens; Memorial for Orkney, p. 117. Addit. to **MARK,** q. v. V. **MERK.**

To **MARK,** v. a. and *n.* To aim, try, strive; implying purpose or endeavour to attain some end. Addit. to **MARK,** q. v.

This wretchit wolf weipand thus on he went,
Of his menyie *markand* to get remeid.
Henryson, Parl. of Beistes, l. 241.

MARMAKIS, s. A kind of cloth.
"Et in septem peciis de marmakis xcjli. vjs. viijd." Exch. Rolls, Scot., I. 381.

MARQUESITT, MARQUISIT, s. Marcassite or fire-stone, a mineral that has an odour of sulphur: there are two kinds, yellow or gold m., and white or silver m.

". . wherein I find fixed lead ore, and some *marquesitt*, accompanied with keelle, sparr, and brimsteue," &c. Early Records of Mining in Scotland, p. 114.
". . I find unknown mynneralls and *marquesitts*," &c. Ibid. p. 114.
Fr. *marcassite*, from Arabic *marcazat;* Brachet. V. also **COTGRAVE.**

MART, MAERT, MAIRT, s. A cow, etc. V. **DICT.**

In the Exchequer Rolls of Scot. frequent mention is

made of various kinds of *marts*; as, *custom-marts, entry marts, fodmarts* or *mart fodellis, fogmarts, fulemarts, grassum-marts, lardenar-marts, malemarts, rynmarts*, and *stukmarts*. The meaning of some of these terms, such as *custom-marts, entry-marts, grassummarts, male* or *mail-marts*, is obvious; but of the others no satisfactory account can be given. Various attempts to explain them have been made; but even the best of them are only guesses; for the terms have long ago passed out of use.

MARTHYRIT, *part. pt.* Bruised, sorely wounded; Douglas, III. 42, 11, Small's ed. V. under MARTIR.

MARTOUN, *s.* Houlate, l. 213. V. MORTON.

MASK-RUTHER, *s.* Same as MASK-RUNG, q. v.; Burgh Recs. Glasgow, I. 129.

MASSILON, MASSILYON, *s.* V. MASHLIN.

MATE, MAYT, *v.* and *s.* V. *Mait.*

MATTEYNE, MATHEYNE, *s.* Ruffian, rascal, blackguard; Burgh Recs. Glasgow, I. 77, Rec. Soc.

This term occurs in a list of opprobrious names applied to a Glasgow bailie in 1579. It is of French origin: from *mâtin*, a mastiff; O. Fr. *mastin*, "A mastiue, or Ban-dog; also, a rude, filthie, currish, or cruel fellow." Cotgr.

MAUCH, MAUCHY, *adj.* Same as MOCH, MOCHY, q. v.; "*mauch* mutton," Dunbar and Kennedy, l. 241.

MAUKIN, *s.* A half-grown female, etc. V. DICT.

This entry should be combined with the preceding one: it presents simply another meaning of the same word. *Maukin*, the pron. of MAUDKIN, dimin. of MAUD, i.e. MATILDA, is precisely the same word as *malkin* or *maukin*, a hare. It also means a maid, and a maid's mop. The etymologies given by Jamieson must therefore be deleted.

MAWIS, *s.* A form of MAUSE, q. v. Alex. Scott.

MEAN, *adj.* Held in common or in equal shares by the owners or tenants: as when a field or farm is so held. Addit. to MEIN, MENE, q. v.

". . in that with both their consentis their wes ane piece of *mean* grass betwixt them, dealt and evened, and dealt the mean betwixt them." Corshill Baron-Court Book, Ayr and Wigtown Arch. Coll., iv. 166.

"*dealt*," divided.

MEANER, MEENER, MENARE, *s.* A mediator, adjudicator, adjuster; one who divides and marks off in equal portions land which is held by joint-tenants.

MEAR, MEER, *s.* A mare. V. *Meir.*

GREY MEAR, GREY MEIR, GRAY MERE, *s.* Used metaphorically for a wife who is truly the better half, i.e., who rules the house: as in the common proverb,—" The *grey mere's* the better horse."

"But there's ae thing sair again ye—Rob has a *grey mear* in his stable at hame."

"A grey mare?" said I. "What is that to the purpose?"

"The wife, man—the wife—an awfu' wife she is. She downa bide the sight o' a kindly Scot, if he come frae the Lowlands, far less of an Inglisher, and she'll be keen for a' that can set up King James, and ding down King George." Scott, Rob Roy, ch. 26.

MEAT, MEITT, *s.* "*Wild meitt*," game, wild fowl, venison, &c.; Burgh Recs. Edinburgh, II. 92, Rec. Soc.

MEDICIANE, *s.* An apothecary, a doctor; Spald. Club Misc., I. 133.

MEET, *adj.* Measured. V. *Mete.*

MEETING, *s.* V. *Meting.*

MEID, MEIDE, MEDE, *s.* Meed, reward, recompense; Douglas, III. 50, 30, Small's ed.; also, bribe, gift, present; Charters of Peebles, 4 Feb. 1444-5, p. 11.

A.-S. *méd*, meed, merit, reward; M. E. *mede, meed*.

MEIN, MEEN, *s. v.* and *adj.* V. under MENE.

MEIND, MEINT, *adj.* Mixed: "*meind grass*," a mixed crop of rye, beer, and oats used for fodder. V. MEING.

Meind-grass was a common crop on poor lands, raised chiefly as food for the horses on the farm. In its green state it was cut and used as ryegrass is now used; but of the portion that ripened and was thrashed the grain was given to the horses, and the straw (which was still called *meind-grass*) was used for bedding, thatching, &c. This explanation is necessary in order to understand the following record:—

John Picken of Netherlobertland sued Alexander Dickie of same place for, inter alia, "twenty shiling for *meind grass*." But Alexander "upon his oath declared that he never received any straw from him save ane bottle which he brought into him;" and the bailie "therfor assoilized him therfrae." Corshill Baron-Court Book, Ayr and Wigtown Arch. Coll., iv. 160-1.

MEIR, MEER, MERE, MEYR, *s.* A large tress or tressle used by builders in erecting scaffolding. Addit. to MEIR, q. v.

"Item, to Robert Graye for timmer to be ane *meir*, iij s. Item, to Thomas Hannayo for making aue band of irne to it, ij. s." Accts., 16 Nov. 1577, Burgh Recs. Glasgow, I. 465, Rec. Soc.

MEIRSWYNE, *s.* V. MERESWINE.

To MEIS, etc., *v. a.* To mitigate. V. DICT.

Meis is short for *ameis*, from O. Fr. *amesir*, which is from L. Lat. *admitiare*, to mitigate—from Lat. *mitis*; see AMESE in Murray's New Eng. Dict.

MEKLEWAME, MEIKLEWAME, MUKLWAME, *s.* The stomach of an animal, but generally applied to the stomach of a cow.

". . in place of potis and sik scithing vesselis,

the painches of ane ox or ane kow they vset cheiflie. Gif necessaitie vrge, this day thay take the hail *mekle-wame* of ane slain ox, thay turne and dicht it, thay fill it partlie with watir, partlie with flesche, thay hing it in the cruik or a sting, eftir the maner of a pott, and sa thay kuik it very commodiouslie vpon the fyre." Leslie's Hist. Sect., p. 94, S.T.S.

The term is still used in country districts where the people have not yet given up making a big haggis. The common or wee haggis is contained in the stomach of a sheep,—generally called a sheep's bag; but the big haggis is contained in a *meklewame*; and it was to such a specimen that Burns addressed the famous lines.

The groaning trencher there ye fill,
Your hurdies like a distant hill,
Your pin wad help to mend a mill
   In time o' need;
While thro' your pores the dews distil
   Like amber bead.

The "*pin*" is the wooden skewer by which the mouth of the bag is tightly closed.

To MELL, MELLE, MELE, *v. n.* The following are additional meanings. V. DICT.

1. To speak, act, undertake; Gol. and Gaw., l. 69.

2. To match, equal, compare, compare favourably.

Simon he's a strappin' chiel,
For looks wad *mell* wi' ony bodie;
In height twa eli but an' a span,
An' half as braid is Simon Brodie.
                        Whistle Binkie, I. 269.

This peculiar application of *mell*, to mix, mingle, etc., is still in use. It is an extension of the meaning to mix or mingle with others on an equal footing; thus, " He *mells* wi' the best in the town," not only means that he mixes with them on an equal footing, but implies that he reckons himself equal with them, and quite a match in comparison with any one of them. *Mell* is derived from O. Fr. *mealer*, to mingle, Mod. Fr. *mêler*. Jamieson gives the form *meller* on the authority of Rudd.; but this is an error; see Gloss. to Doug. Virgil. The assertion that Fr. *mêler* is of Goth. origin is also an error; for it can be traced directly to Latin: Mod. Fr. *mêler*, O. Fr. *mealer*, then through regular modifications to Low Lat. *misculare*, frequent. of Lat. *miscere*, to mix. It has therefore no relation to the Teut. words cited in DICT.

MELYIE, *s.* V. DICT.

The deriv. of this word is correctly given as Fr. *mailis*, a small copper coin; but its relation to the Teut. words cited is a mere fancy. See explanation under *Mail*, *s.*

To MEMER, *v. n.* To stammer; also, to mumble. Errat. in DICT. V. MEMER.

This term implies speaking in a low or indistinct manner, as when a person thinks aloud, or mumbles to himself. It is allied to M. E. *mameren*, and *mamelen*.

MEN, MENE, *s.* Mien, demeanour, bearing; Douglas, III. 197, 20, Small.

MENARE, *s.* V. DICT.

Not from Teut., but from O. Fr. *moienneres*, later *moyenneur*, a mediator. V. Burguy.

MEND, *part. pt.* Mended, improved, amended, atoned for, made up.

For I have heard chirurgeons say,
Oft times deferring of a day
Might not be *mend* the morn.
         Montgomery, Cherrie and Slae, s. 36.
"The morn," to-morrow, next day.

MENDS, MENDIS, MENSE, *s.* Amendment, means of amendment; cure, healing, remedy; also in pl. sense applied to simples, salves, &c., as curatives: as, "I see nae signs o' a *mends* yet; ye'll get nae *mendis* for that ill; ye hae the *mense* in your ain han'."

The birth that the ground bare was broudyn on bredis,
With gerss gay as the gold, and granis of grace,
Mendis and medicine for all mennis neidis.
                        Houlate, l. 29, Bann. MS.

Addit. to MENDS.

To MENSE, *v. a.* To amend, increase; improve, heal, cure: also, to make up for, atone for; as, "Your giein' now canna *mense* for your takin' then;" West of S.

"But, when vnder this patronage pretence they eyther pinche the patrimony or yet the kirk-place, of Laik patrones they become but lawlesse publicans, lyke Hophnees with elcrookes to minche, and not Samneles to *mense*, the offerings of God." Blame of Kirkburiall, ch. 19.

MENEKIN, *adj.* V. MINIKIN.

MENEWITH, *prep.* Right against or flush with: similar to *inwith*.

The King to souper is set, served in halle,
Under a siller of silke, dayntily dight,
With al worshipp and wele, *menewith* the walle.
         Awnt. Arth., 27, 3, MS. Douce.

Wrongly printed *mewith* in Pinkerton's ed. and adopted by Jamieson. That entry must therefore be deleted.

To MENGE, *v. a.* Prob. only a form of *mend*, *mene*, remember, make mention of, intercede for. Addit. to MENGE, q. v.

And *menge* me with mattens and masses in melle.
         Awnt. Arth., st. 25, 3, MS. Douce.

Not defined in DICT., but a meaning is suggested which is wrong. The etym., however, is correct. A.-S. *mengan*, to make mention of; M. E. *mengen*.

To MENIS, MINIS, MINCHE, *v. a.* To minish, diminish; part. pt. *menist*, Douglas, II. 247, 12, Small's ed.; *minche*, Bl. of Kirkburiall, ch. 19. See quot. under *Mense*, *v.*

Fr. *menuiser*, to minish; Lat. *minutiare*, from Lat. *minutus*, small; M. E. *menusen*. V. Skeat's Etym. Dict.

MENSE, *s.* and *v.* V. MENDIS.

MENSE, *s.* Sense, mental ability, skill: "Had he the *mense* as he has the manners, we micht mak him our deacon." West of S. Addit. to MENSE, q. v.

MENSELESS, *adj.* Senseless, stupid, unskilful: "He's no sae *menseless*, seeing he's waled sae guid a wife." Addit. to MENSKLES, q. v.

MENSTRIE, s. A menstruum or flux used in smelting and refining metals; also, testing the fineness of a metal by flux; Early Records of Mining in Scotland, p. 167.
Lat. *menstrua*, the menses; Low Lat. *menstruum*, a flux, a term in alchemy adopted by the old philosophers, in the belief that solvents could be prepared only at certain stages of the moon.

MENT, *part. pt.* A form of *meint* or *mengt*, mixed or mingled. V. MENG.
Iris then sprent on swiftlie as a vyre,
And throw the cluddis hir trace, quhar scho went,
Schupe like a bow of diuers hewis *ment.*
Douglas, Virgil, v. ch. 11.
A.-S. *mengan*, to mix, mingle.

MENYIE, MENYNG, MAYNYE, s. Moan, complaint; also, the cause or ground of complaint, i.e., ill-usage, wrong, misfortune, etc. V. MENE, MENYNG.
With bludie skalp and cheikis bla and reid,
This wretchit wolf weipand thus on he went,
Of his *menyie* markand to get remeid:
To tell the king the cace wes his intent.
Henryson, Parl. of Beistes, l. 241.

MENYNG, s. Meaning, intention, purpose. V. MENE, *v.*
For faith nor aith, word nor assurance,
Trew *menyng*, await or business,—
Full littil or nocht in luve dois availl.
Imitation of Chaucer, Bann. MS. fol. 282 b.

MERCHION, MERSCHION, MARCHION, s. A marquis; originally an officer of the marches; Houlate, l. 685, 328.
L. Lat. *marchionem*, acc. of *marchio*, a prefect or warden of the marches.

MERE, s. A meeting-place, a place appointed for meeting; Gol. and Gaw., l. 1237. Addit. to MERE, q. v.

MERES, MEREST, s. A morass. V. MARES.

MERLION, MERLYEON, s. V. MARLEYON.

MERS, s. The round top in a ship; Accts. L. H. Treas., I. 253, Dickson. Dutch, *mars.*

MERSCHELL, MERSCHIALE, s. A marshal of the household; Accts. L. H. Treas., I. 109, 197: *hors marschael*, a farrier; Ibid. p. 291. The latter was the original meaning of L. Lat. *marescallus.* Addit. to MARSCHAL, q. v.

MERTH, s. Marrow; Rob Stene's Dream, p. 14. V. MERCH.
No doubt this form represents a vulgar pron. of *merch:* but in this instance, and in many others, where the term is read from MS., it is certainly a misreading of *merch.*

MESE, s. V. DICT.
The common form is *Mais* or *Maise,* q. v., for additions and corrections.

To MESTER, *v. a.* Del. this entry in DICT., and see under *Minster.*
This is a misreading in Tytler's ed. The MS. has *mister,* a contr. form of *minister:* but this was not known when I conjectured the proper sense of the word.

MESTOUR, s. Want. V. MISTER.
Represents the pron. of the term in Peebles dist. V. Burgh Recs., p. 115.

MET, METE, METT, METTE, s. A measure-dish of whatever kind; but generally applied to the wooden vessels used in measuring corn, salt, &c. Addit. to MET, METE, q. v.
"Item, that the *mettis* and *mesouris* be assait throw the haile toun, and quhar thai be fundin unrichtuus be distroit, and the avnaris of tham pvnisit be the lawe." *Burgh Recs. Aberdeen,* I. 437, Sp. C.
The *mettis* were the larger wooden vessels used in dry measure, and the *mesouris* were the smaller vessels of tin or pewter used for liquids. The terms occur frequently in our Burgh Records.

METE, MEET, MEIT, MEYT, MEYIT, *adj.* 1. Measure, for the purpose of measuring; as, a *mete*-dish.
2. Measured, adapted, fitting, close-fitting, as applied to articles of dress made to measure.
Apoun his fete put bys *mete* schois hote.
Douglas, Virgil, 258, 40, Rudd.
Small's ed. reads *meyit.*
Mete, meet, etc. as applied to articles of clothing was also used like F. *dress:* as, "a *meet* coat," a dress-coat: which is not properly explained by Jamieson. V. MEET-COAT.

METING, MEETING, s. Measure, fit measure; that which is meet; Bl. of Kirkburiall, ch. 7.

METSOR, METSOUR, MESOUR, MISOUR, MISSOURE, s. A measure or measure-dish of whatever kind; Burgh Recs. Aberdeen, I. 335, Sp. C.

METTER, s. A measurer. V. METSTER.

To METE, *v. a.* To dream, fancy, represent, imagine: pret. *met*, Kingis Quair, st. 73.
And in thare sweuynnys *metis* quent figuris.
Douglas, Virgil, 47, 53, Rudd.
Jamieson defined this term "to paint, delineate," from A.-S. *metan*; but he ought to have added Ruddiman's explanation, "animis obversantur, or rather dream, represent, fancy, in which sense Chaucer uses the word." The context suggests A.-S. *maetan,* to dream, as the correct etym.

METH, METHE, s. V. MEITH.

METURE, s. Measurement, size.

MEWITH. Del. this entry in DICT.
An error in Pinkerton's version for *Menewith,* q. v.

MICHTIS, MYCHTYIS, s. pl. Warriors, chieftains; Gol. and Gaw., l. 1012. V. MICHTIE, *adj,*

MIDDEN-MAVIS, s. A rag-picker: syn. *hauk-gaw.*
Ilk *midden-mavis,* wee black jaudy,
A' dread an' fear ye.
James Ballantine, The Wee Raggit Laddie.

To MIDLE, MIDEL, v. a. Represents a com. pron. of E. *meddle.*

MIDLERT, MYDDIL-ERD, s. V. DICT.
In last para. of this entry near the end, for "*manasedh,* or, the seat of man, *fairghus,* q. fair or beautiful house," read "*manaseths,* seed or race of man, *fairhwus,* world, human society, cognate with A.-S. *feorh,* life."

MIKLEWAME, s. V. *Meklewame.*

MILLOIN, *adj.* Milan: usual form is *millain.* Errat. in DICT.
Jamieson's definition of this word is certainly wrong; but his explanatory note almost corrects it.

MILL-TREE, MILNETREE, s. A beam or spar for a shaft or axle to the running stone of a mill.
"Persued for ane Theiptree, quhich he gave to the defender to carie quhen they were hombringing ane *milnetree* to their master, quhich he lost." Corshill Baron-Court Book, Ayr and Wigtown Arch. Coll., IV. 168.
"Theiptree," a corr. of Threeptree, q. v.

MINAS, s. and v. V. MANAS.

To MINCHE, v. a. To diminish. V. *Menis.*

To MINSTER, v. a. To administer, dispense, render, perform.
Quhat sall I think, allace! quhat reuerence
Sall I *minster* to your excellence.
King's Quair, st. 43, Skeat.
By mistake *mester* in Tytler's ed.: "min[i]ster," as the line requires, in Skeat's ed.: *mister* in MS. This contr. form is occasionally found in MSS. See Note in Skeat's ed., p. 68.
Jamieson, following Tytler's ed., adopted *Mester;* but that entry must now be deleted.

MIRKIN', MIRKENIN', MIRKNIN, s. Darkening, fore-night, gloaming; Shetl. Fireside Tales, p. 132, 133. V. MIRK, MIRKEN.

MIRSORY, s. Prob. a corr. of *mercery,* merchandise. O. Fr. *mercerie.*
"Item of *mirsory* or merchandice, dry or costly guidis, to custome it be the trowne." Burgh Recs. Edinburgh, I. 236, Rec. Soc.

MISCHAWING, s. V. under *Mishaif.*

To MISCHEVE, v. a. To ban, decry, strive to hinder or ruin. Addit. to MISCHIEVE, q. v.
Our curslt craft full mony man *mischevis.*
Henryson, Tod and Wolf, l. 45.

MISCUICKIT, *pret.* and *part. pt.* V. MISCOOK.

To MISHAIF, MISHAUE, MISHAWE, v. a. To misbehave, misdemean: "ye may *mishaif*

yow in sum caice," i.e., may act foolishly or unwisely; Alex. Scott's Poems, p. 18, ed. 1882.
". . wes accusit . . for the iniuring of diuerse nychtbouris and inhabitantes in deid, and sklandering of thame in word, and for *mischawing* of himself in sic sundry wayis, sua that he is ane unlauchtfull nychtbour, and aucht nocht to be sufferit to pas at liberte within this burght." Burgh Recs. Aberdeen, I. 346, Sp. C.
Mischawing is here a bad form of *mishaving;* and, unfortunately, there are in these vols. very many such forms: indicating carelessness both in writing and in reading.
A.-S. *mis,* wrong, and *habban,* to have.

MISK, *adj.* Moist, wet. V. MIST.

To MISMAK, MISMACK, v. a. In the sense of *unmake,* to degrade, depose; and still used in the sense of discompose, blush, or change countenance, as, "He could threep a lee in your face, an' no *mismak* him;" West of S. Addit. to MISMACK.
"Item, that we haid spokine of his Graice that we haid maid his Graice and we wald *mismak* him, quhilk we denye neuir to be thocht be ws, laitt be to apekit," &c. Burgh Recs. Edin., 9 July, 1575, Rec. Soc.

To MISREGAIRD, v. a. To disregard; part. pt. *misregairdit;* Burgh Recs. Edinburgh, IV. 234, Rec. Soc.

MISSAIRT, *part. pt.* V. *Misservit.*

To MISSEME, MYSSEME, v. n. To be unseemly, unbecoming; to ill-become; Douglas, Virgil, 111, 23, Rudd.; part. pres. *myssemand.*
A.-S. *mis,* wrong, and *séman,* to satisfy, conciliate; hence, to suit, become, &c. V. SEEM, in Skeat's Etym. Dict.

MISSERVIT, MISSERUIT, MISSERIT, MISSAIRT, *part. pt.* Not served iu due and proper course, poorly or badly served, ill-supplied.
". . quhilk [regrating of victual] is the occasioun of gryt deartht, and the caus that the pure commounis of this burght ar *misservit.*" Burgh Recs. Aberdeen, II. 54, Rec. Soc.
A.-S. *mis,* wrong; and Fr. *servir,* from Lat. *servire,* to serve.

MISSILRY, s. Leprosy. V. DICT.
Although not defined in DICT., the correct meaning is suggested in the explanatory note. The etym., however, is wrong. This word has no connection with *measles;* it is from M. E. and O. Fr. *mesel,* a leper, but orig. a wretch, from L. Lat. *misellus,* from Lat. *miser,* wretched: and *measles* was borrowed from the Dutch *maselen,* also called *masel-sucht,* "mensellsicknesse," Hexham. In the 14th cent. it appears as *maseles,* which represents the common Scot. pron. still in use.

MISSOUR, MISSURE, MISOURE, s. Measure, a measure, measurement; Burgh Recs. Glasgow, II. 53, 366, Rec. Soc.

This spelling represents the common pron. of the term.

To MISSOUR, MISSURE, v. a. To measure, mete out; Douglas, iv. 105. 19, Small's ed.
O. Fr. *mesure*, from Lat. *mensura*, measure.

MIST, MISK, MISTY, *adj.* Moist, wet; as, *mist* land, *misk* grass, *misty* lea.
By gousty placis, welsche savorit, *mist*, and hair, Quhair profound nycht perpetuall doth repair. *Douglas, Virgil*, vi. ch. 7, Small's ed.

MISTER, *s.* Stale urine; liquid collected from a byre; applied also to the contents of the *midden-hole* of a farm-house. Addit. to MAISTER.
Gael. *maistir*, urine.

To MISTRAM, *v. a.* To disorder, derange, confuse.
"By Kirkburiall kirk bounds are *mistrammed*, and in many places either so eatten up with intaking lles, or the passages so impeshed with thortersome throughes, . . that if they cleaue to that they haue calked, the people that restes must byde at the dore." Left undefined by Jamieson; yet he suggests the right etym., but does not apply it correctly. Prob. he would have accounted for the term fully if he had taken *house* and *room* in the quotations as meaning the interior fittings and arrangements, and not the building or framework. V. MISTRAM.
A.-S. *mis*, wrong, and *trimman, trymian, trymman*, to make firm or right, set in order, array, prepare. From the same root comes E. *trim*.

MITHE, *s.* A batch or baking of loaves. Addit. to MEITH, s.
"Item, for the thryde faut, of ilk *mithe* wantand of the wecht of the lafe vj laffis to be tane and delt to pur fouk." Burgh Recs. Peebles, 1463, p. 150.

MITTEN, MITTAN, *s.* A kind of hawk. V. MITTALE.

To MOCH, *v. n.* To become mouldy or covered with mildew: hence, to rot; applied to articles of clothing, books, &c. Addit. to MOCH, *v.*
". . not onlie sall the maist pairt of thame [the books] *moch* and conswme." Burgh Recs. Aberdeen, ii. 394, Sp. C.

MODERNE, *adj.* Of the present, of this time, at present, that is: a term used after titles of office, rank, &c. Lat. *modernus*.
". . in name of our maist gracious quene *moderne*." Burgh Recs. Aberdeen, 1553, i. 285, Sp. C.
"Quhilkis lytis being presented to my lorde Archibischop of Glasgow *moderne*." Burgh Recs. Glasgow, 1557, i. 62, Rec. Soc.
"Hew erle of Eglingtoune *moderne*, ane noble and potent lorde." Ibid. p. 185.
O. Fr. *moderne*, "modern, new, of this age, of these times, in our time;" Cotgr.

MODYR-HALF, MUDYR-HALF, *s.* Mother's-side: "frendis on the *mudyr-half*," Burgh Lawis, ch. 98, Rec. Soc.

MŒLISCOP, MEIL-COPPIS, *s.* A land measure in Orkney.
"*Coppis* is from Norse *kupa*, a cup, bowl, basin; *meil-coppis* is for *mælis-kupa*, from Norse *mæil*, a measure of grain; and a *meil-coppis* was so much land as would be sowed by a *mælir* of seed." Capt. Thomas, Proceedings Antiq. Soc. Sc., Vol. XVIII., p. 274.

MOIT, *s.* A form of MOTE, an eminence, q. v.; Douglas, II. 110. 11, Small.

MOLAYN, *s.* A form of MOLLAT, q. v.

MOLET, *s.* V. MOLLAT.

MONE, MOYNE, *s.* The moon; the age, the phases, or the changes of the moon; also, the moon-works of a clock, i.e., the mechanism by means of which a clock shows the changes of the moon.
". . . and in likmaner sall mak and repair of new graithit ane orloge and *mone* with all necessaris tharof, kepand just cours fra xij houris to xij houris alswele nycht as day, and just change of the *mone* yeirlie throwout as efferis." Burgh Recs. Stirling, 8 Jan., 1546-7.
". . . to James Scot, payntour, for his bountetht and labouris done be him in cullering of the knok, *moyne*, and orlage and uther commowne work of the towne." Burgh Recs. Glasgow, i. 57, Rec. Soc.

MONEBRUNT, *adj.* Moonstruck, foolish, giddy, light-headed: a polite substitute for *lunatic*, as applied to one who is love-sick, as in "*monebrunt* madynis myld." Alex. Scott's Poems, p. 21, ed. 1882.

MONGIS, MANGIS, *prep.* A contr. for *amongis*, amongst, among: still common in West and South of S.: pron. *mongs* and *mangs*. V. *Amongis*.

MOOSTY, MOOSTIT, MOOSTET, MOUSTED, *adj.* 1. Musty, moulded; covered over with must or mould. V. MUST.

2. Powdered, covered with must or hair-powder.
To think yon birkies i' the town, Wi' ruffil't sark and *moostet* crown, Play siccan tricks on countra bodies, *W. Watson's Poems*, p. 32.

MORISE, *s.* A morris-dance: pl. *morisis*, Douglas, Virgil, xiii. ch. 9.

MORIS-BELLS, MOREIS-BELLS, *s. pl.* Small bells used by morris-dancers; they were attached to the cap, wrists, and ankles of the performers.
"*Moreis bellis* the groce . . xxxs." Halyburton's Ledger, p. 259.
For particulars regarding morris-dancing see Strutt's Sports and Pastimes, pp. 223, 247, 254, ed. 1841, and Brand's Pop. Antiq., pp. 137-152, ed. 1877.
In Edinburgh, in olden times, during the procession of the patron saint on St. Giles Day, June 10th, the most attractive portion of the convoy was a set of morris-dancers in full costume. A humorous account

of the last of these processions is given by John Knox in his Hist. of the Reformation.
Span. *Morisco*, Moorish: from Lat. *Maurus*, a Moor. The term is frequently given as from the Fr. *moresque*.

MORKIN, MORKEN. 1. As an *adj.*, rotten, rotting, as applied to a sheep, etc., that has died afield.

2. As a *s.*, a dead sheep,—one that has died afield: also, the skin of such an one; but when used in this sense the term is generally pl., *morkins;* Halyburton's Ledger, p. 306.

This term is still frequently used as an *adj.*, as, "a *morkin* sheep," which Burns gave as the definition of *braxie*.
Icel. *morkinn*, rotten, decayed; applied to meat, fish, etc.

To MORSE, *v. a.* Errat. for *nurse*, in the sense of foster, cherish, plan, devise; Sir W. Scott.

"Nay, an thou would'st try conclusions," said Christie of the Clinthill, "I will meet thee at daybreak by St. Mary's well."
"Hardened wretch!" said Father Eustace, "art thou but this instant delivered from death, and dost thou so soon *morse* thoughts of slaughter?" Scott, The Monastery, ch. 10.
This is a most interesting example of how such mistakes may be entirely overlooked in popular literature: may be read and repeated as most suitable expressions by generation after generation; and, by so doing duty for the proper words, may at last come to be regarded as correct and genuine elements of our language. The work in which this misprint occurs was first issued in 1820. Thousands of editions have since then been published at home and abroad; and each one in turn has repeated the error without remark and without detection. Not until the summer of 1884 was the mistake suspected and recorded.
When preparing the word for entry in this Suppl., and while still puzzling over its meaning, Prof. Skeat called my attention to a communication in Notes and Queries, s. vi., vol. ix., p. 507, in which *morse* is challenged as a misprint for *nurse*. This was probably the first time that public attention was called to the word.
Having read that communication and several others which followed in reply, and being still dissatisfied with the result, I wrote to Messrs. A. & C. Black, the well-known publishers of Scott's works, for further advice. They could give no information on the subject, which was quite new to them; nor could they understand why *morse* should be doubted; but they very kindly promised to try if the word written by Sir Walter in his MS. of the *Monastery* is *nurse* as clearly as writing can make it." Such an answer is final.
Strange to say, the Centenary ed. of 1871 has *nurse*, while later eds. have *morse*.

MORT-BELL, *s.* The dead-bell: a handbell which was rung through the streets to warn the inhabitants that a funeral was about to take place.

"The provost, baillies, and counsall hes gevin thair twa commoun bellis, viz., the *mort* and skellit bellis, togidder with the office of pwnterschipe, to George Johnstoune, for ane yeir to cum, and that for the

soume of thrie scoir pundis." Burgh Recs. Glasgow, i. 153, Rec. Soc.
The *mort-bell* here mentioned was the old St. Mungo's bell, that had been used for many generations as the dead-bell of Glasgow. For nearly twenty years after the Reformation it remained in the possession of the keepers who had been appointed to the office previous to that event; but after their death the magistrates bought it from the heirs, and it became the property of the town.
The following extract is the record of this transaction; and it is given in full, as it recalls some interesting particulars of old burghal life.
"The provest, baillies, and counsall. with dekinnis, coft fra Johne Muir, sone to vmquhill James Muir, and Andro Lang, the auld bell that yed throw the towne of auld at the buriall of the deid, for the sowme of ten pundis money, quhilk thai ordane Patrick Glen, thair thesaurare, to paye to thame, and als grantit the said Andro to be maid burges gratis; quhilk bell thai ordanit in all tymes to remane as commoune bell to gang for the buriall of the deid, and to be gewin yeirlie to sic persouu as thai appoynt for anys in the yeir, takand cautioun for keiping and delynering thairof at the yeris end.
"And the said Andro Lang, as sone to vmquhill maister Robert Layng, is maid instantlie burges as ane burges sone, gratis, for the said caus of the bell, and hes gewin his aitht of fidelitie to the toun and als for obserwing of the statutis thairof." Burgh Recs. Glasgow, 19 Nov. 1577, i. 64, Rec. Soc.
This old bell remained in use till 1640, and proved to be a very profitable investment for the town. In that year the Dean of Guild was instructed "to caus mak ane new deid bell to be rung for and befor the dead wnder hand." Ibid. p. 424. And that considerable importance was attached to this ceremonial of burial in those days is shown by an order of the magistrates in 1612, when a new bellman was appointed. They allowed him to have the "for ane persoun of age xiijs. iiijd., for ane barn, vjs. viijd.; and ordanis the said Thomas to cleith him self in blak apparell, as is requirit in him in respect of the nature of his office." Ibid. p. 326.

MORT-CAPE, MORT-CAIP, *s.* A mourning cope worn by priests at a funeral; Burgh Recs. Edinburgh, II. 359, Rec. Soc.

MORT-CHARGE, *s.* Now called *deadfreight:* the sum which a merchant has to pay for goods which he has failed to ship; Burgh Recs. Edinburgh, 1 Dec. 1553, II. 184, Rec. Soc.
The term occurs also in an earlier record given on p. 105 of the same vol.

MORTMALLIS, *s. pl.* Skins of sheep found dead afield; also called *morkins;* Halyburton's Ledger, p. 14.
Fr. *mort*, dead, and *mal*, disease.

MOT, MOTE, MOOT, MWT, *s.* and *v.* V. MUTE, MOOT, *s.* and *v.*, and *Mute.*

To the meanings given under MOTS, in DICT., add the following:—1. A meeting place for a court or parliament; an assembly, a law court, a parliament; also in pl. *motis*, the pleas or actions of a law court, and frequently so used in reference to burgh courts and barouy courts; Burgh Lawis, ch. 44, 75, Rec. Soc.; and see under MUTE and *Mute.*

MOT, *part. pt.* Sued or tried in a court of law; Fragments of Old Laws, ch. 8, Rec. Soc.

MOT, MOTE, MOOT, *s.* Lit. a word; hence, signal, call, sign. Also a note or musical sound; hence, a bugle or trumpet call, the cry or call of bird or beast, the strain of the huntsman's horn, the yell of a pack of hounds; and sometimes used for the hunt, hounds, or pack. Addit. to MOT, q. v.

To MOT, MOTT, MOOT, *v. n.* To give the call or sign, to wind a horn or blow a trumpet by way of call; to pipe or call as a bird or beast utters its peculiar sound.
Now the blak kokke *mootis* in his fluthir delpe,
The rowntre rokis the revin to alclpe.
Hogg, Bridal of Polmood.

To MOUBAND, MOUBAN', *v. a.* To put into words; to express, utter, speak, recite; Hogg's Tales, I. 34, ed. 1884.
Fr. *moue,* the mouth; and *bander,* to put together, as in architecture.

MOU'D, MOU'T, MOUIT, MOWITT, *adj.* Mouthed; as, "muckle-*mou'd* Kate." V. Mow.
And shangy-*mou'd* halucket Meg.
Blythsome Bridal, st. 5.
". . ane hors, blak-broune *mowitt,* with ane bell in the forrett." Burgh Recs. Aberdeen, I. 282, Sp. C.

MOULDES, *s. pl.* V. MULDE.
Commonly pron. *mools.*

MOUTER, MUTER, *s.* 1. Multure, q. v.
Now, miller and a' as I am,
This far I can see through the matter;
There's men mair notorious to fame,
Mair greedy than me for the *muter.*
Song: Tak' it Man, Tak' it.

2. A familiar name for a miller.
Wi' him, the lang *mouter,* mysel', an' the soutar,
Hae aften forgather'd an' had a bit spree.
Rhyming Rab, Whistle Binkie, i. 340.
Fr. *molture, mouture, meuture, multure:* from L. Lat. *molitura,* a grinding.

MOY, *s.* Help, assistance: as in "*moy* nor hatrance," i.e., help nor hindrance; Burgh Recs. Aberdeen, I. 171, Sp. C.

MOYT. V. DICT.
This entry must be deleted. The term is a misreading of "*mo y^t,*" which is found in the earlier editions of the Kingis Quair; and Jamieson's suggestion regarding it is wide of the mark.

MUDE, MUYD, MOYD, *s.* Temper, disposition, mood; Douglas, I. 91. 17, II. 273. 18, Small. Addit. to [MUDE], q. v.
The form *muyd* occurs in Douglas Virgil, i. ch. 2, l. 17. V. Small's ed.

MUDYR-HALF, *s.* V. *Modyr-half.*
(Sup.)
X

MUGWEED, MOGWEED, *s.* Mugwort; West of S. V. MUGGART.

MUIR, *s.* Waste land, a common, as, "the burgh *muir*"; the common form is *moor.* Also hill or heath pasture common to all the Skathalds of a district; Memorial for Orkney, p. 117. Addit. to MURE, q. v.

MULD, *s.* A mould for lead bullets; also, a mould or pattern of the bore of a gun.
"Item, for *muldis* to cast the plumbis in," . . viijs." Accts. L. H. Treas., I. 295, Dickson.
". . to a man to tak mesour of *muldis* of diuers gunnys, to send in Frans to mak pellokis of irne, . . xvjd." Ibid. p. 320.

MULDIS, *s. pl.* Fragments or portions of the dead preserved as relics: "haly *muldis,*" sacred relics, or relics of saints: Dunbar and Kennedy, l. 378. Addit. to MULDE, s. 3.

MULLION, *s.* A shoe made of untanned leather; same as RULLION, q. v.
This term occurs in the modern and much condensed version of "The Rock and the Wee Pickle Tow," given by Robert Chambers in his collection of "Songs of Scotland prior to Burns." The term used by Ross in the original song is *rullion.*

MULTIPLIE, MULTIPLE, *s.* Abundance, expanse; Leslie's Hist. Scot., p. 41, S. T. S. Addit. to MULTIPLE, q. v.
"In some places is funde *multiplie* of Tinne and that of fyne tinne." Idem, p. 7.

To MUM, MVM, *v. n.* To act as mummer or mute at a funeral; to pretend or act a part: part. *muming,* Douglas, I. 104. 27, ed. Small.

To MUMCHANCE, *v. n.* To mum, to play dummy, or harlequin; to move about silently, as if dumb through grief: *mumschance,* Burgh Recs. Edin., IV. 229, Rec. Soc. V. MUM CHAIRTIS.
"In steed of humane teeres that best can expresse the owne smart, some will haue trumpets; and in steed of mourning in the dust, as they did oft-tymes, we *mumchance* and murgeon in such delicate duillis, better featad for wowing nor woing, that hoires or widowes never dallies more nor vndor their duilles." Blame of Kirkburiall, ch. 7.
The use of this term is said to have been introduced through the game at dice called Mumchance. See under Chance in Cotgrave.

To MUMMER, MUMER, *v. n.* Same as *Mammer,* q. v.

MUNNA. Must not. V. MAUNA.

MUNT, *v.* and *s.* Mount.
This form represents the pron. of the word in the West of S.: thus, "*to munt heuks,*" to mount or dress fishing hooks; *muntibank,* a mountebank; &c.

MUNTH, MWNTHT, s. V. MONTH.

MURE, adj. Short for demure; "manswet and mure," gentle and demure; Houlate, l. 83, Asloan MS.
O. Fr. de mure, short for de bons murs, of good manners.

MURTHER-HOLES, MURDREIS-HOILLIS, s. pl. Slits, loopholes, &c., pierced in the walls of a building for the purpose of shooting through, as in castles of the olden time: murdreis-hoillis; Burgh Recs. Edinburgh, III. 239, Rec. Soc.
"And although to beligger the lodgings of men, for feare of their murther-holes, they wil looke ere they loupe; yet to enforce the kirk-house (as if God had no gunnes), there are many of small feare." Blame of Kirkburiall, ch. xix.
O. Fr. murdriere a l'ouvert, pierced loopholes : lit. murder-hole.
This term has been treated very differently by the French and the English. In French it gradually came to be simply meurtrière, a loophole, and in English louver, it. For brevity the one language adopted the first part of the term, and the other the last. This is well illustrated by a passage in the Romance of Partenay descriptive of the castle of Melusina. In the French original it runs thus :—
Murdrieres il a a l'ouvert,
Pour lancier, traire, et deffendre.
The English translation has :—
At lovers, lowpes, archers had plente,
To cast, draw, and shete, defens to be.

MUSSELL, s. A veil. V. MUSALL, v.
This term was also applied to the face-cloth or muffle worn by lepers when they appeared in public. In Glasgow they were allowed to visit the town twice a week for a few hours; but they had to "gang vpone the calsay syd with thair mussellis on thair faice, and clopperis." Burgh Recs. Glasgow, I. 237, Rec. Soc.

MUTE, s. To s. 2, in DICT. add :—Also, a law court, and the meeting or holding of it; Burgh Laws, ch. 31, 40.

MUTH, adj. V. DICT.
The origin of this term is not made clear. It ought to be Icel. móthr = A.-S. méthe, tired. As Prof. Skeat has pointed out, "There are four distinct Icel. words, (1) móthr, allied to A.-S. mód, E. mood, (2) mœthr = A.-S. méthe, Scot. muth, tired, wearied. Even Vigfusson mixes them up. See his Icel. Dict."

MYCHARE, s. V. DICT.
Del. the last parag. of this entry and substitute the following :—
From mich, to skulk, play truant; M. E. michen, from O. Fr. mucer, mucier, later musser, to hide, conceal. V. Skeat's Etym. Dict.

MYCHTEN, MYCHTYNE, v. pres. pl. Might; Douglas, Virgil; 89, 38, Rudd., and II. 158. 9, Small.

MYDLIT, MYDDILLIT, part. pt. Mixed. V. under MIDIL.

MYDMORNE, s. Six o'clock, a.m.; Burgh Lawis, ch. 73, 75, Rec. Soc.
According to the ancient reckoning midmorn was hora prima or the first hour of the artificial day, and undern was hora tertia or the third hour. These were accounted the lawful hours for beginning work in summer and winter respectively.

MYKKIS, s. pl. Prob. apparatus for levelling guns in taking aim; Accts. L. H. Treas., I. 292, 334, Dickson.
Dutch, mikken, to level at, aim.

MYLUART, s. A miller. V. MILLART.
This form occurs in Aberdeen Burgh Recs. II. 175, Sp. C., but is printed mylvart.

MYMMERKIN, s. V. MEMERKYN.

MYN, adj. Less: "more and myn," high and low, great and little. V. MIN.

MYNEKIN, adj. V. MINIKIN.

To MYNIS, MYNNIS, v. a. To lessen, diminish; part. pt. mynnist, Burgh Recs. Edinburgh, 1511, I. 133, Rec. Soc. V. Menis.

To MYN, MYNNE, MIN, v. a. To think, devise, plan, mention. V. MIND, MYND.

MYNNINGIS, s. pl. Woolen cloths made at Menin near Comtrai ; Exch. Rolls.

MYNORALL, s. Lit. produce of the mine: also, mining, course or process of mining, preparation of the metal.
Richt as the mynour in his mynorall,
Fair gold with lyre may fra the lede weil wyn.
Henryson, Parl. of Beistis, l. 302.
O. Fr. mineral, "a minerall;" Cotgr.: from L. Lat. minare, to lead ; hence, to follow up the leader or lode, i.e., to excavate the ore, to mine.

MYNT, s. Aim, effort, threat. V. MINT.

MYRE, s. A moor. V. MURE.

MYSAVENTOUR, MYSAUENTURE, s. Mischance, misfortune ; Douglas, Virgil, 285, 32, Rudd.
The more common form is mishanter, which represents the pron. of misaunter, short for Fr. mésaventure.
V. MISHANTER.

MYSBELEVE, s. A false idea, belief, or judgment.
For gif thow wenis that all the victory—
May be reduceit and alterat clar agane,
A mysbeleve thou fosteris all in vane.
Douglas, Virgil, x. ch. 11, l. 56, Rudd., Small.

MYSFURE, pret. Miscarried. V. [MISFURE.]

MYSSOUR, s. Measure. V. Missour.

MYTH, adj. and adv. A form of MEETH, q. v.
This form is poet., and in Houlate, l. 693, has been adopted to rhyme with blyth.

N.

NAB, *s.* V. Dict. Add to s. 2, 'a point, projection, promontory'; West of S.

NACHT. For *ne acht*, ought not, was not bound or called upon.

Quha wan the feild, or greitest Camploun,
Or was Victour, I *nacht* decerne that thing.
Rolland, Court of Venus, iv. 606, S.T.S.
"I *nacht* decerne," I was not called upon to decide. Omitted in Gloss.

NACKET, *s.* An impertinent, mischievous, or wicked child: applied also to a precocious child; South and West of S., and in first sense in Orkn. V. NACHET.

NADE, NAD. Had not: for *ne had*.

NAELSTRING, *s.* The navel-string, umbilical cord; South and West of S.
A.-S. *nafela*, navel, and *strenge*, a cord: Du. *navel*, Dan. *navle*, Sw. *nafle*.

NAESLIN, *part.* and *adj*. Fitting into each other, well matched; working or pulling well together, as in double harness; Orkn.
Prob. the local pron. of *nestling*, sitting or fitting closely to each other like young birds in a nest.

NAFE, NAF. Have not: for *ne have*.

To NAG, NEG, *v. a*. To bite, snap, indent or mark with the teeth, seize smartly; also, to nick, notch, or hack with a sharp instrument. In the latter sense, syn. *hag*. South and West of S. Addit. to NAG, q. v.

To NAG, NEG, *v. n*. To be peevish, querulous, or sarcastic, to keep on grumbling, to repeat an action with irritating frequency. Addit. to NAG, q. v.

NAG, *s.* Bite, snap; nick, hack, notch, or indentation made with a sharp instrument; a snappish answer or retort.

To NAGGLE, *v. a.* and *n.* To gnaw; to keep on scolding or rating, to quarrel or continue an angry altercation, to be constantly fault-finding.

NAGGY, NAGGLY, *adj.* Touchy, fretful, sarcastic, quarrelsome, ill-natured: a person of such disposition is said to be "as *naggy* as a thorn-stick."

Nag and its derivatives are used in most of these senses in various parts of the North of E. V. Brockett, Peacock.
Sw. *nagga*, to nibble, peck; Dan. *nage*, to gnaw.

NAGUS, *s.* V. Dict.
The etym. suggested for this word, *Negus*, or *Old Nick*, is ridiculous. Connection with the latter is certainly not warranted by the context; and with the former is simply impossible; for, the drink called *negus* was invented by a Colonel Negus in the reign of Queen Anne, or about 200 years after Dunbar's death.

NAIF, NEIF, NEYF, *s.* Lit. a native; a serf, servant; a kindly tenant.
"It is not improbable that the *neyf* or serf by descent—*nativus de stipite*—was distinguished from the bond-labourer, but we cannot tell to what extent, or in what manner." Innes, Legal Antiquities, p. 50.
"— . . *cum nativis*—that is, with natives or *neyfs*, whose name, both here and in England, points to their being regarded as the remains of the native population obliged by the invaders to become serfs." Ibid., p. 50-51.
Of this servile race there were two classes, the *neyf in gross*—that is the out-and-out slave, who could be bought and sold like a horse or an ox, and the *neyf regardant*,—or slave astricted to a certain land, who could not be moved at the mere will of the lord even to another estate. But long after the term *naif* had ceased to represent this subject race, and to imply a degree of bondage, it still carried with it the idea of service, and continued to be used as the appropriate name of a menial and help.

NAIFSHIP, NEIFSHIP, NEYFSHIP, *s.* State, condition, or service of a serf. V. KNAVESHIP.

NAIL. Down on the *nail*, promptly paid, paid in money, ready money.

NAIL, NALE, NAL, NALI, *s.* A weight of 7 lbs., used for wool; Burgh Recs. Aberdeen, I., 416, Halyburton's Ledger, p. 14, 43.
The form *nall* is found only in Halyburton's Ledger, and is improper. Indeed, the spelling found in that work is very misleading.
In Halliwell's Dict. the *nail* is represented as a weight of 8 lbs, used for articles of food.

NAIMCOUTIH, *adj.* V. NAMEKOUTH.

NAIT, *s.* Use, occasion, purpose; other forms are Nate, Nayt, Note. Errat. in Dict.
The def. and etym. given by Jamieson are misleading. No doubt he wrote *neid* in the common Scot. sense of *use, purpose;* but this is a mistake. And this led him into the other mistake of relating *nait* with Icel. *naud, need*, whereas it is from Icel. *neyti*, use, from *neyta*, to use. Besides, *naud* is the Norse form for *need*; it is *nauth* in Icel.

NAIT, NATE, *adj.* Neat, trim; also, deft, skilful, as in "*nait* handis," Douglas, Virgil, xii., ch. 7. Fr. *net*.

NAITRAL, *adj.* Natural, illegitimate. E. *natural.*

NAITRAL, *s.* A person of weak intellect, a silly person, a simpleton : E. *natural.*

Naitral, illegitimate, must be of comparatively modern use : for *natural*, which is really the same word, has almost invariably the meaning of *lawful*, legitimate. V. NATURAL.

NAKIT, *s.* Nakedness.
For this dispyt, quhen he was deid, auone
Was dampnyt in the flud of Acherone
Till suffer hungir, thrist, *nakit*, and cald.
Henryson, Orph. and Eur., l. 529, Bann. MS.

NAL, NALL, *s.* A nale or nail; a weight of 7 lbs., used for wool ; Halyburton's Ledger, p. 14, 43, Burgh Recs. Aberdeen, I. 416, Sp. C.

NALD, NADE. Would not: for *ne wald, ne wad.* V. NOLD.

NAMED, *adj.* Edged, bordered, hemmed; Burgh Recs. Glasgow, II. 297, Rec. Soc.

NANE, *s.* No one, nobody, nothing.
The mitherless bairnie creeps to his lane bed,
Nane covers his cauld back or haps his bare head.
Will. Thom, The Mitherless Bairn.
Is *nane* sa gude as leif of and mak na mair stryffe.
Rauf Coilzear, l. 172.
Is *nane* sa gude as drink and gang to our bed.
Ibid, l. 261.
"*Is nane*," there is nothing.

NANES, NANIS, NANYS, NONIS, NONES, *s.* Nonce: "for the *nanes*," properly, *for then anes*, for the once, i.e., occasion or present. Errat. in DICT.

Jamieson's definition and explanation of this term and phrase are altogether wrong. The whole entry must be deleted.

As explained by Sir F. Madden in his Gloss. to Sir Gawayne, the phrase, "*for the nanes*," is simply the A.-S. *for tham anes*, later, *for them anes*, written *for the nanes*. The *then* standing for *tham*, dat. of the def. article, and the adv. *anes* being used as a noun. This explanation, however, was first proposed by Price in his notes to Warton, II., 490.

NAPKIN, *s.* V. DICT.

Only in the last sentence of the note is there even an approach to the correct etym. In M. E. this word was written *napekin* and *napet*, dimin. forms of O. Fr. *nape*, a cloth, from which also have come *naprie* and *napron*.

NAPLE, *s.* An apple.
Befoir his face ane *naple* hang also,
Fast at his mowth vpoun a twynid [threid].
Henryson, Orph. and Eur., l. 282, Bann. MS.

NAP O' THE KNEE, *s.* Knee-pan; West of S.

NAPRE, *s.* Napery. V. NAIPRIE.

NAPRON, NAPRIN, NAPERON, *s.* An apron.
These forms represent the common pron. in West and South of S. Brockett gives the last form as common in North of England.

Napron is not a corr. of E. *apron*, but the correct form of which *apron* is a corr. It is from Fr. *naperon*, a large cloth, which is a deriv. from O. Fr. *nape*, a cloth (Fr. *nappe*), from L. Lat. *napa*, corr. of Lat. *mappa*, a napkin, cloth. See Apron in Skeat's Etym. Dict.

NARENT, ABBOT OF. The Abbot of Unreason, a merry-making at the bringing in of summer, similar to that of Robin Hood and Little John; Burgh Recs. Edinburgh, I. 176, Rec. Soc.

For particulars regarding these summer games, see Brand's Pop. Antiq., pp. 144-6, ed. 1877.

NASH, NAISH, NESH, NESCH, *adj.* Tender, delicate, fragile, slim.
A.-S. *hnæsce, hnesce*, soft, tender : M. E. *nesh.*

NASK, *s.* V. DICT.
This term is of Celtic origin ; evidently from Gael. *nasg, naisg*, to bind, make fast ; M'Leod and Dewar.

To **NATE, NAIT**, *v. a.* Forms of Note, to use, etc., q. v. Errat. in DICT.
So also regarding Nate, Nait, *s.* V. Note, and *Nait.* These mistakes are due to Jamieson's misuse of *need* for *use*, which is a very common error in Scot. still.

NATRIE, *adj.* V. DICT.
Del. the note in this entry, and see the explanation given under Natterin, and *Natter.*

To **NATTER**, *v. n.* V. DICT.
A simpler and more direct etym. for this term is O. Norse *gnaddr*, to grumble, growl, a freq. of *gnadda*, Norse *gnadra*, Dan. *gnaddre;* all of which are from O. Norse *gnadd*, a grumbling. V. FRITZNER, AASEN, and CLEASBY.

To **NATTLE**, *v. a.* V. DICT.
This is simply a doublet of *Natter*, regarding which see the note above.

NAUCHTIE, *adj.* V. [NOUCHTIE].

NAUST, *s.* V. NOUST.
Noust, which Jamieson obtained from Edmondston's Gloss. of the Shetl. and Orkn. Dialect, does not correctly represent the pron. of this term. It should be written, as it is still pron., in its old Icelandic form, *naust.* V. Dasent's Burnt Njal, p. cxviii.
The *naust* is a slip either natural or artificial into which a boat is drawn up for protection : a *nouster*, is a common landing place for boats : see Arcadian Sketch Book, Gloss.

NAY-SAY, *s.* A refusal, denial: as, "He winna tak a *nay-say.*"
Common in North of E. also. V. Brockett's Gloss.

NAYTED, *part. pt.* Noted, celebrated. V. NATE, NOTE.

NEB, *s.* 1. The face, countenance ; as, "I dinna like his looks: he has a gae dour *neb.*"
A.-S. *neb*, face. And in the Ancren Riwle, p. 90, we find "ostende mihi faciem" (Song of Sol. ii. 14), rendered by "schaue thi *neb* to me.

2. End, termination; mouth, as of a river; as, "the water-*neb*," the river mouth.

Elderly people in Paisley and Renfrew generally call the mouth of the Cart, and the lands near the junction of the Cart and the Clyde, the *water-neb*, the *wattirneb*. Addit. to NEB, q. v.

To NECH, NEGH, NYCH (gutt.), v. a. To tend to or towards, belong to, concern, fall to one by right or duty : pret. *nycht*, *nyght*, Houlate, l. 47. Addit. to NEICH.

Syne to the samyn forsuith thai assent haile,
That sen it *nechit* Natur, thar alleris mastris,
Thai couth nocht trete but entent of the Temperale.
Houlate, l. 276, Asloan MS.

In Bann. MS. *nychlit*, which is probably a mistake of the scribe for *nychit*, intended to be written *nychtit*, according to the practice of the 16th cent. of writing *t* after *ch* and *th*, as in *witht*, *nychtbour*, &c. There are various similar mistakes in this version.

NEDDIRMAIR, NEDDIRMAIST. V. NETHIRMARE.

NEDDY, NED, *s*. A name for a donkey: "a tinkler's *neddy*," W. Watson's Poems, p. 100.

This term is common in London, and in various parts of Eng. as well.

NEED, *s*. This word is frequently used in Scot. in the sense of use, occasion, purpose; as, "I don't *need* it," i.e., I don't use it, or I have no use for it; "There is no *need* for it," i.e., no occasion for it; "To serve my present *need*," i.e., my present purpose. Various mistakes in the DICT. may be traced to the misuse of *need* for use. V. under *Nait*, *Nate*.

NEET, *s*. An egg of a louse, a louse. Addit. to NEET, q. v.

A.-S. *hnitu*, a nit; Du. *neet*, Sw. *gnet*, Dan. *gnid*, M. E. *nite*.

To NEG, *v. n*. A form of NAG, q. v.

NEIF, NEYF, *s*. A serf, servant. V. *Naif*.

NEIFSHIP, NEYFSHIP, *s*. V. *Naifship*.

NEIFTY, NEYFTY, *s*. Condition of a serf; also, the service exacted from a serf; Old Glasgow, p. 49.

To NEIS, NEYS, *v. n*. V. NEESE.

NEKED, NEKID, *s*. Nothing, next to nothing. Lat. *nequid*.

NEK-HERING, *s*. The largest and finest herring, picked fish, that are placed in the neck or top-layers of the barrel to catch purchasers.

Than with ane schout thus can the Cadgear say,
" Abyde, and thow ane *Nek-hering* sall haif,
Is worth my capull, creillis, and all the laif."—
" Bot quhat wes yone the carll crylt on hie—"

" Schir," said the Foxe, " that I can tell trewlie :
He said the *Nek-hering* wes in the creill."
" Kennis thow that bering?" " Yes, Schir, I ken it weill :
And at the creill mouth I had it thryis but dout;
The wecht of it neir tit my tuskis out."
Henryson, The Wolf, Fox, and Cadgear, ll. 139, 165.

To NEM, NEME, *v. a*. To seize. V. NAM.

NENT, NENST, NENS, *prep*. Towards, against, opposite; as, "Turnin' *nent* the east." Short for ANENT, q. v.

To NERE, *v*. To come near, approach, gain upon, come up with.

Bot than the swipir Tuscan hund assais
And *nerys* fast, ay reddy hym to hynt.
Douglas, Virgil, xii. ch. 12.

NERES, NERIS, *s. pl*. V. NEIRS.

NERECRESS, NEIRCREIS, *s*. The fat about the kidneys.

" That na fleschour tak oute of ony mutoune the neris or the *nerecress* [quhyl] the feest of Mychelmess." Burgh Recs. Aberdeen, 4 June, 1444, Sp. C.

This regulation was enforced during the summer months in all the larger burghs ; mutton being then in poor condition. An order to the same effect and in almost the same words is found in the Stirling Recs., of 25th May, 1526.

The Spalding Club vol. prints "*fra* the feest ;" but this is evidently a mistake ; even the date of the statute shows that *quhyl* i.e., until, is required.

Icel. *nyra*, Dan. *nyre*, Sw. *njure*, a kidney ; and Fr. *graisse*, grease or fat.

NERVIT, NERUIT, *adj*. Ribbed, shot, threaded ; "*neruit* with gold," Douglas, Palice of Honour, Pt. I. st. 47.

NESH, *adj*. Soft, tender. V. *Nash*.

NESTLING, NESTLIN, NESSLIN, *s*. The smallest bird of the nest, the weakling.

To NETHER, NETTER, NEDDER, NITHER, NYTHER, *v. a*. and *n*. To gnarl, shrivel ; Houlate, l. 57, Asloan MS., Bann. MS. Addit. to NIDDER, q. v.

NETHERHOLE, NETHERHOLL, *s*. The blackhole, or lowest vault of a prison.

" Item, that na maner of persouns be fund walkand on the gaitt fra x houris furth efter of the nyclit, vnder the payne of putting in the *netherhole* incontinent, exceptand folkis of honesty passand their leifull airands, and at thai haif bowetts or candillis within thair [hands] in taikin thairof." Burgh Recs. Edinburgh, 1498, I. 75, Rec. Soc.

NETHIRMARE, NEDDIRMAIR, *adj*. and *adv*. Lower, still lower, farther downward.

The dog slepit and fell vnto the ground,
And Orpheus attour his wame in stall.
And *nethirmare* he went as ye heir sall.
Henryson, Orph. and Eur., l. 260, Laing's ed.

The term occurs in l. 345. In both cases the Bann. MS. reads *neddirmair*.

NETHIRMEST, NEDDIRMAIST, NEDDIRMAST, *adj*. Lowest : generally used as an empha-

tic or intensive form; as, "Theefs sall be put in the *neddirmaist* hole."
Nethirmare is a double compar., and *nethirmest* a double super. used, like all such forms, to mark emphasis. A.-S. *neothera, neothra,* nether: with suffix *mára,* greater, *mast,* most.

NEVE, NEUE, *s.* Fist. V. NEIVE.

To NEVEL, NEVELL, *v. a.* V. DICT.
Del. the note under s. 1: the statement is wrong.

NEWLINGIS, NEWLINS, *adv.* Anew, over again. Addit. to NEWLINGIS, q. v.
"... and thairfore desyrit the samyne *newlingis* againe to be granted for the honour and lovage of Godis service at thair altar of Sant Cubart." Burgh Recs. Edinburgh, I. 214, Rec. Soc.

NEWRDAY, NEWRSDAY, *s.* New-Year's-Day.

NEWRGIFT, *s.* New-Year's-Day gift.

NEWRNEEN, NEWRSEEN, *s.* New-Year's-Even, the evening of New-Year's-Day.
These terms are still common in the West of S.

NEYF, NEYFSHIP. V. *Naif.*

NICE, NYCE, NYSE, *adj.* Foolish, stupid, ignorant, dull, lazy: also tricky, as in Kingis Quair, st. 155. Addit. to NICE, q. v. V. *Nyce.*
Del. the note which follows Niceté, under this entry in DICT. *Nice* has nothing to do with *niais*, which Hailes and Pinkerton and Jamieson adopted as its etym. Fr. *niais*, is from the Ital. *nidiace*, fresh from the nest, hence, silly; and *nice* is M. E. *nice,* from O. *nice,* simple, lazy, which came from Lat. *nescius,* ignorant. V. Skeat's Etym. Dict.

To NICHT, NYCHT, *v. n.* To stop work for the day, cease from labour when day-light closes. Addit. to NICHT, q. v.
"... all the remanent of the yeir, quhen the day is schort, till entyr to his werk at day lycht in the morwyng, laif at half hour to twelf at none, and *nycht* at ewyn." Burgh Recs. Stirling, 26 Aug. 1520.
This is an extract from the engagement which the magistrates made with their master-mason, and which on certain conditions was to last "enduryng his lyfetyme."
The term is still so used in various districts of Scot.

NICHTING-TIME, NYCHTIN-TIME, *s.* The time when out-door labour ceases during the winter season, i.e., when day-light closes.

NICHTBOUR, *s.* V. NYCHBOUR.

NICHTBOURHEID, NYCHTBOURHEID, *s.* Site or ground adjacent; Burgh Recs. Edinburgh, III. 224. Addit. to NYCHTBOURHEID, q. v.

NICHTBOURSCAPE, NYCHBURSCAPE, *s.* Neighbourship, neighbourliness, the rights and duties of neighbours: similar to Nychtbourheid, q. v.: Burgh Recs. Prestwick, 12 Feb. 1480-1, Mait. C.

NICHTWALK, *s.* A night-wake or nightwatch over a corpse; also called a *lichtwake;* Burgh Recs. Aberdeen, I. 131, Rec. Soc.

NICHTYRTALE, *s.* V. DICT.
Jamieson's explanation of the *yr* in this term is not satisfactory. A simpler and more direct explanation of the term is the following one by Prof. Skeat.
Icel. *nátturthel,* by night, in the night-time. Here the *ar* is the Icel. genitive: and so also in *caterwaul,* the *cater* is equal to Icel. *kattar.*

To NICK, *v. a.* To outwit, balk, trick, befool, deceive: also, to answer in a mocking or insulting manner. V. NECK, *v.*

NICK, *s.* An act of trickery or deceit; a retort, gibe, jeer.
Sw. *neka,* to deny: Dan. *negte.*

NIDDRIT, *part. pt.* V. NIDDER.

NID NODDIN. V. under NOD.

NIDDY NODDY, *s.* and *adv.* Nodding and shaking, like an old or palzied person: also, in the pl. a contemptuous name for assumed airs or fine manners.

To think you birkies o' the town,
Wi' ruffel't sark and moostet crown,
Play siccan tricks on counтrа bodies,
Wha 're tentless o' yer *niddy noddies.*
W. Watson's Poems, p. 32.

An' ere we're half gate wi' our life,
Our head plays *niddy noddy.*
Ibid., p. 38.

To NIE, NYE, *v. a.* To approach. V. NEYCH, NECH.

NIKKY, *s.* V. NICK.

NILD. Errat. for *culd,* could. V. DICT.
This is a mis-reading of Pinkerton's transcriber: the Maitland MS. has *culd.* See Small's ed. of Dunbar's Poems, p. 38, S. T. S.

NILE, *s.* Blue or green mould or fungus, as on cheese: *niled cheese,* moulded or mouldy cheese; Orkn.

NILL, NIL, NYL. For *ne will,* will not: *nill ye will ye,* whether you are unwilling or willing, without consulting you, in spite of you: "An' that I'll do, *nill ye will ye.*"
Jamieson's explanation of this phrase is defective. Like the Lat. form "*nolens volens*" it has various applications.
A.-S. *nyllan,* to be unwilling: made up of *ne,* not, and *willan,* to will.

To NIM, NIME, NYME, *v.* 1. As n *v. a.,* to take or pick up hastily; to steal. V. NAM.

2. As a v. n., to walk quickly, trip along.
A.-S. niman, to take.

NINE, NINES, s. Perfection: *to the nines*, *up to the nines*, to perfection, to the uttermost, in the grandest style: West of S.

NINE-TAILS, NINE-TAIL'D-CAT, s. The hangman's lash.

NIR, NYR, adj. and adv. Near: comp. *nirar, nyrar*; sup. *nirest, nyrast*; Houlate, l. 47, Asloan MS., Bann. MS. V. NER.

NIRLOCK, NURLOCK, s. A small hard lump or swelling, an induration on the skin: mostly on the feet or hands. Dimin. of NIRL, q. v.

To NITHER. V. DICT. Kidder is a misprint for Nidder.

To NIVE, KNIVE, v. a. To pinch, grip; to lay turf on the ridge of a house in order to grip and cover the ends of the thatch; Orkn.

"Weel, troutb, lam, thou'll sthune be richt aneuch. Leuk'st thoo there, Maigie, at that saxcar (six-oared boat) comean frae the haaf fu' tae the wayles (gunwales) o' ling and tosch. Na micht I trive, Maigie, but I see a braw new hoos nived wi' poanes (cut turf), an' na less than twa marks o' laund." Rambling Sketches in the Far North, p. 93.
Dan. knibe, to pinch, grip.

NO, NA, adv. Not: *no far*, not far, near. Addit. to No, q. v.

There's no a lad in a' the lan'
Was match for my John Highlandman.
Burns, Jolly Beggars.

We are na fou, we're no that fou,
But just a drappie in our e'e.
Ibid., Willie Brew'd a Peck o' Maut.

No and *na* are the usual forms of negation in Scot.: a peculiarity which Jamieson has not made plain, although he uses many quotations that illustrate it. *No* for *not* is common all over the country; but in Aberdeen, Banff, etc., *na* and *nae* prevail. In the Lowlands generally, while frequently used with verbs, it is invariably used with nouns, adjectives, and adverbs; but in the S. F. counties it is equally so used with verbs, e.g. I *no* think, I *no* ken. When the negation follows the verb the form *na* is used, and is frequently joined to it, e.g. I ken *na*, I kenna. With aux. verbs this combination is very common, e.g. can*na*, manna, wadna.

NOBUT, adv. Only, just, no more than: as, "I've *nobut* saxpence." V. [NA BUT].

When so used *nobut* has the sense of *nocht but*; and when it occurs at the beginning of a sentence, it has a conjunctive sense and represents *No! however*, as in, "*Nobut*, I canna do that." In this latter sense it is common in the North of E. V. Brockett's Gloss. For explanation of *no* and *but* see Skeat's Etym. Dict.

No FAR, adv. Not far, near. V. *No*.

NODDER, NODDIR, NOUDIR, conj. Neither. V. NOUTHER.

To NOIT, v. a. To use, wear; part. pt. *noited*; "the book's sair *noitit*," i.e., much worn or marked through use: West of S. V. NOTE.
A.-S. notian, to use; Sw. nöta, to wear, to be worn.

NOK. "*A nok*," an oak: a form adopted in alliterative poetry.

My neb is netherit as a *nok*, I am bot ane Owle.
Houlate, l. 57.

NOLL, s. V. DICT.

This word represents simply E. *knoll*, and the meanings noted are all secondary. M. E. *knol*, and A.-S. *cnol*, a hillock, are most prob. of Celtic origin, from Welsh *cnol*, a knoll, hillock, a dimin. form of Celtic *cnoc*, a hill, which in Gaelic means hill, knoll, hillock, and in Irish a hillock, a turnip. In Scot. *now*, *nowe*, *knowe*, which represent the pron. of *knoll*, means a hillock, brae, rounded eminence, the head, crown of the head. Comparing these various meanings, the leading idea which they suggest is that of roundness, not mass or eminence; and this is confirmed by Dutch *knol*, a turnip, and Swed. *knöl*, a bump. Besides the term *knock*, as used in the names of hills, is invariably applied to rounded eminences, and to such only.

NONE-METE, s. Dinner. V. NEEMIT.

NONES, NONIS, s. Nonse. V. *Nanes*.

To NOOL, NULE, v. n. To submit, bow, yield, fawn, cringe: commonly written *Knool*, q. v. V. NOLL, v.

To Knool down at marbles is to place the closed fist on the ground, and expose the knuckles to the nags. Another form of the phrase, which is common in Eng. as well, is *to knuckle down*. V. under NAG.

NOOLED, NOOL'D, NOOLT, NULED, part. and adj. Subdued, crushed, dispirited, henpecked: as, "He's a puir *nool'd* body."

Prob. ouly a var. of *knool, knoll, knull*, to knuckle, bent with the fists, expressing the purpose of, and end gained by, the operation.

NOOL-KNEE, adj. V. *Nule-Kneed*.

NOONSHANKS, NONESHANKIS, NONE-SHANKIS, NUINSCHANKIS, NUMSCHANKIS, s. Afternoon repast; also the time allowed for it. Frequently called *four-hours*. Addit. to NOYN-SANKIS, q. v.

This repast was called *four-hours* from the time at which it was taken; and workmen were allowed half an hour for it. In some districts, however, as the following extract shows, *noonshanks* began at 3.30 p.m.

"The said Jhon haiffand ilk work day ane half hour afor nyne houris afor none to his disjone, and ane othir half hour afor four houris eftyr none to his *nunschankis*." Burgh Recs. Stirling, 26 Aug., 1529.

Such was the arrangement with the master-mason of Stirling so long as he could commence work "ilk day in the morwyng at fiwe houris;" but during the season of shorter days he had no *noonshanks*, and only a short meal-time at mid-day. So also was it with the master-mason of Dundee a few years later; for his engagement, dated 1536, distinctly states that in winter he was to have "na tyme of licence of dennar nor *noneshankis* cause of the shortnes of the dais." Memorials of Angus and Mearns, I. 298.

Noonshanks was originally a *noon-drink*; for we are told that in certain cases labourers were allowed *nonemete*, i.e., noon-eating, and *none-schenche*, i.e. noondrinking: *schenche* being a *s*. from M. E. *schenchen*, to pour out or distribute drink. (See *Nunmete* in Prompt. Parv., and Way's note on it.) And in certain circumstances this allowance of an *afternoon drink* is still kept up.

A.-S. *scencan*, to pour out drink, from which came M. E. *skenken*, *schenken*, or *schenchen*; and from the latter form came *schenche* in *none-schenche*, which in Scot. became *noonshanks*, and in E. *nunchion*. V. Skeat's Etym. Dict.

NOOT, *s*. A shinty ball. V. *Note*.

Also called a *nacket*, that which is nacked or knocked. Properly, however, the *noot* is a ball of hard wood turned and fitted for the game; and a *nacket* is a piece of wood, bone, or stone, used by players who have not a *noot*.

NORTIR, NORTER, *adj*. Northern. V. under NORTH.

NOSE-ON-THE-GRUNSTANE. A simile expressive of the hard grinding of poverty, of the result of improvidence, and of a lazy person compelled to work.

In the second sense the phrase is common in the North of E. V. Brocket's Gloss.

NOT, *s*. Naught, nothing; Court of Venus, ii. 973, 975, S. T. S. A form of NOCHT, q. v.

Prob. written *not* in MS.

NOTE, NOT, NOTT, NOOT, *s*. A knot, knob, ball; head, point, conclusion; also, a tool or weapon: hence, *to the note*, to the head or point, to the hammer, axe, etc.: cf. *neb*. V. NOTE.

Icel. *knútr*, a knot; Sw. *knut*; Dan. *knude*; A.-S. *cnotta*; Du. *knot*; Cf. Lat. *nodus*; Fr. *neud*.

NOTIR, *adj*. Known. V. NOTOUR.

NOTOURLIE, NOTERLIE, NOTIRLIE, *adv*. Well or widely known, publicly, notoriously; Burgh Recs. Edinburgh, I. 113, Douglas, IV. 94-4, ed. Small. V. NOTOUR.

NOUMBLES, NOMBLES, NOWMYLLIS, *s. pl*. The heart, spleen, lungs, and liver of an animal: "*nowmelys* of a beest," Prompt. Parv., q. v.

". . . and at the sellaris thairof [i.e., of fleshmeat] be honestlie habilleit according to thair facultie with honest apronis convenient thairfore, and at thai sell nocht oppinly in the merkat thair nolt heids, *nowmyllis*, nor interallis of thair flesche bot quyetlie in private places." Burgh Recs. Edinburgh, I. 114, Rec. Soc.

This extract shows that the term is not limited to the entrails of a deer, as is sometimes stated. It has not yet passed out of use in the West of S., and may occasionally be heard on winter market-days when farmers' wives are bargaining with the butcher for the materials to furnish a good haggis: a sheep's bag and *nombles* being principal elements thereof.

L. Lat. *numbile, numble:* O. Fr. *nombles*, the numbles, which Elyot defines, "as the hart, the splene, the lunges, and lyuer." V. Note in Prompt. Parv.

NOVATION, NOUATION, *s*. Innovation, novelty; Burgh Recs. Aberdeen, II. 43, Sp. C., B. R. Edinburgh, IV. 141, Rec. Soc.

This term occurs also in the Peebles Recs. in an entry dated 3rd March, 1559. The record is interesting, as it affords a glimpse of that old burgh when the Reformation movement began to stir it. On that day, it is recorded, ". . . the baillies of Peblis passed to the personale presens of John Wallace als apostat, and dischargit him to use ony *novationes* of common prayeris or preiching." They told him also that they would not assist him nor any of his sect or opinion, but would abide under the faith and obedience of their prince for the time. Little did they know about the force of the current that had just reached them. On 20th November of the following year 1560, the baillies of Peebles were commissioned by the inhabitants of the toun to Edinburgh to the Lords of the Congregation to secure the services of a faithful minister. Eight days afterwards, John Dikesone, the first minister in Peebles, was formally installed.

NOW, NOWE, *s*. V. DICT.

These forms represent the Sc. pron. of E. *knoll*, M. E. *knol*: Cf. *bow* for boll, *row* for roll, etc. And all the varieties of meaning given under NOLL and NOW represent simply different applications of M. E. *Knol*.

To NOW, *v. a*. To knuckle, to strike or beat with the fist: a form of NOLL, of which it represents the common pron.

The millar was of manly mak,
To melt him wes na mowis;
Thai durst nocht ten cum him to tak,
So *nowit* he thair nowis.
Chrystis Kirk of the Grene, Bann. MS.

NOWEL, *s*. The central column round which a circular staircase winds; also, in pl. *nowellis*, stones to be used in constructing a newel.

". . . for the wark of the tolbuith steipill, sex score four peice of free aisler stanes of the heughe of Kyngeuddies, thairof thrie scoir sevin peice long wark for lintellis and *nowellis*, and the remanent schort wark for rebbittis." Burgh Recs. Aberdeen, II. 379, Sp. C.

"Newel (Old Eng. forms, Noel, Nowel, Nuel), the central column round which the steps of a circular staircase wind." Gloss. of Terms in Architecture, p. 169, ed. 1882.

O. Fr. *nual*, later *noyau*, "the stone of a plumme, the nuel or spindle of a winding staire;" Cotgr. From Lat. *nuculis*, resembling nuts; hence, applied to a fruitstone, an almond, and, from its central position, to the column of a winding stair.

NOWN, *adj*. Own: a common pron. in Orkn.: *nain* in more southern districts.

NOWS AND THENS, *adv*. Occasionally, at long intervals, rarely. The phrase is used also as a *s*., as in, "He jist comes at *nows and thens*," i.e., at odd or rare times. South and West of S.

This phrase is still used in some districts of the North of Eng. V. Peacock's Gloss. of Lonsdale.

NOWT, s. Cattle, horned cattle. V. NOLT.

NOYNSANKIS, s. Afternoon repast; also, the time allowed for it. Errat. in DICT.
Jamieson's explanation of this term is altogether a mistake: therefore, del. the definition and the explanatory note given in DICT., and see corrections given under *Noonshanks*.

NOYSUM, adj. Hurtful, noxious, deadly; Douglas, Virgil, III. 59, 13, ed. Small.
Made up of M. E. *noy*, annoyance; and E. suffix *some*. *Noy* is short for *anoy*, from O. Fr. *anoi*, vexation. V. Skeat's Etym. Dict.

NUB-BERRY, s. V. DICT.
In last para. of this entry, l. 1, *knoo* is a misprint for *knob*.

NUDYT, NWDYT, part. pt. Naked, stripped, denuded. Lat. *nudare*.
". . . ordains hym to be *nwdyt* of his fredome." Burgh Recs. Prestwick, 30 Jan., 1551-2, p. 62, Mait. C.

NUK, NUKE, NUKIT, NUKKIT. V. under NUIK.

NULE, NOOL, s. A knob, protuberance. V. [KNULE].

NULED, NOOLED, adj. Having a knob or protuberance, swollen: as in a diseased joint.

NULE-KNEED, NOOL-KNEED, adj. Having enlarged or protuberant knee-joints; syn. *knuckle-kneed, knock-kneed*. Errat. in DICT.
Jamieson's definition of this term is misleading: it is really the def. of *knock-kneed*. And while a *knule-kneed* person is generally also *knock-kneed*, he is not necessarily so, and may be otherwise: but, be that as it may, the two words imply totally different ideas. *Nule* has nothing to do with the idea of knocking, but of protuberance; and when *nuled* knees do knock against each other, it is because the protuberances are the results of disease which has so weakened the joints that they bend inward under the person as he moves along.

NULE-TAES, NOOL-TAES, NULE-TAED. V. KNOUL-TAES.

To NULE, v. a. and n. V. KNOOL, *Nool*.

NULED, NOOLT, part. and adj. Mauled, subdued. V. *Nooled*.

NURISKAP, NURICEKIP, s. V. NOURISKAP.

NWREIS, NWRIS, s. A nurse. V. NURIS. (Sup.)

NYCE, NYSE, adj. Ignorant, stupid, rude, offensive; Court of Venus, i. 739: also, full of tricks or capers, as, "the *nyce* ape," Kingis Quair, st. 155; foolish, silly, Ibid., st. 129; Dunbar and Kennedy, l. 177.
Nyse is used in the last sense in Towneley Mysteries, p. 237. It is the M. E. *nice*, foolish, simple, and afterwards fastidious; from O. Fr. *nice*, lazy, simple; originally ignorant, from Lat. *nescius*. V. Skeat's Etym. Dict.

NYCELY, NYSELY, adv. Foolishly; Kingis Quair, st. 12, ed. Skeat.

To NYCH, v. a. V. NEICH, *Nech*.

NYCHLIT. Del. this entry in DICT.
This is certainly a mistake in the Bann. MS. for *nychit*, came nigh to, concerned. The Asloan MS. has *nechit*. V. under *Nech*.

NYDDRIT, NYDRYT, part. pt. V. NIDDER.

To NYE, v. a. V. NEYCH, *Nie*.

To NYE, v. a. To deny, refuse, forbid; pret. *nyt*; part. pt. *nyte*. Fr. *nier*.
And othir sum *nyt* all that case.
Barbour, i. 52.

To NYE, v. a. To annoy, vex, harass, distress, afflict; part. pt. *nyte*, a form of *noyit*, q. v.
The May Thisbe wald tine hir self sa nyte,
Caus Pyramus away and deid was quite.
Rolland, Court of Venus, iii. 229, S. T. S.
"*Wald tine hir self*," resolved to kill herself or to perish. V. TINE.
The rendering of *nyte* given in the Gloss. is certainly wrong.

NYE, s. Trouble, difficulty, harm, distress, injury. A form of NOY, q. v.

To NYME, v. a. To seize. V. NAM, *Nim*.

NYSE, NYSELY. V. *Nyce*.

NYT, pret. Denied. V. NYE.

NYTE, part. pt. Annoyed. V. *Nye*.

NYTE, v. a. A form of NATE, NOTE, q. v.

To NYTE, v. n. V. DICT.
In l. 1, for v. n. read v. a.

To NYTE, v. a. V. DICT.
In l. 1, for No read To.

To NYTTL, v. a. and n. V. DICT.
Add to defin.:—A form of *Nattle*, with slightly different application.

O.

O, *prep.* On; but generally equivalent to E. prefix *a*, meaning *on*, as in *o brede*, abroad, *o newe*, anew, *o right*, aright.

OAT-FOWL, *s.* The snow-bunting; Neil's Tour in Orkn. and Shetl. Addit. to OAT-FOWL, q. v.

OBIUSE, *s.* A corr. of *upheise*, vulgarly pron. *obheise*, a block and tackle, used for elevating heavy bodies; Burgh Recs. Aberdeen, I. 176, Sp. C.

OBSERVATOR, OBSERUATOUR, *s.* Lit. an observatory, an aid or help to observers: a monstrance.

". . . ane *obseruatour* of irue to the ewcharist." Burgh Recs. Peebles, 27 Oct., 1560, Rec. Soc.
Lat. *observare*, to observe, pay respect or adoration to; and the *obseruatour* mentioned in the record was, most probably, an iron case for enclosing and at the same time displaying the host.

OBSTANT, *adj.* Standing in the way of, opposing, resisting, adverse; Douglas, IV, 134, 23, ed. Small, Burgh Recs. Aberdeen, I. 37, Sp. C.

OBUMBRAT, *pret.* Overshadowed, shaded, screened; Douglas, IV. 82, 10, ed. Small. Lat. *obumbrare.*

OCHTLINS, *adv.* V. OUGHTLINS.

ODD, ODDS, *s.* Terms used in golfing.

"(1.) 'An *odd*,' 'two *odds*,' etc. per hole, means the handicap given to a weak opponent by deducting one, two, etc. strokes from his total every hole. (2.) To have played 'the *odd*' is to have played one stroke more than your adversary." Golfer's Handbook, p. 35, ed. 1881.
Some of the other terms used in counting the game will be most easily explained in connection with the foregoing.
"If your opponent has played one stroke more than you, i.e., 'the *odd*,' your next stroke will be 'the like'; if two strokes more, i.e., 'the two more,' your next stroke will be 'the one off two'; if three more, 'the one off three'; and so on." Ibid., p. 35.

ODMAN, *s.* An arbiter. V. ODISMAN.

To O'ERGANG, *v. a.* To oversee, superintend; hence, to treat with indignity, to oppress; West of S. Addit. to OURGAE.

O'ERGANG, OURGANG, *s.* Superintendence, oppression; Ibid. Addit. to OURGANG.

To OERHALE, *v. a.* A form of Ouerheild, q. v.; also, of *Ouerhale*, q. v.

O'ERLAY, *s.* and *v.* V. OURLAY.

OF, *adv.* Corr. of *oft*, often, frequently; "also *of* as neid beis," as often as necessary; Burgh Recs. Aberdeen, I. 125.

OFF-AND-ON, AFF-AN'-ON. 1. As an *adj.;* uncertain, unsettled; as, "I'll hae na *off-and-on* bargain: settle't now."
2. As an *adv.;* more or less; as, "It lasted about twa hours *off-and-on*": also, intermittingly; as, "We had moonlicht *off-and-on* a' nicht."

OFF-GANGIN. 1. As an *adj.*, outgoing, leaving; as in "the *off-gangin* tenant."
2. As a *s.*, the amount or proportion of the crop due to the outgoing tenant who leaves a farm while the crop is growing.

OFTER, *adv.* Oftener; comp. of *oft*.

To OGHT, OUGHT, OGHE, *v. a.* V. AUCHT.

OH WHAN! *inter.* Like, and perhaps the local pron. of *ochone*; but its application is more like that of *man alive!* Orkn.

OIS, OISE, OISS, *v.* and *s.* Use. V. OYSS.

OKE, *s.* The Black-billed Auk *(Alca pica*, Linn.); Neil's Tour in Orkn. and Shetl.
Naturalists are now almost agreed that the Oke is not a distinct species, but merely the Razor-bill in the winter plumage of the first year. V. Rennie's Notes in Montagu's Ornith. Dict., ed. 1831.

OKER, OICKER, *s.* Usury. V. OCKER.

OLES, *adv.* and *conj.* A corr. of *Onless*, q. v.

OLK, OLKLIE. V. OULK, OULKLIE.

To OMBESEGE, *v. a.* V. UMBESEGE.

Om is for *omb=umb*, A.-S. *ymb*, round about. This prefix is very common in M. E. in the form of *um-*.

OMELL, *prep.* Among; Ywaine and Gawin, 1. 136, 2667.

ON, *prep.* Of, about, concerning, regarding; as, "He couldna sleep for thinkin' *on*'t," i.e., of or about it; "I'll tell your mither *on* you," i.e., concerning or regarding you. Addit. to [ON], q. v.

ON, ONE. 1. Forms of the prefix *un*, not, or implying the undoing of the action expressed by the verb, as *ongraithe* for *ungraithe*, to unharness, i.e. to undo the harness.

2. Sometimes *on* is intensive, as in *onstandin*, immovable, determined.

N.B.—Words beginning with this form of the prefix which are not found in the DICT. or Suppl., may be found under the form Un-.

ONBETAKIT, ONBETECHIT, *part. adj.* Unrendered, uncommitted, uncommended: "*onbetechit* hir self to God," without commending herself to God.

". . . and commandit hir to ryss airlie befoir the sone, *onbetechit* hir self to God, and onspokin, and nocht to sayn hir self nor hir sone sowkand on hir breist." Trials for Witchcraft, Spald. Misc., i. 91.

The form *onbetechit* may represent the local pron.; but more prob. it is a mistake for *onbetakit*.

ONBETHANKIT, *part. adj.* Unthanked, unacknowledged; "Here am I *onbethankit* for a' I've done for her," West of S.

ON BREID. V. ON BREDE.

ONBYDREW, *pret.* Withdrew, retired; Douglas, Virgil, xii. prol. 6, ed. Small.

On is here not negative but intensive, as in sometimes is in Latin, and *un* in Eng., as in *unloose*, Mark i. 7. Ruddiman's ed. has *umbedrew*, which is similarly explained. V. Gloss. Another use of *on* will be found in *Onlace*, q. v.

ONCHANCY, *adj.* V. UNCHANCY.

ONCOUTH, ONKOUTH, *adj.* Strange, uncommon: generally *uncouth, unkouth*, but latterly and most frequently written and pron. *unco*. V. UNCO.

While *uncouth* and *unco* are really forms of the same word, they have now very different meanings: *uncouth* implies peculiarity of appearance, dress, manner, or bearing, and *unco* refers to the nature or character of a person or thing.

ONCULYT, ONCULIT, *part. adj.* Uncooled, quite hot, warm; Douglas, Virgil, xi. ch. 5.

ONCUNYEIT, *part. adj.* Uncoined: *uncunyeit gold*, gold in bar or mass, or not prepared for coining; Douglas, Virgil, x. ch. 9, ed. Small.

ONE, *adj.* Single, sole: *hym one*, all by himself; *oure one*, all by ourselves; but such phrases are now expressed by himself, ourselves, &c. There is also an intensive form in which *al* or *all* is prefixed: thus, *al hym one*, entirely himself or by himself.

ONE-OFF-TWO, ONE-OFF-THREE. V. under *Odd*.

ONEITH, ONEISE, *adv.* Lit. not easily; hardly, scarcely, with difficulty. V. UNEITH.

ONERD, *adj.* Uncultivated. V. *Uneared*.

ONFARAND, ONFARRANT, *adj.* Ill-favoured, ill-looking, ugly; Douglas, III. 250, 26, ed. Small; it is also used in the sense of ill-informed, senseless, unmannerly, rude, as in "He's aye been an *onfarant* body." V. UNFARRANT.

ONHERMIT, ONHERMYT, *adj.* Unharmed; Douglas, II. 4, 31, ed. Small.

To ONLACE, *v. a.* Lit. to lace on, i.e. to bind, fix, or fasten, as a sandal, piece of armour, etc.; hence, to put or fit on, bind or fasten firmly.

Enfors the strangly contrar hym to stand;
Rays hie the targe of faith vp in thi hand;
On hed the balsum helm of hop *onlace*;
In cheryte thy body all embrace;
And of devote orison mak thi brand.
Douglas, Virgil, xi. prol., ed. Small.
Rudd. ed. has *vnlace*.

On is here both intensive and adverbial.

ONLAND, UNLAND, *s.* Untilled or uncultivated land, pasture land. Addit. to ONLAND.

This term was left undefined by Jamieson; but its meaning is clearly indicated by the following passage : ". . . terras arabilees *lie corneland*, terras non arabiles *lie unland* . . . moris, marresiis, pratis, terris non arabilibus *lie unerd*." Reg. Mag. Sig., 1546-80, No. 2195.

ONLAW, *s.* and *v.* V. UNLAW.

ONLESS, ONLES, OLES, *adv.* and *conj.* Unless, if not; Spald. Mis., I. 85; *oles na*, unless that.

". . . he sal hafe na other service bot it *oles na* it be nocht ten merkis." Charters of Peebles, 4 Feb., 1444-5, Rec. Soc.

ONMYSURLY, *adv.* Without or beyond measure; Douglas, IV. 147, 29, ed. Small.

ONREST, *s.* Unrest. V. *Unrest*.

ONRICHT, ONRYCHT, *adj.* Untrue, false, defective, unfair, unjust.

". . the deakin of cowperis quha sall have power to challenge all sik wrang and *onrycht* missouris." Burgh Recs. Glasgow, I. 295, Rec. Soc.

ONSAULD, ONSELD, ONSELT, *adj.* Unsold; Spald. Club Misc., I. 193.

ONSET, *s.* An addition to a building either for enlargement or as an outhouse; in the former case it is often called an *outset;* in the latter, a *to-fall*, or *lean-to*.

ONSLAUGHT, *s.* A fierce attack or onset; a bloody fray or battle, Roxb.

"The Swedens disappointed of their *onslaught* retired after his Majestie to their leaguer, and having put a terror to the enemies armie by this defeat he did get some days longer continuation to put all things in good order against their coming." Monro's Exped., P. ii., p. 52.

From *on* and M. E. *slaht*, A. S. *sleaht*, a stroke, blow, formed from *sledn*, to strike. Skeat's Etym. Dict.
Misled by his etymology, Jamieson gave two different entries of this term, in the belief that they were different words ; but they are really the same. Both entries must be deleted.

ONSNED, *adj.* Uncut, unpruned, not trimmed ; Douglas, Virgil, Bk. ix. 11.
In the West of S. some thirty years ago a common street cry was, "Birk besoms ; heather besoms ; sned an' *onsned!*" The hawkers were generally gipsies.

ONSPOKIN, *adj.* Unspoken; without speaking to any one, before speaking to any one. Spald. Mis. I. 91.

ONSPOULYET, *adj.* Unspoiled; Burgh Recs. Aberdeen, I. 316, Sp. C.

ONSTERIT, *adj.* Unstirred, unmoved; Douglas, II. 146, 21, ed. Small. V. STEER.

ONTEINDIT, ONTENDYT, ONTEINIT, *adj.* Untithed : without apportioning or paying the teinds. V. TEIND.
". . for the wrangus takin in of peis *on-tendyt*." Burgh Recs. Prestwick, p. 52, Mait. C.

ONTO, *prep.* Unto, upon, a-top of.
The bestis furth hes tursyt this ilka syre
Onto the altar blesand of hayt fyre.
Douglas, Virgil, xii. ch. 4, l. 30.
This is simply a variant of *unto*. These forms are made up of prep. *to* and O. Fries. *und*, *ont*, unto.

To ONTRAY, *v. a.* Errat. for *Outray*, q. v. V. DICT.
Delete this entry in DICT. altogether, as *ontray* is a misprint in Pinkerton's version of Sir Gaw. and Sir Gal.

ONWISELY, ONUYSLYE, *adv.* Unwisely, foolishly, rashly ; Douglas, Virgil, 124, 39, Rudd.
The writer of the Elphinstoun MS. has omitted this word, and has thereby marred the measure of the line. The editor notes it as only a various reading. V. Small's ed., II., pp. 219, 314.

OOSTING, *s.* An encampment, a camp: also an army in camp. V. OST, OSTING.

OOSTING BURD, *s.* A camp-table.
"Item, giffin for ij tynnyt bandis and viij bowlis for trestis for the *oosting burd*, xxxij d." Accts L. H. Treas., I. 295.

OOTLIN, *adj.* and *s.* V. OUTLAN, *Outlin.*

ORA, ORRA, *adj.* Odd, extra. V. ORROW.

ORCHARD-LIT, *s.* A kind of dye-stuff: prob. the orchella weed (*Roccella tinctoria*) of commerce ; Halyburton's Ledger, p. 321, Burgh Recs. Edinburgh, IV. 155.

ORD, *s.* A point of land, promontory, headland ; as, " the *Ord* of Caithness." V. DICT.
Jamieson's defin. and etym. of this term are incorrect. The word is certainly of English origin.

A.-S. *ord*, beginning, point, edge; Germ. *ort*, a peint of land ; Icel. *oddr*, Dan. and Swed. *od*, *odd*.

ORDINER, ORDINAR, ORDYNAR, *s.* 1. Ordinary ; a title given to Church dignitaries having original jurisdiction.
The bishop of a diocese having original jurisdiction was called the *ordinar* of the diocese ; the archbishop, the *ordinar* of his province.

2. An ordinary, a public or common table or meal, pot-luck ; dinner at a restaurant or inn, or at the table of a friend or neighbour ; also, dinner as a meal ; Rob. Stene's Dream, p. 4.
The following injunctions were given to the common minstrels of Glasgow who were provided with dinner by the householders in rotation.
"Item, that nane of thame have nather boy nor doig with thame quhair thai eit thair *ordiner*.
"Item, that thai stope na friemen that is hable to gif them *ordiner*, nor to tak syluer fra ane to pas to ane vther.
"Item, that thai sall nocht misbehaiff thame selffs in na housss quhair thai sal happin to eitt thair *ordiner*, bot to be content of sic as salbe presentit to thame be thame that thai eit with." Burgh Recs. Glasgow, p. 1. 207, Rec. Soc.
O. Fr. *ordinaire*, "an Ordinarie ; also, an ordinarie table, dyet, fare ;" Cotgr.

ORE, *s.* V. DICT.
Del. last two para. of this entry ; they are altogether misleading. The etym. is simply A.-S. *dr*, grace, favour. On this term, Prof. Skeat remarks :—
"A.-S. *dr* gives *ore*, just as A.-S. *ldr* gives *lore*."

ORLIN, ORLING, *s.* A puny, sickly, or stunted creature ; a form of WORLIN, q. v.
Worlin assumes the various forms of *orlin*, *urlin*, *wurlin*, *yurlin* ; and they are still used in the West of S.

ORNACY, *s.* Ornateness, beauty. Lat. *ornatio*.
This term was generally used in relation to language, composition, and poetry ; but in the following passage it relates to architecture.
"So then, under these three conditions, to wit, of amplitude, *ornacy*, and vnprostitude chastity to any other vse nor the owne, but specially the last, it becommes a Kirk." Blame of Kirkburiall, ch. 17.

ORPIMENT, ORPEMENT, *s.* Orpine, painter's gold ; Haliburton's Ledger, p. 323. Also called ORPHANY, q. v. M. E. *orpiment*, Chaucer.
Orpiment is an arsenical yellow pigment, sometimes called *King's yellow* ; it is a gold colour, but not gold. The name is still used.

ORROW, ORA, ORRA, *adj.* V. DICT.
This is a mere derivative of *over*, and all its various meanings are simply different applications of the primary meaning superfluous, spare.
"*Orrow* is precisely Swed. *öfrig*, remaining, lit. over ; adj. from the prep. Cf. Icel. *yfrinn*, from *yfir*, over ; which often drops *f*, and becomes *œrinn*." Skeat.

OSIL, OSILL, *s.* The ousel. V. OSZIL.

To OSSE, v. a. To offer, Rom. Alexander, l. 2263, 2307.

OSSINGE, s. An offering, Ibid., l. 731, 868.

OSSIGAR, s. V. OZIGER.

OST, s. A sacrifice. V. OIST.

OSTRAGE, OSTAGE, s. An ostrich; also, short for an ostrich-feather or plume.

The glaidest man was gayest for to se,
With scarlet cap, quhairin was *Ostage* thre,
Behoung with gold, and all of cullour blew.
Rolland, Court of Venus, L. 83.

Ostage is perhaps a misprint for *ostrage*; in any case, it is improperly rendered "*feather*" in the Gloss. Anglers almost always call the feathers with which their hooks are dressed by the name of the bird from which they are taken. In their parlance a mallard, a jay, or a golden plover means only a feather from the mallard, etc.

OTHERGATES, OTHERGAITS, adj. Otherwise, by other means, by another road, in another way.

This term is still common in the North of Eng. V. Cleveland Gloss., Brockett. It occurs also in the Townley Myst., p. 10.

OTTERLINE, adj. and s. A form of Etterlin, q. v.: "ane *otterline* cow," a young cow in calf in her second year; Corshill Baron-Court Book, Ayr and Wigton Arch. Coll., IV. 142.

OTTOMALL, OTTOMAIL, OTTOM, OTTUM, s. A corr. of *out-toonmall*, a portion of outfield or pasture land newly put under cultivation: also called *quoyland* and *outbrek*; Orkn. V. [TUMAIL], *Tumall*.

These forms occur in Origines Parochiales, II., pt. 2, pp. 610, 615.

OUDIR, OWDIR, conj. and adj. Either; Burgh Recs. Prestwick, pp. 14, 16, Mait. C. V. OUTHIR.

OUERCARIED, OERCARIED, part. pt. Carried away, overdone, overloaded; Blame of Kirkburiall, ch. 7.

To OUERGET, v. a. To overtake, come up with: *get* is often used in the same sense; West and South of S.

To OUERHALE, OUERHAILE, OUERHAYLE, OURHALE, OURHAILE, OUREHALE, OUREHAILE, OUREHAYLE, OERHALE, OERHAILE, ORHAYLE, v. a. 1. To overspread, cover over, conceal; Douglas, I. 88, 24, Small.

2. To turn over, overhaul; hence, to examine, scrutinize, consider, ponder, reconsider: Kingis Quair, st. 10, 158, ed. Skeat.
Addit. to OUERHAILE, q. v.

To OUERSEE, OUERSIE, OURSEE, OWRSEE, v. a. To overlook, wink at: hence to permit, grant, or allow as a favour.

". . . na mair for salmound tallis heirefter except the pryces following, viz., aught pennis for the tail of ane lytill salmound and sextein pennis for the taill of ane meikle salmound, . . . ; and yeit for the regaird they beir to the said William they will *ouersie* him to tak during thair willis onlie tuelff pennis for the taill of ane lytle salmound, and twa schillings for the taill of ane meikle salmound." Burgh Recs. Glasgow, 13 Apr. 1638. V. *Crumbe*.

This is a peculiar and uncommon use of *oversee:* the usual meaning is *to superintend*.

To OUGHT, OGHT, OCHT, v. a. To own, to owe. V. AUCHT.

OUNCELAND, s. V. DICT.

"The meaning of *ounceland* is that each subdivision of that name paid to the Earl money or produce to the value of one ounce of silver. The *ounceland* was divided into eighteen parts, each of which had to pay one penny, or the value of one penny, and hence was called a Pennyland, a 1d. land."

"It is very probable that the assessment by ounces of silver was made by King Harold Fairhair on his conquest of the Isles; for it is told that in 902 the Earl of Orkney was to pay no skat; from which it is to be understood that the Earl was to retain the whole instead of one-third of the skat collected there : this implies a *skratt-skrá*, assessment or valuation-roll." Proceedings Antiq. Soc. Sc., 1883-4, pp. 258-9.

OUP, prep. and adv. Up: but mostly used as a verbal prefix, as in *oupbig*, *ouphald*; *oupset*, etc. Still used in northern districts.

OUR-CROCE, adv. Across, crosswise; Houlate, st. 27.

To OURDRIVE, OURDRYUE, OURDRYFF, v. a. To resist, battle against, overcome; Dunbar, Tabill of Confessioun, l. 20.

To OUREBY, OURBY. V. OVERBY.

OURELERIT, part. pt. Well instructed, having full knowledge of, learned; Houlate, st. 10, Bann. MS. V. LARE.

OURFRET, OURFRETE, OUIRFRET, OUIRFREIT, part. pt. V. OUERFRETT.

To OURGAE, OURGANG, v. a. To oversee, superintend; hence, to drive, oppress. Addit. to OURGAE, q.v.

OURGANG, s. Oversight, superintendence. Addit. to OURGANG, q.v.

OURGANGER, OURGANG, s. Overseer, superintendent; director of a band of workmen: familiarly called "*the ourgang*."

OURERE, OURRERE. V. ORERE.

To OURHAILL, OURHILE, v. a. V. OUERHALE.

OUR [182] OUT

OURHAND, OUIRHAND, OURHAN', *s.* Upper-hand, superiority, mastery : " I'll hae the *ourhan'* o' ye yet," I'll excel you by and bye.
Mot wyth his ene behald me hym befor,
In hie triumphe, with *ourhand* as victor.
Douglas, iii. 315, 16, Small.
I sall the send as victor with *ouirhand*,
To be maister and to maintene this land.
Ibid., 456, 40, Rudd.

To OURSCHROUD, *v. a.* To cover over, wrap up, enfold ; part. pt. *ourschroud*, enshrouded ; "with body all *ourschroud*," Douglas, Virgil, 385, 23, Rudd.

OURSMAN, OURISMAN, *s.* V. OVERSMAN.

To OURSPINNER, OURSPYNNER, OUERSPYNNER, *v. n.* To glide, fly, run, or bound rapidly over or along : lit. to spin over. V. SPYNNER.
The birdis of hartis with ther heidis hie,
Ourspynnerand with swyft cours the plane vaill.
Douglas, ii. 185, 1, Small.

OURWELTERAND, OUERWELTERAND, OURWALTERAND, *part. pr.* Tossing and tumbling about ; also, overturning, overthrowing. V. WALTER, WELTER.
The rageand storm *ourwalterand* wally seis.
Douglas, iii. 74, 18, Small.
Woddis, heyrdis, flokkis, catale, and men,
Our-welterand with hym in the deip glen.
Ibid., iv. 145, 32.
The prefix *ouer*, *ouir*, *ouyr*, as used by Douglas is a monosyllable and pron. as *our*, which is the prevalent form in the Elphinstoun MS. V. Small's ed.

To OUT, *v. a.* To vent, void, extrude. Addit. to OUT, q. v.
". . . ; and ilk ane of thaim [the heart, the liver, and the brain], has his clengyng plas, quhar he may *out* his superfluities and cleng him."—Ane Tretyse agayne the Pestelens, MS. Adv. Lib.

OUTAK, OWTAK, OUTTAKAND, OWTTAKAND, *prep.* Except. Addit. to OUT-TAK.

OUTANCE, OUTIN, *s.* Same as OUTING q. v.

To OUT-AWE, *v. a.* To owe or be indebted to. V. INAWN, *Inawe*.
". . . and gives and commits to thame full power to give up all debts bothe in-awing and *out-awing* to him and be him to uthers." War Com. of Kirkcudbright, p. 171.

OUTBRECK, OUTBREK, *s.* 1. A portion of outfield or pasture-land newly broken up or prepared for cultivation : also called " quoyland," q. v. Orkn.
"A quoyland or *outbrek* is ane peice of land newly win without the dykes :" that is, a piece of land newly improved and not yet enclosed. Peterkin's Rentals of Orkney, No. ii., p. 2.
"If the quoy was near the *Tun* [i.e., farmstead], it was sometimes called an Umbeset (*Um-bus-settnung*, N.), an outlying homestead, an outset ; or an *outbrek*

(*Ut-brekkr*, N.), an outbrink (of the townland)." Proceedings Antiq. Soc. Sc., 1883-4, p. 256. V. OUTSET.
2. An outcrop ; as when a vein of coal or other mineral appears on the surface of the ground.

OUTBURGES, OUTEBURGES, *s.* A burgess residing outwith the bounds of the burgh : Burgh Recs. freq.

OUTEN-TOUN, OUTTEN-TOWNES, OWTINTOWNES, *adj.* Lying or living outside the burgh bounds, not belonging to the town ; as, *outen-toun* lands, *outten-townes* burgess, *outen-touns* multure.
These forms and meanings occur frequently in our Burgh Records. Jamieson has presented the term as a noun only. V. DICT.

OUTEN-TOWNES MULTURE, *s.* Same as Outsucken Multure, q. v. ; Corshill Baron-Court Book, p. 81, Ayr and Wigton Arch. Coll., Vol. IV.

OUTGANGING, OUTGANGIN, OUTGANG, OUTGAN, OUTGAUN, *s.* Outgoing, removal ; the act of giving up possession of burghal property. Addit. to OUTGANGING, q.v.
Outgang is also used, like *Outgait*, with the meaning *outlet*, *passage*, *egress ;* thus, " Every tenant man has ische and entry, *outgang* and ingang, to his haudin (i.e., holding)." *Outgang* and *ingang* are common terms in Holland.

OUTLAND, OUTLAN, *adj.* Outlying, lying on the borders of a burgh ; as, "*outlan* merchis ;" also, out of or beyond the bounds of a burgh ; as, "*outland* burgesses," i.e., burgesses living outside the burgh. Burgh Recs. Peebles, pp. 208, 217, 219, Rec. Soc.

OUTLANDEMER, OUTLANDIMER, OUTLANDMER, *s.* An overseer of the outlands of a burgh, i.e., the lands lying outside the burgh bounds ; also, the marches or bounds of those lands ; Burgh Recs., Glasgow, I. 13, Rec. Soc. V. LANDIMER.
This term occurs in various forms in our Burgh Records.

OUTLANDER, OUTLAND, OUTLAN, *s.* An alien, a stranger ; an incomer to a burgh or parish ; also, one who lives beyond the bounds of a burgh. Addit. to OUTLAN, q.v.

OUTLER, OUTLAIR, OUTLAR, *s.* and *adj.* V. OUTLYER.
Stone dykes, marches, enclosures for cattle, etc. in rural districts are generally built of *outlers*, gathered from fields, burns, and streams. Addit. to OUTLYER.

OUTLIN, OOTLIN, OUTERLIN, OUTERLING, *s.* The weakling of a brood or family ; the despised, neglected, or neer-do-weel member

of a family, who is treated like an outsider; West of S., Orkn.
Outlan, an alien, although sometimes written *outlin* (V. DICT.), is a different word: it is short for *outlander*, one come from or living beyond the bounds of a burgh or parish. *Outlin* or *outling* (*out* with dim. suffix *ling*), the one that is pushed or kept outside, the weakest or least worth one.

To OUTRAY, OWTTRAYE, *v. a.* To injure, defeat, destroy; Awnt. Arth., l. 310. Addit. to OUTRAY, q. v.

OUTREDANCE, OUTREDDING, *s.* Same as Outred, *s.*, q. v.

To OUTRIVE, OUTRIEVE, *v. a.* To tear up plants, etc. by the roots, to clear land of its growth; also, to encroach upon and break up pasture land for cultivation.
". . . persued . . . for the sowme of sex pond Scotis money for *outrieving* of bent land quhairof David Harper got the profit." Cornhill Baron-Court Book, Ayr and Wigton Arch. Coll., iv. 138.
Icel. *rífa*, to rive; Sw. *rifva*, Dan. *rive*, to tear.

OUTSET, *s.* An addition made to a room or building for the purpose of enlargement; also, an out-house. Addit. to OUTSET, q. v. V. *Onset.*

OUTSTOLLING, part. pt. For *outstollen*, stolen or slipt away.
Strenth is away, *outstolling* lyk ane theif, Quhilk keipit ay the thesaure of estait.
King Hart; Douglas, l. 115, 13, Small.
Although this term has the form of a part. pr., its structure and the sense of the passage indicate that it is the part. pt. of *outsteal*.
A.-S. *út*, out, and *stelan*, to steal; (pret. *stæl*, part. pt. *stolen*); Du. *stelen*, Icel. *stela*.

OUTTAKAND, OWTTAKAND, *part. pr.* as *prep.* Excepting, except; Burgh Recs. Peebles, 19 Jan. 1466, Rec. Soc. V. *Outak.*

OUT-TOLL, *s.* The act of giving up possession of burghal property: also, the payment made to the bailie who transfers such property, by the party giving up possession of it. V. *In-Toll.*
"In our older burgh usages, burghal subjects were transferred by the bailie taking a penny for *in-toll* and a penny for *out-toll*." Innes, Leg. Antiq., p. 91.

OUTUT, *prep.* Outwith. V. OUTOUTH.

OVERLAIKE, OVIRLAIKE, *s.* Failure; Rom. Alexander, l. 1861, 3102.

OVER-LEDDERIS, *s. pl.* Upper-leathers or uppers of boots or shoes; Burgh Recs. Aberdeen, I. 176, Sp. C.

OVER-SEA, OUIR-SE, *s.* A name for the Adriatic; Douglas, Virgil, 245, 39, Rudd.
Lit. the upper sea: Lat. *Mare Superum sive Adriaticum*. V. Rudd. Gloss.

OWER-ANENST, OWER-ANENS, OWER-ANENT, *prep.* and *adv.* Over against, opposite to.

OWER-MICKLE, OWRE-MUCKLE, *adj.* and *adv.* Overmuch, too much.

OWER-MONY, OWRE-MONY, O'ER-MONY, *adj.* Too many: also, too-strong, not to be resisted, as, "He's *owre-mony* for you."
Tibbie Fowler o' the Glen, There's *ower-mony* wooing at her.
Songs Prior to Burns, p. 131.

OWER-NICE, OWRE-NICE, *adj.* Fastidious, dainty; also, shy, backward, as, "Dinna be *owre-nice* now, but mak' yersel at hame."

To OWERSE, OURSEE, *v. a.* To superintend, manage; also, to overlook, neglect, pass over. V. [OUERSENE], *Ouersee.*

OWIRTIRIVE, *v.* V. OURTYRVE.

OWN, OWNE. The *own*, its own or peculiar.
". . euery Nation seruing it selfe with *the owne* vowatie deuise." Blame of Kirkburiall, ch. 4.

OWNE, *s.* An oven. V. OWYNE, OON.

To OWRESAIL, *v. a.* V. OURSYLE.

To OWRSET, *v. a.* V. OUERSET.

OXINBOWYS, *s. pl.* Ox-yokes; Exch. Rolls Scot., VII. 3.
Same as *Oxinbollis* in DICT., and represents the common pron. V. Bow.

OXTERED, *part. pt.* Supported under the arm: steadied or assisted in walking by means of such support; as, "He was *oxtered* hame."

OYD-MAN, *s.* A pron. of *Odisman*, q. v. Burgh Recs. Prestwick, 21 Jan. 1487-8.

OYE, *s.* Lit. an eye: pl. *oyes*, openings for light or windows in the walls of a house; Burgh Recs. Glasgow, I. 347. Rec. Soc.
O. Fr. *oeil*, an eye; pl. *yeux*. In architecture loop-holes in a wall are called *oillets*. V. Gloss. Terms in Arch.

OYSE, *s.* An osier; also, osiers, willow wands for wicker work, scrub cut from the banks of a river; Burgh Recs. Glasgow, I. 303, Rec. Soc. O. Fr. *ozier*.

P.

To PACE, PAS, *v. n.* To pass, go, depart, pass away, die; Kingis Quair, st. 22, 69.

PACK, *s.* An old Norse measure of quantity formerly used in Orkney: is now represented by the terms *piece* and *roll*.
A *pack* of wadmæl contained 10 gudlings, and each gudling contained 6 cuttels or Scotch ells.
Throughout Zetland the cuttel was the fundamental unit of length and of valuation; and a cuttel of wadmæl long bore a standard value of 6d. Scots. Six cuttels were equal to an *eyre* or *eire* of valuation; twenty cuttels, to a sheep; and six score, or a longhundred, to an ox. The value of the cuttel was raised to two shillings by Earl Robert as a means of carrying out his cruel exactions from the natives. V, Memorial for Orkney, pp. 58, 114.

PADELL, PAIDLE, PEDDLE, *s.* Lit. a little *pad* or *pack* : a small leathern bag, pouch, or wallet used by packmen for holding small-wares, odds and ends, etc., and generally carried inside their pack; also, the leathern pouch worn by country housewives as a convenient receptacle for various odds and ends required in their daily work. Addit. to PADELL, q. v.
Not explained by Jamieson; but in a note he quotes Sibbald's definition, which evidently refers to a packman's *padell*, but is not quite correct. The *padell* was not "a bag or wallet containing a pedlar's wares"; for it contained only a portion of them, and in most cases a very small portion of them. It held only the small-wares, odds and ends, etc. of his stock, and was in reality one of the packages of his pack. The housewife's *padell* again was a flat leathern pouch, with one or more pockets according to the fancy of the wearer or the nature of her daily work. It hung by her right side and was attached by bands fastened round her waist.

PAIRN-MEAL, PAIRNS, *s.* The coarsest kind of meal made from bran and siftings of wheat.
Lit. *paring-meal, parings*, i.e., meal made from the parings or castings of the grain.

PAIS, PACE, PES, *s.* Weight, standard or legal weight: *to brek pace, to brek the pais,* to make or sell goods of light weight: *to keip the pace,* to make or sell goods of standard or statute weight. Addit. to PACE, q. v.
These phrases occur frequently in our Burgh Records in connection with the Assize of Bread and in charges against fraudulent bakers.

To PAIS, PACE, *v. a.* To estimate the weight of an article by poising it in the hand: part. pr. *paisan, paisin, paising;* South and West of S. Addit. to PAIS, *v.*, q. v.

PAISAND, PAYSAND, PASAND, *adj.* Weighty, ponderous; Douglas, III. 36, 9, Small.

PAITLAT, PAITLET, PAYTLET, PAITLICH, PAITCLAITH, PAITCLAYTH, *s.* A partlet: a portion of female dress, forming an ornamental covering for the neck and throat. One form of it was like a neckerchief, and was called a *paitclaith*, corrupted into *paitlich*, and sometimes called a *paitlich-gown*.
The change of *partlet* into *paitlet* is somewhat peculiar; but we have a similar change in *paitrick* from *partrick*, a partridge. V. *Paitrick*.
This term is not defined in DICT., and Jamieson's note regarding it is altogether misleading. Lord Hailes' suggestion that it was "a woman's ruff" is so far correct; so also is the suggestion by Skinner that it was "a napkin or neck-kerchief"; but both definitions require explanation, and perhaps the following will suffice. As the gowns of that period were more or less open in front, sometimes even to the waist, some sort of covering for the neck was necessary; and both the kind and form of this covering would be determined by the circumstance and taste of the wearer, as well as by the fashion of the day. And so there were *partlets* or *paitlets* of the most costly materials, ruffled, frilled, or otherwise ornamented, and others of plain material and simple form : in some cases, indeed, it was merely a neckerchief. Such, no doubt, was the *paitlich-gown* bemoaned by the harvest-women when they were driven from the field by an autumnal shower. (See "The Hairst Rig," and the quotation from it given under PAITLICH.)
Planché describes the *partlet* as "a covering for the neck and throat similar to what is now called a habitshirt"; and states that "it sometimes had sleeves attached to it, and was made of stuffs of the most valuable and delicate kind." British Costume, p. 264, ed. 1874.
Partlet, dimin. of *part*, a part or portion, may have been applied to this article of dress because it was one of the smallest portions of the gown; or because of its manifold divisions when ruffed or frilled; as it was when first introduced.

PAITLE, PAITTEL, PADDLE, *s.* and *v.* V. *Patill.*

PAITRICK, PAITREK, *s.* A partridge. V. PARTRIK.
'Twas ae night lately, in my fun,
I gaed a roving wi' the gun,
An' brought a *paitrick* to the grun,
A bonnie hen;
And, as the twilight was begun
Thought nane wad ken.
Burns, *Epistle to John Rankine*, st. 7.

PALE, PAIL, *s.* A paling; Douglas, IV. 185, 24, ed. Small. V. PAILIN.

PALE, PALLE, *s.* Fine cloth. V. PALL.

PALWERK, *s.* Fine cloth, figured or brocaded; Awnt. Arthur, l. 19. Addit. to PALWERK, q. v.

PAD [185] PAN

Lit. *work in palle:* Lat. *pallium,* Fr. *palle, poile,* cloth of silk.
This term was left undefined by Jamieson, but in an explanatory note he suggested a meaning which is misleading.

PADYANE, PADGEAN, *s.*   A pageant.   V. DICT.
Horne Tooke's explanation of E. *pageant,* quoted by Jamieson, is a mistake. M. E. *pagent* orig. meant a moveable scaffold made of wooden planks, a stage for shows or on which plays were acted ; L. Lat. *pagina,* a scaffold, from Lat. *pagina,* a page of a book, a plank of wood. Named from *pactus,* fastened together (p. p. of *pangere*). The term *pagina* afterwards denoted the play itself, as may be seen in the Chester Mysteries, ed. Wright, where the various plays or pageants are entitled *Pagina prima,* . . *Pagina secunda,* . . etc. For an account of those scaffolds, see Sharp's Coventry Mysteries, p. 17, and an interesting note in Prompt. Parv., p. 377.

PAGE, *s.*   A boy.   V. DICT.
Del. the last parag. of this entry. Horne Tooke's explanation is a mistake.
The etym. of this term is still disputed ; but the general opinion is that Fr. *page,* Span. *page,* Port. *pagem,* and Ital. *paggio,* have come from Lat. *pagensis,* belonging to a village.   V. Skeat's Etym. Dict.

To PALL, *v. a.*   Lit. to cause to lose colour, fade, or grow pale: hence, to dull or deaden, frighten, appal: "that doith my wittis *pall;*" Kingis Quair, st. 18.
A contr. form of *appal,* which originally meant to fade, grow pale ; and so even in M. E. The transitive sense is comparatively modern. From O. Fr. *palle, pasle,* pale : whence *pallir, paslir,* and *appalir,* to wax pale, to make pale. V. Cotgrave, Palsgrave, Burguy.

To PALL, *v. n.*   V. DICT.
This is not a modification of E. *paw,* but the same as M. E. *pallen,* to strike ; see Gloss. to Piers Plowman, ed. Skeat.

PALLACH, *s.*   V. PELLACK, POLLACK.

PALLAT, *s.*   V. DICT.
Ruddiman's explanation of this term, quoted by Jamieson, is far-fetched. No doubt *pallat* is sometimes used in the sense of scull ; but prob. this is a secondary sense of M. E. *palet,* from O. Fr. *palet,* a sort of armour for the head (Roquefort). See Way's note in Prompt. Parv., p. 378.

PALM, PAUM, PAUME, *s.*   Lit., the flat of the hand: the blade of an oar, branch of a tree, tine of an antler; Douglas, III. 295, 8, ed. Small.

PALMIE, PALMER, PAUMIE, PAMMIE, *s.*   V. PAWMIE.
M. E. and O. Fr. *paume,* from Lat. *palma,* a palmtree.   V. Palm in Skeat's Etym. Dict.

PALPIS, *s. pl.*   Paps; Douglas, II. 18, 8, ed. Small.
This form is due to a confusion of *alp* with *aup ;* see [PAUPIS].

·(Sup.)   Z

PALSONE EVIN.   V. DICT.
Palsone cannot possibly be for *Passion,* as suggested. It represents a pron. of *Palmsun,* used for *Palm Sunday,* just as *Whitsun* is used for *Whitsunday.*

PALWERK, *s.*   V. under *Pale, Palle.*

PAMPHIE, *s.*   V. DICT.
Johnson's explanation of this term is a mistake. It is simply the Fr. *pamphile,* the usual name for the knave of clubs ; see Littré's Fr. Dict. From Lat. *pamphilus,* the name of a slave.

PAN, PANN, PANNE, *s.* 1. A case, covering, enclosure ; *hern-pan,* the brain-case, contr. to *pan,* the scull, as used by Douglas, I. 104, 5, ed. Small.

2. A candelabrum or frame for candles, used in lighting a church.
"Item, for twa stanis of candil to the *pann* in the mydds of the kirk, and keeping of it, xxv s. iiij d." Burgh Recs. Edinburgh, ii. 351, Roc. Soc.
"Item, for xviij faddome of aue tow to the *pann* xxviij s." Ibid., p. 356.
This term is generally stated to be of Celtic origin : cf. Irish *panna,* Welsh *pan.* It occurs in A.-S. as *panne,* a pan, a broad shallow vessel ; and in L. Lat. as *panna,* a pan : prob. corr. of Lat. *patina.* V. Skeat's Etym. Dict. This supposition is much strengthened by the occurrence of L. Lat. *paneta* as a variant of *patina ;* see Sweet, Oldest Eng. Texts, p. 83, 1. 1489, also Ducange, s. v.

PANDIE, *s.*   V. DICT.
Not from Lat. *pande,* but a playful variation of *hand,* as in the common nursery term *handy-pandy.*

PANE, *s.*   1. A piece of cloth suited for a counterpane ; also, the quantity of material required to make it. Addit. to PANE, s. 3, q. v.

2. A package of furs containing a hundred skins: used as synonymous with *mantil* in the "Book of Customs and Valuation of Merchandise"; Halyburton's Ledger, p. 305. Addit. to PANE, q. v.
Besides, it sometimes means fur, sometimes a skin or piece of fur : see quotations in DICT., also Gloss. Liber Albus. Regarding the number of skins in a *pane,* see under *mantil* in Gloss. to Accts. L. H. Treas., Scot., vol. I., Dickson.

PANE, PAYN, *s.*   V. DICT.
This term is used to represent any kind or degree of pain, grief, penalty, or suffering : hence, *but payn,* without trouble, easily ; *a pane,* with trouble, damage, loss, disgrace, as in Douglas, i. 92, 8 ; in difficulty, danger, disaster, at a pinch, as in Barbour, ix. 64 ; through fear, or arbour, ix. 80 ; with difficulty, hardly, scarcely.
The phrase *a payn* is frequently printed as one word, and under this form it was treated by Jamieson : his explanations, however, are not quite satisfactory.

PANFRAY, *s.*   Errat. for *paufray,* a pron. of *palfray,* a small riding horse.   V. DICT.
The version of the Burrow Lawes from which the

quotation in the DICT. is taken is evidently corrupt. A better rendering of the passage is:—"Bot neuer the less the best *palfra* fallis to the ayr." Ancient Laws and Customs of the Burghs of Scotland, p. 171, Rec. Soc.

PANS, PANSE, PAUNCE, PAUNSONE, *s.* The panzar or gambeson, a wadded and quilted tunic sometimes worn instead of a hauberk. Errat. in DICT. V. PANS.

Prob. Jamieson's mistake arose through confounding the *pans* or *panzar* with the *polein*. According to Sir S. Meyrick the *wambeys* or *gambeson* was a wadded and quilted tunic, made of leather and stuffed with wool. It was worn as a defence by those who could not afford a hauberk; and by persons of distinction it was sometimes worn under the hauberk, like a surcoat. The Northmen, both Danes and Norwegians called it a *panzar* or *panzara*, and for short *panse* or *paunce*, which is frequently but improperly translated coat of mail. V. Plancho's British Costume, p. 91.

O. Fr. *pance*, "the panch, or the great belly of a Doublet"; Cotgr. And *panceron* he renders "the full-stuffed bellie of a doublet."

To **PANSE,** *v. a.* To think, meditate, plan; also, to look to, attend, dress, care for, as a surgeon attends to a wound. V. PANST.

". . . in euring and *pansing* Mathow Welche of ane vlcer in his fute thrie oulkis syne or thairby," etc. Burgh Recs. Edinburgh, 12 April, 1587.

O. Fr. *panser*, to dress, attend, or look unto; Cotgr. Mod. Fr. *penser*.

To **PARALL,** *v. a.* To apparel, deck, adorn, mount; Douglas, I. 87, 27; part. pr. *paraling*, used also as a *s.*

PARALING, *s.* A form of *apparelling*, preparation; hence, fitting, mounting, of any kind. Addit. to [PARALING], q. v.

See Peraling in DICT., and Apparelling in Murray's New Eng. Dict.

PAREGALE, *adj.* V. DICT.

The O. Fr. word is not *peregal*, as given by Rudd., but *parigal*, given by Roquefort and Burguy. The latter, s. v. *ewer*, says it is derived from *par* and *égal.*

PARLASY, *s.* V. PERLASY.

To **PARRIRE,** *v. n.* V. DICT.

This is certainly the O. Fr. *parir*, another form of O. Fr. *paroir*, to appear, and has no connection with Lat. *parere*, to obey.

Burguy gives the forms *paroir, parir, parer, pareier*, to appear, to be visible, to show oneself.

PARSELL, *s.* Parsley.

"Petroselinum, *parsell;*" Duncan's Appendix Etymologiæ, 1595, ed. Small, E. D. S.

To **PART,** *v. n.* To depart, leave; Douglas, II. 146, 72, ed. Small, Kingis Quair, st. 67: part. pt. *partit*, gone from, awaked, as, "new *partit* out of slepe;" Kingis Quair, st. 2.

PARTIK, *s.* Short for Particate, q. v.: Burgh Recs. Prestwick, 5 May, 1511, p. 42, Mait. C.

PASIT, *adj.* Heavy. V. under *Pais.*

PATILL, PAITLE, PAITTEL, PAIDLE, PADDLE, *s.* A scraper. Addit. to PATTLE.

To **PATILL, PATIL, PAITTEL, PAIDLE,** *v. a.* To scrape or clean with a pattle: E. *paddle.*

"Item, for ane *patill* to *patil* the kirk with." Burgh Recs. Edinburgh, ii. 351, Rec. Soc.

"Item, the xv day of Marche 1554, gevin to Thomas Hallis servand for *paittelling* and deichting of all the steppis of the turngryss of the tolbuith, viij d." Ibid., p. 296.

PATRON, PATRONE, *s.* A commander of a small vessel; Douglas, Virgil, v. ch. 4: pl. *patrouns*, Ibid., ch. 3.

Lat. *patronus*, a protector: from *pater*, a father.

PATTIE, *s.* A small pot: dimin. of *pat.* West of S.

PAUMES, *s. pl.* Antlers. V. *Palm.*

PAUNSOME, *s.* Same as *Pans, Panse,* q. v.

PAVEAN, PAVEEN, *adj.* Pretentious, upsetting, vain: lit., peacock-like. In Orkney the pseudo-rich are called "*pavean* bodies." V. PAVEN.

Lat. *pavo*, a peacock.

PAWN, *s.* Another form of Pand, Pan, Pane, v. v. Addit. to PAWN, q. v.

Not Belgic, but French. "*Pan*, a pane, piece, or pannell of a wall; . . . also the skirt of a gown, the pane of a hose;" Cotgr.

PAXIS, *s. pl.* A corr. of *packs*, bundles; Burgh Recs. Aberdeen, I. 436, Sp. C.

PAY, *s.* Del. this entry in DICT.

Pay was a misprint for *gay* in the 1508 ed. of Gawan and Gol. In Pinkerton's ed. the mistake was corrected; but, as the alteration was made without explanation, Jamieson rejected it and held by the earlier reading.

To **PAYRE,** *v. a.* To impair. V. PAIR.

PAYSAND, PAYSIT, part. as *adj.* V. *Pais, v.*

PAYSIT, PASIT, part. as *adj.* Weighted, loaded, heaped up, heavy; Douglas, III. 170, 7, IV. 108, 31, ed. Small.

PAYTLET, *s.* V. *Paitlat.*

PEACE OF A FAIR, *s.* The freedom and security during the time of a fair, which was assured by royal proclamation to all persons attending the fair except traitors and miscreants; also, the public notice, declaration, or proclamation of said freedom and security; Burgh Recs. Glasgow, I. 88, 154.

On the evening preceding the opening of a fair the town-officers by order of the magistrates gave public notice of the event, and proclaimed the *Peace of the Fair* to townsfolk and country-folk. This was called "crying the *peace of the fair*," or simply "*crying the fair.*" How this was done is detailed under *To Cry a Fair*, q. v., and in the Glasgow Burgh Recs. referred to above.

The old burghal law on which the proclamation is based is entitled "Of stabillyng of the pece of fayris," and runs thus :—

"This is the ordinans of the pece of fayris on this halfe the wattir of Forth, that is to wyt, that fra the pece of the fayr cryit thar sal na man be takyn na attachyt wythin that ilke fayr bot gif he breke the pece of the fayr towart it cumande or wythin it duelland or fra thin passand, bot gif he war the kyngis traytour, or gif ho war suilke a mysdoar that gyrth of haly kyrk aw nocht to sauffe hym. And gif ony suilke mysdoar be fundyn, or aic as has brokyn the pece of the fayr, he sal be attachyt and aykerly kepyt till the motis of that ilke fayr, and thare he aw for to byde dome and lauch of the courte." Burgh Lawis, ch. 86, Rec. Soc.

If the latter part of the enactment illustrates the stern justice of our old Scot. laws, the following item on the same subject is a fine example of its tender mercy :—

"Gif ony man fyndis his bonde in the fayre the quhilk is fra hym fled, quhil the pece of the fayr is lestande he may nocht of lauch chase na tak hym." Burgh Lawis, ch. 88, Rec. Soc.

This enactment carries us back to times when serfdom was a recognised and legal institution in our land.

PEAK, PEEK, *s*. A very small quantity, a mere pick; as, "a *peak* o' licht, a *peek* o' fire."

As generally used this is an intensive form of *pick*, a small quantity. V. DICT.

PEAKIE, PEEKIE, *adj*. Petty. V. *Pickie*.

PEAKY, PEEKIE, *s*. One who knits woollen caps, nightcaps, etc.: lit. one who works with *peakies*, i.e. pricks or pointed wires. Also called a *peaky-worker*, and the occupation is called " *the peakies*," Ayrs.

Gael. *pic*, Irish *pice*, a pike, spike. V. PIKESTAFF and [PICKIE] in DICT.

Ayrshire has long been noted for its woollen manufactures; and for at least a century its chief town, Kilmarnock, has been specially noted for its woollen caps, cowls, etc. The knitting of these articles was done almost entirely by females, called *peakies* or *peaky-workers*; and only a few years ago there were in Kilmarnock and the surrounding villages many thousands of these knitters in constant employment. Now, however, no such work can be got, and the occupation of the *peaky* is completely gone; for every variety of knitted cap or bonnet is worked by machinery.

PECE, *s*. A form of *pais*, weight; Burgh Recs. Aberdeen, I. 390. V. PAIS.

To PECE, *v. a.* To appease. V. PEIS, *v*.

PECHER, PECHAR, *s*. A pitcher, breaker.

This form of vessel was much more common long ago than it is now. It was made of earthen-ware or metal, in a great variety of shapes and sizes, from the small pitcher that held the morning's milk and evening's ale, to the large pitcher that held the household supply of spring or well-water, or the larger ones in which the ale-wife kept a convenient supply of her different kinds of ale "*fresh-drawn*" from the tun. It was the ale in her pitchers, not in her tuns, which the *cunners* or tasters examined when they came to test the quality of her ale; and they drew the samples for themselves, as the following extract implies :—

". . . and ane of the cunnaris sall fill a cop of quhat *pechar* he plessis." Burgh Recs. Prestwick, 7 May, 1470, Mait. C.

C. Fr. *pichier*, "a pitcher; a Languedoc word;" Cotgr.: from L. Lat. *bicarium*, a wine-cup. Hence, pitcher and breaker are different forms of the same word, derived from Gk. *békos*, an oarthen wine-vessel.

PECK, PEK, *s*. A corr. of *pack*, a collection, great number: as in "a *peck* o' lees," a pack of lies; "a *peck* o' troubles," many troubles.

Peck is so used in various districts of Scot.; and the phrase, "a *pek* of lyiss," is found in the Burgh Recs. Aberd., i. 159, Sp. C.

PEEL-GARLIC, PILL-GARLIC, *adj*. and *s*. Pale and thin, meagre, stunted, worthless, miserable.

Our gentry's wee *peel-garlic* getts
Feed on bear meal an' sma' ale swats,
Wi' thin beef-tea, an' scours o' sauts,
To keep them pale ;
But altmeal parritch straughts thy guts,
An' thick Scotch kail.
J. Ballantine, The Wee Raggit Laddie, st. 4.

The term is also used as a *s*., as in the phrase, "a puir wee *peel-garlic*," which is not uncommon in the West of S. It has various applications, but they all imply a wan, sickly, wasted, or miserable appearance, and consequently weakness or worthlessness.

Webster's Dict. gives *peeled garlic* as another form. In this form it was an old joke. A man who had lost his hair by disease was called a *peeled garlic*, from his head having the smooth white look of garlic when peeled. And this may be the origin of *pill-garlic* too. Some of the applications of the term, however, imply miserly, niggardly habits in the matter of food, and insinuate that the person referred to is mean enough to eat even his peelings of garlic. In this sense the term has much the same force as *skin-flint*; but as generally used it refers to the appearance of a person, and in a jocular way accounts for it.

PEELIE-WALLY, *s*. A name applied to a tall, slender, sickly-looking young person; also applied to a tall, slender plant or young shoot. Also pron. *speelie-wally*, West of S.

Prob. a compound of *peelie*, thin, meagre, and *wally*, withered, sickly-looking.

PEEN, PIN, *s*. A pane: as, "a *peen* o' glass."

To PEEVER, *v. n.* To tremble. V. PIFFER, *Piver*.

PEGANE, *s*. A corr. form of *pageant*: represents the vulgar pron.; Burgh Recs. Aberdeen, I. 449, Sp. C.

To PEIGH, *v. n.* To pant. V. PECH.

"Anhelo, to *peigh* or pant ;" Duncan's Appendix Etymologiæ, 1595, ed. Small, E. D. S.

To PEIRE, PERE, *v. n.* To be on a par, to equal, match, or mate: "to *peire* with," to pair or compare with; Kingis Quair, st. 110, ed. Skeat. V. PEIR, *s*.

In this passage of the Kingis Quair the MS. has

purerese or *pererese*, which is certainly a mistake, and for which Prof. Skeat has suggested *peire*. See his Note, pp. 80-1.

PEIS, PESE, *s.* A vessel. V. PECE.

PEIS, *s.* Weight. V. under *Pais*.

PELE, *s.* V. DICT.
From Lat. *pila*, a pillar, pile. See *Peel* in Supp. to Skeat's Etym. Dict.

PENITION, PENITIOUN, *s.* Punishment, penalty; Burgh Recs. Stirling, 28 April, 1547; *penissione*, Burgh Recs. Prestwick, 30 Jan. 1551-2, p. 62.
Lat. *panitio*, for *punitio*, punishment: from *pœna*, satisfaction for a crime, punishment.

PENNY. The *maist penny*, the most money, highest price, best advantage; Burgh Recs. Edinburgh, II. 1, Rec. Soc.
Similarly, *the mair'penny* means more money, higher price, better advantage. To sell an article for *the maist penny* is to sell it at its highest market price, or to the highest bidder. To *mak the maist penny* of an article was also used in the same sense.

PENNY-BREID, *s.* The penny-loaf: also, penny-loaves, as in the phrase, "flour for *penny-breid*."
The term *breid* is still used for loaf and loaves as above.

PENNYWORTH, PENNY-WORTH, *s.* Goods, merchandise, saleable wares; "to mak payment with penny or *pennyworth*," i.e., with money or goods equivalent, cash or in kind. V. Burgh Recs. Aberdeen, I. 433, Sp. C., B. R. Stirling, p. 58.
Goods sold *in pennyworths*, i.e., in small quantities, by retail; which is also expressed by *in small*, when opposed to wholesale, which is *in great*.

PENSE, *s.* Thought, instruction, lesson; Burgh Recs. Aberdeen, II. 102, Recs. Soc. V. PENS, *v.*

PENURITIE, *s.* Penury, poverty; Burgh Recs. Glasgow, I. 153, Rec. Soc. Lat. *penuria*.

PERCAICE, PER-CACE, *adv.* Perchance, Douglas, II. 15, 19, II. 243, 17, ed. Small.
Fr. *cas*, from Lat. *casus*, case, event, chance.

PERDURAND, *adj.* Lasting, enduring; Douglas, I. 81, 6, ed. Small.

To PERJURNIE, PERIURNIE, *v. n.* To travel throughout a district, to pass through; Burgh Recs. Edinburgh, III. 218, Rec. Soc.

PERK-TREES, PERK-TREIS, *s. pl.* 1. The poles in a green or garden for supporting the *perk* or clothes-line. V. PERK.

2. Rough or unbarked poles from which green or garden poles are made.

PERPRISE, PERPRISS, PERPRISIOUNE, *s.* Invasion of the rights of a superior, encroachment on the ground of a neighbour; Burgh Recs. Aberdeen, I. 401, Sp. C. O. Fr. *perprison*. V. PURPRISIONE.

PERRYE, *s.* Precious stones; Awnt. Arth., l. 368. Addit. to PERRE, q. v.
A corr. of *pierrery*, from O. Fr. *pierrerie*, jewels.

To PERTENE, PERTEEN, *v. n.* To pertain, Kingis Quair, st. 107; part. pr. *pertenand*, being by right the claimant, succeeding; Lyndsay, Papyngo, l. 414. Lat. *pertinere*.

PERTLY, PERTLI, *adv.* Openly: short for APERTLY, q. v.

PES, *s.* Weight. V. PAIS.

PESE, *s.* V. PECE.

PETER, *exclam.* Marry! Short for "*by St. Peter:*" a form of oath; Rauf Coilyear, ll. 87, 304. See notes to Piers Plowman, C. viii. 182.

PEULDER, *s.* V. PEWDER.

PEVYCHE, PEWECH, *adj.* V. PEUAGE.

PEWDER, PEWDAR, PEULDER, *s.* Pewter; Burgh Recs. Glasgow, I. 83, 129, Rec. Soc.

PEWDERAR, PEWDRER. *s.* A pewterer. V. PEUTHERER.

PEYCHTIS, *s. pl.* The Picts. V. PECHTS.

PHILOMEL, PHILOMENE, PHYLOMENE, *s.* The nightingale, Cherrie and Slae, st. 1, Kingis Quair, st. 62, 110.

PIBROCH, *s.* V. DICT.
"*Pibrochs* or airs" is an expression used by Smollett in Humphrey Clinker; see letter dated Sept. 3. Prob. *pibroch* is merely a Gaelic formation from the E. word *pipe*.

To PICK-FOAL. V. DICT.
This means simply to pitch, i.e., to *cast* a foal. It has, therefore, no connection with Fr. *piquer*, as suggested by Jamieson.

PICKIE, PEEKIE, PEAKIE, *adj.* Diminutive, petty, insignificant, trifling: "The bairn's a puir, *pickie*, wee thing." West of S., Orkn. V. [PICK, *s.*]
The form *peekie* is not a mere variety of pronunciation: it is generally used as an intensive of *pickie*, and applied to very small objects.

PIERRERY, PIERRERIE, PYERRERY, *s.* Precious stones, jewels. V. *Perrye*.
"She . . . had on a ryche coller of *pyerrery*.

. . . His churte was bordered of fyne *pierrery* and pearls." Marriage of James IV. and Margaret of England, Leland's Collect., iv. 300.
O. Fr. *pierrerie*, jewels, precious stones.

To PIGNORATE, *v. a.* To pawn, pledge; part. pt. *pignorat*, taken or put in pawn; Corshill Baron-Court Book, Ayr and Wigton Arch. Coll., IV. 115.
Lat. *pignorare*, to pawn, pledge; from *pignus*, a pledge.

PILE, PYLE, *s.* A small quantity; *a wee pile*, a very small quantity; West of S. Addit. to PILE, PYLE.
A.-S. *pil*, from Lat. *pila*, a pile, pillar.

PILL-GARLIC, *adj.* and *s.* V. *Peel-Garlic*.

PINTO, *s.* A wooden pin or lever for turning a weaver's beam, West of S.

To PIPE, *v. n.* To blow, rush, or whistle as a rising wind.
Scars this wes said, quhen evin at our desyre,
The sesonable air *pipis* vp fair and schire.
Douglas, *Virgil*, iii. ch. 8, ed. Small.
This word is still in use. In the West of S. it is a common saying when the wind is rising, "Hear how it's *pipin* i' the lum-tap." It occurs also in various nautical terms.

PISTOLATE, PISTOLET, *s.* A pistol; Burgh Recs. Stirling, p. 56.

PITTEN, *part. pt.* Put: a pron. of *putten*. V. under *Put*.

To PIVER, PEIFER, PEEVER, *v. n.* To tremble, shake, quiver, as with fear or cold, or like an aged person. Addit. to PIFFER, q. v.
In the West and South of S. *peever* and *peifer* are used: in Orkney, *piver*, as in the following passage descriptive of the fear of a jailor while setting a prisoner free from the jougs.
"Patie was unco sweer tae rise; and sweer was he tae tak the lock aff o' the haas-iron: for he wus terrably jubish o' Brockie's muckle fit. For ye see hid was t'ought a muckle smolie on ony aen wha wus jogged, gin he deud ao' kick the offisher whin he teuk him oot. However, "Patie pat on the key, bit his han's *pivered* wi' faer a' the time. Trath, a' the time he sat he wus *piveran'* like a paedle on a plate." Orcadian Sketch Book, p. 33.
Piver is merely a variant of *liver;* from A.-S., *bifian*, to shake, cognate with Ger. *beben*.

PLAGUES, *s. pl.* Playthings. V. PLAIG, PLAYOKIS.
"Crepundia, bairnes *plagues*;" Duncan, App. Etym., 1595, ed. Small, E.D.S.

PLAIT-LOCK, *s.* A form of lock in which the works are fitted on a thin iron plate; Burgh Recs. Peebles, p. 389, Rec. Soc.

PLAT, *s.* Short for *platform*, and old word for a ground-plan; hence, a plan generally, a plot. Addit. to PLAT, q. v.

PLATES, PLATIS, PLAITIS, *s. pl.* Tablets, memorandum or note book; so called, because they consisted of two or more thin plates of metal attached in the form of a book. They were of various shapes and sizes.
". . . that standis writin in this lytill byll with Master Jon Baryis hand befor Master Jon Bary and Jon Cant in Jon Vakeris hous on the *platis* or he deit." Halyburton's Ledger, p. 51.

PLAYFOOL, *s.* A jester, merry-andrew.
"Morio, a pleasand or *playfool;*" Duncan, App. Etym., 1595, ed. Small, E.D.S.

PLEASAND, *s.* A jester, merry-andrew.
"Morio, a *pleasand* or playfool;" Duncan, App. Etym., 1595, ed. Small, E.D.S.

PLEBAN, PLEBANE, *s.* The parson of a mother church which had other churches or chapels dependent on it. His authority was somewhat similar to that of a rural dean. L. Lat. *plebanus*.
"The said Gylbert constitut the saidis *plebane*, curat, and chaplanis and thair successoris to be kepparis to the archidenis place." Burgh Recs. Peebles, p. 189, Rec. Soc.

To PLENE, PLEIN, PLEYNE, *v. n.* To complain, Douglas, II. 34, 14, ed. Small, Kingis Quair, st. 70, 90, 91. V. PLENYE.
These are contracted forms of *plenye*, *plainyie*. Douglas uses both *plene* and *plenye*; the Kingis Quair has *pleyne*.

PLET, *s.* A plait, a fold; hence, a lappet, a rag.
"Lacinia, a *plet*, or rag;" Duncan, App. Etym., 1595, ed. Small, E.D.S.

PLET, PLETT, *part. pt.* Short for *plettit*, rooved, rivetted; Burgh Recs. Aberdeen, I. 36, Recs. Soc. V. PLET, *v.*

PLEYABLE, *adj.* V. DICT.
This simply means plea-able, and has no connection with A.-S. *pleo, pleoh, plioh,* danger. It is not from Fr. *plaider,* to plead, but from O. Fr. *plai*, a plea, short for *plait,* which is from Lat. *placitum,* as Jamieson remarks under PLEY, *s.* 2.

PLONKET, PLONKETTE, PLUNKET, *s.* A coarse woollen cloth : *plunket* in Halliwell's Dict.
Hir belle was of *plonkette* with birdis full baulde
Botonede with besautes and bokellede full bene
Arout. Arth., l. 366.
"Belle," a mantle.
The Douce MS. reads *blunket.*
These forms are prob. mere varieties of *blanket*. Fr. *blanket*, dimin. of *blanc*, white, from O. H. Ger. *blanch, planch*, white. V. Skeat's Etym. Dict.

To PLOOK, PLOUK, *v. a.* To pluck, pick or pull out; to withdraw smartly or with force : another form is *pook,* q. v. E. *pluck*. West of S.

To PLOOK, PLOUK, PLUKE, v. a. To set the plook or measure-knob on a vessel used as a measure of liquids: part. pr. *plouking*, part. pt. *ploukit*. Cf. E. *plug*. V. PLUKE, s.

". . ordanis the tounschip to be warnit to bryng thair stoupis to be maid and mesourit . . . and ordanis the craftisman to have for ilk pund wecht of pewder working vi. d., and for the only *ploukyng* of vtheria liij. d., and the treyn stoipis to be *ploukit* and merkit lykwys." Burgh Recs. Glasgow, i. 83, Rec. Soc.

In 1599 the magistrates of Stirling issued the following instructions for plooking the pewter measures used in that burgh.

"The counsall hes condiscendit and gewin expres command to Robert Robertsone, peudrar, being present at counsall, that all stoupis, sic as quartis, pyntis, chopines, to be maid be him heireftir, sal be agriabill in mesour to the jug and stampit with the townis stamp, and that the *pluik* be benethe the mouth of ilk stoup as followis, to wit, of the quart stoup and pynt stoup ane inche, and of ilk chopein stoup half ane inch, and that he present the stamp to the counsall yeirlie." Burgh Recs. Stirling, pp. 92-3.

PLOOKIT, PLUKKIT, part. and adj. Same as *plukie*, covered with pimples or *plukes*; also a contr. of *plukie-faced*, fiery-faced, as in "Pluto that *plukkit* duke," Douglas, Virgil, vi. prol.

PLOY, s. V. DICT.
The etym. suggested for this word is certainly wrong. In all senses the term is French; from O. Fr. *ploit*, a variant of *plait*, a plea, which is from Lat. *placitum*; see *plait* in Burguy. V. under PLEY, s. 2.

PLUMROSE, s. A corr. of primrose, West of S.

PLYCHT, s. Danger, obligation, liability; to have *plycht*, to run risk, be made responsible or held liable, suffer punishment, pay the penalty. Addit. to PLYCHT, q. v.
Not defined in DICT.; but the correct meaning is suggested. The term here used is quite different from *plight*, M, E. *plite*, meaning state or condition: it is related to E. *plight*, to pledge, as in "to plight troth;" and is the M. E. *pliht*, danger, also engagement, from A.-S. *pliht*, danger, obligation. See Supp. to Skeat's Etym. Dict.

POACHER-COURT, s. A nickname for the Kirk-Session; Burns, Ep. to Rankine.

PODDASWAY, s. A corr. of *paduasoy*, i.e. Padua silk. Addit. to PODDOSWAY, q. v.
Delete the last para. of the entry in DICT. The explanation is a mistake.

To POIL, v. a. To poll, clip, or shear.
"Tondeo, to clip, to *poil*;" Duncan, App. Etym., 1595, ed. Small, E.D.S.

To POIND, v. a. V. DICT.
The etym. suggested for this word is altogether misleading. *Poind* is simply the A.-S. *pyndan*, to impound, from A.-S. *pand*, a pound, fold; and it has no connection with Germ. *pfand*. Besides, Jamieson reverses the order in deriving the sb. from the verb. See under POUNDLAW.

POINT, POYNT, s. In *poynt*, on the point of; Kingis Quair, st. 168, ed. Skeat. Addit. to POINT, q. v.

POINTMENT, POYNTMENT, s. Appointment, Douglas, II. 100, 10, ed. Small.

POLEMUS, s. Prob. a mistake for *poleinis*, poleyns, long-pointed toes, shoes with long, sharp, or turned-up toes; also called poulaines; Awnt. Arthur, l. 385, MS. Douce. V. PULLAINE.
These *poleyns* must not be confounded with the small plates of iron or steel worn on the shoulders of chain mail, and hence called *epaulières* or *poleyns*: see Planché, British Costume, p. 104. They answer to the L. Lat. *polenae*, poulaines or poleyns, cited by Jamieson under PULLAINE, q. v. Properly, they were long-pointed toes which were fitted to shoes or boots, and imitated in armour; but the name was also given to shoes that were sharp-pointed, peaked, or turned up at the toes.
In the early part of the reign of Ed. IV. "almost all, especially in the courts of princes, had points at the toes of their shoes a quarter of an ell long and upwards, which they now called *poulaines*;" see Planché, Brit. Costume, p. 218. They were restrained by Ed. IV., but not wholly laid aside till the reign of Hen. VIII.

POLK, s. V. DICT.
Polk is for *pokk*, a mode of writing *pouk*, a pouch. In MSS. *kk* is frequently found written as *lk*; this was a device of the scribe to secure ease and speed in writing. See under *Rolk*.
Sometimes also *l* was written for *u*, and was not sounded as *l* consonant.

POLLAC, POLLOCK, POWAN, s. V. DICT.
Regarding these names being applied to different fishes, Prof. Skeat suggests, "If, as is probable, all these forms are from *poll*, the head, as signifying a large-headed fish, this will account for the vague use of the names."
In Webster's Dict. *pollock* means a whiting. The Welsh for a whiting is *gwyniad*, not *gwiniad*, as Jamieson has given it.

PONES, s. Same as POUNCE, q. v.

POOPIT, POWPYTT, s. V. *Pupit*.

To POOR, v. a. To impoverish; pret. and part. pt. *poored*, *pourit*, *powrit*.
Till drink and dice have *poored* him to the pin.
Priests of Peebles.

PORCIUNKLE, s. A small portion, pendicle; Burgh Recs. Prestwick, 7 May, 1470, p. 2, 4, Mait. C. Lat. *portiuncula*.

PORPAPYNE, s. Porcupine; Kingis Quair, st. 155.
Called by Henryson the "*pennit porcupyne*," Parl. of Beistis, l. 109; and in Kingis Quair, "*the werely porpapyne*," the warlike porcupine, in allusion to its fabled power of loosening its quills and darting them at its pursuers.
Other E. forms of this word are *porpin* for *porkepin*, and sometimes *porpentine*.
O. Fr. *porc espin*, the prickle-pig: from Lat. *porcus*, a pig, and *spina*, a thorn. V. Skeat's Etym. Dict.

PORPEN, *s.* A partition: a corr. of *parpane*, q. v.: *ane porpen wall*, a partition wall, Burgh Recs. Edinburgh, II. 297.

PORTAGE, *s.* Travellers' baggage, the personal luggage which a passenger is allowed to take on board a vessel. Addit. to PORTAGE.

PORTATIVES, PORTATIUIS, PORTATIFIS, *s.* A small portable organ formerly used in public processions; Douglas, I. 20, 23, ed. Small, Houlate, l. 765.

Given as Portatibus in DICT., but not explained. In the Bann. MS. of the Houlate, the word is certainly indistinct, but appears to have been originally *portatifis:* in the Asloan MS. it is clearly *portatiuis*, and in the Palice of Honour, Small's ed., it is *portatiues*. This musical instrument was a small organ fitted to be borne about upon a man's back, and to be set down upon a stool when required for use. The carrier then blew the bellows while the performer played.

PORTOUNS, PORTOUS, *s.* V. DICT.

The modern form of this term is *portesse*. In M. E. *portous, porthors*, from O. Fr. *portehors* (from *porter*, to carry, and *hors*, forth), a translation of the Latin name *portiforium*, formed from Lat. *portare*, to carry, *foris*, abroad. See *Portesse* in Skeat's Etym. Dict.

POST AND PAN, POIST AND PAN. Lit. post and tie, or posts and binders: the name given to an old style of building a house. The walls were formed of upright *posts* tied with *pans* or cross pieces of timber; and this framework was filled up with stones and black mortar, i.e., clay or mud.

The "auld clay biggin" mentioned by Burns (Vision, st. 2), was so constructed; and specimens of the style may still be seen in some of our rural villages. *Post-and-pan* building was common in Eng. also in olden times; and specimens of it may still be seen in old towns like Shrewsbury, Ludlow, &c.

". . . the letter of deikinheid grantit to the wrychtis this dayc sall nocht prejuge or hurte ony vtheris that presintlic workis bothe masono craft and wrycht craft, and sic as biggis with *poist and pan* and layes with blak morter." Burgh Recs. Glasgow, i. 206, Rec. Soc.

From Fr. *panne;* see under PAWNS in DICT.

POSTIE, *s.* Power. V. POUSTE.

POT, POTT, *s.* V. DICT.

Pot, in the sense of a pit, a pond, like A.-S. *pyt*, E. *pit*, from Lat. *puteus*.

To POT, POTT, *v. a.* To pit, trench, or mark off by furrow, as in boundaries of land; Burgh Recs. Aberdeen, II. 129, Sp. C.: to plant or set in a pit, as in *potting* march stones: also, to pit and cover, as in *potting* or pitting potatoes, in order to preserve them during winter. V. POT, *s.*

To POURE, *v. n.* To pore, gaze, look intently; "prye and *poure;*" Kingis Quair, st. 72.

Swed. dial. *pora, pura*, to work slowly and gradually, to do anything slowly; Rietz. Dutch *porren*, to poke.

POUT, *s.* The sound made by a pout or chicken, a *cheep: to play pout*, to make the least sound, to utter a word. West and South of S.

POVERT, POUERT, *s.* Poverty; Kingis Quair, st. 3, 5. V. [POUER, *adj.*]

POW-AIX, POW-AX, *s.* A pole-axe; Pitcairn's Crim. Trials, II. 432; Burgh Recs. Prestwick, p. 66, Mait. C.

The earlier E. form of this word was *pollax*, which occurs in Chaucer's Cant. Tales, and is prob. derived from the O. Low. Ger. *pollexe*, from *poll*, the head, and *exe*, an axe. With this the Scot. *pow-aix* certainly agrees. V. under *Poll* in Skeat's Etym. Dict.

POWRIT, *part.* Impoverished. V. *Poor.*

PRACTIK, *adj.* Practical, laborious, requiring skill and application.

Traist wele, to follow ane fixt sentence or mater, Is mair *practik*, difficill, and mair straiter,— Thau for to write all ways at libertie.
Douglas, *Virgil*, Bk. i. prol.

For the various uses of this term as a *s.*, see under Prattik.

PRAME, *s.* A frame, hulk, sidework; Burgh Recs. Aberdeen, I. 142, Sp. C.

PRECAT, PRECCAT, *s.* V. *Pricket.*

To PREJUDGE, PREJUGE, *v. a.* To prejudice, damage, injure; pret. and part. pt. *prejudget*, Burgh Recs. Aberdeen, II. 327, Sp. C.

". . . the letter of deikinheid grantit to the wrychtis sall nocht *prejuge* or hurte ony vtheris." Burgh Recs. Glasgow, i. 206, Rec. Soc. Lat. *præjudicare*, to be prejudicial, injurious, or hurtful.

PRENTISSHED, *s.* Apprenticeship; Kingis Quair, st. 185.

PRESENT, *part. pt.* Presented, brought, offered.

". . . and at the fala stuff be *present* to the provost, baillies, and counsale." Burgh Recs. Edinburgh, 22 Aug., 1533, Rec. Soc.

PRESTLY, PRISTLY, *adv.* Promptly, immediately. V. PREST.

To PRESUME, *v. a.* To assume, pretend, make show of. O. F. *presumer.*

Sum knew hir weill, and sum had na knawledge Of hir, becaus scho was sa deformait With bylis blak ovirspred in hir visage, And hir fair colour faidit and alterait; Yit thay *presumit* for hir hie regrait, And still murning scho was of nobill kin, With better will thairfoir thay tuik hir in.
Henryson, Test. Cresseid, l. 397.

To PRETEND, *v. a.* Lit. to stretch forth, spread out; to set forth or state, as an argument, to arrange in order; to plan, intend, purpose; also, to portend, presage; Douglas, III., 300, 17, Small.

"My Lord of Arrane with soe many horsemen past fordward to follow the Frenchmen, *pretending*, that if they had seen sufficient occasion, to have midled with them." Hist. Estate of Scotland, p. 81, Wodrow Soc. Misc.

PREVAGELY, *adv.* Carelessly, slovenly, untidily; Douglas, III. 28, 18, ed. Small. V. PEVAGELY.

Rudd. ed. of Douglas' Virgil reads *peuagely.* Prob. from Lat. *pervagus*, from *pervagari*, to ramble about, straggle.

PRICK, PRIKE, *s.* Contr. for PRICKET, q. v.

A.-S. *pricu*, *prica*, a prick, point, dot; Dan. *prik*, Swed. *prick*, a dot, mark.

PRICK, PRIK, *adj.* Pointed, erect, upright, as in *prick-ear'd.*

With als felll mouthis carpis scho and beris,
Als mony has scho *prik* vpstandand eris.
Douglas, Virgil, iv. ch. 5, l. 20.

PRICKET, PRIKET, PRYCAT, PREKAT, PREKIT, PREKYT, *s.* Candle or taper holder, fitted with a spike, or spikes, on which the taper was fixed; Burgh Records Aberdeen, I. 75. Also, wax-tapers adapted for such holders; Accts., L. H. Treas., I. 200; and in the *pl.* applied to a *pann* or frame for lights suspended in a church. The contr. form *prick*, *prike*, is also used; Burgh Recs. Edinburgh, II. 354, Rec. Soc.

PRICKIT-WITCH, PRICKAT-WICHE, *s.* A tested and proven witch; Burgh Recs. Stirling, p. 86.

Suspected witches were tested by pricking; for a real witch was believed to bear on her body the witch-mark which was insensible. And the purpose of this pricking was, as James VI. explains, "the finding of the marke, and trying the insensibleness thereof."
The witch-mark is described as "sometimes like a little teate; sometimes like a blewish spot; and I myself have seen it in the body of a confessing witch like a little powder mark of a blea colour, somewhat hard, and withal insensible, so as it did not bleed when I pricked it." See Brand's Pop. Antiquities, p. 591, ed. 1877.

PRIK-MERKIS, *s. pl.* The butts or targets used for archery; properly, marks to shoot arrows at.

Rods or wands were generally used for this purpose, hence the term *prick-wand.* V. Halliwell's Dict.

PRIME, PRYME, *s.* The first hour of day, or the first division of the day; Kingis Quair, st. 171.

PRISE, PRYSE, *s.* A screw-press. Addit. to PRISE, q. v.

"Item, ane *pryse* with ane turning staf." Burgh Recs. Aberdeen, i. 176, Sp. C.

To PRISE, *v. a.* To value, estimate, appraise; part. pt. *prisit*, appraised, Accts. L. H. Treas., I. 200, Dickson.

O. Fr. *priser*, to esteem; from O. Fr. *pris*, price.

PRISE, PRYS, PRYSE, *s.* Lit. taken, captured; a hunter's call; the note of the horn blown when the deer is killed; Gaw. Romances.

Fr. *pris*, *prise*, part. pt. of *prendrs*, to take, seize.

To PRISE, *v. a.* Short for *apprise*, to adjudge goods or property as security for debt; part. pt. *prisit*; Accts. L. H. Treas., I., 315, Dickson.

To PRIVE, PRIUE, *v. a.* To deprive, rob; pret. *privit*; part. pa. *private.*

". . . provest, baillies, counsale, greitt dossane, and deikynis thinkis expedient that he be *private* of his fredome for euir, quhill he recover it again at the townis hand," etc. Burgh Recs. Edin., 24 May, 1492.
Lat. *privare*, to bereave; from *privus*, single, separated.

PROCESS, PROCESSE, *s.* Procedure, proper means or method, as in the phrase, "be *process* of law"; also in Kingis Quair, st. 114; course and sequence of events or things, Ibid., st. 127; *be processe*, in course of time, in due time, and so in st. 143, 192; also, as a law term it is applied to the documents or proceedings in a suit.

PROFIT, PROFFITT, *s.* Interest drawn or paid for the use of money.

". . . and ordanis the sowme of ane hundred merkis to be vpliftit vpon *proffitt* be the theasurer," i.e., to be borrowed at current interest. Burgh Recs. Aberdeen, II. 234, Sp. C.
". . . the soume of ane hundreth merkis borrowit be the toune . . . and to pay the soume of four pundis for the *proffitt* of the said soume for the half yeir past." Ibid., p. 256.
O. Fr. *profit*, from Lat. *profectus*, advanced, made profitable.

PROGNE, PROIGNE, *s.* A poetical name for the swallow; Cherrie and Slae, st. 1. Kingis Quair, st. 55.

Regarding Progne, who was turned into a swallow, see the sixth book of Ovid's Metamorphoses, or the Legend of Philomena as told by Chaucer in his Legend of Good Women.

To PRONYE, *v. a.* To deck, trim. V. PROYNE.

PROTHOGALL, *s.* Protocol: a notary's book in which he entered drafts or abstracts of the instruments drawn by him; Burgh Recs. Aberdeen, II. 182; and in p. 180, *prothocall.*

PROTY, PROTTY, *adj.* V. DICT.
Proty is simply a variety of *pratty*, an old form of *pretty*; and it has no connection with Su.-G. *prud*, which is E. *proud*.

PROVIDIT, *adj.* Arranged, planned, premeditated.

" . . . the greit *providit* slauchteris, oppressiones, and skaithis done to ws." Burgh Recs. Peebles, 4 Oct., 1562, Rec. Soc.
Lat. *providus*, providing for, planning.

PROWDE, *adj.* and *s.* V. DICT.
Merely the E. *proud*, M. E. *prud*, from A.-S. *prút*.

PRYSE, *s.* V. PRISE, *Prise.*

PUITTERNELL, *s.* A corr. of PUTTERLING, q. v.; Burgh Recs. Aberdeen, II. 224, 225.

PUMPHAL, *s.* V. DICT.
This is merely a corr. of M. E. *ponfold*, *pund-fold*, i.e. pound-fold, usually *pinfold*. V. PUND.

To PUND, *v. a.* To pound, impound; pret. and part. pt., *pundit*; Burgh Recs. Stirling, p. 72. V. POIND, PUND.

PUNDING, PUNDYNG, *s.* Poinding, pounding, arresting; Burgh Recs. Abeedeen, I. 380. V. POIND, *v.*, and PUND, *s.*

PUNSES, PUNSYS, *s. pl.* The three foretoes, with the claws, of a bird of prey.

. . . . Jovis byg fowle, the ern,
With hir strang tallonys and hir *punsys* stern.
Douglas, iv. 197, 6, ed. Small.
Rendered *talons* in Gloss; but the talon is properly the *hind*-claw of the bird, as we read in the Book of St. Albans, fol. 8, "The grete clees [claws] behynde, . . . ye shall call hem [them] *Talons*. The clees with-in the fote ye shall call . . . *Pownces.*" The latter term, however, has become obsolete, and *talons* is now applied to all the claws alike; see Skeat's Etym. Dict., and Supp. under TALON. *Punses* has come from Lat. *punctus*, pp. of *pungere*, to pierce.

PUPIT, POOPIT, POWPEIT, POWPYTT, *s.* Pulpit: represents the vulgar pron. of the word; Burgh Recs. Aberdeen, I. 160, Sp. C., Burgh Recs. Stirling, p. 42.

To PURFLE, PURFEL, PURFILE, *v. a.* A term in sewing, implying to make the one edge of a seam spread or fill out over the other: hence, to ornament, deck, or adorn with trimmings, edging, or embroidery; to lay or fix the hem of a gown, etc.; to attach a trimming of ermine, sable, etc.

PURFLE, PURFEL, PURFELING, PURFLING, *s.* Trimming, edging, or embroidery; the edge or trimming of a gown, the filling out of a seam; a trimming of ermine, etc.
O. Fr. *pourfiler*, to purfle, overcast: *pourfileure*, *pourfilure*, purfling, overcasting.
(Sup.)   A 2

PURIS, PURYS, *s. pl.* The poor, paupers.
" . . . so sustene the haill pure of all occupatiounis within this burgh, sic as craftismen, . . . vpoun thair awin proper chargis fra this day furth, sua that the gude touu nor nane resortand thairto sall be trablit with thair *puris.*" Burgh Recs. Glasgow, i. 395.

PURPRESION, PURPRESTURE, *s.* A feudal casualty of forfeiture or fine for encroachment on the highways or commonties belonging to the overlord or superior. Addit. to PURPRISIONE, q. v.

PURSE-MAISTER, *s.* A banker, a moneychanger.
" Argentarius, a bancor or *purse-maister* ;" Duncan, App. Etym., 1595, ed. Small, E.D.S.

PURS-PYK, *s.* V. DICT.
A poetic variation of M. E. *pickpors*, a pick-purse.

PURSY, *adj.* V. DICT.
Jamieson's etym. of this term is a mistake. The M. E. forms were *purcy* and *purcyf*, from O. Fr. *pourcif*, a variant of *poulsif*, which Cotgrave renders "pursie, short-winded." The modern Fr. forms *poulsif* and *poussif*, from *poulser*, *pousser*, to push, thrust, are, as Wedgwood remarks, much truer to the origin, Lat. *pulsare*, to beat, thrust.

To PU' STOCKS. One of the superstitious customs observed on Hallowéen. It is the first ceremony of the series performed by the company met for the occasion.
The ceremony consists in the company passing out together to the kail-yard, and pulling each a *stock* or plant of kail.
"They must go out hand in hand, with eyes shut, and pull the first plant they meet with: its being big or little, straight or crooked, is prophetic of the size and shape of the grand object of all their spells—the husband or wife." Burns, Hallowéen, st. 4, Note.
For particulars see st. 4-5 with accompanying notes.

To PUT, PIT, *v. a.* To put, place, set; part. pt. *putten*, *pitten*, put. Addit. to PUT, q. v.

To PUT *on*, *v. a.* and *n.* V. DICT.
Correct the misprint in this heading.

To PUT *to* or *ta*, PIT *to* or *ta*, *v. a.* To shut, close; "*Put ta* the door ahint ye," i.e., shut the door as you go out. Addit. to PUT *to*, q. v.

PUTTEN, *part. pt.* Thrown, cast. V. PUT, PUTT.

To PYE, PIE, PYE *about*, *v. n.* V. DICT.
Delete the last sentence of the note under this entry. "The remark that *ys* is merely the common prefix is not to the point: for the Welsh *yspio* is merely borrowed from E. *spy*; and the E. *spy* from Fr. *espier*, where *s* is radical." Skeat.

To PYKE, PIKE, *v. a.* To trim and improve by picking out the refuse, as when a gardener *pikes* his flower-beds, vines, and fruit. Also to deck, adorn, beautify, and finish embroidery and tambour-work by dressing it with a pike or picker, and by inserting picks, stitches, or threads of silk, gold, or silver.

PYKERY, PYKRIE, PYCKRIE, *s.* V. PIKARY.

PYK-THANK, *s.* A flatterer, fawner; Douglas, III. 145, 20, ed. Small.

PYLIS, *s. pl.* Down, etc. V. PILE.

PYRNIT, *part. pt.* V. under PIRN.

PYSSANCE, *s.* Power. V. PISSANCE.

Q.

QUAD, QUED, *adj.* Vile, base: compar. *quader;* Court of Venus, ii. 161, 333. Addit. to QUAID, q. v.
Still used, but as a low or slang term, in the West of Scot.
Dutch, *kwaad,* evil, ill.

QUAICH, QUAIGH, *s.* V. DICT.
Quaich is the origin of E. *quaff,* as the following extract shows.
"A *quaff,* that is a curious cup made of different pieces of wood, such as box and ebony, cut into little staves," &c., Smollet, Humphrey Clinker (1771), letter dated Sept. 3.

QUAIR, QUERE, *s.* V. DICT.
Quair is merely E. *quire,* spelt *cwaer* in the Ancren Riwle, from O. Fr. *quaier,* later *quayer, cayer,* and in mod. Fr. *cahier.* The origin of the term is L. Lat. *quaternum,* a collection of four leaves, whence also Ital. *quaderno,* a quire. In Wright's Voc., i. 606, L. Lat. *quaternus* is glossed by O. Fr. *quayer,* and in i. 682, by *quare,* a quire.

QUAIT, *adj., s.* and *v.* Quiet. V. [QUATE.]

QUAITLY, *adv.* Quietly.

QUALITIE, *s.* Qualification.
". . and the said Mr. James Ross acceptit of the said stipend with the *qualitie* and conditioun abone mentioned." Burgh Recs. Aberdeen, ii. 375, Sp. C.

QUAREOR, *s.* A mason: lit. a quarrier.
"Lapicida, a maison or *quareor;* qui lapides caedit;" Duncan, App. Etym., ed. Small, E. D. S.
O. Fr. *quarrieur,* a quarrier; from *quarrer,* to square; Lat. *quadrare.*

QUART, QUARTE, *s.* Health, joy, happiness; Awnt. Arth., l. 256. Addit. to QUERT, q. v.

QUAYR, *s.* A choir. V. QUEIR.

To QUEAK, QUEEK, *v. n.* To squeak or cry, as the young of rats or mice do: part. *queekin,* used also as a *s.*

QUEAK, QUEEK, *s.* A gentle squeak, the weak peeping cry of the young of small animals.
This is prob. an imitative term formed as a dimin. of *quaik, quaich,* the cry of a duck, which in M. E. was *queke, quek.* Icel. *qvaka,* Dan. *qvække,* to quack, croak.

QUED, QWED, *adj.* Bad. V. QUAID, *Quad.*

To QUEEL, *v. n.* V. DICT.
More likely from A.-S. *cŴlan,* to cool, which is still represented by prov. E. *keel.*

QUEEN, *adj.* Few. V. QUHENE, WHEEN.

To QUEESE, QUEASE, *v. n.* To wheeze, wheezle; part. *queesin: "queesin* like an auld bellows." E. *wheeze.*

QUEINE, QUEYN, *s.* V. DICT.
Queine, quean, and *queen,* are simply different forms of the same word.

To QUEITH, QUETH, *v. a.* To pacify; to bid farewell; Douglas, Virgil, v. ch. 2. Icel. *kvethja.*
For particulars regarding this term see DICT. under QUEINTH.

QUERT. *s.* V. DICT.
Quert is simply the neut. *kvirt* of O. Icel. *kvirr,* quiet, which is now spelt *kyrr;* hence *kvirt* is now spelt *kyrt.* Jamieson's references to *kyrt* in explaining this term are therefore quite to the point.

QUETHING, *adj.* Pacifying, composing; Ibid. 60, 21, Rudd. Addit. to QUETHING.

QUENRY, *s.* Womankind, women; also, harlotry, carnal lust; Alex. Scott's Poems, p. 89, ed. 1882. Addit. to QUENRY, q. v.

QUENT, *part. pt.* Quenched, extinguished; Douglas, Virgil, 124, 53, Rudd.
Ruddiman connects this term with Queinth; see DICT. As used in this passage, and by Chaucer, it simply means *quenched,* from A.-S. *cwencan,* to quench, extinguish.

QUERE, QUEYR, *adv.* Exactly, plainly; Douglas, Virgil, 238, 51, Rudd.: *queyr* in Small's ed.
This is a contr. of *perquere,* from Fr. *par cœur,* by heart, accurately, exactly. V. PERQUER.

QUERRELL, *s.* A bolt or arrow for a cross-bow, a dart; Douglas, Virgil, 54, 38, 291, 10, Rudd.
O. Fr. *quarreau, carreau,* from L. Lat. *quadrellum,* a square-headed bolt for a crossbow.

To QUEST, v. n. To give tongue as dogs do in hunting: pret. *questede*, hunted in full cry; Awnt. Arth., I. 48. V. QUESTES.

QUEST, QWEST, s. Inquest; Burgh Recs. Peebles, 2 Nov. 1456, Rec. Soc.

QUHAISILL, s. Weasel; Henryson, Parl. of Beistis, l. 116. A.-S. *wesle*.

QUHALM, s. Destruction. V. QUALIM.

QUHALP, s. A whelp; satirical for son, descendant; Rob Stene's Dream, p. 5, Mait. C.

To QUHAMLE, QUHOMLE, v. a. V. *Quhemle.*

QUHAP, QUHAPE, s. V. QUHAUP.

QUHATEN, QUHATAN, QUHATTANE, adj. What kind of, what or which, when used interrogatively; O what, how great, when used interjectionally, as in
*Quhattane ane glaikit fule am I,
To slay my self with melancoly !
Alex. Scott's Poems, p. 75, ed. 1882.*
This corr. of *quhatkin* is still common in both senses. Addit. to QUHATKIN, q. v.

To QUHEIT, v. a. To white or whittle. V. QUHITE, QUHYTE.

QUHEITNAM, s. A whittle, a pocket-knife; Burgh Recs. Stirling, p. 79.

To QUHELM, QUHALM, v. a. 1. To overturn, turn upside down; Douglas, Virgil, 150, 26, Rudd.: pret. *quhelmit*, Ibid., 36, 49.
The more common form is *quhemle*, with its varieties *quhamle, quhomle, quhumle,* from Su.-G. *hwimla*. V. under QUHEMLE.

2. To turn up and down or from side to side, to toss or tumble about.
*Quhan on-fortune quhelmys the quheil, thair gais grace by.
Gol. and Gawain, I. 1225.*
In M. E. *whelmen* generally means to overturn, and is used like Scot. *whemle, whamle, whomle ;* but this passage shows that it also meant to turn backward and forward or from side to side, to toss; and *whemle* is still so used in the West of S. V. *Quhemle.*

QUHELM, QUHALM, s. Destruction. V. QUALIM.

To QUHEMLE, QUHAMLE, QUHOMLE, QUHUMLE, v. a. To turn backward and forward or from side to side, to toss or tumble about : to *quhemle a boat,* to rock or toss it from side to side; to *quhamle milk*, to cause it to move from side to side of the vessel which holds it, to toss it about; West of S. Addit. to QUHEMLE, q. v.

QUHEMLE, QUHAMLE, QUHOMLE, QUHUMLE, s. A rock, toss; a rocking, tossing. Addit. to QUHEMLE, q. v.

QUHILES, adv. Sometimes, at times, now and then; Lyndsay, Thrie Estaitis, l. 372. V. QUHILE.

To QUHIRL, v. a. To whirl, turn from one point or degree to another; also, to hurl. V. *Whirl.*
And thankit be fortunys exiltree
And quhele, that thus so wele has *quhirlit* me.
Kingis Quair, st. 189, Skeat.

QUHIRLING, s. Whirling, turning, Ibid., st. 165.

QUHIRLY, QUHURLIE, s. A small wheel, a caster; a low truck, used in moving heavy packages; also, contr. for *quhirly-barrow, quhirly-bed.*

QUHISCH, s. A hissing or whizzing noise; Lyndsay, Thrie Estaitis, l. 1926: also applied to a stroke or blow which produces such a noise.

QUHISLE, QUHISSLE, QUHISTLE, QUHISSILL, v. and s. Whistle, pipe, fife; Burgh Recs. Edinburgh, II. 219, Kingis Quair, st. 135.

QUHITELL, QUHITLEM, QUEITNAM, s. A whittle, a pocket-knife. V. QUHITE.

QUHO, pron. Who; Kingis Quair, st. 57: whoever, whosoever; Ibid. st. 78 : *"as quho sais,"* as one might say; Ibid. st. 77. Addit. to QUHA, q. v.

QUHOMLE, QUHUMLE, v. and s. V. *Quhemle.*

QUHY, s. V. DICT.
This is simply E. *why*, and not Su.-G. *hui*, as suggested.

QUHYLUMES, adv. Sometimes, at times, occasionally; Lyndsay, The Dreme, l. 410. A.-S. *hwilum.* V. QUHILUM.

QUHYMPERAND, part. Whimpering, whining, wailing; Douglas, Virgil, 64, 21, Rudd.

QUHYNGAR. V. WHINGER.

To QUHYTE, QUHITE, WHEAT, v. a. V. DICT.
The same as M. E. *thwiten,* from A.-S. *thwitan,* to cut. But E. *whittle,* a knife, is not from A.-S. *hwitel ;* indeed, it has no connection whatever with *whet ;* it is from A.-S. *thwitel,* lit. a cutter, a der. of *thwitan,* to cut. See Whittle in Skeat's Etym. Dict.

To QUIKIN, v. a. To quicken, vivify; to give increase and energy to.
And schortly, so wele fortune has hir bore,
To *quikin* treuly day by day my lore,
To my larges that I am cumin agayn,
To blisse with her that is my souirane.
Kingis Quair, st. 181, Skeat's ed.

QUI [196] QUY

QUINQUIN, s. V. DICT.
This is simply a form of *kinken*, short for O. Dutch *kinneken*, *kindeken*, (corrupted into *kilderkin*), the eighth part of a vat. Regarding this term Skeat says,—"The lit. sense is 'little child,' because the measure is a small one as compared with a tun, vat, or barrel. Formed with dimin. suffix -*ken* (now nearly obsolete), from Du. *kind*, a child, cognate with E. *child*." V. Etym. Dict.

QUISH, QUISHIE, s. Forms of **WHISH,** q. v.
Properly *quishie* is a dimin. of *quish*, and it is sometimes so used in the sense of the slightest sound, the least whisper; but generally it is used with the same meaning as *quish*.

To **QUITE, QUYTE, QWYTE,** v. n. To curl; to hurl a stone along ice towards a mark; part. pr. *quiting*, *quitin*, used also as a s. In the West of S. the old name for the game of *curling* was *quiting*, generally pron. *quitin*.

QUITING-STANE, QUYTIN-STANE, QWYTIN-STANE, s. A curling-stone.
To *quite* is prob. of the same origin as *to quoit*; from O. Fr. *coiter*, *coitier*, *cuiter*, to press, push, hasten; and hence prob. to hurl; V. Burguy. To hurl a stone or iron ring through the air towards a mark is *to coit* or *quoit*; while to hurl or drive a stone over smooth ice towards a mark is *to quite* or *quyte*.

QUITTANCE, s. Clearance, discharge; "has failyeat *quittance*," has failed to obtain or secure discharge; Peterkin's Notes on Orkn. and Shetl., Appendix, p. 35: " under *quittance*," in or during the process of clearance, or, within or during the time allowed for securing acquittance or clearing oneself of a charge; Ibid. Addit. to [QUITTANS], q. v.
One of the records, above referred to in illustration of the second phrase, runs thus :—
"[21 June, 1603]. It is tryit that Magnus-Blance has dyit under *quittance* of the stowt of his nyhbor's peits, and according to the lawis decernis his guilds and gere to be escheit thairfoir." Extract from the Court Book of the Earl of Orkney.

To **QUOFF,** v. a. To buy, purchase. V. COFF.

QUOFFYN, s. Purchasing, bargaining, exchange.
". . . the said George allegit he had gottyn it in *quoffyn* fra the said James." Burgh Recs. Prestwick, Oct. 1515, p. 47, Mait. C.

Icel. *kaup*, Swed. *köp*, Dan. *kiöb*, a purchase; but all are borrowed from Lat. *caupo*, a huckster. V. Skeat's Etym. Dict. under CHEAP.

QUOY, QUOYLAND, s. V. DICT.
Add the following explanation :—
"Quoyland (from Norse *kvi*, an enclosure) was originally a patch enclosed from the moor and cultivated. . . . If the *quoy* was near the *tūn* [farm or homestead], it was sometimes called an *umbeset* [N. *um-bussettnung*), an outlying homestead, an outset; or an *outbrek* (N. *ut-brekkr*), an outbrink (of the townland). Quoyland was exempted from the vicious process of *rundale*." Captain Thomas, R. N., Proc. Antiq. Soc., vol. xviii. p. 256.

QUOY, QUOYE, adj. Quiet, secluded; Douglas, II. 97, 4, 102, 16, Small's ed. V. KOY.
Ruddiman's ed. has *koy* in both passages. O. Fr. *quoy*, *coy*, quiet; Cotgr. : but an older form is *coit*, from Lat. *quietus*, still. See Skeat's Etym. Dict. under COY.

QUYKE, adj. Alive, living; Lyndsay, Papyngo, l. 670. V. [QUIK].

QUYNE, s. A form of **QUEINE,** q. v.

QUYOK, QUYACH, s. A young cow or heifer; Douglas, Virgil, 248, 35, Rudd. Properly a dimin. of **QUEY,** q. v.

QUYTE, QWYTE, v. V. *Quite*.

QUYTT, s. A cute, doit; a small Danish coin worth about one-twelfth of a penny :
"ane Dens *quytt*," Burgh Recs. Aberdeen, I. 333, Sp. C.
O. Dan. *kvitt*, Mod. Dan. *hvid*, a coin, one-third of a Dan. shilling, or about one-twelfth of an Eng. penny : similar in value to the O. Scot. *doit*. Hence, a thing of little or no value was said to be " not worth a *cute*," or, " not worth a *doit* ;" "availyeis nocht a *cute*." Alex. Scott's Poems, p. 11, ed. 1882; " caris nocht thre *cutie*," Ibid. p. 83.
The term occurs also in Dunbar and Lyndsay; see DICT. under CUTE, where the secondary meaning and general use of the term are given, but both etymology and explanation are entirely wrong. In Laing's ed. of Lyndsay the term is rendered "a small piece of straw."

QWEST, s. V. *Quest*.

QWYTE, QWYTIN-STANE. V. under *Quite*.

R.

RABBLEMENT, s. A promiscuous and noisy crowd, a mob: also, incoherent talk or discourse: synon. *rablach.* V. under RABBLE.

RACK, s. The clouds, clouds in motion; the movement, course, or direction of the clouds under the action of the wind: a term common in weather prognostics. Addit. to RAIK, and RAK, q. v.

RACK, s. and v. Wreck; wreckage: more commonly Wrack, Wrak, q. v.

RACKEL, RACKLE, RAUCLE, *adj.* V. DICT.
Del. last para. of this entry.
Rackel, same as M. E. *rakel,* rash, reckless, is related not to Icel. *rackr,* ready, but to Icel. *reikall,* vagabond, from *reika,* to roam about, to wander. It is from Swed. *raka,* older form *racka,* to run about; whence have come Sc. *raik,* to roam, range, and Eng. *rake,* a dissolute man. See Wedgwood and Skeat under Rake.

To RACUNNIS, RACWNNIS, *v. a.* To recognosce, to resume the lands of a vassal on account of a breach of conditions of tenure. Addit. to RACUNNYS, q. v.

"Item, that ilk day [30 January 1456] the balyeis has *racwnnis* the wast land in the North Gat for faut of the Kyngis burroumallis, and for faut of the mallis thai war set for. Witnes the hal curt." Burgh Recs. Peebles, p. 117, Rec. Soc.
The definition given above certainly expresses the general meaning of the term as it is used in our Burgh Records. Skene's explanation, which was adopted by Jamieson, is too limited in its application; but it is not so limited as the following, which is given by Erskine:—"Recognition is the forfeiture arising to the superior from alienation by the vassal of more than half the land without the superior's consent."

RAD, RADE, *adj.* Quick, ready; Awnters of Arthur, st. 23, l. 8, Douce MS. A.-S. *rœde.*

RADE, *adv.* Soon. Errat. in DICT. q. v.
Rade, is a form of *rathe, raith,* soon, as stated in the explanatory note, and is therefore an adverb in the positive degree. It cannot, therefore, be rendered by *rather,* which is a comparative. See next entry; also Raith in Dict.

RADLY, *adv.* Quickly, hotly, fiercely.

To RADDLE, *v. a.* To thrash, beat; lit. to beat with a stick or switch; from *raddle,* a switch. Errat. in DICT., q. v.
This word can have no connection with *riddle* as Jamieson suggested. As used in the passage quoted from Scott's Rob Roy, it certainly means to thrash or beat, and it is still so used in the N. of England. Halliwell states that in Sussex the term *raddle* is applied to long pieces of supple underwood twisted between upright states to form a fence. He also quotes from Harrison, p. 167, regarding the wattled houses of the ancient Britons, that "they were slightlie set up with a few posts and many *radels.*" A *raddle,* therefore, is a small rod, prob. from Du. *roede,* rod, wand, switch ; and to *raddle* is to switch or beat. Atkinson in his Cleveland Gloss. suggests that it may have sprung from A.-S. *wræthian,* to wreathe, weave, wattle.

RADDOWRE, s. V. DICT.
The origin of this word is most probably O. Fr. *roideur,* "stifnesse, . . . violence"; Cotgr.

RADE, RAID, s. V. DICT.
Rade is now generally accepted as from Icel. *reith,* a riding, a road; from Icel. *rītha,* to ride, to be borne on a horse or in a ship. A.-S. *rād* has given E. *road.* See Skeat, s. v. *Raid,* and Wedgwood, s. v. *Ride.*

To RADOUN, *v. n.* V. DICT.
Del. the note under this entry.
Radoun is simply the mod. E. *redound,* from O. Fr. *redonder,* "to redound, ... returne back ;" Cotgr.

RAG-FOOTED, *adj.* Lit., ill-shod: hence, poor, worthless, untenable : " *rag-footed* reasons;" Blame of Kirkburiall, ch. 19.

RAGMAN, s. V. DICT.
Del. definition and notes of s. 3 : they are altogether misleading.
The *ragman* there referred to was a papal bull with many seals of bishops attached. A *ragman* or *ragman-roll* means a document with a long list of names, or with numerous seals. As shown by Wright in his Anecdota Literaria, the name was originally given to a game consisting in drawing characters from a roll by strings hanging out from the end ; the amusement arising from the fitness or unfitness of the characters to the persons who drew them. Hence, from its similarity to the apparatus used in this game, any deed with a number of seals attached came to be called a *ragman-roll;* but the name was specially applied to the collection of deeds by which the Scottish Barons were made to subscribe allegiance to Ed. I. As the Chron. de Lanercost has it—"A Scottis *propter multa sigilla dependentia* ragman vocabatur." The name was afterwards applied to any long, intricate, or stupid story. Lit. a coward's roll or story (from Icel. *rag-menni,* a coward, and *rolla,* the addition of *roll*), and afterwards corrupted into *rigmarole.* See Halliwell, s. v. Ragman; also Wedgwood, and Skeat, s. v. Rigmarole.
The note on *bouched* is altogether a mistake. The word in Piers Plowman is not *bouched* but *bonched,* struck, lit. banged, pushed, knocked about. See Gloss. to Skeat's ed., Clar. Press Series.

RAHATOUR, s. An enemy. V. REHATOUR.

RAIBLE, s. and v. V. RABBLE.

RAID, RADE, s. Spawn. V. RED.

RAID, RADE, s. A cleaner. V. *Red.*

RAID, RADE, s. Counsel, V. REDE.

RAID, RED, pret. Rode. V. RAD.

RAIL, s. V. DICT.
The etym. given for this word is wrong: but it is correctly given under Railly, which is simply another form of the word. A.-S. hraegl, hregl, swaddling clothes: but it has no connection with Icel. roegg, sinus, as suggested. See Wedgwood and Skeat, s. v. RAIL.

RAIL, RAILL, part. pt. Railed, fitted with a railing: "a guid rail stair," a well-railed stair, or, a good stair and railed; West of S.

". . . hes ane sufficient guid dure and foir yett weill wallit and lokit, with ane raill galrie stair and ane turlies upoun the northmost windo thereof." Burgh Recs. Glasgow, i. 148, Rec. Sec.

RAILED, RAILIT, RAYLEDE, part. pt. Set with rails or bars, lined or marked off, enclosed; also set, mounted, adorned.

And thus Schir Gawane the gay dame Gayenour he ledis, In a gletterande gyde, that glemet full gaye:
With rich rebanes reuerssede, who that righte redys, Raylede with rubes one royalle arraye.
Avntyrs of Arthure, st. 2.
"*Raylide*, set; MS. Morte Arthure, f. 87." Halliwell.
Swed. *regel*, a bar, bolt; Ger. *riegel*, O. H. Ger. *rigil*, a bar, bolt, orig. a latch of a door. This latter form is from O. H. Ger. *rihan*, to fasten. Skeat, Etym. Dict.

RAIN-BIRDS, s. pl. A name given to the woodpeckers (genus *Picus*, Linn.), on account of the peculiar cries which they are said to emit on the approach of rain; South and West of S.

RAISITLY, adv. Excitedly, astonishedly; Rob. Stene's Dream, p. 23, Mait. C.

RAISS, RAIS, RASSE, RACE, s. V. DICT.
A more direct etym. for this term is A.-S. *ræs*, a course, race, stream. This is confirmed by M. E. *rees*, *rase*.

RAISTIT, part. and adj. Wrinkled, shrivelled; Burgh Recs. Stirling, p. 47. V. *Reistet*.

RAÏT, part. and adj. V. *Rayit*.

RAIVEL, RAVEL, s. Confusion, state of confusion, a confused speech or story. V. [RAIVEL].

To RAIVEL, v. a. To fit or enclose with railing: part. pt. *raiveld*, *raivilt*, as, "a *raivilt* stair." V. RAIVEL, s.

RAIVELING, RAVELING, REAVELING, s. Addit. to RAIVEL, s., q. v.

RAK, s. A stretcher (pron. *streeker*); an instrument used in stretching and softening leather. V. RACK, RAK, v.

"Item, ane kyst lokit fast, ane scherp *rak* for ledder, ane blunt *rak*." Burgh Recs. Aberdeen, I. 176, Sp. C.

RAK, RAWK, ROIK, ROOK, s. V. DICT.
In his explanation of these forms Jamieson has confused two quite distinct words, and has connected them with a source to which neither of them is related. As generally accepted *rack* or *rak* means light, driving clouds, also the drift of such clouds, and comes from Icel. *reka*, to drive; *rek*, drift, motion, the thing drifted; and the M. E. form was *rak*. On the other hand *roik* or *reek*, is vapour, smoke, and has come from A.-S. *rede*, *réc*, smoke; Icel. *rekyr*, Du. *rook*. And neither set is related to the verb *rack*, to extend. See Wedgwood and Skeat, s. v. Rack, Reek.

To RAKE, v. a. To gather together, to cover, to heap or *hap*. *To rake the fire*, is to gather it, and then heap on coals and cinders so that it may continue burning all night.

RAKING-COAL, RAIKIN-COAL, RAKIN-PIECE, s. The coal or piece of coal used in *raking* a fire: called "*the happin-coal*."
A.-S. *raca*, a rake: and allied to Goth. *rikan*, to collect, heap up.

RAKIS, s. pl. V. RAKKIS, RAX.

RAKKILL, RAKIL, s. A chain. V. RACKLE.

To RALYE, v. n. To rally, joke; pret. *ralyest*, for *ralyeit*, Dunbar, Mar. Wemen and Wedo, l. 149. V. RAILL.

RALYEIT, part. pt. Streaked, striped, barred. V. *Railed*.
This term was left undefined in DICT., q. v.

RAMASSE, s. Collection, summary, resumé; Blame of Kirkburiall, ch. 19. O. Fr. *ramas*, id. V. RAMMASCHE, adj.

To RAME at, v. a. To rhyme or keep repeating the same thing: as when a person always asks the same question, sings the same song, or tells the same story. V. RHAME.

RAME, RAMING, s. That which is constantly or very frequently repeated: also, repetition, iteration; as, "His *rame* o' that sang has spoilt it." Addit. to RAME, q. v.

RAMLIN, RAMMELY, adj. Tall, slender, fast growing. A *ramlin* or *rammely* lad is a tall, fast growing young man. V. RAMMEL, s. 2.

RAMSH, s. V. DICT.
E. *ramsons*; but not allied to Icel. *ramr*, as suggested.

To RAND, RANDER, ROND, RUND, RUN, v. a. To thicken, strengthen, or protect the heels

of stockings by sewing or darning: lit. to shield, protect. V. RANTER.
Rand and *rander* are the forms used in Orkney: from Icel. *rönd*, a rim, border, shield, protection. V. RAND, *s.*
Run represents the *pron.* now generally followed in various districts of Scot.

To RANDER, RANDIR, RANDRE, RAND, *v. a.*
1. To render, return, restore; Burgh Recs. Aberdeen, I. 322, Sp. C.
2. To submit, yield, give up; *to randir them*, to surrender; Compl. Scot. p. 77, E.E.T.S.: pret. *randrit*, surrendered; Ibid., 1, 113.
3. To melt, make liquid: "to *rander* tallow." V. RENDER.
Fr. *rendre*, from Lat. *reddere*, to give back.

RAND, *s.* A melting, as much as may be melted at one time: as, "twa *rand* o' tallow."

RANE, RAYNE, *s.* V. DICT.
In p. 620, col. 2, l. 12, for *Rards* read *Bards*.

RANGAT, *s.* The rabble. V. RANGALE.

RANTRY, *s.* A form of Rantree, q. v.

RANTRY-TREE, *s.* Rowan-tree-wood, wood of the mountain-ash.

I'll gar my ain Tammie gae down to the how,
And cut me a rock of a widdershins grow,
Of good *rantry-tree* for to carry my tow,
And a spindle o' same for the twining o't.
Alex. Ross, The Rock and the Wee Pickle Tow.
"*Grow*," growth.
Regarding the rowan-tree as a charm against witches see under ROUN-TREE. See also Brand's Popular Antiquities, ed. Ellis, vol. ii., p. 80, note 2.

To RAPARAL, *v. a.* To repair. V. REPARELL.

RAPHELL, *s.* Doe-skin. V. RAFFEL.

RASOUR, *s.* Prob. cutting, shred. V. DICT.
The supposition that *rasour* is for *or ras*, Venice stuff, is not satisfactory. Jamieson evidently doubted it, seeing he left the term undefined. It is more like O. Fr. *rasure*, a shaving, cutting, shred; see Cotgrave.

RAT, *s.* V. DICT.
Sc. *rat*, as in *cart-rat*, and E. *rut*, are quite different words. *Rat* has come from Icel. *reita*, to scratch, and so is allied to E. *write;* but E. *rut* has come from Lat. *rupta*, broken, through Fr. *route*, "a rut, way, path;" Cotgrave. See Skeat and Wedgwood.

RATCH, *v.* and *s.* Scratch, line; prob. a dimin. of RAT, *Raut*, q. v.

RATCH, RATCHE, *s.* A hound. V. RACHE.

RATHT, *s.* V. RAITH, *s.*

RATIONABLE, *adj.* Reasonable, sensible, just; Burgh Recs. Edin., I. 4, 82, 83, Rec. Soc.
Lat. *rationabilis*, from *ratio*, reason.

RATTON, *s.* V. DICT.
The generally accepted etym. of this term is Fr. *raton*, dimin. of Fr. *rat*, from L. Ger. *ratus*, *rato*. V. Skeat, Etym. Dict.

RATT-RIME, *s.* Originally, a rhyme or piece of poetry used in charming and killing rats. These rhymes were the merest doggerel, and hence the secondary meaning of the term given in DICT. Addit. to RATT-RIME, q. v.

Jamieson gave only the secondary meaning of this term, and his explanation of it is wrong. A more satisfactory account of it is given in the following passages from a note to As You Like It, iii. 2, 164, Clarendon Press Series.
"The belief that rats were rhymed to death in Ireland is frequently alluded to in the dramatists. Steevens quotes from Ben Jonson's Poetaster, To the Reader:

' Rhime them to death, as they do Irish rats
In drumming tunes.'

" Randolph in his play, The Jealous Lovers, p. 156, ed. Hazlitt, has a reference to the same belief:

' And my poets,
Shall with a satire, steeped in gall and vinegar,
Rhyme 'em to death, as they do rats in Ireland.'

" And Pope in his version of Donne's Second Satire, l. 22:

' One sings the fair; but songs no longer move;
No rat is rhymed to death, nor maid to love.'

"In Scot's Discovery of Witchcraft, the power of magic incantations is said to be claimed by the Irish witches: 'The Irishmen addict themselves wonderfully to the credit and practice hereof; yea and they will not stick to affirm that they can rime either man or beast to death."
These references sufficiently suggest the kind of rhymes that were used for the purpose, and enable one to understand how the term *ratt-rime* came to mean halting metres, doggerel, a tirade of nonsense.

RAUK, ROUK, ROAKY, *adj.* Misty, foggy Same as RAUKY, q. v.

RAUT, RAWT, RAUK, *v.* and *s.* Scratch. V. RAT.

RAVAND, RAUAND, *part.* and *adj.* Ravening, ravenous; "*rauand* sauuage volffis;" Complaint Scotland, p. 2, E.E.T.S. V. RAVIN.

RAVELING, REAVELING, *s.* A rail or hand-rail of a stair; Burgh Recs. Aberdeen, III. 7. Addit. to RAVEL, RAIVEL.
This form of the name is still common in the West of Scot.

To RAVERSE, RAUERSE, *v. a.* To ransack, explore; Blame of Kirkburiall, Dedic. Fr. *renverser*.

RAVESTRE, *s.* V. REVESTRE.

RAY, *s.* A spar, yard, etc. V. RA, REA.

RAYIT, *part pt.* and *adj.* Arrayed, ranged; Douglas, III. 67, 4, Small.

RAYNDOUN, *s.* A straight line or course: in *rayndoun,* direct, directly; Burgh Recs. Peebles. Addit. to RANDOUN.

RE, REE, *interj.* A carter's term meaning to the right, or turn to the right. A similar and more common term is Jee (q. v.), which, however, is indefinite, and often used with the meaning "to the left." V. *Heck.*

Jee implies simply to turn or turn aside: hence the saying regarding an intractable person,—"He'll neither *hick* nor *jee,*" i.e., neither go on nor turn to the side. Another form of the saying is,—"He'll neither *heck* nor *ree,*" i.e., neither turn to the left nor to the right.

READE, *s.* V. *Rede,* REID.

REAP, REAPE, *s.* A rope. V. RAIP.

"Restio, a *reape-*maker, or ane that hangs himselfe;" Duncan App. Etym., 1595, ed. Small, E.D.S.

REAST, *s.* A rest for a musket; Spald. Club Misc. V. 160. V. REIST, s. 4.

REASTED, *adj.* V. REESTED.

REBALD, RIBALD, *s.* A rascal, scamp.

O. Fr. *ribald,* from L. Lat. *ribaldus,* a ruffian.

To REBALK, REBAK, *v. a.* To rebuke, snub, threaten, insult; pret. and part. pt., *rebalkit;* part. pr. *rebakin.* Addit. to RE-BAWKIT, q. v.

". . . that he wranguisly *rebalkit* hym & drew a knyf til him." Burgh Recs. Prestwick, 14 June, 1501, Mait. C.

O. Fr. *rebouquer* (Mod. Fr. *reboucher*), to stop the mouth.

REBATT, REBETT, *s.* V. REBBITS.

REBE, *s.* V. under *Reve.*

RECHAS, *s.* The recheat, a hunting term: the notes blown on the horn to recall the dogs from a false scent. Addit. to RECHAS, q. v. Fr. *rechasser.*

To RECHATE, REHATE, REHAYTE, *v. n.* To wind or blow the recheat; *part. pr. rehaytand,* blowing the recheat, recalling the dogs.

To RECKLES, *v. a.* To abandon, give up, depart from. V. RAKLES.

And *reckles* nocht your eirand for the rane,
Bot cast yow for to cum ane vthir day.
Alex. Scott's Poems, p. 17, ed. 1882.

RECOLL, *s.* A collection, selection; pl. *recollis,* gleanings, memorials, as in "the *recollis* of Troy;" Douglas, Virgil, prol. Bk. i. Fr. *recueil.*

To RECONIS, RECONYSE, *v. a.* and *n.* V. RECOGNIS.

RECOUNSILIT, *part. pt.* Reconciled;

Kingis Quair, st. 90, Skeat's ed. V. [RECONSALE].

RECOVERANCE, RECOUERANCE, *s.* Recovery, hope of recovery; "dispaire without *recouerance,*" hopeless or blank despair; Kingis Quair, st. 87. O. Fr. *recouvrance.*

RED, REDE, RADE, RAID, *s.* A contr. form of *redder,* a clearer, cleaner, cleanser, ridder; as, "That will mak a fine *red* for a pipe." Addit. to RED, q. v.

Raid is so used by Dunbar in a somewhat coarse passage of The Twa Mariit Wemen and the Wedo.

RED, *part. pt.* Lit. counselled, advised: *I'm red,* I am led to think, or inclined to suspect, I am of opinion. Errat. in DICT., q. v.

Dut Davie, lad, I'm *red* ye're glaikit;
I'm tauld the muse, ye hae negleckit.
Burns, Second Ep. to Davie, st. 3.

Jamieson has either missed the sense of *red* in this passage, or has been misled by expressing it by means of *afraid,* as used in Scot. colloquial parlance. *Red* in that sense, however, has nothing to do with *rad,* afraid: it is from *rede,* to advise.

REDDAR OF PLAIES, *s.* An umpire of sports. Addit. to REDDAR, q. v.

"Sequester, a *reddar of plaies;*" Duncan, App. Etym., 1595, ed. Small, E.D.S.

REDE, READE, *s.* A calf's stomach used for rennet. V. REID.

To REDOUN, REDOWN, *v. a.* To make good, atone for. Addit. to REDOUND.

". . . and is ordanit to *redown* the skaitht to the said James anstenit be him." Burgh Recs. Glasgow, I. 61, Reo. Soc.

RED-WAT, *adj.* Dyed red; wet, dyed, or stained with blood, blood-stained. Addit. to RED-WAT, q. v.

This term was very improperly defined by Jamieson; however, the passage in which it occurs is peculiar.

RED-WAT-SHOD, *adj.* and *adv.* 1. As an *adj.,* wet over the shoe-tops with blood, soaked or soaking with blood to the ankles. 2. As an *adv.,* walking in blood over the shoetops, ankle-deep in blood.

At Wallace' name, what Scottish blood
But boils up in a spring-tide flood!
Oft have our fearless fathers strode
By Wallace' side,
Still pressing onward *red-wat-shod*
Or glorious dy'd.
Burns, Epistle to Simpson.

RED-WUD, RED-WOD, *adj.* V. under [REID, *adj.*]

REEF, *s.* The itch. V. REIF.

REEF-SAW, *s.* Salve or ointment for the itch-disease.

REEL-BANE, REELE-BANE, REWEL-BANE, ROYAL-BANE, s. An unknown material of which saddles were supposed to be made.

This term occurs frequently, and under various forms, in the older ballads and romances. In Chaucer, Cant. Tales, l. 13807, it appears as *rewel-bone*; in the romance of Thomas of Ersyldoune, as *roelle-bone*; and in the romance of Young Bekie, as *royal-bone;* but regarding the material so called there is no certainty. Speght supposed it was ivory stained in many colours, from Fr. *riolé*, streaked, rayed.

REFE, REF, s. Robbery. V. REIF.

To REFLOIR, v. n. Lit. to flourish again; to burst, abound, or overflow, as with joy or gladness. O. Fr. *reflourir*.

Laude, reuerence, helth, vertow, and honouris,—
To the Venus I rander euermoir.
And nocht causles: with superabundant
Mirth, melodie, thow dois my hart *refloir*,
As Inuincent, victour, and triumphant.
Rolland, Court of Venus, l. 295, S. T. S.

To REFUGE, v. a. To drive away, scatter, blot out. Lat. *refugere*.

Sen for our vyce that Justyce mon correct,
O King most hie! now pacify thy feid,
Our syn is huge, *refuge*, we not suspect,
As thou art Juge, deluge us of this dreid.
In tyme assent, or we be schent with deid.
Henryson, Prayer for the Pest, st. 11.

REGEMENT, s. Rule, government; Compl. Scotland, p. 2, E.E.T.S. O. Fr. *regiment.*

REHATE, v. and s. V. Rechate.

To REIBILL, v. a. A form of REHABLE, q. v.

REID, s. Fate; synon. *weird*. V. REDE.

REID-RAIP, s. Lit., fate-rope; fatal-rope, gallows-rope.

"Schir," said the Foxe, "God wait, I mene nocht that;
For and I did, it wer weill worth that ye
In ane *reid-raip* had tyit me till ane tre."
Henryson, Wolf, Foxe, and Cadgear, l. 63.

REIDSETT, adj. Errat. in DICT. for *Reuerssede,* q. v.

Delete this entry altogether. The term is a misreading in Pinkerton's version of Sir Gawan and Sir Galogras.

REIM-KENNAR, s. V. DICT.

Regarding this word Prof. Skeat has kindly furnished the following explanation:—"It is obvious that Sir W. Scott has here turned the Icel. *rímkænn,* one skilled in rhyme, into *German spelling;* he has substituted the G. *reim* for Icel. *rím,* and the G. *kenner,* i.e., "knower," for the Icel. adj. *kænn*. This hint is of considerable importance, for I suspect that Sir Walter has done the same thing in numerous instances. He knew a little German, but no Icelandic, and thought (as all did *then*), that it made no difference. This may enable us to explain other words.

To REIR, REIYER, RERE, v. and s. V. REIRD, v.

To REIST, REEST, v. a. To reduce, to set or keep at a lower rate: as "*to reist the* (Sup.) B 2

fire," to bank or damp the fire, i.e., to heap it so as to keep it up all night; Fife, Forfar.

REISTET, REESTIT, RAISTIT, *part. and adj.*

Lit. arrested, stopt, stopt short; hence, as applied to growth or progress, stunted, shrivelled, withered; West of S.; *raistit,* Stirlings.

The word is still so used. Neglected, half-starved children are called "puir wee *reestit* things;" and wood that has become shrivelled or rent is called "*reestit* timmer." So also it was used by Burns in his Address to the Deil, st. 17:—

D'ye mind that day, when in a bizz,
Wi' reekit duds, and *reestet* gizz,
Ye did present your smoutie phiz,
'Mang better folk,
An' sklented on the man of Uzz
Your spitefu' joke!

Reestet gizz, stunted or shrivelled wig: it was with this meaning that Burns used the phrase; see his Glossary. The *gizz* was properly the head-dress by which the *gizars* or mummers disguised themselves, and personated the characters they represented. And it is a clever stroke of Burns to represent the deil as donning the orthodox small-wig of the douce elders and ministers of that time, in order to make his "*smoutie* phiz" more presentable among the "*better folk*" he was to meet "*that day.*"

REIT, s. A device, method; hence, spell, charm; pl. *reittis,* witches' spells, methods of witching; Trials for Witchcraft, Spald. Cl. Misc. I. 148. Synon. *freit.*

Lat. *ratio,* calculation, device; from *ratus,* part. pt. of *reor,* I think, deem, devise.

REIT, *part. pt.* A contr. form of *revit,* reaved, plundered: "thair gudis *reit* and rent;" Sempill Ballates, p. 127. V. REVE, v.

To REKE, v. a. and n. To stretch, extend: part. pr. *rekand;* Burgh Recs. Peebles, p. 144. V. [REEK].

RELAND, *adj.* Rolling: *reland eis,* goggle eyes, also, squinting eyes; Rob. Stene's Dream, p. 8, Mait. C. V. RELE.

To RELENT, v. a. To soften, appease. Addit. to [RELENT], q. v.

Were Fortune lovely Peggy's foe,
Such sweetness would *relent* her,
As blooming spring unbends the brow
Of surly savage winter.
Burns, Young Peggy, st. 4.

The use of *relent* as a trans. vb., although uncommon, is quite in keeping with the origin of the term,—O. Fr. *ralentir,* "to slacken, remit, loosen," &c. Cotgr.: Fr. *ra-* being- put for *re-a-* (Lat. re-ad); and *lentir* from Lat. *lentus,* slack, slow. V. Skeat, Etym. Dict.

Lyndsay used the word in the sense of *assuage, lessen, lighten,* in the passage referred to in DICT.

With siching sair I am bot schent,
Without acho cum incontinent.
My hevin langour to *relent*
And saif me now fra deid.
Thrie Estaitis, l. 391.

To RELESCH, RELESCHE, v. a. To relax, assuage; Kingis Quair, st. 184, Skeat.

To RELESCH, *v. n.* To burst out, gush forth: part. pres. *releschand,* as applied to sound or music, ringing, swelling, resounding. Addit. to RELEISCH, q. v.

The larkis lowd *releschand* in the skyis.
Douglas, iv. 87, 30, ed. Small.

The definition in DICT. is defective; and, in the explanation of the passage quoted, there is no reference to the characteristic of the lark's song, which the poet expresses by the term *releschand.*
O. Fr. *relascher,* "to slacken ease, refresh, remit;" Cotgr. From Lat. *relaxare,* to relax.

RELESCHE, *s.* Relaxation, ease; Ibid., st. 150. O. Fr. *relasche.*

REME, *s.* Cream. V. REAM.

To REMEMBER, *v. a.* 1. To convey or express to a person the sympathy, regards, or good wishes of a friend or acquaintance; as, "*Remember* me kindly to your folk: I'm sure I wish them a' weel."

2. To make allowance for, make good, remunerate, reward; as, "Lend me five pund, man, an I'll *remember* 't to you on term day," i.e., I'll repay it then.

"The prouest, baillies, and counsall lykwayis ordanis Mr. Peter Blakburne, minister, to be *rememberit* for the intertening of the said Mr. George this ten or xii. dayes past in the said Mr. Peteris houa." Burgh Recs. Aberdeen, II. 188, Sp. C.

In both senses the word is still used in various parts of Scotland; and in the first sense it is common in England.

REMEMORANT, *adj.* Mindful, bearing in mind; Compl. Scotland, p. 175, E. E. T. S. *Rememorance,* remembrance, Ibid., p. 2. O. Fr. *remémorer.*

To REMORD, *v. a.* Lit. to bite again; hence, to question, search into, examine, test. Addit. to REMORD, q. v.

. . . . that thay wald pance and prent,
Consider weill, and in thair heid tak tent,
Remord thair mindis quhidder gif Chestitie
Be not mair clene, mair glorious, and his
Triumphant stait, mair digne and eminent
Than Venus warkis with all hir dignitie?
Rolland, Court of Venus, iii. 843, S. T. S.

In the Gloss. to this work, *remord* is improperly rendered "to refresh the memory as conscience does?"

REMYT, *s.* Remission, excuse, forgiveness.
Quho sal be thare to pray for thy *remyt?*
Kingis Quair, st. 195, Skeat.
Lat. *remittere,* to send back, slacken, abate.

RENCH, RENSH, *v.* and *s.* Rinse. V. REENGE.

RENDERED-FAT, RENDERMENT, RENDER, *s.* Dripping; also called *kitchen-fee,* because it is generally a perquisite of the family-cook. V. RENDER.

To RENEW, RENEWE. *v. a.* To make or tell anew, to recount, rehearse; Houlate, l. 708.

RENEWE, *s.* Renewal, repetition; Kingis Quair, st. 125, Skeat.

This form is an example of the tendency to drop the affix which is common in the northern dialect, especially in the case of the part. pt.

To RENFORSE, *v. a.* To supply, succour, reinforce; pret. and part. pt. *renforsit.*

"Be that industreus martial act, he *renforsit* the toune witht victualis, hagbutaris, ande munitions." Compl. Scotland, p. 6, E. E. T. S.
O. Fr. *renforcer,* to reinforce, strengthen.

RENT, RENTE, *s.* Interest, annual payment for the use of money, land, or property.

"The saidis provest, baillies, and counsall, thinkis it now maist meit and expedient that the said soume of five hundrethe merkis salbe imployit on yeirlie *rent,* as it hes bene thir six yeiris bygane, for the help and supporte of the ministrie of Godis worde within this burgh in all tyme cumyng." Burgh Recs. Stirling, Feb. 1612, p. 129.

". . . the soume of ane hundrethe merkis, usuall money of Scotland, to be imployed be the toun on *rent* to the help of the ministrie of this burghe." Ibid., Jan. 1611, p. 126.

O. Fr. *rente,* rent, annual payment. Cf. Ital. *rendita, rent,* a corr. of Lat. *reddita,* fem. of pp. of *reddere,* to render.

To REPERALL, *v. a.* V. REPARELL.

REPET, *s.* A quarrel. V. RIPPET.

REPLADGIATION, *s.* Replevin, act of replevin; Burgh Recs. Peebles, p. 101, Rec. Soc. V. REPLEDGE.

REPORT, *s.* Narrative, story, record.

And than how he [Boece], in his poetly *report,*
In philosophy can him to confort.
Kingis Quair, st. 4, Skeat.

To REPOSSESSE, *v. a.* To give back to the original owner; Blame of Kirkburiall, ch. 19; same as REPONE, q. v.

To REPREHEND, *v. a.* To overtake, apprehend; to take one in the act. Lat. *reprehendere.*

". . . it selbe lesum to quhatsumever nychtbour that *reprehendis* the layaris of the said fulze to tak the veschell that it sell happin to be brocht in, to be keipit quhill thai be punyst for the braking of this statut." Burgh Recs. Aberdeen, i. 156, Sp. C.

REPUDIE, *s.* Repudiation, divorce.

Quhen Diomed had all his appetyte,
And mair, fulfillit of this fair Ladie,
Upon ane uther he set his haill delyte,
And send to hir ane lybell of *repudie,*
And hir excludit fra his companie.
Henryson, Test. Cresseid, l. 74.

O. Fr. *repudier,* to repudiate; and prob. *repudie* is short for *repudiement.*

REPUT, *part. pt.* Reputed, deemed; Blame of Kirkburiall, ch. 6.

RESAVE, RESAUE, RESAWE, v. a. Addit. to RESAIFF, q. v.

RESIGN, RESYNG, RESSYNG, s. Resignation; the act of yielding up property or office to another; Burgh Recs. Peebles, Oct. 1457, p. 120, Rec. Soc.

RESOLUTE, RESOLIT, adj. Resolved, well considered, decided, final.

". . . desyring the saidis burrowis conformitie and *resolute* answer anent the establesching of," etc. Burgh Recs. Aberdeen, II. 191, 194.
". . . and to gif his *resolit* answer thairanent." Ibid., p. 194.
Lat. *resolutus*, from *resoluere*, to loosen, take to pieces; hence to investigate, decide, resolve.

To RESP, v. a. To rub or scratch with a rough surface; to rub or grind away, as with a file. Addit. to RESP, q. v.

RESP, s. A rasp or coarse file.

O. Fr. *rasper* (Mod. Fr. *râper*) from O. H. Ger. *raspôn*, whence Ger. *raspeln*, to rasp. V. Skeat's Etym. Dict.

To RESPAIT, RESPATE, RESPLAIT, RESPLATE, v. a. To respite, delay. V. RESPECT.

". . . the assis *resplaitit* this quhil thai be forthir avisit with men of law." Burgh Recs. Aberdeen, I. 401, Sp. C.
The form *resplatit* occurs on p. 404 of same vol.
The word is still frequently pron. *respate* in the West of S.

RESPATE, RESPAIT, s. Respite. V. [RESPIT].

RESPLAID, part. pt. Intermixed, worked into each other; combined, repeated, varied.

His hois thay war of the reid Skarlet maid,—
Begaryit all with sindrie silkis hew,
Of nedill wark richt richelie all *resplaid*.
Rolland, Court of Venus, i. 121, S. T. S.
In Gloss. improperly rendered, "having the edges of the seams sewed down."
Cf. O. Fr. *replier*, allied to *resploiter* (see Burguy), "to redouble, to bow, fould, or plait into many doublings; to make to turne or wind in and out very often;" Cotgr. Formed from Lat. *replicare*.

To RESPLAIT, REESPLAT, v. a. V. REPLAIT.

RESPONSAIL, s. Response, promise; a reading or forecast of the future, an assurance.

Upon Venus and Cupide angerly
Scho cryit out, and said on this same wyse,
'Allace! that ever I maid you sacrifice,
Ye gave me anis ane devine *responsail*
That I suld be the flour of luif in Troy,
Now am I maid an unworthie outwaill
And all in cair translatit is my joy.'
Henryson, Test. Cresseid, 1, 127.
L. Lat. *responsalis*, a letter written in answer to another: see Ducange. Henryson, however, used the term in the sense of a response or reply of an oracle.

To RETEENE, RETENE, v. a. To retain, keep back, maintain; Blame of Kirkburiall, ch. 4. Lat. *retinere*.

To RETERE, v. a. and n. To retire, withdraw; Compl. Scotland, p. 15, E.E.T.S. V. RETEIR.

RETH, adj. A form of RAITH, q. v.

RETHORIKE, s. Rhetoric; Kingis Quair, st. 196, Skeat.

RETHORIKLY, adv. Rhetorically; Ibid., st. 7.

REU, s. A street; *the plane reu*; the open or public street; Compl. Scotland, p. 182, E.E.T.S. Fr. *rue*.

REUTH, s. Wild mustard seed.

REUYN, part. pt. Riven, torn. V. [REUE].

REVE, s. Errat. in DICT. for *rubie*, ruby; Awnt. Arth., xxxi. 4.

This is a misreading of Pinkerton's version. The MS. has *rebe*, a mistake for *rubie*; but the Thornton MS. has *rubyes*. See Laing's version.

To REVE, REWE, v. a. Forms of RIVE, with meaning to tear up, turn over, delve, plough; part. pt. *revin*, *rewin*, Burgh Recs. Aberd., II. 345, 325, Sp. C.; *rewyn*, Burgh Recs. Glasgow, I. 454, Rec. Soc. Addit. to REVE, REUE.

The use of *rive* in this sense is well illustrated by the passage in Death and Dr. Hornbook, in which Burns pities the poor grave-digger ruined by the skill of the Doctor.

His braw calf-ward where gowans grew
Sae white and bonnie,
Nae doubt they'll *rive* it wi' the plew,
They'll ruin Johnnie!

To REVERSE, REUERSS, v. a. To overlay, to fold or lay back as a facing; part. pt. *reuerssede*, Awnt Arth., ii. 3. Addit. to REVERSE, q. v.

See the quotation under *Railed*.

RHIND, s. V. *Rind*.

To RHUME, v. n. To talk nonsense, to rave; Orkney. A form of RHAME, q. v.

RHYME, s. The covering membrane of the skin, the intestines, etc.; "the *rhyme* side," the grain side or outer surface; Burgh Recs. Edinburgh, I. 29, Rec. Soc.

RHYME-PROOF, adj. Fit or determined to resist all inducements to write poetry; Burns.

Proof here has the same force as in *shot-proof*, or as Burns has it, *prief* o' *shot*, i. e., fit to resist the power of shot, or not to be injured by shot or lead.

RHYMIN-WARE, s. Compositions in rhyme, poetry, poems and songs.

We'se gie ae night's discharge to care,
 If we forgather,
An' hae a swap o' *rhymin-ware*,
 Wi' ane anither.
  Burns, First Ep. to Lapraik, st. 18.
In his Second Ep. to Davie he calls his poems *rhymin clatter*.

RIBUP, RIDUPE, *s.* A musical instrument of the violin kind, and played with a bow; Houlate, l. 759.

Called also a *rebec*, and a *ribibe*. Nares states that it was originally an instrument of two strings, then three, till it was improved into the perfect instrument of four strings. It is said to be a Moorish instrument, Fr. *rebec* and *rebebe*; Arab. *rabáb*, Pers. *rubáb*.

RIBUS, *s.* Errat. in DICT. for *Ribup*, q. v.

This is a misreading in Pinkerton's version. Bann. MS. has *ribup*, and Asloan MS. *ribupe*.

RICE, RYCE, *s.* A twig. V. RISE.

RICK, *s.* V. DICT.

Rick is simply a misprint for *relick*, the letters *e, l*, having probably dropped out. The correct reading sets the metre right also. Laing's ed. reads *relict*; see vol. ii. p. 112.

RIDDIN'-KAIM, *s.* A redding-comb ; so pron. in West of S. V. under RED.

RIDE, REID, *s.* Spawn of fish or frogs. V. RUDE.

RIEF, *s.* Robbery ; plunder. V. REIF.

". . . . the sleest paukie thief,
That e'er attempted stealth or *rief*,
Ye surely hae some warlock-breef
Owre human hearts.
  Burns, Ep. to James Smith, st. 1.

RIEF, REIF, REAF, *adj.* Thieving, given to plundering or robbing; *rief randies*, thievish beggars, plundering gypsies ; Burns.

RIFE, *adj.* Plentiful, abundant, common, prevalent: also used in the sense of apt, ready, quick, much given to, as in "He's unco *rife* wi' his promises," i.e., he is very ready in making promises.

The term is still common in the North of England. V. Brockett's and Peacock's Gloss.

RIG, RYG, *s.* A measure of land extending to 240 paces by 6 paces, or 600 ft. by 15 ft. ; and containing 9000 sq. ft. A firlot of oats was reckoned sufficient seed for a *rig*. Addit. to RIG.

RIGING, *s.* Ridge, crown; "the *riging* of the casey ;" Burgh Recs. Glasgow, II. 236, Rec. Soc. Addit. to RIGGIN. V. under RIG.

RIGMAROLE, *s.* V. DICT.

The explanations of this term suggested by Jamieson are fanciful and unsupported.
"There can be little doubt that it is a corruption of *ragman-roll*, which was used in a very similar sense."

Wedgwood, *s. v.* Skeat gives the same explanation. V. under *Ragman*.

To RIKE, RYKE, *v. n.* To reach. V. REIK.

Let me *ryke* up to dight that tear,
 And go wi' me and be my dear,
 And then your every care and fear
May whistle owre the lave o't.
  Burns, Jolly Beggars.
A.-S. *rǽcan, rácean*, to reach, attain to; Mod. E. *rechen*.

To RIN, RINN, *v. a.* To melt. V. RIND.

This form represents the pron. in the West of S.

RIND, RHIND, RINE, RIN, RING, RONG, RUNG, *s.* Various forms of RAND, ROND, ROON, q. v.

When the list or selvage is narrow, it is generally called a *rind* or *rine:* when it is of medium breadth, it is a *rand, ran*, or *rane*, or a *roond* or *roon ;* and when it is of the widest make, it is a *rund, rung*, or *rong*.

The *rhind* or *rind* is a term in golfing applied to the wrapping of selvage on the handle of a club under the leather, which is put on in order to thicken the grip of the club.

Rinds are plaited or woven into a kind of cloth used for the uppers of light shoes, which are therefore called *rind* or *rine*-shoon. *Rands* or *roonds* is the name generally given to remnants or strips of coarse cloth, carpet, etc. used for the same purpose. *Runds, rungs*, or *rongs*, are the strong selvages of horse-cloths, girths, etc., and are used as straps, bands, or runners. For example, the slips of wood which form the bottom of a bed are attached and kept in position by *rungs*. Addit. to ROON, ROOND.

RIND-SHOON, RINE-SHOON, *s. pl.* V. ROON-SHOON.

RINEL, RINNEL, *s.* A runlet, gutter ; Burgh Recs. Aberdeen, I. 78. V. RINNER.

RING-BANE, *s.* An osseous growth on the pastern joint of a horse : it is generally the result of severe inflammation. E. *ring-bone*.

To RIPE, *v. a.* and *n.* To ripen, to grow or become ripe ; part. pt. *ripen*.

"And to speak truth, I hae been flitting every term these four-and-twenty years ; but when the time comes, there's aye something to saw that I would like to see sawn—or something to maw that I would like to see mawn—or something *to ripe* that I would like to see *ripen*—an' sae I e'en dalker on wi' the family frae year's end to year's end." Sir W. Scott, Rob Roy, ch. vi.

RIPPILL, *s.* and *v.* V. RIPPLE.

RIPPLE, *s.* A painful illness, deadly disease, death-pang. Addit. to RIPPLES, q. v.

Auld Orthodoxy lang did grapple,
But now she's got an unco *ripple* ;
Haste, gie her name up i' the chapel,
 Nigh unto death ;
See how she fetches at the thrapple,
 An' gasps for breath.
  Burns, Letter to Goudie.

RISE, *s.* A steep bank rising abruptly from a level surface.

RIST, *s.* A musical instrument; prob. a small stringed instrument of the lyre kind.
The rote and the recordour, the ribupe, the *rist.*
Houlate, 1. 759, Asloan MS.
That the *rist* was a stringed instrument is suggested by the class of instruments with which it is grouped; and that it was of the lyre kind is made prob. by Wright's Voc., which gives *wreste* as the rendering of Lat. *plectrum*; and the name of the little ivory instrument with which the lyre was played, was often used poet. for *a lyre.* In Mod. E. a *wrest* is the name of the instrument or key used for tuning a harp.

ROAK, ROKE, *s.* Forms of ROOK, RAUK, q. v.

ROARIN'-FOU, *adj.* and *s.* 1. As an *adj.,* in a noisy, boisterous mood through liquor.
That ev'ry naig was ca'd a shoe on,
The smith and thee gat *roarin fou* on.
Burns, Tam o' Shanter.

2. As a *s.,* the noisy, boisterous state of intoxication.

ROBLOKKIS, *s. pl.* Lit., ragamuffins. A contemptuous name for a family, a group of followers or dependants, etc.; Rob Stene's Dream, p. 21, Mait. C. V. RABBLE, RABBLACH.
Gael. *rioblach,* ragged ; *rioblaich,* a ragged fellow.

ROBOUR, *s.* A keg, small barrel; Burgh Recs. Glasgow, I. 450. V. ROUDBURIS.

ROCK, *s.* A distaff; also the stuff on the distaff from which thread was spun by twirling a ball or other form of weight called a spindle.
There was an auld wife had a wee pickle tow,
And she wad gae try the spinning o't ;
She louted her down. and her *rock* took a low,
And that was a bad beginning o't.
Alex. Ross, The Rock and the Wee Pickle Tow.
Rock here means the tow on the rock.

RODE, ROOD, ROODE, *adj.* and *s.* 1. As an *adj.,* red, ruddy. V. RUD.

2. As a *s.,* redness; complexion, or more properly, the ruddy tint of the complexion; Awnt. Arth., xiii. 5. V. RUDE.

RODY, RODDY, *adj.* Ruddy; Kingis Quair, st. 1, Skeat; also used as a *s.* V. RUDDY.

ROE, *s.* V. REW.

ROGH, *adj.* Rough. V. ROCH.

ROIF, ROVE, RUVE, RUFE, RUFF, *s.* Break, pause, cessation ; hence, repose, quiet, peace. Errat. in DICT.
The defin. and deriv. of this term given in the DICT. are certainly wrong. For explanations see under *Rufe, v.*

ROLK, *s.* A form of *rokk,* a rock, frequently found in MSS. Addit. to ROLK, q. v.

Even in the most carefully written MSS. *kk* is frequently written as *lk.* This was simply a device of the scribe to secure ease and speed in writing. Besides, in all such forms the *l* was not sounded.
This explanation applies also to ROULK, which is really the O. Fr. *rauque.*

ROME, *v.* and *s.* Growl, roar. V. RAME.

To **ROND, RUN,** *v. a.* To shield. V. *Rand.*

RONE, *s.* A shrub. V. DICT.
"The etym. of this word is Icel. *runnr,* not *runne,* nor *runn,* as stated." Skeat.

RONNE, *part. pt.* Run, berun: " *blody ronne,*" run over with blood ; Kingis Quair, st. 55, Skeat.

ROOD-BROD, RUD-BROD, *s.* The altarbox, offertory-plate: the plate, box, ladle, or other vessel used in collecting alms in a church. So called from being laid on the altar under the *rood* or cross.
"It is thocht expedient be the provest, baillies, and counsall, that quhatsumevir persone being charget to gaddir with the *Rud brod,* in the nycht preceding, that he that refusis and gadderis nocht that he sall pay of his awin purs als mykle as the samyn gyffis on Sonday nixt preceding, or Sonday nixt following." Burgh Recs. Stirling, p. 68.

ROOD-FAIR, RUIDFAIR, RUDE-FAIR, *s.* The name of an annual fair held in various towns of Scotland, in May or September.
Those held in May were probably so named to commemorate the finding of the Holy Cross by St. Helena, May 3, A.D. 328 ; and those held in Sept., to commemorate the recovery of the Cross by the emperor Heraclius, Sept. 14, 615. These fairs were, in most cases, instituted by the Church, and almost always were under its patronage.
"In 1685 a confirmation by King James VII. of a grant of the Marquisate of Huntly to George, Duke of Gordon, included the patronage of the Church of Kilmanerock, with a yearly fair called the *Ruidfair,* to be held there on the 2nd of September." Orig. Paroch., Vol. II., pt. 1, p. 174.

ROOK, *s.* A pile, small heap: as of hay. V. RUCK.

To **ROOK,** *v. a.* To collect into piles or heaps; part. pt., *rookit.*

ROOM-FREE, ROUM-FRE, ROWME-FRE, *adj.* and *adv.* Free of cost, rent, or duty.
"About 1354 the land and tenement of Westersoftlaw were granted with the privilege of grinding corn *roumfre* at the mill of Mawell, on condition," etc. Orig. Paroch., I. 448, Bann. C.
". . . and als we find at the cornes of Corscunnyngfeld aucht to be *roum fre* in the myln of Peblis to the fourty corne." Charters of Peebles, 18 Feb. 1484-5, Rec. Soc.
Room-free at a mill means *multure-free,* or free of charge for grinding ; and " *roum fre to the fourty corne,*" as in the passage above, means that the multure is fixed at one-fortieth of the melder, or that the cost of grinding does not exceed one-fortieth of the stuff.

To sit *room-free* in a dwelling-house means to sit *rent-free;* and to hold a property *room-free* is to hold it without paying the usual burghal duties.

ROOP, ROOPY, ROOPIT. V. ROUP.

ROSSIN, *part. pt.* Roasted.

". . . *rossin* in his bodye, as gif he hed bene *rossin* in ane vne," etc. Trials for Witchcraft, Spald. Mis., I. 85, 1597.

"Vne," an oven.

ROTE, s. V. DICT.

The musical instrument called the *rote* is really the *crotta* or *crowd*. ¡Ritson's etym. is a mistake. See *Rote* (2) in Skeat's Etym. Dict.

ROTHE, ROYTH, s. The conditions and rights of the Odaller as master of his own house; Memorial for Orkney, p. 118.

ROTHMAN, ROTHISMAN, ROITHISMAN, s. An Odaller; *Rothismen's sons,* Odallers by descent. V. Grievances of Orkney, App. II.

Icel. *rathi*, rule, management.

ROULE, ROWLE, s. 1. A roll or piece of cloth; Halyburton's Ledger, p. 326.

2. A ruler for marking lines; Ibid., p. 310.

O. Fr. *role, roule*, from Lat. *rotulus*, a roll.

ROULK, ROLK, adj. V. DICT.

For explanation of these forms see under *Rolk* above. In l. 2 of note, for "is *sowlpit*" read "as *sowlpit*."

ROUNCE, ROUNCIE, ROUNCY, s. A steed, horse. V. RUNSY.

ROUN-TREE, ROAN-TREE, s. V. DICT.

"The Scand. forms given under this entry are incorrect. It is the Swed. *rönn*, Dan. *rönn*, Icel. *reynir ;* and it has nothing to do with *runes,* as suggested." Skeat.

ROUND, adj. Consisting of lumps, in large pieces, free from dross: generally applied to coal fit for household use.

ROUNDY, adj. In the sense of roundish, i.e., consisting of small lumps suitable for mending a fire; without dross: syn. *crunkly*.

These terms are common in the N. of England also.

ROUND, s. Lit. a turn, course, in convivial gatherings a toast, a simultaneous drinking by a company; Burns.

ROUP. To *Cry a Roup*. V. under *Cry*.

ROWMONT, s. Enrolment, decree, ordinance.

". . . produsyt ane *rowmont* of court of the balyeof kyll." Burgh Recs. Prestwick, p. 60, Mait. C.

O. Fr. *roulement*, that which is made into or entered upon a roll; from Lat. *rotulamentum*.

ROWSE, adj. Contr. for *Rowanis*, of or belonging to Rouen: *Rowse cloth,* cloth of Rouen; Halyburton's Ledger, p. 320. V. [ROWANE].

To ROYNE, RHYNE, v. n. To grumble, growl, mutter discontentedly; West of S. V. QUHRYNE.

RUB ON THE GREEN. A term in golfing, denoting a favourable or unfavourable knock which one's ball may receive during the game, for which no penalty is imposed, and which must be submitted to.

RUBE, s. Ruby; pl. *rubes,* Awnt. Arth., ii. 4, Lincoln MS.; *rybees,* Douce MS.

RUCH, RUGH, adj. Rough. V. ROUCH.

RUCKLE, v. and s. V. *Ruttle*.

RUDIR, s. A rudder, helm; *rudirman,* a helmsman; Compl. Scotland, p. 41, E.E.T.S. M.E. *rother, roder*.

A.-S. *rother*, a paddle, an oar. The rudder was called the *steuer-ruder*, the steer-paddle or steer-oar: vessels having originally been steered by an oar working at the stern. V. Wedgwood's Etym. Dict.

To RUFE, v. n. To break, break off, pause, stop, cease. Errat. in DICT. V. RUFE.

This wid fantastyk lust but lufe
Dois so yung men to madness mufe
That thay ma nowthir rest nor *rufe*
Till thay mischeif thair sellis.
    Alex. Scott's Poems, p. 77, Ed. 1882.

RUFE, RUFF, RUVE, ROVE, ROIF, s. Break, interruption, pause, cessation; hence, repose, quiet, peace; *but roif,* without pause, incessantly.

Gloir to the Fader be aboif,
Gloir to the Sone for our behoif,
Gloir to the Haly Spreit of loif,
  In trenefald vnitie ;
As wes, is, salbe ay, but *roif,*
Ane thre, and thre in ane, to proif
Thy Godheid nevir may remoif:
  Lord God deliuer me.
    Ibid., p. 6.

His mynd aall moif but rest or *ruve*,
With diuerss dolouris to the deid.
    Ibid., p. 79.

Regarding the other forms of the word, see the illustrations given under ROIF in DICT.

The definition and origin of the word there given are certainly wrong, and do not suit the passages quoted, much less do they suit those now given.

Roif and rest is not 'a mere pleonasm,' as Jamieson suggests, but a phrase of frequent occurrence in popular poetry, meaning *peace and rest,* a break or pause in work or worry permitting rest to the wearied or worried one.

Rufe is from Icel. *rjúfa,* to break, pause, interrupt; whence *rof*, a breach, opening, interruption; and from these the secondary meanings of repose, quiet, peace, are easily obtained.

To RUG *to*, v. a. To snatch, seize: *to rug to one,* to seize for oneself. Addit. to RING, q. v.

"Arripio, to plucke, or *rug to* me;" Duncan, App. Etym., 1595, ed. Small.

RUIFF, *s.* Running water, streams.

"... terras suas de Petlevy cum toftis, croftis, pasturis, privilegiis et le *ruiff* ad easdem spectantibus." Reg. Mag. Sig., 1513-1546, No. 2393.
Gael. *ruith*, flowing, act or state of flowing, as a stream; M'Leod and Dewar. It may, however, be related to O. Fr. *ravir*, to bear away suddenly, Lat. *rapere*. Cf. *ravine*, a hollow worn by floods, from O. Fr. *ravine*, rapidity, impetuosity; see Skeat and Wedgwood.

RUN, *part.* and *adj.* Gone, completed, perfected: hence, complete, perfect, thorough, out-and-out, habit-and-repute; as, a *run*-knot, a complete knot, one that is tightly drawn; a *run*-deil, a thorough deil, a person who is thoroughly wicked, also, a youth who is exceedingly troublesome or continually working mischief.

The Ladies arm-in-arm in clusters,
As great and gracious a' as sisters;
But hoar their absent thoughts o' ither,
They're a' *run-deils* an' jads thegither.
Burns, The Twa Dogs.

For men I've three mischievous boys,
Run-deils for rantin' an' for noise.
Ibid., The Inventory.

RUNCHECK, RUNSICK, *s.* Wild mustard; Orkney. V. RUNCHES.

These may be merely local varieties of the term *runches*, by which the plant is known throughout the central and southern counties of Scot. In Shetland it is called *rungy*: see Edmonston's Gloss.

To **RUND**, RUN, *v. a.* To shield. V. *Rand.*

To **RUNG**, *v. a.* To fix rungs or steps in a ladder, or spokes in a wheel; Burgh Recs. Edinburgh, II. 348, 350. V. RUNG, *s.*

RUN-METAL, *s.* Cast-iron: metal that has been run into a mould, as opposed to that which has been forged. Also called *pot-metal, pat-metal.*

RUNTY, *adj.* Short and thick-set, stunted. V. RUNT.

To **RUTE**, *v. n.* To take root, be securely planted. V. [RUTE].

To sels thy sublectis so in lufe and feir,
That rycht and reason in thy realme may *rute.*
God gife the grace agains this gude new yeir.
Alex. Scott's Poems, p. 11, ed. 1882.

RUTILLAND, RUTLANDE, *part. pr.* Croaking. V. *Ruttle.*

This term was left undefined by Jamieson. His suggestion that it refers to the appearance of the raven is a mistake: it refers to its rough voice, and is simply a form of *rattling*, with the meaning implied in *death-rattle.*

To **RUTTLE**, RUTLE, RUTILL, RUCKLE, *v. n.* To rattle; to breathe or speak with a rough rattling sound, as on the approach of death, on account of cold, etc.: also, to croak: part. pr. *rutlande*, Lyndsay, Papyngo, l. 688; *rutilland*, see DICT.

RUTTLE, RUTLIN', RUCKLE, RUCKLIN', *s.* Rattle, rattling; the death-rattle, or any noise occasioned by difficulty of breathing; also, a croak, croaking.

Dutch *ratelen*, to rattle, to make a hoarse or hard rough sound. A.-S. *hrætele*, a rattling.
Ruttle, both as a v. and as a s., is common in North of Eng. also. V. Brockett.

RUWITH, *adv.* Errat. in DICT. for *inwith*, within, inside.

A misreading in Pinkerton's version, as Jamieson suspected. See Note in DICT.

RUYNE, *s.* A growl, curse. V. *Ryne.*

RYCE, RYS, RYSS, *s.* A twig. V. RISE.

RYELL, *s.* A coin. V. RIAL.

RYIM, *s.* Rime, hoar frost; Compl. Scot., p. 59, E.E.T.S. A.-S. *hrím.*

To **RYKE**, *v. n.* To reach. V. *Rike.*

RYNDALE, *s.* A term apparently equivalent to RUNRIG, q. v.

"... et lie Fieldland jacentem *ryndale* in territorio de Cottis." Reg. Mag. Sig., 1513-1546, No. 3186.

To **RYNDE**, RYND, *v. a.* To melt. V. RIND.

To **RYNE**, RHYNE, ROYNE, RUYNE, *v. n.* To growl, grumble, croak, mutter, curse. V. QUIRYNE.

RYNE, RHYNE, ROYNE, RUYNE, *s.* A growl, grumble, croak, curse.

Thus leit he no man his peir;
Gif ony nech wald bim neir,
He bad thaim rebaldis orere,
With a *ruyne.*
Houlate, l. 910, Asloan MS.

RYNIN, ROYNIN, RUYNIN, *s.* Grumbling, croaking, complaining.

A.-S. *hrínan*, Icel. *hrína*, to squeal like a pig, to growl, grumble, complain.

RYN-MART, RYN-MUTTON, RYN-WEDYR, *s.* V. under RHIND MART.

The explanation of these terms offered by Jamieson is not satisfactory; but no better one has been suggested. It is useless to speculate regarding them, for the terms have long since passed out of use. See under *Mart.*

To **RYNSE**, RINGE, REINGE, *v. a.* To rinse, lave, clear, clean, purify. Addit. to REENGE, q. v.

And in Aquary, Cithera the clere
Rynsid hir tressis like the goldin wyre.
Kingis Quair, st. 1, Skeat.

RYNSE, REINGE, *s.* A rinsing, scouring, cleansing, washing. Addit. to RINGE, s. 2, q. v.

RYNSER, RINGER, REINGER, *s.* A rinser. Addit. to REENGE, s. 1, q. v.

S.

'S, 'SE, -S, -SE. Besides the possessive case of nouns, these forms represent—

1. The pronoun *his*; as in "till's ain time comes."

   Had rowth o' gear, and house o's ain,
   And beef laid in an' a'.
   Alex. Wilson's Poems, ii. 369, ed. 1876.

2. The present tense of the verb *to have*, or *has*, which is still used both in sing. and pl.; as in "Thou 'se nathing to fear;" "We 'se got it, an' we 'se keep it," i.e., we've got it and we'll keep it; see under s. 4, below.

   I'll clout my Johnie's gray breeks,
   For a' the ill he's done me yet.
   Song, Johnie's Gray Breeks.

   Wee modest crimson-tipped flow'r,
   Thou's met me in an evil hour;
   For I maun crush amang the stour
   Thy slender stem.
   Burns, To a Mountain Daisy, st. 1.

3. The present tense of the verb *to be*, or *is*, which is still used in both numbers.

   There's nae luck about the house,
   When our guidman's awa.
   Hector Macneil.

   Jenny and her jo's come.
   Old Song.

4. They represent the verb *sal*, Old Northern form of *shall*; and therefore express (in a future sense) purpose, determination, etc. In some cases the present also is included; as in "I'se no do that," i.e., I'll not do that, I shall not do it now or ever.

   But, I'se hae sportin by and by,
   For my gowd guinea;
   Tho' I should herd the Buckskin kye
   For't, in Virginia.
   Burns, Epistle to Rankin.

   In this sense 's, 'se should, more correctly, be written s'; thus, "I s' no do that," i.e., I shall not do that. "He's, probably short for *he sal* (he will); still in use in the North of England." Note to The Two Noble Kinsmen, iii. 2, 22, ed. Skeat, 1875. For further explanation see Dr. Murray on Scot. Dialects, p. 216.

5. In the same sense they express a promise, threat, etc.; as in, "Ye'se get mair than ye bargain for."

   But Mauchline race or Mauchline fair,
   I should be proud to meet you there;
   We'se gie ae nicht's discharge to care
   If we forgather,
   An' hae a swap o' rhymin-ware
   Wi' ane anither.
   Burns, Ep. to Lapraik.

   The following stanza, from the old version of "The Weary Pund o' Tow," is remarkable for the number and variety of the examples of 's and 'se which it contains.

O weel's us a' on our guidman,
For he's come hame,
Wi' a suit o' new claes;
But sarkin he's got nane.
Come lend to me some sarkin,
Wi' a' the haste ye dow,
And ye'se be weel pay'd back again,
When ance I spin my tow.

SACCADGE, *s.* Sack, pillage, plundering.

". . . for the misery inflictd by the Gothes at the *saccadge* of Rome." Blame of Kirkburiall, ch. 2.
Fr. *sac*, ruin, spoil; from Lat. *saccus*, a sack, bag. "From the use of a sack in removing plunder;" Skeat's Etym. Dict.

SACHT, *part. pt.* Reconciled. V. SAUCHT.

SACKLESS, SAKLES, *adj.* V. SAIKLESS.

SACRAND, SACRYNG, SACRYN, *adj.* Sacring, i.e., giving notice of sacred or holy services; "the *sacrand* bell," Dunbar and Kennedy, l. 160; Mait. Club Misc., iii. 203.

Sacrand is the old *sacring*, the pres. part.

"*Sacring bell*, the little bell rung at mass to give notice that the elements are consecrated [i.e., are being consecrated]; see Henry VIII., iii. 2, 295;" Schmidt Shakespeare's Lexicon.

SAGRISTANE, SEGSTAR, *s.* A sexton. E. *sacrist* and *sacristan*.

Sagristane; Burgh Recs. Aberdeen, 1503, i. 72, Sp. C. *Segstar;* Ibid., 1531, i. 143.

SAIG, SAIGE, *s.* Forms of SEGE, q. v.; see also under *Sege*.

To SAIG, *v. a.* To press down. V. SAG, SEG.

SAILLIE, SAILYE, SALLY, *s.* A projection outjutting; applied to a room, gallery, or other building projecting beyond the face of a house or wall.

The *saillie* or *sailye* was a device to enlarge the rooms of houses built in the narrow streets and lanes of olden times; specimens of which may still be seen in many of our large towns. It was adopted also as a means of defence in fortified castles, city walls, &c.; and gave a massive frowning appearance to the battlements. When so used, it was called a *corbalsailyie*, q. v.

O. Fr. *saillie*, a projection; "an eminence, jutting or bearing out beyond others;" Cotgr. Fr. *saillir*, to go out, issue forth, project.

SAIL-STONE, SAILE-STANE, *s.* The stone for sailing by, i.e., the lodestone, magnet.

"*Magnes*, the adamant, the *saile-stone*." Duncan's App. Etym., ed. Small, E.D.S.

SAIM, SEIM, SEEM, SEAM, *s.* Fat, lard; but generally applied to hog's-fat, hog's-lard. V. [SAME].

When used in the sense of hog's fat or hog's-lard, *saim* is short for *hog's-saim*. This is shown by the

SAI [209] SAL

other compounds still in use, such as *hen-saim, goose-saim, swine-saim*. The word is pron. both *saim* and *seam*.
 Saim is not from A.-S. *seim*, as is frequently stated, but from O. Fr. *saïm*, lard, contr. from L. Lat. *sagimen*; cf. *saginare*, to fatten. V. Burguy, s. v.
 "The A.-S. *seim* is easily seen to be a fiction, because the diphthong *ei* is unknown in A.-S. MSS." Skeat.

SAIR, *adj.* Severe, greedy, undue. Addit. to SAIR, q. v.
 "Complaint of the baxteris and maltmen aganis David Graheme, custummair, for trubling of thaim in the wrangus and *sair* taking of thair custum." Burgh Recs. Stirling, 1546-7, p. 46.

SAIR, SAIRIN. V. *Ser.*

SAKAR, *s.* A purser, treasurer.
 "Comperit in the said feussit court dene George Esok, subprior of Cambusschennocht, and dene John Arnot, *sakar* of the said place, and thar requirit the said Duncan Patonsoun to pay thame ane stane of talk or of xvjd., eftir the forme and tenor of thar chartour." Burgh Recs. Stirling, 17 January, 1520-1.
 "It was fundin be the inquest that Duncan Bowsould mak the pot that he keist to dene Johen Arnot, *sakar* of Cambussckennecht, ane gude sufficient pot." Ibid., 23 Oct., 1525.
 L. Lat. *saccus*, a bag, purse; *saccare*, to put into a bag; Ducange.

SALAR, SALER, SALURE, *s.* A salt-cellar. Addit. to SALER, q. v.

SALLAT, SALLET, SELLET, *s.* A helmet. V. SELLAT.

SALLAT-OIL, SELLETT-OYLE, *s.* A coarse kind of oil used in polishing helmets, in cleaning armour, domestic utensils, etc. Rates of Customs, 1612, Halyburton's Ledger, p. 311.
 Frequently called, and written *sallad-oil;* but not to be confounded with the pure, sweet oil now called *salad-oil.* See Palmer's Folk Etymology, p. 338
 O. Fr. *salade*, a sallet or head piece; see Cotgr.

SALMON, *s.* The great and inviolable oath of the Scottish gipsies; a corr. of O. Fr. *sarment*, an oath.
 "She swore by the *salmon*, if we did the kinchin no harm, she would never tell how the gauger got it." Sir W. Scott, Guy Mannering, ch. xxxiv.

SALMON-TAIL, SALMOND-TAILL, SALMONT-TAILL, SAMONT-TAILL, SAUMONT-TAILL, *s.* The tail-piece of a salmon, the portion extending from the vent or anal-fin to the tip of the tail.
 This portion of the fish, being the cheapest, was much in demand by the lower classes in Glasgow. But as the population increased, and the salmon did not, this article of food naturally rose in price : a result which the people stoutly resisted, and which they attributed simply to the greed of the magistrates and of their servant the breaker or salesman of salmon at the public stocks. Troubled by the continued clamour and repeated charges against this public servant, the magistrates at length were compelled to take action; and,
(Sup.) C 2

probably understanding the real cause of the rise in price, and foreseeing that the rise must increase rather than abate, they tried to steer a middle course by drawing out a scale of charges which apparently fixed the price of the article, but at the same time gave opportunity for its advance. The following was their resolution, which was generally accepted throughout the city as "*the law of salmon tails.*"
 "The provest, bailyeis, and counsall, wnderstanding the grait abuse done and committit by William Andersone, present breker of the salmound, in taking sutche grait and exorbitant pryces for the taillis of salmound att his awin pleasour and optioun, far exceeding the prycis that war wont to be takine of old ; for remeiding quhairof it is statut and ordanit that the said William, nor na vtheris the breckeris of salmound att the tounes commoun stock, tak na mair for *salmound taillis* heirefter except the pryces following, viz. aught pennies for the taill of ane lytill salmound, and sextein pennis for the taill of aue meikle salmound, and that vnder the pane of deprivatioun presentlie, the samein being tryit ; and yeit, for the regard thej beir to the said William, they will oversie him to tak, during thair willis onlie, tuelff pennis for the taill of ane lytle salmound, and twa schillings for the taill of ane meikle salmound." Burgh Recs. Glasgow, 13 April, 1638, vol. i., p. 387, Rec. Soc.
 For a time peace was restored, and the sale of the town's salmon went on quietly ; but as the demand far exceeded the supply, the *breker* felt he could get a better price for the *tails*, and was tempted to adopt questionable practices in order to secure it. Fish of medium size he cut slightly above the *crumb* or vent, that their tails might look like tails of "meikle salmound," and so fetch the highest price. Again the outcry against the salmon-breaker was raised, his greed and his malpractices became subjects of public talk ; and the poor, who could no longer be purchasers, declared they were wronged and oppressed. Once more the magistrates were compelled to deal with the case ; and as the breaker was clearly in fault his dismissal was all but resolved on. However, by judicious apologies before the council, and through the influence of powerful friends outside, he was retained in office ; but he was strictly bound down to the law of tails, and to implicit obedience thereto by the threat of instant dismission should he offend again. At the same time the council expressed its sympathy with the people by fixing a now scale of charges, and reducing the highest price of a tail from two shillings to twenty pence, Scotch. There, however, their sympathy ended : for the prices they then fixed were considerable in advance of those of 1638. The ordinance of the council on this occasion was as follows :—
 "The provest, baillies, and counsall, taking to ther consideratioune the great wrongis and abuissis done be the breker of the salmount, in taking far greater and moir exorbitant pryces for the tails of salmount nor hes bein done heirtofoir or allowed be the counsall conforme to the act sett doun theranent vpon the threttein day of Aprill 1638 ; the saids provest, bailleis, and counsall now ordain that he tak no moir for the taile of ilk salmount he breks of the pryce of twentie schilings and benetho but twelff penneis Scotes moneye allanerlie ; and for the taill of ilk salmount he breks that is of the pryce betuixt twentie and threttie schilings, sextein penneis ; and for the taill of ilk salmound that is above threttie or fourtie schilings, or above, of his breking, twentie penneis Scotes moneye ; swa that the dearest tail of salmound that he sall brek sall not exceid the said soume of tuentie penneis moneye. And that he sall be heirby bund and astrictit to lay the tails of the salmount to these partes that he sall brek, that gif it be the buyers will and desyr to have the tail with that pairt of the fische they buy, that the persone sall have it to whom it sall fall

be lot or cavill, the said breker sall rander the samein vpon payment of the pryces on the tails as is above writtin, having respect to the pryces of the salmound as it is above speccfeit. Nather sall it be leasum to him to outt the salmound above the crumbe or any pairte therof. And gif it sall happen him to contravein in any of the premisis heireftor he is presentlie to be dischargeit of his said charge and haill casualties he has therby, and never to be readmitit therto," Burgh Recs. Glasgow, ii. 67-8, Rec. Soc.

Such was the 'Law of Salmon Tails' to which in after years the people of Glasgow frequently appealed. But it is now only a record of the past. The Clyde, which then was one of the best salmon rivers in Scotland, is now noted for something so very different, that from Dumbarton to Rutherglen no salmon could live in it.

To SALLY, SAULLY, *v. n.* To move or run from side to side, as children do in certain games, and as workmen do on board a ship after it is launched; to rock or swing from side to side, like a small boat at anchor; also, to rise and fall, like a ship on a rough sea.

SALLY, SAULLY, *s.* A run from side to side; a rush or dash; a swing from side to side, rocking; a continuous rising and falling, a sail in a small boat over rough water; the swinging or bounding motion of a ship at sea.

Fr. *saillir*, to issue forth, bound, leap.

SALT. V. under SALT-FAT, in DICT.

To the note on *Spilling Salt* add the following:—
Spilling salt at table was formerly reckoned a serious and ominous accident, presaging a quarrel between the person spilling the salt and the person towards whom the spilled salt fell. The seriousness of the quarrel was indicated by the quantity spilled; and the extent or endurance of it by the surface over which the salt spread. The accident was in any case a matter of grave concern to the parties interested; but it was of gravest import if they happened to be relatives, and above all if they were members of the same family and household.

TO CAST SAUT UPO' ANE'S TAIL. This expression is used in various ways, but the most common applications are to take one unawares, to get the better of one in argument, in bargain-making, or by means of some sly, underhand trick.

Burns in fond praise of his faithful, oft-tried, riding mare, Jenny Geddes, said she could outstrip even "the fleet dawn," for he could, with fitting opportunity,—

. . . when auld Phœbus bids good morrow,
Down the zodiac urge the race,
And cast dirt on his godship's face:
For I could lay my bread and kail,
He'd ne'er *cast saut upo' thy tail.*
Burns, Ep. to Hugh Parker

SALUTE, *pret.* and *part. pt.* Saluted.

With ane humble and lamentable chere
Thus *salute* I that goddesse bryght and clere.
The Kingis Quair, st. 93, ed. Skeat.

SALVED, SALUED, *pret.* and *part. pt.* Healed, doctored; Awnt. Arthur, 17, 12.

SAMBUTES, *s. pl.* Housings, saddlecloths; Awnt. Arth., i. 11, MS. Douce. Addit. to SAMBUTES, q. v.

Jamieson's etym. of this term is defective. The word has come from L. Lat. *sambuta*, contracted *sabuta*, "curris vel equi ornatus;" Ducange.

SAMEABILL, SEMLABILL, *adj.* Similar, like; Burgh Recs. Aberdeen, I. 320.

Sameabill is prob. a mistake for *samlabill*: the transcriber having misread a short *l* as an *e*. The form *semlabill* occurs in p. 317 of same vol.

SANAP, *s.* A napkin; Awnt. Arth. 35, 8. Errat. in DICT.

Delete the entry under this heading in DICT. The phrase "*sanapes and salers*" means napkins and saltcellars; and the use of the *sanap* is clearly indicated by the full form of the name—a *savenappe*. The Prompt. Parv. gives, "*sanop*, manutergium, mantile." See Sir F. Madden's ed. of Sir Gawayne.

SAND-BLIND, SAAN-BLIN, *adj.* V. DICT.

As noted by Jamieson, this term has various applications; but it always implies that the person so afflicted is partially blind. Lit. it means half-blind, and is a corr. of O. Eug. *sam-blind*: from A.-S. *sâm*, half, and *blind*, blind. See Palmer's Folk Etymology, p. 339.

SANDE, *part. pt.* V. DICT.

Delete this entry in DICT. *Sande* is a misreading of *Saude*, sewed, embroidered; q. v.

SANDEL, SANDIL, *s.* The sparling or smelt: lit. little sand-fish. West of S.

SANDEL, *s.* Silk. V. *Sendal.*

SANDERS, SAUNDERS, SANNERS, SAUNERS, *s.* 1. Abbrev. of *Alexander.* V. SANDIE.

This abbrev. of the name, in all its various forms, is generally applied to an elderly person; and its equivalent *Sandie* is applied to younger persons. This distinction is almost constantly observed in families where father and son are named Alexander. For example, a wife will say to her husband as he leaves home on some errand:—"*Sanders*, gin you see *Sandie* on the road son' him hame." In a similar way the forms *Sandie* or *Sannie* and *Sannock* are employed.

2. A ludicrous and familiar name for the devil: sometimes the adjective *auld* or *aul'* is prefixed.

Considering the religious bias and upbringing of the Scottish people, it is surprising to find in their vocabulary so many familiar and jocular names for the devil, and so many playful allusions to his abode, his character, and his wiles. In our old popular poetry, but specially in our older proverbs, and in the familiar sayings of every day life, this grim humour is of frequent occurrence; but generally there is an air of geniality about it, and very seldom does it appear in an offensive or irreverent form. See Burns' Address to the Deil, and the following passage of later date.

It had been good for you and me,
Had mither Eve been sic a beauty,
She soon would garr'd *auld Saunders* flee
Back to his dungeon dark and sooty.
Alex. Rodger, Whistle Binkie, i. 127.

SANDS. To tak' the sands, to flee the country, seek safety in flight; Burns.

SANG, MY SANG, MA SANG. A veil'd oath; a corr. of the O. Fr. oath, *La Sangue*, or *La Sangue Dieu*. Addit. to SANG, q. v.
Delete the last para. of the entry in DICT. Jamieson was misled by his etym. of this term, which is a mere fancy.

SANGSTER, *s*. A songster, singer; also, a collection of songs or of song-tunes. V. SANG.
"*Oscen*, qui ore canit; a *sangster*, a singing foule shewing things to come;" Duncan's App. Etym., ed. Small, E.D.S.

SANNOCK, *s*. A dimin. of Sannie, Sandie, &c.; an abbreviation of Alexander.
An' L— remember singing *Sannock*,
Wi' hale breeks, saxpence, and a bannock.
Burns, Letter to James Tennant.

SAP, SAPP, *s*. A bunch, clump; the *sap*, a kind of bait used in eel-fishing, consisting of a number of worms strung on woollen yarn and formed into a bunch or clump; West of S. V. SOP.

To SAP, SAPP, *v. n*. To fish with the *sap*; part. pr. *sapping*.
This mode of fishing for eels is practised in salt water as well as fresh, and is still followed at the mouth of tidal rivers on the east coast of England. There also it is called by the same name *sapping*. V. Life of Frank Buckland, p. 217.
Sap is simply a form of *sop*, a round compact mass, from Icel. *soppr*, a ball; see under SOPPE.

SAP, SAUP, *s*. A quantity, lot: applied to liquids, and generally to liquor. West of S., Orkney.
These are prob. local forms of SOUP, SUP, q. v. The term generally implies a small quantity or lot, and is often used by persons wishing to extenuate the quantity of liquor they have consumed.

SAPE, *s*. Soap. V. SAIP.

SARGE, *s*. A taper; B. R. Aberd., I. 206, Sp. C. V. SERGE.

SARKIE, *s*. Dimin. of SARK, q. v.

SATOURE, *s*. Del. this entry in DICT., and see *Fatoure*.
Satoure is a misreading of *fatoure*, a deceiver; and all the editions of The Kingis Quair have this mistake, except the one by Prof. Skeat, which has *fatoure*. Sibbald reads *feator*, this also is wrong.

SAUCHTER, SAWSCHIR, *s*. Forms of *Sauser*, q. v. Errat. in DICT.
The meaning which Jamieson suggested for these forms is a mistake; so also is the etymology. And very probably *sauchter* is a miswriting or miswriting of *sauchier* or *saucher*. However, the meaning is simply *saucer*, figure or emblem of a saucer, a saucer-shaped cavity. V. *Sauser*.

To SAUCHTINE, *v. a*. To reconcile, make peace between. V. SAUCHT.
Dear laydy, yet thu succure me
And *sauchtine* me and thi sowne,
That I ma cume with hym to wyne
And bruk his blys.—
Barbour, Legends of the Saints.
A.-S. *saht*, reconciliation. The M. Eng. verb to reconcile was *sahtlen*, from A.-S. *sahtlian*. See under SAUCHT in DICT.

SAUDE, *part. pt.* Sewed, embroidered, ornamented.
Here sadel sette of that ilke
Saude with sambutes of silks.
Avent. Arthure, 2, 11, MS. Douce.
Misprinted *sande* in Pinkerton's version.
Sir F. Madden with hesitancy suggested "*served*" as the meaning of this term; but that it is simply a form of *sewed* (indeed, it represents a pron. that is still common), is confirmed by the reading of the Lincoln MS., which is—
Hir sadill semyde of that ilke
Semlely sewode with sylke.

SAUF, SAUFE, *adj*. Safe, secure; as, "in *sauf* keepin'." "Hir worschip *sauf*," her honour being kept safe; Kingis Quair, st. 143, ed. Skeat.

To SAUF, *v. a*. To save, preserve, keep safe, protect. Addit. to SAUF, *v*., q. v.

SAUFFER, SAULFFER, SAIFARE, SAW-SILVER, *s*. Salvage money; Register Priv. Council, VII. 148, 712, 721, 728, 744-5. V. SAFER, SAUGHE.

SAULLY, *v*. and *s*. V. *Sally*.

SAUNIE, SAWNIE, SAWNY, *s*. 1. Abbrev. for *Alexander*. V. SANDIE.

2. A ludicrous and familiar name for the devil. V. under *Sanders*.
She turns the key wi' cannie thraw,
An' owre the threshold ventures;
But first on *Sawnie* gies a ca',
Syne bauldly in she enters;
A ratton rattl'd up the wa',
An' she cry'd Lord preserve her!
An' ran thro' midden-hole an' a',
An' prayed wi' zeal an' fervour;
Fu' fast that night.
Burns, Halloween, st. 22.

To SAUNT, *v. n*. To varnish; Burns. V. SANT.

SAUSER, SAWSER, SASER, SUASER, SAUCHER, SAWSCHIR, *s*. The figure or emblem of a saucer; a saucer-shaped cavity on the top of the march-stones of the lands belonging to the city of Aberdeen, and called 'the town's mark.' The term is also used as an *adj*.
In perambulating the marches on 15th June, 1615, the party came to a place "quhair thay fand ane merche stane perfytelie merkit with the signe of the *sauser*, finding the same to be ane of the towne of

Aberdeines merches of propertie." Burgh Recs. Aberdeen, ii. 322, Sp. C. And having traced the old marchline through the greater part of its course, "and keip and the said aukle merche rod, stane be stane as thay ar merkit with the said signe of the *sauser* . . . till it come to ane great sauser stane merkit with twa *sausers*" (Ibid., p. 325), the party then turned eastward; and still tracing the boundary line they came to "merche stanes merkit with ane *sauser* and ane key," and also to "twa merche stanes merkit with Sanct Peiteris key," which marked the boundary "of auld betuixt the landis of Sanct Peteris hospitall and the said towne of Aberdeines landis." Ibid., p. 326. And soon afterwards the perambulation was completed.
Regarding the origin of this *sauser-merk*, or how it came to be adopted by the burgh, no information can now be obtained; but the following statement in explanation of the mark occurs in the Council Register of 6th May, 1580, in a record regarding the marches of a certain portion of the town-lands. It runs thus:—
"The first me. che of the saidis Justice Mylnis begynnis at the graye stane qubair it is pottit and ingranit the towns common merk vitht ane *sauser*, and awa calht the *sawser* stane, lyand in the burne betuixt the landis of the Justice Mylnis and the lands of Ferrihill."
The term is repeatedly used as an *adj.*, meaning of or with the saucer-mark, saucer-like; and sometimes in the sense of *saucered*, marked with the saucer-mark. Thus:—
". . . to the beid of the den of Murthill quhair thair is ane great *sauser* stane on the south syde of the myir at the heid of the said den; and fra the said marche stane," etc. Burgh Recs. Aberdeen, ii. 323, Sp. C.
". . . quhilk stane wes ordanit to be helpit in the *suaser* mark thairof." Ibid., p. 322.

To SAUSER, SAWSER, SASER, *v. a.* To cut a saucer-shaped mark on a block of wood or stone, to mark or engrave the figure of a saucer: part. pt. *sauserit, saserit,* marked with the figure of a saucer, as in the phrase, "ane *saserit* stane."
". . . quhair thair wes ane merche stane ordanit to be *sawserit* with the townes mark." Burgh Recs. Aberdeen, ii. 322.
A *saucer* was originally a vessel for sauce. O. Fr. *sauce*, from Lat. *salsa*, a thing salted.

SAUT, *s.* and *v.* Salt.

To SAUVE, SAUFE, SAU, SAW, *v. a.* To salve, anoint: also to alleviate, heal, cure.
This term occurs in various Scot. proverbs. "Save a' ye can: it will help to *sauve* a sair fit;" i.e., it will be a means of support in time of need.
"They wha freely set the deil
Hae little to *sau* the sairs o' eil'."
A.-S. *sealf*, ointment: Du. *zalf*: M.E. *salue*.

SAVORCOLL, SAVORCOIL, *s.* A woodcutter or sawyer, a forester; pl. *savorcollis savorcoilis.*
"Ordanis the thesaurer to pay four pundis monie to the agent of burrowis for persnte the werkmen in clachanis and *savorcoilis*; and it sall be allowit be the counsale." Charters of Stirling, Appendix ii. p. 219.
Gael, *sàbhair*, a sawyer or cutter, and *coille*, a wood, forest, or grove. V. M'Leod and Dewar.

SAVOUROUS, SAUOUROUS, SAUORUS, *adj.* Wholesome, nutritious. V. SAVOUR.

Mendis and medicine for all mennis neidis,
Help till hert and till hurt, helefull it was,
Vnder the circle solar thir *saumerous* sedis
Were nurist be dame Nature, that nobill maistres.
Houlate, l. 31, Bann, MS.
Asloan MS. has *sauorus*. In Pinkerton's version it was printed *sanourous*, which Jamieson rendered "healing, medicinal;" see DICT.

To SAW, SAU, *v. a.* To salve. V. *Sauve.*

To SAWE, *v. a.* To save, preserve.
I can nocht say suddanlie, so me Christ *sawe.*
Houlate, l. 120, Bann. MS.

SAWTE, SAWATE, *s.* Safety, protection.
"Euerie man sall bygge his dik sufficiant . . . for *sawate* of thair awin stufe." Burgh Recs. Prestwick, 1572, p. 73, Mait. C.

SAWSTER, *s.* A sausage, pudding. V. SASTER.
"*Farcimen,* a pudding, a *sawster;*" Duncan's App. Etym., ed. Small, E.D.S.

SAXEAR, *s.* A six-oared boat: short for Sixareen, q. v.
Dan. *sex*, six, and *aare*, an oar: Icel. *sex*, and *àr.*

SAXTER, *adj.* Of or belonging to a set or company of six; *saxter-aith,* the oath of a company of six compurgators.
". . . has failzeat quittance of the *saxter*-aith of the stowth of lynis the last zeir, and according to the lawis is decernit to quyte himself thairof this zeir with the twelter-aithe, and failzeing thairof to pay 12 markis and to underly the law thairof as stowtt." In the Lawting Court of theft of July 21, 1603, one is ordained to quit himself of theft by the twelter-aith, because the stowth is great; and another to quit himself of the same theft with the *saxter*-aith only, in respect of his minority. Peterkin's Notes on Orkn. and Shetl., Appendix, p. 35.
According to the old Norse law which ruled in Orkney and Shetland, if an accused person could not clear himself by his oath, which was called "*the lawryt-aith,*" he had to find six compurgators to quit him; and this was called "*the saxter-aith.*" If he failed in this oath, he had to go and find twelve compurgators; and this was called "*the twelter-aith.*"
Icel. *séttar-eithr,* the oath of a company of six compurgators: *séttar* being the gen. of *sétt,* a company of six, and *eithr,* an oath. V. Vigfusson's Icel. Dict. s. v. *Sétt.*

SAY, *s.* A bucket. V. DICT.
Scot. *say,* North of E. *so, soa,* and M. Eng. *soo,* are not derived from Fr. *seau,* as Jamieson has stated. They have come from Icel. *sár,* Swed. *så,* a cask. The final *r* in the Icel. word is merely the sign of the nom. case.
Fr. *seau* is regularly formed from L. Lat. *sitellus,* dimin. of Lat. *situla,* a bucket; and is therefore quite a different word.

SAYER, SEYER, SIRE, *s.* A gutter, drain; Burgh Recs. Glasgow, II., 54, 73, Rec. Soc. V. SIVER.

SCAIRTH, *adj.* V. DICT.
The etym. of this term is simply Icel. *skarth-r,* diminished, scanty.

SCALDRIE, *s.* Scolding, intemperate language. V. SCALD.

"Personis convict for flyting and *scaldrie* adjugeit to be govit on the croce quhill four afternone;" Burgh Recs. Edinburgh, 13th Jan., 1502-3, Rec. Soc.

SCALE, SCALE-DISH, SKEILLIE, *s.* A thin shallow vessel like a saucer used for skimming milk. V. SKAIL, s. 3.

SCANTLING, SCANTLIN, *adj.* Scant, scanty, very scanty.

Burns, in one of his letters to Clarinda, uses this term in the sense of *scanty, small;* but as generally used it is a dimin. of *scant,* and implies *very small, very scanty.*

SCAS, *s.* Del. this entry in DICT.

Scas is a misreading of *cast* in Pinkerton's version of Sir Gaw. and Sir Gal.

SCASHLE, *s.* Scuffle. V. SCUSHLE.

SCAUR, *adj.* Timorous, shy, shrinking. V. SCAR, SKAR.

And tho' yon lowin heugh's thy hame,
Thou travels far;
An' faith! thou's neither lag nor lame,
Nor blate nor *scaur.*
Burns, *Address to the Deil,* st. 3.

SCEBLES, *adj.* Knavish. V. *Skeblous.*

SCERLANE, *s.* A form of *skirling,* screaming; shouting, acclamation. V. SKIRL.

"Item, on the XV Apprill in anno a thousand vi hundred ane yeir, the Kingis Majestie cam to Perth, and that sam day he was made Provost, with ane great *scerlane* of the courteours, and the baneait was made at the crois, and the Kingis Maiistie was set down thereat," &c. Peacock's Annals of Perth, p. 597.

SCHAKELL, *s.* A fetter, bond, handcuff. V. *Shackle.*

To **SCHANK,** SCHONK, *v. n.* To go, depart, run, rush, gush: also, to snap, break, or give way at the shank or handle, as when a hammer or a spear breaks while in use; pret. and part. pt. *schankit, schonkit.* V. SCHANK *aff,* under SCHANK.

Thair speris in splendris sprent,
On scheldis *schonkit* and schent,
Euin our thair hedis went,
In field far away.
Gol. and Gawane, l. 619.

Wallace the formast in the byrneis bar;
The grounden aper thronch his body schar,
The shafft to *schonkit* off the fruschand tre:
Dewoydyde sone, sen na bettir mycht be.
Wallace, lii. 147.

A.-S. *sceacan,* to shake, also to run, flee, fly off: hence *sceanca, scanca,* the shank or lower part of the leg, lit. the runner, that by which the body is moved. Hence the shaft or handle of a hammer, a spear, &c., is called its shank.

SCHAP, *adj.* Skilled, learned, able, accomplished: "ane *schap* clerk," a learned scholar. V. SCHAPYN.

"It is avisit and thocht expedient be the commissaris of burrowis . . . that thar be direct ane *schap* clerk and twa burges merchandis of Iaesoun to the Archeduk of Austrie." Burgh Recs. Aberdeen, 1498, i. 67, Sp. C.

A.-S. *scapan, sceapan,* to shape, form; hence, to train, qualify: pp. *scapan, sceapen,* formed, qualified.

SCHAWIS, SCHEVIS, *s. pl.* Blocks or pulleys: "borrowit thair thre greit *schawis,*" borrowed their three great pulleys, i.e., their set of block and tackle; Accts. Burgh of Edinburgh, 1554-5. V. SCHAV.

SCHEAR, SCHEIR, *s.* The groin. V. SCHERE.

SCHED, *s.* A shade, shadow; "a *sched* but substance," a shadow without substance, a mere shadow; Rob Stene's Dream, p. 3, Mait. C.

SCHEDDIT, *pret.* Shed forth, shone, glowed; Pal. of Hon., Douglas, I. 71, 14, ed. Small.

SCHEIDIS, *s. pl.* Del. this entry in DICT.

Scheidis was simply a misprint for *scheildis* in Pinkerton's version of Gawan and Gol.: hence, Jamieson's explanation of the term is a mere fiction.

SCHEILLEN, SCHEILLING, SCHELLEN, *s.* Same as Shillin, q.v.; Burgh Recs. Prestwick, 1562, p. 66, Mait. C.

SCHENKIT, *part. pt.* Del. this entry in DICT.

This is a misreading of *schonkit* in Pinkerton's version: Jamieson's explanations are therefore useless.

To **SCHERE,** SCHEIR, *v. a.* To clip or dress cloth. Addit. to SCHERE, q. v.

SCHERAR, SCHEIRAR, *s.* A cloth-clipper, a bonnet-dresser.

". . . that in tyme to cum baith the craftis, viz. webstaris, wakeris and *scheraris,* in all tymes of processioun pas togedder and be incorporat vnder ane baner in als formis as thai pleis; . . . and the said *scheraris* and wakeris to pas vnder the banner of the wobstaris quhill thai may gudlie furnis thair awin, and the armys of the said *scheraris* and wakeris to be now put in the webstaris bannaris gif thai may be gudlie formit and gottin thairvntill." Burgh Recs. Edinburgh, 15th May, 1509, Rec. Soc.

Properly, *scherar* is short for *scherar of claith;* and in the Seal of Cause of the Walkers and Shearurs of Edinburgh, the craftsmen are so named:—"the masteris and craftismen of the Walkaris and *Scheraris of claith.*" Burgh Recs. Edinburgh, i. 80, Rec. Soc. About twenty years after the passing of this Seal of Cause, the Bonnetmakers were associated with them; no doubt because walking and shearing were necessary parts of their craft and manufactures; see same vol. p. 198.

SCHETE, SCHIT, *s.* A shoot or by-water of a mill. A.-S. *sceótan,* to shoot.

". . . for dailis to mend the *schete* of the Rude Milne with." Burgh Recs. Peebles, 1535, p. 221, Rec. Soc.

To SCHIRRYVE, *v. a.* A poet. form of *schryve*, to shrive, used by Dunbar in his Tabill of Confessioun, ll. 9, 18, Scot. Text Soc. ed.

This form represents a very common pron. of the word, and accounts for the form *schir* or *schire*, to shrive, which occurs in the Howard MS. version of this same piece, and is adopted in Dr. Laing's ed.; see l. 4. In the Maitland MS. it is *schryve*. However, *schir* may here mean *to share*, *skeir*, i.e., to pour off, separate, in the sense of to purge or cleanse. V. SCHIRE, *v.*

SCHONKIT, To-SHONKIT, *pret.* and *part. pt.* Snapped, broke, broken, gave way. V. *Schank.*

Del. the entry in Dict.

To SCHROUD, SCHRUED, SCHRYDE, *v. a.* To cover, protect, screen, ward off. V. SCHROUD, *s.*

Schruedede in a schorte cloke, that the rayne *schrydes.*
Awnt. Arthure, 2. 7.

A.-S. *scrúd*, garment, clothing; Dan. and Swed. *skrud*, dress, attire.

SCHYNBANDES, SCHYNBAWDES, *s. pl.* Greaves, armour for the legs; Awnt. Arthur, 31, 5.

This term is improperly defined in DICT. The *schynbaud* or *schynband* was a piece of armour for defence of the shank or lower part of the leg, and at first consisted of a single plate reaching from the knee to the front of the foot, and fastened by straps behind. It afterwards became a *jamb* or steel-boot, with a *solleret* or over-lapping plate for the foot. See Planché, British Costume, pp. 132, 150.

SCHYND, SCHOIND, SCHOWND, *s.* An inquest of Thingmen regarding the rights, claims, and settlement of heritage; Orkn. and Shetl.

Originally the finding of this court was given *viva voce*, but after the accession of the Scottish Jarls, it was generally by a Skynd-bref or Schynd Bill. V. Memorial for Orkney, p. 118.

Icel. *skyn*, understanding, judgment; Dan. *skjön*, judgment, estimate.

SCLADYNE, *s.* Errat. for SELADYNE. V. DICT.

So misprinted in Pinkerton's version; and the *seladynes* of MS. Douce is a clerical error for *selandynes*, q. v. The rendering of the term given by Jamieson is, however, correct.

SCLAVIN, SCLAUIN, *s.* A pilgrim's mantle; L. Lat. *sclavina*, O. Fr. *esclavine.*

Al his kingdom he forsoke,
Bot a *sclauin* he him toke;
He ne hadde kirtel no hode,
Schert no nother gode;
Bot his harp he tok algate,
And dede him barfot out atte zate.
Orfeo and Heurodis, l. 229.

To SCOB, *v. a.* To scoop out roughly; Burns. V. SCOB, *s.*

SCOGGERS, SCUGGERS, *s. pl.* Shanks or legs of old stockings used by countrymen to keep the snow out of their shoes. Same as HOGGERS, q. v.

SCOLE, SCOLLE, *s.* The skull, head, brain, understanding, ability. Icel. *skál*, bowl.

"*Thick o' the scolle*" is still used to express dull or slow of understanding : and "*his scolle's crackit*" implies that the person is of weak mind, or lacks in ability.

With mony a noble resoun, as him likit,
Enditing in his fairë latyne tong,
So full of truyte, and rethorikly pykit,
Quhich to declare my *scole* is ouer yong.
Kingis Quair, st. 7, ed. Skeat.

"Not 'school' as Tytler supposed. 'Cranium, *scolle* ;' Wright's Vocabularies, vol. i., p. 179, l. 5." Gloss., ed. Skeat.

To SCON, *v. a.* and *n.* V. DICT.

A more direct etym. for the term is A.-S. *scúnian*, to shun, originally to speed, scud along. From this word *scon* or *scoon* comes the word *schooner*. See Skeat's Etym. Dict.

SCONCE, *s.* The *link* or fixed seat by the side of the fire in the large open chimney of olden times.

SCONE. *The haly stane of Scone,* the coronation stone on which the kings of Scotland were crowned at Scone; Dunbar and Kennedy, l. 277.

This stone was taken from the Abbey of Scone by Edward I, and carried to England. It was placed in the Abbey of Westminster as an offering to Edward the Confessor ; and it is now placed under the coronation chair. See Tytler, Hist. Scot., vol. i. p. 47, ed. 1864.

To SCORE FLESH, SCOIR MUTTON. To make incisions in the breast or buttocks of an over-fed sheep, in order to improve the appearance of the flesh and to reduce its ramp flavour. V. under *Let doun,* s. 3.

"That all flescheouris bring thair flesche to the mercat croce, . . . and that thai blaw nane thairof, nor yet let it doune, nor *score it* under the pane of viij s. Burgh Recs. Peebles, 1555, p. 215, Rec. Soc.

"It is statute and ordanit that thair be na manner *scorit* on the bak nor na pairt thairof, nor yit lattin doun before, bot ane scoir owder befoir or behynd, wnder the pane of viij s. ilk falt." Burgh Recs. Glasgow, 1574, i. 26, Rec. Soc.

This barbarous practice was common all over the country, and was persisted in until comparatively modern times, in spite of all the efforts of the magistrates to put it down. When an over-fed sheep was about to be killed it was thus operated upon, and was then left to bleed slowly for some hours before it was put to death. In some cases salt was put into the wounds to further the process.

SCOSCHE, *s.* A drum. V. SWESCH.

"Item, ane perchement skyn to Robert Mair to cover the *scosche,* iij s. vj d." Burgh Recs. Glasgow, 1574, i. 455, Rec. Soc.

SCOTCH MILE, Scots Mile, s. One thousand nine hundred and eighty-four yards, or two hundred and twenty-four yards longer than an English mile.
While we sit bousing at the nappy,
An' getting fou and unco happy,
We think na on the lang Scots miles.
The mosses, waters, slaps, and stiles,
That lie between us and our hame.
Burns,·Tam o' Shanter.

SCOTINGABLE, Scotinyabil, adj. Lit., able to bear scotting or taxing, fit to be taxed; Burgh Recs. Peebles, 1457, p. 125, Rec. Soc. V. Scot, v.

SCOTTISWATH, s. V. Dict.
For Icel. *vad*, as given by Jamieson, read Icel. *vath*, a ford, and the explanation of the term becomes more simple and direct.

SCOUT-WATCH, Scout-Watche, s. A patrol.
"Ordaines a *scowt-watche* to be keipit nightlie, and that twa horsemen be sent owt, . . . and that ane of the scowtis ryd to David Heislope hows, and the vther scowt to ryd to Gladhows milne dayle, and report newes anent the motiown of the enemie." Burgh Recs. Peebles, 1650, p. 390, Rec. Soc.

SCOWIS, s. pl. Small wattles used in fixing thatch on the roof of a house; Burgh Recs. Edinburgh, I. 221. Addit to Scow, q. v.

SCRANNY, Scrankie, adj. Thin, meagre, wrinkled, withered, as applied to a person: "a *scranny* bit o' meat," a lean, scrappy, or indifferent piece. Addit. to Scranny, q. v.

SCRATTER, s. A coarse scrubber made of heather, used for cleaning pots, pans, &c. Orkn. V. Scrubber.

SCRAUT, Scrawt, s. and v. Scratch. V. Scrat.

SCREED, v. and s. V. Dict.
It is now generally accepted that this term is simply the Northern form of E. *shred*; cf. Sc. *reid* for E. *red*.

SCREIGH, Screech (ch gutt.), Skreigh, adj. Screechy, screeching, shrill, piercing. V. Screigh, v.
Still in common use; see quotation under *Skeer*. Irish *screach*, Gael. *sgreach*, Welsh *ysgrechian*, to shriek.

To SCREW, v. a. A term in golfing: same with *Draw*, q. v.

SCROTCHERTIS, s. pl. Sweatmeats: Burgh Recs. Glasgow, I. 454. V. Scorcheat.

SCROW, Skrow, s. A scroll. V. Dict.
The etym. of this term is O. Fr. *escroue*, "a scroll;" Cotgr. From Dutch *schroode*, a shred. See Skeat's Etym. Dict., s. v. *Scroll*.

SCRUBBS, s. pl. The husks of oats, barley, rye, &c. Orkn.

SCRY, Scrie, s. A great number; a crowd, multitude; West of S., Orkn. Same as Scrow, q. v.

SCUFF, Skuff, s. The nape or hinder part of the neck: also called *scruff*, and *cuff*, and frequently the *cuff o' the neck*, *scuff o' the neck*, or *scruff o' the neck*.
Wedgewood derives this term from Du. *schocht*, *schoft*, atlas, the nape of the neck; and he defines it as "applied to the loose skin on the shoulders by which one lays hold of a dog or a cat." But *scuff* and *scruff* as now used are merely varieties of *cuff* in the sense of flap, fold, or slack: and this idea is confirmed by the fact that the slack skin of the buttocks is also called the *cuff*, *scuff*, or *scruff* of that region.

SCUILL, Scuil, Scule, s. School.
These old forms of the word are common in our Burgh Records, and represent the common pronunciation.

SCULTY, adj. Naked. V. [Scuddy].

To SCUTCH, v. a. V. Dict.

Scutching-Knife, s. A bill-hook, a hedging-knife.

Scutchings, Scutchins, s. pl. Refuse lint or flax that remains after the process of scutching; waste tow.

2. Twigs, thistles, etc., that have been lopped by a scutcher; scrub.

SEA-REVER, Sea-Rewar, s. A sea-rover, pirate. V. Rever.
"*Pyrata*, a *sea-rewar*, a pyrate." Duncan's App. Etym., ed. Small, E.D.S.

SECK, Sek, s. Sack. Lat. *saccus*.
This term, while it has come to us from the Lat., is prob. of Egyptian origin: cf. Coptic *sok*, sack-cloth.

Seck-Claith, Sek-Cloth, s. Sack-cloth; Kingis Quair, st. 109, ed. Skeat.

SECONDER, adj. Secondary, second, of the second rank or grade; Blame of Kirkburiall, ch. 11; *secundare*, Burgh Recs. Edinburgh, I. 46, Rec. Soc.

SECRETEE, s. Secrecy. Lat. *secretus*.
And *secretee*, bir thrifty chamberere,
That besy was in tyme to do seruice.
Kingis Quair, st. 97, ed. Skeat.

SEE'D. 1. Represents a common pron. of *see it*; West of S.

2. A vulgar pret. of *see*: used only by the lowest classes; "I *see'd* him comin."

SEESTU, Seesta, Seestow, v. Seest thou.
These forms represent the old pron. which is still followed in some parts of the country.

SEGE, SAIG, SAIGE, s. Seat, i.e. stool, night-stool, closet, privy. Addit. to SEGE, q. v.

"And also that all maner of personis indwellares in this towne clenge all filth of saiges, and vther filth befor thair lugeings within three dayes heirafter," Burgh Recs. Edinburgh, 1521, i. 204, Rec. Soc.
"Ane stand-bed fixit in the wall of the said chalmer, weill bandeit, ane panttrie dure, and ane saig dure,"—Burgh Recs. Glasgow, 1589, i. 148, Rec. Soc.

SEGSTAR, s. A sexton; Burgh Recs. Aberdeen, i. 143, Sp. C.

SEIL, s. and v. V. SILE.

SEILL, s. The collar by which cattle are bound in the stall; Spald. Club Misc., I. 179. Hence binding cattle in the stall is called *seilling* them.

Icel. *seil*, A.-S. *sœl*, a rope, string.

SEINDILL, SEYNDILL, SENDILL, adv. Seldom; Alex. Scott's Poems, p. 87, Rolland, Court or Venus, ii. 156, S. T. S.

SEKE, adj. Sick; Kingis Quair, st. 58. V. SEIK.

SEKENESS, SEKNESSE, s. Sickness; Ibid, st. 111.

SELANDYNE, s. A chalcedony; Awnt. Arth. 2, 9, MS. Douce.

SELL'D, SELL'T, pret. and part. pt. Sold, did sell.

My plengh is now thy bairn-time a':
Four gallant brutes as e'er did draw;
Forbye sax mae, I've *sell't* awa,
That thou hast nurst:
They drew me thretteen pund an' twa,
The verra warst.
Burns, The Farmer to his Mair Maggie.

SELLET - OIL, SELLETT - OYLE, s. V. *Sallat-Oil.*

SELOUR, SELOURE, SELURE, SEILOUR, s. A canopy; Gawan and Gol., 66. V. SYLOUR, SILLER.

SELY, adj. 1. Seasonable; Kingis Quair, st. 185, ed. Skeat.

2. Innocent, simple; Ibid, st. 134.

Addit. to SEILY and SELY, q. v.

A.-S. *sælig*, timely, seasonable.

To SEMBLE, v. n. To join battle, to fight. Addit. to SEMBLE, q. v.

Now, bot I *semble* for thi saull with Sarazenis mycht, Sall I neuer sene be into Scotland.
Houlate, l. 484, Asloan MS.

SEMLABILL, adj. Similar, like; Burgh Recs. Peebles, 1568, p. 73, Rec. Soc. V. SEMEIBLE.

The form *Semeible*, quoted by Jamieson, is prob. a mistake for *Semlible*, the transcriber having misread a short *l* as an *e*. See under *Sameabill.*

To SEN, v. a. To send, grant, bestow.

Unto the Cok in mynd he said, "God *sen*
That I and thow wer fairlie in my den."
Henryson, Chantecleir and Fox, l. 160.

SEN, s. V. DICT.

This is prob. a misprint for *fen*, mud, filth, which is the reading in the Elphynstoun MS.: see Small's ed. of Douglas, Vol. ii., p. 132.

SENACHIE, SCHENACHY, CHENACHY, s. A reciter of stories, an orator; a recorder, annalist, genealogist: *chenachy*, Houlate, l. 803, Bann. MS.

"At the grave the orator or *senachie* pronounced the panegyric of the defunct, every period being confirmed by a yell of the coronach." Smollet, Humphry Clinker, Letter of Sept. 3.

Gael. *seanachaidh*, a reciter of tales or stories, an historian, genealogist: from *seanachas*, story or event of the past, comp. of *sean*, old, and *cùis*, matter, affair. V. M'Leod and Dewar.

SENCE, s. Incense. This is the O. E. form given in Prompt. Parv. V. SENS.

" Wyth sowne of clarioun, organe, song and *sence*
For the atonis, Lord, Welcum all we cry.
Dunbar, Welcum to Lord B. Stewart, l. 22.

SENDAL, SENDALE, SANDILL, s. Fine silk; Awnt. Arth., 30, 9; *sandeill*, Burgh Recs. Aberdeen, I. 234, Sp. C. Also written *cendal.*

SENSES, s. pl. Faculties, wit, mind, judgment; "out of one's *senses*," deranged, mad; "one's *senses* are in a creel," i.e., where and how they ought not to be, hence, bereft of one's senses, mad, foolish, stupid; another form of this expression is, "one's head is in a creel."

My senses wad be in a creel,
Should I but dare a hope to speel,
Wi' Allan, or wi Gilbertfield,
The braes o' fame;
Or Ferguson, the writer-chiel,
A deathless name.
Burns, to W. Simson, Ochiltree.

SENTENCE, s. Opinion, judgment; Kingis Quair, st. 149, ed. Skeat. Addit. to [SENTENS], q. v.

O. Fr. *sentence*, a sentence, pithy saying, opinion, judgment; from Lat. *sententia*, a way of thinking, formed from Lat. *sentire*, to feel, think.

SENTRICE, s. pl. Centres or cooms: the wooden frames used by builders in constructing arches, vaulting, etc. Errat. in DICT.

The defin. suggested by Jamieson is altogether wrong, and unwarranted by the record from which his quotation is taken. It runs thus:—
". . . Gelis Monro and his compleois tuk on hand to vpbauc (i.e., upheave, hoist into position) the

sentrice of the brig quhilk the spait haid brocht dovne incontineut, quhow sone he mycht gudly, for ane France crovne of gold promest to him; and in the said Gelis defalt the said *sentrice* ar broking, spylt, and away to the see haid in gret skayth and damag of that noble wark: the quhilk skayth extendis to ane hundreth pundis." Burgh Recs. Aberdeen, i. 105, Sp.C.
See also *Centers, Centreis,* and the passages there referred to in Vol. ii.

SEQUELS, *s. pl.* Lit. followers: applied to the children of neyfs or serfs, and to the young of animals. Addit. to SEQUELS.

"*Cum nativis et eorum sequelis* means exactly with neyfs and their followers, just as a horse-dealer now sells a mare with her followers. It implies a transfer of the property of the whole descendants of the neyf for ever." Cosmo Innes, Legal Antiq., p. 51.

To SER, SAIR, *v. a.* 1. To serve, supply: pret. and part. pt. *serd, saird*: "Dail sma', and *sair* a'," i.e., divide into small portions in order to serve the whole company.

2. To be of use, profit, or advantage.

If honest nature made ye fools,
What *sairs* your grammars?
Ye'd better taen up spades and shools,
Or knappin hammers.
Burns, *Ep. to Lapraik*, st. 11.

To SER *out*, SAIR *out, v. a.* To deal, divide, deal out; as, "to *ser out* the puir-siller;" also, to complete, fulfil; as, "The prentice maun *ser out* his time."

SERIN, SAIRIN, *s.* Service, supply, portion, dole; as, "He helps himsell; he neer waits for a *serin*."

SERVIT, *v. pret.* Deserved, was justly liable; Dunbar, Tabill of Confessioun, l. 22. V. SERVE.

SESS, *s.* and *v.* Cess, stent, tax; short for *assess*.

Lat. *ossessus*, pp. of *assidere*, to sit beside; whence *assessor,* one who sat beside the judge and fixed the taxes: from that term was formed the verb to *assess*. V. Skeat's Etym. Dict.

To SET, *v. n.* 1. To face in a dance.

The piper loud and louder blew;
The dancers quick and quicker flew;
They reel'd, they *set,* they cross'd, they cleekit,
Till ilka carlin swat and reekit.
Burns, *Tam o' Shanter*.

2. Short for to *set off,* i.e., slip off, go away.

A countra Laird had ta'en the batts,
Or some curmurring in his guts,
His only son for Hornbook *sets,*
An' pays him well.
The lad, for twa guid gimmer-pets,
Was Laird himsel.
Burns, *Death and Doctor Hornbook*.

SET, *part. pt.* Bent, warped: as applied to wood not properly seasoned.

SET, *s.* A twist or warp.
(Sup.)   D 2

SETS-YE-WEEL. It becomes you well: generally used in a taunting or ironical sense. V. SET, s. 8.

SETTEN, *part. pt.* Set.
This old part. form is still used by the common people; and a few other verbs also retain it, such as *hit, let, put,* &c.

SETTEN-ON, *adj.* Short in growth, stunted, ill-thriven; "He a wee *setten-on* body." V. SET-ON, [Sitten].
All the words and phrases of the foregoing group are common in various parts of the North of England also.

SETOLER, SOTELER, *s.* A player on the citole: Awnt. Arth., 27, 5.

SETTEEN, *s.* A weight. V. SETTING.
Icel. *sáttungr,* a sixth part; being the sixth of a *meil*.

SETTER, *s.* The infield pasture of a *tun* or farm; Orkn. Addit. to SETER, and STER.
Icel. *sætr, setr,* a seat, residence: also, mountain pastures, dairy lands; Vigfusson.

SET UPON SEVIN, SET ON SEVIN. In most cases this expression is spoken of God in allusion to the work of creation; *set* having the meaning of dispose or set in order, as in Pystyl of Susan, xxi. 4, Gol. and Gawan, l. 1045. But sometimes it means to attack, encounter, or meet in battle, as in Gol. and Gawan, l. 668.

I swere be suthfast God that *settis all on sevin*.
Gol. and Gawan, 81, 8.

For thair is aegis in yon saill wil *set vpone sevn,*
Or they be wrangit, I wis, I warne you ilk wy.
Ibid., 40, 3.

In the Towneley Mysteries, pp. 85, 97, 118, the expression occurs in the first sense; and in Mort Arthur, fol. 75b, it occurs in the second. In this latter sense it means to strive to the uttermost, fight or work with all one's might.

SEUTE, *part. adj.* Run out, used up, set aside, out of use; lit. waiting on, kept waiting.

"Ordanis the Vanelaw [a common] to be proclamit waist, *seute,* and banyng," i.e., empty or not in use, close-cropt or run out, and under protection or preservation; Burgh Recs. Peebles, 1571, p. 326, Rec. Soc.
O. Fr. *suite,* in the sense of *in suite,* in waiting, kept waiting; other forms of *suite* are *seute, siute, site*. V. Burguy.

To SEW, SUE, *v. a.* and *n.* To follow, pursue; Awnt. Arth., 6, 2; Kingis Quair, p. 54, l. 4, ed. Skeat.

To SEW, *v. a.* To show, describe, relate.
Now gifs I sall *sew*
The ordour of thair armes, it wer to tell teir.
Houlate, l. 577, Bann. MS.

SEYER, *s.* A gutter, drain. V. *Sayer*.

SEYNDILL, *adv.* Seldom. V. SEINDILL.

To SEYNE, *v. a.* To say, declare, utter; Kingis Quair, st. 27, 38, 42, 98, ed. Skeat.

SEYNITY. Del. this entry in Dict.
As the term is a misprint for *seymly*, the explanatory note is useless.

SHACKLE, SCHAKELL, SCHAKYL, *s.* 1. In the sing. This term means the wrist, as in *shackle-bane*, the wrist-bone, wrist-joint; it is also applied to the ankle or ankle-joint.

2. In the pl. it has the same meanings as in Eng. viz. bonds, fetters, connections; but it is most generally applied to fetters for the wrists and ankles, handcuffs, anklets.
In s. 1. the term is common in the north of Eng. also; see Gloss. of Brockett, Atkinson, Peacock.
In all the meanings of this term two ideas are implied, movement or immovableness, and coupling or connection.
" A.-S. *sceacul*, bond, fetter; Icel. *skökul*, pole of a carriage, from *skaka*; Swed. *shakel*, loose shaft of a carriage; Dan. *skagle*, the same." Skeat.

SHAIRD, *s.* Shred, shard, portion, fragment. V. SHARD.
An' when the auld moon's gaun to lea'e them,
The hindmost *shaird* they'll fetch it wi' them,
Just i' their pouch.
Burns, Ep. to Will. Simpson.

SHANDY, SHANNIE, *adj.* Backward, shy; also, wanting in vigour, push, or energy. For the first sense the synon. is *blate*: for the second, *feckless*. V. SHAN, SHAND.

SHANGY, SHANGIE, *s.* A loop of gut or hide round the mast of a boat into which the lower end of the sprit is slipped; Orkn. Addit. to SHANGAN, q. v.

SHANK, SHANKS, *s.* Short for *Noonshanks*, q. v.

SHANNA. Frequently so written, but properly *sha' na*, shall not.
Similarly *winna*, will not; *dinna*, do not—the *do* being pronounced *di*, with short *i*, as in divide; *minna*, may not—the *may* being pron. *mi*, with short *i*. These have probably been formed in imitation of *canna*, can not, *manna*, man (i.e. must) not.

To SHAP, SHAPE, *v. n.* To begin or set about anything; as, " He shaps to his work like a man ;" to seem, appear, promise: as, " It *shapes* weel to grow a guid beast;" also, to fit, be adapted; as, " The naig 'll *shap* better for the cart nor the plow."

SHAPIN-BROD, SCHAIPING-BUIRD, *s.* A smooth flat board on which a tailor, or a shoemaker, shapes his materials; Burgh Recs. Aberdeen, I. 176, Sp. C.

To SHARGE, SHARG, *v. a.* To sharpen, grind, face.

"That nane *sharge* spaidis nor worklowmes vpon the brig-stanes vnder the pane of xl s. toties quoties." Burgh Recs. Peebles, 1622, p. 361, Rec. Soc.
This word, which is still in use, is prob. a corruption of E. *sharp*. It may, however, be a softened form of E. *shark*. *shark* used iu the sense to sharpen. Similarly a *sharper* is called a *shark*.

To SHAVE, SHAVE, *v. a.* To gall, fret, or ruffle the skin; part. *shaving;* pret. and part. pt. *shaved;* as in wind-*shaved*.

SHAVED, *adj.* Galled, fretted.

SHAVING, SHAUING, *s.* A shaving, fretting, or ruffling of the skin.
" *Intertrigo*, galling, or shauing ;" Duncan's App. Etym., ed. Small, E.D.S.

SHEAL, SCHELE, *s.* V. DICT.
A much simpler and more direct etym. for this term is Icel. *skyli*, *skilli*, *skjól*, shelter, cover; Dan. and Swed. *skjul*. That it is allied to Swiss *chalet*, however, is a mistake; that word is from Lat. *casa*. Nor is it allied to Icel. *sael*; nor to A.-S. *saeld*. V. Skeat's Etym. Dict.

SHEERMEN, SHEARMEN, *s.* Properly and originally cloth-clippers, cloth-dressers; but latterly cloth-workers, including all the crafts engaged in dyeing, fulling, dressing, and finishing cloth. Addit. to SHEERMEN, q. v.
The combination of these crafts, which the general term *sheermen* implies, must have been accomplished gradually; but it appears to have been completed all over the country before the middle of the sixteenth century. In Edinburgh the walkers and shearers of cloth obtained their Seal of Cause from the Magistrates in 1500; and in 1520 the *bonnetmakers* were included, and a new Seal of Cause was obtained in ratification of the contract. From that time the term Shearmen began to be used as a general name for the various crafts so grouped. In the same way the term Hammermen included smiths, wrights, masons, coopers, slaters, goldsmiths and armourers. And these general terms were rapidly brought into use through the proclamations and arrangements that had to be made in connection with the processions and pageants of the crafts at the great popular festivals of Candlemas and Corpus Christi. See Burgh Recs. Edinburgh. i. 80, 198, Rec. Soc., and B. R. Aberdeen, i. 450, Sp. C.

SHEET-MAKER, SCHEIT-MAKAR, *s.* A maker of sheet-iron.
" The baillies hais assignet this day xv days to the dekin and craftismen of the hammermen to prefe gife *scheit makaris* scottis and lottis with thar craft in uder borouis,—that is to say in Edinburgh, Dunde, Glasgow, Sanctiohentoun, or in Abirdene." Burgh Recs. Stirling, 17 Feb. 1521-2.

SHEKYLS, SHAKERS, *s.* A name for ague: also called " the trinles," i.e., the trembles; but the latter term is mostly used in reference to sheep.
Shekyls is not an uncommon term in M. E., as is shown by its use in the Town. Myst., p. 99.

SHEUK, *pret.* Shook, did shake.
He ended ; and the kebars *sheuk*
Aboon the chorus roar ;

SHE [219] SIN

While frighted rattons backward leuk,
And seek the benmost bore.
Burns, Jolly Beggars.

SHEW, *pret.* Showed, did show; stated, explained.

". . . yet the necessitie was neuer absolute, as we *shew* before." Blame of Kirkburiall, ch. 19.

To SHEYL, SHYLE, *v. n.* V. DICT.

A.-S. *sceol*, squint, as in *scēol-edge*, squint-eyed. Cf. *shyle*, and *skelly*.

SHIEL, SCHIEL, SHIELIN, SHEELIN, *s.* A hut, shed, &c. V. SHEAL.

To SHILL, SHOOL, *v. a.* To take the husks off seeds. V. SHEAL.

SHIP-POUND, SCHIP-PUND, *s.* The old standard weight of a barrel bulk in shipping; it contained sixteen and a half stones Troy, or 264 lbs.

"Ilk Barrel [i.e., skipper's barrel] being of weicht ane *schip pund*."
"Ane *schip pound* conteinis sexteene stanes and ane halfe of Scottish Trois weicht."
"Ilk Trois stane conteinis sexteene pound Trois." Skene, De Verb. Sign.

SHIP-RAE, SHIP-RAA, *s.* A sail-yard, the yard of a ship. V. RA, RAY.

"*Antenna*, a *ship-rae;*" Duncan's App. Etym., ed. Small, E.D.S.

SHIP-RAID, SCHIP-RADE, SCHIP-REDE, *s.* A road or haven for ships; Leslie's Hist. Scot., p. 8, 127, S.T.S.

To SHIRE, *v. a.* To pour off. V. SCHIRE, SHARE.

SHOK, SCHOK, *s.* A piece or roll of cloth containing twenty-eight ells.

"Poldaveis the *shok* conteuing xxviii. elnis."
Halyburton's Ledger, p. 318.

SHONE, *s.* A form of *Schynd*, q. v.

". . to be at the Arffhows . . betwixt this and All-hallow-evin next eftir the dait of this present writ, to mak ane lauchfull *shone* and ayrfkest, as law levis." Grievances of Orkney, Append. II.

SHOPE, *pret.* Shaped. V. SHOOP.

SHORT-AIND, SHORT-AINDED, SHORT-ENDED, *adj.* Short of breath, short-winded.

"*Anhelus*, pursie, or *short-ended;*" Duncan's App. Etym., ed. Small, E.D.S.

SHOT, *s.* Share, proportion; as, "He plans ay to get the lucky *shot,*" i.e., the best share: also, each man's share of the *lawin* or score at a tavern.

A.-S. *scot*, shot, payment; Icel. *skattr*, Dan. *skat*, tribute, tax. *Skatt*, an old Danish tax is still paid in Shetland. V. under SKAT, SKATT.

SHREW, *s.* V. DICT.

Jamieson's long and learned note on this term is altogether misleading. The word *shrew* has been clearly traced through M. E. *shrewe* to A.-S. *scredwa*, a shrew mouse: lit. *biter*. And all the various senses in which the term has been used, even the worst of them, are easily accounted for by the very old fable regarding the shrew-mouse, that it had an exceedingly venomous bite.

SHRO, SCHRO, *s.* A shrewmouse.

"*Sorex*, a rotton, a *schro;*" Duncan's App. Etym., ed. Small, E.D.S.

To SHUG, *v. n.* To shake; part. pr. *shuggin, shug-shuggin*, frequently or continuously shaking; Whistle Binkie, ii. 226, 316. V. SHOG.

To SHUGGLE, SHOOGLE, *v. a.* and *n.* Freq. of *shug, shoog*: to shake rapidly or easily, to make a rattling noise by shaking. Addit. to SHUGGLE, q. v.

The moon has rowed her in a cloud.
Stravagin win's begin
To *shuggle* and daud the win/low-brods,
Like loons that would be in.
William Miller, Gree, Bairnies, Gree, st. i.

SIBOW, SYBOW, *s.* An onion. V. SEIBOW.

O. Fr. *scipoulle* (Cotgr.), Ital. *cipolla*, an onion; M. E. *chebole;* all from Lat. *cæpe*, dimin. *cæpulla*.

To SIDDER, *v. a.* To sunder, separate; a corr. of *sinder;* Alex. Scott's Poems, p. 25, ed. 1882.

SIDESMAN, *s.* An umpire, referee. Addit. to SYDESMAN.

SIDE-WIPE, *s.* An indirect, covert, or sly rebuke: a remark implying blame or reproof of a person, and spoken not to him but so that he may hear it.

SIESTER-PEN, *s.* The plectrum or quill used for striking the sistrum. V. SEISTAR.

"*Plectron*, a fiddle-stick, or a *siester*-pen;" Duncan's App. Etym., ed. Small, E.D.S.

SIFE, *s.* A sifting-cloth, sieve. V. SIV.

"*Excerniculum*, a *sife* or boulte-claith;" Duncan's App. Etym., ed. Small, E.D.S.

SILVER-SEIK, *adj.* Moneyless, without funds: also used by Henryson as a *s.* in the sense of one whose money is yet to seek.

Sen I am stewart, I wald we had sum stuff,
And ye ar *silver-seik*, I wait richt weill;
Thocht we wald thig, yone verray churlische chuff,
He wald nocht gif us ane hering of his creill,
Befoir yone churle on kneis thocht we wald kneill.
Henryson, Wolf, Foxe, and Cadgear, 1. 86.

SINDLE, SINNLE, *adj.* and *adv.* Rare, rarely, seldom. V. SEINDLE.

SINGT, SINGET, SINGIT, *part. pt.* Singed. V. SING.

SINGULAR, *adj.* Single, individual, certain.

"Again, of the peculiar sort, sum ar proper to *singular* persons only, and others to mo, yet being of one sort or family." Blame of Kirkburiall, ch. 8.

SIPERS, *s.* Fine crape: so called because it was originally made in Cyprus; Rates of Customs, 1612, Halyburton's Ledger, p. 328.
Of the various kinds of crape then used the most valuable were the *curl sipers, silk sipers,* and *scum sipers,* noted in Rates of Customs of 1612.

SIRE, SYOUR, *s.* A gutter, drain; Burgh Recs. Glasgow, II. 128, Rec. Soc. V. SIVER.

SIRFOOTFEATS, *s. pl.* Fragments left after a banquet or feast, scraps of delicacies.
". . . wine drunk in abundance, glasses broken, *sirfootfeats* casten abroad on the causey, gather whaso please." Rejoicings in Aberdeen, 26 June, 1597. V. Reg. Priv. Council, v. 67, Intro.
O. Fr. *sorfait,* excess, and *fait, faict,* a part, portion, article; *sorfait* having come from Lat. *super* and *facere.*

SISTIR, *s.* The zither. V. SEISTAR.

SIT, SITT, *s.* Pain, ailment. Addit. to SITE, q. v.
Icel. *sút,* pain, suffering.

To SIT, *v. n.* To fit, suit, become. "It *sits* ye weel," is said ironically of a person who attempts what is beyond his power or position. *Set* is used with the same meaning.

To SIT *down on one's knees.* To kneel or bow as a suppliant, to humble oneself in the dust, to assume the posture of contrition and supplication.
This was the first act, which offenders against the law had to perform in doing penance publicly in the parish church, as the following record duly sets forth. In Aberdeen, in the year 1555, John Sandris and his wife were, after due trial, found guilty of "strublens, stryking, and bluiddrawing of Thomas Gellane and his wyfe;" and having been duly bound over to keep the peace, "the baillies modifiit the amends of the said strublens as after following: that is to say thai ordanit the said John and his spous foresaid to pay to the said Thomas Gellane xx s. Scottis, and to pay for the barbour for the mending and curing of his woundis, within vilj dayse; and alse to com on Sonday nixt cuming to Sanct Nicholase parroche kirk, in the queir thereof, in the tyme of hie mess, with ane candill of wax in euerie ane of thair handis, and thair *to sit doune on thair kneis* in presens of the said Thomas and his wyf forgifnes: and gif euer thai be conuickit for siclyk in tyme cumyng, to pay tene markis to be applyit to Sanct Nicholace wark onforgewin." Burgh Recs. Aberdeen, i. 282, 8p.C.
For similar records see Burgh Recs. Aberdeen, i. 27, Burgh Recs. Glasgow, i. 149.

To SIT *on one's knees.* To kneel, remain kneeling, as in prayer.

To SIT *summons.* To sit still when called, to disregard a call or summons, to neglect or disobey orders.
The gude wyfe [was] glaid with the gle to begin, For durst scho neuer *sit summoundis* that scho hard him say.
Rauf Coilyear, l. 99.

SITHOL, SITHILL, *s.* V. CITHOL.

SITTLENESS, *s.* Subtilty; Alex. Scott's Poems, p. 76, ed. 1882. V. [SITTIL].

To SIVE, *v. n.* To drain. V. SIPE.

SKAINYA, *s.* Packthread. V. SKEENGIE.

SKAIRNES, *s.* Scantness, scarcity. V. [SKAIR, *v.*], and SKAIRTH, *adj.*
". . . that the tries [barrels] wer nocht to the extreme quantitie becaus of penuritie and *skairnes* of tymer." Burgh Recs. of Glasgow, i. 153, Rec. Soc.
A.-S. *sceran,* to shear, cut, diminish; Icel. *skera,* Dan. *skære,* Sw. *skära,* to shear, cut short.

SKARCH, *s.* A form of *skars,* an opening between rocks; Burgh Recs. Peebles, 1470, p. 1. 165, Rec. Soc. V. SKAIRS.

SKEBLOUS, SCEBLES, *adj.* Rascally, evil-disposed. V. SKEBEL.
"And everie begger, vagaboun, ydel and *scebles* men and wemen." Burgh Recs. Glasgow, i. 359, Rec. Soc.

SKEER, *adj.* Exciting, rousing, wild. Addit. to SKEER, q. v.
It's no the little thing sae screech and *skeer,* That drunken fiddlers play in barns and booths, But the big saucy fiddle that sae soothes The speerit into holiness and calm, That e'en some kirks hae thocht it mends the psalm.
R. Leighton, Dapteesement o' the Bairn.

SKELLUM, *s.* A worthless fellow, ne'er-do-well. V. SCHELLUM.
She tauld thee weel thou was a *skellum,* A blethering, blustering, drunken blellum; That fra November till October, Ae market-day thou was nae sober.
Burns, Tam o' Shanter.
Du. *schelm,* Swed. *skälm,* rogue, knave, villain. We got this word from the Netherlands early in the seventeenth century.

SKELPIE, *adj.* Lit. fit or deserving to be *skelped* or whipped; an opprobrious term generally applied to a girl. Addit. to SKELPIE, q. v.
This term is often used as a *s.*

SKELPIE-LIMMER, *s.* A mischief-worker that deserves to be *skelped;* an extended form of *skelpie,* but more particular and opprobrious.
This term is generally misunderstood; and it has been misinterpreted and misapplied by various writers on Burns. Jamieson defined it as "an opprobrious term applied to a female:" which, though not absolutely wrong, is certainly a vague explanation. Others have interpreted it as "a mischievous or violent woman;" and Dr. Mackay, in his "Poetry and Humour of the Scottish Language," has explained it as "a violent woman ready both with hands and tongue." Now for obvious reasons these meanings are absurd; and chiefly because the term, if properly used, cannot be applied to a woman at all, for she is too old to be subjected to the chastisement of *skelping,* which the term implies. Besides, as used by Burns, the term was

certainly applied to a young girl, a mere child, whom he calls "*wee Jennie*," who pled for the presence and protection of her grandmother in the daring adventure which she proposed. To such an one the epithet *skelpie-limmer*, mischief-worker deserving to be *skelped*, was most appropriate ; and that she was such an one, and not a woman, will be evident to every one who reads the passage with ordinary intelligence.

Wee Jennie to her grannie says,
 Will ye go wi' me, Grannie !
I'll cat the apple at the glass,
 I gat frae uncle Johnie."
She fufl't her pipe wi' sic a lunt,
 In wrath she was sae vap'rin.
She notic't na, an aizle brunt
 Her braw new worset apron
  Out thro' that night.
"Ye little *skelpie-limmer's* face !
 I daur you try sic sportin,
As seek the foul Thief onie place,
 For him to spae your fortune."
  Burns, Halloween, st. 14.

Both *skelpie* and *skelpie-limmer* are still in use in the West of S.; but they are applied only to young people, and mostly to girls.

SKEMLER, *s.* An attendant, a lacquey. Addit. to SKAMBLER, q. v.

SKEMLIS, *s. pl.* V. SKAMBLE.

SKILLET-BELL, *s.* V. SKELLAT.

SKINKING, *adj.* Thin, liquid, and much boiled ; *skinking-ware*, liquid food, as soups, etc. V. SKINK.

Auld Scotland wants nae *skinking* ware,
 That jaups in luggies ;
But if yo wish her gratefu' prayer,
 Gie her a Haggis.
  Burns, To a Haggis, st. 8.

To SKINK, SKYNK, *v. a.* To give or hand over, to add over and above, make a present of. Addit. to SKINK, q. v.

". . . thai sall content and pay to him ten li. . . . at the compleiting, ending, and vpsetting of the auld ruf, . . . and vpoun his gude warkmane- schip and gyding thai *skynk* him the tymmer of the auld ruf." Burgh Recs. Edinburgh, 30 Sept., 1508, I. 117, Rec. Soc.

To SKLENT, *v. a.* To utter or give forth indirectly, to speak at one in a spiteful or sarcastic manner. Addit. to SKLENT, q. v.

D'ye mind that day, when in a bizz,
Wl' reekit duds an' reestit gizz,
Ye did present your smoutie phiz,
 'Mang better folk.
An' *sklented* on the man of Uzz
 Your spitefu' joke.
  Burns, Address to the Deil.

SKONSCHON, *s.* Scoinson or escoinson ; the interior edge of a window side or jamb. See Gloss. Archit. Terms.

"The dores and chimnayis to be marbillit, and the pend of the windowes and *skonschonis* to be weill layit over with ane blew gray." Acct. for Painting in Stirling Castle, 1628, Mait. Club Misc., iii. 372.
O. Fr. *escons*, hidden, covered, pp. of *esconser*, to hide, conceal ; from Lat. *abscondere*.

To SKOOG, SCOOG, *v. a.* and *n.* V. SKOOK.

SKOOGIT, SCOOGIT, *part.* and *adj.* Concealed, sheltered, shaded.

Now here comes Forgan manse amang the trees,
A cozie spot, weel *skoogit* frae the breeze.
 R. Leighton, Bapteesement o' the Bairn.

SKOUGH, *v.* and *s.* Shelter. V. SKOOK, SKUG.

SKREIGH, SKREECH (*ch* gutt), SCREECH, *adj.* Screeching, shrill, piercing. V. *Screigh.*

To SKRIP, SKRIPE, SKRAP, SKROP, *v. a.* To mock ; Houlate, l. 67. V. SKIRP, SCORP.

The Bann. MS. has *skirp* ; the Asloan, *skripe.*

To SKRYM, SKRYME, *v. n.* To rush, dash, make a feint at ; Houlate, l. 67. Asloan MS. V. SKYRME.

O. Fr. *escrimer*, to fence, fight ; from O. H. Germ. *scirman*, to skirmish.

SLABBER, SLUBBER, *s.* The slop or mud of roads in wet weather: also, the slush or half-melted snow on roads when a thaw sets in.

SLABBY, *adj.* Same as SLABBERY, q. v.

SLACK, *s.* A soft or slimy place ; Sempill Ballates, p. 117. Addit. to SLACK, q. v.

SLAID, *s.* A sledge. V. *Sled.*

To SLALK, *v. n.* V. DICT.

This is a MS. form due to the scribe writing (by way of contraction), *kk* so as to resemble *lk*. There is no such word. It should be *slakk*, rhyming with *wakk* of the previous line.
This method of contracting the writing of double long-letters was fully explained by Prof. Skeat in his Address to the Philological Society in 1896.

To SLAMB, SLAM, *v. a.* To smear, as with lard or ointment: part. pt. *slamd, slamb, slam.*

With coistly furis, lucive and sabile,
With stanis and perle innumerable ;
All gold begaine, a glorius growme,
Slamb ouer with faird and fyne perfwme.
  Rob Stene's Dream, p. 4.

SLAP, *adv.* Suddenly, unawares, unexpectedly : an imitative word, implying sudden appearance or change, as if at a slap or clap of the hand.

O let us not, like snarling tykes,
 In wrangling be divided ;
Till, *slap*, come in an unco loon,
 And with a rung decide it.
  Burns, The Dumfries Volunteers, st. 2.

To SLATE, *v. a.* To set on, hound, incite. Addit. to SLATE, q. v.

"To *slate*" implies more than "to let loose," as given by Jamieson. Comparison of the passage quoted will confirm this.
The etym. is not Icel. *slaeda*, but A.-S. *slatan*, to set

dogs on a bull or other animal, and hence, to hound, incite. See Ælfric's Lives of the Saints, ed. Skeat, vol. i. p. 266, l. 72.

SLAUCHTER, *adj.* For slaughter, to be killed for food.
"Ilk *slauchter* kow passing langis the brig . . ., tua pennies; and ilk fyve sheep cuming they wyes, tua pennies." Burgh Recs. Stirling, 1612, p. 132.

SLED, SLEAD, SLAID, *s.* A sledge: a low cart without wheels used for the carriage of goods.
"*Trahea*, a *slead*." Duncan's Appendix Etym., ed. Small, E.D.S.
Icel. *slethi*, Dan. *slæde*, Sw. *slede*, a sledge.

SLENK, *s.* Del. this entry in DICT.
Slenk is a misprint for *slynge*, a blow, in Pinkerton's version of Gaw. and Gol.

SLEUTH-HUND, SLEWTH-HUND, *s.* V. DICT.
The suggestions regarding the origin of *sleuth* are unsuitable. It is simply Icel. *slóth*, track or trail.

SLIK, SLYKE, *adj.* Such like, such, similar; Rom. Alexander, l. 783.
From A.-S. *swá-llc*; M. Goth. *swaleiks*. The latter is given by Jamieson as the origin of *swylk*: but this is a mistake: it is simply the A.-S. *swilc*, which is made up of *swá* and *llc*.

SLIK, *adj.* Del. this entry in DICT.
Slik is a misreading of *slikes* in Pinkerton's version. V. *Slike, v.*

To **SLIKE**, *v. n.* To slide, slip, glide.
The swerd swapped on his swange and on the mayle *slikes*. *Awnt. Arthur*, 48, 6, Douce MS.
The Lincoln MS. reads *slydys*.

To **SLING, SLYNG,** *v. a.* To cast, throw, dash, strike.

SLING, SLYNG, SLYNGE, *s.* A cast, stroke, blow.

SLOGAN, *s.* V. DICT.
Slogan is not a corruption of *slughorne*, but a more correct form of it. Indeed, *slughorne* is a corr. of *slugorne*, an old spelling of *slogan*, a battle-cry: from Gael. *sluagh-ghairm*, comp. of *sluagh*, people, tribe, army, and *gairm*, a call. *Slugorne* is therefore not a horn at all. See *Slughorn* in Suppl. to Skeat's Etym. Dict.

To **SLOKE, SLOIK,** *v. a.* To slake, quench, satisfy; also, to reduce, pulverize, as by throwing water on lime-shells: pret. and part. pt. *slokit, sloikit.*
". . . with ane onsatiable drouth, quhilk scho culd nocht *sloik*." Trials for Witchcraft, Spald. Misc. I. 88, 1597.

SLOT-STAFF, *s.* A kind of pike, or Jedburgh-staff; Burgh Recs. Prestwick, 1561, p. 66, Mait. C.

SLOUN, *s.* V. DICT.
Sloun cannot be connected with *slowhound*, as suggested. See under *Sleuth-hund*. Most prob. from Icel. *sláni*, "a gaunt and clownish boor;" Vigfusson.

SLUCHT, *s.* A kind of cloak or overcoat, a jupe. V. **SLUG, SLOGIE.**
"To Alex^r. Checkum, commoun poist, fyve pundis to help to by him a *slucht* of blew." Burgh Recs. Aberdeen, ii. 163, Sp. C.

SLUGHORNE, *s.* V. DICT.
A *slughorn* is not a horn at all, but a battle-cry: the etym. given is therefore wrong. For explanation see under *Slogan*.

To **SMACK,** *v. n.* To taste, or smell of a thing.
"*Resipio*, to smell or *smack*." Duncan's Appendix Etym., ed. Small, E.D.S.

SMAK, *s.* A taste, smell, taint.
"*Sapor*, a taist or *smack*." Duncan's App. Etym., ed. Small, E.D.S.

SMARADGE, *s.* A kind of emerald; also applied to any precious stone of an emerald colour; Alex. Scott's Poems, p. 15, ed. 1882.
Lat. *smaragdus*, an emerald.

SMATTRIE, *s.* A large number, flock. V. **SMYTRIE.**

SMIDDIE-GUM, *s.* Small-coal used in a smithy.
In various parts of Scot. dross or small-coal for use in smithies and furnaces is called *gum*, a corruption of *culm*, which in some dialects is *coom* (Halliwell). Brockett defines *smiddy-gum* as "the refuse of a smith's shop, the fragments struck off from the hot iron by the hammer."

To **SMIKE,** *v. a.* To cheat; pret. and part. pt. *smikit*, cheated.
"Becaus it is weill knawin and fund that he *smikit* and defraudit his brother foirsaid, and did siclyck to the said Nicoll his brothir sone." Grievances of Orkney Append. II. V. **SMAIK,** *s.*

SMIT, *s.* Infection, contagion. Addit. to **SMIT,** q. v.

SMITTLISH, SMITLISH, *adj.* Infectious, contagious.

SMITTING-SICKNESS, *s.* An infectious disease, infection.
"*Contagio*, an infection or *smitting-sickness*." Duncan's Appendix Etym., ed. Small, E.D.S.

SMOUTIE, *adj.* Smutty, black, begrimed: merely a poetic form of *smutty*.
D'ye mind that day, when in a bizz,
Wi' reekit duds, an reestit gizz,
Ye did present your *smoutie* phiz,
'Mang better folk,
An' sklented on the man of Uzz,
Your spitefu' joke.
Burns, Address to the Deil.

SMOW, *v.* and *s.* Smile. V. **SMOO.**

SNICK, SNICK-DRAWING. V. under SNECK.

SNIPE, SNYPE, s. A kind of muzzle for a pig, which prevents it from eating the growing corn; Orkn. and Shetl.

To SNIPE, SNYPE, v. a. To muzzle, to put a muzzle on the snout of a pig.

" Anent the swyne of Papa, that thai sall be *snypit* and ringit in tyme of summer and winter also, to the effect that the haill nyebours in thair griss land and cornis may be frie of thair skayth." Peterkin's Notes on Orkn. and Shetl., Appendix, p. 30.

Dan. *snabel*, a snout : cf. O. Du. *snavel*, *snabel*, dimin. of *snabbe*, *snebbe*, a bill, beak.

To SNIRTLE, SNURTLE, v. n. Dimin. of *snirt*; to laugh in a subdued, restrained, timorous, or mocking manner: *to snirtle in one's sleeve*, to snirtle secretly, to chuckle or smile slyly in mockery of a person. V. SNIRT.

Wi' ghastly ee, poor Tweedle-dee
Upon his hunkers bended,
And pray'd for grace wi' ruefu' face,
And sae the quarrel ended.

But tho' his little heart did grieve
When round the tinkler prest her;
He feign'd *to snirtle in his sleeve*,
When thus the Caird address'd her.
Burns, Jolly Beggars.

Snirt, of which *snirtle* is a dimin., is allied with both *sneer* and *snort*, and comes from Dan. *snærre*, to grin like a dog, or show one's teeth at a person. V. Skeat's Etym. Dict., under SNEER.

To SNOWK, SNOUK, SNOCK, v. a. To poke, press into, or turn over with the nose, as a dog or pig does: as, "The pig's *snowkin* out the tatties." Addit. to SNOWK, q. v.

Nae doubt but they were fain o' ither,
An' unco pack an' thick thegither;
Wi' social nose whyles snuff'd and *snowkit*,
Whyles mice and moudieworts they howkit.
Burns, The Twa Dogs.

To SOANE, v. n. To sink down, settle down, fall into place and position, like a hewn stone in a building.

"For as Salomons many thousand artificers were exercised about the building of the materiall temple; so must we, the many millions of the greater nor Salomons men, be occupied in making vp the spirituall, and in squairing our selues as the Lords lyuely stones; that being founded on all sides, we may *soane* aright in the Lords islare work, the which is our edification." Blame of Kirkburiall, ch. 15.

The following interesting account of the etym. of this word is by Prof. Skeat.

"The spelling *soane* suggests an A.-S. form *sd-nan*, from a base *sd-*, Goth. *sai-*, a strengthened form from a root SI. But comparison with A.-S. further suggests that the root should rather be SIG-, as there is a strong verb *sigan*, to sink down; but no such verb as *si-an*. The loss of *g* is not uncommon, as in E. *rain*, *brain*, A.-S. *regn*, *brægen*. This shows that the A.-S. equivalent of *soane* was *sdg-nan*, regularly formed with the passive or intransitive suffix *-nan* from *sdg*, pt. t. of *sig-an*, to sink. But as the A.-S. *sdgnan* is not recorded, we must find its equivalent in other languages. The Icel. form would be *seig-na* (not found),

the Swed. would be *seg-na*, and the Dan. *seg-ne*; and the two latter are found. The Dan. *segne*, is to settle down, sink down gradually; and the Swed. *segna*, though not given in the Tauchnitz Dict., appears in Widegren's Dict. (1788), with a by-form *signa*, to sink down. Further light is thrown on the word by Swedish Dialects. Thus, Rietz gives *siga*, to sink, with the derivatives *signa*, *süjna*, to sink slowly down. These he explains by the mod. Swed. *segna*. Hence to *soane* is to sink down gradually, to settle into a final position."

From the same root we have the forms to *seg*, *sag*, *sog*, to shake, press, or settle down, as in filling a sack with grain or flour. V. SEG, v.

SOBER, SOBIR, adj. Steady, industrious, well-doing; as, "He was a douce, *sober* man," a quiet, industrious man, or, a quiet, well-doing, working-man; *sobir folkis, the sobir estait*, working people, the working class. Addit. to SOBER, q. v.

This meaning of the term, which has not yet passed out of use, was overlooked by Jamieson. It occurs frequently in our Burgh Recs., especially in regulations of rates and charges for the community.

The Town Council of Aberdeen, when fixing the emoluments of the *sacristan* in 1565, agreed to give him a salary of ten merks yearly, and that he should have "of accidentis, of euery mariage, xviijd., of honest or reche folkis, and xijd. of *sobir folkis*; and of baptysme, xij. penneis of honest folkis, and vid. of *sobir* folkis; and for making of gravis of the buriall, xvij penneis of reche and honest folkis, and xijd of the *sobir* estait (alwaise, in all ther thre forsaidis, the puir and indegent to be fre)." Burgh Recs. Aberdeen, i. 361, Sp. C.

To SOG, v. a. and n. To sink or press down. V. SEG, SAG, v.

SOIL, SOILL, s. Sill, base, bottom, support: "the *soillis* of the windois," Burgh Recs. Glasgow, I. 348, Rec. Soc.

A.-S. *syl*, a base, support; Icel. and Swed. *syll*.

SOIL-BURD, SOILL-BURDE, SOILBAND, s. A strip of wood placed on the sill of a window to keep out the rain, Ibid., I. 67.

SOK, SOCK, s. 1. A stock, frame, rest, support; as, "The gun needs a new *sock*."

2. Surety, guarantee, backing, assistance: "to lay *sok* to a warrant," to find or obtain surety for a claim, i.e., security against loss or damage.

To SOK, SOCK, v. a. 1. To stock; to fix or mount on a frame or support.

". . . and als tha ordand the deyne of gild to cause the Hamburght man *sok* the gwns at the blokhouse sufficientlie with ane guid soun sok, one the townis expensis." Burgh Recs. Aberdeen, i. 222, Sp. C.

2. To make sure or secure, to give or find surety against loss or damage: "to *sok* to one's warrant,"· to fall back upon one's surety in case of loss.

"That Theman, goldsmycht, sal sustene na scathe for the brekine of the saide ferthing [of a gold noble], bot deliuor it agayn to the saide Thomas Ryburne, and

he to content Thoman of v s. vi d. agayn, that he gaf him for it, sen it was nocht lachfull nor sufficiande to pass for payment na werk, and the forsaide Thomas till *sok* til his warande, gif he hafe ony, til vpricht him." Burgh Recs. Aberdeen, 1463, i. 26, Sp. C.
The meaning of the last statement of the above award is that Thomas might fall back upon the person from whom he got the gold piece to free him from loss. *Sok* is prob. short for *socor*, O. Fr. *socors*, succour, aid, support, which Burguy records along with *secors* and *sucurs*, from Lat. *succurrere*, to succour, support.

SOLAND, SOLAND GOOSE, s. V. DICT.
The etym. given by Martin and Sibbald are certainly wrong: that given by Pennant, and adopted by Neill is correct, but not complete. *Solan* is simply Icel. *súlan*, the gannet : *n* standing for the def. article in the def. form of Icel. *sula*, a gannet. V. Skeat's Etym. Dict.

SOLE, s. A term in golfing denoting " the flat bottom of the head of a golf-club." Gl. Golfer's Handbook.

SOLEYING, *part.* V. SOLYEING.

To **SOLP, SOWLP,** *v. a.* and *n.* To steep, soak, drench ; pret. and part. pt. *solpit*; Houlate, l. 957, 42, Asloan MS. V. SOWP.

SONGATIS, SONEGATIS, *adv.* According to the course of the sun.
" I find it wilbe ane deir yeir: the bled of the corne growis withersones; and quhan it growis *sonegatis* about, it wilbe ane gude chaip yeir." Trials for Witchcraft, 1597, Spald. Mis., i. 96.

SO'NS, *s. pl.* A contr. form of *sowens*; *butter'd so'ns*, sowens served with butter instead of milk, formed the usual supper of a country company after the amusements of Halloween; Burns, Halloween, st. 28. V. SOWENS.
In his note to this term Burns stated that *butter'd so'ns* is always the Halloween supper. It was so at the time the poet wrote, and in the district with which he was acquainted ; but even then sowens were beginning to give place to potatoes in various districts of Scotland, and now they are almost entirely disused. The usual supper now is heat or mashed potatoes, or as they are usually called *champit tatties*.

SOO, SOO-BOAT, *s.* A small square-sterned boat with a scull-hole, for towing after a larger one, is called a *soo*, or a *soo-boat*; Orkn.

SOOLEEN, *s.* V. DICT.
Dan. *solen*, from which Jamieson rightly derives Shetl. *sooleen*, means "the sun," being the def. form of Dan. *sol*, *sun* ; *en* representing the def. article. A similar form is found in the word *Solan*, q. v.

SOPS DE MAYN, *s. pl.* Strengthening draughts or viands. Addit. to entry in DICT.

SOUCAND, SOUCAN, *s.* A single-ply straw-rope ; when the rope is two-ply it is called a " *simmond* or *simmon*."

SOUSE, *s.* V. DICT.
"O. Fr. *sols*, *sous*, is derived from Lat. nom. *solidus*, like *Charles* from *Carolus* ; but the Mod. Fr. *sou* is derived from Lat. acc. *solidum*." Skeat.

To **SOW, SOUE,** *v. n.* To breathe, murmur, sigh: a form of SOUCH, but implying a lighter, gentler sound, as if it were a dimin. of that term: "The wind scarce *sowed* amang the birks." West of S.

SOW-TAIL, SOW'S-TAIL, *s.* A spoiled knot in binding sheaves; Orkn.
In binding sheaves the ends of the straw band are brought together and twisted into a particular kink ; and if that kink is not properly made, the result is a *sow's-tail*. Prob. so called from the appearance of the band after the knot has slipped.

To **SOWF,** *v. a.* A form of SOWTH, q. v.; Whistle Binkie, I. 123.

SPAC, SPAK, *adj.* Quick, smart : used also as an *adv.*, short for *spacly*, spakly.
His sclauin he dede on al so *spac*,
And henge his harp opon his bac,
And had wel gode wil to gon.
  Orfeo and Heurodis, l. 343.
Now athir stoure on ther stedis strikis togedir,
Spurnes out *spakly* with speris in hand.
  Rom. Alexander, l. 786.
Spac and *spacli* occur repeatedly in Will. and Werwolf. See Gloss.

SPAIKIT, SPAKIT, *part.* and *adj.* Dried on *spaiks*, i.e., bars or flakes of wood, like skins or hides for export. V. SPAIK.
" . . nor skynnis *spakit*, nor hyddis kippit,".i.e., neither dried skins nor salted hides. Burgh Recs. Edinburgh, 1437-8, i. 5, Rec. Soc.

SPAK, SPACK, *pret.* Spoke, spake.
Yestreen I met you on the moor,
Ye *spak* na, but gaed by like stoure ;
Ye geck at me because I'm poor,
But flent a hair care I.
O Tibbie I hae seen the day,
Ye would na been sae shy ;
For lack o' gear ye lightly me,
But trowth I care na by.
  Burns.
This form is still common ; and it is used in the North of England also. V. Brockett's Gloss.

To **SPANYS,** *v. n.* V. DICT.
Not from O. Fr. *espanouir*, as given by Tyrwhitt, but from the shorter O. Fr. *espanir*, to blow, given by Cotgrave, which made the part. *espanise-ant;* and this verb is not Germanic, as Jamieson suggests, but has come from Lat. *expandere*.

SPAR-HALK, *s.* A sparrow-hawk ; Rates of Customs, Haly. Ledger, p. 313 ; Houlate, l. 330, Asloan MS. Bann. MS. has SPERK HALK, q. v.

SPART, SPERT, SPIRT, *s.* A dwarf rush: also, the coarse rush-like grass which grows on wet, boggy land. Other forms of the name are SPRAT, SPREAT, SPRIT, q. v.

SPARTY, SPERTY, SPIRTY, *adj.* Full of spart or rush-grass. V. SPRITTY.

SPAVIE, *s.* The spavin; Burns, The Inventory.

SPAVIET, *adj.* Spavined, having the spavin.
O. Fr. *esparvain*, "a spavin in the leg of a horse;" Cotgr. But this O. Fr. form has come from the L. Lat. *sparvarius*, sparrow-like, from the hopping or sparrow-like motion of a horse afflicted with spavin. V. Skeat's Etym. Dict.

To SPAYN, SPEAN, SPEANE, SPEN, *v. a.* To wean: also to hinder, prevent, suspend: part. pt. *spaynd, speand, spent*. Addit. to SPAIN, q. v.
"*Depello*, to put away, to *speane, lacte depellere* ;" Duncan's App. Etym., ed. Small, E.D.S.

SPAYNING, *part.* and *s.* Preventing, suspending, stoppage. Addit. to SPAINING, q. v.
"That nane of thame tak vpoun hand to tap nor sell darrer [i.e. dearer] . . . vnder the payne of *spayning* fra the occupatioun for yeir and day." Burgh Recs. Edinburgh, i. 164, Rec. Soc.

SPECHT, *s.* The speight, spite, or woodspite, a kind of large woodpecker, better known as the popinjay; *Picus viridis*, Linn.
The *Specht* was a pursevant, proude to apper,
That raid befor the emperour,
In a cot of armour
Of all kynd of colour,
Cumly and cleir.
Houlate, l. 334, Asloan MS.
The *Spite* is one of the Rain-birds. It is called by various names, such as the Awl Bird, High Hoe or Highaw (corr. into He-ha), Yappingale, Yaffle ; see Montagu's Ornith. Dict., p. 385, ed. Rennie.
Cf. O. Fr. *epeiche*, which Cotgrave renders "A Speight ; the red-tayled woodpecker, or Highaw."

SPEELIE-WALLIE, SPEELY-WALLY, *adj.* and *s.* Same as *Peelie-Wallie*, q. v.

SPEENDRIFT, *s.* V. DICT.
To the note appended to this entry add :—
The old sense of *spoon* was a chip of wood, hence *speendrift* means that the spray flew about like chips driven by a storm.

SPEET, SPEAT, SPEIT, *s.* A spit; Burgh Recs. Stirling, 1560, p. 72.

To SPEET, SPEIT, SPEAT, SPAIT, SPATE, *v. a.* To spit, fix on a spit; to stab or run through with a sharp instrument.
He swoor by a' was swearing worth,
To *speet* him like a pliver.
Unless he wad from that time forth
Relinquish her for ever.
Burns, Jolly Beggars.

To SPEIR *in*, SPEER *in*, SPIER *in*, *v. n.* To go in and ask for; as, "*Speir in* at father's as ye gang by :" also, to call at a place to fetch something; as, "*Speir in* at the tailor's for my coat.
(Sup.) E 2

To SPEIR *out*, SPEER *out*, SPIER *out*, *v. a.* To search out, find out, or procure by means of inquiry; "to *speir out* men fitting to be employit," Burgh Recs. Glasgow, II. 157, Rec. Soc.

SPELDER'D, SPELDERT, *part. pt.* Lying with the limbs stretched out : like a dog before a fire. Addit. to SPELDER, q. v.
Hey ! Willie Winkie, are ye coming ben ?
The cat's singing gray thrums to the sleeping hen,
The dog's *spelder'd* on the floor, and diana gie a cheep,
But here's a waukrife laddie that winna fa' asleep.
William Miller, Willie Winkie, st. 2.

SPELING, *s.* Del. this entry in DICT., and see under *Spilling*.

To SPEN, SPEEN, *v. a.* To spean, wean ; to hinder, prevent, stop. Forms of Spain, *q. v.* West of S. V. *Spayn*.

SPERD, SPERDE, *part. pt.* Barred, shut. V. SPAR, *v.*

SPERGE, *v.* and *s.* V. SPAIRGE.

SPERK, *s.* A spark; a gleam of fire, but generally the merest gleam, as in the expression, "No a *sperk* on the hearth," implying that the fire has gone out: also, *sperk o' fire*, a small fire, as "Bide a wee, an' I'll put on a '*sperk o' fire* ;'" hence, like *spark* in Eng., the least portion or degree, as, a *sperk o'* wit, *sperk o'* sense.
Quhareby there haug a ruby, without faille—
That as a *sperk* of lowe, so wantonly
Semyt birnyng vpon hir quhyté throte.
Kingis Quair, st. 48, ed. Skeat.

SPIDARROCH, *s.* Lit. spade-darg, a day's work with a spade, the extent of ground capable of being dug with a spade in one day.

To SPIER, *v. a.* To ask, enquire. V. SPEER.

SPILLING SALT. V. under *Salt*.

SPILLING, SPILLYNGE, *s.* Failure, mistake, loss; Awnt. Arth., l. 253, Lincoln MS. V. SPILL.
MS. Douce, from which Pinkerton's version was taken, has *speling*, which is prob. an error of the scribe. Jamieson rendered the term "*instruction*," a meaning which makes nonsense of the passage. That entry must therefore be deleted. V. *Speling*.

SPITTAL, SPITTAILL, SPITTLE, SPITTALHOUS, *s.* An hospital, leper-house.
Than in ane mantill and ane hevar hat,
With cop and clapper, wonder prively,
He opnit ane secreit yett, and out thairat
Convoyit hir, that na man suld espy,
Unto ane village half ane myle thairby,
Delyverit hir in at the *Spittaill* hous,
And daylie sent hir part of his almous.
Henryson, Test. Cresseid, l. 391.

This is a contr. form of *hospital*, which Henryson uses in the same poem.

Thairfor in secreit wyse ye let me gang
Unto your *Hospitall* at the tounis end.
Ibid., 1. 382.

To SPONE, *v. a.* To dispone, bestow, expend; part. pt. *sponyt:* a contr. of *dispone*.

". . . to goyt hym a sufiand lewyn, and the layf be *sponyt* on the plas qwar mast ned is." Burgh Recs. Peebles, 1456, p. 116, Rec. Soc.

SPONGE, SPOUNGE, SPUNGE, *s.* A brush made of hair, fine heath or heather, &c.; Rates of Customs, Halyburton's Ledger, p. 329.

The name *sponge* was formerly given to any implement used for cleaning, clearing, or dressing, such as a mop, brush, or besom ; and various articles of that kind are still so called : such as the brush with which the artillery-man cleans out his gun ; the mop with which a baker cleans out his oven, &c. And the act or process of cleaning is in each case called *sponging*.

The Rates of Customs of 1612 mention "*spounges or brushes*" of heather, of heath, and of hair ; used respectively as cleaners, as head-brushes, and as brushes for weavers or "for dichting of clothes." And what are now named sponges are there called "watter spounges for chirurgeans," and are rated at twenty shillings the pound weight. See Hal. Led., pp. 292, 330.

SPONTOON, *s.* A kind of half-pike carried by inferior officers in the army: hence, metaph. an officer : "*gilded spontoon*," gaudy officer.

From the gilded *spontoon* to the fife I was ready,
I asked no more but a sodger laddie.
Burns, Jolly Beggars.

Burns represents this *fille du régiment* as ready to welcome any soldier from the gold-braided officer to the humblest bandsman.

Fr. *sponton, esponton,* a kind of half-pike, etc.; from Ital. *spuntone,* derived from *spuntare,* to break off the point, to blunt ; and that again has come from Lat. *ex* and *pungere,* to pierce, prick.

SPORNE, *part.* and *s.* A form of *sporing,* spurring in the sense of hasting, hurrying, setting out on a journey, &c. Errat. in DICT.

Oft in Rominis I reid,
"Airly *sporne,* late speid."
Gawan and Gol., 68, 11.

Delete the entry in the DICT. Jamieson has been misled by the unusual form of the word, else he would have recognised the very common proverb here used. Throughout Scot. its usual form is

The mair haste the waur speed
Quo' the tailor to the lang thread.

Sometimes it has a slightly different form, and runs—

The mair hurry the less speed :
Like a tailor wi' a lang thread.

SPORT-STAFES, *s. pl.* The staves or poles used in the game or sport of quarterstaff.

"Remittis to Johnne Robesoun, travellour, the sextene pundis for his nychtbourheid and burgesship, in respect of the service done be him to the toun the tyme of his Majesteis being in Scotland, in hambringing and taking agane to Edinburgh the *sport stafes* and gownes." Burgh Recs. Stirling, 1 Sept., 1634, p. 172.

SPOUSAGE, SPOWSAGE, *s.* Wedlock ; the state or bonds of wedlock ; *spousbreke, spousbreche,* adultery; "brekar of *spousage,*" an adulterer or an adulteress ; Burgh Recs. Stirling, Stirling, 28 April, 1547.

SPRAINGED, *part.* and *adj.* Dotted, scattered, spread over. Addit. to SPRAINGED, q. v.

The window's *sprainged* wi' icy stars.
Whistle Binkie, ii. 350.

SPRAWLS, *s. pl.* A corr. of *spalds,* pieces, shreds, tatters ; lit. limbs : "rive to *sprawls;*" Whistle Binkie, i. 352.

SPREAGH, SPRECH, *s.* Lit. cattle ; hence prey, booty ; Scott, Rob Roy, ch. 23, 26. Addit. to SPREITH, q. v.

SPRETTY, *adj.* V. SPRITTY.

SPRING, *s.* The degree of suppleness that an instrument, or the handle of an instrument, possesses : used regarding a fishing-rod, the shaft of a golf-club, etc.

SPRING, *s.* "Tak a *spring* o' your ain fiddle," i.e., Follow your own plan and take the consequences. V. SPRING.

This proverb is addressed to persons who propose some questionable plan, or to those who resist good advice.

But sen ye think it easy thing
To mount aboif the moon,
Of your ain fiddle tak a *spring,*
And dance quhen ye haif done.
Montgomery, Cherrie and Slae, st. 66.

"'I can hear no remonstrances,' he continued, turning away from the Bailie, whose mouth was open to address him ; 'the service I am on gives me no time for idle discussion.' 'Aweel, aweel, sir,' said the Bailie, 'you're welcome to a tune on your ain fiddle ; but see if I dinna gar ye dance till't afore a's dune.'" Sir W. Scott, Rob Roy, ch. 29.

To SPRUN, *v. n.* To spur, spring, rise, project.

My beikis ar *spruning* he and bauld.
Dunbar, Petition of Gray Horse, 1. 40.

A.-S. *spura,* a spur ; Ger. *sporn:* hence E. *spur,* to press forward, and *spurn,* to rise superior to, as "'to *spurn* delights.'"

SPULE, SPUIL, *s.* A cope or pirn on which yarn is wound for the weaver; Whistle Binkie, i. 353, Burgh Rec. Edinburgh, i. 122, Rec. Soc. Errat. in DICT.

Not "a shuttle," as Jamieson defined it, but the cope or pirn which carries the yarn in the shuttle ; and the pirn whether filled or empty is so named ; that is, a *spule* or pirn for yarn or a pirn of yarn. Besides, the copes of yarn used in thread-making are called *spules.* E. *spool.*

SPURTLE-BLADE, *s.* A ludicrous name for a sword. V. SPURTILL.

SPYNLE, SPYNYLE, s. A spindle; *mylspynyle*, the spindle or shaft of a corn-mill; Burgh Recs. Prestwick, 6 Feb., 1496. V. SPINNEL.

To SPYRE, v. a. To search, ask. V. SPERE.

SQUADER, s. A squadron, squad, set, party.
"The next *squader* that commes in are captaines of cheef." Blame of Kirkburiall, ch. 19.
O. Fr. *esquadre, escadre*, from Ital. *squadra*, a squadron.

SQUARE, adj. A term in golfing, used to denote the state of a game which stands evenly balanced, i.e., when the players are equal in their count of holes. Gl. Golfer's Handbook.

SRAL, s. V. DICT.
A misprint in Pinkerton's version of Sir Gaw. and Sir Gal. for *Iral*, which is prob. a corruption of *Orielle*, a kind of precious stone described by Sir John Maundeville as "a aton well schynynge;" Voiage, p. 48, ed. 1839. V. Gloss. to Sir Gawayne.
"*Irale*, a kind of precious stone." Halliwell.

STABLE-MEAL, s. The liquor consumed in an inn by farmers by way of remunerating the innkeeper for accommodating their horses during the day: i.e., *stable-mail*.
When thou an' I were young and skeigh,
An' *stable-meals* at fairs were dreigh,
How thou wad prance, an' snore, an' skreigh,
An' tak the road.
Burns, The Farmer to his Mare Maggie.

STADDLIN, STADDLE, s. The foundation or stance for a corn or hay stack; also, the mark left in the grass by a hay-rick which has stood for a long time on account of bad weather. V. STADDLE.

STAG, s. A stake, pile, fixed or for fixing in the ground: E. *stake*. West of S., Aberd.

To STAG, v. a. To stake, to drive stakes in the ground; pret. and part. pt. *staggit*, staked, set on stakes, erected on piles; Burgh Recs. Aberd., II. 300.

STAGGIE, s. Dim. of stag.
Tho' thou's howe-backit now, an' knaggie,
I've seen the day,
Thou could hae gane like ony *staggie*
Out-owre the lay.
Burns, The Farmer to his Mare Maggie.

STAKRAND, part. Staggering; Rob Stene's Dream, p. 8, Mait. C. V. STAKKER.

To STALE, STAIL, v. a. To shun, avoid. V. under *Mait*.
That under cure I got sic check,
Which I might not remove nor neck,
But eyther *stail* or mait.
Montgomery, Cherrie and Slae, st. 16.
Check, stale, and *mate*, are all chess terms. "But eyther *stail* or *mait*," means, "but I must either suffer stale-mate or check-mate," i.e., I must, in any case, get the worst of it. *Stail* is simply E. *stale*, allied to *stall* and *still*.

To STALE, STAIL, STAL, STELL, v. n. and a. To make water, piss; pret. *staild*, Inter. Droichis, Bann. MS., l. 54.
"Item, gif ony *stal* in the yet of the gilde or upon the wall of the gild endurand the gild, he sall gif iiijd. to the mendis." Lawis of the Gild, ch. 10. Ancient Laws of Scot., Rec. Soc.
Lat. *stillare*, to drop, distil.

STALL, STELL, s. A pool or collection of urine, that which has been *staled*.

STANCHER, STANECHER, STANCHEL, s. An iron bar for a window. V. STANSSOUR.

To STAND for, STAND in for, v. a. To engage, be bound, come good for, warrant.
Thou art ane limmer, I *stand for'd*.
Lyndsay, Three Estaitis.
Stand for'd, stand for it.
The expression *stand in for* is used when one party becomes surety for another; as, "He has taen the farm, and his brother *stan's in for him*."

STANDAR, adj. Always standing: "*standar* oliphant*," the elephant that always stands; Kingis Quair, st. 156, ed. Skeat.
"The elephant was said to have only one joint in his legs, so that he could not lie down. He used to lean against a tree to go to sleep; see Philip de Thaun, p. 101; Golding's tr. of Solinus, bk. i. c. 32; E. Phipson's Animal Lore in Shakespeare's Time, p. 146." Ibid., Note, p. 87.
The use of this verbal-adjective form ending in-ar (Eag. er) is in imitation of Chaucer. In his Assembly of Foules we find "the *shooter* ew," and "the *bilder* ook." See Gl. Kingis Quair, p. 109.

STANG, pret. Stung, did sting.
This old preterite of *sting* is common in Mid. Eng.

STANNEL, STANEL, STANYEL, STONEGAL, s. Same as STANCHELL, q. v.

To STAUK, STAWK, v. a. and n. To stalk, to hunt game; also, to walk with high and proud step: part. pr. *staukin*, used also as a s. E. *stalk*.
The last Halloween I was waukin
My droukit sark-sleeve, as ye ken;
His likeness cam up the house *staukin*—
And the very grey breeks o' Tam Glen!
Burns, Tam Glen, st. 7.

To STEAL, v. a. A term in golfing meaning "to hole an unlikely put from a distance." Gl. Golfer's Handbook.

To STEAVE, STEVE, STAVE, v. a. 1. To stiffen, tighten, screw up; pret. and part. pt. *steaved, staved*, stiffened, made firm.

I *steave* up my temper-string gayly,
Au' whiles a bit verse I do chant;
For lasses ye ken, maun be wylie,
To mak up their unco bit want.
W. Watson, The Unco Bit Want, st. 3.

2. To sprain; "He *steved* his wrist and *staved* my thumb." Addit. to STEEVE, v. q. v.

STEDABLE, *adj*. Helpful, ready to give assistance. V. STED, STEDE, v.

"The saide Thomas sall be *stedable* to the saide Willam in all thingis that he has ado." Burgh Recs. Aberdeen, 1467, i. 27, Sp. C.

STEEK, STEK, STIK, *s*. A piece, as of cloth. V. STICKE.

STEEL-BOWED, STEIL-BOWED, *part. pt.* Astricted, devoted, or set apart for a special purpose; guaranteed, assured, inviolate. V. STEEL-BOW-GOODS.

"For as by the foster-father-hood of such high callings, Gods Altar-mens trauels in his own tructh ought to be *Steil-bowed*: so these great-good gifts of nature and grace does plentifully promit that comfort to vs." Blame of Kirkburiall, Dedication.

STEEPFAT, STEPFAT, *s*. A vat in which malt is steeped: "Kyll and *stepfat*," Burgh Recs. Peebles, 1550, p. 204, Rec. Soc.

A *steep-vat* was also called a *malt-coble*; but often it was only "a *coble*." See under COBLE, *Coble*.

To STEKIL, v. a. To straw, scatter, sprinkle; part. pt. *stekillede*.

In stole was he stuffede, that steryn was on stede,
Alle of sternys of golde, that *stekillede* was on straye.
Awnt. Arth., l. 390.

This may be a corr. of *strekle, strinkle*, to straw; but the context rather suggests its connection with M. E. *steken*, to stick in, insert, inlay, of which *stekil* may be a dimin. Hence *stickly*, rough, prickly, on account of small points or objects inserted or inlaid.

STEME, STEM, *s*. A glimpse. V. STYME.

STENCHER, STENSER, STENSEL, *s*. V. STANSSOUR, STENCHEL.

To STENYE, STEYNE, STEN, v. a. and n. To stretch, extend. Forms of STEND, q. v.

A gay grene cloke that will nocht *stenye*.
Wowing of Jok and Jenny.

To STEP, STAP, STOPE, v. a. To step over, pass by, miss, neglect, leave out: syn. *to hip*.

In Scot. burghs long ago, the common minstrel or piper was supplied with dinner daily by the inhabitants in rotation; and he was directed by the magistrates "*to hip nane*." In the list of instructions given to the Glasgow minstrels in 1600, one was,—"Item, that

thai *stope* na Iriemau that is hable to gif them ordiner, nor tak syluer fra ane to pas to ane vther." Burgh Recs. Glasgow, i. 207, Rec. Soc.

A.-S. *steopan*, to bereave, deprive; O. H. Ger. *stiufan*, to deprive of parents, to deprive of anything valuable to one.

To STEP-BAIRN, STEP-BARNE, *v. a.* To treat with partiality, disfavour, or unkindness; to exempt from favour, benefit, or advantage.

"And if otherwise it were, why doe they so partially *step-barne* the pursse-miserable poore from such a soul-helpe?" Blame of Kirkburiall, ch. 19.

STEROP, *s*. A kind of hawk; Houlate, l. 652.

STEWTH, STEWTHE, *s*. Theft: Burgh Recs. Stirling, p. 134. A form of STOWTH, q. v.

To STICK, v. a. To stab, kill, murder: pret. and part. pt. *stickit*; part. pr. *stickin*, used also as a *s*., as, "I wadna trust him wi' the *stickin* o' a cawf."

A.-S. *stician*, Du. *steken*, to stab.

STICKIT, STICKED, *part. pa.* Stabbed, murdered, assassinated.

". . the corps of *sticked* Tarquin to be both bathed and balmed;" Bl. of Kirkburiall, ch. xiv.

STIDDIE, *s*. An anvil. V. STUDY.

"*Incus*, a smith's *stiddie*." Duncan's App. Etym., ed. Small, E.D.S.

STIMY, STEIMMY, *s*. A term in golfing to express the predicament in which a player is placed when he finds that his opponent's ball lies in the line of his *put*.

Prob. a corr. from E. *stem*, to check, stop, block, which has come from A.-S. *stæfn, stefn, stemn*, the stem of a tree: "from the throwing of a tree-trunk into a river, which checks the current. So Icel. *stemma*, Dan. *stemme*, to dam up, from *stemme*, trunk." Skeat's Etym. Dict.

To STINT, STYNT, v. a. To scrimp, curtail, stunt, impoverish; West of S. Addit. to STINT, q. v.

Stint is still so used in the West of Scotland; as in the common sayings, "*Stint* the belly to cleed the back;" "It's ill to *stint* a bairn in his broso;" "A sunless simmer *stints* the corn." As the following entry shows the term was so used in the time of Burns. It is the same as E. *stint*, M. E. *stintan*, but it has a wider range of meaning and application.

STINTIT, STYNTIT, *part.* and *adj.* Scrimped, curtailed, stunted; and in some applications it implies small and grudgingly given, as in the expression, "a poor *stintit* wage." Cf. E. *stinted*.

"Fra *stintit* meat comes *reestit* growth," is a common adage in the West of S.

But now the cot is bare and cauld,
Its branchy shelter is lost and gane,
And scarce a *stintit* birk is left
To shiver in the blast its lane.
Burns, Destruction of Drumlanrig Woods.

That *stint* and *stunt* are closely connected may be seen from the following. M. E. *stintan*, to shorten, cut short, has come from A.-S. *styntan*, formed from *stunt*, stupid, short of wit; and O. Swed. *stynta*, to shorten, has come from *stunt*, short, small, cut short. Skeat, Etym. Dict. In fact, A.-S. *y* is the regular mutation of *u*.

STIRRAP, *s*. A hook, chain, or rod by which an article is suspended: "thre *stirrapis* for the lampys;" Register of Vestments, &c., in St. Salvator, St. Andrews, Mait. Club, Misc. III. 205. E. *stirrup*.

STITHILL, *adv*. Del. this entry in DICT., and take the following one instead.

To STITHIL, STITHILL, STITHLE, STICHTLE, *v. n.* To exert oneself, to toil, journey, voyage, press on; also as a *v. a.*, to dispose, guide, manage, rule.

Mony sege our the sea to the cite socht : Schipmen our the streme thai *stithil* full straught, With alkyn wappyns I wys that was for were wroght.
Gawan and Gol., l. 400.

Jamieson evidently misunderstood this passage, and his failure, if not caused, was at least confirmed by reading *stithil* as an *adj.* or *adv*. V. DICT.
In its active sense it occurs repeatedly in the Green Knight, and in Rom. Alexander, l. 193, 589, 2298.

To STIVEL, STIFFLE, *v. n.* To stumble, stagger; to walk or work like one stupified; part. pt. *stivelit*, *stiffilit*: *al to-stiffilit*, completely staggered or confounded; Gol. and Gawane, st. 49. V. STEVEL.

STOCK, *s*. 1. A plant of colewort or kail, cabbage, etc.
The *stocks* pulled by persons holding Halloween were whole plants.

2. The head or top of the plant, i.e., the edible portion is also called a stock: "Bring in a guid kale-*stock*, and a weel-filled cabbage-*stock* for the broth the day."
Jamieson's defin. of a *stock* is not the one generally used. V. DICT.

3. A stand or rest. The block or table on which a butcher or a fishmonger cuts up his goods; Burgh Recs. Edinburgh, I. 114, B. R. Glasgow, I. 64. Also, a hold, handle, stalk. Addit. to STOCK, q. v.

STOCKIT, STOKIT, *part. pt.* Fitted with a stock or stalk: mounted. V. STOK.
". . . presented vnto thame ane bell, new and *stockit*, quhilk he frielie gevis and mortifies for the vse of the grammer schole." Burgh Recs. Aberdeen, ii. 395, Sp. C.

To STOCK-BAND, STOK-BAND, *v. a.* To mount, fix, and bind a gun on its stock: generally applied to the fixing of a cannon on its carriage.
"[The provost, bailies, and council] ordanis Jhone Harwod, theasurar, to caus *stok band* and mont the townis artalyere, now presentle lyand in the end of the kirk, and to by and caus furnis all thingis necessar thairto, to the effect the samyn may be in reddines preparit and reperallit in cais onye fornae inemyis wald cum and persew this burgh," &c. Burgh Recs. Edin., 9 July, 1567, Recs. Soc.

All the varieties of *stock*, implying a stick or stalk, staff, stem, stump, block, table, frame, stand, etc., may be referred to A.-S. *stocc*, a stock, post; Ger. *stock*, Dutch *stok*, Icel. *stokkr*, Dan. *stok*, Sw. *stock*. See Wedgwood, and Skeat.

STOFE, *s*. A stove, vapour-bath. Addit. to STOVE, q. v.
"*Vaporarium*, a hot *stofe*." Duncan's App. Etym., ed. Small, E.D.S.

STONEGAL, *s*. A kind of hawk. V. STANCHELL.

To STOO, STOU, *v. n.* Same as *stound*; and as applied to the sense of feeling, to ache, smart, thrill; "My finger's *stooin* wi' the pain;" as applied to the sense of hearing, to sound, resound, clang, thrill; pret. *stooit*, *stou't*; part. pr. *stooin*, *stouin*. V. STOUND.

O meikle bliss is in a kiss,
Whyles mair than in a score;
But was betak the *stouin* smack,
I took ahint the door.
Song, The kiss ahint the door.
"*Stouin* smack," loud sounding kiss, or, as Burns called it, "a skelpin kiss;" see The Jolly Beggars.

STOO, STOU, *s*. Acute pain experienced in stings or throbs; a sting, thrill, or throb of pain; also, the feeling produced by a shrill, piercing sound. Same as STOUND, q. v.

STOORIE, *adj*. Restless, romping, frolicsome. V. STURE, STOOR.
Wearied is the mither that has a *stoorie* wean,
William Miller, Willie Winkie, st. 5.

STOUT, STOOT, *adj*. Stout-hearted, haughty, defiant; also, daring.
Stout is frequently so used in Scot. ballads.
And they hae quarrell'd on a day,
Till Marjorie's heart grew wae ;
And she said she'd chuse another love,
And let young Benjie gae.
And he was *stout* and proud-hearted,
And thought o't bitterlie ;
And he's gane by the wan moonlight
To meet his Marjorie.
. . . .
"Oh wha has done thee wrang, sister,
Or dared the deadly sin ?
Wha was as *stout*, and fear'd na dout,
As throw ye o'er the linn ?"
Ballad, Young Benjie.

STOWIN, *part. pt.* A poetic form of *stown*, stolen; Alex. Scott's Poems, p. 25, ed. 1882.

To STRAIK, STREIK, STREK, *v. a.* To strike, start, begin, commence: part. pres. *straikin*, *streikin*, *streking*, used also as a *s.*, as in "the *straikin* o' the licht" (i.e., the break of day), "the *strekin* o' the plews" (i.e., when farmers begin to plough, or, the commencement of spring). Addit. to STRAIK.

". . . tua vesitouris to be maid and chosing perpetualie to vesy yeirlie in tyme cuming all propertels and commonteis pertenyng te the liberte and fredom of burgh at the *streking* of the plewis yerelie, betwix Sanct Lucas day and Mertymes, and at harrowis *streking,* gif ony thairof be telit be nychtbouris adiacent, that the samin may be resistit in tyme." Burgh Recs. Peebles, p. 218, Rec. Soc.

The various entries of STRAIK ought to be combined, as they present mere varieties of meaning.

STRAIK, STRAKE, STREK, *s.* 1. A handful of flax in process of dressing: and when dressed it is made up into a small roll or bundle, called a *straik*, or a *straik o' lint*. V. STREIK, STREEK.

2. A streak, line, trace; as, "a *straik* o' bluid:" a small quantity, a very little, a mere handful; as, "Gie the puir body a *straik* o' meal." West of S.

STRAIK O' DAY, STREIK O' LICHT, *s.* Daybreak, dawn of day: "He was up by *straik o' day.*" Another form is *streek o' day.*

To STRAIT THE PIN, STREEK THE PIN. To tighten the temper-pin of a spinning-wheel, keep it at the right pitch, which implies close attention to the spinning; hence, the order, "*strait* or *streek the pin,*" meant attend to your spinning, mind your work.

Auld luckie says they're in a creel,
And redds them up, I trow, fu' weel,
Cries, "Lasses, occupy your wheel,
And *strait the pin.*"
Keith, The Farmer's Ha', st. 15.

"Auld luckie," the mistress of the house.
"Redds them up," rates or scolds them for their trifling.

STREANE, *v.* and *s.* Strain, sprain. V. STREIND.

"*Stringo*, to *streane*, or wring." Duncan's App. Etym., ed. Small, E.D.S.

STRECHT, STRYCHT, *part. pt.* Bound, attached; Houlate, 1. 652, Asloan MS. V. STRICK, *v.*

STREIPILLIS, *s. pl.* Strapples, small straps; "Ane sadill with *streipillis,*" i.e., stirrup-straps, Aberd. Reg. Cent. 16. Errat. in DICT.

Not *stirrups,* as suggested by Jamieson, but straps for stirrups: and very prob. they were called *small straps* to distinguish them from the larger straps for keeping the saddle in position. There may or may not have been stirrups along with them.
Simply a dimin. from E. *strap*, as in Jamieson's first suggestion.

STREK-BED, STRECK-BED, *s.* A folding bed; Burgh Recs. Edinburgh, I. 91, Rec. Soc. V. STREK, STREIK.

STREKIN, STREIKIN, *s.* V. under *Straik, v.*

To STRET, *v. a.* To bind by promise or oath, astrict; part. pt. *stretit*, bound, astricted, constrained; Spald. Club Misc., i. 95. V. STRAIT.

STRINCATES, *s. pl.* Jewels, trinkets; "tresour, *strincates*, and artalyery;" Burgh Recs. Aberdeen, 1489, I. 45, Sp. C.

Perhaps a corr. of *trinkets*, from O. Fr. *trencher*, to cut, carve, of which Burguy gives as prov. forms *trencar, trinchar, trinquor.* Cf. Sp. *trinchar,* and Ital. *trinciare,* to cut, carve. For further discussion see Skeat's Etym. Dict.

STROAN, *v.* and *s.* V. STRONE.

To STROW, *v. a.* To scatter, spread, cover over; part. pt. *strowit*, strewn; Kingis Quair, st. 65, ed. Skeat.

A.-S. *streowian,* Goth. *straujan,* to strew, scatter. Cf. Lat. *stramen,* straw, lit. what is scattered.

STRUDER, STRUTHER, STROUDYR, STROWDER, *s.* Lane, avenue, walk; Burgh Recs. Peebles, p. 180. V. STROTHIE.

This term is used in various districts of Scot., and is generally applied to a long, straight lane or country-road near the bank of a river.

STRYCHT, *part. pt.* V. *Strecht*, STRICK.

STRYND, STRYNDE, *s.* A strum, a sullen, surly, or pettish fit: same as Strunt, q. v.; Dunbar and Kennedy, l. 55; also, perversity; Alex. Scott, p. 16, ed. 1882.

STRYND, *s.* V. DICT.

"*Strynd*, in the sense of 'race' or 'disposition,' is from A.-S. *strynd*, race, as stated in DICT. But O. Fr. *estraine* is from a Frankish equivalent of it, not from Lat. *extractiv*, as Roquefort suggested." Skeat.

STUDE, *pret.* Stood, did stand.

Similar examples of *u* for Eng. *oo* are found in *gude, fude, blude, rude.*

STUMPIE, *s.* Dimin. of stump: applied to a worn quill.

Sae I got paper in a blink,
And down gaed *stumpie* in the ink.
Burns, Ep. to Lapraik.

In another epistle to the same friend Burns uses the word as an *adj.*, meaning much worn, blunt :—

Sae my auld stumpie pen I gat it
Wi' muckle wark,
An' took my jockteleg an' what it
Like ony clark.

The above meanings are additional to those given by Jamieson.

STY, STIE, STEE, *s.* A narrow way, lane, path; a ladder; Rom. Alexander, l. 5064, 2481. Addit. to STY.

STYEN, *s.* V. DICT.

The etym. given for this term does not explain the final *n.* The A.-S. name was *stigend,* rising, from the part. pres. of *stigan,* to ascend, rise. It was used as short for *stigend edge,* rising eye, which in M. Eng. became corrupted into *styanye,* as if it meant "*sty on eye*"; and afterwards by dropping somctimes *-ye,* sometimes *-anye,* it became *styan,* and *sty.* See Skeat's Etym. Dict., s. v. *Sty.*
This explanation accounts for the expression still common, "*a sty on the eye.*"

SUAIF, SWAIF, *adj.* Suave, sweet, pleasant.

Because I fand hir ay so *swaif,*
Sic favour to that sueit I gaif,
That ay I sall hir honour saif,
And schame conseill;
And for hir sake lufe all the laif
With littill deill.
Alex. Scott's Poems, p. 93, ed. 1882.

SUARE, SWAR, *s.* The neck. V. SWARE.

SUBELL, SUBBELL, *s.* A form of Isobel; Burgh Recs. Glasgow, I. 245, Rec. Soc.

SUD, *pret.* Should; commonly written *suld.*

SUDAR, *s.* A napkin; a portion of the fittings of a church altar; Recs. of Old Dundee, p. 559. E. *sudary.*

Lat. *sudarium,* a napkin: from *sudare,* to sweat.

SUERDOME, *s.* V. under *Sweer.*

SUFFERAGH, *s.* Suffrage; service or prayer for the dead. V. SUFFRAGE.

". . twa markis of obit siluer to be uplift and tane to the feft chaplanis yeirly for *sufferagh* to be donn for the saullis of wmquhill Allexander, lord Elphinstoun and Sir Johen Elphinstoun his fader, of ane land and tenement liand in the Bakraw." Burgh Recs. Stirling, 14 Oct., 1521.
This term most prob. represents the local pronunciation of *sufferage,* a form of *suffrage.* The population of Stirling was at that time chiefly of Celtic origin and familiar with Gaelic; hence the peculiar termination of this word.

SUFIAND, SUFIANT, *adj.* Sufficient, suitable; Burgh Recs. Peebles, 1456, p. 116, Rec. Soc.

A colloquial and equivalent contr. form of *suffisand,* which occurs in Barbour, i. 368. Cf. Fr. *suffire,* which may have been Englished as *suffy.* E. *suffice* is not from the infinitive, but from the stem of the part. pres. *suffis-ant.*

SUGET, SUGGET, *s.* A subject.

SUMMERING, SOMMERING, *s.* An old border custom of making hunting excursions into England during the summer season.

Those gypsy adventures, well outlined in the following extract, were gradually put down after the union of the Crowns.
"Quhairas sindrie of the Ellottis and Armestrangis in Liddisdaill and some other partis of the Middle Shyris of this Iland continewis ane auld custome (whiche wes formarlie keepit be thame whill as these Middle Shyris were divydit under the governement of two severall free Princes), in the sommer tyme repairing to some of these boundis that belong to this kingdome, and thair in hostile maner making thair stay and residence thay destroy the game, cuttis the woddis, and utherwayes committis suche insolencies as could not be weill borne with yf those boundis wer still ane bordour, and sould noway be sufferit in the very middis of this oure kingdom. And thairfore oure pleasour and will is . . . thair forbearing ony suche lyke *sommering* heirefter, under greate pecuniall panes," etc. Letter of James I., 12 April, 1606, Privy Council Records, vol. vii. p. 489.

SUMQUHILE, SWMQUHYL, *adv.* For some time, at one time, some time ago.

"Deponyt that he hym self twk *sumquhyl* ta the Rwd servys tha iiij s. of the sayd landis." Burgh Recs. Peebles, 1460, p. 136.

SUN-HORLOGE, SONE-HOROLAGE, *s.* A sun-dial; "to draw and mak dyellis or *sone horolages;*" Burgh Recs. Aberdeen, II. 158, Sp. C. O. Fr. *horloge.*

SUPPLIE, SUPPLE, *s.* Support, backing; in the sense of taking part with or lending aid to another. O. Fr. *suppléer.*

"Forasmekle as the foresaid lordo is obliat till ws in mantenance and *supplie* to keipe ws in oure fredomes. and infeftmentis for certaine termes." Burgh Recs. Aberdeen, 1462, i. 22, Sp. C.

SURCOAT, SURCOTE, *s.* An upper garment worn by females, a dress or ornamented kirtle. Errat. in DICT.

In his treatment of this word Jamieson has confused the *surcoat* and the *sarket.* The *sarket,* dimin. of *sark,* was a portion of dress worn by both men and women; but the *surcoat* was worn by women only, and it was plain or ornamental according to the rank of the wearer. It is thus described by Planché in his account of female costume in the twelfth century:
"Over the long robe or tunic is occasionally seen a shorter garment of the same fashion, which answers to the description of the *super tunica* or *sur cote,* first mentioned by the Norman writers. In the illuminations it is chequered or spotted, most likely to represent embroidery, and terminates a little below the knee with an indented border. This was the commencement of a fashion against which the first statute was promulgated by Henry II. at the close of this century, but which defied and survived that and all similar enactments." Brit. Costume, p. 81, ed. 1874.

And ane *surcote* she *werit* long that tyde,
That semyt [vn]to me of diuerse hewis,
Kingis Quair, st. 160, ed. Skeat.

To **SURFLE, SURFEL,** *v. a.* To overcast, to gather or spread a wider edge over a narrower one: hence, to ornament or adorn with trimmings, edging, or embroidery; similar to *purfle,* q. v.

SURFLE, SURFEL, SURFELING, SURFLING, *s.* An overcast; a trimming, edging, or embroidery; a border or edging of ermine, sable, &c.; the hem of a gown. V. *Purfle.*

SURGET, *s.* Errat. for *Suget.* V. DICT.

This is, as I suspected, a misreading of *suget* in Pinkerton's version. The Lincoln MS. roads *sugette;* Jamieson's note must therefore be deleted. V. *Suget.*

SURREGENIE, SURREGENRIE, SURRE-
GENRY, s. Surgery, the craft of a surgeon.
"... our said craft of *Surregenie* or Barbour
craft." Seal of Cause to Barbers, Burgh Recs. Edinburgh, i. 102, Rec. Soc.
"... and that na barbour, maister nor seruand,
within this burgh hantt, vse, nor exerce the craft of
Surregenrie without he be expert and knaw perfytelie
the thingis [belonging to the craft]." Ibid. p. 103.
O. Fr. *chirurgien*, "a surgeon;" Cotgr.

SUTE, s. Soot, smut, blacks.
"*Fuligo*, sute." Duncan's App. Etym., ed. Small,
E.D.S.

SUTHRON, *adj.* Southern; English.
Addit. to SOUTHRON, q. v.
We'll sing auld Coila's plains and fells,
Her moors red-brown wi' heather bells.
Her banks an' braes, her dens an' dells,
Where glorious Wallace
Aft bure the gree, as story tells,
Frae *Suthron* billies.
Burns, *To W. Simson, Ochiltree*.

SWAIF, *adj.* Suave, sweet. V. SUAIF.

SWAIRD, s. Sward; Burns.

To SWALL, v. n. To swell, enlarge: pret.
and *part. pt. swald, swale;* still common.
V. SWALD.

SWANE, s. Sweden.
"The said James weddit ane tar barrale that the
Quene grace of Yngland suld mary the King of *Swane*."
Burgh Recs. Peebles, p. 262, Rec. Soc.

SWANK, *adj.* "Stately, jolly;" Burns:
well knit, erect, and bold; and when
applied to a person it means well-formed,
good-looking, manly; West of S. Addit.
to SWANK, q. v.
Jamieson is certainly wrong in his statement that
Burns has improperly explained this word: for it is
still in common use with the meanings which Burns
attached to it. Nay, more: in the passage from Ferguson quoted as proof against him, the word must be
accepted in Burns's sense. Look at it—
Mair hardy, souple, steeve, an' *swank*,
Than ever stood on Tammy's shank.
If *swank* here means "*limber, pliant, agile*," as
Jamieson says, then it has exactly the same meaning
as *souple* with which it is joined, and the line is a
weakling whose testimony is worthless, but let *swank*
mean *stately*, as the author no doubt intended, and the
line becomes one of which even Burns would not be
ashamed. Besides, whatever may be the meaning
which the word has elsewhere, we must grant that
Burns knew the precise sense in which he used it, and
that he expected it would be understood by his readers
in that sense; and surely we may accept his word
for it.
Moreover, the term *swanking*, which is similarly
applied, and which is still common in various districts of
Scotland and of the North of England, means "great,
large, strong and strapping, hearty." See Dicts. of
Halliwell and Wright, and Gloss. of Brockett, Atkinson, Peacock.

To SWARE, v. a. To speak, declare, answer;
Rom. Alexander, l. 674.
A.-S. *swerian*, to swear; also, to speak, declare.

SWDOUR, s. A sudary; Mait. Club.
Misc., III. 204. V. *Sudar*.

SWEAT-HOLE, s. A pore of the skin.
"*Porus*, a *sweat-hole;*" Duncan's App. Etym., ed.
Small, E.D.S.

SWEER, SWEIR. *Sweir-out*, unwilling or
difficult to turn out, hard to draw: a term
applied to a very lazy person.
And for ane jack ane ragged cloak has tane;
Ane sword *sweir-out* and rusty for the rain.
Priests of Peebles.

SWEER, SWEIR, s. A lazy time, a short rest
during working hours, such as fieldlabourers take between meals; Forfars.

To SWEER, SWEIR, v. n. To be lazy, to rest
for a short time during working-hours;
"Come, let's *sweer* now," i.e., let us have a
short lazy.

SWEERDOM, SUERDOME, s. Laziness, un-
willingness to work.
For thi eusampll ma be tane
Of this haly mane, sanct Niniane,
Suerdome and idlenes for to fle
And agane al wite wicht to be.
Barbour, *Legends of the Saints*.
Cf. A.-S. *swœr*, Icel. *svarr*, Ger. *schwer*, heavy, diffi-
cult.

SWIME, SWYME, s. Forms of *soum*, the
relative proportion of cattle or sheep to
pasture, or *vice versa*; Corshill Baron Court
Book, Ayr and Wigton Arch. Coll., iv. 152.

SWING, s. A term used in golfing to denote
the circular sweep of the club when the
player is driving. Gl. Golfer's Handbook.

SWINGEOUR, SWINGER (*g* soft), s. A lazy
lounger; so lazy that he requires to be
swinged or whipt to his work; Burgh Recs.
Glasgow, i. 291, Rec. Soc. V. SWINGE.

SWINGLE, SWINGLE-TREE, s. The movable
part of a flail, which strikes the grain:
more frequently called the *souple*, and by
Burns called the *flingin-tree*.

SWIPE, s. In golfing, a full driving stroke.
Gl. Golfer's Handbook. Addit. to SWIPE,q.v.

SWISCHE, s. A drum; Burgh Recs.
Peebles, 1672, p. 336, Rec. Soc. V.
SWESCH.

To SWIVE, SWIFF, SWYVE, SWYFE, v. a.
Futuere; Burgh Recs. Stirling, 1546, p. 43;
Lyndsay, Thrie Estaitis, l. 162, 318.

SWOOR, SWURE, *pret.* Swore, sware, did
swear.
He *swoor* by a' was swearing worth,
To speer him like a pliver,
Unless he wad from that time forth
Relinquish her for ever.
Burns, *Jolly Beggars*.

To SWYKE, v. a. To deceive, betray, fail, act treacherously; Awnt. Arth., l. 539. Errat in DICT.

Both defin. and etym. as given by Jamieson are wrong. The word occurs frequently in alliterative romances, and always implies deceit, treachery, or failure; as in Morte Arthure, l. 1795.
Swappede owtte with a swerde that *swykede* hym never.
So also in Rom. Alexander, l. 5000, and in Havelok. V. Halliwell's Dict.
A.-S. *swic*, deceit, deceitful; *swican*, to deceive.

SYBO, SYBOU, SYBOW, *s.* An onion; "sybous or ingons," Burgh Recs. Glasgow, II. 146, Rec. Soc. V. SEIBOW.
Sybo was the spelling used by Burns.

SYITH, SYTH, *s.* A scythe.
"*Falx*, a huik or *syith.*" Duncan's App. Etym., ed. Small, E.D.S.

SYLOR, SYLOUR, SYLING, *s.* The ceiling. V. SILING, and *Selour*.
"*Laquear, vel laquiarium*, the *syling* of ane house." Duncan's App. Etym., ed. Small, E.D.S.

SYLORING, SYLLORING, *part. pr.* Lining or covering a ceiling; Burgh Recs. Glasgow, i. 342, Rec. Soc. V. SYLL.

SYMBACLANIS, SYMBILYNE, *s.* A musical instrument; prob. a form of cymbals.
Claryonis lowde knellis,
Portatiuis and bellis,
Symbaclanis in the cellis,
That soundis so soft,
Houlate, l. 766, Asloan, MS.
Quhar cherubyne syngis sweit Ossana,
With organe, tympane, harpe, and *symbilyne*.
Dunbar, Roiss Mary most of Vertew, l. 15.

SYMBLER, *s.* V. SUMLEYR, *Sumlare*.

SYOUR, SIRE, *s.* A gutter, drain; Burgh Recs. Glasgow, II. 128, Rec. Soc. V. SIVER.

SYTH, SYTHE, *s.* A *sey*, sieve, or strainer for milk. V. SYE.

SYTHARIST, *s.* A musical instrument: prob. the harp; Houlate, l. 757, Asloan MS. V. CITHARIST.

T.

TABBY, TAB, *adj.* Striped or brindled, marked like *tabby* (i.e., tabin or tabinet, waved or watered silk, Fr. *tabis*); applied to a cat so marked.

TABBY, TABBIE, TAB, *s.* Short for *tabby-cat*, a tom-cat, male-cat; also a colloq. or pet name for a cat.

The most prob. explanation of these terms is that they stand for *Tibbie*, a pet name for a cat, derived from *Tibalt* or *Tybalt* (coll. for Theobald), which was the proper name for the cat in the Beast Epic of the Middle Ages. In Caxton's Reynard the Fox, printed in 1481, a chapter is devoted to the doings of *tybert the catte*; and more than a century later the English dramatists frequently refer to *Tybert prince of cats*. Ben Johnson uses the term *tiberts* for cats; and in Romeo and Juliet Shakespeare makes Mercutio speak of Tybalt as " more than prince of cats," and addresses him as " good king of cats." V. Folk-Etymology, pp. 383-4, Dyce's Gloss. Shakespeare.

TABUIRIE, *s.* Town-drummer, or, in common parlance, the drum.

"Hes ordanit the *tabuirie* to pas throw the towne discharging the inhabitants of Lauirik, Peibillis, or Peddert, to be ressavitt within this towne be any persoune." Burgh Recs. Glasgow, i. 227, Rec. Soc.
Peddert is here a mistake for *Jeddert*, an old name for Jedburgh.
When the magistrates, or indeed any person, wished to send a public notice through the town, *the drum* or *the bell* was sent, i.e., the town-drummer with his drum, or the bellman with his bell. In the smaller towns all notices were proclaimed by the town-officer, who was bellman as well; and when the notice was to be given by *took o' drum*, the town-drummer accompanied him. In some places, however, the town-officer had charge of both drum and bell.
O. Fr. *tabourin*, "a little Drumme; also the Drumme, or Drummer of a companie of footmen;" Cotgr. From O. Fr. *tabour*, a drum.
Tabuirie, however, may be a colloquial form of *taborer*, a drummer, O. Fr. *taboureur*.

TAED, *s.* A toad. V. TAID.

TAED-SPUE, TAED-RED, *s.* The seed or spawn of toads, found in stagnant water in clots or masses like bunches of grapes.

TAET, TEAT, *s.* A small quantity, a tuft: syn. *pickle, wee pickle*. V. TAIT, TATE.
An' tent them duly e'en and morn,
Wi' *taets* o' hay, an' ripps o' corn.
Burns, Death of Poor Mailie.

TAIGSUM, TIGSUM, *adj.* Hindersome, very tedious, wearisome: short for *taiglesum*: *tigsum*, Gloss. Orcadian Sketch Book.

TAINGS, TAYNGS, *s.* Tongs, smith's tongs or pincers. V. TANGS.
"*Forceps, taynys*"; Duncan's App. Etym., 1595, ed. Small, E. D. S.

To TAIS, *v. a.* To stretch, extend, direct; hence, to bend a bow or set a cross-bow, or generally to make a weapon ready for

(Sup.) F 2

use or to make ready to use it, to take aim. Addit. to TAIS, q. v.

Improperly defined in DICT., and only a secondary meaning is given. The primary meaning is to stretch, extend, from which poise, adjust, and other terms implying "to take aim," are obtained. *Tais* is not of Goth. origin, as Jamieson suggested, but from O. Fr. *teser, toiser*, to stretch, from Lat. *tensus :* see Burguy. In the first passage quoted in DICT., *tais* means "did aim ; in the second, *taisyt* implies fitted and drew, i.e., prepared to shoot; and in the third, *tast* is a misprint for *taisit*, in Rudd., in Elph. MS. *taysit*, meaning hold on the stretch, poised, i.e., aimed.

To TAISE, TAYSE, *v. a.* To tease, toss or tumble about, vex, plague, harass; E. *tease*. V. TAISSLE.

A.-S. *tæsan*, to pluck, pull; Dan. *tæse*. The M. Eng. form was sometimes *taisen*, but more commonly *tosen*. See *Touse* in Skeat's Etym. Dict.

To TAIST, *v. a.* V. DICT.

The etym. given in DICT. is a mistake. It is well known that the Teut. forms referred to by Jamieson are borrowed from the Romance. Hence the words are not "of Gothic origin," but of Latin origin. *Taist* is simply M. E. *tasten*, to test, from O. Fr. *taster*, to handle, test, taste, which, according to Diez and Burguy, answers to a L. Lat. *taxitare*, an iterative form of Lat. *tangere*, derived from p. p. *tactus*.

To TAK, *v. a.* and *n.* 1. To take, bite, or rise at the bait readily; "The trout 'll no *tak* ava the day."

2. To be attractive, to command respect or regard, as, "She's a braw lass an' *taks* weel;" to command a good price or ready market, as, "ne'er saw cowts *tak* better," i.e., sell better, or more readily. Addit. to To TAK, q. v.

TAK, TAKIN, *s.* Capture, catch, or haul; as of fish. Also in the sense of a marketing or bargain-making; as, "She made a guid *tak* when she got the laird." Addit. to TAK, q. v.

To TAK AFF, *v. a.* 1. To set out or depart for; as, "Noo, I maun *tak aff* hame;" and similarly Burns has—

Then homeward all *take off* their several way,
The youngling cottagers retire to rest.
Cotter's Saturday Night.

2. To turn off, stop; as, "*to tak aff* the mill."

3. To quaff, drink all of; as, "*Tak aff* your dram;" Burns, The Earnest Cry. Addit. to TAK AFF, q. v.

TAK AFF, *s.* A piece of mimicry, mockery, or personal ridicule; also, a mimic, punster, practical joker. E. *take-off*.

TAKIN', TAKEN, *s.* A small quantity; "*a wee takin*," a very small quantity: West of S., Orkn.

TAKEN, TAKYN, *s.* A token, sign. V. TAKIN.

TAKENYNG, TAKYNIN, *s.* Token, indication, evidence, assurance; Kingis Quair, st. 176, ed. Skeat. Addit. to TAKYNNYNG. q. v.

TALBART, TALBERT, *s.* V. DICT.

Simply *tabbart* and *tabbert*. The apparent *lb* of MSS. is the usual way of writing contracted *bb*. This style of contraction was adopted in writing doubles of the long letters. For particulars see *Slalk*.

TALBRONE, TALBERONE, *s.* V. DICT.

Should be printed *tabbrone, tabberone*. See under *Talbart*.

TALPING, *part.* A form of *taping*, breaking bulk, retailing. V. *Tape*.

"To pas to Dunbertane to arreist schippis for *talping* of groit salt." Burgh Recs. Glasgow, i. 450, Rec. Soc.

TALPON, TALPOUN, *s.* V. *Tapon*.

TANE, *pret.* Took. Still used by the lower classes.

"Johne Cuthbertson vndertuik to learne John Jemesoun, his college [i.e. colleague], the tailycour craft, sua lang as the counsell sall appoint, because thay oulie *tane* thame tua to be drummeris, and na ma." Burgh Recs. Glasgow, i. 360, Rec. Soc.

TANG, *s.* Taste, gout; syn. *smak*. V. TWANG.

TANG O' THE TRUMP, *s.* Lit. the tongue of the Scottish trump or Jew's harp; but used fig. for the chief or most important person in a company, the principal partner in a firm, the leader of a society or in a public movement.

TANGIE, *s.* A young seal; Orkn. Addit. to TANGIE, q. v.

To TANT, TANTER, *v. n.* To argue or dispute in a captious, quarrelsome manner; to rage; hence, *tantrums*, whims, fits of passion, &c.

To TAPE, TAP, TOPE, TOP, *v. a.* To sell goods in small quantities or by retail; Burgh Recs. Edinburgh, I. 36, 37; B. R. Glasgow, I. 41, 46, 174. Addit. to TAPE, q. v.

TAP, *s.* Short for *tapin, tappin*, dealing out in small quantities: hence, *to sell by tap*, to sell by retail, as opposed to selling *in great*, i.e. wholesale.

Improperly defined in DICT.; but the correct meaning is suggested in the note under the quotation.

TAPPAR, TOPPAR, *s.* Retailer, huckster; Burgh Recs. Glasgow, I. 39, 82.

TAPETE, TAPHET, *s.* A mort-cloth, covering laid over the dead during the church-service; Invent. St. Salv. College, Mait. Club Misc., III. 199.

L. Lat. *tapetum*, "pannus qui feretro insternitur;" Ducange.

TAPON, TAPONE, TAPPONE, TALPON, TALPOUN, TAUPON, TAWPON, *s.* 1. Bung, stopper, plug, &c., of a barrel, also the bunghole; Burgh Recs. Edinburgh, II. 112, 161. V. TAPONE-STAFF.

2. The plug, knob, or measure-mark in the mouth of a vessel used as a liquid-measure. V. PLUKE.

"Fra this day furth haif stowppis of mesour with *tawponis* in the hals." Ibid. 31 Jan., 1543-4.
O. Fr. *tapon*, "bung, stopple;" Cotgr.

TAPPE, *s.* V. TAP O' LINT.

TAPPIE, *s.* A stupid blockhead; Orkn. Prob. a form of *taupie*, foolish, applied to males as well as females. V. TAUPIE.

TAPPIE-TOORIE, *adj.* Tall and pointed, lofty and feathery-tipped. V. TAPPIE-TOURIE, *s.*

'Bonn a' that's in thee, to evin me, sunny Spring –
Bricht cluds an' green buds, and sangs that the birdies sing—
Flow'r dappled hill-side, and dewy beech sae fresh at e'en—
Or the *tappie-toorie* fir-tree shinin a' in green—
W. Miller, Spring, st. 4.

TARFF, *adj.* Harsh, acrid; rough in manner; Orcadian Sketch Book, p. 101.

TARLEATHER, TARLETHER, TARLEDDER, *s.* Lit. belly-leather, or belly-skin: a strip of raw sheep-skin (cut from the belly of the skin when it was newly flayed), salted and dried. It was then like thairm or cat-gut in consistency, and was cut up into thongs for ties or mid-couples of flails. V. MID-CUPPIL.

Dr. Jamieson's definition and etymology of this term are altogether wrong. A strip of bull-hide never could be used as a *tarledder* for a flail; being far too thick and unyielding. However, the following extract puts the question beyond dispute, and clearly shows what a *tarleather* was.
". . as it is menit to the prouest, baillies, and counsall of this burgh . . . that the flescheouris of this burgh cuttis thair scheip skynnis hard by the craig, at the leist in the mid craig, qubairthrow the merchandis wantis samekill of the said skynne at the craig with the best portioun of the woll thairof, quhilk is the fynest woll of the skyn, callit the halslok, and als the saidis flescheouris pullis the hail skin fra the hals doun to the taill throw all the wambe thairof, and cuttis ane *tarledder* of the skyn thairwith, diminisching thairby baith the skynnis and the woll in lenth and breid, quhairby the saidis merchandis ar grytly damnefeit and skaythit. . . For remeid quhairof the saidis prouest, baillies, and counsall hes statut and ordanit that all flescheouris flay all thair scheipe in tyme cuming up throw the haill craig to the luggis, sua that the lug steik with the skin, and neuther pull the woll of the halls, wambe, nor na vther pairt thairof, nor yit to diminische the samyn be cutting of ony

sic pairt as thai call the *tarledder*, vnder the pane of confyscatioun of the skynnis," &c. Burgh Recs. Edin., Dec. 1566, Rec. Soc.
Tarleather occurs frequently in our Burgh Records, but generally in charges or complaints against fleshers. Various definitions and explanations of the term have been given; but all of them are more or less defective or erroneous.

TARLETHERIT, TARLEDDERIT, *part. pt.* Having the tarleather cut off: applied to sheepskins from which tarleathers have been cut; B. R. Edin., iv. 407, Rec. Soc.

Gael. *tarr-leathar*, belly-leather, belly-skin, from Gael. *tarr*, belly, and *leathar*, leather: the latter term, however, is borrowed from M. E. or A.-S.

To TARROW, *v. n.* V. DICT.
The etym. of this word is not A.-S. *teorian*, to fail, as suggested, but A.-S. *tirian*, *tirigan*, *tyrwian*, to vex, irritate, provoke. A.-S. *teorian* gives E. tire, through M. E. *tirien*; while *tirigan*, *tirian*, gives tarry, through M. E. *tarien*, to vex, provoke, tire, hence to hinder, delay. See Wedgwood and Skeat, s. v. *Tire*, and Skeat, s. v. *Tarry*.

TASEE, *s.* A fibula, clasp, button, or tache; Awnt. Arthure, st. 28. V. TASSES.
In Pinkerton's version this word was printed *tasses*, and so it was entered in the DICT.; but it was improperly defined. For explanation see under that heading.

TASSEL, *s.* Same as *Tersel*, q. v.

To TAT, TAUT, TAWT, *v. n.* To mat, tangle, or run into *tates*, locks, or tufts, as wool or hair does: also used as a *v. a.*, as, "Dinna *taut* your hair sa."

TAT, TAUT, TAWT, *s.* A tangle, matted tuft or lock of wool or hair.

TAUTY, TAWTIE, TAUTIT, TAWTIT, *adj.* Tangled, matted, uncombed; "*tautit* hair," Whistle Binkie, II. 220. V. TATTY, TAWTIE.

TATHIS, *s. pl.* Tatters, fragments, shreds: prob. a poetic form of *tates*, small portions. V. TATE.
The trew helmys and traist in *tathis* thai ta.
Gol. and Gawane, st. 71.

TATTIE, TATIE, *s.* A potatoe. V. TAWTIE.

TATTIES AND DAB. Potatoes and salt: one of the simplest and cheapest of meals.
When the potatoes are laid on the table each person takes a quantity of salt and lays it in a small heap before him. Then each potatoe, when pealed, he *dabs* into this heap; and it picks up sufficient salt to make the food palatable. When the potatoes are eaten from the pot, however, it is set on the floor, and the party sit round it. Salt is placed on a stool within easy reach of all, and each one helps himself from the supply by *dabbing* his potatoe on it. The meal when so taken is often called "*dab at the stool.*"

TATTIES AND POINT. A repast consisting of potatoes and a sight of meat or fish; sarcastically said to be common in Ireland.

For this repast a plentiful supply of potatoes is said to be provided, with a small bit of meat or fish, which is merely to be looked at. For the improvement of the potatoes, however, each one before it is eaten is *pointed* at the luxury, i.e., gets a look of it. Evidently this is a joke.

TAUM, TAWM, *s.* A drowsy, sick, or fainting turn. Addit. to TAWM, q. v.

To TAUM, TAWM, *v. n.* To fall gently asleep, to faint, become unconscious. V. DUALM.
Gael. *tamh*, rest, quiet; and as a *v.* to fall asleep, give over.

TAUTIT, TAUTY, *adj.* V. under *Tat, Taut.*

TAVER, *v.* and *s.* V. TAIVER.

To TAWNE, *v. a.* To break down, reduce, overcome, subdue; Blame of Kirkburial, ch. 15. Addit. to TAW, TAWEN, q. v.

TAY, *s.* A tie, cover, wrapping: *tay of the harnes*, the membrane enclosing the brain.
"*Meninx*, the *tay* of the harnes;" Duncan's App. Etym., ed. Small, E.D.S.
O. Fr. *taye*, "a filme;" Cotgr.

To TEAL, TILL, *v. a.* V. DICT.
The following account of these terms is simpler and more direct:—
They represent M. E. *tillen*, to draw, draw out, allure: from A.-S. *tyllan*, found only in the comp. *fortyllan*, to draw aside, lead astray. And this etym. is confirmed by the form *tulle*, which Jamieson quotes from Chaucer. It represents M. E. *tullen*, which is simply another form of *tillen.*

TEAT, *s.* V. TATE, *Taet.*

To TED, TEAD, TEDD, TEDDE, *v. a.* To spread out, arrange in order, smooth, tidy, dress: as, " *Ted* your hair, and *tedd* up the house:" West of S.

TED, TEAD, TEDD, TEDDE, *s.* The act of setting right, arranging, or putting in order; as, "Gie the room a ted up."
This term is prob. of Celtic origin. Cf. Welsh *tedu*, to stretch out, and *teddu*, to spread out.

TEDDER-STAKE, *s.* The stake or pin to which the tether of an animal at pasture is fastened; also, the upright post in a stall to which a cow is fastened.

To TEEM, *v. a.* and *n.* V. DICT.
The etym. of this verb is simple yet interesting, and may be stated thus:—Icel. *tæma*, to empty; from Icel. *tómr*, empty (Scot. *toom*).

TEEN, *s.* Anger, vexation; Burns. V. TENE.

To TEETH, TEETHE, *v. a.* To fix teeth in a spiked instrument, as a rake, a heckle, &c.: part. pr. *teethin*, "*teethin* a heckle," Burns.

TEEWIT, TEEWEET, *s.* The lapwing: also called *peeweet*, and *peasweep*, which are names of imitative origin.

TEIL-RIG, TEILL-RYGE, *s.* The borderridge of land under cultivation, tillagebound. V. TEIL, *v.*
"That na maner of takisman of the tounis land ryif out ony landis within the fredome and saw cornis thairon without thair *teill ryge* of auld without license of the prouest," etc. Burgh Recs. Aberdeen, i. 274, Sp. C.

TEIR, TERE, TER, TOR, TORE, *adj.* Tedious, Tiresome, lingering, exhausting, racking; Gol. and Gawane, st. 17, 70, 104; Awnt. Arthure, st. 10. Addit. to TEIR, q. v.
Allied to Icel. *tor*, difficult. The Icel. prefix *tor-* answers to Goth. prefix *tus-*, and Greek prefix *dus-*.
Jamieson's etym. for this term is unsuitable and impossible.

To TELDE, *v. a.* V. DICT.
In the cross-reference of this entry, for "N. Tyld" read "V. Tyld."

TELL. To *hear tell*, to learn by report or hearsay; *to be heard tell of*, to be made known or talked about.

TELL'D, TELL'T, *pret.* and *part. pt.* Told, warned, advised, reported.

To TELL *on, off,* or *over, v. a.* To count, count over, enumerate, make up sets of a certain number each.
" *Recensco*, to *tell on*, to muster;" Duncan's App. Etym., ed. Small, E.D.S.

TEMERAT, *adj.* Rash, inconsiderate, imprudent. Lat. *temaratus.*
Thocht wemen self be *temerat*,
Thay luve no man effeminat,
And haklis thame bot I wat not quhat,
That can nocht be without thame.
Alex. Scott's Poems, p. 18, ed. 1882.

TEMPER, *s.* Contr. for TEMPER-PIN, q. v.

TENDLE, TENNLE, TENNEL, *s.* Lit. firewood; dried twigs, furze, scrub, &c., gathered for fuel.
A.-S. *tendan*, to kindle; Dan. *tænde*, Sw. *tända.*

TENDLE-KNIFE, TENNLE-KNIFE, TENDALE-KNYFF, *s.* A knife for cutting firewood, a hedge-bill, bill-hook. Addit. to TENDALE-KNYFF, q. v.

TENE, *adj.* Causing pain or sorrow; difficult of passage, perilous, fatiguing; " *tene wais*," perilous ways; Gol. and Gawane, st. 3. Addit. to TENE, q. v.

TENE, *s.* Tithe: " *tene corne*," Burgh Recs. Edinburgh, I. 21, Rec. Soc. V. TEIND.

TENT, TENTER, TENTOUR, *adj.* Tenth: "*tentour* ryk," tenth rig, Burgh Recs. Peebles, 27 May, 1470.

TENT, TEYNT, *s.* A wine of a deep red colour, from Galicia or Malaga; Burgh Recs. Aberdeen, II. 176, Sp. C.; Halyburton's Ledger, p. 335.
Span. *tinto,* tinged, coloured: from Lat. *tinctus.*

TERE, *adj.* Tedious, lingering, weary, exhausting, racking: "panis *tere* ontald," countless weary sufferings; Douglas, Virgil, Prol. 358, 8, ed. Rudd. Addit. to TERE, q. v. V. *Teir.*
This term was left undefined by Jamieson, but the correct meaning is suggested in his note of explanation. Allied to Icel. *tor,* difficult.

TEREFUL, TYREFULL, *adj.* Very tedious, difficult, fatiguing; Houlate, l. 421, Asloan MS. Addit. to TEIRFULL, q. v.

TERSEL, TERSIL, TIRSEL, TIRCEL, TESSIL, TASSEL, *s.* The tercel or male falcon, especially the male of the common falcon, *Falco communis.* The male goshawk also is frequently called a tercel. Rates of Customs, 1612.
Latterly, in the language of falconry, all birds trained for the chase were called tercels or falcons according as they were male or female. And according as the sport was called hawking or falconry, the birds were indiscriminately named hawks or falcons.
A tercel in its first year plumage is of a much deeper colour than the adult bird, and hence is called a *red-tercel* or *red-hawk.*
O. Fr. *tiercelet,* dimin. of *tiers,* third, so called because the third in each nest is said to be a male; but Cotgrave's explanation is—"*Tiercelet:* The Tassell, or male of any kind of Hawke, so tearmed, because he is, commonly, a third part lesse then the female."
E. *tarsel, tassell, tercel, tiercel.*

TETH, *s.* V. DICT.
The etym. suggested is unsuitable. Cf. Icel. *teytha,* a vile, wicked, person, a term of abuse with which Vigfusson connects Icel. *tuddi,* similarly used.

TETHER-TOW, *s.* A hawser, cable; Whistle-Binkie, I. 233.

To TETTER, *v. a.* To hinder, delay; prob. a local pron. of *tether;* Orkn. V. TEDDER, *v.*

TEUGH, TEWGH, *adj.* 1. Tough, strong, tenacious, cohesive; as, *teugh* glue, *tewgh* clay.
"*Tenax,* clamm, *tewgh;*" Duncan's App. Etym., ed. Small, E.D.S.

2. Difficult, laborious, troublesome; as, a *teugh* job. Addit. to TEUCH, q. v.

TEUGHNESS, TEWGHNES, *s.* Toughness, strength, tenacity, endurance, tediousness.
"*Tenacitas,* tewghnes, niggardnes;" Duncan's App. Etym., ed. Small, E.D.S.

TEUK, *pret.* Took; Burns.

THACK-NAIL, THACK-PIN, *s.* A wooden pin used in fastening thatch to the roof of a house.
Common in the north of Eng. also. V. Brockett.

THACK-RAPE, THAK-RAIP, *s.* A straw-rope used in fixing the thatch on a stack of hay or grain, or on the roof of a house.

THAIN, *s.* A vane. V. THANE.

THAK-STAYNE, *s.* V. THACK-STONE.

THAME, THAIM, *s.* V. THEME.

THAN. Prob. the acc. of A.-S. *the.*
The wynde and the wedyrs *than* welken in hydis.
Avent. Arthure, st. 26.
For this form see March, A.-S. Gram., p. 69.
In hydis, which is the reading of Laing's version, is certainly a mistake for *un-hydis,* i.e., cleare. The Douce MS. has "*the welkyn vnhides.*"

THARF, THAIRF, *adj.* Cold, stiff, unsocial; backward, reluctant; South and West of S.
Common in the North of Eng. also; see Brockett, Atkinson.
Prob. from A.-S. *tharf, pres. sing.* of *thurfan,* to need, an anomalous verb. Brockett, however, suggests A.-S. *thrafian,* to urge, compel, which can hardly be right; and Atkinson, O. Norse *thörf,* need, necessity.

THARFISH, *adj.* Of a shy, timorous, shrinking nature.

THARTH, *v.* A form of *thart,* it needs or behoves; *me tharth,* it behoves me, I must; Rauf Coilyear, l. 536. V. [THAR].
The change of *t* into *th* at the end of a word is still common; similarly we find *thurth* for *thurt,* Barbour vi. 121, Edin. MS.; and *scurth* for *scart,* a cormorant, is common in the West of S.

THAVIL, THAIVIL, *s.* A pot-stick. V. THEEVIL.

THAYS, *v.* They are. V. *They's.*

THE, *pron.* Thee; Kingis Quair, st. 15, 129; to thee, Ibid., st. 106, ed. Skeat.
In the following passage of the Kingis Quair, *the* occurs both as an *acc.* and as a *dat.*
And therefor humily
Abyde, and serue, and lat gude hope *the* gye:
Bot, for I haue thy forehede here present,
I will the schewe the more of myn entent.
St. 106.

THEAM, THEEM, *s.* V. THEME.

THEEFS, THEIFS, *s. pl.* Thieves; used also as an *adj.,* as in *theifs-hole,* the lowest or innermost cell of a prison; Burgh Recs. Edinburgh, 7 Sept., 1565.

THEFT-BOOT, s. V. THIFTBUTE.
This form was used by Sir W. Scott in his Rob Roy, ch. 23.

THEVIS-NEK, THEUIS-NEK, s. One fit for or doomed to the gallows; synon. *widdie-nek*, used by Henryson. Addit. to defin. in DICT.
  The Tuchet and the gukkit Golk——
  Ruschit baith to the barr aud ruggit his hair,
  Callit him thrys *thevisnek* to thrawe in a widdy.
      Houlate, l. 822, Asloan MS.
Jamieson must have misunderstood this passage when he set it as an illustration to the secondary meaning of *thevisnek* given in the DICT.

THEIPTREE, s. A pron. of THREEPTREE, q. v.

THERE, adv. Where; *there as*, where that.
  Bot, for the way is vncouth vnto the,
  There as bir duelling is and hir soiurne.
  I will that gude hope seruand to the be.
      Kingis Quair, st. 113, ed. Skeat.

THEY'S, THEYS, THAIS, THAYS, v. n. Lit. they are; but also used for they shall, as in *theys be*, they shall be. When this latter meaning is implied, *s* or *'s* represents *sal*, and should be written *s'*.
  I mak ane vow to Sanct Mavane,
  Quhen I them finde *thays* bear thair paiks :
  I se thay haif playit me the glaiks,
      Lyndsay, The Thrie Estaitis, l. 1877.
These are varieties of the old North Anglian form of the verb *to be*, which is not yet entirely disused. Regarding the second meaning, see under *'S, 'Se*.

THIEF'S HOLE, s. V. under *Theefs*.

THIFT, s. Theft, thievery; *commoun thift*, common theft, also, common thief, as in Lyndsay, Thrie Estaitis, l. 3211.

THIGGAN, part. pr. Begging. V. THIG.
  An' if the wives an' dirty brats
  Come *thiggan* at your doors an' yetts,
  Flaffan wi' duds.
      Burns, Address of Beelzebub.

To THIK, v. a. To thatch. V. THEIK.

THIKFALD, adj. and adv. Manifold, numberless; in close succession, thick and fast.
  O ye my feris and my fremdis bald,
  Thron mony hard perrellis and *thikfald*,
  Throw sa feill stormis bayth on land and se,
  Hiddir now careit to this cost with me.
      Douglas, Virgil, xiii., ch. 2, Small.
A.-S. *thicce-feald*, manifold.

THILKE, pron. That, such, the same, that same.
  Quhen flouris springis and freschest bene of hews,
  And that the birdis on the twistis sing,
  At *thilke* tyme ay gynnen folk renewe
  That seruis vnto loue, as ay is dewe.
      Kingis Quair, st. 119, ed. Skeat.
A.-S. *thylc*, the like, such, that; from *thy*, the, and *lic*, like.

THIMBLE, THUMBLE, s. The game of thimbles, thimbles and pea, thimble-rigging; "a sharper at the *thimble*," i.e., a thimble-rigger.

THIMBLER, THUMBLER, s. A thimble-rigger.
  Mony big loons hae hechted to wyle her awa,
  Baith *thumblers*, and tumblers, and tinklers, an' a';
  But she jeers them, an' tells them, her Willie tho' sma',
  Has mair in his buik than the best o' them a'.
      J. Ballantine, Willie an' Maggy, st. 5.

THIMBLIN', THUMBLIN', part. adj. Thimble-rigging, cheating by means of the thimbles and pea; sometimes used as a general term for gambling.
  Ilk *thimblin'*, thievin,' gamblin' diddler—
  Chase thee like fire.
      J. Ballantine, The Wee Raggit Laddie, st. 9.

THINARE, s. V. DICT.
This entry must be deleted, for there is no such word. The term is a misprint for *thin are*, thy favour; and is short for "I supplicate thy favour." Of this I was not aware when I suggested the meaning given in the DICT. For further explanation see under *Are, s.*, in the Addenda.

To THING, v. a. To stand up for, plead for, support, back.
  With leif of ladeis thocht ye *thing* thame,
      Ressoun;
  Bot eftirwart and ye maling thame,
      Tressoun.
      Alex. Scott's Poems, p. 42, ed. 1882.
A.-S. *thingian*, to intercede for.

To THINK on. 1. To meditate, ponder, consider, plan.
  When I *think on* this world's pelf,
  And the little wee share I hae o't to myself.
  And how the lass that wants it is to the lads forgot,
  May the shame fa' the gear and the blethrie o't.
      Song, Shame fa' the gear, st. 1.
  John,
  Wha ne'er the less was *thinkin on*
      A trap he had prepared
  Upon the road—and how to get
      Advantage o' the laird.
      The Million of Potatoes.

2. To remember, bear in mind, take heed of.
  I sit on my creepie and spin at my wheel,
  And *think on* the laddie that lo'ed me sae weel;
  He had but ae saxpence—he brak it in twa,
  An' he gied me the hauf o't when he gaed awa.
      Song, Logie o' Buchan, st. 4.
  While we sit bousing at the nappy,
  An' getting fou and unco happy,
  We *think na on* the laug Scots miles,
  The mosses, waters, slaps, and stiles,
  That lie between us and our hame.
      Burns, Tam o' Shanter.

3. To recollect, recall to mind, muse over. "It's weel laid by; but I canna *think on* where I put it."
In this sense the expression is very common in Shropshire also.

4. To give heed to, consent to, comply with; "Sic a plan as that I wad never *think on*."

THIR, *pron. pl.* V. DICT.
In l. 2 of quotation, for *Waue* read *Wane*.

THIRD, *s.* A term in golfing ; a handicap of a stroke deducted every third hole ; see Golfer's Handbook.

THO, *pron.* Those; Lyndsay, Exper. and Court, l. 224. Kingis Quair, st. 39, 88, Awnt. Arthure, st. 20.
This term was improperly rendered *these* by Jamieson ; see DICT.

THOCHT, *pret.* and *part. pt.* Thought, imagined, expected.

THOCHT, *s.* Thought, imagination, opinion, expectation : *absent thochts*, opinions regarding a person who is not present, unbiased opinions regarding an absent friend or acquaintance.

The Ladies arm in arm in clusters,
As great an' gracious a' as sisters;
But bear their *absent thochts* o' lther,
They're a run deils an' jads thegither.
Burns, The Twa Dogs.

THOFT, THOFTIN. V. under *Toft.*

THOLE, *s.* V. THOILL.

THONDER, *adv.* Yonder. V. THON.

THOOM, *s.* Thumb. V. THOUM.

THORN, THORN'D, *part. adj.* Filled, supplied, provided, satisfied : applied to bodily wants.

Ye'll eat and drink my merry men a',
An' see ye be weell *thorn* ;
For blaw it weet or blaw it wind,
My guid ship sails the morn.
Sir Patrick Spens, st. 6, Buchan's vers.

When they had eaten and well drunken
And a' had *thorn'd* fine ;
The bride's father he took the cup,
For to serve out the wine.
Sweet Willie and Fair Maisry, st. 24.

Perhaps allied to A.-S. *thearfan, theorfan, thurfan,* to need, avail, profit, an anomalous verb. See Note under *Tharf* in Cleveland Glossary.

THORTERSOME, *adj.* Lying or stretching in all directions ; troublesome, perplexing ; Blame of Kirkburiall, ch. 17. V. THORTER.

THOU'S. Contr. for *thou art, thou hast,* or *thou shalt* or *wilt.* V. under '*S, 'Se.*

THRALY, *adv.* Eagerly, fiercely ; Houlate, l. 489. V. THRA, *adv.*

THRAMMEL, *s.* V. DICT.
That this term is of Gothic origin is very unlikely. Both the form and the meaning of the word suggest that it is simply E. *trammel :* M. E. *tramaile,* which, if not from O. Fr. *tramail,* has with it come from L. Lat. *tramacula,* a fishing-net, which later became *tramallum,* and *tramela.* See Ducange, Skeat, and Wedgwood.

THRAPLE-PLOUGH, THRAPPLE-PLOUGH, *s.* The old wooden plough with one stilt.

" The old *Thraple plough* is now seldom to be seen, except in the remote Highlands, or in the Orkneys. It was also called the Rotheram plough, and was entirely composed of wood, with the exception of the culter and sock, and had but one stilt. It was drawn by four garrons or oxen yoked abreast to a cross-bar, which was fastened to the beam by thongs of raw hide or ropes of hair ; and he who managed the stilt held it close and firm to his right thigh, to protect which he had the skin of a sheep or other animal wrapt around it. To keep the plough sufficiently deep in the earth a person was required to press it down, while another performed the office of driver by placing himself between the two central animals, where he walked backwards, protecting himself from falling by placing both arms over their necks. The mould-board was ribbed or furrowed, in order to break the land ; and old people declare that the soil yielded better crops after being ploughed in this manner than it does by the modern practice. The supposition is, that by the old method the soil was more equally broken up." The Scottish Gael, ii. 95-6, ed. 1876.

To this old *thraple plough,* with its traces of raw-hide or rope, reference is made by the *auld farmer* in his New Year greeting to his *auld mare* Maggie, when he says:

Thou was a noble fittie-lan'
As e'er in tug or tow was drawn !
Aft thee an' I, in aught hours gaun,
On guid March-weather,
Hae turned sax rood beside our han',
For days thegither.
Burns.

This plough was still in common use in Carrick and Galloway in Burns' younger days, and it was not generally abandoned in the lower districts till the beginning of the present century. See Old Stat. Acct. Scotland, Robertson's Agricultural Recollections, Ure's Agric. of Dumbarton.

To THRAW, THRA, *v. a.* and *n.* 1. To rush, press, drive, force.

Off Edinburgh the boyis as beis owt *thrawis,*
And cryis owt ay, " Heir cumis our awin queir Clerk ! "
Then fleis thow lyk ane howlat chest with crawis.
Dunbar and Kennedy, l. 217.

2. To contradict, thwart ; hence, to provoke, enrage, torment ; " I'll thraw him at every turn." Addit. to THRAW, q. v.

THRAW, *s.* Rush, press, crowd ; opposition, struggle, contest ; spite, rage, trouble. Addit. to THRAW, *s.,* q. v.

THRALY, *adv.* Eagerly, fiercely. V. THRA, *adv.*

To THREAP, THREIP, *v. a.* To assert, aver ; pret. *threp, threipit.* V. THREPE.

THREAP, THREEP, THREIP, *s.* V. THREPE.

THREF, THRAFE, *s.* A threave ; B. R. Prestwick, 23 Oct., 1550. V. THRAIF.

To THRESH, *v. a.* To thrash grain, to use the flail ; *to thresh the barn,* to do a man's work with the flail.

This form of the word is common in the Bible; and it was used by Milton, see L'Allegro, l. 103, Paradise Lost, iv. 984; *thrash* is comparatively modern. M. E. *threshen*, from A.-S. *therscan*, to thrash.

THRICH, *v.* and *s.* Thrust. V. **Thrist.**

THRINE, Trine, Trene, Tryne, *adv.* Thrice.

Thrinefald, Thrinfald, Trinefald, Trenefald, Trynfald, *adj.* Threefold, triple; "a *thrinfald* hawbrik," Douglas, Virgil, iii. 6.

> Gloir to the Fader be aboif,
> Gloir to the Sone for our behoif,
> Gloir to the Haly Spreit of loif,
> In *trenefald* vnitie.
> *Alex. Scott's Poems*, p. 6, ed. 1882.

THRIVAND, Thriuand, *adj.* Hearty, successful, prosperous; Gol. and Gaw., st. 27.

Thrivandly, Thriuandly, *adv.* Successfully, prosperously; Gol. and Gaw., st. 34.

Thriven,. Thryuen, *part. pt.* Prospered; also used as an *adj.* meaning good-looking, well-favoured.

Icel. *thrífa*, to clutch, grasp, seize; Dan. *trives*, Swed. *trifvas*, to thrive.

THROAT-BOLE, Throate-Bowle, *s.* The throat-ball, ball of the throat.

"*Frumen*, the *throate-bowle*;" Duncan's App. Etym., 1595, ed. Small, E. D. S.

THROCHT, *s.* A trough, vat. V. **Troch.**

To **THROU,** *v. n.* To go through, pass, make or find a passage; Kingis Quair, st. 63, ed. Skeat. Addit. to **Through.**

To **Throu, Throo,** *v. a.* V. **Throuch,** *v.*

Througate, Throughgate, Throgat, *s.* A lane or passage from one street to another; an entry, close, or common passage from a street to a back-land, a field, or a garden; Burgh Recs. Peebles, p. 117, Rec. Soc. V. **Throughgang.**

Through - Lock, Throu-Lok, Throcht-Lok, *s.* A lock which has the key-hole passing right through; with such a lock the door may be fastened from the inside as well as the outside; Burgh Recs. Aberdeen, i. 237, Sp. C.

THROUTHER, *adj.* V. **Through-Ither.**

To **THROW, Throwe,** *v. a.* To drive, propel. Addit. to **Throw,** q. v.

> Helples allone, the wynter nyght I wake
> To wayte the wynd that furthward suld me *throwe*.
> *Kingis Quair*, st. 17, ed. Skeat.

THRUM, *s.* The extremity of the warp of a web from six to nine inches long which cannot be woven; it has the appearance of a tufted border. Pl. *thrums*, short threads which are kept by a weaver for mending his web; hence, fragments, snatches, as applied to snatches of songs, the purring of a cat; *grey thrums*, ravelled snatches.

> Hey, Willie Winkie, are ye coming ben?
> The cat's singing *grey thrums* to the sleeping ben,
> The dog's spelder'd on the floor, and diana gie a cheep,
> But here's a waukrife laddie, that winna fa' asleep.
> *W. Miller, Willie Winkie*, st. 2.

To **Thrum,** *v. a.* To raise a tufted pile on knitted or woven woollen stuffs, to cover woollen cloth with small tufts like thrums; part. pt. *thrum'd, thrummed, thrummit*.

Thrummed, Thrummit, Thrumit, *part. adj.* Lit. covered with small tufts or thrums: applied to knitted or woven woollen stuffs which have been dressed with a rough, shaggy, or tufted surface; a *thrum'd* cap, a knitted cap with tufted pile; "ane *thrumit* hat," a hat made of very coarse woollen cloth, Burgh Recs. Aberdeen, I. 237, Sp. c.

"A *thrummed* hat was one made of very coarse woollen cloth; Minsheu." Halliwell.

Thrummy, *s.* A very coarse woollen cloth with a rough tufted surface; a *thrummy* cap, one made of *thrummy*.

A person who wore such a cap was called *thrummy-cap*, as in the tale of Thrummy Cap and the Ghaist. In the opening of that story the hero is thus portrayed:

> He was a sturdy bartoch chiel,
> An' frae the weather happit weel.
> Wi' a mill'd plaiden jockey coat,
> And eke he on his head had got
> A *thrummy-cap*, baith large and stoot,
> Wi' flaps ahint (as well's a snout),
> Whilk button'd close aneath the chin,
> To keep the cauld frae cummin in.
> Upon his legs he had gammashes,
> Which sogers ca' their spatterdashes;
> An' on his han's, instead o' glo'es,
> Large doddy mittens, whilk he'd roose
> For warmness; an' an aiken stick,
> Nay very lang but gay an' thick,
> Intil his neive, he drove awa',
> An' car'd for neither frost nor sna'.

THRUST, *s.* Thirst. V. **Thrist.**

THRYS, Thryst, Thryset, *adv.* Thrice.

THUMART, Thumar, Thummart, *s.* Pron. of *fowmarte*, a polecat: *thummart*, Burns, The Twa Herds, st. 6. V. **Thulmard.**

THUMBLER, *s.* A thimble-rigger. V. **Thimbler.**

THURL, *v.* and *s.* V. **Thirl.**

THYKIT, *pret.* and *part. pt.* Thatched. V. **Theek.**

TIBETLESS, *adj.* Benumbed, powerless, useless, as applied to fingers, hands, or feet benumbed with cold. It is also applied to the mind, and as expressive of what one's character or conduct indicates regarding it: hence, senseless, stupid, heedless, foolish, incapable of understanding and acting aright. Addit. to TABETLESS, q. v.

This form represents a very common pron. in the West of S., where the word is still used in tho various senses indicated. The term is very fairly discussed in Cuthbertson's Glossary to Burns, p. 390.

To TICE, TISE, *v. a.* To entice, allure, induce: short for *entice*.

O. Fr. *enticer, enticher.* to excite, entice; M. E. *enticen.* "Tycyn or intycyn. *Instigo, allicio.*" Prompt. Parv.

TIFTING, TIFTIN, *s.* Scolding; a scolding given or received. V. TIFT.

To TIKLE, *v. a.* To stir or move gently; to excite, quicken; part. pr. *tiklyng*, used also as a *s.*, meaning gentle stirring, quickening. Addit. to TICKLE, q. v.

In describing the genial influence of the sun in spring, the poet says—

And with the *tiklyng* of his hete and light,
The tender flouris opayt thame and sprad,
And, in thaire nature, thankit him for glad.
Kingis Quair, st. 21, ed. Skeat.

TILLER, *v.* and *s.* V. DICT.

The etym. given for this term is confusing. Indeed, only the last paragraph is applicable to *tiller*. As the root is A.-S. *telgor*, a shoot, twig, the word cannot be allied to Fr. *tailer*, which has come from Lat. *thallus*; nor is it allied to Icel. *tylle*, nor to Icel. *tilldra*, either in meaning or in origin.

This is one of many instances in which Jamieson offers etymologies which are totally inconsistent with each other.

To TILLY, TILLIE, TILE, *v. a.* To till or dig the ground; part. pr. *tillyin, tileing.* V. TELE.

". . . . tho sowme of 40 s. for land *tileing*." Corshill Baron Court Book, p. 73.

To TIMBER, TYMBER, TYMBIRE, *v. a.* Lit. to build, build up; to work, cause, produce, as in "Thay sall *tymbire* yow tene;" Awnt. Arthure, st. 22.

TIMERSOME, *adj.* Fearful, apprehensive, easily frightened. Addit. to TIMOURSUM, q. v.

TIMMER-HEELS, *s. pl.* Wooden-heels for ladies' winter-shoes; shoes so fitted were called *timmer-heels*, and *timmer-heel't shoon*; see Burgh Recs. Aberdeen, I. 250, Rec. Soc.

TINKLER, *s.* A tinker; *a tinkler-gipsy*, a wandering or vagabond tinker; Burns, The Twa Dogs.

(Sup.) G 2

"*Faber aerarius*, a *tinkler*;" Duncan's App. Etym., 1595, ed. Small, E. D. S.
This term is prob. of imitative origin, from M. E. *tinken*, to tinkle, ring; cf. Du. *tinge-tangen*, to tinklo, Lat. *tinnire*, to tinkle, ring. V. Skeat's Etym. Dict.

TINNY, TINNIE, *s.* A small tin jug.

TINO, *s.* A skewer or spit for fish when drying; Orkn. E. *tine*.

To TINO, *v. a.* To spit fish, to fix them on *tinos*.

A.-S. *tind*, a tooth of a rake; Icel. *tindr*, Swed. *tinne*.

TINT, *s.* Proof, evidence, indication; forecast, foretaste; "The beast's awa, and ye'll ne'er get *tint* or wittins o't," i.e., evidence or information regarding it. V. under TAINT.

But mind ye this, the half-ta'en kiss,
The first fond fa'in' tear,
Is, heaven kens, fu' sweet ameus,
An' *tints* o' heaven here.
William Thom, Whistle Binkie, ii. 43.

Tint is the vulgar pron. of *taint*, short for *attaint*; but it has a much wider range of meaning than that which Jamieson assigned to it; see TAINT in DICT.

TIPPENCE, *s.* Two-pence.

When by the plate we set our nose,
Weel heaped up wi' ha'pence,
A greedy glowr Black Bonnet throws,
And we maun drawn our *tippence*.
Burns, Holy Fair, st. 8.

"Black Bonnet," the elder in charge of the plate for receiving the collection for the poor; not, as an English editor has explained it, "the Elder who holds the alms-dish."

In Burns' day, and for long after, "*the plate*," (also called "*the brod*," "*the kirk brod*," or "*the puir's brod*") was placed on a stool outside and in front of the church door, and the elder in charge of it stood inside a stance like a sentry-box close by.

TIPPENNY, *s.* Two-penny ale, ale at twopence a Scotch pint. V. TWOPENNY.

That *tippenny* was a comparatively weak ale is put beyond doubt by the following particulars. The imperial gallon contains 277·274 cub. ins., and the Scotch pint, or "Stirling Jug," contained 104·2034 cub. ins., or nearly three-eighths of an imp. gall.; consequently such ale cost about 5½d. per gall. And yet, according to the comparative estimate of Burns, it must have possessed very considerable inspiring power—

Inspiring bold John Barleycorn!
What dangers thou canst make us scorn!
Wi' *tippenny*, we fear na evil;
Wi' usquebae, we'll face the D——l.
Tam o' Shanter.

TIRE, TYRE, *s.* A snood or narrow band for the hair, worn by females; an ornamental edging used by cabinet-makers and upholsterers; the metal edging of coffins, which is also called coffin-*tire*.

O. Fr. *tire*, a row, file. But for second and third meanings the origin is prob. M. E. *tir, tyr*, short for *atir, atyr*, attire, ornament.

TIRLESS, TIRLEIS, TERLEIS, *s.* A screen, an enclosure, a space enclosed by a screen, railing, or partition. Addit. to TIRLESS, q. v.

"Item, coft vij jestis to be ane *terleis* to the deid banes at the south kirk-dur." Burgh Recs. Edinburgh, ii. 364, Rec. Soc.
"Item, to Hennislie to cast the deid banes in the west *tirleis*, iij s." Ibid.

TIRSO, *s.* Ragwort, groundsel *(Senecio,* Linn.); Orkn.

TISSUE, TISSEW, *s.* A thin muslin-stuff; also, a skirt or under-garment made of it; Kingis Quair, st. 49, ed. Skeat.

O. Fr. *tissu,* woven; and applied to thin woven stuffs of wool, silk, &c.: from O. Fr. *tistre,* to weave, Mod. Fr. *tisser.*

To TO, *v. a.* To take, receive, uplift: part. pt. *ton,* taken; Sir Tristrem, l. 1484. V. TA.

The truage was com to *to*
Morannt, the noble knicht.
Ibid., l. 947, S.T.S.

TO, TA, *prep.* 1. For; "preparation *to* the graue," Blame of Kirkburiall, ch. vii.; see also ch. xix.

2. In; "made *to* the imitation of," i.e., in imitation of, or after the example of; "set up *to* the mockage of," i.e., in mockery of; Ibid., ch. x.

3. Till, until; "our bodies are lade a-part *to* the resurrection; Ibid. ch. x.

TOCUM. A form of *to cum* with an *adj.* meaning: to come, coming, future; Kingis Quair, st. 14.

TOFORE, TOFOIR, TO-THE-FORE, *adv.* Before-hand, over and above, in hand, laid past. Addit. to TOFORE, q. v.

". . . hir and hir guidman suld newir haue frie geir *to-foir.*" Trials for Witchcraft, Spald. Mis. i. 95.

TOFOROWE, TO-FOROWE, *adv.* Poet. form of *tofore,* with the following meanings:—

1. Before, already.

The way we take, the tyme I tald *to-forowe,*
Kingis Quair, st. 23, ed. Skeat.

2. Before this time, heretofore.

That gudeliare had noght bene sene *toforowe.*
Ibid. st. 49.

3. Formerly, in times past, previously.

And thy reqnest both now and eke *toforowe.*
Ibid. st. 105.

TOFT, THOFT, *s.* 1. A portion of land sufficient for a house and garden, a feu or plot; also, a house with garden or other ground attached.

2. "Land once tilled but now abandoned;"

Memorial for Orkney, p. 119. Addit. to TOFT, q. v.

Icel. *tomt,* a clearing, a portion of land fit for cultivation. See also the notes under TOFT in DICT.

TOFTIN, THOFTIN, THOFTYN, *s.* The house built upon a toft of land; the holding or using of said house; also, the right of so doing.

"Wilyam Mathy, son to Gylbert Mathy, is rentalit in vj's. land in Sandy-Hyllis, be consent of Andro Corsby, the said Andro broukand the *thoftyn* for his tym, and Thomas Mathy the land: " i.e., the one was to enjoy the house and the other the land, during the life-time of Andro, the present holder. Diocesan Registers of Glasgow, 1534, vol. i., p. 105, Grampian Club.

TOGS, *s. pl.* Tails of barley or black oats; prob. the local pron. of *tags,* tails; Orkn.

To TOIT, TOTE, *v. n.* To saunter. V. *Toyte.*

TOK, TOKE, TOKEN, *pret.* Took; Sir Tristrem, l. 223, 447, S.T.S.

TOKENING, *s.* Sign, signal, trumpet-call; Sir Tristrem, l. 506, 518, S.T.S. V. TAKYNNYNG.

TOLKE, *s.* A man, person. V. *Tulke.*

TOLLAR, TOLLARE, *s.* A taker of toll or custom, collector of petty customs in a burgh; Burgh Records Aberdeen, I. 191, Sp. C.

Ine til a town he come forby,
Quare in the tolbuth set Lewy,
That as a *tollare* thare wes sate,
Unlesume wynnynge for to get.
And quha ine hopyue syne is taue
The ewangell callis publicane.
Barbour, Legends of the Saints.

To TOLTER, *v. n.* V. DICT.

Del. quotation and note under this entry in DICT.; the one is unsuitable, and the other is a mistake. The *tolter* of that passage is as follows:—

TOLTER, *adv.* Unsteadily, with tottering motion; *toolter,* Orkn., q. v.

And they were ware that leng[ë] sat in place,
So *tolter* quhilum did sche it to-wrye;
There was bot clymbe[n] and ryght dounward hye,
And sum were eke that fallyng had [so] sore,
There for to clymbe thaire corage was no more.
Kingis Quair, st. 164, ed. Skeat.

This passage was not properly understood by Jamieson. He explained *tolter* as a v. *inf.,* and probably was led into this error through mistaking *to-wrye* as [a simple verb.

TOLYE, *s.* Strife, quarrel. V. TULYE.

TON, TAN, *part. pt.* Taken. V. *To,* TA.

TONEGALL, *s.* A weight equal to 6 stones, referring in the Exchequer Rolls to cheese only.

"Redditus casei etc. scilicet de Forfar xiiij^xx et viij *tonegall.*" Exch. Rolls Scot., i. 50.
". . . *tonegall* valet vj petras." Ibid.
There is still considerable doubt regarding the correctness of this term; see under *Cogall.*

To TOOK, TOUK, TOWK, *v. a.* 1. To tug, pluck, pull, tuck; "Dinna *took* it sae, but tak it up." Syn. *to pook.*

2. To strike, beat, blow, tuck; as, "to *took* the drum, to *towk* a trump." E. *tuck.*

Touk was used also as short for *touk the drum,* as in the following record :—
" Ordanis the drummers *to touk* through the toun weik about, and he quha *touks* for the weik sall onlie have power *to touk* to the haill lords and strangers sall cum to the toune for that weik ;" etc. (i.e., he and he only shall go with the drum during that week). Burgh Recs. Glasgow, 12 Feb., 1642.

3. To nag, taunt, reproach; as, "to *touk* or reproach ane another," Riding of Parl., Mait. Club. Misc., III., 103.

4. To tuck, fold; put on, assume, express: "*Took* up your tails;" "*Touk* it a' roun." "*Towking* outragious countenance;" Riding of Parl., Mait. Club. Misc., III., 102. Add. to TOUK, q. v.

TOOK, TOUK, TOWK, *s.* 1. A tug, pluck, pull: "He gied her sleeve a bit *took.*"

2. A tuck, stroke, blast: "Wi' *took* o' drum;" Scott, Rob Roy, ch. 19; and similarly *touk o' trump,* is used.

3. Taunt, reproach, provocation; pl. *touks, towks,* assumed airs, poutings, mocks; Riding of Parl., Mait. Club. Misc., III., 103.

4. A tuck or horizontal fold, as in a garment: "Run a *took* a' roun." Addit. to TOUK, TOWK, q. v.

TOOLTER, *adj.* Unstable, shaky, off the perpendicular; Orcadian Sketch Book, p. 119. Used also as an *adv.* V. *Tolter.*

TOOMLY, TOOMELY, *adv.* Idly, to no purpose, vainly. V. TOOM.
"Rather to teach as I can, what or what not the Kirk should doe, nor *toomely* to talke what hes beene done abroad by the world in this earand." Blame of Kirkburiall, ch. 5.

TOOT. *To toot on anither horn,* to change the subject of discourse, the tone or manner of speech, or the mode of action.
"Hoot, toot, toot!" the birdie's saying,
"Wha can shear the rigg that's shorn?
Ye've snug brawlie simmer's ferlies,
I'll *toot on anither horn.*"
Whistle Binkie, ii. 340.

TOOTHY, TEETHY, *adj.* Having many or large teeth; biting or given to biting;

crabbed, ill-natured, given to making biting or sarcastic remarks.

TOOZLE, TOOSLE, *v.* and *s.* V. TOUSLE.

To TOP, *v. a.* A term in golfing: to hit the ball above its centre; see Golfer's Handbook.

TOPICKS, TOOPICKIS, *s. pl.* Remedies, local applications, as plasters, bandages, &c., applied to injured or diseased parts of the body; Burgh Recs. Edinburgh, iv. 489, Rec. Soc.
O. Fr. *topiques,* "remedies (as plaisters, &c.), applyed vnto vnsound parts of the bodie :" Cotgr.: from Lat. *topica,* the title of a work by Aristotle.

TOPPIN, TAPPIN, *adj.* Same as TOP, TAP, q. v.

TOPTRIE, *s.* V. TAP-TREE.
This form occurs in Burgh Recs. Glasgow, i. 129, Rec. Soc.

TORE, TOR, *adj.* Forms of *teir,* tedious, tiresome, exhausting.

TORFEIR, TORFER, *s.* V. DICT.
The resemblance, here suggested, between *torfeir* and Fr. *torfaire* is a mere fancy. *Torfeir* is derived from Icel. *for-,* prefix, and verb *fara,* to go : whereas *torfaire=tort-faire,* is from Lat. *tortus,* twisted, crooked, hence wrong, and *facere,* to make, do. The etymologies, therefore, are totally inconsistent.

TORRIS, *s. pl.* For the explanation of this term given in DICT. substitute the following:—1. Towers, bastions.
Throu the schynyug of the son ane clete thai see.
With *torris* and turatis teirfull to tell,
Bigly batollit about with wallis sa he.
Gol. and Gawane, st. 4.

2. High and steep rocks.
The king faris with his folk our firthis and fellis
Feill dais or he fand of flynd or of fyre,—
Bot *torris* and tene wais teirfull quha tellis
Tuglit and travalit thus trew men can tyre.
Ibid., st. 3.
O. Fr. *tur, tour,* from Lat. *turris,* a tower : hence applied to a castle, an isolated conical hill, or a steep rock, which rises like a tower ; cf. Gael. *torr,* a conical hill, tower, castle. It is a familiar term in the uplands of Devon and Derby : e.g., Yes Tor in Dartmoor, and Matlock High Tor in Derby.

TOSH, *adj.* Intimate, familiar, kindly, affectionate; "They're unco *tosh* wi' ither;" West of S., Orkn. Addit. to TOSCH, q. v.

To TOST, *v. a.* To toast.
"*Torreo,* torrefacio ; to rost, to *tost ;*" Duncan's App. Etym., 1595, ed. Small, E. D. S.

TO-STIFFILIT, *part. pt.* Staggered, confounded. V. *Stivel.*

TOUCH, *s.* A small quantity, slight degree, sensation : *a wee touch,* a minute quantity, very slight amount or degree.

TOUCH, Touche, *s.* Short for *touch-wood*, but applied to amadou and other materials used as tinder: "as sharp as *touch*," as quick as touch-wood, quick-tempered.

Touch-Box, Touche-Box, *s.* A tinder-box; Halyburton's Ledger, p. 291, 292.

To TOUSK, *v. a.* To indent, jag or joggle: a term in masonry explanatory of the method of joining one building to another.

". . . that the said Cristan Ra and hir factor sall *tousk*, bowule, and ragall the gawill of the saidis Cristan new hous to the gavill of the said Sir Ailexander hous." Burgh Recs. Stirling, 12 April, 1525.

Gael. *toag*, a tusk; prob. borrowed from A.-S. *tusc*. It may, however, be merely a variation of E. *tusk*.

To TOUT, *v. a.* and *n.* To blow, sound, or give a blast upon a horn or trumpet; to sound, resound: "He *touts* his ain horn," i.e., he praises himself, boasts or brags about his own affairs. Addit. to **Toot**, q. v.

Tout, Touting, *s.* A blast, sound, call of a horn, etc.; a boast, brag, puff. Addit. to **Toot**, q. v.

TOWARD, Towards, *prep.* In the direction of; also, regarding, concerning: "*toward* hir goldin haire," Kingis Quair, st. 46, ed. Skeat.

TOWBUYTH, Tobuith, *s.* Tolbooth, prison. V. **Tolbuthe.**

TOWEIR, *adj.* Wearing, for wearing, to be worn; Burgh Recs. Glasgow, I. 393, Rec. Soc.

Shortly before the meeting of the General Assembly in Glasgow in 1638, the magistrates of that city resolved to do every thing in their power to secure the comfort and convenience of that august body while it remained in session; and one of the many appointments then made was, "three persons ellectit and nominat to keip the kirk dooris and the *toweir* gownis [of the ministers, etc.] in a cumlie maner."

To TO-WRITHE, *v. a.* and *n.* To twist, twist about, wrench, break off.

And tristrem dnelled thare
To wite what nien wald say;
Coppe and claper he bare——
As he a mesel ware;—
So wo was y*o*nde, that may,
That alle sche wald *to-writhe*.
Sir Tristrem, l. 3179, S.T.S.

A.-S. *to-writhan*, to writhe, distort. Ælfric's Glossary has "distorqueo, ic *tó-writhe*." See under *To-Wrye*.

TOWRPYKE, *s.* A spiral stair. V. **Turnpike.**

To TO-WRYE, *v. a.* To turn, twist about rapidly.

In describing how Fortune turned her wheel the poet says,—

So tolter quhilum did sche It *to-wrye*;
There was bot clymbe[n] and ryght dounward hye,
And sum were eke that fallyng had [so] sore,
There for to clymbe thaire corage was no more.
Kingis Quair, st. 164, ed. Skeat.

This term is wrongly entered in Dict. under Wry, as if it were a simple verb. "It is obviously a compound verb with the prefix *to-*; cf. 'distorqueo, ic *tó-writhe*,' Ælfric's Glossary, ed. Zupitza, p. 155." Skeat. V. **To Wry.**

To TOYTE, Toit, Tote, *v. n.* To tot or walk about leisurely, like a weak or old person; also, to totter. V. **Toyte.**

In the Dict., and in many of the glossaries to Burns, this word is improperly defined as "to totter like old age." In Burns' first Gloss., that of the Kilmarnock ed., the definition is, "to walk like old age," i.e. in the sauntering, leisurely way of an old man who is still able to move about, and to attend to the wants of his 'auld, trusty servan'' in the pasture field. And that this was the sense in which Burns used the word will become evident to any one who reads the passage carefully. It runs thus:—

We've worn to crazy years thegither;
We'll *toyte* about wi' ane anither;
Wi' tentle care I'll flit thy tether
To some bahu'd rig,
Whare ye may nobly rax your leather
Wi' sma' fatigue.
The Auld Farmer to his Mare Maggy.

TRAIST, *adv.* Trustily, faithfully; Gol. and Gawane, st. 23, 33.

TRAMP, *s.* 1. A foot-journey in search of work: *on tramp*, travelling from town to town in search of employment.

2. A mechanic travelling in search of employment.

To TRANSLATE, *v. a.* 1. To transform, change; Kingis Quair, st. 8, ed. Skeat.

2. To alter or make up anew, as is done with a piece of dress.

Item, for thre eln Scottis blak bocht be the Queen's Maister of Wardrob to lyn ane gonn of the Queen's that wes *translatit*; ilk eln xiiijs., summa xlijs.

Item, for lyning of thir tua collaris, and *translating* of lynyngis of gownis for caus William Fery [the furrier] web suspect
xs.

Item, for iiij eln gray dames to the grene dames of the Inglis hors covir, in stede of the quhit dames was in it, vli. viijs.

Item, for vjj eln yallo carsay to lyne the said hors covir, xxxijs. vjd.

Item, for *translating* and making of the said hors covir of dames, vs. Accts. L. H. Treasurer, 1502-4.

TRANTLUM. 1. As a *s.*: a trifle, knickknack, toy; generally used in pl. *trantlums*, same as **Trantles**, q. v.

2. As an *adj.*: trifling, little-worth, troublesome; "*trantlum* gear," Whistle-Binkie, I. 128.

TRASHER, TRASCHOR, s. A tracer or liner; a sharp-pointed steel or stile for tracing lines on leather: used by saddlers and leather-cutters; Burgh Recs. Aberdeen, I. 176, Sp. C.
O. Fr. trasser, to trace out, delineate: formed from Lat. tractus, pp. of trahere, to draw.

To TRAUAILE, v. n. To travail, toil. V. [TRAWAILL].

TRAUAILE, s. Toil; Kingis Quair, st. 69, 70, ed. Skeat.

TRAUNT, s. A trick. V. TRANE.

TRAVELLYE, s. Downfall, crash; a fall accompanied with great noise; Orcadian Sketch Book, p. 36, 117.
Dan. travl, busy, rushing; travlhed, act or state of bustling about, commotion; but prob. derived from E. travail.

To TRAW, TRAWE, v. a. To believe. V. TROW.

TRAWE, s. A twist; hence a trick, device, make-believe.
Compasand and castand cacis a thousand
How he sall tak me with a trawe at trist of ane othir.
Dunbar, Tua Mariit Wemen, l. 124.
Trawe is a form of thraw, from A.-S. thrawan, to turn, twist.

TRAYFOL, TROFEL, s. A knot, device, in embroidery; see next entry.

To TRAYFOL, TROFEL, v. a. To ornament with knots or devices: part. pt. trayfolede, trofelyte.
Gawane was graythely graythede on grene,
With griffons of gold engrelede full gaye,
Trayfolede with trayfoles and trewluffes by-twene,
One a stirtande stede he strykes one straye.
Awnt. Arthure, st. 40.
The Douce MS. has "Trifeled with traues;" but the meaning is the same.
The mane in his mantyll ayttis at his mete
In paulle purede with pane, full precyously dyghte,
Trofelyte and trauerste with trewloues in trete.
Ibid., st. 28.
Fr. tréfiler, to wiredraw, make chain-work; formerly tresfiler, from Lat. transfilare, to pass thread through the drawing-frame: tréfileur, formerly tresfilier, a chain-maker, a worker in chain-work.

TREDDER, s. A male or cock-bird, but generally applied to a cock.
A.-S. tredan, to tread; Icel. troda: akin to Lat. trudere.

TREE, TRE, TRIE, s. 1. The wooden portion of a pack-saddle, plough, etc.; Corshill Baron Court Book, Ayr and Wigton Arch. Coll., IV. 134.

2. A straight piece of rough timber used as a pole, lever, prop, or stay, is called a tree: as,

a dyer's-tree, a raising-tree or lever for moving a mill-stone.

3. A last for boots or shoes, any wooden frame, mould or block, as a boot-tree, a hat-tree, a mitten-tree, etc.; "ane pair of buyt-treis;" Burgh Recs. Aberdeen, I. 176, Sp. C.

TREE-LEGGED, adj. Having a timber-leg; Whistle Binkie, I. 159.

TREMEBUND, adj. Trembling, timorous; Alex. Scott's Poems, p. 71, ed. 1882. Lat. tremebundus.

TRENCHER, TRINCHER, adj. Lopped, blunted, pointless: trencher-spear, a pointless spear, tilting pole. V. TRUNCHER SPEIR.
O. Fr. trenché, cut off, blunted; prob. from Lat. truncare, to lop off.

TRENDLE, TRINDLE, TRENLE, TRINLE, TRUNLE, s. The wheel of a barrow, also the wooden portion of the wheel; a small wooden wheel such as is used for a trundle-bed; a low truck or hutch, &c.; a wooden roller on which a heavy block is moved along. Trinnyll, Burgh Recs. Prestwick, 1513, p. 44, Mait. C.
Ae auld wheelbarrow, mair for token
Ae leg an' baith the trams are broken;
I made a poker o' the spindle,
An' my auld mither brunt the trindle.
Burns, The Inventory.

To TRENDLE, TRENLE, TRINLE, TRUNLE, v. a. and n. To trundle, roll, move on wheels or rollers. Addit. to TRINDLE and TRINTLE, q. v.

TRENLE-BED, TRINLE-BED, s. A bed set on trendles or small wheels, that it may be easily run under another bed or drawn out as required: also called a hurly-bed or hurly, a whirly-bed or whirly.

TRENE, TRENEFALD. V. under Thrine.

TRENNAL, TREYNAL, s. Lit. a tree-nail; a wooden peg or pin used in shipbuilding, and other kinds of carpenter-work. E. tree-nail.

TRESSOUR, TRESSURE, s. A species of border detached from the edge of the shield, and borne double, sometimes triple: a term in heraldry.
He bure a lyon as lord of gowlis full gay—
Off pure gold wes the grund quhair the grym hovit,
With dowble tressour about flowrit in fay.
Houlate, l. 370, Bann. MS.
O. Fr. tresser, to plait.
The expression "flowrit in fay" is explained by Planché in his remarks on this term.

"The Tressure has been regarded as a diminutive of the Orle [from Fr. *ourler*, to hem], and is a similar border, only narrower, and borne double, sometimes triple, and generally what is termed flory-counter-flory, as in the arms of Scotland." The Pursuivant of Arms, p. 58.

TRETE, *s.* Treaty, bargain; connection, combination; *in trete,* under treaty; connected, combined, linked together.

The mane in his mantyll . . .
Trofelyte and trauerste with trewloues in *trete.*
Awnt. Arthure, st. 28.
O. Fr. *traite,* a treaty; from *traité,* pp. of *traiter,* to treat.

TREVISS, **TREVESSE,** **TRAVESSE,** *s.* V. DICT.

Two distinct words are mixed up in the common applications of *treviss* and *travesse:* the one is a variant of *traverse,* and the other is a derivative of *trave.* The distinction is perhaps best seen in the use of *travesse* for a partition in a wall, and for the stall itself. In the first application it is a form of *traverse,* from Lat. *transversus,* turned across, laid across; and in the second it is deriv. of *trave,* a shackle, originally a frame of rails for confining unruly horses. The two words have got mixed up; but it is well to point out their different origin.

TREWE, DAY OF TREWE, *s.* A justiciary court held by the wardens of the Border Marches. Addit. to TREW, q. v.

These courts were so called, because, during the time they were convened, there was a truce or cessation of hostilities on both sides of the border. Periodical meetings of this kind were necessary for the purpose of hearing complaints, settling disputes, and administering justice.

TREWLOUE, TREWLUFE, *s.* V. *Truelove.*

TRIACLE, TRIAKLE, *s.* 1. An antidote, remedy, cure. Lat. *theriaca, theriace.*

"*Theriace, triacle,* remeid against poyson;" Duncan's App. Etym., 1595, ed. Small, E. D. S.
Prompt. Parv. gives *treacle,* explained as " halyvey, or boke agen sekenesse." And the editor, Mr. Way, has an interesting note regarding the various kinds of *Theriaca,* and their use as an antidote for the bites of serpents, and for the plague or pest; see p. 500.

2. Trial, test, verdict, decision, settlement: "*triakle* of the truth," decision or settlement of the truth, as a cure of strife, or a means of healing it.

". . . as far as may pertene to the town justlie, ay and quhill the *triakle* of the treuth tharof may be had, bayth for the commoun wele of the town and the said Williamis singlar wele, in sic maner that gif he haif just rycht thairto, and awa being funding, that he may bruik the samyn peaceablie without pley; and gyf the town hes the just rycht thairof and recoweris the samyn, that thai may in likmaner use the samyn as thair awin peaceablie according to justyce." Burgh Recs. Stirling, 1554-5, p. 62.

To **TRIBBLE,** *v. a.* To trouble, annoy; to handle overmuch, hence, to damage; also, to clutch, grasp, or finger, like a person in death-throes; West of S., Orkn.

TRINCHER, *adj.* Pointless, blunted. V. *Trencher.*

TRINE, TRYNE, TRENE, TRINFALD. V. under *Thrine.*

TRINK, TRINCK, *s.* The bed or channel of a river or stream; also, the water which flows in that channel. Addit. to TRINK, q. v.

The definitions given by Dr. Jamieson apply only to a trench or drain; but the term has a much wider range of meaning, as the following extracts show.
"That na channell, stanes, sand, nor any uther thing be cassin in the *trink* of the watter, or within the fluid merk, out of schippis." Burgh Recs. Aberdeen, ii. 77, Sp. C.
"The haill *trinck* of the watter salbe drawn doun the south syd of the Lochfield croft, and to rin at the west syd of the Gallowgett . . . in the auld *trinck,* to be cassin deper and wyder, and that the water *trinck* on the south-vest syd of the said locht salbe stoppit and condamnit." Ibid., p. 239.
The term is still used in both senses.

TRINKLE, *s.* A drop, series of drops, falling or fallen, as from a leaking vessel or a spout; a continuous dropping, or a slender thread of falling liquid; also, a faint line or streak, as a *trinkle* of blood.

TRINKALD, TRINKAILD, *s.* A vessel for trickling or dropping oil, etc., a currier's oil-horn; Burgh Recs. Aberdeen, I. 176, Sp. C.

TRINNEL, TRINNYLL, *s.* V. *Trendle.*

TRISTE, TRYSTE, TRYSTER, *s.* A station in hunting. Addit. to TRIST, q. v.

Ilke a lorde withowttyn lett,
At his *triste* was he sett,
With howe and with barcelett,
Vndir those bewes.
Awnt. Arthure, st. 3, l. 11.
The form *tryster* occurs in ll. 8 and 9 of same stanza in the Douce MS. V. TRISTRES.

TROCH, TRUCH, THROCH, THROCHT, *s.* A trough, vat; a large shallow vessel for holding or conveying water, etc.; pl. *trochs, throchtis,* Burgh Recs. Aberdeen, I. 329, Sp. C.

TROFELYTE, *part. pt.* Knotted. V. *Trayfol.*

TROGGIN, *s.* The merchandise of a pedlar hawker; the articles in which he *trogs* or deals. V. TROG, *v.*

Saw ye e'er sic *troggin !*
If to buy ye're slack,
Hornie's turnin chapman,—
He'll buy a' the pack.
Buy braw *troggin,*
Frae the banks o' Dee;
Wha wants *troggin,*
Let him come to me.
Burns, Draw Troggin.

Trog and *troggin* are merely variations of *troke* and *trokin*. Fr. *troquer*, to exchange. V. TROKE.

TROIS, TROISE, TROISS, *adj*. Troy, of Troy, of Troy-weight: "a *trois* pund of brass," i.e. a one-pound-Troy brass weight; Burgh Recs. Aberdeen, II. 10, Sp. C.

TROKING, *s.* Dealing, intercourse: pl. *trokings*, business dealings, transactions. V. TROKE, *s.*

"This is nae kind of time of night for decent folk; and I hae nae *trokings* wi' night-hawks." R. L. Stevenson, Kidnapped, p. 296, ed. 1886.

TRONE, TRON, *s.* V. DICT.

It is a mistake to connect this word with Icel. *triona*, a beak, or Icel. *trana*, a crane, or C.B. *trwyn*, or Fr. *trogne*. Ducange is correct in tracing it to Lat. *trutina*, a pair of scales, from which it has come to us by L. Lat. *trona*, and O. F. *trone*. See Skeat, s. v. *T'ron*.

TROWAN, TROWANE, *s.* An evil-doer, imp, monster: *tryit trowane*, noted evil-doer; Dunbar and Kennedie, l. 513.

Trowan is lit. one of the devil's brood. V. TROW.

TRUAGE, TRUWAGE, *s.* Tribute; Sir Tristrem, l. 947, 992, S.T.S. O. Fr. *truâge*, *treuâge*.

TRUELOVE, TREWLOUE, *s.* A lover's knot.

Trofelyte and tranerste with *trewloues* in trete. Awnt. Arthure, st. 28.

TRULIS, *s. pl.* The game of troll-my-dames, troll-madame, or *pigeon-holes*; a game of *nine-holes*. Addit. to TRULIS, q. v.

This game was borrowed from the French, who called it *trou-madame*. It is fully described by Nares in his Gloss.; and it is mentioned by Shakespeare, Winter Tale, iv. 2. Its old Eng. name, *pigeon-holes*, was given to it because the holes of the frame through which the balls were rolled resembled the holes in a dove-cot. See Dyce, Gloss. Shakespeare.

TRUNCHMAN, *s.* A dragoman, interpreter. V. TRENCHMAN.

"*Interpres*, a *trunchman*, a translator;" Duncan's App. Etym., ed. Small, E.D.S.
O. E. and O. Fr. *trucheman*, an interpreter. V. Cotgrave.

TRYNE, TRYNFALD. V. under *Thrine*.

TRYPES, *s. pl.* Small intestines.

"*Lactes*, graciliora intestina, the *trypes*;" Duncan's App. Etym., ed. Small, E.D.S.
Of Celtic origin: cf. Welsh *tripa*, intestines, Fr. *tripe*, Span. and Port. *tripa*, Ital. *trippa*, tripe.

TUA OF TEN. A popular name for the taxation of 1630, which amounted to twenty per cent. See Acts of Parl.

"To pay the soume of ten thousand merkis money of this realme for the extent of the *tua of ten* grantit furthe of the annuellis of the termes of Mortimes [1633, Whitsunday and Martinmas, 1634, 1635, and 1636]." Burgh Recs. Stirling, p. 171.

TUCHET, TUQUHEIT, *s.* The lapwing. V. TEUCHIT.

TUEY, TWEY, TUEYNE, TWEYNE, *adj.* Two; Kingis Quair, st. 42, 75, ed. Skeat. V. TWA.

TUGLIT, *part. pt.* Toiled, fatigued; Gol. and Gawane, st. 3. V. TUGGLED.

Tuglit has sometimes the sense of *taiglit*, hindered by difficulties.

TULKE, TOLKE, TOLK, *s.* A man, person: applied to gentle and common, but mostly as a contemptuous term; occurs in Gawayne and Arthure Romances. Icel. *tulkr*.

TUMALL, TUMALE, *s.* A portion of land lately in pasture, but now under cultivation and enclosed. Addit. to [TUMAIL].

The following explanations of this term are worthy of notice:—
"*Tumale*, land enclosed from the common pasture, and tilled; but not included in the original Odal-Tun." Balfour, Odal Rights and Feudal Wrongs, p. 119.
A Tumall "is ane piece of land which was quoyland, but now inclosed within the dykis." Peterkin's Rentals of Orkney, No. ii, p. 2.

TUMBLE-CART, TUMBLE CAR, *s.* The common country or farmer's cart of olden times. The box was set on wooden wheels fixed on a wooden axle, which *tumbled* or turned together. Cf. E. *tumbrel*, O. Fr. *tomberel*.

The *tumble-cart*, *tumbler*, or *car*, continued in use in the upland districts till the beginning of the present century; and in moorland districts of the country even then, the roads were so bad that goods and produce could be transported only by sledges or on horseback. Wheel-carts began to be used about 1700, and prior to that time the only wheeled vehicles for common use were "*tumbler-carts*, which were simply sledges mounted on small wheels about three feet in diameter, made solid—drum-wheels, as archæologists call them—united by a wooden axle, and all turning round together." Murray, Old Cardross, p. 38.

TUNG, *s.* Tongue: *keep a tongue*, keep quiet, refrain from speech.

Thairfoir till our rymes be rung,
And our mistonit sangis be sung,
Lat ouery man *keip* weill a *tung*
And euery woman tway.
Lyndsay, Thrie Estaitis, Bann. MS. fol. 195 a.

TUNG-GRANT, *s.* Confession. V. TONG-GRANT.

TURAT, *s.* A turret; Gol. and Gawane, st. 4. Fr. *tourette*.

TURKAS, TURKES, TURKESSE, *s.* V. DICT.

The O. Fr. words which Jamieson cites from Roquefort are obviously from Lat. *torquere*, to twist; and the instrument is called *twisters*, *pliers*, as well as *pincers*, *nippers*. Indeed the main purpose of the instrument is to twist, wrench, bend, stretch, rather than to pince, nip.

TURMENT, *s.* Torment, Kingis Quair, st. 19, ed. Skeat.
O. Fr. *torment,* from Lat. *tormentum,* an engine for throwing stones or for inflicting torment.

TURNOVER, *s.* A small copper coin, equivalent to a bodle; Burgh Recs. Glasgow, I. 422, Rec. Soc. V. TURNER.
O. Fr. *turnoir,* a copper-coin worth one-tenth of a penny sterling.

TURPYKE, TOWRPYKE, *s.* V. TURNPIKE.

TURRGATE, *s.* A turnpike-gate, or closed fence; prob. a corr. of *tirless-gate;* Accts. Burgh Edinburgh, 1552-3, Rec. Soc. V. TIRLESS-YETT.

TUTIVILLAR, TUTIVILLUS, *s.* A demon, imp, evil-doer; colloq. a term like *devil,* and used in a like variety of senses. Addit. to TUTIVILLAR, q. v.

Tutivillus, i.e., superintendent of evil-doers, is represented as chief of the devils appointed to catch people sinning. His main duty was to note and report the sins that deserve punishment. In the play of Juditium, one of the Towneley Mysteries, he is represented with a great roll, and as come to give in his report. He says :—

Here a rolle of ragman of the rownde tabille
Of breffes in my bag, man, of synnes dampnabille.
Towneley Mysteries, p. 311.

Further particulars regarding this evil spirit may be gathered from the Reader's Handbook by Dr. Brewer, and Laing's ed. of Dunbar, vol. ii., p. 438.

'TWAD, 'TWUD. Contr. for *it wad, it wud,* it would.

TWAL, TWALT, *adj.* Twelfth. V. TWELT.

TWAL-PINT HAWKIE. A cow that yields twelve pints at one milking; Burns, Address to the Deil. V. HAWKIE.

TWANG, *s.* A twinge, throb of pain.

My curse upon your venom'd stang,
That shoots my tortur'd gums alang;
And thro' my lugs gies moule a *twang,*
Wi' gnawing vengeance.
Burns, To the Toothache.

O. Friesic *twinga, thwinga,* to constrain; pt. t. *twang.* Dan. *tvinge,* Sw. *tvinge,* to force, constrain; M. E. *twingen,* to nip, pain.

To TWEEDLE, *v. n.* To work in a trifling, careless, or slovenly manner; to sing, or play on a musical instrument, in a light, careless, or slovenly manner; but most commonly applied to careless or awkward fiddling.

TWEEDLE-DEE, *s.* An indifferent musician, a sorry fiddler.

Her charms had struck a sturdy caird,
As well as poor gut-scraper:
He taks the fiddler by the beard,
And draws a rusty rapier.

Wi' ghastly ee, poor *Tweedle-dee*
Upon his hunkers bended,

And pray'd for grace wi' ruefu' face,
And sae the quarrel ended.
Burns, Jolly Beggars.

TWELTER, *adj.* Of or belonging to a set or company of twelve; *twelter-aith,* the oath of a company of twelve compurgators. V. under *Saxter.*

"In the Lawting Court of July 21, 1603, one is ordained to quit himself of theft by the *twelter-aith,* because the stowth is great; and another to quit himself of the same theft with the saxter-aith." Peterkin's Notes on Orkney and Shetland, App. p. 35.

Icel. *tólft,* a number of twelve; *tólftar-eithr,* the oath of a company of twelve compurgators; and similarly, *"tólftar-kvithr,* a verdict of a jury of twelve neighbours." Vigfusson.

TWISE, *adv.* Twice; Kingis Quair, st. 25. V. TWYIS, TWYS.

In Kingis Quair, st. 25, *twise* must be a dissyllable, and ought to have been written *twies.* See Skeat's Gloss.

TWISTLE, TWISSLE, *s.* A pron. of *tussle,* a shaking, tossing; Burns, The Twa Herds, st. 3.

To TWITTER, *v. n.* To shiver, shake, tremble, as with cold or fear: syn. *chitter.*

'TWUD. Contr. for *it wud,* it would. V. WAD.

TWYST, *adv.* Twice. V. TWYIS.

TYE, *s.* Band, bond, engagement; also the binding-clause in a band or bond: "releive thaim of thair *tye,*" i.c. of their engagement, Burgh Recs. Glasgow, II. 193, Rec. Soc.

TYKE, TYKEN, TYKING, *s.* 1. The case or cover which holds the feathers, wool, or other material of a bed, or a bolster. E. *tick.*

2. Used for the bed or the bolster itself: as, "That's the *tyke* or *tyken* o' the bed: a guid feather *tyke* or *tyken.*"

3. A kind of striped cloth of which the cover of a bed is made.

"*Tyking* of the Eist countrey, the eln—x s." Rates and Customs, 1612, Haly. Ledger, p. 331.

He at the sowing-brod was bred,
An' wrought gude serge and *tyken.*
Alex. Wilson's Poems, p. 42, ed. 1876.

TYKEN, TYKING, *adj.* Of or belonging to the cloth called *tyke* or *tyken.*

This group of words is improperly defined and explained in the DICT. Instead of the cloth giving its name to the case or cover, it is the case that has given its name to the cloth of which it is made. Besides the Su.-G. *tyg* is merely a loan-word from Ger. *tuck,* cloth. *Tyke* (E. *tick*), has come from Du. *tijk,* formed from Lat. *teca, theca,* a case, cover, which came from Gr. *théké,* a case. Regarding E. *tick,* Skeat states that it is the M. E. *teke,* a 14th cent. word, Englished from Lat. *teca, theca.* See his Etym. Dict.

TYME, *s.* Time : *be tyme*, betimes, in good time ; Kingis Quair, st. 122, ed. Skeat.

TYMERAL, TYNNERALL, *s.* The crest or ridge of a helmit, the socket or hold in which the crest is fixed.

All thir bieast in the crope four helmes full fair,
And in thar *tymeralis* tryid trewly thai bere
The plesand povne in a part provde to repair,
And als kepit ilk armes that I said eir.
Houlate, l. 613, Asloan MS.

Bann. MS. has *tynnerallis:* prob. a scribal error in writing to dictation.

O. Fr. *timbre, tymbre,* "the creast, or cognisance that's borne vpon the helmit of a coat of Armes;" Cotgr.

TYNNAKIL, *s.* Small tunic. V. TUNNAKIL.

TYRE, *s.* Errat. in DICT. for *Cyre,* leather, q. v.

TYREFULL, *adj.* Very tedious, tiresome ; a form of *tereful,* q. v.; Houlate, l. 421, Asloan MS. V. under *Tere.*

"*Tyrefull to tell,*" (more commonly *tereful to tell*), very tedious to relate, is in the Bann. MS. "*lere for to tell,*" which is prob. a scribal error for *tereful to tell,* made in writing to dictation. The Bann. MS. bears many indications of having been so written.

TYRRING, *part.* and *s.* Uncovering. V. TIRR.

To **TYST,** *v. a.* To entice. V. TYSE.

TYTTYN, *part. pr.* Pulling. V. TYTE, *v.*

U.

UCHE, UCH, VCH, *s.* An ouch; the clasp, bezel, or socket in which a precious stone is set. Addit. to UCHE, q. v.

Only secondary meanings of this term are given in DICT. The proper form of the word is *nouch ;* M.E. *nouche,* from O. Fr. *nouche, nosche, nusche,* a buckle, clasp, brace ; see Burguy. The L. Lat. form is *nusca ;* but all these forms have come from O. H. Ger. *nusca,* M. H. Ger. *nuske,* a buckle, clasp, brooch.

UDAL, *adj.* V. DICT.

Under this word Jamieson discusses the term *allodial,* and quotes various etymologies that have been proposed, of which all but one are wrong. The word is composed of the adj. *all* prefixed to the O. L. Ger. *ôd,* Icel. *audr,* wealth, and means "belonging to the entire property." See *Allodial* in Murray's New Eng. Dict.

UDDIR, UDER, *pron., adj.* and *s.* Other, each other ; pl. *udderis,* others, one another; Dunbar, Douglas. V. UTHIR.

UG, UGSUM. V. DICT.

These words are not connected with *ogertful,* as stated in DICT. They are from Icel. *uggr,* fear, and allied to Icel. *ugga,* to fear, *ôgn,* terror, *ôgna,* to threaten. For further explanation, see under *Ugly* in Skeat's Etym. Dict.

UGGIN, *part.* and *adj.* Exciting terror, repulsive : same as UGSUM, s. 2. Whistle Binkie, I. 311.

UGLY, VGLY, *adj.* Ugly, frightful, horrid. V. UG, *v.*

Ane *vgly* pit [was] depe as ony helle.
Kingis Quair, st. 162, ed. Skeat.

UIKNAME, *s.* Nickname ; local pron. of *ekename;* Orkn.

ULY, VLY, *s.* Oil. V. ULE.
(Sup.) H 2

UMAST, UMAIST, UMEST, *adj.* V. DICT.

The etym. given for this term in the DICT. is misleading. *Umast* stands for *uvemast,* which is simply A.-S. *ufemest (ufe-m-est),* superl. of *ufa,* above. It is really a double superl., and has nothing to do with Eng. *most,* for which the A.-S. is *mæst,* seldom *mêst,* and never *mest.*

UMAST CLAITH, UMEST CLAITH, VP-MAIST CLAITH, UMEST CLAYIS, *s.* The upper or outer garment, the uppermost article of wearing apparel : a perquisite claimed on certain occasions by vicars and heralds. Addit. to entry in DICT.

The explanations of this term given in the DICT. are altogether misleading, The *umast claith* was not a winding sheet, as defined by Sibbald ; nor the coverlet of the bed, as stated by Jamieson and Laing. Indeed, a moment's reflection will convince any one that, however exacting churchmen might be in claiming perquisites like these from the rich, they would in most cases be unwilling even to receive them from the very poor ; and that therefore the *umast claith* which the clergy exacted, and which proved so oppressive to the common people, must have been something very different from either of these. That it was simply the uppermost article of wearing apparel is clearly stated by Lyndsay in one of the passages in which he inveighs against the exaction ; and from his statement all the other passages in which it is referred to entirely agree. It occurs in Pauper's account of how he was reduced to poverty, which we quote from Laing's ed., vol. ii., p. 103.

" My Father was sa waik of blude and bane,
That he delt, quhairfoir my Mother maid gret maine
Then scho deit within ane day or two,
And thair began my povertie and wo.
Our gude gray meir was baittand on the feild,
And our Land's laird tuik her for his hyreild.
The Vickar tulk the best cow he the heid,
Incontinent, quhen my father was deid.
And quhen the Vickar hard tel how that my motller
Was deid, fra hand he tuik to him ane uther.

Then Meg, my wife, did murne baith evin and morow,
Till at the last scho deit for verie sorow.
And quhen the Vickar hard tell my wyfe was deid,
The third cow he cleikit be the heid.
Thair *umest clayis*, that was of rapploch gray,
The Vickar gart his Clark bear them away.
Quhen all was gane, I micht mak na debeat,
Bot with my bairns past for till beg my meat."

Now, *umest clayis* here can have but one meaning, the uppermost garment of each of the deceased persons; and no doubt the uppermost article of clothing was claimed for the same reason which guided the laird in selecting the horse, and the vicar in choosing the cow, because it was the best that the party possessed. And the vicar so claimed and so acted, because on such an occasion he was by law entitled to take the best cow and the best garment of the deceased, as perquisites of his office.

What this *umast claith* or best garment of the common people of Scotland was in Lyndsay's day is explained in the passage quoted by Jamieson; and by a few slight but masterly touches the poet at the same time reveals the abject poverty which then prevailed. The husband's *umast klaith* was "*the gray cloke* that happis the bed": so poor was his household. The cloak was of *rapploch gray*, or coarse woollen cloth made of home-spun undyed wool. In Laing's ed. it is called a "*gray frugge*," i.e., a loose coat or cloak of gray, like a monk's frock. The wife's upper garment was a "*pure cote*," i.e., a petticoat or kirtle: and it too was of *rapploch*, and had to serve the same purposes as her husband's cloak. And it may be noted in passing, that it was of such a covering that mention is made in the old song, "Tak your auld cloak about ye."

There were other examples of a claim to the uppermost garment as a perquisite, as for instance in connection with the office of herald. At the marriage of James IV. to Margaret Tudor, the English heralds, according to custom, claimed as their perquisite the king's marriage dress; and those of Scotland claimed the queen's. The latter, however, was redeemed next day by a payment of forty nobles. Leland, Collectanea, ed. alt., vol. iv., p. 297. See note, p. cxcvii. of Dickson's Preface to Accts. of the L. H. Treas. of Scotland, vol. i.

UMBE, *prep*. and *adv*. About, around: in comp. *umbe*, *umb*, and *um*. A.-S. *ymbe*.

To UMBECAST, UMCAST, *v. a*. To bind or wrap round, as, "to *umcast* a splice," to fasten it by a wrapping of cord. Addit. to [UMBECAST], q. v.

The term is similarly used in the York Mysteries.
All in cordis his coorse *vnbycast*.
Tyllemakers Play, p. 336, l. 467.

UMBECLIPPED, UMBE-CLIPPED, *part. pt*. Encircled, embraced, surrounded; Awnt. Arthure, x. 2, MS. Douce. V. CLIP, v.

To UMBEDRAW, *v. n*. To draw back or aside, withdraw, retire; pret. *umbedrew*, Douglas, Virgil, prol. 399, 11, Rudd.; in Elphinstoun MS. *onbydrew*. Addit. to UMBEDRAW, q. v.

That *um* is here intensive, as Rudd. pointed out, and not the prep. about, around, as stated by Jamieson, is confirmed by the reading of the Elphinstoun MS. It is simply the verbal prefix *un-* modified to blend with *bedraw*; and *be* is a form of *by*, aside, away.

UMBESET, *s*. Same as *Outbreck*, q. v.

UMBESTOUNT, *adv*. Sometimes.
Till he his poynt saw of the kyng,
That than with all his galeryng
Wes in carrik, quhar *vnbestount*
He vald vend with his men till hount.
Barbour, vii. 398, Camb. MS.
Edin. MS. has "he wes wont."
A.-S. *ymbe*, about, and *stund*, a time.

UMBESTRODE, *part. pt*. Bestrode.

UMBEWEROUND, *part. pa*. V. DICT.
The etym. suggested for this term is simply impossible. *Umbeweround* is a hybrid form obtained by substituting *umbe*- (A.-S. *ymbe*) for the Fr. *en-* in *environner*.

UMBOTHSMAN, *s*. An agent, procurator, for-speaker or advocate; Memorial for Orkney, p. 119. V. UMBOTH, s. 2.
Icel. *umboths-mathr*, a trusty manager; Vigfusson.

UMBRE, VMBRE, *s*. A shadow, shade; hence screen, mask, disguise. Addit. to UMBRE, q. v.
The first passage quoted in DICT. is incorrect: the MS. reads:—
Suich feynit treuth is all bot trechorye,
Vnder the *vmbre* of hid ypocrisye.
Kingis Quair, st. 134, ed. Skeat.

UMBRAGE, VMBRAGE, *s*. A shadow, shade; Douglas, iv. 169, 16.

UMBRAKLE, VMBRAKLE, *s*. An arbour; hence retreat, cell, abode: "dethis dirk *vmbrakle*;" Dunbar, Ballat of our Lady, l. 20, Small.
Lat. *umbraculum*, a bower, retreat: dimin. of *umbra*, a shade. Cf. Ital. *ombraculo*, a shady place.

UMBRATE, VMBRATE, *adj*. Shady: "the *vmbrate* treis," Douglas, Pal. of Honour, prol. l. 40.

UMBRELLS, *s. pl*. A form of *honours* paid to worth or dignity at a convivial gathering, in which the toast was drunk off and glasses inverted.

This was a common custom among the crafts in former days, especially at their annual dinners, or as they were popularly called *bancats*. In the humorous sketch of 'The Deacon's Day,' the retiring Deacon Convener of the Incorporated Trades of Glasgow and at the same time Deacon of the Wrights, thus introduces his successor in office:—
"After what I hae this day spoken in anither place, there's nae occasion again to put the bit through the same bore, or to run the plane o'er a dressed plank, sae I'll gie ye Deacon Convener Wriggles' good health, no forgetting wife and sproots—they'll be a' trees belyve —and may every guid attend him and them; and may he aye be able to keep a guid polish on the face o' our Corporation affairs, and leave them without a screw loose to his successor.—*Umbrells to Deacon Wriggles*."
Whistle Binkie, i. 272.
This name was prob. suggested by the resemblance of the upturned glasses to umbrellas, or the small round fans which were called *ombrelles*. See Cotgrave.

UMBYCLEDE, VMBYCLEDE, *part. pt*. Lit. completely clothed; surrounded, wrapt:

"*vmbyclede* in a clowde;" Awnt. Arthure, st. 2. V. CLEED, *v.*
MS. Douce has *vmbeclipped.*

UNCERSSABIL, *adj.* Unsearchable; Abp. Hamilton's Catechism, fol. 114*b*. V. CERSS.

To UMCHOW, VMCHOW, *v. a.* To eschew, avoid. V. UMBESCHEW.

". . . . to ewaid and *vmchow* trubill of thair innymeis." Burgh Recs. Aberdeen, i. 448, Sp. C.

UNAFFRAID, VNAFFRAID, *adj.* Un-afraid, fearless; Kingis Quair, st. 35, ed. Skeat.

UNANALYIT, VNANALIIT, *adj.* Not disponed, unalienated: a law term, common in Burgh Records. V. ANALIE.

UNBACKED, *adj.* Untamed, not broken, unaccustomed to yoke or saddle.

Though Fortune's road be rough an' hilly
To every fiddling, rhyming billie,
  We never heed,
But tak' it like the *unback'd* filly,
  Proud o' her speed.
      Burns, Ep. to Major Logan, st. 1.

Perhaps Burns used the term here in the sense of *unloaded, unhampered*. In the sense of *unbroken* the term was used by Shakespeare and by Sterne.

UNBODEIT, WNBODEIT, *adj.* Disembodied; Douglas, II, 137, 25, ed. Small.

UNCARING, UNCARIN, *adj.* Free from care, careless, regardless, taking no thought or concern regarding work or duty: "He's an *uncarin* servan."

UNCHERSIABILL, *adj.* Lit. uncherishable; unbearable on account of conduct or manners; careless, offensive.

"Alsua, geyf the said Andro worthis vanton and *uncheriabill* in his common seruis." Charters, &c., Peebles, 28 Jan., 1520, p. 141, Rec. Soc.
O. Fr. *un*, not; *cherissable*, "cherishable, fit to be cherished;" Cotgr.

UNCOFT, *adj.* V. DICT.

The last paragraph of this entry has been accidentally misplaced. It belongs to the following entry, UNCOIST, UNCOST, *s.*

UNCOUTH, VNCOUTH, VNCHUT, *adj.* Unknown; Kingis Quair, st. 63, 113: strange, peculiar; Ibid., st. 66, ed. Skeat. Addit. to UNCO, q. v.

The form *vnchut*, which occurs in the Legend of St. Machar, is prob. a scribal error for *vncuth*. The passage runs thus:—

Bot passyt in *vnchut* land but bad,
Quhare na mane knawing of him had.
      Barbour, Legends of the Saints.

UNCOUTHLY, VNCOUTHLY, *adv.* Strangely; Ibid., st. 9.

UNCUNNAND, VNCUNNAND, *adj.* Ignorant, unskilled, unskilful. V. CUNNAND.

UNCUNYETE, *part. pt.* Uncoined, not prepared for coining; Douglas, Virgil, 336, 26, ed. Rudd.

UNDANTED, UNDANTIT, UNDANTONED, VNDANTONIT, VNDANTONET, *adj.* Unbroken, untamed, not under control; "Lyk wyld *vndantit* horss," Alex. Scott, p. 77, ed. 1882. Also, used in the sense of undaunted, unabashed, daring; Burgh Recs. Edinburgh, IV. 510, Rec. Soc.; Blame of Kirkburiall, ch. 7. V. DANTON.

UNDEID, VNDEID, *adj.* Alive, Douglas, I. 36, 14, ed. Small.

UNDER. In *under*, underneath, completely under; under the surface of, as "*in under* the water," implying complete submersion; Frequently pron. *anunder* and *anonder*, q. v. A.-S. *in-undor*.

Ay tresting for to speid,
I haif my harte ourset,
Quhair that I fynd bot feld
  My laugour for to lett.
I seik the watter hett
In vndir the cauld yce,
Quhair na regaird I gett,
  I fynd yow ay so nyss.
    Alex. Scott's Poems, p. 63, ed. 1882.

To UNDERCREIP, VNDERCREPE, *v. a.* To undermine; hence to vitiate, destroy, or take away.

"And thairby sum persones seikand thair avin commoditie myndis to *vndercrepe* my rycht and tytill," &c.   Bill by Mr. Roche, quoted in Records of Mining in Scotland, p. 59.
". . . it is allegit be sum seiking to *vndercreip* my richt, title, and contract," &c. Idem., p. 61.
A.-S. *under*, under, and *creópan*, to crawl.

UNDER-FOUD, *s.* Formerly an official in every parish of Zetland, who represented the Judge or Governor; Memorial for Orkney, p. 119. V. FOUD.

When Orkney and Shetland became integral parts of Scotland, the Under-Foud was superseded by the Bailie.

UNDERN. V. DICT.

This term occurs under various forms, as *under*, *undre*, *undrone*, *undorn*; but they represent mere varieties of pronunciation.

UNDERSEDYL, WNDERSEDYL, *s.* Subtenant.

"Gyffand and grantand fwll power to mak rasonabyll tenandis and *wndersedyllis* als oft as it is sene speidfwll tyll hym." Burgh Recs. Peebles, 1476, p. 177, Rec. Soc.
Dan. *undersidder*, one who sits or holds property under another; from *under*, under, and *sidde*, to sit.

UNDERSTOND, VNDERSTOND, *part. pt.* Understood; Kingis Quair; st. 127, ed. Skeat.

To UNDERTA, *v. a.* To undertake, become responsible for, promise, pledge.

"Thy fals excuse," the Lyoun said agane,
"Sall nocht availl ane myte, I underta."
Henryson, Lyoun and Mous, l. 44.

UNDERTAK, VNDERTACK, VNDERTAKE.
1. As a *s.* short for *undertaking*, bargain, agreement; Burgh Recs. Glasgow, II. 122, Rec. Soc.

2. As a *part. pt.*: short for *undertaken;* Kingis Quair, st. 63, ed. Skeat.

As pointed out by the editor, *undertake* in the second sense is a Southern form; the Northern is *undertane*. See note in Gloss.

To UNDO, *v. a.* To cut up game: a term in hunting. Addit. to UNDO, q. v.

UNDOUTAND, *adv.* Undoubtedly; Abp. Hamilton's Catechism, fol. 92*b*.

UNDRONE, VNDRONE, *s.* A form of *undern*, nine o'clock a.m. Addit. to UNDERN, q. v.

Faste by-fore *vndrone* this ferly gun falle.
Avent. Arthure, vi. 7.

UNDUORDY, *adj.* V. *Unwordy.*

UNE, *s.* Musty smell; the oppressive closeness that meets one on opening a long-closed room; Gl. Orkn.

Cf. Swed. *ugn*, Dan. *ovn*, an oven.

UNEARED. UNEARD, UNERD, *adj.* Untilled, uncultivated: called also *unland.* V. *Onland.*

". . . terris non arabilibus *lie unerd.*" Reg. Mag. Sig. Scot., 1546-1580, No. 2195.
A.-S. *erian*, to plough; Icel. *erja*, M. E. *eren*. Cf. Lat. *arare*.]

UNEIS, UNESE, *s.* Discomfort, suffering, illness; Dunbar.

UNERD, *adj.* V. *Uneared.*

UNFAIN, *adj.* Unfond, having a feeling of dislike or reluctance; Whistle Binkie, I. 204. V. FAIN.

To UNFALD, UNFAULD, *v. a.* To unfold, expand; also, to explain, expound. V. FALD.

There simmer first *unfald* her robes,
And there the langest tarry.
Burns, Highland Mary, st. 1.

UNFEINYEIT, UNFENYEIT, UNFENYET, *adj.* Unfeigned; Lyndsay, Compl. to King, l. 415; Abp. Hamilton's Catechism, Tabil, ch. 14.

UNFEINYETLIE, UNFENYEITLIE, UNFENYETLIE, *adv.* Unfeignedly; Lyndsay, Thrie Estaites, l. 3459; Abp. Hamilton's Catechism, fol. 26*b*.

UNFILIT, VNFILET, VNFYLIT, *adj.* Undefiled; Douglas, II. 75, 31, ed. Small; Abp. Hamilton's Catechism, fol. 53*a*. Also, as a law term, uncondemned. V. FILE.

UNFORGEVIN, VNFOIRGEVIN, *adj.* as *adv.* Not to be forgiven, remitted, or evaded; and frequently used in the sense of without exception or abatement, without fail.

This term occurs frequently in our Burgh Records in connection with fines, imposts, and penalties.
"Ilk persone contravenand and brekand this present act sall pay ten puudis of vnlaw *unforgevin.*" Burgh Recs. Glasgow, 1588, i. 123, Rec. Soc.
"And that na maner of maister of the said craft lift, hous herbery, nor ressauo ony vther maisteris prentice or seruand, vnder the pane of paying of twa pund of walx to our said alter *vnfoirgevin.*" Cordiners' Seal of Cause, 1509-10, Burgh Recs. Edin., i. 128, Rec. Soc.

UNFORLEIT, VNFORLEYT, *adj.* Unforsaken, not forgotten; Douglas, IV. 51, 14, ed. Small. A.-S. *forlætan.* V. FORLEIT.

UNFULYIT, UNFULYEIT, VNFULYEIT, *adj.* Unsoiled; hence unused, new, virgin. V. FULYIE, *Fulyeit.*

Birdis hes ane better law na bernis be melkill,
That ilk yeir, with new ioy, ioyis ane maik;
And fangis thame ane fresche feyr, *vnfulyeit* and constant,
And lattis thair fulyeit feiris flie quhair thai pleis.
Dunbar, Tua Mariit Wemen, l. 62.

UNGANG, *s.* V. DICT.

To the definition given in DICT. add the word "circuit." The prefix in *ungang*, s., is *ymb* : the A.-S. word being *ymb-gang*, a going round, a circuit, which correctly describes the mode of fishing alluded to in the quotation. For, in each *shot*, or shooting of the net, the boat starts from one point of the shore and sweeps round to another point a few yards distant, in order to enclose the fish. *Ane ungang*, therefore, is a circuit or going round, a range or sweep, an outgo or shot.
In the verb *ungang*, however, the prefix is different; and the explanatory note under that term is correct and sufficient.

UNHABLE, VNHABLE, WNHABLE, *adj.* Unable; Douglas, II. 106, 13, ed. Small.

UNHALIST, *part.-pa.* V. DICT.

This is a misprint for UNHALSIT; see quotation.

UNHAP, VNHAP, *s.* Mishap, misfortune.

Frome sic *unhap* I pray God thee defend.
Lyndsay, Exhort. to King, l. 1117.
Icel. *happ*, hap, chance, good luck.

UNHEILD, VNHELIT, VNHEALIET, *adj.* Uncovered, open, unreserved: also used as an *adv.* in the sense of openly, unreservedly; Burgh Recs. Aberdeen, I. 448, Sp. C. V. UNHEILD, *v.*

UNHELTHSUM, UNHALESUM, UNHALSUM, *adj.* Unwholesome; Lyndsay, Thrie Estaites, l. 4167. Icel. *heill*, hale.

To UNHIDE, Un-hyde, Vnhide, v. a. To take or bring out of hiding; as applied to the weather, to clear.

The wynde and the wodyrs than welken *un-hydis*;
Than vnclosede the clowddis, the sone schane schone.
Awnt. Arthure, st. 26.

The Douce MS. has "*the welkyn unhides.*" See Note under *Than.*

UNHOLD, Vnhold, adv. Unbound, under compulsion, not of good will; Sir Tristrem, l. 986, S. T. S.

UNHONEST, adj. Indecent, impure; Abp. Hamilton's Catechism, fol. 76b. Addit. to Unhonest, q. v.

UNKEND, Unkenn'd, Unkent, Vnkend, adj. Unknown, unrecognised; Blame of Kirkburiall, ch. 10. Still used in the sense of undiscovered, unheard of, as in the expression, "*unkend* in our day;" also in the sense of strange, foreign, as in "*unkent* folk," as applied to incomers to a district. V. Ken.

Vnkend and misterful in desertis of Libie
I wandir, expellit frome Europe and Asya.
Douglas, Virgil, fi. 43, 14, ed. Small.

UNKNAWIN, Vnknawin, part. pt. Unknown; Kingis Quair, st. 105; being unknown; Ibid., st. 45, ed. Skeat.

Douglas used the form *unknaw:* see Dict.

UNKNYGHTLY, Vnknygitly, adj. Unworthy of a knight, disgraceful.

Pity was to hear
The crueltee of that *vnknyghtly* dede.
Kingis Quair, st. 55, ed. Skeat

UNKYND, Vnkinde, Vnkyndlie, adj. Unnatural, hence, spiteful; Sir Trist., l. 2758: "moving *vnkyndlie* weir," Douglas, III. 66, 7, ed. Small.

Full deip ingravin in hir breist *vnkynd*
The jugement of Paris, how that he
Preferrit Venus, displsing hir bewte.
Ibid., ii. 23, 26.

Unkyndlie, Vnkyndlie, adv. Unnaturally, spitefully.

UNLACH, Vnlach, Vnlay, s. Fine. V. Unlaw.

UNLAMYT, Vnlamyt, part. pt. Uninjured, scathless; Gol. and Gawane, l. 442.

UNLAND, Onland, s. Untilled or uncultivated land, pasture land. V. Onland.

". . . terras arabiles *lie corneland*, terras non arabiles *lie unland* . . . moris, marresiis, pratis, terris non arabilibus *lie unerd.*" Reg. Mag. Sig. Scot., 1546-1580, No. 2195.

UNLATTAR, Vnlattar, s. Opposer, hinderer, disregarder.

". . . and the town to be watchit in the nicht tyme, . . . and the *vnlattaris* of this act in ony point thairof to be wardit till they mak satisfactioun." Burgh Recs. Peebles, p. 374, Rec. Soc.
A.-S. *ymb-*, prefix, and *lettan*, to hinder; M. E. *letten*.

UNLEIFSUM, Unlesum, Vnleisum, adj. Unlawful, forbidden; Dunbar. V. Unlefull.

Unleifsumlie, adv. Unlawfully; Lyndsay, The Dreme, l. 230.

UNLEIRIT, adj. Unlearned, ignorant; Abp. Hamilton's Catechism, fol. 4b. V. Lair, Lare.

UNLELE, Vnlele, adj. Disloyal; Gol. and Gawane, l. 1107. Addit. to Unleill, q. v.

UNLUSUM, Unlufsum, Vnlussum, adj. Uncourteous, unseemly: "*vnlussum* lates," unseemly manners; Gol. and Gawane, l. 95. Addit. to Unlussum, q. v.

UNMAIST, adv. A corr. of *ummaist*, i.e., *umest, umaist,* uppermost, foremost. V. Umast, adj.

"That thair baneris of baith the saidis craftis be paynitt with the imagis, figuris, and armis of the webstaris, and principalie becaus thai ar found the eldar craft . . . thair signe of the spule to be *vnmaist* in ilk baner." Burgh Recs. Edinburgh, 1509, i. 122, Rec. Soc.

UNMANYEIT, Unmenyeit, adj. Unmaimed, unhurt; Dunbar. V. Manyied.

UNMEIT, Wnmeit, adj. Unequal; Douglas, II. 110, 28, ed. Small.

UNMERCIABLE, Vnmerciable, adj. Unmerciful, unkind, cruel, merciless. V. Merciable.

Than woxe I sa *vnmerciable* to martir him I thought.
Dunbar, Twa Mariit Wemen, l. 329.

Quhen he repentis be nocht *unmerciable*,
Bot hym ressave agane rycht tenderlye.
Lyndsay, Exper. and Court., l. 2563.

UNMESURLY, adv. and adj. Without measure; as an Adj. disproportionate, as in "of schap *vnmesurly;*" Douglas, Virgil, II. 247, 22, ed. Small.

UNOURCUMABLE, adj. Invincible, unconquerable; Dunbar.

UNPERMIXED, Unpermyxte, adj. Unmixed, completely separate, distinct.

"This Christ, the very Sone of God, and very God and very man also, . . . hauynge two naturas *unpermyxte* and one deuyne person," &c. Conf. of Faith of Swiss Churches, p. 15, Wodrow Soc. Misc.
Lat. *un*, not, *permixtus*, mingled.

UNPISSILIT, Unpysalt, adj. Unrestrained in lust, unpizzled: *unpysalt*; Lyndsay, Thrie Estaitis, l. 2767.

Bot Secularis wantis that lybertie,
The qubilk ar bound in mariage;
Bot thay, lyke rammis in to thair rage,
Unpissilit rynnis amang the yowis,
So lang as Nature in thame growis.
Lyndsay, Exper. and Court., l. 4702.

Reference is here made to a custom still common in pastoral districts where the rams and ewes graze together. For some time before the coupling season each ram is furnished with an apron, called a pizzle-cloth, which is tied over its belly to prevent it getting at the ewes too early. In this state the rams are said to be pizzled. At the proper time for copulation these aprons are removed, and the rams are allowed to have free intercourse with the ewes: they are then said to be unpizzled, as in the passage quoted above.

UNPLANE, VNPLANE, *adj*. Lit. uneven; hence false, untrue, deceitful, lying.

The pleasand toungis with hartis *unplane*,
For to consider is ane pane.
Dunbar, Warldis Instabilitie, l. 11.

UNPONEIST, *part. adj*. Unpunished; Douglas, II. 29, 31, ed. Small.

UNPROSTITUDE, *adj*. Unprostituted, uncorrupted, perfect: "*unprostitude* chastity;" Blame of Kirkburiall, ch. 17.

UNPROVISIT, *adj*. Unprovided, unprovided for; "*unprovisit* deid," unexpected death; Lyndsay, Tragedie of the Cardinall, l. 307. Also, unforeseen, unpremeditated; "*unprovisit* slauchteris," accidental murders; Burgh Recs. Peebles, 1562, p. 280, Rec. Soc.

Lat. *un*, not, and *provisus*, foreseen, provided for.

UNPROVISITLIE, VNPROWYSITLIE, *adv*. Unadvisedly, rashly, recklessly; Douglas, III. 20, 6, ed. Small.

UNQUESTIONATE, VNQUESTIONATE, *adj*. and *adv*. Unquestioned, without question.

The maister portare, callit pacience,
That frely lete vs in, *vnquestionate*.
Kingis Quair, st. 125, ed. Skeat.

UNQUYT, UNQUAT, *adj*. Unfinished, unsettled, unpaid; Dunbar.

UNREDE, UNRIDE, *adj*. V. DICT.

The etym. of this word is not *ungereod*, nor *ungeridu*, but *ungeryd*. See *geryd*, ready, in Bosworth and Toller's A.-S. Dict.

UNREST, ONREST, *s*. Unrest, ceaseless or anxious striving; also, whatever causes unrest or disquiet: pl. *unrestis*, *onrestis*, worries, troubles, misfortunes.

De sa feil wynterys blastis and tempestis,
Ilk al the wayis noysom and *vnrestis*,
And all that horribill was, or yit heny,
Woful, hidduous.
Douglas, Virgil, 456, 53, Rudd.

In Small's ed. *onrestis*, which by mistake is rendered "*restless*" in Gloss.

UNRICHT, VNRYCHT, *adj*. as *adv*. Wrongly, unjustly, unfairly. V. [UNRICHT].

Ye may with honesty persew,
Gif ye be constand, trest, and trew,
Thocht thau *vnrycht* thay on you rew,
Ressoun;
Bot be ye fund dowbill, adew,
Tressoun.
Alex. Scott's Poems, p. 42, ed. 1882.

UNRIDE, UNRUYD, UNRYDE, *adj*. Unrestrained, boundless; hence savage, cruel, dreadful, horrible, terrible. V. UNREDE, UNRUDE.

These forms occur repeatedly in the Allit. Rom. Alexander, in Sir Tristrem, and in the Gawane Romances. See notes under UNREDE and UNRUDE.

UNRIDELY, UNRUYDLY, *adv*. Cruelly, horribly, dreadfully, furiously; Allit. Rom. Alex., l. 638, 566.

UNRINGIT, VNRYNGIT, WNRYNGYT, *part. pt*. Unringed, i.e., not having a ring in the snout.

"For the wrangwis worthyne of thar swyne and *wnryngyt*." Burgh Recs. Prestwick, 1510, p. 42, Mait. C.

UNROCKIT, UNROIKKIT, *adj*. Reckless; used also as an *adv*., rashly, wildy; "Thow ravis *unrockit*;" Lyndsay, Papyngo, l. 969.

"Schir, be the Rude, *unroikkit* now ye raif."
Henryson, The Foxe and the Wolf, l. 116.

A.-S. *récan*, to care: formed from a noun with base *róc*-, care, in M. H. Ger. *ruoch*; whence *ruochen*, to reck, and in O. H. Ger. *róhhjan*. See Skeat's Etym. Dict. s. v. *Reck*.

O. Norse, *urækja*, to be careless; Fritzner.

UNRYCHT, *adj., adv.*, and *s*. V. UNRICHT.

UNRYDE, UNRUYD, *adj*. V. UNREDE, UNRUDE.

UNRYPIT, VNRYPIT, *part. pt*. Unripened; used also as an *adj*., as in "*vnrypit* fruyte," Kingis Quair, st. 14, ed. Skeat.

UNSAWIN, UNSAWN, *adj*. Unsown, uncultivated. V. SAW.

To teill the ground that hes bene lang *unsawin*,
Lyndsay, Thrie Estaitis, l. 1601.

UNSEKIR, VNSEKIR, *adj*. Insecure; Kingis Quair, st. 6, ed. Skeat. V. UNSIKKER.

UNSEKERNESSE, VNSEKERNESSE, *s*. Insecurity; Ibid., st. 15.

UNSELDE, VNSELDE, *adv*. Not seldom; Sir Tristrem, l. 2313, S.T.S. V. SELDYN.

UNSELY, VNCELY, *adj*. Mischievous. V. UNSEL.

UNSET, UNSETE, VNSETE, adj. Unbounded, unlimited, extreme; also, unbearable.
His sorwe was vnsete.
Sir Tristrem, l. 1238, S.T.S.

UNSIVERIT, VNSYVERIT, adj. Unsevered, not separated; Douglas, III., 248, 11, ed. Small.
O. Fr. sevrer, from Lat. separare, to separate, sever.

UNSMART, adj. Slow, dull, spiritless, as applied to a person; slack, limp, springless, as applied to an object.
For as we se, ane bow that is ay bent,
Worthis *unsmart* and dullis on the string.
Henryson, Prol. to Fables, l. 23.
A.-S. *smeortan,* to smart, ache; *smart,* adj. originally meant painful, also pungent, brisk, lively.

UNSOCHT, UNSOGHT, adj. V. UNSAUCHT.

UNSOUND, s. Trouble, sorrow. Addit. to Unsound, q. v.

UNSOUND, VNSOUND, adj. Sorrowful; also used as an adv., sorrowfully, as in "thai sighit *vnsound*;" Gol. and Gawane, l, 638.
Vnsound is similarly used in Sir Tristrem, l. 1175, 3342.

UNSOUNDLY, adv. Sorrowfully, with sad and anxious heart.

UNSOUPIT, adj. Unsupped, supperless; Dunbar and Kennedie, l. 382, S. T. S.

UNSPAYND, VNSPAYNIT, VNSPEYNIT, adj. Unweaned, sucking; Dunbar, p. 248, ed. Small, S. T. S. V. SPAIN, v,

UNSPECKIT, adj. Unsuspected, unlooked for; Sempill Ballates, p. 128.

UNSTONAIT, VNSTONAIT, adj. Unamazed, not confounded; Gol. and Gawane, l, 642. V. STONAY, v.

UNSURE, adj. Uncertain, unsafe, risky, dangerous; Reg. Privy Council, vii. 709, Sc. Recs.

UNTHANKES, VNTHANKIS, ONTHANKS, s. pl. Displeasure, hatred; "at myn *vnthankes,*" in opposition to my will; Awnt. Arthure, 33, 8.
A.-S. *unthances,* perforce.

UNTHRALL, adj. Unenthralled, unsubjected; Lyndsay, Papyngo, l. 924.
O. Northumbrian *thrǣl*, from Icel. *thrǣll*, a thrall, serf. See Skeat's Etym. Dict., s. v. *Thrall.*

UNTOUNIS, VNTOUNIS, adj. Not living in or belonging to the town: "*untounis man,*" a stranger or non-resident.
". . . sall be sauld to ony frieman befoir an *vntounis* man." Burgh Recs. Prestwick, 22 Oct., 1601, p. 85, Mait. C.

UNWAFTED, part. adj. Unwoven, unfilled with waft or woof. V. WAFT.
"If there be a web consisting of more lenth then one pair, ilk weaver is to leave the bounds of a large inch at the end of ilk pair *unwafted*, that the foresaid lenth may be the better observed." Burgh Recs. Stirling, 1662, p. 230.

UNWARS, UNWARSE, UNWARLY, UNWERLY, adv. Unawares, unprepared, without warning; *at unwarse*, by surprise, Burgh Recs. Aberdeen, I, 3, Rec. Soc.; *unwerly,* Lyndsay, Exper. and Court., l. 3466. V. UNWAR.
A.-S. *un,* not, and *wær,* cautious. Cf. Icel. *varligr,* safe.

UNWEETING, ONWEETIN, adj. Unwitting, unknowing: unknown, involuntary; "*unweeting* groan," involuntary groan; Burns. E. *unwitting.*

UNWERLY, adv. V. *Unwars.*

UNWINNE, adj. Lit. not to be mastered or cured, incurable. Errat. in DICT., q. v.
Jamieson's defin., "unpleasant," is evidently unsuitable. The *win* of which this term is compounded means to conquer, as in *winning,* conquest: hence, *unwinne,* invincible, incurable, as given in Gloss. Sir Tristrem, S. T. S.

UNWORDY, UNVORDY, VNDVORDY, adj. Unworthy, unbecoming, unfit; Burgh Recs. Aberdeen, I. 285, Sp. C. V. WORDY.

To UNYARK, UNYERK, v. a. To unbind, unbar, throw open, set free. V. YARK, YERK.
Than yode thai furthe and *vnyarkid* the yates of the cite.
Allit. Rom. Alexander, l. 3210.

UPALAND, UPALOND, VPALAND, s. A rustic, countryman. Addit. to Up-a-land, q. v.
"*Pero, vpalandis* shoone;" Duncan's App. Etym., 1595, ed. Small, E. D. S.

UPART, VPART, adv. Upwards, higher up.
"The mele merket of all grane and cornes fra the Tolbuth vp to Liberton's Wynde; also fra thine *vpart* to the treves the merket of all oottone claith." Burgh Recs. Edin., 1477, I., 35, Rec. Soc.

To UPBOLT, VPBOLT, v. n. To shoot up, rise to the surface; part. pt. *upboltit*, risen to the surface; Douglas, II. 234,14, ed. Small.

To UPBRAID, VPBRADE, v. n. To spring or leap up, rush up. V. BRADE, BRAID.
Syne stickis dry to kendle thar about laid is,
Quhill all in flamb the bleis of fyir *upbradis.*
Douglas Virgil, II. 32, 10, ed. Small.
A.-S. *bregdan, brædan,* to move quickly; Icel. *bregdha,* from *bragdh,* a quick motion. See VIGFUSSON.

UPDOST, Vpdost, *part. pt.* Got up, dressed, decked: "all in duddis *vpdost;*" Dunbar and Kennedie, l. 384. V. Doss, *v.*

To UPDRY, *v. a.* To dry up, evaporate; Lyndsay, Papyngo, l. 138.

To UPHIE, Vphie, *v. a.* To uphold, keep up; Dunbar, I Cry the Mercy, l. 52. Addit. to Up-He, q. v.

UPLY, Uplie, Vplie, *adj.* Lit., lofty, high; lifting: *uplie-stane,* the uplifting or leaping-on stone, a stone in the form of a step for assisting a rider to mount on horseback.

". . . fra the *vplie* stane till Lord Borthikes cloise." Burgh Recs. Edinburgh, 1530-1, ii. 46, Rec. Soc.

Also called *loplystane,* i.e. leaping-on stone: "fra the *Loplystane* till Lord Boirthwikis clos." Ibid., 1531, ii. 51, Rec. Soc.

Prob. from A.-S. *uplic,* lofty, high.

UPON, Vpon, Wpon, Apon, *prep.* Among, to.

". . . ony of the said craft that byis ony fawin flecht or ony falty flecht to tap *apon* nebouris, &c." Burgh Recs. Stirling, 28 April, 1522.

This use of *upon* occurs frequently in these Records, and always after the verb *tap,* to retail, sell in small quantities.

UPPERMAIR, Vppermair, *adj.* and *s.* Upper, higher; the higher point, place, or particular.

Well I considerit na *vppermair* I micht,
And to discend, sa hiddeous was the bicht,
I durst not auenture.
Douglas, *Palice of Honour,* pt. 3, l. 40.

The word is still used in both senses.

UPPLANE, *adj.* Rustic, outspoken. V. Uplands.

Thus sang ane bird with voce *vpplane,*
"All cruly joy returnis in pane."
Dunbar, p. 76, ed. Small, S. T. S.

To UPREILL, Upwrele, *v. a.* V. Up-wreile.

UPRENT, Wprent, *part. pt.* Torn up; Douglas, II. 119, 32, ed. Small.

To UPRICHT, Vpricht, Wpricht, *v. a.* To deal justly by one, or to see that justice is done to him; to indemnify, compensate.

The lord or master was bound to *upricht* his vassal or servant; and the parties engaged in bargain-making were bound to *upricht* each other.

"Theman, goldsmycht, sal deliuer it [a quarter noble] agayn to the saide Thomas Ryburne, and he to content Theman of v s. vi d. agayn, that he gaf him for it, sen it was nocht lachfull nor sufficiande to pass for payment na werk, and the forsaide Thomas til sok til his waraude, gif he haf ony, til *vpricht* him." Burgh Recs. Aberdeen, 1463, i. 20, 8p. C. That is, the said Thomas may fall back upon the person from whom he got the coin, and compel him to give satisfaction. See under *Sok, v.*

The sense "to indemnify or compensate" is implied by the term as used in the following passage:—

"Johne Besat chalansit Androw Atkin as he that hyrit a meyr of his, and Androw Murra yungar for the spilling and hurting of hir in the ryding of hir, throw the quhilkis he wants his mere, and that the saidis persons acht til *vpricht* and asseith him for hir." Ibid. 1480, p. 411.

UPRIGHT, *adj.* In golfing this term is applied to a club whose head is at nearly a right angle to the shaft: see Golfer's Handbook.

To UPROSS, Uproos, *v. a.* To rouse, stir up, move.

It wald *vpross* ane hart of stone,
To se me lost for lufe of one
That suld be myne.
Alex. Scott's Poems, p. 51, ed. 1882.

Swed. *rusa,* Dan. *ruse,* to rush; M. E. *rusen,* to rush out. When a stag broke from covert it was said to *rouse.* However, it is chiefly used as an active verb in the sense of stirring up to instant or vigorous action. V. Wedgwood, and Skeat, s. v.

UPSETTER, *s.* Elevator: "*upsetteris* to the ordinance," elevators of the Host in services of the Catholic Church; Invent. St. Salv. College, Mait. Club Misc., III. 201.

UPSPRED, Vpspred, *part. pt.* Outspread, spread, opened.

New *vpspred* vpon spray, as new spynist rose.
Dunbar, *Tua Mariit Wemen,* l. 29.

To UPTAK, Vptak, Upta, *v. a.* To take up; Douglas, II. 126, 2, ed. Small: begin, lead; "to *uptak* the psalms," to lead the psalmody, to precent or act as precentor. Addit. to Uptak.

"His yeirlie stepend for *vptaking* of the psalmes in the kirk, and eruditioun of the youth-heid in the art of musik." Burgh Recs. Edinburgh, iv. 126, Rec. Soc.

UPTAKER, Vptaker, *s.* Collector; leader; "*uptaker* of the psalms," leader of the psalmody, precentor; Burgh Recs. Stirling, p. 150, 153, 240.

To UPWARP, *v. a.* To cast, toss, or drive up; to haul up; Douglas, Virgil, II. 155, 1, ed. Small.

A.-S. *weorpan, werpan,* to cast; Goth. *wairpan,* Icel. *varpa.*

UPWAXING, Wpwaxing, *part. pr.* Growing up; Douglas, II. 192, 3, ed. Small.

UPWITH, Vpwith, Vp-with, *s.* Point of action or attack; "at the *vp-with,*" at the pinch.

All is bot fruitless his effeir, and falyeis at the *vp-with.*
Dunbar, *Tua Mariit Wemen,* l. 401.

URE, Ore, Eyre, *s.* An ounce: the fundamental unit of all Orkneyan valuation. Addit. to Ure, q. v.

The *ure* is the eighth part of a merk; and when used as a denomination of land-value it is a contr. for *Urisland*, q. v.

URISLAND, *s*. A denomination of land-value equal to one-eighth of a markland, or eighteen penny-lands.

URE, *s*. A kind of haze, &c. V. DICT.
In his explanation of this term Jamieson refers to Lye's "A.-S. *urig*, canus, hoary." It is important to observe that Lye's statement is wrong. Tho A.-S. word is *úrig*, and the sense is 'dewy.' Cf. *ure*, sweat, p. 682 of Vol. IV. DICT.

To URN, *v. a*. V. DICT.
Urn is simply another form of *ern*, to which Jamieson refers; and the etym. which he suggests, but at the same time doubts, is quite correct. *Yern, ern, earn*, and *urn* are corruptions of the M. E. *ermen*, to grieve, from A.-S. *yrman*, to grieve; formed from the adj. *earm*, poor, miserable, wretched. V. Skeat's Etym. Dict., s. v. *Yearn*.

URUSUM, VRUSUM, *adj*. Restless : " the *vrusum* fleis;" Douglas, Virgil, 450, 6, Rudd.
Delete the definition given in DICT. under URUSUM; for the sense is simply *restless* (See note in DICT.), and the allusion is to the ceaseless movement of flies in the air. Cf. Icel. *úrô*, unrest, restlessness; Vigfusson.
The form *uriwm* on which Ruddiman based his etym. does not occur in the passage quoted for it; *vrusum* is the reading of his text, and also of the Elph. MS. See Small's ed., iv., 170.

USANS, *s*. Usage, custom, use.
And thair outrallis behald flekkir and steir.
According the ald *usans* to that effect.
Sum augury to persaif or gud aspect.
Douglas, Virgil, ii. 179, 1, ed. Small.
L. Lat. *usancia*, custom; from *usare*.

USCHERE, VSCHERE, *s*. An usher, a doorkeeper; Kingis Quair, st. 97, ed. Skeat. V. HUSCHER.

O. Fr. *ussier, uissier*, and later *huissier*, an usher or door-keeper; see Cotgrave. Formed from Lat. *ostiarius*, a doorkeeper, a der. from Lat. *ostium*, a door : the O. Fr. form for which was *huis*.
Usher, a door-keeper, is a different word from *usher*, a servant who walks before a person of rank : the latter term being formed from Lat. *exire*, to go forth or before, through the O. Fr. *issir*. See Ische, and *Ush*.

To USH, USHE, USCHE, VSCHE, *v. a*. 1. To clean, cleanse, empty; "to *ushe* the belly."

2. To usher or walk before a person of rank : hence, to lead, guide. Addit. to USHE, USCHE, q. v.

I'll gar our guidman trow
That I'm gaun to play,
If he winna fee to me
Valets twa or three,
To bear my train up frae the dirt,
And *ush* me through the town ;
Stand about, ye fisher jauds,
And gie my gown room.
Song, I'll Gar our Guidman Trow.

(Sup.) I 2

USCHER, VSCHERE, *s*. A servant who walks before a person of rank.
In times not yet remote the provost and magistrates marched to church on Sunday in a body, and were *ushered* or preceded by the town-officers in their official dress bearing their halberts : this procession was called " the town-council and *ushers*." This old custom gradually died out after the Disruption of 1843.

USHIE, USCHIE, USCHIN, VSCHAW, *s*. Issue, emptying ; generally used in pl. *ushies, uschies, uschins, vschawis*, and applied to cleansings or emptyings of every kind thrown out as refuse.
"Item, it is statute and ordanit .... that na fleschouris teyme thair *vschawis* [i.e. filth from the entrails of animals which they have killed] vpone the foirgate, vnder the pane of viij s. ilk falt, vnforgewin." Burgh Recs. Glasgow, 1574, i. 25, Rec. Soc.
O. Fr. *issir*, " to issue ; to goe or depart out, to flow forth ;" Cotgr. From Lat. *exire*, to go out or forth.
However, some of our best scholars believe that the verb *ush* was formed from the noun *usher*, and got mixed up with the verb to *ish ;* and that hence arose the popular etymology of *usher* from *ish*.

USQUEBAE, USQUEBA, USQUEBAUGH, *s*. Whisky ; Burns, Tam o' Shanter, Jolly Beggars.
Gael. *uisge beatha*, also *uisge na beatha*, water of life, aqua vitae. V. M'Leod and Dewar.

USUCAPION, *s*. Proprietary right acquired or established by long and uninterrupted possession ; Blame of Kirkburiall, ch. 19. Lat. *usucapio*.

UTASS, WTAST, *s*. V. DICT.
Only the form *wtast* is a corruption ; *utas* is from a Norman French word corresponding to O. Fr. *oitauves*, octaves ; from Lat. *octo*, eight. Cf. O. Fr. *oit, oyt, uit* (Mod. Fr. *huit*), as given in Burguy.

UTEUCHT, *adv*. Outside. V. UTOUTH.

UTGAE, VTGAN, *s*. Outgoing. V. OUTGAIT, *Outgang*.

UTINLAND, WTINLAND, *s*. The pasture ground, or common, lying outside of the arable land of a township.
". . . heretable infeftment of thair landis quhilk are teillable, and *wtinland* to be sowmit by *gersing*." Burgh Recs. Prestwick, 1579-80, p. 78, Mait. C.

UTRID, VTRID, *part. pt*. Uttered ; "*vtrid* be measure," Kingis Quair, st. 132, ed. Skeat.

UTTER, UTER, VTTER, VTER, *adj*. 1. Extreme, greatest, utmost : "*vter* power," utmost power or ability ; Burgh Recs. Edinburgh, III. 233, Rec. Soc.

2. Outer, outward : " the *uter* door."
"*Femur*, the *vtter* part of the thigh ;" Duncan's App. Etym., 1595, ed. Small, E. D. S.
A.-S. *útor, úttor*, outer, uttor ; compar. of *út*, out.

UTYRANS, VTYRRANS, *s.* V. UTERANCE.

UVERING, UVIRING, UVRIN, *s.* A covering, bedcover.
"In a record of 13th Dec. 1657, John Bickerton is spoken of as a worker of *uvirings*, and John and William Williamson are designated by their trade of brabeners [i.e. weavers].
" *Uviring* from *uver*, upper, is evidently a covering, the weaving of which, in woollen only, ceased to be practised in Newburgh towards the end of the first quarter of the present century." Laing, Lindores Abbey and Newburgh, p. 240.

UVERMAST, UVIRMEst, *adj.* Uppermost, highest: "the *uvirmest* lychtis," the highest windows; Burgh Recs. Stirling, 29 April, 1549. V. *Umast.*

UXTER, *s.* The armpit. V. OXTER.

UYTE, VYIT, *s.* and *v.* V. WITE.

V.

VACAND, VACANS, *s.* Vacancy. V. under *Vake.*

VADDLE, VAADLE, *s.* A shallow pool, a pool at the head of a bay that fills and empties with the flowing and ebbing of the sea. Gl. Shetland.
"On each side oozy pools or creeks replenished every tide, named *vaddles*, find for themselves channels among irregular brown hills of heath." Hibbart's Shetland, p. 540.
Dan. *vad*, a ford, shallow pool ; lit. a wading-place ; Swed. *vad*, Icel. *vath*, A.-S. *wœd*. Cf. Lat. *vadum* : but Dan. *vad* has not come from Lat. V. Vigfusson.

To VAGE, *v. n.* To wander. V. VAIG.

VAGER, VAGAR, *s.* A vagabond; Lyndsay, Thrie Estaitis, l. 3004.

VAIFF, VAFF, *s.* A signal flag, a signal. V. WAFF.

To VAIK, *v. n.* To wake, watch. V. VAKE.

To VAIL, VAILE, VAILL, VALE, VAILYIE, VALYIE, *v. a.* and *n.* To avail, to be of value or service, to serve, benefit, profit; Lyndsay, Thrie Estaitis, l. 355.
The Cat cummis and to the mous hes ee,
What *vaillis* than thy feist and rialtie.
Henryson, Upland Mous and Burges Mous, l. 224.
Bot all in vane, it *vailyeit* him na thing.
Ibid., Lyoun and Mous, l. 122.

VAIL, VAILE, *s.* Extent, space. Addit. to VALE, q. v.
"The *vaile* of xxxv[ti] fud [i.e. feet] at the forepart of breid." Burgh Recs. Prestwick, p. 19, Mait. C.
O. Fr. *valoir*, *valer*, to be of use or worth ; from Lat. *valere*, to be strong.

VAIRSCALL, *s.* V. DICT.
Most prob. this is a misreading of VAIRSTALL. In many MSS. the letters *c* and *t* are exactly alike. See under *Warestall*, Wair Almerie.

VAIT, VATE, *pres.* Know. V. under WAIT, *Wait.*

To VAKE, VAIK, VACE. 1. As a *v. n.*; to grow or become empty; Lyndsay, Compl. to King, l. 188; to disperse, to be dismissed: as, "When the kirk *vaiks*," i.e. when the church is emptying or emptied, or when the people disperse or are dismissed. Also, to be closed or shut for a time: as, "The school *vakis* for the hairst," i.e. it is closed during that season.

2. As a *v. a.*; to vacate, retire or withdraw from ; also to empty, as, "He *vaikit* the kirk," i.e. he scattered the congregation. Addit. to VAIK, q. v.

VAKAND, VAIKING, VACAND, *part.* Falling or becoming vacant ; leaving, going out of, giving up, as " *vaiking* his shop."
"He sal be present and put in and to the first service that sal hapyn *vacand* in thair gouernans." Burgh Recs. Peebles, 1458, p. 120, Rec. Soc.

VAKEN, VAIKEN, VACAND, VACANS, *s.* Vacancy; vacation, as in "the school *vacans* ;" pl. *vacands*, Lyndsay, Thrie Estaitis, l. 998.
"Nixt *vaken* that fallis within the towne of Peblis, that the said Thomas sones sall haif the samin." Burgh Recs. Poebles, 1567, p. 305, Rec. Soc.
Lat. *vacuus*, empty ; *vacare*, to be empty ; *vacuare*, to make empty.

VALD, *s.* Dyer's weed. V. WALD.

VALE, VALYIE, *v.* and *s.* V. *Vail, v.*

To VALE, *v. n.* V. DICT.
Not from Fr. *devaller*, as suggested; but from O. Fr. *avaller*, which Cotgrave renders "to let, put, lay, cast, fell downe ; to let fall downe." Hence *vale* is short for *avale*. See Gloss. King's Quair, ed. Skeat.

VALENTINE'S DEAL, VALENTINE'S DEALING, *s.* The choosing of sweethearts on St. Valentine's Day, Feb. 14th. The names of the various members of the company were written on separate slips,

and were then selected by lot; and the person whose name was so drawn was the drawer's *valentine* for the year: Burns.
See under Valentine in Halliwell's Dict.

To VALK, *v. a.* V. DICT.
Valk should be *vakk*. The form arose from misreading the old symbol for *kk* as *lk*. Even to a practised eye the symbols look almost exactly alike.

VANEGLOIR, *s.* Vain-glory, vanity; Henryson, Chanteclcir and Foxc, l. 78. Fr. *vaine-gloire.*

VANGELL, *s.* Short for *evangell,* the gospel: sometimes used as an *adj.,* as in "the *vangell* lettrin"; Invent. St. Salv. Col. St. Andrews, Mait. Club Misc., III. 201. V. *Evangell.*

To VANT, *v. a.* To vaunt, brag of Douglas, Virgil, II. 57, 9, ed. Small.

VANT, *s.* A vaunt, boasting.
To *Vant* and Voky ye belr this rowm alef;
Bid thame thairin that thal tak thair hyre.
Douglas, King Hart, i. 119, 23, ed. Small.

VANTOUR, *s.* A vaunter, bragger; Ibid. II. 170, 8. Fr. *vanteur.*
O. Fr. *se vanter,* to boast, brag; from L. Lat. *vanitare,* to speak vanity.

VARDOUR, VARDUR, VERDOUR, VERDAR, *s.* V. *Wardour.*

VARESTAW, *s.* V. *Warestall.*

VARIANCE, *s.* Contradiction; Kingis Quair, st. 161, ed. Skeat. V. VARIANT.

VARIORUM, *s.* Constant change, continual variation, medley.
Life is all a *variorum,*
We regard not how it goes;
Let them cant about decorum,
Who have characters to lose.
Burns, Jolly Beggars.
From Lat. *variorum,* gen. pl. of *varium,* varied.

VARITE, *s.* Verity, truth.
Blind ignorance me gaif sic hardiness
To argone so agane the varite.
Dunbar, Bann. MS., fol. 284a.
Fr. *vérité,* from Lat. *veritas,* truth.

VARKLUME, *s.* V. WARKLOOM.

To VARRAY, *v. a.* V. DICT.
Varray for *warray.* See WARRAY, WERRAY.

VATH, *s.* V. DICT.

To VAUCE, *v. a.* V. DICT.
Ruddiman's etym. for this term is unsuitable. Rather from O. Fr. *faulser,* to falsify, forge; also *faulser un escu,* to pierce a shield; whence *faulsé,* pierced. When used in this sense the verb was also written *faussser.* Both forms are from Lat. *falsare,* to falsify, from Lat. *falsus,* false. See under *Faucet* in Skeat's Etym. Dict.

VAUDIE, VADY, WADIE, WADY, *adj.* The meanings and quotations given in the DICT. should be arranged thus : —

1. Great, strong, powerful.
Cummers sled and hurl'd as weel
On ice, as ony *vady* chiel.
Pipvr of Peebles, p. 7.

2. Proud, vain, gay, elated.
Then all the giglets, young and gaudy
Sware . . . . . . I might be *wady.*
Forbes's Dominie Deposed, p. 40.

3. Merry, gay, cheerful.
Thus must we be sad, whilst the traitors are *vaudie,*
Till we get a sight o' our ain bonny laddie.
Jacobite Relics, ii. 70.
She says I'm glad 'at ye're sa *wadie,*
Ye sat sne douff an' dowie a' day
Wi' me the ben.
W. Beattie's Poems, p. 7.

Dr. Jamieson must have been strangely misled regarding the term *vaudie,* when he associated it with E. *gaudy,* der. from Lat. *gaudere.* Even granting that *vaudie* retains its Gothic form, no Lat. *g* over becomes *v* or *w* in Eng. ; and though Teut. *w* may answer to Eng. *g,* there can be no connection between these two words.
Most prob. *vaudie* has come from Icel. *völdugr,* O. Icel. *valdugr,* powerful, strong, and secondarily proud, as in Icel. *völduliga,* proudly. This would give a form *waidy,* which certainly would become *wauily, vaudy, wady, vady,* as in the passages quoted.

VAUTE, VAWT, VOLTE, VOULT, VOUTE, VOWTE, *s.* A vault, secret chamber, den; a vaulted roof, an arch.
"With ane lang transe *voult* betuixt the thrie *voultes.*" Burgh Recs. Aberdeen, ii. 339, 8p. C.
"Made vp little canes or *voltes* for buriall vse";
Blame of Kirkburiall, ch. x.
"*Fornix,* a *vawt* or bordell house"; Duncan's App. Etym., 1595, ed. Small, F. D. S.
"*Camera,* a *voute* ;" Ibid.

To VAUTE, VAWT, VOULT, VOUTE, VOWTE, WOUTE, *v. a.* To vault, arch, roof.
"And sall *voult* oner the nethermost voultis the hight of the tolbuith fluir." Burgh Recs. Aberdeen, 1616, ii. 338, 8p. C.
"Sal mak and *voute* v chapellis on the south syde of the paryce kyre of Edinburgh." Charters of Edinburgh, 29 Nov. 1387, Rec. Soc.
". . . *voutyt* on the maner and the masounry as the voute abovyn Sant Stevinys." Ibid.
O. Fr. *vaute,* later *vaulte,* from L. Lat. *volta,* from Lat. *voluta,* a vault.

To VAX, *v. n.* To wax, grow, become: pret. *vaxit, vox;* part. pt. *vaxen, vaxit;* Dunbar, Tua Mariit Wemen, l. 175.

VCH, VCHE, *s.* An ouch. V. *Uche.*

VEDIS, *s. pl.* Raiment, armour. V. WEDIS.

VEIR, VER, WERE, WAIR, VOR, *s.* V. DICT.

The etym. is Icel. *vdr*, not *vor*, as in DICT. Consequently, that the word is of Egyptian origin is a wild fancy.

VELURE, *s.* Naples fustian, mock-velvet.
"Naples fusteanes tripe or *velure*"; Rates of Customs, 1612, Halyburton's Ledger, p. 307.
Velure is short for *tripe de velours*, mock-velvet; see Cotgr.

VELVOUS, *s.* V. DICT.
"Fr. *velour*," given as etym. for this term, is an error for Fr. *velours*. A better form, however, is O. Fr. *velous*, from Lat. *villosus*, shaggy.

VENGEABIL, VENGIBLE, *adj.* Vengeful, revengeful: "*vengeabil* cruelty;" Dunbar, I cry the Mercy, l. 140. Addit. to [*Vengeabil*], q. v.
"*Dirus*, cursed, *vengible*"; Duncan's App. Etym., 1595, ed. Small, E. D. S.

VENGEAND, *part.* Avenging; Gol. and Gawane, l. 759.
O. Fr. *venger*, to avenge : from Lat. *vindicare*.

VENIM, VENEM, VENNOM, WENEM, *s.* Venom, poison; Spald. Club Misc. I. 93; pl. *vennomys,* drugs, philters.
Quham, revist for his lufe, throu *vennomys* seir,
Circes his spous smate wyth ane goldin wand,
And in ane byrd him turnit fut and hand,
Douglas, *Virgil*, iii. 93, 18, ed. Small.
O. Fr. *venin*, from Lat. *venenum*, poison.

VENNEL, VENNALL, VENELL, VINEL, VYNEL, WENNELL, *s.* Lit. a little street: a lane. V. VENALL.

VENT, *s.* Vending, sale, business; Blame of Kirkburiall, ch. 19. Fr. *vente*, sale.

VENT, VENTIGE, *s*, Pl. *vents, ventiges*, the holes in a flute, flageolot, clarionet, &c. Burns.
The form *ventage* is used by Shakespeare in Hamlet.
O. Fr. *vent*, an opening ; older forms *fent* and *fente*, "a cleft, rift ;" Cotgr. This form is still used : as in the phrase, "a *fente* of a gown."

VENTAILLE, VENTAIL, VENTALLE, *s*. The movable piece over the mouth in front of a helmet; Awnt. Arthure, st. 32, 5, Gol. and Gawane, l. 867. Addit. to VENTAILL, q. v.
Delete the notes given under Ventaill in DICT. : the passage to which they refer is incorrect. See under *Waire*, v.
This portion of a helmet is also called *aventaille*.

VERA, VERRA, *adj.* and *adv.* Very. V. VERRAY.

VERAMENT, VERAYMENT, *s.* Truth. V. VERRAYMENT.

VERDOUR, VERDUR, VERDOR. V. *Wardour.*

Jamieson's defin. and etym. of this term are misleading, and do not apply to the *verdour* mentioned in the quotation. The letter *v* in *verdour* does not represent *v*, but *u* or *w;* and the name of the cloth is not *verdour*, but *werdour*, or more properly, *wardour*. For further explanation see under that heading.

VERNAKELL, *s.* The holy napkin; Invent. St. Salv. College, Mait. Club Misc., III. 204.
Vernacle, dimin. of *Verony*, the cloth or napkin on which the face of Christ is depicted. It is preserved in St. Peter's at Rome, and is said to be the napkin which St. Veronica gave to Christ to wipe his face when on his way to crucifixion, and which thereby received a striking impression of his countenance.

VERRE, VERE, VER, *s.* A glass for liquor; pl. *verres, veris, verrys.* Addit. to VERES, q. v.
With vernage in *verrys* and cowppys sa clene.
Awnt. Arthure, st. 36, 2.

To VERT, *v. v.* To turn up or over ; "*vertand* the earth," turning up the soil, rooting. Lat. *vertere*.
"It sall be lesum to quhatsumewir persone apprehendand the said swyne *vertand* the earth to distroy the samen." Burgh Recs. Aberdeen, 1578, ii. 32, Sp. C.

VERTEW, VERTU, *s.* Power, ability, capability; Kingis Quair, st. 74; vigour, powerful influence; Ibid., st. 20, ed. Skeat. Addit. to VERTER, s. 3, q. v.

VERTIE, VERTY, VAIRTIE, *adj.* Cautious, prudent, careful; hence, industrious, wide awake, eager. Errat. in DICT.
Archie, fu' *vertie*, owre the moorlan' spangs
Ilk strype and stank ; nae doubt he itchin langs
To crack wi' San'.
Tarras' Poems, p. 2.
The explanation given in the DICT. is altogether a mistake. The entry must be deleted.
Vertie is simply short for *averty*, prudent, q. v., the a being dropped, as in *vale* for *avale*, &c.
O. Fr. *averti*, cautious, prudent; from Lat. *advertere*, to turn attention to.

VESCHEL-ALMERY, VESCHALE-AUMRY, *s.* V. WESCHALE ALMERIE.

To VESIE, VESY, VISIE, VISE, *v. a.* To view, see, regard ; Lyndsay, Squyer Meldrum, l. 257, Thrie Estaitis, l. 505 ; part. pr. *vesiand,* viewing ; Ibid., Exper. and Court., l. 1466; *vesyit,* visited, examined, Ibid., The Dreme, l. 386. V. *Visie.*

VESIATER, *s.* A surveyor : same as VESIAR, q. v. Burgh Recs. Edinburgh, I. 167, Rec. Soc.

VESIE, VESIGH, *s.* Sight, view, examination ; "Tak a *vesie* o' the lan'."
"Frier Wynssent, litstar, prior of the Freris Predicatoris of this said burgh, protestit solemnly in presens of the saidis ballies, and in the *resigh* of the haill court, that na proces leid nor to be leid within the said burgh sould hourt tham na thair place of thar anualis awin

thame, bot that tha mycht haue remaid of law."
Burgh Recs. Stirling, 30 Sept. 1521.
O. Fr. *viser*, to look at, regard: from Lat. *visus*.

VEST, *part. pt.* Vested, invested; "*vest* and seasit," Burgh Recs. Glasgow, I. 186, Rec. Soc.

To **VEX,** *v. a.* To vex, trouble, annoy; pret. and part. pt. *vexit,* Kingis Quair, st. 174, ed. Skeat. V. VEX, *v. n.*

VEYLE, *adv.* V. DICT.
To this entry in DICT. add: *Veyle* is a form of *weyle,* for *weil,* well.

VIALL, *s.* A chamber-pot made of glass or glazenware; Halyburton's Ledger, p. 309.
In the section including glass and glazenware in Rates of Customs, &c., in 1612, mention is made of "Glasses called *viallis* or vrinallis."
O. Fr. *fiole,* "a violl of glasse;" Cotgr.: from Lat. *phiala,* a drinking vossel with a broad bottom; but the term evidently came to have a wider application, for, as a L. Lat. word, Ducange renders it by "Fons, aquarum receptaculum." It is, however, of Greek origin.

VICE, *s.* Turn, change, succession; Burgh Recs. Aberdeen, II. 279, Rec. Soc.: also place, post, duty, office; Ibid., p. 283.

VICE-COUNGE, *s.* A hand vice; Customs and Valuations, 1612, Haly. Ledger, p. 332.
Lit. a permission vice; one fitted with a movable nut. O. Fr. *vis,* a screw, or spindle of a press, and *congé,* permission, leave.

VICE-TURCAS, VICE-TURKES, *s.* A bench or table vice; also, ringed or clamp pincers for holding a piece of iron while it is worked on an anvil; Burgh Recs. Stirling, p. 58.
Comp. of *vice* and *turcas.* V. TURKAS.

To **VICIE, WYCIE,** *v. a.* To vitiate, violate; *to vicie the valentine,* to violate the engagement, i.e., to annul it. V. VICIAT.
All birdis he rebalkit that wald him nocht bow,
In breth as a battell-wrycht full of bost blawin,
With vnlowable latis nocht till allow.
Thus *vicit* he the Valentine thraly and thrawin.
That all the foulis with assent assemblit agane,
And plenyeit to Natur
Off this intollerable injure;
How the Howlat him bure
So he and so hautane.
Houlate, st. 71, Bann. MS.
Fr. *vicier,* "to viciate, marre corrupt, etc.," Cotgr.

VIDIMENT, *s.* A small particle, a mere fragment, scrap; applied to anything that is insignificant; Orkn.
Lat. *viduus,* bereft; hence applied to scraps, fragments, &c.: from which prob. the second meaning has come.

VIER, VYER, *s.* V. DICT.
Delete the entry under this heading in DICT. The word *vier* in the first quotation cannot be claimed as a Scot. word; and if *vyer* in the second quotation is a misprint for *uther,* it ought not to be ranked with *vier.*

VIGHT, *adj.* Brave; Gol. and Gaw., l. 325. V. WICHT.

To **VIKE,** *v. n.* To move, budge: prob. a local pron. of FIKE, q. v.; Orkn.

To **VILIPEND,** *v. a.* To slight, undervalue, backbite; Douglas, I. 48, 26, ed. Small; Orkn. Lat. *vilipendere.*

VILIPEND, *s.* An evil-speaker, back-biter; Orkn.

VILITIE, *s.* Vileness, baseness; Lyndsay, Papyngo, l. 376.

VINELL, VYNEL, *s.* A vennel; Burgh Recs. Edinburgh. 1512, I. 137, Rec. Soc. V. VENALL.

VINY, VINIE, *adj.* Winded; old or high tasted; generally applied to game that has been overkept; Orkn.
Prob. only a local pron. of *windy,* colloq. form of *winded,* affected by the wind, old-tasted.
Dan. *vindig,* windy; Icel. *vindugr.*

To **VIRK,** *v. a.* and *n.* To work, ferment. V. *Wirk.*

VIRKING, *s.* Working, influence, control; Kingis Quair, st. 188, ed. Skeat. V. under *Wirk,* v.

VIRROCK, *s.* V. DICT.
In the entry under this heading in the DICT. there is no definition, the quotations are misplaced, and of the last paragraph all but the first sentence is irrelevant. Rearrange as under :—

VIRROK, VIRROCK, VYROCK, WYROCK, *s.* A wart, knot, or bony excrescence on the feet; hardness or callosity of the hands caused by labour; also applied to a hard boil or fiery pimple on the hands or feet. V. *Wirrok.*
Ther is not in this fair a flyrock,
That has upon his feit a *wyrock,*
Knoul taes, or moals in nae degre,
But ye can hyde them.
Dunbar, Evergreen, i. 254.
Dr. Leyden, Gl. Compl. S., justly observes &c. (as in DICT. q. v.).

VIRROK, VIRROCK, VYROCK, VIRROKY, *adj.* Warty, knotted; *virrok tais,* toes with swollen knotted joints.
Ane pyk-thank in ane prelottis claise,
With his wawil feit and *virrok* tais,
With hoppir hippis and henches narrow.
Dunbar, Maitland Poems, p. 110.
A.-S. *wear, wearr,* hardness of the hands or feet caused by labour; *wearrig, wearriht,* callous, knotted; and in Wright's Vocabularies *wearriht* is glossed by "*callosus.*"

VISARD, *s.* A mask; same as Visorne, q. v.
"*Persona,* a person, a *visard*"; Duncan's App. Etym., 1595, ed. Small, E. D. S.

O. Fr. *visiere*, "the viser or sight of a helmet"; Cotgr. From its covering the face like a *visor*, a mask came to be so called; its Fr. name was a *faux visage*, which Cotgrave defines as "a mask or vizard."

VISECK, *s.* A kind of song forming an accompaniment to a dance; Hibbert's Orkney and Shetland, p. 563.

Icel. *vísa*, a strophe, stanza; Dan. *vise*, a song, a ballad.

To VISIE, VISY, VISE, *v. a.* To look at, view, oversee, take oversight of; also, to go to see, visit, look into, examine. Addit. to VISIE, q. v.

"Item, the prouest, baillies, and counsale hes depute thir persones to *vise* the brig and wattor daylie at twa tymes." Burgh Recs. Glasgow, 1574, i. 28, Rec. Soc.

"The sersaris sall pas twys on the daye, viz., in the mornyng and evinnyng, and *visie* and inquyre of ilk hous that nane be seik." Ibid. p. 29.

VISIIT, VISIT, *part. pt.* Looked upon, viewed, examined; Burgh Recs. Aberdeen, II. 114, Sp. C.

VIST, *pret.* Wist, knew.

"Yone is the warliest wane," said the wise king,
"That euer I *vist* in my walk in all this warld wyde."
  Gol. and Gawane, l. 494.

As here used this term represents Eng. *wist*, knew, had experience of: from A.-S. *witan*, to know.

VITTALL, VITTAIL, VITTLE, VITTEL, *s.* Victual, grain of any kind used as food; also, food, as in "*horse-vittle.*"

"*Annonna, far, vittall;*" Duncan, App. Etym., 1595, ed. Small, E. D. S.

To VITTALL, VITTAIL, VITTLE, *v. a.* To victual, supply with provisions: pret. *vittaillit*, Lyndsay, Squyer Meldrum, l. 1102.

O. Fr. *vitaille*, from Lat. *victualia*, provisions, food, the neut. pl. of *victualls*, belonging to nourishment. See Skeat's Etym. Dict., s. v.

VIVELY, VIUELY, *adv.* Vividly, clearly, evidently; Blame of Kirkburiull, ch. 2. V. VIUE.

To VMCAST, *v. a.* V. *Umbecast.*

VNCHUT, *adj.* A form of *Uncouth*, q. v.

VNE, *s.* An oven. V. UNE.

To VOCE, *v. a.* V. *Voice.*

VODURE, *s.* Lit. a voider or emptier; a tray for carrying away the fragments after a meal.

Efter the first paws, and that coors neir gane,
And *voduris* and fat trunscheouris away tane,
The goblettis greit with mychty wynis in hy
Thai fillit, and coverit set in by and by.
  Douglas, Virgil, ii. 63, 14, ed. Small.

O. Fr. *vodeur, voideur, vuideur*, a voider, emptier; from *vode, voide, vuide*, empty: formed from Lat. *viduus*, bereft; hence, waste, empty. See Cotgrave and Burguy.

VOGIE, *adj.* Happy, fond, and free; kindly, fondly, or lovingly caressing; and used also as an *adv.*, implying with happy, fond, or loving ways; Whistle Binkie, II. 111, Addit. to VOGIE, q. v.

VOGUE, *s.* Repute, applause, foremost place or position.

"For many to eternize their soone forgot memory, and to gaine the *vogue* of this vaine world, hes prepared Pyramides of pomp, others pillers of pride, some mousolics of maruel." Blame of Kirburiall, ch. 9.

O. Fr. *vogue*, "sway, authority"; Cotgr.

VOICE, VOYCE, VOCE, WOYCE, *s.* Opinion, advice, or resolution, spoken or expressed.

"Patrik Bell, provest, did intimat to the saidis bailyeis and counsall that his *voyce* and volt was to be cravit in the said assemblie anent bischops and episcopacie." Burgh Recs. Glasgow, 1638, i. 394, Rec. Soc.

To VOICE, VOYCE, VOCE, WOYCE, *v. n.* To speak; to discuss, counsel, or advise orally: as, "to *voice* and vote in council," to speak and vote or to deliberate and determine in council.

"That the said Patrik sould voit that the said asemblie sould sitt and not desolve, . . . and that he sould *woyce* for establishing of the said assemblie judges to the saidis bischops." Burgh Recs. Glasgow, 1638, i. 394.

"To voice and vote" is an expression which frequently occurs in our Burgh Records in connection with discussions in the Town Council and other meetings. Lit. it means to speak and vote; but, as at those meetings the vote was often taken orally, the expression '*to voice*' came to imply both discussion and voting.

VOID, *adj.* Empty; K. Quair, st. 164. V. VODE.

VOID, VOYD, *s.* An empty, vacant, or open space or place; a well or shaft in a building.

"And sall build ane *voyd* hard be the said passage for letting doun the paissis from the knock." Burgh Recs. Aberdeen, II. 341, Sp. C.

To VOID, *v. a.* To make void, dissipate, dispel. Addit. to VODE, q. v.

The infare vnicorne,
That *voidis* venym with his cuour horne.
  King is Quair, st. 155, ed. Skeat.

The following is Prof. Skeat's note on this passage:—
"*Voidis venym*, dispels venom with his ivory horn, *Voidis* does not mean '*ejects*,' as Tytler supposed, not knowing the story. The unicorn's horn was supposed to dispel poison: Mrs. Palliser, in her *Historical Devices*, p. 20, gives an example of a unicorn depicted as dipping his horn into water, with the motto *Venena pello*. In a footnote she shows that the *essai* of unicorn's horn is often mentioned in inventories. Cf. Massinger, *Roman Actor*, ii. 1. 46, and see E. Phipson's *Animal Lore of Shakspeare's Time*, p. 453."

VOIDER, VOYDER, *s.* Dispeller.

The sterne of day, *voyder* of dirknes.
  Dunbar, Sterne of Redemptioun, l. 35.

O. Fr. *voide*, from Lat. *viduum*, acc. of *viduus*, bereft hence, waste, empty. O. Fr. *voider, vuider*, to void.

VOKY, WOKY, *s.* Vanity, vain pride; vanity in dress or vain show. V. VOGIE, *adj.*
To Vaunt and *Voky* ye beir this rowm slef;
Did thame thairin that thai tak thair hyre.
Douglas, King Hart, i. 119, 23, ed. Small.
Pinkerton's ed. reads *woky*. See under VOGIE.

VOLUNTAR, VOLENTAR, *adj.* Voluntary, free-will; "*voluntar* contributioun," Burgh Recs. Aberdeen, II. 361, Sp. C.
Lat. *voluntarius*, willing; O. Fr. *volontaire*.

VOLUSPA, *s.* V. DICT.
For further particulars regarding this term see Cleasby and Vigfusson, a. v. *Völva*.

VOO, *adj.* Sorry, grieved. V. *Woo*.

VOP, *s.* A thread or band. V. WOP.

VOUTE, VOWTE, *s.* and *v.* V. *Vaute*.

VOWBET, *s.* V. DICT.
In both quotations the alliteration shows that this word is, and must be pronounced, *wowbet*.

VOWSTIE, *adj.* Boastful. V. VOUSTY.

VPART, *adv.* Upwards. V. *Upart*.

VTASS, WTAST, *s.* V. DICT.
Delete this entry in DICT., and see Utass and *Utass*.

VTH, *s.* V. DICT.
Delete the entry under this heading in DICT., and see *Vch*.

W.

WA', WA'D, *adj.* Chosen, choice: "*wa'-wight men*," stoutest men, boldest warriors; Pop. Ballads. V. *Waled*.

WACHTER, WAUGHTER, *s.* A guard or convoy ship, a war vessel. V. WACH, *v.*
"Ane wther of the Holland *waughteris*, callit the Greyne Dragon of Amsterdam," Burgh Recs. Aberdeen, ii. 388, Sp. C.
Dutch *wachten*, to watch, guard, oversee, act as convoy; *wachter*, watchman, guard-ship.

To WACHLE, WAUCHLE, *v. n.* To move along with difficulty; hence, to struggle, strive: "Lang may he *wauchle* on through this warld;" Whistle Binkie, I. 96. Addit. to WACHLE, WAUCHLE.

WACHLE, WAUCHLE, *s.* Staggering or unsteady movement; difficult, weary work, struggle, battle: "He has had a sair *wachle* a' his days."

To WAD, WED, *v. a.* V. DICT.
Delete the entry under this heading in the DICT., as it is imperfect and improperly arranged, and substitute the following:—

To WAD, WED, *v. a.* 1. To pledge, bet, wager.
Than Lowrie as ane lyoun lap,
And sone ane flane culd fedder;
He hecht to perse him at the pap,
Thairon to *wed* ane weddir.
Christ Kirk, st. 12. *Chron. S. P.,* ii. 363.
Wad, in Callander's ed.
"Our mare has gotten a braw brown foal,"
—"I'll *wad* my hail fee against a groat,
He's bigger than e'er our foal will be."
Minstrelsy Border, i. 85.

In June they *wad*, or Beltan cam roun,
Craignethan lay in his grave.
Mary o' Craignethan, Ed. Mag., July 1819.
It is similarly used in M. E.
—If ye worken it in werke, I dare *wed* mine earcs
That law shal be a labourer, and leade afelde dounge.
P. Ploughman, Fol. 19b.
In the West of S. *wad* is freq. pron. *wat*, and confounded with *wat*, know, believe : as in the very common expression, "*weel I wat*," well I know, or, well I pledge, promise, or assure you.

2. To promise, to engage, as equivalent to *I'll engage for it.*
But where's your nephew, Branky? is he here?
I'll *wad* he's been of use, gin ane may speer.
Shirref's Poems, p. 75.
. . . . . How was the billy pleas'd?
Nae well, I *wad*, to be sae snelly us'd.
Ibid., p. 35.

3. To wed, marry; pret. and part. pt. *wad*.
At last her feet—I sang to see't—
Gaed foremost o'er the knowe;
And or I *wad* anither jad,
I'll wallop in a tow.
Burns, The Weary Pund o' Tow.
A.-S. *weddian*, to pledge, bargain, wed, marry : from *wed, wedd*, a pledge.

To WADE, *v. n.* To pass, penetrate : "The moon's wading through the clouds."
Sa wondir froschly thai frekis fruschit in feir,
Throw all the barnes that hade,
Baith birny and breistplade,
Thairin wappinis couth *wade*,
Wit ye but weir.
Gol. and Gawain, l. 568.
The word is similarly used in Gray's Elegy—
"To *wade* through slaughter to a throne."

WADNA, WUDNA, *v.* Would not. V. WAD.

WAE, adj. Sad, sorry, pained; Burns. V. WA.
Other forms of this adj. are *Wo, Woo, Voo*.

WAFFER, VAFFER, s. Lit. a wavering: a break, fault, dip, or elevation: a mining term. V. *Waive*.
"It is noch possible to men to myn, cast sinkes, *waffers*, big myls, quha never saw ony siclyk." Early Records of Mining in Scotland, p. 80.
A.-S. *wæfre*, wavering, wandering. Cf. Icel. *vafra*, to waver; *vafr*, wavering, as in *vafr-logi*, a flickering flame.

WA'-GANG, WA'-GAIN, WA'-GAUN, s. Departing for a foreign land, departing this life; parting, leave-taking, taking farewell before such departure; also a social gathering of friends to bid farewell. Addit. to WA-GANG, q. v.
It's dowie in the hin' o' hairst,
At the *wa'-gang* o' the swallow,
When the winds grow cauld, when the burns grow bauld,
An' the wuds are hingin' yellow;
But O ! it's dowier far to see
The *wa'-gang* o' her the heart gangs wi'—
The deadset o' a shining e'e,
That darkens the weary warld on thee.
Hew Ainslie, Whistle Binkie, i. 428.

To WAGE, WAIGE, v. a. To wager, bet; part. pr. *waging, waigin*; Burgh Recs. Aberdeen, I. 285, Rec. Soc. Addit. to WAIDGE, q. v. V. WAGE, s.

WAGIT, WADGET, adj. Working for wages, feed or hired; Burgh Recs. Edinburgh, IV. 345.
". . . to tak or ressave ane vthir masteris prenteis, seruand, or *wagit* man." Ibid., i. 81, Rec. Soc.

To WAIF, WAYFE, WAIP, v. a. and n. To wave; to set aside, divorce. V. WAFF, and *Waive*.

WAIF, WAIFF, WAIP, s. A small flag, signal flag. Addit. to WAFF, q. v.
"And the watch that beis in Sanct Nicholace stepill to pyt on the *waiffs* that he bes to the part of the town he seis thame [the approaching strangers] cumand to." Burgh Recs. Aberdeen, 1530, i. 446, Sp. C.

WAIGE, WAGE, WAGGE (*g* soft), s. A wedge; pl. *wagis*, Burgh Recs. Aberdeen, 1544, I. 195; *waggis*, Ibid., I. 197; *weggis*, Ibid., I. 269. V. WADGE.
A.-S. *wæcg, wecg*, a wedge; from A.-S. *wegan*, to move, cause to move. Dutch *wig*, Icel. *veggr*.

WAIL, WAILE, WALE, s. Choice, in the sense of a number to choose from: hence, plenty, abundance; Gol. and Gaw., l. 223, 1329. Addit. to WALE, s.
It is so used in the old adage, "There be *wail* o' wives gin ye've plenty o' siller." So too in the story told by Dean Ramsay of the Laird of Balnamoon, when he lost his hat and wig on his way home after a dinner party. His servant having picked them up and handed them to him, the laird was satisfied with the hat but demurred at the wig, and refused to have anything to do with it. Persuasion having failed, the servant lost his patience, and remonstrated with his master, "Ye'd better tak it, sir, for there's nae *waile* o' wigs on Munrimmon Moor." V. Rem. Scot. Life and Character, p. 167.

WAILIT, part. and adj. V. *Waled*.

WAILL, WALE, s. Worth, value. Addit. to WAILL, s., q. v.
"Thai leif ane *wod* for the *waill* of tua pekis of beyr." Burgh Recs. Prestwick, 1554, p. 63, Mait. C.

To WAIL, WAILE, v. a. To bewail, deplore, mourn for the loss of. Icel. *væla*.
That all the world sall *waile* thaire gouernance.
Kingis Quair, st. 122, ed. Skeat.

WAINDES, s. A windlass, winch, block-and-tackle; Burgh Recs. Edinburgh, II. 325, Rec. Soc.
Icel. *vinddss*, a windlass; Du. *windas*.

WAINE, pret. V. DICT.
The entry under this heading in DICT. must be deleted. *Waine*, in the Edin. MS. of Barbour, is certainly a scribal error for *was*. The Camb. MS. has *wes*; and, as Jamieson admits in rejecting the reading, all the editions have *was*.

To WAINE, WAYNE, v. a. Err. for *Waiue, Wayue*. V. *Waive*.
This is a common mistake arising from the difficulty of distinguishing between *n* and *u* in the reading of MSS.

WAINSCOT, WANESCOTT, WANSCOT, s. A kind of oak, used in shipbuilding and in cabinet-making; wainscot, panelling; also, boards for panelling; Burgh Recs. Aberdeen, II. 228, 234, Rec. Soc.: used also as an adj., meaning oaken, Ibid., p. 326.
In Halyburton's Ledger, p. 290, in the Rates and Customs of 1612, various kinds of timber are included under the heading Boards; and in that list are,—"Boordes called *Wanescott* of Daneskene," "Boordes called *Wanescott* of Swaden," "Table boordes of *wanescott* or waluute trie;" and in the introduction to that work, p. xxxvii., Cosmo Innes states that, among the many articles brought by sea to Antwerp, there were "ornamental woods, and timber for shipbuilding; especially a sort called *wainscot* (*waghescot*), truly beautiful, and varigated like the walnut."
From Dutch *wagenschot*, wainscot; a corr. of O. Du. *waeghe-schot*, wall-boarding: from O. Du. *waeg*, a wall, and *schot*, a covering of boards. An interesting discussion of this word is given in Supp. to Skeat's Etym. Dict.

To WAIP, v. a. To wave, flutter; Gol. and Gawain, l. 440. V. WAFF, *Waif*, v.
The version quoted by Jamieson reads *waif*. See quotation in DICT.

WAIP, WAP, s. A small flag. V. WAFF, *Waif*.
The forms *waif* and *waip* occur in the same entry. See Burgh Recs. Aberdeen, 1 Mar. 1530, i. 446, Sp. C.

WAIR, *s.* Shelter, hiding; resting-place, abode: *went to wair,* went to his abode, went home. Addit. to WAIR, q. v.

Delete the note under this heading in DICT. *Wair,* in this case, clearly means shelter, place of hiding, rest, or abode; and may be traced to Icel. *væra,* rest, shelter; *væri,* shelter, abode, resting-place. Besides, the story plainly demands that the phrase, '*went to wair,*' be rendered 'went home,' i.e., slipped away without rewarding them. See quotation in DICT.

WAIR, *s.* Sea-weed. V. WARE.

WAIRD, *part.* V. *Ward, part.*

To WAIRDE, *v. a.* To imprison. V. WARD.

WAIRSTAW, *s.* B. R. Edin., 1530, II. 39, Rec. Soc. V. *Warestall.*

WAIT, WAYT, WAYTE, *s.* and *v.* V. [WATE].

WAIT, WATE, *adj.* Difficult, tiresome, perilous. V. WAITII, *s.*

Tuglit and travallt thies trew men can tyre,
Sa wundir *wait* wes the way, wit ye but wene.
Gol. and Gaw., st. 3.

Icel. *váthi,* danger, peril; Dan. *vaade,* danger.

To WAIT, VAIT, WATE, WAT, *v. n.* V. DICT.

Delete this heading in DICT. *Wait* is not and can not be properly used in the infinitive. It is the first and third pers. sing. of the present tense, and means "I know" or "he knows;" but it is occasionally, though incorrectly, used with we, or ye, or they, or even with *thou,* as Jamieson shows. The A.-S. *wát* means "I know," and "he knows;" but nothing else. Therefore, substitute the following heading for the entry :—

WAIT, VAIT, WATE, WAT, *v. pres.* Know.

To WAIVE, WAIUE, WAYUE, WAYFE, WAIFF, WAIFE, WAFF, *v. a.* and *n.* To waive, move about; to set or push aside, up, or down; to raise, remove, as, "to *waive* up a window; to shun, abandon, refuse, desert, as, "He *wayfid* his wyfe and wed another;" also, to strike, smite, beat, as, "He *wayues* at Schir Wawayn als he were wode."

The forms *Waiue, wayue* are frequently misread and misprinted *waine, wayne.* See Stratmann, s. v. *Waiven.*
He wayued up his viser fro his ventalle.
Awnt. Arthure, st. 32.
Pinkerton's ed. has *wayned.*
For bowe he fra the bataille bernys me tell,
Then will he wed another wife and *wayfe* me for ever.
Allit. Rom. Alexander, l. 297.
Streyte on his steroppis stoutely he strikes,
And *waynes* at Schir Wawayn als he were wode.
Awnt. Arthure, st. 42.
Printed *waynes* by Pinkerton and Laing.
Wapp, which is a freq. of *waive,* is still used in this sense : "He *wappit* at or on him."

Similar uses of *waive* are noted by Stratmann, thus—
. to *waiven* up the wiket.
Piers Plowman, B. v. 611, ed. Skeat.
(Sup.)   K 2

But went after the werwolf and *wayued* from the beres.
Will. and Werwolf, l. 2386, ed. Skeat.
Printed *wayned.*
L. Lat. *waviare,* to waive : from Icel. *veifa,* to wave, vibrate, move about. Stratmann gives O. Fr. *weiver,* to waive; but, as Prof. Skeat states, it is only recorded in the latter form *guesver,* to waive, refuse, abandon : see Cotgrave. The M. E. forms were *waiven,* and *waven.*

WAKER, *s.* A fuller. V. WAUK, *v.*

"*Fullo,* a *waker* of claith;" Duncan's App. Etym., 1595, ed. Small, E.D.S.

WAKSTAFF, *s.* The staff with which a burgh officer knocked at the doors of those whose duty it was to serve as the nightwatch. Also, the officer who carried this staff, and turned out the night-watch; Burgh Laws, ch. 81, Rec. Soc.

A.-S. *wacan,* to wake, arise : whence *wacian,* to wake, watch; and A.-S. *staf,* a staff. V. Skeat, Etym. Dict.

WAL, WALL, *s.* A certain weight of wool; forms of *waw,* a wey; Halyburton's Ledger, p. 225. V. WAW.

WAL, WALL, WALLE, WALE, *s.* A well, spring; B. R. Glasgow, I. 390; *wallee,* fountain-head, source of a spring. V. WELL-EY.

WALGARSE, WALL-GIRSE, *s.* Water-cress, water-cresses : *valcarse,* Spald. Club Misc., I. 105. V. WELL-GRASS.

WALINK, WALLINK, *s.* Water Speedwell or Brooklime : *Veronica Beccabunga,* Linn. West and South of S.

WALAGEOUSS, WALEGEOUSS, *adj.* V. DICT.

Delete the first etym. given for this term. It cannot be related to A.-S. The second etym. is correct.

WALD, WAULD, WAUL, WAWIL, *adj.* Plain, flat : as, *wald, wauld,* or *wawil feet,* flat feet, or plain soles; *wald* or *waul fittit,* flat-footed, plain-soled. V. WALD, *s.*

Ane pyk-thank in ane prelottis claiss,
With his *wawil-feit* and wirrok tais,
With hopper hippis and henches narrow,
And bausy handis to beir ane barrow.
Dunbar, Complaint to the King, l. 54.

The Reidpeth MS. has *wauld-feit,* which Laing adopted, and which is certainly the correct reading. Both the term and the passage in which it occurs were misunderstood by Jamieson. He interpreted *wawil-feit* as loosely - knit or shaky-feet; but he was prob. misled by the misreadings of the version from which he quoted. Besides, in that passage the poet is describing not a person with loosely-knit limbs and shaky feet, but a coarse, big-boned, ungainly fellow, with great bausy hands and big clumsy feet. And in order to represent them as altogether clumsy, he paints them as *wawil* or *wauld* feet, i.e. flat-soled ones; with *wirrok tais,* i.e., warty or knotted toes, which generally accompany flat soles, and seldom are found with *wavel-cuits* or shaky feet.

WAL [266] WAN

Besides, the measure clearly shows that *wawil* must be read as *waul*, not as *wavil* in *wavill feet*, shaky or *shachly* feet, quoted under *Wavel*. Cf. *wawil* in *wawil-eyid*, wall-eyed.
A.-S. *weald*, *wald*, a wood, also a plain, a flat or open country. Cf. Icel. *völlr*, a field, plain. In M. E. a down or flat open country was called a *wold* or a *wald*.

WALED, WAILED, WAILIT, WAULD, WA'D, WALE, WAIL, WAULE, WA', *adj*. Picked, chosen, selected; as, *waled* or *wale* men, wa' or wa'd men, i.e., picked or choice men, best or bravest soldiers; Pop. Ballad. V. WALE, *v*.

WALED - WIGHT, WEIL'D - WIGHT, WALE-WIGHT, WALL-WIGHT, WA'-WIGHT, *adj*. Strongest and best, best and bravest: "*waled-wight* men," stoutest men, boldest warriors.

At our lang wars in fair Scotland
  I fain hae wished to be ;
If fifteen hundred *waled wight* men
  You'll grant to ride wi' me.
Ballad, Auld Maitland, l. 15.

O where are all my *wall-weight* men
That I pay meat and fee.
Ballad, Lord Thomas, l. 33.

This form occurs twice in "Earl of Mar's Daughter;" see ll. 115, 127.

The king's ca'd up his *wa'-wight* men
That he paid meat an' fee.
Lady Daisy, Aytoun's Ballads, ii. 173.

Robert Semple of Beltrees, in his account of Habbie Simson, the piper, calls him "a weil'd wight-man," on account of his strength and skill in rustic games.

He counted was a *weil'd Wight-man*,
  And fiercely at Foot-ba' he ran ;
At ev'ry game the gree he wan,
  For pith and speed ;
The like of Habbie was na than,
  But now he's dead.
The Piper of Kilbarchan.

To WALLOW, *v. n.* V. DICT.
In the last para. of this entry Germ. *welwen* is a mistake : Germ. *welken*, to wither or wilt, is the proper term with which A.-S. *wealcian*, is allied. Evidently Jamieson was misled by mixing up *wallow* and *sallow*. No doubt he had heard, as one may still hear, people say of a young plant that had drooped and faded, "it's *wallow'd* ;" but they call it *wallow'd* not because of its yellowish colour, but because it is withered, drooped, dried up. And as a matter of fact the *sallowing* is a further stage : it is a consequence of the *wallowing*. The term, therefore, can have no connection with Germ. *falb*, fallow, or with the Lat. *flavus*, as the note suggests. As Prof. Skeat remarks,—"The radical sense is rather 'to be rolled or shrivelled up ;' cf. A.-S. *wealcan*, to roll (whence mod. E. *walk*)." See Notes to The Kingis Quair, p. 96, S.T.S.

WALLY-GOWDY, WALLIE-GOWDYE, *s*. Jewel of gold, precious thing. V. WALLIES.

My tendir gyrle, my *wallie-gowdye*,
My tirlie myrlie, my crowdie mowdie.
Dunbar, In Secreit Place, l. 45.

WALT, WALTIN, WAT, WATTIN, VAT, *s*. Welt, border, edging, as in a shoe, or in the seams and hems of a gown. E. *welt*.

To WALT, WAT, VAT, *v. a.* To attach the welt to the upper of a shoe, to renew the welt in mending a shoe; also, to guard, strengthen, or ornament the seams and hems of a gown by inserting or attaching a welt : pret. and part. pt. *waltit, vatit*.

". . . ane govne of blak *vatit* witht veluot and lynit witht blak buge." Burgh Recs., Glasgow, 1574 ; i. 32, Rec. Soc.

WALTIN-CORD, WATTIN-CORD, *s*. Cord used in forming welts for seams and hems of gowns. E. *welting-cord*.

Welsh *gwald*, a hem, welt, *gwaltes*, the welt of a shoe ; *gwaldu*, to welt, hem : allied to Gael. *balt*, welt, border, belt. V. Skeat's Etym. Dict., s. v. *Well*.

WAM, WAMME, *s*. A scar of a wound. V. [WEM].

"*Cicatrix*, a *wamme*;" Duncan, App. Etym., 1595, ed. Small, E. D. S.
A.-S. *wam*, *wem*, a spot, fault.

To WAMBLE, WOMBLE, WUMBLE, *v. a*. To undulate or move in an undulating manner, as in rinsing a vessel with water. West of S. Addit. to WAMBLE, q. v.

WAME, *s*. The belly portion of a furskin. Addit. to WAMBE, q. v. V. *Wombes*.

WAMPA, WANPA, WAMP, *s*. The vamp or fore-leather of a boot or shoe; also, a shape or pattern of a vamp; "the *vanpa* for a buytt;" Burgh Recs. Aberdeen, I. 176, Sp. C.

This term is a corr. of Fr. *avant-pied*, "the part of the foot that's next to the toes ;" Cotgr. The M. Eng. forms are *vampay*, *vaumpe*.

WAND, *s*. The sign of an ale-house or small change-house, or country inn. Addit. to WAND, q. v.

"We entered a small change-house, which we only knew to be a public by the *wand* over the door, and bought some bread and cheese from a good-looking lass that was the servant." R. L. Stevenson, Kidnapped, p. 266, ed. 1886.

WANDRECHT, *s*. V. WANDRETHE.

WANE, WAN, *adj* Deficient, wanting, lacking; hence imperfect, weak, empty, void. Addit. to WAN, *adj*., q. v.

Quhy suld I than, with dull forhede and *wane*,
With ruide engine and barrand emptive brane,
With bad harsk spoche and lewit harbour tong,
Presume to write quhar thi sueit bell is rung.
Douglas, Virgil, Bk. i. prol. l. 18, Small.

A.-S. *wana*, *wona*, deficient, wanting ; *wana*, a deficiency. The prefix *wan*-, implying lacking, has the force of *un*, not : as *wancanny*, uncanny, *wanchancy*, unchancy, unlucky ; and sometimes it has the force of *mis*-, wrong, as in *wanhap*, mishap, misfortune.

WANSCOT, VANSCOT, *s*. V. *Wainscot*.

WANT, Wanting, *s.* Besides the usual E. meanings of lack, scarcity, poverty, need, absence of what is needful or desired, these terms are used in the sense of (1) loss, deprivation.

Lo ! thise were thay that in thaire myddill age,
Servandis were to lufe in mony weye,
And diversely happinnit for to deye ;
Sum sorrowfully, for *wanting* of thare makis,
And sum in armes for thaire ladyes sakis.
Kingis Quair, st. 86, ed. Skeat.

2. Search for, inquiry after what is lost or missing.

A mechanic travelling about in search of employment is said to be "in *want* o' wark."

To **WANT,** *v. a.* and *n.* 1. To lack, be destitute of ; to lose, as "to want ane lug out of his heid," Burgh Recs. Glasgow, I. 197, Rec. Soc. ; to have lost, Burgh Recs. Aberdeen, I. 411, Sp. C. ; to give up, resign, Lyndsay, Thrie Estaitis, l. 2825.

So standis thou here In this warldis rage,
And *wantis* that auld gyde all thy vinge.
Kingis Quair, l. 15, ed. Skeat.

2. To search, seek, or enquire for ; to desire, request.

"What do you *want* there?" is asked of one who is searching for something. "Wha is't ye're *wantin'?*" is said to one who has asked for some person. "Ye're aye *wantin',*" is often said to one who is a frequent borrower.

WANTON, Wanty, *s.* The belly-band of a horse. Addit. to Wanton, q. v.

Delete the etym. given for this term in the Dict. *Wanty,* of which *wanton* is a mere corruption, is a corruption of *wame-tie,* a tie or band for the *wame* or belly : comp. of A.-S. *wamb,* the belly, and *téag, téah, type,* a rope. V. Palmer's Folk-Etymology, and Webster's Dict. s. v. *Wanty.*

WANUT, Wannat, *s.* Walnut, walnut-tree.

We sned the treis bringis furth gud birth,
We steir thame not that ar nocht wirth ;
The *wannat* quhan ye ding most sair,
Most fructfull is, as sum declair.
Rob Stene's Dream, p. 7, Mait. C.

To **WAP,** *v. a.* 1. To beat, thrash : "He set to an' *wappit* the puir beast."

2. To beat, overcome, excel : "That *waps* a' your stock." Addit. to Wap, q. v.

WAPPER, Whapper, *s.* The biggest or best of a lot : that which beats the rest. Addit. to Wapper, q. v.

WAPPING, *adj.* Beating or excelling the rest. Addit. to Wapping, q. v.

Wap, like *waff,* is a freq. of *wave,* from Icel. *veifa,* to wave, vibrate.

WAPPINS, Vappins, *s. pl.* Weapons ; Gol. and Gawane, l. 820.

WARANDICE, Varandice, *s.* Warranty ; Burgh Recs. Aberdeen, I. 346, Sp. C.

WARD, Warde, Werd, Werde, *s.* World ; in Buchan dial. *wardle.*

"*Ward,* world, North ;" Grose's Dict :
That was the athill Alexandre, as the buke tellis,
That aghte evyn as his awyne all the *werde* ovirc.
Allit. Rom. Alex., l. 18.

Ward is not uncommon in M. E. : see Lancelot of the Laik, ed. Skeat, l. 3184 ; also Genesis and Exodus, ed. Morris, ll. 32, 1315.

Da. *verden* (of which the *en* represents the article), the world, universe, earth.

WARD, Werd, Waird, *part. pt.* Awarded ; doomed, adjudged, decreed, settled : "It's weel *ward, werd,* or *waird* ye want," i.e., it is right and proper that you get nothing, or that you lose your share. V. Ward, *v.*

This expression is generally applied to one who has forfeited his share, or who grumbles at what is offered to him ; for example, if a beggar grumbles at the dole that is offered, the giver will take it back saying, "Weel, weel, if ye dinna tak that, *it's weel ward ye want.*"

WARDER, Wardrer, *s.* A staff, truncheon : *wardrer,* Allit. Rom. Alex., l. 838.

O. Fr. *warder,* a staffe, baston ; Palsgrave.

WARD-HILL, Wart-Hill, Wardill, *s.* The hill on which the beacon was lighted to give warning of approaching danger ; Memorial for Orkney, p. 120.

WARDOUR, Wardour, Werdour, Werdur, Vardour, Vardur, Verdour, Verdur, *s.* 1. A kind of tapestry used for covering and draping a bed ; hence hangings, drapery, garniture ; Halyburton's Ledger, p. 10, 30.

"Ane lettgant bed furneist witht Flandreis *werdour,* blancattis, scheittis, and coddis." Burgh Recs. Glasgow, I. 32, Rec. Soc.

2. Clothing, clothes, dress.

The three gay ladies carousing in the garden are represented by the poet as—

"Arrayit ryallie about with mony rich *wardour.*"
Dunbar, Mariit Wemen and Wedo, l. 30.

See the quotation in full in Dict. under Wardour, which Jamieson left unexplained.

WARE, *adj.* Wary, aware. V. War, Wer.

WAREIT, *pret.* For *waryit,* cursed. V. Wary.

WARESTALL, Wairstall, Wairsta, Vairstall, Vairstaw, *s.* Prob. identical with Wair Almerie, q. v. ; Burgh Recs. Edinburgh, II. 39, Rec. Soc.

WARETINE, *s.* Warrant, guarantee, ground of claim ; Burgh Recs. Prestwick, 7 May, 1470, Mait. C. V. Warrand.

WARING, *s.* Outlay, expenditure: "at the first *waring*," at first cost, at purchase or cost price; Burgh Recs. Edinburgh, I. 227, Rec. Soc. Addit. to WARE, *s.* q. v.

WARISON, *s.* V. DICT.
Delete the heading under this entry in DICT. *Warison* has no such meaning as that with which Scott used it in the passage quoted. No doubt he meant "note of assault," but he used the wrong word for it. *Warison* is correctly explained in the preceding entry; and further explanation is given under WARYSOUN, q. v.

WARL, *s.* World. V. WARLD.

WARL-WORM, WARL'S-WORM, *s.* A miser, niggardly person; Burns.

WARLY, *adj.* Worldly. V. WARLDLIE.

WARLO, WARLOCK, *s.* V. DICT.
Combine the two entries under these terms in DICT. They represent the same word under different applications.

WARLOCK-KNOWE, *s.* A knoll on which, according to popular belief, warlocks held their meetings.
Meet me on the *warlock-knowe*,
Daintie Davie, daintie Davie,
There I'll spend the day wi' you,
My ain dear daintie Davie.
Burns, Daintie Davie.

WARLY, WARLOK, *adj.* Warlike, fitted for war, i.e. fortified, defended, sturdy, strong: "*warliest* wane," best fortified or strongest mansion, Gol. and Gaw., l. 495.

WARLIEST, *adj.* V. DICT.
To the defin. of this term in DICT. add the statement given above under *Warly*. The proper meaning is given in the explanatory note.

To WARNE, WERNE, *v. a.* To oppose; Barbour, ii. 137: to forbid, prevent; Gol. and Gaw., l. 253. Also used with meaning to warn, forewarn, by Barbour, iii. 451, xvii. 114, Camb. MS. Addit. to WARNE, q. v.
In the note under the entry in DICT. mention is made of the M. E. meaning "to prohibit," but nothing is said to indicate that the word was used in Scot. also.

To WARNIS, WARNYS, *v. a.* V. DICT.
A simpler and more direct etym. for this term is O. Fr. *warnis-*, stem of the part. pres. of *warnir* (later *garnir*), to furnish. From the form *garnir* has come E. *garnish*. See *Garnish* in Skeat's Etym. Dict., and *Garnir* in Burguy's Gloss.

To WARP, *v. a.* To prepare the warp for the loom. Addit. to WARP, q. v.
Warp as a *s.* is found in almost all dictionaries; but as a *v.* it is not found in any of the older dictionaries except Bailey's.

WARPER, *s.* One who prepares the warp for the weaver.

WARPING, WARPIN, *s.* The preparation of the warp for the loom; also the art or craft of preparing the warp of a web, as, "apprenticed to the *warping*."
The cardin' o't. the spinnin o't,
The *warpin*' o't, the winnin o't
When ilka ell cost me a groat,
The tailor staw the lymin' o't.
Burns, The Cardin o't.

WARPIN-FAT, WARPENE-FAT, *s.* A vat in which warps, when arranged for the loom, were steeped for dressing or dyeing; Burgh Recs. Prestwick, 15 Oct. 1565, Mait. C.
In those days, and for long after, the customer-weaver in small communities like Prestwick did all the warping and dressing, and most of the dyeing, of the webs entrusted to him for weaving. In many of the households, however, the females dyed, as well as dressed and spun, the wool which was prepared for home use. In various districts of the Highlands these customs still prevail.

WARPIN-PINS, *s. pl.* The pins on which the warper stretched the warp while preparing it for the weaver.

To WARPISS, *v. a.* To deliver or hand over, barter, give up, betray.
"God forbid that yhe suld, for a litil monee that thir Inglismen has promisait yhou, *warpiss* your gude name, and the reward and thank that yhe have deservide and wonnyn of the king." Letter to the Earl of Ross from the Provost and Council of Aberdeen, 1444, Burgh Recs. Aberdeen, i. 11, Sp. C.
O. Fr. *werpis-*, stem of pres. part. of *werpir* (in Cotgr. *vuerpir*), to deliver, hand over: the more common form, however, is *guerpir*. Formed from O. Fr. *werp*, *guerp*, delivery, which prob. was borrowed from the Scand. In Icel. and Swed. we have *varpa*, to cast, throw, and hence to damage, twist, or put out of shape.

To WARSELL, WERSILL, *v. n.* V. DICT.
Delete the last para. of the entry under this heading in DICT. A more direct etym. is A.-S. *terwœstlan*, to wrestle - a frequent. of *wrœstan*, to wrest, twist about ; O. Du. *wrastelen*, *worstelen*, to struggle, wrestle. The M. E. form was *wrestlen*.

WART, *pret.* Wert; Burgh Recs. Glasgow, I. 304, Rec. Soc.

To WASH, *v..* To *wash the head*, to insult or impose upon a person, to cheat him; to *wash one's head*, or give *one's head to be washed*, to be insulted, cheated, or imposed upon, to allow oneself to be insulted, cheated, or imposed upon.
As the following passage shows, these expressions were common among merchants during the sixteenth and seventeenth centuries. It also tells that it was customary to set up a poor-box on board a vessel in which a company of merchants happened to be returning from the continent; also, that fines were exacted from such of the company as had allowed themselves to be cheated when trading among foreigners; and that these fines went to the poor-box.
"Everie merchand, or sa mony of ane schippis merchandis as *waschis thair heidis* in France, Flanderis,

Danskin, or uther countries, to gif and collect to the said box, to the honour of God, and thair pure and nedie brethrene, and to thair vyffis and bairnis left in poncrtie and distres." Burgh Recs. Aberdeen, ii. 216, Sp. C. See also under *Foud*.
"To give the head for washing, i.e., to submit to insult." Halliwell.
The expression was common in France also; for Cotgrave gives, "*Laver là teste d*. To chide, reprove, taunt, or checke very bitterly."

WASHING THE APRON. The name given to a madcap carouse which apprentices held when a new apprentice was entered to work. The custom was followed till comparatively late times by masons and wrights.

"The whilk day complaint being made to the present deacon conveniar of Glasgow, the present deacon of the wrights of Glasgow, masters and members of the said trad, anent prenteissis and their associattis causing wash (as they term it) ilka new prenteis appron, riving, cutting, and nailling the same upon doors, and theirby drinking to excess, and committing many abuses attour the loss of their masters work. Which being taken to their serious considerationes, eftir matur deliberation theranent for preventing such enormities and abuses in time cuming, heirby probibitts and dischairges any washing of approns, riving and nailling thereof, or drinking in such base maner, in all tim coming, vnder the pain of twentie pounds Scotts to be payed by the committer thairof toties quoties to the present collector, or his successores in office, for the vse of the poor of the wright trad, attour corporall punishment to be inflicted at the will of the magistrattis, and injoyns ilke freeman master within tbis Incorporation to intimatt this act to each new prenteis of his at his entrie to him: and in caice the master concur not and incouradg the prenteis in such a fault, the master is to be lyable in the fyne foirsaid. In testimony quhairof thir presentia, &c." MS. Minutes of the Wrights of Glasgow, July, 1773.

WAT, *s*. A welt; pl. *wattis*, the welting of shoes. Addit. to WAUT, q. v.

Stra wispis hingis owt, quair that the *wattis* ar worne.
Dunbar and Kennedy, 1.213, S.T.S.

To WAT, VAT, *v. a*. To welt, border, bind: pret. and part. pt. *watit, vatit*, welted, bordered, bound, trimmed: "*vatit* with veluot;" Burgh Recs. Glasgow, 1574, I. 32, Rec. Soc. Addit. to [WAUT], q. v.

WAT, *s*. A hap or guard, a loose upper coat or big jacket made of thick woollen cloth: a watchman's coat. V. WATE, *s*.

I coft a stane o' haslock woo'
To mak a *wat* to Johnny o't;
For Johnny is my only jo,
I lo'e him best of ony yet.
Burns.

Various editions read "*coat*;" but *wat* is the word which Burns wrote.
It may have been so called from the name of the cloth: O. Swed. *wad*, stuff, clothing, Icel. *vadmál*, wadmal, a plain woollen cloth, Ger. *wat*, cloth, Fr. *ouate*, wadding. See under *Wad* in Skeat's Etym. Dict.

To WAT, *v. n*. V. DICT.
The quotation and etym. under this heading are misplaced. The quot. should be set under s. 1. of *Wat*,

Wate, *adj*.; and the etym. under s. 2. of the same entry. For the entry in the DICT. substitute the following—

WAT, *v*. Know, knew. V. *Wait*.

Wat, know, is improperly used in all the persons, sing. and pl. of the present tense, as stated under *Wait*; and *wat*, knew, is properly used in all the persons sing. and pl. of the pret. tense; but there is no to *wat*, as given by Jamieson.

To WAT, *v. a*. A colloq. form of *wad*, to pledge, promise, plight one's word, honour, or credit: as, "I *wat* a groat." V. *Wud*.

The expression "*weel I wat*" is frequently used with *wat* in this sense.

WATE, VAIT, *v*. Know; Kingis Quair, st. 50, 129, ed. Skeat: "thou *vait*," thou knowest; Compl. Scot., p. 126, E.E.T.S. V. *Wait*.

In the Kingis Quair, st. 60, *wate* is properly used in the first and third pers. sing.; but in the other passages referred to the word is improperly used, as already explained under *Wait*.
The correct forms are these:—Present, I *wait*, thou *waist*, he *wait*; we, ye, or they *wit*. Past, I *wist*, Part. pt., *wist*. Infinitive, *wit*: or less correctly *weet*. The allied adverb *ywis, iwis* (also written *I-wis*), certainly, is frequently mistaken for first pers. sing. present of the verb.

WATER-FOOT, WATER-FIT, WATER-NEB, *s*. The mouth of a river; used also as the name of a village or town at the mouth of a river; Burns, Holy Fair.

"*The Water-fit*," as used by Burns, was a name for Newtown-on-Ayr. "*The Water-Neb*" is still used in Paisley as a name for the mouth of the Cart; but probably, when it was first used, it was applied to the tongue of land formed by the junction of the two Carts near Renfrew.

WATERMAILE, WATERMAYLE, *s*. The name of a kind of fur: perhaps that of the water-rat or water-vole; pl. *watermailis, watermayllis;* Accts. L. H. Treas., I. 136, 137, Dickson.

For the origin of *maile, mayle*, cf. O. Dutch *muyl*, M. Du. *mule*, muzzle, snout: whence O. Fr. *mulot*, the field-vole or meadow-mouse, so named on account of its long snout; also, Fr. *surmulot*, the Norway rat, lit. the great *mulot* or great long-snout. These examples suggest that *watermaile, watermayle*, may represent the water-vole or water-rat.

WATER-SPONGE, WATTER-SPOUNGE, *s*. A sponge. V. under *Sponge*.

So called because originally used by surgeons, leeches, barbers, etc., in bathing and dressing wounds. In the Customs and Valuation of Merchandises of 1612 the following entry occurs :—
"Brushes or spounges called *watter spounges* for chirurgeans, the pound weght, . . . xxs," Halyburton's Ledger, p. 292, Rec. Soc.

WATH, *s*. V. DICT.
Delete the last line of the entry under this heading in DICT. The etym. is Icel. *vath*, a ford.

WATHE, *s*. Danger. V. WAITHE.

WATHELY, WAITHELY, *adv.* Dangerously, severely, mortally: "*wonded* full *wathely*," Awnt. Arthur, st. 24.
This word was misprinted *woyeley* by Pinkerton, and in that form was entered by Jamieson. V. DICT.

WATIT, VATIT, *pret.* Welted. V. *Wat, v.*

WAT-SHOD, *adj.* and *adv.* Wet over the shoe-tops, wading ankle-deep: *red-wat-shod,* wading ankle-deep in blood, Burns, Ep. to Simpson.

WATTLE, WATTEL, WATTILL, *s.* Originally, a night's meal or refection given by the occupiers of the land to their superior when passing through his territory. After the land was feudalized, the tax was charged as rent in proportion to the extent of land occupied. Addit. to WATTLE, q. v.

Wattle, therefore, may be briefly defined as the Norse form of Conveth or Waytinga. As the original form of this tax had long ceased in Orkney and Shetland, the correct meaning of the term was forgotten even by the natives of those islands; and various suppositions were given in explanation, but even the best of them were felt to be unsatisfactory. Until lately, indeed, the word was a puzzle to philologist and antiquary alike; and elaborate papers appeared at intervals in support of some fancied solution. The correct meaning of the word, however, was found lately in some unpublished Rentals of Shetland of the year 1628, in the General Register House, Edinburgh; and these records clearly show that *wattle* was simply the Norse equivalent for the Scottish *conveth.* Since the discovery was made, these Shetland Rentals have been examined by Mr. Goudie, and their records have been fully discussed by him in a paper printed in the Proc. of the Antiq. Society, vol. vii., N. S.

The following is an extract from the Rentals referred to:—

"Rentall of the wattill as it was in anno 1605.
                   Unst.
Ska . . . . . . ij nychtis wattill
Trowoilie & Saudoill . . ij nychtis wattill
Haroldsweik . . . . ij nychtis wattill
Benorth the vo Ska & Howland iiij nychtis wattill."

Icel. *veita,* to grant, give; *veizla,* an entertainment; "as a law term, the reception or entertainment to be given to the Norwe king, or to the king's 'landed-men,' or his stewards, for in olden times the king used to go on a regular circuit through his kingdom, taking each county in turn; his retinue, the places of entertainment, and the time of his staying at each place being regulated by law; this was called 'veizla' or fara at veizlum, taka veizlu." Vigfusson, Icel. Dict.

WATTLE, *s.* A stout wand, a stick such as is used by drovers for driving their cattle. A.-S. *watel, watul.*

Stridin' ower horse an' yerkin cattle
Wi' noisy glee,
Nae Jockey's whup nor drover's *wattle,*
Can frighten thee.
Ballantine. Wee Raggit Laddie, st. 6.

WAUCHIN, WAUGHIN, *s.* Quaffing, drinking, swilling. V. WAUCHT, *v.*

But now he's a dyvor wi' birlin and *wauchin,*
Whistle Binkie, I. 393.
"Dyvor," a bankrupt.

WAUGHTER, *s.* A guard-ship. V. *Wachter.*

To WAUK, *v. a.* and *n.* To wake, awake, to waken: part. pr. *waukin,* waking; used as an *adj.,* awake.

Hey Johnie Cope are ye *waukin* yet?
Or are your drums a-beating yet?
If ye were *waukin,* I wad wait
To go to the coals i' the morning.
Song, Hey Johnie Cope.

In explanation of the phrase, "*to go to the coals,*" it may be mentioned that the battle-field of Prestonpans, where Cope was defeated by Prince Charles Stuart in 1745, lies in the midst of a coal field, from which the inhabitants of Edinburgh have been supplied with fuel for centuries. And Edinburgh carters going out to the pits for their loads say they are "*going to the coals.*"

WAUKRIFE, WAUKRIF, WAKRIFE, *adj.* Easily wakened, lightly sleeping, not apt to sleep. Addit. to WALKRIFE, q. r.

Abune my breath I daurna speak,
For fear I rouse your *waukrif* daddie.
Tannahill, O are ye sleepin' Maggie.
The dog 's speldert on the floor and disna gie a cheep,
But here's a *waukrife* laddie that winna fa' asleep.
W. Miller, Wee Willie Winkie, st. 2.

WAVEL, WAVILL, *adj.* Slack or loose, as applied to joints; hence shaky. Syn. *shachly.* V. WAVEL, *v.*

Resembles weill thy shaithand knees,
Thy *wavill* feet, thy Reland Eis.
Rob Stene's Dream, p. 8, Mait. C.
A.-S. *wafre,* wavering, restless; Icel. *vafra, vafla,* to waver; *vafl,* hesitation.

WAWIL, *adj.* A form of *Wald,* plain, flat, q. v. Errat. in DICT.

Delete the entry under this heading in DICT., for Jamieson's defin., "loosely knit," is a mistake, through confounding *wavel,* shaky, loose, and *wawil,* which represents a vulgar pron. of *wald, wauld,* plain, flat. Hence, *wawil-fitt* means flat feet, plain-soled feet. See under *Wald.*

Laing's ed. has *wauld feitt,* which is the reading of the Reidpeth MS.

WAWIL-EYID, WAWIL-EGHID, *adj.* Wall-eyed, with blind or diseased eyes.
A wirling, a wayryngle, a *wawil-eyid* shrewe.
Allit. Rom. Alex., I. 1706.
Icel. *vagleygr,* wall-eyed: from *vagl,* a beam, and *eygr,* eyed; see Vigfusson.

WAWLY, *s.* Ornament, decoration, toy, gewgaw: bonnie *wawlies,* beautiful ornaments; Scott's Antiquary, ch. 29. V. WALY.

WAWSPER, WAUSPER, WASPER, WASTER, WESTER, *s.* Lit. a striker: a spear for striking fish, a leister or salmon spear, a fish spear. Addit. to WAWSPER, q. v.

All these forms are still in use: *waster* and *wester* are merely corruptions of *wawsper,* more correctly *wosper,* a striker, applied to a fish-spear, and especially to a leister or salmon spear. From O. Du. *woepen*, later *werpen*, to throw, strike : whence *wosppijl*, *werppijl*, a dart, *woapspeer*, *werpspeer*, a javelin.

To WAYMENT, WAYEMETT, *v. n.* To lament.

It weryit, it *wayemettede*, lyke a womann.
                           Awnt. Arthure, st. 9.
The version quoted by Jamieson reads *wayment*, contr. of *waymented*, lamented. See DICT.

WAYMENT, WAYMYNG, *s.* V. DICT.

Delete *wayment* from the heading in DICT., for in the passage there quoted the word is a verb, not a noun. See quotation in DICT., and compare with the reading given in last entry.
Waymyng is prob. a scribal error for *waymenting*. It may, however, be a contr. form of that word.

To WAYNE. V. DICT.

Delete both entries under this heading in DICT. : Wayne is a misreading of Wayue. V. *Waive, v.*

WAYRYNGLE, *s.* An accursed being; also, one who has the power of the evil-eye, a bewitcher; Allit. Rom. Alex., 1. 1706.
A dimin. from *wary*, to curse, ban.

WAYT, WAYTE, *s.* and *v.* V. [WATE].

WAYTINGA, *s.* A certain duty paid to a superior by the occupiers of his land. It consisted of a night's meal or refection on certain occasions when he passed through his territory. Originally it was called *Conveth*, q. v.

"In the reign of Alexander the Third this word [Conveth] seems to have assumed the form *Waytinga*, and appears in the Chamberlain Rolls of his reign as a burden upon the Thanages." Skene's Celtic Scotland, iii. 232.

To WAYVE, WAYFE, WAYF, *v. a.* V. *Waive.*

WEAR, WEER, WEIR, *v.* and *s.* Wear. V. [WER].

My cloak was ance a guid gray cloak,
  When it was fittin for my *weir*,
But now it's scantly worth a groat,
  For I hae worn't this thretty yeir.
      Song, Tak your Auld Cloak about ye.

To-WEAR, To-WEIR, TOWEIR, *adj.* To be worn on certain occasions, for particular use.

Shortly before the General Assembly sat in Glasgow in 1638, the magistrates of that city made various arrangements for the comfort and convenience of the members; one of them was the appointmend of three officers, who were "ellectit and nominat to keip the kirk dooris and the *toweir* gownis in a cumlie maner." Burgh Recs. Glasgow, i. 393, Rec. Soc.
The distinction between the terms *wearing* and *to-wear* is worth noting. A *wearing* gown is one for regular use or daily wear; a *to-wear* gown is one to be worn on certain occasions. The gowns mentioned above were to be worn by the ministers during the sittings of the Assembly.

WEASON, *s.* Weasand, wind-pipe, throat; Burns. V. WIZEN.

This form of the word is not uncommon in Eng. of the seventeenth and eighteenth centuries. It was used by Dryden; and Cotgrave defined Fr. *sifflet*, as "the *weason* or wind-pipe."
A.-S. *wāsend*, the gullet; prob. put for A.-S. *hwæsend*, part. pres. of *hwæsan*, to wheeze. See Skeat's Etym. Dict.

WED, WEDDE, *s.* A stake in play or gambling; Sir Tristrem, 1. 320. Addit. to WED, q. v.

WEDDERIS, WEDDYRS, WEDYRS, *s. pl.* Bad weather, storms, stormy weather; Awnt. Arthure, st. 26; Rauf Coilyear, st. 2. Addit. to WEDDER, q. v.

Ithand *wedderis* of the Eist draif on sa fast,
It all to-blaisterit and blew that thairin laid.
                      Rauf Coilyear, st. 3.
The term is similarly used in the Towneley Mysteries, p. 98.

WEDE, *adj.* Furious; Awnt. Arth., st. 43. V. WEID.

WEDIS, VEDIS, *s. pl.* Raiment; also, armour: "in glemand steil *wedis*," Gol. and Gawane, 1. 563; and it occurs in the same sense in 1. 855. Addit. to [WEDIS].

WEDOS ENEMY, WEDOWIS INEMYE, *s.* The widow's enemy: a name for the fox; because he steals her poultry; Kingis Quair, st. 156, ed. Skeat.

While the passage in the Kingis Quair prob. alludes to Chaucer's Nonne Prestes Tale, there are various tales in which the fox is represented as "the widow's enemy." And a story similar to the one related by Chaucer is told by Henryson in his Taill of Schir Chantecleir and the Foxe. In the opening of that fable the poet thus describes the violence done to a poor widow by a crafty fox.

Ane lytill fra this foirsaid Wedowis hous,
Ane thornie schaw their wes of greit defence,
Quhairin ane Foxe, craftie and cautelous,
Maid his repair and daylie residence,
Quhilk to this wedow did greit violence,
In pyking of pultrie baith day and nicht,
And na way be revengit on him scho micht.

WEDSETT, *s.* Pledge, pawn. V. WADSET.

WEEK, WEIK, WEYK, *s.* A wick for a candle or a lamp: *rag-weyk*, a wick of soft, loose linen or cotton yarn; *hard-weyk*, one of hard-twined yarn; Burgh Recs. Edinburgh, II. 6, Rec. Soc.

In 1679 the proprietors of the paper works near Edinburgh complained to the Privy Council that they were impeded in their operations by a "faulty custom" in the country of using good rags to make candle-wicks. At their urgent request the Privy Council prohibited rags being used for this purpose.

WEEKIT, WEIKIT, *adj.* Having a wick; "*small weikit*," having a small wick.

"Item, that ale candilmakaris has candile reddy to

sele to ale mane, and thai salbe sellit be richt wecht, the pund for iij d., *small weikit* and dry. Burgh Recs. Aberdeen, 1507, i. 436, Sp. C.
A.-S. *weoca*, a wick; O. Dutch *weicke*.

WEELE, *s.* A whirlpool; *wiel*, Burns. V. WHEEL.
"*Gurges*, a *weele* in a water;" Duncan's App. Etym., 1595, ed. Small, E. D. S.

To WEILD, WELD, WELDE, *v. a.* To enjoy, dispense; Awnt. Arthure, st. 27; to control, direct, manage; Ibid., st. 33; to guard, govern, rule; Gol. and Gawain, l. 1188. Addit. to WEILD, q. v.

WEILD, WELD, *pret.* Possessed, enjoyed; protected, guarded.
The rede blnde with the rout folowit the blaid, For all the wedis, I wise, that the wy *weild.*
Gol. and Gaw., l. 941.
The meaning of the last line may be—"In spite of all the clothing or armour that the knight possessed, or that protected the knight." *Wedis* in the sense of armour is common in the Gawain romances.

WEIL'D WIGHT, *adj.* V. *Waled-Wight.*

To WEINE, WENE, *v. a.* To think, deem, imagine, suppose. E. *ween.*
And all thir teinds ye haif amang your hands, Thay war givin yow for uther causses, I *weine*, Nor mummil motins and haid your clayis cleine.
Lyndsay, Thrie Estaitis, l. 2933.
A.-S. *wénan*, to imagine; from A.-S. *wén*, expectation, Dutch *wanen*, Icel. *vána*, Goth. *wenjan*, to expect, fancy.

To WEIR, *v. a.* and *n.* To wear. V. *Wear.*

To WEIR, *v. a.* To ward, avert. V. WEAR, *to guard.*
In his right hand he had ane groundin speir, Of his father the wraith fra us to *weir.*
Henryson, Test. Cresseid, l. 182.

WEIRLYK, VEIRLYK, *adj.* Warlike. V. WERELY.

WEIRSAW, VEIRSAW, *s.* Point of war; *in weirsaw,* appointed or equipped for war: "with ane schip in *veirsaw;*" Burgh Recs. Aberdeen, I. 241, Sp. C. V. WERE.

WELP, *s.* A whelp; Sir Tristrem, l. 2399, S.T.S.

WEMELES, *adj.* Stainless, spotless; without scar or blemish: hence, unhurt, scathless; Gol. and Gaw, l. 99. Errat. in DICT. V. [WEM.]

WEN, WENE, *s.* Doubt, hesitation, *but wen,* without doubt; Gol. and Gaw, l. 98. Addit. to WENE, q. v. V. [WENE, *v.*]

WENING, *s.* Supposition, fancy, hope; Sir Tristrem, l. 1730, 2658, ed. S.T.S.

WENIT, WENT, WEND, *pret.* Imagined, thought, believed. V. [WENE].
Quhen of the Tod wes hard na peip, The wowf *went* all had bene on sleip,
Dunbar, Tod and Lamb, l. 65.

WENEM, WENIM, *s.* Venom, poison.
". . . the said cow gewe no milk bot lyk wirsum or *wenem,* quhilk na leiwing creatur culd preive."
Trial for Witchcraft, 1597, Spald. Mis. I. 93.
O. Fr. *venim,* from Lat. *venenum.*

WENGIT. Winged; Douglas, II. 59, 13, ed. Small.

WENNELL, WENNALL, WINNALL, *s.* A vennel or narrow street; Burgh Recs. Glasgow, 1574, I. 30, Rec. Soc.; Ibid. Aberdeen, I. 112. V. *Vennel.*

WERD, WERDE, *s.* The world. V. *Ward.*

WERD, *pret.* Wore; Sir Tristrem, l. 3296. V. [WER, *v.*]
This pret. form is still in use.

WERD, *part. pt.* Awarded; adjudged, decreed, settled: a form of *Ward,* q. v.

WERELY, *adj.* Warlike, armed for war, bristling: "the *werely* porpapyne," the bristling porcupine; Kingis Quair, st. 155. Addit. to WERELY, q. v.

WERK, *s.* Prob. a scribal error for *werth,* worth, wealth.
Thocht all the *werk* that evir had levand wicht Wer only thyne, no moir thy pairt dois fall Bot melt, drynk, clais, and of the laif a sicht; Yit to the Juge thow sall gif compt of all.
Dunbar, No Tressour availis without Glaidnes, l. 33.

WERKHOUS, *s.* Workshop; Accts. L. H. Treas., I., 289, Dickson.

To WERNE, WERN, *v. a.* To warn, forbid; Gol. and Gaw., l. 138, 477. V. *Warne, v.*

WET, *pret.* Pierced, penetrated, searched. V. WEIT, *v.*
With vengeand wapnis of were throu wedis thai *wet.*
Gol. and Gaw., l. 759.

WETE, *adj.* Piercing, thrilling.
It yellede, it yamede with vengeance full *wete.*
Awnt. Arth., st. 7.

To WETE, WETTE, *v. a.* To wit, know, learn: *wiete,* meaning mark, consider, Awnt. Arth., st. 19, 3; and meaning experience, endure, Ibid. st. 19, 12. V. WIT.
"Now wo es me! for thi waa," sayd Waynour, "I wysse, Bot a worde wolde I *wete,* and thi will ware."
Awnt. Arth., st. 16, 2.

WEX, *pret.* Waxed, became, grew; Sir Tristrem, l. 14, 3327, S.T.S. *Wox* is also used; and *woux,* and even *wolx.*

[To WEY, v. a.] V. Dict.
For V. WE, *read* V. WEE.

To WEY, WEYE, v. a. To consider, regard, pay heed to. Addit. to [WEY].
Thus maist thou seyne, that myn effectis grete,
Vnto the quhich ye aughten maist *weye.*
No lyte offense, to sleuth is [al] forget.
Kingis Quair, st. 120, ed. Skeat.

WEYTON, VEYTON, s. The whitton tree or water elder.
"I sau *veyton,* the decoctione of it is remcid for ane sair hede." Compl. Scot., p. 67, E.E.T.S.

WHALP, s. A whelp: used also as a term of contempt applied to a young person.

WHALPIT, *part. pt.* Whelped.
His hair, his size, his mouth, his lugs,
Shew'd he was nane o' Scotland's dogs;
But *whalpit* some place far abroad,
Whare sailors gang to fish for cod.
Burns, The Twa Dogs, l. 11.

WHART, WHARTFULL. Forms of QUERT, *Quertfull,* q. v.

WHASIE, s. A weasel; lit., the sharp one. V. WASIE.
"*Mustela,* a *whasie* or whitret;" Duncan, App. Etym., 1595, ed. Small, E. D. S.
A.-S. *hwæs,* sharp; Dan. *hvas,* Sw. *hvass.*

WHAT, WHATT, *pret.* Whetted, sharpened, mended.
Sae my auld stumpie pen I gat it,
Wi' nnuckle wark,
An' took my jocteleg and *whatt* it,
Like ony clark.
Burns, Third Ep. to Lapraik.
A.-S. *hwettan,* to sharpen: from *hwæt,* keen.

WHEEM, WHEME, *adv.* and *adj.* V. QUEEM, QUEME.
From A.-S. *cwéman,* to satisfy, please; hence, to fit.

To WHEEP, v. n. To jerk, shake, move rapidly or fly nimbly from side to side or backwards and forwards. A freq. of *whip,* to act or move nimbly. V. WHIP, v.
Come screw the pegs wi' tunefu' cheep
And o'er the thairms be tryin;
Oh rare! to see our elbucks *wheep,*
And a' like lamb-tails flyin
Fu' fast that day!
Burns, The Ordination, st. 7.

WHEEP, s. A small quantity, a sip, taste. *Penny-wheep,* penny-sip, penny-liquor, small beer; Burns. Dimin. of *Whip,* q. v.
In Lancashire small-beer is called *penny-whip;* and in Lincolnshire, *whip-belly.* See Halliwell.

WHEETIE, WHEETIE-WHEET, WHEETLE-WHEETIE, s. Names applied to a very young bird; *wheetle-wheeties,* young chickens; Whistle Binkie, II., 353. Addit. to WHEETIE, q. v.
(Sup.)   L 2

WHELEN. V. Dict.
Del. this entry in DICT. The term is a scribal error for *whethen* in the Douce MS. of the Awnt. of Arthure, and it was so printed in Pinkerton's edition.

WHETHEN, WHYTHEN, *adv.* Whence, Awnt. Arthure, st. 28.
Lincoln MS. has *whythen;* and Douce MS. has *whelen;* see above.

To WHIDDER, v. n. To run nimbly: a freq. of Whid, and similar to Whitter, q. v. West and South of S.
Whid implies a rush, bolt, or leap, as of a rabbit when startled near its burrow: *whidder* or *whitter* implies running with quick pattering or leaping.

WHIP, WHUP, s. A sip, gulp, or draught of liquor taken hurriedly; West of S. Addit. to WHIP, q. v.

To WHIRL, v. a. and n. Used like E. *wheel;* also, to push or draw a wheelbarrow, to drive or be driven in a cart, car, or other vehicle; to drive rapidly, as, "He *whirled* through the town in a gig."

WHIRL, s. The act of whirling; a drive in a cart, or other vehicle; also, the sound made by a wheeled vehicle, as, "I heard the *whirl* o' his machine."

WHIRLY, WHIRLIE, WHURLIE, s. A small wheel, a caster; a low truck used in moving heavy packages; also, contr. for whirly-barrow, whurlie-bed.

WHISKIN, *adj.* Large and tufted; "a *whiskin* beard."
A *whiskin* beard about her mou,
Her nose and chin they threaten Ither;
Sic a wife as Willie had,
I wad na gie a button for her.
Burns, Willie Wastle, st. 2.
"*Whiskin* or *whisking,* adjectively is great, applied to almost every thing, as floods, fire, winds." Thoresby. Bailey's Dict. gives " *Whisking,* great, swinging."
Dan. *visk,* a wisp, rubber; Swed. *viska,* a whisk, small broom.

WHISKY, WHISK, s. A gig; a light, two-wheeled carriage; lit. that which *whisks* along.
Mention is made of this machine in the story told by Dean Ramsay of the Laird of Balnamoon when he lost his wig in Munrimmon Moor. V. Rem. Scot. Life, ch. vi.

WHISSONDAY, WISSONDAY, WYSSONDAY, s. Whitsunday, the May term. These pron. are still common.

WHISTLE, WHISSILL, WHISSEL, s. A flute, fife, or flageolet.
"*Whissillis* for Tabernaris the dozen . . . xx s." Customs and Val. 1612, Halyburton's Ledger, p. 332.

To WHIVER, WHIUER, v. n. To quiver, flutter, wave.

"Men ranking themselves vnder stately standerts, and punicall pinsels, displayed for *whiuering* in the winde." Blame of Kirkburiall, ch. 7.
A.-S. *cwifer*, eager, brisk ; O. Dutch *kuiveren*, to quiver ; Kilian.

WHUP, s. and v. Whip.

WICK, adj. Evil or ill ; hence, difficult, hard to be done. Errat. in DICT.

Morgan is *wick* to slo,
Of knights he hath gret pride.
                 Sir Tristrem, 775, S.T S.
This is the obsolete M. E. adj. *wikke*, evil. It answers to A.-S. *wicca*, a wizard, which is a corruption of *witga*, short for *witega*, prophet, magician, sorcerer.

WICK, WEEK, s. V. WEIK.

WICKAR, WICKER, WIKKER, s. A wicker, or pliant twig, M. E. *wiker*: osier twigs ; as in the phrase, "to cut *wicker*," and so used by Dunbar ; also, used as an *adj.*, as " a *wicker* mawn."

Aye wav'ring like the willow *wicker*,
'Tween good and ill.
                 Burns, Poem on Life.

" *Vimen*, a *wickar* ; *qunsi vincimen*, a *vinciendo vel a viendo.*" Duncan, App. Etym., 1595, ed. Small. E.D.S.
A.-S. *wican*, to give way, bend ; Swed. dial. *vekare*, *vikker*, willow, from *veka*, to bend, ply.

WIDDERSINNIS, &c., adv. V. DICT.

This term is frequently confounded with *widdersones*, *withersones*, contrary to the sun's course ; and that mistake was made by Jamieson himself in his defin. of Withershins, q. v. While under the form Widdersinnis he clearly states that the term has no connection whatever with the sun ; and while he correctly cites the Middle Dutch *wedersins*, otherwise, contrariwise, as its equivalent, he fails to point out the root of the word.
It has come from O. Icel. *vithr*, against contrary to, and *sinni*, of which the orig. meaning was way, direction, journey, as in Icel. *d sinnum*, on the way. Hence its meaning is simply *contrariwise : sinnis* being an old genitive form used as an adverb.

WIDDY, VIDDY, s. In the *s.*, the latch of a door ; in the *pl.*, the fastenings of a door, including both latch and hinges. Addit. to WIDDY, q. v.

" . . for cuttyn the *viddyis* of the dur." Burgh Recs. Prestwick, 15th Nov., 1513, p. 45, Mait. C.
In some parts of the Highlands and islands of Scotland doors fastened with *widdies* or wand-ropes may still be seen ; and such fastenings were not uucommon in the Lowlands at the beginning of this century.

WIDDIEFOW, WIDDIEFU', adj. Altogether like a widdie, full of crossness or thrawnness; hence, as applied to one's person, crooked, deformed ; and, as applied to the mind or temper, cross, cantankerous, ill-tempered. Addit. to WIDDIEFOW, q. v.

As used by Burns and Lyndsay in the passages quoted by Jamieson, this word refers not to *widdie*, the gallows, but to *widdie*, a rope or band of twigs formed by twisting or plaiting. It implies *full of crossness* or *thrawnness* ; and is in keeping with the common saying, "*as thrawn as a widdie*," which is applied to personal appearance and to temper. And any one who has seen a *widdie* will fully appreciate the simile used by Burns in drawing the contrast between the crookit, crossgrained, churlish laird, and the strappiu', ruddy, kindhearted miller.

The Laird was a *widdiefu'*, bleerit, knurl.
                 Song, Meg o' the Mill.
As applied to bodily appearance *widdiefu'* has much the same meaning as *rigwiddie*, which Burns used to describe the unshapely hags that Tam o' Shanter saw in Alloway Kirk.

WIDDIE-NEK, s. Gallows-neck, in the sense of E. *gallows-bird* ; one doomed to be hanged. V. WIDDIE.

For ever we steill, and ever alyke ar pure,
In dreid and schame our dayis we endure,
Syne *widdie-nek* and crak-raip callit als,
And till our hyre hangit up be the hals.
       Henryson, Tod and Freir Wolf, l. 48.

WIDE-WHARE, WYDQUHARE, adv. Widely, far and near, everywhere ; Pop. Ballads.

And eftyre scalit ware *wyd quhare*,
To wyne the folk to Cristis fare.
       Barbour's Saints, Leg. iii. prol. l. 142.
Compound of A.-S. *wid*, wide, and *hwar*, *hwar*, where.

To WIETE, v. a. To know, wit ; Awnt. Arth., st. 19. V. WETE.

This word occurs twice in the same stanza : in l. 3, where it means *know* in the sense of mark, consider ; and in l. 12, where it means *know* in the sense of experience, endure.

WIFIKIE, s. Dimin. of Wifock, q. v.

WIGHT, VIGHT, adj. Brave, powerful ; " ane *vight* weriour," Gol. and Gaw., l. 325 ; *wa'-wight*, *wall-wight*, stalwart, bravest; Pop. Ballads. V. *Waled-Wight*, WICHT.

WILCAT, s. The wild cat, polecat : applied to an ill-natured, spiteful person.

WILD, VILD, WYLD, WULL, WYLE, adj. Fierce, savage, as a *wild*-cat, *wull*-cat : short for wild-beasts, beasts of the chace, game, as *wyld*, *wyld*-meat ; B. R. Edin. II. 6 : extravagant, unreasonable, as a *wyle*-say, *wull*-say, a foolish story : dangerous, risky, hazardous, chance, as *wild aunters*, *wild aventouris*, applied to adventure vessels or cargoes to or from foreign ports. V. under *Aventour*.

WILFIRE, WULFIRE, s. Wild-fire, Will o' the Wisp. Addit. to WILD-FIRE, q. v.

WILL. *To come in will* to a person, to promise submission to him, to put one's self at the mercy of another ; freq. in Burgh Recs.

"Johne Cowan *com in will* to the provest and counsall for the furthputting of Marioun Cowan his dochter to kirk and merkat without licence of the provest or baillies, and gif ony danger cumis tharthrou or ony of his hous, to be at the said provest and counsalis *will.*" Burgh Recs. Stirling, 3 Nov. 1548.

WILL OF REDE, WILL OF WANE. V. under WILL, *adj.* s. 1.

WILLIE, WILLY, WULLY, *adj.* Willing, wishing; as, *weel-willie*, kindly disposed, friendly: also, hearty, with a will, and hence large, immense; as, a "a *willie*-waught," a hearty drink, or, as in common parlance, a hearty pull.

WILSUM, WILLSOME, *adj.* Wandering. V. under WILL.

WILTU, WILTOW, *v.* Wilt thou: "What *wiltow* lay?" what wilt thou bet? Sir Tristrem, l. 312, S.T.S.
—— Soon his face wad mak you fain,
  When he did sough,
"O *wiltu, willu*, do't again,"
  And graned and leuch.
    Ramsay, Patie Birnie.

WIN, WYN, WIND, WON, *part.* and *adj.* Won; also, quarried, quarried, rough-dressed: "*win werk*," cut, blocked, or quarried stones; Burgh Recs. Glasgow, I. 307, II. 132; "may be *wind*," may be quarried; Ibid. II. 151, Rec. Soc.
In the first sense the term is thus used by Burns,—
Like fortune's favours tint as *win*.

To WIN till, *v. a.* To attain. V. WIN to.

WINNIE, WIN and LOSS, *s.* The name applied to the set of games at marbles in which there are stakes or forfeits; West of S.

WINDBANDS, WYNDBANDIS, *s. pl.* The nave-bands of a wheel; Accts. L. H. Treas., I. 287, Dickson. V. WUND-BAND.
"Item, for jᵉ nalis to the *wyndbandis* of the axtreis, xvjd." Ibid., p. 259.
A.-S. *windan*, to turn, revolve.

WINDED, WINDIT, *adj.* Tainted; used with reference to butter, meat, &c. Cf. E. *vinnewed.*

WINDEDNESS, WINDEDNES, *s.* Taint, tainted state.
"*Rancor,* vitium carnis, *windednes;*" Duncan App. Etym., 1595, ed. Small, E. D. S.

WINDIN-CLAITH, WINNOW-CLAITH, WINNEL-CLAITH, *s.* A cloth used in winnowing grain; Burgh Recs. Edinburgh, II. 136, Rec. Soc. Also called a *winnow-claith,* in W. Watson's Poems, p. 59; and a *wonnow-clayth,* in B. R. Glasgow, I. 129, Rec. Soc.

To WINDOW, *v. a.* To winnow; pret. and part. pt. *windowit.* A.-S. *windwian.*
"Quha ansuerit the, that ther was na wind *to window* ony malt; and thow said thow euld get wind anuch to do thi turn." Trials for Witchcraft, Spald. Misc., i. 92, 1597.

WINLY, WYNLY, *adv.* Pleasantly, agreeably, kindly, with delight; "welcummyt thaim *wynly,*" Houlate, st. 51, Asloan MS. V. WIN.

WINNA, WANNA, WONNA, WUNNA. Will not; "I *winna* gang, and he *wanna* come."
  Bonnie Jockie, blythe and gay,
  Kiss'd young Jessie making hay;
The lassie blush'd, and frowning cried, "Na, na, it *winna* do;
I canna, canna, *winna, winna,* mauna buckle to."
    Song, Within a mile o' Edinburgh Town.
The older version has *cannot, wonnot,* and *munnot,* in the last line. This song, however, which has long been a favourite in Scotland, is not of Scottish origin: it was composed by Tom D'Urfey, and set to music by James Hook, a brother of the celebrated Theodore Hook. The verses first appeared in *Wit and Mirth,* a collection of songs published in 1698.

WINNAIL, *s.* A windmill; "the *winnail* dyk," Burgh Recs. Prestwick, 1507, p. 40, Mait. C.

WINNEL-CLAITH, *s.* V. *Windin-claith.*

WINNING, WINNIN, *s.* The winding of yarn on pirns for the weaver; the process or craft of so winding yarn.
  The cardin' o't, the spinnin' o't,
  The warpin' o't, the *winnin* o't;
  When ilka ell cost me a groat,
  The tailor staw the lynin o't.
    Burns, The Cardin' o't.

WINNING, WYNNYNG, VYNING, *s.* Profit, gain, interest; Halyburton's Ledger, p. 106, 151. Addit. to WINNING, q. v.
"All thingis contit betwix Master James Comyng and me, excep the *wynnyng* off his part off his mony." Ibid., p. 102.
"Sic a burges, bot na vther persoun, marrow him with ane maister of substance, and lay his penny to his, and sua far as it will reik the pennyvorthis to be bocht betwixt them, and thai to dele thairvpoun *ryning* and tynsell as effeiris, and sua far as ilk pairt reikis." Burgh Recs. Edinburgh, 1488, i. 55, Rec. Soc.
Winning is similarly used in Chaucer's Prol., l. 277.

WIRD, *s.* Fate, destiny. V. WEIRD.

To WIRK, *v. a.* and *n.* To drive, move, as, "the horse *wirks* the mill;" to influence, control, as, "She can weise or *wirk* him as she likes;" also, as a *v. n.,* to work, ferment, as, "It's *wirkin* like barm." Addit. to WIRK, q. v.

WIRKING, WIRKIN, VIRKING, *s.* Working, driving, influence, control; *virking,* King's Quair, st. 188, ed. Skeat.

WIRLING, WIRLIN, s. Same as WORLIN, q. v. A vulgar pron. is *urlin*.

WIRM, VIRM, s. A worm; Compl. Scot., p. 67, E.E.T.S.

WIRMIN, WERMIN, WORMING, s. Worms, vermin.

"Item, for clynging Brocks-holl, and burning the *worming* furth thairof eftir the wyf wes removed qua deid thairin, xijs." Burgh Recs. Peebles, p. 417.

A.-S. *wyrm*, a worm; and *wirmin*, *worming*, are cognate with O. Fr. *vermine*, which Cotgr. defines "Vermine; also, little beasts ingendered of corruption and filth."

WIRMET, VIRMET, s. Wormwood; Compl. Scot., p. 67, E.E.T.S. A.-S. *wermód*.

The name *wormwood*, applied to Artemisia Absinthium, Linn., has no reference either to *worm* or to *wood* : it is a corr. of A.-S. *wermód*, which in M. E. was first *wermode*, then *wormode*, and later *wormwood*. The plant was perhaps called *wermód*, preserver of the mind, (A.-S. *werian*, to defend, and *mód*, mood or mind), from a supposed belief in its virtues. V. Skeat, Etym. Dict.

In Earle's Eng. Plant Names, it is called *wormwod* in the list taken from a Nominale of the fifteenth cent.; but in the earlier lists it is named *wermod* and *weremod*, *wormod* and *wormode*.

WIRROK, WIRROCK, WY-ROK, s. A wart, knot, or bony excrescence on the feet; also applied to a hard boil or fiery pimple on the hands or feet; Dunbar, Amendis to Teylouris and Sowtaris, l. 18.

WIRROK, WIRROCK. adj. Warty, knotted: "*wirrok* tais," toes with swollen, knotted joints; Dunbar, Compl. to the King, l. 54.

A.-S. *wearrig*, *wearriht*, horny, knotty, rough : from *wear*, *wearr*, knot, wart; hardness of the hands or feet caused by labour.

To WIRRY, v. a. To worry, devour, eat ravenously. M. E. *wirien*.

WIRRIER, s. A worrier, devourer.

"And being admonished that as he should be torne by birds and beasts, did roiyre a taunt in requyring a cudgell to be coutched beside, wherebly to weare his *wirriers* away." Blame of Kirkburiall, cb. 6.

A.-S. *wyrgan*, as in the comp. *awyrgan*, to harm; Dutch *woorgen*, Ger. *würgen*, to strangle. M. E. *wirien* orig. meant to strangle, as in the expression, "dogs worry sheep."

WIRSET, WIRSAT, WORSET, WORSAT, s. and adj. Worsted, worsted cloth; also, made of worsted, as, "a *worset* apron." Addit. to WORSET.

These forms and meanings are common all over the country. *Wirssat* occurs in Accts. L. H. Treas., I. 202, Dickson.

WIRSUM, s. Foul purulent matter; Spald. Mis. I. 93. V. WORSUM, WOURSUM.

To WIS, v. n. Del. the entry in DICT.
There is no such verb. The infinitive is *to wit*.

WISE, WIS, s. Way, manner; Kingis Quair, st. 97, 117; also method, means, instrument.

for word is noght
Bot gif thy werk and all thy besy cure
Accord thereto; and virid be mesure,
The place, the houre, the maner, and the *wise*,
Gif mercy sall admitten thy seruise.
Ibid., st. 132, ed. Skeat.

The form *wis* occurs frequently in comp., as, *langwis*, lengthwise, *endwis*, endwise.

To WISE, WYSE, WYSSE, v. a. To tell, teach, show. Addit. to WISS, q. v.

Mak that course cruel, for Crystis lufe of hevin !
And syne wirk as I *wise*, your vappins to welld.
Gol. and Gaw., l. 820.

I rede thou wirk as I *wise*, or war the betide.
Ibid., i. 1033.

Also, it is used in the sense of to declare, assert, assure :—

"Now we is me ! for thi wus," sayd Waynour, "I *wysse*; Bot a worde wolde I wete, and thi will ware."
Awnt. Arthure, st. 16, l.

WISLE, WISLING, s. V. WISSEL.

WISP, WOSP, WUSP, s. Bunch, bundle, handful; as, "a *wisp* of straw or hay;" also, a packet, package. Errat. in DICT.

In the passages quoted in DICT., *wisp* certainly means bundle, bunch, package. And a *wisp of steel*, or as it is in L. Lat. *garba aceris*, is explained in Fleta as consisting of thirty pieces. See note by Dickson in Accts. L. H. Treas., i. 447. The term *wisp* was applied to a package of clasps (see Rates and Customs, 1612, Halyburton's Ledger, p. 293); and prob. various other articles of hardware were similarly packed and named.

ALE-WISP, ALE-WOSP, AIL-WOSP, s. The bush, branch, or wand, that formed the sign of a tavern or ale-house.

I will na prelatis for me sing,
Dies illa, dies ire ;
Na yit na bellis for me ring,
Sicut semper solet fieri ;
Bot a bag pipe to play a spryng,
Et unum *ail wosp* ante me ;
In stayd of baneris for to bring
Quatuor lagenas ceruisie,
Within the graif to set sic thing,
In modum crucis juxta me,
To fle the fendis, than hardely sing
De terra plasmasti me.
Dunbar, Test. Andro Kennedy.

Wisp in this sense means bunch of twigs, bush; and in many places a bush is still the sign of a tavern. The word was used by Shakespeare in this sense in the Epilogue to As You Like It, in the adage, "Good wine needs no *bush*." And the term *bouchon* is defined by Cotgrave as "A stopple; also a wisp of strawe;
. . . also, the bush of a tauerne, or alehouse."

In M. E. there were two forms of this term, *wisp*, and *wips*, which is the older form : hence a connection with the verb *to wipe* is suggested. Cf. Norweg. *vippa*, a wisp; Swed. dial. *vipp*, a little sheaf or bundle; L. Ger. *wiep*, a wisp.

WISSLE, WISSIL, WYSSIL, WYSSYLL, s. Exchange, the Exchange; Halyburton's Ledger, p. 60, 135. Addit. to WISSEL, q. v.

"Ressauit xv lycht crownis. Sald tham in the *Wissil* off Brugis for 3 li. 6 s. 5." *Ibid.* p. 173.

To **WITCHAFE**, WITCHAFF, v. a. V. *Witsaufe*.

WITH, WI, *prep.* With. In common speech this prep. is frequently redundant, especially after verbs implying working, acting, or doing; thus, "I hae na siller to buy it wi'." "Hae ye a bit string to tie 't wi'?" "Surely, ye hae een to see wi'." And evidently this verbal connection of *with* is an idiom of the North Anglian speech : for it appears in the earliest specimens of that form of Eng. It is common in the Kingis Quair. See st. 16, 174, 190, 111, ed. Skeat.

WITHERSHINS, *adv.* V. DICT.
Delete the second portion of the defin. given for this term in DICT. ; it is a mistake. See under WIDDER-SINNIS, and *Widdersinnis*.

WITHERSONES, *adv.* Contrary to the course of the sun ; Spald. Misc., I. 96. V. *Withershins, Widdersinnis*.

WITHGANG, *s.* Opportunity, implying occasion, circumstance, or means suitable; chance or means of acting. Addit. to WITH-GANG, q. v.
Richt swa in service other sam exceidis,
And thay half *withgang*, weltb and cherissing,
That thay will lychtlie Lordis in thair deidis.
Henryson, Wolf and Wedder, l. 149.

WITHOUT, WITHOUTE, *adv.* Over and above, besides, in addition to ; Accts. L. H. Treas., I. 145, Dickson.

WITRIFE, WITRYF, WITRYFF, *adj.* Very knowing, of great cunning; Spald. Club Misc., I. 122.
Generally used in a sarcastic or contemptuous sense, regarding a person who pretends to be very learned or clever. The term is a comp. of *wit*, knowledge, and *rife*, abounding in.

To **WITSAUFE**, WITCHAFFE, v. a. To vouchsafe; part. pr. *witchaffing*, Burgh Recs. Aberdeen, II. 260, Sp. C.
"That for the worschipe of the king and the gude of the realme, yhe *wotsaufe* to louse and deliuer frely the said Inglismen." Ibid. i. 11.
These forms represent corr. pron. of *vouchsafe*, which originally was written *vouch safe*, i.e. warrant as safe ; from O. Fr. *voucher*, to vouch, *cite*, and *sauf*, safe, which was formed from Lat. *salvus*.

WITSON, WITSUN, VYTSON, *s.* and *adj.* Whitsun, Whitsunday : "*vytson*, veddyinsday," Whitsun Wednesday ; Compl. Scot., p. 168, E.E.T.S.

WLONK, *adj.* and *s.* As an *adj.* it means grand, fair, comely, beautiful; superl. *wlonkest*; Awnt. Arthure, st. 1, 27, 54, Douce MS. As a *s.* it is applied to a lady in the sense of fair one, fair lady, haughty dame ; Dunbar, Twa Mariit Wemen, l. 150. Errat. in DICT.
Jamieson's defin. of this term is a mistake, into which he was probably led by the poet. phrase, *wlonkest in wedis*. *Wlonk* has primarily no connection with dress : it is simply A.-S. *wolonc, wlanc, wlenc*, grand, spirited, proud, splendid ; and refers to spirit, manner, bearing or appearance. See Wright's Vocabularies, and Dicts. of Bosworth and Ettmüller.
The last para. of the entry in DICT. must also be deleted ; for, that *wlonk* is the origin of the term *flunkie*, a servant in livery, is very improbable. Even granting that *flunkie* means "gaudily dressed one," as suggested by Jamieson and confirmed by Wedgwood, but discarded by Webster and others, it cannot be derived from a root that has no relation whatever to dress or dressing.

WNE, *s.* Ane oven. V. UNE.

WO, WOE, WOO, VOO, *adj.* Sad, sorry, sorrowful, pained, miserable. Addit. to WA, WAE, q. v,
"That byr Grace with her chyldryn and husbond cannot resort to the merchys of Ynglond. . . I am ryght sory and *voo* therfor." Douglas, vol. i. p. xxiii., ed. Small.
For luif of the, for thar dyseys was *too*.
Ibid., iv. 221, 13.

WOD, *s.* A wed, pledge; B. R. Prestwick, 1554, p. 63, Mait. C. V. WED, *s.*

WOD, WUD, *s.* Woods ; as in the expression, "Tak to the *wood*," i.e. go into hiding or concealment.

WOD-CRAFT, WODCRAFTIS, *s.* Skill in arts of the chace : Gawain Rom.

WODFANG, WODFAING, *s.* The right to cut and carry away wood, i.e. firewood, from a forest. V. FANG.
"The wod and *wodfaing* only being acceptit, provyding alwais that the samyn be cuttit and tane away be the said ——." Crossraguel Charters, i. 184, Ayr and Wigton Arch. Coll.
Comp. of *wod*, wood, and *fang*, to seize, take.

WODHAG, *s.* The annual cutting of wood in a forest ; Crossraguel Charters, I. 195,. Ayr and Wigton Arch. Coll.
Comp. of *wod*, wood, and *hag*, to cut.

WOD-LYND, *s.* Foliage of the woods ; "under *wod-lynd*," i.e. living in the woods; Gol. and Gaw., l. 123.

WODROISS, *s.* V. DICT.
As Jamieson suggested, the word in the Bann. MS. is *wodrciss*. In the Asloan MS. it is *werthis*, in error, however, regarding *wethis* : it is *wechis* in the Bann. MS., and *watchis* in the Asloan. In the next line *drable* is err. for *terrable*, Bann. MS., or *terrible*, Asloan MS. In the following line, *ferfull* is *feidfull* iu Bann. MS., and *ferd full* in Asloan.
As Pinkerton's version is so inaccurate, and as the Bann. version has evidently been written to dictation, we quote the passage as it stands in the Asloan MS.

The rouch *Wodwoys* wyld, that bastounis bare,
Our growin grysly and growe grym in effeir ;
Mair awfull in all thing saw I never air,
Baith to walk and to ward as watchis in weir.
That terrible felloun my spreit affrayd
So ferd full of fantasy,
I durst nocht kyth to copy
All other armes thar by.
Houlate, st. 48.

In the second line *growe* is prob. an error of the scribe. The word is redundant.

WODWISS, WODWYS, *s*. A satyr, faun; Houlate, st. 48. A.-S. *wude-wase*. V. *Wodroiss*.

WODROME, WODROAM, WODDRAM, *s*. Furious madness; a disease to which cattle are subject, and which causes them to rush about furiously: Orkn. and Shetl.

"The said sickness was taken off the said Marion, and casten upon a young cow of the said John's, which took *wodrome* and died within twenty four hours." Hibbert's Shetland, p. 594.

Comp, of *wod*, mad, and *roam*, to run about. A.-S. *wod*, mad, raging, to which has been added M. E. *rom*, *ram*, from *romen*, *ramen*, to run about.

WOD-WRATH, WOD-WRAITH, *adj*. Lit. madly-wrath, mad-angry; furiously enraged. V. WOD.

Than schir Golagrase for grief his gray ene bryut, *Wod-wraith* as the wynd his handis can wring.
Gol. and Gaw., st. 60.

"Wrath as the wind" is an old proverbial expression common in M. Eng. It occurs in Piers Plowman, iii. 328, ed. Skeat. Evidenly the allusion is to the wind's fury.

WOKE, *pret*. Watched; Henryson, p. 198, ed. Laing: *wook*, Accts. L. H. Treas., I. 294, Dickson. V. WOUK.

WOKY, *s*. See under *Voky, s.*

To WOLDE, *v. a.* To rule, govern, control, direct. A form of WALD, q. v.

The wirchipe of Wales to welde and to *wolde*.
A wnt. Arthure, st. 52.
The Douce MS. reads "*at wolde*," at will or pleasure, as one would.
A.-S. *waldan*, to rule.

WOLENE, VOLENE, *adj*. Woollen; "ane *volene* lwyme," a loom for weaving woollen cloth; Burgh Recs. Prestwick, 15 Oct., 1565, p. 69, Mait. C. V. WOLL.

WOLRONN, *s*. Thief, robber. Fr. *voleron*. Addit. to WOLROUN, q. v.

Because that Scotland of thy begging irkis,
Thow scapis in France to be a knycht of the felde ;
Thow has thy clainschellis, and thy burdoun kelde,
Wnhonest wayis all, *wolronn*, that thou wirkis.
Dunbar and Kennedy, l. 432, S.T.S.
"A knycht of the felde," a highwayman.

WOLSOME, *adj*. Wandering; implying homeless, houseless ones. Addit. to WILSUM.

To hungre meit, nor drynk to thirsty gaif,
Nor veseit the seik, nor did redeme the thrall,
Harbreit the *wolsome*, nor nakit cled at all,
Nor yit the deid to bury, tuke I tent.
Dunbar, I cry the mercy, l. 29.

WOMANHEDE, *s*. Womanhood; Kingis Quair, st. 117, ed. Skeat.

WOMBES, WAMES, *s. pl*. Bellies or bellyportions of furskins.

"Beaver bellies or *wombes* the peice, viii s." Rates and Customs, 1612, Halyburton's Ledger, p. 305.

To WON, WONNE, *v. a.* To quarry ; to cut, dress, or raise stones in a quarry. V. WIN, *v.*

"Licens to John Colquhoun of Kenmuir to *won* alsmony lymstanes in the lyme craig at the Channownmos as he can with ane mell quhill Mertimas nixtocnin, and to *won* and away tak the samyn to his awin vse for tuentie merkis money." Burgh Recs. Glasgow, 1630, i. 374.

WONDER, WONDIR, WONDRE, WONNER, WOUNDER, WUNNER, *s*. 1. A wonder, something to be wondered at.

And the schot als so thik thar was,
That it wes *wonder* for till see.
Barbour, xvii. 383, Camb. MS.

Also used as a contemptuous term.

Our Whipper-in, wee blastit *wonner*,
Poor worthless elf, it eats a dinner,
Better than ony tenant man
His Honour has in a' the lan.
Burns, The Twa Dogs.

2. Used as an *adj*., wonderful, grand; Barbour, xix., 398.

3. Used as an *adv*., wonderfully, extremely, magnificently; Ibid., i. 323, x. 620; "*wonder* sad," Kingis Quair, st. 96; "*woundir* sair," Douglas, II., 113, 11, ed. Small.

To WONDER, WONNER, WUNNER, *v. n*. To wonder. Also used as a *v. a.*, meaning to be curious or anxious to know, as in, "I *wonner* what's in that letter."

WONDERLY, WONDIRLY, *adv*. Wondrously ; Barbour, iii. 562, i. 269, Camb. MS., Gol. and Gaw., l. 162.

WONDRING, *s*. A marvel, wonder. V. WOUNDRING.

A.-S. *wundor*, a portent, wonder ; a thing which inspires awe; allied to A.-S. *wundian*, to turn aside from, to respect, revere. V. Skeat's Etym. Dict.

WONDING, WONDLE, WONNLE, *adj*. Winding, wrapping, infolding; as, a *wonding*-sheet, a winding-sheet for the dead; also called a *wondle* or *wonnle* sheet; West of S.

"Item, for ane *wonding* scheit and kist [i.e., a coffin] at the prouoist command to ane lipperman, xlviij s." Accts. Burgh of Glasgow, 1624-5, Rec. Soc.

WONE, *s*. Prob. a poet. form of *wonde*,

wending, journey, march, travels; *in wone,* during the journey or march. V. WONDE, *v.*
    And all thair vittalis war gone,
    That thay weildit in *wone ;*
    Itesset couth thai find none,
    That suld thair bute bene.
            Gol. and Gaw., l. 37.

WONK, *pret.* Winked, Lancelot of the Laik, l. 1057, ed. Skeat.

WONNELS, *s.* A form of WINNLES, q. v.

WONT, WOND, *pret.* Weened, thought, imagined.
    First quhen I did persew,
    I *wont* ye had bene wyss ;
    But now fair weill, adew,
    I fynd yow ay so nyss.
       Alex. Scott's Poems, p. 64, ed. 1882.
A.-S. *wénan,* to ween, imagine ; from A.-S. *wén,* expectation ; Dutch, *waan,* Icel. *ván,* Goth. *wens.*

WOOK, *pret.* Watched. V. WOUK.

WOONE, WONE, *adj.* Woollen. V. WOUN.

WOORSOME, *s.* V. WOURSUM.

To WORP, *v. a.* To warp, to prepare the foundation of a web for the loom ; part. pr. *worping,* used also as a *s.*; Burgh Recs. Stirling, 1662, p. 240. V. *Warp.*

WORP, *s.* Warp of a web.
A.-S. *weorpan, werpan,* to cast ; Goth. *wairpan,* Icel. *varpa.*

WORRIE-BALDIE, BALDIE WORRIE, *s.* A ludicrous name for an artichoke ; quasi, worry (choke), Archie (Baldie) ; Gall.

WORT, WIRT, *s.* Snout, trunk.
"That nay swyne be haldin within this toun vtteuche band or ane ring in thair *wort.*" Burgh Recs. Aberd., i. 436, Sp. C.

To WORT, WORTH, WIRT, *v. a.* To turn up the earth with the snout, as a pig does ; part. pr. *worting, wortin, worttyne.* Addit. to WORT, q. v.
". . . for the wrangwis *worttyne* of thar swyne and wnryngyt." Burgh Recs. Prestwick, 1510, p. 42, Mait. C.
A.-S. *wrót,* a snout ; from which is formed *wrótan,* to turn up with the snout, to root.

To WORTH, WORTHE, WOURTH, *v. n.* To be, to happen ; Gol. and Gaw., l. 1096 ; *worthes, worthis,* is, becomes, will or shall be ; Ibid., l. 332, 833. Addit. to WORTH, q. v.

WORTHELETH. V. DICT.
As suggested by the editor, this term is an errat. for *worthelich.* It was so misprinted in Pinkerton's version. The Bann. MS. reads *worthelich ;* and the Asloan MS. *wortheliche.*

WOSP, WOSPE, *s.* A wisp. V. *Wisp, s.*

WOT, WOTE, *v. pres.* I know: "wele I *wote*;" Kingis Quair, st. 47. V. WAT, WAIT.

WOUD, WOOD, *adj.* Forms of WOD, q. v.

WOUGH, *adj.* Ill, wrong, false ; Sir Tristrem, l. 1730, S.T.S. V. WOUGH, *s.*

WOUIN, WOVIN, *adj.* Woollen. V. WOUN.

WOUND. V. DICT.
Delete this entry in DICT. As the editor suggested, the term is an error for *woundir* or *wonder* used as an *adv.* It was misprinted *wound* in the ed. of 1508, and Jamieson accepted it as a genuine word.

WOURDIS. A form of *worthis,* becomes, will become ; Gol. and Gaw., l. 822. V. WORD, WORDIS, *v.*

To WOW, *v. a.* To vow, swear, take or give oath upon ; E. vow. Also used for *avow,* confess, own, grant.
". . . allegand the samyn to be hir awin . . . and *wowis* the possessioun thairof." Burgh Rec. Glasg., 11 March, 1577-8.

WOWBAT, *s.* A feeble, decayed person ; Alex. Scott's Poems, p. 88, ed. 1882. V. WOBAT, WOUBIT.

WOYELEY, *adv.* V. DICT.
Del. this entry in DICT. The term is a misprint for *wathely* in Pinkerton's version of Gaw. and Sir Gal.

WRAK, WRAKE, *s.* V. Vengeance. V. WRAIK.

To WRASTLE, WRASSEL, *v. a.* and *n.* To Wrestle. V. WARSELL.
"*Luctor,* to *wrastle* ; Duncan, App. Etym. 1505, ed. Small, E.D.S.
This form is common in M. E.; and is found in Gower and Chaucer. The latter, in his description of the miller in Cant. Tales, says,—
    "At *wrastling* he wold bere away the ram."
A.-S. *wræstlian,* to wrestle ; a freq. of *wræstan,* to wrest, twist about.

To WRAY, WRAIE, WREY, WRIE, *v. a.* To accuse, slander ; Sir Tristrem, l. 2126, 2179, S.T.S.
    Thou seyst y gan the *wrie,*
    Men sets thou bi me lay,
    Ac thei ich wende to dye,
    Thine erand y schal say.
            Ibid., l. 2146, S.T.S.

WRAIER, *s.* Accuser, slanderer ; Ibid., 3288, S.T.S.
A.-S. *wréyan,* to accuse. Cf. Icel. *rœgja* (for *vrœgja*), to slander. From this source we have E. *bewray,* M. E. *bewraien, biwreyen.* V. Skeat's Etym. Dict., s. v.

WRAIGHLY, *adv.* Evilly, slanderously ; Gol. and Gaw, st. 13 : prob. a form of *wraietly.* Errat. in DICT.

WRAIGLANE, *adj.* Wriggling: "wan *wraiglane* waep"; Dunbar and Kennedy, l, 195.

WRAN, VRAN, *s.* The wren; "The cutty *wran*," the little wren : *vran*, Compl. Scot., p. 39, E.E.T.S.: and frequently called *wrannie*.

WRANGUS, VRANGUS, *adj.* Wrongful; Compl. Scot., p. 80, E.E.T.S. V. WRANGWIS.

To WREATH, WREETH, WRETH, *v. a.* and *n.* To twist, swirl, eddy, wreath; Watty and Meg, st. 1. V. *Writh.*

WREATH, WREETH, WRETH, *s.* A wreath, drift, as of snow or sand.
  Ae night the storm the steeples rocked
  Poor labour sweet in sleep was locked,
  While burns wi snawy *wreeths* upchoked
    Wild eddying swirl,
  Or thro' the mining outlet bocked,
    Down headlong hurl.
      Burns, A Winter Night, st. 2.

WRETHING, WRAITHIN, *part.* and *s.* Twisting, twining, as in "*wrethin*' strae-rapes:" swirling, eddying, wreathing; as "The snaw was *wraithin* in the glen." Also, turning, varying, variation, change, as in "*wrething* lesse or more." V. *Writh.*
  And how so be [it], that sum clerkis trete
  That all your chancē causit Is tofore
  Heigh In the hevin, by quhois effectis grete
  Ye movit are to *wrething* lesse or more.
      Kingis Quair, st. 146, ed. Skeat.

WRECHIT, *adj.* Wretched; Kingis Quair, st. 167. V. WRETCH.
  A.-S. *wrecca*, an outcast, an exile: from *wrecan*, to drive, urge, hence to exile. M. E. *wrecche*.

To WREST, *v. a.* To twist, rack, wrench; hence, to torture: part. pt. *wrest*. Addit. to WREIST, q. v.
  And all myn auenture
  I gan oure-hayle, that langer slepe ne rest
  Ne myght I nat, so were my wittis *wrest*.
      Kingis Quair, st. 10, ed. Skeat.
  A.-S. *wræstan*, to twist forcibly, wrench.

WREUCH, *adj.* Sorrowful, sorely grieved, wretched.
  Robene murnit, and Makyne leuche ;
  Scho sang, he sichit sair :
  And so left him bayth wo and *wreuch*,
    In dolour and in cair,
  Kepand his hird under a huche,
    Amangis the holtis hair.
      Henryson, Robene and Makyne, l. 125.
"Wretchedness," which is Sibbald's defin. of *Reuch*, adopted by Jamieson, is not correct: the word is an adj. It seems to be the Icel. *hryggr*, afflicted, grieved, distressed; corresponding to the A.-S. *hreowig*, and E. *rueful*. V. VIGFUSSON.

To WREY, WRIE, *v. a.* To slander. V. *Wray.*

To WRING, *v. a.* To wring the hands, lament; Kingis Quair, st. 57.

To WRITH, WRYTH, WRETH, WREETH, WREATH, *v. a.* 1. To turn, twist, sway; hence to govern, control, direct; Kingis Quair, st. 107. Also, to turn aside, withdraw, remove, unfold.
  Or I sall, with my fader old Saturne,
  And with all hale oure hevinly alliance,
  Our glad aspectis from thame *writh* and turne.
      Ibid., st. 122, ed. Skeat.

2. To twist, pluck up, thrust or drive out.
  The Lady was wow'd, but scho said nay
    With men that wald hir wed ;
  Sa suld we *wryth* all syn away,
    That in our breist is bred.
      Henryson, The Bludy Serk, l. 107.

3. To swirl, eddy, drift, wreath, like snow or sand : hence, to overlay, bank or block up.
  Keen the frosty winds were blawing,
  Deep the snaw had *wreath*'d the ploughs.
      Alex. Wilson, Watty and Meg, st. 1.
A.-S. *writhan*, to twist about ; Icel. *rítha*, Dan. *vride*, Swed. *vrida*, to wring, twist, turn.

WROKKIN, *part. pt.* Avenged, Henryson, Wolf and Lamb, l. 45. V. WROKEN.

To WRY, WREYE, *v. a.* V. DICT.
  Delete the quotation from Kingis Quair and the accompanying note under the entry in DICT. *To-wrye* is there a compound verb with the prefix *to-*; cf. "*distorqueo, ic tó-writhe*," Ælfric's Glossary, ed. Zupitza, p. 153. See note in Gloss. to Kingis Quair, ed. Skeat.

WRY, WRYE, *adj.* Twisted, turned aside: hence crooked, uneven. *On wry,* awry ; Barbour, iv. 705, Camb. MS., Kingis Quair, st. 73.

To WRYTH, *v. a.* To twist. V. *Writh.*

WSCHA, WSSAY, *s.* Issue, completion, close. V. *Ushie,* ISCHE.
  "That day was the *wssay* of the chamerlan ayr."
    Burgh Recs. Peebles, 1437, p. 124.
  The term here implies the making up of the records, accounts, and claims of the court.

WTINLAND, *s.* Pasture land. V. *Utinland.*

WUD, WID, *pret.* Would. V. WAD.

WUDDLE, *v.* and *s.* V. WIDDLE.

WUGH, *s.* Woe. V. WOUCH, WOUGH.

WUMBLE, WOMBLE, WOMMEL, *s.* A wimble, auger. V. WUMMIL.

WUN, WYNE, *part. pt.* Kept under control, subdued. V. WON, *v. n.,* WIN, *v. n.*
  Fra raige of yowth the ryuk hes rune,
  And ressone tane the man to tune,
  The brukle body than is *wyne*,
  And maid ane veschell new.
      Alex. Scott's Poems, p. 77, ed. 1882.

WUST, *pret.* Wist, knew. V. WOST.

WY, WYE, WYGH, WYGHE, WAY, *s.* Man, soldier, knight; pl. *wyes, wyis, wyghes.* Occurs freq. in Gawain Romances, and applied to God in Green Knight, l. 2441. The pl. form *wayis* occurs in Houlate, st. 39, Bann. MS. A.-S. *wiga*, a warrior.

WYANDOUR, *s.* V. DICT.

Regarding Macpherson's note under this word in his Gloss. to Wyntown, it may be remarked that, while the 1501 ed. of Chaucer has *viended*, supplied with meat, the MSS. have *envyned*, i.e., furnished with wine.

To WYCIE, *v. a.* To vitiate; Houlate, st. 71. V. *Vicie.*

WYDQUHARE, *adv.* V. *Wide-Whare.*

WYG, WYGG, WYGGE, *s.* A kind of bread. V. WIG.

WYLD AVENTOURIS, WYLD AUNTOURIS, *s. pl.* V. *Aventour.*

To WYLE, WILE, *v. a.* To select. V. WILE, WALE.

WYLECOT, WYLYCOAT, *s.* V. WILIE-COAT.

WYN, *s.* Pleasure, delight. V. WIN.

WYNLY, *adv.* Pleasantly. V. *Winly.*

To WYN, WYNE, *v. n.* To dwell, abide. V. WON.

WYND, *s.* V. DICT.

Delete the entry in DICT.: *wynd* simply means wind. Jamieson was misled by a mistake in the version from which he quoted. In the second line of the quotation Pinkerton printed *and* for *ad*, which in the ed. of 1508 was a misprint for *as*. The line originally ran thus:—
Wod-wraith as the wynd, his handis can wring.
Gol. and Gaw., l. 770.

WYNDES, WYNDLES, *s. pl.* Winch, windlass, block and tackle; Burgh Recs. Aberdeen, II. 321, 335; *wyndles*, II. 342, Sp. C.; Burgh Recs. Edinburgh, I. 99, Rec. Soc. Addit. to WINDIS, q. v.

WYNING, VYNING, *s.* Gain, profit, interest. V. *Winning.*

WYSSIL, *s.* Exchange. V. *Wissle.*

To WYT, *v. a.* V. DICT.

Delete this entry in DICT. *Wyt*, in the passage quoted, is an error for *wyth*, with, in the sense of against. MS. has *wy*^t. The same error occurs in vii. 621 of the same work. See Skeat's ed. of Barbour, p. 175, footnote.

To WYTE, *v. n.* To escape, go, depart, vanish.

For alle the welthe of this warlde thus awaye *wytis.*
Awnt. Arthure, st. 17.

Lat. *vitare*, to shun, avoid, escape.

Y.

Y, *pron.* I; Sir Tristrem, l. 764, 811.

Y-, *prefix.* The same as I-, q. v. Words of modern Eng. form with this prefix have not been included in the following lists, except when some peculiarity of meaning or use is attached to them.

YADE, YAID, YAUD, YAWD, YAWDE, *s.* Common pron. of *jade*, when used as a familiar or contemptuous name for a female-servant, or a female of slovenly habit or vicious nature: "*freris yawde*," used in last sense in Burgh Recs. Stirling, 1545, p. 41. Addit. to YAD, q. v. Icel. *jalda*, a mare.

YAD-SKYVAR, *s.* Del. the entry under this heading in DICT., and take the following.

YADSWYVAR, *s.* A vulgar name for the man who leads about a stallion during the covering season: used also as a contemptuous term for a lazy, mean fellow; Dunbar and Kennedy, l. 246.

A comp. of *yad* and *swive*, which Allan Ramsay misprinted *yadskyvar* in his Evergreen, from which it passed into the DICT.

YAF, *pret.* Gave; Sir Tristrem, l. 226, 265, S.T.S.

YAID, YADE, *pret.* 1. Went; Lyndsay, Papyngo, l. 560. Mod. Sc. *gaed.* V. YEDE, *Yeid.*

2. Used as an *adj.*, meaning spent, worn-out, wasted, done, as in "ane auld *yaid* aver," i.e. an old worn-out horse; Dunbar, Petition of the Gray Horse, l. 25.

YAILL, *s.* A gable; Burgh Recs. Stirling, 1597, p. 86. V. *Gal, Gayl.*

This may be a misreading of *gaill*, or a local pron. of it. *Gable* is the O. Fr. *gable*, from L. Lat. *gabulum*,

(Sup.) M 2

which came from H. M. Ger. *gabele*, a fork, *gebel*, a gable.

YAIP, YAIPE, *adj.* Eager, keen; Houlate, l. 602. V. YAPE.
Before the etym. given in DICT. under YAPE set the following:—A.-S. *gedp*, wide, spacious.

YAIR, *adj.* Ready. V. YARE.

To YAIRN, YARN, YARNE, *v. a.* To yearn. V. YARNE, *adj.*, *Yearn*, *v.*

YALOW, YALLOW, *adj.* Yellow; Kingis Quair, st. 95, ed. Skeat, S.T.S.; Douglas, III. 82, 13, Small.

YALT, *pret.* Yielded; Sir Tristrem, l. 261, S. T. S. V. YALD, *Yelde*.

YANE, YEN, *adj.* One.

YANCE, YENCE, *adv.* Once.

YANESELL, YANSELL, YENSEL, *s.* One's self.
These forms represent the pron. still common in the West and South of Scot., and in the North of England.

YARD, YAIRD, *s.* A yard, court-yard, enclosure; the uncovered grounds of a public work, as a tan-*yard*, boat-*yard*, wood-*yard*. Addit. to YARD, q. v.
" Item, for drawyng of the lang treis fra the bate to the *yard*, - - viijd."
" Item, giffyne for sorten of the tymmyr in the *yard*, . . iijs. iijd." Accts. L. H. Treas., i., 248, Dickson.

YARD-FOOT, YAIRD-FUT, *s.* The lower end of a garden : the opposite end was called the *yaird*-*heid*.
"It is statut and ordanit . . . to clois vp thair *yaird futtis* within the closis." Burgh Recs. Peebles, 1572, p. 343, Rec. Soc.

YARE, YAR, *adv.* Yore; *yare syne*, long since, long ago.
A.-S. *gedra*, yore, formerly. *Yare* being simply the Northern form of *yore*.

To YARK, YERK, *v. a.* To wrench or twist forcibly, to jerk; "He *yarkit* it out o' my han'." Addit. to YARK, YERK, q. v.

YARKING-FAT, YERKING-FAT, *s.* The vat or vessel in which malt was *yarked* or fermented in former days. V. YERK, *v.*
". . . a masking fat, a wort stane, a saa, a *yarking fat*." Reg. Mag. Sig,, 1424-1513, No. 812. Rec. Ser.

YARM, *s.* The loud, wild cry of a cat; Orcadian Sketch Book. V. YIRM.

To YARM, *v. n.* To howl, yell, cry like a wild beast; part. pr. *yarmand*, howling. V. YIRM.
M. E. *yarmen*, to howl, cry; Stratmann. Cf. Icel. *jarma*, a bleating.

Yirm, as its meaning indicates, is a weakened form of *yarm*: see under YIRM in DICT.

YARNUT, *s.* An earth-nut. V. ARNUT.

YATE, *s.* Gate. V. YET.

YATE-CHEEK, YATE-STOOP, *s.* The post or side of a gate. V. YET-CHEEK.

YAUE, YAF, *pret.* Gave, bestowed ; Sir Tristrem, l. 502, 226, S.T.S.

YAUK, *v.* and *s.* Ache. V. YAIK.

YAUKING, YAUKIN,*part.*, *adj.*, and *s.* Aching: as " *Yaukin* banes are sair to bide;" West of S.
Yeuken is sometimes used in this sense, but probably through carelessness. Burns, however, so used it when he wrote, "If Warren Hastings' neck was *yeukin*;" for he certainly implied *aching* or *quaking* with fear, afraid of his neck. V. under *Youk*, *Yeuk*.

YAULD, *adj.* Sprightly, strong. V. YALD.

YAUMER, YAWMER, *v.* and *s.* V. YAMER.

YAWD, YAWDE, *s.* V. YAD, *Yade*.

YBAIK, *part. pt.* Baked, seasoned; Douglas, Virgil, IV. 52, 13, Small.

YBE, *part. pt.* Been ; Douglas, Virgil, IV. 11, 21, Small.

YBERYIT, *part. pt.* Buried; Douglas, Virgil, II. 84, 2, Small.

YBETE, *v. n.* To beat, fall heavily ; Kingis Quair, st. 116, ed. Skeat, S.T.S.

YBRINT, *part. pt.* Burnt; Douglas, II. 181, 7, Small.

YCACHT, YCAGHT, YCAHT, *part. pt.* Caught. V. *Cacht*.

YCALLIT, *part. pt.* Called ; Kingis Quair, st. 170, ed. Skeat, S.T.S.

YCLEPED, YCLEPIT, *part. pt.* Called ; Sir Tristrem, l. 1674, S.T.S.; Douglas, II. 123, 13, Small.

YCONOMUS, YCONIMOUSE, *s.* V. ICONOMUS.

YCONQUEST, *part. pt.* Conquered ; Douglas, Virgil, iv., 15, 14, Small.

YDANTLY, YDENLY, *adv.* Industriously, continuously ; Leslie, Hist. Scot., p. 111, S. T. S. V. YDANT.

YDEOTRYE, YDIOTRY, *s.* Idiocy, state of idiocy ; Accts. L. H. Treas., I. 238, 239, Dickson ; Orig. Paroch., II. pt. 2, 662.
The *Brief of Ydiotry* mentioned in the Treasurer's Accounts was "a writ directed from Chancery to a sheriff, or other judge competent, to ascertain by the

verdict of an assize the state of mind of an individual alleged to be incompetent to manage his own affairs; and also who was his nearest agnate or relative on the father's side, of proper age (twenty-five years), and capable of having the charge devolved upon him."

YDRED, *part pt.* Dreaded; Douglas, Virgil, iv. 106, 7, Small.

YEALINGS, YEALINS, YEELINS, *s. pl.* Coevals. V. YEILDINS, EILDINS.
Most prob. a der. from *eild*, age; but also said to be a corr. of *yearling*.

To YEALP, YALP, *v. n.* To yelp as a dog.
"*Gannio*, to *yealp* like a dogge;" Duncan, App. Etym., 1595, ed. Small, E.D.S.

YEAR, *s.* Year, years; used for the plural as well as the singular: as, "He was a prentice for five *year*." To *yeir*, this year, now, at present; Douglas, II. 198, 12, Small.
The word is so used in the N. of England also; see Brockett's Gloss.

To YEARN, YAIRN, YARNE, YARN, *v. a.* and *n.* To desire, long for, crave, claim; Lyndsay, Thrie Estaitis, l. 941, Complaynt, l. 50: also, to sue for or strive for secretly; Dunbar, We Lordis hes Chosin, l. 26.
Quhen kirkmen *yairnis* na dignitie,
Nor wyffis no soveranitie;
Wynter but frost, snaw, wynd, or rane,
Than sall I geve thy gold agane.
Lyndsay, Compl. l. 471.
A.-S. *gyrnan*, to yearn; from *georn*, desirous; Icel. *girna*, to desire, from *gjarn*, eager.

YEID, YED, *pret.* Went; Gol. and Gawane, l. 228; Compl. Scot., p. 159, E.E.T.S; *yed*, Accts. L. H. Treas., i. 249; Mod. S. *gaede*, *gaed*. V. YEDE.

YEILD, YEIL, *adj.* Bare, bald. Addit. to YELD, YEALD, q. v.
"*Glaber*, *-bra*, *-brum;* bald, *yeild*, depilis;" Duncan, App. Etym., 1595, ed. Small, E. D. S.

To YELDE, YEILD, *v. a.* To yield, give up; Sir Tristrem, l. 936, 2317; pret. *yeld*, *yalt*, *yold*, *yolde*, Ibid., l. 3248, 261, 307, 1987, S. T. S.; *yeild*, yielded, gave way, belched out, Lyndsay, Thrie Estaitis, l. 4364: part. pt. *yoldin*, yielded, rendered; Gol. and Gawane, l. 1126; Douglas, I. 97, 18, Small.

YEMAN, YOMAN, YYMAN, *s.* An official next in rank to a gentleman of the household; Accts. L. H. Treas., I. 55, 268. Addit. to YEMAN, q. v.
"Item, gevin to Vchiltree, *yeman* of the Kingis stable, passando to Dore for a hors to the King, . . xxs."
"Item, gevin to Desert, *yeman* of the Qwenis stable, passando certane chargis to Dunkeldin, . . vj s."
Ibid., p. 50.

In the royal household there were two grades of officers below the *yemen* or *yomen:* first the groom, and below him the page.

YER, YOR, *poss. adj.* Your: "*yer* ain father," i.e., your own father.

YERSELL, YER-AIN-SELL, *s.* Yourself.

YERB, YARB, *s.* An herb. Addit. to YIRB, q. v.

YERD, YERDE, *s.* A rod or staff, a wand, as, 'the king's *yerd*,' the king's wand, i.e., the sceptre.
A.-S. *gyrd, gierd*, a rod, twig; Du. *garde*.

To YERE, YERRE, *v. n.* To yell, scream; forms of YIRR, q. v.
Prob. an intens. form of *yirre*, to snarl or growl like a dog. A.-S. *georran, gyrran*, to creak: cf. Lat. *garrire*.

YERKING-FAT, *s.* V. *Yarking-fat*.

YERN, YERNE, *adv.* Quickly; Sir Tristrem, l. 3065, S. T. S. V. YARNE.

YE'S, YE'SE, YEIS, *s.* A contr. form of *ye sal*, which was the Old Northern form of *ye shall*. The 's should, more correctly be written *s*'. V. under S, 'S.
Come lend to me some sarkin,
Wi' a' the haste ye dow,
And ye'se be weel pay'd back again,
When ance I spin my tow.
Song, The Weary Pund o' Tow, O. V.
I gang this gait with richt gude will;
Sir Wantonness, tarie ye still.
And Hamelines the cap *yeis* fill,
And beir him cumpanie.
Lyndsay, Thrie Estaitis, l. 537.

To YET, YETT, *v. n.* To shed; "*yettand* teris;" Douglas, II. 140, 8, Small: to gush, rush, dash; as, "the spate *yet* owre the linn." Addit. to YET, q. v.

YETLING, *s.* Applied to various articles made of cast-iron; pl. *yetlingis*, cast-iron guns; Burgh Recs. Edinburgh, IV. 51, Rec. Soc. Addit. to YETLAND, YETLIN, q. v.

YETERIE, YETRIE, *adj.* Same as Eterie, Etrie, q. v. Also, severe, excessive, tormenting; as, "a *yetrie* yisking," a severe or tormenting hiccup; also applied to a severe, troublesome spit accompanying a cough.
The expression *yetire yoskingis*, excessive or deep sobs, occurs in Allit. Rom. Alex., l. 5044, ed. Skeat.

YETIN, YETEN, *s.* A giant: forms of Etin, q. v. Icel. *jötunn*.

To YEUE, *v. a.* To give; Sir Tristrem, l. 2921: pret. *yaue, yaf;* Ibid., l. 502, 226: imper. *yeueth, yif;* Ibid., l. 2265, 1650, S. T. S.

YEW, s. A ewe. V. Yow.

YFALLE, part. pt. Fallen; Sir Tristrem, l. 1937, S. T. S.

YFEDDE, part. pt. Fed, well fed; Sir Tristrem, l. 448, S. T. S.

YFOLD, pret. Felled, smote.

Beliagog the bold,
As alende he faught;
Tristrem hif neighe he sold,
As tomas hath ous taught;
Tristrem smot, as god wold,
His foot of at adraught;
Adoun he fel *yfold*,
That man of michel maught.
Sir Tristrem, l. 2790, S. T. S.

Fel here means many : a form of Fele, q. v.

YGADRED, part. pt. Gathered; Sir Tristrem, l. 2369, S. T. S.

YHIGHT, part. pt. Promised; Sir Tristrem, l. 1966, S.T.S.

YHOLD, part. pt. Held; Sir Tristrem, l. 949, S.T.S.

YIF, YIUE, conj. If; Sir Tristrem, l. 275, 725, S.T.S. V. GIF.

YIF, YIFSTOW, v. V. *Yiue, v.*

YIFT, s. Gift; Sir Tristrem, l. 627: pl. *yiftes*, l. 502, S.T.S.

YINGLING, s. A young person, youth, maiden; Douglas, III. 343, 25, Small. V. YING.

To YIRN, YIRNN, v. a. and n. V. YEARN.

YIS, adv. Yes; Sir Tristrem, l. 436, S.T.S.

YIT, adv. Yet, still; Kingis Quair, st. 63, ed. Skeat, S.T.S.

YIUE, conj. If. V. *Yif.*

To YIUE, YIF, v. a. To give; Sir Tristrem, l. 606, 1830; *yifstow*, givest thou, Ibid., l. 1851; imper. *yif*, give, Ibid., l. 1650, 1925, S.T.S.

YLACHT, YLAGHT, YLAHT, part. pt. Caught, taken, captured. V. *Lacht.*

YLE, s. An island; "the braid *Yle* of Bretane," Lyndsay, The Dreme, l. 791.

O. Fr. *isle*, later *ile*, an island : from Lat. *insula*, an island.

YLERD, part. pt. Taught, informed; Sir Tristrem, l. 3036, S.T.S.

YLIKE, adv. Alike; Kingis Quair, st. 70, ed. Skeat, S.T.S.

To YLL, v. n. and a. To become ill, sicken; to make ill, harm, injure, damage; pret.

yllit; Burgh Recs. Prestwick, 1528, p. 52, Mait. C. V. ILL.

To YMAGYN, v. a. To imagine; pret. and part. pt., *ymagynit*; Kingis Quair, st. 13, ed. Skeat, S.T.S.

YOID, pret. Went; a form of YODE, q. v.

YOK, YOIK, s. Yoke, bondage, service; "in lnfis *yok*," Kingis Quair, st. 193, ed. Skeat, S. T. S.; Compl. Scot., p. 101, E. E. T. S.; *yoilk*, Ibid., p. 31. Addit. to YOK, q. v.

The *lk* in *yoilk* is an example of *kk* in the old contracted form of writing. Indeed, the word ought to be printed *yoikk*. See under *Rolk.*

YOKING, YOKIN, s. A day's work of a carter or farm-servant; Whistle Binkie, I. 131. Addit. to YOKING, q. v.

YOLD, YOLDIN. V. under *Yelde.*

YON, YONE, adj. Yon, that; Kingis Quair, st. 88; those, as, "Bring *yon* books;" and so in Kingis Quair, st. 83, ed. Skeat, S. T. S.

YOND, YONT, adj. Opposite, farther, farther off: as, "Take the *yond* or *yont* side o' the hill." Comparative, *yonder, yondir*; Burgh Recs. Prestwick, p. 8, Mait. C. V. YOUND.

YOND, YONT, adv. Yonder; Kingis Quair, st. 57, ed. Skeat; Sir Tristrem, l. 355, 468, S. T. S.; also, farther on, farther over, from one place to another : as, "Gang *yont* to the next farm;" "Lie *yont*;" "Hirsel *yont*;" "Bring't wi' ye when ye come *yont*." V. under YOUND.

YOND, prep. Beyond, past. V. YONT.

YONMEST, adj. Farthest off; Burgh Recs. Glasgow, I. 286; superl. of *yon*.

YONG, adj. Young; Kingis Quair, st. 7, ed. Skeat. V. YING.

YONGKER, YONGKEYR, YOUNGKER, YONKER, s. A stripling, young person; Douglas Virgil, 23, 5, Rudd., II. 40, 3, Small.

This is properly not an English word, but borrowed from Dutch. Cf. Du. *jonker*, also written *jonkheer* (= *jong heer*, young sir).

YONGLING, YONGLYNG, YOUNGLING, s. Young person; young man, youth; Sir Tristrem, l. 859, S. T. S.: young woman : Douglas, IV., 52, 22, Small. Also used as an *adj.*, as in "the *youngling* cottagers;" Burns, Cot. Sat. Night.

YONG FROW, s. A block without a sheave, forming part of the rigging connected with

the round top in a ship; pl. *yong frowis*, Dutch *jonkvrouw*.
"Item, gevin to Johne Lam for boltis, chenyeis, *yong frowis*, and collaris, seme and rufe to the bote, . . . iij. li. xiiij. s." Accts. L. H. Treas., i. 254, Dickson.

YOPINDALE, YOPINDAIL, YOWPINDALL, *s.* A popular name for the Joachim thaler, a silver coin of the sixteenth century, which varied in value from fifteen to twenty shillings Scots; Balfour, Oppr. in Orkn. and Shetl., pp. 37-48. Errat. in DICT.
Jamieson's rendering of this term is a mistake, for which it is impossible to account. The passages quoted by him certainly indicate that the *yopindail* was a coin in common use : see quotations in DICT. It is frequently mentioned in documents of the sixteenth century, and appears to have been much in use in the northern counties of Scotland, and in Orkney and Shetland. In the last named district it was rated at fifteen shillings Scots in 1541 ; but it was afterwards raised by Earl Robert to the value of twenty shillings Scots ; and at this rate we find it current in 1572: see Gloss. Balfour's Odall Rights. Although perhaps best known as the Austrian dollar, it really was a Joachim thaler, as it was minted at Joachimsthal, a free mining town of Bohemia, in the Erzgebirge, in 1518. V. Proc. Soc. Antiq. Scot., 1883-4, p. 285.
The name is evidently a corr. of *Yokimdale*, i.e., *Joachim-dale*.

YORE, YOIR, *adj.* Ready. V. YARE.

YORE, *adv.* Readily; Sir Tristrem, l. 2182, S. T. S.

YOUDITH, *s.* V. DICT.
The M. Eng. form was *youthe* : but there were older forms, *yuvethe*, and *yuyethe*, from which *youdith* was obtained by the insertion of *d*.

To YOUK, YEUK, YUKE, YUCK, *v. n.* To have an uneasy feeling, to have a feeling of fear, dread, or eager desire ; hence, to be stirred, moved, or influenced by feeling or circumstance. Addit. to YOUK, q. v.
The meanings of YOUK are similar to those of E. *itch* : and sometimes it is used in the sense of *yauk*, *yaik*, to ache, as when Burns wrote, "If Warren Hastings' neck was *yeukin*," i.e., if he wore afraid of his neck, or had an apprehension that he might be executed. And indeed "*the neck yeuking*" is invariably used in the sense of *dreading the gallows*—not longing for it, as Jamieson explained the phrase ; see under YOUK. No doubt *yeuking* generally implies liking, longing, desire for, and is used as a sign of satisfaction, pleasure, delight ; but the context always makes clear which of the meanings is intended, as in the passage—
And aft as chance he comes thee nigh,
Thy auld —— elbow *yeuks* with joy,
which Burns wrote to express the delight of Satan at the prospect of another capture. V. Poem on Life.

YOURE ALLERIS. Of you all : "*youre alleris frend* ;" Kingis Quair, st. 113, ed. Skeat. S. T. S.
In his note on this expression Prof. Skeat says :—

"*Aller* is for A.-S. *ealra*, gen. pl. of *eal*, all. Hence *alleris* is formed by the needless addition of the pl. suffix *is*. . . . Your was originally the gen. pl. of the personal pronoun." Ibid., p. 81.

To YOW, *v. n.* Errat. in DICT. for *Yowl.*
V. YOUL, *Yowl.*
In the quotation the word is printed *yowl*, and as both text and context support the reading, it must therefore be retained. *Yowl*, or *youl*, is the M. Eng. *goulen*, to howl, caterwaul.

YOWILL, YOWELL, *s.* V. YULE.

YOWISWORTH, YOWSWORTH, A proportion of odal-land equal to one-tenth of a pennyland ; Gloss. Balfour's Odall Rights and Feudal Wrongs.

YOWL, *v.* and *s.* Howl, caterwaul; Galt, Ann. of the Par., ch. xlv. Addit. to YOUL, q. v.
Allied to *gowl*, *goul*, M. Eng. *goulen*, from O. Icel. *gaula*, to gowl, howl, bellow.

YOWLLIS YALD, *s.* V. under *Yule*, *s.*

YPLET, *part. pt.* Plaited, folded ; Douglas, IV., 99, 20, Small.

YPOCRAS, *s.* A drink composed of white or red wine and spices ; spiced wine.
I kneillit law and vuheillit my held,
And tho I saw our ladyis twa and twa,
Sittand on deissis, familiars to and fra
Seruand thame fast with *ypocras* and meid,
Delicait meitis, daintcis seir alswa.
Douglas, *Palice of Honour*, i. 45, 15, Small.
Ypocras, Mod. Eng. *Hippocras.* "A cordial made of Lisbon and Canary wines, bruised spices, and sugar ; so named from the strainer through which it is passed, called by apothecaries *Hippocrates sleeve*. Hippocrates in the middle ages was called *Ypocras* or *Hippocras.*" Brewer, Dict. Phrase and Fable.

YPOTHEGAR, *s.* An apothecary ; Burgh Recs. Edin., 2 Jan., 1509-10, Rec. Soc.

YREN, YRN, YRNE, *s.* Iron ; Sir Tristrem, l. 2229, 2236, S.T.S. ; Compl. Scot., p. 10, 28, E.E.T.S.

YSCHAPPIT, *part. pt.* Shaped.
The vmbrate treis that Tytan about wappit,
War portrait and on the cirth *yschappit*
Be goldin bemis viuificative.
Douglas, *Palice of Honour*, prol. p. 2, 21, Small.

YSCHROWD, *part. pt.* Shrouded, dressed, decked ; Douglas, IV., 69, 24, ed. Small.

YSE, Y-SE, *v. a.* See, behold ; Sir Tristrem, l. 1337, S.T.S. ; pret. *yseighe*, saw, Ibid., l. 2062 ; *part. pt. ysene*, Ibid., l. 1052.
Marke seyil :—" Wayleway
That ich it schuld *y sene*
Swiche thing !"
Ibid., l. 1141, S.T.S.
Schuld y sene has here the force of *should have seen*, which is commonly pron. *shuld 'a seen.*

YSEL, YSIL, ISEL, ISIL, s. A hot ember or cinder, a fire-spark, a spark. V. AIZLE, EIZEL.
A.-S. *ysel, ysele*, a fire spark, spark.

YSLAWE, *part. pt.* Slain; Sir Tristrem, l. 3335, S.T.S.

YSONDER, YSOWNDIR, *adv.* Asunder; Douglas, ii. 29, 19, Small.

YSOPE, *s.* Hyssop; Compl. Scot., p. 67. E.E.T.S.

YSOWPIT, *part. pt.* Steeped, soaked, moistened; Douglas, Virgil, III. 75, 13, Small. V. SOWP.

YSPRAD, *part. pt.* Spread over, stocked; Sir Tristrem, l. 442, S.T.S.

YSTEKE, *part. pt.* Stuck, stabbed, pierced,
Mine hert bye hath *ysteke*,
Brengwain bright and fre,
That frende ;
Blithe no may ich be,
Til y se that hende.
Sir Tristrem. l. 2999, S.T.S.

YSTOND, *part. pt.* Stood; Sir Tristrem, l. 973, S.T.S.

YTHES, ITHES, *s. pl.* Waves, waters, the sea; Allit. Rom. Alexander, l. 1039, 63.

YTHRUNGIN, *part. pt.* Pushed together, thrust: "vp *ythrungin*," thrust upwards; Kingis Quair, st. 165, ed. Skeat, S.T.S. V. YTHRANGIN.

YTINT, YTENT, *part. pt.* Lost'; Sir Tristrem, l. 3321 : *ytent*, l. 1911. V. TINE, *v.*

YUCK, YUK, *v.* and *s.* Itch. V. YOUK.

YUCKY, YUIKY, *adj.* Itchy, itching. V. YOUKY.

YUDE, YHUDE, *pret.* Went; Gol. and Gawane, l. 304, 577. V. YEDE.

YULE, YUIL, YOWL, *s.* Short for Yule gift, Yule reward, Yule livery, &c. Addit. to YULE, q. v.

The term is frequently so used in Burgh and Household Accts. It was a general custom to give presents, rewards, liveries, &c., to officers, servants, and dependants at the season of Yule or Christmas; and whatever the party received was called his or her *Yule*, just as we still call similar gifts one's Hogmanay or New Year. In the case of household servants this gift very naturally came to be reckoned as part of their hire, and was often called their *Yule-wages*. Even the dumb animals were not forgotten at this festive season, for it was customary to prepare favours, trappings, or "*trappouris*," of various kinds for the decoration of carriage and riding horses; and among the lords and ladies of the Scottish Court there was considerable rivalry as well as skill called forth by these honours and displays at Yule. But to courtiers and dependants alike, as each season came round, the receipt of Yule from their master gave assurance of royal favour and bounty; while to be left Yuleless implied neglect or disgrace.

YULELES, YUILLIS, YOWLLIS, *adj.* Yuleless, i.e. with no Yule; getting or having got no Yule present, reward, or favour: hence, neglected, unworthy, despised, or cast off : "ane *Yuillis* yald," an old castaway horse for whom there is no Yule favours.

Now lufferis cummis with largess lowd,
Quhy sould not palfrayis thane be prowd,
Quhen gilletis wilbe schomd and schroud,
That ridden ar baith with lord and lawd?
Schir, lett it nevir in toun be tald
That I sould be ane *l'uillis* yald.
Dunbar, Petition of the Gray Horse, l. 6.

In other words, when all other horses are rejoicing in their honours and decorations of Yule, don't let it be said that I have got none. So wrote Dunbar on one occasion when he found he was overlooked and left Yuleless, i.e., had got no Yule present from his master the King. Although he had long submitted to the comparative pittance allowed him, he could not bear to be neglected or cast off. So, in the character of an old horse grown gray in his master's service, he appeals to the King to deal fairly with him; and, whatever he did, not to deprive him of his accustomed Yule favours; for, to be known as a *Yuleless yald* meant to him ruin as well as neglect : he would then be a poor, despised, castaway, fit only for the coalheavers. And he deserved better treatment ; for, old and stiff as he was, and poor as his previous rewards had been, he still loved his master and liked his service; or as he puts it—

The Court hes done my curage cuill,
And maid me ane forridden muill;
Yett, to weir trappouris at this Yuill,
I wald be spurrit at everie spald.
Schir, latt it nevir in toun be tald,
That I sould be ane *l'uillis yald.*

That Dunbar's petition to the King was that he would not leave him Yuleless, i.e., without the customary Yule favours, must be evident to every one who reads the poem with ordinary care ; and that it was so understood by the King, or by Dunbar in the King's name, (for by which of them the reply was written is still doubtful), is shown by the Responsio Regis, which directs the Treasurer to give Dunbar Yule favours of the very best kind. It runs thus :—

Eftir our wrettingis, thesaurer,
Tak in this gray horse, Auld Dunbar,
Quhilk in my aucht with schervice trew
In lyart changeit is in hew.
Gar howss him now aganis this Yuill,
And busk him lyk ane beschopis muill;
For with my hand I have indost
To pay quhat euir his trappouris cost.

Various attempts have been made to explain the expression *Yuillis yald;* but none of them satisfies the context. Pinkerton misread it *ane howllis hald*, and suggested the interpretation "an owl's habitation." Sibbald, reprinting from Pinkerton, altered it into *ane outler hald*, and gave for meaning something equally suitable. Even Dr. Laing's note on the passage is not very helpful : that *Yuillis* means *Yuleless* does not seem to have occurred to him, else he would not have concluded that the poet's meaning is somewhat uncertain. No doubt the full meaning of the expression is now lost ; but the purport of the poem and the customs of the times to which it refers fully warrant the meaning which is given for it above.

YURLIN, YURLING, *s.* A puny, stunted creature : a form of WURLIN, q. v.

YVOR, YUORE, YVERE, YUERE, YVOR-BONE, YUORE-BONE, s. Ivory: *yuere*; Sir Tristrem, l. 1888, S.T.S.
"Ebur, the *yuore-bone*;" Duncan, App. Etym., 1595, ed. Small, E.D.S.
Ivory is properly an *adj.* form : having come from O. Fr. *ivurie*, later *ivoire*, from Lat. *eboreus*, made of ivory, from Lat. *ebor-*, stem of *ebur*, ivory. The Scot. form *yvor* is closer to the Lat. root than the Fr. form is ; but *yvor-bone* tells of the *adj.* use of the term in Sc. also.

YWALLIT, *part. pt.* Walled; Kingis Quair, st. 159, ed. Skeat, S.T.S.

YWIS, I-WIS, *adv.* Surely; Sir Tristrem, l. 17, 989, S.T.S. V. [IWIS].
Frequently explained "I know :" but this is a mistake. V. under *Wis*.

YWYMPILLIT, *part. pt.* Wrapped, rolled, or folded up; Douglas, IV. 52, 14, Small. V. WIMPIL, *v.*

To YYM, *v. a.* To keep. V. YIM, YEME.

Z.

ZEIL, *s.* Zeal; Compl. Scot., p. 6, E.E.T.S.
ZELATUR, *s.* A zealot, zealous person; Ibid., p. 76.

Zeil is M.E. *zele*, from O. Fr. *zele*, which came from Lat. *zelus*, zeal, derived from Greek *zēlos*, ardour. The form *zelatur* has come from O. Fr. *zelote*, zealous, from Lat. *zelotes*, Gr. *zēlōtēs*, a zealot.

ADDENDA.

A.

A, *v. aux.* Have; represents a pron. of *ha, hae;* as, "I micht *a* seen 't."
This pron. of *have* is used in all the persons, sing. and pl. of the pres. tense, and also in the imperative mood.

And ilka egg the wee bird laid,
It might *a* been a bird.
Laird of Logan, p. 561.

It occurs also in William of Palerne, and in the Allit. Rom. Alexander.

A B BROD, *s.* A thin slip of board having the alphabet pasted on it for the use of children at school.

They gied me first the *A B brod*,
Whilk ser't for shool, for book, for rod.
Sillar, Gloss. Laird of Logan.

This old primer was also to be had mounted on a slip of horn. This form was called a *horn-book*.

ABITS, A' BITS, *adv.* In pieces, S.
If his anger should rive him all *abits*.
William Guthrie's Sermons, p. 43.

Still in common use. The second form is used to represent "*all in bits*," as in "His jacket was torn *a' bits*."
A.-S. *a*, on, in; and *bita*, a bit, morsel, from A.-S. *bltan*, to bite, separate.

ABLENESS, ABILNES, *s.* Ability.
". . . bot all my *abilnes* mone cum of the."
Abp. Hamilton's Catechism, Fol. 149, a.

To ABSTENE, *v. n.* To abstain, refrain from, desist; Gude and Godly Ballates, p. 140, Laing; Abp. Hamilton's Catechism, Fol. 186, a.
O. Fr. *abstener*, from Lat. *abstinere*, to refrain from.

AFT, *adv.* Oft, often. A.-S. *oft*.
Aft hae I rov'd by bonnie Doon,
To see the rose and woodbine twine.
Burns, The Banks o' Doon.

AFTER, *adv.* Oftener, more frequently: "*after* than ance;" Leslie, Hist. Scot., p. 49, S.T.S.

AIR, *s.* Descent, extraction: "an hauke of noble *air;*" Sir Tristrem, l. 313, S.T.S.
O. Fr. *aire*, "an airie or nest of hawkes;" Cotgr.: hence, figuratively, descent, extraction.

(Sup.) N 2

To AIR, AYR, AIRE, AYRE, *v. n.* To go, travel, journey, hie. V. AIR, *s.*
In early M. Eng. this verb was common to all the Northern Dialects; and although long obsolete in Scot. we have still a record of it in the sb. *air*, a circuit, as in the term *justice-air*. It occurs repeatedly in the Arthur and Gawain Romances, and frequently in the Allit. Rom. Alexander; but, strange to say, it is unnoticed in the New Eng. Dictionary by Dr. Murray. See Gloss. to the Wars of Alexander, ed. Skeat.
O. Fr. *eirer*, from L. Lat. *iterare*, to journey.

AIRIE, *s.* A shealing; hill pasture, or summer residence for herdsmen and cattle; a level green among hills; Scottish Gael., II. 65. Gael. *àiridh*.

To AKE, AK, *v. a.* and *n.* To pain, ache: "su *akis* me the wame;" Allit. Rom. Alex., l. 538.
A.-S. *œce, ece*, pain; *acan*, to pain; M. E. *aken*.

ALANE, *adj.* as *s.* Self. Addit. to ALANE, q. v.
"I saw the King's Majesty and umquhil Mr. Alexander Ruthven, my Lord's Brother, go furth at the Hall Door their *alanes*." Gowrie Conspiracies, p. 64.
The later form which is still in use is *lane*, pl. *lanes*, and sometimes *lane*, as my *lane*, his *lane*, your *lanes* or your *lane*, their *lanes* or their *lane*. V. under LANE.

ALE-WISP, ALE-WOSP, AIL-WOSP, *s.* The bush, branch, or wand, that formed the sign of an ale-house; Dunbar, Test. Andro Kennedy. V. under *Wisp*.

ALMOUS, AMOUS, *s.* An amice: a sort of cowl or hood; Houlate, l. 210, Asloan MS.; Bann. MS. has. *awmous*. V. *Amyt*.
The amice was a sort of cowl formerly worn by the superior clergy. It was fitted to wear on the head or to rest on the shoulders.
O. Fr. *amis, amit, amict*, an amice: from Lat. *amictus*.

AND, AN, *conj.* Than; as, "Ilk was madder *and* ither," i.e., each was more enraged than the other: so also in Allit. Rom. Alex., l. 1258.

ANE, *s*. Hate, hatred, malevolence.
Thair dwelt a lyt besyde the king
A fowll gyane of *ane*;
Stollin he bes the lady ying,
Away with hir is gane.
Henryson, The Bludy Serk, st. 3.
O. Fr. *haine*, hate, malice, ill-will: from *hair*, to hate.

ANOUR, *s*. Honour, mark of honour; Sir Tristrem, l. 164, S. T. S.

ANUICH, *adv*. Enough. V. ANEUICH.

ANUNDER, ANINDER, *prep.* and *adv*. Under, underneath, under the surface; Ballad, Kempy Kaye, l. 35. Addit. to ANONDER, q. v.

ANSTERCOIP, *s*. Errat. in DICT. for *Austercoip*, q. v.

APNE, *adj.* and *v*. Open. V. APEN.

APPREIF, APREFE, *s*. Approval, consent. V. APPREUE.

APYNING, APPYNING, *part. pr*. Opining, deeming, believing, supposing.
". . . satled and pacefied thame . . . *appyning* that the saidis merchandis and thair associate suld haif na farder insist to have bereft the saidis complenaris of thair liberties." Burgh Recs. Stirling, p. 175.
O. Fr. *opiner*, from Lat. *opinari*, to suppose, opine.

ARE, AR, *adv*. Before, ere; Sir Tristrem, l. 932, S. T. S. V. AIR.
Of playe *ar* he wald blinne,
Sex haukes he yat and yaf.
Ibid., l. 329.

ARE, *s*. Honour, grace, favour, mercy, protection; Sir Tristrem, l. 1816, S. T. S.; Rom. Alex., l. 5362. *Thyn are, thin are*, of or with thy favour, of or of thy mercy, and generally implying supplication: printed *thi nare* in Sir Tristrem, l. 2135, ed. S.T.S., and *thinare* in older editions. Another form of this term is ORE, q. v.
Thin are, or *thin ore*, thy favour (I beseech), is not uncommon. Mätzner, s. v. *are*, refers to it, and quotes this line of Sir Tristrem as an example. It occurs in Chaucer, C. T., l. 3724, and Tyrwhitt has noted and explained the passage.
A.-S. *ár, áre*, glory, honour, respect, reverence; Icel. *æra*, an honour, but Vigfusson states that the word first appears in Icel. about the end of the thirteenth century; Dan. *ære*.

To ARERE, *v. a*. To rear, build up; Sir Tristrem, l. 2834, S. T. S.
A.-S. *ræran*, to rear.

To ARGH, ARCH, *v. n*. To dread, quake or tremble with fear. Addit. to ARGH, ARCH, q. v.

AROCHAR, AROTHAR, *s*. A corr. of *aratre*, a ploughgate of land, i.e., 104 acres.

". . . a plough of land (quæ Scotice vocatur *arochar*)." Orig. Paroch., i. 46.
Although in various districts of Scot. *th* is pronounced like *ch*, *arochar* is prob. a misreading of *arothar*; and this supposition is strengthened by the occurrence of the term in p. 27 of same vol., under the form *harothar*.
L. Lat. *aratrum*, a ploughgate : from Lat. *aratrum*, a plough.

ARSOUN, ARSOUNE, *s*. For defin. in DICT. substitute the following:—a saddle-bow; also, a saddle.
After quotation add—"Each saddle had two arsouns, one in front, the other behind; the former called the *fore-arsoun*, as in Richard Cœur de Lion, l. 5053." Halliwell.
O. Fr. *arson*, also *arceau*, "a little bow; bought; arch; also, a saddle-bow;" Cotgr.

ARST, *adv*. Erst, previously; Sir Tristrem, l. 2644, S.T.S.
A.-S. *ærst*, superl. of *ær*, soon.

ASAUT, *s*. Assault; Sir Tristrem, l. 1442, S.T.S. O. Fr. *assalt*.

AT, *inf. part.* To.
So des this world, y say,
Y wis and nought *at* wene,
The gode ben al oway
That our elders haue bene.
Sir Tristrem, l. 17, S.T.S.
The use of *at* as the sign of the inf. mood is peculiarly a Northern idiom. It is common to Icel., Swed., Dan., &c., and some traces of it remain even in Mod. Eng., as in the word *ado*=*at do*, to do.

ATHARIST, *s*. Del. this entry in DICT.
A misprint for *cithariet* in Pinkerton's version.

ATOUR, *s*. Outfit, equipment, accoutrement.
This term was left undefined by Jamieson, but its general meaning and etym. are correctly stated in his explanatory note: see DICT. Regarding O. Fr. *atour*, *ator*, see Burguy s. v. *tor*.

ATTE. A contr. form of *at the*: "atte riue," at the bank or brink; Sir Tristrem, 1369.
This pron. of *at the* is still common in various districts of Scotland.

ATWINNE, ATVINNE, *adv*. In two, asunder; Sir Tristrem, l. 325, 2548, S.T.S.
A.-S. *a*, on or in, and *twin*, from *twegan*, two.

ATWIX, ATWIXT, *prep*. Betwixt, between.
V. ATWEEN, ATWEESH.

AULD, *s*. V. DICT.
This entry must be deleted. On the authority of the passage quoted from Abp. Hamilton's Catechism, Dr. Jamieson was misled into treating *auld* as a subst.; but he had overlooked the Errata which makes it clearly an adj. by the direction "eftir this word auld, eik aige."

AULD, *adj*. Oldest, eldest: "the *auld* son," the eldest son; Scot. Ball. Child, III. 102. Addit. to AULD, q. v.
This use of *auld* is still common; and similarly *young* is used for *youngest* : "the *young* son," meaning the youngest of the sons.

AUMOUS, AWMOUS, adj. Of, for, or pertaining to alms; "an *aumous* dish;" Burns, Jolly Beggars. V. ALMOUS, s.

AUSTERCOIP, AUSTERCOP, AUSTERCUP, EYSTERCOP, s. A fine similar to the Scot. *grassum* that was formerly exacted in some districts of Orkney and Shetland.

This fine was paid every third year at each renewal of the tack or setting of the smaller islets. Latterly it was assumed to be equivalent to the Scot. *grassum*; but in some districts both burdens were sometimes exacted. See Balfour's Oppressions in Orkney and Shetland, p. 126, Mait. C. Series. This term has been frequently misprinted Anstercoip, and in this form it was presented by Jamieson. V. DICT. Its O. Norse form was *ey-setr-kaup*, the fine or payment at the letting of island lands: being a comp. of Icel. *ey*, an island, *setr*, a setting or letting of land, and *kaup*, bargain or payment.

AUTER, s. An altar. V. AWTER.

To AWEDE, v. n. To go mad, become insane; Sir Tristrem, l. 3181, S. T. S. Addit. to AWEDE, q. v.

This term was left undefined by Jamieson, but in his explanatory note he suggested the correct etym., and almost the correct meaning.
A.-S. *awédan*, to be mad, to go or wax mad: from *wōddan*, to rave, to be mad.

To AWINNE, v. a. To attain, arrive at; Sir Tristrem, l. 2060, S. T. S. V. WIN.

To AWREKE, v. a. To avenge, pret., *awrake*, Sir Tristrem, l. 3337; part. pt., *awreken*, Ibid., l. 2446, S. T. S.

A.-S. *wrecan*, to wreak, revenge; pret. *wræc*, part. pt. *wrecen*: Dutch *wreken*.

B.

To BA, BAA, BAY, v. n. 1. To utter a low continuous sound like the cry of a sheep: "Him preach! he can only *baa*." Also, to sound, resound; as, "The waves came *baaing* in."

2. To hoot, mock, howl at.
Of grace or manners they are void:
For like the bill amang the kye,
They *baa* at us as we gang by.
An Ayrshire Rhyme.
Sum bird will *bay* at my beike.
Houlate, l. 66, Asloan MS.
These are merely imitative words, and different from *bay*, to bark.

BAIGE, s. A badge, token, livery; Abp. Hamilton's Catechism, Fol. 135, b.

BAIL, BAILLE, s. A farm house, farm; or, as formerly called, a farm-town.

"On the old system, a quarter davach [of land] was reckoned a sufficient possession for a gentleman, and this quantity was generally attached to every *baille* or farm town." Scot. Gael, ii. 82.
Gael. *bail*, a place, residence; M'Leod and Dewar.

BAIRDIE, s. A loach. V. BEARDIE.

To BAKE, BAIK, v. a. To cure, preserve, kipper.

"Ordines the thesaurare to caus *baik* thrie salmond to be sent to Edinburgh." Burgh Recs. Stirling, 1618, p. 149.
These salmon were sent by the Magistrates of Stirling as a present to their three law-agents in Edinburgh. The Glasgow Magistrates sent year by year a barrel of salt-herring to each of their Edinburgh agents. See B. R. Glasgow, i. 369, Burgh Rec. Soc.
A.-S. *bacan*, to bake, roast; Icel. and Swed. *baka*.

BANE, BANE-CAME, s. A bone-comb, a small fine-toothed comb made of bone, very necessary for family use.
Whare horn nor *bane* ne'er daur unsettle,
Your thick plantations.
Burns, Address to a L——
"Horn," i.e., a horn-comb, or redding-comb.

BANERECH, s. V. Suppl.
To the etym. given for this term in Suppl. add—
"or, *éiric*, early, a ransom, forfeit, fine."

BANKIT, BANCAT, s. Banquet, feast.
This term occurs frequently in our Burgh and Trades' Records. O. Fr. *banquet*, a dimin. of *banc*, a bench or table, which was borrowed from M. H. Ger.

BARTISING, BARTISHING, s. Forms of *bartizan*, a battlement: also called a *bartise*, or a *bartish*; Orig. Paroch., I. 59. V. BARTIZAN.

BASARE, s. Executioner, headsman, hangman.
The Ape was *basare*, and had him sone ascend,
And hangit him, and thus he maid aoe end.
Henryson, The Fox Tryed, l. 286.
O. Fr. *baisser*, *baissier*, for *abaisser*, *abaissier*, to lower, lessen; hence, decapitate, execute.

BASTEL-HOUSE, s. A blockhouse; Orig. Paroch., I. 294. Addit. to *Bastalye*, q. v.

BATE, BAIT, s. Strife, contention; short for *debate*.
Sa your fader befoir
Held me at *bait* als with bost and scholr.
Henryson, Wolf and Lamb, l. 42.

BAU [292] BIC

To BAUCHLE, v. a. To bungle, spoil, or mar a work or plan; L. R. Stevenson, Kidnapped, p. 87. Addit. to BAUCHLE, q. v.

BAWELL, s. V. BOAL, BOLE.

BEARMEN, s. pl. Carriers, bearers; applied to the bearers of ensignia in a procession, to mason's labourers, etc.

"The smyths and hemmermen to furneiss the *Bearmen* of the Croce." Burgh Recs. Aberdeen, 22 May, 1531.

BED, pret. A form of *bade*, abode, encountered.

Than gelly Johine come in a jak,
To feild quhair he was feidit;
Abone his brand ane bucklar blak,
Baill fell the bern that *bed* it.
Alex. Scott's Poems, p. 29, ed. 1882.

To BEEK, v. a. and n. To bask. V. BEIK.

BEES, BEIS, BES, BESE, v. n. Be; used in the pres. ind., with a future sense, and in the imperat.; Book of Univ. Kirk, p. 190, 197, 199. Addit. to BEIS.

Jamieson's explanation of this term is a mistake. In the Northumbrian dialect *beid* was used in all the persons sing. and pl.; and it was so used in the West of Scot. at the beginning of this century. *Bees*, however, properly means "will be," just as A.-S. *beś* commonly means "I will be." It occurs in the Allit. Rom. Alex., l. 892, 1355.

To BEET, BEAT, v. a. 1. To bundle or put up in bundles; to sort, arrange, or put up in order the several parts of a whole: "to *beet* a web," is to prepare it for the weaver, by making up the several parts into bundles; part. pt. *bet*, arranged, assorted.

2. To mend, repair, improve: "He was quietly *beetin* his net on the green." Addit. to BEIT, q. v.

BEETING, BEETIN, BEATING, s. Mending, material for mending: as, "*weaver's beating*," thread or yarn for mending or repairing his web; Alex. Wilson, II. 68, ed. 1876. Addit. to BEITING, q. v.

As used in the quotations given in DICT., *beiting* means enlarging, extension; but, in the days of handloom-weaving the assortment of bundles which the weaver carried home from the warehouse was called the *beating* of his new web. When the bundles happened to be improperly sorted, the web was said to be *misbet*: see The Deacon's Day, in Whistle Binkie, i. 273.

To BEGOUK, BEGOWK, v. a. To befool, outwit, overreach. Addit. to BEGOUK, q. v.

Tak the right or tak the wrang,
I'll *begouk* ye if I can.
Nursery Rhyme.

"Ah, but I'll *begouk* you there. Play me false, I'll play you cunning." R. L. Stevenson, Kidnapped, p. 76.

BELCHEIR, s. Eulogist, recorder, bard.

When James IV. visited Tain in 1506, he gave "xiv s. to the harper of the bishop of Caithness, xxviii s. to the king's *belcheir* in Tain, and ii s. to the pure folkis be the gait." Orig. Paroch., vol. ii., pt. ii., p. 837.
Gael. *beulchair*, flatterer, eulogist.

BELD, pret. Housed, i.e., laid to rest, buried.

Thar lois and thar lordschipe of as lang dait,
That bene cot-armouris of eild,
Tharin to harrald I held,
Bot sen that the Brus *beld*:
I wryt as I wait.
Houlate, l. 425, Asloan MS.

Delete Jamieson's note on this term; the meaning which he proposed is wide of the mark, and not even suggested by the context. Besides, there are various errors in the passage quoted in DICT.; but these are due to Pinkerton's version.

BELLE, s. A mantle, cloak.

Hir *belle* was of plonkette with birdis full baulde,
Botonede with besantes, and bokellede full bene.
Awnt. Arthure, st. 29.

It occurs also in Wright's Seven Sages, pp. 78, 84.
See Halliwell. Compare Chaucer, prol. 265, where a semi-cope is compared to a *belle*, from its shape.

BELL-WARE, s. The Fucus vesiculosus, Linn. A sea-weed formerly much used in the manufacture of kelp: hence, also called *Kelp-wrack*. Errat. in DICT. V. *Bell-Weed*:

The defin. given in DICT. is a mistake. The *Zostera marina* is not properly a sea-weed, but a flowering plant. Perhaps its common name, *Grass-Wrack*, was the origin of the mistake.
The *Bell-Ware*, however, is a sea-weed, and is so called on account of the bells or bladders with which its fronds abound.
A.-S. *wâr*, sea-weed; prov. E. *wore*.

To BENGE, BENJE, v. n. To cringe. V. BEENGE.

BEST-MAN, s. The friend of the bridegroom who assists him in arranging for the wedding, directs and arranges the party at the ceremony, and superintends the wedding-feast and the rejoicings after it.

This term is improperly defined in the DICT. The *best-man* has nothing to do with the arrangements of the bride or waiting on her: these are attended to by the *best-maid*—the bride's-maid if there is only one, or the chief bride's-maid if there are more than one. In Scotland the friend of the bridegroom is seldom if ever called a *bride-man* or *bride's-man*: at least where the marriage ceremonies are after the Presbyterian fashion.

BETTIR CHEIP, BEST CHEIP. V. under *Cheip*.

BICHT, s. A cross, ill-natured, or troublesome person: generally applied to a child or an aged person; Roxb.

Prob. only another form of BILCH: see s. 2.

BIL [293] BOW

To BILEVE, BILEUE, BYLEUE, v. n. To remain, abide; Sir Tristrem, l. 1086: pret. *bileft*; Ibid., l. 591, *bilaft*, l. 387, ed. S.T.S.

BIRD-MOUTHED, BIRD-MOU'D, *adj.* Softly-spoken, given to speaking in a quiet undertone, afraid to speak out. Generally applied to persons who speak in a quiet kindly manner, or to statements so made. Errat. in DICT., q. v.

Bird-mouthed, lit. with the mouth or manner of a bird, i.e., peeping, soft and low, is altogether different from *mealy-mouthed*. It refers entirely to the manner of speaking, or to the way in which a statement is made; and it always implies softness and kindness. But *mealy-mouthed* refers to what is said, to the words used, and how they are used; and it implies a want of plainness or directness of speech, fear to speak plainly and boldly or to tell one's mind freely.

BIRTH, *s.* Crop, produce. Addit. to BIRTH, q. v.

Regarding the district of Garioch Leslie says "that yeirlie sik a *birth* it beiris . . . that thay cal it the commoune Barn or garnel of Abirdine thair nychtbour citie." Hist. Scot., p. 48, S.T.S.

Als blyth of the *birth*
That the ground bure.
Houlate, l. 25, Asloan MS.

To BITAKE, *v. a.* To bequeath, hand over. V. *Betake.*

BLAWN-LAND, BLAWIN-LAND, *s.* Light sandy land, liable to be damaged by the wind; Peterkin, Rentals of Orkney, No. 1, p. 80, 85.

BLEYNT, *pret.* Yielded. V. BLIN, *v.*

BLIND, BLYND, *part. pt.* Blinded, made blind.
Sa be sorcery *blind* was he.
Barbour's Saints, Peter, l. 367.

BLINKS, *s.* Short for *water-blinks*, the common name for water-chickweed: *Montia fontana*, Linn.

BLUID, BLUDE, *s.* Short for bloodshed, effusion of blood; also, the crime or charge of bloodshed. Addit. to BLUID, BLUDE, q. v.

"Chaingis thair ordinar court-day, being Fryday, to the Saturday for civill caussis onlye in the hour of caus; and trublances, *bludis*, and injuries to be judgit ony uther day, for bettir keiping of the Sabothe." Burgh Recs. Stirling, 1648, p. 194.

BLYTHER, BLYTHAR, *s.* Gladdener, rejoicer. V. BLITHE, *v.*

Hail *blythar* of the Baptist within [the] bowallis
Of Elizebeth thi ant, aganis natur!
Houlate, l. 731, Asloan MS.

Both MSS. read "*thi*" bowels: but this is most prob. a scribal error.

"*Blythar of the Baptist*" is a name applied to Christ on account of what happened at the meeting of Mary and Elizabeth. See Luke, i. 41.

BOFTE, *pret.* and *part. pt.* Buffeted, struck; Barbour's Saints, Paul, l. 21. V. BEFF, *v.*

BOGIE, *s.* Lit. a bend or bender: a small instrument formerly used in plaiting straw; Orkn.
Icel. *bogi*, a bow, arch, bend; A.-S. *boga*.

BOGLE, BOGGIL, *adj.* Neat, small, handy: among coopers *boggil-wark* was the name given to the smallest sizes of vessels which they made.

BOGLES, BOGGILS, *s. pl.* Small wooden vessels of cooper-work for use in household or dairy work.

"This act is declairit to be including of *boggils* and vther small couper work, als well as great, and ordainit to stand vnviolable in all tym coming." MS. Minutes of the Coopers of Glasgow, 11 May, 1704.
Gael. *biogail*, of small size, neat, elegant.

BONDAGER, *s.* One who performs bondage service, but latterly applied only to the female field-worker that each cottar or farm-tenant is bound, by the conditions of his tenancy, to supply to do regular field-work on the farm. V. BONDAGE.

"When we lived in Springfield the house-rent was paid by finding one shearer for the harvest . . . also an outfield worker, winter and summer, for the farmer. [This servant], called the *bondager*, was paid tenpence per day." A. Somerville's Autobiography, p. 6.

BORDLAND, *s.* Land that was bound to supply *guest-quarters* to the King or Jarl: it was therefore exempt from skatt; Oppressions in Orkn. and Shetl., p. 125.
Icel. and Dan. *bord*, table, board; *lood*.

BORROW, BOROWE, BOROW, BORWE, *s.* Pledge, security; hence, protection, protector: to *borrow*, as or for a pledge, security, or protection: "with sanct Jhone to *borrow*," i.e., with St. John for a protection; Lyndsay, The Dreme, l. 996. V. under BORCH.

BOSUM, *s.* Inlet, loch: applied to the sea-lochs on the W. of Scotland. A.-S. *bósm*.

"Among the Lochis or *bosumis* of the Sey, that abundanthe flowis in al kynd of fishe." Leslie, Hist. Scot., p. 40, S. T. S.

". . . farther twa gret *bosums* ar in the sey, quhilkes we commonlie call lochis of salte water." Ibid., p. 13.

BOW, BOWE, BO, BOU, BUE, *s.* 1. Bend, curvature; bend of the arm or of the leg: the loin, thigh, buttocks; a limb, a leg. V. BEUGH.

2. A fold, knot, bunch, as "a *bow* or *bou* of ribbons." Addit. to BOW, *s.*, q. v.

BOWIT, BOWD, BOUIT, BUIT, *part. adj.* Made up in the form of knots or bunches; ornamented with knots or *bows*.

"His gown suld be of all guidnes,
Begareit with fresche bewtie,
Buit with rubanis of richtuusnes,
And perfewit with prosperitie."
Garmond of Gude Ladeis, Banu. MS., p. 657.

To BOWBRAID, BOWBREID, BOWBRED, *v. a.* To prick, pierce, or cut an animal in the loin, thigh, or buttocks; part. pt. *bowbredit;* part. pr. *bowbreding*, used also as a *s.*

Till comparatively late years it was a common practice among fleshers to beat or goad an ox to madness before killing it; this they called *raising the beast;* and in spite of every effort of the magistrates to prevent such cruelty, the practice was persisted in under the belief that it helped to make the flesh more tender. The pricking or goading of the animal was directed chiefly to the flanks, thighs, and buttocks, in order to make it most effective; hence it was called *bowbrailing* or *bowbredin*, i.e., braiding or pricking the *bow* or hough. The following records refer to the brutal custom.

"That thair be na muttoun scoirit on the bak nor na pairt thairof, nor yit lattin doun . . . wnder the pane of viij s. ilk falt; and that na martes be *bowbredit* nor lattin doun vnder the said pane." Burgh Recs. Glasgow, i. 26, Rec. Soc.

"Dauid Lyll and James Robesoun, fleschouris, ar decernit in amerchiament of court for *breiding* of mairtis contrair to the actis maid thairanent." Ibid., i. 119.

"Anent the wrang done be the flescheouris in *bowbreding* of flesche, Johnne Mure, flescheour, for him selfe and in name and behalfe of the haill bretherin of the said craft, is cumin in the baillies will for the *bowbreding* of flesche contrair the actis and statutis maid thairanent." Ibid., i. 122.

Icel. *bógr*, Swed. *bog*, Dan. *bov*, the shoulder of an animal; and Icel. *broddr*, a spike; Swed. *brodd*, Dan. *broad*, *brod*.

BOWALLIS, *s. pl.* V. SUPPL.

Delete the heading of this entry in SUPPL., and substitute the following :—

BOWELLS, BOWALLIS, *s. pl.* Confines, interior, bounds; Book of Univ. Kirk, p. 176.

To BOWELL, *v. a.* To disembowel, embalm: part. pr. *bowelling*, used also as a *s.*

"1610, May 26. Item, to Marcoun Steward, spous to James Inglis, provest, for wyne and vther expensis furnist be hir and for *bowelling* of the lard of Howstoun, provest, xxxvij li. xs." Burgh Recs. Edinburgh, 476, Rec. Soc.

O. Fr. *boel*, from Lat. *botellus*, dimin. of *botulus*, a sausage, intestine; see Burguy.

BOWEL, BOWELL, *s.* A bole or aperture. V. BOAL.

BOWMAN, BOUMAN, BOOMAN, *s.* A farmer or tenant who is steelbowed; Kidnapped, p. 194. V. STEELBOW GOODS.

Particulars regarding *bowmen* will be found in Innes, Leg. Antiq., p. 266.

BOWS, BOWIS, *s. pl.* Papal Bulls.

For to live chaist thay vow solemnitly,
Bot, fra that thay be sikker of thair *bowis,*
Thay live in huirdome and in harlotry.
Lyndsay, Thrie Estaitis, l. 3402.

"My Lords, how have ye keipit your thris vows !"
"Indeid, richt weill till I gat hame my *bows.*"
Ibid., l. 3418.

BRADE, BRAID, BRED, *s.* 1. A spike, a sharp-pointed instrument like an awl, a goad: synon. *brog*. Also, a splint, splinter, shred: "The stick was dung to *braids.*"

2. A prick, a thrust or job with a sharp-pointed instrument. V. BROD, *s.*

To BRADE, BRAID, BREID, BRED, *v. a.* To prick, pierce, job, thrust, goad; part. pr. *brading, breiding, breding,* used also as a *s.*

"Dauid Lyll and James Robesoun, flescheouris, ar decernit in amerchiament of court for *breiding* of mairtis contrair to the actis maid thairanent." Burgh Recs. Glasgow, i. 119, Rec. Soc.

Cf. Icel. *brydda*, to prick; from *broddr*, a sting, prick.

BRAIDFA', *adv.* Scattered about, in disorder, not in proper place or position: "The things are a' lyin *braidfa'*."

BREAK, BREK, *s.* A branch, offset, as in mining; a sprout, offshoot, as in a bulb or root; a band, company, division, separated from the main body, as "a brek o' the sheep." Addit. to BREAK, *s.*

BREIR, BREER, BRIER, *s.* A short twig, spray. Addit. to BREER, q. v.

Belief that Lord may harbary on thy bairge,
To make braid Britane blyth as bird on *breir.*
Alex. Scott, New Yeir Gift to Q. Mary, st. 26.

BRETAGE, *s.* and *v.* V. BRETTYS.

Occurs in both forms in Allit. Rom. Alex., ll. 1416, 1152. Lat. *bretechia*, wooden towers used in assaults.

BRIE, *s.* Eyebrow, brow. V. BREE.

BRINI, BRENY, BRENE, *s.* Breastplate, corslet; Sir Tristrem, l. 3264, S.T.S. V. BIRNIE.

BRONSTANE, *s.* V. BRUNSTANE.

To BROOZLE, *v. a.* To bruise, crush; part. pt. *broozled*, also used as an *adj.* V. BROIZLE.

BRONT, BRUNT, *s.* Impetus, force; *in bront,* in fierce contest; Houlate, l. 492, 498.

"*Brunt,* insultus, impetus;" Prompt. Parv.

BROTH, BROTHE, BROE, *s.* Brine; liquor which has been thickened or strengthened.

"Thomas Anderson cited, accused for drawing *brothe* to his panne on the Lord's day, confessed that he drew some three or four buckettfull in the morning ; ordained to satisfie according to the Act."

"The 'brothe' above mentioned was the salt water contained in the reservoir known as the 'bucket-pat,' a structure of stonework erected on the seashore for the supply of the salt pans." Culross and Tulliallan, i. 221.
These "bucket-pats" were set where they could be filled by spring-tides only; and between spring-tides the sea-water which they contained was allowed to evaporate, and consequently became denser and salter. In this state it was called *broth* or *broe*, and was transferred to the pans or boilers.

BROUN, BROWNE, *part. pt.* Brewn, brewed; Leslie, Hist. Scot., p. 6, S.T.S.

BRUCKET, BRUCKIT, BRUCHTY, *adj.* V. Brocked.

To BRUIK, *v. a.* To win, capture, take by force. Addit. to BRUICK, q. v.

The armies met, the trumpet sounds,
The dandring drums alloud did touk,
Baith armies byding on the bounds
Til ane of them the feild sould *bruik*.
Ballad, Battle of Harlaw, l. 140.

BURRACH, *s.* V. BOURACH.

To BUY, BIE, *v. a.* To buy, pay for, atone or suffer for, expiate. V. ABY. Addit. to BY, *v.*, q. v.

Think, ye may *buy* the joys o'er dear.
Burns, Tam o' Shanter.

Thou slough my brother morgan
At the mete full right,
As I am doubti man,
His death thou *bist* to night.
Sir Tristrem, l. 2329, S.T.S.

To BYLEVE, *v. n.* To remain. V. *Bileve.*

To BYTECHE, *v. a.* V. BETECH.

C.

CACHT, CAGHT, CAHT, *pret.* Caught, seized. V. CAUCHT.

CACHT, CAGHT, CAUCHT, *s.* A hold, grip: "I canna get a *cacht* o't."

CADDO, CADDOIS, *s.* V. CADDES.
These terms as used in Orig. Paroch, vol. ii., pt. 1, pp. 156, 161, imply some fixed and well-known quantity of woollen cloth, prob. a piece or web. Thus, in p. 156—". . . ane braid hewit *caddo*, and failyeing of ane hewit *caddo*, ane fyne braid quhyte *caddo*."

CALIVER, *s.* A culverin; Scot. Ball., Child, vii., 116. V. CULRING.

CALVEL, CALVILL, *s.* Forms of CAVEL, q. v.: "a *calvill* of irne," an iron rod; Burgh Recs. Stirling, p. 43.

CAPERNOITIE, *adj.* Add to definition in DICT.: whimsical, witless.

CARAGE, CARAGES, *s.* V. CARRITCH.

CARKNET, *s.* A necklace. V. CARCAT.
He gae me a *carknet* of bonnie beads
And bade me keep it agane my needs.
Ballad, Cospatrick.
"Carcanet. A necklace, or bracelet." Halliwell.
See Carcanet in Skeat's Etym. Dict.

CASHLICK, *adj.* Careless, rash, regardless: "a *cashlick* fellow," South of S.

CASMER, CASMAR, CASSMER, *s.* Cashmere, a fine woollen cloth: also written *Kasmer,* q. v.

CAVELS, *s. pl.* Pieces, bits, splinters; "ding to *cavels,*" drive to pieces, is still used regarding a wooden vessel. Addit. to CAVEL, q. v.
The term occurs in the same sense in Allit. Rom. Alex., l. 799.

CEARN, *s.* A foot-soldier. V. KERNE.

CHEAT, CHEIT, CHAIT, CHAYT, *v.* and *s.* Contr. forms of *escheat,* common in Burgh Records; see B. R. Lanark, 9 Nov., 1563, B. R. Dunfermline, 9 Sept., 1536.

CHEATRIE, CHEITRIE, CHETTRY, *s.* The casualty of oscheit; also, the revenue arising from said casualty; Oppressions in Orkney, Gloss.
Short for *escheatrie,* from O. Fr. *eschet,* rent, that which falls to one; formed from part. pt. of *escheoir,* derived from L. Lat. *excadere,* to fall in with, meet. V. Skeat, Etym. Dict., s. v. ESCHEAT.

CHEIP, *s.* A booth or stall: "ane *cheip* or pentis;" Records of Old Dundee, p. 153.
A.-S. *céapan,* to sell.

CHESS, *s.* A jess or strap for a hawk's legs; Pop. Ballads. A corr. of E. *jess.*

CHICKSTANE, CHISKIN, *s.* The chitstone, stone-chit, stone-chatter, (Saxicola rubicola); a bird like the flycatcher. See Montagu's Ornith. Dict.

CHIVE, CHEEVE, *s.* A slice; Scot. Ball., Child, iii., 290. Commonly written *sheeve.* V. SHAVE, SHEEVE.

CHRISTENTYE, CHRISTENDIE, s. Christendom; Pop. Ballads.

O. Willie brew'd a peck o' maut,
And Rob and Allan came to see;
Three blyther hearts that lee-lang night,
Ye wad na found in *Christendie*.
Burns.

CLACHT, CLAGHT, r. and s. V. CLAUCHT.

To CLENK, v. a. V. CLINK, *Clinkit*.

CLINKET, CLENKETT, part. pt. Rooved or riveted: "*clenkett* work," rivet-work, clinker-build. V. CLINK, s. 3.

I haif a littill Fleming berge
Off *clenkett* work, hot scho is wicht.
Sempill, Bann. MS., p. 348, Hunt. Soc.

CLINT, s. A cliff, a high steep rock, a precipice, the steep side of a mountain. Addit. to CLINT, q. v.

The term is so used in the S. W. of Scotland.

CLINTED, CLINTIT, adj. Caught among the cliffs.

"*Clinted* on a dass" is said of a sheep that has leaped down upon a ledge of a cliff and cannot get back." V. under *Dass*.

CLIPMALABOR, s. A senseless, silly talker, applied to a thoughtless country wench.

Quoth the wylie auld wife; "The thing speaks weel;
Our workers are scant—we hae routh o' meal;
Gif he'll do as he says—be he man be he deil—
Wow! we'll try this Aiken-drum."
But the wenches skirled: "He's no be here!
His eldritch look gars us swarf wi' fear;
An' the feint o' ane will the house come near
If they think but o' Aiken drum."—
"Puir *clipmalabors*! ye hae little wit;
Is't na Hallowmas now, an' the crap out yet?"
Sae she silenced them a' wi' a stamp o' her fit—
"Sit yer wa's down, Aiken-drum."
W. Nicholson, Brownie of Blednoch.

Some versions have *slipmalabors*, slovenly prattlers, which gives the passage a slightly different meaning; and both terms are still in use.

Gael. *clipe*, deceit, *maol*, silly, and *labhar*, noisy, loquacious.

To CLYTH, CLY, v. a. To conceal, abstract, pilfer: part. pt. *clyit*.

Fy on the telyour that never wes trew,
Fra claith weill can thow *clyth* ane clowt;
Of stowin stommokis baith reid and blew,
Ane bagfow anis thow bur abowt.
Sowtar and Tailyour, Bann. MS., p. 305.
I thame beseik thay be nocht wraith,
Suppois they *clyit* half parte of claith;
Bot seek the cauns and leif the deid,
And blame the scheiris that raif the skreid.
Rowlis Cursing, Bann. MS., p. 305.

Gael. *cleith*, to conceal, hide, keep secret; M'Leod and Dewar.

CO, s. A sea-cave. V. *Cove*.

COBLE, s. A ferry-boat, ferry. Addit. to COBLE, q. v.

"Gives power and commission to Lowrie at Drip *coble*, to collect and receave the custome of all bestiall and other goods passing at the Drip *coble*, or any other foord of Forth neir thereto." Burgh Recs. Stirling, 1660, p. 233.

To CO'ER, COUR, v. a. To cover, conceal: "to *co'er* their fuds;" Burns, Jolly Beggars.

THE COMMON GUDE, COMMON GUID, s. The general welfare or benefit of a community; also, the public property, funds, and revenues of a town or burgh.

In the latter sense *the common gude* of a town means the property, whether in lands or funds, held by the magistrates, and the revenues payable to them, for behoof of the community; as distinguished from property under their management for special purposes, and usually administered under statutory authority. Such property can be applied only to the particular objects for which it was authorised; but *the common gude* of a burgh, which generally consists of lands and customs anciently conferred by royal charter, accumulations of burgh revenues, or property mortified to or acquired by funds of the burgh, must be kept for the common profit of the burgh, and expended on common and necessary things of the burgh, as the following Act of Parl. directs.

"It is statute and ordained anent the common gude of all our Soverane Lordis burrowes," that it "be observed and keiped to the common profite of the towne, and to be spended in common and necessarie thinges of the burgh, be the advise and councell of the towne for the time and deakons of craftes quhair they are; and inquisition yeirly to be taken in the chalmerlaine aire of expenses and disposition of the samin." Act of Parl., 18th May, 1491.

Various enactments of Parl. and regulations by the Convention of Burghs have since been passed for the proper application of *the common gude*. The statute at present in force is Act 3, Geo. IV. cap. xci. (1822); and under it no part of *the common gude* can be sold, or let on lease for more than a year, except by public roup.

To CONCREDIT, v. a. To entrust, confide, trust.

"I thought your Majesty would have *concredited* more to me, nor to have commanded me to await your Majesty at the door, gif ye thought it not been to haue taken men with you." Gowrie Conspiracies, p. 59.
"I repeit this same Bearer to his Lordship, to whom you may *concredit* all your heart in that, as well as I." Ibid., p. 104.

Lat. *concredere*, to entrust.

To CONFIDER, v. n. To confederate, ally; Leslie, Hist. Scot., p. 88, S. T. S. V. CONFIDER, adj.

COOP, COPE, s. A small cone of yarn or thread: the material is wound into this form to facilitate the process of twining or weaving. Syn. *spule*, q. v.

CORONACH, s. The band of wailers at a Highland funeral: composed of women who wail and chant the dirge. Addit. to CORANICH, q. v.

"The old gentlewoman was carried on poles by the nearest relatives of her family, and attended by the *coronach* composed of a multitude of old bags, who tore their hair, beat their breasts, and howled most hideously. At the grave the orator or senachie pro-

nounced the panegyric of the defunct, every period being confirmed by a yell of the *coronach*." Smollet, Humphry Clinker, Letter of Sept. 3.
The etym. given for this term by Jamieson is a mistake. It is the Gael. *corrannach*, lit. a howling together : from *comh*, together, and *ranaich*, a howl, from *ran*, to howl, cry. See M'Leod and Dewar.

COTTRAL, *s.* A cottar, farm-servant, field-labourer.

". . . his and thair subtennentis, *cottrallis*, servandis, and assignayes." Croasraguel Charters, i. 120, Ayr and Wigton Arch. Coll.
This is an unusual word. However, as there were several classes of cottars, the ones here named may have been those who were farm-servants or fieldlabourers. Named from L. Lat. *cotura*, a form of *cultura*, field-labour. See Ducange, and for description of the *cottar* see Innes' Leg. Antiq., p. 267.

COUPLE, **Cupill**, **Cuppill**, *s.* A measure of length, extending to twelve feet : used in measuring building, and the area which it covers or encloses. Addit. to *Cuppil*, q. v.

"A piece of land or particute of the cemetery of the cathedral church, partly built and partly waste, extending to the space of 100 feet, or 8 *cupill* bigging in length, reckoning 12 feet as one *cappill* bigging, and to the space of 5 ells in breadth." Orig. Paroch., vol. ii., pt. ii., p. 572.

COVE, **Co**, *s.* A cave, sea cave ; also applied to a narrow inlet or recess on a steep rocky coast.

Both terms are still common in the west of Scot. ; but on the Carrick and Galloway coasts a sea-cave is invariably called a *co*.
A.-S. *cofa*, a cell, a cave ; Icel. *kofi*.

COWSWORTH, **Kowsworth**, *s.* A proportion of odal-land equal to one-tenth of a penny-land ; also called a *yowsworth* ; Oppressions in Orkney, Mait. C.

CRAPOTE', *s.* The toad-stone : Chelonitis, a precious stone.

Hir selle it was of reole bone,
Full semely was that syghte to see!
Stefly sett with precyous stones,
And compaste all with *crapotd*.
Thomas of *Ersseldoune*, l. 24.
O. Fr. *crapaudine*, "the stone Chelonitis, or the Toad-stone ;" Cotgr. From Fr. *crapaud*, a toad, lit. the creeper ; but of Germ. origin : cf. Icel. *krjúpa*, to creep.
Reele-bone, also *ruele-bone*, *rowel bone*, and *royal-bone*. See Gloss. Scot. and English Ballads, by Prof. Childs.

CROSS-TARRIE, *s.* V. **Croishtarich**.

CRUE, **Cru**, *s.* A fish trap ; Orig. Paroch., II., ii. 612. Addit. to **Crue**, q. v.
Colloq. form and contr. of *cruve*.

To **CRYSTE**, *v. n.* To vaunt, bounce, brag, boast ; part. pr. *crystan*, *crystin*: "crackin' an' *crystin*' by the ingle cheek." V. **Creyst**, *s.*

Lit. to raise or show one's crest, as male birds do when strutting and posing before the female. A.-S. *croesta*, a crest, tuft, which, like O. Fr. *creste*, is prob. from Lat. *crista*, a crest.

(Sup.) O 2

CUITIE, **Cuitie-Boyn**, *s.* V. **Cuttie-Boyn**.

CUMLYNE, *s.* A stranger ; lit. an incomer ; Babour's Saints, Peter, l. 649. Addit. to **Cumlin**, q. v.

"*Comelynge*, new cum man or woman ;" Prompt. Parv.

CUNIAK, **Cunniak**, *s.* A corner, an angle. West and South of S.

This is not a dimin. of *cunyie*, a corner, which has come from Lat. *cuneus*, a wedge, through O. Fr. *coin*. It is of Celtic origin, from Gael. *cuinne*, a corner, an angle.

To **CURE**, *v. a.* To attend to ; hence, to work, dress, prepare ; "to *cure* land," to till it.

I have an aiker of good ley-land,
Ba, ba, ba, lilli, ba,
Which lyeth low by yon sea-strand,
The wind hath blown my plaid awa.
For thou must *cure* it with thy horn,
Ba, ba, &c.,
So thou must sew it with thy corn.
The wind, &c.
Ballad, The Elfin Knight, l. 45.
O. Fr. *cure*, attention ; from Lat. *cura*.

CURROUR, **Cursor**, *s.* A ranger, collector. Addit. to *Curror*, q. v.

"Each ward had a ranger or *currour* (cursor), who collected the reuts and accounted for them to the exchequer, and who appears also to have had a general charge of the royal interests within his ward." Orig. Paroch., i. 240.
"The office of *cursor* or ranger of the ward of Ettrick." Ibid., i. 263.

CURSELL, *s.* V. **Dict.**
Delete the entry under this heading in **Dict.**
Cursell is a misreading of *Tursell*, a form of *Trussell*, the upper die used in stamping money. The etym. suggested for *cursell* is also a mistake. V. under *Trussell*.

CUTE, *s.* A small Danish coin worth about one-twelfth of a penny, and similar to the O. Scot. *doit*; Alex. Scott's Poems, pp. 11, 83, ed. 1882 ; Lyndsay, Sq. Meldrum, l. 294. Addit. to **Cute**, q. v.

Only the secondary meaning is given in **Dict.**, and both etymology and explanation are wrong. See note under *Quytt*.
O. Dan. *kvitt*, Mod. Dan. *hvid*, a small coin, one-third of a Dan. skilling, or about one-twelfth of an Eng. penny.

CUTTEL, *s.* A measuring rod of the length of a Scotch ell, used in Shetland ; an ell.

"The *cuttell*, quhilk is thair mesour or elwand, quhair with thai mett thair clayth callit Wadmell." Oppressions in Orkney, p. 18.
The *cuttel* was the fundamental unit of length and valuation in Shetland. A *cuttel* of wadmel long bore a standard value of 6d Scots : 6 *cuttels* being equal to a ure or ounce of valuation ; 20 *cuttels* equal to a sheep ; and six score or a long hundred, to an ox. The value of the *cuttel* was raised to 2 shillings by Earl Robert. See Gloss. Oppressions in Orkney.

CYPRESS, *s.* Crape, gauze. V. *Sipers*.

D.

To DANDER, DANNER, v. n. To make a loud rattling or reverberating sound: part. pr. *dandering, dandring, dannering*, used also as an adj., as in "the *danderin* drum." A weakened form of DUNNER, q. v.

<blockquote>The armies met, the trumpet sounds,
The *dandring* drums alloud did touk.
Ballad, Battle of Harlaw, 1. 138.</blockquote>

DANDER, DANNER, s. A loud rattling or reverberating sound; also, a stroke or blow that produces such a sound.

DASS, s. A ledge on a precipice. Addit. to DASS, q. v.

<blockquote>A sheep is said to be "clinted on a *dass*," when, having leaped down upon a ledge after fresh herbage, it cannot get back.</blockquote>

DAVACH, DAVOCH, s. An extent of land fit to be worked by four ploughs, and hence equal to 416 acres; Scot. Gael., II., 80; Innes, Leg. Antiq., p. 273. V. under DAWACHE.

DED-THRAWYNG, s. Death-struggle, agony of death; Douglas, III., 348, 18, Small. V. DEDE-THRAW.

To DEFAR, v. a. and n. To submit, withdraw; Bann. MS., p. 410, Hunt. Soc. Addit. to DEFER, q. v.

To DEFEND, v. a. To prohibit, forbid. Addit. to DEFEND, q. v.

<blockquote>Syne 1 *defend* and forbiddis every wicht,
That can nocht spell thair Pater Noster richt,
For till correct or yit amend Virgyle,
Or the translatar blame in his vulgar style.
Douglas, Virgil, Prol., Bk. i.</blockquote>

It is used in the same sense by Shakespeare in Rich. III., iii. 7.

To DEIS, DAIS, v. a. To desk, fit with a desk; to enclose, surround: *to deis a form*, to fit it up as a pew. V. DEIS, s.

<blockquote>"And the foir furmes in the Trongaitt Kirk in all pairtis to be *deissit*." Burgh Recs. Glasgow, 1625, i. 345, Rec. Soc.</blockquote>

To DEME, v. a. To judge, criticise; to think or speak evil of, defame; also, to sift, cleanse.

<blockquote>Bot wist thir folkis that vthir *demiss*,
How that their sawis to vthir semiss,
Thair vicious wordis and vanitie,
Their tratling tungis that all furth temiss,
Sum wald lat thair deming be.
Dunbar, Musing Allone, 1. 36.</blockquote>

DEMAR, DEMER, s. Judge, critic; censor, evil-speaker, defamer; Ibid., l. 42.

DEMING, DEMYNG, s. 1. Judgment, opinion, evil-speaking, defamation. Addit. to [DEMYNG], q. v.

<blockquote>For thocht I be ane crownit king,
Yit sall I not eschew *deming*;
Sum callis me guid, sum sayis I lie,
Sum cravis of God to end my ring,
So sall I not vndemit be.
Ibid., l. 7.</blockquote>

2. Dust, rubbish, refuse: "the *deming* of coals," the siftings or refuse of coal; Records of Old Dundee, p. 107.

DERFT, adj. Determined, stolid, dogged. V. DERF.

<blockquote>But with ane heily heart both doft and *derft*.
Priests of Peebles.</blockquote>

DETESTIVE, DETESTINE, adj. Detestable, to be detested, pernicious, obnoxious; also, despiteful, contemptuous.

<blockquote>Than said Vesta, that did Scriptour deuine
Of the Euangell, and the law positiue,
It did suspend, and haldis as *detestive*.
Rolland, Court of Venus, iii. 369, S. T. S.</blockquote>

In order to suit his rhymes the same poet adopts the form *detestine*.

<blockquote>. . . but bad me sone pas hine
Vnto the nine nobillis of excellence,
Quhair I gat not be ansueir *detestine*.
Ibid., ii. 975.</blockquote>

In the S. T. S. version these lines (and many others) are incorrectly punctuated, whereby the sense is spoiled; but with the setting here given the meaning is clear enough.

In the Gloss. *detestine* is rendered '*definite*,' which is certainly a mistake.

O. Fr. *detester*, to detest, loathe; Lat. *detestari*, to execrate.

To DIFFER, v. n. To disagree, dispute, contend, quarrel. Addit. to DIFFER, q. v.

DIFFERENCE, DIFFER, s. Dispute, contention, quarrel: "They had an angry *differ* about their father's siller." Addit. to DIFFERANCE, q. v.

To DISCURE, v. a. To discourse of: hence, to relate, tell, discover, reveal. Addit. to DISCURE, q. v.

<blockquote>Beware quhome to thy counsale thow *discure*,
Ffor trewth dwellis nocht ay for that trewth appeiris:
Put not thyne honour into aventenre;
Ane freind may be thy fo as fortoun steiris.
Dunbar, To dwell in Court, l. 9.</blockquote>

DISTRIBIT, DISTRUBIT, part. pt. Distributed, apportioned.

<blockquote>These forms represent the common pron. of *distributed*; and the following passage shows that it was prevalent in the middle of the sixteenth century.
". . . and wyll gyf na parte of thair benefice for the sustentatioun of pure peple within thair</blockquote>

paryschyng. For doubtles thay ar bot dispensatouris or stewartis of the same, to be distrublit to thaim self sa far as thai myster to thair honest sustentatioun, and also to the pure peple of thair awin perrochyne in speciall, and in reparationn of thair queir quhen it nedis." Abp. Hamilton's Catechism, fol. 59a.
This word was overlooked by Jamieson, and it does not appear in the very full and careful Gloss. of the Clar. Press ed. of Hamilton.

DOCK-MAILL, *s.* Harbour dues, anchorage; Orig. Paroch., II. pt. 2, p. 638.

DOFT, *adj.* Stupid, senseless. V. DOFART.
But with ane belly bert both *doft* and derft
They aye begin where that their fathers left.
Priests of Peebles.

DOLE, DALE, DULE, *s.* Service, portion, piece, lump, quantity. Addit. to DAIL and DOOL, q. v.
In the West and South of Scotland *dale*, or *dail*, is frequently used with the meaning quantity, amount, as in "There's a *dale* o' confused feedin in a sheep's head." A.-S. *ddl*, variant of *ddel*, a share, portion : M. E. *dole, dale.*

DOLLOP, DOOLUP, DULLIP, *s.* A large piece, portion, or service ; "a dawd o' scone and a *dollop* o' cheese;" also, a quantity, number, collection, assortment; "There's the hail *dullip* or *dollop* to you."
Perhaps *dollop* is a corr. of *dollock*, dimin. of *dole*, used in the loose, general, and sometimes opposite senses in which dimins. are used : for instance, *lassock* or *lassie* seldom means a little lass, and sometimes means a biggish one, as in the expression, "a lump o' a *lassock*," or "a lump o' a lassie."
In the sense of number, collection, assortment, however, the term appears to have got mixed up with Gael. *dislam*, collection, gathering, gleanings.

DONE, DON, *part.-pt.* This auxiliary, when followed by a vb. in the inf., forms an intensive part. pt. of that vb. : thus, " He has *done* settle," he has settled ; lit., he has caused to be settled.
As he hes plainlie *done* declair himsell,
As thou may reid in his halie Evangell.
Lyndsay, Thrie Estaitis, 1. 3584.
This Parliament, richt aa, hes *done* conclude.
Ibid., 1. 3939.

DORMOND, *s.* A joist: "*dormonds* and ribbs," i.e., joists and couples ; Records of Old Dundee, p. 161.
Lit. a sleeper : Fr. *dormant*, part. pr. of *dormir*, to sleep ; cf. L. Lat. *dormitor*, a large beam or sleeper, from Lat. *dormire.*

DORP, DORPE, DROPE, *s.* A village: another form is *thorp.*
"This trie, in testimonie heirof, to the kirke of the nychtbour *dorpe* was brocht, and thair laid vpe, and evin to his tyme, he affirmes, hes bene keipit." Leslie's Hist. Scot., p. 61, S.T.S.
"Priestes, quha may to the lai peple betuene *dorpe* and *dorpe*, and toune and toune, minister the blist Sacrament." Ibid., p. 106.

The form *drope* occurs in Bann. MS., p. 868, Hunt. Soc.
Du. *dorp*, a hamlet ; A.-S. *thorp*, Sw. and Dan. *torp.*

DOT-AND-GO-ONE. V. DICT.
This expression is a record of the old method of teaching and working arithmetic in our parish schools. Fifty years ago it was in common use in country districts of the North of Scotland. *Dot*, i.e., put down the mark or figure, *and go one*, i.e., and carry one. Its application to unequal motion is therefore apt and expressive.

DOUD, DUDE, DUID, DWID, DUIT. Do it : "But he canna *duit.*"
The Bann. MS. here reads *dwid*, in the primary text, and *doud* in the duplex. See Bann. MS., p. 135, Hunt. Soc. These forms represent pron. which are still common.
" Art thow contrite and sorie in thy spreit
For thy trespas ?" " No, Schir, I can nocht *dude.*"
Henryson, The Tod's Confessioun, 1. 86.
Thow mon be hureit in thy hude,
Thy windinscheit is nocht in weir,
Thy airis ar of eild to *duid ;*
Do for thy self quhill thow art heir.
Dunbar, Do for thyself, 1. 55, ed. Laing.

DOUGHTY, DUGHTIE, *adj.* Valiant, brave ; noble, great ; powerful, strong ; Ajax' Speech, st. 1. V. DOUCHTY.

DOUGHTELY, *adv.* Valiantly, Barbour, xv. 319, ed. Hart. V. DOUCHTELY.
A.-S. *dohtig, dyhtig,* valiant.

DOUTII, DOUTIIE, *s.* The nobility, nobles, knights ; also, a noble family, race ; Gaw. and Alex. Romances.
A.-S. *duguth,* excellence ; also, the nobility, noble band of men.

DRAUNT, *v.* and *s.* V. DRANT.

DRAUNTING, DRUNTING, *adj.* Whining, complaining, grumbling.
But lest you think I am uncivil,
To plague you with this *draunting* drivel.
Burns, Poem on Life, st. 8.

DRAIGIE, *s.* V. DREGY.

DRAVE *on, pret.* Passed away. V. *Drive on.*

To DRAW *on, v. n.* To draw near ; as, "The time 's *drawin on.*"

To DRIVE *off* or *aff, v. a.* To put away, banish, defer ; Abp. Hamilton's Catechism, fol. 110b.

To DRIVE *on, v. n.* To pass away, pass rapidly ; pret. *drave, drove.*
The night *drave* on wi' sangs and clatter,
And ay the ale was growing better.
Burns, Tam o' Shanter.

DUGHTIE, *adj.* Valiant. V. DOUCHTY.

DUID, DWID, DUDE, DUIT. Do it. V. Doud.

DULL, s. A goal. V. DULE.

To DUNCH, v. n. To strike, knock, thump, dash, crash: "The boat *dunched* on the rock." Addit. to DUNCH, q. v.

DUNCH, s. A smart blow, a crash, shock.
"It [i.e. the ship] struck the reef with such a *dunch* as threw us all flat on the deck." R. L. Stevenson, Kidnapped, p. 118.

DUNG, part. pt. Driven, beaten, battered, knocked about, as, "*dung* to bits;" also used as a *pret.* in all the senses of DING, q. v. Addit. to DUNG, q. v.

DYSING, s. Dicing, gambling: "carting and *dysing*;" Abp. Hamilton's Catechism, fol. 36a.

DYVOUR, DYVOR, DIYOR, s. Evil-doer, ne'er-do-well, blackguard; Alex. Wilson, Watty and Meg. Addit. to DYVOUR, q. v.

The term is still so used in the West of S., and without the slightest reference to bankruptcy : indeed, it has now almost lost that meaning.
It is besides frequently used as an adj., as in the phrase "a *divor* loon :" and in the following passage by Galt it is so used.
"A sorner, an incomer from the east country, that hung about the change-house as a *divor* hostler, that would rather gang a day's journey in the dark than turn a spade in daylight, came to him as he stood in the door, and went in with him to see the sport." Annals of the Parish, ch. 19.

DYVOUR HABIT, DYVOUR'S HABIT, s. The dress or badge of a bankrupt, a yellow cap. V. DYVOUR.

A Debtor who granted to his creditors a disposition upon a *cessio bonorum*, when set at liberty required, if his creditors insisted upon it, to wear for the future a particular *habit* appropriated by custom to dyvours or bankrupts. This was a yellow cap. See Act of Sederunt, 17 May, 1606.
By Act of Parliament, 1696, ch. 5, dyvours were prohibited from dispensing with *habit* unless they proved that bankruptcy was owing to misfortune. In 1813, however, Lord Meadowbank declared that "condemnation to the *dyvour's* habit is now undoubtedly done away."

E.

EALD, EALDINS, EALINS. V. under EILD.

EASTLAND, ESTLAND, s. and adj. The Baltic countries; from the Baltic; Halyburton's Ledger, pref. p. 83, 107; Tucker's Report, p. 44; B. Recs. Stirling, see Gloss. Addit. to EASTLAND, q. v.

EELINS, EALINS, adj. and s. V. EILDINS.

ELDIN, s. Fire; burning coals, called *kindling*, or *kindling-coal*; also, lightning. Addit. to ELDIN, q. v.
"Wilyem Strayquhon fermer in Aberdeen sittane in his howris the leyft beand full of *eldin*, fell on him and he departit the xi. day of aug' the year of god 1578 yeris." Reg. of Births, Deaths, &c., Aberdeen, 1568 to 1592.

ENDED, ENDIT, pret. and part. pr. Forms of *ainded*, breathed; Leslie, Hist. Scot., p. 29, S. T. S. V. AYND.

ENDER, ENDRE, ENDRES, adj. Past, goneby: *ender*-day, *endres*-day, past day, other day; Scot. Ball., Child, I. 98.
Icel. *endr*, past, in time past, formerly.

ERDLIK, ERDELIK, adj. V. ERDLY.

To ERM, EARM, IRM, v. n. To whine, complain. V. YIRM.
A.-S. *earn*, miserable; *earmian*, to grieve : M. E. *ermen*. By vowel-change of *ea* to *y*, the A.-S. *yrman*, to grieve was formed, from which the words *irm* and *yirm* have come, and also the corruptions *yern* and *yirn*. See Skeat's Etym. Dict. under *Yearn*.

To ESCHEW, v. a. and n. To issue, let out, go out: a form of *issue*. V. ESCHAY, s., and ISCH, v.
"He opened the Door thereof to *eschew* himself, and to let his Majesty's servants in." Gowrie Conspiracies, p. 53.

EVANGELL, EWANGELL, VANGELL, WANGELL, VANGILE, s. The gospel, the Gospels, the New Testament.

EYSTERCOP, EISTERCOWP, s. An ancient land-burden in Orkney and Shetland. V. *Austercoip*.

F.

To FA', *v. a.* 1. To get, obtain, suffer, endure.

> Through misfortune he happen'd to *fa*', man.
> *Sheriffmuir, Hogg's Jacobite Relics*, ii. 1.

2. To attempt, accomplish; to strive to do or to obtain; as, " Ye canna, and ye needna *fa*' that."

Addit. to FAW, q. v.

FA', *s.* Story or complaint of what has befallen one. Addit. to FAW, q. v.

> Now isna that Lady Maisry
> That makes sic a dolefu' *fa*'.
> *Buchan's Ballads*, ii. 228.

FAID, FADE, *s.* Feud, quarrel; Leslie, Hist. Scot., p. 92, 93, S. T. S. V. FAID, *v.*

Gael. *faed*, aversion, displeasure.

FAILRATH, *s.* V. *Fuilrath*.

To FAILYE, FALYIE, FALYE, *v. n.* To fail in duty, fault, do wrong. Addit. to FAILYE, FALYE.

> ". . . and the contraveneris als oft as thai *falyie* sall pay the penalties foirsaidis." Burgh Recs. Stirling, p. 133.

The term occurs frequently in our Burgh Records in this sense.

FAILYIE, *s.* A form of FULYIE, q. v.; Burgh Recs. Stirling, p. 133.

FALCAGE, *s.* Cutting, mowing; the right of cutting grass in wood or meadow; Orig. Paroch., I. 375.

L. Lat. *falcagium*, the right of cutting in wood or meadow; Fr. *fauchage*. From Lat. *falx, falcis*, a sickle.

FA'N, *part. pt.* Fallen.

FA'N *fra the gled.* All in disorder, like prey dropped by a hawk: applied to a slovenly dressed female; "There's our Jennie as she had *fa'n* frae the gled."

FA'N *fra the lift.* Fallen from the sky; applied to unexpected, sudden, or startling events, and generally used as an *adv.*

To FARK, *v. n.* V. *Ferk*.

FASIANE, FASANE, *s.* A pheasant; Leslie, Hist. Scot., p. 39, S. T. S. M. E. *fesaun.*

O. Fr. *fasian*, a pheasant: from Lat. *phasiana*, a pheasant. It was so named because it was brought from the river Phasis in Colchis.

FATOUR, FATOURE, *s.* A deceiver.

> Ryght so the *fatoure*, the false theif, I say,
> With suete tresonn oft wynnith thus his pray.
> *The Kingis Quair*, st. 135, ed. Skeat.

Sibbald reads *feator*; but the correct word is *fatoure*, as in Skeat's ed. All the other editions have the misreading *satoure*.

O. Fr. *faiteor*, from Lat. *factorem*, a doer, maker, agent. Hence it took up the sense of pretender, impostor. Spelt *faytour* in P. Plowman. V. Gloss.

FAULCON, FAUCON, *s.* A falcon, hawk; Halyburton's Ledger, p. 313.

FAUTOR, *s.* Agent, promoter, partisan.

"Sundry practices and devices in hand by the queen of Scotts' *fautors* and ministers here." Sir H. Norris to Queen Elizabeth, Paris, 30 Sept., 1570, Preface to Nau's Memorials of the Reign of Mary Stewart, p. clxvii.

O. Fr. *fauteur*, "A fautor, fauourer, furtherer, helper;" Cotgr. Lat. *fautor*, from *favere*.

FEE, *s.* Wild animals, as deer, &c.; Scot. Ball., Child, I. 100, 107. Addit. to FE, q. v.

FEIDELANDS, *s. pl.* Rich pastures on which cattle are fed both winter and summer; Hibbert's Shetland, p. 507.

A compound of *feedy*, abounding in food.

FERMABILL, FERMEABILL, *adj.* Able to be closed, capable of being shut in. V. FERME, *v.*

"For making of the well *fermeabill* in tyme comeing, for preventing of danger that might happen to young bairns living near by the samyne." Culross and Tullieallan, i. 317.

To FERK, FARK, *v. n.* To start, proceed, march; Allit. Rom. Alex., l. 926, 545.

A.-S. *fercian*, to assist, help, support.

To FICHE, FISCHE, FYSCHE, *v. a.* To set, fix, fix upon, adduce, invent; part. pa., *fichyt, fischit, fyschit*, Barbour, xx. 178.

"Sa and a man mycht haif lauchfully infiit his nychtbouris wyfe, he mycht a *fischit* ane cause to his wife, to put hir away," i.e., he might have fixed, fastened, or invented a cause against her; Abp. Hamilton's Catechism, fol. 72, b.

Jamieson gave only the form *fichyt* from Barbour, Edin. MS. The Camb. MS. has *fyschit*; and the third form, *fischit*, is shown in the above extract from Abp. Hamilton.

FIDDLE, *s.* To find a fiddle, to come upon something very amusing. Addit. to FIDDLE, q. v.

This expression is now generally applied to a person who is extraordinarily merry without apparent cause.

FIN, *s.* A cape, headland; lit. end. Addit. to FYNE.

> It's even ower by Aberdour,
> There's mony a craig and *fin*,
> And yonder lies Sir Patrick Spens,
> Wi' mony a guid lord's son.
> *Ballad, Sir Patrick Spens, Child*, iii., 342.

To FINYIE, v. a. To feign, pretend, imitate.
"Thay dryue the pray now on this syd now on that syd of the riuer : and beyonde the water thay *finyie* a dwble passage, that in troding of the fute thay may be deceiued." Leslie, Hist. Scot., p. 21, S. T. S.
O. Fr. *feindre*, to fashion, feign ; from Lat. *fingere*, to make, fashion.

FITTIE, adj. Nimble, agile ; able to use the feet well and nimbly. Errat. in DICT.
Delete both defin. and note given under this heading in DICT.: they are mistakes. Indeed, the whole entry may be deleted, as the term is previously explained under FIT, a foot. It is not pronounced *feetie*, but *fittie:* as in the *fittie-lan*' of Burns.

FLAN, s. A small plate or piece of metal from which a coin is made. V. under *Trussell*.
O. Fr. *flanc*, "a planchet, or plate of mettall readie to be stamped on, or coyned ;" Cotgr.

FLEIKWANDS, s. Same as FLAIK-STAND, q. v.; Burgh Recs. Glasgow, II. 424, Rec. Soc.

FLEIS, FLEISH, s. Fleece ; a sheep.
Five hundred *fleis* now in ane flok.
Wowing of Jock and Jenny.
Fleish represents the vulgar pron. still in use ; and it may be remarked that shepherds still talk of, and sum their flocks, as so many *fleis* or *fleish*. A.-S. *flys*, a fleece ; Du. *vlies*, Germ. *fliess*.

FLIEDLIE, adv. In fear, timorously, shyly; Leslie, Hist. Scot., p. 25, S. T. S. V. FLEIT.

To FLIKKER, v. n. To flap about, flutter, quiver, struggle like one in agony; part. pr. *flikkerand*.
Doun duschit the beist deid on the land gan ly,
Sprewland and *flikkerand* in the deid thrawis.
Douglas, ed. Small, ii. 252, 25.
This is a freq. form of *flick, flik,* weakened from *flack, flak,* to hang loosely ; M. E. *flakken,* to flap about. From the base *flac-* of A.-S. *flac-or*, flying, roving ; Icel. *flakka,* to rove ; *flaka,* to flap. V. Skeat, Etym. Dict., s. v. Flicker.

FOCH, FOSH, pret. Fetched. V. *Fotch*.

FOTCH, FOCH, FOSH, FUISH, pret. Fetched. V. FUSH.

FOOT-PACK, s. A pedlar's pack; Priests of Peebles.

FORE-AGAINST, FORGAINST, FORE-AGAINS, FORAGANES, FOR-GAINS, FOR-GANES, prep. Directly opposite; Records of Old Dundee, p. 153 ; Leslie, Hist. Scot., p. 87, S. T. S. Synon., *fore-anent*. Addit. to FOREGAINST, q. v.

FORINSEC, adj. Foreign; *forinsec service*, foreign service, or service abroad : also, extraordinary.
A grant of William, Earl of Ross, in 1366, is for "yearly payment of a penny of silver in name of bleuch ferme, in lieu of every other service except the *forinsec* service of the king when required." Orig. Paroch, vol. 2, pt. 2, p. 406.
The term is thus explained by Cosmo Innes in his Legal Antiquities, p. 62 : "*Servitium forinsecum* or *Scoticanum*—service without or within Scotland, corresponded to the old Saxon *utwer* and *inwer.*"
It also meant the payment of extraordinary aid, as opposed to the common and ordinary duties within the lord's court. See Kennet's Gloss., and Cowel.

FORK, s. A prong, a gibbet, gallows.
"Gif ony of thir be conuicte of falshet, lat him end his lyf vpon ane *fork*, and kastne by vnyerdet." Leslie, Hist. Scot., p. 121, S. T. S.
O. Fr. *fourche*, a fork, prong, gibbet.

To FORTUNE, v. n. To happen, befal ; Abp. Hamilton's Catechism, fol. 40b. Addit. to FORTOUN, q. v.

FOUD, FOWD, s. President, justiciar, captain, or chief of a company during a voyage or excursion. Addit. to FOUD, q. v.
"All merchandis passand to thair voyages furth of Scotland to ony forane cuntrie, at the electioun of thair *foud* or justiciar, in thair wayages furth and hame, the *fowd* and his clerk that vayage sall be ansuirabill to the said box [i.e., the poor-box of the merchants] of all unlawis and convictionis of merchandis for swering, banning, or tacking the Lordis name in waine, all unlawis incurrit be the saidis merchandis for pleying, misperconning, iniurring, or bludevict, betuixt merchand and merchand in thair saidis wayages ather be land or be sey, the almess collectit ilk day or ilk secund or third day in the sey efter Goddis service and ordinar prayeris in the morning, all sowmes of money promesit, and conditiones to the pure, in tymes of distres and storme of wether, in perell and danger of thair lyvis, be the merchandis ; everie merchand or as mony of ane schippis merchandis as waschis thair heidis in France, Flanderis, Danskin, or uther cuntries, to gif and collect to the said box to the honour of God and thair pure and nedie brethrene, and to thair vyffis and bairnis left in pouertie and distres." Burgh Recs. Aberdeen, 1600, ii. 215, Sp. C.

To FRAK, v. n. To burst, break, rush or pass quickly over. L. Lat. *fractare.*
Than quho sall wirk for warldis weak,
Quhen flude and fyre sall our it *frak*,
And frely fruster feild and fure
With tempest kene and biddouss crak ?
Dunbar, Quhome to Sall I Complene, 1. 77.

To FRESE, FRESLE, v. a. To undo, unbend, slack, as "to *frese* a bow ;" to furl, as "to *frese* a sail ;" to untwine, untwist, as "to *fresle* out a cord."
O. Fr. *fresler*, " to furle, to slacken or undo ;" Cotgr.

FRUG, FRUGGE, s. A loose upper or overcoat, a cloak or mantle of coarse cloth : also a coverlet, rug, or other covering. V. FROG.
The pure Cottar lykand to die—
And lies twa ky, but ony ma,
The Vickar must haif ane of thay,
With the gray *frugge* that covers the bed,
Howbeit the wyfe be purelie cled.
Lindsay, Thrie Estaitis, l. 2731.

Frugge here evidently means the wife's gray cloak, which was also used as a coverlet by night: the poet thus indicates the poverty of the family.
O. Fr. *froc*, from Lat. *frocus*, a monk's frock : hence any loose upper garment or covering.

FUFFY, *adj.* Short tempered, huffy. V. **FUFF.**

FUFFILY, *adv.* Huffily; scornfully.

FUILRATH, FAILRATH, *s.* Court of bloodwits, i.e., *wites* or penalties for shedding blood; also, right to hold such courts; Celtic Scotland, III. 217.

"Earl Malcolm granted the lands . . . , with court of bloodwits, which is called in Scotch *failrath*. Orig. Paroch., I. 35.
Gael. *fuil*, blood, family, tribe, and *ràith*, appeal, umpire.

FUISH, FOSII, *pret.* Fetched. V. *Fotch*, **FUSII.**

FULLE, *adj.* Foul, base, shameful: "a *fulle* deid," a foul death. V. **FULYIE.**

FULLELIE, *adv.* Foully, shamefully.

Ane croce that was baith large and lang,
To beir thai gaif that blissit Lord;
Syn *fullelie*, as theif to hang,
Thai harlit him furth with raip and corde.
Dunbar, The Passioun of Christ, l. 51.
A.-S. *fúl*, foul; Icel. *fúll*, Sw. *ful*, Dan. *fuul.*

FUR, *s.* A furrow. *To hold the fur,* to keep in the furrow, to plough straight. Addit. to **FUR,** q. v.

Gif that he [the bishop] commis not in at the door,
Goddis plough may never *hold the fur*.
Priests of Peebles.
That is, the true work of the Church can never prosper under a false bishop.

FURE, *pret.* Fared, fed; A.-S. *fóron,* pt. pl. of *faran.*

And of thair merry cheer what make I mair,
Thay *fure* as well as any folk might fare.
Priests of Peebles.

G.

GABART, GABBART, GAUBART, GAUBERT, *s.* A gabardine: a coarse frock or upper garment: applied also to the close-fitting cloak worn by travellers, which was really a loose greatcoat. Addit. to **GALBERT,** q. v.

"Item, ane *gaubart* of russat, xx s.; item, ane hagtoune of rayit clayth, xviij d." Burgh Recs. Stirling, 1521, p. 13.
The loose great-coat or cloak worn by the old chartered beggars called "*bluegowns,*" was often called a *gabart* or *gabardine*.
The form Galbert given by Jamieson is merely graphic, and does not represent the sound. The *lb* is really an old way of writing *bb* ; and the true form of the word is *gabbart*.
Span. *gabardina*, a coarse frock : an extension of Span. *gaban*, a great-coat with a hood. See Skeat's Etym. Dict. s. v. *Gabardine*.

GAIRDONE, *s.* Prob. for *guerdon*, recompense, reward.

Na grome on ground my *gairdone* may degraid.
Henryson, Aige and Yowth, st. 3.
Not defined in DICT.; and Jamieson's suggestion as to meaning is wrong. He is right, however, in reading *grume* for *growine*: Laing's ed. has *grome*.
O. Fr. *guerdon*, from L. Lat. *widerdonum*, corr. from O. H. Ger. *widarlôn*, a recompense, lit. a back-loan, A.-S. *wither-lean*.

GAIT DICHTING. GEAT DYCHTYNG, *s.* A burghal tax or custom to pay for keeping the streets clean; also, the proceeds or income obtained from that tax.

Like most of the burghal taxes, this one was paid in kind. The person who undertook to keep the streets clean got a ladle-full of every boll of grain or victual brought to the market for sale; hence, this tax was also called "*the ladle.*" But as the burgh increased in population this custom became more and more valuable, and the authorities made the most of it by letting it annually to the highest bidder. In the larger burghs, indeed, it was a most important source of income. In Stirling, for instance, this custom, which was let for £12 in the year 1520, at the close of that century realized £120; and fifty years later it was let for twice that amount. But as the custom increased in value and importance as a source of revenue, it pressed more and more heavily on the merchants and dealers, and various attempts were made to limit its claims or to evade its imposition.
Early in the seventeenth century the spirit of opposition to this custom was very strong in large burghs; but the dispute was brought to a head, and to the test of law, by the action of the burgess dealers in Stirling, who claimed exemption from the impost on the ground that—"the layddell dewtie of the said burgh of Sterling, and of all uther burrowis of this kingdome, utherwyse callit the *geat dychtyngis*, gevin fra the begInyng to the burrowes for keiping of the geattis of the burghes cleine, is onlie extendit aganes unfremen who presentis thair victuall to the mercatis of the saidis burrowes allanerlie and na farder." Burgh Recs. Stirling, 1636, p. 176.
The Lords of Secret Council, however, decided against this claim, asserted the lawfulness of the custom, defined its scope and extent in the following terms:—"That the act foirsaid anent the custome of the laidill is lauchfullie maid for the weil of the said burgh, and ordenis the same to rossave executioun, with this interpretatioun, limitatioun, and restrictioun alwyse, that the said act salbe extendit only againes suche persones inhabitantes of the said burgh who buyes and bringis vituall to the said burgh and sellis the same over againe in that kynd, space, and sort as it was bocht ; and that the same he nocht extendit to na victuale brocht in ather bi sey or land belongand to fremen for the exercese of thair awin tredd."

GANGARRIS, GANGERS, s. pl. V. DICT.
Delete the entry under this heading in DICT. Jamieson here followed Pinkerton who read *gangarris* for *gang garris*. The line runs thus :—
"His gang garris all your chaluneris schog." And the meaning is, "His tread makes all your chambers shake." See Laing's ed. of Dunbar, vol. ii., p. 296.

GANTAR, *adj.* Poverty-stricken, pauper.
"And among the sums given yearly out of the bishoprick includes 18 bolls of victual and £10 paid to *gantar* men of Nyg and Terbat." Orig. Paroch., vol. ii. pt. ii., 445.
Gael. *gann*, scarce, mean, poor; *gannlachd*, *ganntar*, scarcity, poverty, want.

GAUBERT, GAUBART, *s.* V. GALBERT, *Gabart.*

GAUDON, *s.* Prob. a corr. of *guidon*, a banner.
"Item, tua *dragonis* for the *gaudons*." Invent. Vestments, &c. in St. Salv. Coll. St. Andrews, Mait. C. Misc., iii. 199.
O. Fr. *guidon*, a banner, from L. Lat. *guido*, id.; but both are of Teut. origin, and prob. allied to Goth. *witan*, to watch, observe, A.-S. *witan*, to observe. Cf. Icel. *viti*, a leader, signal: the primary use of the banner being that of a guide or sign. See under *Guide* in Webster and Skeat.

GEIR, *s.* A green strip of land; Recs. Old Dundee, p. 242. E. *gore.* A form of GAIR, s. 2, q. v.

GIEN, GINE, *part. pt.* Given. V. GIE.

GINGER-NUTS, *s. pl.* Short for *gingerbread nuts*, small gingerbread-biscuits.

GIRTHS, GIRTHES, *s. pl.* Rods or poles from which barrel-hoops are made. Addit. to GIRTH, q. v.
Coopers still call their hoops *girrs*, and the rods from which they are made *girths*.
"If ony outintounsman cum to Glasgow to sell ony rungs, staps, stings, or *girthes*, qubaireiver he hes thame ather be sea or land, and comes to ony brother of craft to sell the samyne." MS. Minute Book of the Coopers of Glasgow, 14 May, 1632.

GLECK, *s.* Vanity: applied to an idol. A form of Glaik, a pretence, image, toy: see s. 11 in DICT.
"We will not fall down and worship the dol that Nebuchadneassar has set up: if our God please he can deliver us; but whether he will deliver us or not, we will not bow down to your *Glecks*." Sermons by Mr. William Guthrie, p. 13.

GLYED, *adj.* Squint-eyed. V. GLEY'D.

GOOD-SON, *s.* V. GUD-SONE.

GORGETT, *s.* A neckerchief, cover for the bosom; Scot. Ball., Child, iii. 246.
O. Fr. *gorge*, the throat: from L. Lat. *gorgia*, id

GOS, Goss, *s.* Short for *goshawk*, a falcon.
Swift as the *gos* drives on the wheeling hare.
Burns, The Brigs of Ayr.

GOUDIE, *s.* An office-bearer of an incorporation who keeps one of the keys of the Box; also, the name of the office. Syn. *boxmaster.*
In each of the incorporated trades of Glasgow there were two such officers; and they were always selected from the Master Court: one was chosen by the Deacon, the other by the freemen of the trade. The incorporation of Cordiners is perhaps the only one which still retains this old term; and the following are its rules regarding appointments to the office.
"One Master, to hold office for one year, shall be nominated and appointed by the Deacon, and be called the Deacon's *Goudie*, or keeper of a key of the Box.
"A Trade's Goudie or keeper of a key of the Box, from among the nine Masters, to hold office for one year." Rules and Regulations of the Incorporation of Cordiners in Glasgow, p. 3.

To GOUL, GOWL, *v. n.* To howl, roar, rave, as the wind. E. *yowl.* Addit. to GOUL, q. v.
"When the wind *gowls* in the chimney, and the rain tirls on the roof." L. R. Stevenson, Kidnapped, p. 271.

GOWL, *v.* and *s.* V. GOUL.

GRANDRIE, GRANDERIE, GRANDORIE, *s.* A septennial court anciently held in Shetland for the purpose of abating nuisances and punishing local abuses; also, nuisance, abuse.
"Giff na man compleins upon swyne ruting, it aucht not to be tane up be way of *Granderie*. Yet nevartheles, the Laird, contrair the law and practik of the cuntrie, put it up as ane article of the *Granderie*." Oppression in Orkney, p. 46.
Icel. *grand*, hurt, injury, evil-doing; and *rof*, review, court of review, lit. reversal of judgment.

GRAVAT, GRAVIT, *s.* A woollen neck-tie or scarf, a cravat: *the hemp-gravat*, the hangman's rope. A corr. of E. *cravat*, from Fr. *cravate.*
"Tie a green *gravat* round his neck,
 And lead him out and in,
 And the best ae servant about your house,
 To wait young Benjie on."
 Ballad, Young Benjie.
Cravats were introduced into France in 1636, being worn by the Croatians, who were called *Crovates* or *Cravates* by the French. V. Skeat's Etym. Dict.

GRAVIL, *s.* The plant graymill or gromwell, of the genus *Lithospermum*, anciently used in the cure of gravel: hence its name.
This plant was said to be used also in procuring abortion; and in this connection it is mentioned in some of our older ballads.

 O! why pou ye the pile, Margaret,
 The pile o' the *gravil* green,
 For to destroy the bonny bairn
 That we got us between.
 Ballad, Tam-a-Line.
Its French name is *grémil*, from which has come the popular name *graymill.*

To GREATH, *v. a:* To prepare. V. GRAITH

GRESSING, GERSING, s. Grazing, pasturing; right to graze or pasture.

"The loch of Garloch with the fishings of the same; the forest, pasturage, and *gressing* of Glaslatter, &c." Orig. Paroch., vol. ii., pt. 2, p. 407.
". . heretable infeftment of thair landis quhilk are teillable, and the utinland to be sowmit be *gersing* [i.e. according to their right to graze]." Burgh Recs. Prestwick, p. 78, Mait. C.

GREY MEAL, GRAY MEIL, s. The refuse and sweepings of a meal-mill, used for feeding poultry : properly, dirty meal.

"John Braedine, in Kilbirnie, was called before the Presbytery of Irvine in 1647 for calling his minister's doctrines *Dust and Gray Meal.* He was ordained first to make confession of his fault on his knees in presence of the Presbytery ; and also before his own congregation in the place of public repentance." Laird of Logan, p. 578.

GROFFE, adj. Coarse, rough; Leslie, Hist. Scot., p. 94, S.T.S. Addit. to GROFF, q. v.

GRULE, GRULL, s. Dry peat that has to be worked like mortar. Addit. to GRULL, q. v.

"When peats have to be made from *grule*, "a quantity of it is puddled in water till it assumes a proper consistency, when it is formed into convenient pieces and spread abroad to dry." Laird of Logan, p. 584.

GUEST QUARTERS, s. Board and lodging which *bordland*-holders were bound to supply to the King or Jarl when he was passing through the country; also, the occasional residence of the King or Jarl as guest of his husbondi ; Oppressions in Ork. and Shetl., p. 126.

H.

HABBIE-GOUN, s. A loose upper garment, a monk's frock.

Cum on, Sir Freir, and be nocht fleyit,
The King our maister mon be obeyit,
Bot ye sall have na harme :
Gif ye wald travell fra touu to toun,
I think this hude and *habbie-goun*
Will hald your wame outr warme.
Lyndsay, Thrie Estaitis, l. 3636.

Rendered "*habergeon, coat of mail,*" in Gloss. to Laing's ed.; but it certainly means a monk's frock or habit.

HAGTOUN, s. An acton. V. HOGTONE.

HALFER, HAUFER, HAWFAR, s. One half; pl. *halfers, hawfaris :* in *halfers,* in half shares.

"The said day, the wyf of Patry Walcar grantit acho had ane young swyne in *hawfaris* betuix hir and Ellene Crippill, quharfore the said Elene protestit for the profittis of the half of the said swyne." Burgh Recs. Aberdeen, 24 July, 1517, Sp. C.

HANAPER, HANEPAR, s. Hamper, crate, or basket; Orig. Paroch., I. 479.

L. Lat. *hanaperium,* a basket to keep cups in : from O. Fr. *hanap* (which in L. Lat. became *hanapus*), a cup. The origin of the term was prob. O. H. Ger. *hnapf,* a cup : cf. A.-S. *hnæp,* a cup or bowl.

HANCH, HANCHE, s. "*hanche* bane,*" haunch or thigh bone, Leslie, Hist. Scot., p. 46, S. T. S. V. HAINCH.

HARATHOR, s. A corr. of *Aratre,* q. v.; Orig. Paroch., I. 27.

HASAN, s. A young seal: a more common name is *tangie,* dimin. of *tang;* Orkn.

(Sup.)   P 2

HAVERPENNY, AVERPENNY, s. Money paid by a vassal to provide *averia,* i.e., beasts of burden, for his superior ; Cal. Doc. Scot., I. 247, Rec. Series.

HAWS, s. pl. Low flat lands near a river, as, "The *Haws* o' Cromdale ;" Scot. Ball., Child, vii., 234-5. V. HAUGH.

HAYBOTE, HEYBOTE, s. The repairing of hedges ; hedge-wood, material for mending hedges.

"They shall have reasonable estovers, viz., husbote, *heybote,* and firbote in the granters' woods in said bounds." Cal. Doc. relating to Scot., i. 290, Rec. Series.
A.-S. *hege,* a hedge, and *bót, bóte,* remedy, repair.

HE JO, *interj.* and *v.* Rejoice ; shout with joy.

Favour is fair in luvis lair,
Yit freindschip mair bene to commend :
Bot quhair despair bene adversar ;
Nothing is thair bot wofull end.
Off men I mene, in scheruice bene,
Of Venus quene but conforting ;
Be thame I wene that mon sustene
The kairis kene of Cupeid king.——
Hir court *he jo* quhair evir thay go
The lyfe is so echo dois thaume len ;
Quhair bis bes wo withowttin bo,
He is sic so till faythfull men.
Alex. Scott's Poems, p. 67, ed. 1882.

HEMINGES, s. pl. Pieces of deer-hide of which rullions were made ; Sir Tristrem, l. 476, S. T. S. Improperly defined in DICT. under HEMMYNYS, q. v.

HEND, HENDE, HIND, HYND, adj. Kind,

mannerly, courteous: Pop. Ballads; Douglas, II. 267, 15, Small; Sir Tristrem, l. 55, 62: also freq. used as a *s.*

HENDLAIKE, HINDELAIKE, HYNDLAIKE, *s.* Courtesy, kindness.

HENDLY, HENDELY, *adv.* Kindly, gently, courteously.
A.-S. *hendig,* skilful; Dan. *hændig,* dexterous, *haandelag,* handiness, dexterity.

HERS, HERSS, *s.* Addit. to *Hearse.*
". . . for furnessing of candillis to the baill *herssis* in the kirk, and als to the pulpitt; and siclyk ordanis that in all tyme cumming the maister of kirk for the tyme sall caus furneiss the haill commoun lichtis and candillis of the kirk, to vit, the *herssis,* pulpitt, and redaris lattroun, togidder with the principall and chief daskis of bayth the kirkis quhair the magistrattis and counsall usais to sitt." Burgh Recs. Aberdeen, ii., 207, Sp. C.

To HERY, HERE, *v. a.* To honour, revere: pret. and part. pt. *hered, herid,* honoured; used also as an *adj.* reverend; Allit. Rom. Alex., l. 1637.
A.-S. *herian,* to praise, commend: from A.-S. *here,* praise, fame.

HET, HETE, *s.* and *v.* Hate.

HETRENT, HETTRENT, HETTRAND, *s.* Hatred. V. HATRENT.

HICHTY, *adj.* Haughty. Addit. to HICHTY, q. v.

HICHTINES, s. Haughtiness, overbearing.
"Of this cumis thair pryd and *hichtines,* and boasting of thair nobilitie." Leslie, Hist. Scot., p. 96, S.T.S.

HILIE, *adj.* Proud. V. HELIE.

HODDLE, *s.* Step, pace, jog-trot. *To hune one's hoddle,* to slack one's pace; Laird of Logan, p. 585. V. HODDLE, *v.*

HORN, *s.* 1. Short for *snuff-horn,* also called a *mill* or *mull*: "Freend, hau' roun' your *horn.*"

2. Short for *horn-comb,* a large-toothed comb, a redding-comb.
Whare *horn* nor bane ne'er dare unsettle
Your thick plantations.
Burns, Address to a Louse.

3. The shod, tip, or point for a lace or thong.

To HORN, HORNE, *v. a.* To tip or point; to fasten the shod or tip, i.e., the *horn,* on a lace or thong.
"That nane within the said burt freinyie or pasment gluiffis, schaip or *horne* pointis, schaip or mak purssis nor bald servandis to do the same." Eik to the Seal of Cause of the Skinners of Glasgow, 5 Feb., 1605.

HOUSBOTE, HUSBOTE, *s.* The repairing of houses; house-wood, material for repairing one's house; Cal. Doc. Scot., i. 290, Rec. Series. See under *Haybote.*
A.-S. *hús,* a house, and *bót, bóte,* remedy, repair.

HOWLLIS HALD, *s.* Del. in DICT.: a misreading of *Yowllis Yald,* q. v.
This extraordinary misreading occurs in Pinkerton's version of Scottish Poems from the Maitland MS.

HOWNE, HUNE, *s.* Delay; forms of HONE, *s.,* q. v.

HUIT, *s.* and *v.* Heap. V. HUT.

HUSSCE, HUSSE, *s.* The dog-fish. Addit. to HUSH, q. v.
The skin of this fish was used for trimming arrows.
"*Hussces* skins for fletcheris, the skin . . . vi s."
Rates and Customs, 1612, Halyburton's Ledger, p. 315.
"Skins called *husse* skins for fletchers, the skin . . . vi s." Ibid., p. 328.

HYNE, *s.* A hind: fem. of hart; Leslie, Hist. Scot., p. 19, S.T.S.

I.

INDIFFERENT, *adj.* Without difference, like, alike, similar, the same.
Until almost the present century *indifferent* and *indifferently* were invariably used in their literal sense in Scot.
"The consultaris with the saidis wicked abusaris . . . are na lesse gilty be the lawis of God and man then thay actuall witcheis, . . . and meritis with thame *indifferent* and equall punishment." Reg. Privy Council, 1597, v. 410.

To INLOW, *v. a.* To allow, grant, pay.
"Gif it hapin common wer of Inglismen and the saidis landis be destroit, the forsaide lady oblisis her to *inlow* to the said Alex. . . . as uthir lordis *inlowis* to thair tenandis." Reg. Mag. Sig., 1424-1513, No. 473.
Prefix *in-* with the force of *ad-,* and O. Fr. *louer,* to hire, rent, grant. See Cotgr. O. Fr. *louer* in this sense = Lat. *locare.*

INTEST. V. DICT.
Delete the entry under this heading in DICT. *Intest* is an error in Pinkerton's version of the Houlate for *in test.,* a contraction for *in testamento,* in the testimony or declaration, an old law form equivalent to "in his schedule or application." Hence it was unnecessary to state his case orally, since it was fully told in his application to the court. And as the court to which

the owl appealed was a consistory court, its jurisdiction was testamentary.

INTHROW, *prep.* Within, in the interior of: used in referring to a district of country. Addit. to INTHROW, q. v.

"I would rather have one of yon sufferers that is bred in Christ's school *inthrow* Clydesdale yonder, than a hundred of you to join with me. You have no weight with God, no grace, no scholars at Christ's school, and therefore ye are but dead folk." The Lord's Trumpet, p. 7.

To INTRAIT, INTRATE, *v. n.* To treat of; Abp. Hamilton's Catechism, fol. 79 b. Addit. to *Intreit*, q. v.

To INTYSE, INTYST, *v. a.* To entice.

"Or gif ony of thame wald *intyst,* counsel, and draw the to ony unlesum thing, in sa mekil that gif thow do nocht thair counsel and bidding, thow sall tyne thair favour." Abp. Hamilton's Catechism, Fol. 40b.

O. Fr. *enticer, enticher, enticier,* to excite, entice; see Burguy.

To IRM, *v. n.* To whine, complain. V. YIRM.

To ISS, *v. n.* and *a.* To pass out, retire, withdraw. Addit. to ISCHE, *v.,* q. v.

"The sissouris suorn, hawand God before, *issit* and come in again, delineris and findis," &c. Burgh Recs. Dunfermline, 2 Sept., 1488.

J.

JERFALCON, GERFAULCON, *s.* The gyrfalcon, peregrine falcon; Rates of Customs, Halyburton's Ledger, p. 313.

O. Fr. *gerfault,* "a Gerfaulcon, the greatest of Hawkes; called also Faulcon gerfaut;" Cotgr.

To JOG, JUG, JUGG, *v. a.* To pierce, job, rip or cut into, with a sharp-pointed instrument, as a flesher may damage a skin in flaying: part. pt. *joggit, juggit.* V. JAG, *v.*

Jog and *jug* are intensive forms of *jag,* to prick, job.

JOIST, *s.* A plank of wood, a spar; Gowrie Conspiracies, p. 44, 57. More commonly JEEST, q. v.

JURR, *s.* A female servant, a menial, a profligate; prob. a corr. of *char,* short for *charwoman,* one who does odd jobs or turns.

As for the *jurr,* poor worthless body,
She's got mischief enough already.
Burns, *Adam Armour's Prayer,* st. 7.

As here used by Burns the term implies a low worthless female, a profligate.

Perhaps from A.-S. *cerr, cierr, cyrr,* a turn: whence M. E. *cher, char,* a turn, turn of work.

K.

KAIL-PAT WHIG, *s.* A person who does not go to church, but stays at home on Sabbath days; Clydes.

During the reign of Prelacy in Scotland those who would not go to church were called Whigs. And since then, those who stay at home to prepare the family meal, or because they have no inclination for church, are called *kail-pat whigs.*

KAIMING - STOCK, KEAMING-STOCK, KEMING-STOCK, *s.* The stock or frame on which the combs were fixed for dressing wool, rippling lint, and breaking flax.

Twa kits, a cogue, a kirn there ban,
A keam, but and a *keaming-stock,*
Of dishes and ladles nine or ten,
Come ye to woo our Jennie, Jock?
The Country Wedding, Herd's Coll., ii. 89.

He fell backward into the fyre,
And brack his head on the *keming-stock.*
Wyf of Auchtirmuchty, l. 84.

In the Glossary to vol. viii. of Child's English and Scottish Ballads this term is by mistake rendered "*back of a chimney grate.*"

To KAITHE, *v. a.* To toss, toss up, cast, throw. V. *Cat, Cathe.*

"He regardet nocht bot walde clate him with his cluifes or *kaithe* him on his hornes." Leslie, Hist. Scot., p. 30, S. T. S.

This is simply a form of *cathe,* to toss. For explanation see under *Cat.*

KARK, *s.* A load, burden. V. CARK.

KASTNE, KASNE, *part. pt.* Forms of *casten,* cast; Leslie, Hist. Scot., p. 121, S. T. S. See under *Fork,* above.

KAX, KEX, *s.* V. CACKS.

KECHING, *s.* V. KITCHEN, *Kitchen.*

KEEP IN YOUR HAN'. 1. Don't strike: used as a command or a threat.

2. Don't spend your money so freely; don't be so ready to help.

KEMING-STOCK, *s.* V. *Kaiming-Stock.*

KENAR, *s.* V. *Kaner, Canare.*

KENDE, KENNE, *s.* Kin, kindred, family; Sir Tristrem, l. 2413, 1233, S.T.S.
Vnkinde were ous to kis
As *kenne.* *Ibid.*, l. 2759.

To KERE, *v. a.* A form of *Kever*, q. v.

To KEVER, KEUER, KERE, *v. a.* To recover, accomplish or gain an end : " *kevered* him," recovered himself ; Awnt. Arth., st. 48.

KILLING, KILLINE, *s.* V. KELING.

KIRK-BRED, *s.* Plate, box, or other vessel for receiving alms in church ; also, churchfunds or money collected for church purposes; Spald. Club Misc., V. 33. See under *Bred.*

KIRK-REEKIT, *adj.* Church bigotted ; Laird of Logan, p. 586.
This term is applied to bigotted churchmen, and to persons who have ill-will against sectaries. Of one who has more zeal than religion it is said,—"He's no very kirk-greedy, but he's gae *kirk-reekit.*"

KIRTLE, KIRTIL, KYRTIL, *s.* A kirtle, gown, skirt, petticoat; also applied to a loose upper garment, tunic, or short mantle. In the older Scot. ballads the term is found in nearly all these senses.
"My Lord Bischop, will ye thairto consent?"
"Na, na ! never till the day of judgment :
We will want nathing that we have in use,
Kirtel nor kow, teind lamb, teind gryse, nor guse."
Lyndsay, Thris Estaitis, l. 2826.
A.-S. *cyrtel*, a tunic ; Icel. *kyrtill*, Dan. *kiortel*, Sw. *kjortel.* *Kirtle* is prob. a dimin. of *skirt.* V. Skeat's Etym. Dict.

KITCHEN, KITCHING, KICHING, KECHING, *s.* Allowance, perquisite, emolument. Addit. to KITCHEN, *s.*, q. v.
Kitchen, short for *kitchen-fee*, dripping, which is reckoned a perquisite of the cook, is still metaph. used, especially by female servants, for the allowauces, perquisites, or other droppings of income connected with a situation. And the word was similarly used by Winzet (see Tractates, p. 8), when ho blamed the Scottish nobles for "appropryng the Kirk landis to thair awin *kechinges.*" So also in the following passage by Archbishop Hamilton :—
"And giffis ane benefice with sic conditioun that the *kepar* of the said benefice sall haif bot ane sober pensioun, that the giffar of that benefice may get in the laif to thame self and thair *keching.*" Catechism, fol. 60a.

KITH, *s.* V. DICT.
Under this heading in DICT. delete the definition and the first quotation given for s. 2: they relate to KYTHE, not to KITH. Delete also the first sentence of the last paragraph : it too relates to KYTHE.
Then substitute the following definition :

2. Native land, country, home ; Awnt. Arth., st. 12.
For this defin. the quotations from Brunne and Langland are very suitable.

KITH, *s.* Appearance, countenance, bearing. Addit. to KYTHE, *s.*, q. v.
The king cumly in *kith* coverit with croune,
Callit knychtis sa kene.
Gaw. and Gol., st. 25.
This is simply a form of *kythe*, from A.-S. *cythan*, to make known, der. from *cúth*, known.

KITTIE-STICK, *s.* A small rod on which pirns are put in order that the thread may be wound off them. Also called a *pirn-stick.*
V. [KITTIE-SWEERIE.]

KLIBBAR, *s.* A packsaddle. V. CLIBBER.

To KNICK, NICK, *v.* 1. As a *v n.:* to click, crack; to make a clicking sound ; "He can gar his fingers *knick.*"

2. As a *v. a.:* to cause to click or crack.
May Margaret sits in the queen's bouir,
Knicking her fingers ane by ane,
Cursing the day that she e'er was born,
Or that she e'er heard o' Logie's name.
Ballad, The Laird o' Logie, l. 10.

KNIR, KNIRR, KNUR, KNURR, *s.* A knot in wood : an old, wizened, or decrepit person, a dwarf. V. KNURL.
Lot's wife was fresh compared to her ;
They've Kyanised the useless *knir*,
She canna decompose—uae mair
Than her accursed annuity.
George Outram, The Annuity.
Although *knur* and *knurl* are similarly used, *knurl* is properly a dimin. of *knur*, M. E. *knor*, a knot in wood : from O. Dutch *knorre*, a hard swelling.
Knir or *knur* is the same word as in the famous Northern E. game of *knurr and spell*, i.e., ball and bat. The *knurr* is a wooden ball, made out of a hard and knotty piece of wood. V. KNURLS.

KNOCKIN-MELL, *s.* A wooden mall or beetle with which linen cloth was beaten after it was bleached. Addit. to KNOCKIN MELL, q. v.

KNOCKIN-STANE, *s.* A large flat stone on which linen cloth was beaten after it was bleached. Addit. to KNOCKIN-STANE, q. v.

KNULLED, *pret.* and *part. pt.* V. *Knool, v.*

KYNEYERDE, *s.* A king's *yerd* or wand, i.e., a sceptre; Ballad, Sir Simon Fraser, l. 68. V. *Yerd.*

To KYTHE, *v. a.* To work, perform ; Abp. Hamilton's Catechism, fol. 52 a, 109 a. Addit. to KYTHE, q. v.

L.

To **LACHE**, Lacche, *v. a.* To take, catch, seize; pret. and part. pt. *lacht, laght, laught;* Gol. and Gaw., st. xlviii., xlix., lix.

M. Eng. *lacchen*, to catch: from A.-S. *læccan*, to seize, catch hold of.

LACHFASTING, *s.* Keeping land lying lea, i.e., in grass or uncultivated.

"The linkis of Lythis is maisterfullie and againe the law attour *lachfasting* ilk yeir thir xx yeiris bigan occupiit be the uthalmen of Akiris and Lythis and nathing payit for the samin. Thairfor remember to tak law therupoun." Peterkin, Rentals of Orkney, No. 1., p. 22.

Icel. *ljá*, grass, grass-land; and *festa*, to fasten, keep or hold fast; *festing*, a fixing, fastening.

LAGHT, Laught, *pret.* Seized. V. *Lache*.

LAIL, Laill, *adj.* Lawful, right, proper. V. Leil.

"*Laill* advisement being given to the saids baillies theranent." Culross and Tulliallan, i. 280.

LANDSETTERCOP, *s.* A fee or fine paid by the tenant at the letting or reletting of a farm; Oppressions in Orkn. and Shetl., p. 126.

Icel. *landsetr-kaup*, payment at the setting or letting of land.

LANDSKYLD, *s.* An old name for the rent of a farm in Shetland; like Scot. *landmale;* Oppressions in Orkn. and Shetl., p. 126.

Icel. and Dan. *landskyld*, land-tax, field-rent, rent of a farm.

LANER, Lanare, Lanret, *s.* The lanneret or long-tailed hawk; Rates of Customs, Halyburton's Ledger, p. 313.

O. Fr. *laneret*, a species of hawk: dimin. from Lat. *laniarius*, a butcher.

By some authors the lanner or lanneret is said to be the young of the peregrine falcon: by others it is represented as a distinct but allied species. V. Jardine's Birds of Europe.

LANG, *adj.* as *s.* Length, extent; as, "the *lang* and the braid o't," i.e., the length and the breadth of it: "a butt-*lang*, a butt-length, i.e., the length of a pair of butts or targets, or the distance between them; pl. butt-*langs*, Gowrie Conspiracies, p. 57. V. Butelang.

LATE-WAKE, *s.* A corr. of Lyke-Wake, q. v.; Annals of the Parish, ch. 24.

LAUCHTY, *adj.* Long, tusky, projecting: made or fit for seizing or tearing. V. *Lache*.

She had *lauchty* teeth an' kaily lips,
An' wide lugs fu' o' hair.
 Ballad, Kempy Kaye, l. 37.

LAUMER, *s.* Amber. V. Lammer.

LAW-DAYS, *s. pl.* A Border assize: "to keep the *Law Days*," to hold an assize, or to be present at one.

From Edinburgh Queen Mary "went to Jedburgh to keep the *Law Days*, which are wont to be held there every year, with the intention of bringing the Borders into order, and punishing the thieves who live in the neighbouring mountains." Stevenson, Translation of Nau's Memorials of the Reign of Mary Stewart, p. 30.

LAWRIGHTMAN, *s.* An official chosen by the Vard-Thing, and charged with the custody and application of the Standard of Weights and Measures, and bound to represent his Herad or Parish in the Law-Thing. In modern times this name was given to the local umpires called rancelmen: Memorial for Orkney, p. 116. Addit. to Lagraetman.

LAY, *adj.* Fallow: a form of Lea, q. v.

To **LAY**, *v. a.* To bet, wager: "I *lay* a groat:" "I dar *lay*;" Dunbar, p. 165, ed. Small.

Lat Symone one fer stand fra the bede,
And ye sal se I *lay* wede,
The fendis craft sone onbyde.
 Barbour's Saints, Peter, l. 486.

This application of *lay* no doubt arose from the custom of bettors placing or laying down their bets by way of guarantee.

LEAR-STANE, *s.* A sort of pillory for the punishment of liars.

In the Burgh Court of Dunfermline on the 17th of March, 1499, "Ellyn of Walwode" was found by an assize to be "ane strubler of Robyn Gibson be detraccione," and doom was given accordingly. Cases of this kind had probably been on the increase at that time, for on the same day an assize considered what ought to be done to suppress such conduct, and their deliverance is thus recorded:—"The quhilk day it was delyverit be ane assise that the *lear-stane* suld be set againe in the place where it was wont to stand, or els ane als gude stane."

The *lear-stane* was therefore an old institution in Dunfermline; and, as burghal life was then very much alike all over the country, this mode of punishment was prob. as well known in other districts. Like the pillory, jougs, etc., this stone was most prob. set near the Tolbooth. See Burgh Life in Dunfermline in the Olden Time, p. 16.

LECCAM, *s.* Body. V. Licaym.

LESQUE, *s.* A pasture; Leslie, Hist. Scot., p. 27, S. T. S. A.-S. *leswe*. V. Lesuris.

LETTGANT, LETTGANT-BED, s. A camp-bed; a portable or travelling bed. A corr. of Fr. *lit-de-champ.* V. [LETACAMPBED].

"Item, ane *lettgant bed* furneist witht Flandreis werdour, blancattis, scheittis and coddis, witht all maner of wtheris necessaris, pryce xx lib." Burgh Recs. Glasgow, i. 32, Rec. Soc.

To LEVE, LEUE, v. a. To believe, credit; Awnt. Arth., st. xxxvii. V. LEIF.

LEVER, LEWER, LEWAR, s. Vent, windows, or similar opening in the roof of a house. V. *Livra.*

With that the Cok over the feildis tuke his flight,
And in at the Wedowis *lewar* couth he licht.
Henryson, Chantecleir and Foxe, l. 189.

LICHAM, LICHE, LIKE, s. The body. Addit. to LICAYM, q. v.

To LIPPEN, v. a. and n. *To lippen in,* to confide in; Abp. Hamilton's Catechism, fol. 131 b: *to lippen to,* to depend or rely upon; Ibid., fol. 76 a: *to lippen with,* to entrust with, in the sense of handing over to another, as, "I'll *lippen* ye wi' my siller." Addit. to LIPPEN, q. v.

LITHER, LYTHER, LETHIR, adj. Evil, wicked, base.

LITHERLY, LETHIRLY, adv. Wickedly, basely.

And ilkane nycht as day cane daw,
As he mycht heyre the cok craw,
Thane wald he think quhow *lethirly*
That he his master outh deny.
Barbour's Saints, Peter, 1. 59.

A.-S. *lyther, lythre,* bad, wicked. Cf. Icel. *leidr.*

LOWIS, s. pl. Lochs: "*the Lowis,*" the Lochs or arms of the sea on the west coast of Scotland; Act. Parl. Scot., III. 309, Rec. Series. Errat. in DICT.

This term, which occurs frequently in the Exchequer Rolls and in the Acts of Parl., was until lately generally understood to mean the islands of Lewis; and it was so rendered by Jamieson. This, however, has been found to be a mistake; and Dr. Burnett has shown that it was the name applied to the Lochs on the west coast. See Exch. Rolls Scot., Vol. IX., Pref., p. 74, Rec. Series.

LUFRAY, s. V. *Luvery.*

To LUIT, LUTE, LUK, v. a. and n. To bend, bow, bow down. V. LOUT.

Jok said, Forsuth I yern full fane
To *luk* my heid, and sit doun by yow.
Wowing of Jok and Jenny, Bann. MS.

Luk here represents a corr. and vulgar pron. of *lout,* which is still common in those districts in which *t* is sounded as a guttural. In the modern version of the Wowing printed in Herd's Scot. Songs, ed. 1776, with the title, The Country Wedding, the passage runs thus:—

Ay, dame, says he, for that I yern.
To *lout* my head, and sit down by you.

For further illustration of this pron. of *t,* see *Lichis,* in Suppl.

LUVERY, LUVRIE, LUFRAY, s. Forms of *livery,* a gift, present. V. LEVERE'.

Grit G⁻d releif Margaret our quene;
For and scho war as scho hes bene,
Scho wald be lerger of *lufray,*
Than all the laif that I of mene,
For lerges of this New Yeirday.
Stewart, Lerges, lerges, Bann. MS., p. 276, Hunt. Soc.

M.

To MAGG, v. a. To mangle, cut up; a form of MANG, q. v.

To MAK. Add the following:—

1. To Mak *awa wi',* v. a. To carry off; to expend, spend, waste; also, to kill.

2. To Mak *mens.* To make amends.

3. To Mak *ower,* v. a. To pass quickly over a wall, river, etc., in order to escape. To *mak aff ower* is also used.

MALATOUT, s. A special tax claimed by the king.

"Saving to the king the custom called *malatout.*"
Orig. Paroch., vol. ii., pt. ii., p. 561.

O. Fr. *mal-toute, maltoulte, maletoste,* "an exaction, imposition, toll, a new or extraordinarie taxation;" Cotgr. So called, because held as *mal tollué.* The name was first applied to an extraordinary tax levied by Philip le Bel in 1206; see under *Maletoste* and *Maletoulte* in Cotgrave, and under *Maltôte* in Littré.

The form *maletoste* is corrupt. Littré shows that it was at first *male-tolte* or *male-toulte,* where *tolte* represents L. Lat. *tolta,* fem. pp. of *tollere.*

To MANCHLE, v. a. To maim, mangle, injure; in reference to documents, to vitiate, alter, corrupt. Frequent. form of MANK, q. v.

"Memorandum to tak the salmond the third, not as it is rentallit, bot as it givis, for this rental is *manchlit.*"
Orig. Paroch., vol. ii., pt. ii., p. 512.

Anglo-Fr. *mahangler,* to maim: freq. of O. Fr. *mahaigner, mehaingner,* to mutilate, from *mahain, mehaing,* imperfection. See Skeat's Etym. Dict. under *Mangle*; and Burguy's Gloss. under *Mahain.*

MAND. A form of *man it,* manage it, accomplish it: like *duid* for *do it.*

MAND, MANT, MAUNT, *pret.* and *part. pt.* Managed, accomplished, attained; "He mand or mant to do't." V. MAN.
> Death's *maunt* at last to ding me owre,
> An' I'll soon hae to lea' ye.
> *Alex. Wilson, Calimphitre's Elegy.*

MANLY, *adj.* Manlike, human.
> "Al thir paynis tholit he for us in his *manly* nature and nocht in his godly nature." Abp. Hamilton's Catechism, fol. 102 b.

To MANURE, MANOR, *v. a.* To till or cultivate, as, to *manor* the land; to work at, practice, to follow as a profession, as, to *manure* justice, i.e., to practice or follow law.
> "In thame ar mony noblemen, and almaist all bot cheiflie the mersmen, thay *manure* justice and thay studie to politike effaires." Leslie, Hist. Scot., p. 10, S. T. S.
> *Manure,* short for *manœuvre;* from O. Fr. *manœuvrer,* to hold, occupy, possess; lit. to work by hand; from L. Lat. *manuopera, manopera,* handiwork.

MARISCALL, *s.* V. MARSCHAL.

MARISEALLACH, *s.* Marshalship, stewardship.
> ". . . together with the coronership and stewardship of those fifteen marklands of his own heritage, . . . and the just fourth part of the *Mariseallach* of the whole." Orig. Paroch., vol. ii., pt. 1, p. 99.

MARK-SHOT, *s.* The distance between the marks or targets in archery; Scot. Ball., Child, I. 274: synon. *butt-lang.*

MAUNT, *pret.* and *part. pt.* V. *Mand.*

MEGIRTIE, *s.* Same as MEGIRKIE, q. v.
> Delete the entry under this heading in DICT., and combine the term with MEGIRKIE, of which it is a variety.

MELLERING, MELLERIN, *s.* Waste meal, the sweepings of a meal-mill; properly the waste-meal gathered after a *melder* or milling. V. MELLER.
> She said—"Gude e'en, ye nettles tall,
> Where ye grow by the dyke;
> If the auld carline, my mither was here,
> Sae weel's she wou'd you pyke.
> "How she wou'd stap ye in her pock,
> I wot she won'dna fail;
> And boil ye in her auld brass pan,
> And of ye mak gnde kail.
> "And she wou'd meal you with *mellering,*
> That she gathers at the mill,
> And mak ye thick as any dough,
> Till the pan it was brimfill."
> *Ballad, Earl Richard,* Scot. vers.

MEMMIT, MEMT, *part. pt.* Errat. for *nemmit, nemt,* named, associated. V. DICT.
> Delete the entry under this heading in Dict., and also the following one under MEMT. *Memmit* is evidently a mistake for *nemmit* in the passage quoted; and Jamieson's explanation is not supported by the context. Besides the word is printed *nemmit* in the 1882 ed. of Alex. Scott's Poems.

MESWAND, *s.* A bar, ingot: "a *meswand* of gold," an ingot of gold; Abp. Hamilton's Catechism, fol. 61b. Addit. to MESWAND, q. v.
> Although left undefined by Jamieson, his suggestions regarding it are correct. The Vulgate renders the term by "*regulam auream.*"

METULAT, *part. pt.* A corr. form of *mutilat,* mutilated.
> ". . . Henry Fennesoun schot in the thie with ane dart, Michaell Smyth schot throw the hand and *metulat* of his formest fingare." Burgh Recs. Glasgow, i. 103, Rec. Soc.

MIND, MYND, *s.* Inclination, desire; *a gude mind,* a strong desire; *of gude mynd,* very desirous, strongly inclined. Addit. to MIND, q. v.
> "His Majestie being *of gude mynd* that the said Sir George be satisfeit of the saidis debursmentis, as ressone requyris." Reg. Privy Council Scot., vi., 40, Rec. Soc.

MING-MANG, *adv.* Confusedly mixed, in disorder: "The things in the drawers were a' *ming-mang.*" V. MING, *v.*

MIRLIN, *s.* V. *Merlion,* MARLEYON.

To MISBEET, *v. a.* Lit. to mis-bundle, to disarrange, mis-assort, mis-match; pret. and part. and part. pt. *misbet.* To *misbeet* a web is to tie up the wrong bundles of warp and weft in giving it out to the weaver. V. *Beet* in Add.
> "Dear me, freens, what's that I hear? The very weans on the street crying—gude day to you Deacon." "No, no, Deacon, it's Hawkie crying a hanging speech, or maybe his cure for ill wives."
> "Is that a'? Weel, lads, that wad be better than Solomon's Balm—for wise as he was he couldna help himsel when he got his web *misbet.*" The Deacon's Day, Whistle Binkie, i. 273.

To MISTER, MYSTER, *v. n.* To be useful for, to minister to: as, "to *mister* to ane's needs," in which sense it is used in Abp. Hamilton's Catechism, fol. 59a. Addit. to MISTER, q. v.

To MOUP, MOOP, *v. a.* and *n.* To moult as a bird: hence, to drop, cast off, or part with. Addit. to MOUP, q. v.
> *Moult* is very commonly expressed by *moup* in the West of Scot.; and that the word is widely used in the sense of to drop, cast off, or part with, is shewn by the popular remark to an unmannerly person: "It's weel seen ye were bred in the mill, ye hae *moupit* a' your manners." V. Henderson's Scot. Proverbs, p. 97, ed. 1881.

MOYNE, *s.* Moon. V. *Mone.*

MUGGANS, *s.* A name for the plant *Mugwort*; Renfrews. V. MUGGER.
> In Caithness and Orkney it is called BULLWAND, q. v.

MUNT, s. and v. Amount. Addit. to *Munt*, q. v.

"Schatt silver and teinds to his Majestie, according to the rentell, quhilk to our knawledge can not be valued nor *munted* heigher nor it is alreddie." Peterkin, Rentals of Orkney, No. III., p. 94.

MURREAN, s. A morion; a kind of helmet without visor or beaver, intended as a covering for the crown of the head.

"Harnes called *murreanes* or heid peices graven the peice, iiili." Rates and Customs, 1612, Halyburton's Ledger, p. 314.

Fr. *morione*; from Span. *morrion*, from *morra*, the crown of the head.

N.

NAEKIN, NAKIN, NAEKINS, *adj*. Of no kind, none at all. Addit. to NAKYN, q. v.

NAGNAIL, NANGNAIL, s. An ingrown nail on the toe; West of S. A corruption of E. *agnail*, which see in Murray's New Eng. Dict.

To NAITE, NAYTE, v. a. To use. Addit. to NATE, q. v.

NARE, s. *Thi nare*, a MS. form for *thin are*, thy favour; Sir Tristrem, l. 2135, S.T.S. See under *Are*, s., in Addenda.

The transfer of final *n* to the word following is frequently found in MSS. It has been the cause of many mistakes; and in the present instance it gave rise to the false form *thinare*, which Sir Walter Scott printed, and which was entered and explained in the DICT.

NASCH, NASCHE, *adj*. Soft, marshy, wet: a form of *nesh*, tender, soft. Addit. to *Nash*, q. v.

". . . and fra the said stane calsay at the end of the hill foirsaid, keipand betuix the *nasche* and the hard north and north eist." Reg. Mag. Sig., 19 Dec., 1584, Rec. Series.

A.-S. *hnæsce*, *hnesce*, soft, tender; Goth. *hnaskwus*.

NAUGHTIE, NOGHTIE, *adj*. Bad, insufficient. Addit. to NOCHTIE, q. v.

". . . buyeth insufficient worsett, . . . and litts [i.e. dyes] the same with *naughtie* cullouris." Burgh Recs. Stirling, 1662, p. 239.

NEAR, NEIR, NERE, NER, *adv*. Nearly, almost: *gae near*, very nearly or narrowly: "He *near* missed it; aye, *gae near*."

NEARLINS, NEIRLINS, NERLINS, *adv*. Nearly, almost: like *near-han*, *ner-han*.

NEIK, NEAK, s. and v. A form of EIK, q. v.

NEIKIT, NEAKIT, *part*. Patched, mended; forms of *eikit*.

"The samyne is decayit and *neakit* in mony places." Culross and Tulliallan, I., 131.

NEST, s. *To look ower the nest* is an expression used regarding young persons when they begin to act for themselves.

To NICK, v. a. To catch, capture, trap; pret. and part. pt. *nicked*, *nickit*. Addit. to *Nick*, q. v.

I think, quo' she, ye're fairly *nicked* now.
Nae hauf sae far, he says, as ye wad trow.
Ross, *Helenore*, p. 169, ed. 1868.

NIRR, s. A knot in wood; a dwarf. V. NURR, *Knir*.

NOMBLES, s. pl. V. *Noumbles*.

To NYAFF, v. n. V. DICT.

NYAFFET, s. A diminutive, conceited chatterer; Laird of Logan, p. 591.

NYAFFING, s. Idle talk or chatter; Ibid.

NYTHE, s. Wickedness, malice; Scot. Ball., Child, VI., 275. A.-S. *níth*, *nýth*.

O.

O, s. A light, or small window; a form of *Oye*, q. v.

"Gevin out of the box to Thomas Pottar to buy glasse and leid to putt ane litle window in the seat, three punds Scottis." MS. Minutes of the Hammermen of Dumbarton, 17th Oct., 1659.

"Thomas Pottar gaue in his accompt concerning the *O* above the seat, quhilk extendis to nyne shillingis six pence sterlingis; 10d. of quhilk is payid to the said Thomas." Ibid., 7th Nov., 1659.

Although the window called an *O* is often found in the form of a circle, it was not so named because it resembles the letter O. For the etym. of the term see under *Oye*. It is simply short for Icel. *auga*, eye.

OCHANIE, *interj*. Alas!: an expression of grief still in use.

Gael. *ochain*, alas!

OGART, *s.* Accusation, evil-speaking, contempt. Addit. to OGART, q. v.

Delete the note under this term in DICT.: the etym. suggested is unsuitable. *Ogart* is from Gael. *agairt*, accusation, fault-finding; from *agair*, "to plead, claim, crave, accuse; require, demand." M'Leod and Dewar.

OGARTFUL, OGERTFU', UGERTFUL, *adj.* Exacting, fastidious, difficult to please: "He's an *ogertfu'* body." Addit. to OGERTFUL, q. v.

OLORINE, *s.* Same as OLOUR, q. v.; Leslie, Hist. Scot., p. 45, S. T. S.

OMNEGATHRUM, OMNIGADDRUM, *s.* A name given to the unincorporated craftsmen of a burgh.

In the larger burghs of Scotland there were three classes of burgesses: the merchants or guild brethren, the incorporated craftsmen, and the unincorporated craftsmen. The last named were deemed a lower order by the other two sections, and, when spoken of as a class, were called the *omnigatherum*. In the burghs generally this name was only occasionally used; but in the royal burgh of Stirling it was almost the only name given to that class during the sixteenth and seventeenth centuries. For example, in the Burgh Records under date 16th July, 1604, regarding a certain taxation to be made, we find: ". . . thairof the merchandis the ane half, and the craftismen and *omnigaddrum* the uther half." And a few months later, under 17th Dec., 1604: "Thair salbe joyned yeirlie to the counsall of this burgh tua of the ald baillies, and tua of the *omnigaddrum*, as extraordinar personesof counsall, conforme to use and wount."

Again, under date 28th Nov., 1642, the arrangement for the salary of the town drummer is: "Of the quhilk thrie scoir foure punds the toun sall pay yeirlie £4, guild brethren £20, the crafts £20, the maltmen £10, and the *omnigadrum*, viz., the wrichtis, maissones, coupares, litstares, glassin-wrichtis, sklaitteris, gairdneris, the soume of ten pundis yeirlie." See Burgh Recs. Stirling, p. 112, 184.

The E. term is *omnium-gatherum*, applied to any very mixed assembly or company.

ONCET, ONEST, *adv.* Once.

ONDE, *s.* Malice, envy; Scot. Ball., Child, VI., 275.

A.-S. *onda*, zeal, envy, malice.

ONFREIND, ONFRIND, *s.* An enemy. V. UNFRIEND.

To **ONHIDE, ONHYDE,** *v. a.* To disclose, expose; Barbour's Saints, Peter, l. 487: also, as a *v. n.*, to become clear, as applied to the weather. V. *Unhide.*

ONKEND, ONKENT, *adj.* and *adv.* Unknown. V. *Unkend.*

ONSICCAR, ONSICKER, ONSIKKER, *adj.* Unsecure, uncertain. V. UNSIKKIR.

ONSPERD, ONSPERT, *adj.* Unasked, unquestioned: also, as an *adv.*, without asking or making enquiry, without having to ask the way. V. *Unspeird.*

With lusty hairt than suld I gif ane loip,
And cum to yow, I ken the gait *onsperd.*
Bann. MS., p. 641, Hunt. Soc.

The adverbial use of this term is still common.

ORGMOUNT, *s.* Singed, sodden, or pealed barley: "sodne beir or *orgmount;*" Leslie, Hist. Scot., p. 98, S. T. S.

For an account of the ancient method of cleaning or peeling grain, see under GRADDAN in DICT., and The Scottish Gael, ii. 103.

O. Fr. *orge*, barley, and *mondé*, cleansed, peeled.

ORTHORT, *prep.* A form of OURTHORT, q. v.

OSTER, OSTIR, *s.* An oyster; Leslie, Hist. Scot., p. 13, 42, S. T. S.; Henryson, Pract. Medecyne, l. 71.

O. Fr. *oistre*, from Lat. *ostrea, ostreum*, an oyster: in Mod. Fr. *huître.*

OTTOUNYR, OTTONYR, *adj.* Pertaining to the *out-town* or out-field lands; Orig. Paroch., Vol. II., pt. 2, p. 671. V. *OutenToun.*

OURDIRKIT, *part. pt.* Darkened, obscured, overcast. V. DIRK.

Ourdirkit with the sable clud nocturn.
Dunbar, The Sterne is rissin, l. 26.

To **OURGIVE, OURGIE,** *v. a.* To bestow, assign, bequeath; pret. *ourgeff;* part. pt. *ourgiffin, ourgien;* Orig. Paroch., II., pt. 2, p. 726.

OUSET, OUSSET, *adj.* Worsted, woollen; "an *ouset* apron." A colloq. form of *worsted.*

Ye ar the lanterne and the sicker way,
Suld gyd sic sympill folk as me to grace;
Your hairfelt, and your *ousett* coull of gray,
Schawis full weill your perfyt halynace.
Henryson, Fox and Wolf, Bann. MS., p. 967, Hunt. Soc.

OUTGANG, OUTGAN, OUTGAE, UTGAE, *s.* Outgoing, giving up tenure; also, the way out, exit. V. OUTGAIT.

To **OUTHAVE, OWTHAE,** *v. a.* To transport, export: lit. to have or fetch out.

"Sinder inhabitants of the toun of Taine occupirs merchandis in buying, sellyng, tappyn,* and *owthawing* of merchandice." Orig. Paroch., II., pt. 2, p. 431.

". . . quhar sic guddis is *owthad* be shippyn of vthirwayis." Ibid.

* Misprinted *cappyn.*

Sup.   Q 2

PAL [314] PIC

P.

PALE, PAIL, PEIL, s. A stake; a stripe, band, bar: also, a limit, boundary.

To PALE, PAIL, PEIL, v. a. To stake; to fix or stretch by means of stakes: as, "to *peil* nets;" hence, to surround, enclose, separate; to stripe, band, or bar; part. pt. *paled palyt*, also used as an *adj.*

"Item, sax courtenes of singill worsat *palyt* of red and grein and yhalou befor the bee altar and about the same for feriall." Invent. Vestmenta, etc., in St. Salv. Coll., St. Andrews, Mait. C. Misc., iii. 199.
O. Fr. *pal*, a pale, stake: from Lat. *palus*, a stake, which is derived from Lat. *pangere*, to fix, fasten.
It may be noted that, in heraldry, *pale* was used with reference to a vertical stripe only. This is probably implied when speaking of the *courtenes* of the altar.

PANE, PAYN, PEEN, s. A pane, panel, division.

To PANE, PAYN, PEEN, v. a. To panel; to cut, divide, or form into panes or panels; to arrange in panels, to quarter, marshal; part. pt. *paned, paynit, peen'd,* arranged in panes or divisions.

"That baith the craftis, viz., webstaris, wakeris and scheraris, in all tymes of processioun . . . be incorporat vnder ane baner, to be maid in this wys, that thair baneris of baith the saidis craftis be *paynitt* with the imagis, figuris, and armis of the webstaris, and principalie becaus thai ar found the elder craft and first placit; and with the ymagis, figuris, and armys of the said scheraris and wakaris quarterlie rynnand togedder; and the armes of the wobstaris . . . to be vnmaist in ilk baner." Burgh Recs. Edin., 1500, i. 122, Rec. Soc.
O. Fr. *pan*, "a pane, piece, or pannell;" Cotgr.; from Lat. *pannus*, a cloth, patch.

PANTENS, s. pl. A corr. of *pattens.* V. under [PATYNIS].

PARLEY, PARLY, s. V. PARLIAMENT-CAKE.

PARLICUE, s. V. PURLICUE.

PARTISING, s. Departure, separation: "libel of *partising*," bill of divorce; Abp. Hamilton's Catechism, fol. 165b.
Fr. *partir*, to part, depart, remove.

PARTY, PARTI, *adj.* Apart, separate, different.

Also used as a *s.* meaning opposition, the opposite side or party; as, "the *parti* Canados tok he," i.e., Canados took the opposite side; Sir Tristrem, l. 3236, S. T. S. Addit. to PARTY, q. v.

PATELAND, s. Particle or portion of land.
"With the *pateland* called John Clerks land, . . . as the said auchtant part and *pateland* . . . lyis in lenth and braid." Orig. Paroch., vol. ii., pt. 2, p. 512.
This is simply a corr. of *partland*, like *patelet* for partlet.

PAULLE, s. Rich cloth; Awnt. Arth., st. 28. V. PALL.

PEEN, s. A pane, as in " a *peen* o' glass;" also, the narrow edge of a hammer head, as in " a *peen* hammer." E. *pane.* V. *Pane.*

PEEVER, s. The pitcher or flat stone with which the children's game of *beds* or *pallall* is played; the game is therefore sometimes called "*peever*" or "*the peever.*" West of S.

To PEILL, v. a. A form of *pail*, to stake; to fix, erect, or fasten by means of stakes: "to *peill* nettis," to stake nets; Reg. Mag. Sig., 25 Aug., 1584, Rec. Series. V. *Pale.*

To PERFEW, v. a. To purfle: part. pt. *perfewit*, for *purflewit,* purfled; Bann. MS., p. 657, l. 36. V. *Purfle.*

To PERFILE, PERFLE, PERFLEW, PERFEW, v. a. V. *Purfle.*

To PERISH, PERISCH, PERISS, v. a. and n. 1. As a v. a.: to destroy, waste, squander, bring to naught; as, "He has *perish'd* his pack."

For mony a beast to dead she shot,
And *perish'd* mony a bonny boat.
Burns, Tam o' Shanter.

2. As a v. n.: to come to naught, become weak, helpless, powerless.

The night was foul, he was all wat,
And *perished* of cauld.
The Mare of Collingtoun, Watson's Coll., i. 40.

PERKINS, s. pl. A species of gingerbread formed into thin round cakes like biscuits, with a piece of almond in the centre of each.

To PERVISE, PERVYSE, v. a. To examine carefully, test, consider. Lat. *pervisere.*
"Their haill travells and work . . . sould be revysit and *perrysit* be some brethren, digestit and disposit in convenient order, to be thereafter presentit to the Assemblie." Book of Univ. Kirk, 1577, p. 163.

PHINK, s. A finch: but the translator of Leslie's Hist. Scot. uses the term as meaning a swan: see p. 40, ed. S. T. S.

PICCADEL, PICKEDAILL, s. An ornamental band, border, or ruff attached to the collar of a doublet; a high ruff; pl. *piccadellis, pickedaillis.*

PIL [315] POU

"Nathir yit that ony marchand by, to top or sell, ony handwork belanging to craftismen, sic as brydill bittis, brydillis, stirrep irnes, stirrep ledderis, maid girdls with buckillis, irn born cambis, spurris, baittis, schone, pantenes, and *pickedaillis*, nor na uthoris handye work maid within this burgh belanging to ony craftismen qnhatsumover, in hurt and preiudyce of the saidis craftismen, under the pane foirsaid of confiscatioun of the same to the tounes use." Burgh Recs. Stirling, 1616, p. 144.

The *piccadel*, from O. Fr. *piccadilles* (which Cotgrave defines as "the seuerall diuisions or peeces fastened together about the brimme of the collar of a doublet"), was an ornamental neck-piece made up in various ways, but generally in the form of a band or ruff to fit the collar of a doublet; and it was so made that it could be taken off at the pleasure of the wearer. The term, however, appears to have had a wider application, for Blount defines it as "the round hem, or the several divisions set together, about the skirt of a garment or other thing; also, a kind of stiff collar made in fashion of a band."

The high ruffs worn in the early Stuart times were called *piccadillies*; but in earlier times, and especially during the reign of Elizabeth, the fine peaked lace used for edging was called *piccadilly lace*, either because it was chiefly used for edging the *piccadilly* or high ruff, or because of its fine spear-like points. And Piccadilly, in London, is said to have derived its name from a noted warehouse which stood there called Piccadilla Hall, which was the chief depot for this kind of lace. Pennant, however, says the Hall was so named because "*piccadillas* or turnovers were sold there." See Brewer's Dict. of Phrase and Fable.

Piccadel, or *piccadilla*, is a dimin. of Span. *pica*, a pike, *picada*, a prick.

PILE, PYLE, *s.* The punch or die for stamping the obverse of a coin; the obverse face of a coin; also, the impression stamped upon the obverse.

The die used for the opposite or reverse face of the coin was called a *trussell* or *tursell*: hence, money was said to be struck or printed with "*pyle and tursell*:" see Acts James VI., 1597. In the 1814 od. of the Scotch Acts, from which Jamieson quoted this phrase, it is misprinted "*pyle and cursell*:" from this source and on this authority the mistake found its way into the Dict.

O. F. *pile*, "the pile or vnder-yron of the stampe wherein money is stamped, and the pile-side of a piece of money;" Cotgr. From Lat. *pila*, a pillar.

PIRKLE, *s.* A kind of muzzle (consisting of a leather band with projecting nails), which is fixed on the nose of a cow that is given to sucking her teats; Orkney.

Prob. only a corr. of *prickle*.

PIRLICUE, *s.* The conclusion of a discourse, the application of a sermon. V. PURLICUE, s. 3.

"And if you distaste the sermon, I doubt the *pirlicue* will please you as little." Kidnapped, p. 245.

PITCHER, *s.* The flat roundish piece of stone with which children play their game of *beds* or *pallall*; hence the game is often called *pitcher* or *the pitcher*; West of S.

So called from the stone being *pitched* or tipped along by the foot of the player.

PITLARICHIE, *s.* Uproar, turmoil; cry and confusion of a disorderly crowd.

The first ae straik that Forbes strack,
He gar'd MacDonnell reel;
And the neist ae straik that Forbes strack,
The brave MacDonnell fell.
And siccan a *Pitlarichie*
I'm sure ye never saw,
As was amang the Hiclandmen,
When they saw MacDonnell fa'.
Ballad, Battle of Harlaw, l. 61.

PLAIT-SLEEVES, PLATE-SLEEVES, PLET-SLEEVES, SLEEVES OF PLAIT, *s. pl.* Mail or armour for the arms; Gowrie Conspiracies, p. 47.

"Ordanis to haue ane lans, ane steill-bonnet, and ane pair of *pletsleuis*, and ane hagbuit." Burgh Recs. Peebles, 1624, p. 364, Rec. Soc.

PLICHT-ANKER, PLYCHT-ANKIR, *s.* Sheet anchor, the principal anchor of a vessel.

Scho tuke Presence *plicht ankers* of the barge,
And Fair Callyng that wele a flayn could schute,
And cherissing for to complete hir charge.
Dunbar, Goldyn Targe, l. 187.

"Lat this faith be thi *plycht ankir*, and doutless thow sall be saiffit fra all the dangeir of syn." Abp. Hamilton's Catechism, fol. 103 b.

Du. *plechtanker*, sheet-anchor: lit. deck-anchor; *plecht*, signifying deck.

PLIE, *s.* and *v.* Plea. V. PLEY.

PLOUGHGATE, PLOUGH-LAND, *s.* V. PLEUCH-GATE.

POLDAVY, POLDAVYE, POLLDAVIE, POLDAUY, *s.* A coarse kind of canvas used for sailcloth and sacking; Burgh Recs. Stirling, p. 144.

"*Poldaveis* the shok contening xxviii. elnis, . . . xv. li." Halyburton's Ledger, p. 318.

To POOK, POUK, POWK, *v. a.* To pull, pluck, or pick with the fore-finger and thumb; as, "I'm *pookin* the hairs out o't": hence, to lift or take in small quantities; as, "He just *pouks* at his meat." Addit. to POOK, q. v.

POOK, POUK, *s.* A pick, a very small quantity: "a *pouk* o' oo," a pick or minute tuft of wool; "a *pook* o' meat," a very small quantity of food. E. *pick*. V. POOKS.

A dimin. from *poo*, *pow*, to pull, pluck, pick, and generally applied to action with the fore-finger and thumb; hence, a very small quantity.

PORTASE, PORTUS, PORTUIS, *s.* A breviary; Invent. St. Salv. Col., St. Andrews, Mait. C. Misc. Addit. to [PORTOUNS], q. v.

Perhaps the form *portouns*, given by Lindsay in the Three Estaitis, represents a vulgar pron. of the period: or, it is a mere scribal error of *portouus* for *portous*.

POUNDLAND, PUND-LAND, *s.* A portion of land extending to four oxgates, or half a ploughgate, or 52 acres.

"That four oxgait of the saids lands extendis and sall extend to ane *pund land* of auld extent in all tyme to cum." Decision of Lords Auditors of Exchequer in 1585, Innes' Leg. Antiq., p. 283.
By this decision it was settled that a ploughland or ploughgate was equal to a forty-shillingland of Old Extent.

PREACHINS, *s. pl.* Sermons, discourses. Communion occasions in Scotland are called *preachins*, from the number of sermons then delivered ; Laird of Logan, p. 592.

PRICK-WAND, *s.* A wand set up as a mark or prick to shoot at. V. PRICK.

The *prick-wand* was often used at contests in archery as a test of skill. In the ballad entitled Adam Bel, Clym of the Cloughe, and William of Cloudeslie, it is recorded that—

Wyllyam went into a fyeld,
And his to brethren with him,
There they set vp to hasell roddes,
Twenty score paces betwene.
" I hold him an archar," said Cloudeslè,
" That yonder wande cleveth in two : "
" Here is none suche," sayd the Kyng,
" Nor none that can so do."
" I shall assaye, syr," sayd Cloudeslè,
" Or that I farther go : "
Cloudeslè, with a bearyng arrow,
Clave the wand in to.
Ritson, Pieces of Pop. Poetry.

PRICKET, *s.* A spire, spike, taper. Addit. to *Pricket*.

"Ane steeple and *pricket* of ashler-wark upon the east neuk and cunyie." Records of Old Dundee, p. 150.

PRICKET SANG, PRIKAT SANG, *s.* Music pricked or noted down, musical notation. Addit. to PRICKSANG, q. v.

"The said Sir John sall study continualie quhill he be cunnand in *prikat sang*." Burgh Recs. Stirling, 1556, p. 70.

PROOF O' SHOT, *adj.* Incapable of influence or impression, heedless, regardless, insensible.

A lover speaking of his heart says:
'Tis *proof-o' shot* to birth or money,
But yields to what is sweet and bonny.
Song, There's my Thumb.

PYE-TREES, *s. pl.* Cross-trees or poles for drying nets, yarn, &c.

" . . . to haill, schutt, peill, and draw nettis on all pairtis usit and wont within the said boundis, and dry the said nettis upon the *pye treis* as said is." Reg. Mag. Sig., 25 Aug., 1584, Rec. Series.
See also under PIE, *s.* 7, in Halliwell's Dict.

Q.

To QUARREL, *v. a.* As in E.: also, to point out or check a fault, find fault with ; as, "He *quarrelled* me for coming late": to challenge, call in question, disapprove of ; as, "He *quarrelled* every plan I proposed": to plea at law, oppose, resist; as, "He *quarrelled* my claim in the Court of Session." Addit. to QUARREL, *v.,* q. v.

QUARRELLABLE, QUARRALLABLE, *adj.* Able to be challenged, opposed, or resisted ; hence, faulty, defective.

"Quhilk gift is not confirmed, neither wes the successors ever in use off presenting ; . . . and so his right is most *quarrallable*." Peterkin, Rentals of Orkney, No. III., p. 14.

QUARRELSOME, *adj.* Fault-finding, given to contradiction, litigious : " He's a *quarrelsome* body ; he's never satisfied."

QUEIR, *s.* Church ; Abp. Hamilton's Catechism, fol. 59a. Addit. to QUEER, q. v.

Lit., quire or choir of a church ; but frequently applied to the whole building. It is so used in the passage quoted.

QUETIIE, *s.* Cry, clamour, sound.

QUHATTINE, QUHATNE, QUHATNA, *adj.* What kind of ; Leslie, Hist. Scot., p. 119, S. T. S. V. QUHATKYN, *Quhaten.*

QUITHER, QWETHIR, *v.* and *s.* Forms of WHITHER, q. v.

QUOSCHE, *s.* A hollow, haugh.

" . . . excepting the turnouris croft . . . with the medo and *quosche* adjacent thereto." Orig. Paroch., vol. II., pt. 1, p. 142.
Gael. *còs,* a hollow, crevice, recess; M'Leod and Dewar.

To QWAITE, *v. n.* A form of *wait,* short for *await,* to befal, happen.

Wait is still used in this sense, and examples of this peculiar form are occasionally found : see Allit. Rom. Alex., l. 1109, and cf. Troybook, l. 13245.

R.

RACHE, *part. pt.* Rated, reckoned, ranked. V. RAIK, REKE.

"Lat the burial of a deid persone be preparet accordeng as the persone is *rache*." Leslie, Hist. Scot., p. 123, S. T. S.

RAIL, *s.* 1. Band, bar; as, the *rail* of a stair, i.e., the hand-rail, also called the *railin*.

2. A row, line; as, "a *rail* o' tackets," a row of hobnails.

They pn' and rax the lingle tails,
Into their brogues they ca' the nails;
Wi' hammers now, instead o' flails,
They mak great rackets,
And set about their heels wi' *rails*
O' clinkin tackets.
Keith, The Farmer's Ha', st. 5.

To **RAIL**, *v. a.* 1. To fit with a band, bar, or border, and hence to enclose; as, "to *rail* a stair," i.e., to fit it with a hand-rail in order to prevent accidents.

2. To set in a row; as, *to rail shoon*, to fill the soles with rows of iron nails.

O. H. Ger. *rigil*, a bar, bolt, from O. H. Ger. *rîhan*, to fasten (Ger. *reihen*, to put in a row, connect). See Skeat's Etym. Dict.

To **RAVE**, RAUE, *v. n.* 1. To roam, wander.

"He lang had *rauet* and wandirit, at last he arriuet in Numidie." Leslie, Hist. Scot., p. 71, S. T. S.
This term is formed from the sb. *raver*, a reavor, robber, in the same way as *rove* from *rover*.

2. To emit a wild rushing sound, to roar, rage; as, "The wind's *ravin* in the lum-head."

Rave in this sense is most prob. from Lat. *rabere*, to rage. See Skeat's Etym. Dict.

To **RED**, REDD, *v. a.* To set in order; hence, to arrange, prepare, provide; as, "I'll sort the place an' *red* the things to your han." Addit. to RED, *v.*, q. v.

RED, REDD, *s.* Arrangement; the act of arranging, preparing, organizing; aiding and abetting. Addit. to RED, *s.*, q. v.

"Ye delete . . . his name furth of the Summons of Treason and Forfaulture raised and executed against him for being art, part, *redd*, counsel and counselling of the late Treason." Gowrie Conspiracies, p. 35.

REDE, *s.* A road for ships. V. RADE.

RED-HAWK, REID-HALK, *s.* A hawk in its first year, but generally applied to the male goshawk or tercel of that age.

The tercel does not reach maturity till its second year, and until then its plumage is of a deep brown colour, and has a much ruddier tint than that of an adult.

Your clerkis ar seruit all about,
And I do lyk ane *reid halk* schout
To cum to lure that lies no leif,
Quhair my plummy is begynis to brek out:
Excess of thocht dois me mischeif.
Dunbar, Schir, yit remembir, st. 2.

Although so printed in the editions of Laing and Small, the second last line of this passage is faulty: *gynis* for *begynis* would greatly improve it.

Reid-halks, i.e., young hawks, however hungry or clamorous for food, were not allowed to "come to lure," or to feed, with the adult or trained hawks. Dunbar, as an old and faithful falcon to the King, complains that he is still treated as if he were only a *reid-halk*.

It may be observed that *halk* is a mere graphic form, and that the *l* is not sounded. Indeed, the *lk* is a contracted form of *kk*, which here represents *uk*, as the preceding vowel is sounded long. See under *Walk, Walk, Wauk, v.*, in Addenda.

REEK-HEN, *s.* The name of an ancient house-tax paid to the landlord; also, the hen given in payment of it. Errat. in DICT.

From every fire-house or reek on his estate the landlord claimed a hen by way of yearly custom. Hence the name *reek-hen*. See Gloss. Orkn. and Shetl., and Innes, Legal Antiq., p. 257.

Under Reik-Hen in DICT. delete s. 1, and the para. which follows it, and combine the remainder of the entry.

REEK-MAIL, REEK-MAILL, *s.* An ancient name for house-rent; dues payable by a householder to his superior; Burgh Recs. Stirling, p. 308. V. under *Reek-Hen*.

REFYNE, *part. pt.* Riven, torn; Barbour's Saints, Peter, l. 23. V. RIVE.

Icel. *rifa*, to rive, tear; pret. *rif*; part. pt. *rifinn*.

REPALINGIS, *s. pl..* Prob. an error for *reperalingis* or *reparalingis*, fittings, furniture.

"A feather bed, and two saddles, with their *repalingis*." Orig. Paroch., i. 185.
See Reparel in Halliwell.

REPRISE, *s.* A renewed effort, attempt, or attack; repetition, resumption.

"The unhappy condition wherein the Church and State of Scotland were plunged during the minority of King James the Sixth, and that not once or twice but in frequent *reprises*." Gowrie Conspiracies, p. 14.

O. Fr. *reprise*, "resumption, repetitiou;" Cotgr. This is the fem. of *repris*, part. pt. of *reprendre*, to resume.

RESATE, RESAT, *part. pt.* Received, accepted, engaged and entered for service.

". . . and ten merks for ane friemans sone befoir he be *resat* frieman, attour the wonted dewes for the poor. Item, . . . the present Clerk and his successors shall have 13s. iiijd. for the buikeing, and ten shillings for the serveand so *resat*." Recs. Incorp. of Tailors, Glasgow, 1648, p. 8.

REST, *s.* A hinge for a door; pl. *restis*; perhaps so called because the door wrests or turns upon them; Douglas, III. 93, 8, ed. Small.

A.-S. *wræstan*, to writhe, twist; M. Eng. *wresten*.

To RING, *v. a.* To put a ring in a swine's snout; to fit with a ring: part. pt. *ringit*, fitted with a ring, as "a *ringit* sow." V. under *Snipe*.

RINNAN BILL, *s.* A furious or mad bull; West of S.

To RIP *out*, RIP *down*, *v. a.* To take down work that is insufficient, or that has been wrongly done; as, "To *rip out* a stocking." When such work is taken down loop by loop it is often called *rippling out*.

RIPPIN, RIPPISH, *adj.* Given to *riping*, i.e., searching, turning over, cleaning out: hence, industrious, cleanly, fastidious. V. RIPE, *v.*

But a new-made wife, fu' o' *rippish* freaks,
Fond o' a' things feat for the first five weeks,
Laid a mouldy pair o' her ain man's breeks
By the brose o' Aiken-drum.
Nicholson, Brownie of Blednoch.

Dan. *rippe*, in the sense of *oprippe*, to rip up, turn over.

To RISP, *v. n.* To dirl, rattle, knock; "*risp* at the manse door;" R. L. Stevenson, Kidnapped, p. 4. Addit. to RISP, q. v.

ROCHT, *pret.* Recked, regarded.
For he had thame inflammyt awa,
That naue of thaime vald part hyme fra,
For his luf to de that ne *rocht*   .   .   .
Barbour's Saints, Prol., l. 105.

A.-S. *récan*, to care; pt. t. *róhte*; formed from a sb. with base *róc*-, found in M. H. Ger. *ruoch*, O. H. Ger. *ruch*, care, heed, whence M. H. Ger. *ruochen*, G. H. Ger. *róhhjan*, to reck; see under *Reck* in Skeat's Etym. Dict.

ROITTING, *s.* Rooting. V. *Rutting*.

ROUCH-RIDER, *s.* A performer of feats on horseback, a circus-rider; Laird of Logan, p. 594. Addit. to ROUCH-RIDER, q. v.

To RUBAN, RUBEN, *v. a.* To fit, bind, deck, or ornament with ribbons: part. pt. *rubanit;* Garmond of Gude Ladeis, Bann. MS., p. 657, Hunt. Soc. V. RUBEN, *s.*

RUITH, RUECH, *s.* A cattle-run, hill-pasture, summer-sheiling; Scot. Gael, II. 82.

Gael. *ruigh*, *ruighe*, lit. arm, forearm; applied to the lower slopes of mountains on which cattle are pastured during summer; hence the secondary meaning, hill-pasture.

RUTTING, ROITTING, *s.* Rooting, turning up the soil as pigs do in search of food; Oppressions in Orkney, p. 88, 4. V. [RUTT.]

S.

SAHT, *part. pt.* Reconciled. V. SAUGHT, *Sacht*.

SAIR, *s.* and *v.* Savour, smell. V. SARE, SAWER.

SAIRING, *part.* and *adj.* Smelling, as, "sueit *sairing* flouris;" Leslie, Hist. Scot., p. 44: stinking, as, "*sairing* like a brock."

To SAPPLE CLAES. To steep or soak clothes in soapy water. V. SAPPLES.

To SAUD, *v. a.* To make solid. V. SAD, *v.*

To SAUGHTILL, *v. a.* and *n.* To reconcile; Awnt. Arth., st. lii. V. *Sauchtine*.

A.-S. *sahtlian*, to reconcile, make peace: from *saht*, peace.

SAY, *s.* and *adj.* Assay. V. SAY, *v.* and SEY, *s.*

SAYLCH, *s.* A seal. V. SELCHT.

SCALE-DRAKE, SKEEL-DUCK, *s.* V. SKAILDRAKE.

SCARE, *s.* The narrow part of the head of a golf-club, by which the head is glued to the handle; Gl. Golfer's Handbook. Addit. to SKAIR, q. v.

This is a special application of Skair, a splice: see s. 2 of that term in DICT.

To SCHEND, *v. a.* To shame, disgrace: part. pt. *schende;* Sir Tristrem, l. 3289. Addit. to SCHENT, *v.*, q. v.

SCHENDSCHIP, SCHENSCHEPE, *s.* Shame, confusion, ignominy; Burgh Recs. Peebles, 1450, p. 15, Rec. Soc.

And tha that tynt had wittis fyffe,
Thai restoryt thaime allswa
Fra *schenschepe* of oure fulone fay.
Barbour's Saints, Prol. l. 119.

A.-S. *scendan*, to confound, shame; O. Du. *schenden*.

SCHIELDRAKE, Shieldrake, *s.* V. Skaildrake.

SCHIPREDE, *s.* A road or anchorage for ships; Leslie, Hist. Scot., p. 127, S. T. S. V. Rade.

SCHUFE, *pret.* Shoved, placed, stuck; Barbour's Saints, Peter, l. 158.
A.-S. *scúfan*, to shove; *pt. t. scéaf.* M. Eng. *schoven.*

SCHULE, *s.* A shoal. V. Skule.

To SCLUFE, *v. n.* V. Skluffe.

To SCOSCHE, *v. a.* To view, examine, search, test: hence, to reject things that are defective.

"That ane persoun be yeirlie elected at Michaelmes to *sconche* all skynis cuttit, hollit, or tuigit in the nek, within this burght, with the decoun of the skynnaris, quha sal haue aue penny for his panis of ilk skyn sua fundyn, to be payet be the byar." Burgh Recs. Glasgow, 28th August, 1613.
This looks very like the old custom of Scawage or Showing to which merchants had to submit on bringing their goods to market, and for which a small custom rate was charged. In the Liber Albus, where it is frequently mentioned, it is thus defined :—" And be it made known, that Scavage is so called as being a 'shewing;' because it behoves the merchants that they shew unto the Sheriffs the merchandize for which the custom is to be taken, before that any of it be sold." Mun. Gildhallm Lond., vol. iii., p. 58, Rolls Series, and see Gloss. also.
A.-S. *scedıcian*, to look at, view, or search.

SCRAE, Skrae, *s.* Short for Skrae-Fish, q. v.

Scrae or *scrae-fish*, especially those that are sweet-salted, i.e., slightly salted, are generally eaten without being cooked.
Scrae, when it appears in Orkney rentals, represents a payment in kind, of which the money value ranges from 3 to 5 shillings per mille.

To SCUG, Scoog, *v. a.* To hide, cover, conceal; also, to expiate, atone for. Addit. to Skug, q. v.

" And aye at every sax years' end,
Ye'll tak him to the linn :
For that's the penance he maun dree,
To *scug* his deadly sin."
Ballad, *Young Benjie.*

Scug, Scoug, Scoog, *s.* Hiding, shelter. V. Skug.

SCULL-CAP, Scull-Hat, *s.* A close-fitting cap or hat.

A sword, a sweel, a swine's bladder,
A trump o' steel, a feather'd lock,
An auld *scull-hat* for winter-weather,
And meikle mair, my Jeunie, quoth Jock.
The Country Wedding, Herd, ii. 91, ed. 1869.

The winter *scull-cap* was generally made of coarse woollen stuff, and was fitted with ear-flaps which could be tied under the chin : the summer *scull-cap* commonly had no ear-flaps, and was made of lighter material.

SCUTTLE DISH, Skiddle Dish, *s.* A large flat dish set below the spigot of an ale-barrel to catch the drops. V. Scuttle, *v.*

In the account of a witch's nettle-kail given in the ballad entitled Earl Richard, the following passage occurs :—

And she would meal you with millering,
That she gathers at the mill,
And msk you thick as any daigh ;
And when the pan was brimful,
Would mess you up in *scuttle dishes*,
Syne bid us sup till we were fou ;
Lay down her head upon a poke,
Then sleep and snore like any sow.
Scot. Ballads, Child, iii. 273.

In the old Scot. alehouses the *scuttle dish* was generally a large wooden bowl or basin, and most probably it is to such dishes that reference is made in the ballad. They were also called *skiddle dishes*.

SEAL OF CAUSE, Seile of Cause, Sele of Cause, *s.* The technical name of a writing granted by a royal burgh, and having the common seal (or common seal of cause, as it was more usually called,) appended by way of verification, confirming the privileges of a body of craftsmen or of a society, and having the effect of a charter of incorporation.

"We have approveit, ratefeit, admitit for us, and in as far as in ws is, or that we haue power, confirmes the said bill in all pointtis and articles. . . . And for the mair verificatioun and strenth of the samyn we haif to hungin oure commoun *seall of caus* for the said burghe of Edinburghe." Seal of Cause to the Hatmakers, 1473 : Burgh Recs. Edinburgh, i. 28, Rec. Soc.
The power of the Scottish Burghs to constitute subordinate incorporations has been recognised by the Supreme Courts, and appears to have been freely exercised. In Glasgow nearly all the incorporated trades have still in preservation Seals of Cause granted to them by the magistrates and council. For the most part they were confined to the older incorporations ; but not exclusively. In 1780 the magistrates of Glasgow granted a Seal of Cause to the Running Stationers or Cadies ; in 1790, to the Society for managing the Sunday Schools in Glasgow ; in 1791, to the Glasgow Society of the Sons of Ministers of the Church of Scotland ; and in the same year to the Governors of Archibald Millar's Trust.
In the application for the Seal of Cause to the Cadies it was set forth " that the members of the said Society would serve the public by going messages by night or by day to any parts of the city and suburbs, or to any places in the country, by hiring as servants by the job, or by the day, week, or month, to serve either in town or country, or during journeys to the country, or otherwise ; by assisting at balls, dinners, suppers, and public entertainments ; and by every other mode practised by the Cadies of Edinburgh ; therefore praying that the Lord Provost, Magistrates, and Council, in virtue of the powers vested in them for erecting societies of that kind, would grant them a Seal of Cause, and erect them into a regular Corporation." MS. Council Records of Glasgow, vol. 34, p. 38-9.

SEEN, Sene *to, part. pt.* 1. Cared or provided for, attended to; trained, disciplined : " The bairns hae been weel *seen to* by their uncle." V. Beseine.

Statements of this kind are made to express what has been done in the past for the support, upbringing, or education of the persons referred to; or what provision has been made for their present or future wellbeing.

2. Short for *beseen*, equipped, skilled, experienced.

> Gude Sir Alexander Irving,
> The much renownit laird of Drum,
> Nane in his days was bettir *sene*,
> Quhen they war semblit all and sum.
> *Ballad, Battle of Harlaw*, l. 219.

To SELE, *v. a.* To spread, cover; a form of SILE, q. v.

SENNACHIE, *s.* V. *Senachie.*

SENT, *s.* Scent, smell: *to sent*, to follow scent, for scenting, to discover or track by scent; Leslie, Hist. Scot., p. 20, S. T. S.

To SET *Up*, *v. a.* To commence, begin, open; *to set up booth* or *buith*, to commence business, open a shop; Hammermen's Seal of Cause. Addit. to SET, q. v.

To SEY, SEGH, *v.* To wend, go. Addit. to SEY, q. v.

SHAFTMON, SHATMOND, *s.* V. SCHAFTMON.

SHANNA, SANNA, SUNNA, *v.* Forms of "shall not."

To SHIRP, *v. n.* To waste or pine away in body. Addit. to SHIRP, q. v.

SHIRPET, *adj.* Shrunk, shrivelled, wasted; as, a *shirpet* face, a *shirpet* leg. Errat. in DICT.

Jamieson's definition of this term is a mistake, and it is not borne out by his quotation.
Gael. *searg*, to fade, wither, pine away.

SHOKLE, SCHOKLE, *s.* A small portion, piece, or point; "*schokles* of yce," icicles; Leslie, Hist. Scot., p. 46, S.T.S.

This term relates only to ice: it is improperly used otherwise.
"Evolved from *ice-schokles*, corruption of *ice-yokles*. The spelling *ysyokels* occurs in MS. of Piers Plowman, B. xvii. 227." Skeat.
Icel. *jökull*, a dimin. of *jaki*, a piece of ice; A.-S. *gicel*, i.e. *is-gicel*, an icicle; L. Germ. *jokel*. See Vigfusson.

To SIC, SIK, *v. n.* To sigh; part. pr. *siccin*, *sikkin*: "*siccin* and sabbin," sighing and sobbing. V. SIKE.

To SIGNE, *v. a.* A form of *sing*, to singe; part. pt. *signet*, singed; Leslie, Hist. Scot., p. 95, S. T. S.

SIMPLESSE, SIMPLESE, *s.* Simpleness, simplicity. O. Fr. *simplesse*.

> Go litill tretise, nakit of eloquence,
> Causing *simplese* and pouertee to wit;
> And pray the reder to have pacience
> Of thy defante, and to supporten It.
> *Kingis Quair*, st. 194, ed. Skeat.

SKAILDRAKE, *s.* V. DICT.

Delete the second last parag. of this entry in DICT. The deriv. from Su.-G. *skael* is a mistake; and Grose's explanation is correct.
Skaildrake is for *skaild-drake*, i.e., shield-drake, hence, M. E. *sheld-drake*, and Mod. E. *sheldrake*. In M. E. *sheld* meant a shield, like a shield, barred, flecked, party-coloured: hence, *sheld-drake* meant variegated or spotted drake. A.-S. *scild* is defined by Grein as a shield, and applied also to the appearance of a bird's plumage. Cf. Icel. *skjöldungr*, a sheldrake.

SKEIFE, *s.* Prob. section, division, applied to a mass or body of immense size. V. SKELVE, SKELF.

"Upoun the penult day of Junij, appeared in the sight of the Castell of Sanctandrois twontiy ane French galayis, with a *skeife* of an army, the lyik whairof was never sein in that Fyrth befuir." Knox, Reform. in Scot., i. 203, ed. Laing, Wodrow Soc.

SKET, SKETE, *adv.* Quick, quickly; Sir Tristrem, l. 559, 896, S.T.S.

SKIR, SKYR, SKIRRIE, *s.* A rock in the sea, a small rocky islet; also, a cluster of rocks. Addit. to SKERR, q. v.

SKIRGE, *s.* A scold, termagant, brawling woman; Laird of Logan, p. 597.

This term is prob. a corr. of E. *scourge*, a lash: from O. Fr. *escorgie*, a scourge, which has come from Lat. *excoriata*, flayed off, hence a strip of raw hide or leather for a whip.

To SLIP, SLIEP, *v. a.* To slit, cut, lay open with a sharp point. Prob. a corruption of E. *slit*.

SLIP, SLIEP, *s.* A slit, cut, incision.

"Also discharges all manner of cutting or carving of kine or oxen, except only one *sliep* on one of the soulders and one squint cutt on one of the hinder legs; and also all cutting of sheep except an even in score in the shoulder and a *sliep* in the rumpell, and that under the paine of six shillings 8d. for each cutt in a sheep and 40s. for each cutt in a lamb. And ordains the bailies to give one half of the fines to the poor of the toun, and the other half to the poor of the trade that need." Annals of Dunfermline, 1703, p. 374.

SLOGHORNE, *s.* V. under *Slogan.*

That *sloghorne* or *slughorne* meant simply a battle-cry is attested by the following passage from John Knox's account of the affray at Solway Moss.
"Great was the noyse and confusion that was heard, while that everie man calles his awin *sloghorne*." Hist. Reform. Scot., i. 87, ed. Laing, Wodrow Soc.

SLOTTING, *part.* and *s.* Slitting or cutting: "*slotting flesh*," cutting animals that are about to be slaughtered, for the purpose of bleeding them; also called *scoring flesh*, and *letting doun flesh*; Burgh Recs. Stirling, 1647, p. 193. V. under *Score*, and *Let down.*

SMARAGDYNE, *adj.* as *s.* Emerald; Kingis Quair, st. 155, ed. Skeat. V. *Smaradge.*

SMERT, *s.* Pain, suffering, as in "the lover's *smert*:" short for *smert-siller*, or *smert-money*, i.e., smart-money; as, "He listed wi' the sodgers, but paid the *smert* and wan hame." V. [SMERT, *v.*].

SMOCH, *adj.* Broken; hence, cast-away, rejected, left: a form of SMUSH, q. v.

Thow wald be fane to gnaw, lad, with thy gammis,
Wudir my burde, *smoch* banis behind doggis bakkis.
Dunbar and Kennedy, l. 364.

Bann. MS. reads *snoch.*
Swed. dial. *smask,* a slight report, noise, smash: from *smakka,* to throw down noisily, to smack, smash. O. Du. *smacken,* to collide, smash; *smacke,* a smack, smash.

To SNITE, SNYTE, *v. a.* Same as SNOIT, q. v.: with addit. meaning, to taunt, gibe; Laird of Logan, p. 597.

These three forms are simply varieties, and should have been united. The primary meaning is to clean or clear the nose; Sw. *snyta,* Dan. *snyde,* from Sw. *snut,* Dan. *snude,* the snout, nose; and "to snuff a candle," as given by Jamieson, is only a secondary meaning. Cf. Dutch *snuiten,* to blow one's nose, to snuff a candle.

SOK, *s.* A ploughshare; a plough. V. SOCK.

SOK AND SYTH, *adj.* Arable, fit to be plowed and reaped.

"*Sok and syith* lande, that is sik lande as may be tilled by ane plouch, or may be mawed with ane syth." Skene, De Verb. Sig., s. v. *Husbandland.*

SOLEMPNE, SOLEMPT, *adj.* Solemn.

And therewith-all thir peple sawe I stand,
With mony a *solempt* countenance.
Kingis Quair, st. 79.

This is the reading of the MS.; but *solempt* should be *solemp[ni]t* to suit the measure. It is so printed in Prof. Skeat's edition.

Very probably King James wrote *solempne* or *solempnit*; for there is no example of his putting only eight syllables in a line.

SOMER, *s.* A sumpter: applied to both men and horses. V. SUMER.

SOO, SOU, *v.* and *s.* Ache, throb, thrill, tingle, as with pain or the sensation produced by a shrill, piercing sound. Addit. to Soo, Sow, q. v.

SOU, SOWE, *s.* A bride's outfit or *braws.* Addit. to Sow, a stack, heap, q. v.

This term is now used only by the fisher-folk of the N.E. of Scot. from Nairn to Buckie.

SOUGH, *s.* Sound, talk, report, fama. Addit. to SOUGH, *s.*

"Before the *sough* gaed abroad about Mr. Alexander." R. L. Stevenson, Kidnapped, p. 50.

SOUN, *s.* Sound, noise; Douglas, Pal. (Sup.) R 2

Hon., I. 34, 8, Small; Kingis Quair, st. 13, 152, Skeat; also, report, rumour; West of S.

SOYT, SOYTE, *s.* Lit. a following, following another, but in different senses:—

1. A suit at law, lawsuit.

2. Company or following under the jurisdiction of a court, or of a lord or overlord.

Regarding a "Chalmerlan Air" in a burgh, it was enacted—"At ye ger be brocht thar that tym al the names of *soyt* of court of the forsaide burgh." Iter Camerarii, ch. 1, Ancient Laws of Scotland, Rec. Soc.
"Item, thar salbe askit the roll of the *soyt* of court, alswell within as vtouth duelland." Ibid., ch. 3.

3. Attendance at the court of the king or of the overlord; see s. 2, in DICT.

4. A suit of clothes or other articles in sets; also, dress, livery.

And eftir this, the birdis euerichone
Tuke vp an othir sang full loud and clere,—
We proyne and play without dout and dangere,
All clothit lu a *soyte* full fresch and newe,
In luñs seruice besy, glad, and trewe.
Kingis Quair, st. 64, ed. Skeat.

Addit. to SOIT, SOYT, *s.*, q. v.
Fr. *suite,* a following of any kind.

SPAININ-BRASH, *s.* Milk-fever; West of S. V. SPAIN.

SPAN, *pret.* Spun, did spin.

SPEIL, SPELL, SPELD, *s.* Forms of SPALE, q. v.

These forms represent the pron. of *spale* in various districts of Scot. In the North of Eng. the old game of *cat and bat* or *ball and bat* is called *knurr and spell.* See under KER, above.

SPLITS, SPLITTIS, *s. pl.* 1. The divisions of a weaver's reed.

2. Rough or undressed staves for barrels.

"Statute and ordaine that they nor nane of thame wndor quhatsumever cullour or pretext sal buy any runges, stinges, *splittis,* or stappis, from the saidis four personnes, nor from any vthoris quho goes betuix the said trade and thair bargaines in all tyme heireftor." MS. Minute Book of the Coopers of Glasgow, 11 June, 1664.

Addit. to SPLIT, *s.*, q. v.

SPONGE, SPOUNGE, SPUNGE, *s.* A mop, brush, or bundle of fibres used for brushing or cleansing.

That this term was formerly synon. with brush, and used in a much wider sense than now, is shown by the name which certain kinds of brushes still bear. For example, the mop with which a baker cleans out his oven is called a *sponge*; so also is the brush with which an artillery-man cleans out his gun after it has been fired; and a sailor boy, when directed to wipe some water from the deck with his mop, is told to *sponge* it up. And in the Rates and Customs of Merchandise in 1612, we find the entries "Brushes or Spoungse," and "Spounges or Brushes," and each entry contains a list of the various kinds then in use. V. Halyburton's Ledger, pp. 292, 329.

HAIR-SPONGE, HAIR-SPOUNGE, s. The name formerly given to the various kinds of brushes made of hair.

"*Spounges* or brushes *of hair* called rubbing brushes, . . . keame brushes, . . . weaveris brushes."
"*Spounges* or brushes *of hair* for dichting of clothes."
Rates and Customs of 1612, Hal. Ledger, pp. 329, 330.

HEATH SPOUNGE, HADDER-SPOUNGE, s. A brush made of heath or heather.

"*Spounges* or brushes *of heath* called heid brushes." Ibid., p. 329.
"*Spounges* or brushes *of hadder* course [i.e. coarse]."
" " *of hadder* fyne.
" " *of hadder* called rubbing brushes." Ibid., p. 329.

WATER-SPONGE, WATTER-SPOUNGE, s. The name by which a sponge was formerly called.

"Brushes or spounges called *watter spounges* for chirurgeans, the pound weight, . . . xx s." Ibid., p. 292.

In his story of The Tua Mariit Wemen and the Wedo, Dunbar makes the widow reveal to her gossips the following secret regarding her use of a water-spounge :—

Quhen frendis of my husbandis behaldis me on fer,
I haif a *water-spunge* for wa, within my wyde clokis,
Thau wring I it full wylely and wetis my chekis:
With that wateris myn one and welteris doune teris,
Than say thai all that sittis about, "Se ye nought, allace!
Yone lustlese led so lelely soho luffit hir husband:
Yone is a pete to euprent in a princis hert,
That sic a perle of plesance suld yone pane dre !"
ll. 436-443.

STAG, *adj.* Dried, hung, raw or unseasoned: applied to the skins of animals that have been simply dried, by being stretched or suspended in the open air.

In the Rates and Customs of 1612, the terms *stay* and *raw* are used synonymously in opposition to *seasoned* or cured as applied to furakins. See Halyburton's Ledger, p. 305, 306.

O. Du. *staken*, to stretch, suspend.

To STAINCH, STAINCHE, *v. a.* V. STANCHE.

STALLAGE, s. V. under STALLENGE.

The older name of this duty was *borghalpeny*, or *borthalpeny*, i.e., the halfpenny paid at fairs and markets for erecting boards or stalls. See Gloss. Liber Custumarum, p. 702, Rolls Series.

STAY-RIG, s. A border or boundary rig; a ridge or strip of land running at right angles to the other ridges, and so forming a border or boundary to them.

"At the tails of all their rigs to make ane *stayrig* upon the auld bounds of the said acres." Records of Old Dundee, p. 242.

STEMBOD, s. A symbol of citation: for ordinary meetings a staff was used; in matters of urgency or haste, an arrow; for a court of justice, an axe; for ecclesiastical or religious affairs, a cross. See Gloss. Oppressions in Orkney.

Icel. *stefnuboth*, a summoning to a meeting: from Icel. *stefna*, later *stemna*, a summons, and *both*, a message, call. See Vigfusson.

STENT, s. Extent, space, measure: hence, limits, bounds, requirement; and still used in the sense of fixed or stipulated amount of work, task. Addit. to STENT, s., q. v.

"Allsua the land liand betuix the estir oxgang and the orchard of the said Dauid and the march of canil [be] comon to bath the partes. Alsua bath the partyes sel kepe lauchful *stent* and noth exceed it." Charter, dated 31 July, 1437, quoted in Annals of Dunfermline, p. 152-3.

STIFHARTIT, *adj.* Obstinate, hard hearted; Abp. Hamilton's Catechism, fol. 46b.

STONIT HORSE, STONYT HORSE, STANE-HORSE, s. A stallion ; Douglas, Virgil, Bk. iv., prol. l. 59.

STOUK, s. A portion of land dedicated to a Saint, and called by his name: as, St. Augustin's *stouk*, St. Duthus' *stouk*. Addit. to STOOK, q. v.

"The foundation of this schoole [the *sang schoole* of Kirkwall] of auld was Sanct Augustin's *stouk*, worth fyve chalder of wictuall be yeir, set out of auld be the Prebendare, and now in his Majestie's possession. . . . That thair is ane *stouck* callit St. Duthus *stouck* within the parochin, and quarter of ane myll distant from the cathedrall kirk." Peterkin, Rentals of Orkney, No. III., p. 35.

STRANGLON, s. The disease called strangles, a tumour or swelling in a horse's throat; Burgh Recs. Stirling, 1555, p. 64.

O. Fr. *estrauguillons*, the strangles : from O. Fr. *estrangler*, to strangle, choke, from Lat. *strangulare*, allied to *stringere*, to bind.

STRENYIE, STRIENYIE, s. A strain, sprain; Watson's Coll., i. 60. V. STRENYIE, *v.*

STURE, STURRE, s. Dust, quarrel. V. STOUR.

STUTHT, s. Same as STUHT, q. v.

STY, s. Pl. *styes*, steps, stages; Sir Tristrem, l. 400, S.T.S. Addit. to STY, q. v.

SUCCINE, s. Amber; Leslie, Hist. Scot., p. 47, S. T. S. Lat. *sucinum, succinum*.

SWAIF, SWAF, s. A sweep, a long swinging stroke or blow; "wi' a *swaif* o' the scythe:" also a gust, blast, swirl; "It was thrown owre wi' a *swaf* o' wind." A variant of *swap*, q. v., West of S.

Under the form *swayfe* this term occurs in the Allit. Rom. Alex., l. 806.

Allied to A.-S. *swdpan*, to sweep along, rush, swoop; Icel. *sveipa*, to sweep, swoop. See under *Swap* in Skeat's Etym. Dict.

SWAIL, SWAILL, SWALE, s. A hollow between two ridges or gently sloping banks;

also, a gentle rising of the ground with a corresponding declivity; Burgh Recs. Aberdeen, II., 324, Sp. C. V. SWAILSH.

"Keipand the strype quhill it enter in Beildeis *sweill*, and keipand and ascendand upwith the said *swaill* quhill it cum to the littill stane calsay, . . . and fra the said stane calsay at the end of the hill foirsaid, keipand betuix the nasche and the hard north and north eist." Reg. Mag. Sig., 19th Dec., 1584, Rec. Series.

SWEIRT, SWEERT, *adj.* Forms of SWEIR, q. v.

SWIMMING, SWOMENG, *adj.* Flooded, flowing, filled; as, "The road's *swimming* wi' water": abounding, teeming; as, "The loch's *swimming* wi' fish." Also used as an *adv.*, as in the phrase, *swimming full*, i.e., abundantly, copiously full or filled, well stocked.

"Linlythgwe, decored with the kings palice . . . and a pleasand Loch *swomeng* full of fyne perchis, and vtheris notable fische;" Leslie, Hist. Scot., p. 23, S. T. S.

SWYKDOM, SWYKEDOM, *s.* Deception, treachery. V. SWYK.

SWYNE-TAIL, *s.* A corr. of *seying-tale*, sifting-measure, of which the modern name is *a milking-caup:* a small cog or ladle for transferring the milk from the milking-pail to the *sey-dish* or strainer.

Ane milk-syth with ane *swyne-taill*.
  Wooing of Jok and Jynny, l. 23.

In the modern version of this piece given in Herd's Collection, and called *The Country Wedding*, this line is rendered—

A sey-dish and a milking-cap.

T.

TABLES, TABLIS, *s.* A tablet or note-book: the school-*tables* were in the form of a double or folding slate: also called *table-books*; Rates and Customs, 1612: and sometimes *plates*, as in Halyburton's Ledger, p. 51.

To TAILE, *v. a.* V. DICT.

To this entry in the DICT. add the following:
There is probably some scribal error in the reading, *he wald him taile*, found in the Edin. MS. But in any case the reading, *he thoucht all hale*, is in every respect a better one; and although Jamieson deemed it unwarranted, it is found in the Camb. MS., as well as in the printed editions.

TAINT, *s.* Notice, attention; a form of TENT, q. v.; Gowrie Conspiracies, p. 39.

To TARY, TARYE, *v. a.* V. DICT.

By mistake the definition and illustration of *s.* 2 of this verb are set *after* instead of *before* TARY, TARYE, *s.* Delete the definition there given, and substitute the following:—

2. To bear, suffer, endure, as in times of trial, oppression, persecution, &c.: "Thy father wald have *taryed* four suche," i.e., would have borne or stood as much as four of you.

TEARER, TEERER, *s.* The boy who stirs, breaks, and spreads the colour for a calico-printer.

This term has been explained as a corr. of *steerer*, a stirrer; but this is a mistake. What the calico-printer requires is not merely that the colour be stirred, but that it be thoroughly mixed, broken, of equal consistency, and smoothly spread; and all this the *tearer* does by spreading and working the colour over the cloth-sieve with his brush.

A.-S. *teran*, to tear, rend, break up; M. Eng. *teren*.

TELDID, *part. pt.* Built, erected. V. *Tild*.

TEMED, *pret.* Appealed; Sir Tristrem, l. 431, S. T. S. Errat. in DICT.

A.-S. *tedman*, to cite, summon, contend: from *team*, an issue, result.

To TERBUCK, *v. a.* and *n.* V. *Trebuck*.

TEU, TEW, TEU-AIRN, TEU-YRON, *s.* The nozzle or tube of the bellows of a forge or furnace.

"To be discharged of their worke by stryking out of thair *teu iyron*, and thair other workloums to be disposed upon our pleasour." Culross and Tulliallan, ii. 166.

O. Fr. *tuyau*, a pipe, quill: older form *tuyel*, from Lat. *tubellus*, dimin. of *tubus*, a tube: see Brachet. Some, however, refer it to O. H. Ger. *tûda*, a tube: see Littré.

TEW, TUE, *s.* An instrument for pulling, drawing, tightening; a tug.

The long pincers with which a blacksmith draws a piece of iron from his forge, is called a *tew* or *tew-iron*. The *tews* of a drum are the leather-catches by which the cords are tightened; but the name is often applied to both cords and catches.

"And altho' the drummer to get als many new *tews* as will serve the drum." Culross and Tulliallan, ii. 90.

A.-S. *taw*, an instrument; from *tawian*, to work, prepare, taw, dress.

THAME, THAIEM, *s.* Thirlage. V. THEME.

THEMSELF, THAMESELF, THEMSEL, THAIMSEL, THAME-SEL, *pron.* Used for himself or herself: as, "Every ane for *themsel.*" Also used for *themselves:* as, "They care na for ocht but *themsel.*"

THOLING, THOLYNG, s. Permission, grace, will, authority; a more common form is *tholance*. V. under THOLE.

"This appoyntment made at Dunfermelyn [25 July, 1457], betwix a venerabill fader in crist, Rechart, be godds *tholyng* Abbotte of Dunfermelyn, and the convente of that ilke on the ta pairt . . ." Regist. Dunferm., No. 451, p. 344, quoted in Annals of Dunfermline, p. 160.

To THORN, *v. n.* To satisfy one's appetite, to eat heartily; part. pt. *thorned, thorn*, refreshed with food.

When they had eaten and well drunken,
And n' had *thorn'd* fine,
The bride's father he took the cup,
For to serve out the wine.
Scot. Ballads, Child, ii., 335.

"Ye'll eat and drink, my merry men a',
An' see ye be weill *thorn*;
For blaw it weet, or blaw it wind,
My guid ship sails the morn."
Ibid., iii., 339.

THOUGHT, THOCHT, s. Grief, sorrow, trouble, affliction: "That wild son has been a sair *thocht* and a heavy burden to his mother."

The word is similarly used in the English ballad of The Nutbrowne Maide; see Child's Eng. and Scot. Ballads, iv. 147.

THUMB, THOUM, s.

To the examples under this heading in DICT. add the following:—

1. *To keep thoum on*, to hide, keep secret: "Mind, noo, *keep thoum on* that." *To keep one's thoum on*, to keep to one's self, in one's power, or for one's own benefit: "Y'ed better *keep your thoum on't*."

2. *Under thoum*, similar to underhand, and used as an *adj.* or an *adv.*; secret, in secret, furtively: "The bargain was made *under thoum*."

"Thay war invaded be that potent natione of the peychtes throuch counsel of the Britanis quyetlie *vnder thoum*." Leslie, Hist. Scot., p. 81, S.T.S.

3. *Under one's thoum*, in one's own hand, possession, or power; also, under the power, control, or subjection of another, as, "His father keeps him *under his thoum*."

Whan I've a saxpence *under my thum*,
Then I'll get credit in ilka toun;
But ay when I'm poor they bid me gang by;
O! poverty parts good company.
Tullin Hame, Herd's Coll., ii. 106.

THRUMS, *s. pl.* Shreds, stumps; "legs o' *thrums*," mere stumps of legs. Addit. to THRUM, q. v.

She's crined awa' to bane an' skin,
But that it seems is nought to me;
She's like to live—although she's in
The last stage o' tenuity.
She munches wi' her wizened gums,
And stumps about on legs o' *thrums*,
But comes—as sure as Christmas comes—
To ca' for her annuity.
George Outram, The Annuity.

TILD, TILDE, s. Cover, tent, roof: hence, house, castle, or building of any kind. V. TELD, TYLD.

A.-S. *teld*, tent; Icel. *tjald*, Dan. *telt*. From A.-S. *teld* comes E. *tilt*, the cover of a cart.

TILSALL, s. A form of *tinsall*, loss; Burgh Recs. Stirling, 1519, p. 2.

TIRE, TIRITNESS, TYRITNES, s. Tiredness, weariness, exhaustion.

". . . with *tyritnes*, service or bondage, sicknes, dolour or dede, or ony displeasour of body." Abp. Hamilton's Catechism, Fol. 110b.

In the text this word was printed *tyrdnes*, but in the Errata corrected to *tyritnes*, and so it is printed in Law's edition.

Both *tire* and *tiritness* are still used; but *tire* is the more common form.

To TIRL, *v. n.* To patter, beat, batter. Addit. to TIRL, *v. n.*, q. v.

"When the wind gowls in the chimney, and the rain *tirls* on the roof." L. R. Stevenson, Kidnapped, p. 271.

To TIRVE, *v. a.* To tear, uncover, strip. V. TIRR.

"The consulis commandit him to be *tirvit* nakit and skurgit with wandis. . . . The mair this man cryit, the serjand maid him to be the mair bastelic *tirvit* of his claithis." Bellend. Livy, b. ii., ch. 23.

TO, TA, *prep.* Regarding, concerning; in opposition to, against. Addit. to *To, Ta*.

"Sa, and a man mycht haif lauchfully luffit his nycht-bouris wyfe, he mycht a fyschit ane cause *to* his wife, to put hir away and tak ane uther, or sche also qnhen sche deayrit ane uther, wald mak faltis *to* hir husband, to get hir leif." Abp. Hamilton's Catechism, Fol. 72b.

TO-BOOT, TOOBOOT, TOBUIT, TABOOT, s. Excess, addition, difference in exchange; anything given in excess of an even niffer or exchange. A.-S. *tó bóte*.

"Pursued for the sowme of four pond scotis money, and that as the niffer of ane horse in *tooboot*." Corshill Baron Court Book, Ayr and Wigton Arch. Coll., iv. 91.

TO-BRIG, TA-BRIG, s. A draw-bridge; also called a *fa'-brig*, i.e. a *fall-bridge*.

"*Tu-brugge*, a draw-bridge;" Halliwell.

The name *to-brig* or *ta-brig* is mostly applied to a movable bridge over a canal or a railway, constructed of two leaves or sections swung from opposite banks, and joining or locking in the middle.

TOR, s. A terminal knob or peak, formerly used in the ornamentation of chairs, cradles, canopies, &c. Addit. to TOR, q. v.

Belinkin he rocked,
And the fause nurse she sang,
Till a' the *tores* o' the cradle
Wi' the red blude down ran.
Ballad, Lambert Linkin, l. 43.

TOUST, TOWST, *s.* A tax, toll, impost. Errat. in DICT.

Delete the entry under this heading in the DICT.: both definition and etymology are wrong. *Toust* has no connection with *towage*, and its meaning is not limited to a tax on ships. It primarily meant an impost or levy, and is formed from O. Fr. *toste*, a corrupted form of *toulte*, "an exacting or extorting of subsidies;" Cotgr. The same corruption occurs in O. Fr. *maltoste*, a later form of *maltoulte*, which is explained by Littré, s. v. *Malôte*. V. under *Malatout*.
In the Reg. Privy Council Scot., vol. vi. (see Index), there are records of *tousts* for repairing bridges, harbours, piers, &c.; and in each case the term is synonymous with taxation. It is so also in the following quotations:
"And that gif ony *towst* sould be taken of their guids." Records of Old Dundee, p. 115.
"From the *towst* the Perth vessels were to be exempted." Ibid., p. 122.

To TRAIK, *v. a.* To hinder, prevent, withhold, restrain.

"And the King said, 'What *traiks* albeit ye take off your hat?' and then Mr. Alexander took off his hat." Gowrie Conspiracies, p. 50.
Dan. *trække*, to draw, drag, hinder; Du. *trekken*.

To TREBUCK, TRABUCK, TRIBUCK, TERBUCK, *v. n.* and *a.* To make a false move in play; to check an opponent for making a false move in play, to catch one tripping.

In these forms this term is still common in the West of Scot.; and the following statement will illustrate its use. If a person, on making a false move in a game of skill, calls out *trebuck* or *trabuck me* before his opponent, he has the right to move again; but if his opponent is the first to call out *trebuck* or *terbuck you*, the player is checked and must pay the forfeit.
Both as a vb. and as a sb. the word is accented on the second syllable.

TREBUCK, TRABUCK, TRIBUCK, TERBUCK, *s.* A slip or false move in play; a check or trip in a game of skill.

O. Fr. *trebucher*, "to stumble, or trip; to slip; . . . also, to offend, misdoe, mistake; also, to overweigh, or beare downe by weight;" Cotgr.
"*Trébucher* dans une affaire, y faire une fausse démarche;" Littré.

TRIBOCHET, *s.* An engine of war used in the middle ages for throwing great stones. Addit. to TREBUSCHET, q. v.

O. Fr. *trebuchet*, "an old-fashioned engine of wood, from which great and battering stones were most violently throwne." Cotgr. From L. Lat. *trebuchetum*.

TROKE, *s.* Dealing, intercourse, companionship; same as *Troking*, q. v. Also, palaver, toying, fondling; as, "Thae twa hae an unco *troke* wi' ither." V. TROKE, *v.*

With this term cf. Mod. E. *truck*, to barter.

TRUAGE, TROUAGE, TRUWAGE, *s.* Tribute, gifts, presents; Sir Tristrem, l. 947, 992, S. T. S. Addit. to TREWAGE, q. v.

O. Fr. *trüage, treüage*, "a toll, custome, tax, imposition;" Cotgr. From O. Fr. *treud, treut, treu*, tribute, from Lat. *tributum*; see Burguy.

TRUE, *s.* A pledge, compact, treaty, truce; Leslie, Hist. Scot., p. 75, S.T.S. Addit. to TREW, q. v.

A.-S. *tredwa, trúwa*, a compact, pledge. In connection with this term it may be noted that the word *truce* is really a misspelling of *trues* or *trews*, pl. of *true* or *trew*, a pledge of truth: from A.-S. *tredwe*, true.

TRUFINGE, *s.* Deception; Barbour's Saints, Peter, l. 242. V. TRUFF.

TRUSSELL, TURSELL, *s.* The upper or reverse die formerly used in striking or stamping money.

As the opposite or obverse die was called the *pyle*, money was said to be stamped or printed with "*pyle* and *trussell.*"
"That thair salbe ane hundroth stane wecht of copper vnmixt with ony vther kynd of mettale, wrocht and forgeit in ane miln, and be the said miln maid reddy to the prenting eftir the accustumat forme of his maiesties cunyiehouse, with pyle and *tursell*, quhair throuch the same be not counterfute." Acts James VI., 1597.
This phrase was entered in the DICT. and explained as "*pyle and cursell;*" but Dr. Jamieson was led into this mistake by the misprint of *cursell* for *tursell* in the 1814 ed. of the Scotch Acts, from which he quoted.
The old method of striking money is thus described by Dr. R. W. Cochran-Patrick, author of The Coinage of Scotland:—"The obverse of the coin was engraved on a die, which was firmly fixed into a large block of wood. This was called the 'pile' or 'standard.' Upon this was placed the prepared piece of metal called the 'flan.' The moneyer, holding in his left hand the upper die (or 'trussell') by a twisted willow, placed it upon the flan, and then struck it firmly with all the force of the hammer held in his right hand."
This primitive method of coining was continued in Scotland till near the middle of the 17th century.
O. Fr. *troussel, trovsseau*, "a troussell; the vpper yron or mould thats vsed in the stamping of coyne;" Cotgr. Lit. the trusser, packer, or driver-home; the termination *-el* denoting instrument.

TRYNE, *s.* 1. A train, retinue, company.

"After that the Quene was somewhat satisfyed of hunting and other pastyme, sche cam to Abirdene, whair the Erle of Huntley met hir and his Lady with no small *tryne*, remaned in court, was supposed to have the greatest credyte, . . ." Knox, Hist. Scot. Reform., ii., 353, ed. Laing, Wodrow Soc.

2. Course, conduct or method of dealing, trade, practice, traffic.

"And als desyring ane ordour to be put amangis the merchandis fraternitie and gild brethir of this burgh for the *tryne* of merchandice, the gud and commone weill of the haill merchandis of the realme, . . . tendis als weill to the dayly augmentatioun and incressing of the *tryme*, ordour, and gud reull of merchandice, policy, riches, amitie, and gud luf amangis the saidis merchandis and gild brethir. . . . And attour, sall haif power to imput, lift, and rais taxtis and extentis

. . . to dispone for the commone werkis and erandis of the forsaidis merchandis and thair successouris, and *tryne* of merchandis alswell on the partis beyond sey as on this syde." Seal of Cause to Merchants, Burgh Recs. Edinburgh, i., 181-3, Recs. Soc.

This is simply a form of M. E. *train*, from O. Fr. *train*, "a (great mans) traine, retinue, or followers; . . . also, any way, course, worke, dealing, trade, practise, traflicke vsed, or entred into ;" Cotgr. It has come from Lat. *trahere*, to draw, through the L. Lat. *trahinere*, to drag or trail along.

To TUG, Tugg, Tuig, *v*. 1. As a *v. a.* : to pull, pluck, twitch, tweak, tear ; " He *tuggit* it to bits."

2. As a *v. n.* : to rend or tear by pulling ; "It *tuggis* in holes," i.e. it rends, tears, or goes in holes when tugged.

"Twynit and small, the best of thame all
May weir the claith for woll and threid,
Bot in the walkmill the wedder is ill,—
Thir ar nocht drying dayis in deid ;
And gif it be watt, I hecht for that,
It *tuggis* in hollis and gais abbreid.
R. Semple, Bann. MS., p. 356, Hunt. Soc.

"*Abbreid*," asunder, in pieces.

TUGGIT, TUIGIT, *part. pt.* Torn, rent, mangled.

"To scosche all skynis cuttit, hollit, or *tuigit* in the nek." Burgh Recs. Glasgow, 28th Aug., 1613. V. under *Scosche*.

The skins here referred to were such as had been damaged by the flesher during the process of flaying. In the minutes of the Skinners of Glasgow there is an entry regarding this search for damaged skins in the market ; and, what the above entry calls *tuigit*, is there called *juggit*, i.e. jobbed, or cut into by the point of the flayer's knife. V. *Jog*.

TUMPH, TUMPHIE, *s*. V. TUMFIE.

TURSELL, *s*. A form of *Trussell*, q. v.

To TYNE, *v. a*. To cause to lose or fail ; hence, to thwart, obstruct. *To tyne* a person at law is to cause him to lose his case. Addit. to TINE, TYNE, q. v.

Is nane so wyiss can him defar,
Quhen he proponis furth ane ple ;
Nor yit sa hardy man that dar
Sir Penny *tyne* or dissobey.
Sir Penny, Bann. MS., p. 410, Hunt. Soc.

U.

UMGANG, *s*. Circuit, bounds, extent. Addit. to UNGANG, *Ungang*, q. v.

"Becaus the said hous, smedy, orchard, and yarde ar within the yettis and *umgang* and wallis of the said abbay." Crossraguel Charters, i. 63, Ayr and Wigton Arch. Coll.

UNBRACHTE, VNBRACHTE, *adj*. Unmatched, unyoked, unattached ; Leslie, Hist. Scot., p. 104, S.T.S.

Prefix *un-*, not ; and *brachte*, braced, matched, yoked, from O. Fr. *brace*, the two arms ; hence a brace, a grasp, yoke. See Skeat's Etym. Dict., s. v. *Brace*.

UNDERLOWT, VNDERLOWTE, *s*. Underling, inferior, servant. V. UNDERLOUT, *adj*.

To thole for Criste as *vnderlowte*.
Barbour's Saints, Peter, l. 128.

UNDERN, *s*. V. DICT.

To the entry under this heading in Suppl. add the following.

The etym. for this term given under the form Orntren in Dict. is confused and unsatisfactory. It does not account for the different meanings which the term has borne, nor the different periods of the day which it has been used to represent. In A.-S. times *undern* meant the third hour, (i.e. about nine a.m.), or a meal taken at that time ; later, it meant a part of the forenoon, or a forenoon meal ; and still later, a period between noon and sunset, or an afternoon repast. Now by deriving the term from A.-S. *under*, which originally meant *between*, like Germ. *unter*, all this becomes clear : *undern* then means the intervening period, and may be applied to any time of the day ; and the different applications of the term may safely

be referred to the changes that have taken place in the social habits of the people.

UNDOLVIN, VNDOLVINE, *adj*. Unburied ; Barbour's Saints, Peter, l. 198. V. *Dolven*, DOLLYNE.

UNICORN HORN, UNICORNE HORNE, *s*. The horn of the narwhal was so called. It was used as a test of the presence of poison in meat or drink.

"Item, a serpent toung and ane *vnicorne horne* set in gold." Accts. L. H. Treas. i. 84, Dickson.

"Under this name the horn of the narwhal was much valued in the fourteenth, fifteenth, and sixteenth centuries, on account of its reputed superiority to all other tests of the presence of poison in meat or drink. It occurs in most inventories of mediæval plate, either mounted with gold, silver, and jewels as an *épreuve*, or set in fragments in drinking cups and other vessels." Ibid., Gloss.

UNJORNAIT, UNIORNAIT, *adj*. Without being summoned to appear in court on a particular day. V. JORNAT.

In 1542 King James V. granted to Hector M'Clane of Dowart and 40 of his friends or others permission to go and come to the King at Edinburgh or elsewhere from the 24th of Feb. to the 25th May, "vnburt, vnharmit, vnattechit, vnarrestit, *vniornait*, vncallit, vnpersewit, vnwexit, vudistrublit." Orig. Paroch., ii., pt. 1, p. 310.

UNLACED, UNLAISSIT, VNLAISSIT, *adj*. Ungirded, unharnessed.

Sall neuer my likame be laid *vnlaissit* to sleip,
Quhill I haue gart yone berne bow,
As I haue made myne avow.
Gol. and Gaw., st. 23.

UNRIDE, UNRYDE, *adj.* V. UNREDE.

UNSPEIRD, UNSPEIRT, VNSPERD, *adj.* Unasked, unquestioned; also as an *adv.* without asking or making enquiry, as, "I fand the gait *unspeird*;" without being asked to do it, as, "He did it *unspeirt*." V. SPERE, SPEIR.

UNWYN, *s.* Pain, suffering, sorrow. V. WIN.
A.-S. *un*, neg. part., and *wyn*, pleasure, delight.

UNYERDIT, VNYERDET, *adj.* Unburied.
V. YIRD, *v.*

UPSPRING, VPSPRING, *s.* Offspring, offshoot.

"Princes are haldne in bichest digrie, and worthilie, because thay ar sa neir *vpspring* of the kingis blude."
Leslie, Hist. Scot., p. 112, S.T.S.

To UPTRIM, VPTRIM, *v. a.* To adorn, embellish; Leslie, Hist. Scot., p. 117, S.T.S.

V.

VERDOUR, *s.* V. SUPPL.
To the entry under this heading add—
"That is to say, three *verdour* beds, and an arras bed, three pairs of sheets, . . . two *verdour* beds, a pair of fustian blankets, a ruff and curtains," etc.
Orig. Paroch., i. 184-5.

VICE, *s.* A screw; applied also to various articles fitted or worked with a screw: thus, the screw of a press, and a screw-press are each called a *vice*; also, a screwed cap or stopper for a flask is so named. Addit. to VYSE, q. v.

"Flagones of glase with *vices* covored with leather, the dozen . . . xii li." Rates of Customs, &c., 1612, Halyburton's Ledger, p. 305.

VITTALLAR, *s.* A provision-ship, storeship. V. VICTUAL.

"The navy was such as never was sein to come fra France, for the supporte of Scotland; for besydis the galayis, being twenty twa in nomber, thei had threscoir great schippis, besydis *vittallaris*." Knox, Hist. Reform. Scot., i., 216, ed. Laing, Wodrow Soc.

VUIR, *adj.* A form of *uvir*, upper; Leslie, Hist. Scot., p. 14. V. UVER.

W.

WA, *s.* A wave; pl. *wais*, waves.
"Oft fleitande with gret surges and wanes like the *wais* of the scy." Leslie, Hist. Scot., p. 30, S.T.S.

To WAIRN, *v. a.* To give notice; to summon: part. pr. *wairnin*, used also as a *s.*
V. [WARN].
In the south and west of S. *warn* is commonly so pronounced.

WAITSKATH, WATESKATHE, *s.* Lit., watchscathe, in the sense of dread or shun injury, and hence equal to coward, craven. V. [WATE].
So saw he cumand a littill than from thence
A worthy doctour of diuinitie,
Freir Wolf *Waitskath*, in science wondrous ele,
To preche and pray was new cum of clostir,
With beidis in hand sayand his Paternoster.
Henryson, Fox and Wolf, l. 54.

To WALK, WAKK, WAUK, *v. a.* and *n.* V. DICT.
This entry should be arranged thus :—To Wakk, Wauk, Walk ; for the form *walk* is a variant or false form of the other two. The apparent *lk* of MSS. is really a contracted form of *kk*, and represents *kk* or *uk* according as the preceding vowel is sounded short or long. A similar arrangement should be followed with the derivative forms Walkin, Walken, and Walkrife. For further explanation see under *Polk* and *Rolk* in Suppl.

WANDAND, *part. adj.* Timorous, shy, backward. V. WANDYS.
Be nocht our hamely in to presens,
Nor yit our *wandand* in to secreit wiss.
Mersar, Bann. MS. p. 604, l. 10.
A.-S. *wandian*, to fear : M. E. *waulien*.

WANE, *s.* Crowd, band, company. Addit. to WANE, q. v.
With that ther cam an arrowe hastely,
forthe off a myghtte *wane*;
Hit bathe strekene the yerle Duglas
In at the brest-bane.
Chevy Chase, l. 74.

To WAR, WAUR, *v. a.* To excel, exceed, beat; to requite evil with evil, as, "I'll *war* ye as muckle for that ere long," i.e., I'll re-

pay you for that ill-turn before long. Addit.
to WAR, q. v.

"Bot Wigtoune *waris* the vthir 2 baith in citizenis
and riches." Leslie, Hist. Scot., p. 13, S.T.S.

WAWSPER, WAUSPEK, *s.* V. *Wawsper*.
For the note under this heading in Suppl. substitute
the following :—
All these forms are still in use: they are merely
corruptions of *warpspear*, more correctly *worpspear*, a
spear for casting or striking, applied to a fish-spear, and
especially to a leister or salmon-spear.
O. Du. *worpspere*, *werpspere*, a javelin : from *worpen*,
later *werpen*, to throw, cast, strike; and *spere*, a spear.

WEEBIS, WEBIS, WEIBIS, WYDIS, *s.* Ragwort. Addit. to WEEBO, q. v.
Prob. from Gael. *uibe*, a mass, clump; *uibeach*,
massy, clumpy ; and so called on account of its shape
and manner of growth.

WEIRLIE, VEIRLIE, *adj.* Warlike, given to
war, fierce, turbulent: "a *weirlie* peple," Leslie, Hist. Scot., p. 14; "*weirlie* armies,"
Ibid., p. 72. V. WEIR, WERELY.

WENE, *s.* V. WANE.

To WERN, WERNE, *v. a.* To refuse. V.
WARNE.

To WERP, *v. a.* To cast, throw, utter;
Douglas, II., 252, 26, ed. Small. V.
WARP.

WEYNG, *s.* A wing : pl. *weyngis* ; Barbour's
Saints, Peter, l. 562.
Icel. *vængr*, a wing ; Dan. and Swed. *vinge*.

To WHIP-THE-CAT, *v.* To go from house
to house to work ; the expression is still applied to jobbing or itinerant tailors.
The custom of *whipping the cat* was in former years
very common both in Eng. and Scot. ; but it is now
comparatively seldom followed except in remote country
districts. The expression is still used in Prov. Eng.
See Halliwell and Webster.

WOK, WOLK, WOLKE, *s.* A week. V.
WOK, WOUK, *Woulk*.

WOULK, WOULKE, WOLK, WOLKE, *s.* A
week. V. WOUK, WOUKE.
These are merely scribal or MS. forms of *wouk*,
woukke, *wokk*, *wokke*. The apparent *lk* of MSS. is really
a contracted form of *kk*, and represents *kk* or *uk* according as the preceding vowel is sounded short or long.
See under *Walk*, *Wakk*, *Wauk*, above.

Y.

To YACHLE, YAUCHLE, *v. n.* To walk in
an awkward, shuffling manner, like a person
with loose joints: hence, to walk with difficulty; part. pr. *yachlin*, *yauchlin*, used also
as an *adj.* and a *s.* West of S.

YOUNG, YONG, *adj.* Youngest; and similarly *ald* is used for *oldest* : as, " the *young*
son and the *ald* ane."

BY PRIVATE SUBSCRIPTION.

Impression, 400 Copies Demy Quarto, and 100 Royal Quarto on Whatman's Paper. Each Copy Signed and Numbered.
UNIFORM WITH JAMIESON'S SCOTTISH DICTIONARY.

Re-issue and Completion
of
Chalmers' Caledonia

THE welcome accorded to the Publisher's re-issue of JAMIESON'S SCOTTISH DICTIONARY proves that there is a widely prevalent desire to possess good texts of works that may be regarded as national in their interest and importance. He is therefore encouraged by the success of JAMIESON to venture on a similar undertaking—the republication of GEORGE CHALMERS' Caledonia. At the time when the distinguished Scottish Lexicographer was occupied in the preparation of his national Dictionary, another patriotic worker, equally qualified for the department which he undertook, was engaged in the cognate task of recording and illustrating the History and Topography of his native Scotland, and bringing to bear upon it as much sound learning, earnest zeal, and patient labour as JAMIESON was devoting to the Scottish Language. It is not a little to the credit of the Northern Kingdom that she possessed at the same time two such sons, qualified and willing to rear for themselves memorials so conservative of the past and valuable for the future as the SCOTTISH DICTIONARY and the Caledonia. Each of these works may be regarded as the complement of the other, and no Library possessing a Scottish department can afford to dispense with either. They mark an important era in the national history. The time at which they appeared was one of transition, when old landmarks, of Language and of Topography alike, were being effaced by the rapid march of modern progress. Although, as we gather from the Dissertation on the Scottish Language prefixed to the DICTIONARY, and from other sources, the two writers were by no means agreed in their opinions as to certain points common to both undertakings, each was successful in producing a work which in many respects can neither be improved nor superseded. Not a few features of Scottish Language and Scottish Localities familiar to our fathers would have disappeared for ever but for the preservative labours of JAMIESON and CHALMERS. The old order has given place to the new, but as we turn over the pages of these writers the past rises before us in vivid and comprehensive, yet minute, detail.

GEORGE CHALMERS was a voluminous author, but his great work was the Caledonia. It is not too strong a statement to affirm that every important work on Scottish History or Topography published since it appeared refers to CHALMERS and owes not a little to his labour. Entering on a field which had been opened up by Father Innes and John Pinkerton, and freely availing himself of their researches, he discovered many treasures which to them were unknown and inaccessible, and accumulated a store of information which is as complete for Scotland as is the great work of Camden—with which the Caledonia has often been compared—for England. Indeed, as Allan Cunningham testified, "In deep research and heaping together of matter, the *Britannia* of Camden fades away before it." No student of Scotland's Family or Local History, of its Institutional or Archæological Records, or of its Ecclesiastical and Civil History and Topography, can afford to dispense with the results of the immense labour and research contained in this work. Later writers may have dissented from the Celtic theories of CHALMERS or disputed some of his conclusions, but none have questioned his ability, his unwearied industry, his painstaking study of authorities or the scrupulous desire for accuracy of statement, which he brought to bear upon his work.

Unlike Jamieson, CHALMERS did not live either to complete the work he set before him, which was to review the entire field of Scottish History, Antiquities and Topography, or even to see in print all that he had prepared for the press. Three volumes only were published which treat of the Counties South of the Forth, and these are all that have hitherto been available to the general student; but it is well known that a considerable amount of manuscript, perhaps even more interesting and important than any of the volumes published, has lain since the Author's death on the shelves of the Advocates' Library. It is somewhat remarkable and scarcely creditable to the Book-printing Clubs and Publishers of Scotland that so valuable a manuscript has not been printed before now. Mr. Allibone, in his *Dictionary of Authors*, in referring to CHALMERS, expresses a desire which has often been felt when he asks: "Will it be thought impertinent in an American to urge one of the Literary Clubs which do such credit to Great Britain to worthily distinguish itself by publishing the remaining manuscripts of this great work?"

To this desire the Publisher now proposes to give effect by publishing CHALMERS' Caledonia IN COMPLETE FORM.

With this object he has made application to the Curators of the Advocates' Library for permission to print the unpublished portion of the Caledonia, and he is glad to be able to announce that they have given their consent in a very cordial way.

It is intended to issue the work in (probably seven) convenient volumes of 500 pages each. References to the pages of CHALMERS are so frequent in the more recent historical and topographical works on Scotland that it has been decided to retain the original *paging*.

In paper, typography, and general appearance, the new edition will be similar to the recent re-issue of JAMIESON'S DICTIONARY, and will in these respects be a great improvement on the first.

Much of the value of the original issue of the Caledonia was lost through the absence of a complete INDEX; and the trouble of hunting up special information through its pages has often been complained of. To obviate this a COMPLETE CLASSIFIED AND ANALYTICAL INDEX will, in the new edition, be added to the entire work, and every care taken to make the work easily available for reference.

The large MAP and PLATES of the original will be carefully reproduced.

The copies offered for subscription will be strictly limited to 400 Demy 4to, at 25s. per vol., and 100 Royal 4to, on WHATMAN's Paper, at 40s. per vol. No special edition will be printed for America, the Colonies, or the Continent. The Foreign, as well as the Home Supply, must, therefore, be drawn from the above number, and it is reasonable to anticipate that, as soon as the announcement of the issue reaches the book-buying community, the entire impression will be at once taken up.

ALEXANDER GARDNER, PUBLISHER, PAISLEY.

www.ingramcontent.com/pod-product-compliance
Lightning Source LLC
Chambersburg PA
CBHW020234240426
43672CB00006B/529